Read + Control of Diplomacy
Chapt. V.   P. 193 — 197

INTERNATIONAL POLITICS

INTERNATIONAL POLITICS

An Introduction to the Western State System

BY

FREDERICK L. SCHUMAN

Assistant Professor of Political Science, University of Chicago;
Author of "American Policy toward Russia since 1917,"
"War and Diplomacy in the French Republic," etc.

FIRST EDITION
FIFTH IMPRESSION

McGRAW-HILL BOOK COMPANY, INC.

NEW YORK AND LONDON

1933

THE MAPLE PRESS COMPANY, YORK, PA.

TO
KARL AUGUST

PREFACE

BOOKS on subjects usually designated as "political," "social," or "economic" fall into two classes: those meant to be read but not taken seriously, and those meant to be taken seriously but not read. Textbooks are in a class by themselves, for they are commonly designed neither to be read nor taken seriously by people in general, and to be both read and taken seriously by their unfortunate victims who have no choice in the matter. The present work strives to attain what to many will seem an impossible ideal. It is designed to be readable for people in general and to be taken seriously by those not under academic compulsion. It purports to be a general presentation of the recent history and present problems of international relations. To the degree to which it achieves this objective it should prove stimulating and useful—both for the factual data which it contains and for the suggestions and interpretations which it offers—to everyone who is consciously aware of the portentous omens hanging over the muddled world of the twentieth century.

Rare indeed is the book which can fulfill such a function and at the same time prove valuable in college and university classes as a basis for courses in the subject it covers. To describe any book as a "text" is equivalent to telling the average reader that it is unreadable and thoroughly useless. To describe any book as "popular" is equivalent to telling the average pedagogue that it is unscholarly and worthless as a text. These judgments are perfectly substantiated by experience and tradition. But it has nevertheless seemed worth while to the present author to attempt a general work on international relations which would at least aspire toward a combination of accuracy, thoroughness, and scholarship with interest and readability.

As a student and teacher, as a research scholar and pedagogue, the author has been painfully impressed with the fact that American textbooks in the social sciences, by common agreement between writers and publishers, are expected to be dull compilations of meaningless and noncontroversial factual material, with a minimum of attention value and no new ideas whatever in their make-up. A textbook, moreover, is expected either to furnish harmless entertainment for readers on an adolescent level of sophistication or to constitute a vehicle whereby the author can achieve narcissistic gratification by parading his erudition through elaborate documentary citations, bibliographies, and appendices.

This conception of the textbook is completely repugnant to the present author. The present volume represents the fruition of six years of teaching experience with American undergraduates in a midwestern university of deservedly high repute. It is not intended to insult the intelligence of its readers by assuming that they are afflicted with cerebral paralysis. Neither is it intended to flatter the vanity of the author by demonstrating that he can outdo his competitors in putting on each page innumerable footnotes which are meaningless and listing at the end of each chapter innumerable books that he has not read. The work is intended to present, in interesting and intelligible fashion, a body of factual material and to provoke thinking, on an adult level, about the phenomena described. It assumes that facts devoid of ideas are more worthless than ideas unsupported by facts, and that tentative or even wrong ideas are more stimulating intellectually than no ideas at all.

A few other respects in which the volume differs from its predecessors may be suggested;

1. The analysis of international politics attempted in the following pages does not postulate the inevitability of sweetness and light or support the illusion that the law of the jungle in the international anarchy has, by some late magic, been superseded by the morality of the millennium. The approach is rather that of *Realpolitik*, characterized by Machiavellian detachment and an earnest effort to delve beneath phraseology to underlying realities. The implications of this approach are clearly stated in Chapter XIII, but they underly the treatment of every topic. The contemporary efforts to insure peace through idealistic verbiage and international organization are evaluated in the light of the fundamental patterns of power in the Western State System.

2. The futility of dealing with politics without dealing, at the same time, with the "social" and "economic" configurations of human relations is recognized. A conscious effort has been made to interpret political forms and forces against the background of the whole social and economic order of the western world.

3. The study of political geography is treated as an indispensable prerequisite to the study of international relations. The outline maps in the present volume are in no sense a substitute for an adequate historical and political atlas. But it is hoped that they will prove suggestive and will be found to differ from most maps appearing in American-made books in that they make some pretense at clarity and relevance to the text.

4. Footnotes have been reduced to a minimum. The writer is of the opinion that general readers and undergraduate students are usually pained and bored by laborious citations of documentary and secondary sources. For specialists, this display of the paraphernalia of erudition is

unnecessary, for specialists are already familiar with sources. For laymen, it is a nuisance and an impediment, serving no useful purpose whatever.

5. Bibliographical compendia have been studiously eschewed. A general interpretation of international politics cannot at the same time be a bibliography of international politics. The literature of the field is too enormous to be crowded into footnotes and book lists. There are no learned citations in the ensuing pages to books and articles in French, German, Scandinavian, or Sanskrit, for the book is intended for readers who have no immediate intention of delving into foreign bibliographies. There are no exhaustive compilations of unread and unreadable works. At the close of each chapter a short reading list will be found, containing a few of the outstanding and readily available books in English dealing with the general subject matter of the chapter. Those who propose to do research in international relations are advised to consult the card catalogues of libraries, the numerous indices of periodical literature, and the many excellent bibliographical compilations which are to be had at every well-equipped university. There is no proper place for such material in a general work of this type.

Two general limitations which confront everyone who writes of contemporary politics are necessarily conspicuous in the present work. One arises from the fact that it is impossible to deal with the events of one's own generation from a long perspective and that it is correspondingly difficult to arrive at evaluations and conclusions which will stand the test of time. As Voltaire wrote to M. Bertin de Rocheret (April 14, 1732), "Whoso writes the history of his own time must expect to be attacked for everything he has said, and for everything he has not said: but those little drawbacks should not discourage a man who loves truth and liberty, expects nothing, fears nothing, asks nothing, and limits his ambition to the cultivation of letters."

The other difficulty arises out of the circumstances that a work which deals primarily with the present (and even with the future) can have no neatly defined terminal point, since life goes on—rapidly and kaleidoscopically—and soon outmodes even the most up-to-date book. Since the present work has gone to press, three momentous happenings have taken place, all on March 5, 1933: (1) the culmination of a new financial panic in the United States with the temporary closing of all American banks and the suspension of gold payments by the United States Treasury; (2) the completion of the Japanese seizure of Jehol with the fall of Chengtieh to the invaders; and (3) the victory of Adolph Hitler's Fascists in the German election. The first event inaugurated a new phase of the Great Depression, possibly foreshadowing world-wide abandonment of the gold standard and world-wide inflation. The second completed the conquest of Manchuria and promised new international conflicts in the

Far East. The third sounded the death knell of German democracy and of the General Disarmament Conference and brought measurably closer the "inevitable" next war between the revisionist States and the *status quo* bloc. These developments confirm the general line of interpretation adopted in the present volume. Their specific results cannot, of course, be forecast accurately. All that can legitimately be hoped for is that the present analysis will suggest the various possibilities of the years to come.

No preface is complete without the usual acknowledgments and confessions of guilt for sins of omission and commission. None of the following chapters has been read by any of the author's academic colleagues. He is consequently not indebted to anybody in particular for the customary "invaluable criticisms and suggestions." He can make only general acknowledgments for stimulating and fruitful exchanges of views with that fraternity of scholars which constitutes the University of Chicago—and he is happy to observe that not all the scholars are on the faculty, and not all the faculty members are scholars.

More specific expressions of appreciation are due to a small and alert group of youthful collaborators, all at Chicago: to Miss Dorothy Blumenstock—for spending endless hours in close cooperation with the writer in gathering factual material, in preparing tables and charts, in criticizing content and style, in reading proof, and in concocting the index; to Miss Brita Berglund—for invaluable and invariably efficient stenographic and clerical assistance; to Mr. Gabriel Almond—for incidental assistance with the appendices; to a host of students, graduate and undergraduate, in the author's classes, from whose "term papers" he has cheerfully filched many useful data and a few suggestive thoughts; and, more particularly again, to Mr. David Blumenstock for assisting with the index and drawing outline maps, and to Mr. George Brodsky for the lettering and shading of the maps under the author's direction. To Mr. Brodsky is largely due whatever merit the maps may possess.

It goes without saying (but by the traditions of the profession, it must always be said nevertheless) that the author is solely accountable for all mistakes of fact or of interpretation. In a work of such wide scope and large size the possibilities of error are multitudinous, despite the most painstaking care in checking facts and weighing conclusions. The author would, in any case, not wish to deprive reviewers of the pleasure of pointing out that a word here is misspelled, that a date there is in error, and that a figure elsewhere is of dubious validity. These opportunities, it is hoped, will not be numerous. But the author accepts full responsibility for all lacunae, all misstatements, and all misjudgments. For the rest, the readers to whom this preface is addressed must arrive at their own verdict.

FREDERICK L. SCHUMAN.

A PREFACE FOR SOCIAL SCIENTISTS

THE literature of international relations is already staggering in volume and overwhelming in complexity. This circumstance imposes an imperative obligation upon every author who hurls another tome on top of the pile: that of justifying his conduct to his own conscience and to the decent opinions of mankind. This justification should be clearly stated at the outset and not merely implied in the text. The present volume is less a work of "research" than a work of synthesis, interpretation, and "popularization." Among the pedants and pedagogues of Academicia, "research" is a holy word, to be spelled with a capital "R" and pronounced in an awed voice, with appropriate incantations. The word "popularization," on the other hand, is anathema, for it is supposed to denote intellectual slovenliness and a cheap truckling to public bad taste. However justified these evaluations may be, it is nevertheless the curse of American social scientists in general, and of students of international relations in particular, that the collection of dull and meaningless facts in articles, monographs, and dry-as-dust treatises has thus far completely overshadowed the more important and laborious process of thoughtful reflection on the significance of the facts which are so assiduously gathered. Only by reflecting and taking thought can one compare, analyze, and synthesize the raw data and draw from them, through the almost lost art of generalization, their broad social implications. The chapters which follow contain a large mass of factual material on the contemporary phenomena of international politics. But the major purpose of the book is less to present new facts than to organize and interpret the known facts in terms of a new approach to the whole field.

Since the ultimate value of the book, for teachers, students, and general readers, rests upon the utility of this new approach (and of the scheme of organization and interpretation to which it has led), it should be helpful to state clearly, in brief compass, the underlying assumptions of this attempt at synthesis. The study of international relations has traditionally been monopolized by historians and by international lawyers. The historians have dealt with the phenomena in question in terms of time sequences and the simple cause-and-effect relations of diplomatic chronology. The lawyers and jurists have dealt with international relations in terms of the principles of public international law. In recent years the historians of diplomacy have been primarily concerned with the question of "war guilt"—and such general treatments of international politics as they have presented have for the most part been characterized by the usual word jugglery and the intellectual acrobatics habitually indulged in by those who conceive of social science as a vehicle for dispensing moral judgments. This procedure has been fruitful in so far as it has promoted scholarly investigation into the facts of diplomatic history. It has not, however, resulted in any significant formulation of concepts which can be utilized for the description and analysis of the great dynamic forces moving States to action in the international arena. The lawyers and jurists, on the other hand, have been primarily interested, in the post-war period, in formal and legalistic dissections of the contemporary fabric of international organization—or "international government," as some prefer to call it. This procedure has likewise been fruitful in that it has clarified the legal nature of the structural forms of international cooperation. But legal concepts and principles also offer no clue to the inner nature and significance of the established patterns of behavior in the relations between States.

In the present study an effort has been made to escape from the limitations of the traditional approaches and to deal with the subject from the point of view of the new Political Science. The adjective is used advisedly, since the old Political Science—still all-too-prevalent in the centers of higher learning—has been circumscribed by barren legal and historical concepts. The approach adopted here assumes that Political Science, as one of the social sciences, is concerned with the description and analysis of relations of power in society—*i.e.*, with those patterns of social contacts which are suggested by such words as rulers and ruled, command and obedience, domination and subordination, authority and allegiance. An adequate treatment of these patterns would require the invention of new concepts and the devising of a new vocabulary, for the old Political Science has little to offer which is helpful. The political scientists of the old school who have dealt broadly with international relations have either wandered up the blind alley of legalism or have contented themselves with elaborate fact gathering on a variety of scattered topics which they are unable to put together into any unified scheme of interpretation. The present work does not pretend to offer the new concepts and the new vocabulary which are necessary to escape entirely from these frustrations. This is a task for the future—and one not to be undertaken in a work intended for fairly wide consumption. The vocabulary employed in the following pages will not sound strange, even to the uninitiated. But a certain degree of originality may, in all modesty, be claimed for the general orientation of the study.

This orientation assumes that the phenomena of international politics can be dealt with most fruitfully if they are envisaged as aspects of the whole pattern of political behavior and power relations which has developed in western civilization. This pattern may be designated as the "Western State System"—*i.e.*, the total complex of attitudes, values, habits, and behavior patterns which have a bearing on the contacts between the States of the western world. This State System has had its antecedents in earlier cultures, and it will doubtless have its successors in future civilizations as yet unborn. The particular and specific problems of contemporary international politics can be dealt with meaningfully only if they are considered in the light of the whole State System of modern world society.

The function of the present work is to describe the Western State System realistically and objectively in terms of its cultural origins, its institutionalized forms, its dynamic forces, and its apparent prospects. The four major divisions of the volume are devoted to these several tasks. This conception furnishes a framework for the analysis and interpretation of all the major events of international relations. The framework is broader than the traditional orientation of the diplomatic historian and international lawyer, for it enables the student and the observer to view diplomatic history and international law in their proper perspectives, as parts of a vast design. The nature and meaning of the design itself become clear only when it is looked upon as an indivisible whole, the various parts of which are significant only as aspects of the total cultural context. It is the author's conviction that all of the existing general works on international relations fall short of their objective, because they are fragmented, particularistic, and limited by the partial views inherent in narrow traditional concepts and approaches. It is the author's hope that this work will be judged, by reviewers and readers alike, by the extent to which it accomplishes its purpose of synthesizing and interpreting the raw data, of presenting a whole picture of the field, and of stimulating thought regarding the implications of particular institutions, forces, and problems in terms of the whole pattern of the Western State System.

FREDERICK L. SCHUMAN.

UNIVERSITY OF CHICAGO,
April, 1933.

CONTENTS

BOOK ONE—ORIGINS

CHAPTER I

CHAPTER II

CHAPTER III

BOOK TWO—FORMS

CHAPTER IV

CONTENTS

CONTENTS

CONTENTS

LIST OF MAPS

LIST OF CHARTS AND TABLES

[xxi]

BOOK ONE
ORIGINS

INTERNATIONAL POLITICS

AN INTRODUCTION TO THE WESTERN STATE SYSTEM

CHAPTER I

STATES AND STATE SYSTEMS OF THE PAST

1. MAN AND THE STATE

> Nature, the art whereby God hath made and governs the world, is by the "art" of man, as in many other things, so in this also imitated, that it can make an artificial animal . . . For by art is created that great "Leviathan" called a "Commonwealth," or "State," in Latin *civitas*, which is but an artificial man; though of greater stature and strength than the natural, for whose protection and defense it was intended; and in which the "sovereignty" is an artificial "soul," as giving life and motion to the whole body.—THOMAS HOBBES, *Leviathan*.

SOME twenty-two centuries ago the observation was made by the Greek philosopher, Aristotle, that man is a political animal. Successive generations of political scientists from that day to this have been engaged in laborious efforts to describe and comprehend that portion of the behavior of the human animal described by common consent as "political." Meanwhile the great mass of human beings everywhere has acquiescently paid taxes, obeyed laws, served in armies, and wielded such powers over its own destinies as interest and opportunity permitted. People have seldom been moved to speculate overmuch upon the nature of politics and the State except when the burden of rulers upon ruled has become intolerable or when social and economic disasters have led to political convulsions and revolution. Men and women in general have usually accepted government as a fixed and immutable feature of the way of life ordained for them upon the earth. So universally has this been true that one might almost say of the State what Voltaire said of God: if it did not exist, it would be necessary to invent it.

Because of its very antiquity and universality, however, this man-made machine of men known as the State can scarcely be regarded as an invention in the usual sense of the word. Like the proverbial Topsy, the State "just growed." Its origins are lost in the mists which enshroud the beginnings of the first civilized human societies. The political philosophers of the eighteenth century wrote in ignorance when they assumed that the State had originated through a contract entered into by people living previously in a pre-civil state of nature. Modern archaeology and anthropology would seem to indicate that almost all human societies on all levels of cultural development have possessed some regularized procedures of command and obedience comparable to the State or government of civilized peoples. The social pattern of the State, like other arrangements and devices common to many cultures and civilizations, probably arose independently at some extremely remote period in various human communities throughout the world, though it is not impossible that it had a single place of origin—perhaps early Egypt—from which it spread over the globe. But in view of the dubious paternity of the State and the mysteries of its birth, no one can speak as yet with much assurance regarding its genesis.[1]

It might indeed appear futile to raise such a question at the outset of a treatise on international politics. The justification for so doing is that there is no field of human problems in which it is easier for the wandering observer to lose sight of the forest because of the trees than in contemporary international relations. If one is to perceive the true configuration of the landscape and the outlines of the strange vistas which stretch forth on every side he must withdraw a bit from the scene about him in order to secure a perspective on the whole confusing panorama. Such a perspective can best be secured by looking into the past, by observing earlier scenes which appear simple in comparison to the chaotic complexities of the twentieth century world because they are farther removed from the conflicting pressures of the here and now. The "lessons of history," to be sure, are a snare and a delusion, for, as wits have often observed, the only lesson which history teaches is that history teaches no lessons. But the known record of the human past may still be useful in affording an orientation and a point of view toward the crowded present and the unknown future. With this purpose in mind, it will be of value to raise the question of the origin of the State, to examine the nature of international politics in the cultures which preceded our own, and to trace through more recent centuries the development of those relationships between States which are peculiar to western civilization.

At first sight it might appear that international relations began as soon as human beings organized themselves into States and these States established contacts with one another. But where, when, or how this first took place is a mystery which neither the historian nor the ethnologist has fully succeeded in solving. Although large land areas of the earth have apparently been inhabited for many hundreds of thousands of years by

---

[1] See Robert H. Lowie, *The Origin of the State*, 1927; W. C. MacLeod, *The Origin and History of Politics*, 1931; and R. M. MacIver, *The Modern State*, 1926.

isolated groups of more or less human beings, the dim record of skulls and cave-dwellings, stone implements and bits of pottery, throws little light upon social and political organization during the major portion of man's life upon the planet. The earliest written records now available were the work of writers who lived some seventy centuries ago. They show that the people who left them were already members of complex societies and had long since been organized into States. Obviously, the transition from primitive, preliterate and unpolitical communities to the cultures of the early States must necessarily have been a very gradual one, extending over many generations and taking place at different times among different peoples. Even in the twentieth century of the Christian era, preliterate societies on a primitive level of culture and political organization still survive in those regions of the globe most remote from the influence of western civilization. These societies reveal something of the type of social life which must have prevailed everywhere during the long millenniums antedating written history. The feeble light of historical and archaeological evidence is insufficient to dispel the shadows of this distant dawn.

However States came to be established, however this transition came to be achieved, the result may be viewed as a process whereby the authority of immemorial custom, imposed by the whole community upon its members, was replaced by the authority of law, imposed by government upon subjects bound together in a common group life, not by ties of kinship, tribe, or clan, but by common habitation within a given territory. There is no reason for supposing that any animals which can properly be called human ever lived upon the earth under conditions in which each individual was entirely a law unto himself, in splendid isolation apart from his fellows. Whether man is a political animal in the sense that his innate biological drives impel him to political activity may be doubted. But that he is a gregarious animal is not open to question. Even the higher apes live in groups and all the humans of prehistory, from the ape-like pithecanthropus to the more complex peoples of the paleolithic and neolithic periods, must necessarily have lived in communities. The race itself presumably became humanized by the progressive development of communal living which enhanced the survival prospects of the group in the face of the hazards of a hard environment. Out of this early community life there somehow developed the symbols of language as tools of communication and the gradual accretion and enrichment of a cultural heritage which could be transmitted from generation to generation. Primitive man was the slave of this heritage as it crystallized into habits, customs, folkways, *mores* from which the group brooked no departure. The group, moreover, was a tribal group, an extension of the family, a unit by virtue of common ancestry and ties of blood and kinship, with no sense of citizenship in a territorial community. The civilized State emerges only when the chieftain

—warrior, magician, medicine man, or "king" with power to lead and to enforce the law of custom—becomes also an embodiment of the authority to make law for the common guidance of all the inhabitants of a defined territory, without reference to blood relationships. Custom then becomes law, territorial propinquity replaces kinship as the basis of social cohesion, and "government," emerging out of the now established distinction between rulers and ruled, symbolizes a type of social control quite different from that which existed hitherto. In short, the State is born.

This process was apparently contemporaneous with the rise of towns and the stratification of primitive society into social classes. The first States of which anything is known were city-states. Which was cause and which effect is doubtful, but it is certain that political organization, as well as most other elements of every literate culture, appeared simultaneously with the contacts and interactions of urban life. Nomads and hunters have seldom developed a true State. Government as we know it arose when agriculture attached man to the soil and made possible the gathering together of large numbers of people within a small territory. At the same time castes and classes made their appearance, in some cases doubtless because of the effects of technological and economic changes, in others because of wars of conquest in which hunters and herdsmen of the mountains and deserts imposed their rule upon the peoples of the plains. The Shepherd Kings of early Egypt were conquerors of this type who imposed a landowning aristocracy of warriors upon the vanquished. Private property replaced communal ownership. Those who acquired property and economic power became the rulers and usually the exploiters of those less fortunate. Breadgivers became lawgivers. Every early State had its nobility and its priesthood. The essence of the State lay in the institutions and practices by which the ruling class maintained its authority over the ruled. Politics emerged as a struggle for power between groups and individuals striving to control and direct these institutions and practices to their own purposes. Government at worst was a process by which the rich and strong dominated the poor and weak to the advantage of those who wielded authority. At best it was a process by which some central symbol and embodiment of communal solidarity arbitrated between conflicting groups and classes within the territory of the State. In either case city life and class cleavages went hand in hand with statehood.

While international relations as we ordinarily think of them arose out of contacts between fully organized States, in another sense they preceded and accompanied the formation of States. It is quite probable that geographically separated communities had contacts with one another long before their cultures contained anything resembling the State as we know it now. These communities were neither nations nor States, but they made war upon one another and sometimes, in a small way, traded with one another as do the nation-states of the modern world. It is not unreasonable to suppose that the members of such primitive communities achieved a highly developed sense of solidarity precisely through such contacts with alien out-groups. Nothing unifies a body of people so readily as conflict with another community. Social cohesion is enhanced by war, and war was the normal relationship between separated communities in primitive times. War's demands for cooperation and leadership may well have been the chief incentive to political organization in early societies. Some authorities would insist that the relations between conquerors and conquered gave rise to the first forms of political authority and to the first procedures and institution of domination and obedience which we call the State.[1] In any case, the waging of war was the chief function of the early State and it is likely that its formation was much influenced by the exigencies of hostile contacts with enemy communities. It is at least arguable, therefore, that international relations in this sense preceded State-building and played a significant rôle in the process. Once States were established, their relationships with one another became more complex than the relationships between primitive, prepolitical communities and the conditions were present for the development of the first State Systems of ancient times.

2. CITY-STATES AND EMPIRES OF THE ANCIENT NEAR EAST

All history is but a seamless web; and he who endeavors to tell but a piece of it must feel that his first sentence tears the fabric.—SIR FREDERICK MAITLAND.

The earliest States known to modern scholars were the small city-states which appear at the dawn of written history in the fertile river valleys of the Nile, the Tigris-Euphrates, the Indus, and the Yangtse-Kiang, each the cradle of a great civilization. While the historical literature of the west contains little regarding the State Systems of ancient China and India, those of Mesopotamia and Egypt have been the objects of intensive investigation by historians and archaeologists. The earliest remains of these communities suggest that their inhabitants had already advanced far along the road from the primitive tribal group to the civilized territorial State generations before their development became a matter of written record. Somewhere between the Stone Age and the period when the use of metals became prevalent, groups of farmers along the Nile and the Tigris-Euphrates had gathered together in towns and had become members of already complex societies, with kings, warriors,

---

[1] See Franz Oppenheimer, *The State*, 1908. Also: "The State owes its origin to war. . . . Agriculture, slavery, and territoriality are the primary factors underlying State formation, but the force which actually welded them together to produce the State was war." M. R. Davie, *The Evolution of War*, 1929, pp. 174–175.

jurists, and administrators, nobles, priests, commoners, and slaves. The governments of these city-states were almost invariably monarchical and despotic in form, with supreme power vested in the sacred kingship, supported by a landed aristocracy and an established church.

With the internal political and cultural history of these early city-states we are not here concerned. It will suffice for present purposes to indicate the general nature of the relations between them and the type of State Systems which evolved out of these relations. The attitudes and policies which they adopted toward one another seem to have been much the same in the early State Systems of Egypt, Mesopotamia, India, and China, in spite of these regions being widely separated seats of very different cultures. The explanation of this similarity is to be found not in the internal structure of the States themselves, nor in contacts between the cultures leading to imitation and diffusion of a single pattern, but rather in the general conditions which inevitably prevail wherever a number of independent communities have political relations with one another.

These relations, for the most part, were those of war—so much so, in fact, that war came to be regarded as the normal and natural relationship between States. In all likelihood, the early States were the creations of war and warriors and the whole institution of government was from the beginning an embodiment of coercive power exercised by rulers over ruled for the economic advantage of the ruling caste and for the common defense of the community against outside enemies. The first city-states, and most of the later and larger States of the ancient world, were little islands of civilization in a sea of savagery, little centers of culturally advanced farmers and town dwellers surrounded by a wilderness peopled by barbarian nomads only too eager to emerge from their hills and forests to sack the cities of the rich valley lands. "Stranger" meant "enemy" and the relations between the city-states themselves, no less than their relations with the forces of outer darkness, were usually those of conflict. Each State sought to increase its security and enhance its power by expanding its territory, by subduing its neighbors, by plundering and enslaving the near-by peoples unable to defend themselves against armed attack. This competitive struggle for power took the form of almost incessant combat. In the land of the two rivers north of the Persian Gulf the original Sumerian inhabitants of the south were gradually conquered by Semitic invaders and settlers from the north. In both areas the *patesi* or ruler of each city-state—Ur, Erech, Adab, Lagash, Kish, Umma, and the rest— was more than likely to be engaged in hostilities with his neighbors. When he conquered adjacent communities, he usually assumed the more pretentious title of *lugal* or king. But these kingdoms were unstable structures, constantly dissolving and reforming under the impact of war, rebellion, and outside invasion. A similar situation probably prevailed through many centuries among the early cities of the Nile Valley, though at a remote period these communities were united, doubtless by conquest, into a single monarchy.

In such a situation there emerged very early a pattern of political relationships between the States which could be described in modern language as a "balance of power." The scantiness of existing records makes it impossible to indicate when and how the balance-of-power principle first appeared either in the early State System of Mesopotamia or in that of Egypt. But it is in the very nature of such State Systems that each unit should seek not merely to extend its own power at the expense of its weaker neighbors but to protect its own independence and existence against the menace of stronger rivals. Weak States thus allied themselves against strong States in order that no one might become sufficiently powerful to conquer the others. This practice was successful for many centuries in preserving the independence of each city-state of the Tigris-Euphrates area and preventing the political unification of the whole region by any one preponderantly powerful State. Not until the time of the Semitic conqueror, Sargon (about 2637–2581 B.C.), ruler of Agade and Kish, was it possible for one ruler to bring under his control most of the valley, and this only in the face of chronic rebellions. The work of unification continued under Sargon's grandson, Naram-Sin, "king of the four regions of the earth, conqueror of nine armies in one year," but this early empire soon fell to pieces from internal dissension and the raids of invaders from the mountains. Ultimately, after many vicissitudes, the balance of power between independent city-states came to an end with the establishment of the Babylonian Empire, whose illustrious king, Hammurabi (1947–1905 B.C.), conquered all his neighbors. Two centuries later Babylon fell before the Hittites from Asia Minor. In Egypt the epoch of the warring city-states was apparently shorter and the first dynasty of the Empire was established about 3200 B.C.

International politics among these early city-states, however, was not entirely a struggle for power between them through war. Peace prevailed from time to time when neighboring cities found it expedient to establish alliances or pacific relations between themselves by treaty. And it may be assumed that at such times commerce flourished and political contacts were maintained through the exchange of diplomatic emissaries. Little is known, however, of the peace-time practices of these States, since their annals are filled with tales of war and conquest. But it is clear that treaty agreements were frequently concluded and furnished the basis for peaceful relations. The earliest treaty of which any written record remains is one concluded about 3000 B.C. between the kings of Umma and Lagash who were involved in a boundary dispute. The controversy was submitted to the arbitration of Mesilim, King of Kish, who, with the aid of the appro-

priate deities, was successful in adjusting the difference between his
neighbors. The stone-carved text of a somewhat later treaty between the
same States is preserved upon the "stele of the vultures" in the Louvre.[1]
Knowledge of these early treaty negotiations is confused and fragmentary,
but enough is known to justify the conclusion that treaties were regularly

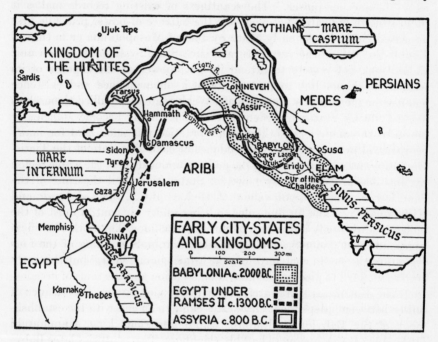

entered into between the city-states and that arbitration for the pacific
settlement of disputes was not an unfamiliar procedure.

Following the political unification of the city-states of the great river
valleys and of the plateaus of the Near East, there developed a larger
State System and a new balance of power between the early oriental
monarchies—Egypt, Assyria, the smaller States of the eastern Mediterranean littoral such as Mitanni, Syria, and Phoenicia, and the Hittite
State in Asia Minor whose armies overwhelmed Babylon about 1750 B.C.
For several centuries these States engaged in chronic conflicts with one
another, each seeking its place in the sun through the conquest of its
neighbors. The weaker States preserved their independence by playing
off the more powerful against one another. Coalitions and alliances formed
and dissolved in anarchical confusion within the area between the Sahara
and the Caucasus, the Black Sea and Arabia. The borderlands and buffer
States between the major contestants were frequently the scenes of bloody

[1] See L. W. King and H. R. Hall, *Egypt and Western Asia*, 1910, pp. 170–173.

combats between rival hosts. The Egyptians and the Hittites were the most formidable of the empire-builders and war between them for control of the eastern Mediterranean seacoast was endemic, with neither side enjoying a decisive advantage. After many changes of fortune, Hattushilish III, King of the Hittites, negotiated a treaty with Rameses II, in order that he might be at peace with his southern enemies in the face of attacks upon his dominions by the Assyrians from the east.

This Hittite-Egyptian treaty, which was apparently concluded about 1280 B.C., is of unusual interest, less so because of its political significance at the time than because of the fact that it is one of the few early treaties of which the text has been preserved. Two incomplete copies of the Egyptian version and a fragment of the Hittite version are extant, both taken from the original in Babylonian, which was seemingly the diplomatic language of the day. It was a treaty of peace and alliance, "witnessed by the thousand gods, by the male gods and the female gods." Like most early treaties, including those of the early modern period of the Western State System, it provided for perpetual peace between the parties. The obvious impermanence of such a pledge led to the general abandonment of this formula in the nineteenth century, though it was revived in modified form in the Pact of Paris of August 27, 1928. The treaty between Rameses and Hattushilish reveals these monarchs renouncing war as an instrument of national policy thirty-two centuries before the days of Kellogg and Briand:

There shall be no hostilities between them forever. The great chief of the Hittites shall not pass over into the land of Egypt, forever, to take anything therefrom; Rameses, the great chief of Egypt, shall not pass over into the land of the Hittites to take anything therefrom, forever. . . . If another people (or state) shall come, as an enemy, against the lands of Rameses, the great chief of Egypt, and he shall send to the great chief of the Hittites, saying "Come with me with your army against him," the great chief of the Hittites shall come, and the great King of the Hittites shall slay his enemy. But if it shall not be the desire of the Great Chief of the Hittites to come, he shall send his infantry and his chariotry, and shall slay his enemy. Or, if Rameses, the great chief of Egypt, be provoked against delinquent subjects, when they have committed some other fault against him, and he shall come to slay them, then the great chief of the Hittites shall act with the lord of Egypt.

This obligation, constituting a treaty of alliance for mutual defense and the suppression of revolution, was made reciprocal, as was also the provision for the extradition of fugitives from justice:

If any of the great men of the land of Egypt shall flee and shall come to the great chief of the Hittites, from either town, or . . . of the lands of Rameses, the great chief of Egypt, and they shall come to the great chief of the Hittites, then the great chief of the Hittites shall not receive them, but the great chief of the Hittites shall cause them to be brought to Rameses, the great chief of Egypt, their lord.

[11]

This arrangement evidently contemplated the extradition of political offenders, who were regarded then as more dangerous than common criminals, though they are now usually exempted from the operation of extradition conventions.[1] Some years after the conclusion of this agreement Hattushilish paid a state visit to the land of the pyramids and his daughter was married to the Egyptian monarch. International peace was thus reinforced by matrimonial bliss—an arrangement which has commended itself to many reigning houses in other periods and civilizations.

In all probability the treaty of 1280 B.C. was in no way unique, but was typical of similar agreements between these and other States, the records of which have been lost. Here, as always, contacts between independent political communities led to the evolution of a more or less elaborate system of treaty relationships and a high development of the art of diplomacy, as well as of the science of war. The passing generations brought great changes in the equilibrium of power between the units of this State System, with old States giving way to new and the uncontrolled ebb and flow of international politics creating new situations with the unrolling years. The Hittite Empire in Asia Minor collapsed at the end of the thirteenth century B.C. under the assaults of migrating hordes from the west. Egypt itself narrowly escaped conquest by invaders from the Libyan desert. It declined in power until it became a mere appanage of the new Asiatic empires of a later period. Freed from the pressure of stronger rivals, the Aramaeans, the Philistines, and the Hebrews established States in Syria and Palestine which warred upon one another in traditional fashion. The long reign of Solomon (c.975–935 B.C.) found the Israelites masters of this region under the rule of a monarch who achieved as much by diplomacy as by war. He brought brief glory to his State by exploiting the subject peoples of his realm, promoting trade, and forming astute political engagements with his neighbors. His kingdom disintegrated after his death, however, and the rising star of Assyria began to cast its light over the entire international arena. The ambitious kings of these eastern peoples conducted a long series of successful military campaigns, extending over several centuries, and ultimately reduced to vassalage most of the surrounding States, which failed to combine effectively against the newcomer. In this fashion the whole State System of the Near East came temporarily to an end and gave way to the first of the "world empires"—an imposing military and administrative structure which, in its palmiest days, extended from the Persian Gulf to southern Asia Minor and from the mountains south of the Caspian Sea to the first cataract of the Nile.

---

[1] See on the text of this treaty the article by Langdon and Gardiner in the *Journal of Egyptian Archaeology*, VI, 1920, pp. 179ff.

The Assyrian Empire, to be sure, disintegrated under the combined attacks of new enemies, among whom the Medes who came out of the east were the most formidable. The capture and destruction of its capital, Nineveh, in 612 B.C., completed the process of dissolution. Assyria proper was annexed to the Median Empire. Egypt and Babylon resumed their independence and fought for the control of Syria which the Babylonians finally conquered. In 586 B.C. Jerusalem was stormed, sacked, and razed by the great Babylonian monarch, Nebuchadnezzar, and from that day to this Palestine has remained under foreign rule. Many decades of confused conflict followed between States, principalities, and nomad hordes, until the military might of the Persians, under Cyrus, Cambyses, and Darius, enabled them to build a new "world empire," even larger than that of Assyria and covering all of the civilized world from the Indus to the Aegean. The end-point in the evolution of the early State Systems of the Near East was thus the military conquest and the destruction as independent political entities of all the weaker States by the most powerful. City-states, principalities, and kingdoms became administrative districts or satrapies of a single great State, semi-feudal and unstable in its political organization, but wielding authority over vast areas inhabited by culturally diverse peoples and bringing peace and order out of the anarchical diversity of the earlier State Systems. World-wide imperialism became in fact the prevalent form of political organization as an alternative to a system of competing independent States struggling with one another for territory and power.

3. THE GREEK STATE SYSTEM

Man is the measure of all things.—PROTAGORAS.

For this is the bond of men in cities, that all shall rightly preserve the laws.—EURIPEDES.

During the centuries of war and empire-building in western Asia there had developed in the eastern Mediterranean another great culture—the fairest and brightest of all in the ancient world in the memory of later ages. The story of its growth and fruition has been told a thousand times and is in no need of repetition here. Its political institutions and the new State System which it evolved, however, are of immense interest to all students of international relations because, like so many other aspects of this civilization, they exhibit patterns of thought and action which have a striking resemblance to corresponding developments in contemporary western culture. Sir Henry Maine doubtless exaggerated when he said that everything that lives and moves in the modern world, excepting only the blind forces of nature, is Greek in its origin. Nevertheless, the debt of western civilization to the culture of ancient Greece is enormous. As later artists, poets, and philosophers all found inspiration in the aesthetic and

[13]

intellectual legacy of the Greeks, so statesmen, diplomats, and political theorists have similarly found much that is worthy of their close attention in the political life and international relations of these remarkable people of the Aegean.

In the Greek peninsula and its adjacent islands, as in the early civilizations of the Nile and Tigris-Euphrates valleys, the city-state was the primary unit of political organization. Throughout its history the Greek State System remained an aggregation of city-states. The citizens of these urban communities, however, were from the beginning bound together by a greater sense of cultural unity than usually prevails under such conditions, for they had developed a common language, a common religion, and common conceptions of social and political organization before they settled the peninsula and constructed their cities in its valleys and on its coasts. Before their coming a great pre-Hellenic civilization had arisen in the eastern Mediterranean, with its center on the island of Crete, and had flourished for a thousand years (c.2400–1400 B.C.). In the days of its decline successive waves of semi-nomadic peoples entered the region from the north, came into contact with the more highly developed Minoan culture, and created in course of time the civilization of the Homeric period, so called from the great epic poems of the *Iliad* and the *Odyssey* in which are described, presumably by Homer, the heroic episodes of the war with Troy and its aftermath. It was this civilization, imposed upon Minoan-Mycenaean society, which prevailed in the peninsula when the earliest city-states became known to written history.

Existing evidence indicates that the Greek city-states emerged as definite political entities through war and that the exigencies of war largely dictated their social and political organization. The original tribal organization of the Greek peoples disappeared as they settled down to agricultural life and the primitive monarchy gave way to an aristocracy of landowners. The early Spartans, in the building of their communistic military State, became the ruling class in the commonwealth which they had created by conquering their neighbors and reducing them to the rank of *helots* or peasant serfs and of *perioikoi* or merchants. These subject classes had no political rights in a State ruled by the citizen-warriors who owned the land. By war and diplomacy Sparta eventually created a confederacy of city-states within the region over which Spartan power could be effectively exercised. Athens similarly seems to have emerged out of the fusion of petty communities and the extension by military means of the power of the dominant group over all of Attica. The relationship of the classes within these early States, in terms of the distribution of wealth and political power, reflects the military origins of the States themselves. Politics within the State revolved about the forms of institutionalized authority through which the wealthy aristocracy of the nobles, descend-

[14]

ants of the original conquerors, administered public affairs. The subject classes and the poor wrested privileges from their rulers from time to time, but even in the brightest days of Athenian "democracy," Greek society was a hierarchy of classes resting at bottom upon slavery. Politics between the city-states, here as in every State System composed of independent political entities, was a struggle for power in which the larger units strove to conquer the smaller and the weak combined against the strong for mutual protection. Commercial advantages throughout the eastern Mediterranean and overseas colonies, scattered as far as Sicily and the coasts of Italy and Spain, were means for the enhancement of State power and they figured prominently among the stakes of diplomacy and warfare among the city-states.

These general characteristics of the Greek State System remained fairly constant throughout its history. Sparta and Argos were hereditary rivals in the south, until the former established its supremacy over the Peloponnese by defeating its enemy decisively about 494 B.C. Wars between the city-states were interspersed with hostilities against the Persians to the east, but the disunity and lack of effective cooperation between the various Greek cities and colonies opposing Darius weakened their strength. When the menace of Persian conquest became imminent, Athens, Sparta, and their respective confederates and allies joined forces and defeated the foe at Marathon in 490 B.C. When the external threat waned the city-states resumed their feuds. The resumption of the assault by Darius' successor, Xerxes, led to the formation of the Hellenic League for common defense, though not without internal wrangling and some disaffection. Greek sea power prevailed over the invaders at Salamis (480 B.C.) and in the following year at Plataea a new Persian army was beaten back and the war carried into Asia Minor. At the same time an attack by Carthage on the Greek colonies in Sicily was frustrated. The Etruscans were no more successful in their efforts to conquer the Greek colony-cities on the Italian mainland. By the first quarter of the fifth century Hellenism was triumphant throughout the whole Mediterranean area. The disappearance of the Persian menace was accompanied by a recrudescence of the rivalries which always disrupted the leagues and confederations of the city-states.

Without attempting to trace in detail the later history of the Greek State System, it should be noticed that the century following the Persian wars was marked by a tendency on the part of the more powerful city-states to extend their dominion over their weaker neighbors and allies to a point where their possessions assumed imperial dimensions by the standards of the time. An almost incessant military struggle for supremacy ensued among the various leagues and "empires" which were established. Under Themistocles, Athens built up a maritime league—the Delian

Confederacy—which ultimately became an instrument through which the Athenians, by adroit use of diplomacy and military force, imposed their authority upon the other members. Sparta was likewise the center of the Peloponnesian league and the two great coalitions, in their rivalry for control of the lesser cities, drifted toward war. The Athenian Empire under Pericles, with its allied States and dependencies, covered northeastern Greece, portions of the Peloponnesus, most of the Aegean islands from Euboea to Rhodes, the coasts of Thrace and Asia Minor, and the shores of the Sea of Marmora. An attempt to wrest Egypt from Persia

ended in disaster in 454 B.C. Conflicts with Sparta took place from time to time, as well as wars against disgruntled allies. In 445 B.C., following Athenian reverses, the two leagues reached an agreement to submit future disputes to arbitration. The attempt of Pericles to establish a powerful land empire ended in failure, but the Athenian empire of the sea was increased by new conquests and colonies.

In 431 B.C. the truce was broken and the great Peloponnesian War began, with the Athenians striving to establish their hegemony and the Spartans professing to fight to free the Greeks from enslavement by Athens. Some States joined Athens, others Sparta, while a few remained neutral. After many vicissitudes of battles, sieges, blockades, and diplomatic moves and counter-moves, the Athenian cause was weakened by the disastrous expedition against Syracuse, the Sicilian colony of Corinth. Finally the Peloponnesian land and sea forces, under Lysander of Sparta, overcame the Athenians and obliged them to surrender in 404 B.C. Spartan hegemony was transitory, however, for the discontent of her allies, coupled with new wars with the Persians, led to a coalition against Sparta and her confederates on the part of Athens, Corinth, Argos, and Thebes. The last-named State achieved a position of equally temporary supremacy, followed by further chaos throughout Hellas which opened the way to foreign conquest by the Macedonians to the north. After preliminary conquests and diplomatic maneuvers Philip of Macedon crushed the Greek forces at Chaerona in 338 B.C. and established his power throughout the peninsula. With this event the Greek cities lost their independence for all time and the Greek State System came to an end.

While the most obvious characteristic of this State System was the incessant struggle for power between its members and the constant resort to military coercion and diplomatic trickery to attain the ends of State, it developed certain international practices and institutions for pacific collaboration which were far in advance of their counterparts in earlier State Systems. Although the Greeks all acknowledged primary allegiance to their local State and were jealous of its sovereignty and power, they were also aware of themselves as members of one race with the same gods and a common culture, quite distinct from that of the outer "barbarians." This circumstance promoted intimate relations between them even when they were not threatened by a common enemy. The network of treaties which the States concluded with one another brought them at times very close to the conception of peace as a normal relationship between them. Treaties were always, in form at least, between equal and independent sovereignties, and were sanctioned by Zeus, the guardian of oaths. They established the conditions of peace between the parties, sometimes in perpetuity, sometimes for a term of years. Commercial treaties were common and a great variety of other subjects was dealt with in the numerous agreements which the city-states entered into. As early as the remote period of the Homeric epics, ceremonials had developed about the making of treaties which are described in the *Iliad* in the account of the compact between the Trojans and the Achaeans setting forth the conditions of the combat between Menelaus and Alexander for the love of Helen.[1] The di-

---

[1] The ceremonial embodied (1) a preliminary announcement by the heralds, (2) an invocation to the gods to bear witness to the transaction, (3) a declaration of oath, (4) a recital of the conditions of the engagement, (5) the offering of a sacrifice, (6) a libation of wine, (7) joining of hands, (8) the utterance of the imprecation: "Zeus, most glorious, most mighty, and ye other immortal gods! Whosoever shall first commit wrong contrary to their pledges, may their brains and their children's be dispersed on the ground, like this wine, and may their wives prove faithless." See Coleman Phillipson, *The International Law and Custom of Ancient Greece and Rome*, I, pp. 386–387.

vine sanction of treaties was always recognized by solemn oaths and imprecations. Heralds, ambassadors, secretaries, and a technical terminology became a regular part of the proceedings. Negotiations were usually public, though private conferences and even secret treaties were not unknown. Each party retained a copy in its own dialect, duly signed by the negotiators and stamped with the public seal of the signatory States. Treaty texts were often engraved on marble or bronze and kept in the temples. Hostages were frequently exchanged, especially in treaties of alliance, to insure the execution of the compact. Treaties might legitimately be broken by one of the parties only if an inconsistency existed between two engagements, if enforcement would lead to hostilities with a friendly third State, or if a complete change of circumstances had taken place.

The principles and procedures governing the exchange of diplomatic representatives also reached a high degree of development in the Greek State System. While permanent embassies were not exchanged, a hierarchy of diplomatic agents developed in terms of rank and prestige. Only fully independent States had the right to send and receive ambassadors. Refusal to receive an envoy was analogous, in modern terms, to non-recognition of the sending State or to a rupture of diplomatic relations foreshadowing war. Envoys were received and dispatched by the popular assemblies, which likewise drew up their instructions. Only persons of distinction, wisdom, and ripe years were chosen. From an early period all diplomatic representatives and their attachés enjoyed inviolability and exemption from local authority and were recognized to have the right to come and go as they pleased in the execution of their duties. The principles of diplomatic immunities were not always carefully observed with respect to non-Greek peoples. When the envoys of Darius came to Athens and Sparta to demand earth and water as a sign of submission, they were thrown into a ditch by the Athenians and into a well by the Spartans. But subsequently two Spartan nobles offered their lives to Xerxes in atonement for this lawless act of violence. The Persian monarch, with singular magnanimity, replied that he would not follow the example of his foes in breaking the common laws of mankind. A rudimentary consular service was likewise developed in the form of the institution of the *proxenoi*, who were permanent officials appointed to furnish commercial information to their home State and to give advice and assistance to its citizens abroad. These officials, however, unlike most modern consuls, were citizens of the State where they exercised their functions rather than of the State which appointed them. They had a wide variety of duties, both political and commercial, and they often served as diplomatic representatives and arbitrators.

While Greek scholars, jurists, and writers, including the prolific and versatile Aristotle, never treated in systematic form any body of law and custom comparable to modern international law, the actual practices of the city-states, as has already been suggested, were based upon general recognition of a body of rules and principles binding upon the members of the State System. There was assumed to exist a universal "law of nature" or of reason to which all men were bound. Although there was, in regard to many matters, one law for the Greeks and another for the barbarians, the relations among the Greek States themselves were regulated by principles which closely approximate modern international law. The details of this somewhat inchoate system of jurisprudence cannot be dealt with here, but it covered such subjects as personal and property rights as affected by conflicting laws of various States ("private international law" in modern terminology), naturalization, status of aliens, right of asylum, extradition, alliances, treaties, diplomatic privileges and immunities, and the like. The international law of war was no less developed than that of peace. Cleinias, in Plato's *Laws*, declares that "in reality every city is in a natural state of war with every other," but in spite of this prevalent view peace was often regarded as a normal relationship. War was condemned as an evil, not to be suffered without a just cause and then only after the exhaustion of diplomatic expedients and a formal declaration. The rules of warfare were designed to mitigate the horrors, cruelties, and barbaric practices which had usually prevailed in the conflicts of the Asiatic States with one another, though there was little uniformity of behavior on the part of the Greeks in this respect. While instances of harshness and savagery can be found, temples, priests, envoys, and captives were usually spared, prisoners were ransomed and exchanged, truces were observed, and treachery and needless destruction were deplored. The neutralization of certain localities, ordinarily the sites of shrines and sanctuaries, was not uncommon and certain rudimentary principles of neutrality were widely recognized.

Another feature of the Greek State System deserving of special mention was the extensive development of arbitration and of permanent institutions and agencies of international cooperation, foreshadowing what has come to be described as "international organization" in the Western State System of the contemporary period. The pacific settlement of disputes by submission to an impartial third party was a procedure familiar to the Greeks from the earliest times. It came to be resorted to so frequently and was developed to a point so far in advance of previous practice that it may well be regarded as one of the most significant contributions of the Greek State System to its successors. Disputes were often submitted to the arbitration of the Delphic oracle, the Amphictyonic Council, a third State, or a tribunal of individuals picked by the litigants.

Treaties of alliance frequently contained "compromise clauses" providing for the submission to arbitration of such disputes as might arise between the parties. From an alliance to a confederation was but a step and the Greek confederations and leagues often served as agencies for the peaceable adjustment of controversies between their members and for the promotion of cooperation in dealing with matters of common interest. The earliest confederations or amphictyonies were religious in character and were devoted to worship in common temples and the communal celebration of religious festivals. The antiquity of the Delphian Amphictyony, later called the Amphictyonic League, is attested by the fact that it was an association not of cities but of the twelve kindred tribes of the Greek peoples, each with two votes in the semiannual councils at Delphi and Thermopylae. This organization has sometimes been described, not without reason, as the Greek prototype of the League of Nations. In the course of its long history it promoted religious unity among the Greeks, diminished the barbarities of war, arbitrated disputes, and subsequently became an instrument of Macedonian, and later of Roman, hegemony over the peninsula. The other Greek leagues and confederacies were true organizations of city-states, though in some cases they were approximations to modern federal governments and in others they were the means through which a powerful State dominated its weaker allies.[1] Such were the first and second Athenian leagues, the Peloponnesian League, and the Achaean League.

That the Greek State System never attained stability, unity, and peace, and finally collapsed before foreign foes was due to the fact that its members, despite their common cultural heritage, were never capable over any long period of time of subordinating the special and particular interests of the local *polis* to the general interests of the Greek peoples as a whole. The procedures of diplomacy, the principles of international law, the machinery of arbitration, and the institutions of international organization never developed to a point where a true international government emerged, capable of keeping the peace and safeguarding the security of each through the cooperation of all. The ruling class of each State pursued its own interests at the expense of its rivals and engaged in an incessant diplomatic and military struggle with its neighbors for economic advantages and political preponderance. The resulting balance of power was easily upset and conflict was inevitable so long as no single State was able to reduce all the others to subjection. Under these circumstances the collectivity of States was incapable of harmonizing rival claims to power on the basis of the general interest. While the clash of

[1] In 1863 the English historian, E. A. Freeman, published his *History of Federal Government from the Establishment of the Achaean League to the Dissolution of the United States of America.*

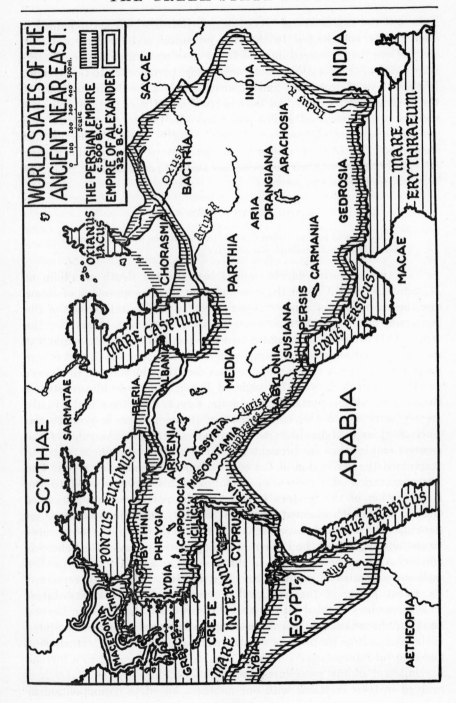

WORLD STATES OF THE ANCIENT NEAR EAST.

THE PERSIAN EMPIRE c. 500 B.C.

EMPIRE OF ALEXANDER 323 B.C.

Scale

0 100 200 300 400 500 mi.

arms and the exaltation of city-state patriotism which accompanied it undoubtedly contributed to the rich profusion and fertility of Greek civilization, they rendered impossible the development of a type of inter-state political organization which could assure permanence to the System. In their days of decadence and exhaustion, when the bright radiance of the great creative period had burned itself out, the city-states fell easy victims to the power of Philip and Alexander of Macedon, rulers of a younger and more vigorous people to the north. Amid all the political changes of the ensuing centuries in the eastern Mediterranean they never fully recovered their independence and the peace between them was kept by the foreign conqueror.

4. THE ROMAN WORLD STATE

Wars are to be undertaken in order that it may be possible to live in peace without molestation.—CICERO, *De Officiis.*

The two centuries which elapsed between the death of Philip of Macedon in 336 B.C. and the establishment of the supremacy of Rome saw the emergence of a new State System in the Near East out of the fragments of the great empire created by Philip's son, Alexander the Great. This extraordinary young man was perhaps the most spectacular military and administrative genius of all time. In his hands the art of war became for the first time an applied science. His Macedonian phalanxes overthrew and destroyed the might of Persia and made him master of Greece, Asia Minor, Syria, Mesopotamia, Egypt, Babylonia, and a vastly greater territory to the east extending through what is now Persia, Turkestan, and Afghanistan to the borders of India. As ruler of the greatest empire thus far brought under the control of a single State, he sanctioned the deification of the royal office and became as a god. The interpenetration of cultures which followed his conquests led to the Hellenization of the western Orient and the partial orientalization of Greece. But death claimed youth in 323 B.C. and the vast imperial structure which he had reared went with him to the tomb. Out of its ruins arose the Kingdom of the Ptolemies in Egypt, the realm of the Seleucids north of Arabia, the Kingdoms of the Arsacids and the Bactrians farther east, and a number of smaller States in Asia Minor. Macedonia remained the Great Power of the west, still dominating the Greek city-states, which were now divided into two rival federations, the Aetolian League and the Achaean League. Out of the struggles between the succession States of the Alexandrine Empire a new balance of power emerged. The turbulent and colorful international politics of the Hellenistic Age led to a further development of the procedures and practices which earlier States had evolved in their relations with one another. An effete cosmopolitanism accompanied the intermingling of the decadent cultures, and the passing generations saw the twilight of a long decline slowly settling down over the peoples of the eastern Mediterranean basin.

Meanwhile, far to the west, a new sun was rising which was eventually destined to shine over the whole of the western civilized world. The remoter origins of the Roman State are obscure. It would appear that between the eighth and the fifth centuries B.C., when central Italy was dominated by the Etruscans, an alien community established itself on the banks of the Tiber. Myth and tradition later attributed its creation to the fabled Romulus and Remus or to wandering Trojans, survivors of the war with the Greeks, whose probably imaginary exploits were so beautifully described, many centuries later, in the great epic of Rome's greatest poet, the *Aeneid* of Virgil. The villages and towns of the Tiber achieved political unity under a monarchy whose later kings were conquering Etruscan despots. The peoples of the region had gradually emerged from tribal life into a society dominated by a landowning aristocracy (patricians) which ruled over the mass of peasant farmers and artisans (plebeians). The early monarchy was overthrown in 509 B.C. by a joint rising of the patricians and plebeians against the Etruscans, after which the patricians seized all political power for themselves and established a "republic." About 493 B.C. the Roman city-state formed an alliance with the Latin League of city-states to the south for mutual protection against Etruria which was at length conquered by the Romans. Rome's allies gradually lost their independence after the Latin War of 338 B.C. New wars followed against the Samnites, Gauls, Etruscans, and the Greeks of the coast cities. By 265 B.C. Roman power was unchallenged throughout Italy. Through military prowess, the construction of roads, and the planting of colonies in conquered territory, the city-state on the Tiber had become mistress of the peninsula.

While the internal history of Rome during the ensuing period was a story of the foundation of Roman law and the gradual increase in political power of the plebeians at the expense of the ruling patrician class, its external history revolves about the great contest with Carthage and the subsequent extension of Roman power over the Mediterranean. The Roman conquest of Italy disrupted the balance of power between the other States of the central Mediterranean area. Rome was viewed with alarm by the great maritime State in north Africa which dominated the coast from Gibraltar to Egypt and exercised authority over southern Spain, the Balearic Isles, Sicily, Malta, and part of Sardinia. Roman intervention in the affairs of Syracuse led to the first open clash of arms in 264 B.C. After a long and exhausting combat, Carthage made peace in 241, agreeing to evacuate Sicily, to abstain from any attack upon Syracuse, now Rome's ally, to surrender Roman prisoners without ransom, and to pay an indemnity. In 238 Rome took advantage of a mutiny in the Carthaginian army to seize Sardinia and Corsica and thus win, the undying hatred of her hereditary foe. Carthage sought compensation by expansion in Spain. The second Punic War opened in 219 B.C. The greatest of the Carthaginian generals, Hannibal, led a formidable host from Spain over the Alps into Italy itself. Three-quarters of the Roman army were destroyed in the first great battle at Trebia. Disaster followed disaster and the dilatory guerrilla tactics of Q. Fabius, who was made dictator, were without decisive results. On the field of Cannae, in 216, Hannibal's superb cavalry almost annihilated a Roman army of 80,000 men. Many of Rome's Italian allies deserted her, while Macedonia allied itself to the enemy and threatened to invade Italy. But Rome joined forces with Pergamum and the Aetolian League, both at war with Macedonia, and thus frustrated this plan. For ten years Hannibal was held in check in southern Italy and in 207 an army of reinforcements under his brother, Hasdrubal, was crushed by the Roman legions at Metaurus in the north. Four years later Hannibal withdrew to Carthage, his invasion of Italy a final failure. Spain was wrested from the enemy by Scipio, who carried the war into Africa and compelled the Carthaginians to sue for peace in 202 B.C. Carthage was compelled to pay a huge indemnity, to be spread over fifty years, was deprived of Numidia and of all her non-African possessions, and was forbidden to wage any future wars without Rome's permission. Rome was now master of the middle sea and had achieved the position of the greatest military power of the ancient world.

Had the remaining independent States of the Mediterranean basin appreciated the ultimate menace to themselves which the Roman victory over Carthage represented, had they combined their forces against the strongest unit of the State System as balance-of-power considerations dictated, the legions of Rome might not have been able to achieve triumph after triumph along the road of empire and deprive them, one by one, of their independence. But this union of the weak against the strong was never consummated. Macedonia and Syria conspired to deprive Egypt of her possessions and in the resulting complications Rome found her opportunity to interfere in the East. In 200 B.C. war was declared on Macedonia, with Rhodes, Pergamum, and the Greek leagues on the Roman side. In 197 B.C. the phalanx was conquered by the legion at Cynoscephalae and Macedonia was compelled to accept a Roman peace. When the Aetolian League invited Antiochus, King of Syria, to assist it in checking the power of Rome, war followed once more, with Rhodes and Pergamum again Roman allies (191). Antiochus was defeated and deprived of Asia Minor. In 146, following further conflicts, Macedonia was destroyed as an independent State and became a Roman province, while Rhodes and Pergamum were shortly afterward reduced to a similar status. The Greek leagues were dissolved and though the fiction of the independence of certain of the city-states was retained for another century, Roman power was supreme in the Hellenic world. In 146 B.C. there also took place the last Punic War, culminating in the complete destruction of Carthage. The insistent injunction of Cato in the Senate— "Carthago delenda est!"—was thus at last fulfilled and the territory of Rome's erstwhile enemy became the province of Africa.

Internal constitutional struggles between parties, factions, and classes within the metropolis hampered the further progress of imperial expansion, but only temporarily. In the Jugurthine War (112–106 B.C.) Numidia was almost lost and Italy itself was menaced by a new invasion of the Gauls from the northern forests. In both cases the day was saved by Marius, seven times consul of the Republic. The revolt of Mithridates VI, King of Pontus, led to a general rebellion of the Greeks against Roman rule, but under the leadership of Sulla the legions reestablished Rome's power in the Near East. Pompey completed the task which Sulla had begun and formed the First Triumvirate with Caesar and Crassus as its other members. Caesar, operating in Gaul (59–49 B.C.), carried Roman power to the Rhine and the Channel and even led his soldiers into Germany and Britain. Like his predecessors and rivals, Caesar used his military prestige to advance his political fortunes, overthrowing Pompey and making himself master of the Roman State. At the time of his murder in 44 B.C. Rome was already a world empire. At the close of the civil war which ensued, Octavius Augustus made himself *princeps* or "First Citizen" (27 B.C.–14 A.D.). He extended Roman power over Egypt and the region south of the Danube and restored peace, order, and prosperity to the Roman world. The simplicity of the early republic had already given way to the gaudy glory of military imperialism. "Princeps" became "Imperator." The name "Caesar" was taken as an imperial title and the government of the Roman State become more and more absolutist. During the middle period of the third century Franks, Goths, Moors, and other barbarians made damaging incursions into the Empire, but the great World State was reorganized, on the basis of the personal despotism of the emperor, by Diocletian (284–305 A.D.). Under Constantine (306–337) the capital was transferred to Byzantium (Constantinople) and in 392 Theodosius made Christianity the state religion. Three years later the Empire was completely divided into east and west, with one capital at Constantinople and the other at Milan or Ravenna, each with its own emperor.

As a universal State, Rome had no international relations. It had no contacts with the States of the Far East and few with those of India, while its relations with the quasi-states of the outer barbarians were never on a basis of equality. During its earlier history, however, before its legions had transformed the Mediterranean State System into a world empire, it had developed certain procedures and practices in its dealings with other States which are worthy of brief notice. Like most ancient peoples the Romans for a long period regarded themselves as being at war with all States with which no treaty of peace had been concluded. From the early days of Rome decisions of war and peace and the negotiation of treaties were entrusted to the College of Fetials (*collegium fetialium*). All wars were "just wars," declared and conducted in accordance with elaborate ceremonial rules and only after efforts at a pacific solution of the controversy had failed. If the *pater patratus* of the Fetials, acting as negotiator, failed to achieve a peaceful settlement, he so reported to the Senate. In the event of a decision for war, he hurled a bloody spear on the soil of the enemy to the accompaniment of appropriate oaths and invocations to Jupiter and other deities. As Rome expanded, the Fetials were represented by envoys and the ceremony of hurling the spear was performed, in purely symbolic fashion, on the Campus Martius or, later, before the temple of Bellonus. The Fetials were also entrusted with the conclusion of treaties, but foreign envoys had audiences with the Senate during the month of February in the *Grecostasis*, an open tribune near the Capitol. In the imperial period, the Emperor took over these functions. Almost all Roman treaties were unequal and in perpetuity in the sense that they imposed upon the other party a permanent status of dependence. The *ius gentium* of the Romans was not a body of true international law, but a set of legal principles adapted to the problems arising out of the relations of Roman citizens with citizens of other States which were friends or allies of Rome. Despite the influence of Greek models upon them, the Romans never developed any conception of international law or relations based upon a system of independent States dealing with one another as equals. All was judged by Roman standards. The vision of world dominion was at all times, consciously or unconsciously, inherent in the attitudes and practices of the Roman State in its dealings with other peoples. The World Empire in its final form rested upon the extinction of the earlier States and State Systems by Roman military power. While it was a huge international or cosmopolitan structure made up of very diverse elements, its whole organization and indeed its very existence precluded the possibility of those customs, procedures, and institutions of international intercourse which inevitably develop within a society of equal and independent political entities.

It was not without cause that the peoples of later ages came to view this great World State of the Caesars as the most magnificent political structure ever reared by the hand of man. At the time of its greatest territorial extent, under Trajan (98–117 A.D.), its forty-four provinces stretched from the borders of Scotland to the frontiers of India, from the Pillars of Hercules to the Black Sea and the Caucasus, from the Danube to

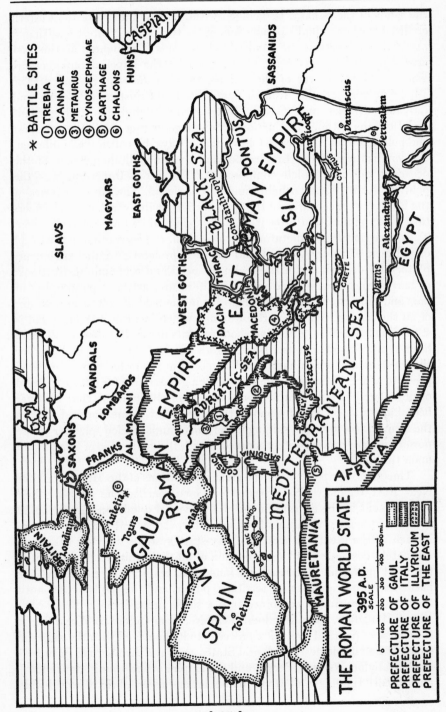

BATTLE SITES

* ① TREBIA
  ② CANNAE
  ③ METAURUS
  ④ CYNOSCEPHALAE
  ⑤ CARTHAGE
  ⑥ CHALONS

THE ROMAN WORLD STATE
395 A.D.
SCALE
0 100 200 300 400 500 mi.

PREFECTURE OF GAUL
PREFECTURE OF ITALY
PREFECTURE OF ILLYRICUM
PREFECTURE OF THE EAST

the sands of the Sahara. It included within its confines all of the western civilized world and had a population, in the time of its greatest wealth and prosperity, of perhaps one hundred million souls. Throughout all this vast area, threaded by well-built roads, ruled by the imperial bureaucracy, guarded by the power of the legions, the *Pax Romana* prevailed. The administrators of the Roman law meted out justice to Latins and Libyans, Greeks and Gauls, Britons and Babylonians, Egyptians and Illyrians without distinction of language or race. Military conquest and political unification were followed, as always, by cultural assimilation. The civilization of the Empire became a cosmopolitan mélange of the decadent cultures which composed it. The great Imperium was the political form of the twilight time of Classicism. The later centuries of the Empire were centuries of that progressive decline which seems to overtake every civilization after it has fully achieved its own self-realization. They were centuries of dictatorship, despotism, and corruption in the world of politics; of slavery, bread and circuses, proletarian impoverishment, plutocratic degeneracy in the realm of social and economic institutions; of barren and bizarre dilettantism in literature, art, and philosophy; of fads and fancies and neurotic religiosity in the field of cults and worship; of all the phenomena, in short, of an age which has run its course and is stumbling toward the gathering shadows of its doom. But despite all these later symptoms of *malaise*, here was an empire which had endured for six centuries and which had brought more of unity, order, prosperity, and peace to a larger human community over a greater area for a longer period of time than had ever been known before—and, be it added, than has ever been known since. Small wonder, therefore, that Rome lingered long in the memories of men as a shining imperium of unparalleled splendor whose power and glory were contemporaneous with the golden age of humankind upon the earth.

Thus the State Systems of the great civilizations of the Mediterranean-Near East region which preceded our own reached the close of their development in the establishment of a universal dominion embracing all civilized humanity within its frontiers. The pattern had run true to form in each of the great cultures. The city-state systems in every case were ultimately destroyed by the subjection of all their units to the control of the most powerful. The resulting kingdoms, empires, or confederations battled with one another for territory, power, and the spoils of war until they, too, were finally combined into a single great domain. From city-state to kingdom, from kingdom to empire, from empire to World State, the course of political evolution proceeds to its final goal with the majestic sweep of inevitable destiny. World States arise and disintegrate in succession—Babylon, Assyria, Persia, and the empire of the young Alexander—until finally the might of Rome builds an enduring fabric of world-wide

[28]

political organization in which all independent States have been merged. Throughout all these centuries, viewed in retrospect, international relations and the various State Systems in which they developed were but the phenomena of the slow transition from the city-state to universal empire, so well epitomized by the history of Rome itself. The final imposing structure continued to give political unity to all of western mankind until the paralysis of senescence and the irresistible pressure of rude, young, and vigorous peoples from the east brought about its final collapse along with the gradual dissolution and disappearance of the great civilizations which had produced it.

SUGGESTED READINGS

Breasted, J. H.: *Ancient Times*, Boston, Ginn & Company, 1916.

Chapot, V.: *The Roman World*, New York, Alfred A. Knopf, 1928.

Davie, M. R.: *The Evolution of War*, New Haven, Yale University Press, 1929.

Homo, L. P.: *Roman Political Institutions*, New York, Alfred A. Knopf, 1929.

Jouguet, Pierre: *Macedonian Imperialism*, New York, Alfred A. Knopf, 1928.

Lowie, R. H.: *The Origin of the State*, New York, Harcourt, Brace & Company, 1927.

MacLeod, W. C.: *The Origin and History of Politics*, New York, John Wiley & Sons, 1931.

Moret, A.: *From Tribe to Empire*, New York, Alfred A. Knopf, 1926.

Oppenheimer, F.: *The State*, Indianapolis, Bobbs-Merrill Company, 1912.

Phillipson, C.: *The International Law and Custom of Ancient Greece and Rome* (2 vols.), London, Macmillan & Co., Ltd., 1911.

Tod, M. N.: *International Arbitration among the Greeks*, Oxford, Clarendon Press, 1913.

CHAPTER II

THE EMERGENCE OF THE WESTERN STATE
SYSTEM

1. THE MEDIEVAL IDEAL OF UNIVERSAL EMPIRE

The Moving Finger writes; and, having writ,
Moves on: nor all your Piety nor Wit
 Shall lure it back to cancel half a Line,
Nor all your Tears wash out a word of it.
     —EDWARD FITZGERALD, *Rubaiyat.*

THE tragic epic of the decline and fall of Rome has inevitably impressed itself upon the modern mind as the greatest collective catastrophe which has ever overtaken humankind. Of all the similar disasters which have befallen past civilizations, it lies nearest in time and space to the great new culture which slowly grew up on the ruins of Rome and became the matrix of modern man. The dissolution of the Roman World State has inspired the work of innumerable historians, both before and since the great Gibbon who best retold the tale. It has stirred the imagination of poets and artists of all succeeding generations and it has challenged all students of human affairs to explain how the vast society and the majestic Imperium which gave it governmental unity came to be destroyed. From the point of view of the modern observer of international relations the drama is chiefly significant for the light which it throws upon the process whereby the political unity of western mankind was forever shattered and the wide dominion of the Caesars was gradually dissolved into a chaos of petty States, principalities, and feudal kingdoms, out of which emerged, a millennium later, the State System of contemporary western civilization. In the present chapter an effort will be made to sketch the broad outlines of that process and to indicate how the foundations of the Western State System came to be laid. The motifs of the piece are to be found in the fascination which the idea of imperial unity continued to exercise over the minds of men for centuries after the reality had vanished, in the failure of successive attempts to restore what had disappeared for all time, and in the final recognition by later generations, more aware of the living present than of the dead past, of the new political configuration of the western world.

That the Roman world did not undergo long centuries of slow, undisturbed decay after the fires of creative energy had smoldered out among its peoples was due to a vast westward movement of nomadic barbarians out of the *terrae incognitae* beyond the Rhine and the Danube. Somewhere, far off in north central Asia, there began at a remote time a series of migrations among peoples of the wilderness who have left no written records of their wanderings. Some change of climatic conditions, some unchecked expansion of population, or some other combination of misfortunes apparently made it increasingly difficult for the nomads of the great plains and plateaus to sustain their flocks and herds and to carry on their primitive agriculture. Sparse as were these populations, compared to those of today, they were seemingly unable (because of the low level of their arts and the rude simplicity of their economic activities), to adjust themselves to the new situation. They found it easier to move away to more fertile lands and to plunder and push aside such enemy peoples as barred their way. To the east were barren plains stretching to the shores of the impassible Pacific and to the north lay the land of eternal snow. To the south the paths toward China and India were beset by enormous mountain ranges and vast deserts. Only to the west lay an open road toward the forests and steppes of Eurasia. As the barbaric ancestors of the peoples of modern Europe moved into this region from the east, its inhabitants in turn found it easier to wander farther westward than to offer stout resistance to the newcomers. This constant westward movement of population had perhaps gone on sporadically over thousands of years before the beginnings of written history. During the period of the rise and expansion of Roman power in the Mediterranean successive waves of migrants continued to flow into Europe out of Asia. Various Celtic tribes or Gauls strove periodically to swarm over the fertile countryside and into the gleaming cities of Greece and Italy, only to be beaten back by the superior military strength of the more civilized peoples of the south and to find their way finally into northwestern Europe. Behind the Gauls came the Germans—Teutons or Goths—behind the Germans the Slavs, and behind the Slavs the Finns, Huns, Avars, Magyars, Tartars, Mongols, and Turks.

The submergence of the Roman Empire by these wanderers from the east was a slow and gradual process, almost imperceptible in its early stages and finally completed in the fifth century only because the Empire itself had already become thoroughly permeated by barbarian peoples. From the time of Marcus Aurelius the Emperors had settled barbarian captives on the land as *coloni*, had taken them into the army when the Romans themselves had lost enthusiasm for military service, and had entered into alliances with the barbarians on the frontiers. When, in 376 A.D., the Emperor Valens admitted into the territory of the Empire a great horde of Visigoths who had been driven from their lands by the Huns, he was merely following the well-established policy of his predecessors. But the Visigoths rose in revolt, slew the Emperor and his legionaries, and ravaged Macedonia and Thrace to the gates of Constantinople. Theodosius made peace by settling them south of the Danube. Thirty years later another Visigothic chieftain, Alaric, led his warriors across the Alps, devastated Italy, and sacked Rome (410 A.D.). The elevation of Alaric's successor, Atolf, to the command of the imperial armies by the Emperor Honorius is indicative of the impotence to which the Roman State had been reduced. Britain was evacuated by the legions and the distant frontiers crumbled before new foes, while barbarian hosts wandered almost unopposed through the provinces. Out of the east came the dreaded Huns under Attila, bent upon the complete destruction, of the Empire and the creation of a great barbarian dominion. After Attila's hordes were beaten at Châlons-sur-Marne in 451, they invaded Italy, only to withdraw again into the eastern wilderness. The Vandals carried fire and sword through Gaul and Spain, occupied north Africa, crossed the sea, and sacked Rome once more in 455. In 476 the little six-year-old Emperor, Romulus Augustus, the last of the Emperors of the west, was deprived of his throne by Odoacer, chief of the mercenaries, and the imperial insignia were sent to Constantinople with the request that the Emperor Zeno permit Odoacer to administer Italy as a province of the Eastern Empire. This final "fall of Rome" was but an incident in a century of turmoil, but it marked the end of the Western Empire as a political entity.

But Rome dead was more powerful than Rome alive. The city itself remained the seat of the Papacy, which asserted and gradually established its spiritual supremacy over the Christianized barbarian kingdoms. The unity of western Christendom which had been disrupted by the collapse of the old Empire was revived by the growing power of the universal Church. The memory of the vanished universal State lingered on in the minds of the barbarians. The *pax Romana* of the lost golden age became an ideal ever more desirable in the eyes of medieval mankind as it became ever more impossible of restoration. Catholic Christianity and this vision of order and peace under a universal State were the two great legacies which classical civilization left to its heirs. The religious and political history of the long springtime of western civilization—traditionally misnamed "the middle ages"—is largely the story of the Church and the "Empire"—the former a living reality of medieval life, the latter the unfulfilled dream of a vanished past which could never be quite recovered. The new State System which rose on the ruins of Roman power was ever under the spell of the magic of the Popes and the legend of the world-wide Imperium of the Caesars.

So effectively did this legend stir the thoughts and acts of those who inherited the faded fragments of the imperial purple that attempts were repeatedly made to restore in one form or another the political unity of the western world which the barbarian invasions had destroyed. Amid centuries of gloom and chaos, when western Europe was afflicted with all the misfortunes of war, famine, and political disorder, the dream of world empire and the humanizing mission of the Church were the two great guiding lights of an age in which one civilization had died and another had not yet been born. The brief but brilliant gesture of the Eastern Emperor, Justinian (527–565), was without permanent results. In the middle of the fifth century his able generals, Belisarius and Narses, wrested Africa from the Vandals, Italy from the Ostrogoths, and parts of Spain from the Visigoths. But the recovered provinces were soon lost and the west sank deeper into anarchy. The later Eastern Emperors, secure in colorful Byzantium and its hinterland, abandoned the effort and contented themselves with safeguarding themselves against the Persians and other Asiatic foes. The Byzantine Empire was destined to endure for another thousand years, until the final capture of Constantinople by the Turks in 1453, but the restoration of the Western Empire seemed an idle dream.

In time, however, as the barbarians settled on the land, absorbed the remnants of Roman culture, and embarked upon state-building, new kingdoms and principalities emerged and conditions were ripe for the development of a new system of independent territorial States. But the vision of unity persisted and reached partial fulfillment three hundred years after the end of the Western Empire. The Kingdom of the Franks, established in what had been Roman Gaul, allied itself with the Papacy and gradually extended its power over its neighbors. The rise of the Frankish kingdom was contemporaneous with the appearance of a great new civilization in the Near East in the wake of the founding of Mohammedanism. When the armed apostles of Islam, having conquered Egypt, north Africa, and Spain with spectacular rapidity, pushed on to the north, it was the Franks who saved Christendom from Moslem conquest by defeating the Saracens at Tours in 732. At the end of the century the greatest of the Frankish kings, Charlemagne, had so widely extended his control over the pagans that his realm reached from northern Spain to the Baltic and from the Atlantic to the Oder. In 799 he restored Leo III to the Holy See in Rome by frustrating the schemes of the Pope's rivals and enemies. On Christmas day, 800 A.D., in the church of St. Peter at Rome, the grateful Leo placed an imperial crown upon the head of the Frankish monarch, while the populace shouted, "To Charles, the Augustus, crowned by God, great and pacific emperor of the Romans, life and victory!" Thus, with the sanction of the Papacy, the Empire was at length restored by the power of Frankish arms and one emperor ruled again over most of western Christendom.[1]

[1] David Jayne Hill aptly characterizes the significance of this ceremony as follows: "The two figures before the high altar of St. Peter's on that Christmas day form a sym-

This restoration was ephemeral, however, and the medieval "empire" was not finally established until another century and a half had elapsed. The realm of Charles the Great fell to the weakest of his sons, Lewis the Pious, in 814, and was promptly divided among the grandsons. Internecine wars and further partitions followed, with the eastern or German portion definitely separating itself from the western or French portion and with both halves set upon during the ninth century by new invaders—Vikings from the north, Magyars from the east, and Saracens from the south. New rulers were crowned "emperor" by the Popes, but their authority was feeble. The imperial crown was finally transferred to a German king in the person of Charles the Fat in 881. When Henry the Fowler, Duke of the Saxons (the grave and stately monarch of Wagner's *Lohengrin*), was elected king in 919 by the Saxon and Franconian nobles, he renounced imperial ambitions and busied himself with beating back the Magyar invaders and restoring some degree of order in his domains. His son Otto continued the work with such success that he was able to extend his power into Italy and in 962 was crowned Emperor by the Pope. The compact between the Roman bishop and the German king laid the basis for what later came to be called the "Holy Roman Empire of the German Nation" —a curious political structure with a double sovereignty, resting upon the notion that the Empire and the Papacy were respectively the temporal and spiritual agencies designated by the divine will for the governance of Christendom.

To trace through the subsequent history of his ramshackle creation of medieval statesmanship would be of little value here except to reveal the persistence with which the ideal of imperial unity was adhered to during many generations. The imperial crown passed to the House of Hohenstaufen and later to the House of Hapsburg, where it remained until the extinction of the Empire in 1806. The theory of the Empire as the successor of the Roman World State was not much modified either by the great conflicts between Popes and Emperors for supremacy or by the fact that

---

bolical picture of the whole course of history since the time of the Caesars. The Roman and the German, the overshadowing past and the potential present, the universal and the individual, the majesty of law and the vigor of liberty, the world of the spirit and the world of actuality, imperial right and barbarian energy—all these are present, and all are henceforth to be combined as if swallowed up in one new creation. But it is the German who kneels in pious devotion, the present which humbles itself before the past, the individual who feels the power of the universal, the vigor of liberty which yields to the majesty of law, the actual which seeks strength from the spiritual, and the barbarian who has been conquered by the Empire. It is the Roman who bestows the crown, the Roman who speaks in the name of the divinity, the Roman whose transfigured republic is to profit by Rome's latest conquest; for after centuries of suffering, toil, tragedy, it is the triumph of Rome's work which is before us." *A History of Diplomacy in the International Development of Europe,* I, pp. 95-96.

the Empire had no effective authority outside of the German States and Italy. Even in these regions the imperial power was constantly flouted by the great dukes, the unruly principalities, and the turbulent free cities. Such powers as the Emperor wielded he derived less from his imperial office than from the lands and subjects which he controlled as a German king among many kings. It could almost be said of the Empire from the beginning what Voltaire said of it in the eighteenth century: that it was neither Holy nor Roman nor an Empire. It existed in the world of theological speculation and political metaphysics rather than in the world of fact. It was the most perfect expression of medieval mysticism and scholasticism applied to world politics. It was the ghost of ancient Rome which would not be laid, but insisted upon stalking ceaselessly across the stage of the middle ages between classical and modern civilization. The firm hold which the theory of imperial unity secured on the hopes and imaginations of men is explicable in terms of a deep yearning for peace and order in a world of endless war and confusion. But the political and social structure of western society in medieval Europe doomed that yearning to perpetual frustration. The medieval political theorist and statesman became a new Tantalus, constantly groping for that which lay beyond his reach, constantly striving to realize an ideal which the conditions of the time put past all realization.

Nowhere in medieval political literature is this tragedy more poignantly expressed than in the *De monarchia* of Dante Alighieri, jurist, statesman, poet, and author of the immortal *Divine Comedy*. His great political essay has accurately been described by Lord Bryce as the "epitaph of the Holy Roman Empire." It is indeed a last cry of despair, a last plea for unity in a world of inescapable diversity. It represents both the culmination and the close of medieval political theorizing on international relations. A brief consideration of its message and of the circumstances which produced it will constitute an appropriate conclusion to this discussion of the medieval ideal of the world-wide Imperium.

The *De monarchia* was written about 1309, twelve years before Dante's death, at the period of the "Babylonian Captivity" of the Papacy, when the Popes were residing at Avignon under the surveillance of the French monarchy, when no Emperor had visited Italy for over half a century, and when the Italian city-states were waging chronic war upon one another for power and territory. Great hopes were entertained that the newly elected Emperor, Henry VII, would come to Italy for his coronation and would restore peace to the land. Dante, as a practical student of law and government and as one who had served on several Florentine embassies and who was not, therefore, unfamiliar with diplomatic problems, shared this hope and wrote his famous essay as a defense of the Empire and as an appeal for general recognition of its supremacy. In allegorical and scholastic style, he presented the arguments in favor of his ideal.

Whole heaven is regulated by a single ruler—God. It follows that the human race is at its best state when it is ruled by a single prince and one law. So it is evidently necessary for the welfare of the world that there should be a single monarchy or princedom, which men call the Empire. Whenever disputes arise, there must be judgment. Between any two independent princes controversy may arise and then judgment is necessary. Now an equal cannot rule over his equal, so there must be a third prince of wider jurisdiction who is ruler over both, to decide the dispute. This third ruler must be the monarch or Emperor. And so monarchy is necessary for the world. . . . Moreover, the world is ordered best when justice is most powerful, and justice is most powerful under a monarchy or empire.

Dante cited the age of Augustus as the golden age of mankind and concluded with a dramatic exhortation, colored by pessimism and a half-confessed realization of the futility of the poet's aspirations.

But how the world has fared since that "seamless robe" (the Roman Empire) has suffered rending by the talons of ambition, we may read in books; would that we might not see it with our eyes. Oh, race of mankind! What storms must toss thee, what losses must thou endure, what shipwrecks must buffet thee, as long as thou, a beast of many heads, strivest after contrary things! Thou art sick in both thy faculties of understanding; thou art sick in thy affections. Unanswerable reasons fail to heal thy higher understanding; the very sight of experience convinces not thy lower understanding; not even the sweetness of divine persuasion charms thy affections, when it breathes into thee through the music of the Holy Spirit: "Behold how good and how pleasant a thing it is, brethren, to dwell together in unity!"

But the hope was vain. Henry came to Italy and was crowned by agents of the Pope at Rome. He brought not peace, but a sword. Rome itself was torn by the struggles between Guelfs and Ghibellines. The Emperor and Pope, whom Dante had envisaged as two facets of a single perfect entity, quarrelled violently in words and in arms. Henry was placed under the ban of the Church by Clement V at Avignon, who was supported by the King of France in rendering aid to Robert of Naples and the cities of the north which resisted the imperial power. Henry laid unsuccessful siege to Florence and died in 1313, carrying with him to the grave all prospects of restoring the prestige of the Empire in Italy. The peninsula, like all Europe, was a welter of warring States, with the Empire but a specter of half-forgotten yesterdays.

2. REALITIES OF THE MEDIEVAL STATE SYSTEM

All nations of the west are of dynastic origin. In the Romanesque and even in Early Gothic architecture the soul of the Carolingian primitives still quivers through. There is no French or German Gothic, but Salian, Rhenish, and Suabian, as there is Visigothic (northern Spain, southern France) and Lombard and Saxon Romanesque. But over it all there spreads soon the minority, composed of men of race, that feels membership in a nation as a great historical vocation. From it proceed the Crusades, and in them there truly were French and German chivalries. It is the hallmark of Faustian peoples that they are conscious of the direction of their history.—OSWALD SPENGLER, *The Decline of the West,* II.

The plea of the great Italian poet for unity and peace through the reestablishment of the Empire was a typically medieval appeal in behalf of an ideal which had long since become something less than the shadow of a dream. Almost all the thinkers of the middle ages who indulged in speculation on international affairs looked backward in similar fashion to an age long dead and to a scheme of world organization which was never to be restored. This constant preoccupation with the legacy of ancient Rome precluded any objective examination of the State System which had grown up out of the Dark Ages. This State System, by its very nature, made impossible any recovery of the political unity of Christendom. Its nature was unperceived—or, if perceived, deplored, because of the painful contrast between its anarchical violence and the peace and order of the *pax Romana.* Blinded by the glory of the ancient Roman Empire, reflected dimly down the centuries of chaos and confusion, the medieval scholars and statesmen lived in their memories, only half aware of the world about them. Here, as in so many phases of medieval thought, a wide chasm yawned between ideal and reality, theory and practice, literature and life, spirit and flesh. But the business of living went on, undisturbed by this dilemma, until finally the visionaries and scholastics returned to earth and awakened from their melancholy reminiscences to find themselves living on a new earth under a new heaven.

For a thousand years before this awakening, there had been developing a new State System and a new international life no less rich and colorful for having been largely ignored by the intelligentsia. As soon as the Western Empire dissolved into political fragments and the barbarian kingdoms were established in its stead, the stage was set for a drama not dissimilar to that which had been played by the independent States of the Mediterranean basin before Rome became supreme. Again there were contacts between States which were, for all practical purposes, independent, despite theories of imperial vassalage entertained by their rulers. Again geographically separated communities, uncontrolled by any single central authority, were free to bargain, trade, and fight with one another.

Out of their relationships emerges the old design of the ancient State Systems, overlaid by the pattern of the dead Rome of the Caesars and the living Rome of the Popes.

As early as the fifth century, the barbarian kings played a wary diplomatic game with one another and with Byzantium to the east, despite the fact that Odoacer in Italy, Euric in Spain, Gondobad in Gaul, and Genseric in Africa continued to do homage to the Empire that had been. Theodoric the Goth conquered Italy from Odoacer in the name of the Emperor, but he ruled as an independent king who extended his power by diplomacy, by war, and by marriage. He exchanged envoys with his neighbors and chose illustrious men for his diplomatic service.[1] Latin forms were used in letters of credence and instructions. Latin remained the language of diplomacy, as it was the language of learning, throughout the middle ages. Diplomatic ceremonies were imitated from the court of Byzantium and the old principle of diplomatic immunity and inviolability was generally observed. But the instability of the barbarian kingdoms made the development of an enduring fabric of international contacts between them impossible. The empire of Charlemagne which emerged out of the turmoil maintained diplomatic relations with the Eastern Empire until Charles, in resentment at the refusal of the Emperor Nicephorus to treat him as an equal, broke the ties between them. Charles was friend and ally of Haroun al-Raschid, the Caliph of Bagdad, who ceded to him the Holy Places of Palestine. He likewise maintained diplomatic contacts with the Moslem Princes of Africa, the Scottish kings, and the rulers of the Avars and the Bulgarians. The semi-independent Republic of Venice for a time played off the Franks and the Byzantines against one another, but finally became a vassal of Charles the Great.

Following the rise of the institutions of feudalism throughout western Europe during the ninth and tenth centuries, the medieval State System became a congerie of feudal principalities whose contacts with one another were overlaid by complex feudal relationships. Feudalism was at once a form of land tenure, a scheme of government, and an economic and social system. With the disappearance of all central authority through internal conflicts and new barbarian invasions following the death of Charlemagne, political power in each locality passed to those who were mighty with sword and mace. The mass of the population sought safety from marauding bands by subordinating itself to those able to afford protection. The warrior class became the landowning class and this new ruling caste

---

[1] Theodoric's great adviser, Cassiodorus the Elder, says: "If indeed every embassy requires a wise man, to whom the conservation of the interests of the state may be trusted, the most sagacious of all should be chosen, who will be able to argue against the most crafty, and to speak in the council of the wise in such a manner that even so great a number of learned men will not be able to gain a victory in the business with which he is charged." Quoted in D. J. Hill, *History of Diplomacy*, I, p. 39.

transformed itself into a true feudal aristocracy. Barons, dukes, counts, and bishops administered their land like private estates. Royal authority almost vanished and power rested with the local nobility, lay and ecclesiastical. In the German States, in the French provinces, and in England, the hierarchy of the feudal pyramid reared itself on the foundation of the manor with its peasant serfs, its military ruler, and his knights. The king, at the apex, granted lands to the great barons in return for military service; the barons were the overlords of lesser barons and knights, who likewise held their fiefs in return for rendering the aid in war which was due from the vassal to his superior; each great landowner owed fealty to him from whom he had received his lands and had under him such henchmen and men-at-arms as he could afford to maintain by subdividing his own estates; at the bottom were the peasants, bound in serfdom to the land, and obliged to render goods and services to the lord of the manor in return for military protection. Such towns as survived the general decay of commerce and industry likewise owed allegiance to local dukes or barons. The whole system reduced central authority to impotence and fostered chronic anarchy and neighborhood warfare. In the absence of large territorial units under the power of a single effective government, there could obviously not develop any well-established system of international intercourse between States. Throughout Europe the fragmentation of economic and political power made war and diplomacy matters of concern to each noble and his neighbors rather than to well-defined political entities possessing the attributes of statehood. Each tiny unit was far smaller in size and power than the units of a city-state system and the result was an incredibly complex and anarchical jungle of feudal confusion.

Despite these characteristics of the feudal age, the most powerful of the nobles became kings, established dynasties, and gradually built up aggregations of power which were the foundation stones of the later national monarchies. This process was resisted at every step by the great barons who, while vassals of the king, regarded him only as *primus inter pares* and were in no degree disposed to see their own power as local magnates diminished by accretions to the royal authority. Yet, little by little, in England, in France, in Spain, and in the German principalities and electorates, the reigning houses extended their estates, subdued their unruly vassals, and created the realms out of which the States of modern Europe have been built. These States had extensive contacts with one another, even in the feudal period, though the medieval State System was unlike its predecessors and successors in that its units were not fully independent entities, but were bound over to one another by complex relationships of vassalage and allegiance. The Norman kings of England, for example, were vassals of the king of France, but the normal relationship between them was not one of rulers and ruled but rather one of rivalry for control of the lesser barons and knights of the provinces. Both acknowledged vaguely the overlordship of the Emperor, to whom, in theory, all other Christian princes were vassals, and both were periodically at odds with the Papacy no less than with the Emperor. Notwithstanding these complexities, the modern States of western Europe slowly emerged out of feudalism. They first assumed clear outlines in the fifteenth and

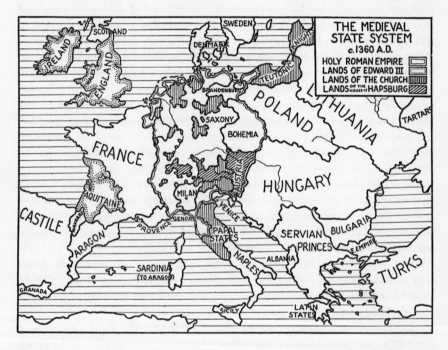

sixteenth centuries, when the kings, with the support of the burghers of the growing cities, demolished the power of the feudal baronage and made themselves absolute monarchs over unified nations. By this time the rudiments of international practice were well-established and the Western State System had been born.

The rôle of the Church in this process was of great significance. It long continued to symbolize the unity of the Christian world. The Pope was not merely the spiritual head of Christendom, but exercised temporal powers as well, both as ruler of the Papal States in central Italy and as the Vicar of Christ upon earth with power over emperors, kings, and princes. As kings were crowned by the bishops of the Church, the Emperor was crowned by the Pope himself. He who gives is superior to him who receives. The Papacy not only asserted its authority over temporal rulers in all matters, both lay and ecclesiastical, concerning the administration of their realms, but offered its services as arbitrator to settle disputes between them. Such offers were often coupled with insistence upon acceptance, which gave to papal arbitrations the character of interventions. This arbitral procedure was widely utilized, particularly as between the princes of the Italian States. The national monarchies of the west likewise resorted to it. Among the more famous of the papal arbitrations were those between Philip le Bel and the English king (1298), between Philip le Long and the Flemings (1319), between the Emperor Maximilian and the Doge of Venice in the fifteenth century, and between Spain and Portugal regarding their claims in the New World in 1494. Nonecclesiastical arbitration was also developed as a means of settling disputes by the Swiss cantons, the cities of the Hanseatic League, the German States, and even by the English and French monarchies,[1] but the Papacy may properly be regarded as having made the greatest contributions to the institution of international arbitration during the period.

The Church likewise played an important part in the development of diplomatic practices and of the rudimentary international law which gradually came to be recognized by the various European States. From early times the Popes had dispatched envoys (*legati*) to attend Church councils and had regularly maintained ambassadors at the Byzantine court known as *apocrisiarii* until relations were severed between Constantinople and the Holy See in consequence of religious differences. Similar representatives were exchanged between the Vatican and the exarch at Ravenna. Later the Popes sent special envoys to the Emperor and to the courts of England, France, Naples, Hungary, Aragon, Castile, and other States. Ecclesiastical influence was also considerable in the development of Byzantine diplomacy which, in turn, greatly influenced the diplomatic practices of the Italian city-states in the fourteenth century. As regards international law, the archbishop of Seville, St. Isadore, was writing as early as the seventh century, in his *Etymologies*, of the *ius gentium* of the Romans as a body of law having to do with "wars, captivities, enslavements, the recovery of rights of postliminy, treaties of peace and others, the scruple which protects ambassadors from violence, and prohibition of marriage between persons of different nationality." The efforts of the Church to restrict private warfare and protect noncombatants led to a marked development of what later came to be known as the international law of war and neutrality. In insisting upon the observance of the "Truce of God," the Church forbade fighting on Sunday. In the eleventh century efforts were made to extend the period of Sabbath peace from Wednesday evening to Monday morning and to apply it to religious holidays and to the whole period of Lent. In 1095 Pope

---

[1] See J. H. Ralston, *International Arbitration from Athens to Locarno*, 1929, pp. 176–178, for types of medieval arbitration treaties.

Urban II decreed it for all Christendom in this form. The *pax ecclesiae* forbade fighting in the vicinity of church buildings or against clerics, pilgrims, merchants, women, or peasants, thus neutralizing certain areas and protecting certain categories of persons from the rigors of war.

If ecclesiastical anathemas and excommunications were not always effective in restraining the pugnacity of the embattled baronage, these efforts were nevertheless of great influence on later thought and practice and, coupled with certain other developments of the period, contributed toward the weaving together of the warp and woof of customs, laws, practices, and institutions which are the fabric of modern diplomacy. As neighborhood warfare declined under the pressure of clerical persuasion and kingly power, towns grew and waxed prosperous through the wider commercial contacts which peace made possible. The Hanseatic trading cities of the north and the city-states of the Mediterranean maritime leagues built up a flourishing commerce which they fostered by exchanging commercial or consular representatives and by concluding numerous commercial treaties with one another. Political representatives followed on the heels of trading agents and therewith the modern diplomatic service was established. International maritime law also evolved out of these relationships and received its first clear statement in the *Consolato del Mare* of the fourteenth century, which the Italian mercantile States accepted as a guide in their trade relations. Another development contributing to the same result was the launching of the great Crusades to rescue the Holy Land from the infidels. These high adventures brought the rough warriors of western Europe into conflict with Saracen knights who fought like gentlemen. Chivalry was born and war became no longer a matter of cruel bludgeoning, rapine, and wanton destruction, but a science and an art to be practiced in accordance with fixed rules. Travel increased with trading and crusading. Feudal provincialism declined and governments were brought into closer contact with one another. The dream of imperial unity gradually faded, while the new city-states and national monarchies dealt with one another as equal and independent political entities. Out of these new contacts between larger territorial units emerged a further development of the procedures and institutions of diplomacy, the usages and practices of international law, and the attitudes and values which underlie modern statecraft.

3. RENAISSANCE ITALY AND MACHIAVELLI

We are much beholden to Machiavel and others, that write what men do, and not what they ought to do.—FRANCIS BACON, *Proficience and Advancement of Learning*.

Modern diplomacy was born in northern Italy. Here there existed from the twelfth century onward a microcosmic State System that was in almost all respects save size a miniature of the larger State System of western Europe as a whole which made its appearance some two centuries later. The Italian city-states of the later middle ages and the Renaissance created the matrix in which modern statecraft was conceived. Here there prevailed on a small scale political conditions comparable to those which later, on a larger stage, furnished the scenery and the plot of the great drama of international politics throughout the western world. Here, where feudalism had never struck deep roots, there had developed at an early period a number of independent principalities whose inhabitants were brought into intimate relations with one another because of their geographical proximity and whose rulers, undeterred by such pleas for peace and unity as Dante had voiced, struggled lustily with one another and with Popes and Emperors for power, prestige, and the greater glory of their realms. Here the great aristocratic commercial families amassed fortunes which enabled them to patronize the arts and sciences and to reach out for political power and greater wealth. Here sculptors, painters, and architects embellished the glittering cities of the peninsula until they shone like jewels against the drab background of the poorer and more primitive societies north of the Alps. Princes maintained colorful courts, sent and received envoys, married for reasons of state, sought to trick one another out of lands and subjects, and carried on warfare through the services of a swashbuckling mercenary soldiery. The fascinating history of this miniature State System throws so much light upon the genesis of contemporary international relations that a brief summary of its evolution is indispensable for an understanding of all that has followed it across the international stage.

During the ninth and tenth centuries the Emperors, who claimed suzerainty over Italy and who sought allies in their struggles with the Popes, began the process of granting the cities of Lombardy and Tuscany imperial charters which conferred upon them a large degree of autonomy and self-government. With the weakening of imperial authority, the cities became for all practical purposes independent republics whose citizens were imbued with a strong consciousness of civic pride and local patriotism. Milan, Genoa, Parma, Bologna, and Ravenna became centers of a vigorous political life in the north. To the east the descendants of the fugitives who had fled to the islands of the Adriatic for refuge from the barbarians founded Venice, which carried on extensive commerce with Byzantium and other eastern cities and became a leading maritime power. To the south in Tuscany, Florence, Pisa, Lucca, and Siena became flourishing city-states which ignored Pope and Emperor alike. In 1112 Milan and Pavia concluded a treaty of alliance in which they pledged themselves to protect "their persons and their possessions against every mortal born or to be born." Leagues and alliances became the order of the day as the city-states strove to assert their independence by playing off papal supporters and imperialists against one another. During the third quarter of the twelfth century Frederick Barbarossa attempted, with temporary success, to restore imperial absolutism over the Italian municipalities. A generation later Innocent III raised the Papacy to a position of supreme authority, not only over the Italian States, but over all of Christendom. But in both cases the reassertion of central power was transitory and the city-states went their own way, striving with one another for land and power, and keeping the peninsula in turmoil by their diplomatic trickeries and tumultuous brawls. Frederick III's final effort to crush the independence of these petty States led to a combination against him of the Lombard League, the Tuscan League, the Umbrian League, and the Papacy, and he died in 1250 with his ambition unrealized.

From the thirteenth century onward the States of Italy were free alike from any effective threat of external control and from any possibility of unification by any one of their number. Under these circumstances they inevitably evolved a complex pattern of relationships with one another and developed the art of diplomacy to a higher level than had ever been known elsewhere in western Christendom. The Republic of Venice—"school and touchstone of ambassadors"—perhaps contributed most to this development because of its far-flung commercial interests and its contacts with the sophisticated, if decadent, Eastern Roman Empire. At a remote period the Venetian authorities began the practice of registering treaties, keeping diplomatic archives, and maintaining an elaborate system of commissions, written instructions, records, and dispatches in their contacts with diplomatic representatives abroad. By a law of 1268 a Venetian ambassador was forbidden to take his wife along on missions, lest she divulge his business, but required to take his cook along, lest he be poisoned. The *Consolato del Mare*, based upon the ancient "Tables of Amalfi," was solemnly approved by the Venetian representatives in Constantinople in 1255 as the basis of maritime international law and was later adopted by Pisa, Genoa, Naples, Aragon, and the States of northern and western Europe. The ceremonies which the Venetians developed for the reception and dispatch of diplomatic representatives influenced the practice of other States to a great degree. Envoys were carefully selected from the ranks of the nobility, until Venetian ambassadors became models of honesty, competence, and *savoir faire*.

In other states as well the diplomatic profession attracted to it the service of distinguished and learned men. The diplomatic service of Florence during the thirteenth and fourteenth centuries included such illustrious names as Dante, Petrarch, Boccaccio, and Guicciardini. Diplomatic missions were at first limited to two or three months' duration and later extended to several years. Not until the middle of the fifteenth century did the practice become prevalent of maintaining permanent and regular diplomatic posts at the seats of foreign governments. The first clear instance of this kind was the establishment of a permanent embassy at Genoa by Milan in 1455. Various ranks of diplomatic agents were recognized, though there was much confusion on this point and no uniformity of practice.

This structure of diplomatic practices and usages was, of course, based upon the existence of a number of independent territorial States, free from external control and able to pursue their own interests by bargaining and fighting with one another. Here, as always in such a State System, each unit pursued such objectives as best served the interests of its ruling class and these objectives involved in each case a maximum extension of the territory and power of the State at the expense of its rivals. International politics was a competitive struggle for power, a war of each against all, an uneasy equilibrium in which the weak combined against the strong in order to maintain a balance of power in which no one State could become so powerful as to threaten the independence of the others. Dante might deplore the resulting chaos and plead for unity. Other reflective souls might call, despairingly, for solidarity, as did an obscure priest of Milan: "And thou, Milan, thou seekest to supplant Cremona, to overthrow Pavia, to destroy Novara. Thy hands are raised against all, and the hands of all against thee. . . . Oh, when shall the day dawn in which the inhabitants of Pavia shall say to the Milanese: 'Thy people are my people,' and the citizen of Novara to the Cremonese: 'Thy city is my city'!"[1] All in vain. Each prince pursued his own interests. Each community was fired with local patriotism and looked upon its neighbor as a potential enemy or as a possible ally against an enemy still more dangerous. Republicanism gave way to princely absolutism as each city, in constant rivalry with its neighbors, perceived the advantages of concentrating diplomatic and military power in a single hand. Diplomacy and war were the means to power. War required money and the services of the *condottieri*. Diplomacy required secrecy, espionage, plot and counterplot, and a nice sense of the imponderable interrelationships and the fleeting opportunities for the enhancement of the power of the commonwealth. The prestige and power, the glory and aggrandizement of the local State became the supreme concern of government and all means thereto were justified.

At last a great spokesman emerged who, first among political observers, comprehended the realities of the State System in which he lived. His name has become a symbol and his work may well be regarded as marking the conscious beginning both of modern diplomacy and of political science. Niccolo Machiavelli was born in Florence, May 5, 1469, into an ancient

[1] Quoted in Hill, *op. cit.*, I, p. 359.

and honorable family which had long and faithfully served the State under whose authority it resided. Under Lorenzo di Medici, called "the Magnificent," young Niccolo began the diplomatic career which gradually matured his agile mind and left with him that fund of mellowed and practical political wisdom which he incorporated in *The Prince*. This work was written about 1513, probably to commend its author to the Medicis for future service in their cause. It is the most famous of his political writings—and indeed has come to be regarded as belonging among the greatest political treatises of all time—though Machiavelli also set forth his views in other works, such as the *Art of War* and the *History of Florence* which he completed in 1525, two years before his death.

The Prince has earned for its author the opprobrium of all right-thinking moralists and has come to be viewed as the most eloquent exhortation to the vices of trickery, treachery, unscrupulousness, and dishonesty to which modern diplomacy has fallen heir. In fact, it was nothing more than a realistic account of the behavior of States toward one another, with a wealth of contemporary and historical illustrations, coupled with a set of maxims for the guidance of rulers seeking power in the type of State System with which Machiavelli was familiar. It contains, in small compass, as he declares in his dedication to Lorenzo, "all the experience I have acquired during many years of continual meditation and suffering in the school of adversity." Far from being immoral, it is entirely unconcerned with ethics and regards the State as beyond good and evil—an end in itself for the service of which all means are legitimate. Political expediency rather than morality is the criterion of State action. Machiavelli discards completely the mysticism of the scholastics and the vague aspirations toward a vanished unity so well represented by Dante. Holy Scripture and the sweetness of divine persuasion are alike irrelevant, not because he is *advocatus diaboli*, but because he is a coolly objective realist, weighing States and princes as dispassionately as a physical scientist manipulating inanimate matter. The Italian State System, declares the Florentine, is thus and so; since it is thus and so, princes desiring to further their fortunes must act accordingly. To pass judgment upon reality is futile; to deplore facts is useless. Machiavelli is neither judge nor idealist, but merely analyst and diagnostician. His little treatise is a book of prescriptions in the political methods which his keen observation had convinced him would prove effective in serving the ends of State. He is not a philosopher, for he is unconcerned with ends and values. He accepts his political universe without question. But in accepting, he dissects, analyzes, and probes until he is able to describe the State System about him with an assurance born of empirical observation and experience, and to indicate with complete objectivity the political tools which princes must use to attain their objectives.

Machiavelli opens his work with a description of different types of States and of the problems involved in state-building. A prince may establish firm control over newly conquered lands by colonizing his own people on them, by establishing garrisons, by playing off neighboring princes against one another, and the like. Those who are injured thereby should be disposed of with dispatch, lest they become dangerous enemies —for a man "may revenge a slight injury, but a great one deprives him of his power to avenge." Desire for aggrandizement is a natural characteristic of rulers. "Nothing is so natural or so common as the thirst for conquest, and when men can satisfy it, they deserve praise rather than censure. But when they are not equal to the enterprise, disgrace is the inevitable consequence." And the power for which princes strive is a relative quantity: "The prince who contributes toward the advancement of another power, ruins his own." Monarchies must be conquered by superior force, and then can be easily held, since once the reigning dynasty is disposed of, none remains to oppose the conqueror. Aristocracies can be conquered by intrigue among the nobles, but once in power the conqueror will encounter "an infinity of difficulty, not only from the conquered, but from those who have assisted in the enterprise." Free States may be subdued only by ruining them, by colonizing them, or by permitting them to remain in the enjoyment of their own laws. The difficulties of rulership which princes encounter vary with the means by which they have acquired power. "The usurper of a State should commit all the cruelties which his safety renders necessary at once, that he may never have cause to repeat them . . . for when time is allowed for resentment, the wound is not so deep; but benefits should be frugally dispensed, and by little at a time, that they may be the better relished."

The Florentine next discusses the problems of defense, military establishments, and mercenary troops, concluding that the latter are usually untrustworthy and to be avoided. "The first cause of the decline of the Roman Empire arose from taking the Goths into their pay, which brought these barbarians into repute at the expense of the Roman soldiery. . . . There is nothing so weak as a power that is not supported by itself, that is to say, that is not defended by its own citizens or subjects. . . . Princes ought, therefore, to make the art of war their sole study and occupation, for it is peculiarly the science of those who govern. . . . By neglect of this art it is that States are lost, and by cultivating it they are acquired." A wise prince will not only make himself a master of warfare, but will win over his subjects to him by being liberal, without being prodigal, and merciful without being weak. "It is safer to be feared than be loved, for it may truly be affirmed of mankind in general, that they are ungrateful, fickle, timid, dissembling, and self-interested." But the prince must avoid earning the hatred of his subjects. This can be achieved by respecting his subjects' property and the honor of their wives, "for it is certain that men sooner forget the death of their relations than the loss of their patrimony."

Since force and trickery are twin tools for the acquisition and retention of power, the prince must make the lion and the fox his models. "A prudent prince cannot and ought not to keep his word, except when he can do it without injury to himself, or when the circumstances under which he contracted the engagement still exist." It is unnecessary that a prince should possess many good qualities, but indispensable that he should appear to have them, "as men in general judge more from appearances than from reality. All men have eyes, but few have the gift of penetration. . . . The vulgar are ever caught by appearances, and judge only by the event. And as the world is chiefly composed of such as are called the vulgar, the voice of the few is seldom or never heard or regarded." A prince should choose his ministers with care and avoid flatterers. The volume closes with an exhortation to Lorenzo to free Italy of foreigners, meaning the French invaders. "Every war that is necessary is just; and it is humanity to take up arms for the defense of a people to whom no other recourse is left."

The long shadow which *The Prince* of Machiavelli has cast down the succeeding centuries is attributable less to the influence of the work on the thought of its day or to the pith and pungency of the author's wit and wisdom than to the fact that his maxims and shrewd observations reflected the fundamental nature of the new Western State System which existed in miniature in the Italy of the Renaissance. That State System rested upon the unlimited and uncontrolled sovereignty of the territorial State and upon the principle of the balance of power through which each State checkmated its rivals. The ruler of each unit inevitably strove to protect and further his own interests by force, when force was expedient, by trickery, when force was unnecessary. "To reign is to dissimulate," declared Louis XI of France. "If they lie to you," he admonished his ambassadors, "lie still more to them." The power of the State justified all means necessary for its enhancement. The political relations between States had again become a competitive struggle for power while the vision of imperial unity receded into the past. The old pattern, characteristic of all State Systems made up of independent territorial units, had re-emerged, first in Italy and later throughout western Europe. The new national monarchies dealt with one another precisely as did the Italian city-states—and neither Pope nor Emperor could say them nay. The Empire was by now a phantom. The Papacy was impotent—in part because the Renaissance Popes were themselves rulers and diplomats who used the same methods for increasing their power as did the lay princes, in part because the forces of revolt against papal Catholicism were already gathering about the person of a German monk, Martin Luther, in preparation for the last great schism of the Reformation which was to shatter for all time the ecclesiastical unity of the Christian world. The great States of the modern age were in process of being born—and the politics which they practiced toward one another were then, and have ever been since, "Machiavellian politics" in the broadest sense of a much abused phrase. In this fashion *The Prince* symbolized a new dispensation, and the humble servant of the magnificent Lorenzo became the prophet of a new epoch.

4. THE GENESIS OF SOVEREIGNTY

> It is evident from the law of nature, that all men being naturally free and independent, they cannot lose these blessings without their own consent. Citizens cannot enjoy them fully and absolutely in any State, because they have surrendered a part of these privileges to the sovereign. But the body of the nation, the State, remains absolutely free and independent with respect to all men, or to foreign nations, while it does not voluntarily submit to them.—EMERICH DE VATTEL, *Droit des Gens.*

The concept of State sovereignty and the politics of the balance of power may be regarded as the two cornerstones upon which the Western State System has come to rest. These features have characterized all State Systems in which independent political communities have struggled with one another for predominance, for they are inherent in the pattern of relationships which inevitably emerges in such situations. Only in the State System of contemporary western civilization, however, have they been clearly and consciously formulated and verbalized. The one has been elevated to the dignity first of a political theory and later of a juristic concept underlying the whole structure of modern international jurisprudence; the other has become an avowed principle of foreign policy, accepted and acted upon so consistently by all the great States that it may well be viewed as the central theme about which modern diplomatic history revolves.

In the historical development of the concept of sovereignty scholars, statesmen, and jurists have always been concerned with two problems, separate in reality, but usually considered together: (1) that of the location of supreme power within States in relation to the various groups of population and the various agencies of government, and (2) that of the relations between States as they affect their freedom of action and independence. Only the second of these problems is of immediate interest here, though both of them must be dealt with if the evolution of sovereignty as a concept of international law and policy is to be understood. In classical civilization the idea of sovereignty was never clearly formulated. Both Plato and Aristotle, however, recognized the existence of a supreme power in every State and classified States as monarchies, aristocracies, and democracies on the basis of whether that power resided in one person, in the few, or in the many. Similiarly the legal and administrative system of Rome rested upon the notion of supreme power residing first in the whole body of the citizens of the Republic and later in the person of the Emperor, who commanded the armed forces of the State, made war and peace, conducted negotiations, legislated, heard lawsuits, appointed officials, and controlled the great priesthoods. The Emperor at length came to be invested with the attributes of divinity and became as a god, though the idea of the ultimate authority of the people was never wholly lost.

Academic interest in the nature and location of sovereignty in the State was revived with the study of Roman law in the twelfth and thirteenth centuries. While no complete theory of sovereignty was worked out until the rise of the national monarchies, the prevalent conception of the problem during the medieval period may be described in terms of what later came to be called "popular sovereignty." To Thomas Aquinas and his fellow scholastics, government rested upon the consent of the governed. The Emperor ruled by the consent of his subjects and the sanction of the Church. The Pope was regarded as having derived his authority directly from God, though in the Conciliar movement of the fourteenth century the argument for the popular basis of power was applied to ecclesiastical as well as to lay government and was used against the Papacy itself by its critics within the Church.

Theories of government, however, are usually rationalizations of those who govern or of those who resist government. It was not until powerful aggregations of centralized power had been built up by the western dynasts that a systematic presentation of the philosophical basis of political authority became possible. The turbulent feudal aristocracy was gradually subordinated to the authority of absolutist kings and princes who preserved the ruling class and protected its interests without permitting it to interfere with an effective central administration. As soon as the new monarchs sought ethical justification for their policies, they found jurists and scholars at hand to supply them with the ideational paraphernalia requisite to make the cause of absolutism intellectually respectable. While Machiavelli postulated the absolute sovereignty of the territorial State in relation to its neighbors, he did not discuss the location of sovereign power within the State, nor was he interested in the problem from a legal and juristic point of view. It fell to the French scholar, Jean Bodin, to formulate the first systematic presentation of the concept of sovereignty in its modern form in his *De republica* of 1586—a title which must be literally translated as "Concerning Public Affairs," since its author, far from being a republican, was an apologist of the purest absolutism. Bodin, in fact, devised the political theory upon which the French monarchy was to rest its case for unlimited and autocratic central power.

Sovereignty he defined as "unlimited power over citizens and subjects, unrestrained by law." This power, he insisted, is by its nature absolute, unqualified, perpetual, and indivisible and resides not in the whole State but in the body of the citizenry in a democracy, in the estate of the nobility in an aristocracy, and in the person of the king in a monarchy. Rulers rule by divine right, but are subject to the laws of God, of nature, and of nations, and also to the "laws of the kingdom"—a vague adumbration of constitutionalism. These limitations upon supreme power, however, are ethical rather than legal or political. The ideal form of government is a kingship in which unlimited sovereign power is exercised personally by the monarch.

While Bodin's view of the nature of sovereignty became prevalent everywhere in Europe among the apologists of absolutism, it was not unchallenged. In fact two conflicting schools of thought battled for supremacy until their differences were in part reconciled in the formulation of the concept suggested by Hugo Grotius, "the father of international law." The first great challenge to absolutism came from that school of political philosophers known as the Monarchomachs—spokesmen for the most part of the persecuted sects of the period of the wars of religion who were anxious to justify resistance to tyranny and oppression. This group insisted upon the original and inalienable sovereignty of the people and argued that government had come into existence as a result of a written or tacit contract between rulers and ruled for the mutual convenience of both as an escape from the anarchy of a pre-civil state of nature. In the event of a ruler violating the compact by indulging in outrageous and despotic misgovernment, his subjects are *ipso facto* released from the obligation of obedience and may engage in revolution, depose the monarch, or even assassinate him under extreme provocation.

Johannes Althusius, one of the leading Monarchomach theorists, defined sovereignty in his *Politics Systematically Considered* (1609) as "the highest and most general power of administering the affairs which generally concern the safety and welfare of the soul and body of the members of the State." This power, according to his view, could be neither absolute nor supreme, since it is limited by the laws of God, the laws of nature, and the terms of the contract with the people, who remain the ultimate, original, and permanent source of sovereignty. This conception was obviously sharply at variance with that of Bodin, though Thomas Hobbes in his *Leviathan* (1651) later used the contract theory of the origin of the State as the basis for the most imposing intellectual justification of monarchical absolutism which has ever been presented.

Grotius resolved the issue, so far as international law and relations are concerned, by defining sovereignty as "that power whose acts are not subject to the control of another, so that they may be made void by the act of any other human will." For the great Dutch jurist, sovereignty was not absolute, but limited by divine law, by the law of nature, and by the law of nations, and also by agreements between rulers and ruled. It is likewise capable of division and resides simultaneously in the government and in the State. Subjects, however, may alienate their portion of sovereignty entirely to their ruler. The important thing to Grotius is the fact that a State is sovereign in relation to other States when it is free from outside control and capable of exercising its will without outside interference. This conception has become the foundation of the whole structure of modern international law.

Despite the great interest which necessarily attaches to the question of the location of sovereignty within the State, its importance in the development of the Western State System lies rather in its application to the relations between States. The aristocratic and courtly followers of Bodin and Hobbes valiantly defended the principle of personal and divine-right autocracy, while the bourgeois successors of the Monarchomachs, such as Locke, Montesquieu, and Rousseau further elaborated the contract theory in justification of the behavior of the middle-class rebels who engineered the Great Rebellion in England and the American and French Revolutions. "Popular sovereignty" has finally triumphed with the rise to political power of the bourgeoisie. Modern democratic theory vests internal sovereignty either in the legislature, as in England, or in the mass of the voters who express their will in a written constitution, as in the United States and other countries. But in any case, each independent political community in the society of modern States is sovereign with respect to all the rest—that is to say, has exclusive and omnipotent jurisdiction over its own territory and nationals and enjoys complete freedom to legislate within its frontiers and to deal as it wishes with States outside of its frontiers, subject only to its own agreements and the customary principles of international law. It is subordinate to no higher authority of any kind. Each State is thus a law unto itself, free from all external controls except those dictated by political expediency and the accepted usages of international intercourse. The sovereignty of the territorial State thus underlies the whole complex superstructure of international law and relations.

This conception obviously grew out of the political realities of international contracts in the formative period of modern diplomacy. If carried to its logical extreme, it would result in a situation which can only be described as international anarchy. With the breakdown of the authority of Pope and Emperor, the national monarchies of the west, no less than the city-states and principalities of Italy and Germany, went their sovereign way, each striving against the others for territory, power, and prestige, each employing force, trickery, and bargaining in its quest. The provincial chaos of feudalism was replaced by an international chaos of national States, struggling with one another as the embattled knights and barons had once struggled in an earlier age. In this anarchic jungle of sovereign political communities, each State pursued its own ends in disregard of the interests of others, redressing its wrongs by self-help, acting as prosecutor, judge, jury, and sheriff combined, and hotly resenting any suggestion of allegiance or responsibility to any superior power. Here, indeed, was a pre-civil state of nature as Hobbes had described it, in which life was "solitary, poor, nasty, brutish, and short"—in which might makes right—in which power is to the strongest, and the devil takes the hindmost.

That modern international society has often seemed to possess these characteristics is not strange in view of the concept of State sovereignty upon which it rests, for a society of competing sovereign States can, by its nature, be no different. The implications of the persistence of the ideas of national sovereignty and independence into an era in which technology and economics have made States internationally interdependent units of a world society will be examined in other connections. Here it is enough to note the fact that while sovereignty may, in fact, have become a myth, as some commentators affirm,[1] it nevertheless remains a myth enormously potent to stir peoples and governments to action in international affairs. The absolute and unqualified sovereignty of States has, to be sure, long since disappeared, if indeed it ever existed, for modern States are constantly obliged by agreement, to accept limitations upon their freedom of action to acknowledge their responsibility to the whole society of States for their breaches of international law, to consider the rights and interests of others as the sole means of protecting their own, and to recognize in other ways that stubbornly irreducible facts have imposed a thousand checks upon unrestricted sovereignty in the old sense. But the theory lingers on, buttressed by the newer enthusiasms of national patriotism which exalt the sovereign nation-state to the skies. The dead hand of the past is heavy and men are moved as much by inherited attitudes and behavior patterns as by a rational conception of present interests. The sovereignty of the territorial State remains in the twentieth century, as in the sixteenth, the basis of international intercourse and the most characteristic feature of the entire Western State System.

[1] Francis Delaisi, *Political Myths and Economic Realities*, 1930.

5. THE BALANCE OF POWER

> The balance is a word that has subdued the whole world, by the light
> in which it was considered of its securing a constant possession; and yet,
> in truth, this same balance is no more than a bare word, an empty sound;
> for Europe is a family in which there are too many bad brokers and quarrel-
> some relations.—FREDERICK THE GREAT, *Confessions*.

If sovereignty is the mast to which the sails of modern statecraft are attached, the principle of the balance of power is the wind which drives the vessel over the stormy seas of international politics. The one has become the central concept of national political organization and of international law. The other has become the most important single pattern of political action in the international arena. Both existed in latent form in early State Systems. Both received their first clear formulation in the sixteenth century—tentatively at the hands of Machiavelli and more definitely by his successors.

The principle of the balance of power as an unformulated guide to State action is of great antiquity, as has been suggested in the preceding chapter. It has emerged more or less clearly in every system of States in which the units have engaged with one another in a competitive struggle for power. Apparently all States known to history have at one time or another striven to extend their power over the lands and peoples in their vicinity, for these are sources of additional wealth and power to the ruling class of the State. As such they furnish the basis for a further enhancement of State power which makes possible still greater conquests. It has been said truly that a large empire is the best possible reason for a larger empire. State power tends to spread outward from the central nucleus and to increase as it spreads. But power is local. Its efficacy within a given area varies inversely with the distance from the State which is wielding it. A single State, encountering no other obstacles, would normally extend its power over as wide an area as it could conquer and control effectively with the technological, military, and administrative tools at its disposal. But in practice obstacles are encountered almost invariably in the form of other States, similarly striving to expand their power. A struggle for power consequently arises, in which each State endeavors to overcome its competitors. The power of a State—*i.e.*, its ability to conquer other States or to bend them to its will—is necessarily relative to the power of its rivals. Since State power is a relative quantity, any enhancement in the power of one State automatically produces a diminution in the power of its neighbors.

It is because of this fact that the pattern of balance-of-power relationships emerges in every State System. Whenever three States are in contact with one another, the prerequisite conditions for its appearance are present. If one postulates a State System composed of the three units, *A*, *B*, and *C*, it is obvious that an increase in the power of any one of them involves a decrease in the power of the other two. Should State *A* conquer State *B*, or deprive it of a portion of its territory, State *C* would immediately be adversely affected, for *A* has now enhanced its power at the expense of *B* and is in a better position than before to impose its will upon *C*. If the authorities of State *C* are wise, therefore, they will attempt to forestall this result by coming to *B*'s assistance against *A*, not because of any sympathy or solicitude for the fate of *B*, but because considerations of self-interest make any enhancement of the power of *A* dangerous to *C* itself. In such a situation *B* and *C* have a community of interests in opposing *A*, for each realizes that any increase in *A*'s power creates a potential threat to its own independence or existence. By the same token any attempt by *B* to increase its power at the expense of *C* must be resisted by *A* and any enhancement of *C*'s power at the expense of either *A* or *B* must be resisted by the other. Consequently each unit in this hypothetical State System will inevitably tend to throw its weight into the balance behind either of the other two States menaced by the third. If the principle is consistently applied by all three, no one State will be able to overcome another and all will preserve their independence. In its elementary form, therefore, the balance-of-power principle is designed not to preserve peace or to contribute toward international understanding, as later rationalizations would have it, but simply to maintain the independence of each unit of a State System by preventing any one unit from so increasing its power as to threaten the rest.

This pattern of political relationships characterized all of the State Systems which antedated the contemporary State System of western civilization. It is clearly apparent in the early city-state systems of the Tigris-Euphrates valley and in the relations of the great oriental monarchies of the ancient Near East. It likewise appears very distinctly in the international politics of the Greek city-states and also emerges in the larger State System of the whole Mediterranean basin during the second and third centuries B.C. In every case, however, the resulting balance of power was an unstable one and in the final event the balance was disrupted by the rise of a preponderantly powerful State which succeeded, in spite of all combinations against it, in imposing its will upon its rivals. The extinction of the classical State System through the establishment of the world empire of Rome came about through the breakdown of the early balance of power between the Mediterranean States. In the absence of an effective coalition to check the rising power of the Roman State, the legions were able to dispose of one rival after another in piecemeal fashion, to deprive all other States of independence, and to create a universal dominion.

The wars of the middle ages, such as the Hundred Years' War between England and "France," waged while the latter was still an inchoate congeries of principalities, did not exhibit the characteristics of a true State System, since the contestants were not well-defined territorial units, but were feudal structures, linked to one another in complex relationships of vassalage and fealty. But as soon as definite territorial States came into being and competed with one another for power, the balance-of-power pattern reemerged. This took place first, as has been noted, in Italy where the Kingdom of the Two Sicilies, the Papal States, Milan, Venice, Florence, Genoa, and lesser Powers struggled with one another and against outside invaders, German, French, or Spanish, who were attracted to the peninsula by the wealth of its cities. Each pursued its own interests, for, as Machiavelli observed, "the prince who contributes toward the advancement of another power, ruins his own." Invariably the weak combined against the strong and no one power, whether local State or foreign invader, was able to bring the whole peninsula into subjection. The national monarchies of the west—England, France, and Spain—and the smaller States and principalities of central Europe were similarly engaged in a competitive struggle for power in which the same principle inevitably operated. When the House of Hapsburg under Charles V attained such vast domains that its power seemed a menace to other States, they combined to check its ascendancy. When Spain under Philip II aspired to hegemony it was checked in turn by hostile coalitions. Later France became the most powerful State of Europe—a position which it held for over two hundred years. International politics accordingly assumed the form of coalition after coalition against *la Grande Nation*, from the time of the league formed by William of Orange to frustrate the ambitions of Louis XIV, to the quadruple alliance which humbled Napoleon at Leipzig and Waterloo. Another balance of power, involving Sweden, Russia, Poland, Prussia, and Austria, developed in eastern Europe and became an integral part of the whole European State System in the latter half of the eighteenth century.

These developments will be examined in some detail in the following chapter. Suffice it to say here that balance-of-power considerations began to dominate State policies as soon as the Western State System came into being. So perfectly has the principle of equilibrium operated subsequently that, with few exceptions, each of the major aggregations of political power of the sixteenth century has been able to preserve its existence as an independent State up to the present time. No State has thus far succeeded in repeating in the Western State System the achievements of Rome in classical times. Each of the successive aspirants for universal dominion— the Hapsburg dynasty, the French monarchy, the first French Empire, and imperial Germany—has been frustrated by coalitions of weaker

States allied against the stronger. The four centuries of development of the Western State System are, to be sure, but a short period compared to the many centuries of evolution of earlier State Systems. At some future time the balance of power may be disrupted and the State System may go the way of its predecessors, as Napoleon anticipated when he declared that some day Europe must be either all French or all Cossack. But up to the present time the balance of power has operated with almost mathematical precision, each weight finding its counterweight, each coalition creating its counter-coalition, with no State succeeding in imposing its power permanently on the others.

During the fifteenth and sixteenth centuries the States of western Europe pursued balance-of-power policies toward one another, without the principle itself receiving any clear and conscious formulation. In the early 1500's Francis I and Cardinal Wolsey, the great adviser of Henry VIII, both hinted at the principle in their declarations. But not until the time of Louis XIV does the concept emerge in definite form in the statements of diplomats and the literature of international relations. Lord Bolingbroke, who was responsible for English foreign policy during the last years of the War of the Spanish Succession (1701–1713), was one of the first English ministers to attempt to build his program with the deliberate purpose of preserving the continental equilibrium. In the negotiations which preceded the signature of the Treaty of Utrecht he was instrumental in arranging the solemn and public declarations of Philip V and the Dukes of Orleans and Berry by which, in the interest of maintaining a balance between the Powers of Europe, they renounced all ambitions of attempting to unite France and Spain under a single crown. In the words of one of Bolingbroke's friends, these renunciations "lay down the balance of power in Europe as their foundation, expressing that Spain ought not to be united either to France or to the House of Austria."[1]

[1] The Duke of Shrewsbury to Bolingbroke, Paris, March 23, 1713. Bolingbroke himself stated the principle as follows: "The scales of the balance of power will never be exactly poised, nor is the precise point of equality either desirable or necessary to be discerned. It is sufficient in this as in other human affairs, that the deviation be not too great. Some there will always be. A constant attention to these deviations is therefore necessary. When they are little their increase may be easily prevented by early care and the precautions that good policy suggests. But when they become great for want of this care and these precautions, or by the force of unforeseen events, more vigor is to be exerted, and greater efforts to be made. But even in such cases, much reflection is necessary on all the circumstances that form the conjuncture; lest, by attacking with ill success, the deviation be confirmed, and the power that is deemed already exorbitant become more so; and lest, by attacking with good success, whilst one scale is pillaged, too much weight of power be thrown into the other. In such cases, he who has considered, in the histories of former ages, the strange revolutions that time produces, and the perpetual flux and reflux of public as well as private fortunes, of kingdoms and states as well as of those who govern or are governed in them, will incline to think, that if the scales can be brought back by a war, nearly, though not exactly, to the point they were at before this great deviation from it, the rest may be left to accidents, and to the use that good policy is able to make of them." *The Works of Lord Bolingbroke*, 1841, II, p. 291.

Some years later the French philosopher and political writer, Fenelon, discussed the balance as essential to maintain the liberty, tranquillity, and public safety of Europe. At the opening of the War of the Austrian Succession (1741), Sir Robert Walpole stated the principle with even greater clarity:

> The use of alliances . . . has in the last age been too much experienced to be contested; it is by leagues well concerted and strictly observed that the weak are defended against the strong, that bounds are set to the turbulence of ambition, that the torrent of power is restrained, and empires preserved from those inundations of war that, in former times, laid the world in ruins. By alliances . . . the equipoise of power is maintained, and those alarms and apprehensions avoided, which must arise from vicissitudes of empire and the fluctuations of perpetual contest. . . .
>
> The firmest bond of alliances is mutual interest. Men easily unite against him whom they have all reason to fear and to hate, by whom they have been greatly injured, and by whom they suspect that no opportunity will be lost of renewing his encroachments. Such is the state of this nation (England) and of the Austrians. We are equally endangered by the French greatness, and equally animated against it by hereditary animosities, and contests continued from one age to another; we are convinced that, however either may be flattered or caressed, while the other is invaded, every blow is aimed at both and that we are divided only that we may be more easily destroyed (*Parliamentary History*, XII, pp. 168–169).

Frederick the Great likewise paid lip-service to the principle, though his expansionist policies upset the balance and led to new wars to check Prussian power. The English philosopher, David Hume, in his *Political Discourses* (1751), dwells upon the efficacy of Britain's balance-of-power policy in checkmating French efforts to establish hegemony on the Continent. The Swiss jurist, Emeric de Vattel, who based his *Droit de gens* (1758) on the work of Wolff, was one of the first text-writers to consider the principle as a problem of international law:

> Europe forms a political system in which the nations inhabiting this part of the world are bound together by their relations and various interests into a single body. It is no longer, as in former times, a confused heap of detached parts, each of which had but little concern for the lot of the other, and rarely troubled itself over what did not immediately affect it. The constant attention of sovereigns to all that goes on, the custom of resident ministers, the continual negotiations that take place, make of modern Europe a sort of republic, whose members, each independent, but all bound together by a common interest, unite for the maintenance of order and the preservation of liberty. This is what has given rise to the well-known principle of the balance of power, by which is meant an arrangement of affairs so that no State shall be in a position to have absolute mastery and dominate over the others. (E. de Vattel, *The Law of Nations*, translation of edition of 1758, Washington, 1916, pp. 248f.)

Vattel argued that the balance of power could best be preserved through alliances and confederations to check the ascendancy of any one

Power which seemed likely to upset the equilibrium. He denied that balance-of-power considerations give a State any absolute right of armed action against another, but he conceded that "one is justified in forestalling a danger in direct ratio to the degree of probability attending it and to the seriousness of the evil which is threatened."

If an unknown man takes aim at me in the middle of a forest, I am not yet certain that he wishes to kill me; must I allow him time to fire in order to be sure of his intent? Is there any reasonable casuist who would deny me the right to forestall the act? But presumption becomes almost equal to certitude if the prince who is about to acquire enormous power has already given evidence of an unbridled pride and ambition. In the imaginary case mentioned above, who would have dared counsel the European States to allow Louis XIV to make such a formidable addition to his power? (*Ibid.*)

Vattel also sought to present the balance of power as a guarantee of the liberty and independence of States. His wide influence led to general acceptance of this view. It is a substantially accurate characterization of the pattern, though it is obvious that the balance may sometimes be preserved by the partition of a weak State among its stronger neighbors, as happened in the extinction of the independence of Poland at the end of the eighteenth century by Russia, Austria, and Prussia. In any case, the balance-of-power principle has been recognized as an integral feature of the Western State System by Rousseau, Kant, and a host of later writers, as well as by the great majority of diplomats and statesmen.

6. THE RISE OF INTERNATIONAL LAW

It remains now that I briefly explain with what aids, and with what care, I undertook this work. In the first place, it was my object to refer the truth of the things which belong to natural law to some notions, so certain, that no one can deny them, without doing violence to his own nature. . . . What cannot be deduced from certain principles by solid reasoning, and yet is seen and observed everywhere, must have its origin from the will and consent of all.—HUGO GROTIUS, *De Jure Belli ac Pacis.*

With the general acceptance of the concept of sovereignty by the States of western Europe and the general adoption of the balance-of-power principle as a guide to State policy, the foundations of the Western State System in its modern form were established. There remains only to be noted the emergence of international law out of a confused and unformulated body of customs and usages into a definite system of jurisprudence regulating the relations between States. This development likewise took place in the later sixteenth and early seventeenth centuries, though it was foreshadowed by many centuries of preparation during which international law existed and evolved as a practical basis for defining the legal rights and obligations of States long before it attracted the attention of scholars and jurists.

As has been suggested above, even the earliest States of the ancient world appear to have recognized the utility of observing certain usages and formalities in their dealings with one another. These international folkways, if they may be so described, were mutually advantageous to those who observed them and they became customary and traditionalized by virtue of their general acceptance. War was almost incessant and international politics was a struggle for mastery between rival powers. But it was none the less expedient for States to act in conformity with such habits and customs of international society as slowly developed to replace the law of the jungle in its crudest form. The sanctity of treaties and the inviolability of diplomatic representatives were among the first principles of international usage to receive general recognition. In the State Systems of classical and pre-classical civilization, however, these habits and customs never attained the dignity of "international law" or of "international morality," but remained on the level of rules of etiquette which were observed when States found it convenient to do so and were disregarded frequently without serious consequences. Not until the State System of western civilization had emerged out of medieval feudalism did a true international law come into existence.

In view of the large amount of popular confusion which still prevails regarding the nature of international law, it may be well to indicate at the outset how it differs from custom, etiquette, and morality, on the one hand, and from other types of law, on the other. All early law would appear to be an outgrowth of habits and customs which have grown up more or less unconsciously to regulate the relations between members of a community. To utilize the terminology of modern sociology, it may be said that when the violation of a custom meets merely with the disapproval of the community, such a custom is still part of the folkways, *i.e.*, of the established ways of doing things to which conformity is expected by the group, but not imperatively demanded as a matter of necessity. When the violation of a custom meets with the moral condemnation of the community and with organized punishment, it is part of the *mores* of the group which feels not only that its standards of propriety have been departed from, but that its moral values have been outraged. In both cases religious sanctions are likely to attach to the custom in question. In primitive societies there is seldom any recognized distinction between custom, morality, religion, and law. Early legal codes, like that of Hammurabi or the Mosaic laws, are usually looked upon as divinely inspired, if not actually handed down from on high, and consist of verbal formulations of the group's sense of what is right and just.

The concept of "law," however, has inherent in it the idea of deliberate fabrication, of a supreme power representing the community which has authority to lay down somewhat flexible rules for the guidance of its members and to impose penalties for nonobservance. As John Austin expressed it, law is a "command issued by a political superior to a political inferior with power to enforce it by penalties for disobedience." Law thus comes to express the will of the rulers, of the sovereign power in the State. It defines the rights and obligations of citizens or subjects with respect to their relations toward the State and toward one another. It furnishes a basis for the orderly settlement of disputes between individuals and it designates as "crimes," *i.e.*, injuries against the community or the State, such acts as offend the prevailing sense of justice and the prevailing moral values. It is enforceable to the degree to which it harmonizes with popular attitudes and opinions. It has become distinct from the folkways and the *mores*, for it consists not of mere usages nor yet of moral precepts, but rather of rules of conduct laid down by the political authorities and enforced by the coercive power of the State.

It is obvious that international law is not "law" in this sense. It is derived from customs and usages, but it is concerned not with the relations between individuals nor between the individual and the State, as is national or municipal law, but with the relations between States. And since States are sovereign, independent, and equal, with no State subject to the control of another, there is no political superior, no supreme authority, no superstate to legislate for the members of the "international society." Neither is international law an outgrowth of anything which can properly be called international morality, for morality has to do with the relationships between individuals within a social group the members of which have built up a moral code on the basis of their common interests and the common conscience which reflects these interests. States in their dealings with one another have as yet no "conscience" and no common interests comparable to those which unite individuals into groups on the basis of a sense of right and wrong. The State is, by its nature, beyond good and evil, as Machiavelli so clearly perceived. International law, therefore, is not concerned with ethical or moral values and it is in no sense the pronouncement of any sovereign power. It grows out of the practices and usages which States find useful and expedient to observe with respect to one another. These practices and usages become international law when, in any State System, all or nearly all of its members attach so much importance to them that they tend to hold each particular State answerable for departures from them. When this situation prevails, the practices and usages become verbalized into "principles" which define the legal rights and obligations of the units of the State System. Consequently international law may best be defined by describing it as the body of rules and principles of conduct generally observed within the society of civilized States for the violation of which States are habitually held responsible. Responsibility is enforced by the whole body of States, and the competitive struggle for power which is the essence of international politics goes on as before within the new legal framework.

International law as a distinct branch of legal science received almost no recognition among lawyers and jurists before the fifteenth century, despite the practical development of international customs and usages in the medieval State System. Vittoria (1480–1546) and Ayala (1548–1584) made early efforts to integrate these usages into a consistent system of law, while the Spanish Jesuit, Suarez (1548–1617), endeavored to discover the basis for such a system in "natural law" or reason. Gentilis (1552–1608) likewise attempted on a more pretentious scale to set forth the principles governing the relations between States. In this period of groping toward a logical basis for an international jurisprudence two schools of thought were distinguishable: one looked for guidance to international practice and sought to make international law the written customs of States; the other tried to formulate principles on the basis of ethics, theology, reason, and common sense. The former school relied much upon the *ius gentium* of Roman law, while the latter searched for light in the *ius naturale* or law of nature which was the current symbolization of what seemed rational and just. These two fountain-heads of wisdom have ever since been supplementary sources of international law in its subsequent development.

The task of reconciling the two schools and of erecting an imposing edifice of legal principles worthy of being called a true "law of nations" was first performed by the versatile and erratic Dutch genius, Huig van Groot or Hugo Grotius, in the Latinized version of his name. So significant was his contribution and so profound has been his influence that later generations of jurists conferred upon him the title of "the father of international law." Born at Delft, April 10, 1583, son of the burgomaster of Leyden, he wrote Latin verses at the age of nine, entered the university at twelve, and was a learned editor at fifteen, when he accompanied a Dutch embassy to Paris. After winning his LL.D. at the University of Leyden, he devoted himself to writing Latin dramas and poems and practicing law. At twenty he was appointed official historiographer by the States General, in which capacity he began work on his *De jure praedae* (1604) which was the basis of his later treatise. As advocate of the Dutch East India Company, he defended the capture of a Portuguese galleon in the Straits of Malacca by the Dutch captain, Heemskirk, with the argument that the Portuguese claim that all eastern waters were under Portuguese jurisdiction was unsound and contrary to the accepted practice of nations. His part in this early controversy over freedom of the seas won him further fame and he embarked upon a promising diplomatic career which was rudely cut off in 1619—fortunately, perhaps, for posterity, for had he continued to occupy himself with the practical work of diplomacy he might never have found leisure to compile his monumental work.

Grotius' great treatise, *De jure belli ac pacis* ("Concerning the Law of War and Peace") was in part written in the prison fortress of Louvestein, where the poet-jurist was incarcerated in 1619 on a life sentence because of his unpopular religious views. The bloody Thirty Years' War had just broken out in Bohemia. It was to mark the culmination of the religious conflicts of the century. Young Hugo was a theologian no less than a lawyer and, like Erasmus a hundred years before, he pleaded for toleration and sought to mediate between the warring sects of Remonstrants and anti-remonstrants. He was jailed for his pains and had his property confiscated, but prison life was not unbearable, for he was permitted to live with his gifted wife and to continue his studies with the aid of many large chests of books which were periodically brought to him by his guards. In 1621 his wife nailed him up in a book chest and in this appropriate disguise he escaped from his cell and fled to Antwerp and Paris, where Louis XIII granted him a small pension. In 1625 his treatise was completed and published. It brought him no profits, but insured him immortal fame, for it was the most adequate and comprehensive statement of the principles of international law which had yet appeared. He subsequently became Swedish Ambassador to France and died at Rostock in 1645.

The *De jure belli ac pacis* was largely inspired by the author's revulsion at the horrors and excesses of the wars of religion which were devastating the Europe of his day. In his Prolegomena he declared:

The civil law, both that of Rome, and that of each nation in particular, has been treated of, with a view either to illustrate it or to present it in a compendious form, by many. But international law, that which regards the mutual relations of several peoples, or rulers of peoples, whether it proceed from nature, or be instituted by divine command, or introduced by custom and tacit compact, has been touched on by few, and has been by no one treated as a whole in an orderly manner. And yet that this be done, concerns the human race. . . .

I, for the reasons which I have stated, holding it to be most certain that there is among nations a common law of rights which is of force with regard to war, and in war, saw many and grave causes why I should write a work on that subject. For I saw prevailing throughout the Christian world a license in making war of which even barbarous nations would have been ashamed; recourse being had to arms for slight reasons or no reason; and when arms were once taken up, all reverence for divine and human law was thrown away, just as if men were thenceforth authorized to commit all crimes without restraint.

He therefore attempted, with signal success, to compile the principles by which States are, or ought to be, governed, deriving them from the law of nature or dictates of right reason, as set forth by philosophers, historians, poets, and orators, and also from the law of nations which he sharply distinguished from the other as consisting of the practices of States and the resulting principles of law binding upon them by virtue of their having consented to them.

Grotius here laid the foundations upon which subsequent jurists were to build. He combined custom and reason as sources of international law, as did such notable successors as Bynkershoek, Wolff, Vattel, and Wheaton. The Naturalist school, represented by Puffendorf, Thomasius, and Rutherford, continued to give precedence to reason or natural law, while the Positivist school of Selden, Zouch, Bentham, Martens, and others emphasized the actual customs and practices of States as the best possible criteria of their legal rights and obligations. The Grotian view, which was a synthesis of the two, has now come to prevail and has in turn influenced the practice of States and led to the erection of the imposing structure of modern international jurisprudence, the basic principles of which will be reviewed in a later chapter.

Many observers, particularly in recent years, have been struck by the apparent anomaly presented by a State System in which a great body of legal concepts has developed to define the rights, obligations, and procedures of States in their mutual relations and in which, at the same time, these States continue to be engaged in a competitive struggle for the stakes of diplomacy, involving the maintenance of an unstable equilibrium of power and periodical resorts to armed violence. This anomaly disappears, however, in the light of a fuller appreciation of the peculiar nature of international law. Within national societies, law is a substitute for force in the settlement of disputes. Private law defines the rights and remedies of individuals and groups and provides means for the pacific settlement of differences through litigation and adjudication. Public law defines the structure of the State and the procedures of government and makes of politics no longer an armed struggle for power as it was in the feudal period, but a peaceable process of competition, discussion, and compromise between parties, factions, classes, and other associations organized for political action. Domestic peace within the State is normally maintained by the coercive power of government, resting upon the acquiescence of the great mass of the governed who are willing to subordinate special interests to general interests and to submit to the result of the process of politics. International law has no such coercive power upon which to rely and it does not rest, except to a very limited degree, upon any willingness upon the part of sovereign States to subordinate their interests to the interests of the whole society of States. It is not, therefore, a substitute for force in the relations between States, however much enthusiastic jurists would like to give it this function. Neither does it insure the pacific settlement of disputes, though it supplies a set of concepts for the legal definition of the subject matter of disputes and it specifies what procedures are permissible, both in pacific and in non-pacific settlement. It consists merely of a set of rules which States have found it useful and expedient to observe.

These rules relate quite as much to the conduct of warfare, *i.e.*, to the application of violence by State against State, as to non-violent discussion and compromise. Being based upon the actual behavior of sovereign States, they take cognizance of the realities of that behavior. They are not concerned with the purposes, goals, and objectives of State behavior, but only with its forms. International law, unlike municipal law, does not deprive those to whom it is addressed of the right to protect their interests by their own power, though in recent years efforts have been made, with results as yet uncertain, to outlaw war and to require States to resort only to pacific means of settlement. International politics, unlike national politics, has not yet been transformed from a violent to a pacific process by virtue of the evolution of a system of jurisprudence governing the relations between the contestants. The international law of the Western State System simply lays down the rules which the contestants are expected to follow. Within the limits of these rules there goes on as before that perpetual struggle for prestige and influence which is the distinguishing pattern of an international politics resting upon State sovereignty and a balance of power. The general course of that struggle during the past three centuries will be sketched in the next chapter, with the following book devoted to a description and analysis of the forms—legal, procedural, and administrative—into which the political relations between States have been cast.

SUGGESTED READINGS

Bryce, J.: *The Holy Roman Empire*, New York, The Macmillan Company, 1914.
Cambridge Medieval History, New York, The Macmillan Company, 1913.
Dunning, W. A.: *History of Political Theories* (3 vols.), New York, The Macmillan Company, 1920.
Hill, D. J.: *A History of Diplomacy in the International Development of Europe* (3 vols.), New York, Longmans Green & Co., 1924.
Laski, H.: *Foundations of Sovereignty*, New York, Harcourt Brace & Company, 1921.
Machiavelli, N.: *History of Florence*, London, George Bell & Sons, 1906.
————: *The Prince*, New York, E. P. Dutton & Co., Inc., 1908.
Merriam, C. E.: *History of the Theory of Sovereignty*, New York, Columbia University Press, 1900.
Munro, D. C.: *The Middle Ages*, New York, Century Company, 1928.
Oman, C. W.: *A History of the Art of War in the Middle Ages* (2 vols.), London, Methuen & Co., 1924.
Sellery, G. C., and A. C. Krey: *Medieval Foundations of Western Civilization*, New York, Harper & Brothers, 1929.
Thompson, J. W.: *Economic and Social History of the Middle Ages*, New York, Century Company, 1928.
————: *An Economic and Social History of Europe in the Later Middle Ages*, New York, Century Company, 1931.
Thorndike, L.: *History of Medieval Europe*, Boston, Houghton Mifflin Company, 1917.
Villari, P.: *The Life and Times of Niccolo Machiavelli*, London, T. Fisher Unwin, 1892.
————: *Mediaeval Italy from Charlemagne to Henry VII*, London, T. Fisher Unwin, 1910.

Chapter III

THE EVOLUTION OF THE WESTERN STATE SYSTEM

I N ONE of his frequent moments of cynicism, the German philosopher, Nietzsche, observed that "the earth hath a skin; on this skin are diseases—for example: man." Without necessarily accepting the unsavory implications of this figure of speech, one may nevertheless legitimately compare the spread of man and of man's culture over the terrestrial globe with the spread of a thin film of parasitic organic matter over the skin of, let us say, an orange. Microscopic living beings appear where conditions are most favorable in the crevices of the surface; they reproduce, expand, and create societies or colonies; these societies spread in the direction of the most favorable opportunities and the least resistance; they come into contact with one another, intermingling and at the same time changing their own character; new societies emerge out of the fusion; old ones die and wither away. First one area and then another nourishes a rich growth and the process goes endlessly on until the orange is no more, or until the condition of its skin no longer supports life among the organisms which have made it their home.

If an observer on the moon, gifted with great longevity and remarkable powers of vision, could watch the course of man's history upon the globe of the earth, as men on the earth can observe the growth of bacteriological cultures on an orange, he would behold during the course of recent centuries the rise of a great culture in a relatively small but variegated area of the earth's surface known as Europe. He would notice further the gradual spread of this culture over the entire sphere until it had covered the whole and had, to a greater or lesser degree, superimposed itself upon the older cultures of other areas. If our imaginary observer on the moon were familiar with the past development of life upon the planet, and with the earlier spread of other and now vanished human cultures, he would see in this process a certain resemblance to what had happened many times before. Were he philosophically inclined, he might even venture to set forth the "laws" of cultural evolution and the principles of cultural emergence, growth, expansion, and decline. These laws, if carefully formulated on the basis of accurate observation, would apply to all the cultures of the earth from that distant dawn when civilized human societies first appeared in the river valleys and plains to that even more remote twilight time of the far future when, in the words of Anatole

[66]

France, "the last man will stumble face foremost into the snow and breath forth into the glacial air, hateless and loveless, the last human breath." But in so far as our lunar observer was concerned with the living present, he would be impressed by the fact that no previous culture had developed with such intensity and rapidity or had extended itself so completely over the globe as that which arose a thousand years ago in western Europe.

The history of the Western State System is but a phase of the history of western European civilization. The history of that civilization, in its later phases, is the chronicle of its gradual spread outward in all directions from Europe until it has come in contact with all other civilizations and imposed itself upon them. This long and complex course of growth and expansion is almost too vast to be encompassed as a whole by the finite intelligence of those who are themselves part of the process. But its various aspects and phases may readily be studied separately. The present study is concerned with a particular aspect of the process, *i.e.*, with the organizations and activities of the "States" into which European civilization has somehow divided itself, with the interrelationships between these States, with the attitudes, behavior patterns, procedures, and institutions to which these interrelationships have given rise, with, in short, the particular complex—bewildering enough in itself, but simple in comparison with the larger whole—which has here been designated as the Western State System. In the present chapter an effort will be made to sketch the rise of the more important of the States comprising the System, to indicate the general course of their relationships, and to show how the System has been transformed from a European System in the sixteenth century to a World System in the twentieth through the world-wide diffusion of the culture out of which it has grown.

1. THE EUROPEAN SYSTEM TO 1648

It may be observed, that provinces, amid the vicissitudes to which they are subject, pass from order into confusion, and afterwards recur to a state of order again; for the nature of mundane affairs not allowing them to continue in an even course, when they have arrived at their greatest perfection, they soon begin to decline. In the same manner, having been reduced by disorder, and sunk to their utmost state of depression, unable to descend lower, they, of necessity, reascend; and thus from good they gradually decline to evil, and from evil again return to good.—NICCOLO MACHIAVELLI, *History of Florence.*

From the point of view of international relations, the history of western Europe between 1500 and 1650—the age of the Renaissance, the Reformation, and the Wars of Religion—is the history of the transition from a Europe of confused, fragmented feudal principalities to a Europe of well-defined and consolidated territorial States. It is the period of the definite emergence of the Western State System. Europe as a whole becomes the larger stage upon which is played the same drama of power conflicts between States as had already been played with gusto and finesse on the smaller stage of medieval and Renaissance Italy. While Italian princes sought to outwit one another through diplomatic trickery and to overcome one another by unleashing their hosts of mercenary *condottieri*, kings and burghers elsewhere were checking the unruly power of the feudal nobility and preparing the way for royal absolutism. Gunpowder had rendered the armored knight and the fortified keep both obsolete. The English nobility was decimated by the Wars of the Roses and when the despotic Tudors ascended the throne they brought order and peace to a sorely troubled land. In France royal power was similarly in the ascendancy. In Spain other monarchs had at length pushed the Saracens out of Granada (1492) and united Aragon and Castile into a single kingdom. In the great central European plain, beyond the Low Countries and south of the Scandinavian kingdoms, there still existed a confused congerie of small States, in which the Mark of Brandenburg, the Kingdoms of Saxony, Bavaria, and Bohemia, and the Austrian possessions of the House of Hapsburg constituted the most notable aggregations of political power. Farther to the east lay the Kingdoms of Sweden and Poland and the Grand Duchy of Muscovy, and in the south, in the great Danubian plain, lay the Kingdom of Hungary. These were the border States of the emerging European System, for beyond them loomed dimly the world of Asia— the world of the Tartar hordes of Genghis Khan, who beat fiercely at the gates of Europe in the thirteenth century, and the world of the Ottoman Turks who likewise sought to storm the portals in the early sixteenth century under the leadership of Suleiman the Magnificent. In both cases these waves of Asiatic invaders from the east and south were ultimately turned back and Europe was left free to follow out its own destiny.

In the world of the west the old unity of Christendom was already gone, for the Church had decayed after the Great Schism. The Popes had become princes not of peace but of diplomacy and war. Luther, Calvin, and Zwingli toppled over the structure of the universal Church during the first half of the sixteenth century. In the ensuing battle of Reformation and Counter Reformation the warring sects fell upon one another with a zest and ferocity worthy of the soldiers of Islam. In this turmoil of religious struggle the kings and princes of the north seized upon ecclesiastical wealth and waxed more powerful on the profits of Protestantism, while other sovereigns in the south rushed to the defense of a reinvigorated and militant Catholicism. Organized Christianity became divided into "national" churches. Civil and international war followed in the wake of theological strife. In the flame of conflict territorial States were definitely precipitated out of the formless, feudal mass of petty political fragments. These States were for the first time all involved in a great continental struggle during the Thirty Years' War. At its close, Europeans found themselves in the new world of the "modern" age. The State System of modern Europe was still in embryo when Columbus set forth across the Atlantic to seek a new route to the Indies. It was a lusty and turbulent infant when, fifteen decades later, the princes and diplomats of all Europe met in solemn conclave in Westphalia to redraw boundaries and to redistribute territory in accordance with the verdict of arms in the first general European war.

To retell in detail the oft-told tale of the stirring events of this period is no part of the present task. But the tyranny of time hangs heavy over every present and the Western State System in its contemporary configuration is intelligible only in terms of the past out of which it has come. Like all complexes of attitudes, behavior patterns, and institutions within a culture, it is a product of long growth, is indeed nothing more than the sum of its past translated into the living present. This will be abundantly apparent in every phase of the System which is examined in succeeding chapters. But by way of completing this introduction, it should be useful to attempt to secure that wider perspective on the present which a consideration of the past affords.

International politics in Europe at the beginning of the sixteenth century and throughout the whole Baroque period of western European history was primarily a struggle for power, prestige, and territory between the rival dynasties which forged the States of modern Europe. Within each State the reigning house relied for support upon the new burgher class and upon that portion of the landed nobility which was willing to occupy the position of a titled ruling caste within the limits imposed by monarchical absolutism. Each dynasty strove to enforce its authority upon the still unruly remnants of the feudal aristocracy. Each king and prince endeavored to consolidate the power of his house over the realm by imposing unity upon the medieval, feudalized diversity of his heritage— ecclesiastical and religious unity, linguistic unity, judicial unity, fiscal unity, administrative unity, military unity. And between the rival dynasties of nation-builders there was constant struggle, with each pursuing its own interests and seeking to expand its lands and its influence through marriage, war, and diplomacy.

The rivalries between the dynasts were first focused in Italy. The Italian peninsula, itself the cradle of modern diplomacy, became the first of many subsequent arenas of combat between the great national monarchies of the north and west. Throughout the whole history of the Western State System the clash of conflicting Powers has ever been most acute in rich regions where the local States are powerless to resist outside aggression and where no outside State is able to establish its own undisputed control. Such a region was Italy between 1450 and 1550. The

Hundred Years' War between England and France was just drawing to a close, with the victory of the French monarchy already in sight. The death of the Duke of Milan in 1447 was followed by the first of a long series of French interventions in Italian affairs. Charles VII of France secured control of Genoa, but was hampered by fear of continued English aggression against his own lands and by difficulties with his own vassals. His successors embarked upon an active policy of establishing French hegemony in Italy which met with stout resistance from Spain, Austria, and the Italian States themselves. Louis XI, "universal spider" and astute proponent of the methods of diplomatic trickery and deceit which the Italian States had perfected, spun his web with care, but he was deflected from his purpose and devoted himself to overthrowing Charles the Bold, Duke of Burgundy, and incorporating into the French monarchy such of the Duke's lands as he could seize upon and hold. But in 1494 young King Charles VIII embarked in earnest upon the French conquest of Italy. He entered Rome and seized control of Naples, but this menacing extension of French power raised up against it a hostile league of Spain, Austria, Venice, and lesser States which finally compelled Charles to quit the peninsula empty-handed. These events have properly been described as marking the beginning of modern European diplomacy. As one commentator puts it, "the expedition of Charles VIII may justly be regarded as the last great mediaeval adventure and the first military campaign of modern times. With equal truth, it may be taken to mark the birth of international politics."[1]

Louis XII of France continued the Italian policies of his predecessors and built for himself a structure of European alliances which he hoped would enable him to achieve his purposes. By 1499 he could count on the support or benevolent neutrality of England, Scotland, Spain, Portugal, Norway, Denmark, Sweden, the Pope, Venice, Archduke Philip of Austria, and certain electors of the Empire. Milan fell to the French and Louis forthwith proceeded to form alliances with Poland and Hungary in order to surround his most dangerous enemy, the Emperor Maximilian, with an unbroken ring of French satellites. In 1500 the Kingdom of Naples was partitioned between France and Spain, but the partitioners quarrelled over the spoils and fell upon one another in bitter combat. Louis was obliged to renounce his ambitions of making himself master of a united Europe in which the Hapsburg and Valois dynasties should divide the Continent between them. His diplomatic blunders, so well described by Machiavelli, were to cost him Italy as well. Alexander VI, perhaps the most Machiavellian and worldly-minded of the Renaissance Popes, played off France and Spain against one another until his death in 1503. Five years later the "League of Cambray" was formed as a secret military

[1] Hill, *op. cit.*, I, p. 209.

alliance between the Pope, the Emperor, Louis XII, and King Ferdinand of Spain for the dismemberment of Venice, but the clever Venetian diplomats set the allies by the ears, detached Pope Julius II from the conspiracy, and provoked the intervention of Henry VIII of England against France. The Tudor monarch, along with the Emperor Maximilian, finally entered the "Holy League" of 1511–1512, in alliance with the Papacy and the Spanish monarchy for the purpose of isolating Louis and expelling the French from Italy. The French troops were driven from Milan by the Swiss and Louis' designs were frustrated, but when Julius died in 1513 it was clear that the allies, as usual, had fallen out among themselves and that Italy was to remain a bone of contention among the States which had striven for control of the peninsula. Francis I (1515–1547) attempted at once, in alliance with Venice, to recover Milan for France and a new French invasion of Italy was forthwith launched. The success of this venture caused England, Spain, the Empire, and certain of the Swiss cantons to take up arms against the French king, but in 1517 general peace was temporarily reestablished.

The drama thus opens with France occupying a position of continental predominance which later came to be regarded as traditional and inevitable by the rulers and diplomats of *la Grande Nation*. But here, as always in the European State System, each great aggregation of power is sooner or later confronted with a counterweight in the form of an opposing aggregation whose leaders are prepared to check the ambitions of the one Power which seems a menace to all. The various leagues against France represented such counterweights. But in 1519 an immensely greater concentration of power appeared in the House of Hapsburg whose new representative, young King Charles of Spain, fell heir to estates vaster and richer than those held by any other Christian ruler. Charles' mother was Joana, daughter of Ferdinand of Aragon and Isabella of Castile, from whom he inherited Spain, Naples, Mexico, Peru, and the Indies, East and West, far across the seas. His father was Philip of Hapsburg, son of the Emperor Maximilian and Mary, Duchess of Burgundy, from whom he inherited the seventeen provinces of the Netherlands, Franche Comté, Austria, Styria, Carniola, Carinthia, the Tyrol, and other scattered possessions in Germany and Italy.

This pyramid of power was crowned in 1519 by the election of the young king as Charles V, Holy Roman Emperor—an honor which he wrested from his rival candidates, Francis I of France and Henry VIII of England, by a liberal resort to bribery, made possible by the aid of the great banking house of Fugger. Charles' brother, Ferdinand, made the Hapsburg power even more formidable by securing for himself the crowns of Bohemia and Hungary. Here was a magnificent imperial realm which created the possibility of one dynasty establishing its undisputed hegem-

ony over Europe. But here, as always, the pretender to universal dominion was eventually frustrated by a combination against him of all States
threatened by his power. Elaborate bargainings had gone on between
Charles, Francis, and Henry, with the last, under the influence of his
great minister, Cardinal Wolsey, seeking to preserve the balance between
France and the Empire. Henry had met Charles both in England and on
the Continent and had exchanged elaborate amenities with Francis in
1519 on the "Field of Cloth of Gold" near Calais. But once the lines of
rivalry were clearly drawn, a struggle in arms appeared inevitable and
England under Wolsey began that balance-of-power policy which has
ever since characterized her foreign relations. The international politics of
the first half of the sixteenth century revolves about the combat between
Charles V and the various coalitions which France erected against him,
with England seeking to preserve an equilibrium between the contestants.

War opened in Italy in 1521, with the imperial armies driving the
French from the peninsula, invading southern France, and then retiring
to Milan in the face of a new French invasion. In 1525 Francis I was defeated and captured at Pavia. He was left, he wrote his mother,
"nothing in the world save his honor and his life." Francis was taken to
Spain and later released on condition of his marrying the Emperor's sister
and surrendering all claims to Burgundy, the Netherlands, and Italy—
but no sooner was the French monarch free than he formed a new coalition
against Charles with the aid of the Pope, Florence, Venice, and Milan.
In 1527 the imperial armies captured and sacked Rome and compelled the
Pope to sue for peace. The Peace of Cambrai (1529) registered a deadlock
between the belligerents. Charles was master in Italy and was there
crowned Emperor by the Pope in 1530—last of his line to receive this
honor. Francis made alliances with the Scots, the Swedes, the Danes, the
Protestant princes of north Germany, and even the Turks in his efforts
to thwart the Hapsburg power, but the later contests were indecisive.
Charles retired in 1555–1556, exhausted by the cares of kingship and
disappointed over his failure to crush the Reformation in Germany. In
France Henry II (1547–1559) continued the struggle until the Peace of
Cateau-Cambresis of 1559. In the final result France had been driven from
Italy, but had checkmated the Hapsburg power and had extended its
own territory eastward toward the Rhine by acquiring Metz, Toul, and
Verdun.

The next phase of the incessant rivalries of the dynasties centers about
the son of Charles, Philip II (1556–1598), who inherited Spain, the
Netherlands, Franche Comté, the Two Sicilies, Milan, and the American
colonies of Spain, while his uncle Ferdinand secured the eastern possessions of the House of Hapsburg. Philip's power was scarcely less
formidable than his father's and his active championship of the Counter

Reformation aroused Protestant Europe against him. During his reign Spain, enriched by the booty of Mexico, Peru, and the Indies, annexed Portugal (1580), rose to brief ascendancy over Europe, and then gradually fell to the position of a secondary Power. Philip was hampered in his foreign policy by various revolts within his realm—that of Aragon against Castilian domination (1591), that of the Moriscoes in the south who attempted, unsuccessfully, to restore the independence of Granada (1568–1570), and, finally and most significant, that of the Protestant Netherlands (1566–1648) which rose in rebellion under the leadership of William the Silent, Prince of Orange, and ultimately established their independence as the United Netherlands—a new member in the European constellation of States. England and France were the logical counterpoises of Spain, but both were similarly hampered by internal strife resulting from religious disturbances.

Philip sought to extend his influence over both England and France for ecclesiastical and political reasons. His marriage with Mary Tudor (1553–1558), who temporarily restored England to the Catholic fold, promised well for his designs, but Mary's successor, the Protestant Queen Elizabeth, gave him endless trouble. The Spanish king, in his efforts to achieve his purposes, alternately tried offers of matrimony, diplomatic trickery, machinations against the English throne, and, finally, armed force—all equally in vain. The religious wars in France and the bitter civil strife of Bourbons and Guises likewise offered an opportunity for Spanish intrigue, for the power of the royal house (dominated by Catherine de Medici during the reigns of her three weak sons, Francis II, Charles IX, and Henry III) was constantly menaced by the nobles and by the Protestant Huguenots. In 1585 Philip entered into a compact with the French Catholic leader, Henry, Duke of Guise, whereby he agreed to assist him in wresting the French crown from King Henry III and his other rival, the Protestant Henry of Bourbon, King of Navarre and legitimate heir to the kingship of France by indirect descent from St. Louis. The success of this scheme would have given Philip a controlling influence at the French court. But in the "war of the three Henries" Queen Elizabeth assisted Henry of Navarre and in 1588 Henry III caused Henry of Guise to be assassinated. In the same year the vast Armada which Philip had gathered for the conquest of England was defeated and wrecked in the Channel. This event symbolized the decline of Spanish sea power and the rise of England to commercial and naval supremacy. King Henry of France was assassinated the following year and Henry of Navarre became the first of the Bourbon kings as Henry IV (1589–1610). He pacified France by accepting Catholicism in 1593 and fought Philip to a draw until the Treaty of Vervins (1598) confirmed the terms of Cateau-Cambresis of forty years before. Philip of Spain had lost the Netherlands and failed in his efforts against England and France. His cooperation in crushing Turkish sea power in the Mediterranean (1571) was small compensation for the decline of Spanish power and prestige in western European affairs.

By the second decade of the next century a definite pattern had emerged in the closely woven fabric of dynastic rivalry, religious conflict, and clashing national ambitions. Europe was in process of transition from an aggregation of separate States which had isolated and incidental contacts with one another to a State System in which each member is directly concerned with the relations between all the rest. This interdependence of political relations between the Powers was vaguely appreciated in the days of Elizabeth, Henry, and Philip. By 1648 it was a fixed feature of European international politics. The first general European war had intervened as a dramatic and bloody climax to the religious struggles of the preceding century. In its flames medieval Europe was consumed. The modern State System, fully matured, emerged from the ashes.

The causes and events of this great combat are too involved to be dealt with here. Suffice it to say that it was at once a contest for supremacy between the Bourbon and Hapsburg dynasties, a death grapple between Protestantism and Catholicism, and a conflict (between the Emperor and the princes) over control of the German States. In 1618 the Calvinist nobles of Bohemia revolted against their new Hapsburg king, Ferdinand II (1619–1637), and thus began a struggle which was eventually to draw all Europe into its vortex. Ferdinand's general, Count Tilly, soon restored Hapsburg power in Bohemia, whose unfortunate "winter king," Frederick, was driven out and compelled to see his lands in the Palatinate transferred to Maximilian of Bavaria. This expansion of Bavaria, however, upset the balance of power which had prevailed between Protestant and Catholic Germany since the Peace of Augsburg of 1555. The Protestant Princes accordingly took up arms and welcomed the intervention of the Lutheran King Christian of Denmark who received financial aid from England for his invasion of Germany in 1625. The Danes and their allies were defeated by Tilly and Wallenstein, whose motley horde of plundering freebooters became an effective military machine under the command of their great leader. But Gustavus Adolphus, King of Sweden, who had already wrested territory from Poland and Muscovy, now turned his attention to north Germany in his endeavor to enhance the power of his State and save the Protestant cause. At the same time the opportunity which the situation presented for weakening Hapsburg power was not lost upon Cardinal Richelieu, the great statesman who dominated France during the reign of Louis XIII (1610–1643). Richelieu concluded an alliance with Gustavus and supplied him with arms and money for his invasion of Germany. This union of Catholic churchman and Protestant king for reasons of high politics was characteristic of a new era.

The Swedish monarch landed in Pomerania in 1630, allied himself with the electors of Brandenburg and Saxony and other Protestant princes, defeated the imperial armies, and invaded Bavaria. Tilly having been killed in battle, the Emperor restored Wallenstein to his service and concluded an alliance with his kinsman, Philip IV of Spain. At the battle of Lützen (1632) the Swedish king was slain, though his armies defeated Wallenstein's forces. Owing to growing suspicions regarding his loyalty to the Emperor, Wallenstein was assassinated in 1634. Vast areas of the Germanies were in ruins, and peace now seemed possible between the

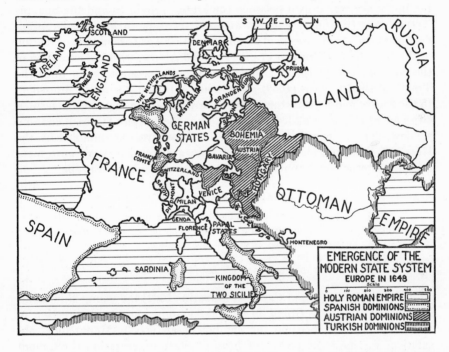

exhausted combatants. But in 1635 Richelieu sent the French armies across the Rhine to deliver the *coup de grace* to Austria and the Empire. Despite initial reverses, they pressed the fight (under the generalship of Condé and Turenne) against both Spanish and Austrian Hapsburgs. Richelieu's successor, Mazarin, held steadfast to the policy which had been embarked upon. With French encouragement the Portuguese revolted against Spain and recovered their independence in 1640. The French intervention in central Europe compelled Ferdinand and his German allies to sue for peace and left France in a position of diplomatic and military hegemony over the Continent.

The Peace of Westphalia of 1648 was the first of the grand territorial and political settlements which have incorporated the verdict of arms into the public law of Europe after every general war among the Powers.[1] At the close of the prolonged and tedious peace conference which opened in 1642, three treaties were concluded: one signed at Münster, January 30, 1648, between Spain and the Dutch, another signed at Münster, October 24, 1648, between the Empire, France, and the German princes, and a third of the same date, signed at Osnabrück, between the Empire and Sweden. Mutual toleration between Catholics and Protestants was provided for and the wars of religion were at long last brought to a close. The independence of Switzerland and the Netherlands was acknowledged and the boundary was drawn between the Dutch provinces and the Spanish Netherlands (Belgium). Sweden annexed territory in Pomerania; Brandenburg began that process of expansion which was to lead to the creation of the Kingdom of Prussia; France annexed Alsace, with the exception of the city of Strasbourg, and continued the war against Spain until the Treaty of the Pyrenees (1659) gave to her Artois to the north, Roussillon to the south, and a protectorate over Lorraine on the east. In this fashion two new States were added to the System, the Empire was reduced to a shadow of its former self, the House of Hapsburg was humbled by the House of Bourbon, and an enlarged France stepped forward once more into the international arena as arbiter of the destinies of Europe.

2. EUROPE AND THE WORLD, 1648–1815

> The future of the west is not a limitless tending upwards and onwards for all time towards our present ideals, but a single phenomenon of history, strictly limited and defined as to form and duration, which covers a few centuries and can be viewed and, in essentials, calculated from available precedents.—OSWALD SPENGLER, *The Decline of the West*, I.

Following the death of Cardinal Mazarin (1661) the young king, Louis XIV (1642–1715)—*le Grand Monarque*—assumed personal direction of French policy and became the symbol of an epoch. Monarchical absolutism was now the prevalent form of State organization throughout

---

[1] The great German historian, Treitschke, characterizes the situation as follows: "Although the medieval Christian world possessed the vision of an ideal unity, the interests of the different States were in actual fact severed by difficulties of communication and backwardness of civilization. A community of interests, or a System of States, were still undeveloped. A war might go on for a hundred years between Germans and Italians, quite distinct from a contemporaneous struggle between English and French, without the remaining Powers having any idea of intervening. The idea of a practical comity of States had not yet penetrated into the flesh and blood of the nations. . . . In the seventeenth century the Congress of the Peace of Westphalia offered the astonishing spectacle of a conference of ambassadors from every State, laying down the frontiers for the individual countries. The Peace of Westphalia came to be looked upon like a *ratio scripta* of international law: everyone uttered thanksgiving that some sort of *status quo* had now been established. People began to feel themselves part of an organized European society, and all the sovereign States began, as it were, to form one great family" (*Politik*, translated by Dugdale and de Bille, II, pp. 567–570).

Europe, though in England the Great Rebellion and the civil war of Cavaliers and Roundheads imposed limits upon the royal prerogative, despite the Stuart restoration of 1660. In France the old unruly aristocracy had become an ornamental and submissive ruling caste of titled and privileged nobles, who now perceived that their class interests were intimately bound up with the kingship. The bourgeoisie constituted willing servants and patient subjects of the great king who declared himself the State. The masses of peasants and artisans were inarticulate and politically of no consequence. The theory of divine-right monarchy was perfected and accepted by all men of substance save a few critics and cranks. The period was the great age of French letters. Artists, scientists, poets, and dramatists helped to make the Court at Versailles the envy and the model of the western world. The able ministers and generals which Louis XIV gathered about him—Colbert, Louvois, Vauban, Turenne, and Condé—led the French monarchy forward along the paths of power and glory in diplomacy and arms. France was the first State of Europe in peace and in war. The international politics of the age of Louis XIV therefore revolved about the attempts of France to impose its will upon the Continent and the counter-efforts of numerous coalitions of weaker States to thwart this ambition and preserve the established equilibrium.

The development of the Western State System since the seventeenth century, however, is no longer the story of the States of an isolated Europe. It is constantly complicated by the rivalries of the Powers for control of growing overseas possessions. Between northwestern Europe on the one side and Africa and Asia on the other lay the great Ottoman Empire, whose warriors had crossed the Dardanelles to seize Constantinople in 1453 and had subsequently extended their conquests over all of southeastern Europe, north Africa, and the eastern Mediterranean. This circumstance played its part, though not as important a one as was once supposed, in causing the enterprising merchants of Italy and the Atlantic seaboard States of Europe to seek other routes to the distant Indies with which a profitable trade had already developed. The competition for the eastern trade between the Italian, Spanish, and Portuguese merchants was also a factor encouraging the search for new sea routes to the Orient. Daring Italian captains sailed southward around the huge hulk of the dark continent and westward toward the setting sun. These first slender filaments were to link Europe to a vast new world. The Vikings, to be sure, had reached America in the middle ages, but the memory of their wanderings had been lost. Not until Columbus, under Spanish auspices, reached the Antilles in 1492 was there begun a systematic exploration of the great unknown across the Atlantic. The rounding of Africa by Vasco da Gama in 1497 and the first circumnavigation of the globe by Magellan shortly afterwards opened new seaways to southern Asia. Here an ancient and

[77]

highly developed native civilization made easy conquest and settlement by Europeans impossible. But the Amerindian aborigines who lived in the wilds of the western continents could offer no effective resistance to European explorers, conquerors, and colonizers, even where they had evolved great civilizations of their own as in Mexico and Peru. As tools for the exercise of political power the bow and arrow, the lance, and the canoe were no match for the blunderbuss, the horse, and the sailing vessel. The superior technology of European civilization enabled the Powers to conquer or disperse the native peoples of the new world and to carve out vast empires from the wilderness. Explorers, colonizers, treasure-seekers, and empire-builders jostled one another in quest of adventure, gold, and power, and their respective States were not slow to support claims to territory and to quarrel with one another for new dominions.

Portugal and Spain were first in the field. Following the Turkish conquest of Egypt in 1517 most of the eastern trade was diverted to the new route around the Cape of Good Hope, to the profit of Spanish and Portuguese merchants and shippers. This shift of sea routes gradually transferred commercial supremacy from the Mediterranean States to the Atlantic coast States of Europe and here, as always, political power and prestige followed in the wake of economic hegemony. Portugal claimed all of Africa, southern Asia, and Brazil, by right of discovery. The papal arbitration and the Treaty of Tordesillas (1494) had recognized Portuguese claims in the new western world which came to be named after the Portuguese navigator, Americus Vespucci. But the annexation of Portugal to Spain in 1580 led eventually to the conquest of much of the Portuguese colonial empire by the Dutch. As for Spain, Cortez had conquered Mexico in 1519 and in 1531 Pizarro similarly added Peru to the Spanish-American possessions. The ruthless exploitation of this enormous colonial domain contributed to the brief ascendancy of Spain over Europe in the reign of Philip II. Following the revolt of the Netherlands, the seafaring Dutch covered themselves with glory by plundering Spanish and Portuguese commerce in the Indies, seizing ports in Africa and India, acquiring the Spice Islands in the South Seas, occupying Brazil until 1654, when a revolt restored it to Portuguese control, establishing Dutch Guiana in South America, and exploring and settling the Hudson River region in North America—all in the first quarter of the seventeenth century.

By this time the English and French Governments had similarly turned their attention toward the lands beyond the seas. The explorations of Cabot, Frobisher, Hudson, Baffin, Chancellor, Hawkins, Drake, and a score of other navigators and piratical adventurers furnished the basis for English territorial claims, while Verrazano and Cartier performed the same service for France. Conquest and settlement followed exploration. A New Spain, a New Netherlands, and a New England came into being.

Extravagant territorial claims were made to the wilderness, and colonial rivalries contributed to the causes of conflict between the European Powers. By the time of Louis XIV the English had conquered the Dutch in North America (1664) and had laid the foundations of an empire along the Atlantic seacoast of the western continent. French posts had been established in the St. Lawrence valley toward the end of the century and French missionaries and explorers, such as LaSalle, Marquette, and Joliet extended "New France" to the Great Lakes region, the Ohio and Mississippi valleys, and the vast plains of "Louisiana." At the same time friction developed for control of the ports and markets of India. France and England became the great contestants for colonial supremacy in southern Asia no less than in North America.

This clash of imperial aspirations played a major rôle in the long duel between the English and French which was about to open in Europe. In the middle period of the seventeenth century, when France was crushing the Hapsburgs and extending her frontiers to the Pyrennes, the Alps, the Rhine, and the Meuse, England was torn by the internal disturbances of the Great Rebellion, the civil war, the Commonwealth, and the Restoration. But when Louis XIV sought to acquire still more territory and to establish French hegemony over the Continent, England actively joined his enemies both to preserve the balance of power in Europe and to challenge French pretensions in Asia and America. Louis took advantage of a naval war between the English and the Dutch to invade the Spanish Netherlands (Belgium) in 1667 on the ground that they had devolved upon him through his wife, daughter of Philip IV of Spain. England and Holland at once made peace and joined Sweden in the Triple Alliance of 1668, which checkmated France and compelled Louis to content himself with the annexation of a few frontier towns in the Peace of Aix-la-Chapelle of 1668.

The French king now determined to conquer the Dutch, who had frustrated his designs, and with this end in view he bought off England and Sweden by mercenary secret alliances. In 1672 he launched the attack. His soldiery soon overran the Low Countries, but in the face of this menacing extension of French power England soon withdrew from the alliance with France. The Empire, Spain, and the Duchy of Lorraine joined the Dutch to resist the aggressor. The Treaties of Nymwegen (1678) preserved the equilibrium, though France acquired Franche Comté and Valenciennes, Cambrai, and Ypres on the frontiers of the Spanish Netherlands. In 1681 Louis seized Strasbourg in Alsace and strengthened his hold upon Lorraine. His further efforts at aggrandizement led to the creation of the League of Augsburg (1686), composed of the Dutch, Spain, the Empire, Sweden, Brandenburg, and other German States, which strove to check French power. When William III of Orange secured the English crown in the "Glorious Revolution" of 1688, he brought England into the grand alliance against the French, and inaugurated the policy which the British Government has ever since pursued of opposing by armed force all efforts on the part of continental Powers to seize control of the Low Countries and the mouth of the Scheldt. The war which followed was fought in America as well as in Europe and was known as King William's War on the western side of the Atlantic. After a long and indecisive struggle, peace was made at Ryswick in 1697. Louis was again forced to relinquish the Spanish Netherlands, but he retained control of Strasbourg.

The issue was now complicated by the impending death of the childless Charles II of Spain, whose two brothers-in-law, Louis XIV of France and Leopold I of Austria, were likely to lay claim to the Spanish empire and thus upset the delicate balance once more. William III labored to achieve an equitable and pacific partition of the Spanish legacy in the treaties of 1698 and 1700, but Austria rejected the proposed arrangements and Louis insisted upon observance of the will of the Spanish monarch who left his lands in toto to the second grandson of the French king. When Charles died in 1700, Louis sent the young man to Madrid as Philip IV of Spain and asserted that the Pyrenees were no more. Here was an enhancement of the power of the House of Bourbon so enormous as to raise up against France a coalition of almost all the States of Europe save Bavaria, which was Louis' only ally. Just before his death William created the second grand alliance of Great Britain, Austria, and the Netherlands for the purpose of detaching such outlying Spanish possessions as the Spanish Netherlands, Milan, Naples, and Tuscany and thereby reducing the dominions of Louis' grandson to reasonable proportions. The War of the Spanish Succession (1701–1713) was long and costly. Again the English and French fell upon one another in America in Queen Anne's War. At Blenheim (1704) the French were defeated and driven from the Empire. Prince Eugene of Savoy expelled Louis' forces from Italy (1706) and the Duke of Marlborough freed the Netherlands from French occupation (1706–1709). France was invaded, but Louis rallied his troops to resist the allies among whom dissension had already arisen. After a decade of bloodshed and destruction it was clear that France could not be conquered by the coalition and that Spain would not renounce Philip IV.

The peace conference at Utrecht (1712–1713) took cognizance of these facts in the seven treaties which its members drew up. Here was another great international settlement, comparable to that of Westphalia in 1648, and destined to endure in its main features for more than a century. Philip was recognized as Spanish king, but it was stipulated that France and Spain were never to unite, since "the most destructive flame of war which is to be extinguished by this peace arose chiefly from

hence, that the security and liberties of Europe could by no means bear
the union of the Kingdoms of France and Spain under one and the same
King" (Article 6 of the Anglo-French treaty of April 11, 1713). The
Spanish Netherlands were transferred to Austria, to which Louis was
obliged to give up Ypres and Tournai. Austria also acquired Naples,
Milan, and Sardinia, while England secured Gibraltar and Minorca from
Spain. The Duchy of Savoy (Piedmont) was recognized as a kingdom and
permitted to annex Sicily, which it later exchanged for Sardinia. The
Elector of Brandenburg was similarly recognized as King of Prussia. As
for America, England acquired Acadia (Nova Scotia), Hudson Bay, and
Newfoundland, and trade concessions from Spain. With France checked
and Spain stripped of portions of her territory, the other Powers were
content to permit Bourbon kings to reign both at Paris and Madrid. The
European equilibrium was preserved, though the contest between England
and France for mastery of India and the new world was still undecided.
It should be noted that the contemporaneous eastern wars between
Charles XII of Sweden, and Russia, Denmark, and Poland were fought
and terminated almost without reference to the relations between the
western European States. But after Utrecht, the European State System
became an indissoluble unity and all States, east and west, were involved
in every contest between any of its members.

The settlement at Utrecht was followed by an interlude, marked by
new wars in the east (Austria against Turkey, 1715-1718, and Sweden
against Russia, 1715-1721) which were not ignored by the western Powers,
but in which they did not actively intervene. In 1719-1720 England and
France joined forces to prevent Philip V from upsetting the terms agreed
upon at Utrecht. The next general war arose out of international controversy over the election of a king of Poland. In the War of the Polish
Succession (1733-1738) Austria and Russia, supporting the candidacy
of the Elector of Saxony, defeated France which supported Stanislaus
Leszczinski, father-in-law of Louis XV. England remained neutral and
Spain seized the opportunity to wrest the Kingdom of the Two Sicilies
from Austria and to place a Bourbon upon the throne of her recovered
dependency. These conflicts, however, produced no fundamental changes
in power relationships between the States of the European System. The
next serious disturbance was a result, on the one hand, of rivalry between
England, France, and Spain for colonial dominions and, on the other, of
the rise of a new Power to ascendancy in north Germany—the Kingdom
of Prussia under the Hohenzollern dynasty.

Great Britain fought a brief, indecisive, and localized war with Spain
in the Caribbean in 1727. In 1739 the struggle was resumed in the "war
of Jenkin's ear" which opened in American waters and led to hostilities
on the frontier between the British colony of Georgia and the Spanish

colony of Florida. Walpole knew that the conflict could scarcely be localized because of the Bourbon "Family Compact" of 1733 which constituted an alliance between France and Spain. Difficulties were in the offing, moreover, regarding the throne of Austria, for there was little assurance that Great Britain, France, Spain, and Prussia would abide by the arrangement which they had made to guarantee the succession to Maria Theresa, daughter of Charles IV. In December of 1740, following the death of Charles, Frederick II of Prussia, surnamed "the Great," sent his armies into Austrian Silesia to expand Prussian power at Maria

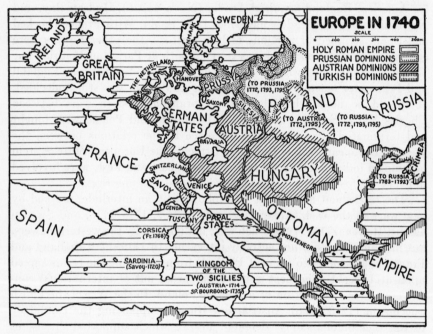

Theresa's expense. France, Bavaria, Saxony, and Spain joined Prussia in a league of plunder to despoil the young Queen of her possessions. England, supported by the Netherlands, joined Austria in the combat to preserve the continental equilibrium and to continue the struggle against France and Spain in the new world. The War of the Austrian Succession (1740–1748), known to the transatlantic colonists as King George's War, was fought in America and in India as well as in central Europe. In all the arenas of conflict it was indecisive. In the Peace of Aix-la-Chapelle of 1748, Great Britain and France restored the *status quo ante bellum* in India and America. Frederick managed to retain Silesia, and Austria also lost certain Italian dependencies, but Maria Theresa averted the partition of her realm. With Austria determined to check the Prussian menace in Germany and with Great Britain no less bent upon a final reckoning with

France, the peace was but a truce. The great Prussian King perceived that Russia might be drawn into the coalition which Maria Theresa was striving to form against him. He therefore devoted himself to preparing for the inevitable, for to him:

Politics is the science of acting always by convenient means conformably to one's own interests. To act conformably to one's interests, it is necessary to know what they are; and to arrive at this knowledge requires study, research, and application. The politics of sovereigns have two parts: one, which is concerned with internal government, comprises the interests of the State and the maintenance of its system of government; the other, which embraces all the System of Europe, labors to consolidate the safety of the State and to extend as much as is possible by customary and permitted means the number of its possessions, the power and consideration of the prince. (*Die politischen Testamente der Hohenzollern*, II, p. 33.)

Frederick likewise perceived that Anglo-French relations dominated the whole European scene.

Christian Europe is like a republic of sovereigns which is divided into two great parties. England and France have for a century given the impulse to all movements. When a warlike prince wishes to undertake anything, if both Powers are in agreement to keep the peace, they will offer their mediation to him and compel him to accept it. Once it is established, the political System prevents all great robberies and makes war unfruitful unless it be urged with greater resources and extraordinary luck. (*Ibid.*, p. 54.)

Under these circumstances the stage was prepared for the next general war which was to decide whether Austria must permit Prussia to dominate north Germany and whether Britain or France would rule North America and India. In 1754 Anglo-French hostilities broke out in the Ohio valley in the so-called French and Indian War. In the "diplomatic revolution" of 1756 England became the ally of her erstwhile enemy, Prussia, which was now set upon from all points of the compass by Austria, France, Russia, and Sweden. The military genius of Frederick enabled him to defeat the French and Austrians at Rossbach and Leuthen (1757), but the Russians invaded East Prussia and occupied Berlin in 1759. After initial successes the French cause fared badly outside of Europe. Wolfe wrested Quebec from Montcalm in 1759. In India the British forces under Robert Clive outwitted Dupleix and seized most of the French strongholds. These failures, coupled with reverses in Brunswick, caused Louis XV to call to his aid the other Bourbon States, Spain and the Two Sicilies (1762). The Spanish intervention was overbalanced, however, by the accession to the Russian throne of the mad Tsar, Peter III, who deserted Austria, joined Prussia, and restored to Frederick the conquests of his predecessors. He was at once superseded by his wife, Catherine II, who refused to give active assistance to either side. Austria now despaired of recovering Silesia and ruining Prussia.

The Treaty of Hubertsburg (1763) put an end to the Seven Years' War in Europe, with Austrian acknowledgment of Prussian title to Silesia. European frontiers remained unchanged, but the House of Hohenzollern had successfully despoiled and defied the House of Hapsburg. With magnificent irony, Frederick placed upon the pinnacle of the New Palace at Potsdam three female figures supporting the Prussian Crown—Madame de Pompadour of France, Maria Theresa of Austria, and Catherine of Russia. The combined efforts of these ladies to consummate his destruction had left his State and his dynasty more powerful than ever. The Treaty of Paris, also of 1763, established peace between Britain and France. The English were masters of Canada and of the east coast of India. Louis XV was compelled to yield up to the victor almost the whole of New France in America east of the Mississippi, retaining only a few islands in the West Indies and off Newfoundland and French Guiana in South America. Spain was obliged to cede Florida to Britain and received as compensation from her ally all that remained of the French claims on the North American mainland, i.e., the wilderness of Louisiana west of the Mississippi. French power in India was similarly broken by the peace terms. By the provisions of these settlements, Prussia attained the position of a new Great Power in the European galaxy and England definitely triumphed over France in the long contest for commercial, colonial, and naval supremacy in America and the Orient.

Between the Seven Years' War and the great revolutionary upheaval of 1789–1815, which was temporarily to subvert the European State System, two developments took place which produced significant changes in the relationships between the Powers. One was to lead to the creation of a new State in the System on the other side of the Atlantic. The other was to lead to the extinction of an old State in eastern Europe. Such were the results of the "American Revolution" and the partition of Poland. In the former case the outbreak of rebellion against British rule in 1775 and the declaration of America's independence in the following year offered an opportunity to Britain's continental enemies to recover some of their lost prestige and to contribute toward the weakening of British power. France concluded a military alliance with the American rebels in 1778 and was soon joined in the war against England by Spain and the Netherlands. The British Government was at length obliged to sue for peace and by the treaties of 1783–1784 the United States of America became an independent member of the family of nations, Spain recovered Florida, France reacquired minor possessions in the West Indies and Africa, and Holland lost to Britain a portion of her Asiatic empire. The British overseas dominions were thus reduced, but they still constituted an imposing imperial edifice. The United States, despite its vast territory and resources, was still too young and feeble to play a decisive rôle in the relations between the European Powers.

Meanwhile, Frederick of Prussia connived with the Tsarina Catherine in 1772 to relieve the weak and disorderly Kingdom of Poland of part of its territory. In order to counterbalance this enhancement of Prussian and Russian power, Austria intervened and annexed Polish Galicia. This bargain at Poland's expense was the means of preventing a general war threatened by Austrian resistance to Russian aggrandizement against the Turks in the Balkans. When Austria later made additional claims to Polish territory, Frederick objected. The balance of power was peaceably preserved by the extinction of the Polish State, Prussia and Russia taking fresh slices in 1792, and all three of the Powers dividing up the remainder in 1795.

By the last quarter of the eighteenth century, then, the Western State System comprised five major Powers on the European Continent, a large number of minor Powers, and a new State across the Atlantic, born of European colonialism. Of the States which might have been described as Great Powers in 1648, England, France, and Austria retained their former position. Spain had declined in wealth and in diplomatic and military prestige and had fallen to the rank of a second-rate Power, in spite of the vast colonies which she still held in the Americas and the East Indies. Holland and Portugal likewise retained extensive overseas possessions, but they had long since passed the halcyon days when they could cope with other Powers as equals. Following the failure of France to establish her supremacy over the Continent, the new State of Prussia, founded on the Mark of Brandenburg, had emerged in central Europe as the dynastic creation of a line of able kings. It had successfully withstood an assault by the other Powers upon the newcomer and had asserted its right to be regarded as their equal. In the more remote east, the Tsardom of Muscovy had extended its dominions eastward, southward, and westward. Under Peter the Great (1682–1725) Russia became partially "westernized" and made itself a member of the European System. Under Catherine the Great (1762–1796) it became a Great Power. Its expansion pushed the Swedes from the eastern shores of the Baltic and the Turks from the northern shores of the Black Sea. Sweden fell to the rank of a third-rate Power and the Ottoman Empire, never really a part of the European System, was already in decay. The end of Poland brought the enlarged States of Russia, Prussia, and Austria into closer relations with one another. The petty States of Italy and Germany remained pawns among their greater neighbors. The first great struggle for overseas empire was ended and the Powers had achieved an equilibrium of power which seemed reasonably permanent and stable.

Beneath the surface of European society, however, there had long been germinating new forces and pressures now ready to burst forth in a political and social revolution which was not only to overturn the whole social and political structure of the Continent but also to demolish temporarily the whole European State System and replace it once more by universal empire. The slow expansion of industry and trade, the growth of cities, and the extension of commercial contacts between the States of Europe and between Europe and the world had all led to a great increase in numbers and wealth of those who were neither peasant serfs nor landowning nobles, but who constituted the great urban middle class of the bourgeoisie. As this class in the European social order acquired economic power and became aware of its peculiar interests, it endeavored to secure political influence and to supersede the nobility and the clergy as a ruling caste. The political and social order of the *ancien régime*, resting upon monarchical absolutism and the privileges of the titled aristocracy, was rudely challenged by the will-to-power of the new class, whose intellectual weapons of assault were furnished by the philosophers of the eighteenth century "enlightenment" and whose aspiration toward political power had already been reflected in the Great Rebellion in England and in the American Revolution. These upheavals preceded corresponding developments on the Continent. The first blow fell in 1789 where the old order was weakest and where the new forces were most powerful: the France of Louis XVI. Within three years the bourgeois revolutionaries had abolished the privileges of the nobles, confiscated the feudal estates, overturned the monarchy, executed the king, and involved themselves in war with all of Europe.

The alarm with which the French Revolution was viewed by the other Governments of Europe was the natural reaction of the rulers and beneficiaries of an old social order in the face of the menace of a new. However much Bourbons and Hanoverians, Hohenzollerns and Hapsburgs might quarrel among themselves for territory and power, however bitterly the aristocrats of the great States might struggle against one another for the prestige and glory of king and country, they were united in opposing the assault of the Jacobins upon what they regarded as the very foundations of civilized life. Official Britain, with Burke as her spokesman, shrank shudderingly from the violence of the Paris mobs. The Bourbon kings of Spain and the Two Sicilies were outraged by the attack upon their Bourbon brother in France. The House of Hapsburg was horrified by the dethronement of Marie Antoinette, the Hapsburg wife of the French king. That the old Europe would strive to crush the new and to restore absolutism and privilege in France was only too apparent to the French radicals who took the initiative by declaring war upon Austria and Prussia in April of 1792. Under the revolutionary tricolor and to the strains of the Marseillaise and much shouting of "*liberté, égalité, fraternité*," the apostles of the new dispensation steeled themselves to save the fatherland and to emancipate Europe from despotism by force of arms.

Before a year had elapsed, the French monarchy was demolished, the king and queen were guillotined, and the Republic was fighting not only Austria and Prussia, but Britain, Holland, Spain, and Sardinia, which constituted the "first coalition." The new energies which revolutionary enthusiasm gave to its people made France more than a match for her enemies. In 1795, after the French armies had conquered the Austrian Netherlands, reached the Rhine, and transformed Holland into the Batavian Republic, Spain sued for peace and Prussia withdrew from the conflict to complete the carving of Poland. War continued with Britain, Austria, and Sardinia while the Reign of Terror waxed and waned in France and the National Convention gave way to the Directory. In 1796–1797 a young commander of the revolutionary armies, Napoleon Bonaparte, swept the Austrians from north Italy, compelled Sardinia to cede Nice and Savoy to France, marched on Vienna, and imposed the Treaty of Campo Formio on the Hapsburg monarchy. France annexed the Austrian Netherlands while Austria, in compensation, received Venice, whose ancient independence was thus extinguished. With England the only remaining enemy of the Republic, Bonaparte invaded Egypt in 1798 in a wild scheme to sever communications between the British Isles and India. When he returned, he found the Directory bankrupt and its armies hard pressed by the forces of the Second Coalition of Great Britain, Austria, and Russia. Hailed as the savior of the Republic, he overthrew the Directory in 1799 and made himself First Consul. The French bourgeoisie, with the approval of the masses, sacrificed democracy and parliamentarianism upon the altar of militant national patriotism. Napoleon became the symbol of *la patrie* and high priest of the new cult of the nation in arms. Under his banner the people's armies of France set forth upon the paths of glory which were to lead to the conquest of Europe.

In the light of the historical evolution of the Western State System, the era of Napoleon is significant chiefly because it represents the most nearly successful effort at the restoration of universal empire which has ever been made by a single State. The power of earlier aspirants toward ascendancy over Europe—Charles V, Philip II, Louis XIV—was feeble and ineffective compared to the military might and diplomatic prestige of France under the first Bonaparte. Napoleon had at his back the richest and most populous nation of the Continent, welded into a solid phalanx by the new fire of patriotic fervor. His battalions were no longer the small, professional forces of the eighteenth century, but were made up of conscript armies drawn from the man power of the whole population. His revolutionary predecessors had already invented military conscription as a means of defending France against Europe. His enemies were likewise obliged to resort to universal conscription, which has ever since been the basis of continental military organization. But the mailed fists of his soldiery were so effectively supplemented by his own military genius and diplomatic astuteness that no State or combination of States could stand against him. The old balance of power was completely disrupted. In 1804 he made himself Emperor—and his Empire seemed likely to include all of western Europe within its limits. For a decade it appeared possible that the Western State System, like all its predecessors, had reached its end and was about to be superseded by a world-wide dominion of its most powerful member.

The temporary triumph and final failure of this imperial adventure throw a flood of light upon the fundamental nature of the State System which ultimately proved to be more powerful than its conqueror. From 1800 to 1812 French power rose dizzily in an almost uninterrupted ascent. The diplomacy of flattery induced Tsar Paul to withdraw Russia from the Second Coalition. Austria was crushed in Germany and Italy and obliged to come to terms. At Amiens (1802) England also made peace. But fourteen months later the British Government, with the support of the merchant classes, resumed the war in the conviction that British maritime, commercial, and colonial supremacy were dangerously menaced by French ambitions. Napoleon accepted the challenge in the equally firm conviction that the power of England must be broken before France could feel secure on the Continent. With England crushed, he could take up the task of rebuilding the French overseas empire and of winning for the French bourgeoisie a position of mercantile hegemony throughout the world. Pitt countered Napoleon's preparations for the conquest of England by strengthening British sea power and building up another continental coalition. The allied French and Spanish fleet was destroyed at Trafalgar (1805). Henceforth British naval predominance was assured and Napoleon had no means at his disposal for the invasion of England. But the Third Coalition was smashed by the French armies. In December, 1805, the Austrian and Russian forces of the Emperor Francis II and Tsar Alexander I were crushed at Austerlitz. By the Treaty of Pressburg Austria was required to cede Venetia to the newly created French satellite kingdom of Italy and to surrender much of her territory in Germany to Bavaria and Württemberg, which were also Napoleonic puppet States. Prussia entered the lists, only to be defeated at Jena (1806).

Napoleon, who now entered Berlin, had already abolished the Holy Roman Empire and organized the west German States into the Confederation of the Rhine as a French protectorate. The Russians were in turn beaten at Friedland in 1807. At Tilsit Napoleon met Alexander and the two Emperors almost literally divided Europe between them. The Third Coalition was destroyed. Austria was reduced to a second-rate Power and

Prussia was humbled to the dust. A truncated Poland was revived in the form of the Grand Duchy of Warsaw as a French dependency. Russia seized Finland from Sweden and the latter State also became a French appanage. By 1808 Napoleon was Emperor of a France that extended from the Pyrenees and the Alps to the North Sea and the Rhine. He was also King of Italy and his relatives, friends, or admirers held the thrones of Naples, Spain, Holland, Denmark, Sweden, and lesser States. Even England seemed likely to be brought to terms by the Continental System which was to close the European market to British goods and compel the "nation of shopkeepers" to sue for peace.

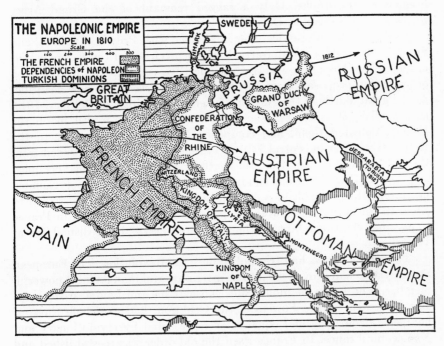

That Napoleon failed in this purpose and lived to see the destruction of the whole fabric into which he had woven so much blood and treasure was due primarily to the continued ascendancy of British sea power and to the intense national consciousness which foreign conquest evoked among the subject peoples of France. In 1808 Napoleon deposed the Spanish Bourbons and made his brother Joseph King of Spain. But a popular insurrection broke out almost at once against the usurper, which led Great Britain to occupy Portugal and send Wellington to assist the Spanish rebels in harassing the French in the Peninsular War (1808–1813). A national uprising took place in Austria in 1809 which Napoleon suppressed with difficulty. The Prussian Government introduced various internal reforms, civil and military, and bided its time. Napoleon was still master of Europe, nevertheless, and might have remained so had he not quarrelled with Tsar Alexander and taken up arms against him in an effort to compel him to enforce the Continental System against Great Britain. By 1812 the French Emperor had gathered together an international army of 600,000 troops for the subjugation of Russia. The Russian forces withdrew before him and he entered Moscow in September. But the capital was burned under his eyes and as the Russian winter descended the enemy soldiers and peasant irregulars assailed the French communications in the rear. The city was abandoned and the retreat from Moscow became a catastrophe. Only a ragged remnant of the Grand Army recrossed the Niemen in December.

Early in 1813 Alexander, now in alliance with Prussia, England, and Sweden, launched a counter-attack which precipitated the German War of Liberation. Napoleon won further indecisive victories, but his rejection of mediation proposals from Vienna added Austria to the new coalition. At the great Battle of the Nations, fought near Leipzig in October, 1813, the Swedish, Russian, Prussian, and Austrian forces closed in on the French, defeated them, and compelled Napoleon to withdraw to the Rhine. His power in central Europe collapsed. France was invaded from the east by the allies and from the south by Wellington who had occupied all of Spain. Despite furious and brilliant resistance, Paris was surrounded in March, 1814. Napoleon was compelled to abdicate and was exiled to Elba. In the spring of 1815 he escaped and returned to power in France to play out the tragic farce of the "Hundred Days" to its dismal end at Waterloo.

The *ancien régime* had triumphed over the Revolution. The European State System had proven itself to be more powerful than its most powerful member. The forces of monarchical absolutism and feudal aristocracy, as represented by the Powers of the Coalition, had overcome those of bourgeois democracy and equality as represented by revolutionary and Napoleonic France. In France itself the old order was reestablished and the Bourbons were restored to the throne in the person of Louis XVIII. At the great international Congress of Vienna (September, 1814–July, 1815) emperors, kings, princes, and diplomats met in brilliant assemblage to restore dynasties in the name of legitimacy, to rebuild the Europe of 1789, and to consider "the disposal of the territories given up by his Most Christian Majesty (Louis XVIII) . . . and the relations from whence a real and permanent balance of power is to be derived" (Article I of the Separate and Secret Articles of the First Treaty of Paris, May 30, 1814).

Under the inspiration of the Austrian statesman, Metternich, the delegates set to work, only to discover that the old Europe had been smashed beyond all hope of complete restoration and that Humpty-Dumpty could not, after all, be replaced in his old position on the wall. Bargains and compromises were necessary to adjust conflicting interests and ambitions. France was obliged to renounce her rights of sovereignty and protection over some 32,000,000 people who had been brought under Napoleon's power, but she recovered the boundaries of 1792, with some slight additions. By the second Treaty of Paris, November 20, 1815, France was obliged to cede a number of strategic posts to the allies, to pay an indemnity of 700,000,000 francs, and to submit to the occupation of eighteen fortresses for three to five years. Most of the Grand Duchy of

Warsaw was given to Russia, which also retained Finland and Bessarabia, conquered respectively from the Swedes and the Turks. Prussia received Swedish Pomerania, two-fifths of Saxony, and extensive territories on both banks of the Rhine. In the rest of Germany it was scarcely feasible to restore either the defunct Holy Roman Empire or the hundreds of petty principalities which Napoleon had abolished. A German Confederation of thirty-eight States was therefore established, with Austria securing the presidency of its Diet. Austria gave up the Austrian Netherlands (Belgium), which were annexed by the Dutch, and also gave up a large part of her territories in Germany proper. In return she was awarded north Italy (Lombardy-Venetia), Illyria, the Tyrol, and Salzburg. The

Papal States and the Kingdom of Naples were restored and Italy remained a "geographical expression." In the north, Norway was taken from Denmark and joined to Sweden, under whose control it remained until it secured independence in 1905. Great Britain secured Heligoland in the North Sea, Malta and the Ionian Islands in the Mediterranean, and other fruits of victory overseas from the remnants of the French and Dutch colonial empires: Cape Colony in South Africa, Ceylon, St. Lucia, Tobago, Trinidad, etc.

All these bargains having been struck, the religious Alexander I of Russia induced his fellow sovereigns of Prussia and Austria to join him in the "Holy Alliance," by which they pledged themselves to act as good Christians and to cooperate to preserve peace and to suppress revolution wherever it might appear. This "piece of sublime mysticism and nonsense," as Castlereagh termed it, became the symbol of the post-Napoleonic decade, but it was of less political significance than the Quadruple Alliance of November, 1815, to which France was admitted as the fifth member at the Congress of Aix-la-Chapelle in 1818. This union of the five Great Powers of Europe was formed to preserve the new *status quo* by putting down all new revolutions, maintaining the new frontiers and the new distribution of territory and power among its members, and preserving peace through periodical congresses to consider international problems. When revolution broke out in Naples in 1820, in Piedmont in 1821, and in Spain in 1823, the new organization was put to the test and found to be effective, at least temporarily. Congresses met at Troppau (1820), Laibach (1821), and Verona (1822). Austria was authorized to suppress the Italian revolutions and France was given a mandate to restore absolutism in Spain by armed intervention. Revolution was liquidated, but Great Britain withdrew from the alliance. Her government did not favor armed action to suppress continental bourgeois liberalism and her merchants viewed with alarm the possibility of international action to restore to Spain her lost Latin American colonies, which were becoming a profitable market for English exports.

A final word regarding events in the western hemisphere during the Napoleonic epoch: The new republic of the United States embarked upon its spectacular career of territorial expansion by purchasing Louisiana from France in 1803—a region which the First Consul had reacquired from Spain in 1800, but which he was happy to sell when developments in Europe and the West Indies made a restoration of the French colonial empire impossible. American expansionists next turned their attention to Florida and Canada, but the issue was obscured by long and bitter controversies over blockades, impressments, contraband, and neutral trading rights between the United States on the one hand and Great Britain and France on the other. In 1812 the United States declared war on England in the name of "freedom of the seas" and moved at once to occupy Canada and Florida. In spite of continental preoccupations, England was easily able to defend Canada from American attacks. The United States was invaded, its capital burned, and its commerce swept from the seas. The Treaty of Ghent (1814) restored the *status quo*. At no time since has the United States resorted to force in its controversies with Great Britain. Spain, however, was a weaker rival and a skillful policy of browbeating and bargaining induced Madrid to sell the Floridas to the United States in 1819. Meanwhile the Latin American colonies of Spain had secured their independence and a whole series of new nations was thus added to the Western State System. The United States, no less than Great Britain, was opposed to any restoration of these States to European control. Canning "called in the New World to redress the balance of the Old," as he put it, and the result was the Monroe Doctrine of 1823 by which the United States, with British approval, expressed its intention to resist any further colonization, interposition, or extension of control by European Powers over the American continents. At the very outset of Latin American independence, therefore, the United States asserted its claim to hegemony over the western hemisphere.

3. THE EPOCH OF CAPITALISM, NATIONALISM, AND IMPERIALISM

> In the social production of the means of life, human beings enter into definite and necessary relations which are independent of their will— production relations which correspond to a definite stage of the development of their productive forces. The totality of these production relations constitutes the economic structure of society, the real basis upon which a legal and political superstructure arises and to which definite forms of social consciousness correspond. . . . With the change in the economic foundation, the whole gigantic superstructure is more or less rapidly transformed.—KARL MARX, *Capital*, I.

The century between Waterloo and Sarajevo will probably always remain, in a peculiar sense, a unique era of world history. The population of the world doubled and that of Europe quadrupled during the hundred years between 1815 and 1914. The system of technology which had prevailed with few changes for many millenniums was completely revolutionized. The old economic order was replaced by a new, the like of which had never before been known on the planet. The bourgeoisie, masters and beneficiaries of the new technology and the new economy, became the ruling class in almost all the States of the western world. A new social group—the industrial proletariat, child of machine industry and the factory system—prepared to contest the dominance of its masters. Commerce and industry expanded with astounding rapidity in what appeared to be the triumphant and uninterrupted march of "progress." European civilization was carried throughout the five continents and the seven seas through a thousand new channels of travel and trade. New nations were born in the Near East, in Asia, in Africa, and in the Americas. In Europe two new Great Powers appeared on the international stage: Italy and Germany. Across the Atlantic the United States grew from a feeble infant to a young giant, with vast resources and an enormous population at its disposal. In eastern Asia another Great Power emerged: Japan. The European State System became a World State System. The entire globe was divided, partitioned, and subjected to the control of the Powers, whose citizens were fired with a new patriotism and whose governments struggled with one another for territory, for markets, and for a "place in the sun" until their rivalries culminated in the greatest and most destructive of all wars. All of these developments were without parallel or precedent in the past. Out of them has evolved the world society of the twentieth century.

These amazing transformations of western civilization are of interest here because of their bearing upon the equally amazing transformations of the Western State System which accompanied them and were part of the whole process of change. The most significant modifications of European society—those which underlay and in large degree occasioned the other changes—were in the realm of technology and economics. During the last quarter of the eighteenth century there had already begun that progressive utilization of new inventions and technical devices to expand the production and distribution of commodities and services which has continued to the present day. The gradual accumulation in the hands of the bourgeoisie of the profits of a slowly growing commerce and of a simple industrial economy made it possible for enterprising entrepreneurs to launch more profitable business ventures through the use of expensive machines which the individual handicraft artisan of an earlier age could never afford to own. The machine and the factory made their appearance together—first in England and later on the Continent and in North America—the one as the god of a new industrial age and the other as the temple in which the god performed his miracles under the direction of a new priesthood and with the aid of a new order of toiling wage-earners. Those who possessed wealth erected mechanical monsters and employed laborers to turn out goods at an enormously accelerated rate—with undreamed-of profits accruing to the organizers of the new industrialism. Profits begot more profits and the technological revolution was soon in full swing. The steam engine, the steam loom, the steamboat, and the steam locomotive followed one another in rapid succession, completely transforming manufacturing, transportation, and communication.

Countless thousands of new inventions succeeded one another with bewildering rapidity, each new device treading upon the heels of its predecessor, each making enormous profits for those who acquired and exploited it, each at first displacing thousands of workers and later expanding human wants and multiplying goods and services to meet those wants at an ever more rapid rate. Iron and coal turned to gold at the touch of the engineer, the manufacturer, and the merchant. Production leaped upward in every line of economic endeavor which was touched by the new magic. The new agencies of distribution reached out and down for wider and more inexhaustible markets in which to sell the products pouring forth from the factories. The wheels of industry ground faster and faster to meet the insatiable demand for profits and greater profits. Motors whirred, dynamos hummed, dividends mounted, wages rose, on and on in endless rhythm until observers wondered whether the machine was the slave of man or man had become the slave of the machine.

The new economic order which arose on the basis of the new technology has usually been described as "Capitalism." It rests at bottom upon the age-old institution of private property. The most productive form of property in the machine age is not land—the basis of economic life in all pre-industrial societies—but capital goods: machinery, factories, mines, mills, banks, stores, railroads, and shipping lines. The capitalists who own such property wield vastly greater economic power over the lives and destinies of their wage-earning subjects than was ever wielded by the landholding aristocracies of earlier societies. This power they wield for private profit. Private acquisitiveness is the mainspring of economic activity in capitalistic society. Each entrepreneur who perceives an opportunity to profit borrows capital, establishes an industrial unit, employs engineers to build, administrators to organize, and workers to toil, and hopes to find a market in which he can sell his product for more than it cost to produce. An elaborate mechanism of production, distribution, and exchange is set up, with "supply" and "demand" determining prices, prices determining profits, and profits determining the allocation of land, labor, and capital among various productive enterprises.

As the use of machinery increases and machines become more complex and costly, individuals and partnerships are replaced by great corporations and trusts, able to mobilize huge financial resources, to take great risks, and to plan mass production and mass sales on a vast scale over long periods of time. A correspondingly complex series of banks and credit institutions is developed to meet the needs of expanding industry and commerce. The bonds and stocks issued by the great magnates of the new industrial feudalism afford an opportunity to all who have money to invest and speculate on a nation-wide and world-wide scale. Productivity is enormously enhanced and the standard of living of all communities touched by the magician's wand rises to ever greater heights. Those with economic power take the lion's share of the proceeds and those who work for wages take what they can out of the remainder. Fabulous wealth becomes concentrated in the hands of the few to a degree never before possible and the many suffer from the evils of poverty, unemployment, and economic insecurity resulting from the endless alternation of prosperity and depression in the planless competition of capitalistic economy.

These are commonplaces in a period in which capitalism is still the predominant form of economy throughout the western world. The implications of these changes for the relations between States are perhaps not so obvious. And yet the attitudes and policies and patterns of behavior which are designated by the vague terms "nationalism" and "imperialism"— leading motifs of the discordant symphony of international politics in the machine age—are intimately and directly connected with the technological and economic transformations which have been referred to. The main features of these relationships can perhaps be suggested by a few generalizations which, like all generalizations, are false to the extent to which they oversimplify complex situations, but which will nevertheless be recognized as describing fairly accurately what has occurred in the political sphere in the epoch of capitalism.

The most obvious political consequence of the technological and economic revolution was to bring into power a new ruling class in every State in which the new economy struck deep roots. That class consisted of the capitalistic entrepreneurs who, as organizers and beneficiaries of the new order, possessed economic power and soon aspired to political power as well. Breadgivers are ever lawgivers in every society and political power ultimately resides with those who have most of the goods of the world. So long as land was the most productive form of wealth, the landowning aristocracy which had survived from the age of agrarian feudalism remained secure in its titles and privileges and continued to exercise political power in its own interests through the forms of divine-right monarchy. As soon as capitalism gave to the bourgeoisie a preponderance of economic power, it was certain that the new class would react against the position of political inferiority to which it was subjected under the *ancien régime*. It would strive to attain control of the machinery of the State for itself in order to throw off the irksome mercantilist restrictions of the preceding century and inaugurate a régime of laissez-faire individualism and economic liberty. The upheavals of the seventeenth century in England and of the eighteenth in America foreshadowed the future. The French Revolution, the revolt of the "Third Estate" against monarchy and aristocracy, sounded the death knell of the old order. Temporarily beaten by the military forces of reaction, the new aspirants to power retired underground after 1815.

But time and tide and the logic of the new economics were with the revolutionists and the storm burst forth irresistibly with increasing popular support. Even the peasantry and the new proletariat learned to respond to the catch words of democracy, universal suffrage, civil liberty and equality, and constitutional limitations upon the powers of government. In England the process was a pacific one. The great parliamentary reform bills of the nineteenth century transformed the English State from one in which the squirocracy still dictated public policies in 1800 to one in which manufacturers, merchants, bankers, and shopkeepers held the reins of power a century later. In the United States a great civil war, involving the threat of the dissolution of the federal union into two independent nations, was fought before the western farmers and the northern manufacturers crushed the power of the slaveholding landowners of the south. On the European continent the shift was achieved through a series of revolutions which swept over the nations in 1830 and 1848. In part by violence, in part by slow imperceptible change, democracy and constitutionalism were established and extended from State to State. By 1870 the bourgeoisie was at last firmly seated in the saddle in every capitalistic State.

This shift in the sources of political control within the States of the Western State System was accompanied, wherever it occurred, by an unprecedented efflorescence of national patriotism. This coincidence was not accidental. The bourgeois middle class in European society was first conditioned to patriotism in its modern form because of its economic position in society. It produced, bought, sold, and exchanged not in the self-sufficing isolated community of the medieval manor, nor yet in the local neighborhood or province, but in the wider market of the nation. It supported royal absolutism in the interest of order and prosperity throughout the nation and it rejected royal absolutism when the dynasties had built the nations and had fulfilled their historic function. While the titled aristocracy of the age of the despots pursued political power for personal, family, and dynastic reasons, the bourgeoisie identified itself with the nation as a whole. The "fatherland" became its symbol of social cohesion and the fatherland became a well-integrated, closely organized aggregation of citizens in the period of the railroad, the steamship, the automobile, the telegraph, the telephone, and other devices of easy communication and transportation which diminished distances and broke down parochialism and provincialism. *Fraternité*, no less than *Liberté* and *Égalité*, was the battle cry of the bourgeois revolution. And as nationalism is always bred of war, the impact of people upon people in the great Napoleonic conflicts intensified national consciousness at the very time when the bourgeoisie was rising to grasp power from kings and aristocrats. The revolutions of the mid-century were led and supported by middle-class patriots for whom the achievements of national unity and of democratic constitutionalism were but two facets of the same liberal program. The tide of nationalism in almost every State rose in proportion to the economic and political ascendancy of the bourgeoisie. Nationalism and democracy were everywhere corollaries, for true national unity is impossible without that common participation in public life which political democracy implies, and democracy is unworkable on a national scale in a population whose members are not imbued with a sense of national consciousness and solidarity. In the era of the triumphant bourgeoisie, nationalism became a creed and a way of life, shaping the attitudes and actions of millions of people and scores of governments throughout the western world.

The major political effects of this phenomenon upon the relationships between the members of the Western State System need only be suggested here, for they will be considered in some detail below. The older political entities of Europe, such as England, France, and Spain, ceased to be dynasti~ creations and became nation-states whose people were bound together by popular patriotism, by a high degree of linguistic homogeneity, and by stereotyped national symbols and traditions. The linguistic groups of Europe which had not yet achieved political unity and independence strove mightily to attain the destiny which national patriots had marked out for them. Devotion to the fatherland filled the peoples of old States with a new pride of place and sense of power, and inspired the peoples of new States (and of States not yet born) to gain for themselves a position of honor and glory in the family of nations. The fervor of patriotism flowed like strong wine through the veins of the western world. In Germany, in Italy, in the Balkans, and in many lands beyond the seas the process of national emancipation and unification proceeded apace, with earth-shaking reverberations upon the power relationships between old and new States alike.

The progressive dissolution of the Ottoman Empire presented an opportunity to the Slavic Christians of southeastern Europe to achieve liberation and statehood. The Serbs gained autonomy in 1815. The revolt of the Greeks began in 1821 and culminated a decade later in the attainment of Greek independence through the intervention of Great Britain, France, and Russia against the Turks. Belgium rose up against Dutch control in 1830 and nine years later her independence as a perpetually neutral and inviolate State was recognized by the mother country and by the Powers. In the 1830's Russia sought to establish a protectorate over Turkey, but was frustrated by British and French opposition. The apprehension of the western States over the extension of Russian power at the expense of "the sick man of Europe," as Turkey came to be called, led to the Crimean War (1854–1856) in which Great Britain and France, with the aid of little Sardinia, fought Russia to a draw in the Black Sea. Russian domination of Constantinople and the Straits was prevented by admitting the Sublime Porte to "the advantages of the public law and system of Europe" (Treaty of Paris, March 30, 1856), and by guaranteeing the independence and integrity of Turkey. In 1877 Russia waged war on Turkey again, now using the Slavic nationalities still under Turkish rule as pawns in her game of imperial expansion. The Powers again intervened and Russia yielded once more, this time without a trial of armed strength. The Treaty of Berlin of 1878 created Bulgaria as an autonomous principality, while Serbia, Montenegro, and Rumania were all recognized as independent and granted additional territory at Turkey's expense. In 1912 the Balkan States waged war upon Turkey and further extended their frontiers, only to fall out among themselves to the detriment of Bulgaria which was set upon by Serbia, Montenegro, Greece, and Rumania in the Second Balkan War (1913) and deprived of many of her conquests. Balkan nationalism thus created six new States (Albania was established by the Powers in 1913) and made the Balkans an arena of the conflicting ambitions of the Great Powers. The interaction between Balkan nationalism and Great Power politics in this region furnished the immediate occasion of the Great War of 1914.

Nationalism effected even more significant changes in the political organization of central Europe after 1815. The people of Italy were divided into seven States and those of Germany into thirty-nine States. In both spheres Austrian power was predominant. In both, the impact of the Napoleonic wars had given rise to a rich growth of national sentiment under the influence of which middle-class patriots strove to attain political unity and nationhood. Since Austria refused to yield pacifically to such a disadvantageous modification of the *status quo*, war seemed the only road to unification, particularly after 1848, when the German liberals failed miserably in their efforts to create a German nation by peaceful means and when diplomatic efforts to achieve Italian unity proved of no avail. In both regions the new nation was forged in the heat of battle, with the Kingdom of Sardinia (Piedmont) under Cavour playing the same rôle in Italy as the Kingdom of Prussia under Bismarck was to play in Germany. In 1858 the new Bonaparte Emperor at Paris, Napoleon III, formed an alliance with Sardinia against Austria on condition of the return to France of Nice and Savoy, conquered by the first Napoleon but lost in 1815. War followed in 1859 and Sardinia was able to annex Lombardy. Nationalist revolutions in central Italy increased the territory of the new State while Garibaldi's filibusters added Naples and Sicily in the south. In 1861 King Victor Emmanuel of Sardinia took the title of King of Italy.

Three years later Prussia under the "Iron Chancellor" joined Austria in war against Denmark and promptly proceeded to quarrel with her ally over the spoils—Schleswig-Holstein. In the Seven Weeks' War of 1866 Prussia defeated Austria and assumed the presidency of the new North

German Confederation, while Italy took her chance to wrest Venetia from the control of Vienna. This enhancement of Prussian power was viewed with alarm by Napoleon III who played into Bismarck's hands by precipitating the Franco-Prussian war of 1870. With the withdrawal of French troops from the Papal States, Italy occupied Rome and the new Italian nation was complete, save for *Italia Irredenta* ("Italy Unredeemed"), *i.e.*, the provinces of the Tyrol and the Trentino, still under Austrian rule. The French armies were meanwhile crushed by the Prussian military machine. Napoleon III lost his throne and the Third French Republic was compelled to return Alsace-Lorraine to German control. Since the south German States had joined Prussia in the war, the German Empire was proclaimed at Versailles during the siege of Paris, January 18, 1871. Two new Great Powers were thus created at the cost of the defeat and humiliation of France and the exclusion of Austria from German and Italian affairs. Austria and Hungary had already joined themselves together in the Dual Monarchy in 1867, but this political edifice, composed as it was of an incongruous congeries of German, Magyar, Latin, and Slavic peoples, was not a national State, but a composite structure which the rising tides of nationalism threatened to engulf.

The mid-century decades of national emancipation and unification, which completely upset the arrangements established by the Congress of Vienna, were followed by a new era of colonial expansion in which almost all of the non-European world was seized upon and partitioned by the Great Powers during a short span of thirty years. The unprecedented rapidity with which the vast colonial empires were created was a direct result of the effects of capitalism and nationalism upon western civilization. The continuing technological and economic revolution going on in every industrial State produced an enormous pressure for expansion in quest of markets for goods and investments and sources of raw materials to supply the needs of machine industry. It placed at the disposal of every capitalistic State, moreover, weapons of power undreamed of in earlier centuries. The steamship, the railroad, the telegraph, the cable, the automobile, the rifle, the machine gun, and the new artillery enabled the States whose citizens and soldiers possessed these devices to impose their control with ease upon the technically backward peoples of Africa and Asia. Missionaries, merchants, and conquerors followed one another in rapid succession. Distant lands across once remote seas could now be conquered, administered, and exploited with a speed impossible in the pre-machine age. Nationalism, moreover, filled the home populations of the imperial States with pride in overseas expansion and insured popular acquiescence in the colonial ventures engineered by diplomats, investors, army officers, and merchants.

The great States of the west, old and new alike, took to the path of empire once more and gained larger territories and more imposing dominions in a single generation than their ancestors had won during the three centuries following the circumnavigation of Africa and the discovery of America. The impact of European culture upon the older civilizations of the East and upon the primitive peoples of the tropics resulted in almost every instance in the loss of political independence and in social and economic disorganization among the societies which were the victims of imperialism. One outstanding exception stood out in brilliant contrast. The medieval island empire of Japan was opened to western influences by an American naval expedition under Admiral Perry in 1854—but instead of falling prey to the western Powers as did the other States of Asia, Japan adopted western technology, western economics, and western nationalism and emerged forty years later as a great nation-state in her own right, the latest addition to the Western State System and the only one of the Great Powers whose population is not of European origin.

The imperial expansion of the Great Powers assumed its most spectacular form in Africa. It may be said to have begun in its modern phase in 1881, with the French conquest of Tunis on the north African coast. Prior to this time, the Dark Continent was an unknown wilderness. France held Algeria in the north, occupied in the 1830's, and scattered bits of coastline farther south. Egypt had been jointly controlled by Great Britain and France in the interests of their investors since 1879. England also held strips of the coast and Cape Colony on the southern tip, north of which the independent Dutch Boer communities of Transvaal and the Orange Free State had been established. Portugal held coastal strips on the western side south of the equator and on the east coast opposite Madagascar. The entire interior was, for the most part, *terra incognita*, unknown and unclaimed by European States and largely inhabited by savage tribes except for the Coptic Kingdom of Abyssinia in the northeast and the State of Liberia on the west coast, founded by freed slaves from the United States. The French Seizure of Tunis in 1881 and the British "occupation" of Egypt in 1882 initiated a general scramble. In the heart of equatorial Africa King Leopold II of Belgium, acting under international auspices, founded the Congo Free State, which was recognized by the Powers in the Berlin Conference of 1884–1885 and was transformed into a Belgian colony in 1908. The Soudan was conquered by the British, who also acquired British Somaliland, British East Africa, Nigeria, Rhodesia, Bechuanaland, the Boer Republics, and smaller areas elsewhere. France seized upon Madagascar, larger in area than France itself, and created a vast empire in the northwest, comprising as additions to Algeria and Tunis the entire Sahara region, Senegal, the Ivory Coast, the French Congo, and Morocco. Portugal carved out Angola and Portuguese East

[101]

Africa. Germany and Italy came late into the field, but the former secured German Southwest Africa, German East Africa, and the Cameroons, and the latter seized upon Eritrea, Italian Somaliland, and Tripoli. By 1911 every square mile of the huge African continent had been partitioned among the States of Europe with the exception of Liberia and Abyssinia, which managed to retain a precarious independence. Compared to this achievement, the most far-flung conquests of the legions of the Caesars fade into insignificance.

The partition of Asia was a scarcely less impressive process. In 1815 Great Britain already held most of India, southeastern Australia, and scattered islands in the South Seas. The Dutch retained the Sunda Islands, including Sumatra and Java, and part of Borneo and the Celebes. France held a few remnants of her Indian empire. Spain held the Philippines and other islands to the east, while Russian power already extended across north Asia to the Bering Sea and Alaska. Great Britain and France in the first and second Opium Wars (1840–1842 and 1856–1860) compelled China to open her ports to European trade. The lopping off of the dependencies of the Celestial Empire soon followed. The British took Hongkong in 1842. In 1863 France annexed Cambodia, to which she added Annam and Tonkin in 1885 to form French Indo-China. Russia seized the Amur River coastal region in 1858–1860. Japan annexed Formosa in 1895. In 1898 Germany seized Kiaochow, France Kwangchow-wan, and Britain Weihaiwei. Russia then took Port Arthur, Dairen, and the whole of Manchuria, but was dispossessed by Japan in 1905. Korea became a Japanese dependency five years later. Only the dissensions among the Powers and the championship of Chinese independence and integrity by the United States in the "Open Door" policy prevented the complete partition of the empire of the Manchus at the turn of the century. In the south Great Britain consolidated and rounded out her Indian Empire and annexed Burma in 1885. Only Turkey, Persia, Afghanistan, Siam, and a truncated China were left in the enjoyment of an uncertain independence on the Asiatic mainland.

The course of empire-building between 1881 and 1914 was marked by numerous minor wars between the European States and native African and Asiatic communities and by one open conflict between Great Powers: the Russo-Japanese War of 1904–1905, in which Japan ousted Russia from South Manchuria and the Liaotung peninsula. The minor wars are almost too numerous to list, but mention may be made of the French war against China of 1884–1885 which was inconclusive, of the Sino-Japanese War of 1894 in which Japan made her first successful bid for empire, the Italian war against Abyssinia of 1896 which was unsuccessful, the Boer War of 1898–1900 in which Great Britain finally conquered the stubborn Dutch settlers of South Africa in the face of heroic resistance, and the

Italian war against Turkey of 1911 which resulted in the Italian annexation of Tripoli. These and innumerable other conflicts were waged by Great Powers against the feeble States of Africa and the Orient. The rival claims of the Powers themselves were usually adjusted by diplomacy and conference.

That the Americas did not also become an arena of imperialistic aggrandizement on the part of the European States was due primarily to the preponderant power of the United States in the western hemisphere. After the promulgation of the Monroe Doctrine in 1823 no European State made any permanent addition to its American possessions. The United States, on the other hand, annexed Texas in 1845, waged war upon Mexico and relieved her of almost half her territory in 1846, and purchased Alaska from Russia in 1867. Napoleon III had taken advantage of the American Civil War of 1861–1865 to attempt to carve out a French Empire in Mexico, but the venture failed dismally. In 1898 the United States resumed its expansion by annexing the Hawaiian Islands and by relieving Spain of Porto Rico, Cuba, and the Philippines after the Spanish-American War. It subsequently converted Cuba, Panama, Haiti, Santo Domingo, and Nicaragua into protectorates and made the Caribbean an American lake, much to the alarm of the Latin American Republics which bitterly resented the hegemony of the "Colossus of the North." The United States, no less than Great Britain, France, Germany, Italy, and Japan, thus carved out an overseas empire at the expense of weaker nations. By 1914 the political map of the world had largely become the map of the colonial possessions, protectorates, and spheres of economic influence of the great States which dominated the international scene.

These remarkable transformations of the Western State System, which was now literally a World System, greatly enhanced the power of its members, enormously extended their territories and resources, and knit them together into compact national units. But they did not modify the fundamental nature of the System, or change the character of the competitive struggle for power between its members. They rather extended the struggle over the globe and intensified it to a great degree because the stakes of diplomacy were larger than ever before. The balance of power now depended no more upon power relationships in Europe than upon developments all over the earth. The "Concert of Europe" operated fitfully to keep the peace in the race for empire, but rapid shifts in power relationships as a result of national unification and colonial expansion were constantly threatening to upset the equilibrium.

Bismarck's system of alliances to preserve the *status quo* of 1871 was superseded by new arrangements. Italy joined Germany and Austria-Hungary in the Triple Alliance of 1882 out of pique over the French seizure of Tunis, but her ambitions in the Near East and her hope of recovering Italia Irredenta made her an unreliable member of the combination. France, bent upon recovering the territory and the prestige lost in the war with Prussia, won Russia to her side in the Dual Alliance of 1894. After serious friction over the partition of Africa and Asia, France entered into the Entente Cordiale with England in 1904, which the Anglo-Russian agreements of 1907 converted into the Triple Entente. Through these arrangements and the alliance with Japan of 1902, Great Britain sought security from the menace of the growing commercial and naval power of Germany. France sought the *revanche* and Russia strove to

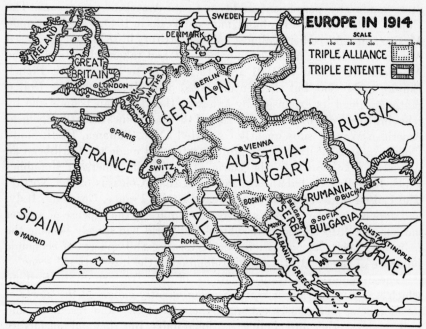

extend her influence in the Near East and the Balkans in competition with Germany and Austria-Hungary. The Central Powers in turn similarly hoped to achieve security, expansion, and a place in the sun by close cooperation with one another. The two great military coalitions, cemented by common interests and secret treaties, faced one another across the armed frontiers and competed with one another in a race of armaments and a struggle for colonial possessions. Each diplomatic conflict—the Franco-German controversies over Morocco of 1904–1905, 1908, and 1911, the Austro-Russian disputes in the Balkans of 1908, 1912, and 1913 and many lesser frictions—thus became crises between the alliances. An unstable equilibrium between these immense aggregations of power was maintained for some years, only to break down in a gigantic combat of nation-states in 1914, which marked the beginning of the end of an epoch.

4. THE WESTERN STATE SYSTEM IN THE TWENTIETH CENTURY

Solutions and panoramas as yet unimagined await the unveiling. Light will be thrown on the dark questions which underlie dread and longing—those deepest of primitive human feelings—and which the will-to-know has clothed in the "problems" of time, necessity, space, love, death, and first causes.—OSWALD SPENGLER, *The Decline of the West*, I.

The Great War marked the culmination of the competitive struggle for power in which the States of the coalitions had engaged for the preceding twenty years. It emerged out of the tangled complex of tensions which had arisen between the Powers as a result of the ambitions of conflicting nationalisms, the striving of competitive imperialisms, and the rivalries of acquisitive capitalistic societies. It must necessarily furnish the point of departure for any consideration of the Western State System in the contemporary period. With its background and events we need not here concern ourselves, for thousands of historians have flooded the world with minutely detailed accounts of its every phase. Suffice it to say that it was occasioned by the assassination at Sarajevo in June of 1914 of the heir to the ancient throne of the Hapsburgs by a Pan-Serbian terrorist whose fellow patriots were eager to enlarge their State by incorporating into it the South Slav provinces of Austria-Hungary. Serbia was confident of Russian support in the pursuit of this ambition. The Dual Monarchy, provoked beyond endurance by the constant menace to its integrity which Serbian nationalist agitation represented, decided to repress the danger by war. Since the extinction or reduction of Serbia would spell the end of Russian influence in the Balkans and since this in turn would constitute a disastrous diminution of the power and prestige of the Entente coalition, the Russian Government determined to resist this action by force. Behind Russia stood her ally, France. Behind Austria stood her ally, Germany. Neither side could afford to yield to the other without making an intolerable sacrifice of its power interests. The hopes of victory which each side cherished in the event of a trial of armed strength made such a sacrifice unthinkable. At the end of a tragic July the Continent was in flames. Germany's invasion of France through Belgium made it easy for the British Government to win popular approval for intervention on the side of France and Russia. Italy, valuing Italia Irredenta more than hypothetical colonial gains, deserted the Triplice, sold herself to the highest bidder for her support, and joined the Allies in 1915. Japan, in alliance with Great Britain since 1902, seized the German possessions in the Far East. All of the Great Powers of Europe and Asia were thus involved in the most catastrophic resort to armed violence between nations which had ever taken place in the history of western civilization.

From the point of view of the relationships of power between the major belligerents, the outstanding fact which emerged almost immediately was that the military might of Germany had been underestimated by both sides. The German Empire, as the most highly mechanized industrialized society on the Continent, was more than a match for the superior populations and armies of her enemies. As the struggle wore on, it became clear that Germany and her allies, with their superior military and economic organization and with the advantage of interior lines of communication, possessed a growing strategic preponderance over the Allies. At the very outset the Teutonic troops carried the war into enemy territory by repulsing the Russian invasion of East Prussia, conquering

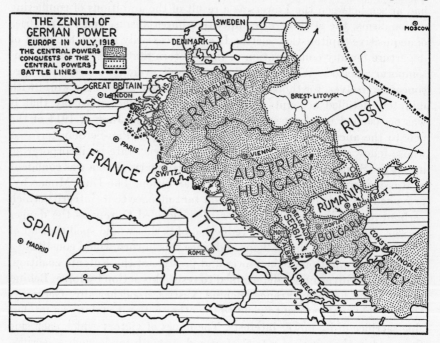

Belgium, and deeply invading northern France. In the sequel the old balance-of-power principle operated with almost mechanical precision to preserve the equilibrium between the contending forces. While Germany and Austria-Hungary were joined by only two small States—Bulgaria, bent upon revenge against Serbia, and Turkey, already a sphere of German economic influence—the ranks of the Allies were swelled by the entrance of State after State into the combat against the Central Powers. The conquest of Serbia in 1915 and the prospect of complete Germanic domination of the Balkans brought Rumania in on the Allied side in 1916. The conquest of Rumania, the defeat of Russia, and the collapse of the Tsardom in political and social revolution, followed by a separate peace, further enhanced the chances of victory of the German coalition. But more and more units of power were thrown into the scales on the Allied side to preserve the balance. The only Great Power which had remained neutral, the United States, joined forces with Great Britain, France, and Italy in 1917 and more than outweighed the defection of Russia. Other States of Latin America and Asia entered the Allied coalition until twenty-three sovereignties were united in fighting the four Central Powers. In the face of these overwhelming odds the last desperate efforts of Germany to achieve victory on the western front in 1918 were frustrated and the balance was finally overturned completely with the defeat and collapse of the central European belligerents.

The Paris Conference of 1919 met amid the ruins of a blasted world. Like its historical predecessors, the Congress of Westphalia, the Conference of Utrecht, and the Congress of Vienna, it sought to incorporate into the public law of Europe and the world the verdict of arms and the new distribution of power resulting from the war. But while its predecessors for the most part restored a *status quo* existing prior to the conflicts which they terminated, the Paris Peace Conference found the European System of 1914 so completely shattered by the great struggle and its aftermath that it was obliged to reconstitute the System in an entirely new form. The Treaties of Versailles with Germany, St. Germain with Austria, Trianon with Hungary, and Neuilly with Bulgaria furnished the basis for the relations between the victors and the defeated States.[1] Among the defeated States was Russia which fell under the control of the Communists as a result of military disaster and social upheaval. The Allied Powers made an unsuccessful effort to destroy the revolutionary Soviet régime by armed intervention in the Russian civil war of 1918–1921. Despite the final triumph of the Red Army over the White Armies and the Allied forces, the Russian State lost sovereignty over Finland, the Baltic States, and Poland, and also over Bessarabia which was annexed by Rumania with Allied approval. Germany, officially designated in the treaty as responsible for the war, was deprived of her army and navy, her overseas colonies, Alsace-Lorraine, and parts of Silesia and West Prussia annexed to Poland, and was subjected to partial military occupation and a colossal war indemnity of indeterminate amount. The Dual Monarchy of Austria-Hungary was completely destroyed as a political entity and the House of Hapsburg, like the Hohenzollern and Romanov dynasties, passed into the shades. Republican Austria survived as the severed head of a truncated imperial body and was forbidden to join Germany. Hungary was reduced to the position of a small landlocked State, having lost most of its territory

[1] The Treaty of Sévres with Turkey was repudiated by the Turkish Nationalists who succeeded in driving the Greeks out of Asia Minor and in playing off the imperial ambitions of Great Britain and France against one another. The final Treaty of Lausanne of 1923 was consequently much more favorable to the new Turkish State than would otherwise have been the case.

to its neighbors, Jugoslavia (Serbia), Rumania, and Czechoslovakia. Bulgaria was cut off from the Aegean Sea by the expansion of Greece, while Turkey was deprived of control over Arabia, Palestine, Syria, and Iraq (Mesopotamia).

A tremendous explosion of nationalism in 1918 and 1919 led to the political fragmentation of central Europe in the name of self-determination. As a means of further reducing the power of the defeated States, the Allies approved the resurrection of an enlarged Poland which was granted Austrian Galicia, part of German Upper Silesia, and the corridor to the sea between East Prussia and the rest of Germany. In 1920 Poland extended her frontiers eastward by waging war upon Russia and by annexing Vilna, the ancient capital of Lithuania. The Allies likewise sanctioned the restoration of the independence of Bohemia in the new State of Czechoslovakia. They acquiesced in the creation of a Greater Serbia, into which Montenegro was incorporated, and they approved the enlargement of Rumania at the expense of Hungary and Russia. To the north of the Succession States of Austria-Hungary appeared the new Russian border States, Lithuania, Latvia, Esthonia, and Finland, each with a total population smaller than that of the capital cities of the great States of the west, but each intensely jealous of its new sovereignty and independence.

In terms of power relationships, the chief effect of the war and the peace was to upset completely the old equilibrium between the pre-war coalitions and to replace it by the imposition upon the Continent of the military and diplomatic hegemony of France and her new allies in the east. The post-war alliances between the beneficiaries of the new distribution of power—France, Belgium, Poland, and the Little Entente States of Czechoslovakia, Jugoslavia, and Rumania—created a new coalition for the preservation of the *status quo* to which no adequate counterweight has yet appeared. Germany, disarmed and diminished in size and population, is reduced to diplomatic impotence. Hungary and Austria remain powerless. Italy has become master of the Adriatic by the annexation of territory at the expense of Austria and Jugoslavia and by the imposition of an Italian protectorate on Albania. She has become a potential enemy of France and the Little Entente because of still unsatisfied territorial, colonial, and naval aspirations which can be fulfilled only by an alteration of the *status quo* disadvantageous to her neighbors. But she is incapable of realizing these ambitions unaided. The resentments of the past and the tensions of the present have thus far prevented any effective diplomatic combination between Italy and the other revisionist States which have a similar interest in modifying existing treaties and frontiers. Friction has developed between Great Britain and France over colonies, debts, reparations, and armaments. A naval race has started between France and

Italy. Russia (the Union of Soviet Socialist Republics) has held aloof from the international politics of the bourgeois States. These circumstances have all made it impossible for Great Britain and Italy either to support the dominant continental bloc or to create effective counterweights against it. Up to the time of writing, therefore, almost every new clash of power interests between the European States has resulted in an enhancement of the prestige of France and her satellites, which together dominate the Continent more completely than has any similar combination of States in the past.

In the world outside of Europe the post-war period has been marked by equally striking transformations in the power relationships between States. All the colonial possessions of Germany were taken from her by the victors. These territories, as well as the areas of the Near East detached from Turkey, were not annexed outright by the Allies, but were converted into "mandates," to be administered under the supervision of the newly established League of Nations. The result was nevertheless to increase greatly the territory and the populations under the political control of the British Empire and France. Italy gained minor "rectifications" of the frontiers of her African colonies, but failed to obtain any new possessions of a magnitude sufficient to satisfy the colonial aspirations of her patriots. The United States, having turned the scales of battle in the Great War and having, through President Wilson, exerted an important influence in the drawing up of the terms of peace, withdrew into isolationism in 1919 and repudiated the League, the treaty, and all the works of the Peace Conference. It none the less emerged from the war with fewer losses and greater additions to its wealth and power than any of the other belligerents. The increase in American naval forces, coupled with the destruction of the German navy, left the United States the second largest naval Power of the world. The billions of dollars loaned to the Allies by the American Government for war purposes and the additional billions of American private capital invested abroad transformed the United States from the greatest debtor nation to the second largest creditor nation of the world. Japan similarly suffered little from the conflict and even more obviously increased her power and prestige in the Far East, securing control of the German islands north of the equator and becoming the third largest naval Power of the world. Japanese efforts to expand on the Asiatic mainland at the expense of China and Russia were frustrated, in part by American opposition. But Japan achieved naval supremacy in the western Pacific and attained a position of preponderance in Asia which augured well for a further enhancement of the power of the Empire of the Rising Sun.

Many of the subsequent pages of this study will be concerned with the confusing cross currents and conflicting forces of international politics

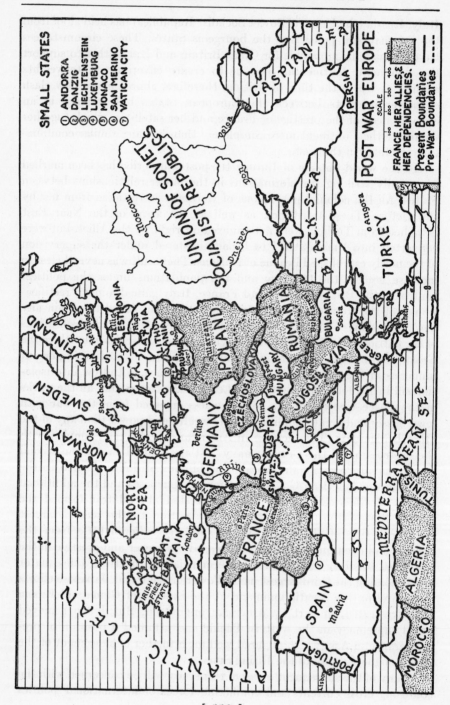

in the post-war period. The Great War and its aftermath constituted such a revolutionary modification of the power relations between States, such a gigantic castastrophe for all of western civilization, that the results may well be regarded as a decisive turning point in the history of the Western State System and of the whole culture complex of which that State System is a part. The prospects of the future will be suggested in the closing book of this volume, after the institutional forms and the dynamic forces operating within the System have been examined. This chapter may be appropriately concluded with a brief survey of the sovereign States which compose the System at the present time—not with the object of describing their culture, their forms of government, or their foreign policies, but simply for the purpose of presenting in résumé the major aggregations of political power in the contemporary world and of naming the *dramatis personae* of the most recent act of the long drama of international politics which has not yet played out its end.

The Western State System in the third decade of the twentieth century is distinctly a world system, consisting of some threescore sovereign States scattered over the five continents. These States are the " persons " of international law and of international politics. Some of them are huge in area and population: China with 450,000,000 people and 4,280,000 square miles of territory; the Soviet Union, with more than 165,000,000 people and 8,240,000 square miles; the United States, with 126,000,000 people and 3,685,000 square miles. Others are almost microscopically minute particles, like Liechtenstein, with 10,000 people and 65 square miles, Andorra in the high Pyrenees with 5,000 people and 191 square miles, or the Vatican City, covering only a hundred acres peopled by 639 persons. Between these extremes are all possible variations. The accompanying chart ranks the States of the world by the population of their metropolitan areas, exclusive of colonies. From the point of view of contemporary international relations they may be ranked more significantly, in terms of their political influence and power, as Great Powers, Secondary Powers, and Minor States.

The Great Powers of the System were reduced from eight to seven by the dissolution of Austria-Hungary. Five of the seven have their capitals and their major centers of wealth, population, and political influence on the European continent where western civilization and the Western State System were born. Of the other two, one—the United States—centers in the great land mass at the heart of the North American continent and the other—Japan—rests upon the islands off the east coast of Asia. The three western European Powers—Great Britain, France, and Italy, each with a population of roughly forty millions of people in its home territory—have all succeeded in extending their sovereignty over large portions of the non-European world. Great Britain controls the largest and most populous of the colonial empires, France possesses the second largest imperial dominion, and Italy falls far behind her two rivals. Germany, with a population of 65,000,000, is still the largest of the western continental Powers, both in area and in population, despite her losses in the Treaty of Versailles, but she has been deprived of all her overseas possessions. The Soviet Union, with a population larger than that of any three of the western Powers combined and with an expanse of contiguous territory under its control in Europe and Asia which is about three times the land area of all the remainder of Europe, is clearly the greatest of the Powers in the number of its citizens and the size of the domain under its jurisdiction. To the east lies the Japanese Empire, the home islands of which are relatively small in area, but upon which reside some 64,500,000 of the Mikado's subjects. Directly across the Pacific lies continental United States, second in size and population only to the Soviet Union and the greatest of the Powers in terms of wealth and industrial productivity.[1]

Considerations of national pride and the variety of the criteria which may be employed make it difficult to classify the other States accurately as Secondary Powers or Minor Powers. For the purposes of a general survey, there can be little objection to placing arbitrarily in the second rank all States, aside from the Great Powers, with populations larger than ten millions. Five States on the European continent fall into this category: Spain, rich in the memories of a vanished empire, but poor in the goods of the machine age; Poland, resurrected and triumphant in the possession of her newly conquered lands; and the three Little Entente countries which have inherited most of the lost realm of the Hapsburgs—Jugoslavia, the dream come true of the pre-war patriots of Serbia; Rumania, more than doubled in size as a result of the war; and Czechoslovakia, emancipated from Austrian rule and a shining citadel of Slavic culture in the heart of central Europe. Hungary has been reduced to the rank of a Minor Power with fewer than 9,000,000 people, while German Austria is an even smaller aggregation of population which would fain join its fortunes with those of Germany, but is prevented from so doing by the terms of the peace. Belgium and the Netherlands are approximately equal in size and population, with about 7,500,000 subjects each, while Portugal, farther south on the Atlantic seaboard beyond France and Spain, has about 5,000,000 citizens. These three States alone among the Minor Powers of Europe have important colonies in Africa and Asia as legacies of their imperial past. Switzerland, perched in the Alps on the crossroads of the Continent, has about 4,000,000 citizens. Bulgaria and Greece in the southeast have about 5,000,000 and 2,500,000 inhabitants respectively. In the north Sweden, Denmark, and Norway constitute a Scandinavian triumvirate,

---

[1] For the colonial possessions and economic status of the Great Powers see below, pp. 382f. and 519f.

the first named having about 6,000,000 subjects, the second about 3,500,-
000, and the third only 2,750,000. Finland's population is approximately
equal to Norway's. The remaining States of Europe have still smaller
populations. Of the three Baltic States, Lithuania has some 2,500,000
citizens, and Esthonia and Latvia fewer than 2,000,000 each. Albania,
appanage of Italy; Iceland, independent, but united with Denmark in a
personal union under a common king; Luxemburg, also independent, but
united with Belgium in a customs union; and the Free City of Danzig all
have fewer than a million inhabitants, while the political microcosms of
Andorra, San Marino, Monaco, Liechtenstein, and the Vatican City each
has considerably less than 1 per cent of that figure as the total number of
its citizens.

The Secondary and Minor Powers of Africa and Asia are fewer in
number. On the former continent only Abyssinia, with about 12,000,000
people, and Liberia, with 2,000,000, retain full political independence,
though Egypt has been nominally independent since 1922. In the Near
East, between the Dardanelles, the Indian Ocean, and the borders of
Tibet, are several Moslem States, survivors of the once mighty dominion
of Islam. Three of these might be classified as Secondary Powers on the
basis of the criterion of population suggested: Turkey, with 14,000,000
people, Persia with about 10,000,000, and Afghanistan whose Emir rules
perhaps 12,000,000 subjects. The Arabian States in the south, comprising
Hejaz, Nejd, Yemen, Oman, and Kuwait, have probably less than
7,000,000 people taken together. The Kingdoms of Hejaz and Nejd are
united in a personal union. Oman is also independent. Iraq entered the
League as an independent State in September, 1932. At the opposite
extremity of the continent lies Siam, with 10,000,000 inhabitants, and to
the north looms the huge hulk of China, unconquerable by its vastness,
but torn by chronic civil strife and the aggressions of the Powers. In the
high Himalayas, between British India and Chinese Tibet, lie the two
States of Nepal and Bhutan. The latter has about a third of a million
inhabitants. Since it is a British protectorate, it cannot be included in any
enumeration of independent sovereignties. Nepal, on the other hand, with
its 5,500,000 inhabitants, is a fully independent State.

In the Latin American area of the western hemisphere, the most
populous States are Brazil with more than 30,000,000 people, Mexico
with 14,500,000, and Argentina with 10,000,000. Among the Central
American republics, only Guatemala and Salvador have more than a
million inhabitants, with Honduras and Nicaragua having between a half
and three-quarters of a million, and Panama and Costa Rica having fewer
than half a million each. On the islands between the Caribbean and the
Atlantic are the three American protectorates of Cuba with about 3,000,-
000 people, Haiti with 2,500,000, and the Dominican Republic with

900,000. In South America, Colombia with its 6,000,000 people, Peru with 5,500,000, and Chile with 4,000,000 rank next to Brazil and Argentina. Bolivia, Venezuela, Ecuador, Paraguay, and Uruguay all have fewer than 3,000,000 citizens each.

There are then in the third decade of the twentieth century 61 independent sovereignties in the Western State System, excluding from this total the very minute States of Europe, the Free City of Danzig, India, and the self-governing Dominions of the British Commonwealth of Nations, in spite of the fact that these entities are in certain respects international persons in their own behalf. Seven of the 61 are Great Powers, 5 in Europe, 1 in America, and 1 in Asia.[1] Of the 15 Secondary Powers, 5 are located on the European continent, 5 in Asia, 3 in America, and 2 in Africa.[2] Of the 39 Minor Powers, 17 are European, 17 Latin American, 4 Asiatic, and 1 African.[3] Of these 61 sovereign States, 50 are members of the League of Nations, which also includes among its membership Luxemburg and 6 units of the British Empire: India, the Irish Free State, the Dominion of Canada, the Union of South Africa, the Commonwealth of Australia, and New Zealand.[4] The remaining 11 States remain outside of the new scheme of international organization superimposed upon the Western State System at the Paris Peace Conference.[5]

This World State System of the twentieth century is as truly a result of the spread of the political patterns of western European culture over the earth as was the "world" empire of classical civilization a consequence of the diffusion of Graeco-Roman patterns over the Mediterranean basin and the adjacent lands. In the latter case, there evolved ultimately a single sovereignty exercising jurisdiction over all of the areas of the western world whose peoples were no longer barbarians. In the former case there has finally been created a multiplicity of sovereignties covering the entire land surface of the planet with the exception of the uninhabitable polar caps. The resulting State System is west European in its origins, forms, and driving forces. Its system of international law, its agencies of diplomacy, its political attitudes and values, even its languages, its religions, its economy, and the forms of the States which compose it, all arose in western Europe. All were diffused over the world in a fashion which has either

[1] Great Britain, France, Italy, Germany, U.S.S.R., the United States, and Japan.

[2] Spain, Poland, Czechoslovakia, Jugoslavia, Rumania, Turkey, Persia, Afghanistan, Siam, China, Mexico, Brazil, Argentina, Abyssinia, and Egypt.

[3] Minor Powers: European—Austria, Hungary, Belgium, The Netherlands, Portugal, Switzerland, Albania, Bulgaria, Greece, Norway, Sweden, Denmark, Iceland, Finland, Esthonia, Latvia, Lithuania; Latin American—Cuba, Haiti, Dominican Republic, Guatemala, Honduras, Salvador, Costa Rica, Nicaragua, Panama, Colombia, Venezuela, Peru, Bolivia, Uruguay, Paraguay, Chile, and Ecuador; Asiatic—Hejaz-Nejd, Oman, Nepal, Iraq; African—Liberia.

[4] See pp. 258f. below.

[5] The United States, U.S.S.R., Ecuador, Brazil, Costa Rica, Iceland, Egypt, Hejaz-Nejd, Oman, Nepal, and Afghanistan.

destroyed indigenous non-European cultures or has overlaid upon them patterns of thought and action derived from western European civilization. The great core of the System still remains the European continent, where are located almost half of the independent States of the world. Only two of the Great Powers—the United States and Japan—are located outside of Europe and of these the United States has a population which is preponderantly of European extraction. These two Powers are the only non-European States of the world possessing overseas colonial empires. From the point of view of racial composition, it is noteworthy that only five of the sixty-one sovereign States have populations which belong to biological stocks differing fundamentally in physical characteristics from the stocks of Europe, though the Latin American Republics all have populations which represent a fusion between European stocks and the native Amerindians. China and Japan have Mongoloid populations, while Haiti, Liberia, and Abyssinia are made up primarily of Negroid peoples. Even these populations, as well as the countless millions of other non-European peoples who live under the political control of European States, have in greater or lesser degree incorporated western European civilization into their native cultural patterns, until the influence of Europe extends far beyond the boundaries of race, language, or political frontiers. The European State System has thus at last become the nucleus of a family of States girdling the globe.

SUGGESTED READINGS

Abbott, W. C.: *The Expansion of Europe*, New York, Henry Holt & Company, 1918.
Barnes, H. E.: *World Politics in Modern Civilization*, New York, Alfred A. Knopf, 1930.
Beard, C. A. and M. R.: *The Rise of American Civilization*, New York, The Macmillan Company, 1930.
Bowman, I.: *The New World, Problems of Political Geography*, Yonkers-On-Hudson, New York World, 1928.
Buell, R. L.: *Europe, A History of Ten Years*, New York, The Macmillan Company, 1928.
———: *International Relations*, New York, Henry Holt & Company, 1929.
Coolidge, A. C.: *The United States as a World Power*, New York, The Macmillan Company, 1921.
Cresson, W. P.: *The Holy Alliance*, New York, Oxford University Press, 1922.
Fay, S. B.: *The Origins of the World War* (2 vols.), New York, The Macmillan Company, 1929.
Gibbons, H. A.: *An Introduction to World Politics*, New York, Century Company, 1922.
Gooch, G. P.: *History of Modern Europe*, New York, Henry Holt & Company, 1922.
Gottschalk, L.: *The Era of the French Revolution*, Boston, Houghton Mifflin Company, 1929.
Hayes, C. J. H.: *A Political and Cultural History of Modern Europe* (2 vols.), New York. The Macmillan Company, 1932.
Hick, A. C.: *Modern World History—1776–1926*, New York, Alfred A. Knopf, 1928.
Hicks, F. C.: *The New World Order*, New York, Doubleday, Page & Company, 1920.
Hodges, C.: *The Background of International Relations*, New York, John Wiley & Sons, 1931.
Moon, P. T.: *Syllabus of International Relations*, New York, The Macmillan Company, 1925.
Morse, H. B. and H. F. MacNair, *Far Eastern International Relations*, Boston, Houghton Mifflin Company, 1931.

Mowat, R. B.: *The European State System*, New York, Oxford University Press, 1923.
Rippy, J. F.: *Latin America in World Politics*, New York, Alfred A. Knopf, 1928.
Schmitt, B. E.: *The Coming of the War—1914* (2 vols.), New York, Charles Scribner's Sons, 1930.
Simonds, F. H.: *Can Europe Keep the Peace?* New York, Harper & Brothers, 1931.
Slosson, P. W.: *Twentieth Century Europe*, Boston, Houghton Mifflin Company, 1927.
Toynbee, A. J.: *Survey of International Affairs*, New York, Oxford University Press, Annual.

THE TWENTIETH CENTURY

THE SOVEREIGN STATES OF THE WORLD

State	Capital City	Area, square miles	Population (estimated as of 1933)
1. China	Nanking	4,277,655	450,000,000
2. Union of Soviet Socialist Republics	Moscow	8,241,921	165,000,000
3. United States	Washington	3,685,382	126,000,000
4. Japan	Tokyo	147,593	66,000,000
5. Germany	Berlin	180,985	65,300,000
6. Great Britain	London	89,041	46,200,000
_a._ India	Delhi	1,819,000	353,000,000
_b._ Canada	Ottawa	3,690,043	10,300,000
_c._ Union of South Africa	Cape Town	471,917	8,100,000
_d._ Australia	Canberra	2,974,581	6,500,000
_e._ Irish Free State	Dublin	26,601	3,000,000
_f._ New Zealand	Wellington	103,410	1,512,000
_g._ Newfoundland	St. Johns	162,734	275,000
7. France	Paris	212,659	41,840,000
8. Italy	Rome	119,710	41,500,000
9. Brazil	Rio de Janeiro	3,275,510	40,275,000
10. Poland	Warsaw	139,868	32,000,000
11. Spain	Madrid	190,050	23,000,000
12. Rumania	Bucharest	122,282	18,000,000
13. Mexico	Mexico City	767,198	16,500,000
14. Czechoslovakia	Prague	54,207	14,800,000
15. Egypt	Cairo	383,000	14,200,000
16. Jugoslavia	Belgrade	96,134	14,000,000
17. Turkey	Angora	294,416	13,700,000
18. Siam	Bangkok	200,234	11,700,000
19. Argentina	Buenos Aires	1,153,119	11,500,000
20. Abyssinia	Addis Ababa	350,000	10,000,000
21. Persia	Teheran	628,000	10,000,000
22. Hungary	Budapest	35,875	8,700,000
23. Belgium	Brussels	11,752	8,000,000
24. Netherlands	Amsterdam	12,603	7,920,000
25. Colombia	Bogota	447,536	7,850,000
26. Austria	Vienna	32,369	6,720,000
27. Greece	Athens	50,257	6,315,000
28. Afghanistan	Kabul	245,000	6,300,000
29. Portugal	Lisbon	35,490	6,200,000
30. Peru	Lima	532,047	6,150,000
31. Sweden	Stockholm	173,146	6,140,000
32. Bulgaria	Sofia	39,814	5,475,000
33. Nepal	Kathmandu	54,000	5,400,000
34. Chile	Santiago	285,133	4,300,000
35. Héjaz-Nejd (Saudian Arabian Kingdom)	Mecca	150,000	4,000,000
36. Switzerland	Berne	15,940	4,000,000
37. Finland	Helsingfors	132,589	3,660,000
38. Cuba	Havana	44,164	3,640,000

THE EVOLUTION OF THE WEST

State	Capital City	Area, square miles	Population (estimated as of 1933)
39. Denmark	Copenhagen	16,576	3,500,000
40. Venezuela	Caracas	393,874	3,200,000
41. Bolivia	La Paz	514,155	3,000,000
42. Iraq	Bagdad	177,148	2,900,000
43. Norway	Oslo	124,964	2,800,000
44. Ecuador	Quito	275,936	2,500,000
45. Liberia	Monrovia	43,000	2,500,000
46. Lithuania	Kovno	21,489	2,370,000
47. Haiti	Port-au-Prince	10,304	2,300,000
48. Guatemala	Guatemala	48,353	2,000,000
49. Uruguay	Montevideo	72,153	1,900,000
50. Latvia	Riga	24,400	1,900,000
51. Salvador	San Salvador	13,176	1,440,000
52. Dominican Republic	Santo Domingo	19,332	1,200,000
53. Esthonia	Tallinn	18,353	1,120,000
54. Albania	Tirana	10,629	1,000,000
55. Honduras	Tegucigalpa	44,275	860,000
56. Paraguay	Ascuncion	61,647	850,000
57. Nicaragua	Managua	51,660	750,000
58. Oman	Muscat	82,000	500,000
59. Costa Rica	San José	23,000	470,000
60. Panama	Panama City	32,380	468,000
61. Iceland	Reykjavik	39,709	109,000
Small States:			
A. Danzig (Free City)	Danzig	754	410,000
B. Luxemburg	Luxemburg	999	300,000
C. Monaco	Monaco	370	25,000
D. San Marino	San Marino	38	13,000
E. Liechtenstein	Vaduz	65	10,000
F. Andorra	Andorra	191	5,000
G. Vatican City	Vatican City	....	700

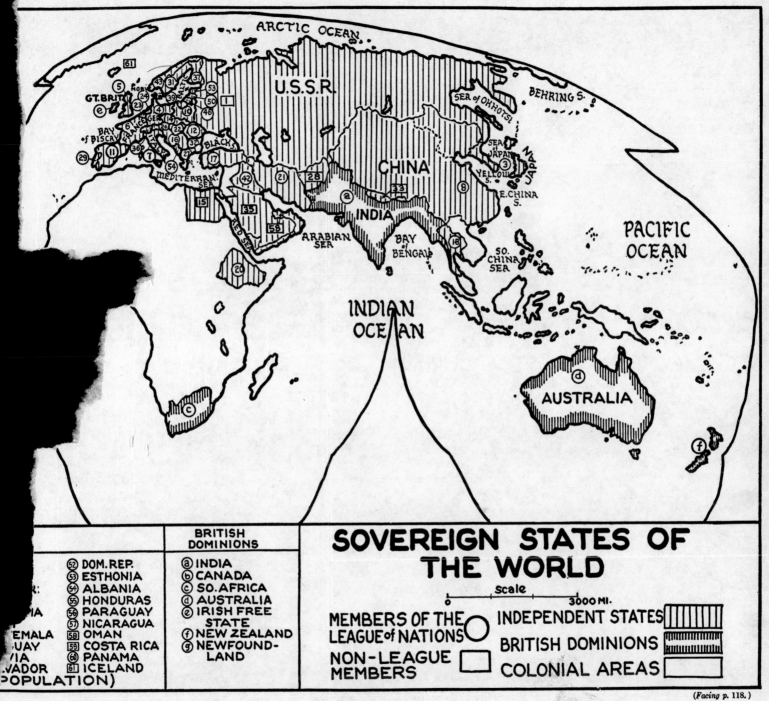

SOVEREIGN STATES OF THE WORLD

BRITISH DOMINIONS

52 DOM. REP.
53 ESTHONIA
54 ALBANIA
55 HONDURAS
56 PARAGUAY
57 NICARAGUA
58 OMAN
59 COSTA RICA
60 PANAMA
61 ICELAND

ⓐ INDIA
ⓑ CANADA
ⓒ SO. AFRICA
ⓓ AUSTRALIA
ⓔ IRISH FREE STATE
ⓕ NEW ZEALAND
ⓖ NEWFOUND-LAND

scale
0 _____ 3000 MI.

MEMBERS OF THE LEAGUE of NATIONS ◯

NON-LEAGUE MEMBERS ☐

INDEPENDENT STATES ▦

BRITISH DOMINIONS ▦

COLONIAL AREAS ☐

(Facing p. 118.)

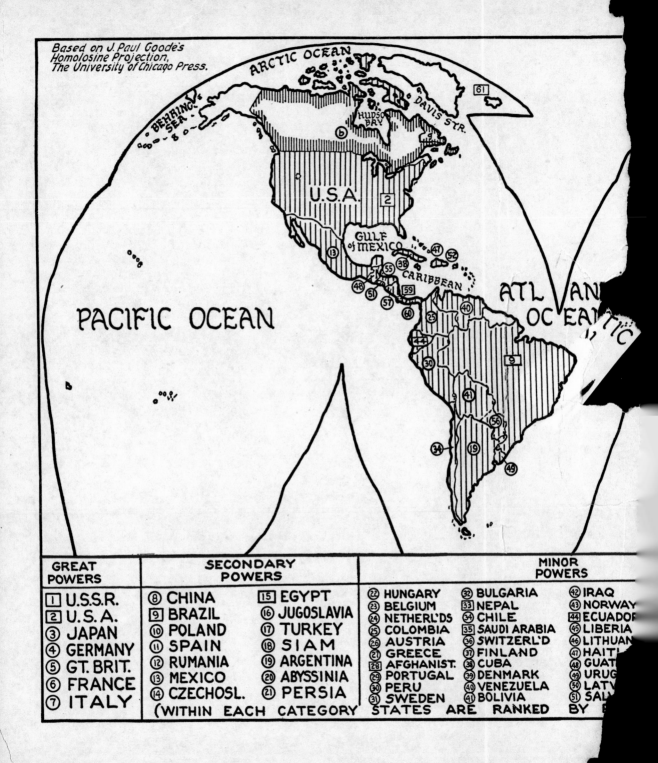

Based on J. Paul Goode's
Homolosine Projection,
The University of Chicago Press.

ARCTIC OCEAN

BEHRING SEA

DAVIS STR.

HUDSON BAY

U.S.A.

GULF of MEXICO

CARIBBEAN

PACIFIC OCEAN

ATLANTIC OCEANIC

GREAT POWERS	SECONDARY POWERS		MINOR POWERS		
① U.S.S.R.	⑧ CHINA	⑮ EGYPT	㉒ HUNGARY	㉜ BULGARIA	㊷ IRAQ
② U.S.A.	⑨ BRAZIL	⑯ JUGOSLAVIA	㉓ BELGIUM	㉝ NEPAL	㊸ NORWAY
③ JAPAN	⑩ POLAND	⑰ TURKEY	㉔ NETHERL'DS	㉞ CHILE	㊹ ECUADOR
④ GERMANY	⑪ SPAIN	⑱ SIAM	㉕ COLOMBIA	㉟ SAUDI ARABIA	㊺ LIBERIA
⑤ GT. BRIT.	⑫ RUMANIA	⑲ ARGENTINA	㉖ AUSTRIA	㊱ SWITZERL'D	㊻ LITHUAN
⑥ FRANCE	⑬ MEXICO	⑳ ABYSSINIA	㉗ GREECE	㊲ FINLAND	㊼ HAITI
⑦ ITALY	⑭ CZECHOSL.	㉑ PERSIA	㉘ AFGHANIST.	㊳ CUBA	㊽ GUAT
			㉙ PORTUGAL	㊴ DENMARK	㊾ URUG
			㉚ PERU	㊵ VENEZUELA	㊿ LATV
			㉛ SWEDEN	㊶ BOLIVIA	⑸ SAL

(WITHIN EACH CATEGORY STATES ARE RANKED BY

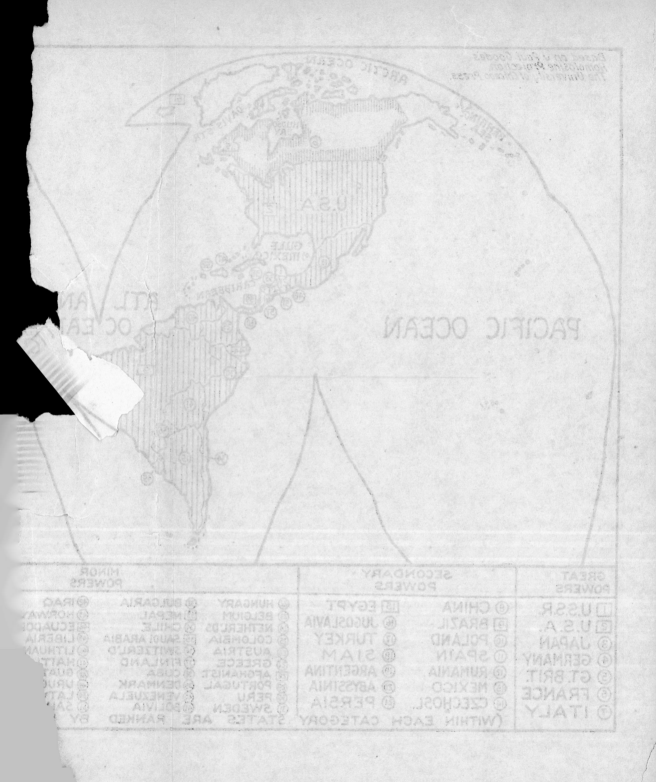

BOOK TWO
FORMS

INTRODUCTION TO BOOK TWO

The present study is based upon the assumption that it is useful to view international politics against its immediate background, *i.e.*, the States of western civilization and the complex of attitudes, behavior patterns, institutions, and procedures which they have evolved in their dealings with one another. This complex has here been designated as the Western State System. Since international politics revolves about the competitive struggle for power and prestige between the units of the System, it is comprehensible only in terms of the general nature of the System and the specific habits and patterns of action which have grown out of the interrelationships between its units.

These habits and patterns have been dealt with historically in the first section of the volume. In the remaining sections they will be dealt with descriptively and analytically. For this purpose, they may be classified into two general types, here called "Forms" and "Forces." By Forms is meant the legal and institutional foundations of the System, the established principles of law observed by its members, the agencies of diplomacy, and the mechanisms of international intercourse and cooperation. These highly formalized and stereotyped behavior patterns will be described in the present section. By Forces is meant the drives, motives, and purposes inherent in the attitudes of the governments and peoples which compose the System, impelling them to action within the limits imposed by the framework of Forms.

Forms are structural and static. Forces are functional and dynamic. The study of Forms is the anatomy of international politics. The study of Forces is its physiology. Forms are laws, procedures, and institutions— the rules and tools of the game of international politics. Forces are the purposes, motives, and objectives which move the players to action. Forms shape the relations between States. Forces arise within States and determine the content of the policies behind the Forms. The two obviously interact upon one another, and any sharp distinction between them must be somewhat artificial. But for descriptive purposes, it seems legitimate to separate them and to deal with each in turn—Forms in the present section and Forces in the third section of the book. The four chapters which follow will take up in order the basic principles of the system of international jurisprudence which determine the legal rights and obligations of States; the customs, practices, and agencies of diplomatic intercourse between States; the various methods which have been developed for the settlement of international disputes; and the existing machinery of international cooperation and organization.

CHAPTER IV

THE ELEMENTS OF PUBLIC INTERNATIONAL LAW

1. SOURCES AND SANCTIONS

It follows that we make enquiry into that most general and universal rule of human action, to which every man is obliged to conform, as he is a reasonable creature. To this rule custom hath given the name of natural law, and we may call it likewise the law universal or perpetual, the former in regard that it binds the whole body of the human race, the latter because it is not subject to change, which is the disadvantage of positive laws.— SAMUEL PUFFENDORF, *De jure naturae et gentium.*

Another species of law is positive (instituted or voluntary) law, which derives its origin from will and is either human or divine. Human positive law includes civil law, which proceeds from the power of the State, the law of nations, which receives its binding force from the will of all nations or of many, and law which does not emanate from the power of the State though subject to it, such as the commands of a father or a master.—HUGO GROTIUS, *De jure belli ac pacis.*

FOR the past three centuries the States of the Western State System have played the game of international politics in accordance with certain generally recognized rules which have usually been regarded as binding upon all the members of international society. These rules were first systematically formulated and set down as principles of the "Law of Nations" by Hugo Grotius at the beginning of the seventeenth century. Like many rules of law, however, they had been developing for many centuries before they were reduced to written form. Once put into writing and made the object of scientific study, they developed at a much more rapid rate than before. They have now become a well-defined and logically integrated set of principles indicating the rights and obligations of States in almost every conceivable international situation. The mere recital of these principles in any complete fashion would fill many hundreds of pages. Since the days of Grotius, innumerable scholars and jurists in all lands have written elaborate textbooks and treatises for the purpose of describing these rules and relating them to one another. Hundreds of judicial tribunals, both national and international, in countless thousands of cases, have developed international law by an endless process of adapting established rules to new situations. Thousands of treaties and conventions between States have made more specific the conceptions of rights and obligations which have grown out of custom and usage. This constant adaptation, re-interpretation, and elaboration of principles have created a vast body of international jurisprudence which could not be described adequately in many volumes, much less in one chapter of a single volume. This circumstance, coupled with the fact that the great textbooks are available in almost every part of the world, makes it necessary for the purposes of the present study to undertake only a brief and simple sketch of the basic concepts underlying the whole structure.

Since the present study is concerned with the relations of States to one another, rather than with the legal rights and obligations of individuals, attention will be devoted only to that portion of international law which applies to States, *i.e.*, "public" international law, as distinct from "private" international law. The former has to do with States as legal and political entities. It consists of the rules and principles which the whole society of States habitually expects its members to observe in their relations with one another. It seeks to deduce from these rules and principles the legal rights and obligations of States in each particular situation. Private international law, on the other hand, is concerned primarily with individuals rather than with States. It has to do with the rights and obligations of individuals as they are affected by differences in the legislation of States. The name "conflicts of laws" is often applied to this body of legal principles, for it deals with situations in which the legal status of persons or property is in doubt because of overlapping jurisdictions and divergencies of national legislation. If the American Government becomes involved in a dispute with the French Government over the respective rights of the two States to German reparations payments, or over the territorial claims of the two States in the islands of the Pacific, the rights and obligations of the parties will be defined by public international law. But if an American citizen, with property in Germany, marries a French wife, with an estate in Java, his rights will be defined by the principles of private international law. Such situations are fascinating to the lawyer and the jurist, but are of only incidental interest to the statesman and the diplomat. The principles which govern them need scarcely be considered by the student of international politics. Public international law, however, is of fundamental importance to any understanding of the patterns of relationship between the sovereign States of the modern world.

Inasmuch as public international law differs in many respects from other types of law, as has been suggested above, it will be useful to consider at the outset the problem of its sources and sanctions. Every statesman, diplomat, and jurist who is confronted with a legal problem concerning the relations between States must know where to look for the principles, precedents, and established rules and procedures which will indicate the rights and obligations of the parties in the particular situation. In dealing with problems of national or "municipal" law, as it is sometimes called, this problem is comparatively simple, for lawyers and jurists can readily "find the law" in written constitutions, in statutes passed by national or local legislatures, or (in Anglo-Saxon countries) in past judicial decisions which furnish precedents for future cases. Once the law has been determined upon and a decision has been reached, the judgment will be carried out by the court, the sheriff, or, if need be, by the whole force of the State. In criminal cases, the convicted offender is fined, sentenced to jail, or sometimes executed for his crime. In civil cases, the injured party is awarded damages at the expense of him who has committed the injury. In international law, however, the situation is quite different. The law is not usually reduced to statutory form, and there is no judge, jury, sheriff, or police force to insure its execution. In both its sources and its sanctions, *i.e.*, the means available to insure its enforcement, it differs markedly from other types of law.

The sources of international law may be divided into four categories in order of their importance: (1) agreement, (2) custom, (3) reason, and (4) authority. In every international law case, the best and most conclusive source of information regarding the rights of the parties are the written agreements, treaties, conventions, protocols, and the like, which the States involved have concluded with one another. Such written agreements, if properly signed and ratified, are unqualifiedly binding upon the parties. All modern States have hundreds of treaties with other States, dealing with an enormous variety of matters. The texts of these treaties are usually published by the signatory parties in a national treaty series.[1] There is also available a large number of privately published compilations of treaty agreements, though the best single source of recent treaties is the League of Nations Treaty Series, which now consists of over one hundred volumes, containing the texts of more than 2,000 treaties arranged by years in alphabetical order of countries.[2] States are always free to make international law between themselves by treaty, providing they do not violate the rights of third States. In this way they agree upon the rules and principles which they propose henceforth to follow in dealing with one another. If such agreements cover the case in hand, it is unnecessary to look further for sources of law, for specific agreements supersede all other possible sources.

[1] Treaties of the United States are issued in pamphlet form in the State Department Treaty Series. *Cf.* also Malloy (ed.), *Treaties, Conventions, Protocols, etc., of the United States* (2 vols.), 1909, and a third volume issued in 1923.

[2] Article XVIII of the League of Nations Covenant specifies that "Every treaty or international agreement entered into hereafter by any member of the League shall forthwith be registered with the secretariat and shall as soon as possible be published by it. No such treaty or international engagement shall be binding until so registered." The only recent treaties not contained in the series are those concluded between non-member States, which are few in number.

But if existing agreements do not cover adequately the situation under consideration, it is necessary to look further for enlightenment as to the rights and duties of the parties. The established customs, practices, and usages of States in dealing with analogous problems in the past furnishes the next best guide. Differences of opinion are obviously more likely to arise regarding rights based exclusively upon customary international law than is the case where rights are specifically defined in written agreements. But the great bulk of modern international law is based upon custom and practice. When it can be clearly shown that a particular principle or practice has been generally observed by the majority of States over a long period of time, no question will ordinarily be raised regarding its legal validity. When, for example, the United States Supreme Court was obliged to pass upon the legality of the capture of a Spanish fishing smack by American gunboats during the Spanish-American War, it held the capture unlawful on the ground that "at the present day, by the general consent of the civilized nations of the world, and independently of any express treaty or other public act, it is an established rule of international law, founded on considerations of humanity to a poor and industrious order of men, and of the mutual convenience of belligerent States, that coast fishing vessels, with their implements and supplies, cargoes and crews, unarmed, and honestly pursuing their peaceful calling of catching and bringing in fresh fish, are exempt from capture as prize of war" (*The Paquete Habana*, 175 U.S. 677). The court further held that a practice which had originally been a matter of custom or comity could readily become an established rule of law through securing the general assent of States. This view has been followed by practically all courts, arbitral tribunals, jurists, and textwriters.

When appeals to agreements and to customs both fail to indicate the rights and obligations of States, recourse is had to reason and to authority, *i.e.*, to logical deductions from established general principles, and to arbitral awards, the decision of courts, and the opinions of textwriters and jurists. Novel situations are constantly arising in contemporary international relations with regard to which no agreements have been concluded and no customs have developed. These are ordinarily dealt with by seeking to apply to the new facts a line of reasoning resting upon established general rules accepted as *a priori* premises. If, by this procedure, a definition of rights and obligations can be arrived at which appears to be in harmony with the whole body of international jurisprudence, it is more than likely to be accepted by the parties as a source of law in the novel situation. Similarly the judgments of judicial tribunals, national or international, and the views of widely recognized authorities are constantly relied upon as guides to the law, chiefly to support the conclusions to which a consideration of agreements, customs, and reason has already led.

Judicial decisions and arbitral awards are binding only upon the parties to the disputes of which they are settlements, but taken as a whole they indicate to all States the prevalent conception of rights and duties accepted in international society. Agreement and authority are written sources of international law. Custom and reason are unwritten only in the sense that they are not incorporated in treaties or decisions. The precedents, practices, and usages out of which they emerge, however, are to be found in the diplomatic correspondence and State papers maintained in governmental archives.

To illustrate the relative importance of these four sources of international law, mention may be made of two typical cases. By a treaty of February 29, 1893, an arbitral tribunal was set up by the American and British Governments to pass upon the legality of the seizure on the high seas of certain Canadian fishing vessels by the American Coast Guard authorities attempting to enforce the legislation of the United States designed to protect the Behring Sea seal herds from extermination. In the hearings before the tribunal, the attorneys for the United States argued that the treaty agreements of 1824, 1825, and 1867 between the United States, Great Britain, and Russia conferred upon the United States a property right in the fur seals which entitled the American Government to prohibit pelagic sealing in all waters frequented by the animals. It was also argued that the customs of nations and the reasonableness of the motive justified the American action. The tribunal decided, however, that the treaties in question did not confer the right alleged and did not cover the case in hand. It likewise decided that custom and reason did not support the American contentions. It therefore reached a conclusion based upon the long-accepted and generally recognized principle that States have no jurisdiction beyond the three-mile limit of territorial waters and consequently no right to enforce their legislation on the high seas against the vessels of other States. Since the United States was unable to show that this established rule had been superseded by specific agreements or in any other fashion, the award was against it and it was subsequently obliged to pay damages of $473,151.26 for the vessels seized.[1]

The Permanent Court of International Justice was similarly called upon to determine the sources of law when, on May 19, 1931, the Council of the League of Nations requested it to deliver an advisory opinion on the legality of the projected customs union between Germany and Austria. Here, however, the question before the court was not whether the proposed arrangement was contrary to customary international law—and still less whether it was desirable on economic or political grounds—but simply whether it was or was not contrary to Article 88 of the Treaty of St. Germain, which forbids Austria to alienate or compromise her inde-

---

[1] *Cf.* J. B. Moore, *International Arbitrations*, I, pp. 755–961.

pendence, or to the Financial Protocol of 1922, which obliges Austria to "abstain from any negotiations or from any economic or financial engagement calculated directly or indirectly to compromise (its) independence." The specific agreements between the parties covered the situation. It was not necessary for the Court to inquire into custom, reason, or authority, except for the purposes of interpreting the agreements. By an eight to seven vote, it held on September 5, 1931, that the customs union (which Germany and Austria had in fact already agreed to abandon) was in violation of Austria's obligations under the Financial Protocol. Here the treaty terms were sufficient to decide the issue, the only difference of opinion being with regard to the meaning to be given to them.

The sanctions of international law may be classified, in order of their importance, as (1) habit, (2) expediency, (3) good faith, and (4) organized force. Those rules and principles which have been habitually observed for the longest period of time are obviously most likely to be observed in the future, since the whole force of inertia lies behind them, and States, no less than individuals, are prone to do things in ways which are easy because traditional. The principle of the immunity and inviolability of diplomatic representatives, for example, has been generally observed by States for more than 2,500 years and is almost never willfully violated at the present time. Considerations of self-interest and political expediency are also influential in securing the observance of established principles, particularly as regards the international law of war. At the outbreak of the American Civil War there was some disposition in Union circles to treat captured members of the Confederate armies not as prisoners, in accordance with the laws of war, but as rebels who might be punished for treason, arson, murder, and other individual acts. Once it was realized, however, that the Confederacy would promptly retaliate on Federal prisoners and that the Union cause would be injured rather than aided by the contemplated departure from established rules, the intention was abandoned and the usual principles governing the conduct of hostilities were observed on both sides during the conflict. A more farsighted view of military and political expediency on the part of the German High Command would similarly have dictated observance of agreements forbidding the use of poison gas in the Great War. After the first use of gas by the Germans in 1915, events revealed that the Allied armies were not merely prepared to retaliate, but possessed more adequate facilities for gas manufacture and enjoyed the advantage of the prevailing westerly winds on the Western Front.

Good faith as a sanction is doubtless of increasing importance in the era of democracy and organized public opinion, but numerous instances can still be found in which States adhere to the Machiavellian view that agreements and established customs should be observed only so long as it is expedient to do so. As for organized force, there has not as yet been developed in the Western State System any effective machinery for applying international coercion to lawbreaking States, in spite of the hypothetical scheme embodied in the Covenant of the League of Nations. Thus far, when force has been utilized to insure observance of international law, it has always been the force of State against State, with the enforcer often pursuing ulterior political objectives disguised by a façade of morality and sanctimonious solicitude for the observance of international obligations. Organized force thus remains the least effective of the four types of sanctions mentioned.

2. STATE AND GOVERNMENT

There is annexed to the sovereignty the right of making war and peace with other nations and commonwealths; that is to say, of judging when it is for the public good, and how great forces are to be assembled, armed, and paid for that end; and to levy money upon the subjects to defray the expenses thereof.—THOMAS HOBBES, *Leviathan*.

Since States are the persons of public international law, it follows that international law is concerned primarily with such sovereign political entities as are generally recognized as "States" within international society. With certain exceptions which will be noted below, no individual or corporation, no community or territorial group can claim rights under international law unless it is regarded by the members of the State System as a State, independent and co-equal with other States. It is generally agreed that a State, in order to be worthy of the name, must possess citizens or subjects and a well-defined territory. Since land was the most important form of wealth and power, and sovereignty was associated with territorial property at the time when the foundations of international law were being laid, a territorial basis has always been regarded as a prerequisite to statehood. But the question of whether a particular political entity does or does not constitute a State in fact (*de facto*) is not, in itself, a problem of international law at all. A "State" may exist for a long period of time as a sovereign political entity, but it does not become a State in the legal sense until it has been received into the family of nations as a recognized member. Switzerland and the Netherlands before 1648, the United States between 1776 and 1778, Japan prior to 1854, and Turkey prior to 1856 all constituted *de facto* States without being persons of international law, *i.e.*, without being formally admitted as full-fledged members into the Western State System. States are initiated into the society of States only by the process of diplomatic recognition extended to them by other States.

When and under what circumstances established States shall recognize new States is entirely a matter of policy. That is to say, the granting of recognition to new States is entirely discretionary, and not mandatory, on the part of other States already established and recognized. It may be granted at once, it may be delayed, or it may be withheld indefinitely for legal reasons, for political reasons, for good, bad, or indifferent reasons. A new State seeking recognition has no means of compelling other States to grant it. Considerations of convenience and the obvious utility of maintaining diplomatic contacts with a *de facto* State, however, will usually dictate its recognition by other States as soon as its existence and independence are firmly established. New States may be recognized individually or collectively by other States. Greece was recognized collectively by the Powers at the London Conference of 1830. Belgium was likewise recognized collectively in 1831, Montenegro, Serbia, and Rumania in 1878, and Czechoslovakia and Poland in 1918. The Allied Powers jointly recognized the independence of the Baltic States of Esthonia, Lithuania, and Latvia in 1919, but the United States, for reasons connected with its policy toward Russia, withheld recognition until 1922.

Recognition may be granted in a variety of ways, but once granted is irrevocable. When granted, it dates back, so far as legal rights and obligations are concerned, to the date of the establishment of the new State. Normally, one State recognizes another by a formal declaration to this effect, followed by an official exchange of diplomatic representatives. Both the dispatch and reception of a diplomatic agent constitute recognition. The reception of the consular agents of a new State through the granting to them of exequaturs authorizing them to assume their functions is also equivalent to recognition, though the sending of a consular agent to receive an exequatur from the authorities of a new State does not necessarily imply recognition on the part of the sending State.[1] The signature of an international agreement, a salute to the flag, or any other similar act authorized by the responsible authorities of the State whose officials take such action likewise constitutes recognition. In the United States, as in all other countries, the power to recognize new States and governments is vested in the executive, *i.e.*, the President and the Secretary of State. Congress has no power to grant, or to compel the granting of, recognition, and the courts never question executive discretion in such matters.[2] The United States has usually recognized new States by official proclamation of the President or Secretary of State.

If an outside State recognizes the independence of a new State during a period of conflict in which the new State's claim to independence is still being contested by the State formerly having jurisdiction over its territory, the act of recognition takes on the appearance of intervention or

[1] See pp. 174–175 below.
[2] See *Williams v. Suffolk Insurance Co.*, 13 Pet. 415; *Jones v. U. S.*, 137 US 202; *Foster v. Nielson*, 2 Pet. 253.

unlawful interference in the domestic affairs of another State. The injured party may legitimately regard such premature recognition as a hostile act. France recognized the independence of the United States by signing treaties of alliance and commerce with American representatives at Paris on February 6, 1778, when Great Britain was still making active efforts to subdue her rebellious colonies. Great Britain consequently declared war against France and later against Spain and the Netherlands for the same reason. Had the European Powers recognized the independence of the Confederacy during the American Civil War, this action similarly would have been regarded as a *casus belli* on the part of the Union. The recognition of Mexico and the other Latin American republics by the United States in 1822 and 1823 was granted at a time when Spain still asserted claims to her lost empire, but when all prospects of her recovering it had vanished. The recognition was not therefore premature. The recognition by the United States of the independence of Panama in November, 1903, on the other hand, was a definite violation of the rights of Colombia, since the revolution which established Panama's independence was organized in Washington and carried out with the cooperation of American marines. Colombia subsequently was paid $25,000,000 by the United States in accordance with the terms of the treaty of 1914, ratified by the Senate in 1925. This money payment was implicitly, though not expressly, an act of reparation to Colombia for American violation of her rights in 1903. Japan's recognition of the Manchurian puppet State of Henry Pu-Yi on September 15, 1932, was likewise a violation of the territorial integrity of China and might have been treated as an act of war by China had the latter been in a position to offer resistance. In every such case, the State whose rights are violated by premature recognition has a valid complaint against the recognizing State which has thus sanctioned the partition of its territory before the alleged new State has in fact established its independence.

Almost all of the foregoing observations are also applicable to the recognition of new governments within States already recognized. A revolution within a State normally terminates its diplomatic relations with other States. The State continues to be a person of international law, but in the absence of the recognition of its new government by other governments it has no means of communicating with outside States. Recognition of revolutionary governments, no less than recognition of new States, is a question of policy on the part of other governments. During the period from 1793 down to the first Wilson administration, the United States usually adhered to the so-called *de facto* theory of recognition, which holds that new governments should be recognized as soon as they are in fact in control of the State, in contrast to the *de jure* theory, which denies the right of revolution and holds that only legitimate, constitutional governments are entitled to recognition. When Washington's Cabinet in 1793 granted an official reception to the new French Minister, Citizen Genêt, *i.e.*, extended diplomatic recognition to the revolutionary régime in France, it did so on the basis of Secretary of State Jefferson's view that the only relevant question was whether the new régime was in effective control of France and therefore in a position to represent the French State and discharge its international obligations. The *de facto* theory was followed by the United States quite consistently with respect to the various revolutions in Europe and Latin America throughout the nineteenth century.

These two divergent *theories* of recognition should not be confused with *de facto* and *de jure* recognition. The former phrase is applied to diplomatic recognition of a new State or government not followed at once by an exchange of diplomatic representatives. Great Britain, for example, extended *de facto* recognition to the Soviet régime in Russia by signing the trade agreement of March, 1921. *De jure* recognition was not extended until February of 1924, when regular diplomatic agents were exchanged. The United States has never extended either *de facto* or *de jure* recognition to the Soviet Government, in spite of the fact that the Communists have been in control of the Russian State since November 7, 1917. This policy has been defended on the ground that the Soviet régime is unwilling to discharge the international obligations of the Russian State, as shown by its repudiation of the debts of the Tsarist and Provisional Governments, its confiscation of foreign property in Russia, and its alleged encouragement of subversive propaganda directed against other States. These reasons are rationalizations of the established policy of nonrecognition rather than explanations of it.[1] The policy in question, as well as American recognition policies pursued toward the republics of Central America, represents a departure from the *de facto* theory of recognition, despite official allegations to the contrary, for it involves the use of recognition as a weapon to achieve diplomatic objectives unrelated to considerations of the convenience and utility of maintaining contacts between established governments.[2] All governments are free, however, to grant or withhold recognition of revolutionary governments in other States at their option, though it is obvious that any general use of the power of recognition as a tool of diplomacy inevitably results in an unfortunate interruption in the official relations between the members of the State System.

In summary, the rights and obligations of international law are in general applicable only to States recognized by the members of the family

[1] See F. L. Schuman, *American Policy toward Russia since 1917*, 1928; and Louis Fischer, *Why Recognize Russia?*, 1931.

[2] In 1923 the United States persuaded the Central American Republics to sign a treaty in which they pledged themselves not to recognize governments set up by revolutionary means. Except for the cases of these States and the Soviet Union, the United States now follows the *de facto* theory of recognition.

of nations and States can deal officially with other States only through recognized governments. In both cases recognition is a discretionary political act of the executive authorities of other States. There are, nevertheless, certain "persons" of international law which are not true States and yet which enjoy a certain qualified legal status. Members of confederations and other unions, while not sovereign States, may have their own diplomatic representation abroad and may be granted certain customary rights under international law by outside States. Such is the peculiar position of the self-governing Dominions of the British Commonwealth of Nations. Neutralized States, protectorates, and suzerainties are sovereign only in part, but they may be recognized as States by third parties. Insurgents and belligerents, *i.e.*, groups of armed individuals conducting hostilities for public purposes, are also entitled to the usual rights of the international law of war, providing that they observe the reciprocal obligations. When outside States recognize a condition of "insurgency" in a particular State, they take cognizance of hostilities in which they are bound to refrain from interference. The local State remains answerable for the acts of the insurgents. When a state of "belligerency" is recognized, on the other hand, either by the State confronted with civil war or by outside States, the international law of war applies in full to both combatants and the local State is released from responsibility. In these instances a qualified status under international law is granted to entities which are not genuine States.[1] With the exception of these special cases, however, international law is concerned only with recognized States and governments.

3. FUNDAMENTAL RIGHTS AND OBLIGATIONS

Nations being free, independent, and equal and having a right to judge according to the dictates of conscience, of what is to be done in order to fulfill its duties; the effect of all this is, the producing, at least externally, and among men, a perfect equality of rights between nations, in the administration of their affairs, and the pursuit of their pretensions, without regard to the intrinsic justice of their conduct, of which others have no right to form a definitive judgment; so that what is permitted in one, is also permitted in the other, and they ought to be considered in human society as having an equal right.—EMERICH DE VATTEL, *Droit des gens.*

In so far as the whole structure of public international law can be deduced from elementary principles, it may be said to rest upon certain broad concepts inherent in the idea of the sovereignty of the State which

[1] It is sometimes said that individuals have rights but no remedies in international law, in the sense that individual rights may be affected by State action but that the individuals so affected have no means of compelling observance of their rights unless they are protected by a State which takes diplomatic action in their behalf. In the Central American Court of Justice (1907–1917) the citizens of the five Central American Republics were granted the right of bringing suit in the court against the States themselves, but this arrangement is anomalous and exceptional.

lies at the basis of the whole Western State System. A State which is sovereign is not subject to the will of any other State. It exists as an independent entity, co-equal with other sovereignties and with exclusive jurisdiction over its territory. From this elemental fact it follows that every State possesses certain fundamental rights and obligations with respect to other States. It possesses, for example, a right of existence or self-preservation and an obligation to recognize that other States enjoy the same right. It possesses a right of independence and an obligation to respect the same right in other States. It possesses a right of legal equality with other States and a right of exercising its power and enforcing its legislation within its frontiers, *i.e.*, a right of jurisdiction. It is sometimes said that States also possess fundamental rights of property and of intercourse. In view of the logical relationship between these fundamental rights and the whole superstructure of rules and principles, it will be legitimate for the purposes of the present survey to suggest the superstructure by an examination of the meaning of the fundamental rights.

The right of existence or self-preservation is obviously the most important and elementary of these fundamental rights. That every sovereign State is free to take any action which may be necessary to preserve its existence as a political entity, even to the extent of infringing upon the rights of other States, has long been recognized as an axiomatic principle. This right must be strictly construed, however, for no State can lawfully violate the rights of others on the basis of vague and general allegations that its existence is menaced by acts taking place outside of its own frontiers. An attack upon an innocent third party, for example, can never be justified on the plea of self-preservation. The German invasion of Belgium in 1914, in violation of the neutralization treaty of 1839, was defended on the ground that it was the only procedure available to Germany for attacking France effectively and thus meeting the threat to Germany represented by the Franco-Russian alliance. But since the existence of Germany was by no conceivable stretching of the imagination jeopardized by any act of Belgium, the invasion was unlawful. The German Chancellor, Bethmann-Hollweg, recognized this in his address to the Reichstag of August 4, 1914, in which he declared, "We are in a state of necessity and necessity knows no law." A State can allege self-preservation as a justification for an infringement of the rights of other States only when it is directly and immediately menaced by some action in the other State which can be thwarted in no other way.

This principle has been laid down in its classic form by Secretary of State Daniel Webster. During the Canadian rebellion of 1838 a body of insurgents gathered on the American side of the Niagara River, seized guns from American arsenals, occupied an island in midstream from which they fired shots into Canadian territory, and prepared to recross in the

American ship *Caroline* to continue hostilities against the Canadian forces. In this emergency British troops crossed into New York State, broke up the expedition, sent the *Caroline* over Niagara Falls, and returned to Canada. This violation of the territory of the United States evoked a strong protest from Webster in which he demanded an apology and repara- tion unless the British Government could "show a necessity for self- defense, instant, overwhelming, leaving no choice of means, and no moment for deliberation. It will be for it to show also that the local au- thorities of Canada, even supposing the necessity of the moment author- ized them to enter the territories of the United States at all, did nothing unreasonable or excessive, since the necessity of self-defense must be limited by that necessity and kept clearly within it."[1] In this instance the British Government had no difficulty in justifying its action, since an instant and overwhelming necessity menacing the existence of the estab- lished government in Canada did undeniably exist and the action taken was limited to meeting this threat. Under such circumstances the right of self-preservation renders legitimate any reasonable action to safeguard the existence of the State or of its government.[2]

The right of independence entitles a State to formulate its own foreign policy within the limits of the rights of other States and to conduct its domestic affairs as it sees fit, provided that it does not ignore the obliga- tions which international law imposes upon it. "Independence" as to domestic affairs is subject to the qualification that a State is responsible for injury to aliens within its territory, is required to maintain some de- gree of law and order, and is bound to maintain some authority answer- able to foreign governments. A State must exercise due diligence in the protection of aliens who are entitled to at least the same degree of protec- tion as it affords to its own citizens. It is responsible for any obvious miscarriages of justice in its courts. An interesting case involving these questions arose between the United States and Italy in 1891. On March 14, 1891, eleven persons of Italian origin were taken from jail, where they were confined on charges of complicity in the murder of the chief of police, and were lynched by a mob in New Orleans. The local authorities made no effort to afford them protection. The Italian foreign minister at once instructed the Italian Minister in Washington "to denounce immediately to the United States Government the atrocious deed of New Orleans, requesting immediate and energetic steps . . . to protect the Italian colony endangered, and to punish severely the guilty." Secretary of State Blaine reminded the Governor of Louisiana that the treaty of 1871 guaranteed reciprocal protection of persons and property, but no action

---

[1] See W. E. Hall, *International Law*, 1924, pp. 323–324.

[2] See also the case of the *Virginius, Foreign Relations of the United States*, 1874, pp. 922–1117, and Moore's *Digest*, II, pp. 895 f.

was taken to punish the lynchers and no indemnity was paid to the relatives of the victims. In protest, the Italian Minister was recalled from Washington, while Blaine intimated that the federal government of the United States had no constitutional authority to compel action by the State officials of Louisiana. The Italian Government denied the relevancy of this allegation and on April 12, 1892, Blaine offered an indemnity of 125,000 francs, the acceptance of which was followed by a full resumption of diplomatic relations.[1] Every State must maintain central authorities responsible for the fulfillment of its international obligations. While the right of independence carries with it the reciprocal obligation of respecting the independence of other States, the Great Powers have frequently violated the independence of small and weak States when conditions of domestic disorder have led to damage to foreign lives and property. The extent to which States are justified in taking such action is much disputed, but the general principles indicated are universally accepted.

The right of equality has reference only to legal rights and obligations and not, of course, to territory, population, power, or political influence. The sixty-one sovereign States of the world differ enormously among themselves in these characteristics, with the seven great States having power vastly disproportionate to that of the lesser countries. But before the law, all sovereign States are equal. Nicaragua enjoys the same rights and is bound by the same obligations as those of the United States. The minute City of the Vatican occupies the same international legal status as the British Empire. All States have equal opportunities to protect their rights and to demand that other States observe their obligations. All have an equal right to make treaties, wage war, maintain or sever diplomatic relations with other States, and the like. From the principle of State equality is deduced the rule of unanimity in international conferences, according to which each State has one vote and no State can be bound without its consent. In practice, however, it has long been conceded that theoretical legal equality is inconsistent with actual political disparity. When controversies over conflicting claims lead to a resort to coercive measures, small, weak States are obviously less capable of protecting their rights than large powerful States. So long as self-help and coercion are the ultimate means of protecting State rights, equality under international law, in a system of unequal States, will remain almost as tenuous as individual equality in domestic law, in societies in which economic power is unequally distributed among the citizenry. Anatole France once marvelled at that majestic equality of the law whereby the rich and poor alike were forbidden to steal bread or to sleep under the bridges at night. This principle is paralleled by the comparable principle of equality among States in international law in a State System in which there appears at

[1] *Foreign Relations of the United States*, 1891, pp. 658–728.

[134]

times to be one law for the Great Powers and another for the lesser nations. The principle of State equality is, nevertheless, a logical corollary of the concepts of sovereignty and independence, and States always resent hotly any suggestion that they are not the equals of their neighbors.

Any act by one State which infringes upon the sovereignty, the existence, the independence, or the equality of another State is an act of intervention and is *ipso facto* unlawful. Intervention is usually defined as any act of dictatorial interference by a State in the internal or foreign affairs of another State or any effort to coerce another State in its State action. "With the right of independence goes the correlative *obligation* of *nonintervention, i.e.,* of refraining from all acts that would forcibly limit the freedom of another State."[1] By its very nature intervention is a violation of international law, unless it has been authorized by specific treaty agreements, as is the case in the relations between the United States on the one hand and certain Caribbean States on the other—notably Cuba, Haiti, the Dominican Republic, and Panama. In all other cases intervention is necessarily unlawful, though under peculiar circumstances it may be justified if it is essential to protect the fundamental rights of the intervening State. It is generally agreed that a State may infringe upon the rights of another without incurring liability for paying damages to the victim if its existence or independence is menaced and it is acting, in Webster's words in the *Caroline* case, under an instant and overwhelming necessity of self-defense, leaving no choice of means and no moment for deliberation. If an act of intervention in such a situation is limited to meeting the immediate danger, it may be permissible, though the burden of proof is always on the side of the intervening State.

In spite of the indisputable logic of this principle, interventions have frequently been resorted to on a variety of other grounds. The colonial empires of the Great Powers were largely created by intervening in, and extinguishing the independence of, small or weak States incapable of resisting imperialistic aggression. The United States, during the past half century, has intervened repeatedly in the affairs of the States of the Caribbean. Interventions, individual and collective, have been embarked upon by States in the name of upholding international law, enforcing treaty rights, preserving the balance of power, maintaining humanitarian principles, insuring the payment of debts, affording protection to the lives and property of citizens abroad, etc. Since international law rests no less upon custom than upon reason, it might be contended that a general right of intervention had been established by these practices. This is scarcely a tenable position, however, since every act of intervention unauthorized by treaty terms is clearly a violation of the rights of the victim and no amount of practice can establish it as a principle of law

[1] G. G. Wilson, *International Law*, 8th ed., 1922, p. 87.

that States have a right to violate the rights of other States. The doctrine laid down by Webster would appear to indicate the only legitimate grounds upon which intervention is justifiable. If this principle is not always adhered to, it is because States, in the pursuit of the objectives of high politics, do not always limit themselves to actions permitted by the accepted principles of law and because the existing machinery of international government is not yet adequate to insure protection to the rights of States incapable of defending themselves by self-help.

It is sometimes said that intervention may be justified by its own success. This is simply another way of saying that after a successful intervention the victim may be reduced to such a condition that he is in no position to protest or protect his rights. If State *A* intervenes in State *B* and extinguishes its independence there will be no one left to protest the intervention. Or if State *A* intervenes in a civil war between faction *X* and *Y* in State *B*, in order to bring about the triumph of faction *X*, it is clear that in the event of the intervention accomplishing its purpose the Government of State *B*, now dominated by faction *X*, will not complain over the fact that State *A* assisted it in securing power. If, on the other hand, the intervention fails and faction *Y* comes into power, it will demand reparation from *A* for the intervention. This was, roughly, the situation in the Allied and American intervention in the Russian Civil War of 1918–1921, which took the form of supporting the reactionary White Armies against the Red Army and of attempting to overthrow the Soviet Government. Had the intervention succeeded, the White régime which would have secured power in Russia would have expressed only gratitude to those who assisted and subsidized its cause in the conflict. But the intervention failed and the Soviet Government at the Genoa Conference of 1922 presented counter-claims for damages to the amount of sixty billions of dollars, in response to the Allied claims of thirteen billions on account of pre-revolutionary debts and claims repudiated by the Soviet Government. The Soviet Government refused to pay the debts of its predecessors unless the Allied Governments recognized the illegality of their intervention and made compensation for the destruction of life and property resulting therefrom. Neither side was able to compel payment by the other, but the intervening States have, in effect, been obliged to pay damages to the extent of their claims for repudiated debts and confiscated property.

A powerful State, like Russia in this instance, can usually thwart intervention and compel respect for its rights. Small States, like the Latin American republics, or weak States, like China, are unable to protect themselves from intervention or to enforce payment of damages for violations of their rights. The rights are the same in both cases, and the interventions in question may be equally unlawful, but since international law is still enforced primarily by State action, the remedy which a State has available in such circumstances is likely to depend on its size and power. Other States may lend it moral support, or may refuse to recognize the results of the intervention, as did the United States and the members of the League of Nations on behalf of China in the Sino-Japanese conflict of 1931–1932, but the time is not yet when a State can rely exclusively for the protection of its rights upon the organized force of international society.

4. JURISDICTION

> A thing may become our property by acquisition, original or derivative. Original acquisition formerly, when the human race could meet together and agree, might be made by division; at present it is only made by occupation.—HUGO GROTIUS, *De jure belli ac pacis.*

Jurisdiction—literally authority to "say the law"—is the right to exercise State authority. It is a corollary of the rights already discussed. States have the right to exercise their jurisdiction, *i.e.*, to legislate and to impose their power, over the territories in which they are recognized as sovereign and over the persons who are their nationals. Conflicting claims put forward in the name of territorial jurisdiction and in the name of personal jurisdiction have been a fruitful source of international controversy in the past, for if States, as was once the case, insist both upon exclusive jurisdiction over their own territory, including all persons within it, and also over all their citizens or subjects, wherever they may be abroad, it is clear that difficulties will result. In the twentieth century the principle of the territorial basis of jurisdiction has in almost all countries been granted precedence over the idea of personal jurisdiction. A State, therefore, has jurisdiction over all persons within its territory, whether they be nationals or aliens, and possesses no general right to claim jurisdiction over its nationals who happen to be on the territory of other States. The two forms of jurisdiction, nevertheless, persist. It will be convenient to consider the various problems of jurisdiction in terms of (1) territorial jurisdiction, (2) personal jurisdiction, and (3) exemptions from jurisdiction.

A State may acquire territorial jurisdiction by discovery and occupation, by prescription, by accretion, by cession or leasehold, or by conquest. Discovery of hitherto unknown and unclaimed land is no longer regarded as conveying valid title to the State of the discoverer unless it is followed by effective occupation. In the sixteenth century the maritime States of Europe laid claim to vast regions of the new world on the basis of discovery alone. England granted "sea-to-sea" charters to the Atlantic seaboard colonists who occupied only the coastal strip and had no notion whatever as to the location of the other sea or the extent of intervening land. As late as the nineteenth century Germany sought, unsuccessfully, to lay down the "hinterland doctrine" with respect to Africa, according to which a State occupying a sea-coast could claim all of the unexplored interior region drained by its rivers. It is now conceded, however, that only effective and continued occupation conveys title to newly discovered lands. This basis of title differs little from prescription, which refers to a situation in which a State secures title to territory by virtue of long-continued occupation acquiesced in by other States. Similarly, if the natural processes of accretion build up deposits on a seacoast or create new land by other means in the immediate vicinity of an adjacent State, the latter has title to the new territory. The normal method of acquiring territorial jurisdiction during the past century, following the exploration and partition of the entire inhabitable globe by the colonial Powers, has been by treaties of cession. Such cessions may take the form of sales or exchanges of territory, with pecuniary or territorial considerations attached, or they may be the result of war and conquest, with the victors relieving the vanquished of their possessions. Conquest, in the form of military occupation so prolonged as to be permanent, may confer title even when not followed by a treaty of cession, though the League of Nations Covenant, in protecting the territorial integrity of all members (Article 10), and the Kellogg-Briand Pact of August 27, 1928, in prohibiting recourse to nonpacific means in the settlement of disputes (Article 2), both seek to outlaw military conquest as a means of acquiring territory. In accordance with the new dispensation, the United States, on January 7, 1932, declared to the Chinese and Japanese Governments that "it cannot admit the legality of any situation *de facto* . . . and it does not intend to recognize any situation, treaty, or agreement which may be brought about by means contrary to the covenants and obligations of the Pact of Paris." Whether this procedure will prove to be effective in preventing territorial conquests in the future remains to be demonstrated. Finally mention may be made of leaseholds as a means of acquiring territory. The status of the Panama Canal Zone and of certain treaty ports and "concession" areas in China is based upon agreements by which the territories in question were leased to an outside State by the State originally having jurisdiction.

Almost all of these methods of acquiring territory have been employed by the United States in the course of its expansion. The original boundaries of the new State were fixed by the treaty of 1783 with Great Britain, which recognized the independence of the United States and bounded it roughly by the Atlantic coast, the St. Croix-St. Lawrence-Great Lakes line, the Mississippi River, and the line of 31° on the south. The vaguely defined territory of Louisiana was secured by a treaty of purchase concluded with France in 1803, under the terms of which the United States paid $15,000,000 to the Government of the First Consul. East and West Florida, which were periodically subjected to American military occupation between 1806 and 1819, were acquired by treaty with Spain in 1819, on terms requiring the United States to meet claims of $5,000,000 on the part of American citizens against Spain. This treaty likewise defined the western boundary of Louisiana from the Sabine River northwestward to 42° of latitude and thence to the Pacific. This line was confirmed by the treaty of 1832 with Mexico. Texas, having declared independence of Mexico in 1836, was annexed by joint resolution of the American Congress in 1845, followed by similar action on the part of the Texan Congress. At the close of the Mexican War, during which the southwest was conquered and subjected to military occupation, the Treaty of Guadaloupe Hidalgo was signed, February 3, 1848. By its provisions, Mexico was obliged to cede a vast area of its northern provinces to the United States for $15,000,000, plus the assumption by the United States of claims of its citizens against Mexico to the amount of $3,250,000. This acquisition was rounded out in 1853 by the Gadsden purchase, for which the United States paid $10,000,000. Meanwhile the northeastern and northwestern boundary disputes with Great Britain were settled respectively by the Webster-Ashburton Treaty of 1842 and the Oregon Treaty of 1846. The first annexation of noncontiguous territory by the United States was provided for by the treaty of 1867 with Russia, by which the United States secured Alaska for $7,200,000. The Hawaiian Islands were acquired by joint Congressional resolution of July 7, 1898, acquiesced in by the independent native government, following the failure of earlier treaty negotiations. At the close of the Spanish-American War, Spain was obliged by the Treaty of Paris of December 10, 1898, to cede to the United States the Philippine Islands, Guam, and Porto Rico for $20,000,000. Tutuila, in the Samoan Islands, was acquired by a treaty of partition with Great Britain and Germany, signed December 4, 1899. The Panama Canal Zone was secured by the Hay-Bunauvarilla Treaty of December 7, 1903. By its terms the United States established a protectorate over the Republic of Panama, to which $10,000,000, plus $250,000 annually, were paid for sovereign rights in the Canal Zone. The Virgin Islands in the Caribbean were purchased from Denmark in 1917 for $25,000,000. The American empire was thus created by a mixed process of occupation, conquest, purchase, and cession.

The next problem deserving of consideration is that of the extent of territorial jurisdiction, particularly with reference to air and water boundaries. The question of aerial jurisdiction assumed great importance in the period of extensive international air communication, and many treaties have been signed regarding it.[1] All of these are now based upon the uni-

[1] See Kenneth G. Colgrove, *International Control of Aviation*, 1930.

versally accepted principle that a State has absolute jurisdiction over the air above its territory and its territorial waters, extending out into the farthest reaches of space. It is generally recognized, however, that as a matter of comity a State should grant a right of innocent passage through its air to foreign aircraft, subject to such reasonable regulations as are necessary to insure observance of local laws relating to customs duties, immigration, public safety, national defense, and the like. Jurisdiction over the waters adjacent to a State, on the contrary, does not extend out indefinitely, but is limited to a zone within three miles from the coastline. The three-mile limit of territorial waters or maritime jurisdiction, established at a time when three miles represented the effective range of coast artillery, is now recognized by almost all States. The waters beyond the three-mile limit are "high seas" and are not subject to the jurisdiction of any State, except for purposes of punishing pirates who may be proceeded against by all States. Coast-guard vessels may, however, pursue foreign ships suspected of violating local laws out into the high seas, provided that the pursuit is begun within territorial waters and is continuous. This so-called "doctrine of hot pursuit" has been extended by treaty so far as the United States is concerned for the purpose of enabling the American Government to enforce more effectively its legislation prohibiting the importation of intoxicating liquors. The prohibition enforcement treaties which the United States has concluded with some twenty States authorize American prohibition authorities to exercise jurisdiction over foreign vessels suspected of rum-running outside of American territorial waters but within a zone defined as one hour's sailing distance from the shore.[1] Such an extension of maritime jurisdiction is, of course, entirely a matter of treaty arrangement and may not be applied to vessels of States not

[1] Article 2 of the Convention between the United States and Chile for the Prevention of Smuggling of Intoxicating Liquors, signed at Washington, May 27, 1930 (Treaty Series 829), reads as follows: "The Chilean Government agree that they will raise no objection to the boarding of private vessels under the Chilean flag outside the limits of territorial waters by the authorities of the United States, its territories or possessions, in order that enquiries may be addressed to those on board and an examination be made of the ship's papers for the purpose of ascertaining whether the vessel or those on board are endeavoring to import or have imported alcoholic beverages into the United States, its territories or possessions, in violation of the laws there in force. When such enquiries and examination show reasonable ground for suspicion, a search of the vessel may be initiated. If there is reasonable cause for belief that the vessel has committed or is committing or attempting to commit an offense against the laws of the United States, its territories or possessions, prohibiting the importation of alcoholic beverages, the vessel may be seized and taken into a port of the United States, its territories or possessions, for adjudication in accordance with such laws. The rights conferred by this article shall not be exercised at a greater distance from the coast of the United States, its territories or possessions, than can be traversed in one hour by the vessel suspected of endeavoring to commit the offense. In cases, however, in which the liquor is intended to be conveyed to the United States, its territories or possessions, by a vessel other than the one boarded and searched, it shall be the speed of such other vessel, and not the speed of the vessel boarded, which shall determine the distance from the coast at which the right under this article can be exercised."

consenting to it. Within territorial waters privately owned foreign vessels are subject to local laws, though they are ordinarily granted a right of innocent passage and are exempt from interference by the local authorities except where a violation of local law occurs of such a nature as to disturb the peace of the port. Foreign public vessels, *i.e.*, war vessels and other ships owned by foreign governments and engaged in public business, are exempt from local jurisdiction and may not be boarded for any purposes by local authorities, since the foreign sovereign is directly responsible for their conduct which may, if objectionable, be made a matter of diplomatic representations.

Other water boundaries, like land frontiers, are usually defined by treaty. In the absence of treaty arrangements to the contrary certain general rules are applied. River boundaries between two States follow the *thalweg* or deepest navigation channel of the stream. If a boundary river shifts its bed gradually by accretion, the boundary shifts likewise, but where a sudden change by avulsion takes place, the boundary remains in its old position. Rights of navigation and of water diversion for irrigation or power purposes are always dealt with by treaty provisions. Rivers, lakes, and canals which are entirely surrounded by the territory of one State are completely within its jurisdiction in the absence of treaty arrangements to the contrary. The Boundary Waters Convention of 1909 between the United States and Great Britain opens navigation on Lake Michigan to British vessels. Straits less than six miles in width are within the jurisdiction of the shore State or States, though the vessels of other States have a right of navigation, subject to reasonable local regulations and duties for safety, the upkeep of lighthouses, and the like. The right of Denmark to levy tolls upon vessels passing through the Danish Sound connecting the North and Baltic Seas was successfully resisted by the United States and other Powers and abandoned in 1857, though it had been exercised since 1368. The Bosphorus and the Dardanelles, surrounded by Turkish territory, were opened to Russian merchant vessels by the treaty of 1774 and to foreign war vessels by the Treaty of Paris of 1856. The Treaty of Lausanne of 1923 made elaborate provision for the neutralization of these waterways and for freedom of navigation through them. The Suez Canal was partially demilitarized and opened freely to all vessels, public and private, both in war and in peace, by the convention of 1888. The Panama Canal is similarly open on a basis of equality to vessels of all States by the Hay-Pauncefote Treaty of 1901, though it is controlled and fortified by the United States. Gulfs, bays, and estuaries opening out onto the high seas are within the jurisdiction of the State enclosing them, with the line of maritime jurisdiction parallel to a line drawn from headland to headland, if the mouth is not more than six miles wide. Other arrangements have often been made by treaty, however, and more recently a ten-mile limit for width of mouth of territorial bays has been recognized.[1]

Jurisdiction over persons, as distinct from jurisdiction over land, sea, and air, has been claimed by States under two different theories which are still only partially reconciled. Under the rule of *ius soli* (right of the soil) States have claimed as nationals all persons born within their territorial limits. Amendment 14 to the American Federal Constitution declares "All persons born or naturalized in the United States, and subject to the jurisdiction thereof, are citizens of the United States and of the State wherein they reside." Under the rule of *ius sanguinis* (right of the blood), States have claimed that all children of their nationals, wherever born, are their nationals by virtue of parentage. The legislation of States regarding the bases of nationality varies considerably and no general international agreement has yet been reached regarding these questions. Most States, however, now adhere to the rule of *ius soli*, with certain qualifications. American legislation, for example, bestows American citizenship on children born abroad of American parents provided that the parents have resided at some time in the United States. Almost all States now permit their citizens to expatriate themselves, *i.e.*, to become nationals of other States, and also provide for the "naturalization" of foreigners who desire to become citizens of the local State. Many States provide that women acquire the nationality of their husbands at marriage, though the American law of 1922 permits an American woman marrying a foreigner to retain her citizenship and does not automatically confer American citizenship on alien women marrying Americans. Foreigners who have resided in the United States for five years may become American citizens by taking out citizenship papers. Collective naturalization is often provided for in annexation treaties. Aliens, in general, are entirely subject to the jurisdiction of the State where they reside. Aliens who are fugitives from justice may be delivered up to the authorities of the State from which they have fled by the process of extradition. This procedure is almost invariably provided for by treaties which specify the crimes for which extradition shall be granted and the categories of persons subject to extradition. Political crimes, short of attempts at assassination, are normally exempted by specific provisions of such treaties.

Because of differences in the nationality laws of various States, it is possible for an individual to be a national of two States simultaneously, or to lose his nationality entirely by taking some action which forfeits his citizenship in one State without entitling him to citizenship in another. Such unfortunate individuals (*heimatlosen*, in the German phrase) have no

[1] See the award of the arbitral tribunal in the North Atlantic Fisheries dispute between the United States and Great Britain, 1910, in G. G. Wilson, *Hague Arbitration Cases*, pp. 180 f.

State to afford them diplomatic protection abroad. Such problems of personal jurisdiction make it desirable that the nationality laws of the various States be made more nearly uniform. Such uniformity can be achieved in this field, as in others, only through the process usually referred to as the "codification of international law," *i.e.*, the conclusion of general international conventions in which States agree upon the principles involved and pledge themselves to put their own national legislation in harmony with the agreement. The legal experts of the League of Nations prepared a draft nationality convention which was considered by the First Conference on the Progressive Codification of International Law which met at The Hague in March and April of 1930. The conference on April 12, 1930, adopted four instruments: (1) a convention on certain questions relating to the conflict of nationality laws; (2) a protocol relating to military obligations in certain cases of double nationality; (3) a protocol relating to a certain case of statelessness; and (4) a special protocol concerning statelessness. The first of these engagements has been signed by some forty States, but none of them has as yet received general ratification.

Certain common exemptions from local jurisdiction are universally recognized. Sovereigns traveling abroad in their official capacity are entirely exempt from the jurisdiction of the States through which they pass and may not be arrested, proceeded against, or interfered with on any ground, either as to their own persons, their families, their retinue, or their effects. Diplomatic representatives are similarly exempt from the jurisdiction of the State in which they reside. The buildings and grounds of embassies and legations are regarded as "extraterritorial," *i.e.*, as part of the territory of the foreign State maintaining them rather than of the local State. They may not be taxed or entered by the local police without permission, and local laws may not be enforced within their precincts. Diplomatic agents, along with their families, staffs, and servants, are immune from local laws and enjoy complete exemption from local civil and criminal jurisdiction, local police and administrative regulations, taxes and duties, jury and witness duty, and the like. They may not be arrested, subpoenaed, or otherwise interfered with in the exercise of their functions. Consuls ordinarily enjoy certain limited exemptions from local jurisdiction in order to enable them to carry on their work effectively. Foreign armies granted a right of passage through a State and foreign public vessels within its territorial waters are likewise exempt from local jurisdiction. In certain oriental States, notably China, special treaty arrangements have been imposed by the western Powers, whereby western nationals, when defendants in cases brought by natives, are exempt from local jurisdiction and are usually tried in consular courts maintained by their own governments. The recent efforts of China to terminate extraterritoriality of this type have not yet met with success, except as regards the Soviet Union, which voluntarily relinquished this right for its nationals, and Germany, which was compelled to renounce the right by the terms of the Treaty of Versailles.

5. TREATIES AND TREATY-MAKING

> In contracts, nature requires equality, and in such a way that, from inequality, he who has the worse share, acquires a right. This equality consists partly in the act, partly in the matter concerning which the act is, and in the acts both precedent and principal.—HUGO GROTIUS, *De jure belli ac pacis.*

The making of treaties between States regarding matters of mutual interest is a practice of great antiquity. It has been resorted to in all State Systems of which any record remains. The practice developed very early in the evolution of the Western State System and has been followed with increasing frequency by all of its members during the past few centuries. The States of the world are now bound to one another by thousands of international agreements covering almost every conceivable subject of international interest and assuming a wide variety of forms. Early treaties were almost always bilateral, *i.e.*, between two States. More recently many treaties are multilateral, *i.e.*, between three or more States. The growing frequency with which States enter into treaty engagements is revealed by the treaty history of the United States. Since July 4, 1776— or, more accurately, since February 6, 1778, when the first treaties between the United States and a foreign State were signed—the United States has entered into no less than 850 formally ratified international engagements, exclusive of executive agreements.[1] Of these only 59 were concluded prior to 1838, 110 during the next thirty years, 134 in the following three decades, and the remainder during the period since 1898. The record of most other States would show a comparable growth of treaty engagements during the past half century.

Since treaties and similar instruments constitute legally binding obligations between the signatory States, a large body of legal principles has developed with regard to their negotiation, conclusion, ratification, interpretation, and termination. The somewhat confusing problem of terminology may be considered first. The word "treaty" is sometimes loosely applied to all types of international engagements, other than executive agreements. The latter are not legally binding compacts between States, but merely arrangements entered into by executive authorities. An executive agreement binds only the administration which has concluded it, though it may be continued in force at the option of the succeeding administrations. The "Gentlemen's Agreement" of 1908 between the

[1] See U. S. Department of State, *Treaty Series.*

United States and Japan remained in force until 1924 when it was abrogated by the immigration act passed in that year by Congress. In the United States executive agreements are easily distinguishable from treaties by the fact that they are concluded by the President or his agents and are not submitted to the Senate or formally ratified. They thus assume the character of personal promises, rather than of solemn contracts or "treaties" binding upon the State. In a narrower sense, "treaties" are State agreements relating to important political questions. "Conventions" are usually agreements relating to more specific and technical matters, though there is no uniformity of practice in this regard. A particular agreement may be designated as a treaty or a convention at the discretion of the negotiators. The term "protocol" is applied sometimes to any type of agreement less formal than a treaty or a convention, sometimes to preliminary drafts of agreements signed in anticipation of the preparation of more formal documents, and sometimes to the signed official minutes or *procès verbal* of the sessions of an international conference. "Declarations" are multilateral engagements, setting forth a common conception of certain principles of international law, such as the Declaration of Paris of 1856, though the word is likewise applied to formal statements of policy on the part of particular governments. A declaration of the latter type, such as the Monroe Doctrine, is, of course, not an international agreement at all. "Sponsions" are agreements, subject to subsequent approval, signed by representatives who have not been properly commissioned or who have exceeded their authority. "Cartels" are agreements entered into between belligerents for such purposes as the exchange of prisoners of war. An "armistice" is an agreement between belligerents for the suspension of hostilities. A "compromis" is an instrument by which two States submit a dispute to arbitration. Letters, memoranda, and exchanges of notes may also under certain circumstances be given the effect of true international obligations.

The making of treaties and other inter-State instruments has been elaborately formalized and involves adherence, with minor variations, to a well-established sequence of procedures which must be followed if the resulting agreement is to be valid. The first step is (1) the meeting of the negotiators and the "exchange of full powers" between the plenipotentiaries. Upon meeting, the agents of each State submit documentary credentials to the agents of the other, showing that they have been regularly authorized (given full powers) to negotiate the contemplated agreement. Next follows (2) the actual negotiation and signing of the agreement. Prior to the nineteenth century, treaty texts usually began with an invocation of the Deity. A preamble ordinarily sets forth the general purposes of the agreement and gives the names of the heads of the signatory States and of the negotiators whom they have appointed to sign.

There follow the numbered articles of the compact, the conditions of ratification, the place and date of signature, and the signatures and seals of the agents.[1] Signatures are usually attached in accordance with the principle of the alternat, whereby each State receives a copy of the treaty signed first by its own delegates. Multilateral treaties are often signed by the delegates in alphabetical order of the names of the States, in French. Many treaties are drawn up in French, still the traditional language of diplomacy, as well as in the languages of the signatory States, either in separate versions or in parallel columns. The next step is (3) ratification of the signed agreement by the constitutionally designated authorities in the signatory States. Under the American Constitution, all treaties are ratified by the President, acting "by and with the advice and consent of the Senate . . . provided two-thirds of the Senators present concur" (Article II, Section 2, §2). Ratification may be withheld or amendments and reservations may be attached, if irregularities have taken place in the negotiations or if the agreement is regarded as unsatisfactory, though in the latter case friction and misunderstanding are likely to result, since States normally assume that a treaty which has been negotiated and signed by accredited representatives, in accordance with their instructions, ought to be ratified as a matter of course. Amendments and reservations attached by one party are not binding unless accepted by the other. (4) The exchange of ratifications is a formal ceremony whereby the parties indicate to one another that ratification has taken place and solemnly guarantee to one another the execution of the terms of the contract. This ceremony consists in the exchange of the executive acts of ratification and the preparation of a *procès verbal* registering this fact. Treaties subsequently ratified are normally binding from the date of signature, unless some other arrangement is specified. (5) The execution of the agreement is the final step whereby the terms agreed upon are carried out by the parties. In the United States execution is preceded by a formal proclamation of the treaty in the name of the President.

In order that an international agreement may be legally binding upon the signatory States, certain conditions are essential. The parties must first of all be legally competent to contract the engagement, *i.e.*, they must be free under the terms of their constitutions and of earlier treaties to enter into the agreement which has been made. The treaty, moreover, must in form and substance be a proper State agreement on the part of all of the signatories. The plenipotentiaries must have been fully accredited and must have acted within the scope of their authority. There must be freedom of consent on the part of the negotiators, with no hint of fraud, bribery, or coercion. Coercion invalidates a treaty if it is applied against the persons of the negotiators, but not if it is applied against a State.

[1] For types of treaty texts, see Appendices pp. 857–889 below.

Treaties of peace imposed by victors upon vanquished, like those of 1919, are usually accepted under duress, but so long as the coercion is of the State and not of its representatives, the agreement is binding. Finally, international agreements must be in conformity with international law and must not involve any infringement of the rights of third States. If, in any particular case, it can be shown at any step in the proceedings that these essential conditions have not been complied with, the agreement in question can be regarded as void by either party.

States which are not parties to an international agreement are, of course, not bound in any way by its terms, since treaties are contracts which specify rights and obligations only for the signatory States. Outside States may protest against a treaty only if it violates their own treaty rights or is contrary to accepted principles of customary international law. States not parties to a treaty may express their *approbation* of the agreement, by which they indicate approval of its terms without in any way becoming a party to them; or they may announce their *adhesion* to it, by which they agree to abide by its principles, also without becoming a party; or, finally, they may announce their *accession* to the engagement, in which case they formally become parties to the engagement.

In the interpretation of treaties the real intention of the parties is usually accepted as a basis for definition of terms, rather than grammatical deductions from the language employed. The intention of the parties may be ascertained through *procès verbaux*, notes, memoranda, and other exchanges of communications at the time of the negotiations. If such documents are exchanged and accepted by both sides prior to the exchange of ratifications, they bind the parties to the interpretation of the treaty terms which they set forth. In the controversy over the meaning of the Clayton-Bulwer Treaty of April 19, 1850, between the United States and Great Britain, relating to the rights of the parties in Central America with respect to a proposed interoceanic canal, it appeared that Bulwer on June 29 (five days before the exchange of ratifications) had written Clayton to the effect that the provisions of the agreement for reciprocal renunciation of territorial claims had no application to British Honduras "and its dependencies." The United States was obliged to accept this interpretation, in spite of its reluctance to do so. The language of treaties is construed in the ordinary sense of the words employed, unless evidence of a contrary intention is adduced. In conflicts between clauses of a single treaty, special clauses prevail over general clauses and prohibitory clauses prevail over permissive clauses. Cessions of sovereignty are always strictly construed. As between two conflicting treaties between the same States, the later one prevails. In general, treaties are so construed as to be self-consistent and as not to violate international law and the rights of third States.

Treaties may come to an end by the expiration of a specified time limit, by the complete fulfillment of their terms, by an express agreement of the parties, or by renunciation of the rights granted. A new treaty, expressly superseding an earlier one, is the most common and satisfactory form of termination. Treaties are likewise terminated by the disappearance of one of the parties. When the independence of a State is extinguished, all of its treaties with other States are terminated unless provision to the contrary is made by the new State acquiring its territory. A declaration of war terminates political treaties between the belligerents, suspends all agreements of a permanent nature such as commercial and extradition treaties until the close of hostilities, and brings into operation such agreements as may relate to the conduct of war. Nonfulfillment of the terms of a treaty by one party, if persisted in despite diplomatic representations, makes it voidable by the other party. In all other cases, treaties cannot ordinarily be denounced by one party without the consent of the other, unless their terms make provision for such a procedure. Under the American Constitution the President or Congress or both may denounce a treaty without the consent of the other party. The French treaties of alliance and commerce of 1778 and the commercial convention with France of 1788 were abrogated by act of Congress of July 7, 1798. The Chinese exclusion acts of 1888 and 1892 were in violation of earlier American treaties with China relating to immigration. In 1911, in the face of Congressional demands, President Taft abrogated the commercial treaty of 1832 with Russia. Under international law, however, it is doubtful whether one party to a treaty ever has a legal right to terminate it without the consent of the other unless the treaty itself provides for this. Under the principle of *rebus sic stantibus* (conditions remaining the same), it has been contended that fundamental changes of conditions authorize one party to a treaty to terminate it by unilateral action. The Chinese Republic in recent years has endeavored unsuccessfully to escape from the obligations of the so-called "unequal" treaties of the nineteenth century on this ground. But the other party almost invariably protests against such a contention and it cannot be said that this principle is part of accepted international law.

6. THE LAW OF WAR

"You will observe the rules of battle, of course?" the White Knight remarked, putting on his helmet too. "I always do," said the Red Knight, and they began banging away at each other with such fury that Alice got behind a tree to be out of the way of the blows.—LEWIS CARROLL, *Through the Looking Glass.*

The preceding discussion constitutes only a fragmentary presentation of the most important principles of the international law of peace. The international law of war may, for purposes of the present survey, be dealt with in an even more cursory fashion, not because it is less important, even in an age when war is supposed to have been outlawed, but because its underlying principles can be indicated quite briefly and its details involve technical questions of interest only to military and naval commanders. Grotius' textbook of 1625 devoted primary attention to the law of war and most of his early successors gave approximately an equal number of pages to the two great branches of international law. In recent years, notwithstanding the innumerable legal problems created by the Great War and its aftermath, there has been a disposition on the part of textwriters to give less attention to the law of war as compared with the law of peace. On the other hand, a large proportion of the international law of war has been codified in the form of multilateral agreements between States, such as the conventions drawn up at the first and second Hague conferences of 1899 and 1907. It might almost be said that States have found it easier to agree upon the principles of law which they will observe in fighting one another than to agree upon common principles governing the problems of peace. Here it will be sufficient to suggest a few of the elementary principles of the law of war which are of general interest.

From the point of view of international law, war may be defined either as a properly conducted contest of armed public forces, or as a condition or period of time during which inter-State relations are regulated by the law of war instead of by the law of peace. International law does not justify or sanction war, but recognizes it as a fact of international politics and seeks to restrict and mitigate its cruel and destructive features. Any literal "outlawry of war" would be a step backward rather than forward, if, contrary to the hopes of the proponents of such schemes, armed conflicts between States continued under conditions permitting them to act as if the international law of war had become non-existent. Such a development is quite unlikely, however. Even in the Sino-Japanese hostilities of 1931–1933 in which both sides refused to admit the existence of a legal state of war, the usual principles of international law governing the conduct of hostilities were reasonably well observed, despite appearances to the contrary. Here, as in the Great War and in most other international conflicts, public attention tends to be centered on the occasional violations of international law which occur, creating the false impression that all customary restraints have been thrown to the winds and that the international law of war has been scrapped by the belligerents in their desperate efforts to overcome one another. In fact, the great body of rules and principles which have been developed to regulate the conduct of warfare are almost always fully observed because of considerations of expediency and fear of retaliation.

A state of war involves both an intention to wage war on one or both sides and overt acts of hostility. Hostile acts, unaccompanied by an intention to wage war, create a state of war in the legal sense only if they are regarded as inaugurating war by the victim or by third States. A legal state of war may exist without hostilities if the parties have expressed an intention to deal with one another as belligerents. But hostilities, unaccompanied by the intention and not treated as war either by the contestants or by outside parties, do not in themselves create a state of war. They constitute reprisals, retaliation, or intervention, but the rights and obligations of the parties continue to be determined by the law of peace. In recent wars it has been customary for States to issue formal declarations of war, making clear their intentions and specifying the time at which a legal state of war shall be regarded as having commenced. The Hague Convention of 1907 with regard to the opening of hostilities[1] forbade the signatory States to commence hostilities without warning, through either a declaration or an ultimatum. At the opening of the Great War the belligerents in every case specified in a formal declaration the exact hour and minute of the commencement of war, a formality particularly useful to prize courts in determining the legality of captures. Declarations of war usually require legislative action under most modern constitutions. In the United States they require the approval of a majority of both houses of Congress, but such approval has never been withheld when the President has recommended war, nor has Congress ever declared war in opposition to the wishes of the executive.[2]

As for the general principles underlying the law of war, it may be said that war suspends all nonhostile intercourse between the belligerent States and their citizens. Diplomatic and consular relations are severed, along with contacts of trade and travel. Political treaties between the belligerents are terminated, other treaties are suspended for the duration of the conflict, and agreements relating to the conduct of hostilities are put into operation. Relations between the belligerents are henceforth subject to the international law of war and their relations with outside States not participating in the struggle are governed by the international law of neutrality. From the legal point of view, the purpose of war is to bring about the complete military subjection of the enemy in the shortest possible time with the least possible loss of life and property. This conception of the objective of hostilities is shared by the jurist and the strategist, but under modern conditions differences of opinion necessarily arise as to

[1] Article 1. The contracting Powers recognize that hostilities between them must not commence without a previous and explicit warning, in the form of either a declaration of war, giving reasons, or an ultimatum with a conditional declaration of war.

Article 2. The existence of a state of war must be notified to the neutral Powers without delay, and shall not be held to affect them until after the receipt of a notification, which may, however, be given by telegraph. Nevertheless, neutral Powers may not rely on the absence of notification if it be established beyond doubt that they were in fact aware of the existence of a state of war.

[2] On the effects of the Pact of Paris of 1928 on the legal status of war, see p. 685 below.

the implications of such a statement. It is agreed that mere wanton destruction and slaughter, having no reasonable relation to the military subjection of the enemy, is unlawful. The older view of the continental States of Europe was that war should, as far as possible, be limited in its effects to armed public forces. Great Britain, and more recently the United States, have regarded it as permissible to attack the commercial resources and the food supplies of the whole enemy population through naval blockades, a view which has now received general acceptance. During the Great War, Germany developed the theory of *schrecklichkeit* or frightfulness, according to which, in its extreme form, it is legitimate to attack the entire civilian population of the enemy State by all possible means in order to break its will to resist. In spite of the general condemnation of this view at the time, it is the logical corollary of universal military conscription, of the mobilization of industrial resources, and of the decisive importance of civilian morale in a long-drawn-out war of attrition. It may consequently be expected to receive general acceptance in the wars of the future, however appalling may be the results.

This development is tending to break down the well-established legal distinction between soldiers and civilians. Nevertheless, it is still correct to say that for the purpose of ascertaining the legal rights and obligations of individuals in war time they are divided into the two general categories of combatants and noncombatants. Combatants may be fired upon at sight and if taken alive are entitled to be treated as prisoners of war. In this category are members of the regularly authorized military, naval, and air forces of the State, officers and crews of merchant vessels resisting capture, and members of levies en masse and of popular civilian uprisings against invaders, provided they carry arms openly, obey the laws of war, wear emblems or uniforms and are under a definite command.[1] Noncombatants are all persons not participating in hostilities, not members of fighting forces, and not belonging to any of the special classes mentioned below. Civilian enemy aliens found within a State at the outbreak of war may be expelled, interned, permitted to depart, or permitted to remain unmolested. In the Great War most of the belligerent States interned enemy aliens within their jurisdiction, sometimes for their own protection against mob violence. Noncombatants in occupied territory or in the zone of military operations are free from violence, constraint, or injury except what is dictated by military necessity or what may befall them through actual hostilities. Finally, notice should be taken of certain exceptional classes of persons who are neither combatants nor noncombatants, but are subjected to special treatment. Officers and crews of merchant vessels taking offensive action against other merchant vessels may be punished by death for piracy since the abolition of privateering

[1] *Cf.* Hague Convention of 1907 on Laws and Customs of War on Land, Article 1.

by the Declaration of Paris of 1856. Guerrillas, *i.e.*, individuals not in the armed forces of the State who engage in military operations without State authorization, may likewise be punished for their individual acts. They are not entitled to be treated as prisoners of war, but may be tried and sentenced for murder, arson, and other crimes which are not individually punishable when committed by soldiers, sailors, or aviators acting under orders. Similar treatment is accorded to spies, *i.e.*, individuals in disguise who act under false pretenses behind the lines or in occupied territory to secure information for the enemy. They are entitled to a trial and if found guilty are usually executed.

As regards the treatment accorded to property in war time, the general rules applied are relatively simple, though their specific application in complex situations often involves tangled legal problems. Public real property in an enemy State or in occupied territory, *i.e.*, property owned by a belligerent government within the jurisdiction of an enemy belligerent or in a region under hostile military occupation, may be taken over and administered during the war for the benefit of the State in control, but may not be confiscated. Public movable property, with the exception of works of art, science, or education, is subject to confiscation, but enlightened opinion has been increasingly averse to the exercise of this right, except in occupied territory. During the Great War, however, the American Government seized the German patents in the United States under conditions which amounted to confiscation. Private property of enemy nationals was formerly considered to be subject to confiscation wherever found. This harsh rule has now been modified in a variety of ways. Private property of enemy aliens found within a State at the outbreak of war is now usually unmolested or held under bond by the local government for the duration of the war to prevent its being used to the advantage of the enemy State. Private enemy property in occupied territory may no longer be taken by the occupying forces without compensation, though if military necessity requires its destruction no compensation need be paid. The Treaty of Versailles, however, required Germany to pay compensation to the victors for all civilian damages, on the theory that the Great War was a result of German aggression.[1] Forces of military occupation

---

[1] Article 231: The Allied and Associated Governments affirm and Germany accepts the responsibility of Germany and her allies for causing all the loss and damage to which the Allied and Associated Governments and their nationals have been subjected as a consequence of the war imposed upon them by the aggression of Germany and her allies.

Article 232: The Allied and Associated Governments recognize that the resources of Germany are not adequate, after taking into account permanent diminutions of such resources which will result from other provisions of the present treaty, to make complete reparation for all such loss and damage. The Allied and Associated Governments, however, require, and Germany undertakes, that she will make compensation for all damage done to the civilian population of the Allied and Associated Powers and to their property during the period of the belligerency of each as an Allied or Associated Power against Germany

may levy taxes on the local population for local purposes and may assess fines and penalties on communities where it is clear that the municipal authorities have been negligent in fulfilling their obligations to maintain order and to prevent civilian participation in hostilities. In all other cases, as in the levying of money contributions upon the local citizenry, the requisition of food and other materials needed by the occupying forces, or the sequestration of vessels, vehicles, and the like, a receipt must be given to the owner as a promise of eventual compensation.

Property at sea is dealt with in accordance with principles differing somewhat from those applicable to property on land. Enemy property at sea is, in general, subject to capture and condemnation. Save for ships engaged in humanitarian, educational, or scientific enterprises, there are no exceptions to this rule for public enemy property, *i.e.*, battleships and other vessels and goods owned by the enemy State. With regard to enemy property owned by private individuals, however, various qualifications to the general right of capture have received general acceptance. Enemy merchant vessels in port at the outbreak of hostilities are normally accorded a specified number of days of grace within which they may escape to sea. Religious, scientific, and philanthropic vessels are exempt from capture, as are hospital ships, fishing vessels, and small coastwise vessels of all types. Under the Declaration of Paris of 1856[1] it is no longer lawful for belligerents to issue letters of marque and reprisal to private vessels (privateers) authorizing them to capture enemy merchant ships. The Declaration likewise specifies that goods of neutral ownership found on enemy ships shall be exempt from capture, and that goods of enemy ownership found on neutral ships shall also be exempt, contraband of war being excepted in both cases. The signatory Powers further declared that a proclamation of a blockade cannot give an indiscriminate right of capture of neutral vessels unless it is, in fact, effectively enforced. Enemy vessels are subject to capture wherever found, even in the absence of a blockade. In the exercise of the right of capture all vessels are regarded as enemy vessels which fly an enemy flag, which have been transferred to a neutral flag to escape capture, which are under convoy of belligerent war

---

by such aggression by land, by sea, and from the air, and in general all damage as defined in Annex I hereto.

Under these provisions Germany was required to pay compensation for all civilian injuries and deaths and for all Allied military pensions. She was likewise obliged to assume the entire war debt of Belgium.

[1] The plenipotentiaries who signed the Treaty of Paris of the thirteenth of March, one thousand eight hundred and fifty-six, assembled in conference . . . have adopted the following declaration: (1) privateering is and remains abolished; (2) the neutral flag covers enemy's goods, with the exception of contraband of war; (3) neutral goods, with the exception of contraband of war, are not liable to capture under enemy's flag; (4) blockades, in order to be binding, must be effective—that is to say, maintained by a force sufficient really to prevent access to the coast of the enemy. . . . April 16, 1856.

vessels, or which resist search. Captured enemy vessels may be destroyed if there is no means of taking them into port for condemnation, but provision must be made for the safety of passengers and crew. The inability of submarines to make such provision led to widespread criticism (from enemy and neutral governments) of their use by Germany in the Great War. In the great commercial wars of modern times, the naval Powers have usually attempted, in accordance with the general right of capture, to sweep enemy commerce from the seas. The pursuit of this objective has usually led to attacks upon neutral commerce as well. The problems resulting therefrom will be suggested in the following section.

A large number of well-defined principles have grown up regarding the actual conduct of hostilities. The more important of these were codified in the Hague Conference Conventions of 1899 and 1907 relating to the laws and customs of war on land. The details of their application are of interest only to military technicians, but their more general features may be indicated briefly. These principles are for the most part designed to mitigate the horrors and cruelties of war as much as possible. They are usually well-observed, since considerations of expediency dictate their observance on both sides of the battle line. Wanton and unnecessary destruction of life and property is forbidden, as is the use of poison, dumdum bullets, the refusal of quarter, resort to assassination, deliberate perfidy and treachery, and attacks upon undefended towns. Sick and wounded are to be cared for and prisoners of war must be humanely treated. Civilian populations are, so far as possible, to be spared from the incidents of war. Hospitals, churches, schools, museums, public buildings, and the like are to be spared, unless used for military purposes. Naval and aerial bombardment of undefended cities is usually viewed with disapproval. During the Great War the established principles dealing with the relations between the armed forces were reasonably well-observed, in spite of the introduction of poison gas, liquid fire, and other novel weapons. The rules designed to protect civilians, however, were in many instances ignored, particularly by the Central Powers which were strategically in a position to strike at enemy centers of population through air raids and long-range artillery for the purpose of disorganizing manufacturing and transport and breaking down morale through terrorism. These departures from established rules designed to protect civilians are logically dictated by military necessity under the contemporary economic, social, and psychological conditions attending large-scale combats between national States. In future wars there is every reason to anticipate intensive and persistent attacks upon civilians by weapons of unprecedented destructiveness. If such catastrophes are to be averted, it will be through the abolition of war itself, rather than through further efforts at limiting weapons or setting up new legal safeguards which are certain to be brushed aside in suicidal conflicts of the magnitude of the war of 1914–1918.

7. THE LAW OF NEUTRALITY

In Agathias, we read, that he is an enemy who does what the enemy wishes: and in Procopius, that he is reckoned to be in the army of the enemy, who helps the enemy's army in matters which are properly of military use.—HUGO GROTIUS, *De jure belli ac pacis.*

In most of the wars between members of earlier State Systems and in the early wars in the Western State System as well, the notion that an outside State might refrain from participation in a conflict between its neighbors was an unfamiliar one. What is now known as the international law of neutrality developed very slowly and did not reach its mode,n form prior to the nineteenth century. As recently as the War of the American Revolution, it was regarded as legitimate for a "neutral" State to rent out its troops to belligerents without violating its obligations. The Hessian mercenaries of Great Britain were secured in this fashion. In the early period, textwriters, from Grotius onward, emphasized the rights of neutral States to be free from interference by belligerents, since such rights were frequently ignored. Later, after neutral rights had been more clearly defined, emphasis was shifted to the obligations of neutral States to refrain from participation in hostilities. In the most recent period the great controversies over neutrality have again centered about neutral rights as related to trading privileges. The United States neutrality code of 1794 was one of the first clear formulations of the modern conception of neutral obligations. As the first member of the Western State System outside of the European continent, the United States could more easily hold itself aloof from European wars than could the States of Europe. It has accordingly played a large rôle in the subsequent development of the principles of neutrality.

Neutral obligations may be summarized in terms of abstention, impartiality, and prevention. It is now customary for States to declare their neutrality upon the outbreak of war by a formal proclamation issued by the head of the government. A State which has declared itself neutral has a right to have its neutrality respected by the belligerents. It is correspondingly obliged to enforce its neutrality by conducting itself impartially toward the belligerents, by abstaining from any participation in the conflict, and by preventing its citizens from engaging in certain acts regarded as breaches of neutral obligations. A neutral State may not permit its territory to be used as a base of hostile operations by either belligerent against the other. It may not permit its armed forces to be employed to the advantage of either belligerent, nor may it officially loan money or sell war supplies to warring governments. It is not obliged, however, to prevent its nationals from lending money or selling war supplies, providing that they are legally free to sell to both sides on equal terms. Between 1914 and 1917, the period of American neutrality in the Great War, hundreds of millions of dollars worth of Allied war bonds were sold in the United States and billions of dollars worth of munitions were sold to the Allied Governments by American manufacturers and exporters. The German Government complained that in fact this trade was entirely one-sided, since the Allied blockade prevented American munitions from reaching the Central Powers. In law, however, there was no breach of neutral obligations on the part of the United States, since the American Government was not responsible for the Allied blockade and Americans were free to sell to both sides on equal terms at their own risk.

A neutral State must prevent the enlistment of troops for war purposes on its territory and it must intern belligerent troops and aircraft forced into its jurisdiction. It may grant a right of innocent passage through its territorial waters, however, to belligerent warships. Neutral governments are likewise obliged to prevent their nationals from making their territory a base of hostile operations. Neutral nationals may be permitted to sell war supplies to warring States, but they must be prevented from fitting out, in neutral ports, vessels designed to take part in the war. The failure of Great Britain to fulfill this obligation during the American Civil War caused the Geneva Arbitration Tribunal, created by the Treaty of Washington of 1871, to award $15,500,000 to the United States for damages committed by the "Alabama," the "Florida," and other Confederate cruisers constructed in British ports. A neutral State may not, in the course of a war, modify its neutrality regulations to the advantage of one belligerent. It must use due diligence to insure observance of its obligations and it cannot extend its protection to its citizens who engage in "unneutral service," i.e., who commit hostile acts against belligerents and thereby render themselves liable to treatment as enemy nationals.

During the past century the most acute controversies over neutral rights have arisen as a result of the efforts of belligerent States to cut off commercial contacts between the enemy State and neutral States. A belligerent State is recognized to have a right to intercept such commerce on two grounds. It may proclaim a blockade of enemy ports and if such a blockade is effectively enforced, i.e., if it is not merely a "paper blockade," it entitles war vessels of the blockading State to capture neutral vessels seeking to enter or leave the blockaded ports. At the same time, in the absence of any blockade, belligerent war vessels may capture neutral goods and ships falling in the category of contraband of war, i.e., goods of neutral ownership, found on the high seas, of use in war, and destined for the enemy. Neutral vessels may be condemned if more than half of the cargo consists of contraband, as measured by volume or by value. All other neutral commerce with States at war is theoretically legitimate and not to be interfered with. Neutral commercial States have always insisted vehemently upon "freedom of the seas" and neutral trading rights. Belligerent States, on the other hand, have always been disposed to interpret their rights to intercept neutral commerce as broadly as possible, through the extension of the contraband list and the "doctrine of continuous voyage."

The doctrine of continuous voyage or "ultimate destination" was developed by Great Britain at the end of the eighteenth century, utilized by the Union in the American Civil War, and employed by both the British and American Governments in the Great War. It holds that neutral vessels going from one neutral port to another may be captured if there is presumption of eventual enemy destination of the cargo.[1] In the Great War the British Admiralty applied this doctrine both to contraband and to blockade. It went so far as to allot quotas of foodstuffs and other supplies to the Scandinavian neutrals and to confiscate all neutral cargoes bound for Scandinavian ports in excess of the quotas, on the ground that there was reasonable presumption that the cargoes were destined for transshipment to Germany, either as contraband goods or in violation of the blockade. The retaliatory measures of the German Government took the form of a submarine blockade of the Allied States. By their very nature, the U-boats were obliged to strike and flee, without regard to the safety of life and property aboard torpedoed vessels. The ensuing controversies with neutrals over the legitimacy of this method of enforcing a blockade furnished the pretext for the entrance of the United States into the war on the Allied side. In addition to devising novel methods of enforcing blockades and applying the doctrine of continuous voyage, belligerent States in recent wars have extended the list of contraband goods to a point where almost all neutral commerce with the enemy is swept from the seas. Originally only war supplies were regarded as contraband, but the British contraband lists of 1914 and 1915 included practically every conceivable commodity. This procedure was defended on the ground that all the industrial and commercial resources of Germany had been mobilized for war purposes. The Allied navies cut off the Central Powers from almost all commercial contacts with the outside world. Neutral ships and cargoes of every nature, destined either for German ports or for other neutral ports near Germany, were captured and condemned in wholesale fashion. The United States and other neutrals protested against these practices, but resorted to them with even greater enthusiasm after becoming belligerents.

These developments raise serious and still unsettled questions regarding the status of neutral commerce in future wars. The use of submarines

---

[1] *Cf. The Maria,* 5 C. Rob. 365, 368; *The Kim,* L. R. 215 (1915); *The Hart,* 3 Wall. 559–560.

and airplanes to enforce blockades, the enormous expansion of the contraband list, and the application of the doctrine of continuous voyage to both contraband and blockade are all devices whereby desperate belligerents seek to establish legal justification for a policy of severing all trading relations between the enemy and neutral States. They may be resisted by neutrals, but the law is still much confused and such protests are usually of little avail except to embroil the neutrals in controversies and sometimes in war with the belligerents. In recent years the traditional American championship of "freedom of the seas" and neutral trading rights has raised doubts as to whether members of the League of Nations can even apply economic sanctions to a Covenant-breaking State without involving themselves in a serious risk of diplomatic difficulties with the United States. The League of Nations Covenant and the Kellogg-Briand Pact, if taken literally, go far in the direction of abolishing neutrality completely as a feasible policy and a defensible legal status. Neutrality implies a large degree of isolation and aloofness from the issues of a war on the part of a neutral State. In a world of interdependent States, in which all States have, in principle if not in practice, renounced war and in which no State can view with indifference a war between any other two States, it may be doubted whether such isolation and aloofness are any longer possible. Here again international law as a means of protecting the rights of States appears to have reached the limits of its development, pending the effective outlawry of war itself.

SUGGESTED READINGS

Evans, L. B.: *Leading Cases on International Law*, Chicago, Callahan, 1922.
Fenwick, C. G.: *International Law*, New York, Century Company, 1924.
Hall, W. E.: *A Treatise on International Law*, Oxford, Clarendon Press, 1924.
Hershey, A. S.: *Essentials of International Public Law and Organization*, New York, The Macmillan Company, 1927.
Hyde, C. C.: *International Law. Chiefly as Interpreted and Applied by the United States* (2 vols.), Boston, Little, Brown & Company, 1922.
Lawrence, T. J.: *The Principles of International Law*, Boston, D. C. Heath & Company, 1923.
Malloy, W. M.: *Treaties, Conventions, International Acts, Protocols and Agreements between the United States and other Powers* (3 vols.), Washington, Government Printing Office, first 2 vols., 1909, 3rd vol., 1923.
Moore, J. B.: *Digest of International Law* (8 vols.), Washington, Government Printing Office, 1906.
Oppenheim, L.: *International Law* (2 vols.), New York, Longmans, Green & Co., 1928.
Westlake, J.: *International Law* (2 vols.), Cambridge University Press, 1910–1913.
Wilson, G. G.: *International Law*, New York, Silver, Burdett & Company, 1922.
American Journal of International Law (Quarterly).
British Yearbook of International Law.
League of Nations Treaty Series.
Proceedings of the Grotius Society (Annual).
United States Department of State, *Executive Agreement Series.*
United States Department of State, *Treaty Series.*

CHAPTER V

THE PRACTICE OF DIPLOMACY

1. THE DEVELOPMENT OF DIPLOMATIC INSTITUTIONS AND PROCEDURES

> The late Duke of Tuscany, who was a remarkably wise and enlightened
> prince, once complained to the Venetian Ambassador, who stayed over
> night with him on his journey to Rome, that the Republic of Venice had
> sent as resident at his court a person of no value, possessing neither judg-
> ment nor knowledge, nor even any attractive personal quality. "I am not
> surprised," said the Ambassador in reply; "we have many fools in Venice."
> Whereupon the Grand Duke retorted: "We also have fools in Florence,
> but we take care not to export them."—M. DE CALLIÈRES, *On the
> Manner of Negotiating with Princes*, 1716.

EARLY in the seventeenth century Sir Henry Wottan inscribed
in Christopher Flecamore's album a definition of an ambassador
which has since become famous: "An ambassador," he wrote, "is
an honest man sent to lie abroad for the good of his country." This conception of the function of diplomacy is reminiscent of Machiavelli and Louis
XI. While it is now frowned upon by those who urge openness and honesty
in international relations, it nevertheless suggests the fundamental nature
of the State System in which modern diplomacy has arisen. In a System
of independent sovereign units, engaged in a perpetual struggle with one
another for territory, power, and prestige in an oft-times violent if not
entirely lawless fashion, diplomacy and war are inevitably regarded as
means to the greater glory of the State. A State may enhance its power at
the expense of its rivals through violent coercion or through discussion,
compromise, and bargaining which may well involve unscrupulous trickery,
deception, and misrepresentation. The end is the same. Which means it is
most expedient to use in a given situation depends upon circumstances.
But in any case modern diplomacy, like military might, is a weapon for
the enhancement of State power quite as much as a means for the orderly
discussion of international problems.

In the present chapter, however, attention will be directed to the
mechanisms of diplomacy rather than to its purposes. The mechanisms
have been created to achieve the purposes, for in the process of political
and administrative invention, no less than in technology and organic evolution, structure reflects function. But the purposes of diplomacy are no
longer limited to the enhancement of the power of the State at the expense
of its neighbors. The functions of diplomats have become varied and

[159]

multitudinous to the same degree to which the contacts between States in the machine age have become enriched and bewilderingly complicated. Sir Ernest Satow, in his great work, *A Guide to Diplomatic Practice*, defined diplomacy as "the application of intelligence and tact to the conduct of official relations between the governments of independent States" (2d ed., 1922, I, p. 1). In the contemporary period the number of problems which fall within the purview of the official relations between governments is enormously greater than it has ever been before. A correspondingly complex set of diplomatic procedures and institutions has been developed to meet the needs of the international world society of the modern age of western civilization.

Modern diplomacy, invented in Renaissance Italy and embellished and enriched by the practice of the national monarchies of western Europe in the epoch of the great discoveries and of the Reformation, was first subjected to a crucial test of its efficacy as an instrument of international collaboration at the Peace Congress of Westphalia which concluded the Thirty Years' War. The circumstances attending this first great gathering of European diplomats revealed clearly the necessity of establishing fixed rules of diplomatic etiquette and ceremonial. The long delay of six years in the conclusion of the peace was due in large part to the absence of such fixed rules in the international practice of the period. A Venetian offer of mediation was ignored because the Republic had addressed Queen Christina of Sweden as "Sérénissime" and had failed to add "Très-Puissante" to her title. The Venetian Ambassador at Paris apologized for this omission to Grotius, then Swedish Ambassador to France, but the war went on. Not until the close of the year 1641 were arrangements made between the belligerents for the summoning of a peace conference. Innumerable procedural difficulties arose at once. The Swedes refused to send delegates to Cologne as the Pope had suggested or to any other place where Sweden's ally, France, might be regarded as having precedence. The mountain refused to go to Mohammed and Mohammed refused to go to the mountain. After much wrangling it was decided that the Swedes would negotiate with the enemy at Osnabrück and the French at Münster, both cities in Westphalia about thirty miles apart and roughly halfway between Paris and Stockholm. While the war continued, the two towns, as well as the route between them, were neutralized by international action to afford security to the delegates. New controversies arose over the forms of the documentary credentials of the plenipotentiaries. The Count d'Avaux, representing France, refused to accord the title of Emperor to Ferdinand III, and Salvius, the Swedish delegate, would not have the King of France named before his Queen. Finally, each delegate in his credentials gave first place to his own rulers. Next the Emperor refused to ratify the preliminary treaty which was concluded. It recognized the rulers of France and Sweden as his equals, he complained; his own name did not appear first in the document; the neutralization of Westphalia was derogatory to his dignity.

Not until July of 1642 were arrangements for the Congress finally completed, and another thirteen months elapsed before any of the delegates arrived on the scene. Since the full powers of some of them were questioned, no business was done till June of 1645. "If," wrote Ogier, friend of the French delegate, Abel Servien, "they create in the substance of the business delays proportioned to those hitherto, I do not know that the unborn child Madame Servien is expecting can hope to see the end of a treaty to which our adversaries create such extraordinary obstacles."[1] Long wrangles ensued over titles, places of honor in processions, and seating arrangements at the conference. Most of the States of Europe were represented, except England, Russia, and Turkey. So numerous were the delegates that one observer declared that "one could not look out the door without seeing ten ambassadors." Each delegate stood upon his dignity at all costs. All wanted to be at the head of the conference table. When a round table was at length agreed upon, more quarrels arose over the honor of occupying the place nearest the door. So tedious and complicated were all the details of the negotiations that the records fill many volumes. Eight years elapsed before the terms of peace were finally settled and embodied in the treaties of 1648.

Each succeeding international conference of European States has accomplished its work in a progressively shorter period of time. The congress at Utrecht, 1713–1714, required only two years to complete its task. The Congress of Vienna of 1814–1815 lasted only fourteen months. The Paris Peace Conference of 1919 required less than six months to draw up the treaties of peace which closed the Great War, despite the fact that the problems under consideration were of world-wide significance and the issues were enormously more complex than in earlier negotiations. The expediting of the business of international conferences was made possible by the gradual development of established rules of precedence, etiquette, and ceremonial which may appear needlessly elaborate and even silly to the layman, but which are essential to insure the conduct of diplomatic business with dispatch.

Among the most important of these rules are those relating to the ranks and titles of diplomatic representatives. During the fifteenth century States began the practice of exchanging permanent diplomatic agents with one another. With the appearance of diplomats of lesser rank than ambassadors, such as envoys, ministers, residents, and the like, confusion and controversy arose over questions of dignity and precedence, until general agreements could be reached regarding the principles to be

[1] D. J. Hill, *History of European Diplomacy*, II, p. 594.

applied to such problems. At the Congresses of Vienna and Aix-la-Chapelle of 1815 and 1818, respectively, rules were formulated regarding the relative rank of State agents[1] which have since been accepted by all States. Four classes of diplomatic agents are now recognized in order of rank:

1. Ambassadors extraordinary and plenipotentiary, and papal legates or nuncios, accredited to sovereigns or heads of States.

2. Envoys extraordinary and ministers plenipotentiary, also accredited to sovereigns or heads of States.

3. Ministers resident, likewise accredited to sovereigns.

4. *Chargés d'affaires, ad hoc* when the agent so named is the permanent head of a diplomatic mission, *ad interim* when he is an official left temporarily in charge of an embassy or legation; accredited to the Minister of Foreign Affairs.

These ranks are significant chiefly for ceremonial purposes and serve to prevent most of the difficulties and embarrassments which hampered the work of the Congress of Westphalia. The third rank has now become of minor importance, since most States now confer the title of envoy extraordinary and minister plenipotentiary upon their ministers abroad, whether they are sent on special missions or reside permanently at their posts. In general, only sovereign States may send diplomatic agents. When States not fully sovereign are accorded this privilege, it is usually on the basis of the treaty arrangements which limit their sovereignty. Since the Great War the British Dominions have exchanged diplomatic agents of their own with a considerable number of foreign States. The

---

[1] The protocol of March 9, 1815, and the articles adopted at Aix-la-Chapelle, November 21, 1818: "In order to prevent in future the inconveniences which have frequently occurred, and which may still occur, from the claims of precedence among the different diplomatic characters, the plenipotentiaries of the Powers who signed the Treaty of Paris have agreed on the following articles, and think it their duty to invite those of other crowned heads to adopt the same regulations: Article I. Diplomatic characters are divided into three classes: that of ambassadors, legates, or nuncios; that of envoys, ministers, or other persons accredited to sovereigns; that of chargés d'affaires accredited to ministers for foreign affairs. Article II. Ambassadors, legates, or nuncios only shall have the representative character. Article III. Diplomatic characters charged with any special mission shall not, on that account, assume any superiority of rank. Article IV. Diplomatic characters shall rank in their respective classes according to the date of the official notification of their arrival. The present regulation shall not occasion any change respecting the representative of the Pope. Article V. There shall be a regular form adopted by each State for the reception of diplomatic characters of every class. Article VI. Ties of consanguinity or family alliance confer no rank on their diplomatic agents. The same rule also applies to political alliances. Article VII. In acts or treaties between several Powers that admit alternity, the order which is to be observed in the signatures of ministers shall be decided by lot. Article VIII. It is agreed between the five courts that ministers resident accredited to them shall form, with respect to their precedence, an intermediate class between ministers of the second class and chargés d'affaires." Article VIII of these regulations was adopted in 1818, the others in 1815. While theoretically binding only upon the signatories, they have in practice been accepted by all States. *Cf.* G. G. Wilson, *International Law*, pp. 164–166.

Papacy from time immemorial has likewise enjoyed the right to send diplomatic agents (nuncios and legates) who have usually been accorded the position of "doyen" or "dean" of the diplomatic corps in States receiving papal representatives. The doyen is otherwise the senior diplomat of highest rank. While the Papacy was not a sovereign State between 1870 and 1928, it should be noted that it again has jurisdiction over territory and subjects (the Vatican City) under the recent agreement with the Italian Government.

Before diplomatic agents are appointed, it is customary to ascertain whether the person about to be chosen is personally acceptable to the sovereign and foreign minister to whom he is sent. A diplomatic agent who, for any reason, is displeasing to those with whom he is expected to maintain friendly relations can obviously be of no great utility. All States are free to refuse diplomatic agents of other States on the ground of their being *persona non grata*. No reasons need be given for such refusal, and if trivial or irrelevant reasons are offered, irritation is likely to result.[1] The rule of reciprocity is ordinarily followed by States in the rank of diplomatic representatives exchanged. Ambassadors are exchanged between the Great Powers and between some of the Secondary Powers. Since they were once regarded as representatives of royalty, the republican government of the United States sent only representatives of lesser rank, *i.e.*, ministers and chargés d'affaires, for over a century after its establishment. In view of the fact that such representatives were literally obliged "to take a back seat" at foreign courts in deference to agents of the first rank, Congress authorized the President to exchange ambassadors with foreign States in 1893.[2] Every diplomatic representative is entitled to bring with him to the capital to which he is sent a suite, the members of which share his privileges and immunities. The official suite of an ambassador or minister usually comprises a counselor, various secretaries, military, naval, and commercial attachés, interpreters and dragomans,

---

[1] In 1885 the Italian Government refused to receive Mr. Keiley as American minister on the ground that he had denounced the overthrow of the temporal power of the Pope. The Austrian Government subsequently refused to receive him on the ground that his wife was a Jewess and his marriage was only a civil one. In the one case he was too good a Catholic to be *persona grata;* in the other he was not a sufficiently good Catholic. President Cleveland showed his displeasure by refusing to appoint a new minister. "I have made no new nomination," he told Congress, "and the interests of this government at Vienna are now in the care of the secretary of legation, acting as chargé d'affaires *ad interim*" (First annual message, 1885).

[2] "Whenever the President shall be advised that any foreign government is represented or is about to be represented in the United States by an ambassador, envoy extraordinary, minister plenipotentiary, minister resident, or special envoy or chargé d'affaires, he is authorized in his discretion to direct that the representative of the United States to such government shall bear the same designation. This provision shall in no wise affect the duties, powers, or salary of such representative." Law of March 1, 1893, 27 U. S. Statutes at Large, c. 182.

clerks and accountants, a chaplain, a physician, etc. The unofficial suite includes the family, servants, private secretaries, etc., of the head of the mission.

Every diplomatic agent receives a letter of credence, a special passport, and a set of instructions before starting on his mission. The letter of credence is issued by the head of the State to ambassadors and ministers and by the Minister of Foreign Affairs (Secretary of State in the United States) to chargés d'affaires. It authorizes the agent to undertake his duties. The standard form employed by the United States is as follows:

LETTER OF CREDENCE

....

President of the United States of America

To [President, King, Emperor, or (for chargés d'affaires) Minister of Foreign Affairs of the foreign State]

Great and Good Friend:

I have made choice of [name of the agent], one of our distinguished citizens, to reside near the Government of Your [Majesty or Excellency] in the quality of [ambassador, minister, or charg' d'affaires]. He is well informed of the relative interests of the two countries and of our sincere desire to cultivate to the fullest extent the friendship which has so long subsisted between the two Governments. My knowledge of his high character and ability gives me entire confidence that he will constantly endeavor to advance the interest and prosperity of both Governments, and so render himself acceptable to Your [Majesty or Excellency].

I therefore request Your [Majesty or Excellency] to receive him favorably and to give full credence to what he shall say on the part of the United States, and to the assurances which I have charged him to convey to you of the best wishes of this Government for the prosperity of [name of the foreign State]. May God have Your [Majesty or Excellency] in His wise keeping.

Written at Washington this...day of...in the year...

Your good friend,

....

By the President   (Signature of the President)

....

Secretary of State.

A diplomatic mission is commenced with the formal ceremony of the presentation and acceptance of the letter of credence. The agent is received for this purpose by the head of the local State, if he is an ambassador or minister, and by the Minister of Foreign Affairs if he is a chargé d'affaires. Diplomats of the first and second rank are usually received in a solemn public audience. They present their letters and make a short address, to which a formal reply is given. A diplomatic mission may be terminated in various ways, as by the expiration of the period for which the letter of credence or full power is granted, the change of grade of the representative, or the fulfillment of the purposes of a special mission. In all of these conjunctures, as well as in the case of the death of a diplomat, his resignation, or his recall or dismissal for personal reasons, a new letter of credence is required by his successor. Diplomatic missions are also terminated by a declaration of war or by recall or dismissal for political reasons in a situation of strained relations leading to a rupture. Such a severance of diplomatic contacts is not always followed by war, but war is invariably preceded or accompanied by a diplomatic rupture. On August 3, 1914, Ambassador von Schoen, German representative in Paris, appeared at the Quai d'Orsay for the last time to inform Foreign Minister Viviani of the declaration of war against France by Germany and to ask for his passports. On February 3, 1917, Count von Bernstorff, the German Ambassador in Washington, was handed his passports by President Wilson as a protest against the resumption of unrestricted submarine warfare on the part of Germany four days previously. At the same time James W. Gerard, American Ambassador in Berlin, was recalled to Washington. On April 6, 1917, the American Congress declared war on Germany in accordance with the President's recommendations.

The outbreak of a successful revolution, either in the home State of a diplomat or in the State where he is serving, also terminates his mission under ordinary circumstances and raises the question of the diplomatic recognition of the new government as a prerequisite to the resumption of relations between the States. Sometimes, however, this principle is not observed. On March 17, 1917, David R. Francis, American Ambassador to Russia, reported to the State Department the overthrow of the Imperial Government and the abdication of the Tsar. His request that he be authorized to recognize the new Provisional Government was granted by Secretary of State Lansing two days later. On March 22, Francis called on Miliukov and the new Council of Ministers and presented his new credentials. Shortly afterward, George Bakhmetev, Tsarist Ambassador in Washington, resigned his post and was replaced by Boris Bakhmetev (no relation to his predecessor) whose credentials were received by Lansing on June 19. On November 7, 1917, however, the Provisional Government was overturned by the Bolshevist coup d'état which set up the present Soviet régime in Russia. In this instance recognition of the new Government was withheld. Francis received no new credentials to the Soviet authorities and his mission was presumably terminated, though he remained in Russia and continued to enjoy diplomatic privileges and immunities until his departure on July 25, 1918, from Vologda to Archangel, already held by forces hostile to the Soviet Government. The new revolution would normally have been regarded as terminating the diplomatic missions of the agents of the defunct Provisional Government abroad, but the State Department in Washington continued for several years to deal with Boris Bakhmetev as the accredited and official representative of the State of Russia, though he represented no authority in Russia save, for a time, that of the counter-revolutionary White Guard leader, Admiral Kolchak, who was executed after the destruction of his régime in Siberia by the Red Army. Bakhmetev resigned in 1922, but his financial attaché, Serge Ughet, still appears on the rolls of the State Department as Russian diplomatic representative, despite the fact that the government which appointed him vanished from the face of the earth sixteen years ago. This situation is anomalous and contrary to general practice. When, in 1919, Mr. Martens, the newly appointed Soviet Ambassador to the United States, sought to present his credentials to the State Department, they were refused and he was arrested and deported.

A diplomatic representative who is officially received is entitled to the benefit of the usual privileges and immunities during his entire mission. As a matter of general practice and comity, he is usually accorded the same privileges during the interval between his departure from his own State and his arrival in the foreign capital and likewise, in the event of his return, dismissal, or recall to his own State, during the interval between his departure from his post and his safe arrival home. Diplomatic ceremonial at the present time has been somewhat simplified as compared with the current practice in the eighteenth century. No diplomat can claim honors above other diplomats of the same rank. As between diplomats of the same rank, the one who has served longest at his post receives precedence. At diplomatic dinners, the host sits at the head of the table. The first place on his right is the place of honor accorded to the ambassador who has served longest; the next ambassador in order of service occupies the first place on the left, the third the second place on the right, and so on. When all the ambassadors are thus placed, the ministers plenipotentiary are seated in the same order, followed by the ministers resident and the chargés d'affaires. In processions the place of honor is sometimes the first place and sometimes the last. Diplomats of the first rank are entitled to be addressed as "Your Excellency," to remain covered in the presence of the sovereign or head of the State, to use a coat of arms over the door of the embassy, to receive military and naval honors, to be invited to all court functions, and the like. Ambassadors traditionally receive salutes of nineteen guns, ministers plenipotentiary of fifteen, ministers resident thirteen, and chargés d'affaires eleven. The legal privileges of diplomatic agents, suggested in the preceding chapter, comprise inviolability of person, family, suite, and residence, extraterritoriality and exemption from local civil and criminal jurisdiction, freedom from personal and general property taxes, and liberty of worship.

Somewhat more flexible rules have been developed with regard to the conduct of international conferences, which have been held with increasing frequency during the past century. The conference method of dealing with international problems was largely limited in the formative period of the Western State System to issues of war and peace. It has now become a normal and institutionalized procedure for dealing with questions of all kinds. During the calendar year 1931, for example, the United States participated in no less than forty-eight different international conferences, covering a bewildering variety of subjects of international interest.[1] The number of States represented at such conferences depends of course upon circumstances. The first Hague Conference of 1899 consisted of representatives of twenty-eight States and the second Conference of 1907 was participated in by forty-four States. The London Naval Conference of 1908–1909 was restricted to ten States. At the Paris Peace Conference of 1919 twenty-seven States were represented, in addition to the British Dominions and India. The four defeated States were not permitted to participate in the negotiations, but sent agents to accept the terms of peace dictated to them by the victors. The Washington Arms Conference of 1921–1922 was participated in by the eight States accepting the invitation of the American Government. The annual Assemblies of the League of Nations are participated in by the representatives of fifty or more States, while the General Disarmament Conference of 1932 had practically all of the sovereign States of the world represented at its sessions.

The State or States issuing invitations to an international conference must assume responsibility for the membership and for the proposing of a list of topics to be dealt with. On the basis of such proposals every international conference draws up an "agenda," representing the consensus of opinion among the delegates present as to what subjects should be discussed. Every conference similarly determines its own organization and

[1] The mere listing of these conferences is extremely revealing of the scope and importance of the international conference as a method of dealing with contemporary international problems. The list, taken from the annual *Register of the Department of State*, January 1, 1932, pp. 298–310, is as follows:

Advisory Committee on Traffic in Opium and Other Dangerous Drugs
International Conference for the Unification of Laws on Bills of Exchange, Promissory Notes, and Checks
International Committee on Liberia
First Conference of Representatives of Central Police Offices
Second Pan-American Conference of Directors of Health
International Colonial and Overseas Exposition
International Coffee Conference
Conference of Wheat-exporting Countries
Fourth International Conference of Labor Statisticians
Seventeenth Plenary Assembly of the International Parliamentary Conference of Commerce
International Technical Consulting Committee on Radio Communications
Conference on the Limitation of the Manufacture of Narcotic Drugs
Thirteenth International Housing and Town-planning Conference
Fifteenth International Congress of Agriculture
Second International Hospital Congress

rules of procedure. Usually the organization of an international conference resembles that of a national legislative body, with presiding officers, secretaries, committees, plenary sessions, and committee meetings. The principle of State equality, however, requires that each State have one vote and that all action be by unanimity, since no sovereign State can be bound to an agreement without its consent. In most cases, the agreements reached are subject to ratification on the part of the participating States. In the League of Nations, the International Labor Organization, and the various public international unions, the conference method of dealing with international problems has been institutionalized in a fashion which will be described in a later section.

2. DIPLOMATS AND CONSULS: FUNCTIONS

A correct man punctually executes the orders he has received; but to this quality must be joined ability. Now, in order to execute a political commission well, it is necessary to know the character of the prince and those who sway his counsel; to attach himself to those who can procure him ready access to the prince, for there is nothing difficult to an ambassador who has the prince's ear; but it is above all things necessary to make himself esteemed, which he will do if he so regulates his actions and conversation that he shall be thought a man of honor, liberal and sincere.— NICCOLO MACHIAVELLI TO RAPHAEL GIROLAMI, Ambassador to the Emperor.

Modern States maintain official contacts with one another through far-flung networks of agents scattered over the globe. Each of the sovereign entities of the Western State System sends permanent diplo-

Sixth International Congress of Military Medicine and Pharmacy
Sixth International Conference on High Tension Electric Systems
Eleventh Session of the Journées Médicales de Bruxelles
Conferences Relating to the Moratorium on Intergovernmental Debts
Sixth Congress of the International Association of Agriculture of Tropical Countries
European Conference on Rural Hygiene
International Congress for the Protection of Nature
International Congress of Wood and Sylviculture
Forty-second Congress of the Royal Sanitary Institute
Ninth International Dairy Congress
Sixth Congress of the International Seed-testing Association
Thirteenth International Congress of Secondary Instruction
Seventh International Congress of Agriculture and Fisheries
Third Congress of the Pan-American Medical Association
Eighth International Dental Congress
Sixth International Congress on Industrial Accidents and Diseases
First International Congress of the New International Association for the Testing of Materials
International Congress for Studies Regarding Population
Eighteenth International Congress of Orientalists
Committee on the Regulation of Whaling
Fifteenth Congress of the Permanent International Association of Navigation Congresses

matic and consular officers to foreign capitals and cities and receives similar officers into its own territory from other States. The number of such officers has greatly increased during the last century with the growth of contacts between States and the transformation of the Western State System into a world system. Into the foreign office of every State come reports, queries, and official dispatches from agents scattered over the six continents and the seven seas. Out of each Foreign Office go elaborate instructions to the widely dispersed field agents in scores of foreign States. To use a familiar analogy, the foreign offices constitute the brains and higher nerve centers of the States in their dealings with one another. The field agents are the nerve endings and sense organs, through which impressions of the outside world are received and impulses are transmitted and translated into action in the game of world politics. According to the Department of State of the United States an efficient foreign service officer:

Creates good will and common understanding, and, with restrained and critical leadership born of mature experience and profound knowledge of men and affairs, uses these as instruments for enhancing international confidence and cooperation among governments and people.

Promotes and protects the interests of the United States and of its citizens.

Negotiates, with tact, sound judgment, and intimate knowledge of conditions at home and abroad, protocols, conventions, and treaties, especially regarding international intercourse, tariffs, shipping, commerce, preservation of peace, etc., in strict conformity to Government instructions.

Establishes and effectively utilizes personal contacts in farsighted ways for the benefit of his Government and of American citizens.

Analyzes and reports on political and economic conditions and trends of significance to the United States.

Twentieth Session of the International Institute of Statistics

International Congress of Geography

Discussions Relative to an Armaments Truce: Held in the Third (Disarmament) Committee of the Assembly of the League of Nations

Twenty-seventh Conference of the Interparliamentary Union

Fourth Pan-American Commercial Conference

Second International Conference on the Rat

Third Congress of the Pan-American Postal Union

Fourth General Conference on Communications and Transit

Second Congress of Comparative Pathology

Discussions Relative to the Application of the Pact of Paris to the Sino-Japanese Controversy: Held in the Council of the League of Nations

Bangkok Conference on Opium Smoking in the Far East

Discussions Bearing on Treaty Rights and General Interests of the United States in Connection with Developments in Manchuria

Only a few of these conferences, obviously, dealt with "political" questions in the narrower sense of the term. The United States was represented at all of them, however, by governmental delegates or observers, in some cases by members of the regular diplomatic or consular services, in others by special appointees, and in the remainder by officials in various other branches of the governmental service.

Exercises skill in following prescribed form and routine procedure when possible; and displays discriminating judgment, as may be necessary in more complicated situations requiring investigations, careful accumulation of information, or professional understanding of laws, customs, conditions, etc.

Administers an office in a business-like and efficient manner.[1]

To revert to the well-established distinction between diplomatic and consular agents, the former may be described broadly as political representatives and the latter as commercial representatives, although there are certain functions performed by both. Diplomatic agents maintain contacts between governments, *i.e.*, between the foreign offices, while consular agents are entrusted with duties relating to trade relations, the protection of citizens abroad, the enforcement of customs and immigration laws, and the like. At the present time a diplomatic representative is entrusted in general with the business of directing the internal business of the embassy or legation of which he is in charge, of conducting negotiations with the proper authorities of the State to which he is accredited, of making reports to his home government, and of rendering various services to the nationals of his own State. These duties are likely to prove extremely arduous and expensive at an important foreign post, as Walter Hines Page, Ambassador to Great Britain before the war, discovered shortly after assuming the functions of his office. In a much-quoted letter of December 22, 1913, he described his impressions as follows:

If you think it's all play, you fool yourself; I mean this job. There's no end of the work. It consists of these parts: Receiving people for two hours every day, some on some sort of business, some merely to "pay respects"; attending to a large (and exceedingly miscellaneous) mail; going to the Foreign Office on all sorts of errands; looking up the oddest sort of information that you ever heard of; making reports to Washington on all sorts of things; then the so-called social duties—giving dinners, receptions, etc., and attending them. I hear the most important news I get at so-called social functions. Then the court functions; and the meetings and speeches! The American Ambassador must go all over England and explain every American thing. You'd never recover from the shock if you could hear me speaking about education, agriculture, the observance of Christmas, the navy, the Anglo-Saxon, Mexico, the Monroe Doctrine, co-education, woman suffrage, medicine, law, radio-activity, flying, the Supreme Court, the President as a man of letters, the hookworm, the Negro—just get down the encyclopædia and continue the list! I've done this every week-night for a month, hand running, with a few afternoon performances thrown in. I have missed only one engagement in these seven months; and that was merely a private luncheon. I have been late only once. I have the best chauffeur in the world—he deserves credit for much of that. Of course, I don't get time to read a book. In fact, I can't get time to keep up with what goes on at home. To read a newspaper eight or ten days old, when they come in bundles of three or four—is impossible. What isn't telegraphed here, I miss! and that means I miss most things.

I forgot, there are a dozen other kinds of activities, such as American marriages, which they always want the Ambassador to attend; getting them out of

[1] *The American Foreign Service*, State Department Publication 235, 1931, pp. 4–6.

jail when they are jugged (I have an American woman on my hands now, whose four children come to see me every day); looking after the American insane; helping Americans move the bones of their ancestors; interpreting the income-tax law; receiving medals for Americans; hearing American fiddlers, pianists, players; sitting for American sculptors and photographers; sending telegrams for property owners in Mexico; reading letters from thousands of people who have shares in estates here; writing letters of introduction; getting tickets to the House Gallery; getting seats in the Abbey; going with people to this, that and t'other; getting tickets to the races, the art galleries, the House of Lords; answering fool questions about the United States put by Englishmen. With a military attaché, a naval attaché, three secretaries, a private secretary, two automobiles, Alice's private secretary, a veterinarian, an immigration agent, consuls everywhere, a dispatch agent, lawyers, doctors, messengers—they keep us all busy. A woman turned up dying the other day. I sent for a big doctor. She got well. As if that wasn't enough, both the woman and the doctor had to come and thank me (fifteen minutes each). Then each wrote a letter! Then there are people who are going to have a fair here; others who have a fair coming on at San Francisco; others at San Diego; secretaries and returning and outgoing diplomats come and go (lunch for 'em all); niggers come up from Liberia; Rhodes Scholars from Oxford; presidential candidates to succeed Huerta; people who present books; women who wish to go to court; Jews who are excited about Roumania; passports to sign; peace committees about the hundred years of peace; opera singers going to the United States; artists who have painted some American portraits—don't you see?[1]

This first-hand account of the functions of a diplomat would undoubtedly receive the hearty endorsement of foreign representatives of the first rank in all of the great capitals of the world. Social functions, speeches, routine duties, and favors done to follow countrymen consume the major portion of a diplomat's time, despite the popular notion that he is primarily concerned with high and mighty affairs of State. While negotiations between States are now almost incessant and cover a bewildering variety of topics, the diplomat as negotiator is much less important than he was a century ago. He is no longer isolated at his post and obliged to make important decisions at his own discretion as he was in the days of the sailing vessel and the stagecoach, when instructions from his government came slowly, infrequently, and sometimes not at all. The diplomat is now in daily—sometimes in hourly—communication by cable and telephone with those from whom he receives his orders. In Mr. Dooley's phrase, he has become "merely a highly paid messenger boy, and not always a very efficient one at that!" Very seldom is he placed in a situation where he must make an important decision without being able to consult the foreign office in his own capital. His importance is further diminished by the current practice of having treaties negotiated by special representatives chosen for the purpose, rather than by the regularly accredited diplomatic representatives. Foreign ministers and heads of

[1] See *The Life and Letters of Walter Hines Page* for other interesting comments on the diplomatic function.

States, moreover, are now in much more frequent and direct communication with one another than was ever possible before the Industrial Revolution. During the twelvemonth between June, 1931, and June, 1932, Secretary of State Stimson made two separate trips abroad—to London, Paris, Berlin, Rome, and Geneva—for the purpose of consulting with the foreign ministers and prime ministers of the States he visited. In the same period Premier Laval of France and Foreign Minister Grandi of Italy both visited the United States and were received by President Hoover and Secretary Stimson. On the European continent there were almost innumerable conferences between foreign ministers, most of them at Geneva through the Council and Assembly of the League of Nations and others at London, Paris, Berlin, and elsewhere. Under such circumstances the professional diplomat ceases to be the formulator of policy and the master of the destinies of nations that he was some generations ago. Nevertheless, he still serves as a permanent official who transmits communications between governments, who discusses current problems and differences of interests and policies with responsible authorities, and who still plays a not insignificant rôle in negotiations.

The less spectacular functions of the diplomatic agent, on the other hand, have expanded steadily during the same period. The duties connected with supervising the administration of embassies and legations have grown with the increase in the staffs of diplomatic missions. An ambassador or minister at an important foreign capital will frequently have a score or more of subordinates working under his direction, comprising a counselor, various grades of secretaries, military, naval, financial, and commercial attachés, interpreters, translators, clerks, stenographers, doormen, janitors, flunkeys, and lesser fry. He is responsible for organizing and coordinating their activities in order that the work of the mission may be performed with neatness, dispatch, and economy. He has minor disciplinary authority over his subordinates and he is answerable for the custody of the archives, the handling of diplomatic correspondence, and the keeping of records of the work of the mission. He is likewise responsible for reporting regularly to his home government the policies of the State to which he is accredited and the current political and economic developments affecting the relations between the States. His relations with his fellow nationals consume most of his time and that of his subordinates. He is constantly being called upon to do them all sorts of favors, from getting them out of jail to giving them letters of introduction to local officials, entrées to libraries and museums, and admission cards to the sessions of the national parliament of the State where he resides. He visas passports of aliens contemplating journeys to his own State and he may issue passports, certifications of nationality, and travel certificates to his own fellow citizens under certain circumstances. He transmits from his own government to the government to which he is accredited, requisitions for the extradition of fugitives from justice who have fled into the State where he resides. In cases of extraditions from his own State of nationals of the State to which he is accredited, he transmits the certification that the papers submitted as evidence are properly and legally authenticated. He may likewise be authorized to perform certain notarial acts and he must, in general, strive to be of service in every possible way to his fellow citizens traveling or residing in the State where he is performing his duties.

The functions of consular representatives are, if possible, even more varied. From the point of view of the historical development of the foreign service, the States of the Western State System exchanged consular representatives before they exchanged diplomatic agents, for merchants had contacts with one another across political boundaries before governments entered into negotiations with one another regarding high affairs of State. Here, as in so many other respects, politics was the handmaiden of economics. The first consuls of the medieval period were apparently chosen by communities of merchants residing abroad to exercise extraterritorial jurisdiction over them and to represent their interests in dealing with the State where they resided. The office of consul was fully established by 1200 A.D. The Hanseatic city-states and the Mediterranean trading States exchanged consuls at an early period, with the national monarchies of western Europe presently following their example. The political functions of consuls were gradually diminished, however, with the development of a diplomatic service and they have lost their extraterritorial jurisdiction except in a few oriental countries. On the other hand, the constant growth of commercial contacts between States has increased the duties of consular officers and led to a great multiplication of their numbers.

The duties of consuls are determined by custom, treaty stipulations, and the provisions of exequaturs or consular credentials. A consular officer, unlike a diplomatic agent, does not act as the spokesman of his government to a foreign government, though he may sometimes exercise quasi-diplomatic functions. He labors primarily to serve the business interests of his own State abroad and to perform incidental services for his fellow citizens. His concern is with markets, sales opportunities, and profits for traders and investors. In the epoch of economic nationalism and keen competition between rival merchant groups, each enlisting governmental support in its quest for the elusive dollar, pound, franc, or mark, even diplomatic agents must keep a sharp eye open for bargains. But this has been consuls' work for centuries. A consul makes detailed reports to his home government on economic opportunities, tendencies of trade, conditions of navigation, price trends, conditions of competition, etc. These reports are published for the information and guidance of exporters and investors back home interested in foreign markets. The consul is expected to exert himself to insure the observance of commercial treaties and to make certain that invoices of shipments going to his own State are properly submitted and that shipments are made in accordance with the laws and regulations of his own State. He has also such supervision over merchant vessels of his own State in the port where he is serving as custom and the laws of his State grant to him. The papers of such ships are deposited in his office while the ship remains in port. He usually has authority to supervise the transportation, wages, relief, and discharge of seamen, the recovery of deserting seamen, the care of the effects of deceased seamen, and sometimes the adjustment of disputes between masters, officers, and crews. The function of protecting citizens abroad is shared by consular and diplomatic agents, though in situations not involving political questions the problems which arise are handled by consular representatives. Consuls arbitrate private disputes voluntarily submitted to them, intercede with local authorities on behalf of citizens, administer property of deceased citizens of their own nationality, assist in the enforcement of the immigration laws of their own States, and perform sundry minor services for such of their fellow citizens as solicit them. In certain oriental States consuls also have extensive civil and criminal jurisdiction in cases involving fellow citizens under the provisions of extraterritoriality treaties.

Consular agents enter upon their duties when they have been granted an exequatur by the authorities of the State to which they are sent. These documents correspond to the credentials of diplomatic representatives, except that they are issued by the State receiving the consul instead of by the sending State. When a consul is appointed, his commission or patent is transmitted to the diplomatic representative of the appointing State who applies to the foreign office for an exequatur for the consul. The issue of an exequatur may be refused for cause. It may subsequently be revoked, though it is more usual to request the recall of the consul who gives offense. Exequaturs are usually issued in the name of the head of the State. In the United States the form is as follows:

FULL PRESIDENTIAL EXEQUATUR

. . . .

President of the United States of America

To all whom it may concern:

Satisfactory evidence having been exhibited to me that [name of consular official] has been appointed [title of office: consul general, consul, vice consul, etc.]. I do hereby recognize him as such, and declare him free to exercise and enjoy such functions, powers, and privileges as are allowed to [title of officer].

In testimony whereof, I have caused these letters to be made patent, and the Seal of the United States to be hereunto affixed.

(SEAL OF THE UNITED STATES) Given under my hand at the City of Washington the... day of......, A.D., 19..., and of the Independence of the United States of America, the...

....
(Signature of the President)

By the President,

....
Secretary of State.

The granting of a consular exequatur usually signifies diplomatic recognition of the State or government of the recipient by the granting State, but the reception of a consular exequatur does not have this effect. Should American consuls in the Union of Soviet Socialist Republics, for example, receive exequaturs from the Soviet foreign office, this action would not constitute diplomatic recognition of the Union of Soviet Socialist Republics by the United States. If, however, the President of the United States should issue exequaturs to Soviet consuls in the United States, this would constitute diplomatic recognition of the Union of Soviet Socialist Republics by the United States. In point of fact, there are at present no consular agents of either State in the other. A severance of diplomatic relations between States, either through a rupture or through revolution followed by nonrecognition of the new régime, usually terminates consular as well as diplomatic missions. Both are normally terminated by war. Consular missions may likewise be terminated by the recall of the agent, by the sending State or by the revocation of the exequatur by the receiving State.

Consular privileges and immunities are less extensive than those of diplomatic agents, particularly when, as is still sometimes the case, the consular officer is a citizen of the State where he exercises his functions. Certain immunities, however, are well-defined by custom and are frequently extended by treaty.[1] These include the inviolability of the archives and other official property, exemption from arrest save on criminal charges, exemption from witness duty, taxation, military charges and service, etc. In general, consuls are entitled to those privileges and immunities which will enable them to perform their duties without personal inconvenience. In oriental States where extraterritoriality prevails, consuls usually enjoy the same privileges and exemptions from local jurisdiction as diplomatic representatives.

[1] See Appendix IV, pp. 874–883 below.

3. DIPLOMATS AND CONSULS: ORGANIZATION

The art of negotiation with princes is so important that the fate of the greatest States often depends upon the good or bad conduct of negotiations and upon the degree of capacity in the negotiators employed. Thus monarchs and their ministers of state cannot examine with too great care the natural or acquired qualities of those citizens whom they despatch on missions to foreign States to entertain there good relations with their masters, to make treaties of peace, of alliance, of commerce or of other kinds, or to hinder other Powers from concluding such treaties to the prejudice of their master; and generally, to take charge of those interests which may be affected by the diverse conjunctures of events.—M. DE CALLIÈRES, *On the Manner of Negotiating with Princes.*

To describe in detail the structure of the diplomatic and consular services of all of the sixty-one sovereign States of the world is obviously impossible within the limits of a single volume. Neither is it necessary, since the patterns of organization are fairly uniform for all States. For the purpose of revealing the general nature of these patterns, attention will be concentrated on three of the Great Powers: the United States, Great Britain, and France.

The United States Government maintains 56 diplomatic posts abroad.[1] Of these 15 are embassies, *i.e.*, posts headed by ambassadors, and the remainder are legations headed by diplomatic agents of lesser rank. The United States exchanges ambassadors with all of the Great Powers with which it has diplomatic relations—Great Britain, France, Germany, Italy, and Japan—and it would exchange ambassadors with the Soviet Union in the event of its recognition. It likewise exchanges ambassadors with Mexico, Cuba, Argentina, Brazil, Chile, and Peru among the American republics, and with Belgium, Poland, Spain, and Turkey among overseas States. Envoys extraordinary and ministers plenipotentiary are exchanged with all other States, save Abyssinia, where a minister resident is maintained, and Iraq, with which chargés d'affaires are exchanged. A single minister plenipotentiary represents the United States in its dealings with Esthonia, Latvia, and Lithuania, and the American ambassador to Belgium acts as minister plenipotentiary to Luxemburg. Only consular agents are exchanged with the Free City of Danzig, Palestine, and Syria. The total number of officials in the foreign service of the United States, including heads of missions and consular as well as diplomatic agents, but excluding the officials in the State Department in Washington and subordinate employees, is over 1,300. In small States only a half dozen or so representatives are usually maintained—6 in Albania, for example, 4 in Bolivia, 7 in Bulgaria, 7 in Ecuador, 9 in Esthonia, and so on. In Great Britain and her Dominions, colonies, and

[1] As of January 1, 1932.

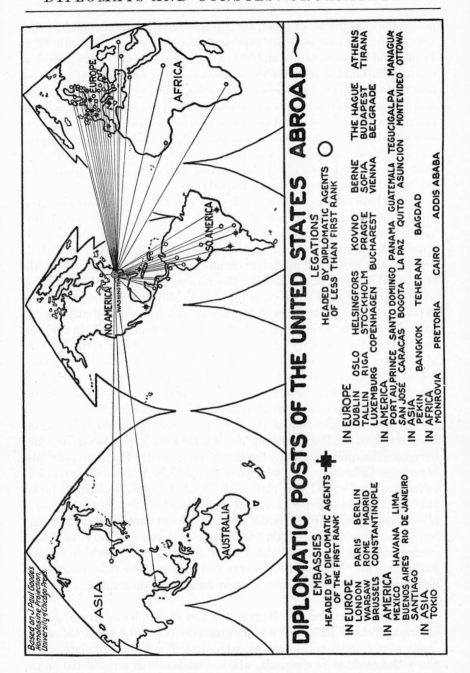

Based on J. Paul Goode's Homolosine Projection. University of Chicago Press.

DIPLOMATIC POSTS OF THE UNITED STATES ABROAD

EMBASSIES
HEADED BY DIPLOMATIC AGENTS ✦
OF THE FIRST RANK

IN EUROPE
LONDON   PARIS   BERLIN
WARSAW   ROME   MADRID
BRUSSELS   CONSTANTINOPLE

IN AMERICA
MEXICO   HAVANA   LIMA
BUENOS AIRES   RIO DE JANEIRO
SANTIAGO

IN ASIA
TOKIO

LEGATIONS
HEADED BY DIPLOMATIC AGENTS ◯
OF LESS THAN FIRST RANK

IN EUROPE
DUBLIN   OSLO   HELSINGFORS KOVNO   BERNE   THE HAGUE ATHENS
TALLIN   RIGA   STOCKHOLM   PRAGUE   SOFIA   BUDAPEST   TIRANA
LUXEMBURG   COPENHAGEN   BUCHAREST VIENNA   BELGRADE

IN AMERICA
PORT AU PRINCE SANTO DOMINGO PANAMA GUATEMALA TEGUCIGALPA MANAGUA
SAN JOSE   CARACAS   BOGOTA QUITO   ASUNCION   MONTEVIDEO OTTOWA

IN ASIA
PEKIN   BANGKOK   TEHERAN   BAGDAD

IN AFRICA
MONROVIA   PRETORIA   CAIRO   ADDIS ABABA

possessions, on the other hand, the United States maintains no less than 152 diplomatic and consular representatives, as compared with 86 in France and her possessions, and 69 in Germany. The staff of the American embassy in London includes the ambassador, the counselor of embassy, four first secretaries, two second secretaries, military, naval, commercial, and agricultural attachés, two assistant military attachés, three assistant naval attachés, two assistant commercial attachés, and a score or more of stenographers, clerks, messengers, and other subordinate employees. Some of these officials are maintained by departments other than the State Department. A similarly elaborate organization is maintained in the capitals of other States of major importance.

The administration of this small army of 1,300 civil servants involves difficult problems of recruitment, salary classification, promotion, retirement, and efficiency ratings. All foreign-service officials are formally appointed by the President and confirmed by the Senate, though in practice the President no longer names appointees to any except the highest diplomatic posts. During the nineteenth century foreign posts were frequently filled by incompetent local politicians who received such appointments as their share of the loaves and fishes distributed by the party in power in accordance with the "spoils system." Early in the present century the necessity of professionalizing the service in the interests of efficiency was appreciated and steps in this direction were taken through executive orders issued by the President. In 1906 the consular service was placed under civil-service rules and in 1909 the lower positions in the diplomatic service were similarly classified. The most important measure for the professionalization of the foreign service was taken by Congress when it passed the Rogers Act of May 24, 1924. This statute was designed to replace the spoils system by the merit system and to lay down principles of personnel administration which would enable the American Government to have at its disposal diplomats and consuls who might compare favorably in competence, experience, and professional *savoir faire* with those of other Great Powers. Perhaps the most significant contribution of the act was the amalgamation of the diplomatic and consular services into a single "Foreign Service of the United States," within which capable individuals may achieve a life career and may transfer from consular to diplomatic posts and *vice versa* as their own inclinations and the needs of the service dictate.

Under the terms of the Rogers Act and of supplementary executive orders all "classified" foreign-service officers (*i.e.*, all officers below the heads of embassies and legations, who are still political appointees, and above the grade of vice consuls, who are unclassified) are selected on the basis of competitive civil-service examinations. Since ambassadors and ministers are expected to represent the views of the administration in power, there is much to be said for having them appointed on a political basis. But the lesser officials perform administrative duties of a routine nature and have no policy-determining functions. It is more important, therefore, that they be professionally competent than that they be sympathetic with the political party in office at Washington. Considerations of professional efficiency have led to an increasing tendency to fill even the higher posts by promotion from the lower ranks. The lower posts are filled, in order of merit, by those who pass competitive examinations designed to test the applicants' knowledge of international, maritime, and commercial law, arithmetic, modern languages, history, economics, and economic geography. About 70 per cent of the present foreign-service officers of the United States are college graduates. Only 7 per cent have had no college training. The examinations are given periodically (at least once a year) in the principal cities of the United States and are open to all persons between the ages of twenty-one and thirty-five who have been American citizens for at least fifteen years.[1] As for salaries, ambassadors receive $17,500 annually and ministers $10,000, though the heads of missions at important foreign capitals are likely to spend a good deal more than they receive and must usually be people of independent means. The foreign-service officers proper are divided into nine classes, with salaries ranging from $2,500 to $10,000. The senior clerks are divided into five classes, with salaries from $3,000 to $4,000 and the junior clerks into three classes, with salaries from less than $2,500 to $2,750. Compensation is increased with years of service and allowances are granted for travel and living quarters. Retirement is obligatory at sixty-five, with a variable pension paid out of a retirement fund. Promotions from one class to another are based upon efficiency ratings. Appointments are made not to particular posts or positions but to one or another of the designated classes, the members of which are assigned their posts at the discretion of the President and the Department of State.

The tasks of recruitment and personnel administration in the American foreign service are entrusted at present to four agencies which are part of the State Department. The board of examiners, under Executive Order 5642 of June 8, 1931, consists of three assistant secretaries of state, the chief of the division of foreign service personnel, and the chief examiner of the Civil Service Commission. It prepares the written and oral examinations which candidates for admission to the service are required to take. The board of foreign service personnel prepares and submits to the Secretary of State lists of foreign-service officers, graded as to their efficiency and value to the service, recommends promotions and transfers, considers

---

[1] The rules and regulations governing admission to the foreign service, as well as copies of sample examination questions, are contained in the pamphlet, *The American Foreign Service,* which is mailed out to applicants by the State Department upon request.

controversies and delinquencies and recommends disciplinary action, and passes upon recommendations for dismissal from the service made by the division of foreign service personnel. The latter agency interviews applicants for admission to the service, collects data relating to personnel, recommends appointments to subordinate positions, keeps efficiency records, and, in general, acts in a supervisory capacity for the development and improvement of the service. The foreign service officers' training school is maintained for the instruction of new appointees and is open only to those who have successfully passed the entrance examinations.

This general scheme of organization is paralleled in the British and French foreign services, although they have long been professionalized whereas sound principles of personnel administration have been introduced into the American service only comparatively recently. The British Government exchanges ambassadors with 14 States—the United States, the Soviet Union, France, Germany, Italy, Japan, Spain, Belgium, Poland, Turkey, Portugal, Argentina, Brazil, and Chile. In addition it maintains legations, headed by envoys extraordinary and ministers plenipotentiary, at the capitals of 33 other States, and several hundred counselors of embassy, first, second, and third secretaries, naval, military, and air attachés, commercial counselors and secretaries, and sundry subordinate officials. The total number of representatives abroad of the British Foreign Office is over 1,000, of which 14 are ambassadors, 37 ministers, 298 lesser diplomatic officers, and 768 consular officers.[1] Admission to the diplomatic service and to the Foreign Office is by open competition through general cultural examinations, similar to those given to applicants for the highest posts in the general civil service. Recruitment to the service is supervised by a board of selection and by the Civil Service Commission, which grants certificates of admission to successful candidates. Ambassadors receive £2,250 or £2,500, ministers £2,000, counselors abroad £1,200 to £1,500, and first secretaries abroad £800 to £1,000, plus liberal expense allowances and living quarters. Appointments to the higher diplomatic posts may be made on recommendation of the Secretary of State to the King without regard to membership in the diplomatic service or to claims based on seniority, although promotion from the ranks is the general rule.

The diplomatic and consular service of the French Republic includes over 600 officials, not counting the subordinate agents and employees at foreign posts who are recruited locally. This total includes 15 ambassadors, 62 ministers, 37 consuls general, 217 consuls, and a host of lesser agents. Competitive entrance examinations were first introduced in 1856 for the post of student consul and have subsequently been extended to all the lower posts. As shown in the accompanying chart, a single examination is

[1] The *Foreign Office List* for 1931.

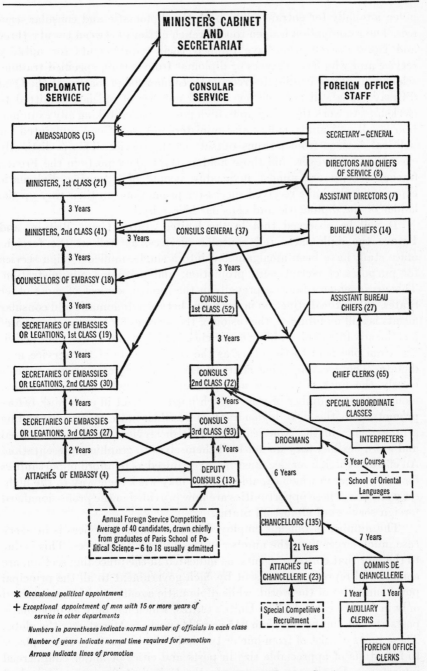

The Personnel Hierarchy in the French Foreign Service.

given annually for entrance into both the diplomatic and consular services. The examination is open to all French citizens between twenty-three and twenty-seven who have fulfilled their requirements for military service and who have degrees or diplomas from certain specified training schools. Accepted candidates receive three months' probation at the Quai d'Orsay. It is still possible for a small number of officials admitted to clerkships to work their way up to high posts without taking any examination at all and ambassadors and ministers are sometimes appointed for political reasons from persons outside of the service. This is distinctly exceptional, however, and those holding the highest posts in the French foreign service are almost invariably people of extensive diplomatic experience who have received successive promotions on their way up the ladder of the diplomatic and consular hierarchy.[1]

It will be observed that in the United States, Great Britain, and France the diplomatic and consular services, as well as the foreign-office staff, have been amalgamated into a single, unified foreign service for purposes of recruitment, promotion, and personnel administration. This arrangement likewise prevails in the foreign services of most other States. While the distinction in functions between diplomatic and consular agents is still maintained, the fusion of the services for personnel purposes has the advantage of enabling experienced officials to transfer their activities from one field to the other as the requirements of the service may dictate. The accompanying chart of the French foreign service reveals clearly the lines of transfer and promotion throughout the hierarchy, along with the number of years which must be spent in each rank before promotion to the next higher rank is possible. Since the corresponding arrangements in the American and British services are less formalized and more flexible, they do not lend themselves to graphic representation. An efficient foreign service must be so organized as to afford opportunities for a life career in which capable officials may work their way to the highest positions. These opportunities are now provided in the professionalized foreign services of almost all States.

The number of officials employed in the consular services is in every case much larger than the number in the diplomatic services. This is due to the fact that consular agents, as indicated in the preceding section, are commercial representatives sent by each government to all the principal ports and cities of the world, while diplomatic agents need be maintained only in foreign capitals. The United States, which has only 56 diplomatic posts abroad, has no less than 345 consular posts scattered over the globe. These posts consist of from one or two individuals in a few remote places to full staffs of appreciable size in ports and cities of major commercial importance. In Albania, for example, the United States maintains only 2

[1] *Cf.* F. L. Schuman, *War and Diplomacy in the French Republic*, 1931, pp. 40–45.

vice consuls in the capital, Tirana. In Brazil there is a consul general, a consul, and 2 vice consuls at Rio de Janeiro, a consul general and 3 vice consuls at Sao Paulo, and 5 additional consuls at other points, supplemented by 6 vice consuls or consular agents. In Canada the United States maintains 89 consular representatives at 34 different posts scattered throughout the Dominion. In China there are 66 American consular officials in 14 cities; in France 57 in 15 cities; in Germany 53 in 10 cities; in Italy 40 in 11 cities; in Japan 26 in 8 cities; and in Great Britain 50 in 17 cities. All of the Great Powers maintain a similar network of consular representatives at the principal cities and ports of all other States, while the lesser Powers send abroad as many consuls as their commercial interests appear to warrant.

Since there is no general international agreement in regard to consuls corresponding to that of 1815–1818 in regard to diplomatic agents, each State is free to determine for itself the ranks of its consular representatives and the organization of the service. The United States divides its consular representatives into five categories: (1) consuls general at large, who are traveling inspectors of consular posts; (2) consuls general, most of whom reside at the 36 supervisory consular offices to oversee the work of the consular service in their respective areas; (3) consuls; (4) consular agents, exercising consular functions at posts other than those at which full officers are located; and (5) vice consuls, acting as subordinate officers, assistants, and substitutes at the principal consulates. Most officers in the first two categories fall into Classes I to IV of the foreign service and receive from $6,000 to $9,000 a year. Most of the consuls are placed in classes IV to VIII and receive from $3,500 to $6,000. Consular agents were abolished by the Rogers Act, but a few still survive and are for the most part paid out of fees. The vice consuls are unclassified and receive from $2,500 to $3,000 a year. In the British consular service the ranks are: inspectors-general of consulates, consuls general, consuls, vice consuls, consular agents, and proconsuls. The last are individuals appointed to administer oaths, take affidavits or affirmations, and perform notarial functions. Most of the British proconsuls, consular agents, and vice consuls and some of the consuls are unsalaried. The French consular service consists of consuls general, consuls of three classes, and deputy consuls. These variations in the organization and rank of consular representatives seldom give rise to difficulties, since consuls are ordinarily nonpolitical agents who are not hedged about with the pomp and ceremony attaching to diplomats.

4. FOREIGN OFFICES

No diplomatist can succeed in his foreign task unless he is well supported by his own government and given every opportunity to understand its policy. . . . Without such knowledge he will certainly go astray, and without a constant contact with his home government the conduct of diplomacy cannot possibly prosper in his hands.—M. DE CALLIÈRES, *On the Manner of Negotiating with Princes.*

Consuls and diplomats of all States perform their work under the direction of the department of their own government charged with the administration of foreign affairs. They may be assisted and supplemented by agents maintained abroad by other departments of the national administration. Military attachés are sent out by ministries or departments of war, naval attachés by navy departments, financial attachés by treasury departments, and commercial attachés by departments of commerce. Departments or ministries of commerce frequently maintain extensive foreign services of their own with far-flung commercial agents scattered over the globe to assist business men and perform sundry functions not very different from those of consuls. These recent developments represent a devolution of authority over the foreign representatives of States away from the departments expressly charged with foreign affairs to other branches of the national administration. But it still remains true that each State maintains a single department or ministry which is primarily answerable for the conduct of the State's relations with other sovereignties. This department or ministry is under the control of the head of the State—President, Premier, King, or Emperor—and is directed by a minister or secretary who always occupies first place in the Cabinet in terms of honor and prestige. Into the foreign offices, state departments, or ministries of foreign affairs, as they are variously designated, go all the diplomatic and consular reports from abroad; out of them go the instructions to the hundreds of field agents in scores of foreign cities. Within the foreign offices are formulated the foreign policies of the States of the world. Between them the great game of international politics is played. Here again, for illustrative purposes, it will be sufficient to deal with the American, British, and French foreign offices, for the functions performed and even the administrative pattern of divisions, boards, and bureaus is much the same in all States.

The Department of State of the United States is located in the State, War, and Navy Building which is situated just west of the White House on Pennsylvania Avenue and G Street, Washington, D. C. It is headed by the Secretary of State who is appointed by the President, with the confirmation of the Senate. He is first in rank among the members of the Cabinet and he succeeds to the presidency in the event of the death of the President and Vice President. He has at his disposal a personal assistant, a special assistant, a private secretary, a stenographer, a chauffeur, and a small staff of aides. Next in authority under him is the under-secretary of state who acts for the secretary in matters not requiring his personal attention and who is acting secretary in the absence of his superior. The under-secretary aids in the formulation and execution of policies and directs the work of the department and of the foreign service. The first assistant secretary of state is charged with the general administration of the department and the foreign service and with supervision of matters relating to personnel and management. He is also the fiscal officer of the department who prepares estimates of necessary appropriations, submits them to Congress, and makes allotments of appropriations which have been approved. He likewise has supervision over consular affairs, passports, visas, foreign-service buildings, and international conferences. He is chairman of the foreign service personnel board, the board of examiners for the foreign service, and the board of the foreign service school. The three other assistant secretaries of state are charged with such duties as are assigned to them by the secretary.

The subordinate agencies of the department, which employ about 900 people in Washington, fall into three broad functional categories: those concerned with the internal administration of the department and its field services; those which receive, gather, and summarize factual information and advise the secretary on the formulation of policy; and those which deal with international travel, *i.e.*, with passports and visas. The legal adviser of the department, whose office falls into all three categories suggested and who has about 30 assistants and clerks working under him, drafts and interprets treaties and other international agreements, gives advice on questions of municipal, foreign, and international law, handles diplomatic claims of American citizens against foreign States, and of foreign citizens against the United States, defends the United States in claims cases before arbitral tribunals, deals with questions of the legal rights of aliens in the United States and of Americans abroad, and with all questions of diplomatic privileges and immunities, citizenship, naturalization, expatriation, extradition, insurgency, belligerency, and neutrality. Among the other offices which fall within the category of agencies concerned with internal administration there may be mentioned first that of the chief clerk and administrative assistant who supervises the clerical personnel and property of the department and has charge of appropriations, salaries, expenses, classification of positions, and efficiency ratings. Under him are the appointment section, the stenographic section, the mail section, and the supply section. The four agencies mentioned in the preceding section as charged with the recruitment, training, and personnel management of the foreign service, are likewise part of the

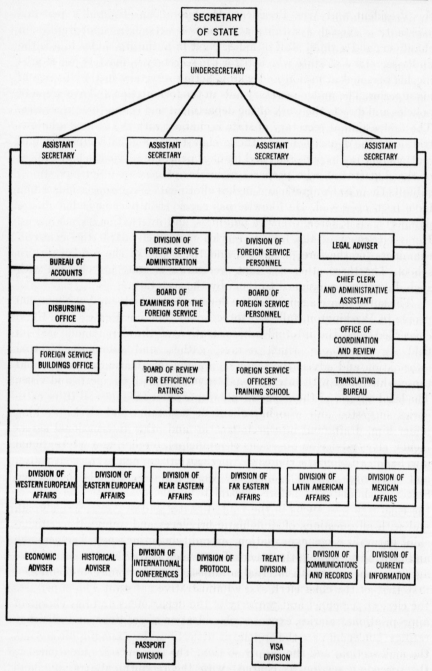

Organization of the American Department of State.

internal administrative machinery of the department. In the same category are the division of foreign service administration (divided into sections for administration, property, shipping, notarials, documentation, welfare, and miscellaneous, with four dispatch agencies at New York, New Orleans, San Francisco, and London) and the two district accounting and disbursing offices in Ottawa and Mexico City. The bureau of accounts, the translating bureau, the office of coordination and review, the foreign service buildings office, and disbursing office, and the board of review for efficiency ratings might likewise be placed in the same general category.

Among the fact-finding and policy-determining agencies are the six geographical divisions and various other agencies required to deal with particular matters of general interest. For purposes of receiving and filing dispatches and reports there are maintained the divisions of Far Eastern affairs, Near Eastern affairs, western European affairs, eastern European affairs, Latin American affairs, and Mexican affairs. The chief of each of these divisions must familiarize himself with the problems of his area and be in a position to advise the Secretary of State regarding current developments. The great mass of reports and dispatches coming into the department daily from its field agents all over the world is classified and filed according to these divisions. The economic adviser gathers information and makes recommendations regarding American economic interests abroad. The historical adviser similarly gives advice on the historical and geographical aspects of current problems. His office likewise has charge of the publication of diplomatic correspondence and of all of the work of the former division of publications, such as the editing of the *Foreign Relations of the United States, Treaties and Other International Acts of the United States*, the *Statutes at Large*, the *Register of the Department*, the *Foreign Service List*, *Press Releases*, etc. Its work is divided between an administrative office, a geographic section, a research section, an office for territorial papers, a library, a publishing section, a special documents section, a law section, an archives section, and a treaty section. The division of current information prepares news items for the press, receives and replies to inquiries from newspaper correspondents, and furnishes to officials daily press summaries and special articles. The division of international conferences is charged with arrangements for international conferences, congresses, expositions, and conventions in Washington and abroad, including appointment of delegates, preparation of estimates of expenses, allotment of appropriated funds, preparation and distribution of reports of American delegations, etc. The recently established division of protocol is charged with the arrangement of ceremonials, receptions, and official social functions, the supervision of the forms of diplomatic correspondence, and all questions of the honors, privileges, rights, and immunities of heads of States, diplomats, consuls, military and naval officers, and distinguished foreign visitors. The treaty division assists in the drafting of international agreements, keeps lists and records of international engagements, and furnishes information regarding the content, interpretation, and status of all international instruments. The large and important division of communications and records, which has over 150 members, is charged with the receipt and dispatch of all telegraphic correspondence of the department. It prepares codes and ciphers, codes and decodes messages, audits telegraph accounts, administers the telephone service, and classifies, records, distributes, and preserves all correspondence.

Two agencies of the department deal with the formalities of international travel. The passport division passes upon applications presented by American citizens for passports and for registration of individuals as American citizens in American consulates abroad. It issues passports and letters of introduction and deals with correspondence relating to citizenship, passports, registration, and rights of individuals to diplomatic protection abroad. It is made up of a correspondence reviewing section, a research section, a fraud section, a correspondence section, an examining section, a cashier's office, an information and record section, a transcribing section, a passport-writing section, and a passport-mailing section. It maintains passport agencies for the convenience of American citizens desiring to travel abroad in New York, Chicago, Boston, San Francisco, and Seattle. The visa division is charged with the administration of American immigration laws, "in so far as they concern the Department of State and its officers abroad." All American citizens going abroad must have an American passport, upon which is affixed a "visa" by a consul of the State which they plan to visit, authorizing them to enter its territory. Foreign nationals, similarly, are admitted to the United States only when their own passports have been visaed by American consuls abroad. This power to grant or refuse visas is used as a means of enforcing American immigration legislation.

This general pattern of organization is found, with minor variations, in other foreign offices. The British Foreign Office, located on Downing Street in London, is headed by the Secretary of State for Foreign Affairs, who is assisted by a permanent under-secretary of state, two parliamentary under-secretaries of state (both members of the House of Commons), a deputy under-secretary of state, two assistant under-secretaries of state, three legal advisers, a finance officer, a press officer, twelve counselors, and sundry other high assistants and secretaries. The subordinate staff in London has about 500 members, with several hundred additional officials and employees in the department of overseas trade, which is jointly administered by the Foreign Office and the Board of Trade. The agencies of internal administration include the chief clerk's department,

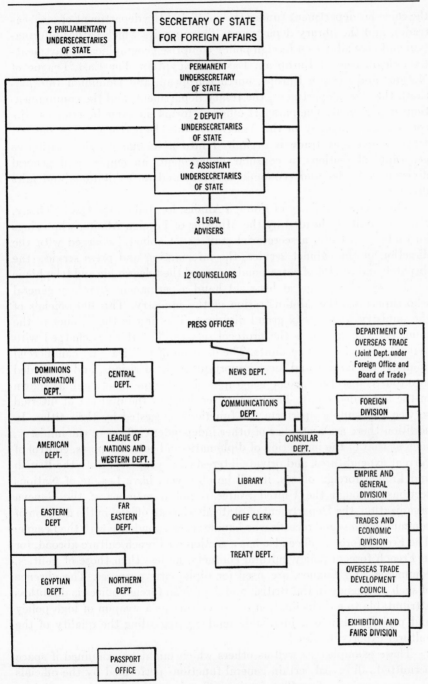

Organization of the British Foreign Office.

the consular department (under the control of the department of overseas trade), and the library department. The agencies which gather information and give advice on foreign policy comprise geographical departments (American, central European, Eastern, Egyptian, Far East, League of Nations and western Europe, north European, and Dominion Information), the news department, the treaty department, and the communications department. The passport office performs the same functions as the corresponding agency in the American State Department. The department of overseas trade is organized into a foreign division with five geographical sections, a consular department, an empire and general division, a trades and economic division, and an exhibitions and fairs division.

The French Ministry of Foreign Affairs, located on the Quai d'Orsay, Paris, is similarly headed by the Minister of Foreign Affairs, who brings into office with him a secretarial staff or "Cabinet," charged with the direction of the cabinet service, the information and press service, the dispatch and receipt of correspondence, and the telegraphic and telephonic service. He always has at his right hand a permanent secretary-general who supervises the administration of the ministry. The 400 officials of the ministry work in six grand divisions. The first is the cabinet of the minister. The second is the protocol service. The third is charged with personnel service and accounts. The division of political and commercial affairs is the largest and most important of the divisions, and is divided into fourteen sections, some geographical and some functional, as shown in the appended chart. The archive service and the division of internal service and supplies perform the functions suggested by their titles. In addition there are a number of other independent offices in the ministry, such as that of the inspection of diplomatic and consular posts, control of current expenditures, and private interests and property. Both the British and French foreign offices, it will be observed, have League of Nations sections. Though the United States is not a member of the Geneva organization, the Department of State also has an official in the division of communications and records who handles correspondence with the League. The French foreign office also has a section on French culture abroad, for in French foreign policy cultural contacts, no less than those of politics, commerce, and finance, are used for diplomatic purposes. The absence of such an agency in the British and American foreign offices is doubtless attributable to a disinclination to use culture as a weapon of high policy and perhaps also to a justifiable modesty regarding the quality of the cultural exports involved.

These examples, as well as others which might be examined if space permitted, all reveal certain general functions performed by the officials of every foreign office. The foreign office is in the first place a liaison agency between the executive branch of the government and the diplomatic and consular agents in the field. As such, it dispatches instructions, receives reports, keeps files and archives, and furnishes the secretary or minister with authoritative information and advice on developments in all parts of the world affecting the interests of the State. It likewise does

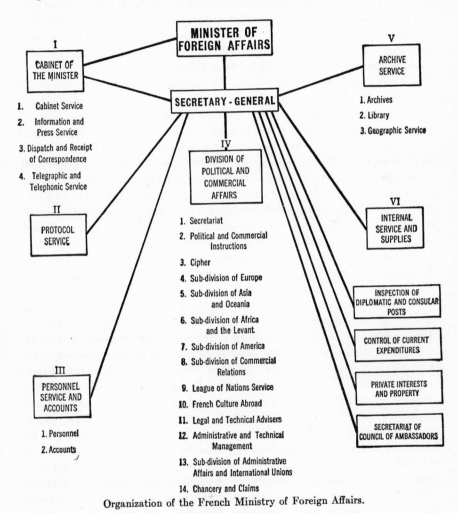

Organization of the French Ministry of Foreign Affairs.

what is necessary to facilitate communication with agents abroad and it acts as a recruiting, examining, and training agency for the foreign service. In the second place it is a liaison agency between the secretary or minister, on the one hand, and the public and the press on the other. Parliamentary under-secretaries, press officers, and sections of current information all function in this capacity. In the third place it serves as an expert staff through which the secretary or minister may secure such information and advice regarding the conduct of foreign affairs and the formulation of policy as does not come directly from the foreign-service officers abroad. Legal, economic, and historical advisers perform these services. Finally, it performs certain functions for citizens of the State: the issuance of passports, the publication of consular reports, the protection of nationals abroad, and the promotion of the economic interests of citizens in all parts of the world. Practically all of the functions of every foreign office fall into one or another of these broad categories.

It goes without saying that in all well-organized foreign offices the staff is part of a permanent bureaucracy which plays an important rôle in the determination of foreign policy, in spite of the fiction that the temporary political head of the department formulates the policies which his subordinates carry out as part of their routine administrative duties. A Secretary of State or a Minister of Foreign Affairs in most governments adhering to the forms of democracy is likely to be an amateur who may have had no diplomatic experience. He secures his position in the Cabinet by virtue of political services rendered to the party or parties in power. In all the technical duties of his office (and his duties are increasingly of a highly technical nature) he is, therefore, dependent upon the information and advice supplied by his professional expert subordinates who will in most cases have had extensive diplomatic experience and who will have become the custodians of tradition and the keepers of precedents. Since in most governments (though less so in the United States than elsewhere) there is an interchangeability of personnel between the foreign office and the foreign service, and since both are increasingly professionalized, the officials in the capital and the officials in the field are likely to see eye to eye on most important questions. The secretary or minister is usually constrained to accept the advice offered to him or to run the risk of making blunders or of creating friction between himself and his subordinates. The heads of important divisions often change with changes of administration, just as do ambassadors and ministers abroad, but the constant and insidious pressure of the permanent bureaucracy upon the formulation of policy can scarcely be overestimated. This is no less true at Washington than at Downing Street, Wilhelmstrasse, or the Quai d'Orsay. Those who are nominally charged with the formulation of foreign policy are thus hedged about on all sides by those who are in theory simple administrators. It is not astonishing then that the secretaries or ministers frequently become rubber stamps and that the permanent bureaucrats, acting behind the scenes, really determine policies. Here is one among many sources of power and pressure lying beneath the surface of foreign affairs which must be borne in mind constantly by all who would understand the dynamics of international politics.

5. CONSTITUTIONAL CONTROLS OF DIPLOMACY

> Foreign politics demand scarcely any of those qualities which a democracy possesses; and they require, on the contrary, the perfect use of almost all those faculties in which it is deficient.—ALEXIS DE TOCQUEVILLE, *Democracy in America.*

Quite apart from the influences brought to bear upon a foreign minister from within the ranks of his own subordinates and agents, there are pressures playing upon him constantly from without. These pressures operate through his colleagues in the cabinet, the president, the prime minister, or head of the State, the national legislature, the courts, the press, private lobbying agencies of all kinds, and "public opinion," The nature of the process by which foreign policy is formulated through the interaction of these pressures will be examined later in connection with the forces which drive States to action. Here, however, notice may be taken of the constitutional and legal forms which have developed within States for the conduct of foreign affairs. These forms determine the relationship between the foreign office and the other branches of the national government and they set up certain fixed patterns of procedure which must be complied with in the day-to-day handling of international business.

As has already been suggested, the foreign office in every State is always one of a dozen or more executive departments or ministries of the national administration. The head of it is always appointed by and is removable by the head of the national administration—by the President in the American governmental scheme, by the prime minister in the name of the king or president in parliamentary governments, by him who, in one capacity or another, wields the executive power in dictatorships. In parliamentary governments the prime minister may assume the post of foreign minister himself if he so desires, as did Ramsay MacDonald in the first Labor Cabinet in Great Britain in 1923. Chancellor Bruening of Germany also assumed the post of foreign minister, following the resignation of Foreign Minister Curtius in the fall of 1931. Many French premiers have taken for themselves the portfolio of the Quai d'Orsay. In any case, the foreign minister is the first official in the cabinet even when he is not the head of it. In parliamentary governments he will usually be a prominent leader of the party in power, or of one of the parties in a coalition, and he will have a seat in the national legislature. In so-called "presidential" governments, like that of the United States and most of the Latin American republics, he will not be a member of the legislature, but he will be a prominent party leader close to the president. In either instance he must perform the duties of his office in accordance with the provisions of the constitution and statutes dealing with the conduct of foreign affairs.

In almost all States, the national legislature is given a considerable measure of control over foreign relations. In the period of monarchial absolutism, the handling of foreign affairs was normally an exclusive prerogative of the executive, *i.e.*, of the king and his ministers. In the period of bourgeois democracy, the executive has been made responsible either to the legislature or to the voters and has been obliged to share this, as well as other functions, with representative, popularly elected assemblies. The American Constitution of 1787 was one of the first of modern constitutional documents to give large powers over foreign relations to the national legislature. Under its provisions, Congress has power over diplomatic appointments, treaties, and declarations of war. The President "shall nominate, and, by and with the advice and consent of the Senate, shall appoint ambassadors, other public ministers, and consuls" (Article II, Section 2, §2). Diplomatic and consular appointments are thus subject to the confirmation of a majority of the upper chamber of Congress, except where Congress, by statute, has vested this power in the President alone or in the Secretary of State, as has been done with regard to all the subordinate positions in the foreign service. The President has power "by and with the advice and consent of the Senate, to make treaties, provided two-thirds of the Senators present concur" (Article II, Section 2, §2). In practice the President and his agents in the Department of State and the foreign service negotiate treaties without legislative participation in the process, but he may not constitutionally ratify treaties without the approval of two-thirds of the Senators. The President is commander-in-chief of the army, the navy, and the militia, but Congress has power to raise and support armies, to provide and maintain a navy, and to declare war by a majority vote of both houses (Article I, Sections 8, 11, 12, 13). In all of these respects, Congress is given express power over foreign affairs by the Constitution. Its general powers of legislation and appropriation have also been used to influence foreign relations. General Congressional resolutions on foreign policy may be ignored by the President, but Congress may grant or withhold money for diplomatic missions and for the enforcement of treaties and it may, by legislation, carry out treaties, refuse to carry them out, or abrogate them.

It is now well established as a matter of general constitutional practice that all powers over foreign affairs not expressly granted to the legislature by the Constitution are exercised by the executive. The diplomatic recognition of new States or governments and the issuance of neutrality proclamations, for example, are both functions performed by the President and Secretary of State without Congressional participation. Even with regard to those powers which the President must share with Congress, the course of developments has tended to place more and more power in the President's hands. President Washington, taking the Constitution very literally, endeavored to collaborate with the Senate in the negotiation of treaties as well as in their ratification. But when, in 1796, the Senators manifested a desire to have him withdraw his imposing presence from the chamber in order that they might consider by themselves the negotiation of an Indian treaty, he walked out and said he'd be damned if he ever came before them again on such business. None of his successors has ever consulted the Senate as a body during the course of treaty negotiations. Prior to 1815 the President submitted to the Senate for confirmation the names of special diplomatic representatives named to negotiate important treaties. But ever since the Senators embarrassed President Madison by refusing to confirm the appointment of Secretary of the Treasury Gallatin as one of the negotiators of the Treaty of Ghent, the President has ordinarily made such appointments without consulting the Senate. Treaties are now submitted to the Senate only after they have been signed. As Secretary of State Hay once observed, they are like bulls going into the arena, with no assurance that they will emerge alive. Friction between the President and the Senate over treaties has been chronic in the conduct of American foreign affairs, for two-thirds of the Senators are never of the President's party. But if an international engagement does not require legislation or appropriations, the President can escape the constitutional requirement of Senatorial ratification by concluding an "executive agreement" which may achieve the same purpose. Similarly, the power of Congress over declarations of war means less in practice than in theory, for the President, as spokesman of the nation and as commander of the armed forces, can easily create diplomatic or military situations which leave Congress no genuine freedom of choice. On innumerable occasions American forces have engaged in hostilities abroad without Congressional authorization of any kind. All of the formally declared wars in which the United States has engaged, with the possible exception of the Spanish-American War, were embarked upon at the initiative of the executive branch of the government. In practice, therefore, the conduct of American foreign affairs is in the hands of the President, subject to constitutional checks which often lead to friction between the executive and legislature, but which give Congress no real authority to initiate and direct diplomatic action.

Much the same situation prevails in parliamentary governments, though the responsibility of the executive to the legislature leaves less room for friction than is possible under the American check-and-balance system and the legislature is nowhere given such extensive control as in the United States. In Great Britain, the Cabinet has full authority over foreign affairs, though the House of Commons may, of course, vote it out of office if it is dissatisfied with its foreign policies. This is true of all parliamentary governments, but this power of the legislature is obviously not a very effective or subtle weapon for controlling foreign relations. Diplomatic appointments in Great Britain are not confirmed by the legislature. Treaties are made and ratified by the Cabinet in the name of the King, but important political treaties are sometimes submitted to Parliament for discussion and approval before the act of ratification takes place. Parliamentary objections to the Anglo-Soviet agreement of 1924 led to the fall of the first Labor Cabinet in the autumn of that year. Decisions of war and peace are also made by the Cabinet. As a matter of well-established convention Parliament is always consulted before a formal declaration of war is issued, though hostilities are frequently embarked upon in the absence of a formal declaration without parliamentary authorization. The French Constitution of 1875 gives the President of the Republic, *i.e.*, the Cabinet, acting in the President's name, the power to negotiate and ratify treaties, to appoint diplomatic representatives, and to dispose of the armed forces of the State (Law of July 16, 1875, Article 8; Law of February 25, 1875, Article 3). Certain treaties are valid only when approved by a majority of the Senators and the Deputies: those relating to territory, peace, commerce, finances, and personal and property rights of Frenchmen abroad. It is significant that important political engagements, like treaties of alliance, do not require legislative approval and may even be kept secret for long periods of time. In France as elsewhere initiative and control in foreign affairs rest with the executive, with legislative checks being of less practical importance than the Constitution might seem to indicate.

A word or two may be added regarding the position of the courts in foreign relations. The American Constitution (Article VI, Section 2) declares that all treaties made under the authority of the United States shall be regarded, along with the Constitution itself and laws of the United States which shall be made in pursuance thereof, as "the supreme law of the land; and the judges in every state shall be bound thereby, anything in the constitutions or laws of any state to the contrary notwithstanding." This means that all American courts, both state and federal, enforce treaties as law in cases which come before them requiring their application. State statutes contrary to treaties are held unconstitutional by the federal courts. As between a conflicting federal statute and a treaty, the courts enforce the most recent in point of time, since the Constitution places treaties and federal laws in the same category and Congress clearly has the right, under American constitutional law, to abrogate treaties by legislative act. In accordance with the "doctrine of political questions," however, the federal courts accept the interpretation placed upon treaties by the political branch, *i.e.*, the executive branch, of the government. The same applies to the enforcement of customary international law in American courts. In most other States treaties and international law are likewise enforced in the courts, though sometimes only when they have been enacted into statutory form. In the absence of the judicial review of legislation in most other governments, the executive and the legislature are fully responsible for the observance of the international obligations of the State.

In summary, the constitutional arrangements of most modern States require some form of legislative participation in diplomacy, but initiative and control still remain for the most part in the hands of the executive. Whatever degree of "democratization" of foreign policy has been attained has been achieved by imposing legislative checks upon the freedom of action of the executive and by making the executive responsible to the legislature as in Great Britain, France, and Germany, or to the electorate, as in the United States. Direct popular control over foreign affairs is by its nature unworkable. In Switzerland, to be sure, certain treaties must be ratified by popular referendum and the Utopian French Constitution of June 24, 1793 (which was never put into operation in this respect), required a vote of popular assemblies in the communes for all declarations of war. Popular referenda on questions of foreign policy are, by common consent, impracticable. Such responsibility to the electorate as exists is enforced through legislative action and through the popular election of policy-determining officials. In both cases, such responsibility is vague and intangible and control continues to reside in the executive officials and in the diplomatic bureaucracy of the foreign offices and the field services.

SUGGESTED READINGS

Corwin, E. S.: *The President's Control of Foreign Relations*, Princeton, Princeton University Press, 1917.

Dangerfield, R. J.: *In Defense of the Senate*, Norman, Okla., University of Oklahoma Press, 1933.

Dunn, F. S.: *The Practice and Procedure of International Conferences*, Baltimore, Johns Hopkins Press, 1929.

Fleming, D. F.: *The Treaty Veto of the American Senate*, New York, G. P. Putnam's Sons, 1930.

Flournoy, F. R.: *Parliament and War*, London, King, 1927.

Heatley, D. P.: *Diplomacy and the Study of International Relations*, New York, Oxford University Press, 1919.

Hill, N.: *The Public International Conference*, Palo Alto, Stanford University Press, 1929.

Lay, T. H.: *The Foreign Service of the United States*, New York, Prentice-Hall, Inc., 1932.

Mathews, J. M.: *American Foreign Relations, Conduct and Policies*, New York, Century Company, 1928.

Ponsonby, A.: *Democracy and Diplomacy*, London, Methuen & Co., 1915.

Poole, D. O.: *Conduct of Foreign Relations under Modern Democratic Conditions*, New Haven, Yale University Press, 1924.

Satow, E.: *A Guide to Diplomatic Practice*, New York, Longmans, Green & Co., 1922.

Schuman, F. L.: *War and Diplomacy in the French Republic*, New York, McGraw-Hill Book Company, Inc., 1931.

Wright, Q.: *The Control of American Foreign Relations*, New York, The Macmillan Company, 1922.

Young, G.: *Diplomacy, Old and New*, New York, Harcourt, Brace & Company, 1921.

CHAPTER VI

THE SETTLEMENT OF INTERNATIONAL DISPUTES

IN THE evolution of the Western State System there have been developed patterns of procedures and institutions for the settlement of controversies between States no less worthy of the attention of the observer of international politics than the principles of law and the forms of diplomacy which have been reviewed. Some of these methods for the adjustment of international disputes have already been suggested. In the present chapter an effort will be made to survey existing mechanisms and procedures in logical sequence, from the crude and primitive methods which were first utilized by States to the complex and highly developed institutions of arbitration and adjudication of recent times. In terms of such a sequence, the available methods can conveniently be divided into five categories: (1) enforcement of rights by self-help, (2) settlement by negotiation, (3) settlement by methods approaching arbitration, (4) arbitration, and (5) adjudication. These categories will form the divisions of the present chapter, which will be concluded with a résumé of the provisions of recent treaties for the pacific settlement of disputes.

It should perhaps be noted at the outset that the five categories suggested involve five more or less distinct methods of dealing with controversies between States. In the first—self-help—each party seeks to impose its will on the other by coercive measures. In the ensuing clash of wills, might makes right and the weaker yields to the stronger. In settlement by negotiation, the disputants discuss and bargain over their differences and seek to arrive at a mutually satisfactory adjustment. Negotiation may also involve pressure and threats of coercion and the result will usually reflect the relative power of the States concerned. But, in form at least, dictation is replaced by compromise and mutual concessions. In the use of methods approaching arbitration, the parties to the controversies appoint special agencies to conduct discussions or investigations for them in a spirit of impartiality and to make recommendations for the settlement of the dispute. The bargaining here is not directly between the diplomatic representatives of the disputing States, but between delegates who have been made members of commissions entrusted with the task of ascertaining the facts and of making a report on the basis of their findings. In true arbitration the parties agree in advance to submit the dispute to the judgment of an impartial third party, either a third

State or a tribunal of individuals set up for the purpose, whose award will be accepted as binding upon the litigants. In adjudication, the most recent and advanced method of settlement, the parties have recourse to a permanent judicial agency which examines the facts, hears the arguments, and hands down a judgment accepted as final by both parties in accordance with their preliminary agreement. These methods of dealing with differences between States correspond to the historical development of methods of settling controversies between individuals: first, the duel, or trial by battle; second, discussion and compromise; third, settlement outside of court through a meeting of agents; fourth, resort to friends or neighbors as impartial moderators; and finally, recourse to courts, with juries to find facts and judges to apply the law of the land. In both cases, the progression is from a primitive procedure in which the disputing parties seek to browbeat one another into submission to a complicated procedure of litigation and judicial settlement through permanent institutions established for this purpose.

1. SELF-HELP

> Fury said to a mouse that he met in the house, "Let us both go to law:
> *I* will prosecute *you.*—Come, I'll take no denial: we must have the trial;
> for really this morning I have nothing to do." Said the mouse to the cur,
> "Such a trial, dear sir, with no jury or judge would be wasting our breath."
> "I'll be judge, I'll be jury," said cunning old Fury; "I'll try the whole
> cause and condemn you to death."—LEWIS CARROLL, *Alice in Wonderland.*

The rights and obligations of States received reasonably clear definition long before there existed any established procedures for their enforcement. It is sometimes held to be a principle of private law that there is no right without a remedy. If this notion were applied to international law, it would mean that States had no genuine rights at all throughout the whole formative period of modern international jurisprudence. It would be more accurate to say, however, that the observance of the rights of States depended upon their power and ability to compel respect on the part of other States. In the development of private law, remedies were established simultaneously with rights and even in some cases antedated clear definitions of rights. In international law, on the other hand, because of the peculiar nature of the relations between independent sovereignties, legal rights were recognized long before adequate remedies for their protection came into being. In the absence of a superstate or a supreme international authority to enforce international law, in the absence even of settled procedures for the enforcement of rights between particular States, all States were obliged to rely upon their own strength and upon their ability to resist and coerce their neighbors as means of protecting themselves. The promptings of ambition, the will to power, the lust for conquest, the pursuit of national interests all dictated coercion as a method of dealing with other States quite as much as did considerations of legal rights. States sought (and still seek) security and the realization of their aspirations by efforts to impose their will upon one another by force. Each State resorts to self-help, *i.e.*, to its own power and resources, in its attempts to protect its rights and interests.

War is obviously the ultimate means of coercion in interstate relations. In war the belligerents each act as policeman, judge, jury, sheriff, and executioner all in one. Questions of legal rights and obligations may be raised on both sides at the beginning of war as excuses, rationalizations, pretexts, or plausible formulations of interests in the pursuit of which war seems preferable to surrender or compromise. War is a means of settling disputes only in the sense that after an appropriate interval of bloodshed and destruction, the weaker party will be disposed to yield to the stronger or both will fall exhausted and agree to a compromise settlement which seemed unacceptable so long as each felt optimistic about imposing its will on the other. The terms of peace will set up new legal relationships between the disputants, reflecting the verdict of arms and destined to be more or less durable, depending upon the wisdom of the victors, the weakness of the vanquished, and subsequent shifts of power relationships. If neither side has succeeded in imposing its will on the other, the terms of the peace may make no reference to the original dispute at all. Such was the case with the Treaty of Ghent in 1814, which terminated the Anglo-American War of 1812. Under such circumstances, the dispute is "settled" by common agreement to say no more about it. In other instances, the dispute is not settled at all, is disposed of by the subjugation of one of the parties, or disappears in the face of new disputes arising out of the war and the peace. That war is the most completely unsatisfactory method of settling disputes scarcely calls for demonstration in the third decade of the twentieth century. If war were to be judged on such grounds, it would have been banished long ago. But States generally resort to war not in the conviction that it represents the best mode of adjusting a controversy, but because armed coercion is an instrument of State power and a means of protecting and promoting the political interests of the State, quite apart from questions of legal rights.

There are various methods of hostile redress short of war which also involve a resort to self-help and an element of coercion. These may be broadly classified as threats of force, acts of retorsion, and acts of reprisal. Threats of force may take the form of military, naval, or aerial maneuvers, mobilization, the dispatch of an ultimatum, the severance of diplomatic relations, and the like. None of these is either injurious in fact to the other party or a violation of his legal rights, but is a more or less violent gesture designed to frighten the other party into a more tractable frame of mind. Needless to say, most wars break out after one or both parties to a controversy have made threats of force which fail to produce the desired result, but which cannot be revoked because of considerations of national honor and vital interests. Acts of retorsion are definitely injurious to the other party, though not in violation of his legal rights. Such measures are always within the bounds of customary international law and are performed entirely within the jurisdiction of the State taking such action. Discriminatory tariff duties or penalties, the suspension of commercial intercourse, and the use of an economic boycott are common examples. In 1808–1809 the Jefferson administration enforced an embargo on American trade with Great Britain and France as a means of bringing their governments to terms in the controversies over neutral rights. In this case the measure of retorsion was unsuccessful and the United States suffered more than its victims. In recent years China has frequently resorted to economic boycotts against the western Powers with varying results. The anti-Japanese boycott of 1931–1932 was an act of retorsion in retaliation for the Japanese military occupation of Manchuria. Such acts are not, in and of themselves, violations of the customary legal rights of the victim State, though they sometimes involve breaches of treaty obligations and often lead to violent incidents. When the victim retaliates in kind, grave consequences may easily ensue.

Acts of reprisal, as distinct from retorsion and threats of force, are in patent violation of the legal rights of the other party. Prior to the abolition of privateering by the Declaration of Paris of 1856[1] it was usual for States to authorize private reprisals by issuing "letters of marque and reprisal" to their nationals with unsatisfied financial claims against a foreign State. Such individuals were then free to plunder the commerce of the other State up to the amount of their claims. In 1832 President Jackson urged Congress to authorize the seizure of goods from French vessels on the high seas as a means of compelling France to meet her financial obligations to the United States. Reprisals of this type are, happily, no longer permissible. Public reprisals, however, are still recognized as a legitimate method of redress. They may take the form of hostile embargoes, pacific blockades, acts of intervention, and acts of overt hostility indistinguishable from war in everything but name. An embargo is hostile, i.e., a violation of the rights of its victim and therefore an act of reprisal rather than of retorsion, when it takes the form of the seizure of the ships or goods of nationals of the other State. This practice is now looked upon with disfavor and even on the outbreak of war enemy merchant vessels in port are usually allowed "days of grace" within which they may depart unmolested. A blockade consists of action by naval forces to intercept commerce. A war blockade may be applied to vessels of

[1] See above, p. 153.

all States entering or leaving the blockaded ports. A "pacific" blockade, however, must be limited in its enforcement to the vessels of the parties to the controversy and cannot lawfully be extended to vessels of third States. The first modern instance of this practice was the pacific blockade of Greece by the Powers in 1827. This led to the great naval battle of Navarino, in which the Turkish-Egyptian fleet was destroyed, but war was not declared and the blockade was applied only to Greek and Turkish vessels and to those of the flag of the blockading States. New Granada was subjected to a pacific blockade by Great Britain in 1836, Mexico by France in 1838, Greece by Great Britain in 1850, China by France in 1884, Greece by Great Britain, Germany, Austria, Italy, and Russia in 1886, Zanzibar by Portugal in 1888, Crete by the Powers in 1897, Venezuela by Great Britain, Germany, and Italy in 1902, Soviet Russia by the other Powers in 1918–1921, etc. Most pacific blockades are directed by Great Powers against small ones, too weak to resort to war or to retaliate effectively. Those directed against strong States usually lead to war.

All acts of intervention are acts of reprisal, when they are resorted to as a means of bringing diplomatic pressure to bear upon their victim and when they are unaccompanied by any intention of creating a legal state of war. In 1914 the United States bombarded and occupied Vera Cruz and two years later it sent a military expedition into northern Mexico, in both instances disclaiming any intention of making war. The American interventions in the Caribbean States have been similar in character. The attack of the Powers upon the Shimonoseki forts (Japan) in 1863, the allied expedition against Pekin in 1901, and the Italian bombardment of Corfu in 1923 are other examples. The military occupation of the Ruhr valley in 1923 was likewise an act of reprisal for German nonpayment of reparations, though the French and Belgian Governments insisted that they were authorized to take such action by the Treaty of Versailles. In January and February of 1932 Japanese military and naval forces, in retaliation against the Chinese boycott, bombarded and occupied Shanghai, after several weeks of severe fighting. In every such case, the victim whose rights are violated may regard the act as a *casus belli* and resort to war. The act itself does not automatically create a state of war, regardless of how much fighting takes place, unless one party or the other expresses an intention to make war. These various forms of pressure may thus be indistinguishable in fact from actual war, but they are "pacific" in the sense that a legal state of war is not inaugurated by them.[1]

[1] On the present legal status of war see p. 685 below.

2. NEGOTIATION

All government, indeed every human benefit and enjoyment, every virtue and every prudent act, is founded on compromise and barter.—
EDMUND BURKE, *On Conciliation with America*, March 22, 1775.

If the parties to a dispute are disposed to discuss their differences rather than to threaten one another or to fight about them, they will resort to negotiation as a means of settlement. Negotiations may be conducted through diplomacy, through conference, or through the services of third States offering good offices or mediation. In the first instance the regular diplomatic channels may be utilized for an exchange of views in an effort to reach an adjustment. The foreign minister of either State may call in the ambassador or minister of the other for consultation. Or the two foreign ministers may confer with one another directly. Or they may appoint special agents, publicly or secretly, to carry on discussions. If an agreement is reached it may be incorporated into an exchange of notes or some more formal international engagement. If negotiations are unsuccessful, other methods of settlement may be resorted to. The conduct of negotiations is essentially a bargaining process, for there can be no successful settlement by this method without give-and-take on both sides. Legal rights will be argued, but considerations of State power, equity, and political expediency will also be thrown into the scales. Each side will necessarily strive to attain maximum advantages with minimum concessions to the other. The respective foreign offices formulate their own claims and, by a more or less prolonged exchange of diplomatic correspondence, fence and parry with one another until some consensus of views is reached or until the negotiations break down in failure. In all negotiations the contending States remain judges of their own cases. The time consumed, however, allows an interval for popular passions to cool and facilitates compromise. When negotiations are conducted openly and irreconcilable claims are made public, it frequently becomes impossible for foreign ministers or diplomats to recede from the position which they have taken, particularly when patriotic zeal has been aroused over the controversy. Secret diplomacy obviates this difficulty, though it may lead to others even more undesirable. The great majority of international disputes are settled by diplomacy and it may be viewed as the normal method of dealing with international differences.

In the settlement of disputes by conference, as distinct from diplomacy, recourse is had to special representatives, specifically chosen to deal with the particular controversy, rather than to the regular diplomatic service. It is also customary in international conferences to draw up an agenda or list of subjects to which the discussion is to be limited, while in diplomatic correspondence each side may draw into the case the whole range of national interests, including many matters subsidiary to, or even irrelevant to, the main question at issue. States participating in international conferences frequently insist upon the exclusion from the agenda of certain problems upon which they are especially sensitive. The United States, for example, has frequently refused to discuss the Monroe Doctrine or the international law of intervention at the Pan-American Conferences. In the Washington Conference of 1921–1922 Japan insisted upon excluding the status of Shantung and the famous twenty-one demands of 1915 from the discussion. This limitation of the agenda often serves to expedite a settlement, though it is not always easy to exclude extraneous questions from the proceedings and when they are so excluded irritation and resentment may be engendered rather than reduced. Settlement by conference has become increasingly common, as has been pointed out above.[1]

When two States are unable to reach any agreement with regard to a pending controversy, and relations between them become "strained," it is permissible for outside States to offer their services in an effort to facilitate a settlement. If such interposition is dictatorial in character, it constitutes intervention. But if it is purely advisory, it cannot be regarded as an unfriendly act. Neither can the third State take offense if its offer is declined. A "tender of good offices" is usually nothing more than a mere polite inquiry as to whether the third State can be of service in preserving or restoring peace. It is often extended at the request of one of the parties to the controversy and is frequently made after a rupture of diplomatic relations or in the course of a war, as a means of restoring communication between the parties. If a tender of good offices is accepted on both sides, the third State may transmit suggestions for a settlement between the parties or may make such suggestions itself. In the latter case, true mediation occurs. Good offices consist of an invitation to resume discussions. Mediation, which normally follows an acceptance of good offices, consists of the actual transmission of suggestions. The mediating State does not seek to impose a settlement on the parties, but attempts rather to create the atmosphere and the means necessary for a settlement. In 1813 the Russian Government offered its mediation to Great Britain and the United States in an effort to terminate the war which had broken out in the preceding year. The United States at once accepted the offer and sent commissioners to St. Petersburg to negotiate, but the British Government declined to reciprocate. Peace negotiations were finally opened by direct conversations between the parties. In 1905 President Roosevelt made a tender of good offices to Russia and Japan, then at war. The offer was accepted on both sides. The United States then acted as mediator and arranged a peace conference at Portsmouth, New Hampshire. Its sugges-

[1] See pp. 166–168 above.

tions were instrumental in enabling the belligerents to come to an agreement and frame a peace treaty.

The first Convention of the first Hague Peace Conference of 1899 contained a number of provisions regarding good offices and mediation, in addition to providing for the creation of the Hague Permanent Court of Arbitration. In its revised form, as amended by the second Conference of 1907, it provided that the contracting Powers "agree to have recourse, as far as circumstances allow, to the good offices or mediation of one or more friendly Powers" in cases of serious disagreements or disputes between them. All Powers were recognized to have the right to offer good offices and mediation to disputants. "The exercise of this right shall never be regarded by one or the other of the parties in conflict as an unfriendly act."[1] The function of a mediator was declared to be that of "reconciling the opposing claims and appeasing the feelings of resentment which may have arisen between the States at variance." It was made clear that mediation is purely advisory and that the function of the would-be mediator is at an end as soon as his suggestions are declined by either party. The convention likewise made provision for a plan of mediation (never subsequently utilized) whereby disputing States were to refer the controversy to two designated mediating Powers which would have exclusive control over efforts to achieve a settlement for a period of thirty days.

The term "conciliation" is frequently used to refer to the sequel of successful mediation, i.e., to the process whereby an outside party promotes an agreement between contending States. This procedure has been institutionalized in the League of Nations Covenant, which makes the Council an agency of conciliation.[2] The members of the League agree by Article 15 to submit to the Council "any dispute likely to lead to a rupture which is not submitted to arbitration or judicial settlement." The Council is authorized to endeavor to settle the dispute. If its report is unanimously agreed to by its members, other than the representatives of the disputing States, the "members of the League agree that they will not go to war with any party to the dispute which complies with the recommendations of the report." In the absence of unanimity, "the members of the League reserve to themselves the right to take such action as they shall consider necessary for the maintenance of right and justice." The dispute in question may be referred to the Assembly of the League and must be so referred at the request of either party, if the request is made within fourteen days after the submission of the dispute to the Council. Only one dispute has been referred from the Council to the

[1] Article 11 of the League of Nations Covenant declares that it is "the friendly right of each member of the League to bring to the attention of the Assembly or of the Council any circumstance whatever affecting international relations which threatens to disturb international peace or the good understanding between nations upon which peace depends."

[2] See Covenant, Articles 10 to 17, Appendix VI, pp. 900–903 below.

Assembly in this fashion—that between China and Japan of 1931–1932, which came before the extraordinary session of the Assembly of March, 1932. Since the Council is a smaller and more expeditious body, it is unlikely that the Assembly will succeed in settling a dispute when the Council has failed, and this proved to be the case in the instance cited. While the Assembly's Committee of Nineteen did succeed in bringing about the signature of an armistice and the Japanese evacuation of Shanghai, it failed, as the Council had failed, to achieve a settlement of the Manchurian problem which was the original cause of the conflict.[1]

3. METHODS APPROACHING ARBITRATION

It becomes a wise man to try everything that he can do by words, before having resort to arms.—TERENCE, *Eunuchus.*

With respect to certain types of international controversies, States are willing to resort to methods of settlement which are in advance of negotiation in the sense that recourse is had to more or less impartial tribunals of adjustment, but which fall short of arbitration or adjudication in that the disputants are unwilling to bind themselves in advance to accept such recommendations as may be made. These procedures can conveniently be described as methods approaching arbitration. In every instance the parties remain free to accept or reject the solution proposed by the agencies which they have created. These procedures fall into the categories of mixed commissions, commissions of inquiry, and commissions of conciliation.

A mixed commission is a body of representatives chosen by two disputing governments to make recommendations for its settlement. It consists of an even number of delegates, half chosen by each side—an arrangement which compels the members either to agree to disagree or to come to a definitive settlement. The members of mixed commissions are usually technical experts, qualified to ascertain the facts of the controversy. One of the most interesting instances of recourse to this procedure is presented by the Alaska boundary dispute between the United States and Great Britain. The American Government, after its purchase of Alaska from Russia in 1867, interpreted the treaty of cession and the Russo-British treaty of 1825 to mean that the "pan-handle" boundary shut off Canada from access to the sea north of 54° 40′. The Klondike gold discoveries of 1897 made access to the sea appear extremely desirable to Canadian prospectors and to the Government of the Dominion. The Canadian authorities therefore disputed the American contention. Both sides refused to yield. President Roosevelt declined to arbitrate the dispute, but in 1903 finally agreed to submit it to a mixed commission of three Americans and three Britishers. Of the Britishers, two were Canadians and one, Lord Alverstone, was an Englishman whose views, President Roosevelt

[1] See pp. 782–791 below.

felt certain, were favorable to the American claim. The American case was argued before the commission by John W. Foster, a former Secretary of State, after Ambassador Choate, American representative at the Court of St. James, refused to act as the American attorney on the ground of the diplomatic impropriety of his appearing in such a rôle. In the decision of October 20, 1903, the three American members voted solidly to sustain the American view and the two Canadians voted to sustain the Canadian view, both groups thus acting as political representatives rather than as impartial experts. Lord Alverstone voted in favor of the American contentions, which were consequently supported by a vote of four to two. This recommendation was not, of course, legally binding, but it was accepted on both sides as the basis for a settlement.

A commission of inquiry differs from a mixed commission in that it usually consists of an odd number of members and limits itself to fact-finding. Its findings are again purely recommendations. This method of settlement was first provided for by general international agreement in the Convention for the Pacific Settlement of International Disputes drawn up at the first Hague Conference. The convention declared in part:

> In differences of an international nature involving neither honor nor vital interests, and arising from a difference of opinion on points of fact, the signatory powers recommend that the parties who have not been able to come to an agreement by means of diplomacy should, as far as circumstances allow, institute an international commission of inquiry, to facilitate a solution of these differences by elucidating the facts by means of an impartial and conscientious investigation. (Article 9.)

The scheme of settlement here proposed was based upon a procedure whereby the parties to a dispute would, by special agreement, set up a commission of inquiry, designate the questions to be put to it, and indicate the rules to be followed. The commission would make an investigation, hear both sides, call witnesses and experts, and prepare a report limited to a statement of facts, leaving the parties "entire freedom as to the effect to be given to the statement." This procedure was first applied in the Dogger Bank affair of 1904. A Russian squadron, proceding through the North Sea on its way to the Far East in the course of the Russo-Japanese War, fired upon a number of British trawlers under the impression that they were Japanese torpedo boats. In Great Britain, ally of Japan since 1902, a popular clamor for war commenced at once and the Government demanded immediate explanations and reparations from Russia. The two States agreed to submit the questions of fact connected with the incident to a commission of inquiry of five members, consisting of British, Russian, American, and French naval officers with a fifth member (an officer in the Austro-Hungarian navy) chosen by the other four. The commission met at Paris and published its report on February 25, 1905. It found the

Russian squadron at fault and the Russian Government paid an indemnity of £65,000. The same procedure was resorted to by Germany and the Netherlands with regard to responsibility for the sinking of a Dutch steamer in 1916. The commission here found that the vessel was sunk by a torpedo fired by a German submarine and an indemnity was likewise paid. Resort to the procedure outlined in the Hague Convention was not in any sense obligatory and the commissions were not permanent agencies, but merely *ad hoc* bodies set up for each particular controversy.

In an effort to institutionalize this procedure the United States, through Secretary of State Bryan, proposed to other States in 1913 the negotiation of a series of bilateral treaties which should set up permanent boards or commissions of conciliation to which all disputes, without exception, should be submitted. These commissions were to consist of five members: two nationals of the parties, two chosen by the parties from among foreign nationals, and the fifth selected by agreement. The commissions were to be given a year's time to report, during which period the parties agreed not to resort to hostilities. Thirty of the so-called Bryan "cooling-off" treaties were negotiated and twenty-one came into force— nine with European States, eleven with Latin American States, and one with China. Only ten commissions were set up. None of them was ever utilized for the settlement of any dispute and the entire scheme has been allowed to lapse. This effort to create permanent commissions of conciliation thus bore no immediate fruits, although the principle in question reappears in a number of post-war treaties.

4. ARBITRATION

It is impossible to attack as a transgressor him who offers to lay his grievance before a tribunal of arbitration.—ARCHIDAMUS, King of Sparta.

If a difficulty should arise between the aforesaid cities, which cannot easily be settled by themselves, it shall be decided by the arbitration of the Sovereign Pontiff; and if one of the parties violates the treaty, we agree that His Holiness shall excommunicate the offending city.—Treaty between Venice and Genoa, 1235.

In all of the procedures sketched above, the disputing States remain free to accept or reject the recommendations made. It is of the essence of true arbitration that the parties bind themselves in advance to submit their differences to an impartial arbitrator or to an arbitral tribunal and to accept the award as binding. Article 37 of the Hague Convention for the Pacific Settlement of International Disputes defined arbitration as follows:

International arbitration has for its object the settlement of disputes between States by judges of their own choice, and on the basis of respect for law. Recourse to arbitration implies an engagement to submit in good faith to the award. (Article 37 of the first convention of 1907.)

This definition involves four elements which are the distinguishing features of genuine international arbitration: (1) settlement of disputes between States through their own voluntary action, (2) by judges of their own choice, (3) on the basis of respect for law, and (4) with an obligation to accept the award as binding. The last-named element distinguishes arbitration sharply from the methods dealt with above, in which recommendations are purely advisory. The phrase "respect for law" implies that arbitrators are free to consider extralegal aspects of a controversy, if this will contribute toward a settlement, and are not bound to apply the strict letter of international law to the case before them. C. C. Hyde defines international arbitration as "an impartial adjudication according to law, and that before a tribunal of which at least a single member, who is commonly a national of a state neutral to the contest, acts as umpire."[1] This suggests that the process of arbitration is identical with that of adjudication except as to the method of choosing judges. In practice, arbitral tribunals have usually acted as judicial bodies and have applied the principles of international law to the controversies submitted to them. It remains true, nevertheless, that arbitrators have more discretion than judges of a court and may apply principles of equity and justice, as well as political considerations, in making their award—a procedure inadmissable in a genuine judicial body.

Arbitration as a method of settling international disputes is of great antiquity. As was pointed out in the first chapter of this study, the earliest treaty of which any record remains was an arbitration treaty and the practice of arbitration was extensively resorted to in the State Systems preceding the present one, particularly among the Greeks. During the medieval period there were numerous papal arbitrations and an appreciable number of secular arbitrations between temporal rulers. Between 1500 and 1800, however, arbitration went out of fashion as a mode of adjusting differences, except for a few seventeenth century English arbitration treaties negotiated by Cromwell. The practice was revived in the Jay Treaty of 1794 between Great Britain and the United States. By this instrument, four commissions were set up: to locate the source of the Mississippi, to settle the St. Croix River boundary, to pass upon the claims of British subjects for pre-revolutionary mercantile debts confiscated by the United States, and to judge of reciprocal claims arising out of the seizure of American vessels by British cruisers and the capture of British merchantmen by French privateers fitted out in American ports. These commissions were really arbitral tribunals, with the exception of the first, which might be better described as a commission of inquiry. The first failed in its object. The second located the St. Croix River to the

---

[1] *International Law Chiefly as Interpreted and Applied by the United States*, II, pp. 111–112.

satisfaction of both parties, subject to certain later readjustments of the boundary. The third failed to agree upon an award, but by the convention of 1802 the British Government agreed to accept $2,664,000 in settlement of the claims in question. The fourth awarded $11,650,000 to the American claimants and $143,428 to the British claimants. Between 1794 and 1900 it has been estimated that there were no less than 400 international arbitrations, of which the most spectacular was doubtless the arbitration at Geneva, under the terms of the Treaty of Washington of 1871, of the claims of the United States against Great Britain for violations of neutral obligations during the American Civil War.[1] Since 1900 recourse to arbitration has become even more frequent, until it is now one of the best established procedures for the settlement of international controversies.

In its simplest form arbitration involves the negotiation by the parties to the dispute of a bilateral treaty, known as a *compromis*, in which they state clearly the question to be arbitrated, name the arbitrators or specify the method of their selection, and set forth the rules of procedure and the principles of law or equity to be applied. This arrangement is still used in many instances, particularly for the settlement of financial claims.[2] General rules of arbitral procedure have gradually been developed, however, which now render it unnecessary to specify in detail how a particular tribunal shall act. In 1875 the Institute of International Law drew up a code of arbitral procedure and in 1889 the first Pan-American Conference prepared a complete scheme of arbitration, which was not adopted, however, at that time. When a dispute is not submitted to the judgment of a single arbitrator, such as the sovereign of a third State, a tribunal is set up, consisting usually of one or two nationals of each of the disputing States, plus one or more nationals of outside States. These may be named in the *compromis* or chosen by the other members of the tribunal. One of the outsiders usually acts as umpire. The tribunal—almost invariably consisting of an odd number of members—meets at some designated place, organizes itself, and proceeds to hear both sides of the controversy. Each party argues its case through attorneys, who present briefs in the form of cases and counter-cases. The exchange of written arguments may be followed by oral pleading and the summoning of witnesses, though there is no use of a jury. The tribunal then reaches its decision by a majority vote and submits a written statement of the award, with the reasons therefor, to the respective disputants. Minority opinions may be rendered by the members of the tribunal who differ with the majority, but they are without legal effect.

An arbitral award is binding upon the parties and constitutes a final settlement of the controversy. States sometimes expressly reserve in the

[1] See p. 156 above.
[2] For an example, see Appendix II, pp. 862–864 below.

compromis the right to demand a reconsideration on the basis of the discovery of some new fact of vital importance, unknown to the tribunal or to the party making the demand at the time of the award. Arbitral awards may also be rejected on certain other grounds. If the arbitrators exceed their authority under the *compromis*, the award is not binding. In 1827 the United States and Great Britain submitted to the arbitration of the King of the Netherlands the question of the location of the "highlands" mentioned in the treaty of 1783 as marking the American-Canadian boundary between Maine and Quebec. The arbitrator drew a compromise line through a valley located between two sets of highlands and both parties rejected the award on the ground that "highlands" could not be situated in a valley and that the arbitrator had exceeded his instructions. The subsequent discovery of fraud, bribery, or coercion in the course of an arbitration also invalidates the award, but such cases are rare. In general, arbitral awards are almost always accepted in good faith and loyally carried out, for States refrain from submitting questions to arbitration unless they are prepared to accept whatever settlement the tribunal may reach.

In the development of arbitral procedure, the next step beyond *ad hoc* agreements providing for the submission of a particular dispute to a particular tribunal was the inclusion in other treaties of provisions for the submission to arbitration of disputes arising thereunder. In addition to this arrangement, States also began to negotiate general arbitration treaties, specifying that all future controversies of a designated character between the signatories would be submitted to arbitration. During the nineteenth century the number of general arbitration treaties and of arbitral clauses in other treaties steadily increased. Prior to 1855 only 6 such treaties were in operation. Thirty were negotiated between 1865 and 1894, 50 in the ensuing decade, and 123 between 1905 and 1914. Such treaties provide for what is known as "compulsory" or "obligatory" arbitration. These adjectives are somewhat misleading, since the treaties referred to merely constitute a voluntary pledge that the parties will in future submit to arbitration certain specified types of disputes. They frequently contain such broad qualifications and exceptions as to leave the parties almost complete liberty of action with regard to any particular controversy. Many pre-war general arbitration treaties, modeled after the Anglo-French treaty of October 14, 1903, specified that all cases should be excluded from their operation which involved "national honor, independence, vital interests, or the interests of third parties." "These phrases are vague and indefinite and lend themselves to the purposes of any statesman who may desire to proceed to extremities. An interest becomes vital when a government chooses to consider it as such, and there is no fixed criterion of national honor."[1] Prior to 1917 thirty-six

[1] T. J. Lawrence, *The Principles of International Law*, 7th ed., 1923, p. 579.

bilateral treaties had been signed providing for the submission to arbitration of any dispute whatever between the parties, without qualification. The first of these was the treaty of May 28, 1902, between Argentina and Chile. Nineteen other treaties provided for the arbitration of any dispute not involving constitutional questions. But no general treaty of this kind had been entered into between any two of the Great Powers. Projects of general compulsory arbitration treaties were defeated at both the first and second Hague Conferences of 1899 and 1907. The Hague Convention for the Pacific Settlement of International Disputes bound the parties to resort to arbitration only "in so far as circumstances permit" (Article 38, convention of October 18, 1907).

Despite American championship of arbitration, the actual practice of the United States has been measurably behind that of other Powers. This has been due in part to the divergent attitudes of successive administrations and in part to the opposition of the Senate. The American Government has arbitrated numerous controversies, particularly with Great Britain, through *ad hoc compromis* agreements. It has likewise included arbitration clauses in numerous other treaties, but has not always availed itself of the opportunities provided in this fashion. Article 21 of the Treaty of Guadaloupe Hidalgo with Mexico of February 2, 1848, for example, specified that the parties would "consider" the arbitration of all future difficulties not settled by diplomacy, but when Mexico in 1916 proposed the arbitration of current controversies between the two governments, the United States declined the suggestion and instead resorted to reprisals by capturing and occupying Vera Cruz. Again in 1927, when the dispute over the alleged confiscatory effects of Mexico's land and oil laws became acute, a widespread popular demand for arbitration appeared in the United States and even won the support of the Senate, but the administration declined to resort to this mode of settlement.

As for general treaties, providing for "compulsory" arbitration, so many obstacles have been encountered that the United States has long been in the rear of the procession of States entering into arrangements of this kind. In 1896, following the successful arbitration of the boundary dispute between Great Britain and Venezuela, the British Government proposed to the United States a general treaty providing for obligatory arbitration. Secretary of State Olney, who insisted that arbitration should be made "automatic," was even more enthusiastic than Lord Salisbury and on January 11, 1897, a treaty was signed which went far in the direction of such an arrangement. The Senate, however, rejected the treaty and nothing came of the proposal at the moment. The American delegates to the first Hague Conference of 1899 were instructed to champion arbitration and to work for the establishment of an international court of justice, but anything in the nature of compulsory arbitration was ruled out by the Conference. Only voluntary arbitration was provided for, as will be noted below. Following the Russo-Japanese War of 1904–1905 and the Anglo-French arbitration treaty of 1903, the United States signed a number of general treaties for the obligatory arbitration of questions of a legal nature, which, with the exception of controversies involving national honor, independence, vital interests, or the interests of third States, were to be submitted to the Hague Permanent "Court" of Arbitration. Here, as in all such treaties, it was of course contemplated that each *compromis* for the submission of a particular dispute to arbitration would not be a formal treaty requiring ratification, but merely an administrative agreement under the terms of the general treaty. But the Senate insisted that each *compromis* must be expressly approved by it as a "treaty" before the arbitration could proceed. President Roosevelt declared that this was "mere nonsense" which made the general treaties "shams." The administration therefore withdrew the treaties from Senate consideration and abandoned the whole enterprise. In Europe the formulation of a *compromis* under general arbitration treaties has always been regarded as a merely procedural matter, for unless it is so regarded there is no value in the general treaties.

In 1908 Secretary of State Root revived the negotiations and concluded some twenty-five treaties containing the provisions demanded by the Senate. In fact, as John Bassett Moore pointed out, the treaties represented a step backward in one sense, since prior to 1908 pecuniary claims had often been arbitrated without concluding a formal treaty with the foreign government, while under the new arrangement a treaty had to be concluded for each arbitration.[1] This feature, added to the exceptions of independence, national honor, and vital interests, made the treaties little more than meaningless gestures. In 1911–1912 another group of general arbitration treaties was negotiated by President Taft and Secretary of State Knox. They abandoned the exceptions of vital interests and national honor and pledged the parties to arbitrate all differences "which are justiciable in their nature by reason of being susceptible of decision by the application of the principles of law and equity." These treaties provided for a joint high commission of inquiry to determine whether a particular controversy was "justiciable." The Senate objected to this arrangement, struck it out, and inserted numerous reservations prohibiting the arbitration of a whole series of cases—with the result that President Taft declared of the treaties, after the Senate had finished with them, that "their own father would not recognize them." In disgust he dropped the whole project. Except for the Bryan conciliation treaties,

[1] See his *Principles of American Diplomacy*, p. 331, and *International Law and Some Current Illusions*, p. 86.

nothing more was done by the United States, prior to the outbreak of the Great War, in the direction of perfecting international machinery for the pacific settlement of disputes.

The post-war arbitration treaties of the United States are for the most part based upon the treaty with France of 1928.[1] They omit the exceptions of national honor and vital interests, but contain exceptions of cases within the domestic jurisdiction of the parties, involving the interests of third parties, depending upon or involving "the maintenance of the traditional attitude of the United States concerning domestic questions, commonly known as the Monroe Doctrine," or involving the observance of obligations under the Covenant of the League of Nations. Each *compromis*, moreover, must take the form of a separate treaty which must be submitted to the Senate. The exceptions are almost as flexible as those in the pre-war treaties. In other words, the United States in its general arbitration treaties has said no more than that it will enter into special treaties for the arbitration of particular disputes if it regards them as suitable for arbitration, *i.e.*, not falling within the exceptions, and if the Senate, in its wisdom, sees fit to approve ratification of such special treaties. The General Treaty of Inter-American Arbitration of January 5, 1929, to which the United States and most of the Latin American Republics are parties, obligates the signatories to submit "juridical" questions to arbitration by special treaty, subject to reservations of questions affecting domestic jurisdiction and third States. In addition, a long series of individual reservations were attached by particular States. An appended "protocol of progressive arbitration" made provision for the voluntary abandonment of the exceptions and reservations by the signatories,[2] but no steps of any significance have been taken in this direction thus far. This arrangement, too, is little more than rhetorical verbiage. The American Government is obviously not prepared to commit itself to arbitrate particular controversies automatically, unless the language employed is so vague and flexible that loopholes can readily be discovered through which disputes can be excluded from the operation of the general treaties if considerations of political expediency dictate such action. While many other States have entered into general arbitration treaties which really pledge them to arbitrate certain types of disputes, the United States has reserved its liberty of action to such a degree that its general arbitration treaties are little more than empty words.

The most important step thus far taken toward the institutionalization of arbitration was the creation of the Permanent Court of Arbitration by the first Hague Conference of 1899. This agency is neither "permanent" nor a "court," for its members are not required to reside and work

[1] See the American-Italian Treaty of April 19, 1928, Appendix I, pp. 857–860 below.
[2] See J. B. Scott, *International Conferences of American States,* 1931, pp. 458–462.

at The Hague, nor do they collectively constitute a judicial body. Its name was due to the confusion between arbitration and adjudication which prevailed at the time of its establishment. It came into being through the signature and ratification by a large number of States of the Convention for the Pacific Settlement of International Disputes. This multilateral engagement required each of the signatory Powers to designate for a term of six years "four persons of known competency in questions of international law, of the highest moral reputation, and disposed to accept the duties of arbitrators." The list of arbitrators so compiled is kept at the international bureau of the "court" at The Hague as a panel from which States may pick an arbitral tribunal for the settlement of particular controversies. A new tribunal is picked for each dispute by means of a *compromis* between the parties. Only the panel is permanent. Resort to this procedure is entirely optional and voluntary. At the second Hague Conference of 1907, it was provided that of the two arbitrators appointed by each party, "only one can be its national, or chosen from among the persons selected by it as members of the Permanent Court." This insures a majority of neutral members on each tribunal.

This institution is nothing more than a list of arbitrators and a secretariat. It has doubtless received more attention than its practical importance warrants. It did, nevertheless, stimulate general interest in arbitration and it has performed a useful, if limited, function in disposing satisfactorily of a number of disputes submitted to it. The United States has resorted to its services six times, Great Britain six times, and France nine times. Between 1903, when the United States and Mexico established the first tribunal to deal with the "Pious Funds" case, and 1914, fifteen cases had been arbitrated in accordance with the procedure outlined in the convention. These included international claims against Venezuela, the right of the Dhows of Muscat to fly the French flag in the face of British objections, the Norway-Sweden maritime boundary dispute, the Anglo-American North Atlantic Fisheries controversy, a Dutch-Portuguese boundary dispute on the island of Timor, the Franco-German dispute over the Casablanca deserters, two Franco-Italian disputes, a Russo-Turkish dispute, and other cases of lesser importance. Most of these disputes were of little political significance, though arbitration achieved a settlement where diplomacy had failed. Since the war, most of the cases which would have been arbitrated in this fashion have been adjudicated by the World Court. From the record of the years, as well as from the logic of arbitral procedure itself, it is clear that arbitration, taken by itself, is no substitute for war, but merely a convenient device for settling certain types of controversies with regard to which the parties are willing to accept the decision of an impartial third party. The international controversies which lead to war are precisely those involving questions which States are unwilling to submit to arbitration or to adjudication or, for that matter, to any form of pacific settlement which obliges the contestants in advance to subordinate their special and exclusive interests to the will of impartial international agencies.

5. ADJUDICATION

> In concerning the office of an arbiter, we must consider whether he be elected into the place of a judge, or with some laxer power, which Seneca speaks of as the proper power of an arbiter: "The judge is limited by rules of law: the umpire is left quite free, and can soften law and justice by kindness and mercy." So Aristotle says, "that a fair man will rather go to an arbiter than to a judge, because the arbiter looks to equity, the judge to law."—HUGO GROTIUS, *De jure belli ac pacis.*

If it be true, as seems likely, that arbitration in the future will not progress much beyond its present status, the cause is to be found both in the unwillingness of States to submit politically important disputes to arbitral tribunals and in the fact that disputes which are regarded as suitable for such treatment will be increasingly settled by adjudication rather than by arbitration. The two procedures have in the past been much confused. But it is now permissible, and indeed essential for clarity of thought, to distinguish sharply between them. Arbitration and adjudication are both modes of settlement whereby disputing States voluntarily submit their differences to an impartial outside agency. In both cases the parties agree in advance to abide by the award or decision. But in arbitration, even under The Hague procedure, the agency of settlement is an *ad hoc* tribunal specifically chosen by the parties for the purpose of dealing with a single controversy. The tribunal gathers evidence, hears arguments, and makes an award on the basis of respect for international law, taking into account such extralegal and political considerations as the arbitrators may think useful to achieve a settlement. In true adjudication, on the other hand, the agency of settlement is a permanent and continuous judicial body, not chosen by the parties but existing independently of them, and not weighing considerations of equity or politics but applying quite literally to the cases before it the established principles of international law. A true court proceeds from case to case, builds up precedents, and gradually creates a consistent body of case law. Arbitral tribunals, lacking continuity and corporate existence, are unable to act in this fashion.

The adjudication of international disputes is obviously impossible without the prior creation of a permanent international court to which they may be submitted. Numerous unofficial proposals were put forward in various States during the nineteenth century for the creation of an international judicial tribunal. But apparently insuperable obstacles stood in the way of the fulfillment of the vision. The principle of State equality seemed to require that all States be represented on any world court—an arrangement which would require a court of impossible size. Regional courts would have only regional utility. There were disputes, moreover, arising from differing national interpretations of certain moot points of international law. What legal principles should such a court apply? How were cases to be brought before it if it were created? What authority, if any, would such a body have to enforce its decisions?

These problems were discussed at the first Hague Conference, but without result. The Permanent Court of Arbitration there established was a court in nothing but name. They were again discussed, more fruitfully but again unsuccessfully in the final event, at the second Hague Conference of 1907. Elihu Root, Secretary of State of the United States, instructed the American delegates to work for the "development of the Hague tribunal into a permanent tribunal composed of judges who are judicial officers and nothing else, who are paid adequate salaries, who have no other occupation, and who will devote their entire time to the trial and decision of international causes by judicial methods and under a sense of judicial responsibility." This proposal met with the support of the British and Russian delegates, who likewise presented projects for a world court. A plan was drawn up for the creation of a Permanent Court of Arbitral Justice which should be a true judicial agency sitting permanently at The Hague. Unfortunately, however, no agreement could be reached regarding the number of the judges and the method of their selection. For all of the forty-four participating States to be "represented" on the court was out of the question and the minor Powers were unwilling to establish a court which might be dominated by the Great Powers. The whole scheme therefore failed, with the Conference recommending the adoption of the plan when an acceptable method of selecting the judges could be devised. A similar fate overtook the project of an international prize court which was also discussed at the second Hague Conference. An agreement was reached to set up a court to pass upon the legality of captures in naval war. The tribunal was to consist of fifteen judges, with the eight Great Powers having permanent appointees on the bench and the lesser Powers sharing the remaining seats by a process of rotation. The court was to hear appeals from national prize courts, with both States and individuals having a right of recourse to it. Thirty-three States signed the convention for its creation, but difficulties developed over the fact that much of the international law of prize is unsettled. The British Government rejected the plan for this reason, and the lesser naval Powers and the land Powers accordingly suspended further action. The London Naval Conference of 1908–1909 sought to codify the law of prize and drew up the Declaration of London. But this in turn was rejected by the House of Lords and failed of ratification. Both of these efforts to establish an international court thus failed, in the one instance because of disagreement as to the method of choosing judges, in the other because of disagreement over the international law to be applied.

The first genuine international court to be fully established on a working basis was the creation of the United States and five republics of Central America. Under the inspiration of the American State Department, the Central American Peace Conference of 1907 set up the Central American Court of Justice, consisting of five judges, one each for Costa Rica, Nicaragua, Salvador, Honduras, and Guatemala. The signatory States agreed to submit all questions to it for decision, without qualifications or reservations, unless they could be settled by negotiations. Its jurisdiction was thus "compulsory." This remarkable international agency had an even wider jurisdiction than the Supreme Court of the United States in that private citizens might bring suits against States before it. It was established for a ten-year period and went out of existence in 1917, after a decade of useful service, under somewhat peculiar circumstances. Costa Rica and Salvador had brought suit against Nicaragua, whose puppet government, supported by American marines, had negotiated the Bryan-Chamorro Treaty of 1916 with the United States.[1] By this agreement the "Colossus of the North" was given canal rights along the San Juan River, which divides Nicaragua from Costa Rica, and also the right of fortifying Fonseca Bay, which commands the Pacific coast not only of Nicaragua, but also of Salvador and Honduras. The other States alleged that Nicaragua was legally incompetent to conclude such a treaty without their consent, since it affected their rights adversely and Nicaragua could not lawfully cede away what she did not possess. The court accepted this view and decided the suit against Nicaragua. The latter, however, with the tacit approval of the State Department at Washington, refused to abide by the decision. The other States then took the entirely reasonable view that there was nothing to be gained by maintaining a court if its members were free to ignore its judgments. They accordingly declined to renew the arrangement. What Washington had created it likewise destroyed and this fruitful experiment thus suffered an untimely demise. The Conference on Central American Affairs at Washington in 1923 put into effect a new scheme, but this is modeled after the Hague Permanent Court of Arbitration and is not a true court in any sense.

Not until the Paris Peace Conference at the close of the Great War was it possible to create a permanent international judicial agency of wide jurisdiction. President Wilson regarded the creation of a world court as a necessary feature of the peace settlement. Article 14 of the Covenant

[1] See p. 409 below.

of the League of Nations entrusted to the Council of the League the task of formulating and submitting to its members plans for the establishment of a "Permanent Court of International Justice." The court was to be competent to hear and determine any dispute submitted to it by the parties and to give advisory opinions upon any question referred to it by the Council or Assembly of the League. In accordance with this provision, the Council in 1920 appointed a commission of jurists, upon which Elihu Root served for the United States. The commission prepared a "Statute" or constitution of the proposed court, which was submitted first to the Council and then by the Council to the Assembly and the members of the League. The Statute became effective not through any action of the Council or Assembly, but through its ratification on the part of the member States. The first panel of judges was elected in September of 1921. On February 15, 1922, the judges convened at The Hague and the ceremonies of its official establishment were performed in the Great Hall of Justice of the Peace Palace which had been erected by Andrew Carnegie for the Hague tribunal of arbitration created twenty-three years before. The same strange irony which made President Wilson a prophet without honor in his own land has made the United States, long an ardent proponent of international adjudication, one of the few States not members of the Court. Successive administrations have been endeavoring ever since 1923 to secure American adhesion to the Statute, but the reservations to the protocol of adhesion attached by the Senate in 1926 have been of such a character as to render an international agreement regarding them impossible up to the time of writing.[1]

The thorny problem of the selection of judges was ingeniously solved in the Statute. Eleven judges and four deputy judges were originally provided for, but the amendments of 1930 increased the number of judges to fifteen. All have nine-year terms. Candidates for these positions are nominated by the national groups of the Hague Permanent Court of Arbitration, each group having the right to name four candidates, only two of whom may be of its own nationality. The Secretary-General of the League prepares an alphabetical list of the persons so nominated and transmits it to the Council and Assembly of the League. These bodies, each voting independently, elect the fifteen judges and four deputy judges by majority vote. In the event of disagreement, recourse is had to a conference of six members, three from the Council and three from the Assembly, for the purpose of submitting to their respective bodies one name for each vacant seat. If it is still impossible to reach an agreement, the judges already chosen fill vacancies from the candidates who have been voted for in the Assembly or in the Council. Large and small States alike thus have an equal voice in the selection of judges and the

[1] See pp. 806f. below.

dilemma of 1907 is resolved without creating a court of unwieldy size. At the first election of September, 1921, eighty-nine candidates were nominated and all places were filled by majority vote of the Council and Assembly after three days of balloting. At the second election (1930), forty-nine candidates were nominated. Eleven ballots were cast by the Council and Assembly for judges and six ballots for deputy judges before an agreement was reached.[1]

The equally difficult question of the jurisdiction of the Court has been solved with equal ingenuity. The commission of jurists which drafted the Statute recommended compulsory or obligatory jurisdiction with respect to the disputes mentioned in Article 13 of the League Covenant and Article 36 of the Statute, *i.e.*, disputes as to (1) the interpretation of a treaty; (2) any question of international law; (3) the existence of any fact, which if established, would constitute a breach of an international obligation; or (4) the nature or extent of the reparation to be made for the breach of an international obligation. This arrangement was rejected by the Council and the Assembly on the ground that Article 14 of the Covenant contemplated a court with voluntary jurisdiction. In general, the Court has jurisdiction only over such disputes as member States are willing to submit to it. Article 36 of the Statute, however, was trans-

---

[1] Article 9 of the Statute provides that "At every election, the electors shall bear in mind that not only should all the persons appointed as members of the court possess the qualifications required, but the whole body also should represent the main forms of civilization and the principal legal systems of the world." The present composition of the Court is as follows:

Judges

M. Adatci (Japan)
M. Anzilotti (Italy)
M. Fromageot (France)
Sir Cecil Hurst (Great Britain)
M. Altamira y Crevea (Spain)
M. Van Eysinga (Netherlands)
M. Guerrero (Salvador)
M. Urrutia (Colombia)

Baron Rolin-Jaequemyns (Belgium)
Mr. Kellogg (United States)
Count Rostworowski (Poland)
M. Schücking (Germany)
M. Wang Chung-Hui (China)
M. de Bustamente y Sirven (Cuba)
M. Negulesco (Rumania)

Deputy Judges

M. Erich (Finland)
M. DaMatta (Portugal)
M. Novakovich (Jugoslavia)
M. Redlich (Austria)

The Court thus has upon its bench seven members of Latin European or Latin American origin, two of Teutonic origin, two of Anglo-Saxon origin, two Orientals, three Slavs, a Belgian, a Dutchman, and a Finn. The members are, of course, in no sense representatives of their nations, but international judicial officials. The United States has had a judge on the court from the beginning—first John Bassett Moore, then Charles Evans Hughes, and now former Secretary of State Frank Kellogg. Needless to say, these gentlemen were nominated by national groups on the Hague tribunal panel other than the American group, since the United States, as a non-member State, plays no official rôle in nominations or elections.

formed into an "optional clause" which member States may accept or reject as they wish. Those accepting it recognize the jurisdiction of the Court to be compulsory, without special agreement, for the four categories of disputes mentioned, providing both parties to the dispute have adhered to the "optional clause." In other words, they agree in advance to submit all disputes in these categories to the Court for settlement. States not accepting the clause remain free to submit, or refuse to submit, such disputes to the Court as they choose. Almost forty States have thus far adhered to Article 36 of the Statute for varying terms of years.

The Permanent Court of International Justice represents the most important and successful effort thus far made to establish an international judicial tribunal for the adjudication of controversies between States. Its record during the ten years of its existence has revealed it to be a body of very great value, both as a tribunal to render judgments between litigating States and as an agency to advise the Council of the League on the legal aspects of international problems. All of its judgments and advisory opinions have been accepted in good faith and only rarely, as in the Austro-German customs union opinion of September 5, 1931, have its members been criticized for placing their national prejudices above the impartial logic of the law. It is engaged in building up a body of legal precedents of great utility for the solution of future international cases of a justiciable character. If it is not a panacea for war, nor a means of settling all international disputes—and assuredly it is neither of these things as yet—the cause lies in the fact that States do not regard all disputes as justiciable and that the realm of international law is not coterminous with the realm of international politics.[1]

6. EXISTING METHODS OF PACIFIC SETTLEMENT

> Every Christian prince must take as his chief maxim not to employ arms to support or vindicate his rights until he has employed and exhausted the way of reason and of persuasion. It is to his interest also to add to reason and persuasion the influence of benefits conferred, which indeed is one of the surest ways to make his power secure, and to increase it.—M. DE CALLIÈRES, *On the Manner of Negotiating with Princes.*

The years since 1919 have been marked by the conclusion of more international agreements for the pacific settlement of international disputes than were negotiated during many decades prior to the Great War. Between November 11, 1918, and November 11, 1928, no less than 130 treaties of investigation, conciliation, arbitration, or adjudication were signed, exclusive of those between the Union of Soviet Socialist Republics and its neighbors. Fifty-two States are bound by the obligations of these instruments. Five of them were multilateral and 125 bilateral in charac-

[1] On the organization and work of the Court and the relation of the United States thereto, see, pp. 765f. and 806f. below.

ter. Ten contain provisions for investigation, 92 for conciliation, 96 for arbitration, and 56 for compulsory adjudication. Seven permanent commissions of investigation and 81 permanent commissions of conciliation have been established in this fashion. The great majority of these engagements have been signed since 1924 and are eloquent testimony to the world-wide yearning for peace and security. The texts of these agreements fill almost 1,000 pages of a good-sized book. While limitations of space make it obviously impossible to analyze these arrangements in detail, it will be useful to conclude the chapter with a résumé of their major provisions.[1]

The first and most ambitious of the post-war arrangements for the pacific settlement of international disputes is that embodied in the Covenant of the League of Nations. While the forms of this scheme can be adequately considered and evaluated only after the structure of the League itself has been outlined in the following chapter, the nature of the obligations assumed by the signatories may be sketched at this point. The members of the League agree in the first place to respect and preserve as against external aggression the territorial integrity and existing political independence of all other members. "In case of any aggression, or in case of any threat or danger of such aggression, the Council shall advise upon the means by which this obligation shall be fulfilled" (Article 10). There is here no provision for the settlement of disputes, but rather a kind of alliance or pledge of international cooperation against any State violating the integrity or independence of a League member. Under Article 11 of the Covenant, any war or threat of war is made a matter of concern to the whole League, which may "take any action that may be deemed wise and effectual to safeguard the peace of nations." The Council takes the initiative in such action and any member of the League may bring to the attention of the Assembly or the Council any circumstance threatening peaceable relations between States. Article 12 obliges the League members, in all disputes likely to lead to a rupture, to submit the matter to arbitration or judicial settlement or to inquiry by the Council. The members of the League agree not to resort to war until three months after the arbitral award, the judicial decision, or the report by the Council. Arbitration and adjudication are thus not made obligatory, but the members are obliged either to resort to these procedures or to conciliation through the Council. War is not prohibited, but must be delayed for three months. By Article 13 the members of the League agree to submit to arbitration or judicial settlement such disputes as they recognize to be suitable for arbitration or judicial settlement, a statement which comes

---

[1] The material of this section is in part based upon Max Habicht's excellent compilation and analysis of *Post-war Treaties for the Pacific Settlement of International Disputes,* 1931, 1,103 pages.

dangerously close to saying nothing. The second paragraph, however, declares that "disputes as to the interpretation of a treaty, as to any question of international law, as to the existence of any fact which, if established, would constitute a breach of any international obligation, or as to the extent and nature of the reparation to be made for any breach, are declared to be among those which are generally suitable for submission to arbitration or judicial settlement." The Permanent Court of International Justice is named as the agency for adjudication. The members agree to carry out in good faith any award or decision which is rendered and pledge themselves not to go to war against a member of the League which complies therewith.

Article 15 of the Covenant outlines the conciliation procedure of the Council. If the Council agrees unanimously (with the exception of the disputants) to a proposed solution of an international controversy submitted to it, the members of the League agree not to go to war with either party which complies with the Council's recommendations. Article 16 declares that any member of the League which goes to war in violation of the foregoing provisions shall be deemed to have committed an act of war against all other members of the League, which undertake to apply military and economic sanctions against the Covenant-breaking State. Article 17 deals with disputes between members and non-members. If a non-member State, upon invitation, refuses to accept League membership for the purpose of settling the dispute and resorts to war against a member of the League, "the provisions of Article 16 shall be applicable as against the State taking such action."[1]

The League system for the settlement of disputes is thus compounded of arbitration, adjudication, conciliation, and the application of organized international force against Covenant-breaking States.[2] The League members have accepted obligations not to resort to war in certain specified contingencies, but they have not renounced war under all circumstances. On the contrary, they have, in theory at least if not in fact, accepted obligations to wage war collectively against States which break the peace. War is still possible under the Covenant in the following situations: (1) when one or both parties to a controversy refuse to abide by an arbitral award, a judicial decision, or a unanimous recommendation of the Council; (2) when the Council fails to reach a unanimous decision, in which case the League members "reserve to themselves the right to take such action as they shall consider necessary for the maintenance of right and justice" (Article 15, Paragraph 7); (3) when the dispute is found by the Council to be solely within the domestic jurisdiction of one of the parties; (4) when there is unreasonable delay in arriving at an award,

---

[1] See the text of the Covenant, Appendix VI, p. 902 below.
[2] On sanctions see pp. 716f. and 791f. below.

decision, or recommendation of the Council; (5) when the dispute is between non-members of the League; and (6) when sanctions are applied against a Covenant-breaking State. In case (1) war is permissible. In case (6) it is presumably obligatory, though the sanctions have never in fact been applied. It is clear, moreover, that the obligations of the Covenant not to resort to war refer to war in the legal sense.[1] They have not as yet been successfully applied to acts of retorsion, reprisal, or intervention short of war, though these may easily lead to fighting between States on a large scale.

Even more comprehensive, though much simpler in its provisions—so simple, indeed, as to be almost naive—is the Kellogg-Briand Pact of Paris of August 27, 1928.[2] The Pact is primarily a negative gesture of renunciation and is, thus far, entirely unimplemented. It provides no mechanisms or procedures for the settlement of international disputes and need not, therefore, be discussed in connection with the general topic here under consideration.[3] But the differences between the Pact and the Covenant and the efforts to reconcile them should be noted. The applicability of both engagements to hostile acts short of war is highly questionable and controversial. In 1931–1932 Japan wrested Manchuria from China by military force and conducted active hostilities at Shanghai. She claimed, nevertheless, that she had violated no obligations under either the Covenant or the Pact, since no state of "war" in the legal sense was recognized on either side. This claim has not been successfully controverted up to the time of writing. The Pact, however, clearly purports to outlaw all war (in the legal sense), while the Covenant permits and even requires war in the circumstances mentioned above. At the Tenth Assembly of the League (1929) the British Government proposed a series of amendments to close the "gap" in the Covenant. The Assembly referred the matter to a committee of eleven members, who presented a report suggesting modifications of Articles 12, 13, and 15. The proposed changes would eliminate the three months' delay provision and bind members to apply only pacific means for the settlement of all disputes. They would be bound unreservedly to refrain from war against a State complying with an arbitral award or a judicial decision and to accept a unanimous report of the Council without qualification. Disagreements arose, however, regarding certain features of the proposed changes, due in part to uncertainty over the future attitude of the United States and in part to the reluctance of some States to make the vague and qualified commitments of the Pact definite obligations. The Locarno treaties and the alliances between France and her eastern satellites impose military obligations in

[1] On this distinction see pp. 149–150 above.

[2] The Pact is very brief, containing only two articles of importance. The full text is given on p. 678 below.

[3] On the meaning and significance of the Pact see pp. 680f. below.

the event of war which are inconsistent with the proposed amendments to the Covenant, but which were excepted from the operation of the Pact by various "interpretations." To incorporate the interpretations into the Covenant would deprive the proposed changes of most of their significance. To omit them would not merely write the Pact into the Covenant, but would put the sanctions of the Covenant behind the Pact, in its original and unqualified form, and thus oblige the members of the League to accept obligations more extensive than those assumed by them in signing the Pact. The effort, therefore, failed and the whole matter is still hanging fire at the present time.

A number of other general or regional agreements for the pacific settlement of international controversies may be mentioned. The efforts of the League of Nations to promote disarmament led to a realization that no substantial reduction of armaments was possible without guarantees of security. The Cecil-Requin Draft Treaty of Mutual Assistance of 1923 sought to obligate its signatories to guarantee peace by taking cooperative action against an aggressor State, as contemplated in Article 16 of the Covenant. The Council of the League was to designate what State was the victim of aggression and therefore entitled to assistance. Owing to the refusal of the British and other governments to pledge themselves to come to the aid of victims of aggression under the terms of such far-reaching commitments, the treaty failed of adoption. There followed an effort to link arbitration, security, and disarmament in a new arrangement. The Geneva Protocol, adopted by the Fifth Assembly of the League and opened for signature October 2, 1924, pledged the signatory States to secure amendments to the Covenant to achieve its purposes and meanwhile bound them to renounce war in favor of pacific settlement. Compulsory arbitration and adjudication were provided for. If a State refused to resort to these procedures or refused to abide by an award or decision or a unanimous report of the Council, it was to be judged an aggressor by the Council. All League members would then be bound definitely to apply sanctions against the aggressor. Plans for disarmament were to follow.[1] The British Government opposed the Protocol and it likewise failed of adoption.

The failure of these general schemes led to negotiations for regional arrangements. On August 16, 1925, representatives of Great Britain, France, Germany, Italy, Belgium, Poland, and Czechoslovakia met at

[1] "Compulsory arbitration for every kind of dispute; aggression defined in such a way as to give no cause for hesitation when the Council has to make a decision; the indissoluble binding up of the whole system with a conference for the reduction of armaments; no arbitration or security without disarmament, and no disarmament without arbitration and security." This summary of the meaning of the Geneva Protocol is contained in the *League Handbook: The Reduction of Armaments and the Organization of Peace*, 1928, p. 56. *Cf.* Habicht, *op. cit.*, pp. 929–936.

Locarno and agreed to seven historic treaties which were subsequently signed at London, December 1, and ratified by all the parties. The first— a treaty of mutual guarantee—obligates France and Belgium on the one side and Germany on the other to renounce war against one another except in self-defense and under certain treaty provisions, and to settle all their controversies by pacific means, *i.e.*, adjudication, conciliation commissions, or the Council of the League. This agreement guarantees the inviolability of the frontiers between Germany, France, and Belgium as fixed by the Treaty of Versailles. In the event of unprovoked aggression, as ascertained by the Council, all the signatories, including Great Britain and Italy, are pledged to come to the defense of the victim. Two treaties of mutual guarantee between France and Poland and between France and Czechoslovakia provide for mutual assistance against Germany in the event of her violation of the obligations mentioned above. Four treaties of compulsory arbitration and conciliation complete the series—between Germany on the one side and France, Belgium, Poland, and Czechoslovakia on the other. They oblige the parties to submit all disputes of every kind "with regard to which the parties are in conflict as to their respective rights" to a permanent conciliation commission, arbitration, adjudication, or to settlement by the Council. While the eastern frontiers of Germany are not guaranteed, all the parties are bound to resort only to pacific methods of settling disputes. Germany's entrance into the League of Nations in 1926 followed the conclusion of these agreements.

Through the instrumentality of the League of Nations, other steps were taken in the direction of establishing general arrangements for the pacific settlement of disputes. Various draft conventions relating to arbitration, adjudication, and conciliation were woven together at the Ninth Assembly of the League (1928) into a General Act which provides for the submission of disputes not settled by diplomacy to a permanent or special conciliation commission of five members, including three neutral members, set up by the parties. "All disputes with regard to which the parties are in conflict as to their respective rights shall, subject to any reservations which shall be made . . . be submitted for decision to the Permanent Court of International Justice, unless the parties agree to have resort to an arbitral tribunal" (Article 17). The act specified in the remainder of its forty-seven articles the details of the judicial or arbitral procedure to be followed. All States may accede to the Act, in whole or in part, and the Secretary-General of the League maintains a list of acceding States between which the terms of the act are binding. Some fourteen States have acceded to the General Act up to the time of writing. Three bilateral conventions for arbitration, conciliation, and adjudication and three draft treaties of nonaggression were also prepared by the 1928 Assembly as models which member States might follow. Numerous bilateral treaties have been concluded on the basis of these drafts. The 1928 Assembly likewise prepared a draft convention for the granting of financial assistance in the form of guaranteed loans to States threatened with aggression. This draft was completed and signed by twenty-eight States in September of 1930. Its operation was made contingent upon the adoption of a general plan for the reduction of armaments under Article 8 of the Covenant. The members of the League thus have available a great variety of arrangements which they may, at their option, enter into if they are so minded. Eventually, some of these arrangements may be placed in the Covenant and become binding upon all members. In the meantime, each State picks and chooses the particular type of arrangement suitable to its own interests and prejudices.[1]

Meanwhile several general treaties have been entered into by the States of the western hemisphere. The Inter-American Conciliation Treaty of 1923, to which sixteen States including the United States are parties, provides for conciliation commissions or commissions of inquiry, which are, however, given no final authority to settle disputes. The Central American Commission of Inquiry Treaty, to which six States including the United States are parties, gives the commission created by it authority to recommend settlements, but is limited to certain types of disputes. The Inter-American Conciliation Convention and the General Inter-American Arbitration Treaty of 1929 are also limited as to the cases which are subject to pacific settlement and as to the authority conferred upon the commissions set up by them. In addition to these general or regional arrangements, there have been concluded in the past decade a great many other bilateral or multilateral treaties for the pacific settlement of international controversies. They are far too numerous and bewildering in their profusion to be reviewed here. Only a few generalizations regarding their nature may be ventured. The United States concluded twenty such treaties in 1928–1929 with non-American States. They provide for conciliation or for the arbitration of disputes other than those involving domestic jurisdiction, the interests of third parties, the Monroe Doctrine, or the Covenant of the League of Nations. Other new treaties have been negotiated, closely resembling the Bryan treaties of 1913–1914.

Many other States have gone considerably further than this in the direction of providing for the pacific settlement of disputes. Numerous treaties provide for the arbitration or adjudication of justiciable disputes and for various forms of conciliation procedure for nonjusticiable disputes. A few treaties (France-Luxemburg, 1927, Italy-Switzerland, 1924)

[1] Professor Eagleton aptly observes: "When one considers that a State may sign the optional clause, or the general act, or a variety of bilateral treaties, the resulting hodgepodge of obligations seems an unnecessary sacrifice to the whims of nations." Clyde Eagleton, *International Government*, 1932, p. 341.

provide for the submission of all disputes to arbitration or adjudication. Various methods of pacific settlement are provided for: submission to an international commission for impartial investigation prior to new negotiations, submission to a commission of conciliation which both investigates and recommends a solution, submission to arbitration or to adjudication. These treaties run from three to twenty years and make all possible combinations of the various modes of procedure. Reservations are less numerous than they were in the pre-war treaties. The traditional reservations of independence, vital interests, and national honor have largely been abandoned. The United States still reserves questions affecting the Monroe Doctrine which, as always, remains extremely flexible in definition. Latin American treaties usually reserve cases affecting constitutional principles. Many treaties reserve disputes falling within domestic jurisdiction. There is an increasing tendency, however, to provide for the interpretation of reservations by some impartial agency rather than at the option of the parties.[1] In short, all of the pre-war methods of settlement have been further developed, clarified, and refined and various novel methods have been devised.

The significance for international politics of this amazing proliferation of forms and procedures for the pacific settlement of differences between States can be accurately evaluated only by future historians, blessed with a perspective upon the Western State System in the twentieth century which is necessarily denied to those too close to the events. If these ingenious arrangements are taken out of their setting and studied separately, as is so frequently done, they may lead the observer to the conclusion that international peace is henceforth securely established on a permanent basis for all time to come. If they are viewed through the cynical and sophisticated eyes of those too familiar with the ways of diplomats and with the ingrained habits of the centuries, they may be regarded as empty gestures and scraps of paper for the misleading of the unwary. Since the future of social and political phenomena is so largely unpredictable, one guess may be as good as another. Certain considerations bearing upon this problem of evaluation will be reviewed in the final portion of this study.

Here it may merely be suggested that exaggerated optimism regarding the efficacy of these schemes to keep the peace is as unwarranted as is the pessimism which would dismiss them as meaningless. Their very existence is evidence of a widespread and determined effort to devise methods of pacific settlement. If pledges and procedures were sufficient to achieve the end, there could be no doubt of the outcome, for all the States of the world are now pledged in one way or another to procedures to keep the peace. But men have ever been deceived by words without content and

[1] Habicht, *op. cit.*, pp. 971–1058, analyzes these provisions in detail.

CHAPTER VII

PUBLIC INTERNATIONAL ORGANIZATION

1. LEAGUES OF NATIONS IN THEORY AND PRACTICE

The middle ages were a period when everything was broken up; when each people, each province, each city, and each family, had a strong tendency to maintain its distinct individuality. At the present time an opposite tendency seems to prevail, and the nations seem to be advancing to unity . . . The consequence is, that there is less difference, at the present day, between the Europeans and their descendants in the new world, than there was between certain towns in the thirteenth century, which were only separated by a river.—ALEXIS DE TOCQUEVILLE, *Democracy in America.*

THE cry for peace between nations has ever been a powerful appeal to people everywhere to bestir themselves to thought and action designed to promote pacific cooperation between States. The development of international law, the evolution of diplomatic practice, and the elaboration of procedures for the settlement of disputes have all been stimulated by the quest for a warless world. Of equal significance in the building of these forms of international intercourse have been the practical exigencies of cooperation between States in dealing with common problems not always directly related to questions of war and peace. On the one hand pacifists and idealists have theorized about the law of nations, the functions of diplomats, and the utility of arbitration and adjudication as a means of promoting peace. On the other hand, the growth of commerce, travel, and communication between States has obliged practical statesmen to face new problems of common interest to all States and to devise agencies for their solution. The forms which the members of the Western State System have created to facilitate their dealings with one another all reflect these two sources of inspiration: theory and practice, spirit and substance, ideal and reality. In international affairs, no less than in other human relations, the patterns of social action which men devise to achieve their purposes embody both Utopian aspirations and the concrete experience of the past. Specific and tangible national needs which could only be served by international cooperation have contributed as much to the final design as vague yearnings for an ordered and orderly international society. The net result in the nineteenth and twentieth centuries has been the emergence and development of habits and institutions of cooperation between States to which it is now customary to apply the terms "international organization" or "international government."

[231]

As a descriptive phrase to refer to these habits and institutions "inter national organization" seems preferable to "international government.' "Government" implies sovereignty, territory, subjects, and an aggregation of power in the hands of those who rule. In the existing pattern of international cooperation there are as yet no central agencies which possess sovereignty or territory in their own right and no institutions through which international political power is effectively exercised by one group of people over another. "The parliament of man and the federation of the world" may be in process of creation, but they have not yet been built except in a narrow and restricted sense. What has taken place in reality is that the sovereign States of the world, still retaining their full claims to sovereignty, independence, and equality, have in the past century come to cooperate with one another in so many ways and with respect to such a variety of common problems that they have found it useful to institutionalize their cooperative efforts. They have, in short, set up permanent agencies through which they may more adequately serve their common purposes. These agencies are still very far from constituting a "government" of the world as a whole. They have been set up by treaty agreements between the sovereign States which govern the world, each within its own frontiers. With rare exceptions these agencies have no authority of their own over people or territory, but only such authority over the States which create and compose them as these States have voluntarily granted to them. The number of such international agencies has been growing constantly since 1850. Since 1919 they have been knit together into a coordinated organization, almost world-wide in its scope, with its headquarters in Geneva and its members scattered over the globe. In the present chapter a brief description of the historical development and the present structure of these agencies will be undertaken. Their significance for the future of the Western State System will be evaluated in the last book of the study.[1]

The term "international organization," as used here, will be limited to public agencies of international cooperation established by States and working on States, by States, and through States. The word "organization" implies conscious and purposeful action between independent units for common ends. The word "system" which has here been applied to the whole pattern of inter-State relations in contemporary western civilization, implies a set of relations in which each unit acts in its own character and for its own ends. The resulting "system" is a consequence of the unplanned interaction of the units. Prior to the nineteenth century, the States of Europe comprised a System, but they possessed no common international institutions to achieve common purposes, unless the decrepit Holy Roman Empire—once the embodiment of the common purposes of

[1] See pp. 823f. below.

Christendom—could be regarded in this light. At present, however, the States of the world have established a large number of such institutions. The ultimate consequences of the imposition of the new pattern of international organization upon the old pattern of the Western State System are still unpredictable. But the new pattern may readily be described and analyzed. This pattern of public institutions of cooperation established by States has followed upon the emergence of a vastly greater number of so-called "international organizations" which are private in character. The League of Nations *Handbook of International Organizations* lists some 300 structures of this type. The International Chamber of Commerce, the International Tourists' Organization, the International Federation of Trade Unions, the Amsterdam International of Socialist Parties, the Moscow International of Communist Parties are all "international organizations" in the sense that they are agencies of cooperation which transcend national frontiers. But they are composed not of States but of private individuals, organizations, groups, parties, and the like. They do not therefore fall within the scope of the present chapter. The same is true of such public organizations as the British Commonwealth of Nations or the United States of America. The units of these organizations are "States" or "Dominions," but the units lack sovereignty. They are parts of a larger sovereign whole. The public international organizations to which attention will here be directed are those made up of fully sovereign States.

It has been suggested above that certain of the State Systems of the past developed the rudiments of international organization.[1] The Amphictyonic Council and the various confederations of the Greek city-states were noteworthy prototypes of their modern counterparts. The State Systems of ancient China and India also had approximations to Leagues of Nations and other forms of institutionalized international cooperation. The world State of Rome and the medieval ideal of imperial unity both precluded the possibility of international organization as here defined. Dante's speculations on world organization were overshadowed by the imperial ideal.[2] His contemporary, Pierre Dubois, to be sure, was more realistic. His *De recuperatione sanctae terrae*, published in 1305, was the first clear formulation of a plan for international organization. He proposed a temporal union of the princes of Europe with a council and a court and cooperative action to rescue the Holy Land from the infidel. But it was not possible to envisage the creation of common agencies of cooperation between States until sovereign territorial units had emerged out of feudal confusion and built up through their contacts with one another a new system of independent political entities. Even after this

[1] See pp. 19–20 above.
[2] See pp. 35–36 above.

development had taken place the States of the Western State System were for centuries so exclusively occupied in struggling with one another for power and prestige that they had no common interests requiring institutionalized cooperation. The periodical wars to which this struggle gave rise, however, caused scholars and thinkers in many States to reflect upon the possibility of establishing international institutions to keep the peace. The result was the fabrication of a long series of theoretical and Utopian schemes to link together the States of the world into some kind of conference or league. None of these schemes was put into operation and all were without immediate results. But this early outflowering of thought and theory was destined to bear fruit ultimately in the field of practical statesmanship. It is worth while, therefore, to survey the more interesting of these hypothetical arrangements.

Two of these schemes appeared about the time that Hugo Grotius published his great treatise on international law. An obscure monk, Emeric Crucé, issued *Le nouveau Cynée* in 1623 as the first significant proposal for international organization since Dubois. Crucé's scheme contemplated the formation of a world union of States, including China, Persia, and the Indies, which should strive to promote freedom of trade among its members, foster the construction of interoceanic canals, and keep the peace through an elaborate structure of negotiation and arbitration, embodying a world assembly and a world court. The other scheme—the "Grand Design" of Henry IV—is described by the Duc de Sully in his memoirs and is attributed by him to the great French King who assumed the throne in 1593 and died by the dagger of Ravaillac in 1610. Sully alleges that Henry had already devised the outlines of the plan when he took the crown and even negotiated with Queen Elizabeth regarding it. It was based upon the assumption that no State of Europe could permanently establish its ascendancy over the others and that all should therefore cooperate to keep the peace. This was to be achieved by dividing Europe into fifteen Powers which would have nothing for which to envy one another. There would be six hereditary monarchies: England, France, Spain, Sweden, Denmark, and Lombardy. There would be five elective monarchies: the Empire, the Papacy, Poland, Hungary, and Bohemia. Finally, there would be four republics: Venice, Italy, Switzerland, and The Netherlands. These States would form a general council modeled after the Amphictyonic Council of the Greeks. The council would consist of four commissioners for each of the Great Powers and three for each of the lesser ones, all to be chosen for a three-year term. This body of commissioners would discuss all problems and pacify all quarrels between the nations and would be supplemented by six regional councils, from whose decision appeal could be taken to the general council. The latter would have at its disposal an international army and navy to enforce its decisions and keep the peace. Premiers Tardieu and Herriot of France made this same proposal for the League of Nations at the General Disarmament Conference of 1932. The scheme of King Henry was aimed primarily at reducing the power of the House of Hapsburg. The Tardieu proposal was aimed at preventing any forcible revision of the 1919 peace settlement by Germany, Austria, or Hungary. Both projects failed of adoption.

Toward the end of the seventeenth century the Quaker missionary, theologian, and colonizer, William Penn, propounded an even more ingenious, if less practicable, plan of international organization in his "Essay toward the Present and Future Peace of Europe" (1693). He proposed a general diet, estates, or parliament of all European princes to meet periodically for the purpose of establishing rules of international law and settling international disputes. "If any of the sovereignties that constitute the imperial States shall refuse to submit their claim or pretensions to them, or to abide and perform the judgment thereof, and seek their remedy by arms, or delay their compliance beyond the time prefixed in their resolutions, all the other sovereignties, united as one strength, shall compel the submission and performance of the sentence, with damages to the suffering party, and charges to the sovereignties that obliged their submission." Since all war, argued Penn, is waged to keep, to recover, or to conquer territory, the imperial diet can keep the peace by adjusting territorial controversies. He suggested that representation and voting strength in the international parliament be based upon national wealth: twelve units for the Holy Roman Empire, ten each for France and Spain, eight for Italy, six for England, three for Portugal, ten each for Turkey and Muscovy, etc. This scheme would have numerous advantages. Peace would be preserved, friendship among princes would be promoted, they would be enabled to marry for love instead of for reasons of State, and, not least important, "the reputation of Christianity will in some degree be recovered in the sight of infidels." This scheme, too, needless to say, failed to receive serious consideration from any of the governments of the day.

At the time of the Conference of Utrecht the learned Abbé Saint-Pierre published his "Project of Perpetual Peace" which he communicated to the French minister, Fleury. The statesman commented drily: "You have forgotten an essential article, that of dispatching missionaries to touch the hearts of princes and to persuade them to enter into your views." The good Abbé proposed an alliance of all States which should guarantee the territory of all its members, suppress revolutions, and maintain monarchs on their thrones. The alliance would oppose by force of arms any Power which should refuse to give effect to its judgments or make treaties contrary to them. Utrecht was to be designated as the City of Peace. Each State would maintain agents there who would constitute an assembly, authorized to keep the peace and to enact, by majority vote, all laws necessary and proper to give effect to its decisions and to achieve the objects of the alliance.

Jean Jacques Rousseau, vagabond philosopher of Geneva, used the Abbé's essay as the basis for his own interesting contribution to the literature of international organization. In his *Extrait du projet de paix perpetuelle de M. l'Abbé de Saint-Pierre* (1761), he came closer to an accurate analysis of the fundamental problems involved in organizing the world for peace than any of his predecessors. The imperfections of governments, he declared, are due less to their constitutions than to their foreign relations. The care which ought to be devoted to internal administration and security is withheld owing to the need of external security. Men have prevented little wars only to kindle greater ones and the only solution is a federation of nations by which States, no less than individuals, are made subject to laws. The balance of power is at best an uneasy and unstable equilibrium. Without a community of interests between States, asserted Rousseau, there can be no stability or lasting peace. All the Powers of Europe must therefore be brought together in a solid confederation, with a common tribunal to pass laws and regulations binding upon its members. The confederation must have coercive power to enforce its decisions and it must be able to prevent members from seceding as soon as they imagine their particular interests to be contrary to the general interest. Rousseau accordingly proposed an international agreement of five articles for the purpose of achieving "A Lasting Peace Through the Federation of Europe." The first article would establish a perpetual and irrevocable alliance, working through a permanent diet or congress where all disputes would be settled by arbitration or judicial pronouncement. The second would deal with membership, finances, and officers. Each State would have one vote in the diet, the presidency of which would be rotated, and each would contribute its share to the expenses. By the third article, the federation would guarantee to all its members their territorial integrity and present form of government. Article 4 specified that any State breaking the treaty would be placed under the ban of Europe, proscribed as a public enemy, and proceeded against in arms by all of the other members. By Article 5, the plenipotentiaries in the congress would have power, by a three-quarters majority, to frame common rules for the guidance of all.

Jeremy Bentham, who apparently was the first to use the word "international" in 1780, followed Rousseau's footsteps in his "Principles of International Law" (1786–1789). He argued that war, which he defined as "mischief on the greatest scale," can be prevented by defensive alliances, general guarantees, disarmament, and the abandonment of colonial imperialism. By agreement the forces of the several nations comprising the European System are to be reduced and fixed and the distant dependencies of each State are to be emancipated. Secret diplomacy and the deeper causes of war must be eliminated and conditions must be created appropriate to the establishment of a tribunal of peace with power to enforce its decisions on refractory States. Tariff barriers, bounties, and colonies must alike be abolished. "Mark well the contrast," declared Bentham. "All trade is in its essence advantageous—even to that party to whom it is least so. All war is in its essence ruinous; and yet the great employments of government are to treasure up occasions for war, and to put fetters on trade." Unless governments can be induced to desist from these activities, there can be no hope of peace.

Not least in the list of contributors to the Utopias of international organization was the celibate philosopher of Königsberg, Immanuel Kant. In 1795 he published his essay *Zum ewige Frieden* ("Toward Eternal Peace") which begins, in good Kantian fashion, with the postulate that the highest of all practical problems for the human race is the establishment of a civil society administering right according to law, *i.e.*, the reconciliation of power and liberty. The external relations of States must be regulated through an international federation. "Every State, even the smallest, may thus rely for its safety and its rights, not on its own power, nor on its own judgment of right, but only on this *foedus amphictionum*— on the combined power of this league of states, and on the decision of the common will according to laws." Man is civilized, but not yet moralized. No true or lasting league of nations is possible without a long process of internal improvement within States to create the proper moral atmosphere. On the basis of these observations, Kant drew up articles of perpetual peace between States. His scheme rested upon the maintenance of the independence of all States, the acceptance of the principle of nonintervention, and the gradual abolition of standing armies. His articles provided for republican constitutions for all States, world citizenship, and a federation of free States for the protection of international rights. At the close of his *Rechtsehre* Kant likewise dwelt on the necessity of a universal union of States, voluntary in character, through which the idea of public rights among nations might become real and differences might be settled by civil process instead of by war.

Since the beginning of the nineteenth century the number of theoretical plans of international organization has multiplied manyfold. If the recent thinkers who have formulated such programs have been less distinguished than their more famous predecessors, they have been no less earnest and ingenious in the presentation of their proposals. Every general war has given rise to a rich crop of plans for perpetual peace. Those referred to above were inspired, successively, by the wars of religion, the conflicts between Louis XIV and his neighbors, the Seven Years' War, and the American and French Revolutionary Wars. The Napoleonic Wars and the Great War led to such a profuse output of schemes to keep the peace that the mere enumeration of them would require many pages. It is significant that all of these schemes were directed toward the prevention of war. All of them embodied some form of international league, confederation, or alliance, operating through a representative body of delegates for the discussion of international problems and the settlement of international disputes. Almost all of them envisaged the application of international coercion against peacebreaking States. And it is equally significant that "practical" statesmen and governments, traditionally engaged in the pursuit of exclusively national objects, were uniformly uninterested in such schemes except in situations where tangible political interests could be served by organizing international support behind them.

Sincere and conscientious reformers frequently discover that their proposals are put into operation by those more interested in their own personal advancement than in serving humanity and that the final result is a pathetic perversion of their original noble intentions. This tragic paradox is strikingly apparent in the field of international organization. For centuries writers and philosophers pleaded in vain for a federation of the world to keep the peace. Their pleas were unheeded until special circumstances produced situations in which States and governments perceived possibilities of gain to themselves in the creation of the institutions and agencies which the reformers had advocated. They were then set up, not by the reformers but by politicians, and were utilized, not to achieve the reformers' purposes but to serve the immediate political interests of those who established them. Twice within a century have such situations arisen. At the close of the Napoleonic Wars and again at the close of the Great War the victors banded together for the purpose of preserving the fruits of victory and maintaining the new *status quo*. In both cases international organization was translated from the sphere of Utopian speculation into the sphere of practical politics. In both cases the Western State System had superimposed upon it a framework of forms and procedures of institutionalized international collaboration. In the earlier instance, the result was the so-called "Holy Alliance" and the "Concert of Europe." In the later instance the result was the establishment of the League of Nations. This comparison is not meant to suggest that the two schemes are analogous as to purposes, procedures, or permanence. But in both cases the proposals of reformers were put into operation only when considerations of national interests and political expediency led States to perceive the advantages of such action. The origins and forms of the League of Nations will be dealt with below. Here the earlier effort will be briefly reviewed for the light which it throws upon the nature of the whole problem.

Prior to 1815 international organization was a vision of dreamers rather than a concern of statesmen. Only when the existing European

System had been all but demolished by the impact of revolutionary and Napoleonic France did States perceive the necessity of permanent institutions of cooperation to avert a recurrence of catastrophe. The victors of Leipzig and Waterloo represented triumphant reaction. They were bent upon restoring what had been destroyed and determined to preserve what had been restored. To achieve these objects they banded themselves together into a rudimentary type of organization to maintain the *status quo,* keep the peace, and suppress revolution wherever it might raise its head. Under the provisions of the final act of the Congress of Vienna, June 9, 1815, and of the second Treaty of Paris, November 20, 1815, Great Britain, Prussia, Austria, and Russia established the Quadruple Alliance which became the Quintuple Alliance in 1818 through the admission of a chastened and reactionary France. For the first time all of the Great Powers of Europe had joined forces to serve their common interests. The organization which they created functioned through periodical congresses called to deal with emergencies as they arose. At the insistence of Tsar Alexander I the structure was crowned by the Holy Alliance agreement of September 26, 1815, between Alexander, Francis of Austria, and Frederick William of Prussia. In this romantic and religious document the three sovereigns, "in the name of the Most Holy and Indivisible Trinity" pledged themselves "to take for their sole guide the precepts of that holy religion, namely, the precepts of justice, Christian charity, and peace," to "remain united by the bonds of a true and indissoluble fraternity," to consider themselves all as "members of one and the same Christian nation," and to receive "with equal ardor and affection into this holy alliance" all other Powers subscribing to its sacred principles.

Behind this façade of mysticism there existed here the first genuine approximation to international organization in the history of the Western State System. The organization was partial, incomplete, fragmentary, and lacking in permanent agencies—legislative, executive, or judicial. Its purposes were reactionary and ran counter to the great dynamic forces of bourgeois nationalism and constitutionalism which were destined to undo its work and bring it to ruin. Nevertheless, it was a true international organization, existing in fact and not merely in the minds of Utopian theorists and it did function successfully for a time under the leadership of Metternich, its guiding genius. Congresses were summoned at intervals to devise means of keeping the peace and suppressing revolution. At Vienna and Aix-la-Chapelle European political problems were discussed and rules of diplomatic precedence and procedure were drawn up. At Troppau, in 1820, Metternich proposed international intervention to put down the revolts which had broken out in Naples and Spain. At Laibach, in 1821, Austria was granted a mandate by the Powers to intervene in Italy. With its action thus sanctioned by international authority the

[239]

Austrian Government sent troops to restore monarchical absolutism in Naples and Piedmont. At Verona in 1823 France was similarly given a mandate to suppress the constitutional movement in Spain. Great Britain withdrew from the organization, however, and joined the United States in opposing any extension of its activities to the western hemisphere. The organization failed to act in the Greek insurrection of 1821 and had become moribund by the time of the French and Belgian revolutions of 1830. The revolutions of 1848 led to its final collapse and disappearance.

The causes of its failure are fairly obvious in retrospect. It was composed of governments whose ruling classes were striving to preserve their privileges through political forms which social and economic changes had rendered obsolete. It was created to resist change either in the internal structure of its members or in the international *status quo* of Europe. No political structure, domestic or international, which is dedicated to resisting modifications of the existing distribution of power can hope for permanency in a world changing so rapidly as is contemporary western civilization. The international organization of 1815–1830 made no provision for the pacific alteration of the *status quo*. When the forces making for such alteration attained ascendancy, they achieved change by violence and swept the organization into the discard. The organization itself, moreover, was lacking in machinery to achieve its purposes, even had they been possible of achievement. Its only organ was the periodical congress of representatives, called *ad hoc* to deal with problems as they arose. It had no secretariat, no central headquarters, no permanent central agencies capable of functioning in the intervals between the congresses. It acted as a unit only when circumstances rendered it expedient for its member States to take joint action, each in its own interests. It failed to act when these circumstances did not exist. It had no authority superior to that of its member States and was therefore only as strong as its weakest link. Like all international organizations, it made possible only such a degree of cooperation as the interests and attitudes of the members permitted. When these interests diverged, the organization was paralyzed.[1]

If any "lesson" is to be drawn from this unsuccessful experiment, it is that the success of such an organization is determined by the extent to which its members feel themselves bound together by common purposes which can best be served by cooperative action. In the absence of common purposes and a disposition to cooperate, the organization can achieve nothing. Its efficacy, within these limits, depends upon the degree to which cooperative action is definitely institutionalized through permanent central agencies and upon the provisions made for the peaceful and orderly modification of the *status quo*. These are the criteria which must be applied to the evaluation of all international organization. They will be

[1] See pp. 90–92 above.

discussed at greater length elsewhere.[1] Suffice it to say here that the "Holy Alliance," when tested by these criteria, was found wanting and came to a timely end.

The disappearance of the Holy Alliance was followed by the development of a habit of consultation between the Powers which came to be referred to as the "Concert of Europe." Here was no international organization, but merely a disposition on the part of States to confer with one another in international conferences at such times as their interests dictated. The Concert of Europe emerged out of the efforts of the Powers to deal with the "Eastern Question" and it functioned fairly successfully in supervising the gradual dissolution of the Ottoman Empire. The independence of Greece was recognized by the Powers, acting jointly, in 1829. The concert was disrupted by the Crimean War, but was reconstituted at Paris in 1856 and at the Congress of Berlin in 1878. The Powers likewise acted in concert in the recognition and neutralization of Belgium and in the partition of Africa and Asia among the great imperial States. But the conflicting interests and policies led to discord. In crises, when its services were most needed, it was non-existent, for it had no permanent organs or procedures and each State determined for itself, in each situation, whether it would cooperate or not. In 1870, when Count Beust of Austria failed in his efforts to arrange a conference to prevent the Franco-Prussian War, he exclaimed, "I cannot find Europe!" Whenever the exclusively national interests of the States of Europe reasserted themselves in the face of the general interests of all States, the concert ceased to function. And yet it represented the only approximation to institutionalized cooperation between the Powers in dealing with questions of high politics during the whole period between the dissolution of the Holy Alliance and the outbreak of the Great War in 1914.

2. THE PUBLIC INTERNATIONAL UNIONS

> The postal union, having by its birth effected a revolution in the constitution of the society of nations, has had a forty years' history of placid obscurity, unworthy of the notice of patriots, and rarely recognized as a herald of the millennium by an occasional pacifist.—L. W. WOOLF, *International Government.*

If the members of the Western State System were not sufficiently bound together by their political interests to make possible the building of an enduring structure of international organization to serve these interests, they were nevertheless constrained by the economic and social developments of the nineteenth century to cooperate closely with one another for the protection and promotion of interests of lesser importance. This cooperation developed rapidly after the middle of the century and

[1] See pp. 791f. below.

assumed the form of the establishment of permanent international agencies of an administrative character, usually called "public international unions." These agencies for a long period of time had no influence upon international politics in the narrower sense of the term. Neither did they bear much resemblance to the Utopian schemes of international organization put forward in earlier periods. International organization first achieved reality and permanence not as a result of the agitation of pacifists and reformers, nor yet as a result of international collaboration in dealing with the great issues of international politics, but as a consequence of the urgent necessity of international action in dealing with technical and routine matters of no particular interest to pacifists, patriots, or politicians. The public international unions fulfilled admirably the limited functions which they were called upon to perform and their very existence promoted habits of cooperation between States in dealing with other international difficulties. The experience gained thereby was of great significance in the later re-establishment of international organization in the political sphere at the Paris Peace Conference of 1919. These circumstances make it desirable to survey these institutions before considering the present-day pattern of international organization centering at Geneva.

The need for international action leading to the creation of the public international unions grew out of that amazing and unprecedented transformation of western society usually designated as the Industrial Revolution. Within a few decades the new technology of the machine age introduced greater changes in the techniques of production, distribution, transportation, and communication than had occurred during the preceding millennium. These changes resulted in a tremendous increase of international trade and travel, leading to the economic integration of the western world on a scale never before thought possible. The political ascendancy of the bourgeoisie in the era of commercial and industrial capitalism led in turn to a democratic revolution, a nationalist revolution, a military revolution, and a humanitarian revolution of vast scope and dimensions. People everywhere in the western States were obliged, willy-nilly, to cast off the habits of localism and provincialism and to become members of a great cosmopolitan world society. In every field of human interest and endeavor, local organizations were merged into national organizations and national organizations, transcending political frontiers, became parts of international associations and societies of all kinds. Lawyers, legislators, doctors, social workers, business men, labor leaders, financiers, educators, farmers, philanthropists, missionaries, scientists—all these and scores of others—formed private international organizations of every conceivable type, representing every conceivable interest. But the new needs and interests could not be served adequately by purely private organizations, nor were they matters of indifference to governments. In part as a consequence of the pressures brought to bear by private associations, national or international, in part as a result of the obvious utility of intergovernmental collaboration, States themselves began to follow the example set by individuals and private organizations and to create public international agencies for dealing with an increasing variety of problems.

Problems of international communication were among the first to command the attention of governments. With the growth of trade and travel, the international regulation of waterways, railroads, telegraphy, and postal service became imperative. In 1856 a number of States established the bases of the European Commission of the Danube, composed of representatives of the members, for the purpose of facilitating and regulating traffic on the great waterway of southeastern Europe. The Commission was established by international agreement as a permanent administrative agency with authority to maintain and improve the navigability of the lower Danube, to fix, collect, and apportion tolls, to enforce navigation rules and to license tugs, lighters, and pilots. On fundamental matters of principle, the Commission acts only by the unanimous consent of its members, but on administrative questions it acts by simple majority decisions. The organization has been modified by many subsequent agreements. The supplementary International Commission for the Danube, set up by the Treaty of Versailles, now cooperates with the European Commission to improve transportation facilities. Many other commissions to deal in similar fashion with other waterways have been established from time to time. The Rhine River Commission, the Congo River Commission, the Straits Commission, the Elbe River Commission, and various Chinese river commissions have functioned successfully in the same way. The International Commission for Air Navigation, set up in 1922, under the Air Convention of 1919, similarly functions as an international agency for the regulation of aerial navigation.

Telegraphic communication across national frontiers likewise involves numerous problems which can be dealt with effectively only by international action. These problems were first handled through bilateral treaties between neighboring States. Austria and Prussia concluded the first of such treaties in 1850. France, Belgium, and Prussia followed suit. In 1852 most of the continental States signed a multilateral convention to regulate telegraphic communication. In 1856, at an international conference at Paris at which twenty States were represented, the International Telegraphic Union was established as a permanent regulatory agency. A multilateral convention set forth the general principles of the new structure and a *règlement* specified in some detail the administrative rules to be followed by the signatories and applied by the organization. A conference of diplomatic representatives was provided for to discuss common problems and amend the *règlement* by unanimous vote as necessity might require. A permanent administrative bureau was established at Berne, Switzerland, to gather and distribute information regarding telegraphic communication and to carry out the provisions of the agreement. Most of the member States—over sixty in number at the present time— maintain government monopolies of telegraphic communication. Such States as the United States, in which telegraphy is in private hands, frequently send representatives to the conferences, but are not members and have no vote. In 1906 twenty-nine States sent delegates to Berlin, where another convention and *règlement* were signed establishing the International Radiotelegraphic Union, consisting of a conference of plenipotentiaries to revise the convention, an administrative conference to deal with modifications of the *règlement*, and a bureau which is identical with that of the Telegraphic Union. The second conference of this organization was held in London in 1912 and, in view of the greatest of all sea disasters in peace time—the sinking of the liner *Titanic* in April, 1912, as a result of its collision with an iceberg in the north Atlantic, devoted much attention to wireless communication on ships. The third International Radiotelegraphic Congress was held in Washington in 1927. It was attended by representatives of seventy-nine contracting administrations who drew up a new convention and two appended sets of regulations, allocating radio wave-lengths to various services by international agreement and dealing in detail with various problems of broadcasting and transmission.

The problems of international postal communication led to the creation in 1874 of the best-known of the public international unions—the Universal Postal Union. In 1817 France and the Netherlands signed the first bilateral postal convention. Other treaties followed, but each State sought to place the burden of postal charges on the other. Rates were high and uncertain and there was no uniformity of national regulations regarding charges, routes, weights, registry, etc. On August 4, 1862, Montgomery Blair, Postmaster-General of the United States, invited other postal administrations to take remedial action. "Many embarrassments to foreign correspondence," he wrote, "exist in this, and probably in other postal departments, which can be remedied only by international concert of action. . . . Without entering into details, it is evident that the international adjustment of a common basis for direct correspondence, and for intermediate land and ocean transit, and for an international registry system, and for the exchange of printed matter, is clearly of the first importance to the commercial and social intercourse between this and other nations." A meeting was held in Paris in May, 1863. No definite action was taken, but thirty-one regulatory articles were agreed upon and submitted to the governments represented. Many difficulties remained, however. The Austro-German Postal Union of 1850 was a model of successful cooperation and in 1868 Herr Stephan, Director-general of Posts of the North German Confederation, proposed the organization of a universal postal union, embracing all civilized States. The Franco-Prussian War interrupted the negotiations, but a few years later the government of Switzerland, at the suggestion of the German, Belgian, and Dutch Governments, invited the Powers to send delegates to a conference at Berne. In September, 1874, representatives of twenty-two States assembled and began discussion of various projects and suggestions. Within a few weeks a convention and a *règlement* were drawn up and the General Postal Union (later renamed the Universal Postal Union) was created.

This remarkably successful organization is based upon the principle that all of the member States form a single postal territory for the reciprocal exchange of mail. Uniform rates for foreign correspondence are fixed and charges are normally borne by the State of origin. Transit charges on mail matter passing through a State are based on total net weight and mileage. Detailed regulations deal with registered articles, return receipts, prepayment, reply coupons, exemptions from postage, prohibitions on sending certain articles through the mails, etc. Under the original arrangements a congress of plenipotentiaries, to meet every five years, was given authority to amend the convention or the *règlement*, while questions of technical detail were to be dealt with by a periodical conference of administrators. An international bureau was set up at Berne to collect, publish, and distribute information on postal questions, to issue a journal, and to act as an international clearing house for the settlement of accounts. The bureau also circulates proposals for changes in the convention or the *règlement*, which may be made by any administration during the intervals between the congresses and conferences, provided that two other administrations concur. Votes on such proposals are taken by the bureau. Sixteen of the thirty-nine articles of the convention can be amended only by unanimity and the rest by majority vote. Every State, colony, and territory in the world, with the exception of Northern Rhodesia, Nigeria, Afghanistan, and a few small islands, now belong to the union, though many of these are grouped together for purposes of voting in the congresses. The principle of State equality is departed from by giving additional votes to colonial postal administrations. Great Britain thus has seven votes, France four, Japan, the United States, Portugal and The Netherlands three each, and Italy two. The expenses of maintaining the bureau are apportioned among the member States on the basis of area, railway mileage, and volume of postal traffic. States in Class I pay 25 units, those in Class II, 20 units, those in Class III, 15, and so on down to Class VII, the members of which pay only one unit.

In practice the conference has ceased to exist and all the work of the organization is done by the congress and the bureau. At the periodical congresses decisions are really arrived at by majority vote. Members may refuse to sign or ratify proposed amendments, but since the practical disadvantages of withdrawal are so great that small comfort can be derived from abstract rights of independence and sovereignty, this is a theoretical rather than an actual danger. The cooperating postal administrations frequently put proposed changes into operation without waiting for formal ratification on the part of the political authorities entrusted with treaty-making. The congresses, of which the ninth was held in London in 1929, have always functioned through discussion and compromise and have shown a willingness to make exceptions to general rules in special cases. In 1906 Persia, for example, requested the right to levy charges on incoming mail as well as outgoing mail, contrary to the general principles of the union. The Persian postal authorities, it appeared, derived very little revenue from outgoing mail, but were put to great expense to distribute by camel caravan the large quantities of Bibles sent into the country by Christian missionary societies. Persia was consequently granted the right to tax all incoming printed matter. The Universal Postal Union has kept postal rates throughout the world at a minimum level and has made possible what could never have been achieved by national action: cheap and rapid postal communication between all parts of the globe under the supervision of a permanent international agency capable of securing uniform regulations and of dealing effectively with all new problems as they arise.

Problems of health, sanitation, commerce, finance, and humanitarian reform have led to the creation of public international unions no less significant in their respective fields than those dealing with international communication. These organizations are far too numerous to be described here individually. Reinsch, in his book of 1911 entitled *Public International Unions*, listed forty-five such organizations, of which over half had permanent administrative bureaus or commissions. The term should not be applied, however, to international arrangements for cooperation which do not set up permanent central organs, for these differ in no particular from ordinary multilateral conventions. The *Handbook of International Organizations* published by the League of Nations lists some two dozen associations of States, outside of the League itself and its subsidiary agencies, which are true international organizations. All of these have been established since 1850 and nine of them have come into existence since 1914. They cover a wide range of interests. Brief mention may be made of a few of the more important.

The International Bureau of Weights and Measures (the Metric Union) was established in 1875 for the purpose of maintaining at the common expense of the parties an international body of scientific experts at Paris, working under the direction of an international commission and a general conference, who should prepare and maintain standard prototypes of the meter, the centimeter, the millimeter, the kilometer, the gram, the milligram, the kilogram, and all units of the metric system. These are decimal multiples or fractions of the meter, originally considered one ten-millionth part of the earth's meridian quadrant through Paris. The international prototypes, prepared with the utmost care and kept under constant conditions of temperature and humidity, are constantly being compared with national standards, which are thus verified and made as accurate and uniform as possible. The Bureau of Trade Marks, Copyrights, and Patents makes possible the international registration at Berne of these industrial and literary property rights—a procedure which entitles them to legal protection in all of the contracting States. The International Union for the Publication of Customs Tariffs publishes at the common expense "the customs tariffs of the various States of the globe and the modifications that may, in future, be made in these tariffs" (Article II of the convention of July 5, 1890). The International Institute of Agriculture, established in Rome in 1904, collects, publishes, and distributes information relating to the production and movements of crops and livestock, studies agricultural cooperation, credit, and insurance, and recommends measures for the protection of the economic interests of farmers. The Geneva conventions of 1864 and 1868 established the International Red Cross for the amelioration of the condition of the wounded in war time. The Union for the Suppression of the African Slave Trade (1890), the Union for the Regulation of the African Liquor Traffic (1890), and the International Opium Commission (1909) were likewise created to deal with social and humanitarian problems. Finally mention may be made of the "Union of American Republics," composed of the United States and the Latin American nations of the western hemisphere. This organization operates through periodical conferences of American States and has as its secretarial bureau the Pan-American Union, located at Washington. At the sixth conference at Havana in 1928 a Convention of the Pan-American Union was drawn up to define more clearly by international agreement the functions of the bureau, which hitherto had been maintained only on the basis of the resolutions of the conferences. The bureau operates under the direction of a governing board. It compiles and distributes information regarding commercial, industrial, agricultural, social, and educational developments throughout the American republics. It is a nonpolitical body which is intended to promote good will and cooperation between the member States. The conferences have dealt with a variety of matters of general interest but have usually avoided delicate political questions underlying the chronic suspicions entertained by many Latin Americans toward the "Colossus of the North."

The broader significance of the public international unions has given rise to considerable difference of opinion among students of these organizations. They are sometimes described as the forerunners of a new era in international relations in which all international problems will be considered by experts through permanent international institutions. By others they are dismissed as convenient administrative devices to deal with technical problems which have little or no bearing upon the forces and frictions of world politics. Since the ultimate place of international organization in the Western State System is not yet fixed, differing evaluations of what has already been achieved are inevitable. It may be suggested, however, that the international unions exhibit interesting departures from traditional attitudes and behavior patterns in a number of respects. In almost every instance the member States, by agreement, have in effect surrendered a portion of their sovereignty and independence and have transferred power to an international body over what was once a "domestic question." In the practical operation of the unions, moreover, the obstructive principles of State equality and action by unanimity have been largely abandoned and decisions are reached by majority vote of the member States. These concessions are prerequisites to successful international collaboration. The structure of the unions is such that broad questions of principle are dealt with by diplomatic representatives meeting in periodical congresses, and problems of administrative detail are dealt with by the actual administrators meeting in conferences or working through the permanent bureaus. The national administrations are geared together into an effective international administration. Problems which were formerly discussed and quarrelled about by diplomats in terms of national honor, prestige, and sovereignty are removed from the sphere of *politics* and made problems of *administration*, to be considered by administrative experts in terms of efficiency, economy, and the progressive adaptation of means to ends. Organized social intelligence is applied to the fullfillment of human needs. An anarchic and individualistic system of relationships in which each State pursues its own interests, with resulting inconvenience and loss to all, is replaced by organization and planning through which all cooperate to serve the common interests.

It may well be doubted, however, whether this form of collaboration is adaptable to all problems of international concern. The great sources of tension and conflict between States, the great problems of power, prestige, territory, armaments, and markets, cannot readily be transferred from the political sphere to the administrative sphere so long as national attitudes toward these things remain what they have been in the past. The public international unions have functioned successfully in dealing with matters of no particular interest to patriots or politicians. They have dealt with problems with regard to which there has been an obvious, urgent, and generally appreciated necessity of international cooperation. Their member States were willing to create the instrumentalities of such cooperation because they had nothing to lose thereby in power-and-prestige values, and much to gain in other respects. The problems in question, furthermore, have been of a character which made possible a precise definition of the general interests of all States. These interests have been clear and reasonably uniform for all the participants. It has been easy, therefore, to relegate them to a nonpolitical level of treatment. International politics deals with vague, half-formulated imponderables and with interests which are envisaged as being exclusive and national, not general and international. States are quite prepared to regard questions of postal service, weights and measures, sanitation, and telegraphy as matters of international concern which they can safely and advantageously submit to international regulation. But they are not yet prepared to deal in the same fashion with questions of armaments, colonies, or economic opportunities in "backward" areas and they are not at all prepared to submit to international control their decisions regarding tariffs, immigration, security, or territorial claims. The problems involving "national honor" and "vital interests" are those which States are unwilling to submit to arbitration or adjudication. They are the same problems which States are reluctant to submit to agencies of international organization and administration.

Here, in the last analysis, is the limiting factor which prevents the extension of the methods and procedures of international organization to cover all international problems. To apply to the question the familiar distinction already suggested between *politics* and *administration*, one may say that politics on all levels, local, national, and international, is concerned with the determination of public policies, with the formulation of programs of action through discussion, compromise, and conflict between divergent interests, adhering to differing views and presenting differing demands. Administration, on the other hand, is concerned with the practical task of carrying into execution such programs of action as have already been agreed upon by policy-determining agencies. There can be no administrative treatment of a problem unless there is prior agreement among those interested as to what their common interests are and what can be done to serve these interests most advantageously. International politics is the process by which States pursue their separate and divergent interests and arrive somehow, by diplomacy or war, at an equilibrium of forces or a general consensus of views. International administration is the process whereby States put into practice their common views regarding common interests with regard to which they have already reached an agreement. Administration postulates prior agreement

[249]

upon common interests and upon the best mode of furthering such interests. Politics postulates disagreement and divergencies of interests and views. It is therefore impossible to apply administrative solutions to political problems, for these are precisely the problems upon which there is no agreement and no consciousness of common interests. It may well be that the whole function of contemporary international organization is to bring about agreement on an increasing number of common interests and in this way to reduce an ever larger number of problems to a level where they can be handled administratively rather than politically. But, despite the long strides which have been taken in this direction, this ideal is still very far from achievement. Only when the political issues which divide States from one another have been reduced to the vanishing point will it be possible to extend international administration in an effective fashion over the whole range of international relations. Meanwhile international organization functions most successfully with respect to administrative problems. As for problems which are still "political," international organization can only serve to provide agencies for discussion and pacific settlement through which "national interests" may perhaps be integrated into international interests and eventually reduced to terms where administrative solutions become feasible.

3. THE COVENANT OF 1919

An effective society of nations neither presupposes nor anticipates the creation of a super-State. It does envisage a loosening of the political fetters of the nationalist era in order that an essentially cooperative civilization may survive. . . . The society of nations has been established not to override the independence of the nation-state, but to avert the deterioration and submergence of the national contribution in a world where frontiers have lost so much of their economic, cultural, and intellectual validity.— FELIX MORLEY, *The Society of Nations.*

The establishment of the League of Nations at the Paris Peace Conference of 1919 represents the most recent and the most ambitious effort ever made to extend the method of international organization into the sphere of political relations between States. Between the collapse of the Holy Alliance and the outbreak of the Great War, enormous numbers of people throughout the western world organized themselves in their private capacities to promote cooperation across national frontiers in the pursuit of a great variety of economic, scientific, religious, and aesthetic interests. At the same time States organized public institutions and agencies of cooperation between governments to deal with problems of transportation, communication, commerce, finance, health, sanitation, social problems, and the like. But during this entire period no effort was made to set up an international organization of States to deal with broader political questions. The Concert of Europe functioned fitfully and the Hague Conferences of 1899 and 1907 offered vain promise of peace on earth, good will to men. No permanent procedures of political collaboration were set up, however, until the world-shattering cataclysm of 1914–1918 brought disaster to all nations alike and led to a world-wide demand for a league of States to keep the peace. This demand, personified in Woodrow Wilson and buttressed by the desire of the victors to create an international federation to maintain the new *status quo*, led to the framing of the Covenant of the League of Nations.

The League of Nations may be regarded as having been founded by America's war President. If it was not his invention (and the process of political invention is at best ill-understood) it was at any rate the project upon which he, more than any of the contemporary statesmen, had set his heart. He played a large part in writing into the Covenant the ideas of others and the experience of the past. He insisted emphatically, moreover, upon the creation of the League at the Peace Conference and upon the incorporation of the Covenant into the peace treaties. Had it not been for his active leadership, it is quite possible that the League would not have been established. In a broader sense, however, the League was the work of the long line of Utopian theorists whose work has been reviewed above. It was a synthesis of the ideas of many people in many lands and it embodied into a single structure all of the past experience of the States of the world in establishing and maintaining international organizations. That experience was supplemented by the efforts of the Allied Governments during the war to work out methods of joint action for the purpose of coordinating their activities in the fields of shipping, food supplies, munitions, and military affairs.[1] The League was not, then, the creation of a single man or of a single generation of men, but was the culmination of a long process of practical and theoretical preparation for the building of an enduring structure of cooperation between States.

Popular interest in the possibilities of a League began to manifest itself in the United States shortly after the outbreak of the great conflict and grew rapidly during the period of American neutrality. A "League to Enforce Peace" was established by a group of prominent public leaders, including many outstanding figures in the Republican party, headed by ex-President William Howard Taft. This organization held a

---

[1] Not until the spring of 1918, when the great German offensives threatened to break through the western front, did the Allied Governments finally agree to appoint a single commander-in-chief of their armies in the person of Marshal Foch. It was only in the face of this supreme emergency that the Allied Maritime Transport Council, the Munitions Council, the Food Council, and the other coordinating agencies began to function effectively. Here, as in the public international unions, success was attained when the problems at stake were dealt with directly by administrators as administrative problems, instead of by diplomats as political problems. *Cf.* Arthur Salter, *Allied Shipping Control*, 1921, *passim.*

conference in Independence Hall, Philadelphia, in June of 1915, and adopted a four-point program which received wide publicity. The program called for the submission of all justiciable international disputes to arbitration, the submission of all other disputes to a council of conciliation, the application of economic and military force by all States against any State resorting to war without submitting its disputes to pacific settlement, and the convocation of periodical congresses to codify international law. This program was a synthesis of the Hague arbitration system and the Bryan "cooling-off" treaties, with a new element of sanctions added to them. At the end of May, 1916, the organization held another conference in Washington "to devise and determine upon measures for giving effect" to these proposals. This meeting was widely attended by leaders in all walks of life. Mr. Taft, as president of the League, presided. Alton B. Parker, Democratic candidate for the presidency of the United States in 1908, was vice president of the organization, with Edward Filene, Hamilton Holt, and Theodore Marburg serving as vice chairmen. The speakers included the presidents of the United States Chamber of Commerce, of the American Federation of Labor, and of Harvard University, as well as Senator Henry Cabot Lodge, Secretary of War Baker, and President Wilson himself. The speeches, in retrospect, were not without a certain ironic significance, for Senator Lodge exhibited much more enthusiasm for a league of nations than did President Wilson. The Senator declared that "the limits of voluntary arbitration have been reached" and that international force must be placed behind peace.

I know the difficulties which arise when we speak of anything which seems to involve an alliance. But I do not believe that when Washington warned us against entangling alliances he meant for one moment that we should not join with the other civilized nations of the world if a method could be found to diminish war and encourage peace.[1]

President Wilson, though more restrained, definitely committed himself to the major purposes of the organization:

"We are participants, whether we would or not, in the life of the world," asserted the American President. The peace of the world "must henceforth depend upon a new and more wholesome diplomacy. Only when the great nations of the world have reached some sort of agreement as to what they hold to be fundamental to their common interest, and as to some feasible method of acting in concert when any nation or group of nations seeks to disturb those fundamental things, can we feel that civilization is at last in a way of justifying its existence and claiming to be finally established." Right must prevail over selfish aggression. Cooperation and understanding must be achieved on the basis of certain fundamental principles. We believe, first, that "every people has a right

[1] Full text in "League to Enforce Peace," *Enforced Peace*, 1916, *passim*.

to choose the sovereignty under which they shall live"; second, "that the small States of the world have a right to enjoy the same respect for their sovereignty and for their territorial integrity that the great and powerful nations expect and insist upon "; third, "that the world has a right to be free from every disturbance of its peace that has its origin in aggression and disregard of the rights of peoples and nations. . . . So sincerely do we believe in these things that I am sure that I speak the mind and wish of the people of America when I say that the United States is willing to become a partner in any feasible association of nations formed in order to realize these objects and make them secure against violation."[1]

The activities of the League to Enforce Peace were supplemented by those of a number of other organizations, both in the United States and abroad. The "League of Free Nations Association" was formed in New York as an organization of more liberal minded people than those in the League to Enforce Peace. Both organizations cooperated, however, and finally endorsed the League of Nations Covenant as achieving their purposes. After the war the League of Free Nations Association transformed itself into the New York Foreign Policy Association. In England, the Fabian Society and the League of Nations Society both played active rôles in organizing peace sentiment behind the project of a league, with George Bernard Shaw and James Bryce taking the initiative in the respective groups. In France a League of Nations Society was likewise formed under the leadership of Leon Bourgeois. The French group emphasized the necessity of military sanctions and defense against outside attack. A corresponding German group was led by Erzburger, and similar organizations appeared in the neutral countries.

On January 22, 1917, President Wilson addressed the American Senate on a "World League for Peace."[2]

In every discussion of the peace that must end this war it is taken for granted that that peace must be followed by some definite concert of power, which will make it virtually impossible that any such catastrophe should ever overwhelm us again. Every lover of mankind, every sane and thoughtful man, must take that for granted. . . . It is inconceivable that the people of the United States should play no part in that great enterprise. To take part in such a service will be the opportunity for which they have sought to prepare themselves by the very principles and purposes of their polity and the approved practices of their Government, ever since the days when they set up as a new nation in the high and honorable hope that it might in all that it was and did show mankind the way of liberty. They cannot, in honor, withhold the service to which they are now about to be challenged. They do not wish to withhold it. But they owe it to themselves and to the other nations of the world to state the conditions under which they will feel free to render it. That service is nothing less than this—to add their

[1] *Ibid.*
[2] See Congressional Record, Senate, January 22, 1917; International Conciliation, Official Documents Looking toward Peace, Series II, 111, February, 1917.

authority and their power to the authority and force of other nations to guarantee peace and justice throughout the world.

In resounding Wilsonian rhetoric, the American chief executive proposed that the United States take the initiative in organizing the world for peace. A durable peace, he argued, must be a "peace without victory."

Victory would mean peace forced upon the loser, a victor's terms imposed upon the vanquished. It would be accepted in humiliation, under duress, at an intolerable sacrifice, and would leave a sting, a resentment, a bitter memory, upon which terms of peace would rest, not permanently, but only as upon quicksand. Only a peace between equals can last; only a peace the very principle of which is equality and a common participation in a common benefit. The right state of mind, the right feeling between nations, is as necessary for a lasting peace as is the just settlement of vexed questions of territory or of racial and national allegiance. . . . I am proposing, as it were, that the nations should with one accord adopt the doctrine of President Monroe as the doctrine of the world: That no nation should seek to extend its policy over any other nation or people, but that every people should be left free to determine its own policy, its own way of development, unhindered, unthreatened, unafraid, the little along with the great and powerful.

I am proposing that all nations henceforth avoid entangling alliances which would draw them into competition of power, catch them in a net of intrigue and selfish rivalry, and disturb their own affairs with influences intruded from without. There is no entangling alliance in a concert of power. When all unite to act in the same sense and with the same purpose, all act in the common interest and are free to live their own lives under a common protection.

I am proposing government by the consent of the governed; that freedom of the seas which in international conference after conference representatives of the United States have urged with the eloquence of those who are the convinced disciples of liberty; and that moderation of armaments which make of armies and navies a power for order merely, not an instrument of aggression and selfish violence.

These are American principles, American policies. We can stand for no others. And they are also the principles and policies of forward-looking men and women everywhere, of every modern nation, of every enlightened community. They are the principles of mankind and must prevail.

Less than a week after these brave words were uttered, the German Government announced the resumption of unrestricted submarine warfare and President Wilson responded by severing diplomatic relations between Washington and Berlin. On April 6, 1917, the American Congress, on the President's recommendation, declared war against Germany. In his war message President Wilson again insisted that peace in the future could never be maintained except by a world-wide partnership of democratic nations. "It must be a league of honor, a partnership of opinion." Wilson's facility at phrase-making made him an invaluable asset to the Allied cause and the chief interpreter of Allied war aims to a weary and blood-sickened world. Throughout the summer and fall of 1917 he clarified his views regarding the purposes of the "war to end war" and the struggle to "make the world safe for democracy" in a series of public addresses. Early in January, 1918, he received two pleas for a concise restatement of war aims which would have popular propagandist value. One was from Lord Balfour, British Foreign Secretary, who was worried over the restlessness of the British trade unions. The other was from Edgar Sisson, representative in Russia of the United States Committee on Public Information, who was trying to feed peace propaganda into Germany and to inspire the exhausted peasants and workers of Russia to continue the hopeless battle against the Central Powers. In response to these appeals, President Wilson, on January 8, 1918, issued his famous program of fourteen points, the last of which declared, "A general association of nations must be formed under specific convenants for the purpose of affording mutual guarantees of political independence and territorial integrity to great and small States alike." In the following September, Wilson asserted "the constitution of that league of nations and the clear definition of its objects must be a part, in a sense the most essential part, of the peace settlement itself." On November, 11, 1918, came the armistice and peace, not without victory, but with an overwhelming Allied triumph, and in January of 1919 the great Peace Conference opened in Paris.

By this time numerous plans for a league, both official and unofficial, had been put forward. In March, 1918, a committee of the British Foreign Office, with Lord Phillimore as its chairman, had prepared a draft convention for the creation of a league. Three months later, Colonel House, President Wilson's confidential adviser, prepared another draft on the basis of Wilson's own ideas. In July of 1918 Wilson typed out his own first draft. In December General Smuts of South Africa proposed a plan containing the germs of the Council and the Mandate System. At the same time Lord Robert Cecil prepared a new draft on the basis of the Phillimore report. Wilson prepared his second draft on January 10, 1919, and his third draft ten days later to submit to the Peace Conference. Meanwhile the British delegation to the conference had combined the Cecil and Smuts drafts into an official British draft of January 20, 1919. Since the third Wilson draft and the British draft diverged at a number of points, they were submitted to Cecil Hurst, legal adviser of the British delegation, and to David Hunter Miller of the American delegation, for revision. The result was the composite Hurst-Miller draft of February 3, 1919, which was used as a basis for discussion by the League of Nations Commission of the Peace Conference.

Wilson insisted, in the face of the indifference or opposition of Clemenceau and Lloyd George, that the conference should give its attention to the league project before taking up territorial and political settlements. Following the adoption of the British resolutions of January 25, appointing a commission to work out the details of the constitutions and functions

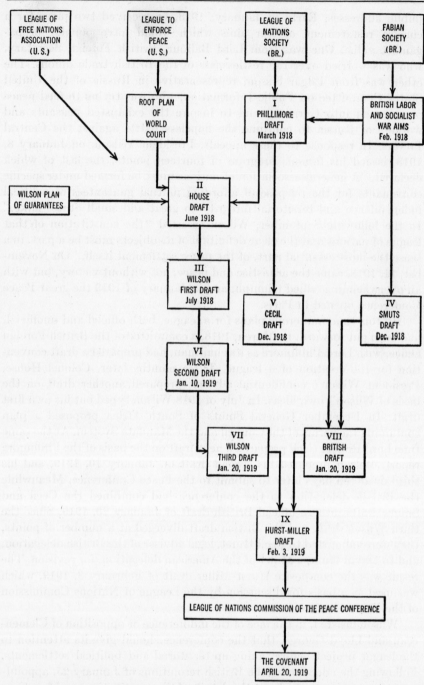

The Genesis of the League Covenant. (*Adapted from Ray Stannard Baker, "Woodrow Wilson and the World Settlement," Vol. I.*)

of the proposed organization, Wilson declared that the league is "the central object of our meeting. Settlements may be temporary, but the actions of the nations in the interests of peace and justice must be permanent. We can set up permanent processes. We may not be able to set up permanent decisions." A commission of nineteen was chosen, with the small Powers in a minority of one. Wilson assumed the chairmanship of the commission and the work was rapidly pushed forward by the combined efforts of the British and American representatives. On February 14 the tentative draft of the covenant was presented to the conference as a whole for its consideration. "A living thing is born," asserted the American President. "While it is elastic, while it is general in its terms, it is definite in the one thing we are called upon to make definite. It is a guarantee of peace. It is a definite guarantee by word against aggression. Armed force is in the background in this program, but it *is* in the background, and if the moral force of the world will not suffice, the physical force of the world shall. But that is the last resort, because this is intended as a constitution of peace, not as a league of war. . . . (But) it is not in contemplation that this should be merely a league to secure the peace of the world. It is a league that can be used for cooperation in any international matter."

A few subsequent changes were made in the Covenant and on April 28, 1919, the revised document was accepted unanimously at a plenary session of the conference. The other terms of the victors' peace were gradually hammered out and on June 28 the German delegates were called into the Hall of Mirrors in the great château of Louis XIV and compelled to attach their signatures to the Treaty of Versailles. The first twenty-six articles of the Treaty contained the Covenant of the League of Nations. The Covenant was likewise incorporated into the Treaty of St. Germain with Austria of September 10, 1919, the Treaty of Neuilly with Bulgaria, November 27, 1919, the Treaty of Trianon with Hungary, June 4, 1920, and the Treaty of Sèvres with Turkey, August 10, 1920. The last-named agreement was repudiated by the Turkish Nationalists. The four other treaties were ratified. On January 10, 1920, the League of Nations came officially into existence with the deposit at the Quai d'Orsay of eighteen ratifications of the Treaty of Versailles.

4. THE GENEVA LEAGUE: ITS NATURE, SCOPE, AND STRUCTURE

> The world is a stupendous machine, composed of innumerable parts, each of which being a free agent, has a volition and action of its own; and on this ground arises the difficulty of assuring success in any enterprise depending on the volition of numerous agents. We may set the machine in motion, and dispose every wheel to one certain end; but when it depends on the volition of any one wheel, and the correspondent action of every wheel, the result is uncertain.—MACHIAVELLI, *On Fortune, Chance, etc.*

The organization thus created is in so many respects a departure from all its antecedents and counterparts that it is not strange that statesmen, scholars, and commentators have differed appreciably in their evaluations of its fundamental nature. In the various efforts which have been made to place the League in established legal and political categories, it has been described as an alliance, a confederation, a partnership, a superstate, and a corporation. In fact, while it possesses certain characteristics of each of these, it resembles none of them very closely. The League is scarcely an alliance between its members, for it possesses central administrative agencies whereas all past alliances have achieved their purposes exclusively by State action. Neither is it a confederation, federation, or superstate, since its central organs reach decisions only by unanimity and it has no jurisdiction in any sense over individuals. It operates on States, by States, through States. While its central organs exist independently of the members, they are sustained only by contributions from the members. They have no authority except that conferred upon them by the members and, in general, they can take no action which is not at the same time action by the member States. Comparisons with partnerships and corporations are equally strained, since these entities are creations of municipal law and have the legal status of persons in courts, while the League was created by international agreement and cannot itself sue or be sued before any judicial tribunal, national or international. The League bears closest resemblance to the public international unions and like them is a true international organization of States which have set up joint institutions of cooperation to achieve their common purposes. The purposes served by the League, however, are wider than those of any of the other international organizations and one of its major functions is that of coordinating their activities. The general purposes are set forth in the preamble to the Covenant in the following language:

The HIGH CONTRACTING PARTIES,

In order to promote international cooperation, and to achieve international peace and security

    by the acceptance of obligations not to resort to war,

    by the prescription of open, just, and honorable relations between nations,

by the firm establishment of the understandings of international law as
the actual rule of conduct among Governments,
and by the maintenance of justice and a scrupulous respect for all treaty
obligations in the dealings of organized peoples with one another,
Agree to this Covenant of the League of Nations.

The first four words of this statement of purposes and of means
thereto make it clear that the League is a creation and agency of the
States ratifying the Covenant. Emphasis is placed upon *international*
cooperation and *international* peace and security. All domestic questions
are thus excluded from the scope of action of the League, but in the sphere
of international relations the language employed is broad enough to cover
the whole field of contacts between States. The "obligations not to resort
to war" have been suggested in the preceding chapter and will be considered at some length below. The phrase "open, just, and honorable
relations between nations" is reminiscent of the first of the fourteen
points: "open covenants, openly arrived at." Article 18 of the Covenant
provides for the registration and publication of all treaties concluded
by member States. The proceedings of the League itself are public and are
published in its *Official Journal*. The "understandings of international
law" suggests the origins of international jurisprudence in custom and contract. "Respect for all treaty obligations" implies the perpetuation of the
peace settlements of 1919, though Article 19 of the Covenant makes provision for the reconsideration of treaties which have become inapplicable. As
for the articles of the Covenant itself, the first seven deal with membership
and structure, 8 to 21 with the League as an agency to keep the peace, and
22 to 25 with the League as an agency of international cooperation.[1]

If the League be defined functionally, it may be regarded as fulfilling
three fundamental purposes. It is in the first place an agency for the
enforcement of certain provisions contained in the peace treaties and in
other supplementary agreements following the Great War. In this
capacity the League is intended to preserve and maintain the *status quo*
established by the Peace Conference. It is entrusted with certain administrative and supervisory functions usually exercised by the victors themselves at the close of a war, but here conferred upon an international
agency. Among these are the protection of national minorities,[2] the supervision of the Free City of Danzig,[3] the administration of the Saar valley,[4]
and the operation of the mandate system.[5] In the second place, the League
acts as a means of promoting international cooperation in dealing with
problems of health, social questions, finances, transportation, communica-

[1] See text of the Covenant in Appendix VI, pp. 897–906 below.
[2] See pp. 309–324 below.
[3] See pp. 748–750 below.
[4] See pp. 745–748 below.
[5] See pp. 609–621 below.

tion, and the like.[1] In this capacity it serves to integrate and coordinate the activities of the existing public international unions. In the third place, the League is an agency for the prevention of war and the pacific settlement of disputes. All threats to peace are within its competence and all controversies between its members are, in theory at least, submitted to the procedures of arbitration, adjudication, or conciliation provided for in the Covenant.[2] These functions will be dealt with in some detail below and an effort will be made to evaluate the present position of the League in the Western State System. Here it will be enough to deal with League membership and to sketch the structure of the League and its subsidiary organizations.

Article 1 of the Covenant provides for membership and withdrawal.[3] The Covenant, as incorporated in the Treaty of Versailles, was signed by 31 of the 32 States named in the annex. The thirty-second, China, became an original member by signing the Treaty of St. Germain. Of these 32 signatories, 3 failed to ratify the treaties: Ecuador, the Hejaz, and the United States. By January 10, 1920, 19 ratifications had been deposited at the Quai d'Orsay and by April of 1920 a total of 42 States had become original members of the League, comprising the 29 Allied and Associated Powers which ratified the peace treaties (including Canada, Australia, South Africa, New Zealand, and India along with the 24 fully sovereign Allied belligerents) and the 13 neutrals invited in the annex to accede to the Covenant. Mexico, Costa Rica, and the Dominican Republic were not mentioned in the list of neutrals, because their governments were not at the time recognized by all of the Allied and Associated Powers. India and the self-governing Dominions of the British Empire were given full status as members, though by a curious error of phraseology in the annex Great Britain itself was referred to as the "British Empire," with the Dominions and India listed separately below. Of the 42 original members, one, Brazil, ceased to be a member in 1928, following notice of withdrawal

---

[1] See pp. 752f. below.

[2] See pp. 762f. below.

[3] Article 1. 1. The original members of the League of Nations shall be those of the signatories which are named in the annex to this Covenant and also such of those other States named in the annex as shall accede without reservation to this Covenant. Such accessions shall be effected by a declaration deposited with the Secretariat within two months of the coming into force of the Covenant. Notice thereof shall be sent to all other members of the League.

2. Any fully self-governing State, dominion or colony not named in the annex may become a member of the League if its admission is agreed to by two-thirds of the Assembly, provided that it shall give effective guarantees of its sincere intention to observe its international obligations, and shall accept such regulations as may be prescribed by the League in regard to its military, naval, and air forces and armaments.

3. Any member of the League may, after two years' notice of its intention to do so, withdraw from the League, provided that all its international obligations and all its obligations under this Covenant shall have been fulfilled at the time of its withdrawal.

given in 1926. Seventeen other States have since been admitted to membership.[1] Of these, one, Costa Rica, withdrew in 1927, following notice given in 1925. In March of 1928 the Council invited Costa Rica to consider renewing its membership. A favorable reply was received, but the legislature of Costa Rica has taken no further action in the matter, and Costa Rica consequently remains a non-member. By 1933 there were, therefore, 57 members of the League.

The States of the world which are not members of the League fall into three categories: States applying for membership but not admitted, States which have withdrawn, and States never making application. The first class includes only very minute States or States at present nonexistent as independent political entities. Applications were refused from Montenegro (now part of Jugoslavia), and from Armenia, Georgia, and the Ukraine (now parts of the Soviet Union). San Marino, Andorra, Monaco, and Leichtenstein also applied for admission, but in view of their microscopic size, no action was taken on their applications. Iceland and the Vatican City might be placed in the same category, though neither has ever applied for membership. Only two non-member States have withdrawn from former membership: Brazil and Costa Rica. The States which have never applied for membership include two Great Powers—the United States and the U.S.S.R.; one Latin American State—Ecuador; one central Asiatic State—Nepal; and four Moslem States of the Near East—Afghanistan, Egypt, Oman, and Hejaz. It is significant that Persia, Turkey, and Iraq are the only Moslem States in the League. In the other independent Moslem communities the League has been regarded as the creature of western imperialism. The failure of Ecuador to ratify the Covenant was apparently due to indifference. As for the United States, the American Senate refused to ratify President Wilson's work and the statesman who played the largest single rôle in the drafting of the Covenant was repudiated in his own country. This was due to a popular recrudescence of isolationism, to partisan rivalry between the Republican and Democratic parties, and to the personal animosity of Senator Lodge and his fellow irreconcilables toward the Democratic war President.[2] The Communist rulers of Russia have from the beginning looked upon the League as a hostile association of bourgeois States, doomed to failure and unworthy of serious attention.

The structure of the League can be described in terms of its major organs: the Assembly, the Council, and the Secretariat. The Assembly is the representative and deliberative organ of the League, consisting of all

[1] In 1920 Albania, Finland, Bulgaria, Austria, Costa Rica, and Luxemburg were elected as members; in 1922 Esthonia, Latvia, and Lithuania were admitted; in 1923, Hungary, Abyssinia, and the Irish Free State; in 1924 the Dominican Republic; in 1926 Germany; in 1931 Mexico; and in 1932 Turkey and Iraq.

[2] See pp. 802f. below.

its members, with each entitled to one vote in accordance with the ancient principle of State equality. The Assembly meets annually, usually in the Hall of the Reformation in Geneva, and has thus far held three special sessions, one in March, 1926, to deal with the admission of Germany to the League, and two in 1932–1933, to deal with the conflict between Japan and China. Each member State is entitled to have not more than three delegates and several alternates at the Assembly meetings. The delegates from each State collectively cast the vote to which the State is entitled, in accordance with their instructions. Delegates are ordinarily chosen, like other diplomatic representatives, by the executive authorities of the State, though in many recent Assemblies prime ministers and foreign ministers have themselves acted as delegates. The Assembly elects its own presiding officers and makes its own rules in harmony with the provisions of the Covenant. Its agenda is prepared in advance by the Secretary-General and is subject to modification by the Assembly itself. Its organization resembles that of a legislative body in that it follows the usual principles of parliamentary procedure and operates through committees. It maintains six regular standing committees—on constitutional and legal questions, on technical organizations, on reduction of armaments, on budgetary matters, on social and humanitarian questions, and on political questions —and it is free to appoint special committees for particular purposes.

The functions of the Assembly are very broad, even if somewhat vague. Article 3 of the Covenant declares that it "may deal at its meetings with any matter within the sphere of action of the League or affecting the peace of the world." In practice it has exercised three general types of powers: electoral, constituent, and deliberative. In the exercise of its electoral functions, it elects new members to the League by a two-thirds vote, as occasion may arise; it elects annually three of the nine non-permanent members of the Council by a majority vote; and, in conjunction with the Council, it elects every nine years by majority vote the fifteen judges and four deputy judges of the Permanent Court of International Justice. It also approves by majority vote the Council's nominations for the post of Secretary-General. As a constituent body, it amends the Covenant in accordance with the provisions of Article 26.[1] In this capacity, it acts by majority vote, but amendments must be approved unanimously by the Council and are subject to the ratification of the member States. As a deliberative body, the Assembly considers general political, economic, and technical questions of international interest, advises the reconsideration of inapplicable treaties under Article 19 (it has never exercised this

[1] Article 26. 1. Amendments to this Covenant will take effect when ratified by the members of the League whose representatives compose the Council and by a majority of the members of the League whose representatives compose the Assembly.

2. No such amendment shall bind any member of the League which signifies its dissent therefrom, but in that case it shall cease to be a member of the League.

power), supervises the work of the Council and of the technical organizations, and prepares the annual budget of the League. The budget has usually totaled about $5,000,000, which, it has been pointed out by pacifists, is about one-fifth the cost of a single modern battleship. The budget is prepared by the Secretariat, subject to revision by the Assembly, and is divided into three major parts, one for the Secretariat and special organizations, one for the International Labor Office, and one for the Permanent Court of International Justice. The 1932 budget was larger than usual and totaled about $6,735,000.[1] The Assembly has provided for the apportionment of these expenses among the members in accordance with a scale totaling 1,000 units, on which Great Britain pays 105 units, France and Germany 79 units each, Italy and Japan 60 units each, India 56 units, China 46, Spain 40, and so on down to one unit each for such small States as Albania, Haiti, Liberia, Luxemburg, etc. These important functions have made the Assembly the dominant organ of the League, though because of its nature and size it cannot, of course, act as swiftly and expeditiously as the Council.

The Council of the League was designed to be a small body on which the Great Powers should have permanent seats, with the other seats rotated among the lesser Powers. It was originally contemplated that it would consist of five permanent seats to be occupied by the United States, Great Britain, France, Italy, and Japan, and four non-permanent seats, assigned temporarily in 1920 to Belgium, Brazil, Spain, and Greece, with their successors to be chosen periodically by the Assembly. The refusal of the United States to join the League reduced the ratio of Great Powers to small Powers to four to four. In 1922 two additional non-permanent seats were added, making a Council of ten members. The admission of Germany to the League created a "Council crisis" which necessitated further reorganization. The German Government agreed to enter the League only on condition of being received on a basis of complete equality and of receiving a permanent seat on the Council. Brazil, Spain, and Poland presented demands for permanent seats at the same time, which were resisted by Germany and other States. While Germany could be admitted to the League by a two-thirds vote of the Assembly, it could secure a permanent seat on the Council only by unanimous vote of that body. An impasse was created which the special session of the Assembly in March, 1926, was unable to resolve. On March 18 the Council set up a special committee to study the problem. In accordance with its recommendations, subsequently approved by the Council and the Assem-

[1] 33,687,994 Swiss francs, apportioned as follows: Secretariat and special organizations 19,174,317; International Labor Office, 8,792,290; Permanent Court, 2,663,702; Nansen international office for refugees, 297,763; buildings at Geneva, 1,748,899; and pensions, 1,011,023. *Monthly Summary of the League of Nations*, XI, 9, September, 1931, p. 256.

bly, the Council was enlarged by establishing nine non-permanent seats, three to be filled annually for three-year terms by the Assembly. By a two-thirds vote the Assembly may declare non-permanent members re-eligible, may fix rules for the election of non-permanent members, and may, if it chooses, elect *in toto* an entirely new group of non-permanent members. Under the terms of this compromise Germany was admitted to a permanent seat on the Council. Poland was satisfied to be declared re-eligible to a non-permanent seat for another three-year term. Brazil and Spain, however, gave notice of their intention to withdraw from the League. Spain later reconsidered her intention, but Brazil ceased to be a member in 1928.

Since 1926, then, the Council consists of five permanent and nine non-permanent members. At the 1926 Assembly Poland, Chile, and Rumania were elected for three years. Colombia, the Netherlands, and China for two years, and Belgium, Salvador, and Czechoslovakia for one year. A petition from Belgium to be declared re-eligible was rejected by the Assembly in 1927. Poland and Spain were declared re-eligible for another term of three years in 1928. The subsequent composition of the Council is shown below.

PERMANENT MEMBERS OF THE COUNCIL
Great Britain
France
Italy
Japan
Germany

NON-PERMANENT MEMBERS OF THE COUNCIL
(By years of election)

Election	1926	1927	1928	1929	1930	1931	1932
For three years.	Poland Chile Rumania	....	....	Poland Jugoslavia Peru	....	....	Poland Czechoslovakia Mexico
For two years.	Colombia Netherlands China	....	Spain Persia Venezuela	....	....	Spain China Panama	
For one year.	Belgium Salvador Czechoslovakia	Canada Cuba Finland	....	....	Irish Free State Norway Guatemala		

The functions of the Council are as broad as those of the Assembly. It meets about four times a year, or oftener as occasion may require, usually in the Palace of the League in Geneva, which also houses the Secretariat. Like the larger body, it may deal "with any matter within the sphere of action of the League or affecting the peace of the world" (Article 4). Its powers may be expanded by treaty agreements between States. The minorities treaties conferred special powers on the Council in regard to the supervision of the enforcement of their obligations. The Treaty of Lausanne of 1923, between the Allied Powers and Turkey, similarly gave the Council jurisdiction over the Mosul dispute. The Council is free to refuse to assume such special duties, but it has never thus far done so. In practice, the most important function of the Council has been the settlement of international disputes. It shares this function with the Assembly, but the latter has intervened only once in such matters—in the spring of 1932, when it sought to achieve a settlement of the Sino-Japanese conflict after the Council had failed. The Council also has executive, administrative, and supervisory functions in connection with Danzig, the Saar valley, the mandates system, etc. Under Articles 10 to 16 of the Covenant it has authority to mobilize the sanctions of the League against a Covenant-breaking State, but this power has never yet been exercised. The Council likewise carries out recommendations of the Assembly, prepares plans for disarmament, nominates the Secretary-General, and approves his appointments to subordinate positions in the Secretariat. All other League functions are shared concurrently by the Council and the Assembly. All efforts to describe the relations between the two bodies in terms of those between the two chambers of a legislature, or in terms of those between the cabinet and the legislature in parliamentary governments are strained and misleading. The respective functions of the Council and the Assembly can be understood only by an analysis of the Covenant and of the operations of the two bodies in practice.

It should be noted that while the Council and the Assembly are both, in theory, expected to reach decisions only by unanimity, many practical departures from this rule have taken place.[1] Article 5 declares that on matters of procedure, as distinct from "decisions," action may be taken by majority vote. In practice, the moral pressure brought to bear on small minorities is frequently sufficient to compel acquiescence in action which is technically by unanimity, but in fact is by majority vote. In the Assembly, moreover, a clear distinction has been made between recommendations and decisions. In the former case, action is by a simple majority. Most of the acts of the Assembly take the form of recommendations or *voeux* (wishes). There is likewise the well-established rule of law that no

[1] Article 5. 1. Except where otherwise expressly provided in this Covenant, or by the terms of the present treaty, decisions at any meeting of the Assembly or of the Council shall require the agreement of all the members of the League represented at the meeting.

2. All matters of procedure at meetings of the Assembly or of the Council, including the appointment of committees to investigate particular matters, shall be regulated by the Assembly or by the Council and may be decided by a majority of the members of the League represented at the meeting.

3. The first meeting of the Assembly and the first meeting of the Council shall be summoned by the President of the United States of America.

one shall be judge in his own case, which means that in the consideration of international disputes the litigating parties are not permitted to vote. The Covenant itself makes additional qualifications to the unanimity principle. Non-members are admitted to the League by a two-thirds vote of the Assembly. Amendments to the Covenant are passed by a majority vote of the States in the Assembly. Judges of the Permanent Court are elected by majority vote. It may be argued that all League actions are in any case only recommendations, since the League cannot bind any State without its consent, and all League acts are legally subject to ratification by the members before they become binding obligations. In view of these developments, the rule of unanimity, which in the past has constituted a serious obstacle to effective international cooperation, has become of theoretical rather than of practical importance.

The Secretariat is the permanent administrative organ of the League and consists of an international civil service of some 500 expert officials and subordinates residing at Geneva. It bears the same relation to the League as a whole as do the bureaus of the public international unions to their respective organizations. The Secretariat is headed by a Secretary-General, appointed by the Council with the approval of the Assembly. Sir Eric Drummond of Great Britain held this office from 1920 to 1933 and was largely responsible for the establishment and organization of the Secretariat. He was succeeded by M. Joseph Avenol of France. The Secretary-General appoints his subordinates with the approval of the Council. His immediate subordinates are a Deputy Secretary-General and three under-secretaries. Thus far one of each of these higher posts has been held by a national of each of the five Great Powers in the League. The body of the Secretariat is divided into a dozen sections, as indicated in the appended diagram, two of which (political questions and international bureaus) are headed by under-secretaries, with the rest in charge of directors. The officials of the Secretariat are not recruited by civil-service examinations, but are chosen by the Secretary-General on the basis of professional competence, with a proper regard for the distribution of posts among the various States. The officials are in no sense governmental representatives, however, but are responsible only to the Secretariat itself. They are charged with the compilation and publication of information on all of the complex problems which come before the League for consideration and with the secretarial work of the Council and Assembly, which includes the preparation of agendas, the translation of speeches into French and English (the two official languages of the League) and the preparation and publication of the Assembly and Council minutes in the *Official Journal*.

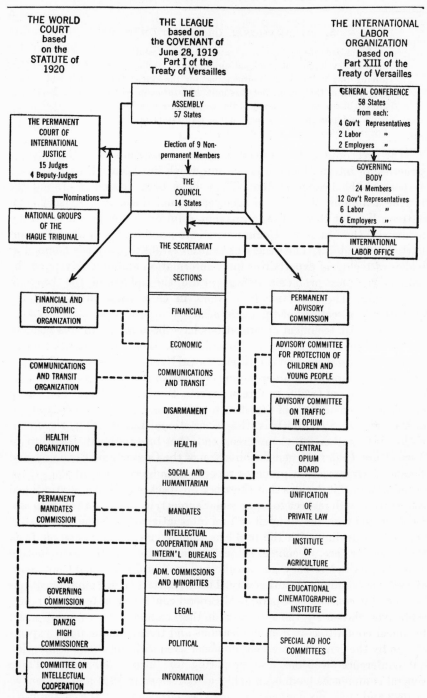

THE WORLD COURT based on the STATUTE of 1920

THE LEAGUE based on the COVENANT of June 28, 1919 Part I of the Treaty of Versailles

THE INTERNATIONAL LABOR ORGANIZATION based on Part XIII of the Treaty of Versailles

THE ASSEMBLY
57 States

GENERAL CONFERENCE
58 States
from each:
4 Gov't Representatives
2 Labor   "
2 Employers   "

THE PERMANENT COURT OF INTERNATIONAL JUSTICE
15 Judges
4 Deputy-Judges

Election of 9 Non-permanent Members

THE COUNCIL
14 States

GOVERNING BODY
24 Members
12 Gov't Representatives
6 Labor   "
6 Employers   "

—Nominations—

NATIONAL GROUPS OF THE HAGUE TRIBUNAL

THE SECRETARIAT

INTERNATIONAL LABOR OFFICE

SECTIONS

FINANCIAL AND ECONOMIC ORGANIZATION

FINANCIAL

PERMANENT ADVISORY COMMISSION

ECONOMIC

ADVISORY COMMITTEE FOR PROTECTION OF CHILDREN AND YOUNG PEOPLE

COMMUNICATIONS AND TRANSIT ORGANIZATION

COMMUNICATIONS AND TRANSIT

DISARMAMENT

ADVISORY COMMITTEE ON TRAFFIC IN OPIUM

HEALTH ORGANIZATION

HEALTH

CENTRAL OPIUM BOARD

SOCIAL AND HUMANITARIAN

PERMANENT MANDATES COMMISSION

MANDATES

UNIFICATION OF PRIVATE LAW

INTELLECTUAL COOPERATION AND INTERN'L BUREAUS

INSTITUTE OF AGRICULTURE

SAAR GOVERNING COMMISSION

ADM. COMMISSIONS AND MINORITIES

EDUCATIONAL CINEMATOGRAPHIC INSTITUTE

DANZIG HIGH COMMISSIONER

LEGAL

COMMITTEE ON INTELLECTUAL COOPERATION

POLITICAL

SPECIAL AD HOC COMMITTEES

INFORMATION

(Solid lines indicate appointment and source of authority; broken lines indicate advice or collaboration)

5. INTERNATIONAL ORGANIZATION TODAY

> Organized international cooperation is a manifestation and an embodiment of developing international unity, not an engine for creating or enforcing this unity. It is indispensable for the proper formulation and expression of that unity, but it is in its best forms merely a natural outgrowth of the maturing unity of this cosmopolitan world. As such it is the body and raiment of the soul of the civilization of the future.—P. B. POTTER, *International Organization*.

The preceding sketch conveys only a very partial idea of the complex structure of international organization which has been set up at Geneva as part of the League system. There have been organized around the League a number of technical agencies, commissions, and advisory committees. Two of these—the Permanent Advisory Commission on Armaments and the Mandates Commission—are provided for in the Covenant (Articles 9 and 22). The others have been established by the Council as bodies of technical experts to supply information and give advice on the various complex problems falling within the sphere of the League's competence. These organizations work in close cooperation with the corresponding sections of the Secretariat.

Three great technical organizations have been set up in this fashion: the Economic and Financial Organization, the Communications and Transit Organization, and the International Health Organization. The first of these is composed of an economic committee and a finance committee, each consisting of twelve to fifteen experts, to which was added in 1927 a consultative committee of fifty-two members, comprising representatives of the two other committees, the International Labor Office, the International Chamber of Commerce, and the International Institute of Agriculture. Under the general direction of the Council, the Economic and Financial Organization prepares reports on subjects submitted to it for examination. If it decides that there is a prospect of effective international cooperation with respect to a particular subject, it prepares a program and recommends that the Council call an international conference to draft a convention dealing with the problem. Such conventions as emerge from this procedure are, of course, subject to ratification by the participating governments before they go into effect. The World Economic Conference of 1927 was summoned in this way. The Organization for Communications and Transit consists of a periodical general conference of technical representatives chosen by the members of the League, and an advisory and technical committee on communications and transit, made up of experts chosen by the general conference and entrusted with the duties of carrying out conference decisions and preparing for future conferences. Three general conferences have been held—at Barcelona in 1921 and at Geneva in 1923 and 1927. Six conventions have been drawn up by the conferences, dealing with freedom of transit, navigable waterways, railways, ports, hydraulic power, and the international transmission of electric power. The Health Organization consists of the health section of the Secretariat, the health committee of twenty members, and the advisory council, which is identical with the permanent committee of the International Office of Public Health at Paris. The health committee draws up resolutions on international health problems on the basis of the data prepared by the health section and transmits them to the advisory committee for consideration. The latter makes recommendations to the Council. The organization is supplemented by numerous committees, joint commissions, subcommittees, subcommissions, and the like, dealing with health insurance, maternity, smallpox, tuberculosis, sleeping sickness, malaria, preventive medicine, etc. The public-health activities of the member States are thus coordinated and a basis is laid for the conclusion of international conventions dealing with health problems.

In addition to the three great technical organizations numerous permanent or temporary committees have been set up from time to time by the Council, often on the basis of Assembly resolutions, to deal with special problems. The Committee of Experts for the Progressive Codification of International Law and the Preparatory Committee for the Disarmament Conference are good examples. The social and humanitarian work of the League has also required the creation of the necessary organizations of experts. The first Assembly established the Advisory Commission on the Traffic in Opium and other Dangerous Drugs, which has been instrumental in securing more effective enforcement of the Hague Opium Convention of 1912 and has organized international conferences in 1924 and 1925 at which a new opium convention (1925) was drawn up, to regulate the production and distribution of opium on a world-wide scale. In 1921 a conference on the so-called "white slave traffic" drew up a final act, later embodied in the International Convention for the Suppression of the Traffic in Women and Children. The Council created an Advisory Committee on the Traffic in Women and Children, reorganized in 1925 as the Advisory Committee for the Protection and Welfare of Children and Young People. Various other organizations have been established to deal with the traffic in obscene publications, slavery and the slave trade, and the repatriation of war prisoners and refugees. In 1922 the Council set up the International Committee on Intellectual Cooperation to coordinate the work of such bodies as the International Research Council, the International Academic Union, the Institute of International Law, etc. In 1924 the Council accepted an offer of the French Government to establish in Paris an International Institute of Intellectual Cooperation to act as the secretariat of the committee.

[269]

The judicial agency of the League—the Permanent Court of International Justice—has been referred to in the preceding chapter.[1] This tribunal renders decisions and "orders" in such cases as are submitted to it by member States in accordance with the provisions of the Statute and it also gives advisory opinions to the Council on the legal aspects of such questions as the Council wishes to submit to it. The Assembly may also request advisory opinions, but has never in fact done so. The Court meets annually at The Hague and consists of fifteen judges and four deputy judges elected by majority vote of the Council and Assembly. The deputy judges act as substitutes for the regular judges in their absence. Nine judges constitute a quorum. All the judges are strictly international officials and in no sense representative of their States, though this principle is departed from in the provision that in every case the parties are entitled to have a judge of their own nationality on the bench. When no judge or deputy judge of the required nationality is a member of the Court, a "national" judge may be added to the body for the purpose of the case. All the regular judges and deputy judges hold office for nine years and vacancies are filled by election for the unexpired term. The justices are expected to devote their entire time to the work of the Court and are forbidden to hold any political or administrative position, to engage in any other profession, or to act as agent or counsel in any case. The judges receive 45,000 Dutch florins ($30,000) annually, plus traveling expenses and liberal allowances. The Court choses its own president for a three-year term and draws up its own rules of procedure. Each party in the cases before it is represented by an agent and proceedings are both oral and written, with witnesses summoned, but no use of a jury. Decisions and opinions are reached by majority vote and are always publicly printed with a statement of the reasoning upon which the judgment is based. Judges who differ with the majority are free to publish dissenting opinions. Special chambers hear cases relating to communications and transit and to the International Labor Organization under Parts XII and XIII of the Treaty of Versailles. There is little difference in procedure as between decisions and advisory opinions. The latter are not legally binding, but are usually accepted as a basis of settlement by the Council.[2]

The International Labor Organization has its headquarters at Geneva and while it is distinct from the League proper, it is an integral part of the whole League system. Its creation was due to an effort on the part of the Paris Peace Conference to satisfy the demands of organized labor and to provide a mechanism for dealing internationally with labor problems which would present the appearance of fulfilling the pledges made to labor by the various belligerent governments during the war period.

[1] On the jurisdiction and method of election of the judges, see pp. 219–221 above.
[2] On the work and practical significance of the court see pp. 765–771 below.

Article 23 of the Covenant of the League defines the general purposes of the organization.[1] Its constitution was embodied in Part XIII of the Treaty of Versailles. It may be amended by a two-thirds vote of the conference, subject to ratification by all States on the League Council and three-fourths of the members of the League. The organization consists of three parts. The General Conference consists of four delegates from each State (two representing the participating governments, one chosen by the governments to speak for the most representative employers' organization in their respective countries, and one chosen to speak for the most representative workers' organization). The General Conference assembles annually at Geneva. The delegates vote individually and deliberate upon the items of the agenda prepared by the Governing Body. They draw up, by a two-thirds majority, recommendations or draft conventions on labor legislation which are supposed to be submitted within a year to the national legislatures for ratification. The Governing Body, which meets every three months, consists of twenty-four members chosen for a three-year term. Twelve are appointed by the member governments, eight of these representing the States of chief industrial importance (Great Britain, France, Germany, Italy, Japan, India, Canada, and Belgium) and the remaining four being picked by the Conference. The other twelve members of the Governing Body are chosen half by the employers' delegates at the Conference and half by the workers' delegates. The Governing Body prepares the agendas of the conferences, appoints the director of the International Labor Office, and supervises its work. The International Labor Office consists of some 350 experts appointed by the director and is the secretariat of the organization. It gathers and publishes information on labor legislation and assists the governing body in preparing for the conferences. M. Albert Thomas was its director from its establishment until his death in April, 1932. Harold Butler has been named his successor. The expenses of the International Labor Organization are met out of the League budget.

The primary purpose of this agency is to promote uniformity of labor legislation throughout the world. National governments are frequently reluctant to enact adequate protective legislation for wage-earners because the States granting such protection are alleged to be placed at a competitive disadvantage in world markets in comparison with States where employers are free to exploit labor without legislative hindrances. The problem involved can be dealt with adequately only by inter-

---

[1] Article 23. Subject to and in accordance with the provisions of international conventions existing or hereafter to be agreed upon, the members of the League:

(1) Will endeavor to secure and maintain fair and humane conditions of labor for men, women, and children, both in their own countries and in all countries to which their commercial and industrial relations extend, and for that purpose will establish and maintain the necessary international organizations. . . .

national action. It cannot be said, however, that the International Labor Organization has achieved very much in this direction. Draft conventions and recommendations are binding only when ratified by the member States. More than fifty such proposals have been made, but many have not received general ratification and some have not even been submitted to the national legislatures. The methods provided for ensuring the execution of such conventions as are ratified have not prevented violations. The Governing Body may give publicity to violations and it may ask the Secretary-General of the League to appoint commissions of inquiry to investigate alleged violations. If one of the parties is dissatisfied with the report of such a commission, appeal may be taken to the Permanent Court which has authority to render a final decision. Economic sanctions against a violating State may be authorized by the commissions or by the Court, but they have never been applied. The organization provides an international forum for the discussion of labor legislation; it prepares the way for the formulation of international standards of labor legislation, and constitutes a useful agency for the collection and publication of labor statistics; it promotes the crystallization of attitudes and policies on the part of governments, employers' associations, and labor unions in the member States. But its actions are purely advisory and its achievements, in the opinion of many observers, have not been proportionate to the time and energy devoted to its work. In no sense is it a panacea for the conflicts in modern industrial societies resulting from the divergent economic interests of those who own the means of production and organize industry for their profit and those who work for wages under their employers' direction.

Finally, mention may be made of the Bank for International Settlements. This is not a League organization, but its creation may conceivably mark the beginning of an international coordination of the activities of central banks in various States. The Bank was created in 1930 as part of the Young Plan for the "final" settlement of Germany's reparations obligations under the Treaty of Versailles. Its primary function is that of acting as a trustee and agent for the creditor governments in the collection and allocation of indemnity payments. The Bank is located at Basle, Switzerland, and has a stock of $100,000,000, underwritten by the central banks of Great Britain, France, Italy, Germany, and Belgium, a consortium of Japanese banks, and a syndicate of private banks in the United States. The American Government refused to permit the Federal Reserve Banks to participate and the United States remains outside of the institution, as it is outside of the League of Nations, the Permanent Court, and the International Labor Organization. The Bank is controlled by a board of sixteen directors, made up of the governors of the central banks and persons appointed by them. The suspension of all payments of reparations and interallied debts in June of 1931, under the Hoover moratorium, and the subsequent cancellation of the reparations obligations may foreshadow the dissolution of the organization. On the other hand, it has already demonstrated its utility as an agency for international cooperation between central banks and it may continue to function in this capacity.

There has thus come into existence since the Great War an elaborately integrated structure of international organization far in advance of anything which existed prior to 1914. This structure reflects an enormous multiplication of the common interests and purposes of States. It is without precedent or parallel in earlier State Systems. It represents a culmination of the forms which have been evolved in the Western State System for the regulation of the relations between States and the promotion of international cooperation. It provides an opportunity for the international control of a large number of technical, economic, and social problems through international conventions based upon the advice of professional specialists and through permanent institutionalized cooperation between the administrative officials of the nation-states. It likewise provides an opportunity for the constant discussion of international political problems and the pacific settlement of disputes between governments. It constitutes an embryonic international government which may develop into a true world federation if the members of the Western State System are capable of integrating their particular national interests into world-wide international interests.

But the "if" is large and involves a fundamental modification of the attitudes, values, and behavior patterns which have controlled State action in the past. The degree to which these opportunities will be used constructively for the building of a better world depends upon the willingness of States to subordinate special and exclusive goals and purposes to general international goals and purposes. And this in turn implies revolutionary transformations in the dynamic forces which have shaped international politics and conditioned the relationships of power between the States of the West for the last five centuries. No judgments of the present structure of international organization, no reasoned evaluations of its functions and its future, are worthy of attention unless they are based upon a careful examination of the rôle of the forces of international politics in the past and at present. The next book of this study will undertake such an examination. When it is completed, further attention will be given to international organization in functional and dynamic, rather than structural and static, terms.

SUGGESTED READINGS

Baker, R. S.: *Woodrow Wilson and the World Settlement* (3 vols.), New York, Doubleday Page & Company, 1922.

Barnes, G. N.: *History of the International Labor Office*, London, Williams and Norgate, 1926.

Barrett, J.: *The Pan-American Union: Peace, Friendship, Commerce*, Washington, D. C., Pan-American Union, 1911.

Bassett, J. S.: *The League of Nations*, New York, Longmans, Green & Co., 1928.

Eagleton, C.: *International Government*, New York, Ronald Press Company, 1932.

Einzig, P.: *The Bank for International Settlements*, New York, The Macmillan Company, 1930.

Hill, N. L.: *International Administration*, New York, McGraw-Hill Book Company, Inc., 1931.

Howard-Ellis, C.: *The Origin, Structure, and Working of the League of Nations*, New York, Houghton Mifflin Company, 1928.

Hughan, J. W.: *A Study of International Government*, New York, Thomas Y. Crowell Company, 1923.

Lansing, R.: *The Peace Negotiations*, Boston, Houghton Mifflin Company, 1921.

Marburg, T.: *Development of the League of Nations Idea* (2 vols.), New York, The Macmillan Company, 1932.

Miller, D. H.: *The Drafting of the Covenant*, New York, G. P. Putnam's Sons, 1928.

Mower, E. C.: *International Government*, Boston, D. C. Heath & Company, 1931.

Perigord, P.: *The International Labor Organization*, New York, D. Appleton & Company, 1926.

Phelan, E. J.: *The International Labor Organization*, Geneva, 1925.

Potter, P. B.: *An Introduction to the Study of International Organization*, New York, Century Company, 1928.

Rappard, W. E.: *International Relations as Viewed from Geneva*, New Haven, Yale University Press, 1925.

Reid, W. A.: *The Story of the Pan-American Union*, Philadelphia, Dorrance & Company, 1924.

Reinsch, P.: *Public International Unions*, Boston, Ginn & Company, 1911.

Salter, J. A.: *Allied Shipping Control, an Experiment in International Administration*, New York, Oxford University Press, 1921.

Sayre, F. B.: *Experiments in International Administration*, New York, Harper & Brothers, 1920.

Temperley, H. W.: *History of the Peace Conference*, 6 vols. London, Hodder & Stroughton, 1920–1924.

Woolf, L.: *International Government*, New York, Brentano's, Inc., 1916.

York, E.: *Leagues of Nations, Ancient, Medieval, and Modern*, London, Swarthmore Press, 1928.

See also references at end of Chapter XVIII, p. 821 below.

BOOK THREE
FORCES

INTRODUCTION TO BOOK THREE

The preceding chapters of this volume have been concerned with the historical origins of the Western State System and with the principles of law, the practices of diplomacy, and the procedures and institutions of international collaboration which have been developed by its members to serve their common needs. The remaining chapters will be concerned with less tangible and more controversial material—with the values, behavior patterns, attitudes, and purposes of peoples and governments; with the "forces" impelling them to action in dealing with one another and conditioning their interaction; and with the consequences which flow from this interaction. Some of these "forces" have already been suggested in the description of "forms." All which make for international collaboration and organization, all which are vaguely described by the term "internationalism" have been reflected in the forms depicted above. Certain of these will receive additional treatment below in other connections. But in the present portion of the study, attention will be given to the "national" forces, *i.e.*, to those which divide States from one another and set them against one another in the arena of international politics—national patriotism in its political and economic aspects; imperialism as a frame of mind and a governmental policy; and the patterns and values of Great Power politics which have grown up in consequence of the rivalries between the imperial nation-states.

These phenomena are obviously not susceptible of objective description and analysis in the sense in which this is possible for the "forms" of the international society. The social sciences have not as yet achieved a level of development at which it is feasible to pretend that there is general agreement among their devotees regarding the nature and significance of the "forces" which move States to action. Psychologists, historians, sociologists, economists, and political scientists have all endeavored in one way or another to describe and analyze these forces, but the results in terms of valid scientific conclusions are not impressive. The observers are too much a part of the phenomena under observation to enable them to achieve that calm detachment which is supposed to characterize scientific objectivity. The observers are not merely observers, but also Englishmen, Frenchmen, Germans, or Americans, ultra-patriots, mild nationalists, internationalists, or cosmopolites, bourgeois individualists or proletarian collectivists, conservatives, liberals, radicals, or revolutionaries, imperialists, anti-imperialists, pacifists, or apostles of preparedness. The attainment of objectivity is a process whereby the observer stands off from his material and deals with it in terms of concepts and categories not inherent in the material itself but part of some larger frame of reference and some wider universe of discourse. Particulars are generalized and fragments of knowledge are synthesized into a larger whole, which in turn may become part of some still larger synthesis. All objectivity is relative. Truth, like beauty, is for the most part in the eye of the observer. The great driving, dynamic forces of the Western State System have necessarily been studied by those who are a part of the system and who are rarely capable of seeing its parts against some broader background affording a basis for objective evaluation. Students of international relations have therefore taken refuge in easy descriptions of forms or in speculation and impressionistic interpretations which have been widely divergent and highly controversial.

There can be no pretension that the chapters which follow are the work of one who has somehow broken through the circle and achieved a sufficient breadth of view and precision of insight to justify a claim to detachment. They constitute a particular interpretation—one among many—and their ultimate validity depends upon future developments which involve so many variables as to make all prediction hazardous. Indeed, the very organization of the present study (and of all others of a similar character) is based upon a particular set of assumptions and evaluations. Much of the recent literature of the field is based upon the tacit or admitted assumption that the forces making for international cooperation and world unity are more significant than those making for international differences and conflicts. The present interpretation is based upon the opposite assumption—so much so that the following treatment of forces will be largely limited to those values, attitudes, behavior patterns, and policies leading to tensions and rivalries between States. Only the observer of a generation or two hence can properly pass judgment upon the soundness and accuracy of the divergent interpretations of the present day. Only the events of the next half-century can furnish a basis for definite conclusions regarding the significance of contemporary social and political phenomena. But at least it may be claimed that the particular line of interpretation adopted here rests upon a broad historical perspective of the past and upon an effort to interpret the present which is free from the emotional bias inherent in deeply rooted provincial or national allegiances. It is self-consistent and its concepts and conclusions, when tested pragmatically by application to events in progress, will, it is hoped, be found to "work," *i.e.*, to offer a reasonably satisfactory explanation of the phenomena under discussion. With this preliminary apologia and word of caution, the analysis may proceed.

Chapter VIII

THE CULT OF THE NATION-STATE

1. THE MAKING OF PATRIOTS

He who loves not his country can love nothing.—LORD BYRON, *The Two Foscari.*

TO AN observer from Mars or the moon, to an observer resurrected from the ancient world or from early medieval Europe, and even to an observer of today from the "backward" or unwesternized parts of the earth, the outstanding and distinctive characteristic of the peoples of the Western State System would doubtless appear to be their devotion and allegiance to the "nations" into which they have gotten themselves divided. The western world is a world of nations. The Western State System is essentially a system of nation-states. The western peoples and their oriental and African imitators are keenly aware of themselves as "nationals" of particular nation-states, already in existence or striving to be born. They have identified themselves with the other members of their national groups. They have achieved like-mindedness with those of their fellows who speak their own language, who cherish their own traditions, who are a part of their own national culture as fellow citizens and fellow patriots. They have acted together with their fellows for so long a period in war and in peace, they have made themselves so much a part of the collective national community of the fatherland, that they have become emotionally bound together into solidly integrated national blocs. The members of each of these communities have beeen conditioned to certain symbols of group solidarity which serve as stimuli to action and emotion. National flags, national anthems, national heroes, national traditions of glorious memory, all play their part as symbols of identification and as stimuli to various types of behavior. "Nationalism" is the primary force in the Western State System shaping the attitudes and the actions of its members toward one another.

This has not meant that western peoples have ceased to be aware of themselves as members of other types of groups or have ceased to identify themselves with other interests. People continue to differ from one another in scores of ways quite unrelated to differences in nationality. These differences are in part biological and in part social and cultural. All people are obviously either men or women—and the modern cult of feminism indicates that collective interests based upon common sex often furnish

[277]

a basis for organization and social action. All people are obviously either white, black, yellow, red, brown, or mixed—and racial differences continue to furnish symbols of identification, slogans of solidarity, and stimuli to cooperative behavior. All people are Christians, Moslems, Jews, Buddhists, Brahmanists, Confucionists, atheists, etc.—and these categories are further divided into innumerable sects and denominations. Common religious interests are still the sources of powerful forces influencing human behavior. People are likewise employers, employees, capitalists, wage-earners, farmers, professional men, carpenters, bankers, fishermen, physicians, shopkeepers, miners, butchers, bakers, candlestick makers, etc., *ad infinitum*. Common economic interests, common class interests, common professional interests, have perhaps created greater solidarity within each of the numerous vocational groups into which modern society is divided than ever existed in earlier civilizations. People are also baseball fans, tennis players, nudists, bridge addicts, football enthusiasts, billiard sharks, marksmen, swimmers, and philatelists. Thousands of different avocational interests in the realm of sports, recreation, and athletics bring people together from all parts of the world. All of these and many other common interests have little relationship to nationality, political frontiers, language, or patriotism.

But in the nineteenth and twentieth centuries the relations between the States in the Western State System have been influenced to a greater degree by the "national" interests of their citizens than by any others. Millions of people are influenced more in their emotions and behavior by a sense of national solidarity and fellow feeling with their fellow nationals than by their racial, religious, economic, aesthetic, or recreational interests. This becomes most apparent in war time, when governments demand and usually receive unswerving and undivided allegiance to the nation. All other interests are in form, if not always in substance, subordinated to the supreme end of saving the fatherland, chastising the national foe, and enabling the nation to impose its will on the enemy nation. In 1914 throughout the European continent, labor leaders forgot their slogans of class solidarity, pacifists forgot their crusade against war, churchmen forgot the Prince of Peace, socialists forgot the general strike of the workers of the world which would make war impossible. Merchants, munition makers, and militarists had less to forget. All rallied to the unfurled banners of the nations in arms. All hurled themselves into the fiery furnace, chanting hymns of hate against neighbor nations. But war merely brings to the surface and makes plain through pathological exaggeration what already exists in peace: an almost universal disposition to place the nation before all other human groupings, to give precedence to national interests above all other interests, to look upon national patriotism as the highest type of loyalty and allegiance.

[278]

This phenomenon is something new under the sun. Nationalism is a development of the modern period of western civilization. In its contemporary mold it arose, in its rudiments, in the western Europe of the fourteenth century. It influenced, and was influenced by, the emergence of the national monarchies. It burst forth into flaming flower in the revolutionary and Napoleonic epoch, and it bore its full fruits in the nineteenth and twentieth centuries. It became a universal cult among western peoples and spread over the world in the period in which the bourgeoisie rose everywhere to political power. In earlier ages and in earlier State Systems nationalism in its modern aspects was practically unknown. There has always necessarily been a large degree of social solidarity and certain forms of political loyalty wherever there have been States. But common nationality was seldom the basis of solidarity and allegiance. Early "patriotism" was local or provincial or little more than submissiveness to the personal leadership of kings and warriors. The ancient city-states and world empires aroused loyalty and enthusiasm among great masses of people, but in no case did these attitudes center in a "nation" or a national community. In the early medieval period, nationalism was unknown. Loyalties to feudal overlords, to provincial communities, to free towns, to the universal Church, to guild and clan and class loomed constantly larger than any loyalty to king or country. From the point of view of world history, nationalism is a phenomenon characteristic of a particular period in the evolution of a particular civilization. It appeared slowly and it will fade slowly. But it is temporary and limited in space and time.

This fact renders absurd all efforts to explain nationalism as an "instinct" of people everywhere, or as a set of attitudes and behavior patterns characteristic of all peoples in all cultures. "Instincts"—however they may be defined and however much sociologists and psychologists may dispute about them—are unlearned responses, innate patterns of reaction which all members of the human species must possess if the term is to have any meaning. The complex of symbolic stimuli and stereotyped responses called nationalism can by no stretch of the imagination be regarded as falling within this category. The stimuli may and do evoke responses which appear to be related to tendencies deeply rooted in the human organism: toward gregariousness, self-assertiveness, pugnacity, submissiveness, and the like. The tendencies clearly have some relation to the primal drives of hunger and sex or of security, new experience, recognition, and response, or of any other of the four or seven or nine or eleven categories of "instincts" or elemental yearnings into which ingenious scholars are prone to divide innate human impulses. But nationalism is far too complex, variegated, temporary, and localized, to be reduced to such terms. It must be regarded, not as an element of the biological inheritance of *homo sapiens*, but of his *cultural* inheritance—and specifically of the inheritance of a particular culture in a particular time and place. If it is to be explained at all, it must be explained in terms of cultural history and of social psychology, rather than in terms of largely imaginary traits which human beings everywhere and always are supposed to possess.

Patriots are not born but made. The values, attitudes, emotions, and ideologies of patriotism are instilled into people in every nation by an elaborate process of education and inculcation. Nationalism is an inseparable component of the cultural heritage handed down from generation to generation in every modern society. Upon the fresh and eager minds of little children, as upon a blank slate, are writ at an early age the large characters of "mother," "home," and "heaven," "flag," "fatherland," and "patriotism." The first impressions of the great society outside of the family, the neighborhood, and the kindergarten are associated with national emblems, national heroes, national myths and traditions. Every child in the western world, before he has learned how to read and write his national language, has learned how to respond to the gayly colored banner which is the flag of his fatherland, to the stirring rhythm of the song which is his national anthem, to the names and legends of the great nation builders who are revered as men like gods. Awe, respect, reverence, and enthusiasm toward the nation-state and its symbolic representations are inculcated from infancy in the home, in the school, and in the church. Next comes the primer, with its quaint little tales of national glory and achievement, and after that the elements of national history and geography. In later childhood there is nationalistic history with a vengeance, patriotic exercises, flag-day celebrations, festivals and fun for independence day, or constitution day, or Bastille day or Guy Fawkes' day. Puberty brings membership in the Boy Scouts or the Girl Scouts, outings and parties and training in citizenship. In adolescence the young citizen enters secondary school. He becomes acquainted with the alien tongues and customs of enemies and strangers. He studies the national literature, the national history, the national *kultur*. He becomes politically conscious and emotionally inspired by a fuller appreciation of his identity with his fatherland. *La patrie* becomes father, mother, mistress, or lover in the heart of the youthful patriot and he (or she) is taught to swear undying allegiance to that which is more sacred even than truth, honor, or life itself. And at length, in early adulthood, comes, in most lands, military service for the young man, romantic attachments to soldier lovers for the young woman, the right to vote and pay taxes, and a deep sense of loyalty and devotion to that half real, half mystical entity which is the nation-state. Thus through the seven ages of the patriot, national sentiment is systematically inculcated into the citizens of every State—with the home, the church, the school, the army, the press, the

[280]

political party, the business enterprise, and the State itself all contributing mightily to that process through which children and raw youths are transformed into ideally loyal and patriotic good citizens.

The mechanisms, procedures, and techniques of education and propaganda through which this result is attained have been analyzed in many States by a score of assiduous scholars.[1] The primitive initiation ceremonies of the tribe or clan through which the rising generation is made a participant in the social group are repeated with elaborate variation in the educational processes of every modern nation. Youth is conditioned to allegiance—no longer to the tribe, the clan, the class, the caste, the province or the city, but to the nation which demands an allegiance above all other allegiances and a loyalty requiring, if need be, the supreme sacrifice on the altar of patriotism. What youth has been taught, age seldom forgets—and all modern States are nations of patriots whose rulers may ordinarily rely upon the unswerving devotion of the great masses of the citizens to the mighty traditions of the national past. Each State thus develops and enriches its own personality by perpetually recreating itself in its own image. Each State perpetually models its figures of earth and gets them more and more to its liking. Each State becomes symbolized as an anthropomorphic deity to which are attributed the national virtues and vices, the national achievements and frustrations. Each patriot, like a new Narcissus, is enthralled by the beauty of his own image, which he sees reflected in the national mirror, and he feels himself to be one with the nation. Here, beneath the world of forms and structures, beneath the external trappings of government and sovereignty, are the reality of the nation and the essence of nationhood instilled into the minds and hearts of the millions who make "France" because they feel themselves Frenchmen, the millions who make "Germany" because they feel themselves Germans, and the millions who make "America" because they feel themselves Americans.

2. THE NATURE OF NATIONALISM

Breathes there a man, with soul so dead,
Who never to himself hath said,
This is my own, my native land!
—SIR WALTER SCOTT, *Lay of the Last Minstrel.*

An understanding of the process of manufacturing patriots, however, does not in itself serve to explain why national patriotism has come to occupy such an all-pervading place in the culture and ideology of western civilization. This is perhaps one of the mysteries which western man, in

[1] See C. E. Merriam, *The Making of Citizens*, 1931, the concluding volume of the series which includes Elizabeth Weber, *The Duk-Duks*; C. J. H. Hayes, *France, a Nation of Patriots*; John Gaus, *Great Britain: a Study in Civic Loyalty*; S. N. Harper, *Civic Training in Soviet Russia*; and Oscar Jaszi, *The Dissolution of the Hapsburg Monarchy.*

his ceaseless efforts to understand himself, can never quite comprehend.[1] Neither the historian, the sociologist, the political scientist, nor the psychologist has succeeded in offering any satisfactory explanation of the origins and causes of the strange fervor of nationalism which has now become the dominant pattern of group loyalty and political allegiance in the contemporary world. While this is not the place to offer new answers to old riddles, certain suggestions may nevertheless be made regarding the circumstances under which national patriotism sprang up in western Europe. These suggestions are purely tentative and are of value only in so far as they correspond to historical reality and help to explain the content and significance of nationalism at the present time.

Cultural anthropologists have observed that in almost every pre-literate society there develops a pattern of attitudes, values, folkways, and *mores* which may be collectively designated as "ethnocentrism." This pattern gives unity and cohesion to the group, identifies it and distinguishes it from other groups, and involves on the part of its members a feeling of fellowship toward other members and a corresponding feeling of strangeness toward members of outside groups. Ethnocentrism implies friendship with the members of the "in-group" and hostility toward members of all "out-groups." The in-group is the focus of all social life. Each new generation is initiated into the rituals and ceremonies which symbolize its solidarity. Law, language, art, religion, government, morality, family institutions, economic activities are all phases of the group culture, all strands in the ties which bind the individuals into a social whole. These fruits of social living are enjoyed only by the members of the group and are denied to outside groups, even though they may be extended to individual aliens in accordance with the ancient custom of hospitality. Through them the community is made aware of itself as a collective entity set apart from outside communities. "Stranger" is usually "enemy" and foreign cultures are strange and hostile.

Nationalism may be regarded as an advanced form of ethnocentrism, in which the limits of social solidarity and cohesion are coterminous with the bounds of the language and culture of people in a large community inhabiting extensive territories. A "nation" consists of a relatively large number of people spread over a relatively large area and bound together by common ties of language and culture. The communities which com-posed the civilizations of the Near East and the Mediterranean basin in

[1] "What has given great vogue to nationalism in modern times? We really do not know It is a pity that we do not know, for if we did, we could probably make some fairly accurate guess as to the future of nationalism. As it is, we have to content ourselves with hypotheses and suggestions. Of these the most plausible would appear to be the underlying tendency in modern times to regard the national state as the medium through which civilization is best assured and advanced." C. J. H. Hayes, *The Historical Evolution of Modern National-ism*, 1931, p. 302.

ancient times were, for the most part, not nations in this sense. In their political organization they were city-states, military monarchies, or "world empires," consisting either of small communities of culturally homogeneous people or of large aggregations of culturally diverse peoples brought under unified control through war and political subjugation. The same was true of the peoples of the western world in the early medieval period. Group solidarity, civic loyalty, and political organization rested not upon national communities but upon smaller or larger units. Nationalism appeared only as "nations" came into existence and attained awareness of their own identity.

This process was made possible by the peculiar conditions prevailing in western Europe in the feudal period. Here, in a small but extremely variegated portion of the world, a number of linguistically and culturally diverse peoples were thrown into intimate contact with one another. These peoples were the descendants of the migrating barbaric tribes which had settled down upon the land and developed, each within its own sphere, the various dialects which came to be fused into national languages, the customs and institutions which came to be fused into national cultures, and the sense of kinship and fellow feeling which is the psychological prerequisite of nationhood. Had each group been living in complete isolation from different neighboring groups, its members would probably have developed no sense of their identity. Had all the groups been different in language and culture, but small as to numbers and as to the areas which they inhabited, with no basis for unified political control, they likewise would probably have developed no sense of their identity on a national scale but would have remained divided into particularistic communities inspired by local and provincial loyalties. In Italy and the Germanies such a situation prevailed for many centuries before cultural interpenetration and assimilation, combined with the pressure of foreign invaders, produced a sense of nationhood. But in the west an English nationality, a French nationality, and a Spanish nationality emerged out of the diffusion of language and culture over wide areas and out of the imposition of unified military and administrative control over these areas. War against neighboring out-groups, political unification under national kings within the in-group, and a transition from local manorial economy to provincial or national economy were doubtless the three factors of major importance in laying the foundations of nationalism.

It seems probable that conflicts between culturally divergent populations played a significant rôle in producing within each community that sense of its own identity, that feeling of solidarity and common interest, that conception of the personality or ego of the group which is of the essence of national patriotism. Contacts of war would seem to be more effective than any other kind in producing the type of group cohesion which lies back of nationalism. No emotion unifies a group so readily as hatred for a common enemy. Group hostility to the foreign foe arouses the most elemental types of defensive behavior which serve to give the primitive group a solidarity it could never attain otherwise. International relations in the formative period of nationalism were for the most part those of war. Anglo-Saxon England attained a degree of national unity for the first time when Alfred the Great rallied his subjects to resist the Danish invasion. Norman England was already an embryonic national State, with a national government of considerable power and authority and with a population increasingly impressed with its "English-ness" by virtue of chronic conflicts with the Scots, the Irish, and the French. In France, localism and provincialism gave way to a common consciousness of "French-ness" in the course of the Hundred Years' War, when its inhabitants at long last organized themselves for effective resistance against the English invaders and found a fitting symbol of the national cause in the person of the first great heroic figure of the French nation, Jeanne d'Arc. In Spain, constant warfare against the southern Saracens gave birth to Spanish nationalism and produced that blending of patriotic sentiment and crusading Catholicism which became its distinctive characteristic. In every case nationalism was born of war against alien groups.

All of the later nationalisms between the fifteenth century and the twentieth were similarly born of conflict situations between societies already differing from one another in language, religion, and institutions, and made more aware of these differences by increased contacts with aliens. Dutch nationalism attained full flower in the long struggle against Spanish rule of the Netherlands. Swiss nationalism emerged out of conflicts with Austria. Sweden became a nation through conflicts with Russians and Poles and Germans. American nationalism was generated by the War of the Revolution. In the nineteenth century, Italian nationalism attained political unity for Italy as a result of common resistance to foreign invasion and common conflicts against Austria. The German nation became a unified State through conflict with Danes, Austrians, and Frenchmen, after Napoleonic domination and the "war of liberation" earlier in the century converted Prussians and Bavarians and Suabians and Württembergers into "Germans." The peculiarly intense and fanatical nationalism of the Balkan peoples has been the product of armed revolt against the Turks and of the presence within the peninsula of a large number of divergent linguistic and religious groups, each of which became aware of itself through contact and conflict with its neighbors. Irish nationalism, Turkish nationalism, Japanese nationalism, Indian nationalism, and Chinese nationalism were likewise products of conflict against alien rulers, alien invaders, or alien foes across the frontier.

This suggests that the process whereby a community acquires a sense of its own identity and national personality bears a certain resemblance to the process whereby an individual growing up in society acquires a self or ego of his own. Social psychologists are generally agreed that an individual growing up to biological maturity in complete isolation from his fellows would not have a complete human "personality." The individual becomes humanized by social contacts and interactions with his fellows. His innate impulses are inhibited, directed, and conditioned through social pressure—until his personality becomes, in the language of the psycho-analyst, a fusion of instinctive biological drives (the "id"), unconscious controls and repressions of these drives (the "super-ego"), and the conscious thinking and acting self (the "ego") which is built up out of the other elements.[1] The individual becomes aware of himself and develops distinctive personality traits by "taking the rôle of the other,"[2] by socialized experience with other persons.

Similarly, a nation acquires its ego by contacts with other nations, and it seemingly becomes acutely aware of its own identity to the degree to which such contacts are intimate, rich, and varied. Contacts of war would seem to promote national solidarity more effectively than contacts of peace, for war requires cooperation and cohesion in the interest of self-preservation. It emotionalizes and dramatizes the symbols, the flags, the songs, the slogans, the traditions, and the leaders which give unity to the group and distinguish it from other groups. National patriotism is the most complete expression of ethnocentrism. Its devotees are imbued with an intense consciousness of the collective personality of the national community, and this collective personality emerges out of social contacts and interactions between divergent groups not dissimilar to those contacts and interactions between single human beings which produce and enrich the individual personality. The history of this process remains to be written by social psychologists with historical training or by historians who are also social psychologists.

3. MY COUNTRY, RIGHT OR WRONG!

Our country! In her intercourse with foreign nations, may she always be in the right; but our country, right or wrong!—STEPHEN DECATUR, April, 1816.

Nationalists everywhere exalt the nation-state as the highest form of political and social organization. The national community must achieve political independence. It must incorporate within its frontiers all peoples speaking the language and having the culture of the national society.

[1] See Franz Alexander, *Psycho-analysis of the Total Personality*, 1930.
[2] This phrase was frequently used by the late professor George H. Mead in his lectures on social psychology at the University of Chicago.

It must compel conformity to the dominant language and culture on the part of alien groups within its frontier. It must attain unity, uniformity, solidarity. It must assert its rights vigorously and protect its interests energetically in contacts with other national groups. It is the all-in-all, the *ne plus ultra*, the final and perfect embodiment of social living for all loyal patriots. It is beyond good and evil, right or wrong, for its interests are supreme and paramount and all means toward its greater glory and power are justified by the end. "A true nationalist places his country above everything; he therefore conceives, treats, and resolves all pending questions in their relation to the national interest."[1] His object is "the exclusive pursuit of national policies, the absolute maintenance of national integrity, and a steady increase of national power—for a nation declines when it loses military might."[2] To the patriot the nation-state is a great goddess to be worshipped, to be loved, to be served—and all sacrifices in her service are noble and heroic. She calls out to her worshippers:

Citizens, it is I (the Great Mother, *la Patrie*) that undertakes to protect your personal safety, your peace, your property: What wilt thou give me in return for constant benefit? If it happens that I am in peril, if unnatural children torment my bosom . . . wouldst thou abandon me in these stormy moments for the price of my invariable protection? . . . No! . . . There are times when I would command the sacrifice . . . even of thy life which I have so steadily protected.[3]

It is not without significance that nationalism has flowered most luxuriously in the period since the French Revolution, during which the bourgeoisie has risen to political power in most of the western States. The nation-states of western Europe were originally dynastic creations of warrior kings. Loyalty has been transferred from king to State, from monarch to fatherland only since the rise of modern mechanized economy. Machine industry brought social integration and interdependence on a national scale. Bourgeois democracy and parliamentarianism inspired che majority of the citizens of the nation-state with the attitudes, ideals, and values of popular patriotism. Of the three great passwords of the middle class revolution—"liberty, equality, fraternity"—only fraternity, *i.e.*, national solidarity, was fully achieved, for liberty and equality in a social order of economic inequality and insecurity have remained dreams only partially fulfilled. Out of the gigantic efflorescence of mass patriotism in Napoleonic France, out of the military impact of Napoleonic France upon Europe, was born a nationalist awakening of the ascendant middle classes throughout the Continent. During all of the nineteenth century, liberalism and nationalism were the two faces of the bourgeois revolt

[1] Charles Maurras, in *Action Française*, June 10, 1908, p. 969.

[2] Maurras, quoted in C. J. H. Hayes, *The Historical Evolution of Modern Nationalism*, p. 165.

[3] Barrère in *Procès-Verbal de l'Assemblée Nationale*, No. 699, pp. 7–8, cited in Hayes, *op. cit.*, pp. 69–70. This and the preceding quotations all refer to French nationalism, but the values and ideology which they suggest are typical of all nationalisms.

against the *ancien régime* throughout the western world. Only in the old Germany and the old Russia did the landowning aristocracy retain a large degree of political power—and even here the members of this class became more patriotic than the bourgeois patriots. The same observation might be made of contemporary Japan. Patriotism places allegiance to the whole national community and to its political symbol, the national State, above allegiance to caste or class or party. But it is nevertheless true that nationalism as a cult and a way of life became a mighty driving force in the hands of bourgeois patriot-liberals and that it has received general acceptance in the period during which merchants, bankers, and industrial entrepreneurs—the ruling classes in the epoch of capitalism— took political power unto themselves in the great nation-states. This historical coincidence need not be taken to mean that nationalism is of significance only as a manifestation of the attitudes and ideology of the bourgeoisie. But it is clear that this class has in most States played the largest rôle in the elaboration and inculcation of the attitudes and ideology of nationalism.

Not only is the period of the highest development of nationalism the era of the bourgeoisie, but it is also the epoch of political democracy and representative government on a national scale. Constitutionalism and parliamentary democracy were part of the bourgeois program of political reform from 1789 onward. But the achievement of the program has a significance for nationalism in another connection. Nationalism and democracy have marched hand in hand because they both require a popular state of mind in which the inhabitants of a State are willing to subordinate their lesser and local interests to the interests of the nation as a whole and are prepared to cooperate in a common national life. The general prevalence of patriotism (or of some equivalent pattern of social cohesion) is a prerequisite to the successful operation of democratic government on a national scale. Experience in operating democratic government contributes in turn toward the substitution of national loyalty and allegiance for localism and particularism and makes for national solidarity and popular patriotism. Economic life in the machine age binds together the provinces or districts of every nation more closely than they could ever be bound together in the localized handicraft economy of the pre-industrial period. This economic integration of the nations has been followed by greater political integration. This political integration on a national scale has made possible the development of the forms of democratic government and the worship of the national State, which is the essence of contemporary patriotism.

The cult of nationalism has its high priests, its rituals, and its theology no less than other cults. The rites and symbols are too familiar to the citizens of all states to require labored exposition here. The emotional responses of nationalism are evoked by stereotyped representations of the power and glory of the State. These representations have become stimuli to patriotic action because they have been associated in the minds of the citizens of all States with the social "instincts" and emotions. The process of making patriots is largely a process of building up such associations, of conditioning individuals to respond to the desired stimuli, of inducing individuals to identify themselves with the "nation" and with the symbols of the nation, of directing innate impulses into socially acceptable forms of expression by identifying them with the collective life of the national group. The more common of these associations and identifications are about us on every hand. The patriot has learned reverence for the land of his ancestors—for merrie England, America the beautiful, *la Patrie*, or *das Vaterland*. This involves both ancestor worship and territorial fetichism. The great nation-builders and national leaders of the past are revered as men of heroic mold whose deeds were drama of epic grandeur and whose words were wisdom handed down from on high. All criticism, all deflation, all "debunking" of the national heroes is unpatriotic—and the same charge is often hurled at "objective" historians and at history textbooks which fail to manifest the appropriate degree of adoration for the sacred dead. Living political leaders are judged by the degree to which they appear to come up to or fall short of the traditional standards set by the departed figures of national myths and legend.[1]

Similarly, the patriot worships the land of his nation—the hallowed soil, watered by the tears and blood of heroes, the towns and country-side, the cities and villages, the mountains, rivers, lakes, and valleys, the rocks and rills and templed hills which are the physical symbols of the nation.[2] The national flag is everywhere a peculiarly sacred symbol, always to be respected and never to be defiled. The emotions evoked by the Star-spangled Banner, the Union Jack, and the tricolor are obviously not due to virtues inherent in colored bits of cloth, but to an inculcated reverence for the flag as a symbol of the nation. The thrill produced by the martial music of national anthems is likewise not attributable to their musical excellence, but to a rich variety of pleasing associations which they evoke. Other symbols call forth the responses of patriotism to an only slightly lesser degree: the marching soldiery, the roaring battle planes, and the majestic cruisers and dreadnaughts of the forces of national defense; the king, emperor, or president; the royal palace or execu-

[1] "Our manner of thinking, determined in first instance by our fathers and mothers, retains hold of all that our ancestors have been; these are dead only in appearance. They maintain in our nature the character which has been marked in them in other days. . . . The living expression of French nationalism is the result of the vigor of the good and pure blood which we have received from our fathers and mothers." Charles Maurras, *La Politique Religieuse*, xxxiii–xxxiv, 18–19, cited in Hayes, *op. cit.*, p. 205.

[2] "The cult of the sacred soil . . . has started; from year to year it will grow; it will be a factor in the renaissance of *la Patrie*." Maurras, *ibid.*, cited in Hayes, *op. cit.*, p. 205.

tive mansion; the pictured representations of the national capital; the battlefields and shrines and memorials recalling the glorious past; governmental ceremonies and rituals; traditionalized shibboleths and slogans; the tariff to which is mystically attributed national prosperity; the Monroe Doctrine, which few Americans understand but which all Americans are prepared to fight for; "imperial preference," "national security," "a place in the sun," etc. These are but a few of the symbols and stimuli which can always be relied on to touch off the fireworks of patriotic enthusiasm.

No less interesting and influential are the multitudinous rationalizations which flow from the pens of patriotic pamphleteers. A whole library would not exhaust the literature of national self-justification and glorification. Every field of ideas, every realm of intellectual endeavor is called upon to do homage to the greater glory of the State, to extol the virtues of its citizens, to explain convincingly the eternal rectitude of the national ambition. Philosophy, history, political science, sociology, geography, and even the natural sciences and the arts are pressed into service. This has perhaps taken place on the largest and most impressive scale in Germany, with Fichte, Hegel, Treitschke, Schlegel, Schopenhauer, Nietzsche, Wagner, and even such universal geniuses as Goethe and Beethoven becoming symbols, if not apologists, of the national *kultur*, which to the German patriot is manifestly superior to that of all other nations. Patriots in all other States have similarly glorified the national culture, and hosts of pseudo-scientists and pseudo-historians have contributed to the intellectual mythology of nationalism. Mystical virtues are attributed to the national personality.[1] Aphorisms are coined to characterize the national traits.[2] Allegedly scientific doctrines are worked out to explain and justify the national delusions of grandeur. Patriotic historians prove the national greatness of the country by the evidence of its past. Patriotic geographers evolve theories of "natural frontiers" and of

[1] The French scholar Bonald, in describing "the most enlightened and reasonable people of Europe," *i.e.*, the French, declared, "I observe with attention this people, compounded of Romans, Gauls, and Germans; and I think I perceive in its character the national pride of the Roman, the impetuosity of the Gaul, the candor of the German; as I find, in its manners, the urbanity of the first, the vivacity of the second, the simplicity of the third. It is all soul, all sentiment, all action: it feels when others think; it acts when others deliberate; with it, action precedes thought, and feeling precedes action. Terrible in its errors, extreme in its virtues, it has less vice than passion; frivolous, yet capable of constancy; proud, yet capable of docility; impetuous, yet capable of reflection; confident even to the point of insolence, active so as even to perform prodigies, courageous to the point of foolhardiness, its good qualities are its own, and too often its faults are due to those who govern it." *Legislation Primitive*, I, p. 295, cited in Hayes, *op. cit.*, p. 99.

[2] For example: one Englishman equals correctness, two Englishmen fastidiousness, three Englishmen Parliament; one Frenchman equals politeness, two Frenchmen a duel, three Frenchmen hegemony; one German equals boredom, two Germans organization, three Germans *das Vaterland;* one Russian equals a genius, two Russians intoxication, three Russians a brawl, and so forth.

"manifest destiny" to lend plausibility to territorial aggrandizement. Patriotic philologists glorify the national language—and in newly created States delve into the forgotten past to revive or to invent a national language if one is not already in use. Patriotic anthropologists elaborate popular concepts of national and racial purity and superiority, and lend credence to patriotic desires to hold the alien in contempt. Discriminatory immigration policies, schemes to assimilate minorities, and such far-reaching programs of national expansion as Pan-Germanism, Pan-Slavism, Pan-Anglianism, and the like are given a façade of intellectual respectability. To examine and criticize all these ideological super-structures of nationalism would be a task as gigantic as it is thankless and unnecessary. Suffice it to say that they are the blossoms which adorn the tree of patriotism—and the fact that the flowers may be artificial makes them no less attractive to the patriotic passers-by.

The net result of all these phenomena is to glorify the nation-state as no other type of political community has ever been glorified in the past. In each country the ruling classes couch their interests and attitudes in the symbolism of national unity and national welfare. The masses identify themselves with the nation. The nation and its interests, real or imaginary, become the criteria by which all is judged. Political leaders are good if they serve the nation and contribute to its greater power and glory. Wise politicians in all lands have long ago acquired skill in wrapping themselves in the national flag and in proclaiming from the housetops their undying devotion to the fatherland. Economic institutions and practices are evaluated, not in terms of productivity and welfare, but in terms of the unity, self-sufficiency, and power of the national State. Entrepreneurs and profit-seekers long ago acquired skill in disguising their own motives with the phraseology of patriotism and the catchwords of nationalism. Service to the national State is the touchstone of character, the test of goodness and wisdom, and the criterion of social utility. And the national State itself is a metaphysical embodiment of all virtue and perfection which stands above all criticism and questioning. It is its own glory and justification. It is the highest creation of human effort in the realm of politics. It is at once the creation of the people of the nation and the great protector and guardian of its subjects. It is beyond all morality and not subject in its collective behavior to the standards applicable to individuals or to lesser groups.

The more recent manifestations of this cult have been aptly character-ized by Professor Hayes, astute student of patriotism in all its forms, as "integral nationalism."[1] This doctrine differs not at all from earlier forms

---

[1] See Hayes, *op. cit.*, pp. 164f., "Integral nationalism is hostile to the internationalism preached by humanitarians and liberals. It makes the nation, not a means to humanity, not a stepping-stone to a new world order, but an end in itself. It puts national interests

MY COUNTRY, RIGHT OR WRONG

of nationalism in its fundamental postulates and values, but it requires its devotees to take their nationalism with deadly seriousness and to apply themselves in all earnestness to serving and glorifying the nation. Integral nationalism is best represented in the contemporary world scene by the *London Morning Post*, the *Action Française*, or French Ultra-national Royalists, the "National Socialist" followers of Adolph Hitler in Germany, the Fascismo of Italy, and the military bureaucracy of Japan. American counterparts of these groups are to be found in the American Legion, the D.A.R., the National Security League, the Defenders of America, and other associations of professional patriots, as well as in such papers as the *Chicago Tribune* and the dailies of the Hearst press. The various patriotic groups and organizations in many lands which are somewhat vaguely described (usually by their enemies) as "fascists" are ordinarily made up of "integral" nationalists. The point of view of these organizations perhaps represents the logical development of nationalism to its ultimate end, and the latest and most extreme form of the nationalist philosophy. The germs of this final formulation of the gospel of the nation-state were latent in all the earlier manifestations. But the gospel has been purified of all irrelevancies, purged of all elements of thought or feeling running counter to the glorification of the nation, and applied as a categorical imperative to all phases of contemporary political and economic life.

Extreme nationalism of the Fascist or quasi-Fascist variety has various faces in various countries, but it has everywhere certain common characteristics which deserve to be noted. Like nationalism in its earliest form, it is born of war and conflict between nations. It has emerged out of the world-wide international bitterness and friction engendered by the Great War and it has fed upon the intensified resentments between nations in the post-war period. It is most acute and widespread in "unsatiated" States like Italy, Germany, Hungary, and Japan, whose patriots are obsessed with a sense of national injustice or fascinated by ambitions of national expansion. It is everywhere directed against past, present, or future "enemy" nations. Perhaps its most striking characteristic is its divorce from nineteenth century bourgeois liberalism. It is still for the

---

alike above those of the individual and above those of humanity. It refuses cooperation with other nations except as such cooperation may serve its own interests real or fancied. It is jingoistic, distrusts other nations, labors to exalt one nation at the expense of others, and relies on physical force. It is militarist and tends to be imperialist. In the face of it, a league of nations or any international sense of peace and security is threatened with sterility and destruction. Besides, in domestic affairs, integral nationalism is highly illiberal and tyrannical. It would oblige all citizens to conform to a common standard of manners and morals and to share the same unreasoning enthusiasm for it. It would subordinate all personal liberties to its own purpose, and if the common people should murmur it would abridge democracy and gag it. All these things it would do 'in the national interest.'"
Op. cit., pp. 165–166.

most part bourgeois in terms of the social and economic status of its devotees. But it is the bourgeois nationalism of an age in which the position
of the bourgeoisie as a ruling class is everywhere challenged by enemies
within and without. Since the challenge must be met and the enemies must
be suppressed, emphasis is placed, not upon liberty, equality, and laissez-
faire individualism, but upon law and order, discipline, national unity,
and salvation through ultra-patriotic dictatorship:

> Liberty is not an end but a means. As a means it must be controlled and
> dominated. This involves force . . . the assembling of the greatest force possible,
> the inexorable use of force whenever necessary—and by force is meant physical,
> armed force. . . . When a group or a party is in power it is under an obligation
> to fortify itself and defend itself against all comers. . . . Liberty is today no
> longer the chaste and austere virgin for whom the generations of the first half
> of the last century fought and died. For the gallant, restless, and bitter youth
> who face the dawn of a new history there are other words that exercise a far
> greater fascination, and these words are: order, hierarchy, discipline. . . .
> Fascism has already stepped over, and if it be necessary it will turn tranquilly
> and again step over, the more or less putrescent corpse of the Goddess of Liberty.[1]

In accordance with this philosophy, "strong" government is called for
to suppress all "national enemies," in which category are usually placed
all racial or linguistic minorities and all political groups aiming at
changing the existing distribution of wealth and political power. The most
common objects of attack are Socialists, Communists, labor leaders,
liberals, Jews, aliens of all kinds, and all who by virtue of race, language,
religion, or political doctrines fail to conform to the highest standards of
patriotic respectability. "Strong" government is likewise called for to
discipline and organize the nation, to regulate and coordinate all economic
activity, to regiment the entire population in order to give greater power
to the State. Fascist Italy represents the most complete example of the
political and economic forms which extreme nationalism has devised to
achieve its purposes.

No less marked is the close association between integral nationalism
and military glory. Extreme nationalists are invariably advocates of
military preparedness, of heavy armaments, of "strong" foreign policies,
of the exclusive pursuit of national interests by military means. The army,
the navy, and the air fleet are the visible symbols of the power of the
nation and the instrumentalities through which it suppresses internal
dissent and attains its goals in international politics. They are, therefore,
the objects of particular solicitude on the part of ultra-patriots everywhere. On its negative side, extreme nationalism is anti-foreign, anti-
pacifist, anti-liberal, and counter-revolutionary. On its positive side, it is
ultra-patriotic, militaristic, and collectivistic to the degree required to
preserve the established bourgeois economic order and to enhance the

[1] Benito Mussolini in "Forza e Consenso," *Gerarchia*, March, 1923.

power of the nation. Here again Italian Fascism represents this doctrine in its purest contemporary form. Its greatest spokesman, Il Duce, contends that "with regard to the future development of humanity and aside from expediency and political considerations, Fascism does not believe either in the possibility or usefulness of perpetual peace and rejects pacificism as cowardice and denunciation of struggle. Only war carries human energy to the highest tension and prints the seal of nobility on the peoples which have the virtues to confront it. All other proofs of quality are substitutes which never make a man actually confront himself with the alternatives of life and death. Doctrine, therefore, which is prejudiced in favor of peace is foreign to Fascism."[1]

The implications of these values and attitudes for the relations between the nations of the Western State System are sufficiently obvious to call for no extended commentary. It is the paradox of the twentieth century that in a world of increasingly interdependent nations in which the procedures and institutions of international cooperation have been elaborately developed, Fascist nationalism is everywhere rising in a great flood tide to glorify the national state and to set nation against nation in an ever more acute struggle for power and prestige. With its glorification of the national State and its emphasis upon the exclusive and paramount interests of the nation, Fascist nationalism offers no hope for that strengthening of world views and world interests which is the prerequisite to international peace and harmony. It envisages a world in which each State will pursue its own ends by its own might, strive to make itself as self-sufficient as possible, and reject as impotence, folly, or treason all that smacks of internationalism or of international cooperation in the interests of all. In the face of international organization, it would return with a vengeance to the conditions of international anarchy. In the face of efforts to organize peace, it would indulge in armament building, sword rattling, and military adventures. In the face of an imperative necessity for international economic coordination, it would aim to make the nation-state a self-contained economic unit, using its commercial and financial power as weapons of diplomacy and as means of strengthening and enriching the State or its ruling classes. As nationalism was born of the peculiar conditions of intergroup contacts prevailing in the formative period of the State System of the modern world, so it remains today in its latest form the greatest force conserving the traditional values and patterns of that State System and preventing its transformation into something other than a competitive congery of rival nation-states.

[1] Benito Mussolini, in "Politics and Social Doctrine," *Popolo d'Italia*, August 4, 1932.

SUGGESTED READINGS

Desjardins, P.: *French Patriotism in the Nineteenth Century*, Cambridge, Cambridge University Press, 1923.

Dominion, L.: *Frontiers of Language and Nationality in Europe*, New York, Henry Holt & Company, 1917.

Drinkwater, J.: *Patriotism in Literature*, New York, Henry Holt & Company, 1924.

Gaus, J. M.: *Great Britain: a Study in Civic Loyalty*, Chicago, University of Chicago Press, 1930.

Gooch, G. P.: *Nationalism*, New York, Harcourt, Brace & Company, 1920.

Hayes, C. J. H.: *Essays on Nationalism*, New York, The Macmillan Company, 1926.

————: *France, a Nation of Patriots*, New York, Columbia University Press, 1930.

————: *The Historical Evolution of Modern Nationalism*, New York, Richard R. Smith, 1931.

Herbert, S.: *Nationality and Its Problems*, New York, E. P. Dutton & Co., Inc., 1919.

Kohn, H.: *A History of Nationalism in the East*, New York, Harcourt, Brace & Company, 1929.

————: *Nationalism and Imperialism in the Hither East*, New York, Harcourt, Brace & Company, 1932.

Kosok, P.: *Modern Germany*, Chicago, University of Chicago Press, 1932.

Merriam, C. E.: *The Making of Citizens*, Chicago, University of Chicago Press, 1931.

Schneider, H. W. and S. B. Clough: *Making Fascists*, Chicago, University of Chicago Press, 1931.

CHAPTER IX

PATRIOTISM AND POWER

1. NATIONALITY, RACE, AND LANGUAGE

> The home of a language means merely the accidental place of its forma-
> tion, and this has no relation to its inner form. Languages migrate in that
> they spread by carriage from tribe to tribe. . . . It is impossible, there-
> fore, to draw conclusions as to the fortunes of the race side of peoples from
> mere place names, personal names, inscriptions, and dialects.—OSWALD
> SPENGLER, *The Decline of the West*, II.

NATIONALISM is a force in international politics only in so far as
it influences the behavior of States, and of peoples striving toward
Statehood, in their relations with one another. If the sentiments,
ideals, attitudes, and values of nationalism influenced human thought
and action only in the supposedly nonpolitical realm of literature, art,
folkways, and social institutions, it would be unnecessary for political
scientists to devote much attention to these phenomena. And if nationalism as a political attitude and doctrine were limited in its effects to
matters of domestic concern within each State, it would be unnecessary
for students of international relations to consider it seriously. But no
such divisions exist. Even in the fragmented, confused, and pluralistic
twentieth century, western culture is still an indivisible unity in which the
ubiquitous cult of the nation-state, with its millions of patriot devotees,
influences every phase of human interests, political and nonpolitical alike.
And a nationalism limited in its political effects to the internal politics
of a State is inconceivable, for the very attitudes and values of which it
consists are the product of international contacts and conflicts. International politics began before nations were aware of themselves as national
communities. Kings and dynasties in their pursuit of power created the
nation-state. They conquered and gave political unity to large areas. The
conflicts to which their rivalries led, engendered patriotic sentiment
among those who furnished the soldiers and paid the bills. These sentiments have become the common legacy of the whole population of modern
States, and they have in turn come to influence and determine State
policy in countless ways.

Everywhere modern nationalism, as a cult and a political dogma,
postulates the political independence of the national community as its
original goal and its ultimate ideal. To all patriots throughout the world,

[295]

no truth is more elementary than that the nation must be "free" to govern itself, to work out its own destiny, to formulate its own foreign policy. The nation must therefore attain statehood, *i.e.*, become an independent and sovereign political entity. If existence and independence are the most fundamental rights of States under international law, they are likewise the most fundamental values of national patriotism. Nothing engenders patriotic fervor among a people more effectively than foreign control or oppression. Nothing seems more supremely desirable to the patriot, or more in accordance with the most obvious principles of justice and common sense, than the political independence of the nation. The cry of national self-determination is accordingly the most poignant and insistent demand put forward by the nationalists of all countries. Each nationality demands political independence for itself, though it is seldom willing to grant the same right to the subject nationalities under its control. Each nation-state expresses its will to power in international politics no longer in terms of dynastic interests, but in terms of "national" interests. The nation must be served by enhancing its power and prestige in every way possible, and all of its nationals rejoice in this adventure. The resulting tensions, the ensuing conflicts of interests and policies have been perhaps the most fruitful sources of international friction during the past century and the most important factors underlying the attitudes of governments and peoples toward one another.

This demand for self-determination, for the political independence of the national community, obviously raises questions, as soon as attempts are made to translate it into action, of what *is* the national community. Of whom does it consist? What persons are "nationals," to be included within the frontiers of the nation-state, and what persons are aliens? What territories shall the national community insist upon including within its political boundary? What is the criterion of nationality? These questions have been variously answered by the patriots of various lands. Of absolute truth regarding them there is none. It is easy—doubtless too easy—to apply the test of the pragmatist to such queries and to say that all individuals are to be regarded as members of a given nationality who so regard themselves. A German is one who proclaims himself a German. A Czech is one who announces himself a Czech. A Chinese is one who declares himself a Chinese. In each case the individual in his proclaiming is presumably expressing a desire to live under the sovereignty of the nation-state representing his nationality. This is the test of workability which lies behind the device of the plebiscite as a means of ascertaining national allegiance. But the subjective attitudes of individuals are in turn conditioned by generally accepted associations and symbols which deserve examination. In the contemporary world, two criteria of nationality have received general acceptance: race and language.

[296]

The test of race is a thoroughly unsatisfactory criterion of nationality, but it is frequently emphasized by patriots, largely as a result of their efforts to rationalize designs of aggrandizement or discriminations against disliked minorities. The veriest novice in biology knows that "racial purity" is entirely nonexistent among the nations of the earth and that mankind can be classified into races only in the crudest and most unscientific fashion. If "pure races" ever existed in the human family, they have long since disappeared as a result of migrations, wars, conquests, travel, intermarriage, and miscegenation on the grandest scale over thousands of years. And as for biologically pure national stocks, there are none. The population of every modern nation is made up of a large number of mingled strains, each of which was itself originally a mixture of earlier stocks. "Englishmen" are for the most part descendants of Celts, Romans, Angles, Saxons, Danes, Normans, and other lesser breeds. "Frenchmen" are descendants of Cro-Magnons, Gauls, Romans, Franks, Goths, Huns, Vikings, and lesser groups. "Italians" are the sons and daughters of Romans, Gauls, Goths, Vandals, Lombards, Norsemen, and others, and each of these in turn was a mingling of mixtures. "Americans" are so obviously products of a melting-pot of races that even the most ardent 100 per cent patriot has difficulty in proving the existence of any American race save the dispossessed red Indians. *Homo sapiens* is hopelessly mongrel, and all attempts to dig up pure pedigrees for any of the sons of Adam are doomed to failure. Equally absurd are most popular notions of racial differences and race prejudice. People may easily be conditioned by their cultural environment to dislike members of an alien race, particularly where there is a clash of economic interests between the two groups. But that there is any inherent racial prejudices in the human animal is disproved by innumerable instances of perfect interracial harmony and cooperation. People of different races differ in their capacities and achievements, due in large part to differences in economic opportunities, cultural background, climatic stimuli, and social environment. But individual differences are greater than racial differences, and glib generalizations of racial superiority or inferiority are little more than rationalizations of culturally inherited prejudices.

And yet men and women *are* white, black, red, yellow, or brown, with various shadings in between, and within each of these groups there are physical differences of stature, body build, hair, skin and eye color, shape of skull, and the like. These differences are sufficiently marked to enable nationalist doctrinaires to spin finely woven theories of racial virtues and vices, of instinctive racial sympathies and antipathies, and of racial purity as the only proper criterion of nationality. The scientific unsoundness of these theories has not made them less effective in influencing attitudes and behavior. The cult of Aryanism was one of the earliest of the pseudo-scientific rationalizations to gain general acceptance. Professor Max Müller in 1816 developed the myth of the existence of an Aryan race on the basis of the resemblances between the various Aryan or Indo-European languages. Von Jhering, in his *Evolution of the Aryans*, carried this idea a step farther. Gobineau, in his *Essai sur l'inégalité des races humaines* (1884), developed the idea of Aryan superiority and of racial purity as a prerequisite of high civilization. Among the so-called Aryans, however, were obvious physical differences which led to the familiar division of the white race into categories of Nordic, Alpine, and Mediterranean. Houston-Stewart Chamberlain, a Germanized Englishman, first presented persuasively the notion of "Teutonic" superiority. Teutonism, Gallicism, Anglo-Saxonism, were all cut of the same cloth, as is the cult of "Nordic" supremacy which has flourished so amazingly in the backward areas of Anglo-Saxon North America. This most recent of the racial myths has also produced its pseudo-scientific apologists[1] and has evoked in the hinterland the familiar patterns of anti-Semitic, anti-foreign, anti-Negro, and anti-Catholic movements so well exemplified in the recent revival of the Ku Klux Klan. The Hitlerite movement in Germany, with its emphasis upon anti-Semitism, anti-foreignism, and "Aryan" or "Teutonic" purity, is a similar phenomenon.

These efforts to link nationality with race, or to find in racial purity a new basis of social cohesion in contrast to nationality, have had considerable political significance. They have intensified racial and national prejudices. They have influenced the immigration legislation and population policies of national governments. They have lent popular support to imperialism and to the subjugation and exploitation of "backward" peoples by the "superior" races. But they have not resulted in any widespread cult of racialism comparable to nationalism. People in most parts of the world continue to identify themselves as Englishmen, Persians, Germans, Japanese, Italians, Bulgarians, etc., rather than as Nordics, Mediterraneans, Alpines, yellow men, black men, or brown men. Nationality or identification with the national group is an inherent feature of man's cultural heritage in many regions of the globe. It is the product of centuries of political contacts and cultural developments, and it has become a part of the life and soul of people everywhere. Nations have been built by patriots and molded by constant efforts to remodel the nation to the patriot's liking. The biological accidents of racial differences have always been beyond man's control. In dim, far-off times there took place such a migration and mingling and interbreeding of peoples that all semblance of racial purity has long since vanished. Efforts to restore what

[1] *Cf.* Madison Grant, *The Passing of the Great Race*, 1918; Lothrop Stoddard, *The Rising Tide of Color*, 1920, *The Revolt Against Civilization*, and *Racial Realities in Europe*, 1924; C. S. Burr, *America's Race Heritage*, etc.

probably never existed are doomed to futility. And efforts to lend reality to biological myths which have little relation to the content of national cultures are not likely to become a gospel and a way of life for any large number of men and women. People identify themselves much more readily with "nations," religious denominations, and economic classes than with largely imaginary racial groups.

If race has not become the basis of nationality, the same can scarcely be said of language. Race and language obviously have no necessary connection with one another, since the one is a biological phenomenon and the other is part of the cultural legacy of the past. People are born with skin color, eye color, skull shapes, and the other physical marks of race. But the language they learn depends not on their heredity, but upon their cultural environment. Language, while no indication whatever of race, is everywhere the best index of an individual's cultural environment—of the linguistic and cultural group with which he identifies himself and of which he is a member. By the same token, one's mother tongue is everywhere taken as the best criterion of one's nationality. Most of the nations of the earth are nations, not so much because they are politically independent and socially unified, as because their peoples use a common speech which differs from that of other nations. Englishmen, Americans, and British colonials, it is true, all speak variants of a single language. Portuguese and Brazilians use a single language. So do Frenchmen and Haitians, and likewise Spaniards, Mexicans, Chilians, Argentinians, Peruvians, and the other Spanish-Americans. For these people, varying dialects, rather than language, may indicate nationality. On the other hand, Swiss nationals may speak French, German, or Italian and still be Swiss; and Belgians may speak French or Flemish without ceasing to be Belgians. For the most part, however, distinctions of nationality, in the social and cultural rather than in the legal sense, are coterminous with distinctions of language. With few exceptions, Germans are Germans because they *sprechen echt Deutsch*, Frenchmen are Frenchmen because they *parlent la belle langue française*, Englishmen, Englishmen because they speak the King's English. This association between language and national consciousness appears as natural and obvious as the association between race and nationality appears strange and false. The historical circumstances of the establishment of the older national groups have made the association inevitable. Language is almost universally regarded as the most important single criterion of national sentiment and allegiance. In the last analysis, however, nationality is not a matter either of race or of language, but of social attitudes, sentiments, and ideologies.

2. SELF-DETERMINATION AND IRREDENTISM

He is an Englishman!
    For he himself has said it,
    And it's greatly to his credit,
That he is an Englishman!
    For he might have been a Roosian,
    A French, or Turk, or Proosian,
Or perhaps Itali-an!
    But in spite of all temptations,
    To belong to other nations,
He remains an Englishman!
    Hurrah!
For the true born Englishman!
                    —W. S. GILBERT, *The Englishman.*

The fact that the national group is so generally regarded as coinciding with the language group has meant that the aspirations of nationalists are usually envisaged in terms of the common "national" interests of all who speak the same tongue. Common language has come to be the test of nationality—so much so that States like Switzerland or Belgium or the old Austria-Hungary, where more than one tongue prevails, are often spoken of as "non-national" or "multi-national" States. Whatever the location of political boundaries may be at any given time, "nations" in the nonpolitical sense are aggregations of people aware of themselves as units by virtue of linguistic and cultural ties. The national community whose independence is postulated by nationalism is a community whose members employ the same speech. If the language group does not possess independence, it must achieve it. If, having attained independence, it does not include within the nation-state all those who speak the mother tongue, efforts must be made toward their annexation, even at the cost of the dismemberment of neighboring States. If there are those within the State who do not speak the mother tongue, they must be taught, assimilated, and if necessary coerced into abandoning their own language and culture in the name of national unity and power. From these articles of faith of the national patriot flow many of the consequences of nationalism in the realm of international politics.

The most obvious consequence has been the fragmentation of the world into a large number of sovereign nation-states in the name of national self-determination and independence. Each linguistic group, as it has become infected with the nationalist germ (and the malady is extraordinarily contagious), has striven to attain its political independence, to achieve statehood, to set up national housekeeping for itself. The notion that a national language group can live contentedly under the political control of a government representing another and different group is anathema to the national patriot. Frenchmen have resisted English domination, Germans have resisted French domination, Poles have resisted German domination, Lithuanians and Ruthenians have resisted Polish domination. Each national community has asserted its right to political independence as soon as national consciousness has taken root and flourished among its people. In the ancient world and in the middle ages, people differing in language and culture were content enough to live together under a common political control embodied in world empires or in complex feudal state-forms. Not so in the modern era of western civilization. Each distinct linguistic group must build its own State, win its own independence, have its own territory, flag, army, bureaucracy, and all the other trappings of sovereignty.

State after State has been born as a result of this demand: the United States and the Latin American republics in the later eighteenth and early nineteenth centuries; Greece, Bulgaria, and the other Balkan nations in the mid-nineteenth century, as well as Italy and Germany, fused together out of smaller fragments; Poland, the Baltic States, Czechoslovakia, Jugoslavia, and Greater Rumania in the "Balkanization" of central Europe which followed the Great War. Each national group has demanded and attained statehood until the Western State System has become truly an aggregation of nation-states. This aspiration has led in some cases to the building of newly integrated political structures and in others to the disintegration of established States. It has brought about the breakup, complete or partial, of a number of empires and non-national States, for nationalism is a disruptive and centrifugal force in such political entities. The British Empire was split in 1776, for already "Americans" had begun to feel themselves to be distinct from "Englishmen." The Empire has since evolved, more or less peacefully, into a "commonwealth of nations," *i.e.*, a federation of self-governing units. The Spanish and Portuguese empires in the New World similarly dissolved into independent fragments. In these instances the units which became independent did not differ from the mother country in language, but their inhabitants were imbued with a sense of their own identity by virtue of geographical separation, cultural differences, and divergent economic interests. In more recent cases of dissolution, the association between nationality and language has been more marked. The progressive decay of the Ottoman Empire was due to demands, first for autonomy and then for independence, on the part of Greeks, Serbians, Bulgarians, Rumanians, Egyptians, Armenians, Syrians, Kurds, and other linguistic groups. The destruction of Austria-Hungary in 1918 was due to insistence upon independence on the part of each of the major language groups comprising the Dual Monarchy. The partial dissolution of the Russian Empire was similarly a consequence of the demands of the western border peoples for self-government and statehood. On the other hand, in the creation of the States of Germany and Italy in the nineteenth century, a large number of formerly independent communities speaking the same language were brought together into politically unified nations. In the future, as in the past, it will doubtless remain true that the desire of each nationality for statehood will threaten to disrupt multi-national States, and States with large national minorities such as Poland, Czechoslovakia, and Rumania, while it will at the same time bring greater unity and cohesion to States whose nationals already enjoy linguistic and cultural homogeneity.

Demands for national self-determination and independence became peculiarly insistent during the Great War and were utilized by the Allied Governments as a means of encouraging the disruption of the enemy States and of convincing their own citizens that the Allied cause was the cause of justice and liberty. President Wilson, as the most eloquent phrase-maker among the statesmen who formulated "war aims" for popular consumption, constantly emphasized the "rights of small nations." Even before the United States entered the war, he laid it down as a principle "that no nation should seek to extend its polity over any other nation or people, but that every people should be left free to determine its own polity, its own way of development, unhindered, unthreatened, unafraid, the little along with the great and powerful."[1] The "fourteen points" address of January 8, 1918, demanded self-determination for the peoples of central and eastern Europe, and in February, 1918, the American President, in an address to Congress, asserted:

Peoples and provinces are not to be bartered about from sovereignty to sovereignty as if they were mere chattels and pawns in the game. Peoples may now be dominated and governed only by their own consent. Self-determination is not a mere phrase. It is an imperative principle of action, which statesmen will henceforth ignore at their peril.

At the Paris Peace Conference of 1919 the newly emancipated nationalities of central Europe insisted that the slogan of self-determination be translated into political reality, and the Allied Governments gave effect to these demands wherever they found it politically advantageous to do so. It was clear, however, that in many cases political boundaries could not be made to coincide with language boundaries, for the intermingling of tongues in central Europe is so confused, as shown in the accompanying map, that this ideal is impossible of attainment. The independence of Poland, Czechoslovakia, Hungary, Austria, Jugoslavia, Albania, and Greater Rumania, and later of Finland, Esthonia, Latvia, and Lithuania, was accepted as a matter of course. But the boundaries which the new States insisted upon, and the boundary adjustments which the victors

[1] Address to the Senate, January 22, 1917.

demanded for themselves, were dictated quite as much by considerations of economics, strategy, and territorial aggrandizement as by the expressed desire to grant to the populations affected a right of self-determination. When "self-determination" threatened to thwart the territorial ambitions of the victors, it was denied to the peoples in question. Germans were transferred to foreign rule in the Tyrol, in Alsace, and in the Polish corridor, with no opportunity of expressing their preferences. Hungarians were transferred to Rumanian, Jugoslav, and Czech control in a similar fashion. Lithuanians, Russians, and Ukrainians were annexed without their consent by Poland and Rumania. But wherever there appeared a possibility of reducing further the territory and power of the defeated States, self-determination was appealed to and the populations in question were given an opportunity to express their wishes through plebiscites.

The plebiscite, or popular referendum, as a means of enabling peoples to attain national self-determination, has become an increasingly popular device. It has seldom been applied in recent times to an entire national community to determine whether or not its members desire political independence, though the division of Sweden and Norway into independent kingdoms in 1905 was sanctioned by a popular vote, and plebiscites were held in the States of Italy in 1860 and 1861 prior to their amalgamation into the present kingdom. Such referenda have been repeatedly held to ascertain the preferences of the inhabitants of a particular territory as between two outside States seeking control. Napoleon III held a plebiscite in Nice and Savoy prior to their annexation to France in 1859. The Treaty of Ancon in 1883 between Chile and Peru provided for a plebiscite in Tacna-Arica which was never held, in spite of efforts on the part of the United States to make arrangements for a vote in 1923–1925. The plebiscite principle, as a basis for allocating territory, received only partial recognition at the Paris Peace Conference, but the treaties of 1919 nevertheless provided for nine popular referenda: in Schleswig, Allenstein, Marienwerder, Upper Silesia, Eupen, Malmedy, Klagenfurt, Burgenland. and the Saar valley. In most of Schleswig the population voted to remain under German, rather than Danish, sovereignty, and in Allenstein and Marienwerder the East Prussians likewise voted for German rather than Polish control. In Upper Silesia 707,000 votes were cast for Germany and 479,000 for Poland (1921). The League Council, however, divided the area to the great disgust of nationalists in both countries. Eupen and Malmedy, formerly German territories, voted for annexation to Belgium. Klagenfurt, in dispute between Austria and Jugoslavia, voted for Austria. Burgenland voted for Austrian rather than Hungarian rule. The Saar plebiscite is to be held in 1935 to determine whether the inhabitants prefer the return of the valley to Germany, its annexation to France, or a continuation of its international status.

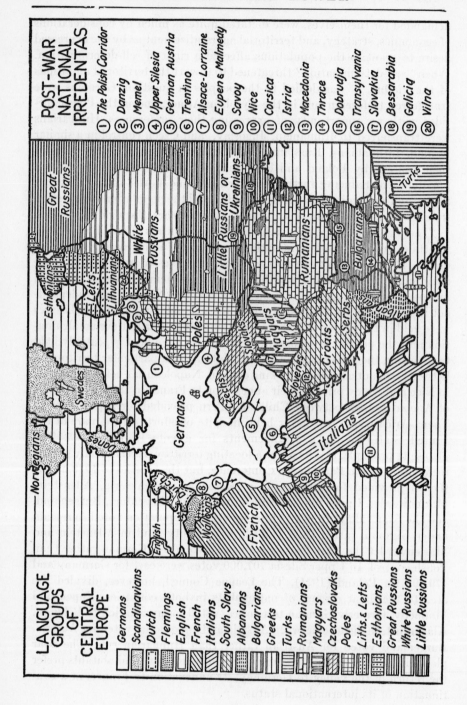

POST-WAR NATIONAL IRREDENTAS

① The Polish Corridor
② Danzig
③ Memel
④ Upper Silesia
⑤ German Austria
⑥ Trentino
⑦ Alsace-Lorraine
⑧ Eupen & Malmedy
⑨ Savoy
⑩ Nice
⑪ Corsica
⑫ Istria
⑬ Macedonia
⑭ Thrace
⑮ Dobrudja
⑯ Transylvania
⑰ Slovakia
⑱ Bessarabia
⑲ Galicia
⑳ Vilna

LANGUAGE GROUPS OF CENTRAL EUROPE

Germans
Scandinavians
Dutch
Flemings
English
French
Italians
South Slavs
Albanians
Bulgarians
Greeks
Turks
Rumanians
Magyars
Czechoslovaks
Poles
Liths. & Letts
Esthonians
Great Russians
White Russians
Little Russians

While the plebiscite method commends itself to idealistic self-determinationists, it is fraught with numerous dangers and difficulties. Even when adequate neutral policing is provided and satisfactory suffrage qualifications and electoral procedures are devised, the referendum itself embitters national feeling, creates temptations of bribery, coercion, and terrorism on both sides, and offers no assurance that the voters will record their permanent national preferences rather than their fears, prejudices, and economic interests at the moment. President Coolidge, as arbitrator of the Tacna-Arica dispute, ordered a plebiscite in that area in 1923. But General Lassiter, American member of the plebiscitory commission, reported in 1926 that the plebiscite was impracticable because of Chilean terroristic tactics and the tense feeling on both sides. In September of 1919 the Allied Supreme Council for similar reasons abandoned its intention of holding a plebiscite in Teschen (in dispute between Poland and Czechoslovakia) and divided the territory between the contestants. The League Council found it impossible to arrange a plebiscite in the Vilna district, which Poland wrested from Lithuania in 1920. It likewise refused to authorize a plebiscite in the Aaland Islands and permitted Finland to retain control of them in the face of protests from Sweden and the local population.[1] It seems unlikely, in view of the difficulties encountered, that the plebiscite can be made a practicable basis for giving effect to the principle of national self-determination, except in isolated cases and under strict international supervision. Territories and peoples continue to be transferred from State to State and to be granted or denied national independence, in accordance with the dictates of political expediency and the verdict of force. And whenever the outcome fails to correspond to the demands of the peoples themselves, local dissatisfaction, international tension, and controversies between neighboring States invariably ensue.

Another phenomenon of nationalism, which may conveniently be characterized as "irredentism," is closely related to the cry for self-determination and has been an equally fruitful source of conflict between the nation-states. The term is of Italian origin. In 1861 Italian nationalists at length achieved the goal which they had pursued for decades. A United Kingdom of Italy was created through the annexation to Piedmont of the lesser States of the south. Venetia was wrested from Austria in 1867 and Rome was added to the new nation in 1870. But a large Italian-speaking community in Trentino and the Tyrol remained under Austrian

[1] In this instance the Council committee declared: "To concede to minorities, either of language or of religion, or to any fractions of a population the right of withdrawing from the community to which they belong, because it is their wish or their good pleasure, would be to destroy order and stability within States and to inaugurate anarchy in international life; it would be to uphold a theory incompatible with the very idea of the State as a territorial and political unity." Report of Commission of Rapporteurs, April 16, 1921, Council Document B. 7, pp. 28–30.

rule. No Italian patriot could regard the task of national unification as completed until these regions were likewise "liberated." They came to be known as *Italia Irredenta* ("Italy Unredeemed"). Toward them were turned the eyes of all patriots. Their annexation became one of the major objectives of Italian foreign policy. The French annexation of Tunis in 1881 threw Italy into the arms of Germany and Austria-Hungary, for Italian patriots had regarded the north African province as a future Italian colony. But in the Triple Alliance of 1882, Italy remained an ally of dubious loyalty, for the demands of nationalism were more appealing than the demands of imperialism. So long as Austria-Hungary retained control of Italia Irredenta, the Italian government could not rest content with the prevailing arrangements. In 1914 Italy remained neutral and sought to bargain with her neighbor and erstwhile ally for possession of the unredeemed provinces as the price of her entrance into the war on the side of the Central Powers. But the Allies were more generous in promises, and by the secret Treaty of London of May, 1915, they pledged Italy the realization of her irredentist ambitions at Austria's expense, on condition of her joining their cause. Italy accordingly declared war upon Austria-Hungary and in the peace settlement was awarded the coveted territories and considerably more besides. National irredentism was thus the guiding star of Italian foreign policy for over half a century.

Such aspirations are almost universal among patriots. Irredentist nationalists invariably strive to incorporate into the nation-state such territories as are inhabited by kinsmen of common speech and culture across the frontier. The claims of nationality and the cry of self-determination supersede the claims of legal right and are assumed to justify annexationist ambitions in such situations. Numerous "irredentas" of this character existed in pre-war Europe. Alsace-Lorraine under German rule was France irredenta, for every French patriot prayed and hoped for the *revanche* which would enable the Republic to take back to its bosom the "lost provinces," snatched away by Bismarck in 1871. Bosnia, Herzegovina, and the Dalmatian coast under Austrian rule were Serbia irredenta, and Serbian patriots were determined, by fair means or foul, to incorporate the South-Slav inhabitants of these regions into a Greater Serbia. Transylvania, under Hungarian rule, and Bessarabia, under Russian rule, were Rumania irredenta, for they were in large part inhabited by Rumanian-speaking peoples whose control by an alien government was intolerable to the peoples themselves and to their fellow patriots within Rumania. Macedonia and Silistria, under Serbian and Rumanian rule respectively, were Bulgaria irredenta for similar reasons. The post-war irredenta are even more numerous. Germany now has her own "lost provinces" and her own irredentas: the Saar valley, Upper Silesia, Pomerelia and Netze (the Polish corridor), Danzig, Memel,

German-speaking Austria, the German Tyrol, the German-speaking areas of Czechoslovakia, and even, in the eyes of the more extreme German nationalists, Alsace-Lorraine itself. No German patriot can regard as permanent the loss of these areas, nor can he rest content until they are recovered, at least in part. Hungarian nationalists are similarly embittered over the dismemberment of the ancient Magyar State and strive to incorporate into a resurrected Hungary the millions of Magyars annexed by Czechoslovakia, Jugoslavia, and Rumania. The Aaland Islands are an irredenta for Sweden, eastern Karelia for Finland, Vilna for Lithuania. Bulgaria has her old grievances and a new irredenta as well in western Thrace, taken from her by Greece. If a nationalist government existed in Russia, the eastern provinces of Poland and Rumanian Bessarabia, with their White Russian and Ukrainian populations, would be a new Russia irrendenta. Such attitudes tend to prevail wherever political frontiers fail to follow the boundaries of language, and they are obviously among the most productive causes of tension and conflict among the nations.

These attitudes and aspirations lie at the root of the various pan-nationalistic movements which have flourished so abundantly. "Pan-Germanism" in the pre-war period contemplated the annexation to a united Germany of all German-speaking peoples in adjacent foreign States. The Pan-German League, established in 1894, strove "to quicken the national sentiment of all Germans and in particular to awaken and foster the sense of racial and cultural kinship of all sections of the German people."[1] Germany's defeat in the Great War led to additional losses of German territory, and the terms of the peace treaties forbidding any *anschluss* or union of German-speaking Austria with Germany constitute a new obstacle to the realization of Pan-German ambition. This union, which is apparently desired by the overwhelming majority of Germans and Austrians, would create a German State of 70,000,000 people. It is opposed by France, Italy, and the Little Entente for obvious reasons of power politics. Pre-war Pan-Slavism was a similar movement, sponsored by Russian patriots and by certain South-Slav groups. It aimed at the "liberation" of the Slavic peoples living under German, Austrian, or Turkish rule, and the formation of a Slavic confederacy dominated by Russia. As early as the seventeenth century, the Croat, Krijanitcha, urged a political union of Slavic peoples. Pan-Slavic congresses were held in 1848, 1867, and 1908. These ambitions played a large rôle in the pre-war foreign policy of imperial Russia. Combined with annexationist designs on Constantinople and the Straits, they caused Russia to come to the defense of Serbia against Austria-Hungary in 1914 and thus precipitated the Great War. The Russian Revolution and the political independence of Poland,

[1] M. S. Wertheimer, *The Pan-German League,* 1890–1914, p. 95.

Czechoslovakia, and Jugoslavia have deprived Pan-Slavism of any present significance. The "Norden Movement" in Sweden, Norway, and Denmark was a comparable Pan-Scandinavian movement. Pan-Anglianism has striven to encourage closer political relations between the English-speaking peoples. Joseph Chamberlain in 1898 advocated an Anglo-American alliance as part of this program. The English-speaking Union has endeavored to promote closer cultural and economic contacts between the United States and the British Empire. Pan-Americanism is a movement of a somewhat different character, for any political union of the Latin peoples of South and Central America with the Anglo-Saxon peoples of the United States runs counter to the national aspirations of all Latin Americans. Pan-Latinism and Pan-Hispanism, however, are much more solidly grounded in national sentiment. They do not reflect irredentist ambitions so much as a feeling that linguistic and cultural ties should be made the basis for closer political and economic relations. Pan-Africanism, Pan-Islamism, Pan-Arabianism, Pan-Turanianism, Pan-Asianism and other movements reflect similar sentiments and ambitions.[1]

The nationalistic aspirations of self-determination and irredentism breed inevitable discontent with all national boundaries which are at variance with the lines of language and culture. Very rarely can these lines be ascertained to the satisfaction of both parties. When they are ascertained, they are often unacceptable for economic or strategic reasons. Italy, for example, recovered Italia Irredenta at the Peace Conference but insisted also on acquiring the Brenner Pass and the southern slope of the Tyrolean Alps for reasons of defense, with the result that 250,000 German-speaking peoples of the Bozen (Bolzano) are are now under Italian rule and constitute an Austria irredenta. Boundaries drawn to conform to considerations of strategy and economics are criticized by patriots as violating the wishes of the population. Boundaries drawn to conform to the wishes of the population are criticized by other patriots (or even by the same ones) for other reasons. In such a situation, no rational basis exists for the demarcation of frontiers. Efforts to minimize tension are frustrated by annexationist ambitions. Each State exerts its power to gain all the territory possible as a means to greater power, wealth, and security. Power considerations are rationalized in terms of self-determination or irredentism or, when these are inapplicable, in terms of other catchwords and symbols. "Historic" frontiers are insisted upon. "Natural" boundaries are demanded. "Manifest destiny" is called upon to justify annexation. When the line of linguistic cleavage is gained, then the next river or mountain range becomes the goal, and when that is attained some line beyond becomes the natural and necessary frontier. Boundaries are fixed by the clash, in peace or war, of the rival wills-to-power of the nation-

[1] See R. L. Buell, *International Relations*, 1929, pp. 76–95.

states. Nationalism spurs the rivalry and furnishes formulas and slogans, in terms of which each national community can reassure itself of the justice and rectitude of its ambitions.

3. THE PROBLEM OF NATIONAL MINORITIES

> A healthy nation is as unconscious of its nationality as a healthy man of his bones. But if you break a nation's nationality it will think of nothing else but getting it set again. It will listen to no reformer, to no philosopher, to no preacher until the demand of the nationalist is granted.—G. B. SHAW, *Preface for Politicians*.

Not only is each nation-state anxious, in its quest for territory and power, to extend its control over the peoples beyond its frontier who speak its language, but it is equally anxious to achieve linguistic and cultural homogeneity among the peoples within its frontiers. "Self-determination" is a phrase used by nationalists only with reference to the oppressed subject peoples of other States. Their "liberation" will weaken the power of the State controlling them and thus enhance that of its neighbor. The neighbor is accordingly solicitous over their fate, particularly when they speak his own language and constitute an irredenta. Patriots are concerned in quite a different way, however, with the minority groups in the population of their own State. These groups must under no circumstances be liberated or granted a right of self-determination. They must be assimilated in the name of national unity and patriotic solidarity. They must be induced or compelled to abandon their own identity and their ties with other peoples beyond the frontier. They must learn the prevailing language, adopt the prevailing customs, and make themselves one with their fellow citizens.

The "problem of national minorities" arises from such nationalistic efforts at assimilation and from the counter-efforts, supported by the national consciousness of the minorities, to resist assimilation at all costs. Except for the sentiments, attitudes, and ideologies of nationalism, there would be no problem. Peoples heterogeneous in language, race, and religion might dwell together peaceably under a single sovereignty, as in the Roman Empire, with no attempts made on the part of the government to impose uniformity of tongues and creeds on its subjects, and consequently no attempts at resistance to such efforts on the part of minorities. But in the age of nationalism, any such rational arrangements are regarded by all patriots as highly undesirable and even dangerous. Unassimilated minorities are viewed with alarm, for they are presumed to be of doubtful loyalty, to constitute an alien and possibly hostile element in the population, and to be peculiarly susceptible to secret conspirings with neighboring enemy nations of their own blood and language. These suspicions may be at first unjustified, but they find justification as soon as efforts are made to extinguish the identity of the minority. People cling doggedly to their language and culture—never more so than in the era of nationalism, when these things are closely associated with the social cohesion and political self-respect of the community. Efforts at assimilation are vigorously resisted with an energy and determination equivalent to the pressure brought to bear by the assimilators. Resistance assumes the appearance of disloyalty, and this in turn justifies the national government, in the eyes of its patriots, in applying more coercion. The greater the coercion, the greater the resistance; and the greater the resistance, the greater the coercion. The outcome of the cycle is persecution, revolt, international complications, and often war. In view of these consequences, the problem is not merely a domestic one, but is of increasingly vital international concern.

In pre-war Europe, the prevalent policy pursued by governments toward minorities might be described as one of forcible assimilation. This policy was adopted, with minor variations, by the four governments of Europe which had the largest minority groups living under their control—those of Russia, Germany, Austria-Hungary, and Turkey. The German census of 1900 showed, in the Empire, 51,880,000 Germans, 3,080,000 Poles, 211,000 Frenchmen, 142,000 Masurians, 141,000 Danes, 106,000 Lithuanians, 100,000 Cassubians, and smaller numbers of Wends, Dutch, Italians, Moravians, and Czechs. While there was no outright persecution of these groups by the central government, representing the dominant German majority, a policy of "Germanization" was steadily carried forward, aiming at the eventual liquidation of the language, culture, and national identity of the minorities. This policy encountered most opposition, and led to the most intense bitterness, in the case of the Polish minorities in East Prussia.

In Russia the "nationalities problem" was much more serious. The Russian census of 1897 (the last nation-wide census taken before the Great War) revealed, in a total population of 129,200,000, 55,673,000 Great Russians, 22,380,000 Little Russians or Ukrainians, 7,931,000 Poles, 5,885,000 White Russians, 5,000,000 Jews, 4,084,000 Kirghiz peoples, 3,737,000 Tartars, 2,496,000 Finns, 1,790,000 Germans, 1,658,000 Lithuanians, 1,492,000 Bashkirs, 1,435,000 Letts, 1,173,000 Armenians, 1,352,000 Georgians, 1,134,000 Rumanians, 1,000,000 Esthonians, and smaller numbers of Mordvinians, Chuvashes, Sarts, and other Asiatic and Caucasian peoples. The half-religious, half-nationalistic creed of Pan-Slavism adhered to by the ruling classes dictated a policy of forcible "Russification" of such minorities as seemed assimilable, and a policy of discrimination, segregation, and persecution against such groups as the Jews, who could obviously never be made good and loyal Russians. The Jewish minority suffered most severely, both because of its religion and race and because the political radicalism bred of oppression flourished most luxuriously among this most persecuted of minority groups. Pogroms, massacres, and assassinations alternated with savage repression, bloody revolt, legalized discrimination, and desperate determination to preserve the ancestral heritage against the assaults of the defiling Gentile. The Finns enjoyed a measure of autonomy prior to 1905, but were ruled and misruled with an iron hand following the unsuccessful revolution of that year. The Poles were even more bitterly persecuted following their abortive rebellion against Russian rule in 1863. The other border peoples on the west, in the Caucasus, and in central Asia and Siberia fared scarcely better.

Austria-Hungary and Turkey exhibited variants of the same general policy. In Austria-Hungary's population of 51,300,000 (1910), no single linguistic group constituted a majority. In Austria the 12,000,000 Germans were the dominant element. In Hungary the 10,000,000 Magyars occupied a similar position. In addition there were 8,500,000 Czechs and Slovaks, 5,500,000 Serbs and Croats, 5,000,000 Poles, 4,000,000 Ruthenians, 3,250,000 Rumanians, 1,250,000 Slovenes, 750,000 Italians, and other smaller groups. In the Austrian half of the Empire, these groups enjoyed a large degree of freedom of language, religion, and education. The Poles under Austrian rule were less subjected to alien pressure than the Poles under Prussian or Russian sovereignty. In the Hungarian portion of the Empire, on the contrary, the government approved a policy of Magyarization, directed against the Rumanians, the South Slavs, the Jews, and others. This policy developed among the minorities self-determinationist and irredentist sentiments in its most extreme form. In Turkey, with its large minorities of Armenians, Kurds, Syrians, Arabs, Bulgars, Greeks, etc., the policy of the government was for the most part one of ruthless persecution, inspired by fears of uprisings and of foreign intervention. With respect to certain of the minorities, notably the Armenians, the physical annihilation of the minority group appears at times to have been the objective of governmental policy. Massacres were frequent—the most notable occurring in 1894–1895, 1904, 1909, 1915, 1922—and provoked the very things they were intended to prevent: bitter resistance, disloyalty, and interference on behalf of the minorities by interested foreign governments.

The pre-war policy of forcible assimilation was, almost without exception, unsuccessful in suppressing the identity of the minorities or in compelling them to adopt the language, culture, creeds, and institutions of the majority group. Indeed, it more frequently intensified to the point of desperation the solidarity of the oppressed groups and thus rendered impossible of achievement its own purposes. The failure of this policy had already received a certain degree of recognition in various treaties which protected minority rights and made forcible assimilation difficult. Religious minorities were the first to receive international protection in this fashion, following the wars and persecutions of the Reformation period. The Peace of Augsburg (1555) and the Treaties of Westphalia both gave to minority religious groups a degree of protection from efforts at persecution on the part of the majority denomination. Here, as always, intolerance gave way to tolerance only when persecution had brought disaster and when the folly of achieving conversion by coercion was evident to all. The Powers exacted pledges regarding the protection of religious minorities in Holland and Greece in 1815 and 1830 respectively, on the occasions of the union of Belgium with Holland and of the recognition of Greek independence. Ethnic and linguistic minorities were in no need of such protection before nationalism became a new religion and led in turn to new efforts at conversion and persecution. By the late nineteenth century, however, the problem was a pressing one. The Treaty of Berlin of 1878 required Bulgaria, Montenegro, Serbia, Rumania, and Turkey to refrain from discriminating against religious minorities. As early as 1839, Turkey had been obliged to pledge equal treatment of its subjects regardless of religion, race, or language. The failure of the Turkish Government to observe this and subsequent pledges, led to repeated diplomatic representations and interventions by the Powers. From time to time international inspectors and supervisors were dispatched to Turkish territory to guarantee the protection of minorities in Armenia and Macedonia. These efforts at treaty protection and international guarantees were largely ineffective, however, and were utilized by interested Powers to further their own designs. They were not applied, moreover, to such powerful States as Russia, Austria-Hungary, and Germany, where the minorities were entirely at the mercy of the local patriots bent upon assimilating them.

The Great War and its aftermath created new minority problems and led to the development of an alternative to forcible assimilation. The new policy may be designated as protection by international guarantees. The breakup of Austria-Hungary and the partial dissolution of the Russian, Turkish, and German Empires, coupled with the redrawing of frontiers in the name of self-determination, reduced the minorities of Europe from 54,000,000 to about 17,000,000. But the new frontiers were based upon economic and strategic considerations and did not in every case follow the lines of language. They were designed to cripple the defeated States as much as possible. Seven and a half million Germans, three million Magyars, and one and a third million Bulgarians were placed under alien rule in France, Poland, Czechoslovakia, Jugoslavia, Rumania, Italy, and Greece, along with half a million Jugoslavs in Italy, four and a half million Ruthenians and Ukrainians in Poland,

NATIONAL MINORITIES

MINORITIES OF CENTRAL EUROPE[1]

State	Date	Total population	Minorities		Percentage of total
Germany...........	1925	62,410,619	61,131,222	Germans	97.95
			356,314	Poles	0.57
			545,698	Polish-Germans	0.87
			50,298	Masurians	0.08
			31,343	Masurian-Germans	0.05
			62,622	Wends	0.10
			10,004	Wendish-Germans	0.01
			30,382	Czech-Moravians	0.05
			16,203	Czech-Moravians and Germans	0.03
			7,494	Danish	0.01
			3,189	Danish-Germans	0.005
			4,208	Lithuanians	0.007
			3,267	Lithuanian-Germans	0.005
			119,671	Others	0.19
			38,604	Others-Germans	0.06
Czechoslovakia......	1921	13,613,172	6,840,261	Czechs }	64.8
			1,979,402	Slovaks }	
			3,218,005	Germans	23.6
			761,823	Magyars	5.6
			477,430	Russians	3.5
			110,138	Poles	0.8
			190,856	Jews	1.4
			14,828	Rumanians	0.1
			14,537	Others	0.1
Austria...........	1923	6,534,481	6,272,892	Germans	96.00
			93,533	Czechs	1.43
			5,170	Slovaks	0.08
			43,383	Slovenes	0.66
			44,771	Serbs and Croats	0.69
			25,071	Magyars	0.38
			47,943	Others	0.73

[1] From *Die Nationalitäten in den Staaten Europas—Herausgegeben im Auftrage des Europäischen Nationalitäten-Kongresses* (edited by Dr. Ewald Ammende, Generalsekretar), 1931, 568 pp.

Czechoslovakia, and Rumania, and several million Russians along Poland's eastern frontier. One-fourth of Jugoslavia's population, one-half of Poland's population, two-fifths of Czechoslovakia's population (not counting the Slovaks as a minority), and over one-tenth of Italy's population consist of linguistic minorities. To permit a reversion to policies of forcible assimilation on the part of the overenthusiastic patriots of the new States would create widespread domestic disorder and international tension throughout central Europe. The Peace Conference accordingly

MINORITIES OF EASTERN EUROPE[1]

State	Date	Total population	Minorities		Percentage of total
Esthonia...............	1922	1,107,059	969,976	Esthonians	87.7
			91,109	Russians	8.2
			18,319	Germans	1.7
			7,850	Swedes	0.7
			4,566	Jews	0.4
			14,508	Others	1.3
Latvia.................	1930	1,900,045	1,394,957	Letts	73.5
			69,855	Germans	3.7
			201,778	Russians	10.6
			36,029	White Russians	1.9
			94,388	Jews	5.0
			59,374	Poles	3.1
			25,885	Lithuanians	1.4
			7,708	Esthonians	0.4
			8,566	Others	0.4
Lithuania..............	1923	2,028,971	1,701,863	Lithuanians	84.2
			153,743	Jews	7.6
			65,599	Poles	3.3
			50,460	Russians	2.5
			29,231	Germans	1.4
			14,883	Letts	0.7
			4,421	White Russians	0.2
			1,592	Others	0.1
Poland.................	1921	27,176,717	18,814,239	Poles	69.2
			3,898,431	Ukrainians	14.3
			2,110,448	Jews	7.8
			1,059,194	Germans	3.9
			1,060,237	White Russians	3.9
			68,667	Lithuanians	0.3
			56,239	Russians	0.2
			30,628	Czechs	0.1
			78,634	Others	0.3

[1] *Ibid.*

devised a new method of international regulation, involving the incorporation of protective guarantees in treaties between the new States and the Allied Powers, and the provision of international machinery through the League of Nations to insure the observance of these obligations.

The first of the minorities treaties was imposed upon Poland and signed June 28, 1919. Other treaties followed, with Czechoslovakia (September 10, 1919), Jugoslavia (September 10, 1919), Rumania

MINORITIES OF SOUTHEASTERN EUROPE[1]

State	Date	Total population	Minorities		Percentage of total
Hungary............	1920	7,980,143	7,147,053	Magyars	89.6
			551,211	Germans	6.9
			141,882	Slovaks	1.8
			23,760	Russians	0.3
			1,500	Ukrainians	
			36,858	Croats	0.5
			17,131	Serbs	0.2
			6,087	Slovenes	
			31,644	Others	0.4
Jugoslavia...........	1921	11,894,911	8,911,509	Serbs and Croats	74.3
			1,019,997	Slovenes	8.5
			176,479	Other Slavs	1.4
			467,658	Magyars	3.9
			505,790	Germans	4.2
			439,657	Albanians	3.6
			231,068	Russians	1.9
			12,553	Italians	0.1
			220,200	Others	1.8
Rumania............	1930	18,024,269	11,545,311	Rumanian	71.9
			1,464,573	Magyars	9.1
			778,094	Jews	4.9
			713,564	Germans	4.5
			500,484	Ukrainians	3.1
			351,328	Bulgarians	2.2
			222,375	Turks and Tartars	1.4
			174,293	Russians	1.1
			133,025	Gypsies	0.8
			52,570	Serbs	0.3
			35,033	Poles	0.2
			26,884	Slovaks	0.2
			5,000	Czechs	
			48,704	Others	0.3
Bulgaria............	1926	5,478,741	4,585,620	Bulgarian	83.7
			607,763	Turks	11.1
			41,563	Jews	0.8
			19,590	Russians	0.4
			12,782	Greeks	0.2
			211,423	Others	3.8

[1] *Ibid.*

(December 9, 1919), Greece (August 10, 1920). The Treaty of St. Germain with Austria, of September 10, 1919 (Articles 62 to 69), of Trianon with Hungary, of June 4, 1920 (Articles 54 to 60), of Neuilly with Bulgaria, of November 27, 1919 (Articles 49 to 57), and of Lausanne with Turkey of July 24, 1923 (Articles 37 to 45), likewise contained clauses for the protection of minorities, largely modeled upon the Polish treaty. The Baltic States and Albania were subsequently induced to accept the same obligations.[1] Fifteen States of central and southeastern Europe, including Finland, Danzig, and Greece, were thus obliged to renounce their efforts at forcible assimilation and to protect the rights of minorities living within their frontiers. In all of these arrangements, six general principles are set forth. (1) The States in question must protect the life and liberty of all inhabitants "without distinction of birth, nationality, language, race, or religion" (Polish Treaty, Article 2). (2) "All inhabitants . . . shall be entitled to the free exercise, whether public or private, of any creed, religion, or belief whose practices are not inconsistent with public order or public morals" (Polish Treaty, Article 3). (3) All persons born within the territory of these States are entitled to rights of citizenship. "All persons born in Polish territory who are not born nationals of another state shall *ipso facto* become Polish nationals" (Polish Treaty, Article 6). (4) "All . . . nationals shall be equal before the law and enjoy the same civil and political rights without distinction as to race, language, or religion. Differences of religion, creed, or confession shall not prejudice any national in matters relating to the enjoyment of civil or political rights, as for instance admission to public employments or the exercise of professions and industries" (Polish Treaty, Articles 7 to 9). (5) "No restrictions shall be imposed on the free use by any . . . national of any language in private intercourse, in commerce, in religion, in the press or in publications of any kind or at public meetings. Notwithstanding any establishment of an official language, adequate facilities shall be given for the use of their [the minorities'] language either orally or in writing before the courts" (Polish Treaty, Articles 3 and 4). (6) The States involved must grant educational facilities for instruction in their own language to minorities in districts where a considerable proportion of the population is of minority speech (Polish Treaty, Article 9). Among these items (1), (2), (3), and (5) are essentially guarantees of individual rights, while (4) and (6) protect the minorities as groups by giving them schools and a share of public funds where they constitute a "considerable proportion" (in practice usually one-fifth) of the population. Lines of race,

[1] A resolution of the First Assembly, December 15, 1920, declared "in the event of Albania, the Baltic and Caucasian States being admitted into the League, the Assembly requests that they should take the necessary measures to enforce the principles of the minorities treaties and that they should arrange with the Council the details required to carry this object into effect" (League of Nations *Records of Assembly*, 1920, I, pp. 568–569).

religion, and language do not of course always coincide and the ultimate test of whether a group is a minority is historical, social, and psychological.

Two means are provided for ensuring the observance of these obligations. In the first place, the guarantees are declared in the treaties to be part of the fundamental law of the States concerned, prevailing over any laws, regulations, or official acts contrary to them. This is a constitutional device for ensuring that the minorities will be protected by national courts. In the second place, and more significantly, the minorities are placed under the protection of the League of Nations.[1] The Council of the League, in a series of resolutions, has worked out a procedure for dealing with minority problems. Only States represented on the Council can bring such problems officially before the body. But States not on the Council and organizations of the minorities themselves may call attention to infractions of the treaties by sending petitions to the Secretariat. The Secretary-General passes upon the receivability of petitions on the basis of five criteria: the petitions must have in view the protection of minorities in accordance with the treaties; they must not be submitted in the form of a request for the severance of political relations between a minority and the State of which it is a part; they must not emanate from an anonymous or unauthenticated source; they must abstain from violent language; and they must contain information not recently the subject of a petition.[2] When a petition is found receivable, it is sent to the interested governments for observations, which are transmitted along with the petition to the Council. Under a Council resolution of October 25, 1920, such petitions, if acted upon by the Council, are submitted to a minorities committee of three members, consisting of the president and two other members of the Council, none of whom is to be a representative of the States concerned or of neighboring States. The committee, in cooperation with the minorities section of the Secretariat, procedes to investigate the complaint (resolution of June 10, 1925). Most petitions never get beyond the committee of three, for investigation, publicity, and suggestions usually suffice

[1] The clauses of the treaties "so far as they affect persons belonging to racial, religious, or linguistic minorities constitute obligations of international concern and shall be placed under the guarantee of the League of Nations. They shall not be modified without the assent of the majority of the Council of the League of Nations. . . . Any member of the Council of the League of Nations shall have the right to bring to the attention of the Council of the League of Nations any infraction or danger of infraction, of any of these obligations. The Council may thereupon take such action and give such direction as it may deem proper and effective in the circumstances. . . . Any difference of opinions as to questions of law or fact arising out of these articles between the government concerned and anyone of the principal Allied and Associated Powers or any other Power, a member of the Council of the League of Nations, shall be held to be a dispute of an international character under Article 14 of the Covenant of the League of Nations. . . . Any dispute shall, if the other party thereto demands, be referred to the Permanent Court of International Justice. The decision of the Permanent Court shall be final and shall have the same force and effect as an award under Article 13 of the Covenant." Polish Treaty, Article 12.

[2] Official Journal of the League of Nations, November, 1923, p. 1426.

to ameliorate the situation. When the case seems to warrant further action, however, the committee refers the question to the Council with recommendations. The Council may take no action if it feels that the petition is not based upon a genuine grievance, or it may call the attention of the offending government to its obligations and suggest remedies. Under the most recent rule, adopted in 1929, the president of the Council may invite four members to join him in the examination of the petitions, instead of the customary two. On September 21, 1922, the Assembly passed four resolutions in which it urged (1) friendly and informal communication as an alternative to direct recommendations by the Council; (2) resort to the Permanent Court for decisions on questions of law or fact; (3) the recognition by the minorities of their obligation to act as loyal citizens of their State;[1] and (4) adoption by States not bound by the minorities treaties of a standard of justice and toleration toward their minorities, at least as high as that expected by the Council from the signatory States.

It is difficult to measure in precise terms the efficacy of these arrangements. There is probably no question in the mind of any unbiased observer but that the minorities have fared better than would have been the case in the absence of such international protection. On the other hand, it cannot be said, nor could it be reasonably expected, that all discrimination and persecution have been eliminated. States not bound by the minorities treaties are free to treat their minorities as badly as they like. A Lithuanian proposal of 1925 to make these obligations universal was rejected. Thus, while Jugoslavia and Austria are bound to protect the rights of Italians, Italy is not at all bound to grant the same protection to its German and Jugoslav minorities. Even in treaty States, minorities in which no government on the Council is particularly interested have not received a full measure of protection. Such has been the situation at times of the Jews in Rumania and Hungary, the Hungarians in Rumania, and the Ukrainians in Poland. Prior to 1926, the Council took official cognizance of only three petitions. It never asked a State to withdraw objectionable measures, but merely expressed the hope that the State would observe its obligations. Since the admission of Germany to the League, the Council has acted on minority questions more frequently and with greater energy. The largest number of petitions has come from the German minority in Polish Upper Silesia, which is perhaps the best organized and most articulate of the minority groups. The petitions, most of which were considered by the Council in 1929, related primarily to minority schools, language

[1] "While the Assembly recognizes the primary right of the minorities to be protected by the League from oppression, it also emphasizes the duty incumbent upon persons belonging to racial, religious, or linguistic minorities to cooperate as loyal fellow citizens with the nation to which they now belong." *Records of Assembly*, 1922, I, p. 186, Resolution II.

instruction, and property rights. Some of these grievances have been remedied by Council action, but permanent harmony is unlikely. Between 1921 and 1925 the Council considered various petitions from Jewish organizations in Hungary, complaining of discrimination against them in the matter of admission to higher educational institutions. The results were somewhat inconclusive. All such disputes, the Council has insisted, are subjects of discussion between the Council and the State concerned, never between governments. But since the Council is a political body, it proceeds with great circumspection and is often tempted to side-step embarrassing issues[1] or to make innocuous or ineffective recommendations. Proposals have been made by Professor Gilbert Murray in 1920, and by the government of The Netherlands in 1928, to set up a permanent minorities commission analogous to the permanent mandates commission, but no action has been taken on this suggestion.

The existing system of international protection is partial, incomplete, and only moderately effective. Its fundamental principle has been assailed as strengthening irredentist aspirations on the part of minorities and encouraging the formation of States within States. Governments not bound by the treaties have shown no enthusiasm for accepting such obligations. Such a system of international protection can be little more than a makeshift in an imperfect world in which patriots insist upon linguistic and cultural homogeneity within their States and in which minority patriots continue to cherish aspirations of independence or of annexation to some neighboring State.

A more drastic solution of the problem has been adopted in the case of certain minorities in the Balkans and the Near East. In 1914 Greece and Turkey entered into an agreement for the voluntary exchange of minorities across the new frontiers resulting from the Balkan wars, but the outbreak of the Great War prevented the execution of this plan. In 1919 Greece and Bulgaria signed a treaty for the exchange of minorities under the supervision of a mixed commission of one Greek, one Bulgar, and two members appointed by the League Council. In January, 1923, at the suggestion of Dr. Nansen, refugee commissioner of the League of Nations, a Turco-Greek convention was signed, providing for the compulsory exchange of their respective minorities, also under the supervision of a mixed commission of four Turks, four Greeks, and three neutral nationals chosen by the League Council. The individuals thus exchanged were to receive property in their new State equivalent to that left behind in the old. This arrangement rooted up hundreds of thousands of people from their ancestral homes. It led to the ruthless expulsion of Greeks from

---

[1] On September 9, 1924, Count Apponyi of Hungary declared before the Council, "A man has obtained justice even though he loses his case; he does not obtain it if his case is ignored."

Turkey and of Turks from Greece. The Greek Government was obliged to care for almost a million refugees, and the entire proceeding was characterized by an enormous amount of hardship and disorder. The exchange of minorities is obviously a permanent solution of the problem only if the eternal permanence of existing frontiers is postulated—an assumption which is, to say the least, rash. The suffering and the social and economic disorganization to which it leads are out of all proportion to the benefit gained. The confused intermingling of linguistic groups in southeastern Europe, moreover, makes this method quite inapplicable as a general solution.

The United States exhibits on the largest scale the most successful application of still another method of dealing with minorities—one which may be termed "voluntary assimilation." The original American Indian population of the United States has been largely confined to reservations where it is cared for (or neglected) by the federal government. The population groups in the United States whose members are of European ancestry have never been regarded as "minorities" in the European sense. The United States has proverbially been the melting-pot of all nations, and millions of immigrants from overseas poured into its territories during the period of its greatest agricultural and industrial development. The peoples in question were not subjected to American governmental authority, American laws, American language and culture by virtue of transfers of territory and changes in boundaries which they had no hand in bringing about. They came voluntarily for their own economic advancement. Most of them did not contemplate returning to their home States, nor did they cherish hopes that the new lands which they occupied would eventually be annexed to their fatherlands. Neither did they cherish aspirations of national independence. No problem of irredentism or of self-determination arose under these circumstances. "Americanization" was rapid and amazingly successful because on the one hand it was not coercive in character, and on the other it did not encounter the resistance of national sentiment among those being Americanized. This process is now, of course, of only historical interest. The "quota law" of 1921 restricted the numbers of each foreign nationality which might enter the United States annually to 3 per cent of foreign-born persons of the same nationality residing in the United States in 1910. The 1924 act reduced the quotas to 2 per cent of those residing in the United States in 1890, in the interest of cutting down immigration still further and of admitting a larger proportion of northern and western Europeans and a smaller proportion of southern and eastern Europeans. The Rumanian and Italian Governments protested against this disguised discrimination, but without result. The "national origins" plan which went into effect in 1929 provides for the admission of some hundred and fifty thousand aliens annually on this quota basis. The new immigrants entering the United States are far too few in number to constitute a problem. Since the onset of the economic depression and the prevalence of widespread unemployment in the United States, American immigration has been reduced almost to the vanishing point by administrative action. The aliens already here are in process of speedy assimilation.

If aliens of European extraction in the United States have not constituted a minority problem, the same cannot be said of the Asiatics and Africans. The twelve million Negroes in the United States are descendants of the slaves of pre-Civil War days who were brought to the New World

UNITED STATES: RACE, NATIVITY, AND PARENTAGE
(United States Census data)

Population groups	1900	Per cent	1910	Per cent	1920	Per cent	1930	Per cent
Total.........	75,994,575	100.	91,972,266	100.	105,710,620	100.	122,775,046	100.
White........	66,809,196	87.9	81,731,957	88.9	94,820,915	89.7	108,864,207	88.7
Negro........	8,833,994	11.6	9,827,763	10.7	10,463,131	9.9	11,891,143	9.7
Mexican......	....	....	....	....	....	....	1,422,533	1.2
Indian........	237,196	0.3	265,683	0.3	244,437	0.2	332,397	0.3
Chinese......	89,863	0.1	71,531	0.1	61,639	0.1	74,954	0.1
Japanese.....	24,326	....	72,157	0.1	111,010	0.1	138,834	0.1
All others....	....	....	3,175	....	9,488	....	50,978	
Native born (all races)..	65,653,299	86.4	78,456,380	85.3	91,789,928	86.8		
Foreign born .	10,341,276	13.6	13,515,886	14.7	13,920,692	13.2		
Native white (total).....	56,595,397	74.5	68,386,412	74.4	81,108,161	76.7	95,497,800	77.8
Foreign born (white).....	10,213,817	13.4	13,345,545	14.5	13,712,754	13.10	13,366,407	10.9

against their will for purposes of economic exploitation. Their emancipation in 1863 and the granting to them of constitutional protection in the Thirteenth, Fourteenth, and Fifteenth Amendments of the federal Constitution have not been followed by their reception into American society on a basis of equality. In all of the Southern States they are denied the right to vote, and throughout the nation they are subjected to so many forms of discrimination and oppression, social and economic if not political and legal, that they continue to constitute a degraded and outcast pariah community. Here again there is no problem of irredentism or self-determination, and the serious problem of racial adjustment is in no sense an international one, for the Negro States of the world—Haiti, Liberia, and Abyssinia—are such feeble midgets compared to the United States that they are in no position to act in a protective capacity, even were they inclined to do so. The only treaties which the United States has ever entered into, regarding Negro rights, relate to the African slave trade. The colored population of the nation continues to be "kept in its place" by the white "Nordic" masters, and the poverty, indignity, and occasional violence and persecution to which it is subjected is a domestic question with which no outside State and no international organization (save the Communist International) concerns itself.

The situation with regard to Asiatics in the United States is somewhat different. Considerable numbers of Chinese were welcomed into the country in the mid-nineteenth century, when labor was scarce in the west. Many of the western railroads were built with the aid of Chinese coolie labor. Later Japanese came to the Pacific Coast as workers and farmers, along with a smaller number of Hindus. Race prejudice and friction developed as soon as changed economic conditions created competition for land and jobs between white and Asiatic workers. The latter were regarded as "unassimilable" because of their physical characteristics. They were prevented from becoming American citizens by the provisions of American naturalization laws, which open citizenship rights to white persons, Amerindians, and persons of African descent, but bar them to all the yellow and brown peoples of Asia. Following outbreaks of mob violence against Chinese in a number of western towns, Congress barred all Chinese immigration to the United States in a series of acts passed in 1882, 1888, and 1892. This legislation was in violation of American treaties with China of 1868 and 1880, but Chinese diplomatic protests were of no avail. Slightly over 70,000 Chinese now reside in the United States.

Diplomatic controversies between the United States and Japan later developed over California legislation barring Japanese children from public schools in San Francisco and forbidding Japanese to own land. In 1907, by the Gentlemen's Agreement concluded between President Roosevelt and the Japanese Government, the latter voluntarily agreed not to issue passports to laborers desiring to go to the United States.[1] This arrangement achieved its purpose without offending Japan. The Japanese

[1] The following extract from the *Annual Report of the Commissioner-general of Immigration for the Fiscal Year ended June 30*, 1908, p. 125, quotes briefly what is understood to be the purport of the Gentlemen's Agreement: " . . . an understanding was reached with Japan that the existing policy of discouraging emigration of its subjects of the laboring classes to continental United States should be continued, and should, by cooperation of the Governments, be made as effective as possible. This understanding contemplates that the Japanese Government shall issue passports to continental United States only to such of its subjects as are nonlaborers, or are laborers who, in coming to the continent, seek to resume a formerly acquired domicile, to join a parent, wife, or children residing there, or to assume active control of an already possessed interest in a farming enterprise in this country, so that the three classes of laborers entitled to receive passports have come to be designated 'former residents,' 'parents, wives, or children of residents,' and 'settled agriculturists.' With respect to Hawaii, the Japanese Government of its own volition stated that, experimentally at least, the issuance of passports to members of the laboring classes proceeding

population of the United States (111,000 in 1920) continued to increase through natural multiplication, but the increase by immigration was only about 500 a year. In 1924, however, Congress placed in the immigration act a provision declaring that "no alien ineligible to citizenship shall be admitted to the United States" (Act of May 26, 1924, §13, Part C). This was an obvious discrimination against Asiatics. It was a violation of the Gentlemen's Agreement, was opposed by the administration and the State Department, and was needlessly offensive to Japanese sensibilities. Had Japan been treated equally with other foreign States and placed on a quota basis, fewer than 200 Japanese could have entered the United States annually. But patriotic fervor and white supremacy dictated discriminatory exclusion despite its evil effects on Japanese-American relations.[1] American treatment of Asiatic minorities has thus created diplomatic friction, though here again there is no problem of self-determination, irredentism, or international protection.

Finally, brief notice may be taken of the solution of the Russian "nationalities problem" arrived at by the Communist Government of the Soviet Union. This solution was that of complete cultural autonomy within the political and economic framework of the proletarian State. All efforts at "Russification" have been abandoned, and each of the many nationalities of the U.S.S.R. is not only permitted, but is encouraged, to use its own language, develop its own culture, and pursue its own way of life. So long as the content of the national cultures and the political and economic institutions of the nationalities are "proletarian" in spirit and substance, the forms may be "national." The 1923 federal constitution of the Soviet Union incorporates this solution into

thence would be limited to 'former residents' and 'parents, wives, or children of residents.' The said Government has also been exercising a careful supervision over the subject of emigration of its laboring class to foreign contiguous territory."

[1] On May 31, 1924 Ambassador Hanihara presented to Secretary of State Hughes an official protest from the Japanese Government against this provision. This protest concluded: "unfortunately . . . the sweeping provisions of the new act, clearly indicative of discrimination against Japanese, have made it impossible for Japan to continue the undertakings assumed under the Gentlemen's Agreement. An understanding of friendly cooperation reached after long and comprehensive discussions between the Japanese and American Governments has thus been abruptly overthrown by legislative action on the part of the United States. The patient, loyal, and scrupulous observance by Japan for more than sixteen years of these self-denying regulations, in the interest of good relations between the two countries, now seems to have been wasted.

"It is not denied that, fundamentally speaking, it lies within the inherent sovereign power of each State to limit and control immigration to its own domains, but when, in the exercise of such right, an evident injustice is done to a foreign nation in disregard of its proper self-respect, of international understandings, or of ordinary rules of comity, the question necessarily assumes an aspect which justifies diplomatic discussion and adjustment.

"Accordingly, the Japanese Government consider it their duty to maintain and to place on record their solemn protest against the discriminatory clause in §13 (c) of the Immigration Act of 1924 and to request the American Government to take all possible and suitable measures for the removal of such discrimination."

the political structure of the State, which now consists of seven federated Soviet Republics (Russia, White Russia, Ukrainia, Trans-Caucasia, Uzbekistan, Turkmenistan, and Tadjikistan), each of which is politically independent and has a right of secession from the Union. The Russian and Trans-Caucasian Republics are themselves federations, composed of numerous autonomous areas and districts. The Central Executive Committee of the Union consists of two chambers, the Council of the Union and the Council of Nationalities. In the latter chamber each constituent republic has five members and each autonomous district, one member. Political unity and social cohesion are given to Soviet society by the All-Union Communist Party which, like the Soviet Government itself, rests upon complete equality for all nationalities and races. These arrangements have put an end to the minorities problem in Russia. In the absence of efforts at assimilation by the majority groups, there is no basis for irredentist or secessionist aspirations among the minorities. In the absence of political, economic, or social discrimination based on lines of race and language, there is no problem of interracial relations.

MINORITIES OF THE SOVIET UNION[1]

State	Date	Total population	Minorities		Percentage of total
U.S.S.R.	1930	161,000,000	81,466,000	Russians	50.6
			32,683,000	Ukrainians	20.3
			4,991,000	White Russians	3.1
			805,000	Poles	0.5
			1,288,000	Germans	0.8
			322,000	Moldavians	0.2
			1,932,000	Georgians	1.2
			1,610,000	Armenians	1.0
			3,059,000	Tartars	1.9
			483,000	Ostiaks	0.3
			644,000	Turcomens	0.4
			1,771,000	Turks	1.1
			966,000	Tadzhiks	0.6
			805,000	Kirghisians	0.5
			805,000	Bashkirs	0.5
			644,000	Kalmuks, Buriats and Yakuts	0.4
			4,025,000	Uzbeks	2.5
			322,000	Ossetins	0.2
			2,737,000	Jews	1.7
			1,449,000	Mordvens	0.9
			1,127,000	Chuvash	0.7
			483,000	Chechenets	0.3
			16,583,000	Others	10.3

[1] Percentages taken from *Soviet Union Yearbook*, 1930.

These various solutions of the problem of national minorities can be judged pragmatically by their results. Their application to other situations must be judged by local circumstances, attitudes, and social philosophies. The pre-war European policy of forcible assimilation was uniformly a failure and will doubtless lead, wherever it is applied in the future, to the same results of bitterness, resistance, and international friction. The post-war European policy of international protection offers hope of avoiding the worst of these evils. The American policy of voluntary assimilation, applied by the United States to European aliens, is applicable only in countries inviting immigration, and there are very few such States left in the world. American discrimination against the Negro and against Asiatics has had the undesirable results which have been noted. The Soviet solution of complete cultural autonomy solved the problem most adequately by removing its causes, but this solution, it should be observed, is based upon the extirpation of nationalism. It is a solution put into effect by Marxian internationalists, whose slogan is "Workers of the world, unite!" and whose fundamental tenet is that the class interests of the proletariat against those of the bourgeoisie transcend all State boundaries and all lines of language, race, or nationality. In the U.S.S.R. the values, attitudes, and ideologies of nationalism as a force of political and social cohesion have been replaced by the values, attitudes, and ideologies of international revolutionary Communism, whose devotees are sworn enemies of nationalism in all its manifestations. This solution, therefore, can have no application in the bourgeois nation-states without a social revolution comparable to that which destroyed the old Russia and created the Soviet Union.

4. PATRIOTISM AND WAR

But war's a game, which, were their subjects wise,
Kings would not play at.
— WILLIAM COWPER, *The Winter Morning Walk.*

We don't want to fight,
But by jingo if we do,
We've got the ships, we've got the men,
We've got the money too.
— English Music-hall Ballad, 1877.

That nationalism and international conflict are concomitant and seemingly inseparable features of international politics in the Western State System is in no need of demonstration to those familiar with the past. States waged war on one another before nationalism in its modern form had come into being. The wars between the dynastic States of western Europe between the fourteenth and eighteenth centuries contributed powerfully to the development of nationalism among their subjects. In a State System of nation-states, wars are inevitably fought between nationalities made aware of their identity through conflict, imbued with national consciousness in the heat of battle, and fused into solidarity by bellicose symbols, gestures, and acts. Common opposition to an alien group, common resistance to an invader, common participation in an attack upon the enemy, fuse national societies together much more effectively than any amount of undramatic collaboration in the tasks of peace. National patriotism, by virtue of its origins, its faith, its deeds, and its symbols, is essentially bellicose and bellivolent. It puts the power interests of each State into terms of nationalistic aspirations. Peace-loving patriots are highly exceptional. A pacific nationalism is almost a contradiction in terms. If all patriots are not warlike, at least all wars are patriotic and serve to raise the enthusiasms of patriotism to fever heat. The cult of the nation-state is a cult of Mars, god of battles—and even in a generation when all the world cries for peace, the various efforts to recondition patriots, to reeducate nationalists, to reform the whole nationalist ideology in the direction of international peace and cooperation have thus far given little promise of permanent success.

Any effort to classify the specific ways in which nationalism has constituted a cause for war is somewhat artificial, since the patriot's creed is so widespread in its ramifications and implications that it pervades the whole pattern of interstate relations. It may nevertheless be useful to refer to certain aspects of nationalism as it translates itself into political behavior and policies which have played a major rôle in setting State against State and creating the situations out of which wars arise. The demand for national self-determination has been a fruitful source of revolution, civil war, and international conflict since the close of the eighteenth century. The earlier wars of the Dutch and the Swiss against Spaniards, Austrians, and Germans were due to comparable ambitions which attained fulfillment in the achievement of national independence after bloody combat with the foreign oppressor. The war of the American Revolution (1775–1783), which involved Great Britain, France, Spain, The Netherlands, and the embattled trans-Atlantic infant, the United States, was clearly a war for national self-determination. The independence of the Balkan States was achieved through a whole series of wars between 1821 and 1913. The unification of Germany as a nation required three wars: with Denmark (1864), with Austria (1866), and with France (1870–1871). The unification of Italy likewise required three wars: with Russia (Piedmont in alliance with Great Britain and France) in 1854–1856; with Austria in 1859, and again with Austria in 1866. The American Civil War (1861–1865) was less a war over slavery than a war for national independence on the part of the Confederacy and for national unity on the part of the Union. Innumerable colonial rebellions and insurrections have been engineered by ardent native patriots striving to cast off the foreign yoke. Such wars, when successful, have multiplied the number of sovereign States, increased the points of international friction and conflict, and prepared the stage for still greater wars. The fever of nationalism has ever been a violently destructive and revolutionary malady within all States with discontented national minorities.

National irredentism has been an equally fertile source of international conflict. It is difficult to mention a single major combat between States in the past century in which irredentist ambitions have not played a significant rôle in the determination of State policy. The greatest and most destructive of all wars—that of 1914–1918—grew out of a welter of clashing national ambitions, largely of an irredentist character. The determination of Serbian patriots to wrest Bosnia and Herzegovina from Austria-Hungary lay behind the terroristic and revolutionary activities culminating in the assassination of the heir to the Hapsburg throne. The alarm of Austro-Hungarian patriots over the dissolution of the Dual Monarchy, threatened by this irredentist agitation, lay behind their decision to chastise Serbia. The attack of Tsarist Russia upon Austria-Hungary and her ally, Germany, was inspired by Pan-Slavic nationalism no less than by imperialistic aspirations. The French Government accepted war without hesitation in the hope of recovering the "lost provinces" of Alsace-Lorraine. Italy remained neutral because Austria-Hungary would not yield up Italia Irredenta and finally joined the Allies when they promised the fulfillment of this dream. Rumania entered the war on the Allied side in the hope of freeing the Rumanian-speaking peoples of Transylvania from Hungarian rule. Greece similarly hoped to wrest Thrace and parts of Asia Minor from Bulgaria and Turkey. The irredentas of post-war Europe are likewise sources of friction and resentment, and if general war ever again engulfs the Continent, most of the belligerents will similarly be striving to recover irredentas and to incorporate into their frontiers their fellow patriots across the border.

Nationalism, moreover, causes its converts to respond approvingly to State policies making for imperialism and for economic rivalries among nations. The patriot in every land rejoices to see large areas of the map painted red, green, or yellow, as the case may be, signifying that his State has carved out a colonial empire overseas. His enthusiasm is not due to economic benefits to himself derived from colonies (unless he happens to be a concessionaire, investor, or export trader), for the man-in-the-street or the ordinary taxpayer usually gains nothing from colonies and often loses heavily. His approval of imperialism is more subtle and less crassly materialistic. He identifies his own ego with his nation. His nation is symbolized by his government. When his government paints the map red, he feels his own personality inflated, his own private aspirations toward mastery and adventure vicariously fulfilled, his own sense of power, self-assurance, and security enhanced by the greater glory of the nation of which he is a part. These associations and reaction patterns render it easy to secure popular approval for policies of colonial expansion. They likewise mobilize public opinion behind policies of economic nationalism and of mercantile imperialism. Prohibitive protective tariffs, dumping, and cut-throat competition in foreign markets are all sponsored by nationalistic governments. Good patriots respond quite as enthusiastically to the slogans of "Buy British," "Made in Germany," or "keep out foreign goods" as they do to the passwords of "manifest destiny," the "Monroe Doctrine," or "a place in the sun." They are easily persuaded that their own economic well-being is furthered by the policies represented by these phrases. International tension is heightened and international conflict made more likely by the resulting imperialistic and economic rivalries between the nation-states. The "Buy American" movement so prevalent in the United States in 1932–1933 is an excellent example of the idiotic and destructive economic policies which profit seekers are able to foist upon patriots in the name of serving the national interest.

The somewhat mystical concept of "national honor," which is an integral part of nationalist ideology everywhere, likewise plays a significant rôle in contributing to war. The "honor" of nations, like the honor of individuals in the days of dueling, usually requires blood-letting for its redemption, once it has been jeopardized or impugned. Questions of national honor are traditionally exempt from arbitration treaties and other forms of pacific settlement, for honor is, by its nature, a value which cannot honorably be compromised or negotiated about, but must be fought over. "Insults" to the national honor must always be avenged by force. Such considerations impelled France to declare war on Prussia in 1870, Austria-Hungary to wage war on Serbia in 1914, the United States to bombard and occupy Vera Cruz in 1916, Italy to bombard and occupy Corfu in 1923, Japan to bombard and occupy Shanghai in 1932. "Honor" is the symbol of the prestige, the dignity, the power, and the self-respect of the nation-state and of all its patriots. It demands vengeance and violence whenever the State is slighted by its neighbors or finds its will thwarted or its pronunciamentos defied. War in defense of national honor always appears to patriots to be preferable to peace with dishonor, even though the actual business of slaughter and destruction may seem to participants and observers alike to be quite without honor when it is viewed calmly in retrospect after passions have cooled.

The values, attitudes, and reaction patterns of national patriotism are in fact inseparably associated with military force, and patriots consequently tend to view with approval resorts to force in the pursuit of national purposes—whether for the protection of citizens abroad, the collection of defaulted loans, the enforcement of treaties, the vindication of national honor, the acquisition of territory or markets, or the settlement of other disputes. The patriot identifies himself with the national community and integrates and develops his own personality by merging it with that of the nation-state. This process flows from a deep human yearning for self-respect, for security, for recognition, for a solid foundation in the common ideals and values of the social group. These values—or the appearance thereof—are easily attained by self-assertiveness, braggadocio, egotism, quarrelsomeness, *i.e.*, by common attitudes of hostility toward the out-group and by common participation in combat against a real or imaginary enemy. Conflict, force, and violence serve to unify and integrate the national group, and the symbols of its unity and group consciousness are in large part the symbols of war. No stimulus is more effective in evoking patriotic sentiment and emotion than an army with banners marching forth to battle. Martial anthems, military heroes, warlike exploits, traditions of strife and sacrifice and glory—these are the stock in trade of patriots everywhere. The power interests of the State are sentimentalized in terms of these symbolic figures and memories. The patriot consequently demands armaments in the name of "preparedness" and "security." In most of the nation-states the ultra-patriots are the most enthusiastic advocates of heavier guns, larger battalions, and more numerous warships and airplanes, and the most vigorous opponents of all proposals for limitation or reduction of armaments. In this atmosphere, pacifists become unpatriotic traitors to the fatherland and competitive armament-building meets with the approbation of all good citizens.

Whether a pacific patriotism is possible may well be doubted, in view of the long past of belligerent exaltation of the nation-state and in view of the current symbols, formulas, and attitudes which the cult of the nation-state has evolved. And it may likewise be doubted whether western civilization, on its present level, can survive the continuation of international strife which belligerent patriotism breeds. The reconditioning of patriots, the reeducation of intransigeant nationalists is perhaps the most critical problem of the twentieth century. Human nature is very flexible and adaptable, and it is quite conceivable that under appropriate conditions the attitudes and values of traditional patriotism may be modified in the direction of international and world interests, making for harmony between States. To substitute for nationalism a new set of emotional responses, associated with a new basis of social integration and affording equally adequate psychic satisfactions, is not, in the abstract, a task which is beyond all imagination and incapable of achievement. But little measurable progress toward its achievement has taken place thus far. On the contrary, the post-war period has witnessed the intensification of belligerent patriotism throughout the western world and its extension to the peoples of Africa and Asia. The rising tide of Fascist nationalism bodes no good for peace and international cooperation—for if patriots continue to sow the dragon's teeth, they will continue to reap the usual harvest of armaments, conflicts, and war.

SUGGESTED READINGS

Burr, C. S.: *America's Race Heritage*, New York, Natural History Society, 1922.

Buxton, N. E., and T. P. Conwil-Evans: *Oppressed Peoples and the League of Nations*, London, J. M. Dent & Sons, Ltd., 1922.

Deniker, J.: *The Races of Man*, New York, Charles Scribner's Sons, 1900.

East, E. M.: *Mankind at the Crossroads*, New York, Charles Scribner's Sons, 1924.

Fawcett, C. B.: *Frontiers, A Study in Political Geography*, New York, Oxford University Press, 1918.

Guerard, A. L.: *Short History of the International Language Movement*, New York, Boni & Liveright, 1922.

Jaszi, O.: *The Dissolution of the Hapsburg Monarchy*, Chicago, University of Chicago Press, 1929.

Josey, C. C.: *Races and National Solidarity*, New York, Charles Scribner's Sons, 1923.

Junghann, O.: *National Minorities in Europe*, New York, Covici-Friede, Inc., 1932.

Ladas, S.: *The Exchange of Minorities: Bulgaria, Greece, and Turkey*, New York, The Macmillan Company, 1932.

Mair, L. P.: *The Protection of Minorities*, London, Christophers, 1928.

Marvin, F. S.: *Western Races of the World*, New York, Oxford University Press, 1922.

Mattern, J.: *The Employment of the Plebiscite in the Determination of Sovereignty*, Baltimore, Johns Hopkins Press, 1920.

Oakesmith, J.: *Race and Nationality*, New York, Frederick A. Stokes Company, 1919.

Perla, L.: *What is "National Honor"?*, New York, The Macmillan Company, 1918.

Rose, J. H.: *Nationality in Modern History*, New York, The Macmillan Company, 1916.

Stocks, J. L.: *Patriotism and the Super-State*, New York, Harcourt, Brace & Company, 1920.

Toynbee, A.: *Nationality and the War*, New York, E. P. Dutton & Co., Inc., 1915.

Wittmann, E.: *Past and Future of the Right of National Self-Determination*, Amsterdam, Van Holkema & Warendorf, 1919.

Young, D.: *American Minority Peoples*, Harper & Brothers, 1932.

CHAPTER X

PATRIOTISM AND PROFITS

1. ECONOMIC NATIONALISM

I understand by economic nationalism the point of view that it ought to be the object of statesmanship in economic matters to increase the power rather than the economic well-being of a given society.—T. E. GREGORY.

THE economic consequences of national patriotism are no less significant for international politics than its "political" manifestations. The traditional division of human motives and activities into "economic" and "political" is at best somewhat artificial and misleading. The "political animal" of Aristotle is no less an imaginary creature than the "economic man" of the classical economists. Men and women in their private capacities have, from time immemorial, striven to gain for themselves the necessities of life, to create wealth, and to increase their material well-being. They have likewise striven to exercise power over one another and to set up common procedures and institutions for the exercise of power, through which their "public" affairs could be regulated and administered. But the line between "private" and "public" affairs is purely arbitrary and relative. The distinction between economics and politics, business and government, profit motives and power motives is useful only for purposes of academic division of labor and not for purposes of analyzing realistically the whole complex of human interrelationships and social behavior. In contemporary western civilization there is no form of economic activity which is not affected by governmental action, and there is no type of political or governmental activity which is not intimately connected with the production and distribution of wealth.

People often "go into" politics, individually or collectively, for private pecuniary gain. And governments often legislate and administer in response to the pressures of economic-interest groups, and for the purpose of affecting the relationships of power between factions, parties, classes, or sections within a State, or between the nation-states themselves, by dealing with the economic foundations of political power. Those with wealth, property, and economic power exercise political power in order to protect or increase their wealth by political action, and those without property frequently organize themselves for political action for the purpose of modifying the existing distribution of wealth and economic

[331]

power. The State mediates between conflicting economic interests, in accordance with the relative political power and influence which the various interests can bring to bear upon its acts.[1] Control of the machinery of the State is usually the decisive element in the relations between economic groups and classes, even in the period of laissez-faire individualism, when those with economic power strove to reduce governmental functions to a minimum. In modern industrial society it is more true than ever that politics and economics are inextricably intertwined.

The complex of sentiments, traditions, symbols, slogans, and policies termed "nationalism" therefore constitutes a force which affects those interests and activities called economic quite as much as those called political. It has quite as much bearing upon the production and distribution of wealth and the relations of economic interest groups throughout the world as it does upon relationships of power and upon political ideas, activities, and institutions within States and between States. From the point of view of a broad historical perspective, the epoch of nationalism is the epoch of the political ascendancy of the bourgeoisie in the western nations. Those who engage in commerce and industry, who become the entrepreneurs of capitalistic industrialism, who acquire vast wealth and economic power enabling them to secure control of governments and bend them to their desires, have ever been the most ardent devotees of the cult of the nation-state. That cult became universal and won over to itself other social classes—nobles, peasants, and workers—only when the bourgeoisie became the dominant group in western society, both economically and politically. Nationalism is the political philosophy of the bourgeois nation-states. While it has permeated other types of States and spread from the western world to other cultures and civilizations, its historical development is intelligible only in terms of the rise of the bourgeoisie to political power. This is not to say that all members of the bourgeois class are patriots, or that all patriots are bourgeois. But it is to say that this class has constituted the matrix of modern nationalism, which is the dominating political philosophy and the most significant pattern of social integration in the era of machine industry, the factory system, and capitalistic economy.

---

[1] The words of the "Father of the American Constitution," James Madison, may be recalled in this connection. He found the source of political parties in the fact of "the various and unequal distribution of property. Those who hold and those who are without property have ever formed distinct interests in society. Those who are creditors and those who are debtors fall under a like distinction. A landed interest, a manufacturing interest, a mercantile interest, with many lesser interests, grow up of necessity in civilized nations and divide them into different classes actuated by different sentiments and views. The regulation of these various and interfering interests forms the principal task of modern legislation and involves the spirit of party and faction in the necessary and ordinary operations of government." *The Federalist*, No. 10, 1788.

The national patriot necessarily thinks of international economic relations, as he thinks of international political relations, in terms of "national interests." He inevitably regards the independent and sovereign nation-state, not merely as the normal basis of human political organization, but likewise as the basis of economic organization and activity. The fatherland to which he grants supreme loyalty is the land which produces his meat and drink, his corn and cabbage, his potatoes and peas. Its fields and farms and vineyards give employment to him or to many of his fellow citizens. Its factories, mills, and mines, its shops and stores and business offices, its ships and railways and airlines are the bases of national prosperity. The maintenance and promotion of this prosperity are the primary concern of government, for the nation which is prosperous presumably becomes wealthy and strong and politically influential in world affairs. The government is accordingly called upon to enact such legislation within the national frontiers as will contribute to prosperity and economic power. It is expected to administer its relations with foreign governments in such fashion as will be most advantageous to the national economy. These assumptions and ideas, and the governmental policies which flow therefrom, can conveniently be described by the phrase "economic nationalism."

It cannot be too strongly emphasized at the outset of any discussion of this aspect of the cult of the nation-state that the economic nationalist is concerned more with the adequacy of the national economy as the basis of the political power of the State than he is with the individual prosperity and well-being of its citizens. Under some circumstances, these two objectives are one and the same, for whatever serves the national economy, whatever promotes the prosperity of the whole nation-state may also be assumed to contribute toward the economic well-being of its citizens. Under other circumstances, the objectives are quite distinct. The economic nationalist would have his government regulate economic activities to achieve purposes couched in terms of the interests and economic power of the whole entity of the nation-state in its relations with other States. These purposes are not concerned with the economic well-being of the mass of the citizenry, except in so far as this is related to national economic power and security. If a proposed measure (say, restriction of immigration when there is no longer a scarcity of labor within the State) both enhances the power of the State (by barring out unassimilable aliens, by excluding foreign radicals, by promoting national unity, etc.) and also contributes to the economic well-being of the citizens (by maintaining high wage levels and high standards of living), no problem arises. The economic nationalist approves the measure. If a proposed measure (say, a prohibitive tariff) enhances the power of the State (by promoting home industries and economic self-sufficiency) at the expense of the economic well-being of the citizenry (by raising prices and making the prohibited goods more expensive in the domestic market), the economic nationalist still approves, because he is more directly concerned with power than with welfare. If a proposed measure (say, the legalization of birth control) promises to promote economic well-being (by limiting the growth of population and raising living standards through reducing the pressure of numbers on resources) at the expense of the power of the State (by cutting down its available military man power), the economic nationalist is against it. Power rather than well-being is the criterion applied to all governmental regulation of economic activity.

Now, this fact calls for explanation. In a sane, rational world, governmental regulation of economic activity would be directed toward welfare rather than power. In the world of the western nation-states, the reverse is the case. Among the numerous explanations of this anomaly which can be suggested, three are particularly worthy of attention. The first has to do with the assumptions of nationalism. National patriotism glorifies and exalts the nation-state and strives to enhance its power and prestige in every way possible. If in a given situation the power of the State and the economic welfare of its inhabitants do not coincide, the patriot must insist that the power and security of the State are paramount and that economic sacrifices are necessary on the altar of the fatherland. The second explanation has to do with war. The patriot regards the interest of his State as being, in many respects, opposed to those of other States. In the competitive struggle for power the decisive elements are population, resources, industries, trade, and investments, and each State must formulate its economic policies accordingly. Wars occur from time to time as a result of clashing national interests which will not be reconciled. The patriot does not shrink from war, even though it involves enormous economic losses, for the power interests and the prestige of his nation are at stake. War is a means of weakening or disrupting the economy of the enemy State and thus of tipping the scales of the balance of power in favor of one's own country. But the incidents of war must be anticipated and the fatherland must be prepared for all emergencies. It must not run the risk of being cut off from essential sources of raw materials or manufactured goods in war time. It must not run the risk of defeat through lack of cannon fodder. It must not permit investments to be made where they will be jeopardized by war, with a resulting diminution of national power and prestige. In anticipation of war the State must maintain its own military industries and have its own sources of supply. It must strive to attain economic self-sufficiency, to make itself as far as possible a strong and self-contained economic system. This may involve a heavy cost, but the exigencies of war require that welfare be sacrificed to power.

The third explanation, which is perhaps most significant from the point of view of the political process by which economic policies are formulated within States, has to do with the relative political power and influence of producers and consumers. Generally speaking, all producers are also consumers and *vice versa*, and in an ideal world there would be no clash of economic interests between them. But in the salesman's and advertiser's world of capitalistic industry, with its great inequalities in the distribution of wealth and economic power, production is organized and managed by a relatively small number of persons whose control over the productive process is out of all proportion to their consuming capacity. The great mass of consumers are employees who work for wages or salaries and who have no control over production. They have an interest in low prices, cheap goods, reduced living costs, more abundant goods and services of all kinds from whatever source, domestic or foreign. But they are inarticulate, unorganized, unaware often of the effect upon them of governmental policies and economic measures. They have no political power or influence over domestic legislation proportionate to their numbers.[1] Those who control production, on the other hand, are the great entrepreneurs, the captains of industry, the business leaders, the owners of the means of production, the bankers, capitalists, and employers of labor. These persons organize production and produce goods and services for profit. Profits are dependent upon prices, and prices are dependent upon the well-known "law of supply and demand." If foreign goods can be shut out or heavily taxed, if domestic industries can be "protected" and subsidized, the domestic producers can monopolize the domestic market and raise prices to enhance profits. Protective tariffs, bounties, and indirect governmental assistance of various kinds are instrumental in bringing about this result. The producers, moreover, are few, highly organized, well aware of their interests, and politically influential in proportion to their economic power. They can usually bring effective pres-

[1] "Power depends for its habits upon a consciousness of possession, a habit of organization, an ability to produce an immediate effect. In a democratic state, where there are great inequalities of economic power, the main characteristics of the poor are exactly the want of these. They do not know the power that they possess. They hardly realize what can be effected by organizing their interests. They lack direct access to those who govern them. Any action by the working classes, even in a democratic state, involves risk to their economic security out of all proportion to the certainty of gain. They have rarely in their hands the instruments necessary to secure their desires. They have seldom even learned how these may best be formulated and defended. They labor under the sense of inferiority which comes from perpetual obedience to orders without any full experience of the confidence which comes from the habit of command. They tend to confound the institutions they have inherited with the inescapable foundations of society. There is, in fact, every reason to expect that a state built upon universal suffrage will be responsible for wider concessions to the multitude than will be granted under any alternative form; but there is no historic reason to suppose that such a state will be able of itself directly to alter at the root the social results of an economically unequal society." Harold J. Laski, *Politics*, 1931, pp. 26–27.

sure to bear to secure governmental aid. In the name of patriotism, national self-sufficiency, and the "full dinner pail" for the working man, they can determine public policies in their own interests and persuade the consumers to acquiesce or even to imagine themselves to be benefited by the process. The patriot and the profiteer work hand in hand. Nationalism, which is a creation of the ideology and the class interests of the bourgeoisie, *i.e.*, the owners and managers of production, continues to serve its creators.

In summary, economic nationalism has become the universal policy of the nation-states, because those who profit by it are politically influential and able to control governmental policy and because all good patriots place national power above economic welfare for reasons of high politics and war. This policy promotes national self-sufficiency, national political power, and producers' profits rather than economic specialization and consumers' welfare through a world-wide exchange of goods and services. It tends increasingly to divide up the world into small, self-contained economic units coinciding in area and population with the political frontiers of the nation-states. Each unit strives desperately to free itself from economic dependence upon the others and each suffocates behind its tariff walls to the common economic detriment of all. The dilemma resulting from this situation will be examined below.[1] Here it will be sufficient to examine the results of economic nationalism as it has influenced governmental policies toward population, raw materials, commodity markets, and capital markets. People, resources, trade, and investments are the decisive factors behind national armaments and national power and all governments have attempted to enhance national power by dealing with these things in such a way as to strengthen the economic (and therefore the political) position of the nation-state.

2. POPULATION POLICIES

Come, Malthus, and in Ciceronian prose
Show how a rutting population grows,
Till all the produce of the soil is spent
And brats expire for lack of aliment.
—Popular English version of the Malthusian thesis.

While population and man power have always been an extremely important element in the fighting strength and the political influence of nations, they have usually not been susceptible of any very effective control through governmental action. The size of a State's population is determined by birth rates, death rates, immigration, and emigration, and these things in turn depend upon resources, economic opportunities, fecundity, and a variety of other uncontrollable factors. The composition

[1] See pp. 544f. below.

of a State's population is similarly dependent upon relative birth and death rates among the various groups which compose it. These things are little affected by legislation and administration—so little, in fact, that it may be doubted whether there has ever been a single clear instance of a nation's population being radically changed, either as to size or composition, through deliberate governmental policies. Governments have nevertheless attempted from time to time to regulate population growth for economic and political reasons. They have sought to subject to organized social intelligence the ebb and flow of peoples, the size and movements of families, the number of births and deaths—not through the impossible method of intervening in the private affairs of each of the millions of homes comprising a nation's population, but through various legislative and administrative devices intended to influence the underlying causal factors determining population growth. These measures are part of the policies of economic nationalism, since they have to a large degree been motivated, not by any rationally devised program of social and economic amelioration, but by power considerations and by various prejudices, superstitions, inhibitions, and stupidities which have furthered the purposes of patriots.

Prior to the nineteenth century, very little attention was paid to population problems, either by patriots, professors, or politicians. In the late Roman Empire, to be sure, various ineffective fiscal and agrarian measures were enacted to check the decline of population, but throughout the whole medieval and early modern period people were born, married, and buried without help or hindrance from the State. The Church officiated on all of these occasions but it had no "population policy" except the Scriptural injunction to multiply and replenish the earth. The growth and decline of populations were in the hands of Providence—which is to say that as many people were born as the endurance of mothers permitted and as many died as famine, pestilence, war, and senescence swept away. These things were regarded as being beyond social or political control. When the Black Death carried off a quarter of the population of western Europe in the fourteenth century, the disaster was attributed to the wrath of God against sinners. When economic prosperity made possible an expansion of population, this was likewise attributed to the beneficence of heaven. Only when the Industrial Revolution enormously increased man's capacity for exploiting the resources of nature and made possible the doubling of the world's population in a single century was serious attention directed toward population problems.

This is not the place to review the economics and the sociology of population, but some general statement of the more important conclusions of specialists is essential to an evaluation of the population policies of economic nationalism. Early in the nineteenth century the English economist Malthus promulgated the discouraging hypothesis (which helped to earn for economics the name of the "dismal science") that there is everywhere a constant pressure of population on resources which tends to keep the living standards of the masses down to a bare subsistence level. According to Malthus, population increases in geometric ratio (1, 2, 4, 8, 16, 32, etc.), while the means of subsistence increase in arithmetic ratio (1, 2, 3, 4, etc.). He could perceive, therefore, nothing but prospects of increasing misery in the rapid growth of population which he saw taking place around him. The Malthusian formulation was in error in that it assumed a constant rate of reproduction and overlooked the effects of technological improvements and industrialization in providing better means of subsistence for vastly greater populations than any ever seen before the age of the machine. It is quite true that the reproductive capacity of the human species is enormously greater than its capacity to provide the means of livelihood for its swarming broods. Given favorable economic conditions, any human population group can double its numbers every twenty-five years. It has been calculated that if a single pair of human beings, at the time of Christ, began reproducing at this rate, and if all their descendants had reproduced at the same rate, the entire land surface of the globe would furnish standing room only for one-eleventh of the living progeny. If the population of the earth had doubled only every fifty years for the past twenty centuries, the descendants would now number one thousand times the world's present population.[1] But the ultimate possibilities of human fecundity are never attained. Positive checks on population growth always operate through famine, disease, and war. Preventive checks likewise operate through birth control and perhaps through a decline in fecundity with higher standards of living and urban life. The population which a given area can sustain does not depend so much on the resources of the area as on the technological devices employed for utilizing those resources. Population growth is thus determined, not by any simple relationship between reproduction and resources, but by (1) the birth rate, which is affected by the number and the fecundity of childbearing mothers, by birth control, and by social habits and customs; (2) the death rate, which is affected by longevity, war, and the control of disease; (3) the natural resources at the command of a given population, which influence both the birth rate and the death rate; and (4) the level of technology, which has a bearing upon all of the three other factors.

Such phrases as "overpopulation," "underpopulation," or "surplus population," glibly bandied about by nationalists and imperialists, have no meaning except as they are related to these factors. Overpopulation in a given area has nothing to do with the size, density, or resources of the population, but can only refer to a situation in which there is sufficient

[1] See E. B. Reuter, *Population Problems*, 1923.

pressure of population on resources to cause a reduction of living standards or to retard their improvement. Underpopulation can only mean a situation in which the number of people available to exploit natural resources is too few for the most profitable exploitation possible. Overpopulation—or underconsumption, or underdeveloped technology (these are all the same thing)—has long existed in large parts of Asia, where the level of technology has been constant for centuries, where contraception has never been generally practiced, and where living standards have been kept down to a bare subsistence level. Famines, pestilences, unemployment, and extensive emigration are typical symptoms of overpopulation of this kind. But an improvement in technology may make it possible for a given area to sustain an enormously greater population on a higher standard of living than was possible on a lower technological level. The present territory of the United States sustained only a million or so Indians in pre-Columbian days, because hunting and fishing and very primitive agriculture were the only means of livelihood. It now sustains 126,000,000 people through intensive agriculture, industry, and commerce. Germany, with 30,000,000 in the mid-nineteenth century was overpopulated, as shown by low living standards and wholesale emigration. Germany, with 60,000,000 people in the early twentieth century, was no longer overpopulated, for the industrialization of the country had intervened. It has long been alleged that Japan and Italy are overpopulated, but no deterioration of living standards had taken place in either country prior to the Great Depression. Density of population per square mile is also no index to overpopulation. The Netherlands has 517 people to the square mile, Belgium 666, England 701, Germany 332, Italy 332, and Japan 383. On the other hand, the United States has 30 people to the square mile, the Soviet Union 21, Argentina 7, Brazil 9, Canada 2, and Australia less than 2. These figures by themselves do not in the least prove that the first group of States is overpopulated, or that the second group is underpopulated, if one measures these conditions by living standards. One can properly speak of overpopulation only in relation to numbers, resources, technology, and standards of living. This phrase is more frequently a rationalization of expansionist ambitions than a statement of economic and social facts.

A rational and scientific population policy, it may be agreed, would be one aimed at securing an economic optimum population, *i.e.*, a population of such size in relation to resources and technology that all of its members could enjoy the highest possible standard of living. Such a policy might call for a larger population in such States as Russia, Australia, and Argentina, in order that existing resources might be more adequately utilized. It would call for a smaller population in highly developed industrial States, where resources have already been fully exploited and where further technological improvements have reached the point of diminishing returns, as measured by unemployment. While expert opinion is not unanimous on this point, it is probable that if economic well-being were the sole test of wisdom in such matters, it would follow that a substantial reduction of population in most of the great States of the world would be advantageous to succeeding generations. Such a reduction is, in fact, impending in northwestern Europe and in North America, but it is viewed with alarm by governments and has taken place in spite of governmental efforts to check it. It is apparently due to a decline of birth rates more rapid than the decline in death rates. The higher the standard of living of a population, the more nearly stationary it becomes. This circumstance, which is sometimes mysteriously attributed to a decline in fecundity, is more probably due, in the western world at least, to the increasingly prevalent practice of contraception on the part of parents for the purpose of limiting voluntarily the size of families. From the point of view of economic welfare, the weight of evidence would seem to indicate the desirability of a general extension of the practice of birth control as a means of making possible the voluntary restriction of population growth.

It is scarcely necessary to point out that the population policies of national governments are not based on such considerations. Military and political power, rather than social and economic well-being, is the immediate objective of the economic nationalists who so largely dictate governmental policies. The patriot tends to regard the size of his country's population as the measure of its power and prestige. He favors all governmental measures that seem likely to increase the rate of population growth. He condemns all that threaten to limit the unchecked growth of population. He is joined in condemnation by many churchmen, who are opposed to birth control for theological reasons. He is also joined by moralists and reformers, to whom liberty means license and to whom compulsions, inhibitions, and prohibitions are preferable to organized intelligence and freedom of choice as roads to the good life. He is joined by many others: the employer of labor, who wants labor to be cheap and who knows that it can be cheap only when it is abundant; the military expert, who feels that men rather than machines win wars; the physician, who would keep the laity in ignorance and profit from the esoteric mysteries of his trade; the time-serving politician, who shouts with the crowd and who would sell his soul to the devil before he would offend the religious and moral sensibilities of his constituents; and by a few sincere sociologists and economists, who view an impending decline of population with apprehension for reasons not directly connected with the economic welfare of the next generation. This combination is overwhelming and decisive, and the voices of the more farsighted physicians, politicians,

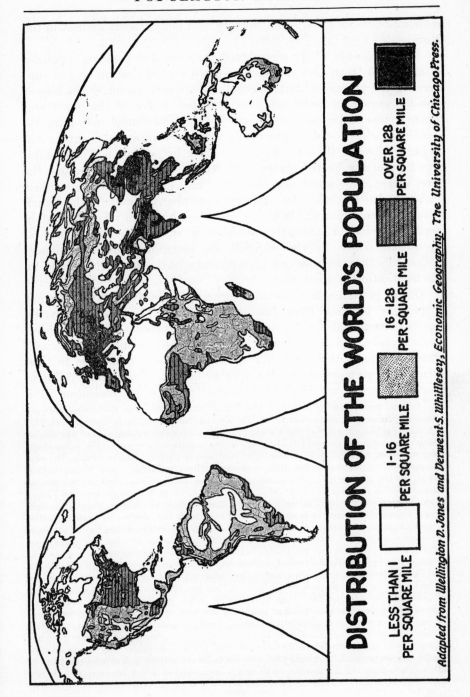

DISTRIBUTION OF THE WORLD'S POPULATION

LESS THAN I PER SQUARE MILE

1-16 PER SQUARE MILE

16-128 PER SQUARE MILE

OVER 128 PER SQUARE MILE

Adapted from Wellington D. Jones and Derwent S. Whittlesey, Economic Geography. The University of Chicago Press.

economists, sociologists, social workers, and labor leaders are lost in the storm.

In consequence of these combined pressures, the population policies of almost all the nation-states are directed toward discouraging or suppressing the practice of birth control and toward promoting the largest possible growth of population. Great Britain is one of the few States where contraceptive information may be freely distributed and contraceptive devices freely sold. In practically all of the continental countries and in Latin America, these things are forbidden by legislation. The prohibitive laws of the United States, both federal and State, are among the most severe in the world, imposing heavy fines and jail sentences for their violation, but like other American laws are observed more in the breach than in the enforcement.[1] In the Orient, where birth control is desperately needed, it is just beginning to make headway in the face of governmental opposition. Only in the U.S.S.R. is parenthood made genuinely optional by the maintenance of governmental birth-control clinics and by the legalization of abortion.

On the positive side, national government has striven with indifferent success to promote large families. President Theodore Roosevelt's vigorous denunciation of "race suicide" finds responsive echoes elsewhere. French political and military leaders have been bemoaning France's stationary population for half a century and have from time to time offered tax exemptions and bounties to fathers of numerous children. German patriots are similarly concerned over every indication of a

[1] Federal and State legislation in the United States makes no distinction between immorality, obscenity, and birth control. The United States Penal Code (Sections 211, 245, 311, 312) prohibits the use of the United States mails for the transmission of any advice concerning contraception and forbids, under heavy penalties, the importation, publication, transportation, sale, gift, or exhibition of all contraceptive information or devices. To send an applicant for information the address of any birth-control clinic is also illegal. Section 245 of the act of March 9, 1909, as amended by the act of June 5, 1920 (41 Statutes at Large, 1060) is as follows: "Whoever shall bring or cause to be brought into the United States, or any place subject to the jurisdiction thereof, from any foreign country, or shall herein knowingly deposit or cause to be deposited with any express company or other common carrier, for carriage from one State, territory, or district of the United States or place noncontiguous to but subject to the jurisdiction thereof, or from any place in or subject to the jurisdiction of the United States through a foreign country, to any place in or subject to the jurisdiction thereof, or from any place in or subject to the jurisdiction of the United States, to a foreign country, any obscene, lewd, or lascivious print or any filthy book, pamphlet, picture, motion-picture film, paper, letter, writing, or other matter of indecent character, or any drug, medicine, or article or thing designed, adapted, or intended for preventing conception or producing abortion or any indecent or immoral use; or any written or printed card, letter, circular, book, pamphlet, advertisement, or notice of any kind, giving information directly or indirectly, where, how, or of whom or by what means any of the herein beforementioned articles, matters, or things may be obtained or made; or whoever shall knowingly take or cause to be taken from such express company or other common carrier any matter or thing the depositing of which for carriage is herein made unlawful, shall be fined not more than $5,000 or imprisoned not more than 5 years or both."

decline in the German birth rate. In Fascist Italy, with its combination of extreme nationalism and Catholicism, the government has made the most determined effort to raise the birth rate. The birth-control movement is rigidly suppressed. Bachelors are penalized by heavy taxes. Heads of large families are rewarded for their labor. Reduced rates on railroads are granted to honeymooners, to encourage matrimony. The Fascist reasoning is perhaps the most complete *reductio ad absurdum* of economic nationalism as applied to population problems. It holds, in effect, that Italy is overpopulated, that it must have more land and colonies for its surplus population, that these can be gained only by war, that success in war requires a large army, and that a large army requires a still larger population! This logic is not different in kind from that of economic nationalists elsewhere.

That these legislative and administrative devices have had any appreciable influence in promoting population expansion may be doubted. The factors entering into population growth are too complex and too ill understood to be much affected by such measures. But it is possible that legal restrictions on birth control have had some influence on the rate of reproduction of different classes of the population in certain countries and have contributed to what is sometimes described as a progressive deterioration of population. When the acquisition of birth-control information is made difficult and when the sale of contraceptive devices is made unlawful, those who are ignorant and poverty-stricken are deprived of the means of limiting their families, while those who are wealthy or clever can easily evade the law. In all the western States, ditch diggers and coal heavers have three or four times as many children as college graduates. To attribute this situation entirely to legislation would be to overlook other factors, but the legislation has not been without influence. It is significant that in Italy, which has a birth rate of 26 per 1,000, the greatest increase of population takes place in the most backward, impoverished, and illiterate areas such as Calabria, Basilicata, and Apulia, while progressive and industrialized Piedmont has a birth rate of only 16 per 1,000. In most countries those sections of the population which from a eugenic point of view ought to contribute the largest contingent to each new generation contribute the smallest, while a less desirable stock breeds without restraint. General dissemination of birth-control information would do much to change this situation. But States and churches alike remain obdurate and continue to cooperate, the one in the name of national power, the other in the name of conventional morality, to make population restrictions as difficult as possible even in a period of world-wide poverty and unemployment.

A final word may be in point by way of showing the failure of such policies in the western nations and by way of suggesting future trends of population growth. The present total population of the world is usually estimated at about 1,800,000,000, of which, in round numbers, perhaps 800,000,000 are white, 500,000,000 yellow, 400,000,000 brown or red, and 100,000,000 black. The white race has in the past century multiplied more rapidly than any of the others and is apparently still in the lead. Authorities are agreed, however, that the unprecedented population growth of the nineteenth and early twentieth centuries will not continue in the future, though the world's population is still increasing at the rate of five-eighths of 1 per cent annually, which means an annual excess of births over deaths of about 11,500,000. Future increments of population depend not upon a simple calculation of the present ratio between deaths and births, but upon the age composition of society and specifically upon the reproduction rate of child-bearing mothers. In northwestern Europe, on the basis of a 1926 calculation, every 100 mothers gave birth to only 93 future mothers.[1] While this population continues to grow slowly because of its age composition, it is already failing to reproduce itself and will soon become stationary or decline. The same situation exists in North America and in Australia. The populations of Italy and Japan, however, show few signs of a diminished rate of growth, and the Slavic peoples of eastern Europe continue their rapid expansion. The population of the Soviet Union, already much larger than that of any other Power, is increasing at the rate of about 3,000,000 a year. The next half-century, therefore, will lead to a stationary or declining population in the western countries and to a growing preponderance of the Slavic stocks over the Teutonic and Romance stocks of the white race.[2]

[1] See Robert R. Kuczynski, *The Balance of Births and Deaths in Western and Northern Europe*, 1929.
[2] See p. 520 below.

3. THE STRUGGLE FOR RAW MATERIALS

Quinquireme of Nineveh from distant Ophir,
Rowing home to haven in sunny Palestine,
With a cargo of ivory,
And apes and peacocks,
Sandalwood, cedarwood, and sweet white wine.

Stately Spanish galleon coming from the Isthmus,
Dipping through the Tropics by the palm-green shores
With a cargo of diamonds,
Emeralds, amethysts,
Topazes, and cinnamon, and gold moidores.

Dirty British coaster with a salt-caked smoke-stack,
Butting through the Channel in the mad March days,
With a cargo of Tyne coal,
Road-rails, pig-lead,
Firewood, ironware, and cheap tin trays.
—JOHN MASEFIELD, *Cargoes.*

If population is the most elementary foundation of national power, the great primary commodities which are indispensable to the operation of modern industry are of almost equal importance in the calculation of statesmen, business men, and economic nationalists. Prior to the Industrial Revolution, in the era of handicraft industry, the economic foundations of State power were to be found in local agriculture, forestry, shipbuilding, and such simple industries as could be supplied with needed raw materials from the national economy. Economic activity was simple and diversified. People traded with one another across political frontiers, but each State was largely sufficient unto itself, for the raw products of its industries could be found within its boundaries. But the introduction of machinery and steam power created an economic order demanding coal and iron in large quantities. The States possessing abundant amounts of these mineral resources—Great Britain, Germany, and the United States— passed most rapidly and completely through the transition from agricultural to industrial society. This transition involved the progressive utilization, for a bewildering variety of productive purposes, of an ever greater number of raw products—cotton, rubber, sugar, oil, nitrates, copper, etc. That industrialized States can with great speed bring enormously greater power to bear in a distant area than is possible for agricultural States is a natural result of the new technology. The fact itself has been amply demonstrated in every great contest of power between States during the past century. Agrarian States have therefore striven to industrialize themselves, quite as much for political and military reasons as for reasons related to wealth production and living standards. The

[345]

struggle for power, for diplomatic and strategic advantages has played a rôle in promoting economic competition between national societies quite as important as that played by "economic" motivations in a narrower sense. Competition has been especially keen with regard to basic raw materials, and governmental policies have been particularly directed toward deriving maximum political and economic advantages from the control of such material. The resulting relationships constitute one of the most interesting phases of economic nationalism in the world economy of the twentieth century.

The problem which arises here can be put in quite simple terms. It is due to the uneven distribution of basic raw materials over the globe, to the determination of competing private producers to derive maximum profit from such materials, and to the determination of national governments to regulate production and trade in such materials in the interests of national power and profits. The basic materials are available only in certain areas and in restricted amounts. The great mineral resources—coal, iron, petroleum, and a variety of metals—are found only in certain regions of the earth and are obviously present in definitely limited quantities. The great vegetable resources—rubber, cotton, sugar, wheat, etc.—can be produced continuously, but only in the regions which are suitable to their cultivation by virtue of soil and climate.

No international struggle would take place if producers and consumers throughout the world were left free to buy and sell in accordance with their needs and inclinations, for such goods would then flow as easily across national frontiers as they now do across provincial or district frontiers within the nation. But large producers, in their quest for profit, and large consumers, in their quest for cheap sources of supply, call for governmental intervention or assistance. And patriotic governments are the more willing to render such assistance out of a desire, inspired by considerations of national power, to utilize such materials as they control for purposes of diplomatic bargaining. They seek to acquire, if possible, independent sources of supply in order to be secure in war time and in order to prevent other governments and national producing groups from charging monopolistic prices. The result is a welter of monopolistic combinations, price-fixing arrangements, export and import duties, quotas, prohibitions, and valorization schemes.

To review all of these measures for all of the basic commodities would take more pages than are included in this volume. The fundamental patterns of policy, with the purposes lying behind them and the results ensuing from them, are more important than the details of special cases. In general, governmental regulation of raw materials takes the form, either of control of exports and imports, or of restrictions on production and marketing. Customs duties or import taxes on goods entering a country are frequently levied for the purpose of barring out foreign raw materials and of raising prices in the domestic market to the advantage of the "protected" domestic producers. Export duties are constitutionally impossible in the United States and are seldom imposed by industrialized countries, but they are much in vogue in colonial regions and in States which are sources of important raw materials for the outside world. Such duties are usually intended to raise revenue or to conserve resources, but they may also be used, by States enjoying a monopolistic position, to raise world prices. India, for example, enjoys a monopoly in the production of jute, used in the manufacture of burlap bagging, and its government imposes an export duty on this commodity, both to raise revenue and to keep up the price. Chile has long raised a large proportion of her public revenues from export taxes on mineral nitrates, the production of which is monopolized by the Cosach combine (*Compania Saliterera de Chile*), formed in 1931 under the leadership of the Anglo-Chilean Consolidated Nitrate Corporation, controlled by the Guggenheim interests. The British East Indies produce a large proportion of the world's rubber supply, most of which is purchased by the American tire industry. The decline of rubber prices led to the adoption of the Stevenson plan of 1922, which provided for a sliding scale of export duties for the purpose of limiting production and raising the price. American rubber importers secured the support of the United States Government in protesting against this arrangement and attempted to find independent sources of supply in the Philippine Islands and in Liberia. In part as a result of American defensive measures, the Stevenson plan failed and was abandoned in 1928. British interests likewise control the world supply of tin, most of which is produced in the Federated Malay States, Australia, Bolivia, and British Africa. The Malay export duties are preferential as regards tin shipped to Singapore, Great Britain, and Australia. These duties have also aroused opposition in the United States, the world's largest consumer of tin. Complete prohibitions or embargoes on the import or export of certain products are sometimes resorted to. After the Great War, Great Britain forbade the importation of coal-tar dyes to cripple the German industry and foster domestic production. Various Canadian provinces have forbidden the export of pulp wood.

In recent years taxes and embargoes, as means of governmental control of raw materials, have been supplemented by various devices to regulate production and marketing. In many instances these schemes are designed to prevent overproduction and to keep up prices. In a few cases governments have themselves gone into business and established State monopolies for purposes of raising revenue and serving "national interests" of an economic and strategic nature. The Japanese Government maintains a practical monopoly of the output of camphor, the bulk of which is produced in Taiwan (Formosa). It restricts production, licenses producers, fixes prices, and makes allotments of exports to other countries. The Spanish Government has at times produced and marketed mercury. More frequently, production of basic raw materials has remained in private hands in States in which private capitalism is the prevailing form of economy, with the government assisting or regulating the activities of the producers, both to increase the power of the State and to enhance producers' profits at the expense of consumers, either within the State or in the world market. In 1902 the Government of Sao Paulo, largest coffee-producing state of Brazil, passed a law limiting coffee planting as a means of reducing exports and keeping up the world price. Subsequently, taxes were levied on exports and government loans were provided for the purchase and storage of coffee in times of surplus supply. In 1921 the Brazilian federal Government took over these functions and established an Institute for Permanent Coffee Protection, which purchases and stores coffee in order to control prices, makes loans to producers, and advertises coffee abroad to promote greater consumption. Since 1931 it has likewise resorted to burning coffee or dumping it into the sea. This "valorization" scheme has at times had an appreciable effect in raising coffee prices. Ecuador has evolved a similar scheme for pegging cocoa prices, Greece for currant prices, the Mexican State of Yucatan for sisal prices, Spain and Portugal for pyrite, Italy for sulphur and citric acid, Chile for nitrates, etc.

Efforts by national governments to fix world prices can obviously be effective only when a State enjoys a monopoly or a quasi-monopoly of the goods in question. As regards goods produced in many countries, the world price of which is determined by a variety of uncontrollable factors, purely national efforts to fix prices are likely to be unsuccessful. Perhaps the most striking instance of the failure of such attempts is furnished by the efforts of the American Government to fix agricultural prices. The McNary-Haugen Bill of 1924 contemplated the establishment of an Agricultural Export Corporation to purchase and hold the exportable surplus of American wheat and other crops until the desired price in the world market could be obtained. This bill was passed by Congress but vetoed by President Coolidge in May, 1928. In the following year, however, Congress and the President created a Federal Farm Board, empowered to buy and sell farm products in the open market with governmental funds, for the purpose of stabilizing prices. In December of 1929 the board took the view that prices of wheat and cotton were too low and it began making loans to cotton cooperatives at the rate of 16 cents a pound on their holdings, and to wheat cooperatives at the rate of $1.18 (Chicago) and $1.25 (Minneapolis) per bushel. The purpose in both cases was to keep up prices by enabling the cooperatives to hold a portion of the crops off the market. Prices continued to decline, however, and the loans could not be repaid. The board then created stabilization corporations which used public money to purchase the wheat and cotton held by the cooperatives at fixed prices above current market quotations. In February, 1930 the board went into the open market as a buyer. When it discontinued purchases in May, 1931, it held 250,000,000 bushels of wheat and 1,300,000 bales of cotton. Prices were still falling. It had sustained losses of $150,000,000. Even had it succeeded in inducing American farmers to curtail the exportable surplus by reducing acreage, it is doubtful whether the scheme could have succeeded, for wheat and cotton are produced in quantity in other parts of the world and world prices are fixed by factors entirely beyond the control of any agencies, public or private, in the United States. National price-fixing schemes for such commodities are unworkable.

Governmental policies dictated by economic nationalism have been directed toward the acquisition of independent sources of basic raw materials as well as toward price fixing and the exploitation of monopolistic advantages. The currency of such phrases as "oil diplomacy," "oil imperialism," "rubber imperialism," and the like is indicative of general recognition of the fact that the territorial and political ambitions of States are greatly influenced by such considerations. The fascinating and intricate story of the international struggle for petroleum resources is too long to be recounted here, but a few of its salient features may be suggested. The rapid adoption of petroleum for power, light, and lubrication and the amazingly large number of products resulting from its distillation have led to its rapid and wasteful exploitation in all parts of the world where it is found. In 1927 the United States was producing 70 per cent of the total world production, with Russia, Venezuela, Mexico, Persia, Rumania, the Dutch East Indies, Colombia, and Peru following next in order. The United States and the Soviet Union are the only Great Powers which have sources of supply within their own territory adequate to meet their own needs. The oil business is conducted on a world-wide scale by a small number of huge industrial combinations, including the Standard Oil (American), the Royal Dutch Shell (Anglo-Dutch), the Anglo-Persian Oil Company (British), etc. The British Government owns the controlling stock in the Anglo-Persian Oil Company and has frequently given diplomatic support to the Royal Dutch Shell, as has the American Government to the Standard Oil and other American oil interests. The United States has protested against the established British policy of excluding aliens from the control of petroleum supplies within the Empire. The Dutch Government pursues a similar policy in the East Indies. French legislation virtually excludes from the French sources of supply all companies not under French control. Powerful governments are able to enforce such policies in the face of foreign protest. Weaker governments, like that of Mexico, are often compelled to abandon such monopolistic efforts under pressure of the Great Powers. The United States has not pursued a discriminatory exclusion policy, except in retaliation against particular States, and has demanded an Open Door policy throughout the world as a means of enabling Americans to enter foreign fields.

The Near East has been a theater of acute international friction for the control of oil resources. There is reason to believe that the unsuccessful British intervention against the Soviet Government in the Russian Civil War was in part inspired by a desire to secure possession of the rich Caucasian oil fields. Prior to 1914 Anglo-German rivalry in the Near East centered about the oil fields of Mesopotamia. On April 14, 1920, at San Remo, the British and French Governments, acting in the interests of military security and on behalf of the prospective profits of their oil corporations, reached an agreement for the division between them of rights to exploit oil resources in Rumania, Russia, Mesopotamia, and elsewhere. The United States protested against this horse-trading in oil-bearing areas, on the ground that it contemplated exclusion of Americans and other foreign nationals from the opportunities for profit in these regions. At the Lausanne Conference of 1923, the local hotels housed more representatives of oil companies than of governments, and the resulting treaties were oleaginous in the extreme. Great Britain insisted successfully upon the abandonment of Turkish claims to the Mosul district, reputed to be rich in oil reserves, in favor of Iraq, under British mandate. The British and French Governments were unable to validate all of their contested claims, but the great game of oil imperialism still goes on, with private producers posing as patriots in order to enlist governmental support for their profit-making schemes and with governments granting such support for reasons of strategy and Great Power politics. The story of oil diplomacy in Mexico, Colombia, and other regions reveals the same basic motives at work, creating the same types of governmental policies. The story of the international struggle for other basic resources differs only in degree and not in kind from that already suggested.

4. NEO-MERCANTILISM AND THE STRUGGLE FOR COMMODITY MARKETS

> Let our city be accounted neither large nor small but one and self-sufficing.—PLATO, *The Republic*.

The policies of economic nationalism, directed toward exclusive national control and monopolistic exploitation of the world's raw materials, are but a phase of the competitive struggle for markets carried on by the nation-states. Trade carried on by producers and merchants would be of little direct significance for international politics if it went on without governmental interference or regulation. But international trade, even more than domestic trade, has almost always been subjected to various forms of State control designed to increase national wealth, to benefit exporters, to enhance the profits of producers, to "protect" or monopolize domestic markets, to invade foreign markets, etc. Competition in international trade is not competition between the governments of the nation-states, for governments seldom engage in production and commerce. It is competition between private producers and merchants who receive governmental support and encouragement in their search for profit. Such support and encouragement are extended because the profit-seekers possess sufficient political influence to control governmental action and because governments seek to enhance national power through striving after markets abroad and economic self-sufficiency at home. In the twentieth century ambassadors, consuls, and commercial agents have become advertisers and promoters of private business. Though they are paid out of the public treasury they devote a large proportion of their time to discovering new markets abroad for private business interests in their own States. Viewed historically, governmental policy toward international trade in the Western State System has passed through three distinct stages which may be designated as the period of mercantilism, the period of laissez-faire or free trade, and the period of neo-mercantilism or tariff protectionism. The first two of these deserve brief examination as a means of understanding the third.

During the seventeenth and eighteenth centuries, the prevailing school of economic thought in western Europe was that of the mercantilists, who held, among other things, that government should regulate trade for the purpose of enhancing national wealth and prosperity. This early philosophy of economic nationalism was based upon a number of serious misconceptions of the nature of international commerce. Trade was regarded less as a mutually advantageous exchange of commodities than as a process in which one party lost what the other gained. Gold was regarded less as a convenient symbol of value and a useful medium of exchange than as an embodiment of riches. A nation's wealth was assumed to be equivalent to its stock of gold. All that would increase the gold stock was therefore good, and all that diminished it was bad. It was observed that when a nation's exporters sold more goods abroad than its importers purchased, the surplus of exports over imports was paid for in gold instead of goods. Since this situation produced a flow of gold into the country, it was looked upon as "favorable"—and ever since an excess of national exports over imports has been called a "favorable balance of trade." On the other hand, it was observed that when importers purchased more goods abroad than exporters sold, gold flowed out of the country. An excess of imports over exports was consequently described as an "unfavorable balance of trade." Inasmuch as gold was assumed to be wealth, governmental policies were directed toward encouraging exports by bounties and subsidies of various kinds and discouraging imports by tariffs, embargoes, and prohibitions. At the same time, colonial trade was monopolized by the nationals of the mother country in order that it too might contribute as much as possible to the national wealth. Domestic trade was likewise subjected to numerous restrictions and regulations.

The decline of mercantilistic policies at the end of the eighteenth century was due less to the demonstrated fallacies of mercantilist logic than to the political ascendancy of the new bourgeoisie born of the Industrial Revolution. The new manufacturers and merchants found the old restrictions a burdensome interference with free profit-seeking. The publication of Adam Smith's *Wealth of Nations* in 1776 and the work of the continental economists, known as the Physiocrats, revealed clearly the *lacunae* in mercantilist reasoning and furnished intellectual respectability to the demand for an end of governmental interference with trade. Gold, it was pointed out, is not wealth, but simply a medium of exchange in terms of which commodities are priced. An inflow of gold into a nation tends to raise the price level, for the purchasing power of gold varies inversely with its quantity. An outflow of gold lowers prices for the same reason. If an excess of exports over imports leads to an inflow of gold, prices rise, domestic costs of production increase, and the nation's exporters are less and less able to compete effectively in foreign markets with producers in other nations where prices are lower. At the same time, foreign exporters, attracted by the higher prices, send in goods in increasing volume. The export surplus consequently tends to vanish and to be replaced by an import surplus, as a result of the effect upon trade of changing national price levels due to gold movements. Conversely, an excess of imports over exports causes gold to flow out, lowers prices, places exporters at a competitive advantage and importers at a competitive disadvantage, with the result that the movement is in course of time reversed. In short, gold movements and price levels tend to keep foreign trade at an equilibrium. It is impossible for a nation, in the long run, to export more than it imports. In the long run a nation's imports and exports, including in these terms not merely commodities, but all the items in the international balance such as shipping charges, insurance premiums, investments, immigrant remittances, etc., must attain parity. Governmental efforts to prevent this are ineffective and mischievous.

Out of this reasoning developed the "free-trade" doctrine of the classical laissez-faire economists, which the new entrepreneurs found to be a plausible rationalization of their own interests and the new bourgeois governments adopted quite generally. In 1846 the Corn Laws (import duties on grain) were abandoned in Great Britain, which then became a free-trade country. The United States adopted lower tariffs between 1830 and 1860. The Anglo-French Cobden Treaty of 1860 provided for French tariff reduction. German tariff duties were almost completely abandoned in the mid-century. The period of untrammeled individualism, with governmental regulation of economic activity reduced to a minimum, was marked by the general abandonment of mercantilist restrictions on foreign trade and the progressive adoption of free-trade policies by many governments. The economic theory of free trade may be succinctly summarized as follows: in the absence of governmental interference with foreign trade, producers, importers, and exporters will buy and sell freely across national frontiers in accordance with the dictates of price and the opportunities for profit. Each nation will specialize in the production of those commodities which, by virtue of climate, resources, and technical skill, it can produce most cheaply. It will sell these goods abroad and receive in exchange goods which can be produced more cheaply abroad than at home. World-wide geographical specialization develops and each nation gains economically by free exchange with all others. The resulting trade is advantageous to all concerned, even to those to whom it is least so. Just as each individual, partnership, or corporation within a State gains by buying and selling freely in an open national market, so each nation in international society gains by buying and selling freely in an open world market. To put this position in American terms, it is economically advantageous for the people of Illinois, Wisconsin, New York, California, and all of the other forty-eight States of the American Union to buy and sell freely across State lines. Anyone who would propose that Indiana could profit economically by taxing or prohibiting imports from Kentucky, Michigan, and Ohio and thus encouraging "home industries" would be regarded as a madman. Similarly, the peoples of the United States, Canada, Mexico, Great Britain, France, Germany, and all of the other States of the world would gain economically, in the long run, by buying and selling freely across national frontiers. But, for reasons which remain to be noted, governmental interference with this process has come to be regarded, not as madness, but as the highest economic wisdom.

In spite of the fact that the logic of free trade has never been successfully refuted, the governments of the nation-states have progressively abandoned it since 1870 and have once more erected higher and higher tariff walls in a new quest for prosperity and economic self-sufficiency. As soon as production began to outrun the market, as soon as competition in all markets became increasingly keen, entrepreneurs began to perceive possibilities of profit through governmental action. They abandoned their former laissez-faire attitude and looked to government to bar out competitors from the domestic market and to assist them in conquering foreign markets. In the United States the tariff "for revenue only" was replaced during the Civil War by a tariff designed to protect national producers from foreign competition and to encourage home industry. The McKinley Tariff of 1890 was enacted to prevent the importation of various foreign goods or to make their prices so high in the American market that they could not compete successfully with similar American goods. The Dingley Tariff of 1897 and the Payne-Aldrich Tariff of 1909 raised duties to still higher levels. The (Democratic) Underwood Tariff of 1913 lowered import duties, but only temporarily. The Fordney-Mc-Cumber Tariff Act of 1922 carried American tariff duties to unprecedentedly high levels, while the Smoot-Hawley Tariff (1930) of the Hoover administration carried protectionism to a point which threatened the complete strangulation of American import trade. In Germany, Bismarck's protective tariff of 1879 inaugurated a permanent policy of high duties on both agricultural and industrial imports. The Third French Republic adopted moderate protectionism in 1881, and subsequently imposed higher and higher duties on imports. These three States set the pace and others followed step by step, until almost all nations in retaliation and self-defense had become protectionist by the turn of the century. The general economic disorganization following the Great War and the determination of the new States of Europe to become economically self-contained led to the erection of higher tariff barriers everywhere, until finally even Great Britain, the last citadel of free trade, abandoned its ancient faith and embraced protectionism in 1931. A large section of the British Liberal party, along with Ramsay MacDonald and the renegade members of the Labor party, followed the example of the American Democratic party in abandoning traditional convictions and championing neo-mercantilism. The Great Depression, which began in 1929, found international trade hampered on every side by almost prohibitive barriers set up by all the governments of the world.

This is not the place to review the various arguments, real and imaginary, for and against protective tariffs. Suffice it to say that most of the economic arguments advanced in justification of neo-mercantilism are wholly unsound and are put forward by profit-seekers and politicians to bamboozle the domestic consumer, who is persuaded that his own welfare is furthered by tariffs and who pays the piper, even when he does not call the tune. Mark Hanna's plea, in the McKinley campaign of 1896, for tariff protectionism as a means of ensuring a "full dinner pail" for the working man was representative of arguments put forward with unfailing zeal by Republican and (since 1924) Democratic politicians in the United States. The tariff is presented as a necessary measure to preserve national prosperity against a flood of cheap foreign goods which, it is argued, would lower prices, drive domestic manufacturers out of business, and produce unemployment and business depression.[1] This argument may be valid in the short run, in the sense that a sudden lowering of tariff walls would drive out of business the uneconomical local producers who are able to make high profits by monopolizing the domestic market despite their high costs. Such action would thus produce a painful period of adjustment before an equilibrium was restored. In the long run, the economic advantages of geographical specialization and free exchange far outweigh the largely imaginary advantages of cultivating a self-contained domestic market. It is likewise argued that a tariff is essential to encourage and support "infant industries" by protecting them against foreign competition until they are able to reduce production costs to a normal competitive level and stand on their own feet. In point of fact, such industries, particularly in the United States, are never willing to have protection withdrawn and constantly clamor for more and more—indicating, perhaps, that they remain in a perpetual state of infancy and in need of a governmental wet nurse. It is further contended that a tariff is essential to promote national prosperity by maintaining a "favorable" balance of trade. This is but a new version of the old mercantilist fallacy. No nation can maintain a permanent excess of exports over imports, and if it could it would lose rather than gain, for a nation's gains from commerce are most assuredly in the goods it takes in and uses rather than in the goods it sends out and loses. No nation can continue to sell if it refuses to buy. These and most other arguments for tariffs are without economic justification in terms of the welfare of the whole national economy.

A sharp distinction must be drawn, however, between economic and political considerations. Almost all of the arguments for protective tariffs

[1] The Republican party platform of 1932 declared: "The Republican party has always been the stanch supporter of the American system of a protective tariff. It believes that the home market, built up under that policy, the greatest and richest market in the world, belongs first to the American agriculture, industry, and labor. No pretext can justify the surrender of that market to such competition as would destroy our farms, mines, and factories, and lower the standard of living which we have established for our workers.

"Because many foreign countries have recently abandoned the gold standard, as a result of which the costs of many commodities produced in such countries have, at least for the time being, fallen materially in terms of American currency, adequate tariff protection is today particularly essential to the welfare of the American people. The tariff commission should promptly investigate individual commodities so affected by currency depreciation, and report to the President any increase in duties found necessary to equalize domestic with foreign costs of production. . . .

"We commend the President's veto of the measure, sponsored by Democratic congressmen, which would have transferred from the President to the Congress the authority to put into effect the findings of the tariff commission. Approval of the measure would have returned tariff making to politics and destroyed the progress made during ten years of effort to lift it out of log-rolling methods. We pledge the Republican party to a policy which will retain the gains made and enlarge the present scope of greater progress.

"We favor the extension of the general Republican principle of tariff protection to our natural-resource industries, including the products of our farms, forests, mines, and oil wells, with compensatory duties on the manufactured and refined products thereof."

which seek to demonstrate that the barring out of imports is economically advantageous to the mass of the population within the domestic market are illogical, false, hypocritical, and based upon surviving mercantilist confusion. If the goal, however, is not the promotion of national economic welfare but the enhancement of national power, the situation is quite different. Welfare arguments are "economic," power arguments are "political." But in all public discussion the two are hopelessly confounded. It is politically inexpedient for the domestic beneficiaries of tariffs to be intellectually honest, either with themselves or with the electorate, and it is good political tactics for patriotic economic nationalists to contend that what contributes to national power also contributes to national welfare. Broadly speaking, protectionist and prohibitive customs duties on imports are in most cases economically indefensible, for they diminish national wealth and prosperity rather than increase them. But such duties may be politically justified if it is assumed that the legitimate objective of governmental regulation of foreign commerce is the enhancement of State power, regardless of the economic cost. It is arguable that the promotion of uneconomical home industries and the attainment of national economic self-sufficiency are politically advantageous to a State, since they diminish its dependence upon foreign sources of supply, lessen the dangers of loss from an economic blockade in war time, and perhaps increase its fighting power by making it self-contained. These political gains are always paid for in economic losses, but the economic nationalists may contend that power and security are worth whatever they cost in welfare.

Great Britain, for example, would probably be better off economically if her manufacturers purchased all of their dye stuffs and chemicals from Germany, whose technicians and industrialists have developed the requisite skills and processes to a point where they can produce such goods more cheaply and efficiently than they can be produced in England. If the British Government bars out or imposes heavy taxes upon such imports and thereby raises their price in the British market and enables inefficient domestic producers to continue in business, it is absurd to argue that Great Britain as a whole benefits economically in consequence of this policy. But it may be maintained that the existence of a British dye and chemical industry, fostered by the profits of a protected domestic market, is strategically necessary for British power in world politics—so necessary that the patriotic British purchasers of dye stuffs and chemicals should be willing to pay higher prices for inferior goods in the name of national security. Or—to take a more extreme and in this instance hypothetical case—it might be contended that the United States would be more secure politically if it developed within its own borders sources of supply of coffee, rubber, and bananas instead of importing these goods from Latin America and the East Indies. Prohibitive tariff duties on these imports might conceivably stimulate their domestic production by raising prices to a level where it would become profitable to grow these plants in hothouses in the United States, since they cannot be grown outdoors in any part of the country. Here the cost of self-sufficiency would be enormous, so much so, in fact, that the American Government has not resorted to any such policy but has preferred to afford diplomatic and military protection to those who purchase the goods in question where they are produced cheaply and abundantly. Tariff protectionism in every case has its price—and this price represents an economic loss which nationalists are prepared to pay for the sake of the supposed political gain resulting therefrom.

But this is only a partial explanation of the paradox of neo-mercantilism. Tariff protectionists invariably insist that restrictions on imports are *economically* advantageous as well as politically desirable, and they have succeeded in convincing a politically effective majority in most modern States that this is really the case. Tariff-making politicians (and this includes most politicians) are perpetually at odds with free-trade economists (and this includes most economists). When a thousand American economists petitioned President Hoover not to sign the Tariff Act of 1930, on the ground that it would bring ruin to American foreign trade, the Chief Executive showed himself to be a politician rather than an economist by ignoring the plea and signing the act. The explanation of such situations is to be found in the domestic economic effects of tariffs and in the nature of the domestic political process as it affects tariff making.

Every protective-tariff duty which actually bars out foreign goods or admits them at higher prices raises the price of the goods in question to consumers in the domestic market, for tariff duties are not paid by foreign producers but by domestic consumers. The domestic producers of such goods are "protected" from foreign competition and can therefore charge higher prices and reap greater profits at the expense of the domestic consumers. Almost every tariff is a device whereby privileged and protected domestic producers are enabled to exploit the domestic market more effectively by charging their customers monopoly or quasi-monopoly prices. It likewise enables inefficient and uneconomical domestic producers to continue production by antiquated methods, since they are protected from more efficient foreign competitors who produce better goods at lower cost. Now it so happens, as has already been suggested, that in bourgeois democratic governments or dictatorships organized producers are politically influential. They are few in number. They know exactly how they may profit from protective duties. They possess wealth and prestige. They contribute to campaign funds, maintain powerful lobbies, and control the acts of legislators and administrators. The ultimate consumers, who pay the bill, are inarticulate, unorganized, multitudinous, without political power, often unaware of where the burden falls, and easily persuaded that their interests as consumers are identical with those of profit-seeking producers attempting to enlist governmental support in exploiting them. Governmental policies are dictated by the few privileged producers who are enabled to profit at the expense of the many. This fact, coupled with considerations of patriotic duty and national self-sufficiency, serves to explain why all important governments are now protectionist. What is an economic loss to the country as a whole is not merely a political gain for the power of the State, but is an economic gain also (at the expense of consumers) for the influential producers who rule the State and shape its policies.

Under these circumstances, tariff making becomes a process in which ever larger numbers of interested producers call loudly for protection, *i.e.*, for higher prices in the domestic market, and pose as patriots promoting national prosperity. Once a tariff wall is set up, vested interests arise behind it and assume that they possess an inalienable right to the profits of patriotic protectionism. They demand more and more protection as a means to greater and greater profits, and other producers' groups soon demand the same privilege. These demands cannot be ignored by politicians, for these groups control political parties. Legislators and executives cannot ignore their master's voice and continue to enjoy the profits and perquisites of holding public office. To raise tariff duties is always politically easy, for those who profit thereby pay generously for such services and those who lose are dumb and voiceless. To lower tariff duties is almost always politically impossible, for the vested interests which profit from them are too powerful to be defied. The resulting process of log-rolling, horse-trading, and patriotic profiteering is most beautifully illustrated in the tariff history of the United States. Most of the senators and representatives who pass American tariff acts are pliant tools of a great variety of profit-seeking producers' groups, and by common consent they support one another in serving those who can make and unmake parties and politicians. When the Fordney-McCumber Act of 1922 required three additional votes in the Senate for its passing, they were gained by adding duties on sugar, fruits, nuts, and other products of California and Louisiana. Senator Hiram Johnson and the Democratic senators from Louisiana then voted for the bill. The Smoot-Hawley Act of 1930 was passed by a combination of Republican and Democratic senators and representatives, each interested in securing protection for the industries of his own State.

At the same time that the protectionist governments of the world have endeavored to exclude imports, they have attempted to promote exports by a variety of devices. The mercantilist doctrine, which regarded an

[358]

outflow of goods as "favorable" and an inflow of goods as "unfavorable," has received new recognition at the hands of entrepreneurs anxious to enhance profits, both by monopolizing the domestic market and by selling their surpluses in foreign markets. Government aid has been solicited by profit-seekers to achieve both of these purposes. It has been freely granted by patriotic legislators who find economic nationalism politically expedient. Government bounties have frequently been paid to exporters. Austria-Hungary began paying bounties on exported beet sugar in 1888, Germany in 1891, and France in 1897. In this instance the importing countries levied retaliatory duties on sugar imports to nullify the effects of the bounties. A general agreement was finally reached in the International Sugar Convention of 1902 to make bounties unprofitable by the systematic imposition by each State of countervailing duties on sugar imports coming from States which paid bounties on exports. Government bounties on exports are often nullified by such retaliatory action. The payment of "drawbacks" is a device with a similar purpose. Manufacturers who import raw materials to be used in the fabrication of goods for export are refunded the tariff duties paid on such materials. More recently, as in the American tariff acts of 1922 and 1930, such manufacturers are often permitted to import goods for eventual export without paying any duty in the first place.

Bounties and drawbacks are only two of the innumerable methods employed by governments to subsidize and encourage export trade. Railway freight rates on exported goods are often reduced. Financial aid from governments to shipping lines is now customary in most commercial States, as a means both of promoting exports and of making available a large tonnage of merchant shipping for use in war. This aid may take the form of direct bounties, of large payments for mail services, or of various disguised subsidies. During the Great War, the American Government operated merchant shipping lines directly, through the United States Shipping Board. Since the passage of the White-Jones Act of 1927, it has subsidized shipping indirectly, following the rejection by Congress of the Ship Subsidy Bill of 1922. Governments have likewise loaned money to other governments or have encouraged private capitalists to lend money to private enterprises abroad, on condition that the proceeds be used for purchasing goods in the lending country. "Concessions" obtained in "backward" countries for railroad construction or other industrial purposes often specify that the goods in question are to be purchased in the country of the concessionaire. Favorable credit facilities and legal privileges of one kind or another are frequently made available to exporters. The United States, France, Spain, Sweden, and other States refuse foreign vessels permission to engage in their coastwise trade. The American Webb-Pomerene Act of 1918 exempts export-trade associations from the operation of the antitrust laws. These and other devices frequently make profitable the practice of "dumping," *i.e.*, of selling goods in foreign markets at a price lower than that charged in the domestic market, either for the purpose of disposing of surpluses, conquering new markets by swamping competition, or limiting domestic supplies to raise prices in the home market.

The policies of economic nationalism pursued by modern governments aim both at the restriction of imports and the promotion of exports. Each of the nation-states whose policies are dictated by bourgeois entrepreneurs strives to make itself economically self-sufficient in the interest of national power and of the profits of domestic producers. It endeavors at the same time, for similar motives, to invade as many foreign markets as possible. The logical end of this policy is reached when the government of each State makes it impossible for its nationals to purchase anything from foreigners and does all in its power to enable them to sell goods to foreigners. Each national unit seeks to sell without buying. International trade is progressively impeded, and each nation-state finds its efforts to promote exports thwarted by the determination of all other States to bar out imports. Out of this situation have emerged commercial treaties, international tariff bargaining, import and export quotas, and the recent acute strangulation of world commerce which has developed since 1930. The nature of this economic dilemma will be examined below, along with national and international efforts to solve the problem.[1] Here it is enough to have noticed how national economic policies in the era of neo-mercantilism have produced a crisis as a result of the collaboration of patriots and profiteers.

5. "DOLLAR DIPLOMACY" AND THE STRUGGLE FOR INVESTMENT MARKETS

> The first duty of a government is to protect life and property. For this, governments are instituted, and governments neglecting or failing to perform it are worse than useless. Protection *in fact* to American lives and property is the sole point upon which the United States is tenacious. . . . The pretense that the United States are plotting or executing invasions for conquests in Mexico is fallacious and absurd.—WILLIAM M. EVARTS.

In the epoch of world economy, of large-scale production and immense accumulations of wealth in the hands of those who look further and further afield for profitable investment opportunities, it is natural that governments should concern themselves with movements of capital across frontiers, no less than with movements of goods. Capitalists and investors, as well as manufacturers and merchants, early perceived the possibility of increasing their profits through enlisting governmental support in their

[1] See pp. 537f. below.

behalf. And politicians and statesmen similarly perceived the possibility of increasing national prestige and achieving diplomatic objectives through an adroit use of investments and loans as weapons of power politics. Governmental regulation of capital movements has accordingly become the order of the day, and the diplomacy of high finance has, like Jehovah, moved in mysterious ways its wonders to perform.

Before discussing the purposes and methods of governmental action in this field, it will be well to suggest the economic origin of the huge volume of foreign loans and investments which now exists throughout the world. From the beginning of the Industrial Revolution, modern capitalistic economy in its periods of prosperity has concentrated greater and greater aggregations of liquid capital in the hands of individual entrepreneurs and proprietors of industrial and commercial corporations, and of the banking institutions which accumulate the savings of millions. On the basis of these accumulations an elaborate and delicate credit structure can be reared and expanded for the purpose of financing new enterprises, extending old ones, and carrying forward the work of producing and selling goods and services. Profits beget more profits, and nothing succeeds like success. While the proceeds of capitalistic production have in prosperous periods been distributed sufficiently widely to permit an almost constantly rising standard of living for the masses in the industrialized States, they have, on the other hand, been sufficiently concentrated to bring about an enormous inequality in the distribution of wealth and income. Those with large fortunes, and those who convert the savings of millions of petty depositors into large fortunes, reinvest their money in industry and commerce to accumulate still larger fortunes through interest, dividends, and profits. The available quantity of liquid or variable capital in the national economy, i.e., of money seeking investment, has thus tended to increase more rapidly than the quantity of fixed capital, i.e., factories, mines, machinery, buildings, etc.

Now it so happens, in accordance with the familiar law of diminishing returns, that the larger becomes the available quantity of one element in the productive process, with the other elements remaining constant, the smaller will be the increment to production resulting from the addition of each successive unit. In the terminology of classical economics, land, labor, and capital are the three elements of production, each of which receives its share of the product in the forms respectively of rent, wages, and interest. When an optimum ratio between the three elements prevails, each will receive the largest possible return. In a given situation, perhaps five units of land (natural resources), five units of labor (applied human power of brawn and brain), and five units of capital (machinery and producer's goods, or the money required to furnish these things) may constitute such an optimum. If all three units are doubled or halved the sellers of each will continue to get the same rate of return. But if only one unit is increased or decreased, a disequilibrium will be created. If, in the case assumed, ten units of labor are added to the five units each of land and capital, the productivity of labor per unit will decline and each individual worker will receive less wages than before. Similarly, if labor and land remain constant and capital is increased to say ten units, the productivity of capital will decline and each successive addition of units of capital will net a smaller and smaller return per unit. Interest and dividends will fall, and the owners of capital will seek more profitable fields of investment. At the beginning of the nineteenth century, the British capitalist who invested his money in Birmingham steel mills or Lancashire textile plants could obtain a handsome return, for labor and resources were abundant and capital was still scarce. By the middle of the century, however, liquid capital had grown in volume more rapidly than resources and labor, and the investor in stocks and bonds of Birmingham or Lancashire enterprises who once got 10 or 15 or 20 per cent on his investment now got only 6 or 8 per cent. By the end of the century he got perhaps 4 or 5 per cent. Capital was now abundant as compared with labor and resources. While those who continued to invest money in old established industries had greater security than ever before, they received smaller and smaller returns.

This process took place successively in all States touched by the magic of industrial capitalism—first in England, later in Germany and other continental countries, and still later in the United States and Japan. Since the investors of capital sought maximum returns, they began investing money in new industries or, more significantly, in foreign States where land and labor were abundant and capital was scarce. The "backward" regions of the earth were those which were economically undeveloped because of lack of capital. Risks were great, uncertainties were numerous, but interest and profits were large and in some cases fabulous. The British capitalist who was certain of 5 per cent on his money in England might secure 8 per cent in the Dominions or in America and possibly 10, 15, 30, or even several hundred per cent if he invested luckily in the exploitation of the rich resources and labor power of Asia, Africa, or South America. The price of capital, like the price of other goods, is determined by the available supply and the effective demand, with the element of risk or insecurity also playing its part in fixing interest rates. Capital is loaned, as goods are sold, where prices are highest. Just as differences in commodity price levels between nations guide the flow of goods across frontiers from innumerable sellers to innumerable buyers, so differences in interest rates on loans and investments control the flow of funds from capitalists, banks, and petty speculators to the multitude of industrial and commercial enterprises throughout the world. Capital has inevitably flowed outward from the capital-rich western States to the capital-poor regions of the European and non-European world, as soon as interest, dividends, and profits in the home country have become less than could be realized by investment abroad.

This outward movement of capital began first, naturally enough, in Great Britain, the cradle of modern industrial capitalism. By 1914 private British capital to the value of about $20,000,000,000 had been invested abroad, with British investments increasing at the rate of $1,000,000,000 a year. In the case of Germany, about $9,000,000,000 had been invested abroad, with an annual increase of perhaps $250,000,000. France was less industrialized and therefore less wealthy in liquid capital than her neighbors, but the stockings of the peasant, the artisan, and the petit bourgeois were long and deep. About $8,000,000,000 of French private capital had found its way abroad by 1914, with an increase of perhaps $500,000,000 a year. Belgian, Dutch, Swiss, Italian, and other investors likewise found it possible to get more for their money by sending it abroad to remote and exotic places than by investing it in domestic industry. From northwestern Europe there flowed outward a golden stream of capital, running like the blood of life through the veins of industry and commerce all over the world. And from the backward and capital-hungry regions there flowed back a steady stream of dividends, premiums, interest payments, and commissions to enrich the lenders from the profits of the borrowers. In the United States, until recently a new, undeveloped country, more foreign capital was absorbed than was exported. Some $4,000,000,000 of European capital were invested in the United States by 1914, though it should be noted that over $2,500,000,000 of American capital had already gone into the Caribbean area, Canada, and Europe.

The Great War and its aftermath produced a complete reversal in the international position of the United States from the point of view of movements of private capital. The American colossus was transformed from the greatest debtor to the second greatest creditor country in the world. One of the first effects of the war was to cause European investors in the United States to sell their stocks and bonds in American industries to Americans, who became increasingly eager to purchase them with the onset of the feverish flush of war prosperity. Some $2,500,000,000 worth of American securities held abroad were repurchased in this fashion. Private investors in the United States, moreover, reaped a rich harvest by lending money to enterprises of all kinds abroad and to the Allied Governments through the purchase of their war bonds. Under the influence of an unprecedented European demand for goods and services at almost any price, American industry, commerce, and finance entered upon a "boom" period which lasted, with minor interruptions, until the great crash of 1929. Twenty-one thousand new American millionaires emerged from the most profitable of all American wars. The newly accumulated hordes of capital in the United States fed the automobile industry, the motion-picture industry, the radio industry, and the stock market—and then looked abroad for still greater profits. After 1924 American loans flowed to Europe, particularly to Germany, in a great flood, and it became possible in the United States to sell at lucrative prices almost any foreign security, public or private, printed on good paper with the requisite gilt edge. American loans and investments in Europe increased from about a third of a billion dollars to over $5,500,-000,000, in Canada from $750,000,000 to almost $4,500,000,000, in South America from $100,000,000 to $3,000,000,000, in Central America from $1,250,000,000 to almost $3,000,000,000. So large was this flow of capital that American investors, by 1931, had exported about eighteen billions of dollars abroad, exclusive of intergovernmental debts. Since 1931, in the face of world-wide defaults and bankruptcies, the outward movement of American capital has practically ceased and many of the loans of the boom epoch have become worthless.

Quite apart from governmental efforts to control these great capital movements they produce in themselves economic and social effects with political ramifications. Some of these effects will be considered below in connection with imperialism, Great Power politics, and the contemporary crisis of capitalism. From the point of view of economic nationalism, the most significant aspect of capital exports and imports is that they have frequently been regulated by governments for the purpose of promoting national power and prestige and attaining diplomatic objectives having no direct relation to the immediate interests of borrowers or lenders. If "free trade" prevailed in the world's investment markets, i.e., if governments permitted investors and borrowers to do as they pleased and if investors and borrowers made no appeals for governmental assistance or support, loans would be made and investments would be placed in accordance with pure and simple profit considerations. Mistakes of judgment would certainly occur, and frauds and swindles might be even more frequent, for brokers and investment bankers are not distinguished from ordinary mortals by excessive wisdom or honesty. But governments would not be at once involved in the results, and capital movements would scarcely deserve consideration in a treatise on international politics. In fact, however, this situation seldom prevails, for the governments of capital-exporting States are disposed to point with pride to a swelling volume of foreign investments and to use the money power of their financiers for political purposes, while the governments of capital-importing States often view with alarm the invasion of the domestic market by foreign capitalists and seek to check their influence in various ways.

The methods employed to control capital exports vary considerably from State to State. The devices used are both positive and preventive.

They aim to encourage private investments in certain States and to discourage them in others. In almost every case some form of official approval is required before foreign stocks and bonds may be listed and sold in the local market. In France all foreign flotations on the Paris Bourse must be approved by the Minister of Finance and the Minister of Foreign Affairs. In Italy, Belgium, Germany, and certain other continental States, similar regulations are enforced. In Great Britain informal contacts are regularly maintained between investment houses and the Foreign Office, and loans disapproved by Downing Street are seldom made. In March of 1922 the American State Department announced "the desire of the Government to be duly and adequately informed regarding (loan) transactions before their confirmation, so that it might express itself regarding them if that should be requested or seem desirable. . . . Subsequently, the President was informed by the bankers that they and their associates were in harmony with the Government's wishes and would act accordingly." This American loan-supervision policy is not based upon legislative enactment, nor does the State Department have any authority to compel bankers to heed its advice. But it would be a rash banker indeed who would float a foreign loan not approved by his government. The implication of governmental supervision is that the government will grant diplomatic support to approved lenders if their interests are jeopardized, while it may withhold such support from loans which have not met with official approval. This fact alone is usually sufficient, in most capital-exporting States, to insure a large degree of governmental control over foreign loans and investments, regardless of the particular devices utilized.

The purposes for which such control is exercised are various and sundry. Considerations of economic welfare would dictate governmental supervision to prevent fraud, dishonesty, and undue risks, and to safeguard borrowers and lenders alike. But considerations of patriotism, power, and profits lead to quite different motives and purposes. At least four specific political objectives have been sought by governments in their regulating activities.

1. Loans are often encouraged to strengthen an ally. The French Government has pursued this objective on the grandest scale. Almost one-quarter of the French foreign investments in 1914 were placed in Russia, either in government bonds or in private Russian enterprises. This was due less to considerations of profit and security than to the deliberate policy of the Quai d'Orsay in bolstering up the Tsardom in order that Russia might push forward her industrialization and her military preparations and thus become a more trustworthy ally. All of these investments were lost in the revolutionary holocaust of 1917. Since the Great War the Quai d'Orsay has similarly encouraged French bankers to loan money to governments or private enterprises in France's

new eastern allies. During 1931 French capital to the amount $21,560,000 was invested in Poland, $22,540,000 in Rumania, $23,520,000 in Czechoslovakia, and $38,220,000 in Jugoslavia.

2. Loans are frequently discouraged to weaken a past or prospective enemy State. Prior to the war, the Quai d'Orsay vetoed participation by French banks in the proposed Bagdad railway consortium because of German interests in the project. Since 1918 the French Government has discouraged investment in the defeated States—Germany, Austria, Hungary, and Bulgaria. Such capital boycotts are frequently ineffective, since funds can ordinarily be secured elsewhere, but they have at times been successfully used as a tool of high politics.

3. Loans are often offered as part of a diplomatic bargain to obtain political concessions from the government of another State. In 1921 and 1922 the American State Department brought pressure on the European governments to refund their war debts to the United States by requesting American bankers to make no loans to governments not taking such action. The post-war financial diplomacy of France, in its dealings both with ally and enemy States, has repeatedly sought to achieve its purposes by offering or withholding loans from French banks. In the spring of 1931, for example, the Quai d'Orsay made it clear that French participation in a loan to the Austrian Government was contingent upon the abandonment of all efforts at treaty revision or *Anschluss* with Germany.[1] In the summer of 1932, Austria was obliged to renounce for twenty years the project of a customs union with Germany as a condition of receiving a new League of Nations loan of $43,000,000. Germany has been refused French loans for similar reasons, while French loans to Poland and Czechoslovakia have cemented the alliances with these States and brought their policies into harmony with those of France.

4. Loans have frequently been encouraged by governments as a means of securing economic and political control of "backward" areas. Governments have protected investors in such regions, and investors have served the purposes of government. Bankers in capital-exporting States have loaned money to impecunious governments or have invested in private enterprises in backward regions, often on usurious terms calculated to exploit the borrower to the limit of endurance. When the repayment of such obligations has been endangered through bankruptcy

[1] In accepting the international League of Nations loan of 1922, the Austrian Government was obliged to pledge itself "not to alienate its independence; it will abstain from any negotiations or from any economic or financial engagement calculated directly or indirectly to compromise this independence." Austria also agreed that in customs matters "she shall not violate her economic independence by granting to any State a special régime or exclusive advantages calculated to threaten this independence" (Protocol I, League of Nations. Official Journal, November, 1922, p. 1471). It was on the basis of this protocol that the Permanent Court of International Justice, on September 5, 1931, denied Austria the right to form a customs union with Germany.

or local revolution, the lenders have appealed for diplomatic or military support to their own governments, which in many instances have encouraged the original loan in order to create such opportunities. Diplomatic support is extended, and the result in many cases is the landing of marines, the collection of customs duties by agents of the bankers' government, and the imposition of a financial and political protectorate upon the defaulting State.[1] This pattern of "dollar diplomacy" is a familiar one in the imperialistic expansion of all of the Great Powers and will be considered in specific cases in the following chapter.

The most significant political results of capital exports have in fact occurred in situations where money is loaned by the financiers of the Great Powers to governments or private enterprises in weak and backward States. A flow of funds from one powerful and stable State to another seldom gives rise to political controversy, even though the governments concerned may, for political purposes, influence the actions of borrowers and lenders. Such loans are likely to be on terms which ensure a fair degree of security, the productive use of the money granted, and a reasonable certainty of repayment. Defaults are rare in times of prosperity. When something approaching wholesale bankruptcy takes place, as in the world economic crisis of 1929–1933, governmental action is demanded and granted, but usually without important effects on the political relations between debtor and creditor nations. But when funds flow from a Great Power to a backward State of Africa, Asia, or Latin America, the political consequences are quite different. Here there is little assurance of stability, productive use, and repayment and sometimes no assurance even of honest intentions on either side. Defaults are frequent, and lenders' demands for diplomatic protection are chronic. There is no parity of power between the governments involved, and the stronger is always tempted to browbeat the weaker and impose its will upon it, both in the interest of the private investors and for the broader political and strategic purposes of Great Power politics. Even when governments do not act, great corporations are often able to make and unmake local administrations in the pursuit of their own objectives. In Mexico and Central America revolutionary disturbances have often been financed by foreign investors and trading companies. In such situations, the native governments, in the words of one commentator, are "almost powerless to protect themselves against the oppression and greed of foreign interests, for

[1] President Taft declared in 1912: "The diplomacy of the present administration has sought to respond to modern ideas of commercial intercourse. This policy has been characterized as substituting dollars for bullets. It is one that appeals alike to idealistic humanitarian sentiments, to the dictates of sound policy and strategy, and to legitimate commercial aims. It is an effort frankly directed to the increase of American trade upon the axiomatic principle that the Government of the United States shall extend all proper support to every legitimate and beneficial American enterprise abroad." Annual Message to Congress, December 3, 1912.

corporations like the great fruit companies and the railway companies are able to bring to the support of their projects financial resources which far exceed those of the local governments or of any group of natives."[1]

Having learned from painful experience that imports of foreign capital often lead to diplomatic pressure from the lenders' governments, and sometimes to loss of political independence, the governments of capital-importing States frequently seek to impose restrictions upon the rights of foreign investors and property owners with resulting diplomatic complications of various kinds. Occasionally such governments may deliberately encourage foreign investments on terms highly advantageous to the investors. This is one means whereby a despotic or dictatorial régime is sometimes enabled to retain power in the face of popular discontent. The Tsarist Government of Russia financed itself on foreign capital and suppressed the revolution of 1904–1906 with French loans. The Khedive of Egypt loaded a huge foreign-debt burden on his State to gratify his personal whims and strengthen his régime. Porfirio Diaz, Mexican dictator from 1874 to 1910, maintained himself in power by selling out the resources of the country to foreign concessionaires. But liberal and "patriotic" governments in backward States are increasingly disposed to restrict imports to foreign capital and often attempt to limit foreign property rights acquired from preceding régimes. All of the foreign loans and investments in Russia were repudiated or confiscated by the Soviet Government. Many capital-importing States require that their nationals own 50 per cent of the stock in companies organized to exploit local resources. China's mining laws contain such a provision. Venezuela and Ecuador provide in their constitutions that no concessions shall be granted to foreigners unless they agree not to invoke the diplomatic aid of their governments in future disputes. Article 27 of the Mexican constitution of 1917 nationalized the mineral resources of the State and declared that all contracts and concessions "which shall have resulted in the monopoly of lands, waters, and natural resources of the nation by a single individual or corporation, are declared subject to revision, and the executive is authorized to declare those null and void which seriously prejudice the public interest."

Such efforts naturally arouse resentment among the investors who feel that their acquired rights—whether honestly obtained or not—are deserving of protection. Their resentment usually manifests itself in agitation in the public press of the local State and of the investors' State against the régime which proposes to interfere with property rights. Revolutions are sometimes organized against it and appeals are made to the investors' home government for protection. Such appeals are usually heeded, both because bankers and investors are politically influential and because the

[1] D. G. Munro, *The Five Republics of Central America*, 1918, p. 314.

[368]

resulting diplomatic controversies offer opportunities for imperialistic expansion. The governments of capital-exporting States may bring varying degrees of pressure upon the governments of backward States in the interests of investors and concessionaires. They may, in the first place, refuse to extend diplomatic recognition to governments which confiscate property, repudiate debts, or otherwise reduce the profit of foreign nationals. American recognition policy in the Caribbean has been largely motivated by such considerations. The United States withheld diplomatic recognition from the Obregon Government in Mexico until 1923, when it agreed not to apply Article 27 of the constitution retroactively. The United States has acted in the same fashion toward Nicaragua, Costa Rica, Honduras, Colombia, Peru, and other Latin American States. The governments of such States are chronically in a condition of financial embarrassment and are usually unable to secure foreign loans without diplomatic recognition. The withholding of such recognition is therefore an effective weapon in the hands of the American State Department. The Huerta régime in Mexico was compelled to abdicate in 1915 for this reason. The United States has withheld diplomatic recognition from the Soviet Union on similar grounds, but without effecting a change of régime or a modification of policy at Moscow.

Governments of capital-exporting States may go a step further in the protection of the interests of their investors by engaging in intervention against the State complained of. Armed intervention and military or naval demonstrations for the collection of debts have been the usual weapon of the Great Powers in their dealings with backward States. Between 1800 and 1927 the United States engaged in no less than seventy interventions in Latin America, many of them for the purpose of protecting investments and collecting debts. Interventions by other Powers in Asia and Africa have been even more numerous. Such interventions are often accompanied by efforts to overthrow the local government and replace it by one more acceptable to foreign interests. Where the victim is weak the intervening Powers usually achieve their purposes. Where the victim is strong or is supported by another Power, success is less likely. The French intervention in Mexico, culminating in the setting up of the Archduke Maximilian on the throne of a new Franco-Mexican empire in 1861, was frustrated by internal insurrection, the exigencies of European politics, and the hostile attitude of the United States. The Allied and American intervention in the Russian Civil War (1918–1921) was designed to overturn the Soviet régime and replace it by a government disposed to pay its debts, recognize foreign property rights, and make Russia safe for capitalism. It was beaten back by the Red Army and failed to achieve its purposes. Seldom can a Great Power, or even a combination of powers, intervene successfully in the affairs of another Great Power. But in dealing with small and weak States such interventions have been frequent and effective. The Latin American governments have endeavored, with little success, to secure general recognition of the principle that all armed interventions for the protection of nationals abroad are illegal (the "Calvo doctrine") or, failing this, that there should be no resort to intervention for the collection of debts (the "Drago doctrine"). At the Hague Conference of 1907 a convention was drawn up in which the signatories bound themselves "not to have recourse to armed force for the recovery of contract debts claimed from the government of one country by the government of another country as being due its nationals," unless arbitration of the dispute was refused. This agreement has had no visible effect in reducing the frequency of such action.

The most extreme measure of protection which a State may take on behalf of the property rights or financial claims of its nationals is to impose its control upon the weak State whose conduct is an object of complaint. Intervention has often led to this result. The degree of control established varies with circumstances. In its mildest form it may involve only the appointment of customs collectors or financial advisers by the intervening Power, coupled with whatever action is necessary—usually the landing of marines—to compel the local government to accept their services. In its ultimate form it involves the extinction of the sovereignty and independence of the victim State and its annexation by the intervening Power. All possible variations between these extremes are observable in the history of financial imperialism. The Caribbean policy of the United States has led to the exercise of financial control over backward countries on the largest scale. The finances of Cuba have from time to time been supervised by an American representative in Havana. The treaty of 1915 between the United States and Haiti authorizes the United States to "nominate" a general receiver of customs and a financial adviser who collects revenues to pay the salaries of American officials, to meet the interest and principal on the public debt, to maintain the American controlled constabulary, and finally, if any revenue remains, to meet the expenses of the Haitian Government. By the treaty of 1907, the United States likewise appointed a general receiver of customs for the Dominican Republic. In 1916 the Republic, along with Haiti, was occupied by American marines. Between 1905 and 1922 the American receiver collected $67,000,000 in customs duties, of which $33,000,000 went to foreign bankers. Under the Bryan-Chamorro Treaty of August 5, 1914, Nicaragua also became a financial protectorate of the United States, which was given authority to supervise the expenditure of the $3,000,000 paid annually by the United States to Nicaragua for canal rights and for the lease of islands as naval bases. In 1922 Bolivia borrowed $33,000,000 from New York bankers at 8 per cent and was obliged to pledge certain revenues for repayment under the supervision of a banker's commission. Salvador is under similar control. Financial experts named by the American State Department have likewise been employed from time to time by Colombia, Guatemala, Honduras, Panama, Peru, and Persia. International financial control was imposed upon Egypt in 1876, upon Turkey in 1881, upon Greece in 1897, and upon China at various times for limited purposes. Through the League of Nations a degree of international financial control has been established over Austria, Hungary, Bulgaria, Greece, Danzig, and Esthonia.

The implications of these phenomena in the development of modern imperialism will be discussed in the following chapter. Consideration will also be given elsewhere[1] to the problem of inter-Allied debts and reparations. These problems involve loans from government to government, or financial claims advanced by governments against other governments. Intergovernmental loans constitute an unusual arrangement in international finance, resorted to ordinarily only in time of war. During peace, governments in need of money borrow it by selling bonds to private investors at home or abroad. All that has been said in the present discussion applies not to intergovernmental loans, but only to loans extended by private individuals or corporations to foreign individuals, corporations, or governments. Here it is sufficient to emphasize again that the power of private bankers and investors to lend or withhold money, to export or to refuse to export capital has been regularly employed by the governments of the Great Powers as an instrument of national policy to achieve diplomatic purposes. These purposes have sometimes reflected directly the pecuniary interests of the lenders and investors; they have almost always served these interests even when they have been inspired by patriots and politicians rather than by entrepreneurs and profiteers.

But more often than not the purposes have been those of *haute politique*, involving larger stakes of diplomacy than interest payments and premiums and reflecting the power-prestige-and-profit goals of the patriotic bourgeoisie as a whole. The interests of particular entrepreneurs, concessionaires, and coupon clippers have been utilized by governments to serve these larger purposes quite as often as they have themselves been the objects of governmental solicitude. In the words of one commentator describing the political rôle of capital exports in pre-war Europe:

Capital was called upon to abstain from investment in the lands of potential enemies. It was urged or commanded into the service of allies. It was encouraged to develop the areas that were within the political system of the country where it accumulated. It was upheld in ventures which sustained a national political ambition or hope. In France and Germany, and within the alliances which they headed, it came to be commonly regarded as a servant of national purposes rather

[1] See pp. 569f. below.

than as ordinary private possession to be disposed of in accordance with the private judgment and on the private risk of the owner.[1]

While nationalistic bankers and investors have found it lucrative to wrap themselves in the national flag, to call upon governments to protect their interests abroad, and to drink deeply of the profits of patriotism, patriotic statesmen in the pursuit of diplomatic prestige, political influence, and imperial possessions have at the same time found bankers and investors willing tools of the politics of power. Here again a mutually advantageous combination of patriots and profit-seekers shapes the policies of economic nationalism and impels the nation-states to action in the international arena.

It is clear, then, that no phase of economic contacts across national frontiers has been left free from governmental interference designed to increase national power and to enhance the profits of those able to bend governments to their will. The reciprocally beneficial cooperation of profitable patriotism and patriotic profiteering which has been designated as "economic nationalism" has shaped governmental policies toward every aspect of human activity affecting the power of States and the production and distribution of wealth. In the acquisitive societies of the machine age, those with economic power and political influence have been able to enlist governmental support in their quest for profits at home and abroad. In the competitive State System of the modern nations, governments seeking to enhance national power have been able to enlist the aid of profit-seekers in their quest for ample military man power, raw materials, national self-sufficiency, and imperial dominions. The values, attitudes, and ideology of patriotism have enabled both the profit-seekers and the statesmen to identify their particular interest with those of the whole national community. And the great mass of patriotic workers, farmers, voters, and taxpayers in each nation have been led to accept this identification and to give their support to all manner of profit-and-power designs, even at their own expense. The resulting conflicts between the nation-states for raw materials, for commodity markets, and for investment markets have contributed powerfully to war and have come perilously close to bringing about a catastrophic collapse of the world economy built up by capitalistic industrialism. But the policies of economic nationalism have served the interests of patriots and profit-seekers, and as long as the nation-states are composed of patriots who permit profit-seekers to dictate governmental policies, economic nationalism will remain one of the permanent patterns of national policy in the Western State System.

[1] Herbert Feis, *Europe: The World's Banker* 1870–1914, 1930, pp. 465–466.

SUGGESTED READINGS

Ashley, P.: *Modern Tariff History*, New York, E. P. Dutton & Co., Inc., 1920.

Borchard, E. M.: *The Diplomatic Protection of Citizens Abroad*, New York, Banks Law, 1915.

Carr-Saunders, A. M.: *The Population Problem*, New York, Oxford University Press, 1922.

Davenport, E. H., and S. R. Cooke: *The Oil Trusts and Anglo-American Relations*, New York, The Macmillan Company, 1924.

Day, C.: *History of Commerce*, New York, Longmans, Green & Co., 1925.

Delaisi, F.: *Oil, Its Influence on Politics*, London, Labour, 1922.

Dennis, A. P.: *The Romance of World Trade*, New York, Henry Holt & Company, 1926.

Donaldson, J.: *International Economic Relations*, New York, Longmans, Green & Co., 1928.

Einzig, P.: *Finance and Politics*, New York, The Macmillan Company, 1932.

Feis, H.: *Europe—The World's Banker*, New Haven, Yale University Press, 1930.

Fisk, G. M., and P. S. Peirce: *International Commercial Policies*, New York, The Macmillan Company, 1923.

Fraser, H. F.: *Foreign Trade and World Politics*, New York, Crofts, 1932.

Gide, C., and C. Rist: *A History of Economic Doctrines*, New York, D. C. Heath & Company, 1915.

Kuczynski, R. R.: *The Balance of Births and Deaths*, New York, The Macmillan Company, 1928.

Leith, C. K.: *World Minerals and World Politics*, New York, McGraw-Hill Book Company, Inc., 1931.

Overlach, T. W.: *Foreign Financial Control in China*, New York, The Macmillan Company, 1919.

Pasvolsky, L.: *Economic Nationalism in the Danubian States*, New York, The Macmillan Company, 1928.

Reuter, E. B.: *Population Problems*, Philadelphia, J. B. Lippincott Company, 1923.

Smith, G. O.: *The Strategy of Minerals*, New York, D. Appleton & Company, 1919.

Spurr, J. E.: *Political and Commercial Geology and the World's Mineral Resources*, New York, McGraw-Hill Book Company, Inc., 1920.

Tawney, R. H.: *Religion and the Rise of Capitalism*, New York, Harcourt, Brace & Company, 1926.

Thompson, W. S.: *Population Problems*, New York, McGraw-Hill Book Company, Inc., 1930.

Harris Foundation Lectures, *Population*, Chicago, University of Chicago Press, 1930.

See also references at end of Chapter XIV, p. 587 below.

Chapter XI

THE QUEST FOR EMPIRE

1. IMPERIALISM OLD AND NEW

Take up the White Man's Burden—
    Send forth the best ye breed—
Go bind your sons to exile
    To serve your captives' need;
To wait in heavy harness,
    On fluttered fold and wild—
Your new-caught, sullen peoples,
    Half-devil and half-child.
                —Rudyard Kipling, 1899.

THAT patriotism and economic nationalism have contributed to the pursuit of policies of territorial aggrandizement on the part of the nation-states has been suggested in the preceding chapter. These policies have led to the most spectacular results in the backward regions of the globe, where native governments have been unable to offer effective resistance to the Great Powers. The latter have succeeded in partitioning most of the non-European world between themselves, sometimes by peaceful bargaining, sometimes by war. More than half of the world's land surface and almost half of its population are included in the colonies, protectorates, mandates, and spheres of influence of the imperial States. For every resident of Great Britain there are ten colonial subjects of the Crown. The colonial empire of Italy is six times as large as the mother country; that of France, twenty times; that of Portugal, twenty-three times; that of Belgium, eighty times.[1] Black men, brown men, and yellow men all over the earth have been subjected to political control by the seven Great Powers and by a number of lesser European Powers (Spain, Portugal, Belgium, The Netherlands, and Denmark) which retain colonial possessions. Political control has been sometimes preceded, and always followed, by economic contact through travel, trade, and investment. The resources and the labor of the backward regions have been exploited by nationals of the home States. Social interaction has led to the diffusion and interpenetration of cultures, with the backward culture in most cases being disintegrated or assimilated by that of the conqueror.

[1] P. T. Moon, *Imperialism and World Politics*, 1926, p. 1.

[374]

"Imperialism" is the collective and all-embracing term usually applied to these and related phenomena. This term, like most words ending in "ism," has a multitude of meanings, none of them clear and precise. Historians apply it generally to all situations in which States acquire colonies or build empires. They usually distinguish this process from that of simple conquest by limiting the application of the term to instances where the conquered are alien in language, culture, or race to the conquerors, or where noncontiguous overseas territory is acquired. Patriots employ "imperialism" as an epithet of opprobrium to describe the territorial ambitions of enemy States. Communists apply it to the historical epoch which they regard as marking the last stage of capitalism. From the point of view of the present study, imperialism is chiefly significant as a phase of the competitive struggle for power between the sovereign units of the Western State System. That struggle typically takes the form of efforts on the part of the nation-states to increase their power by extending their control over new land. In the modern period of western civilization, it has been easier for the States of Europe—and for the non-European States which have adopted the technology of Europe— to acquire new land at the expense of the small weak States or of the politically unorganized natives of the non-European world than to wrest contiguous territory from powerful neighbors. Conquest has followed the paths of least resistance and has reflected the dictates of interest and opportunity. The political partition and the economic exploitation of America, Asia, Africa, and the islands of the seven seas at the hands of the great States constitute the most grandiose and characteristic expression of the will to power in modern times. It is this process, with all its political, economic, and cultural ramifications, to which the term "imperialism" will be applied in the following pages.

Before tracing the historical development of modern imperialism and raising questions on motives, causes, and effects, it will be well to emphasize certain underlying factors which are the prerequisites of all successful empire-building. These factors are primarily technological in character. It may be assumed that all States, by virtue of their statehood, seek to expand their power as widely as possible and that their expansionist ambitions usually involve territorial aggrandizement. That some States succeed in such efforts, while others fail and still others are conquered and absorbed by rivals, is scarcely to be attributed to differences in values and purposes. It is rather due to what may be termed the "technological differential" between the various States and cultures of the world, i.e., to the varying degrees of technical skill and efficiency which prevail over the globe. Imperialism requires the exercise by a State of military and administrative authority at a distance from its centers of population and power. The exercise of such authority is easy or difficult, depending upon the tools of transportation, communication, and warfare available to the imperialists as compared with the tools in the hands of those who resist conquest. Successful imperialism is possible only for States whose technology is more effective for these purposes than the technology of the peoples over whom control is extended. If the level of technology in State *A*, for example, permits it to send troops and administrators with great rapidity and efficiency to distant points to conduct effective warfare in places far removed from its center, to have and to hold remote regions with relative ease by virtue of its superiority in communication and transportation, while State *B* can do these things only slowly, haltingly, and ineffectively, it is clear that State *A* will in all probability be more successful in creating a colonial empire than State *B*. If State *B*'s territory happens to be the object of State *A*'s imperialistic designs, State *B* will lose its territory and perhaps its independence, for its powers of resistance are much less than *A*'s powers of conquest. If the technological differential between the two States is less marked, if each can exert power as effectively as the other, it is unlikely that either will become the victim of the other. In every case the existing technological differential determines the possibilities and the probable success of policies of aggrandizement. These observations are as applicable to ancient or medieval imperialism as to their modern counterpart.

Now it so happens that in the course of the past five centuries the States of western European civilization have developed a technology enormously more effective for distant conquest than that possessed by the non-European cultures of the world. Controversies over the relative inferiority or superiority of civilizations is quite pointless, since no objective standards of judgment are available and each culture judges others by its own values. Whether the civilization of the white peoples of the West, in all of its aspects, is "superior" or "inferior" to that of Orientals, Africans, Amerindians, or Polynesians is a pointless and meaningless query. But that the *technology* which western civilization has developed is much more effective than that of other peoples cannot be gainsaid, for it has enabled the western populations to exploit natural resources, to amass wealth, and to increase production and consumption of material goods on a scale never before attained elsewhere. From the point of view of imperialism, this technology has enabled the western States to extend their power at great distances over remote peoples having a less effective technology. The conquest of the world by the western States can in no sense be attributed to the innate virtues of the white races as compared with black, yellow, red, or brown peoples, nor to the superiority of Christianity over Mohammedanism, Buddhism, Brahminism, or other non-Christian cults, nor to any inherent genius for politics or administration. It is due solely to the circumstance that western technology (and the economic system erected on the basis of that technology) has given to the western States enormously more effective devices of transportation, communication, and warfare than those possessed by non-European peoples.

With this circumstance clearly before us, we may briefly trace through the three major periods of western imperialism: (1) the epoch of commercial and naval imperialism on the part of the Atlantic seaboard States of Europe, dating roughly from 1492, the year of the discovery of America, to 1763, the year of the Peace of Paris; (2) the epoch of the partial dissolution of the old colonial empires and of a diminution of interest in colonies on the part of European governments, 1763–1881; and (3) the conquest of the world by the new imperial Powers and the creation of the present colonial empires during the period since 1881, the year of the French conquest of Tunis and the beginning of the partition of Africa on a large scale.

In the second half of the fifteenth century the peoples of western Europe invented or adapted to their own uses a number of devices which enabled their governments to exercise military and political power overseas much more effectively than had been possible hitherto. The general employment of gunpowder in warfare was perhaps the most significant of these developments. The invention of printing, the construction of larger, sturdier, and more seaworthy sailing vessels, the progress made in the sciences of navigation, geography, and astronomy, the improvements in road-building, carriage construction, and fortifications, and the elaboration of the institutions of banking and commerce also played their part in producing those economic and social changes usually associated with the transition from "medieval" to "modern" times. These devices greatly altered the technological differential between the European and non-European world to the advantage of the former. When competing Mediterranean merchants sought new routes to the Indies in order that they might import more cheaply and sell more profitably the spices, precious stones, drugs, dyes, perfumes, woods, and rare fabrics of the Orient, they found ships and navigators at their service capable of doing what had not been done before—sailing around Africa, crossing the Atlantic, exploring distant sea routes, and finally circumnavigating the globe.

The governments of the European States at once perceived the possibilities of increasing their power and wealth by assisting their merchants in the quest for profits, their missionaries in the quest for converts, their navigators and explorers in the quest for adventure, fame, and fortune. They accordingly organized commercial and colonizing companies, fitted out exploring expeditions, and developed their sea power as a means to the attainment of this purpose. And when Negroes, Hindus, Arabs, South Sea Islanders, or Amerindians offered resistance to conquest, the European States sent out military and naval expeditions to confer upon them by force the blessings of Christianity, to save them from temptation by relieving them of their riches, or in some cases to exterminate them in order that white men might take their lands. The establishment of political control over the newly conquered regions seemed a necessary step to foster commerce and promote economic exploitation. Each European State was determined to monopolize for itself and for its subjects as many of the new opportunities as possible. The tools of resistance available to the victims of these ambitions were no match for the tools of the conquerors. The bow and arrow, the spear, the lance, the canoe, and the small sailing craft could not cope with the blunderbuss, the cannon, the galleon, and the armed man-of-war. The non-European peoples were consequently vanquished and great colonial empires were established by the Atlantic seaboard States which possessed navigators, ships, and sea power and had direct access to the great ocean highways.

If European technology in the sixteenth and seventeenth centuries was superior to that of the non-European peoples, it was still feeble and ineffective by the standards of the twentieth century. The path of empire was arduous and beset with difficulties, delays, and detours of all kinds. Empire-building was accordingly a slow and painful process, requiring not years or decades, but generations and centuries. The old colonial empires were created very gradually. Portugal first rose to brief commercial ascendancy and conquered the Spice Islands in the East Indies, Angola on the west African coast, a strip of East Africa opposite Madagascar, Brazil in South America, and other scattered possessions. Portuguese sea power was unequal to the task of maintaining this empire, however, and it suffered partial dissolution at the end of the sixteenth century. Spain conquered most of the New World, as well as various Pacific islands, and waxed wealthy and powerful with the gold and silver of the Aztecs and the Incas. The old Spanish empire was the largest, richest, and most imposing of the colonial domains, but Spanish power rapidly declined in the sixteenth century, owing to policies of ruthless exploitation, mercantilistic monopoly, and religious intolerance. The destruction of the Armada by the English and the elements in 1588 foreshadowed the end of Spain's overseas domain.

In the first half of the seventeenth century, The Netherlands rose to a position of commercial and naval supremacy. The Dutch conquered most of the Portuguese possessions in the East Indies and established settlements on the Atlantic coast of North and South America. But Dutch sea power was worsted in contests with England, and The Netherlands soon fell to the rank of a second and then of a third-rate power. France entered the lists later and established footholds in Canada, the Great Lakes region, the Mississippi Valley, and India. This large empire was not settled by Frenchmen, but was feebly held by scattered military posts unsupported by adequate sea power. England, having vanquished Spain and The Netherlands, entered the arena last of all, in the early seventeenth century. But the English colonies of North America were settlement colonies with a large and growing white population, and the constant growth of English sea power insured English colonial supremacy. In the long combat with France, England finally triumphed, both in India and in North America. The first great epoch of European imperialism thus came to an end with England holding North America east of the Mississippi and north of the Great Lakes, much of India, and various possessions in the East and West Indies, Africa, and the Pacific. Spain still held most of South America, all of Central America and Mexico, North America west of the Mississippi, the Philippine Islands in the East Indies, and smaller scattered islands. Portugal retained Brazil, the Azores, the Madeiras, the Cape Verde Islands, and portions of the African coastline, while the Dutch held the major portion of the East Indies and the Cape of Good Hope in South Africa. The French colonial empire had all but disappeared.

The period between 1763 and 1880 was a century of the decline of commercial and naval imperialism, the partial dissolution of the old empires, the agrarian expansion of Russia and the United States, and the full flowering of industrial capitalism and nationalism in Europe. Great Britain lost her Atlantic seaboard colonies in the American Revolution. Spain and Portugal lost their western empires in the Latin American Revolutions. Mercantilism and the doctrines of the old colonialism fell into disrepute. France, to be sure, conquered Algeria in the 1830's and Great Britain took control of Australia, New Zealand, South Africa, and other overseas regions. But in general, European governments lost interest in colonies and came to regard them as a wasteful and unprofitable extravagance. While the old empires decayed, two new empires—or, more accurately, two States of continental proportions—came into prominence in world politics. Tsarist Russia continued its land-hungry, military imperialism, pushing eastward and southward into central Asia and toward the Pacific. At the same time, the young giant of the New World, the United States, extended its power across the North American continent at the expense of France, Spain, and Mexico. Other Powers remained quiescent.

Viewed in retrospect, this century was but an interlude between the old and the new imperialism. It was a period during which the western States were revolutionizing their technology and gathering their energies for another epoch of overseas expansion, destined to overshadow completely all earlier achievements. The new drives to imperialism came from the Industrial Revolution and the cult of the nation-state, from the new

[379]

capitalism and the new nationalism, from entrepreneurs, exporters, and investors, and from patriots, thirsty for national power and glory. The advent of the machine industry produced a direct effect upon the technological differential between the western States and the non-European world. In the realm of transportation, the wooden sailing vessel, the stagecoach, and the mud highway were in course of time replaced by the steel steamship, the steam railway, the concrete road, the bicycle, the motor car, the electric line, and the airplane. In the realm of communication, the old modes of dispatching messages by horseback, stagecoach or ship gave way to the telegraph, the telephone, the radio, and modern postal services. In the realm of warfare, the pistol, the blunderbuss, and the muzzle-loading cannon were replaced by revolvers, rifles, machineguns, heavy mobile artilery, armored cars, tanks, dreadnaughts, submarines, bombing planes, and other strange weapons. Formerly difficult or insuperable problems of distant military operation and remote colonial administration became child's play for those with the new technology at their disposal. The non-European peoples now found European technology to be not two or five or ten times more effective than their own, but one hundred or five hundred or even one thousand times more effective. A single modern cruiser could destroy with ease a vast squadron of sailing vessels. A single battery of modern artillery could demolish the strongest fortification of the pre-machine age. A single machine-gun company or a few airplanes could put to flight an enormous army equipped with more antiquated weapons. In short, the Industrial Revolution placed at the disposal of the western States tools of colonial conquest and administration of a range and potency inconceivable in any earlier period.

The indirect economic effects of the new technology have been as significant for imperialism as its direct effects upon the political and military power of governments. The productivity of the new industry was many times greater than that of the old handicraft economy. An enormous flood of goods of all kinds poured out of the mills and factories, seeking purchasers wherever they might be found. Population in the industrial States doubled, trebled, and quadrupled. Standards of living ascended dizzily. Home markets soon became glutted, in spite of increasing populations and rising living standards. Farmers and manufacturers turned abroad for an outlet. The total foreign trade of the world, estimated at $1,400,000,000 in 1800, grew to $4,000,000,000 by 1850, $10,000,000,000 by 1870, $20,100,000,000 by 1900, $40,400,000,000 by 1913, and $65,200,-000,000 by 1927. The great markets of the Orient and of Latin America became spheres of keen competition among rival national groups of entrepreneurs and exporters. The rich natural resources of Africa, Asia, and the Americas were demanded in ever greater quantity to feed the seemingly insatiable hunger of the god of the machine. As fortunes were accumulated by the profit-makers, as great sums of liquid capital were piled up, the new captains of industry and finance turned abroad for investment markets as well as for commodity markets. The backward areas of the earth—rich in resources or in labor power or in consumptive capacity, but poor in capital and undeveloped industrially and commercially—became happy hunting grounds for the profit-seekers of western capitalism. From western Europe, from the United States, from westernized Japan there poured forth a deluge of ships, goods, and money, inundating the rest of the world.

That these economic developments led to a revival of imperialism on a grandiose scale was due to the social and political changes which accompanied them. The economic consequences of the Industrial Revolution brought into political power in every State which it affected the new bourgeoisie of manufacturing entrepreneurs, merchants, exporters, brokers, bankers, capitalists, and concessionaires. The advent of this class to political ascendency meant that it could dictate or influence governmental policies in its own interests. It likewise meant, as has been suggested above, an intensification and popularization of the cult of the nation-state throughout the western world. With the end of laissez-faire individualism came also an end of the old indifference toward colonies. Profit-seekers bent their governments to their own ends and reaped a rich harvest from the exploitation of the backward regions over which their governments established political control. Patriotic statesmen perceived new elements of national power and prestige in overseas possessions and used profit-seekers for the accomplishment of the purposes of high policy. Imperial conquest was easy with new weapons, new ships, new money, and new men, and patriotic voters approved and cheered. The new industrial and financial capitalism of the nineteenth century, combined with the new nationalism, bred imperialism as prolifically as had the old commercial capitalism and the nascent nationalism of the sixteenth century. The new imperialism was an inevitable outgrowth of the economic and political forces generated by the new technology, and the new technology in turn enabled the nation-states to create empires which would have dazzled the imagination of Alexander, Caesar, or Napoleon.

Within the brief period of three decades—roughly from 1880 to 1910— the imperial Powers partitioned the world between themselves. Within a single generation, larger colonial empires were established than had been created during the three centuries of the old imperialism. Great Britain conquered an imperial domain upon which the sun never sets. France created the second largest colonial empire of the world. Imperial Russia pushed onward into Asia. Two new Powers, Italy and Germany, entered the field belatedly and carved out empires of their own in regions not yet seized by their rivals. The United States reached out into the Pacific and the Caribbean for new territory, power, and profits. The new Japan created a colonial empire in eastern Asia and the western Pacific. Lesser States kept what they had (*e.g.*, Portugal and The Netherlands) or carved out new empires (*e.g.*, Belgium). Only Spain lost her remaining overseas possessions. By 1914 the process of peaceful partitioning was practically completed and the new epoch entered upon the phase of armed combat between the empires for world supremacy.

2. THE EMPIRES OF THE NATION-STATES

There was nothing left for us to do but to take them all, and to educate the Filipinos and uplift and civilize and Christianize them, and by God's grace do the very best we could by them as our fellow men, for whom Christ also died. —WILLIAM McKINLEY, to the Methodist Ministers.

To retell the tale of the building of the new empires and to describe the way in which they are governed would require many more pages than can be devoted to the task in a work of this kind. But some general conception of the colonial possessions and the imperial interests of the Great Powers is indispensable to an understanding of the patterns of contemporary international politics. A brief survey of the empires will suffice for this purpose.

The British Empire, or, more accurately, the "British Commonwealth of Nations" as it has been officially designated since 1926, is by far the largest of the imperial domains. It is scattered over the six continents and the seven seas and includes within its frontiers something like one-fifth of the land area of the globe and one-quarter of its population. It differs from the other empires in that its largest units are self-governing Dominions, largely inhabited by the descendants of those who emigrated overseas from the mother country. Viewed as a whole, however, it represents not an empire created by outward-moving settlers, colonizing empty land, but an empire built up by conquest and by the imposition of British rule upon alien peoples. Fewer than seventy million of its four hundred and ninety million inhabitants are of the white race, and of these forty-six millions live in the mother country. Of the white British subjects, several millions are of non-English stock, such as the French in Canada, the Dutch in South Africa, and the Irish of the Irish Free State. If the Empire was not precisely built up inadvertently in periods of absence of mind, as some have alleged, it does nevertheless represent the result of a long process of accretion, expansion, and internal evolution.

The richest and most populous unit of the Empire is India. Early in the seventeenth century trading posts were established along the coasts by the British East India Company, an organization of private merchants who received a charter from the Crown, giving them a monopoly of British trade with India and authorizing them to rule over the natives

THE BRITISH COMMONWEALTH OF NATIONS
(M. = League of Nations Mandate)

Political divisions	Area, square miles	Population
Great Britain..........................	89,041	46,200,000
India................................	1,819,000	353,000,000
Dominions:		
Canada............................	3,690,043	10,300,000
Australia...........................	2,974,581	6,500,000
Union of South Africa..............	471,917	8,100,000
Newfoundland and Labrador.........	162,734	275,000
New Zealand.......................	103,410	1,512,000
Irish Free State....................	26,601	3,000,000
Dominion totals..................	7,429,286	29,687,000
Colonies and Protectorates		
In Europe:		
Cyprus............................	3,584	349,000
Malta.............................	122	233,000
Gibraltar..........................	2	16,000
European totals..................	3,708	598,000
In Africa:		
Anglo-Egyptian Sudan..............	1,008,100	5,606,000
Nigeria...........................	366,781	19,264,000
Tanganyika (M.)...................	373,494	5,000,000
South West Africa (M.)............	322,394	275,500
Northern Rhodesia.................	287,950	1,310,000
Bechuanaland......................	275,000	150,000
Kenya............................	221,089	3,000,000
Southern Rhodesia.................	150,344	1,058,000
Uganda...........................	94,204	3,410,000
Gold Coast........................	91,690	3,120,000
Somaliland........................	68,000	347,000
Nyasaland.........................	47,949	1,360,000
Cameroon (M.).....................	34,236	7,050
Sierra Leone.......................	31,000	1,542,000
Togoland (M.).....................	13,240	276,000
Basutoland........................	11,716	500,000
Swaziland.........................	6,704	123,000
Gambia...........................	4,002	240,000
Zanzibar..........................	1,020	217,000
Mauritius Island and Dependencies.......	809	414,000
Seychelles Island...................	156	28,000
St. Helena Island..................	47	4,000
Ascension Islands..................	34	220
Tristan de Cunha..................	3	130
African totals....................	3,409,962	47,251,900

THE BRITISH COMMONWEALTH OF NATIONS.—(*Continued*)

Political divisions	Area, square miles	Population
In America:		
British Guiana..........................	89,480	310,000
British Honduras.......................	8,598	51,000
Falkland Islands and South Georgia.......	5,618	3,500
Jamaica...............................	4,450	1,000,000
The Bahamas...........................	4,404	61,000
Trinidad...............................	1,862	378,000
Leeward Islands........................	708	125,000
Windward Islands.......................	516	185,000
Cayman Islands........................	225	6,000
Barbadoes.............................	166	170,000
Turks and Calcos Islands................	166	5,000
Tobago................................	114	26,000
Bermuda..............................	19	31,000
American totals.....................	116,326	2,351,500
In Asia:		
Palestine and Trans-Jordan (M.)..........	70,000	1,295,000
Sarawak...............................	42,000	600,000
British North Borneo...................	31,106	295,000
Federated Malay States.................	27,648	1,661,000
Ceylon................................	25,332	5,479,000
Other Malay States.....................	23,355	1,460,000
Brunei................................	2,500	30,000
Straits Settlement......................	1,600	1,135,000
Socotra...............................	1,382	12,000
Hongkong and Territory.................	391	1,075,000
Bahrein Islands........................	250	120,000
Maldive Islands........................	115	70,000
Aden (including Perim).................	80	50,000
Asiatic totals........................	225,759	13,282,000
In Oceania:		
New Guinea (M.)........................	91,300	404,500
Papua Territory........................	90,540	276,000
British Solomon Islands.................	14,600	150,000
Fiji Colony............................	7,435	180,000
New Hebrides (with France)..............	5,700	51,000
Western Samoa (M.)....................	1,133	44,500
Tonga Islands..........................	390	27,000
Gilbert and Ellice Islands...............	180	30,000
Nauru Island (M.)......................	9	2,700
Other Pacific Islands...................	60	300
Oceania totals........................	211,347	1,166,000
Grand totals........................	13,304,429	493,536,400

within their sphere of commercial operation. Since the disintegration of the Empire of the Great Mogul, India had been divided into warring principalities in whose quarrels the Europeans found an excellent opportunity for intervention. The British East India Company and the French East India Company became rivals for commercial and political supremacy, with the former triumphing over the latter in the Seven Years' War (1756–1763) and undertaking all of the functions of government in the portions of the country under its control. Huge profits were made by the members of the company and by its agents, who were almost completely free from governmental supervision prior to 1784 and were then subjected to merely a loose control by parliamentary commissions. The area of British power was gradually extended by conquest. In 1818 the Mahratta Confederacy of Princes was overthrown and its land in central and western India annexed. In 1849 the Sikhs of the Punjab were similarly conquered and brought under British rule. A series of wars on the eastern frontier culminated in the annexation of Burma in 1886. Baluchistan became a province of British India in 1903.

Meanwhile, native resentment at alien control had flamed out in the great Sepoy Rebellion of 1857, which was crushed two years later after extensive fighting and the customary atrocities on both sides. An act of Parliament of 1858 abolished the East India Company and transferred its powers to the Crown. A large part of the country was left under the control of the native princes, with British advisers directing them. The administration of the remainder was placed in the hands of a viceroy, assisted by executive and legislative councils, both appointed by the British Government and acting under the supervision of the Secretary of State for India. Under the pressure of Indian nationalist agitation for autonomy, a limited degree of native participation in the government has been permitted. In the post-war period, constitutional changes in the administration have failed to satisfy nationalist demands for self-government (Swaraj), and under the leadership of Mahatma Gandhi, a native movement of passive resistance, boycott, and non-cooperation has been launched, the final outcome of which is not yet apparent at the time of writing.

In so far as any consciously formulated and consistently pursued purpose has played a part in the creation of the empire, that purpose may be said to be that of safeguarding by all possible means the channels of trade between India and Great Britain. Considerations of trade and strategy along the line from Manchester to Calcutta played a prominent part in the acquisition of coaling stations, naval bases, colonies, and protectorates along the two routes from England to India—one around Africa and the other through the Mediterranean, the Red Sea, and the Arabian Sea. Both routes, before they divide west of Gibraltar, lie along the coast of

Portugal, and Portugal has been more or less under British influence since the early seventeenth century. The southern route circumscribes the African continent. Along its course Great Britain controls Sierra Leone, the Gold Coast, South Africa, Tanganyika territory, Kenya colony, and scattered islands in the south Atlantic and in the western Indian Ocean. The shorter Mediterranean-Red Sea route is of even greater strategic significance. British hegemony in the Mediterranean is assured by the possession of Gibraltar, Malta, and Cyprus, and in the Red Sea by possession of Aden, British Somaliland, and the Sudan, and by effective control of Egypt and the Suez Canal.[1] In the region between the Mediterranean and the Persian Gulf, British power is secured through control of Palestine and Iraq. The security of north-south communications between the two routes has been attained by acquiring Rhodesia, Uganda, and other points in Africa between Cairo and the Cape. The vital line of imperial defense has been extended eastward in two directions to include Malacca, Singapore, Sarawak, North Borneo, British New Guinea, Australia, and New Zealand, on a line from India to the southern Pacific; and Hongkong and Weihaiwei on a line curving northeastward around Asia from Singapore to the Yellow Sea. In the western hemisphere the Empire includes Canada, Newfoundland, British Honduras, Jamaica, the Bermudas, the Bahamas, a string of Caribbean islands, British Guiana in South America and sundry islands in the south Atlantic and the south Pacific.

These segments of the globe-girdling arcs of British imperial power have been put together through a mixed process of settlement and conquest, involving the imposition of British rule upon native peoples, the granting of autonomy to British settlers, or the seizure of territories of other States. From a stategic point of view, Egypt and South Africa may be regarded as the two most important links in the line of imperial defense, for they command the two routes to India. The Suez Canal, the construction of which was begun in 1859, lies entirely within Egyptian territory. The government of the country was heavily indebted to European bankers, who encouraged its extravagant borrowing. In 1876, the Khedive offered to sell a large number of shares of his Suez Canal stock as a means of extricating himself from his difficulties. The British Prime Minister, Disraeli, with an eye open for imperial bargains, purchased the shares for the British Government. In the following year Great Britain and France took over the management of Egyptian finances. In 1882 the disgruntled natives, under the leadership of Arabi Pasha, rallied to the cry of "Egypt for the Egyptians!" and rose in revolt against the Khedive and

[1] In a note of October 7, 1924, Prime Minister Ramsay MacDonald declared "it is no less true today than in 1922 that the security of the communications of the British Empire in Egypt remains a vital British interest and that absolute certainty for the free passage of British ships is the foundation on which the entire defensive strategy of the British Empire rests." Parliamentary Command Papers 2269, 1924.

the foreign bankers. France failed to act, and a British army marched in, quelled the uprising, took control of military as well as financial affairs, and seemingly prepared for an indefinite sojourn. Under Mohammed Ahmed—the "Mahdi"—the fanatical Moslems of the Sudan attacked the invaders in 1885, massacred Gordon and the British garrison at Khartoum, and defied British power for more than a decade, until the dervishes were crushed by Kitchener at Omdurman in 1898. The Sudan became an Anglo-Egyptian "condominium." France relinquished her claims in 1904 and Egypt, still nominally under the suzerainty of the Sultan, passed under British control. It was officially proclaimed a protectorate in 1914. Nationalist agitation for self-government continued, however, and in February of 1922 Great Britain recognized the "independence" of Egypt, subject to reservations regarding the Sudan, the security of communications, defense, and the protection of foreign interests and minorities. Egyptian resentment at these reservations led to further friction, which culminated in the assassination on November 19, 1924 of Sir Lee Stack, British Governor-general of the Sudan and Commander of the Egyptian army. Great Britain dispatched an ultimatum, demanded an apology and an indemnity, seized the customs houses at Alexandria, and compelled Egypt to accept a status which amounts to a disguised protectorate with a British high commissioner and other financial and military advisers always at hand to make Egyptian policy conform to British interests.

South Africa was settled by Dutch colonists in the seventeenth century and remained a Dutch colony until 1814, when it was awarded to Great Britain at the Congress of Vienna. As a result of constant friction between the old Dutch and the new English settlers, the Dutch packed up bag and baggage in 1836 and migrated northward, where they established the two independent Boer republics of Transvaal and the Orange Free State. In 1877 Great Britain announced the annexation of the South African Republic (Transvaal). The Dutch successfully resisted this attack and Great Britain again recognized their independence in 1884. But the discovery of the Rand gold deposits led to a rush of Englishmen into the Transvaal and resulted in the Boers being outnumbered by the Uitlanders or foreigners, who sought to control the government and transfer authority to Great Britain. Cecil Rhodes, millionaire gold and diamond prospector, conspired with Joseph Chamberlain, British Colonial Secretary, to bring on a war which would result in the annexation of Transvaal to the Empire. The spectacular "Jameson raid" of 1895 failed in its purpose but convinced the Boers that they must prepare to resist British aggression. When they refused a British demand that suffrage rights be granted to the Uitlanders, war broke out in 1899. Under the leadership of Paul Kruger, the tiny Boer republics defeated the British and compelled the British

Government to mobilize a large army and to send her ablest generals, Roberts and Kitchener, to South Africa. A British force of 250,000 troops was required to overcome the 40,000 Boer soldiers. The conflict, which Lloyd George called "a war for 45 per cent dividends," cost Great Britain £250,000,000 and 30,000 lives. Not until 1902 was Boer independence extinguished and the Transvaal and Orange Free State reduced to colonial status. In 1906–1907 the new Liberal Ministry granted responsible government to the Boers, and in 1909 the Union of South Africa was created as a federation of the four provinces of the Cape of Good Hope, Transvaal, Orange Free State, and Natal. This grant of dominion self-government to the Boers has insured their loyalty to the Empire, though the future of the Union is clouded by growing unrest among the native Negro population, which greatly outnumbers the whites and is subjected to a status of political, economic, and social inferiority.

The other self-governing Dominions of the Empire, with the exception of Ireland, are "settlement" colonies rather than conquests. Canada, to be sure, was conquered from the French in 1763, but the French Canadians remained loyal during the American Revolution and were subsequently outnumbered by English-speaking immigrants. Following the suppression of the rebellion of 1837, self-government was gradually introduced. On the basis of the report of Lord Durham (1839), the British North America Act of 1867 united all of the colonies except Newfoundland into the present federation of the Dominion of Canada, which consists of nine self-governing provinces and a central government independent in all important respects. Newfoundland is a self-governing Dominion in its own right. New Zealand and the arid island continent of Australia were claimed for the British Crown by Captain Cook at the end of the eighteenth century. Australia was first used as a penal colony and was gradually settled by immigrants from England. In 1900 the six Australian colonies of New South Wales, Queensland, Victoria, South Australia, West Australia, and Tasmania were united into a self-governing federal union. New Zealand was formally annexed to the Empire in 1839. In 1907 it was organized as a self-governing Dominion. Ireland received Dominion status in the Irish Free State Act of 1921. The six Dominions of the Empire are all theoretically subject to control by the Parliament at Westminister, in which they have no representation, and in form their constitutions are simply parliamentary statutes. In fact, however, the constitutions are quasi-treaties which confer upon the Dominions rights of complete local autonomy and self-government. The British Crown remains the symbol of imperial unity, but the royal governors-general in the Dominions occupy the same position with respect to the Dominion parliaments and cabinets that the King occupies with respect to the Parliament and Cabinet of the United Kingdom, *i.e.*, that of a figurehead with power to recommend and to admonish, but with no power to control policy and administration. The Dominions are all independent members of the League of Nations. They maintain their own diplomatic services, enter into treaties with foreign governments, and in general conduct themselves like sovereign States.

The Empire as a whole, including Great Britain, India, the Dominions, the Crown colonies, the protectorates, and the mandates, has gradually evolved away from the form of political organization prevailing before the American Revolution, when Parliament claimed the right to tax and legislate for all the parts, and has become a federation of self-governing units. The new colonial policy of the nineteenth century repudiated the monopolistic economic doctrine of mercantilism and sought to achieve imperial unity through compromise and cooperation rather than through dictation by the home government. That imperial loyalty has been attained is shown by the fact that in the Boer War and in the Great War the Dominions fully supported Great Britain. At the end of the nineteenth century, Joseph Chamberlain pleaded eloquently for imperial federation. In 1887 the first Imperial Conference was held as a means of discussing common problems of trade and defense. Such conferences have been held at fairly regular intervals ever since. The 1926 conference took cognizance of the new constitutional structure of the Empire and gave it its present official name of the British Commonwealth of Nations. This title suggests that the Empire, like the Trinity, is both singular and plural at the same time. At the 1930 conference the Statute of Westminster recognized the equality of the Dominions with Great Britain in the Commonwealth. Thus far the integrating and cohesive forces within the Empire, making for closer imperial relations, would appear to be more powerful than the centrifugal forces making for complete local independence and imperial disintegration. The Imperial Economic Conference at Ottawa in the summer of 1932 adopted measures designed to make the Empire more nearly self-sufficient commercially, but the divergent interests and the protectionist policies of its several units make "imperial preference" a slogan rather than a reality and preclude any complete customs union.

The colonial empire of France is the second largest in the world in area and population. Unlike the British Empire, it represents less a reconstruction and expansion of the old imperial dominions of the eighteenth century than a creation *de novo* of the nineteenth century. The old French colonial empire collapsed under the blows of Britain in the Seven Years' War. By 1815 French overseas possessions included only five Indian ports, French Guiana in South America, Guadaloupe and Martinique in the West Indies, and a few scattered islands. The building of the new empire began with the conquest of Algeria in North Africa in the 1830's. In the face of stout resistance and numerous revolts, French power was pushed into the

THE FRENCH EMPIRE
(M. = League of Nations Mandates)

Political divisions	Area, square miles	Population
France	212,659	41,840,000
Colonies and Protectorates		
In Africa:		
French West Africa	1,440,400	13,542,000
French Equatorial Africa	982,049	2,846,000
Algeria	847,522	6,065,000
Madagascar	228,707	3,600,000
Morocco	223,000	4,229,000
Cameroon (M.)	166,489	1,900,000
Tunis	50,000	2,160,000
Togoland (M.)	21,893	730,500
Somali Coast	5,790	86,000
Reunion Island	970	172,000
Comoro Islands	790	110,000
African totals	3,967,610	35,440,500
In America:		
French Guiana	32,000	44,000
Guadaloupe and dependencies	688	230,000
Martinique	385	245,000
St. Pierre and Miquelon	93	4,000
American totals	33,166	523,000
In Asia:		
Laos	96,500	838,000
Cambodia	62,550	2,500,000
Tonkin	40,530	7,160,000
Annam	39,758	5,172,000
Cochin-China	26,476	4,000,000
Kwangchow	190	208,000
French Indo-China (total)	265,004	19,878,000
Syria (M.)	60,000	3,000,000
French India (Pondicherry, Karikal, Chandernagor, Mahe, and Yanaon)	196	290,000
Asiatic totals	352,200	23,168,000
In Oceania:		
New Caledonia and dependencies	7,650	47,000
Tahiti and other islands in the Eastern Pacific	1,520	31,000
Oceania totals	9,170	78,000
Grand totals	4,547,805	101,049,500

interior. French settlements were established along the Ivory and Guinea Coasts in the 1840's. Under the Second Empire (1852–1870) control of Algeria was consolidated, New Caledonia and adjacent islands in the Pacific were acquired (1853), expeditions were sent into Cochin-China and Annam (1858) to avenge the murder of missionaries, and a French protectorate was established over Cambodia (1863). The attempt to conquer Mexico (1863–1866) ended in disaster.

Upon the foundations laid by its predecessors, the Third French Republic built an imposing colonial edifice to compensate itself for its loss of power and prestige in Europe and to protect merchants, missionaries, investors, and concessionaires. The major fields of French imperial expansion were north and central Africa, the southwestern Indian Ocean, and southeastern Asia. In 1881 French troops descended upon Tunis in the name of protecting Algeria from raiding tribesmen. The interests of investors and of holders of Tunisian bonds were safeguarded by the conversion of the country into a French protectorate. From the foothold already established in Senegal, on the west African coast, expeditions were sent up the Senegal River toward Timbuktu and westward along the Niger Valley. French Equatorial Africa north of the Congo was acquired in 1884. By 1893 Mauretania, Dahomey, and the central Sudan were secured and a broad belt of French power stretched across the Sahara from the Guinea Coast on the south to Algeria and Tunis on the north. On the eastern coast of the Dark Continent France held a small but strategically valuable strip of Somaliland at the head of the Gulf of Aden. The agents of French imperialism pushed westward from Somaliland across Abyssinia and eastward from the French Sudan to converge on the headwaters of the Nile. But this was already a British sphere of influence. Following the meeting at Fashoda between Marchand and Kitchener in 1898, French ambitions yielded before British power and the two segments of the French empire in north Africa remain separated by Abyssinia and the Anglo-Egyptian Sudan. If British resistance to French encroachment in the Sudan was effective, German resistance to French encroachments in Morocco was not, and after several diplomatic crises most of this remnant of the Moslem world became a French protectorate in 1912.

Meanwhile, ancient claims to Madagascar, the huge island lying off the southeast coast of Africa, were vigorously pressed at the instigation of French property owners, naval officers, and expansionist diplomats. In 1885 a treaty of protectorate was concluded which led to endless difficulties, culminating in annexation in 1896. The conquest of Madagascar was completed by the ruthless repression of the native Hovas' resistance to the invaders. In southeastern Asia the government of the Republic utilized its position in Cambodia and Cochin-China to establish a protectorate over Annam and Tonkin in 1884, a procedure which led to an indecisive war with China. The annexation of Laos in 1892 completed the creation of French Indo-China. Among France's other oriental possessions are five ports in India, Kwangchow-wan in China, New Caledonia, Tahiti, and Syria, the last acquired as a mandate in 1922.

THE ITALIAN EMPIRE

Political divisions	Area, square miles	Population
Italy...................................	119,710	41,500,000
Colonies and Protectorates		
Tripolitania and Cyrenaica.................	710,980	800,000
Italian Somaliland........................	190,000	900,000
Eritrea...................................	45,754	510,000
Colonial totals...........................	946,734	2,210,000
Grand total..............................	1,066,444	43,710,000

Italy's imperial career was begun belatedly and was hampered by Italy's relative weakness as compared with Great Britain and France. Italian patriots and imperialists bitterly resented the French conquest of Tunis, but were unable to prevent its successful completion. Italy established a foothold in Eritrea on the Red Sea coast, north of French Somaliland, and in 1889 acquired a larger colony in Italian Somaliland, on the easternmost tip of the African shoreline. Italian designs against Abyssinia were frustrated by the crushing defeat of the invaders at the hands of the natives in the battle of Adowa (1896). A decade later Italy, France, and Great Britain all agreed to respect the independence of the Ethiopian kingdom. The French Government pledged itself not to oppose Italian ambition in Tripoli and in 1911 Italy waged a war upon Turkey which ended in the annexation of Tripoli and Cyrenaica. These provinces were united in the colony of Libya, which has been held with considerable difficulty and at great expense in the face of Arab rebellions. After the Great War its boundaries were extended westward with the consent of France, and eastward with the consent of Great Britain. Italy has acquired no colonial possessions outside of Africa.

The colonial empire of imperial Germany was likewise created belatedly and was lost in its entirety in the Great War. Between 1884 and 1890 Germany acquired Togoland on the Guinea Coast, Cameroon between Nigeria and French Equatorial Africa (extended to the Congo in the Franco-German settlement of 1911), German Southwest Africa between Portuguese Angola and British South Africa, and German East Africa between Lakes Victoria, Tanganyika, and Nyassa on the west and the Indian Ocean on the east. A general native rebellion in German East Africa in 1905 led to great loss of life before German authority was restored by the customary blood and iron methods of imperialists everywhere. In Asia and Oceania, Germany acquired Kiaochow in the Shantung peninsula as a leasehold from China (1899), the Bismarck Archipelago (1884), the Marshall Islands (1885), the Caroline Islands (1899), the Pelew Islands (1899), the Ladrone Islands (1899), and two of the Samoan group (1899). In 1884 Germany annexed the northeastern section of New Guinea (Kaiser Wilhelm's Land). These territories were all seized by the Allies in the Great War and by the peace settlement they passed to the victors as mandates of the League of Nations. Togoland and Cameroon were divided between Great Britain and France. Southwest Africa became a mandate of the Union of South Africa. German East Africa became a British mandate (Tanganyika), with the small western section known as Ruanda-Urundi becoming a Belgian mandate. Kiaochow, seized by Japan in 1914, was restored to China in 1922. The German Pacific islands north of the Equator became Japanese mandates, and those to the south became mandates of Great Britain, New Zealand, and Australia. Kaiser Wilhelm's Land likewise became an Australian mandate. Post-war Germany thus remains without overseas possessions of any kind.[1]

The only other States of western Europe with colonial empires are Spain, Portugal, The Netherlands, Belgium, and Denmark. Spain, once mistress of the greatest of all colonial empires, lost the last of her possessions in America and the Far East in 1898–1899. As a somewhat pathetic and expensive compensation for her losses, she obtained three strips of African coast: Spanish Morocco, opposite Gibraltar, Rio de Oro, opposite the Canary Islands, and Rio Muni on the Guinea Coast. The enormous losses of men and money incurred in the effort to suppress the revolt of Abd-el Krim in Morocco (1920–1925) contributed to the overthrow of the Spanish monarchy in April of 1931. Portugal, whose navigators and explorers first opened Africa to Europe in the fifteenth century, retains only Portuguese East Africa (Mozambique and Zambesia), Portuguese West Africa (Angola), Pourtugese Guinea, and St. Thomas, Prince's Island, the Cape Verde Islands, the Azores, and the Madeiras off the west coast. Portuguese efforts to unite the east and west African possessions were frustrated by Cecil Rhodes and the British Government in 1891. Portugal retains none of her American possessions and has in Asia only the ports of Goa in India and Macao in China. The Netherlands have retained a larger proportion of their old colonial empire, including Dutch Guiana in South America and, in southeastern Asia, Java, Sumatra, most of Borneo, the Celebes, and Dutch New Guinea, with the adjacent islands. The African empire of Belgium was the creation of King Leopold II, who became in-

[1] See table of Mandates, p. 612 below.

terested in the explorations of Livingstone and Stanley in the Congo basin
and who took the initiative in the formation of the "International Association for the Exploration and Civilization of Africa" in 1876. A Belgian
commercial company, the International Association of the Congo, was
formed two years later and in 1885 the "Congo Free State" with Leopold

COLONIAL EMPIRES OF THE MINOR POWERS

Political divisions	Area, square miles	Population
THE NETHERLANDS...........................	12,603	7,920,000
Colonies and Protectorates		
Borneo...........................	206,061	2,194,500
Molucca Islands	192,402	893,000
Island of Sumatra...........................	163,093	7,662,000
Island of Celebes...........................	73,160	4,226,600
Java and Madura...........................	51,057	41,719,500
Timor Archipelago...........................	24,530	1,656,600
Riau-Lingga Archipelago...........................	12,503	298,300
Bangka...........................	4,548	205,400
Bali and Lombok...........................	4,070	1,802,150
Billiton...........................	1,872	73,400
Total Dutch East Indies...........................	733,296	60,731,450
Dutch Guiana (Surinam)...........................	54,291	153,300
Dutch West Indies (Curacao)...........................	403	76,300
Colonial totals...........................	787,990	60,961,050
Grand total...........................	800,593	68,881,050
PORTUGAL...........................	35,490	6,200,000
Colonies and Protectorates		
In Africa:		
Angola...........................	487,071	2,522,000
Mozambique...........................	287,756	3,528,800
Guinea...........................	13,944	344,000
Cape Verde Islands...........................	1,517	150,150
Principe and St. Tome...........................	320	60,000
African totals...........................	787,608	6,604,950
In Asia:		
Timor...........................	7,330	451,600
Portuguese India (Goa, Damoa, Diu)...........................	1,638	570,500
Macao...........................	4	160,000
Asiatic totals...........................	8,972	1,182,100
Grand total...........................	832,070	13,987,050
SPAIN...........................	190,050	23,000,000
Colonies and Protectorates		
In Africa:		
Rio de Oro and Adrar...........................	109,200	500
Spanish Guinea...........................	10,036	140,000
Spanish Morocco...........................	7,700	600,000
Ifni...........................	965	20,000
Fernando Po and Adjacent Territory...........................	795	23,800
African total...........................	128,696	784,300
Grand total...........................	318,746	23,784,300
BELGIUM...........................	11,752	8,000,000
Colonies and Protectorates		
Belgian Congo...........................	900,654	8,500,000
Ruanda and Urundi (M.)...........................	21,429	3,000,000
Colonial total...........................	922,083	11,500,000
Grand total...........................	933,835	19,500,000
DENMARK...........................	16,576	3,500,000
Greenland...........................	46,740	15,000
Total...........................	63,316	3,515,000

as its personal sovereign was recognized by the Powers. Through the atrocious exploitation of native forced labor, Leopold and his fellow investors made millions from the trade in rubber, ivory, and palm oil. In 1908, after numerous scandals, "reforms" were introduced and the shrewd Leopold surrendered the Congo to the Belgian Government for a liberal compensation. The Belgian mandate of Ruanda-Urundi lies just west of the Belgian Congo. Denmark retains a somewhat controversial title to Greenland and is united with Iceland in a personal union under a common king.

Of the other empires of the Powers, the largest is that of Russia. The expansion of the Russian State differed from that of the States of western Europe in that it represented the spreading out over contiguous territory of a land-hungry agrarian population, rather than an imperialism of commerce, sea power, and investments over the ocean highways. The only noncontiguous possession ever acquired by Russia was Alaska, sold to the United States in 1867. This process of expansion brought under Russian power a large number of non-Russian peoples, some of them on a primitive cultural level. The power of the Tsardom was extended over a vast realm stretching from the Baltic and Black Seas to the Pacific, covering eastern Europe and northern Asia and comprising one-sixth of the land surface of the globe. The original Grand Duchy of Muscovy brought most of European Russia under its control by the end of the sixteenth century. The early Tsars of the Romanov dynasty (1613–1917) pushed Russian power eastward across Siberia and reached the Pacific before the end of the seventeenth century. Continued pressure westward and southward for outlets to the sea led to the founding of St. Petersburg in 1721, the annexation of Esthonia and Latvia from Sweden in the same year, the expulsion of the Turks from the north coast of the Black Sea, the partition of Poland at the end of the eighteenth century, the acquisition of Finland in 1809, and the occupation of Bessarabia in 1812. These conquests were followed in the nineteenth century by the penetration of Trans-Caucasia, central Asia, the Amur River region of the Pacific coast, and of Manchuria. Further Russian expansion in eastern Asia was checked by Japan, in central Asia by Great Britain, and in the Balkans and the Near East by Great Britain, France, Turkey, and later by Austria-Hungary and Germany. The Russian Revolution led to the independence of Finland, Esthonia, Latvia, Lithuania, and Poland, and the loss of Bessarabia to Rumania. The new Soviet Union remains, however, the largest of the Great Powers next to the British Empire, both in territory and in population. In Asia it has extended its control beyond the old limits, for the new Soviet spheres of influence include not only northern Manchuria, but Outer Mongolia and an undefined area of Chinese Turkestan north of Tibet.[1]

[1] See map, p. 486 below.

THE QUEST FOR EMPIRE

The American Empire

Political divisions	Area, square miles	Population
United States..............................	3,685,382	126,000,000
Possessions:		
Alaska..................................	586,400	60,000
Philippine Islands........................	114,400	12,200,000
Hawaiian Islands.........................	6,407	368,000
Porto Rico..............................	3,435	1,544,000
Panama Canal Zone......................	549	40,000
Guam...................................	206	18,500
Virgin Islands...........................	133	22,000
American Samoa.........................	76	10,050
Wake and Midway Islands.................	1	35
Total..................................	711,607	14,262,585
Grand total............................	4,396,989	140,262,585

The expansion of the United States prior to the twentieth century resembled that of Russia in that it was the expansion of an agrarian population across a contiguous territory of continental dimensions. Alaska was the only noncontiguous possession of the United States prior to 1898. In the last two years of the nineteenth century the United States annexed the Hawaiian Islands and Samoa, and seized Porto Rico, the Philippine Islands, and Guam as the fruits of victory of the Spanish-American War. Since 1900 the United States has embarked upon an active career of com-

The Japanese Empire
(M. = League of Nations Mandates)

Political divisions	Area, square miles	Population
Japan...................................	147,593	66,000,000
Colonies and Protectorates		
Manchukuo (Manchuria)................	363,610	29,000,000
Korea................................	85,228	21,000,000
Japanese Sakhalin (Karafuto)...........	13,935	295,000
Formosa..............................	13,890	4,600,000
Kwangtung............................	1,444	1,330,000
Marianne or Ladrone Islands (M.)........	....	66,500
Marshall Islands (M.)...................	829 (total)	9,700
Caroline Islands (M.)...................	....	23,400
Pescadores............................	50	....
Colonial total.......................	478,986	56,324,600
Grand total...........................	626,579	122,324,600

[396]

mercial and financial imperialism in the western hemisphere. In 1903 Cuba became an American protectorate as a condition of its independence, and Panama accepted a similar status. The construction of the Isthmian Canal and the growth of American commerce and investments in the Caribbean led to the imposition of American protectorates upon the Dominican Republic (1905) and upon Haiti (1915), the purchase of the Virgin Islands from Denmark (1917), and chronic interventions in the Central American States for reasons of strategy, commerce, and "dollar diplomacy." The American islands in the Pacific and American trade in the Far East led to the projection of a policy of establishing American naval supremacy in the Pacific, but this policy was abandoned and replaced by one of cooperation and consultation with the other Pacific Powers in 1922.

The great rival of the United States for control of the Pacific is, of course, Japan, whose new empire in eastern Asia makes her one of the great imperial Powers. Following the reopening of Japan to contacts with the west in the middle of the nineteenth century, her peoples imported, along with other elements of western culture, industrial capitalism, militarism, and imperialism. In 1894 Japan waged war on China, defeated her, annexed Formosa and the Liukiu Islands, and detached Korea from Chinese control. She was compelled to give up Port Arthur and the Liaotung peninsula under Russian pressure, supported by Germany, France, and Great Britain. Russo-Japanese conflict for control of south Manchuria culminated in war in 1904–1905. A second Japanese victory enabled the Empire to annex southern Sakhalin, acquire Port Arthur and the Liaotung peninsula by leasehold from China (on whose territory war was fought), and free Korea and southern Manchuria from Russian influence. Korea was annexed in 1910. Japan, in alliance with Great Britain since 1902, declared war upon Germany in 1914 and seized Kiaochow, Shantung, and the German islands in the north Pacific. The islands she retained as mandates, but she was obliged, under Chinese, Russian, and American pressure, to give up Shantung, to relinquish her design to establish a protectorate over China, and to evacuate the Russian territory occupied by Japanese troops during the Allied intervention in the Russian Civil War. In the fall of 1931 Japanese troops ousted the Chinese authorities from Manchuria and subsequently set up the independent State of Manchukuo as a Japanese protectorate. The most important issues of international politics in the Pacific and the Far East revolve about the future of Japanese imperialism in eastern Asia.

This brief survey of the empires has dealt primarily with territories which have been openly annexed or brought under the direct control of the imperial Powers. Mention must also be made of the indirect forms of imperialism through which varying degrees of foreign control have been imposed upon States still nominally independent.[1] The leasehold has been a device commonly resorted to for this purpose. The German "colony" of Kiaochow in China was acquired in 1898 through a ninety-nine year lease from the Chinese Government. China was likewise compelled to lease Port Arthur and Dairen to Russia in 1898 for twenty-five years. In 1905 Russia was obliged to transfer these leases to Japan, which coerced China into extending them until 1997 in the twenty-one demands of 1915. Great Britain still holds the leases of Weiheiwei (acquired in 1898 for as long as Russia should hold Port Arthur) and of Kowloon (acquired in 1898 for ninety-nine years). France leased Kwangchow-wan in 1898 for the same period. The United States has also leased naval bases from Cuba, Nicaragua, and Panama. In 1903 the Republic of Panama, established by a revolution against Colombia, instigated in Washington and supported by American naval forces, leased to the United States in perpetuity the Canal Zone for a consideration of $10,000,000 and an annual payment of $250,000. The same agreement made Panama a protectorate of the United States, by giving the American Government the right to use its forces to protect the canal and maintain order. The treaty agreements between the United States and Cuba, Haiti, the Dominican Republic, and Nicaragua also make these States semiprotectorates.

The protectorate as a form of imperial control usually involves the retention of agencies of local self-government on the part of the "protected" State, with the "protecting" State assuming control of the foreign relations, the defense, and sometimes the financial affairs of the victim. "Spheres of influence" represent another device of imperial control. This phrase is usually applied to areas in which imperial Powers are granted economic privileges, while the native States retain sovereignty and political authority. It is also loosely used to describe a situation in which an imperial Power exercises an appreciable degree of control over a region which it has not formally annexed or converted into a protectorate. By the agreements of 1896 and 1904 Great Britain and France divided Siam into spheres of influence. The Anglo-Russian agreement of 1907 divided Persia into British and Russian spheres, with an intermediate zone between them. At the present time Manchuria, Tibet, and the southern provinces of China might be described as spheres of influence respectively of Japan, Great Britain, and France. The territories of Turkey have from time to time been divided into spheres of influence between Great Britain, France, Germany, and Italy. In Africa and Asia annexations and the establishment of protectorates have usually been preceded by the creation of such spheres. In other instances imperial control has been established over backward States through various devices of finan-

---

[1] *Cf.* R. L. Buell, *International Relations,* 1929, pp. 463–495.

cial supervision, tariff regulation, extraterritoriality, military intervention, etc.

The most significant result of the new imperialism for international politics has been the partition of most of the non-European world among the colonial Powers of the Western State System. Only two non-European States possess colonial empires—the United States and Japan—and these are the only States of the world not located on the European continent which can be regarded as Great Powers. Of the colonial States of Europe, all save Belgium and Denmark are, or have once been, Great Powers. Between 1860 and 1914 the non-European peoples have been progressively deprived of their territory, their freedom of action, and often of their independence by the empire-builders. On the African continent only Liberia, Abyssinia, and Egypt remain even nominally independent. All have suffered territorial losses. Egypt still remains, for all practical purposes, a British protectorate, and Liberia has remained independent only because of the interest of the United States in its fate. In Asia only Japan, China, Siam, Nepal, Afghanistan, Persia, Turkey, and the Arabian States have remained independent. Japan has become an imperial Great Power. The other States have remained nominally independent only because their size, resources, or strategic location made them objects of competition between several Powers, no one of which has been willing to permit another to absorb them. All have suffered losses of territory and have been subjected to greater or lesser degrees of foreign control. No independent States remain in the South Sea Islands. The States of Latin America have been free from efforts of the European Powers to control them primarily because of the hegemony of the United States in the western hemisphere. If this hegemony has been instrumental in protecting the American States from Europe, it has at the same time led to Yankee control of the Caribbean, Yankee pressure on Mexico, and general resentment throughout Latin America against "Yankee imperialism."

It is worthy of note that while this new conquest of the world involved innumerable wars against weak States and native peoples on the part of the imperialistic governments, it was for the most part achieved without war between the imperial Powers themselves. The Crimean War of 1854–1856 and the Russo-Japanese War of 1904–1905 were the only open clashes of arms between the Great Powers for control of backward areas prior to 1914. The Spanish-American War of 1898 was waged by a Great Power against a third-rate Power. All other conflicts and controversies between the empire-builders were adjusted pacifically by diplomacy, conference, bargaining over pawns, and horse-trading in territory and populations. War, rebellion, and repression there were in abundance, for the path of empire is red with the blood of its victims. Britishers have fought and beaten Hindus, Egyptians, Arabs, Turks, Afghans, Boers,

Bantus, Bushmen, Chinese, and Polynesians. Frenchmen have fought and beaten Arabs, Syrians, Hovas, Chinese, Siamese, etc. Americans have fought and beaten Filipinos, Haitians, Mexicans, Nicaraguans, etc. But before 1914, with the exceptions noted, the Great Powers did not fight one another so long as native States remained to be conquered and new lands remained unclaimed. But when the world became filled with jostling imperialists, friction between the Powers increased to a dangerous degree. The Great War of 1914, like the wars between the Powers in the days of the old colonialism, was a life-and-death struggle between the great States themselves with the loser, Germany, losing all her overseas possessions to the victors. It is not impossible that the twentieth century may witness a series of suicidal combats between the imperial nation-states for world mastery.

3. THE ART OF EMPIRE-BUILDING

> The legions which [America] sends forth are armed not with the sword but with the Cross. The higher State to which she seeks the allegiance of all mankind is not of human but of divine origin. She cherishes no purpose save to merit the favors of Almighty God. . . . We extended our domain over distant islands in order to safeguard our own interests and accepted the consequent obligation to bestow opportunity and liberty upon less favored people.—Inaugural Address of CALVIN COOLIDGE, March 4, 1925.

If the process of imperialism is to be understood in terms of its actual functioning rather than in terms of preconceived dogmas and theories of interpretation, it must be studied, not through a consideration of abstract generalizations, but through a careful examination of men, motives, facts, and events in particular situations. To examine in detail the process of empire-building in all of its manifestations would obviously be impossible even in a work of many volumes. It is quite out of the question in the present study. It should nevertheless prove illuminating to outline the process in a small number of representative instances which are more or less typical of the imperialistic pattern everywhere. These instances have been chosen from widely separated geographical areas and represent the imperial policies of five different nation-states. The activities of Great Britain in Rhodesia, of France in Tunis, of Italy in Libya, of the United States in Nicaragua, and of Japan in Manchuria will be examined in the present section for the purpose of revealing in concrete instances the rôles of missionaries, merchants, investors, diplomats, soldiers, and colonial administrators in the making of the new empires.

A. Rhodesia

In September of 1870 Cecil Rhodes arrived at Durban on the coast of Natal in South Africa. He was the youngest son of an Anglican pastor. Four of his brothers had gone into the army and three had gone to the colonies. Young

Cecil was destined for the law or the Church, but his health failed and he came to South Africa, as he later said, to escape "the eternal cold mutton." South Africa had a mixed population of Boers (farmers) of Dutch and French extraction, Negro slaves, Bushmen, Hottentots, and Griquas or bastards—half-breed children of Hottentot women and Dutch settlers. Great Britain had occupied Cape Colony in 1806 and secured title in 1814. Rhodes arrived just after the discovery of diamonds in Griqualand to the north of Cape Colony. He set out at once for the prairie plateaus and mountains of the high veldt to make his fortune. He entered into partnership with one C. D. Rudd and began that process of buying up claims, squeezing out competitors, and building up profitable business combinations which made him head of the De Beers Mining Company, with a capital of £2,000,000. By astute financial manipulations, he compelled his chief rival, Barnate, to amalgamate with his own concern. By 1890 he was the leading figure in the De Beers Consolidated Mines, which enjoyed a monopoly of South African diamonds. Transvaal gold also offered opportunities for profit and another Rhodes company—the Consolidated Gold Fields of South Africa—achieved a monopoly of gold mining as well. These and other enterprises netted the clever and acquisitive entrepreneur who had organized them an annual income of a million pounds in the 1890's.

From capitalism to imperialism was but a step. Rhodes perceived possibilities of greater profit through enlisting governmental support for his enterprises. He was, moreover, a convinced imperialist who believed in the right of the Anglo-Saxon race to inherit the earth, who thought "in continents," as he said, and who cherished fantastic dreams of extending British power over Africa, Asia, Oceania, and North and South America. He was quite prepared to assume his share of the white man's burden, providing profits were not forgotten. "Pure philanthropy is very well in its way," he said, "but philanthropy plus 5 per cent is a good deal better." He made fabulous profits in his business ventures and used the proceeds to support the Liberal party, buy up newspapers and politicians, and create opportunities for still greater profit. His immediate objective was to paint all of South Africa red, *i.e.*, to bring it under British control and to link it eventually with Egypt by a Cape-to-Cairo railway. Native Bechuanaland, north of Cape Colony and British Bechuanaland, was the gateway to empire, for it lay between the Boer Republics to the east and German Southwest Africa to the west. He agitated and propagandized for its acquisition and in 1885 the British Government sent in an army and proclaimed it a protectorate. Beyond lay the high table lands inhabited by warlike tribes and coveted by Boers, Portuguese, and Germans. Rhodes persuaded the British high commissioner for South Africa to send a missionary to talk to King Lo Bengula and paid the costs himself. The result was a treaty wherein the King agreed to refrain from negotiations with foreign Powers without British consent. Rhodes, convinced that the region was rich in gold, then sent three of his own colleagues—Rudd, Maguire, and Thompson—who induced the King to grant them "complete and exclusive charge over all metals and minerals situated and contained in my kingdom, principalities, and dominions," along with the right "to exclude . . . all persons seeking land, metals, minerals, or mining rights" therein. In return for this concession, Lo Bengula, who ill understood what he was giving up, received a thousand rifles, some ammunition, a second-hand steamboat, and a monthly stipend of a hundred pounds.

Rhodes now proceeded to organize the British South African Company, and after numerous adroit political manipulations persuaded Lord Salisbury, the Prime Minister, to approve the granting of a charter to the company. The

British aristocracy was won over to the scheme by making the Duke of Abercorn president and the Duke of Fife vice president. British humanitarianism was enlisted in the enterprise by pledges to improve the condition of the natives. The charter of October 29, 1889, gave to the company for twenty-five years the right to make treaties and laws, maintain police, construct roads, develop industries and mines, and in general govern and exploit a vast undefined territory. The promoters took 90,000 shares and 50 per cent of the profits, granted 200,000 shares to the De Beers Company, and sold 710,000 one-pound shares to small investors who were assured by the London *Times* and other papers, for reasons best known to their owners and editors, that the land was fabulously rich in resources of all kinds. Difficulties and discouragements were numerous, but the settlement grew and the company at length sent its troops to attack Lo Bengula, seize his lands and cattle, and convert his kingdom into "Rhodesia." This vast domain was expanded northward and in 1893 a British protectorate was proclaimed over Nyasaland, which the African Lakes Company and the London Missionary Society jointly opened to British occupation. Profits were large, for gold was mined in considerable quantities, but white settlers were slow in coming. By 1921 Southern Rhodesia had 33,600 white inhabitants and 770,000 natives, while Northern Rhodesia had only 3,500 whites and 1,000,000 Negroes. The best agricultural lands were taken by the whites, while the natives were taxed to compel them to work for a pittance with which to pay the taxes. The British Government intervened in the affairs of the chartered company only occasionally, when the ruthless exploitation of the natives became too scandalous.

In 1922 Southern Rhodesia became a "self-governing" colony with settlers, landed proprietors, and mine owners ruling the black peasantry and proletariat. Meanwhile Rhodes and his fellow capitalists had engineered the Jameson raid, precipitated the Boer war, and extended British power over all of South Africa. Rhodes died in 1902, leaving most of his enormous fortune to endow 175 scholarships at Oxford for students from the British colonies, the United States, and Germany. The foundations of the Cape-to-Cairo empire were thus established by a combination of patriotic profit-seekers, Christian missionaries, and bourgeois diplomats. By force native independence was extinguished. By force imperial power was extended. By force rich profits were wrested from the land and the people to whom the civilizing mission of the white man meant political subjugation, compulsory labor, and shameless exploitation.[1]

B. Tunis

The French acquisition of Tunis in 1881 is no less revealing of the motives and methods of modern imperialism. Algeria, Tunis' western neighbor, was already a French possession and considerations of the defense of Algeria furnished a convenient pretext for encroachments on the land of the Bey. In the 1850's the Tunisian Government found itself financially embarrassed and unable to meet payments on its bonds. In 1862 the Bey contracted with foreign capitalists and money-lenders, mostly French, for a loan of 35,000,000 francs, most of which went into the pockets of local officials, financiers, and middlemen. Heavy taxes were of no avail, and the clamor of the new foreign bond-holders for "protection" led to the creation of the Anglo-Italian-French *commission financière* to manage

[1] This summary is largely based on the account in P. T. Moon's *Imperialism*, pp. 160–173. See also Basil Williams' *Cecil Rhodes*, 1921; J. H. Harris, *Chartered Millions*, 1920; P. F. Hone, *Southern Rhodesia*, 1909; and E. D. Morel, *The Black Man's Burden*, 1920.

the Bey's finances. So successful was this management that the Tunisian debt grew by the proverbial leaps and bounds, the finances fell into ever greater disorder, and the French creditors began demanding governmental intervention in their behalf. The Bey meanwhile became involved in bitter disputes with foreign concessionaires and investors regarding land claims, industrial rights, and other contracts. Foreign consuls rushed eagerly to the defense of foreign property owners and profit-seekers. Signor Maccio, the Italian Consul, and M. Rustan, the French Consul, pushed the claims of their respective nationals and became bitter rivals for ascendancy in the Tunisian capital, while the foreign offices at Rome and Paris cast covetous eyes upon the country. Its fate had already become a subject of diplomatic conversations among the Powers. The British Government had assured Paris that it had no objection to the expansion of French influence in Tunis. Rustan sought to extend this influence by championing the economic interests of French nationals, resisting Italian designs, and inducing commercial groups interested in Tunisian trade to subsidize a section of the French press in favor of the establishment of a French protectorate. Rustan was instructed to open negotiations for such an arrangement, but he encountered difficulties. "Authorize me to disembark a company of marines and the Bey will sign," he reported. Premier Freycinet told his successor, Ferry, "The fruit is ripe. You may pick it at the propitious moment." In the early months of 1881 tension between Paris and Rome, and between French agents, merchants, concessionaires, etc., and the Government of the Bey reached the breaking point. Under these circumstances Rustan, Ferry, Barthélemy Saint-Hilaire, French Foreign Minister, and Albert Grévy, Governor-general of Algeria, concocted a scheme to frustrate Italian ambitions, seize control of Tunis, enhance the gains of the profit-seekers, and increase French power in north Africa.

This scheme contemplated a military descent upon Tunis on the pretext of defending Algeria from the raids of frontier tribesmen. Ferry—a conservative patriotic bourgeois Republican—was an imperialist expansionist by conviction. "Colonies," he declared, "are for rich countries a most advantageous place for capital investment . . . eh, oui, pour les capitalistes!" That he should be willing to use the military power of the French State on behalf of concessionaires and investors was a natural result of his background and outlook. The conquest of Tunis was but the first of a series of imperial adventures upon which Ferry embarked. In all of them he was obliged to reckon with the bitter opposition of the extreme Right and the extreme Left in Parliament, and with the attacks of the opposition press. In this instance, as in later ones, his Cabinet resorted to deliberate deception of the press, the public, and Parliament. Early in April, 1881, the Chamber of Deputies and the Senate were asked for credits to finance a military expedition against the Kroumir tribesmen who had crossed into Algeria from Tunis in the course of their cattle-raiding operations. "The Government of the Republic," said Ferry to the Deputies, "does not seek conquests; it has no need of them." But Algeria must be defended and the raiders must be taught respect for the French flag and for French territory. With Parliament convinced that this was the sole purpose of the projected military expedition, the Chambers voted the credits asked, expressed confidence in the Cabinet, and adjourned for four weeks. The prearranged plan then unfolded with clocklike precision. The wandering border tribesmen were scattered without difficulty. An army of 30,000 troops descended by sea upon the capital of Tunis. The Bey and his advisers were terrified and helpless. On May 12, 1881, they were compelled to attach their signatures to the Treaty of Bardo, by the terms of which the French Government assumed control of Tunisian foreign relations, guaranteed the person and the territories of the Bey, imposed a French military occupation upon the country, and undertook to supervise the reorganization of public finances.

On the same day Ferry told the reassembled Deputies and Senators that France was merely demanding "durable guarantees necessary for its security. It is from the Bey of Tunis that we demand them. We desire neither his territory nor his throne. The French Republic has solemnly repudiated all notions of annexation, all ideas of conquest, in launching this expedition; it renews the same declarations at this hour when the end is near." Two days later Barthélemy Saint-Hilaire announced the signature of the treaty to Parliament, explaining that the Bey had become an "ally" of France and presenting a "Yellow Book" of documents prepared at the Quai d'Orsay to justify what had been done. Parliament and the public acquiesced in the *fait accompli*. The treaty was approved and a new gem was added to the crown of the French colonial empire. To be sure, a costly military expedition was required to suppress the national insurrection which broke out in Tunis against the invaders. The Italian Government, furious but impotent, threw itself into the arms of Germany and Austria-Hungary in the Triple Alliance of 1882. The parliamentary opposition, led by Clemenceau the "Tiger," assailed Ferry bitterly for his misrepresentation, for his concealed policy of conquest, for his solicitude for investors and concession-aires, for his spending of the treasure and blood of France on behalf of private capitalistic interests: the Bone-Guelma Railway Company, the Société Marseillaise, the Credit Foncier, and sundry other groups of fortune hunters. Ferry resigned in the face of criticism, but his successor, Gambetta, accepted the conquest.

Tunis became formally a French protectorate by a new treaty of 1883. The French advisers of the Bey established a postal system, built roads, schools, hospitals, and colleges, promoted phosphate mining, and consolidated the Tunisian public debt into 4 per cent bonds. French merchants and investors hastened to develop and exploit the resources of the country. The foreign commerce of Tunis rose from 27,000,000 francs in 1881 to 100,000,000 francs in 1899 and 1,395,000,000 (about 280,000,000 at par) francs in 1921. French importers and exporters reaped most of the profits of this trade, for they were largely exempt from the high protective-tariff duties levied on foreigners after 1897. French settlers were encouraged to enter the country. In 1881 there were only 700 Frenchmen in Tunis, as compared with 11,200 Italians. In 1921 the French numbered 71,000, though they were still outnumbered by the 89,000 Italians. The native population numbered about 2,000,000. Tunis, in short, became one of the most valuable units in France's African empire from the point of view of the profits of traders and investors and of the power-and-prestige considerations of patriots, diplomats, and strategists.[1]

C. Libya

If the Italian Government and Italian patriots hotly resented the French conquest of Tunis, they were still not obliged to give up all hope of securing a place in the north African sun. Between Tunis and Egypt lay the two Turkish provinces of Tripolitania and Cyrenaica, to which the Government at Rome now

[1] *Cf.* F. L. Schuman, *War and Diplomacy in the French Republic*, 1931, pp. 57–77; S. H. Roberts, *History of French Colonial Policy*, 1929, I, pp. 259f.; A. M. Broadley, *Tunis Past and Present—The Last Punic War*, 1882, *passim*.

turned its attention. In 1887 Germany pledged Italy her armed assistance to prevent France from seizing this region. Great Britain, Austria-Hungary, and Spain were likewise disposed to resist further French expansion in north Africa. The French foreign office itself desired to placate Italy, with an eye toward the inevitable clash with Germany. Between 1899 and 1903 Italy was effectively detached from the Triple Alliance by understandings that if Italy would raise no objection to French designs on Morocco, France would grant Italy a free hand in Tripoli. By the secret agreement of Racconigi, October 24, 1909, Russia also consented to the projected Italian conquest of Tripoli in return for a promise of Italian support of Russian designs on the Dardanelles. Tripoli was not coveted by the Italian Government because Italian capitalists had large interests at stake there, or Italian merchants were carrying on a profitable trade, or Italian settlers had gone there in large numbers. The country was largely a barren desert, inhabited by unruly tribesmen, and of no great economic value. The pressure for conquest did not come, in this case, from investors, traders, or emigrants, but from diplomats, politicians, and patriots. Tripoli was desired for reasons of prestige. Italian nationalism demanded that Italy be not left behind in the struggle for colonial empire—for Italy's claims to be regarded as a Great Power rested no less on overseas possessions and imperial pretensions than on population, resources, and armaments. Instead of bankers, merchants, and investors pushing the Italian Government to action to protect their interests and enhance their profits, the Italian Government utilized their services to make possible the realization of its own colonial ambitions, which were motivated less by a hunger for private profits than by a will to national power and prestige in the game of international politics.

The seizure of Tripoli required some plausible pretext, some excuse, some reason which would appear legitimate to the Italian public and to the world at large. Italy, unlike France, had no Algeria whose security demanded the conquest of neighboring territory. But if Italy secured "economic interests" in Tripoli and these interests were in some way jeopardized, a pretext for action would be available. If Italian bankers, merchants, concessionaires, and missionaries would only go to Tripoli, invest money in Tripoli, buy land in Tripoli, establish enterprises in Tripoli, the problem would be simplified. But the country was too barren and forbidding to attract wise profit-seekers, moved only by economic considerations. Bankers and traders remained singularly obtuse to suggestions from the foreign office that it was their patriotic duty to invest in Sahara sands. Suggestions coupled with tangible incentives, however, might bring about a change of mind. A bargain was soon struck. The Banca di Roma and the Banca d'Italia were granted certain discount privileges which they desired and certain legal exemptions regarding their domestic financial operations. In return they invested money in steamship lines, olive farms, oil and soap factories, sponge fisheries, and other enterprises across the Mediterranean. The Italian press waxed eloquent over the prosperous future of Tripoli, and small investors snatched at the golden bait. Presently Italy had "interests" in Tripoli which required "protection." Turkish misgovernment endangered these interests. "Order" must be restored. The Italian flag was "insulted." Italian nationals were subjected to indignities and losses. Italy must protect its nationals and confer the blessings of capitalism and Christianity upon the benighted Arab heathen.

In the summer of 1911 the appropriate "incidents" were manufactured and the army was prepared for action. France, Germany, and Great Britain were locked in the great diplomatic crisis over Morocco. Austria-Hungary had occupied

Bosnia and Herzegovina in 1908, and Turkey was threatened by the Balkan States. In August the Italian Government secretly communicated its intentions to the other Powers, none of which offered serious objection. On September 28, 1911, an astonishing ultimatum was dispatched to the Sublime Court. It declared that Italy had "a vital interest of the very first order" in putting an end to "the state of disorder and neglect in which Tripoli and Cyrenaica are left by Turkey." Italian business enterprises "constantly encounter a systematic opposition of the most obstinate and unwarranted kind," due to the "agitation prevailing against Italian subjects . . . The Italian Government, therefore, finding itself forced to think of the guardianship of its dignity and its interest, has decided to proceed to the military occupation of Tripoli and Cyrenaica." The hope was expressed that Turkey would cooperate and prevent resistance. Turkey replied that while she was not prepared to give up possession of the territory, she was ready to meet all legitimate complaints if the Government at Rome would indicate what was demanded. Italy responded with a declaration of war. Italian troops captured the city of Tripoli and other coast towns, and on November 5 the annexation of the region was decreed. But the Arabs in the interior offered stout resistance and Turkey refused to yield. Italian forces occupied the Dodecanese and other Aegean islands and twice attacked the Dardanelles without success. Fortunately for the Italian cause, the Balkan States seized upon Turkey's embarrassments to prepare an attack upon her and in October, 1912, Turkey made peace. The new conquest was renamed Libya (the name of the province in Roman times) and the hearts of patriots and imperialists swelled with pride over their victory.

Libya constitutes one of the most perfect examples of a colonial possession acquired and held at great cost to the taxpayers of the home country for reasons of diplomatic power and prestige, with only moderate profits accruing to privileged investors and concessionaires and no economic gains whatever accruing to the nation as a whole. The Arab and Berber tribesmen not only resisted the original conquest but engaged in chronic revolt against foreign rule. By the close of the Great War they had driven the Italian forces to the seacoast, and the Italian Government was obliged to reconquer most of the territory by successive military expeditions which have been costly in money and lives. Up to 1924 it was estimated that $600,000,000 had been spent in military operations and in making up the difference between the small revenues and heavy expenses of the Libyan administration. A certain measure of participation in the government was granted to the natives in 1919, as a means of placating them. But the colony has been held only through constant warfare and reprisals. The sparsity of the population, which numbers less than a million, and the poverty of the country have hindered trade and investment. Exports declined after the conquest, though they have increased somewhat since the war. Imports increased, but the total foreign trade was negligible and smaller in value than the annual budgetary deficit. Since the advent of the Fascist régime, the colonial budget has been brought nearer to a balance and Libya has been more firmly held. The "rectifications" of the frontiers at the expense of Tunis and Egypt have given Italy control of certain important caravan routes. Italian patriots still point with pride to the map and contemplate new conquests with enthusiasm. But here, as in most imperial adventures, pecuniary gains go to the favored few, while the nation as a whole pays the piper without calling the tune.[1]

[1] There is relatively little material available in English on Italian imperialism. But see Charles Lapworth, *Tripoli and Young Italy*, 1912, and Luigi Villari, *The Expansion of Italy*, 1930.

D. Nicaragua

American imperialism in the Caribbean since 1900 exhibits a more intimate association between private profit motives and public power-and-prestige motives. By 1914, $1,200,000,000 of American private capital had been invested in the area which was then the most important single field of American foreign investment. Trade between the United States and the Caribbean had likewise increased greatly, for Caribbean products such as sugar, bananas and other tropical fruits, rubber, cocoa, oil, woods, spices, etc., have found a growing market in the United States. This profitable trade, coupled with large investments in various enterprises and numerous loans to Caribbean governments by New York financiers, have given American merchants, bankers, and security-holders a vested economic interest in the region which has constituted an important stake of American diplomacy. The Caribbean policy of the United States has likewise been influenced by strategic considerations growing out of the necessity of defending the Panama Canal, maintaining American naval supremacy, and planning for the possible construction of another interoceanic canal over some alternative route. The interrelationships between these purposes and interests is well illustrated by the policy of the United States toward Nicaragua.

Nicaragua is the largest of the Central American republics in area (49,200 square miles), but it has a population of only 750,000. Most of the population, white, Indian, and mestizo, is concentrated in the plains region between the Atlantic and Pacific seaboards adjacent to the San Juan River and Lake Nicaragua. These waterways constitute an interoceanic highway and a possible canal route. The Conservative party, with its stronghold in Granada, and the Liberal party, centering in Leon, have alternated in control of the Government. Their bitter rivalry frequently led to revolution and civil war in the nineteenth century and provoked foreign intervention. The Conservatives had held office for thirty years when José Santos Zelaya became Liberal President in 1893. For sixteen years he dominated the political scene, ruling by dictatorial methods, selling concessions to foreign investors, and contracting foreign loans with reckless abandon. He became *persona non grata* to the American State Department because of his propensity for making loans with British rather than American bankers, his plans for negotiating with Japan regarding a canal route, and his generally independent and bellicose policies. In October of 1909 Emiliano Chamorro, a prominent Conservative, Juan Estrada, Governor of Bluefields, and Adolfo Diaz, secretary of an American mining company, organized a revolution against Zelaya with the tacit approval of foreign residents and the American State Department. Zelaya's execution of two Americans who were assisting the rebels led Secretary of State Knox to sever diplomatic relations with the Liberal Government and to espouse openly the Conservative cause. Zelaya resigned in favor of José Madriz, who defeated the insurgents. The new President probably would have put an end to the revolt, except for the intervention of American naval forces, which established a "neutral zone" around Bluefields (where the rebel army was besieged) and refused to permit military operations in the vicinity. In August, 1910, Madriz resigned and the Conservatives, under Estrada, took control of the republic with the approval of the United States.

Thomas C. Dawson, American Minister to Panama, was sent to Managua, the Nicaraguan capital, and induced Estrada and his colleagues to agree to a foreign loan, a constituent assembly, and a commission to settle all claims against the Government. The assembly chose Estrada President and Diaz Vice

[407]

President. In January, 1911, they were inaugurated and at once recognized by the United States. The new American Minister, Elliott Northcott, intervened in the quarrels between the Conservative leaders and in May Estrada was forced out and Diaz became President. Following an investigation of the public finances by an American expert recommended by the Washington State Department, the Knox-Castrillo convention of June 6, 1911, was signed, providing for American governmental assistance in securing from American bankers a loan of $15,-000,000 to be used in paying foreign claims, consolidating the debt, stabilizing the currency, and building a railway to the eastern coast. This agreement further specified that during the period of the loan contract, Nicaraguan customs duties would be collected by a collector-general appointed by the Nicaraguan President on the nomination of the bankers and subject to the approval of the American State Department. On September 1, 1911, the Nicaraguan Government signed contracts with Brown Brothers and Company and J. and W. Seligman and Company of New York for a $15,000,000 loan, to be secured by customs revenues. Colonel Clifford B. Ham became collector-general, representing American and European bond-holders and responsible to the Nicaraguan Minister of Finance and the American Secretary of State. The Nicaraguan Government pledged itself not to alter its customs laws and internal taxes without the consent of the American bankers, who further intrenched themselves by taking over a majority of the stock in the national bank and the national railways, by agreeing to act as agents for the English and French bond-holders, and by reserving the right to appeal for protection to the United States Government, whose decision should be final in all controversies.

Further plans for the financial "reconstruction" of Nicaragua were interrupted by the refusal of the United States Senate to ratify the Knox-Castrillo convention and by the outbreak of a new revolution in 1912. General Mena led the opposition to Diaz and to the American interests behind him. Mena got himself chosen President by a hand-picked Assembly and pushed through a new constitution forbidding such contracts as Diaz had made with the bankers. While Diaz appealed to the United States for aid and suggested a treaty giving the United States a right of intervention to maintain and preserve a stable government, the revolt broke out and soon became a new contest between Conservatives and Liberals. In response to the appeals of Diaz and the Brown Brothers, a force of American marines under Major Smedley D. Butler was sent to the capital in August, 1912. By the end of the summer almost 3,000 American troops had been landed on Nicaraguan soil for the purpose of protecting and keeping open the railway, now under the control of the American bankers. The American troops attacked the Liberal rebels, who surrendered their last stronghold, Leon, in October, after much destruction of life and property. The State Department declared that it intended to "lend its strong moral support to the cause of legally constituted good government for the benefit of the people of Nicaragua." After suppressing the revolt the marines remained and were instrumental in persuading the Conservatives to send Chamorro, their presidential candidate, to Washington as minister and to accept Diaz as President. When Diaz was safely elected, the marines were withdrawn, save for a legation guard of 100 at Managua. The Diaz Government borrowed more money from American bankers, who assumed the collection of all revenues, with the national bank as their agent. The outbreak of the Great War produced a financial crisis, and in the autumn of 1914 payments on the foreign debt were suspended. The Conservative Government became increasingly unpopular because of its arrangements with the bankers, and only the firm support given to the régime by the United States prevented revolution. In the election of 1916 the Liberal candidate, Irias, was not permitted to enter the country to conduct his campaign, and the Conservative candidate, Chamorro, was elected with the open support of the American minister.

The new President, while Nicaraguan minister in Washington, had signed the Bryan-Chamorro treaty of August 5, 1914, with the new American Secretary of State. Following the failure of the Knox-Castrillo convention, negotiations had been opened for an agreement to give the United States a hundred-year option on the construction of a canal through the San Juan River-Lake Nicaragua route, a right to fortify in perpetuity the Corn Islands off the Caribbean coast, and a right to construct a naval base on Fonseca Bay on the Pacific coast in return for a payment of $3,000,000 to Nicaragua. This agreement was under discussion when Wilson succeeded Taft and Bryan replaced Knox. Bryan added to it provisions placing Nicaragua's foreign relations under American control and authorizing American intervention at any time to protect life and property and to preserve the country's "independence." The American Senate objected to the protectorate provisions and they were struck out. The Senate approved the treaty containing the other terms indicated, and it was ratified June 24, 1916. Costa Rica and Salvador protested that the treaty violated their rights, since Costa Rica had as much claim to the San Juan River as did Nicaragua, and since an American naval base on Fonseca Bay would constitute a menace to Salvador and Honduras. This controversy was carried before the Central American Court of Justice which held, in September, 1916, that Nicaragua had violated the legal rights of Costa Rica and Salvador. Both Nicaragua and the United States ignored the decision and the court disbanded. The New York bankers now demanded that the $3,000,000 be used to pay arrears on their loans, while the Nicaraguan Government sought to use it to meet its own deficit and to pay off local claimants. After protracted negotiations the State Department arranged a compromise involving new loans by the bankers, to be secured by a second lien on the customs and a first lien on the remaining 49 per cent of the stock of the national railway and the national bank, 51 per cent of the stock of which was already held by the bankers. The total debt of Nicaragua had now reached $17,500,000. The Nicaraguan Government got less than one-third of the $3,000,000 payment under the Bryan-Chamorro treaty.

Under the complicated financial plan of 1917 the public finances of Nicaragua were placed almost entirely under the control of a high commission of two members named by the President of Nicaragua, one on the recommendation of the State Department. Disagreements between them were to be settled by an arbitrator, also named by the State Department. The major purpose of this arrangement was to protect the American bankers and to pay off other claims against the government. The debt was reduced and revenues were increased. By 1919 the American bankers were paid off in full, and the Brown Brothers withdrew. In 1920 the Nicaraguan Government bought back the stock of the national railways. So favorable were the prospects that plans were made for a new loan of $9,000,000. A contract was concluded for this purpose, but it met with such opposition in the American Congress that it was abandoned. The condition of Nicaraguan finances steadily improved, however, under the supervision of the bankers and the State Department, and by 1924 the Government was able to buy back control of the national bank. Meanwhile, prolonged efforts to bring about a federation of the Central American republics ended in failure because of the continued opposition to the Bryan-Chamorro treaty on the part of Costa Rica, Salvador, and Honduras and the refusal of Nicaragua to cooperate. In 1923, under the auspices of the State Department, a series of conventions was drawn up providing for arbitration, neutrality, political stability, extradition, greater freedom of trade, etc., in which American financial and strategic interests were adequately protected, as they would not have been in the projected plan of union sponsored by enemies of "Yankee imperialism." Salvador and Honduras fell into bondage to American bankers at the same time, and American marines intervened in the internal political conflicts of the latter country (1924–1925) to play their customary rôle.

The election of 1924 in Nicaragua inaugurated a new period of American interference. President Diego Chamorro, uncle of Emiliano, died in office in 1923. Control of the election machinery passed to Bartolome Martinez, Conservative successor of Chamorro, who arranged with the State Department for the employment of a group of outside observers in the hope that a peaceable and honest election would be followed by the withdrawal of the marines. The candidates were Emiliano Chamorro, representing one faction of the Conservatives, and Carlos Solorzano, another Conservative, supported by Juan Sacasa, a Liberal and candidate on the same ticket for Vice President. The election was fairly conducted. When the State Department declined to indicate its preference between the candidates, the Martinez Government decided to dispense with the "observers." Solorzano and Sacasa won by 48,000 votes to 28,000. Conservative-Liberal friction in the coalition Cabinet led to difficulties, however, and Chamorro, by a military coup d'etat, compelled Solorzano to dismiss the Liberal ministers. Sacasa fled the country in fear of his life in the fall of 1925. Chamorro became dictator, replaced the Liberal minister at Washington by Castrillo of "dollar diplomacy" fame, induced Congress to banish Sacasa, and assumed the presidency in January, 1926. Despite his pro-American leanings, the State Department refused to recognize him on the ground that he had acquired power by unconstitutional means contrary to the 1923 conventions. Chamorro's efforts to sell the railways and the national bank to American financiers were unsuccessful because of his unrecognized status. In May of 1926 the Liberals began a revolt against the dictator by raiding a branch of the national bank at Bluefields. The company then controlling the bank was incorporated in the State of Connecticut. A request from its manager brought an American cruiser to the scene. A "neutral zone" was proclaimed by American forces and Chamorro recovered control. Sacasa went to Guatemala to direct operations, and hostilities were reopened in August. An armistice was arranged in September through the action of Admiral J. H. Latimer, commander of the American squadron. Lawrence Dennis, secretary of the American legation, attempted to arrange a settlement. Chamorro agreed to resign and the Conservatives supported Adolfo Diaz as his successor, while the Liberals insisted on Sacasa. Diaz was favored by the State Department and the conference broke up with the withdrawal of the Liberals. Chamorro's tool, Uriza, assumed control and persuaded the Congress to elect Diaz President instead of permitting Sacasa, the constitutional Vice President, to fill out the unexpired term. Diaz was recognized by the State Department on November 17, 1926, a week after his election, and American bankers at once loaned his Government $300,000. Diaz denounced Sacasa as a Mexican and Bolshevist agent and asked the United States to take any steps necessary to prevent his activities. Sacasa set up a government at Puerto Cabezas on the east coast and was recognized as constitutional President of Nicaragua by Mexico.

The United States acted at once to prevent the impending civil war. Diaz was supported against Sacasa. Marines were landed, neutral zones were proclaimed, and all possible obstacles were placed in the way of the Liberal forces. The country rallied to the Liberal cause, however, and the Diaz régime was saved only by fifteen American war vessels and the landing of American troops in January, 1927. In response to a storm of criticism in Latin America, Europe, and the United States, President Coolidge and Secretary of State Kellogg defended the constitutionality of the Diaz Government, charged Mexico with anti-American designs, and alleged that Sacasa was the agent of a Bolshevist conspiracy. Costa Rica and Guatemala, both of which had refused to recognize Diaz, offered mediation, which Diaz refused with the apparent approval of the Coolidge administration. Fighting was renewed. Diaz offered to retire if American marines would remain in control, and he proposed an "alliance" with the United States which would make Nicaragua an American protectorate in law as well as in fact. Five thousand American troops were now landed, railroads were occupied, additional neutral zones were created, and the Liberal military campaign was effectively blocked. In February, 1927, the State Department announced the sale to the Diaz Government of 3,000 rifles, 200 machine guns, and 3,000,000 rounds of ammunition for $217,718. In April Henry L. Stimson departed for Nicaragua as special representative of President Coolidge. He conferred with both sides and insisted on retaining Diaz in office. He proposed peace, disarmament, and American supervision of the election of 1928. Since the Liberals could not hope to fight the United States successfully, their commander, General Moncada, was obliged to yield and to disband his forces. All his subordinates except one, Sandino, accepted the terms of disarmament. Sacasa denounced the American intervention and withdrew to Guatemala. Sandino retired to the northeastern jungles, rallied such Liberal forces as refused to accept American dictation, and opened his campaign by seizing an American mine and attacking the American marines at Ocotal in June. While five American bombing planes slaughtered some 300 of his followers, the Government at Washington denounced him as a "bandit." He withdrew further into the wilderness to prepare for guerilla warfare against the Government and the American forces of occupation. In March, 1927, the Diaz Government borrowed $1,000,000 from J. and W. Seligman and Company and the Guaranty Trust Company of New York, secured by a mortgage on new taxes, on the budgetary surplus, and on the stock and dividends of the national bank and the national railways. The State Department appointed William Cumberland, formerly financial adviser to Haiti, to make recommendations regarding the advisability of new loans.

Subsequent developments may be briefly summarized. In preparation for the election of 1928, Emiliano Chamorro consulted the State Department regarding his acceptability as a candidate and learned that the American Government regarded him as constitutionally ineligible and that it would refuse to recognize him, even if elected. The other Conservative leader, Diaz, was also ineligible, since the Nicaragua constitution forbids two terms. The Conservative party now began to criticize the arrangements for American supervision of the election and to accuse the United States of partiality toward the Liberals, whose candidate, General Moncada, was declared *persona grata* to the State Department. A new election law was pushed through to enable American agents to supervise the election adequately. Adolfo Bernard became the Conservative candidate. The election of November 4, 1928, supervised by 7,000 American marines, was apparently conducted fairly without American pressure being exerted for either candidate. Moncada and the Liberal ticket won by a majority of 20,000 in a total vote of 133,663. The Conservatives accepted their defeat with good grace. Moncada, now completely won over to the United States, was inaugurated as President on January 1, 1928, and Sacasa became the new minister to Washington. The American forces were gradually reduced during the course of the year, while a native constabulary was organized and trained under American supervision. In February of 1929 the Tonopah Mining Company of Nevada secured a twenty-five year concession from the Nicaraguan Ministry of Public Works to exploit mineral deposits. In March the American Congress authorized a new survey for an interoceanic canal. Sporadic attacks upon the constabulary and the American marines by the Sandino "bandits" continued, but the State Department refused to approve large-scale military operations to suppress these disorders. In April, 1931, Mr. Stimson, now Secretary of State, advised American citizens "who do not feel secure under the protection afforded them by the Nicaraguan Government" to withdraw from the interior to the coast towns. He added that those "who remain do so at their own risk and must not expect American forces to be sent inland to their aid."

This reversal of the interventionist policy, confirmed by the decision to withdraw all marines after the election of 1932, was due to the comparative state of peace prevailing in most of the country, despite Sandino's activities, and to the fact that the Government in power could now be counted upon to meet the wishes of the United States in all important matters. The election of November, 1932, was won by the Liberals, and Sacasa at last became President. In January, 1933, Sacasa was inaugurated and the American forces were completely withdrawn. A month later, Sandino made peace with the new administration and his followers laid down their arms. Yankee intervention was ended—until such time as American "interests" should again be threatened by the changing course of Nicaraguan politics.[1]

E. Manchuria

Japanese imperialism in Manchuria reveals a pattern of State behavior not dissimilar to those already considered, though one complicated by greater resistance on the part of the victim and by the conflicting interests of other

[1] *Cf.* Isaac J. Cox, *Nicaragua and the United States, 1909–1927,* 1927; D. G. Munro, *The Five Republics of Central America,* 1918; John Parke Young, *Central American Currency and Finance,* 1925; Harold Norman Denny, *Dollars for Bullets,* 1929.

Great Powers. Manchuria is an extensive region covering some 384,000 square miles and larger in area than Germany and France combined. It has a population at the present time of about 29,000,000, of which perhaps 250,000 are Japanese and 750,000 Koreans, with the balance consisting of Chinese who have gone into the region from China in large numbers during the past two decades. Manchuria comprises the three eastern provinces of China or the Northeastern Provinces, as they have been renamed. It was politically a part of China even before the Manchurian conquest, and during the period of the Manchu dynasty (1644–1911) it was of course an integral portion of the Celestial Empire. Following the revolution of 1911 and the commencement of the chronic civil strife which has devastated China ever since, Chang Tso-lin became war lord or military governor of Manchuria. In 1922 and again in 1928 he made gestures of severing the connections between his satrapy and the rest of China, but no permanent separation resulted. Imperialistic intervention by foreign Powers in Manchuria began on a large scale during the last decade of the nineteenth century. By the treaties of 1858 and 1860, Russia had already secured title to all Chinese territory north of the Amur River and east of the Ussur;— a region which became the Maritime Provinces of Russian Siberia, with an excellent harbor and naval base at Vladivostok. In 1876 Japan forced Korea, a suzerainty of China south of Manchuria, to open its ports to Japanese traders. Following the Sino-Japanese War of 1894, Japan compelled China, in the Treaty of Shimonoseki, April 17, 1895, to recognize the independence of Korea, to cede to Japan Formosa and the Pescadores Islands, and to pay an indemnity of $150,000,000. China was also obliged to cede to Japan the Liaotung peninsula in southern Manchuria, but Russia, Germany and France objected to this acquisition and the Japanese Government reluctantly abandoned it.

There followed a decade of Russo-Japanese rivalry over Manchuria which culminated in war. The Tsarist Government contemplated extending the Siberian railway to Vladivostok and acquiring an ice-free port farther south, such as Port Arthur. In 1896 the Russo-Chinese Bank was organized with the aid of French capital, to aid China in paying the indemnity to Japan and to acquire railway and telegraph concessions. The most important railway concession which it obtained was that for the construction of the "Chinese Eastern Railway" across northern Manchuria between Chita and Vladivostok by way of Harbin. A Russo-Chinese railway company, the bonds of which were guaranteed by the Russian Government, was formed to undertake the building of the road which would give Russia control of north Manchuria. In 1898 the Russian Government, following Germany's example at Kiaochow, obtained from China a leasehold of the tip of the Liaotung peninsula, including Dalny and Port Arthur, to be connected by railroad with the Chinese Eastern and the Trans-Siberian lines. A battle of concessions between the Powers ensued, each striving to secure from China railway construction rights for its own capitalists. Chinese resistance to foreign aggression culminated in the Boxer Rebellion of 1899–1900, which was crushed by British, Russian, German, American, and Japanese troops. The Russian troops remained in Manchuria in spite of Japanese protests. Japan concluded a defensive alliance with Great Britain in 1902 and opened hostilities by attacking Port Arthur in February, 1904. Port Arthur was captured, the Russian armies were defeated at Mukden, and the Russian squadrons were destroyed by the Japanese fleet.

The Treaty of Portsmouth, September 5, 1905, transferred to Japan Russia's leasehold of Port Arthur and Dalny (Dairen), the railway from Port Arthur to

Changchun, and Russian coal-mining rights in south Manchuria, which thus became a Japanese sphere of influence. Japan also obtained southern Sakhalin as a result of the war and annexed Korea in 1910. In the same year the Russo-Chinese Bank was merged with the Banque du Nord and renamed the Russo-Asiatic Bank. The shares of this institution, which still held nominal title to the Chinese Eastern Railway, were largely purchased by French financiers. By the understanding of 1907, Japan recognized Russian interests in northern Manchuria. By the Root-Takahira agreement of November, 1908, the United States and Japan agreed to respect each other's possessions and to maintain the *status quo* "in the region of the Pacific Ocean," preserve the independence and integrity of China, and uphold the principle of the Open Door: "equal opportunity for commerce and industry of all nations in China." Japan had checked Russia, secured an impregnable foothold in south Manchuria, and placed herself in a position to embark upon even more grandiose schemes of expansion.

In Manchuria the Japanese Government made the most of its opportunities for political power and for profit for Japanese investors and business men. By the Peking convention of December 22, 1905, China consented to the transfer of Russian rights in south Manchuria to Japan. In an additional agreement China obligated herself to open up sixteen Manchurian towns to foreign trade and to permit Japan to maintain, operate, and improve the Antung-Mukden Railway, the nucleus of the South Manchurian Line, partly owned by the Japanese Government. Japan agreed to withdraw her railway guards simultaneously with the withdrawal of the Russian guards on the Chinese Eastern Line. Tokyo alleged subsequently that China also signed at this time the secret "parallel railway protocols," whereby she pledged herself not to construct other railways competing with the South Manchurian. Japan likewise rested her claim to maintain troops in Manchuria on the Sino-Russian Railway Convention of September 8, 1898, which gave to the Russo-Chinese Bank absolute and exclusive rights of administration over the lands granted to it for purposes of railway construction (Article 6). The Japanese Government contended that it inherited these rights as regards south Manchuria in the settlement of 1905. Under the original arrangement, the Liaotung peninsula leasehold would expire in 1923 and China would have a right to repurchase the Chinese Eastern and the South Manchurian railways in 1939. Japan seized the opportunity provided by the Great War to extend these rights. On January 18, 1915, the famous "Twenty-one Demands" were presented by Japan to China. These demands, in addition to attempting the imposition of a Japanese financial and military protectorate on China, extended the leaseholds and the railway rights for 99 years, canceled Chinese rights to repurchase the South Manchurian Railway in 1939, and provided for preference to Japanese in loans for railway concessions in south Manchuria and Inner Mongolia. China was compelled to accept these arrangements by the treaties of May 25, 1915. The Allied Powers and the United States were too much occupied elsewhere to interfere. By the Lansing-Ishii agreement of November 2, 1917, the Open Door and the territorial integrity of China were reaffirmed, but the United States conceded that "territorial propinquity" gave Japan "special interests" in China. Japan obtained additional railway concessions in Manchuria in 1918, and the Russian Revolution enabled her to oust Russia from north Manchuria as well. The close of the Great War found Japanese forces in occupation of all of Manchuria as well as Shantung, northern Sakhalin, and eastern Siberia.

Japan was obliged to surrender a portion of these gains as a result of the victory of the Red Army in the Russian Civil War and of American pressure exerted at Paris in 1919 and at the Washington Conference of 1921–1922. Shantung was restored to China and Siberia was evacuated by 1925. Under the Nine Power Treaty of 1922, to which Japan was a signatory, the principles of the Open Door and of the territorial integrity and the administrative entity of China were reaffirmed. The Soviet Government in Russia renounced the imperialistic rights of the Tsarist régime in China by the treaty of May 31, 1924, concluded both with the Chinese Government at Peking and the Manchurian Government at Mukden. The new Russia, however, asserted its rights in the Chinese Eastern Railway and China accepted a new arrangement for joint ownership and management, in the face of protests from France, the United States, and the Russo-Asiatic Bank, whose stockholders now found their securities to be worthless. In China the Nationalist revolution, which had overthrown the Manchu dynasty in 1911 by ousting Henry Pu Yi, the boy emperor, and had set up the unstable Republic, led to increasing hostility to foreign interests of all kinds, with resulting international complications. In Manchuria Japan's political and economic position was progressively jeopardized by the refusal of Chang Tso-lin to act as a Japanese puppet and by the construction of Chinese railways in competition with the South Manchurian Railway and its branches. In June of 1928 Chang Tso-lin was killed by the bombing of his train under circumstances suggesting Japanese complicity in the tragedy. His son, Chang Hsiao-liang, was equally unsatisfactory to Japan, for he became a member of the Kuomintang or Nationalist party, acknowledged allegiance to the Government which the Kuomintang had set up at Nanking, and shared its intention of ousting foreign interests. He retained his own army of 350,000 troops, however, and was for practical purposes an independent ruler. His high-handed treatment of the Chinese Eastern Railway led to a clash with the Soviet Union in the autumn of 1929, when Soviet troops entered north Manchuria and compelled the young marshal to respect the agreements of 1924. Japan held aloof from this controversy but determined to safeguard its interests against attack from any quarter and retained its railway guards in the south, despite the withdrawal of the Russian guards.

It is against this background that the course of Japanese imperialism in Manchuria since 1931 must be interpreted. During the summer of that year the view apparently came to prevail among responsible authorities at Tokyo that Japan's position in Manchuria, in which almost a billion dollars of Japanese capital had been invested, could be secured only by ousting Chang Hsiao-liang and by terminating all control of the Nanking Government over the area. The region had been kept free from the civil wars going on south of the Great Wall, but the policies of young Chang seemed to endanger Japanese property, Japanese profits, and the Japanese political domination of the provinces required to protect property and profits. Here, as always, it was not difficult to find "incidents" which would appear to justify forcible action. On June 28, 1931, Captain Nakamura of the imperial army, while traveling as a civilian along the Manchurian-Mongolian border, was attacked and robbed by Chinese soldiers and executed for spying, along with his companions. Friction between Chinese and Korean farmers led to rioting and bloodshed in Korea and along the Machurian frontier. Early in September, Japanese military leaders utilized the Nakamura murder to stir up patriotic sentiment in Japan. Chang replied to Japanese warnings by suggesting a League of Nations investigation. On September 18, 1931, according to the Japanese account, a bomb was exploded on the tracks of the South Manchurian Railway near Mukden by the soldiers of Chang, bent upon tearing up the tracks as the first step in an anti-Japanese campaign. With this as their immediate pretext for action, the Japanese forces at Mukden, under General Honjo, bombarded the Chinese barracks, seized the arsenal, disarmed Chinese troops, and within forty-eight hours took control of Mukden, Changchun, Antung, and other points. Chang offered no resistance to the Japanese attack, and the Chinese Government appealed to the Council of the League of Nations under Article 11 of the Covenant. The Council called upon China and Japan to avoid aggravating the situation and to withdraw their troops. Both agreed, but Japan insisted on direct negotiations with China prior to the evacuation of the cities which had been occupied and the withdrawal of troops into the railway zone—a demand which the Chinese Government refused to accept.

The rôle of the League in the ensuing controversy will be examined elsewhere.[1] Here the major phases of the conflict may be summarized from the point of view of the status of Manchuria. On September 24, and again on October 8, Japanese planes bombed Chinchow, the new headquarters of Chang Hsiao-liang. The Japanese Government defended its action as necessary to protect Japanese lives, property, and treaty rights, and demanded the negotiation of a new settlement with China which would safeguard Japanese interests. The Chinese Government refused to negotiate so long as Japanese troops remained outside the railway zone—an attitude which confirmed the Japanese Government in its determination to set up a new régime in Manchuria. Tokyo returned polite and reassuring replies to the recommendations of the Powers and the resolutions of the League Council, but proceeded with what appeared to be a prearranged plan to take over control of all of southern and central Manchuria. Additional cities were occupied, new pressure was placed upon the forces of Chang to compel them to withdraw behind the Great Wall, and the area of military operations was extended northward and eastward. The dispatch of an engineering corps to repair the Nonni River bridge near Tsitsihar, alleged to have been blown up by Chinese troops, provoked an armed clash culminating on November 19 in the Japanese capture of Tsitsihar. This city, the capital of Heilungkiang province, is north of the Chinese Eastern Railway and well within the Russian zone. The forces resisting the Japanese operations were described in Tokyo as "bandits." By the end of December Marshal Chang was obliged to withdraw his troops behind the Great Wall, and on January 2, 1932, Japanese troops occupied Chinchow. Chinese power in Manchuria was at an end, and under the protection of the Japanese military a new local government was installed. The new "State" was renamed Manchukuo in February. The Manchu boy emperor, Henry Pu Yi, became head of the new régime on March 9, 1932, with Japanese approval and support.

Meanwhile, the action of the Chinese Government in encouraging a boycott of Japanese trade throughout China precipitated large-scale hostilities in the vicinity of Shanghai. Japanese exports to China declined sharply, and it was doubtless felt at Tokyo that an effective blow at Shanghai, China's greatest port, might break the boycott. The navy, moreover, desired to share in the glory which the army was winning for itself in Manchuria. The foreign office perhaps calculated that the occupation of Shanghai would furnish a basis for bargaining with Nanking for a new settlement. Whether what followed was part of a carefully planned program or was due to sporadic incidents is not yet clear. But on January 21, 1932, the Japanese authorities at Shanghai demanded a cessation of anti-Japanese agitation and protested against a mob attack on five Japanese monks. On January 27 a twenty-four hour ultimatum was delivered to Mayor Wu Te-chen. Its terms were unconditionally accepted, but Admiral Shirozawa

[1] See below, pp. 782–791.

nevertheless decided to dispatch Japanese sailors to enforce order and protect Japanese property in the native city of Chapei. This action met with resistance and the Nineteenth Route Army, under General Tsai Ting-kai, ignoring orders from Nanking, beat off the Japanese attack. Chiang Kai Shek, Kuomintang dictator, was obliged by public clamor to abandon his policy of non-resistance and to rush troops to the defense of Shanghai while his Government appealed to

the League under Articles 10 and 15 of the Covenant and called for a special session of the League Assembly. Since the fighting was indecisive, Japan dispatched battleships and troops to Shanghai in large numbers, and on February 18 delivered another ultimatum demanding the cessation of hostilities, the dismantling of all Chinese fortifications, and the withdrawal of the Chinese forces to a line twenty kilometers beyond the International Settlement. This demand was refused, and on February 20 a general Japanese attack by land, sea, and air was launched against Chapei, Kiangwan, north of Shanghai, and the Woosung forts at the mouth of the Yangtse. Heavy fighting continued for

[417]

about two weeks. Chapei was repeatedly bombarded and reduced to ruin. Kiangwan was wrecked, the surrounding countryside devastated, and the Woo-sung forts smashed under a hail of high explosives. Thousands of lives were lost and millions of dollars worth of property destroyed. By March 3, when the Assembly met, the Chinese troops had been forced back and the fighting came to an end. After protracted negotiations, participated in by League representatives and agents of other Powers, a truce was signed on May 5, providing for Japanese evacuation of the Shanghai area.

Manchuria, however, has been converted into a Japanese protectorate through the puppet régime of Henry Pu Yi, which Tokyo has presented as a fulfillment of the self-determinationist ambitions of the Manchurians. The Japanese Government, with the support of patriotic public opinion, is prepared to fight all comers before abandoning this latest and richest addition to the Japanese empire. Desultory military operations continued throughout the spring and summer of 1932, for the purpose of mopping up "bandits" and other elements resisting the authority of "Manchukuo." Japan extended formal diplomatic recognition to the new State by the signature of a treaty of protectorate on September 15, 1932, following the seizure of Chinese customs houses and the liquidation of the last vestiges of Chinese authority in the region.

Acute friction between Japan and the United States resulted from these developments, and on January 7, 1932, Secretary of State Stimson, following the precedent set by the Wilson administration with regard to the Twenty-one Demands of 1915, informed the Chinese and Japanese Governments that the American Government could not recognize the legality of any situation, treaty, or agreement brought about by means contrary to the Pact of Paris or in violation of the Open Door.[1] On March 11, 1932, the League of Nations Assembly declared it "incumbent upon the members of the League of Nations not to recognize any situation, treaty, or agreement which may be brought about by means contrary to the Covenant of the League of Nations or to the Pact of Paris." This policy has had no visible effect up to the time of writing in modifying Japan's purposes in Manchuria. The Soviet Union meanwhile viewed with alarm the Japanese invasion of northern Manchuria and prepared to defend the Siberian border from a possible Japanese attack. Veiled negotiations between the Japanese Government and the Russo-Asiatic Bank were interpreted to foreshadow Japanese seizure of the Chinese Eastern Railway and the extinction of Russian influence in the north. The Chinese Government has continued to protest at the loss of Manchuria and to prepare for prolonged resistance to Japan through boycotts and guerilla tactics.

By January of 1933 it was clear that Japanese power was too securely established in Manchuria to be successfully challenged from any quarter. Local insurrections in the preceding autumn were suppressed. Groups of rebels in the northwest (Barga) and in the southeast (Kirin) were driven across the Soviet frontier, and Japanese military forces held the Chinese Eastern Railway throughout its entire length. The final resumption of diplomatic relations between the Nanking Government and the U.S.S.R. on December 12, 1932, after the refusal of the Japanese Government to sign a non-aggression pact with Moscow, was interpreted in Tokyo as a hostile gesture. But inasmuch as the Soviet régime had no intention either of supporting China against Japan or of resorting to force to defend its interests in Manchuria, this development did not threaten any immediate heightening of Japanese-Russian tension. Japanese attention, for the

[1] See p. 680 below.

moment at least, was directed not toward Siberia, but toward the province of Jehol, a region claimed by Manchukuo but penetrated by the troops of the ousted war-lord, Chang Hsiao-liang, who was safely ensconced in the Peiping-Tientsin area south of the Great Wall. On January 2–3, 1933, Japanese military, naval, and air forces bombarded and seized Shanhaikwan, a port south of the Great Wall of great stretegic importance because of its location with reference to Taku, Tientsin, and Peiping. On January 11, after desultory fighting, Chumenkow, the pass in the Great Wall northwest of Shanhaikwan, was occupied by Japanese troops. The invasion and occupation of Jehol followed, after active hostilities in which the Chinese were as usual defeated. In the spring of the year the Japanese Government was faced with the alternative of resting on its arms within the frontiers of its puppet State or of moving forward toward Peiping to the south and Mongolia to the west. The former policy would enable it to consolidate its position in Manchukuo. The latter policy would involve new hostilities with China and new friction with the Soviet Union.[1]

4. THE PURPOSES OF IMPERIALISM

> Many a man without six feet of earth in which to be buried is swollen with pride because his country "owns" an empire.—NORMAN THOMAS, *The Challenge of War.*

The case studies in the preceding section might be multiplied endlessly over many hundreds of pages. But the instances cited reveal the processes of contemporary imperialism operating in typical fashion. With minor variations of time, place, circumstances, and personalities, the sequence of events is much the same whether one studies the United States in Panama, Haiti, or the Philippines, Great Britain in Burma, Borneo, or Hongkong, France in Siam, Syria, or Madagascar, Belgium in the Congo, The Netherlands in Java, Portugal in Angola, Spain in Morocco, or Japan in Manchuria. All show much the same pattern. Should some new Machiavelli, capable of looking objectively and realistically at this pattern, attempt to set forth the maxims which modern statesmen must follow if they would be successful in empire-building, his precepts might read somewhat as follows:

Choose as your field of operation some area, preferably rich in resources, which is weakly held by a feeble State or has a weak independent government of its own. If your capitalists, traders, and investors already have interests in this area, make a great show of protecting these interests and complain bitterly over every infringement upon them, real or imaginary. If no interests exist, create some by inducing your profit-seekers to enter the region. In either case, act in close cooperation with

---

[1] *Cf. The League and Manchuria*, 1932; W. W. Willoughby, *Foreign Rights and Interests in China*, 1920; M. J. Bau, *The Foreign Relations of China*, 1921; W. C. Young, *Japan's Special Position in Manchuria, Japan's Jurisdiction in South Manchurian Railway Areas, The International Relations of Manchuria*, 1931; Etherton and Tilman, *Manchuria The Cockpit of Asia*, 1931; H. F. MacNair, *China in Revolution*, 1931; G. E. Sokolsky, *The Tinder Box of Asia*, 1932.

private business. Use the power of the State to serve business and use business interests to further political designs. Look about you circumspectly to see what the interests and policies of other Powers are. If they conflict with yours, if they are certain to oppose you when you endeavor to acquire control of the territory, decide whether you can safely defy them or must come to terms. Defiance is dangerous unless you have a great preponderance of power and your rivals are weak or only moderately interested. Coming to terms is more advantageous if you can offer a *quid pro quo* for their acquiescence or support. Diplomacy and war— bargaining and force—are essential means of preparing the ground for action.

When all is in readiness, manufacture a pretext, an incident, a grievance which will make your aggression appear defensive and thus justify it in the eyes of your patriots and of certain opinion groups in other States. Deceive your parliament and press, if necessary, as to your intentions and make much of national honor, vital interests, the sanctity of the flag, the necessity of protecting the rights of your citizens abroad, the blessings of Christianity, and the duties of humanitarianism. It is often possible, by intrigues among the native politicians conducted by your business men, diplomats, and naval officers, to achieve your purposes by cleverly contrived revolutions without an open resort to force. If this seems too difficult, strike swiftly, decisively, with overwhelming strength, in order that you may paralyze resistance, impose your will, and confront your own people and the world with a *fait accompli*. Speak softly to foreign governments which object, but never yield to their objections unless you feel unable to defeat them if they should resort to extreme measures. Secure recognition of your new position in treaties and use the treaty rights as a means of further extending your power if you do not gain all you desire at a blow. Whether you create a colony, a protectorate, a dominion, or merely establish financial and military control over the region depends upon circumstances. In any case, once in power, make firm your control by assisting your bankers to loan money to the local government, by securing concessions for your business men and investors, and by acquiring trading privileges for your merchants and exporters. This economic exploitation of the area will enhance the profits of your business men and make them disposed to cooperate with you in future ventures. Unless carried out too wastefully, it will make the territory a more valuable asset to the State. Placate the local inhabitants wherever possible by granting them small favors and benefits, or even the appearance of self-rule, for long-nursed grievances breed resentment and future trouble. When they will not be placated and offer resistance, stop at nothing to crush their will, for in the eyes of your business men and patriots yours is a mission of enlightenment and civilization.

These maxims of imperialist behavior are not offered in any spirit of cynicism or jesting, but are presented in all seriousness as precepts which imperialist statesmen have followed. They are offered not as praise or condemnation, nor indeed as judgment of any kind, but simply as necessary prescriptions which successful empire-builders must adhere to. These are the methods employed by Great Britain and France in Africa and southeastern Asia. These are the methods utilized by imperial Germany in Africa, Asia, and the South Seas during the creation of the now defunct German colonial empire. These are the methods used by the United States in the Caribbean since the turn of the century, and used by Japan in China in recent years.

As soon as questions are raised regarding the ends behind the means, the deeper motives beneath the technique, the underlying purposes which are served by the practice of the art of empire-building, complex problems of interpretation and evaluation present themselves for solution. These problems are usually resolved by glib formulas which express half-truths but fail to explain imperialism in its totality. "Over-population," "the need for markets," "the white man's burden," "capital investments," "trade follows the flag," "exploitation of subject peoples," and "the monopolistic stage of capitalism," are among the formulas which have gained wide acceptance. Each emphasizes one element in the process whereby the western nation-states have divided the world between them. Each seeks to explain the entire process in terms of this single element, which is regarded at the same time as a clue to motives and purposes and an explanation of results. The validity of each hypothesis can be demonstrated to the satisfaction of its proponents by a careful selection of evidence to prove a case, and each can be as readily disproved by a compilation of negative evidence. Every interpretation and evaluation in the third decade of the twentieth century must necessarily be tentative, for the Western State System is still in the midst of the epoch of imperialism. Whither the road which has been taken will finally lead no one can now say. As one commentator aptly puts it:

The question is too complex, despite its brevity, to be disposed of neatly in a final formula or a facile phrase. The answer can be obtained only by summing up the profit-and-loss account in each of half a dozen departments of activity, and combining the net results. An exhaustive study of each item would require more than one volume and more than a single lifetime. In the end, some of the benefits and evils of imperialism would still be imponderable, and the final judgment would be subjective rather than scientific, for no scientific balance can be devised to weigh ships against schools, raw materials against wars, profits against patriotism, civilization against cannibalism.[1]

[1] P. T. Moon, *Imperialism and World Politics*, p. 526.

The problem of analyzing the purposes of imperialism is made peculiarly difficult by the fact that prior intentions are usually hopelessly confused with subsequent results, both in official apologias and in public discussions. Results are cited in explanation of original motives with which they have no connection at the time of action. If the American occupation of Haiti leads to the construction of roads, schools, and hospitals, the occupation is defended in terms which suggest that its original purpose was to construct roads, schools, and hospitals, despite the fact that those who engineered the occupation had no such purpose in mind. The American annexation of Alaska is justified by gold discoveries, though the very existence of gold in the territory was unknown at the time of the purchase. Prior intentions, moreover, are frequently disguised in such ambiguous verbiage that the outside observer may well wonder whether those who framed and executed policies had any clear conception in their own minds of why they were acting. The arts of dissimulation, misrepresentation, and rationalization are so highly developed that the practitioners are deceived by their own cleverness. After naval strategists had dictated the annexation of the Philippine Islands for reasons of high politics, President McKinley justified the acquisition by solicitude for the little brown brothers "for whom Christ also died." After sugar, investments, and naval policy dictated the conversion of Cuba into an American protectorate, its "emancipation" from Spain was defended in the name of humanity and self-determination. In the age of democracy, profit motives and power motives must be skillfully concealed in terms of humanitarianism, civilizing missions, religious conversion, and material benefits conferred upon the backward peoples, for, as a distinguished Florentine diplomat pointed out some centuries ago, "the vulgar are ever caught by appearances and judge solely by the event." The multitudes of patriots and taxpayers are moved to enthusiasm and self-glorification by the tactics of interested minorities, and the shouts of the multitude move statesmen to action as a means of retaining public favor. In this jumble of slogans, catchwords, and emotional appeals to irrationality, it is next to impossible to separate the honest and the dishonest, the sincere and the insincere, the realities and the illusions.

For present purposes, consideration of the fruits and prospects of imperialism may be deferred to a later chapter, while an effort is made here to demonstrate the irrelevance of many of the alleged motives and to formulate a statement of the whole process in terms of the general interpretation of international politics attempted throughout this volume. The alleged motives may be divided into those which postulate benefits to the home country and those which postulate benefits to the colony. As for the first of these, it is argued that colonies are necessary as outlets for surplus population, as markets for goods produced in the home country, as markets for surplus capital seeking investment, and as sources for the raw materials essential to make the nation self-sufficient and secure. These arguments are at best of the *post hoc ergo propter hoc* variety. At worst they are pure rationalizations of quite other purposes or figments of too vivid imaginations skilled in wish-fulfillment thinking.

A few words may first be devoted to disposing of the naive assumption that colonies are acquired for the purpose of adding to the wealth of the mother country. This statement may be given a number of very different meanings, a few of which bear some relation to the realities of the situation as it actually exists. But if it is assumed to mean that the political control of colonies has been consciously sought as a means of enhancing the economic welfare of the inhabitants of the imperial State, or that it has led to any such result, the statement is on the face of it absurd. The inhabitants of an imperial State, lumped together as a whole, do not build empires or formulate imperialistic policies. Governments are seldom pushed into such policies by an aroused populace which believes that it will benefit in a material sense from the acquisition of colonies. The empire-builders are members of small, aggressive minorities possessing economic power and political influence in the State—merchants, missionaries, militarists, bankers, diplomats, naval officers, capitalists, humanitarians, and investors. In most cases these minorities are not even organized into any single, compact group, but consist of divergent elements no one of which has any interest in colonies as a means of promoting the economic well-being of the mass of their fellow citizens. The fellow citizens, to be sure, may be induced to believe that colonies will have this result, and their acquiescence or approval may be won by such specious arguments, though ordinarily they will respond more readily to non-economic arguments and to appeals to patriotic feeling and national pride.

The establishment of political control over some backward area, moreover, works no magic whereby the wealth of the area is appropriated and distributed piecemeal among the citizens of the imperial State. The type of imperialism which involves the seizure of the goods and chattels of the conquered and the distribution of the inhabitants as slaves among the conquerors has long since disappeared. When a modern State asserts title to a backward region, the property of the inhabitants remains in the hands of its former owners precisely as before, or it is bought up and exploited by interested investors of the conquering State for their own private profit. In the first case, the total population of the State which has asserted title derives no economic benefit whatever from the new status; and in the second, the general benefit, if any, is entirely incidental and completely negligible. The direction of trade and investment, it is true, may be altered by political means, but it cannot be demonstrated that the masses of voters and taxpayers in the mother country gain anything thereby except additional satisfaction for their patriotic impulses.

The value of colonies to the imperial nation-states as outlets for surplus population has thus far been completely negligible, despite the large rôle played by this alleged purpose in imperialistic propaganda in Germany, Italy, Japan, and other supposedly "overpopulated" States. Since most of the empires are located in tropical or subtropical areas unsuitable for residence by Europeans, and since emigrants prefer to go to congenial lands of easy economic opportunity, there has been no appreciable outflow of population from the nation-states to their colonies. In all of the pre-war colonies of Germany there were in 1914, after two decades of imperialism, only 24,000 Germans as compared with hundreds of thousands of Germans who emigrated to the United States and other places. Italy's African colonies have attracted fewer than 30,000 Italians, while other Italians by the millions have gone to France, the United States, and South America. As for Japan, there are only 178,000 Japanese in Formosa, fewer than 300,000 in Manchuria, and less than 400,000 in Korea. Great Britain is the only imperial Power with important settlement colonies. Populations of Canada, Australia, New Zealand, and parts of South Africa are made up largely of immigrants from England. In every other case conquest has not been followed by settlement, and surplus population has gone to other countries instead of to colonies. The "surplus population" argument for imperialism has played its part in convincing patriots of the necessity of expansion, for reasons, facts, and logic are usually conspicuous by their absence in the mental processes of emotional nationalists. It has therefore been utilized effectively by imperialists as a means of securing popular support for their policies. But in view of the results, it can be regarded as an honestly and consciously formulated purpose behind the quest for empire only on the assumption that statesmen are imbeciles or madmen.

It is likewise not difficult to show, despite appearances to the contrary, that most colonies are not acquired by States as markets for goods or for investments, though such motives may influence particular groups of politically influential imperialists and may be regarded as plausible by the citizenry. "Trade follows the flag," cries the imperialist—and the crowd believes and approves. In fact, trade does *not* follow the flag in most cases, and where it does the economic results, while profitable for the traders involved, are of little significance to the people of the home State.[1] The total trade of the colonial empires is reasonably impressive in round numbers—or was before the onset of the Great Depression. During

[1] "One of the purest fallacies is that trade follows the flag. Trade follows the lowest price current. If a dealer in any colony wished to buy Union Jacks he would order them from Britain's worst foe if he could save a sixpence. Trade knows no flag." Andrew Carnegie, quoted in Moon's *Imperialism*, p. 530.

the post-war years when "prosperity" still prevailed, the total foreign commerce of the colonies of the world reached an annual figure of about $15,000,000,000, something less than one-quarter of the world's international trade.[1] The British Empire accounts for three-quarters of this colonial trade, with the United States enjoying 10 per cent of it and the other colonial Powers smaller proportions. Efforts on the part of the imperial States to monopolize such trade for their own nationals have in many cases led to an increased percentage of the foreign trade of the colonies being carried on with the mother country. But only two imperial Powers enjoy over half of the trade of their colonies: the United States and Japan. Even in these cases colonial trade is a negligible fraction of the State's total foreign trade and an infinitesimal fraction of the total domestic and foreign commerce of the State. The larger part of this fraction would in most cases be enjoyed by the imperial State without political control of the territories with which the trade is carried on. To a few industries in the colonial States, *e.g.*, cotton textiles, iron and steel, etc., colonial markets are of considerable importance. In the national economy as a whole, these markets are of minor significance.[2]

The same statement may be made regarding exports of capital. Investment interests have often played a leading rôle in the process of imperialism. "Dollar diplomacy" suggests empire-building on a grand scale. But most of the foreign investments and loans of the imperial States are not made in their colonies, but in foreign countries. Accurate investment figures are difficult to obtain, but there is no question regarding the validity of this generalization for all of the capital-exporting States. Again professions and facts are widely at variance. Again the professions must be regarded as rationalizations, superstitions, and shibboleths, not as accurate verbalizations of the purposes of imperialism.

[1] Moon, *op. cit.* p. 519, gives the following figures for colonial trade:

Colonial powers	Total commerce of colonies, millions of dollars	Commerce with mother country, millions of dollars	Mother country's share in total commerce of colonies, percentage
Great Britain (1923–1924)........	11,079	3,778	34
United States (1923–1924)........	1,524	1,194	77
France (1922)..................	906	441	49
Netherlands (1924).............	898	100	11
Japan (1923)...................	607	430	71
Belgium (1924).................	44	22	50
Italy (1922–1923)...............	21	7	33

[2] See the interesting discussion of this in Moon, pp. 526–535.

Finally, it may be pointed out that the contention that colonies are acquired as sources of raw materials is also without foundation, either in the political process of empire-building or in the economic results of the process. On the one hand, efforts on the part of imperial States to fix world prices of raw materials exported from their colonies, and thus make profits for their own nationals at the expense of foreign purchasers, are largely unsuccessful. On the other hand, none of the imperial Powers derives the major portion of its required raw materials from its colonies. Colonial raw materials are sold to purchasers willing to buy them, and such purchasers are quite as likely to be found in foreign States as in the mother country. Purchasers needing raw materials buy them where they are to be had most cheaply, and the sources of supply are quite as likely to be found in foreign States or colonies as in the territories of the State of the purchasers. Self-sufficiency in raw materials is impossible even for Great Britain, with her vast and variegated Empire, and is quite out of the question for other States. If the empires have been acquired to make the imperial States self-sufficient in such goods, the experiment has failed miserably. In point of fact, this too is not a "purpose" of imperialism, but a phrase employed by profit-seekers and by power-and-prestige politicians to bewilder the uninitiated and win popular approval for policies motivated by considerations of a different character.[1]

In the same fashion, the argument that colonies are acquired for the purpose of civilizing and converting naked pagan savages and of conferring upon them the blessings of western culture is undeserving of serious consideration in any effort to evaluate imperialism in the international politics of the Western State System. Missionaries there are who go out to Africa, Asia, and the South Seas to convert the heathen. And there are colonial administrators who strive, sometimes successfully, to elevate living standards among the people they rule, just as there are merchants who sell them clothes, concessionaires who take away their property, investors who profit from their exploitation, financiers who loan them money, and settlers who go among them to seize their land. But these are small bits in a vast mosaic, and the pattern of the whole is not revealed by the shape and color of any one of the bits. It is no more the "purpose" of imperialism to confer benefits upon its victims than to confer benefits upon the home country. The "white man's burden" rests heavily upon the shoulders of the black men and brown men and yellow men who have been subjugated. The benefits received by the victims have been entirely incidental and they have, moreover, been negligible in quantity, doubtful in quality, and bitterly resented because of their source and the methods employed in conferring them.[2] As for the alleged benefits of Christianity,

[1] See pp. 345–350 above.
[2] The attitudes of the "backward peoples" was well expressed by Señor Luis Cabrera, a member of the Carranza Cabinet in Mexico, in an address delivered at the United States

they have not been accepted. Generations of missionary activity, both Catholic and Protestant, have converted to the Cross only a tiny fraction of the immense non-Christian population of Asia, Africa, and Oceania. As for public education, sanitation, and other social benefits, only a small proportion of colonial budgets is devoted to these functions. The backward peoples have more frequently encountered economic exploitation, venereal disease, social disintegration, and other evils at the hands of the white man.

Now it may very well be contended that this refutation of alleged purposes is beside the point, since each particular purpose plays its rôle in the total complexity of purposes and the entire process has been so confused, anarchic, and disorderly that no clear, single purpose is discernible. This contention is quite valid. The preceding observations have served their end if they have suggested (1) that no "single-purpose" explanation of imperialism is tenable, whether it be couched in political, economic, religious, or humanitarian terms, and (2) that the course of empire-building has been one in which no single directing intelligence has ever played a controlling rôle, save in a few exceptional instances. Generally speaking, scores of divergent interests in the imperial States, by a more or less blind and uncoordinated pushing and pulling, have contributed to a final result not clearly foreseen at the outset by anyone and certainly not representing any consciously formulated and willfully executed program on the part of any single individual or group. Contemporary imperialism is a phenomenon of western civilization in the age of private capitalism, bourgeois individualism, planless economy, parliamentary democracy, and demagogic politics. These aspects of western culture suggest one of its dominant characteristics: pluralism, competition between a bewildering multitude of interests and forces, uncontrolled and uncontrollable economic and political drifting under the impact of pressures released by the Industrial Revolution and not yet brought under the control of organized social intelligence. Out of the interaction of interests and forces certain consequences flow which take on the appearance—which are indeed deliberately given the appearance—of purpose

Embassy in 1917. He declared: "What you people must get out of your minds . . . is the idea that we in Mexico want to be like you. We do not—not in any respect. We don't want your Red Cross coming down here to make us antiseptic. . . . We don't want your sanitary commissions down here trying to change our habits; we don't want your type of education, your kind of religion, your commercialized ideas of living. . . . Our civilization is older than yours by centuries. It suits us. Your paternalism, your continual oversight of Latin American affairs is irritating to us. You assume too much, and the benevolent rôle fools none of us. . . . To a Mexican of education, who knows life in the States, this Pan-American talk is what you say, the bunk! It's nothing but talk, hot air, empty language disproved every day. There is no equality or fraternity possible so long as your people keep your sense of social superiority. . . . Why talk about a unity that does not live? Why keep up all this Pan-American propaganda unless—what we all believe—for your own purposes of exploitation and political dominance." G. Marvin in *The Independent*, January 14, 1928.

and planning on the part of the whole community of the nation-state. But this is appearance only, for the forces which have produced the consequences are part of a chaotic jumble of interests and groups within each nation. "Imperialism" is such a consequence. Its "purposes" are intelligible only in terms of the nature of the political process within and between the nation-states themselves.

The significant thing is that the pushing and pulling of competing political and economic groups, each pursuing its own ends, takes place within the framework of the nation-state. Normally each group, whatever its particular purposes may be, acknowledges allegiance to the nation, identifies itself with the national community, and symbolizes its goals in terms of the attitudes and ideology of national patriotism. The nation-states of the Western State System, like all States in all State systems, are perpetually engaged with one another in a struggle for power and prestige. In this struggle they strive to extend their authority over as wide a territory as possible, for possession of territory is assumed, correctly in most cases, to enhance State power. The western nation-states are usually unable to impose their power on one another, and a "balance of power" results from their conflict. But, owing to the technological differential suggested at the beginning of this chapter, they have been able to impose their power upon the backward peoples of the earth, unable to resist their superior efficiency. Imperialism is intelligible as a factor in international politics only in terms of the imposition by military means of the power of the western nation-states upon the non-European parts of the world.

The specific objectives of this striving for power are necessarily couched in economic terms, since political power always rests upon economic and technological foundations. The objectives necessarily reflect the interests and purposes of those groups within the nation-state which are able to control government and make their own interests prevail in the current conception of the national interests. In the nineteenth and twentieth centuries, bankers, investors, merchants, property owners, entrepreneurs, and profit-seekers of all kinds are usually more successful than other groups in controlling governments and dictating their policies. Imperialism is therefore rationalized in terms of these particular interests and is made to serve the purposes of these groups. Its broader ends are accurately suggested by the adjectives "national" and "capitalistic." But the process itself is an integral part of the pattern of Great Power politics, to be considered in the following chapters. The will-to-power of the western nation-states in the age of machine technology has enabled them to create huge empires and to impose their control upon millions of square miles of territory and hundreds of millions of people. That control is sought not to contribute to the economic well-being, either of the natives or of the home population, but to enhance the power of each imperial State in relation to that of its rivals. And the enhancement of power which is achieved is inevitably utilized for the profit of the ruling classes in the imperial States themselves. This, in the last analysis, is the alpha and omega of the quest for empire.

SUGGESTED READINGS

Beer, G. L.: *Origins of the British Colonial System*, New York, The Macmillan Company, 1908.

Earle, E. M.: *Turkey, The Great Powers, and the Bagdad Railway*, New York, The Macmillan Company, 1923.

Egerton, H. E.: *A Short History of British Colonial Policy*, London, Methuen & Co., 1918.

Elliott, W. Y.: *The New British Empire*, New York, The McGraw-Hill Book Company, Inc., 1932.

Fischer, L.: *Oil Imperialism: the International Struggle for Petroleum*, New York, International, 1926.

Gibbons, H. A.: *An Introduction to World Politics*, New York, Century Company, 1922.

———: *New Map of Africa: a History of European Colonial Expansion and Colonial Diplomacy*, 1900–1916, New York, Century Company, 1917.

Hertslet, E.: *Map of Africa by Treaty*, London, Harrison and Sons, 1896.

Hobson, J. A.: *Imperialism, A Study*, New York, Pott (Gorham), 1905.

Johnston, H. H.: *History of the Colonization of Africa by Alien Races*, Cambridge, Cambridge University Press, 1905.

Jones, C. L.: *The United States and the Caribbean*, Chicago, University of Chicago Press, 1929.

Lapworth, C.: *Tripoli and Young Italy*, London, Swift, 1912.

Lewin, E.: *The Resources of the Empire and Their Development* (British Empire Series, IV), New York, Henry Holt & Company, 1924.

Lucas, C. P.: *Historical Geography of the British Colonies* (6 vols.), Oxford, Clarendon Press, 1898–1907.

———: *Patriotism and Colonization in Africa*, New York, Oxford University Press, 1922.

Moon, P. T.: *Imperialism and World Politics*, New York, The Macmillan Company, 1926.

Nearing, S.: *The American Empire*, New York, Rand School, 1921.

Pasvolsky, L.: *Russia in the Far East*, New York, The Macmillan Company, 1922.

Roberts, S. H.: *History of French Colonial Policy*, 1870–1925 (2 vols.), London, King, 1929.

Shuster, M.: *The Strangling of Persia*, New York, Century Company, 1912.

Torchiana, H.: *Tropical Holland*, Chicago, University of Chicago Press, 1921.

Townsend, M. E.: *Origins of Modern German Colonialism*, New York, Columbia University Press, 1921.

Toynbee, A. J.: *The Western Question in Greece and Turkey*, New York, Oxford University Press, 1923.

Viallate, A.: *Economic Imperialism and International Relations during the Last Fifty Years*, New York, The Macmillan Company, 1923.

Woolf, L. S.: *Economic Imperialism*, New York, Harcourt, Brace & Company, 1920.

———: *Empire and Commerce in Africa*, New York, The Macmillan Company, 1920.

See also Suggested Readings for Chapter XV, pp. 639–640 below.

Chapter XII

THE FOREIGN POLICIES OF THE GREAT POWERS

IN THE four preceding chapters of this survey an effort has been made to suggest the nature of the more important forces which operate within modern States to move them to action on the stage of international politics. While these forces are complex and multitudinous, it has seemed permissible to reduce them to a few general categories of ideas, attitudes, and purposes: the patriot's ceaseless questing for greater power and prestige for his State; the profit-seeker's search for riches in the name of patriotism and national prosperity; and the ambitions of the empire-builders to extend the control of the nation-state over vast undeveloped areas, for reasons of patriotism, power, prestige, and profit. In short, the forces behind the policies of the nation-states have been interpreted in terms of certain of the values, motives, and patterns of behavior associated with "nationalism," "capitalism," and "imperialism."

Out of the interaction between these policies emerges the fluctuating and kaleidoscopic mosaic of "world politics." This familiar phrase is misleading, for the "world" is not a political entity, but only a vast arena in which many political entities, great and small, strive with one another like gladiators for glory and profit. The gladiators are the sovereign nations of the Western State System, and their struggles with one another, in peace and in war, are the sum and substance of international politics. The rules of the game have been sketched in the preceding book. The spirit of the game, the motives of the players, and the prizes at stake have been suggested by looking at the forces within the nation-states determining their foreign policies. Before considering the interrelationships between these policies and the resulting pattern of power politics, it will be useful in the present chapter to outline the recent and contemporary foreign policies of each of the seven Great Powers. The foreign policies of the lesser Powers are equally illuminating and worthy of investigation, but since space is limited and the major trends of international politics are determined by the Great Powers, attention will be concentrated on the States falling into this category. This is not the place to recount the diplomatic history of each of these States, for numerous histories of foreign policies are readily available. But it should prove valuable to trace recent developments and to suggest the stakes of diplomacy which each of the Great Powers is at present pursuing. The summaries which follow are less factual presentations than interpretations of foreign policies, based upon the factual record and in harmony with the general approach toward international politics adopted in the present volume.

1. FRANCE: LA GRANDE NATION

And threatening France, placed like a painted Jove,
Kept idle thunder in his lifted hand.
—JOHN DRYDEN, *Annus Mirabilis*, 1666.

The French nation-state is, with the possible exception of England, the oldest of the Great Powers in the Western State System. It was the first State of continental Europe to attain political unity under its medieval kings. It was in France that royal absolutism and centralized power first triumphed over feudal anarchy and medieval particularism. It was in France, some three centuries later, that bourgeois democracy first triumphed over absolutism and the landed aristocracy. Corresponding changes had taken place earlier in England, but England was across the Channel and was no longer able to act effectively on the Continent after her knights and barons were driven out of Normandy, Aquitaine, and other "French" provinces in the Hundred Years' War (1337–1453). The same conflict which ousted England from the mainland launched France on her career as the largest, richest, and most populous State of Europe. For three centuries—roughly from 1500 to 1815—French kings, statesmen, and patriots took pride in the fact that *la belle France* was ranked first among the nations in military might, in diplomatic influence and prestige, and in the arts of civilization. French hegemony was never successfully translated into the permanent conquest of France's neighbors, for coalitions of weaker States checked Louis XIV and Napoleon I in their ambitions. While the long-coveted Rhine frontier was obtained, efforts to extend French power beyond the Rhine, the Alps, and the Pyrenees and into the Low Countries were frustrated by hostile alliances. But a habit of predominance, a purple memory of glory in arms, a cherished conviction of French superiority and French supremacy in the European State System are such an integral part of the French national tradition that they continue to shape French foreign policy in recent times.

From the point of view of the traditional position of *la grande nation*, it was the tragedy of the nineteenth century that France ceased to be the most powerful State of western Europe. French policy under the Second Empire of Napoleon III (1852–1870) was directed toward imperial expansion and toward preventing the political unification of Germany. If the small, divided, impotent States of central Europe were to be united into a single nation, France would face a neighbor across the Rhine more wealthy and populous than herself. The effort to forestall this misfortune failed. The Franco-Prussian War of 1870–1871 spelled the end of French supremacy on the Continent. In the dust of Sedan and the agony of besieged and captured Paris, there perished the possibility of retaining in the hands of the Quai d'Orsay the reins of power which those hands were no longer strong enough to hold. The Rhine frontier was lost. Alsace-Lorraine was lost. Germany was a united nation. And Italy to the south was also a united nation. French foreign policy after 1871 is intelligible only in terms of a conscious and consistently pursued effort to recover for France what had been lost and to reestablish traditional French hegemony over Europe. How this goal—seemingly impossible of realization—was attained and how French soldiers and diplomats have achieved and preserved a new position of uneasy preponderance over the Continent in the post-war period can readily be indicated by a résumé of diplomatic events during the six decades of the Third Republic.

Viewed in retrospect, French policy from 1871 to 1914 presents the appearance, which is certainly not belied by the facts, of a progressive adaptation of diplomatic and military means to the great end of the *revanche, i.e.*, the recovery of the Rhine frontier and the lost provinces, and the restoration of French hegemony over Europe. This end could be attained only by reducing Germany to subjection. Germany was the largest, wealthiest, most highly industrialized and most efficiently militarized State of the western world. France could never defy Germany alone, nor hope to achieve her purposes without support from beyond her own frontiers. That support was obtained by the building up of a colonial empire which added 60,000,000 subjects to France's 40,000,000 citizens, and by the creation of a series of diplomatic combinations which brought other Powers into the French orbit in common opposition to Germany. The French colonial empire has already been dealt with.[1] In the course of its conquests, French diplomacy came into sharp conflict with other Powers. Humiliating surrenders of claims were at times necessary, but each rebuff was ultimately turned to advantage in the task of restoring a balance of power against Germany. The iron ring of alliances which Bismarck forged to keep France in isolation was at length broken through in the formation of the Dual Alliance with Russia in 1891–1894. The Tsardom was won away from German influence and became France's mainstay in the East. The Alliance was "defensive," and St. Petersburg was cautious and not always reliable. But the secret political understandings and military conventions contemplated eventual cooperation in war against Germany, in the event of a German "attack" upon either of the parties. This afforded a "security" which enabled the Republic to raise its head again, to exercise less circumspection regarding German

[1] See pp. 389–392 above.

sensibilities, and to look with less apprehension upon the danger of another invasion of grey-clad, spike-helmeted Teutonic legions. Imperial expansion in north Africa and southern Asia brought the Republic into conflict with Great Britain—in Siam in 1893 and in the Sudan in 1898. In both cases the weaker party yielded to the stronger, but out of the resulting friction the Republic gained a new ally instead of a new enemy.

Théophile Delcassé, French Foreign Minister from 1898 to 1905, perhaps contributed more to the successful consummation of French diplomatic purposes than any other single individual. He strengthened the Dual Alliance, won Italy away from Berlin and Vienna, and brought perfidious Albion—traditional enemy of France—into the sphere of French designs. He surrendered as gracefully as possible to Great Britain following the clash of the empire-builders at Fashoda in 1898. He then bargained with Downing Street for concessions and support in other spheres. Morocco was coveted to round out France's African empire, but Morocco could not be taken without appropriate diplomatic preparations. Delcassé, past master in the art of give and take, approached Rome in 1900 and made it known that France would not stand in the way of Italian ambitions in Tripoli if Italy would grant France a free hand in Morocco. A bargain was struck, and in 1902, by additional secret commitments, the Quai d'Orsay received what amounted to an assurance of Italian neutrality in the event of war with Germany. Spain was likewise placated by a secret partition agreement regarding Morocco. As for Great Britain, the crisis of 1898–1899 was followed by an unofficial *rapprochement* which culminated in protracted official negotiations regarding colonial claims. In the spring of 1904 the Anglo-French *Entente Cordiale* became a diplomatic reality. Controversies over Newfoundland, West Africa, Madagascar, and Zanzibar were adjusted by compromise, and the partition of Siam into British and French spheres of influence was reaffirmed. Paris withdrew its long-standing objection to British control of Egypt, and London agreed to the partition of Morocco between France and Spain. Not only did the path now seem clear for the taking of Morocco, but British diplomatic support was assured for this and probably for other ventures. The Entente was supplemented by military and naval understandings in 1906, 1910, and 1912. French diplomacy smoothed the way for Anglo-Russian reconciliation, and by the understandings of 1907 the Entente Cordiale became the Triple Entente of France, Great Britain, and Russia, facing the Triple Alliance of Germany, Austria-Hungary, and Italy, with the last State no longer a loyal member of the central coalition, thanks to Delcassé's maneuverings.

Meanwhile, however, Germany remained to be reckoned with, for even the Triple Entente was not yet prepared to defy Berlin. There ensued a series of Franco-German crises over Morocco, where Germany also had interests and ambitions which she was unwilling to surrender, except for a price. When French "pacific penetration" of Morocco jeopardized its independence, Germany came to its defense and challenged the Quai d'Orsay in 1905. Delcassé favored defiance, for he could count on British support. But Russia had been defeated by Japan and was in the throes of revolution. More cautious heads at Paris perceived that defiance could end only in disaster. Delcassé was forced to resign and the French Government was compelled to confer with Germany and the other Powers regarding Morocco in the Algeciras Conference of 1906. This German diplomatic victory, however, merely strengthened the Entente and increased French determination to acquire Morocco. Another crisis of 1908 was indecisive. In 1911 Berlin again championed the sovereignty of Morocco in the face of French encroachments, and a final bargain was struck by Caillaux. Germany now recognized France's rights to establish a protectorate over Morocco in return for the cession to Germany of 100,000 square miles of the French Congo, with a valueless strip of German Cameroon going to France as a sham compensation. This "victory" over Germany in Morocco was dearly bought, and the resulting resentment on both sides increased press recriminations and diplomatic tension. The race of armaments continued, and the French Government strove to bind Russia and Great Britain ever more closely to its cause. President Poincaré visited Russia in 1912 and again in 1914. A series of military and naval agreements cemented the Triple Entente into a solid block, all three members of which were determined to accept no further losses of prestige by yielding to the dictates of Berlin.

While the French Government had no direct interest in the Hapsburg quarrel with Serbia in the fatal summer of 1914, its leaders felt obliged, in the interest of a solid Entente front against the Central Powers, to support Russia in any action she might take to protect her interests in the Balkans. When that action assumed the form of mobilization against Austria-Hungary and Germany, the Quai d'Orsay acquiesced. It accepted the hazards of the "inevitable" war in the conviction that Russian military preparations had now reached a point at which the combined power of France, Russia, and Great Britain was more than a match for Germany and Austria-Hungary. Here was the great day of the *revanche* and the final struggle for mastery. Victory would mean the recovery of the lost provinces, the restoration of the Rhine frontier, the partition of the German colonies, and the crushing of the German military menace. Poincaré the Lorrainer—President and symbol of militant French nationalism—was supported by the Viviani Cabinet in standing steadfast by Russia's side. Queries from Berlin regarding French policy were answered with the statement that "France will be guided by her interests." French mobilization was ordered on August 1. On August 3

Germany declared war on France, and on the following day the French Parliament, without even asking to see the texts of the Dual Alliance and convinced that the Republic was the victim of unprovoked German aggression, gave its patriotic approval to the course which the ministers had embarked upon.

After four years and three months of unprecedented bloodshed and destruction, France achieved the goal which her diplomats and soldiers had pursued since 1871. German military might had been as grossly underestimated as Russian fighting capacity had been exaggerated, and only a world in arms against the Central Powers enabled France to achieve victory in 1918. The Republic's eastern ally had been ground to pieces by the enemy and was in the throes of social revolution. Great Britain, Italy, the United States, and a host of lesser allies stood in the way of a purely French peace. They opposed French annexation of the Rhineland. They opposed outright annexation of the German colonies. They refused to conclude an alliance against Germany for the future. But much had been gained despite these obstacles. Austria-Hungary was destroyed. German military and naval strength was reduced to impotence by the Treaty of Versailles. A crushing indemnity of undetermined amount was assessed against the fallen foe. Germany lost all her colonies. In Europe she was compelled to surrender Eupen and Malmedy to Belgium, Alsace-Lorraine to France, the "Corridor" and part of Upper Silesia to Poland. She was also obliged to give up Danzig and Memel, to surrender the Saar valley to temporary French control, and to submit to Allied military occupation of the Rhineland and the Rhine bridge-heads. The French army became the most powerful force on the Continent. French power and prestige were restored almost, if not quite, to their old status. French hegemony was successfully reasserted. A new distribution of territory and power, embodying the realities of this hegemony, was written into the public law of Europe. If Poincaré and other extreme nationalists were bitter over the "leniency" to the enemy of the most crushing peace settlement between Great Powers in modern times, at least the new Europe offered ample opportunities for the permanent humiliation of Germany and the perpetuation of French ascendancy.

Post-war French foreign policy has been directed almost exclusively toward the attainment of this end, although differences of opinion have developed as to the best means thereto. "Security" became at once, and has remained ever since, the guiding slogan of the Quai d'Orsay. "Security" means assurance against invasion from the east. Assurance against invasion is not to be had, in the opinion of most patriotic Frenchmen, unless the prospective invader is kept in a position of political inferiority and military helplessness and the prospective victim retains such a preponderance of power that the enemy cannot even contemplate a test of strength. No chances are to be taken with German good will, for France has been twice invaded in fifty years. Germany, moreover—defeated, truncated, disarmed—still possesses 63,000,000 people to France's 40,000,000 and a magnificent industrial establishment for the making of modern war. There can be no security unless the Republic possesses overwhelming power to paralyze at once any threatened resort to force on the part of the foe. Since the political, territorial, military, and reparations clauses of the peace treaty afforded a large measure of such security, it was natural that the French Government should not only insist upon their preservation intact, but should interpret them as liberally as possible from the point of view of French interests.

The attainment of French security, *i.e.*, the maintenance of French hegemony over the Continent, requires that Germany be kept weak and that France be kept strong. To achieve this goal, the dismemberment of the German federal State was at first contemplated. "Separatist" intrigues in the Rhineland were indulged in extensively between 1918 and 1925, and were then abandoned when it appeared that the Rhineland was not detachable. The French Government has now given up all reasonable expectations of inflicting further territorial losses upon Germany, or of consummating the political dissolution of the German nation. But the territorial clauses of the Treaty of Versailles must be kept intact, and any union, political or economic, between the Reich and German Austria must be prevented. Germany must be kept disarmed, for a rearmed Germany, bent upon a counter-*revanche*, would be a formidable foe. Germany must be kept diplomatically isolated, for if she gains allies she might conceivably at some future date undo the verdict of 1919, as France, with the aid of allies, was able earlier to undo the verdict of 1871. And Germany must be kept economically and financially prostrate, for without capital and productive capacity no State can achieve military power or diplomatic influence. With this end in view, the French Government, between 1918 and 1924, insisted upon the full execution of the economic and financial clauses of the Treaty. A weak Germany could perhaps pay no reparations, but a strong Germany could threaten French security. Poincaré and his supporters preferred security to reparations. When payments were defaulted in 1923, French and Belgian troops occupied the Ruhr Valley, the industrial heart of Germany, as a means of coercing the Reich.

If these and similar measures have been adopted to keep Germany impotent, corresponding measures have been devised to keep France powerful. New fortifications have been erected along the eastern frontier, and the French army, while reduced in numbers, has been maintained at the highest possible level of technical efficiency. The French Government has steadfastly refused to reduce its armaments further, except in return for an international police force or some alternative arrangement which would afford an equal degree of security. New allies have been sought to replace the old. Tsarist Russia is gone, and French efforts during the Russian Civil War to bring about the overthrow of the Soviet régime were fruitless. But Belgium has become France's ally, and in the east Poland is likewise an ally, for Poland would be menaced even more directly by a German *revanche* than would France. In the southeast the Little Entente—Czechoslovakia, Jugoslavia, and Rumania—is no less resolved to maintain the *status quo*. All of its members are allies of France, and under French guidance and with the aid of French loans they are resolved

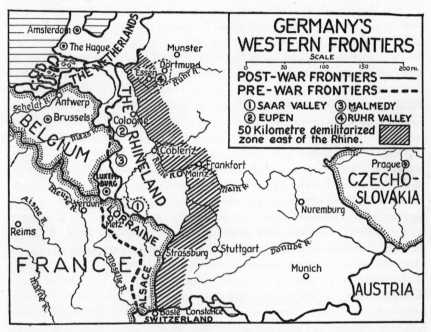

to oppose all efforts to modify the existing distribution of territory and power, whether from Germany to the north, from Hungary or Austria within their midst, from Italy to the west, or from Russia to the east. These common interests have stretched a broad cordon of French power around Germany's frontiers.

Not content to rely only upon this bulwark, the Quai d'Orsay has sought overseas assistance from every possible source. In 1919 the French Cabinet reluctantly abandoned its plan for annexation of the Rhineland in return for a pledge of a Franco-Anglo-American security pact which never materialized. French interest in the League of Nations has been largely motivated by the hope that it can be utilized to ensure enforcement of the peace treaties and place the power of all its members behind the victim of any aggression. The French Government has attempted for a decade, without success, to secure a general British guarantee of European frontiers. Nothing would be more welcome to it (or more improbable of attainment) than a pledge of diplomatic and military support from the United States, in the event of any forcible effort at treaty revision. Despite failures and disappointments, post-war France and her eastern allies have established such a preponderance of power on the Continent that the old equilibrium between opposing coalitions has disappeared and no aggregation of power has emerged as yet which can hope to challenge French ascendancy.

But this "security" has been as uneasy as that of the proverbial head that wears a crown. Seventy million Germans remain in central Europe, and should they ever become politically united and armed, they could overwhelm Poland and Czechoslovakia. Should they ever secure Russian and Italian assistance, they could sweep through all barriers. It has consequently seemed expedient to placate Germany to a certain degree. Following the failure of the Poincaré policy of coercion, the Herriot Cabinet of 1924 consented to the so-called Dawes Plan of reparation payments and to the evacuation of the Ruhr. Reparation obligations were further reduced in the Young Plan of 1930, and in the face of world-wide economic collapse were abandoned entirely in the Lausanne agreements of July 8, 1932. Under the leadership of Briand, a "new era" of Franco-German relations was inaugurated by the Locarno pacts of October, 1925, and by the admission of Germany into the League in 1926. The Rhineland was evacuated in 1930, five years before the required time. Extreme French Nationalists have condemned these concessions as an indication of weakness, a menace to security, and an invitation to Germany to make new demands for treaty revision. More moderate Frenchmen have defended them as necessary steps toward security via conciliation and rapprochement. The "Locarno epoch" closed with the deaths of Briand and Stresemann, and new friction developed over *Anschluss*, armaments, and treaty revision in 1931–1932. In 1935 the Saar valley plebiscite will be held and new difficulties will arise. In any case, French conciliatory gestures must stop at the point where equality in armaments and frontier revision begins, for no French Government can permit any such enhancement of German power. Security demands peace. Peace demands the preservation of the *status quo* in its broad essentials. Preservation of the *status quo* demands the maintenance of French hegemony and, paradoxically, France will fight to maintain peace, *i.e.*, French ascendancy, rather than yield the fruits of victory.

French uneasiness has been increased by the attitudes of other Powers. American non-cooperation in European affairs is deplored. British aloofness and "encouragement" to Germany are deprecated. Italy's ambitions to increase her colonial empire at the expense of France, to extend her influence in the Balkans at the expense of Jugoslavia, to reacquire Nice, Savoy, Corsica, and to achieve naval parity with France in the Mediterranean are viewed with alarm. The strategy of French diplomacy is as much directed toward thwarting these Italian designs as to keeping Germany in a position of subjection. The Little Entente is similarly the weapon whereby Hungarian and Bulgarian irredentist aspirations are frustrated. And in the east there looms the Soviet Union, vast, menacing, incalculable. In 1919 France and the other Allied States sought in vain to destroy the Soviet régime by armed intervention. In 1920 Poland was saved from conquest at the hands of the Red Army only by French assistance. Between France and the U.S.S.R. there are enmity and deep suspicion, despite the resumption of diplomatic relations in 1924. All of these States are potential disturbers of the *status quo*. Each of them must therefore be guarded against, and any combination between them must be prevented at all costs. Thus far French diplomacy has succeeded admirably in its purposes and French financial, military, and political hegemony was never more obvious than in the troubled years following the onset of the Great Depression in 1929.

2. GERMANY: A LOST PLACE IN THE SUN

To harness slowly but to drive rapidly is in the nature of this people.— PRINCE OTTO VON BISMARCK.

The newly created German Empire which imposed the Treaty of Frankfort upon France in 1871 occupied a position in the European State system, during the years which followed, somewhat comparable to that enjoyed a half-century later by the France which imposed the Treaty of Versailles on Germany in 1919. By the Franco-Prussian War the Germany of William I and Bismarck attained national unity and military and diplomatic supremacy on the Continent, just as the France of Poincaré and Clemenceau attained strategic preponderance and political hegemony over Europe by the Great War. Around the chronic conflict between France and Germany, the whole narrative of European diplomatic history might be woven, for French and German armies have fought on opposite sides in every general European war since 1618. The two peoples who were one a millennium ago, and who both look back to Charlemagne or Karl der Grosse as a national hero, have never been reunited since the dissolution of that ancient monarch's realm. Each has gone its own way, developing its own language and its own rich culture. But while France early attained political unity, "Germany" long remained a congeries of powerless principalities. That the strong should expand at the expense of the weak was as natural here as elsewhere, and from Richelieu to Napoleon III the story of Franco-German relations is a tale of the constant territorial expansion of France to the eastward and of constant French invasion of the Germanies. Between the fourteenth and eighteenth centuries the region between the Maas and Moselle valleys and the Rhine was progressively subjugated by French arms, and French incursions across the Rhine were periodical. In the days of the first Napoleon, Prussia was humbled and most of Germany was brought under French control until its release in the "War of Liberation." Under the impetus of a new nationalism, patriotic Germans strove to attain political unity. The Liberals failed in 1848. Bismarck succeeded in 1871, after war with Denmark, Austria, and France. United Germany overshadowed defeated France and bestrode Europe like a new Colossus. It was content with its gains and, like all satiated States, sought only security and the preservation of the *status quo*.

As long as Bismarck remained at the helm (1871–1890), this purpose remained the single aim of German foreign policy. Security required vigilance against the only Power which had an interest in upsetting the new equilibrium. Alone and unaided, France could never hope to challenge Germany. But a France with allies would become dangerous. France must therefore be kept isolated. For twenty years the Iron Chancellor kept France at bay in this fashion. Austria-Hungary, Russia, Italy, and Great Britain were all conciliated by adroit diplomatic moves. Between 1872 and 1878, Hohenzollern Kaiser, Romanov Tsar, and Hapsburg Emperor met in frequent conference in a *Drei Kaiserbund*, although Russian aggression against Turkey in 1877 caused Austro-Russian friction in the Balkans and endangered the Three Emperors' League. In 1879 Bismarck concluded with Austria-Hungary a secret defensive alliance which became the Triple Alliance in 1882 by the accession of Italy. In 1883 Bismarck arranged a defensive alliance between Austria-Hungary and Rumania, to which Germany and Italy subsequently adhered. In 1887 a three-year "Reinsurance Treaty" was concluded with Russia, whereby Germany pledged her support in maintaining the *status quo* in the Balkans and agreed to view with benevolence Russian ambitions to control the Straits of the Dardanelles. France was completely isolated, and while Germany refrained from imperial expansion overseas, Bismarck could afford to encourage French colonial adventures in the hope that they would assuage the bitterness occcasioned by the loss of Alsace-Lorraine and dissipate French energies in Africa and Asia.

The young Kaiser, William II, dismissed Bismarck in March, 1890. This "dropping of the pilot" was promptly followed by the non-renewal of the Reinsurance Treaty with Russia and by the conclusion of the Franco-Russian Alliance. What Bismarck had long feared and successfully checkmated while he remained in power had thus come to pass. Whether other States could be prevented from being drawn into the French orbit depended upon the skillfulness of Bismarck's successors, Caprivi (1890–1894), Hohenlohe (1894–1900), and Bülow (1900–1909). The belated adoption of a policy of imperial expansion and the building up of a battle fleet rendered it inevitable that British hostility toward Germany would be aroused, for German colonialism and German navalism represented, in appearance at least, a threat to Britain's empire of colonies, commerce, and sea power, much more serious than any possible threat from France or Russia. Empire-building and naval armaments were the logical consequences of the impressive growth of German foreign commerce and investment, though the most ardent imperialists and navalists were the ultra-patriotic Prussian Junkers, members of the agrarian aristocracy, rather than the merchants, bankers, and industrialists. But all German patriots were agreed that Germany was now a "world Power," with a future upon the sea and a right to a place in the sun of colonial Africa and Asia. Negotiations for a naval understanding and an alliance with Great Britain were unsuccessful, and the year 1904 found Great Britain no longer in her rôle of splendid isolation, but aligned with France in common opposition to German colonial ambitions. Italy was already won away from the Triple Alliance, though how completely Berlin did not know until later. The Anglo-Russian agreements of 1907 completed the circle. Germany no longer dominated the Continent in serene security, unconcerned over the *revanchard* ambitions of an isolated France. A balance of power was reestablished. The Triple Alliance was confronted by the Triple Entente.

All that happened after 1907 confirmed German fears of "encirclement," for the combined military, naval, and economic resources of Great Britain, France, and Russia heavily outweighed those of Germany and Austria-Hungary. Great Britain and France opposed Germany in Morocco. Great Britain, Russia, and France opposed the Berlin-to-Bagdad railway project. Anglo-German competition in battleship building became increasingly keen with the construction of the new "dreadnaughts," and suspicions and recriminations increased correspondingly, particularly after new naval negotiations broke down in 1908. The three Moroccan crises solidified the Entente. Morocco was lost and France, Britain, and Russia were more firmly united than ever by a web of secret military and naval agreements which appeared the more menacing because of their very secrecy. If Germany was not to be "strangled" by her enemies, she must adopt a "firm" policy and make no more concessions. Above all, she must "protect her interests" in the Near East and strengthen Austria-Hungary in every way possible. When Vienna took advantage of the Young Turk Revolution to annex Bosnia and Herzegovina in 1908, all Serbian patriots were furious, for the provinces were inhabited by South Slavs and were earmarked for incorporation into a greater Serbia. Russia, aiming at the Straits and at a Pan-Slavic hegemony in the Balkans, supported Serbia in the crisis and backed down only when Germany indicated her intention of standing behind Austria-Hungary "like a knight in shining armor." Berlin and Vienna had triumphed in this encounter, but Serbian irredentist ambitions, encouraged by Russia, led to plots and conspiracies which boded ill for the integrity of the Dual Monarchy. The Racconigi bargain between Russia and Italy of 1909 was followed by the Tripolitan war of 1911. Germany's "ally," Italy, with Entente approval, despoiled Turkey, which was already a German sphere of influence. Austro-Italian friction was further increased by the Balkan Wars of 1912–1913. Austria and Russia were soon at swords points over the issue of a Serbian outlet to the Adriatic. The creation of an independent Albania blocked Serbian ambitions and engendered increased bitterness at Belgrade and St. Petersburg.

In view of these developments, the German Government felt that it had no alternative in the crisis of 1914 to supporting Austria-Hungary in her determination to chastise Serbia. Pan-Serbian terrorists, with the connivance of Serbian officials, assassinated the Archduke Francis Ferdinand, heir to the Hapsburg throne, at Sarajevo, capital of Bosnia, on June 28, 1914. The very existence of Austria-Hungary seemed to be at stake, for irredentist and autonomist agitation, encouraged by Serbia, threatened dissolution to an empire composed of diverse national elements. Behind Serbia stood Russia, and behind Russia France, for the Dual Alliance had been "Balkanized" and Paris was tied to the wheels of the Russian chariot in its course toward the Straits. Following an unsatisfactory reply to the ultimatum of July 23, Austria-Hungary declared war upon Serbia on July 28. Two days later the Russian Government mobilized its armies against Austria-Hungary and her ally, Germany. To yield now to Russian pressure would destroy Austrian prestige in the Balkans and pave the way for the disintegration of the Dual Monarchy. If Germany refused to support Austria-Hungary, the Triple Alliance would be weakened and Berlin would remain isolated within a circle of enemies. By the secret terms of the Franco-Russian alliance, mobilization was the signal for war. On July 31 the German Government dispatched a twelve-hour ultimatum to St. Petersburg, demanding the suspension of all Russian war measures. No reply was received. On August 1, 1914, Germany declared war on Russia. The French Government had failed to restrain the Russian mobilization, which transformed the Austro-Serbian war into a general war. France, as a loyal ally, stood as staunchly behind Russia as Germany stood behind Austria-Hungary. War was declared on France on August 3. The German invasion of Belgium as a means of attacking France furnished Great Britain with a pretext for declaring war on Germany on August 4. Italy remained neutral. All

German patriots rallied to the sacred cause of the fatherland, certain that Germany had been attacked by scheming enemies and that their only course was to hack their way to victory through encircling foes.

In the colossal combat which ensued, Germany revealed herself to be the most formidable of all the Powers in military might and more than a match for any three of her major enemies. The defection of Italy left Germany with Austria-Hungary as her only ally. Turkey joined the fray on the German side on November 5, 1914, and Bulgaria followed suit on October 14, 1915. But in this coalition of the four Central Powers, Germany was not only the keystone of the arch but the supporting pillars and the foundation stones as well. German industry and finance, German science and technology, German efficiency and morale proved equal to what seemed at the outset the impossible task of facing overwhelming odds. But here, as always in the Western State System, the coalition which proved itself the weaker was joined by one neutral State after another, alarmed at the prospect of the conquest of Europe by the most powerful State on the Continent. The blunders of German diplomacy contributed to this fatal result. The prodigious feats of German arms were in the end unable to rectify diplomatic mistakes and to turn the tide of battle against an anti-German coalition which included all of the other Great Powers of the world and half of the Minor Powers as well. Imperial Germany conquered vaster territories and won a position of military preponderance greater than that enjoyed by the first Napoleon, but in the end this military empire crumbled to pieces even more rapidly and completely than that of Bonaparte.[1]

The major phases of the struggle need only be sketched here. The original German plan of campaign contemplated a swift and decisive blow at France, which would release the German armies to face the Russian invasion from the east. French resistance was to be broken by a

---

[1] The States at war with Germany and the dates of commencement of war were as follows:

1. Russia, August 1, 1914*	13. United States, April 6, 1917
2. France, August 3, 1914	14. Panama, April 7, 1917
3. Belgium, August 4, 1914	15. Cuba, April 7, 1917
4. Great Britain, August 4, 1914	16. Nicaragua, May 7, 1917
5. Serbia, August 6, 1914	17. Siam, July 22, 1917
6. Montenegro, August 9, 1914	18. Liberia, Aug. 4, 1917
7. Japan, August 23, 1914	19. Brazil, Oct. 26, 1917
8. Italy, August 28, 1916†	20. Guatemala, April 21, 1918
9. San Marino, May 24, 1915‡	21. Costa Rica, May 24, 1918
10. Portugal, March 9, 1916	22. Haiti, July 12, 1918
11. Rumania, August 27, 1916§	23. Honduras, July 19, 1918
12. Greece, November 28, 1916	

* Separate peace, March 4, 1918.
† Declared war against Austria-Hungary, May 24, 1915.
‡ Against Austria-Hungary.
§ Separate peace, May 6, 1918.

gigantic flank attack through Belgium to the north of the great border fortresses. With crushing efficiency and precision the German divisions poured into Belgium, pulverized the Belgian fortifications with heavy artillery, swept aside the Belgian army, defeated the French and English, and descended from the northeast upon Paris. At the Marne, however, the German onrush was stopped early in September, 1914, and the spear-point of the invasion was deflected. In the race for the Channel ports the Allied armies retained possession of the French coast. The German lines were stabilized along the Aisne, and the conflict on the Western front became a long-drawn-out war of attrition characterized by the costly and bloody futility of trench fighting. The decisive blow had failed, but the German armies held Belgium and the coal districts of northern France and could rest on the defensive pending developments elsewhere.

Meanwhile the Russian invasion of East Prussia was crushed at Tannenberg on August 29, 1914, and the war in the east carried into Russian Poland. On May 24, 1915, Italy joined the Entente against her erstwhile allies, but without any marked effect upon the combat. An Allied attack upon the Dardanelles ended in disaster, and the entrance of Bulgaria into the war enabled Germany and Austria-Hungary to conquer Serbia and establish communication with Turkey. While the German command remained on the defensive in the west, the Russian invaders of Austrian Galicia were driven out, Poland was conquered, and Russia itself was deeply invaded. In the spring of 1916 the German armies resumed the offensive on the western front, with a gigantic but unsuccess-ful assault upon Verdun, key to the southern half of the Allied lines. In the summer a great Allied offensive on the Somme similarly broke down. The war in the west remained a stalemate. In the east Rumania joined the Allies by declaring war on Austria, August 27, 1916, but was promptly conquered by the forces of the Central Powers. The German lines were pushed deeper into Russia, and the defeated and discredited Tsarist régime collapsed in revolution in March of 1917. The war in the east went on, but with diminished intensity, for Russian powers of resistance were approaching the vanishing point.

The military ascendancy enjoyed by the Central Powers as a result of greater fighting efficiency, a unified command, and interior lines of communication was nullified by the diplomatic consequences of the war on the sea. Only one great naval battle between the British and German grand fleets was fought—off the coast of Jutland, on May 31, 1916. The German navy inflicted heavier losses on the enemy than it suffered, but the result was indecisive and the German fleet remained in port for the balance of the war. Allied naval superiority held the Central Powers in the grip of an unbreakable blockade, to which they responded by submarine blockades of Great Britain and France. The resulting controversies with neutral governments furnished the ground upon which the United States and other countries entered the war on the Allied side in the spring of 1917. Despite this enormous accession to the power of the Allies, German victory still seemed possible. The German armies remained on the defensive in France throughout 1917, but a disastrous defeat was inflicted on Italy at Caporetto in October and a second revolution in Russia brought peace in the east. The Treaty of Brest-Litovsk of March 4, 1918, was a conqueror's peace, imposed by Berlin and Vienna on a prostrate foe.

If German military might could be concentrated for a decisive assault in the west before American fighting strength could turn the tide, there was still a possibility of success. In March of 1918 a terrific offensive was launched against the British lines in Picardy, which carried the German armies forward fifty miles toward Amiens and the Channel. In April another German attack in Flanders pushed the British back on Ypres. In May a third onslaught against the French resulted in a thirty-mile gain and carried the German forces to the Marne once more. Other attacks followed with less spectacular gains, and by July the struggle had again reached a deadlock. A final German effort to envelop Rheims in mid-July was checked at Château-Thierry. The German effort to break through the western front had failed. An Allied counter-offensive was launched in July, and the German divisions were gradually forced back toward Belgium. Bulgaria, defeated by the Allied armies north of Salonika, sued for peace at the end of September. With Mesopotamia, Syria, and Palestine already lost, Turkey likewise surrendered. Austria-Hungary collapsed into chaos. On November 11, 1918, following a revolution and the overthrow of the Hohenzollern dynasty, the new German Government acknowledged defeat and signed the Armistice which concluded the conflict.

The Treaty of Versailles of June 28, 1919, humbled Germany to the dust and imposed upon her terms so severe as to render her impotent in European international politics for many years. The Reich lost all its overseas colonies, Alsace-Lorraine, the Saar valley, Eupen and Malmedy, the Polish corridor, part of Upper Silesia, and a portion of Schleswig. German investments and property abroad were seized. Germany's coal production was reduced by one-third, and her iron supplies by three-fourths. The German merchant marine was confiscated by the Allies. The German battle fleet was surrendered. The German army was limited to 100,000 men and was forbidden to possess tanks, heavy artillery, or airplanes. The new German navy was restricted to six battleships of not more than 10,000 tons, six light cruisers, twelve destroyers, and no submarines. The left bank of the Rhine and a fifty-kilometer zone on the right bank were demilitarized. The left bank and the bridge-heads were subjected to military occupation for fifteen years. A Reparation Commission was appointed to fix Germany's financial obligations to idemnify the victors for civilian damages, pensions, and the Belgian war debt, on the theory that the war was a result of "the aggression of Germany and her allies."[1] The Kaiser was arraigned "for a supreme offense against international morality and the sanctity of treaties," and provision was made for bringing him to trial, along with other German "war criminals." Thanks to the collapse of Russia and the attitude of President Wilson, the terms of the secret inter-Allied treaties of 1915–1917 for the division of the spoils were not literally executed. But Germany was nevertheless crushed to earth and not permitted to join the League of Nations, which Wilson insisted on including in the peace settlement.

Under these circumstances, German post-war foreign policy has inevitably been directed toward minimizing the losses inflicted by the treaty and striving to recover for the Reich a position of equality in the community of States. Given the prevalent power-and-prestige values which underlie State action, the ultimate diplomatic objective of any German Government must be treaty revision and a restoration of as much as possible of what has been lost. This involves the displacing of French hegemony over the Continent by a new balance of power. The first step toward a new balance of power is the recovery of equality and liberty of action through the breaking down, in whole or in part, of the restrictions contained in the peace settlement. Since these restrictions reflect the power interests of the victors of 1918 and are the bulwark of the political preponderance of France and her new allies, it follows that almost every immediate goal of German foreign policy encounters opposition from the dominant French bloc. With Germany disarmed and helpless, with her former allies even more impotent, with France, Belgium, Poland, Czechoslovakia, Jugoslavia, and Rumania possessing overwhelming power to crush any movement at forcible revision of the treaties, any resort to coercion, open or threatened, is out of the question for Germany. And diplomacy unsupported by potential coercive power is invariably paralyzed in all it attempts. Germany has consequently been reduced to passive resistance and to efforts at dividing the victors, gaining support from other States, and bargaining for concessions through conciliatory gestures. Germany has been reduced to these expedients—largely ineffective—in her efforts to lower or cancel reparation payments, to relieve herself of the onus of war guilt, to terminate the military occupation of her territory, to recover equality in armaments, and to achieve readjustments of frontiers. These are the major purposes of German diplomacy since 1919—imposed upon Germany by the international position to which she was reduced by the peace settlement. The

[1] Article 231 of the Treaty of Versailles. See p. 152 above.

limited means at Berlin's disposal for attaining these objectives have led to varying degrees of success or failure, which can be suggested by a brief resumé of diplomatic developments with regard to each of these problems.

As for reparations, the Allied Governments agreed at Spa in 1920 that France should receive 52 per cent of all German payments, Great Britain 22 per cent, Italy 10 per cent, Belgium 8 per cent, Greece, Rumania, and Jugoslavia 6.5 per cent each, and Japan and Portugal 0.75 per cent each. Even before the total bill was fixed, the Reparation Commission, under French domination, declared Germany in default on the advance payment of 20,000,000,000 marks which were demanded by May of 1921. The Allied Governments had already ordered the occupation of Düsseldorf, Duisburg, and Ruhrort, had set up a tariff wall around the Rhineland, and had levied taxes on German imports as punitive measures designed to ensure payment. On April 27, 1921, the Reparation Commission fixed the total bill at 132,000,000,000 marks, or about $31,000,000,000. Germany was compelled to accept this total, under threat of the occupation of the Ruhr. But the financial condition of the German Government led to huge budgetary deficits, which were met by inflation, with a resulting depreciation of the mark. A temporary moratorium had to be granted to Germany, but at the end of 1922 the determination of the Poincaré Government in France to use force and seize "productive guarantees" was reflected in the action of the Reparation Commission in declaring Germany in voluntary default on timber, coal, and cattle deliveries. In the face of British objections, the French and Belgian Governments ordered engineers and troops into the Ruhr in January, 1923. Germany countered by stopping all reparation payments and organizing passive resistance against the invaders. The forces of occupation resorted to reprisals, arrests, courts-martial, and other repressive measures, but coal could not be mined with bayonets and the occupation was fruitless. The German Government, however, was reduced to bankruptcy, and in August of 1923 Chancellor Stresemann abandoned passive resistance and surrendered. Germany had lost the first great battle in the "war after the war."

The subsequent history of reparations[1] is the story of the progressive abandonment of Allied efforts to collect impossibly huge sums from the defeated enemy. Since the Allied States, in the interests of their security and their position in world markets, had no intention of permitting Germany to develop the great export industry which would make payments possible, they were finally obliged to abandon the bulk of their claims. The Dawes Plan, adopted by all the Powers on August 16, 1924, did not revise the 1921 total, but provided for reduced annual payments.

[1] See pp. 569f. below.

The German Government and German industry borrowed heavily abroad after 1924, chiefly from British and American investors, and met its payments in this fashion. It was obvious, however, that this procedure could not be continued indefinitely, and in June, 1929, the Powers agreed to the Young Plan as a "complete and final" settlement of the reparations problem. Under the terms of the final act of the conference at The Hague, signed January 20, 1930, provision was made for a reduced schedule of annuities, which broke down within a year and a half with the collapse of the structure of international credit and the onset of the Great Depression. By the terms of the Hoover moratorium of June 20, 1931, all reparations and inter-Allied debt payments were suspended for one year. The German Government now felt strong enough to announce both its inability and its unwillingness to pay further reparations—a position which the Allied Governments found it necessary to accept. The final act of the Lausanne Conference of July 8, 1932, expressly abolished the reparation clauses of the Treaty of Versailles and provided for the later payment by Germany of 3,000,000,000 gold marks (about $750,000,000) into a European reconstruction fund in lieu of reparations. Whether even this sum will ever be paid is doubtful at the time of writing, and reparation payments may be assumed to be at an end. This result represents less a triumph for German diplomacy than a recognition of financial realities in a world threatened with economic disaster. The "war-guilt" clause of the treaty, which was the basis of reparations, has not been expressly abrogated, but the Kaiser and the other "war criminals" have never been tried as the treaty contemplated.

Germany's efforts to bring about the end of foreign military control and to secure equality in armaments have been less successful. The Allied occupation of the Rhineland was terminated in June of 1930, five years before the expiration of the period specified in the treaty, and the Allied military and financial control commissions were withdrawn. This was a substantial gain and the fruit of the Briand-Stresemann era of *rapprochement*. By abandoning passive resistance and flirtations with the Soviet Union, by accepting as permanent the Reich's western frontier, guaranteed in the Locarno treaties of 1925, and finally by accepting the Young Plan, Stresemann gained membership in the League of Nations for Germany in 1926 and achieved the end of the military occupation in 1930. But this was a negative victory and only a small step toward that equality of military status which was the prerequisite of effective political equality with other Powers. Germany insisted upon the fulfillment of the pledge of the Treaty of Versailles that the unilateral disarmament of Germany would be followed by general disarmament. In the sessions of the Preparatory Commission for the Disarmament Conference between 1925 and 1929, and in the General Disarmament Conference of the League of Nations which met at Geneva in February, 1932, the German representatives, pleaded eloquently for general disarmament to the German level or, as an alternative, the granting to Germany of the right to re-arm up to the level of her neighbors. France and her eastern allies, with qualified support from Great Britain, have thus far stood steadfast against both demands, for the acceptance of either would destroy the strategic bases of French hegemony and enable Germany to challenge the 1919 *status quo* in other respects. In this regard Germany remains caught in an impasse: without potential force to back up diplomatic demands for equality in armaments, Germany cannot compel her erstwhile enemies to heed her wishes. And without equality in armaments, the necessary

potential force to make the demands effective is lacking. Here is an "encirclement" which the Reich can break through only by secret re-arming, which is difficult, or by open defiance, which is dangerous. Yet this demand cannot well be abandoned, since other objectives cannot be attained without sufficient military force to use at least for bargaining purposes.[1]

In the matter of territorial readjustment, Germany has thus far achieved nothing. In the Locarno treaties she accepted the loss of Alsace-Lorraine, and of Eupen and Malmedy, as permanent. The Saar valley

[1] See pp. 686f. and 698f. below.

she will probably recover as a result of the 1935 plebiscite, unless some alternative arrangement is made in the meantime. But the loss of Danzig, the Polish corridor, and Upper Silesia remains a festering wound in the hearts of all patriots, and none can abandon hope of recovering these territories in the future. Their recovery, however, demands a new dismemberment of resurrected Poland—and behind Poland stands France and the Little Entente, firmly resolved to maintain frontiers as they are. Here is a stake of German diplomacy which can be attained only at the risk of war, and so long as Germany is impotent war cannot be risked under any circumstances. At Locarno, Germany refused to guarantee the eastern frontiers, but agreed not to resort to forcible measures of revision. Stresemann and his successors have consequently been obliged, like Gambetta, to cherish in silence the memory of the new "lost provinces" and to await a more favorable conjuncture of events before assaying their recovery. As for the lost colonies, the most that Germany has been able to attain has been a seat on the Permanent Mandates Commission of the League of Nations. The German Government has made no formal request for a mandate, because of the certainty of refusal, and it has no means of inducing any of the colonial Powers to part with any of their territory. German colonial aspirations remain unfulfilled.

To the south is truncated Austria—purely German in language and culture, strangled by the tariff barriers of its neighbors, unable to maintain itself economically alone, and anxious for union with Germany. Austro-German union—the *Anschluss*—is, and will remain, a major object of both German and Austrian foreign policy. But such a union would create a German State of 70,000,000 people, completely surrounding western Czechoslovakia and bordering upon France, Italy, Jugoslavia, and Poland. All these States are determined to thwart every effort at revising the clauses of the Treaties of Versailles and St. Germain, which forbid political union. In the Financial Protocol of 1922, Austria was obliged, as the price of financial aid from the League of Nations, to renounce all efforts to alienate her economic independence as well. The French bloc, with Italian support on this issue, has thus far been able to enforce the strict observance of these provisions. In March, 1931, Berlin and Vienna announced their intention of entering into a customs union involving the abolition of the tariff wall between them, as a means of saving Austria from economic collapse. Even such an apparently innocuous arrangement as this was regarded in Paris, Brussels, Prague, and Rome as a step toward political union and was vigorously opposed before the League Council. The World Court, to which the Council appealed for an advisory opinion, held on September 5, 1931, by a vote of eight to seven, that the project was contrary to the protocol of 1922 and hence unlawful. Germany and Austria had already been compelled by French diplomatic and financial pressure to abandon the scheme. In the face of this new diplomatic debacle, the German foreign minister, Curtius, was obliged to resign. Austria has subsequently been obliged to renounce the customs-union project for twenty years, as a condition of securing new foreign loans to bolster up her tottering financial structure.[1] So long as France and her allies retain the hegemony of the Continent, the *Anschluss* will remain incapable of realization.

In summary, German post-war foreign policy has encountered a succession of defeats at the hands of France and has attained none of its major objectives. Reparations and foreign financial and military control have been abolished. Germany was admitted to the League in 1926 and granted a position of equality on the Council with the other Great Powers. But these are empty victories so long as the League machinery cannot be utilized to achieve pacifically those revisions of the treaty which Germany's weakness forbids her to attempt by force. Equality in armaments is not yet in sight, and recovery of the colonies and of the eastern provinces is even more remote. *Anschluss* is likewise forbidden. These frustrations of national aspirations, coupled with the economic ruin of the German middle classes, lie behind the rapid growth of Adolph Hitler's Fascist and ultra-patriotic "National Socialist" party since 1930. German Fascism aims at outright repudiation of the treaties and open defiance of France and Poland. But regardless of the form or political complexion of the German Government, these things are not yet within the realm of diplomatic possibilities.

In the last analysis, Germany's hopes of attaining her objectives depend upon diplomatic combinations and alliances with foreign powers, as did the similar hopes of France after 1871. German power *vis-á-vis* France since 1919, as measured by population and economic resources, is much greater than was French power *vis-á-vis* Germany after 1871. But Germany is now disarmed, as France was not in the earlier period. And Germany is confronted not by France alone, but by France plus Belgium, Poland, and the Little Entente. This combination, it is true, is less overwhelming than was the German-Austrian-Russian-Italian combination with which Bismarck confronted France, but it is nevertheless sufficiently formidable to render impossible any single-handed German defiance of French hegemony. Without allies Germany cannot hope to place herself in a position of diplomatic equality with the French bloc, and thus far no allies have been secured. Great Britain holds aloof and opposes German efforts to upset the *status quo*. Italy is in the offing as another "revisionist" State, for Italian interests conflict with those of France in the Mediterranean and Africa, and with those of France's ally, Jugoslavia, in the Adriatic. Italy, however, stands with France in opposing the

[1] See p. 553 below.

Anschluss. Italy holds the German Tyrol—Austria's irredenta—and Germans have not yet forgotten the "betrayal" of 1914–1915. Germany has secured diplomatic support from Italy on questions of finance and armaments, but there is as yet no basis for an alliance. Embittered Hungary is likewise her potential ally, but Hungary is held firmly in the grip of the Little Entente and is so weak as to be a liability rather than an asset. To the east looms the Soviet Union. At the Genoa Conference of 1922 the German Government startled the Allies by extending full recognition to the Soviet Union and concluding with it the Treaty of Rapallo. At various times since, German Nationalists have vaguely threatened France with a Russian alliance. Poland is the common enemy of both Germany and the U.S.S.R., since it holds territory seized from both. Between the Soviet Union and the French bloc, moreover, there are undying enmity and suspicion, for France, as the best friend abroad of the Tsarist régime, has always been the worst enemy of the Communist dictatorship. These common interests have promoted economic collaboration between Germany and the Soviet Union and have led to diplomatic cooperation with regard to armaments and other problems. But the Soviet Union will play the game of bourgeois diplomacy only to the extent required to ensure its own security, and a genuine alliance between bourgeois Germany and proletarian Russia remains unthinkable. A German Delcassé is not yet in sight. Pending his arrival, Germany remains isolated and helpless.

3. ITALY: THE NEW CAESARISM

The Fascist State is a will to power and an empire. The Roman tradition is the idea of force. In the Fascist doctrine, the imperial idea is not only a territorial, military, and mercantile expression, but also one of spiritual and moral expansion. For Fascism, the tendency to the imperial idea means expansion of the nation and is a manifestation of vitality.—BENITO MUSSOLINI in *Popolo d'Italia*, August 4, 1932.

The Kingdom of Italy has always occupied the weakest international position of any of the Great Powers. Many foreign observers have characterized it as a second-class State with aspirations beyond its capacities. Italy's only asset has been a teeming population. This population inhabits a country poor in coal, iron, and other resources essential to modern industry, lacking in capital, and lying in the center of a sea all of whose outlets are held by other States. Behind the façade of ultra-patriotic boastings and threats, Italy remains inferior to other Powers in the economic and strategic prerequisites of an effective rôle in power politics. She has consequently been reduced to adroit maneuverings and complex bargainings to achieve her purposes—and she has repeatedly met with failure and frustration.

The foreign policy of Italy after 1870 was pulled alternately in two directions by two sets of irreconcilable ambitions: the desire to secure Italia Irredenta, and the desire to create an African empire. The first could be achieved only at the expense of Austria, the second only at the expense of France. The French seizure of Tunis precipitated Italy into the waiting arms of Germany and Austria-Hungary in the Triple Alliance of 1882. But Italy remained an unreliable ally, for her nationalistic aspirations in the north and in the Adriatic were more powerful driving forces behind her foreign policy than her hopes of imperialistic aggrandizement in Africa. France, for a price, was prepared to approve the fulfillment of at least a portion of these hopes. In 1896 Italy at last recognized the French protectorate in Tunis, in return for commercial concessions. In 1899 a commercial convention put an end to the long Franco-Italian tariff war. In 1900 France extended assurances that she harbored no designs on Tripoli, while Italy acquiesced in French designs on Morocco. By the agreement of 1902, Italy, acting contrary to the spirit if not the letter of her compacts with her allies, agreed to remain neutral in the event of an attack upon France, even if France should be obliged to take the initiative declaration of war. In 1909 Italy agreed to view with benevolence Russia's designs upon the Straits and Constantinople, in return for Russian approval of her project of seizing Tripoli from Turkey, Russia's hereditary enemy and satellite of Italy's allies, Germany and Austria-Hungary. Tripoli was accordingly seized in the Italo-Turkish war of 1911. But in form Rome retained its commitments to Berlin and Vienna. Italy thus had a foot in both camps and was prepared to bargain for terms in the event of a crisis in which each of the great coalitions should seek her support.

When the Great War came, Italy remained neutral on the specious plea that the war was aggressive and not defensive on the part of her allies and thus did not involve the *casus foederis*. With her long, open coastline exposed to attack by the British and French fleet, Italy had more to lose than to gain by joining the Central Powers, even if eventual victory might enable her to seize a large portion of the French African colonies. During the winter of 1914–1915 the Italian Government, acting frankly on a policy of *sacro egoismo* (holy selfishness), bargained with both coalitions for promise of territorial compensation and agreed to enter the war on the side which promised most. While Germany and Austria-Hungary were lavish with promises of French territory in Africa, they were unwilling to surrender Trieste, the Tyrol, and Trentino as the price of Italian aid. The Allies, on the other hand, promised Rome all of these territories and part of the Dalmatian coast besides, plus compensations in the Near East and "rectifications" of the African frontiers. These terms were embodied in the secret Treaty of London of April 26, 1915, and on May 24 Italy declared war on Austria-Hungary. Italy's military contribution to the Allied cause was not impressive, and when the Italian front collapsed in the disaster of Caporetto in the fall of 1917 and most of Venetia fell into the hands of the enemy, British and French divisions had to be sent to the Piave to stem the German invasion. In the summer of 1918, however, the Italian armies checked an Austrian offensive and counter-attacked with sufficiently telling effect to claim a share in the glory of final victory.

At the Peace Conference Italy found her claims thwarted by Wilsonian idealism, by Serbian annexationist aspirations in the Adriatic, and by French and British reluctance to permit Italy to dominate the Mediterranean. "Rectifications" of the Libyan frontiers were secured, but they were not of sufficient magnitude to satisfy Italian colonial hopes. In the north Italia Irredenta was indeed acquired, plus the Austrian Tyrol south of Brenner Pass, which was demanded for strategic reasons. Fiume was likewise seized, as well as Zara and the island of Lagosta. But the Italian acquisitions included territory claimed by Serbia on grounds of language and self-determination. Italy was faced across the Adriatic by an embittered and resentful Jugoslavia in alliance with France. In the Near East Italy gained nothing save the Dodecanese Islands and the confirmation of her occupation of Rhodes. While Kemal Pasha's Turkish Nationalists frustrated Italian aspirations in Anatolia, France retained Syria and Great Britain acquired Iraq and Palestine. All Italian patriots felt that while Italy had won the war, she had lost the peace. Italy, despite her gains, emerged from the conference an unsatiated State.

This thwarting of patriotic ambitions played its part in the discrediting of parliamentary government, the rise of Fascism, and the establishment of the dictatorship. The Fascist revolution was at bottom a resort to force on the part of the bourgeoisie and the landed proprietors to meet the threat of a peasant-proletarian social revolution under Communist and extreme Socialist leadership. The armed Black Shirts of Mussolini were subsidized by the industrialists of the north and the agrarians of the south, and at first even supported by the weak Cabinet at Rome in their assaults upon Socialist and Communist party headquarters, their destruction of working-class papers, and their suppression of labor unions and cooperative organizations. In October of 1922, when the instrument for the suppression of the social revolution had become more powerful than its creators, the Fascist militia marched on Rome and Mussolini became Premier. In 1925 all the opposition parties were suppressed and the Italian Government has since remained a dictatorial régime in which all power is monopolized by the Fascists.

The Fascist movement has made its appeal, not merely to the economic and social interests of the propertied classes, but to the nationalistic emotionalism of all ardent patriots. Its symbols are those of the Rome of the Caesars. Rome's ancient glories are to be restored. Il Duce is the new imperator and conqueror. Italy is to be made strong, powerful, respected. A new empire is to be won. All other interests are to be subordinated to the supreme end of the power of the fatherland. In the name of national solidarity, the old trade unions have been dissolved and the right to strike has been suppressed. Italian economic life has been rigidly regimented, as a means of securing industrial peace and prosperity. In the name of unity and power, Italian youth has had inculcated into it a fervent anti-foreign, militaristic patriotism. In the name of unity and power, the dictatorship has been defended, rationalized, and sanctified. In the name of unity and power, the Italian State has concluded its long struggle with the Papacy and by the Treaty and Concordat of 1929 restored the temporal authority of the Pope and recognized the Vatican City as the new Papal State.

The foreign policy of Fascist Italy is frankly directed toward territorial expansion at the expense of her neighbors. "Population pressure" is advanced as the chief justification for territorial demands. During the four-year period before the war 3,500,000 Italians emigrated to foreign lands, and at present over 10,000,000 Italians live abroad. Since the war Italian immigration to the United States has been shut off by American legislation, and while Italians continue to go to France, South America, and elsewhere, emigration is no solution of the problem. In any case, Il Duce desires to retain the sons of Italy, for Italy "must appear on the threshold of the second half of the century with a population of not less than 60,000,000 inhabitants. If we fall off . . . we cannot make an empire."[1] Empire-building involves war. War requires man power. Man power requires not emigration or birth control, but a population which will grow to the bursting point. More colonies must be acquired at all costs. Italian power must be extended over the Mediterranean. Only in this way can Italy attain that "place in the sun" to which she has so long aspired.

But the practical political difficulties in the way of the achievement of this program are almost insurmountable, however large Italian population may become and however energetically the nation may be organized for the inevitable conflict. Italy's economic and strategic weakness remains what it has always been—a stubbornly irreducible fact which obliges Italy to temper strong words with cautious acts and to proceed in diplomatic bargainings with the utmost circumspection. British and French naval forces dominate the Mediterranean. British and French interests are dominant in north Africa and the Near East. Italy has nothing to offer either Great Britain or France to induce them to yield to her claims. A resort to force against them would be suicidal. Italy can afford to use

[1] Mussolini to Parliament, May 26, 1927.

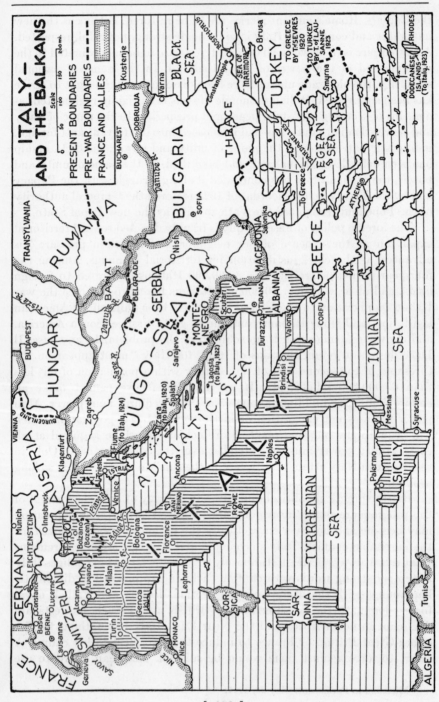

ITALY AND THE BALKANS

Scale
0 50 100 150 200 mi.

PRESENT BOUNDARIES
PRE-WAR BOUNDARIES
FRANCE AND ALLIES

force only against small, weak States. When an Italian general was assassinated by Greek patriots near the Albanian frontier, Italy bombarded and seized the Greek island of Corfu on August 31, 1923, and defied the League of Nations to say her nay. An indemnity and an apology were exacted from Greece, but Corfu was evacuated under British pressure and Italy gained no conquests. By the Treaty of Tirana, November, 1926, Albania became definitely an Italian dependency, to the alarm of Jugoslavia and Greece. But against the prospective enemy in the Adriatic, Jugoslavia, Italy must proceed cautiously, for Jugoslavia is the ally of France and a member of the Little Entente. Fascist Italy has been obliged to modify Theodore Roosevelt's advice to "speak softly and carry a big stick," by speaking softly (occasionally) and recognizing that the Italian big stick is ineffective against the bigger stick of French hegemony over the Continent. Italy, therefore, has become increasingly disposed toward cooperation in the League of Nations and to a favorable attitude toward disarmament.

Since 1930 Franco-Italian friction has centered about Italy's claim to naval parity with France. At the Washington and London disarmament conferences of 1921 and 1930, Italy was conceded theoretical parity with France in battleships. At the London conference Italy claimed parity in other categories of war vessels. The Italian Government has subsequently expressed its willingness to disarm on land and sea to any level which may be agreed upon, providing that Italian armaments are not exceeded by those of any other continental Power. This claim to parity with France has been steadily and successfully resisted at the Quai d'Orsay. The French fleet must be divided between the Atlantic, the Mediterranean, and the colonies. An Italian fleet equal to the French would give Italy supremacy in the Mediterranean and enable her to threaten France's vital line of defense between Marseilles, north Africa, and the Near East. Italy, moreover, does not possess the financial resources to construct a navy equal to that of France. The French Government may therefore rest assured, in opposing the grant of hypothetical parity with Italy, that Italy by her own efforts will remain incapable of jeopardizing French security. The French frontier facing Italy is heavily fortified and French divisions stand guard at the Alps. Franco-Italian relations are further embittered by the Italian hope of recovering Nice and Savoy, ceded to France in 1860, of recovering Corsica, which is in part Italian speaking, and of securing Tunis, in which the Italians outnumber the French. In addition to these sources of friction, anti-Fascist Italian emigrés have been granted a hospitable refuge in France, with resulting "incidents" and press recriminations. Diplomatic efforts to reconcile French and Italian naval policies have thus far been unsuccessful, and tension continues between the two States.

Here again Italy can hope to achieve nothing against France by her own unaided efforts. Allies are indispensable. But powerful allies are nowhere to be found. The Italian-Spanish treaty of August 7, 1926 provided for Spanish neutrality in a Franco-Italian war, but Spain is no longer a factor to be reckoned with in power politics. Albania is less an ally than a stepping-stone to power in the Balkans, if and when Jugoslavia can be checkmated. Since 1924 Italy has entered into mutually advantageous commercial and political relations with the Soviet Union, but Communist Russia will never pull Fascist chestnuts out of the Mediterranean fire. Italy is a "revisionist" State seeking modification of existing treaties and of the present distribution of territory and power. She has, therefore, a community of interests with the other revisionist States of central Europe. Following the signature of the treaty of April 5, 1927, with Hungary, Mussolini expressed sympathy for Magyar irredentist ambitions, but Hungary is not an ally and is too weak to lean upon, in any case. Between Italy and Austria there can be no cordiality so long as 250,000 Austrians in the Tyrol remain under Fascist rule. Behind Austria stands Germany, but Italy is as much opposed as France and the Little Entente to the realization of one of Germany's highest hopes—the Austro-German *Anschluss*. Now, as in the period before 1914, Italy has a foot in both camps, but she is less able than before to bargain advantageously for concessions. Most Germans remain resentful over Italy's past policies and contemptuous of Italian fighting capacity, despite sentimental Hitlerite adoration of the source of inspiration of German Fascism. A fully Fascist Germany could perhaps make common cause against France with Fascist Italy. The probabilities, however, are against such a development. Italy remains without allies. She is reduced to limited diplomatic cooperation with Germany, Hungary, Bulgaria, the Soviet Union—any State which opposes French hegemony—but in this there is as yet no promise of an effective anti-French coalition which might serve Italy's interests. Barring some wild military adventure certain to result in disaster, the restoration of the empire of the Caesars must wait for better days.

4. GREAT BRITAIN: IMPERIAL DEFENSE

English Unionists when asked what they have to say in defense of their rule of subject peoples, often reply that the Englishman is just, leaving us divided between our derision of so monstrously inhuman a pretension, and our impatience with so gross a confusion of the mutually exclusive functions of judge and legislator. . . . The indispensable preliminary to democracy is the representation of every interest; the indispensable preliminary to justice is the elimination of every interest.—G. B. SHAW, *Preface for Politicians.*

England will never be civilized until she has added Utopia to her dominions. There is more than one of her colonies that she might with advantage surrender for so fair a land.—OSCAR WILDE.

Since Great Britain is the heart of a world empire, an adequate summary of British foreign policy would require a treatment of all of the manifold stakes of British diplomacy scattered over the six continents and the seven seas, with additional consideration of the separate but interrelated foreign policies of the Dominions. A task of such magnitude can scarcely be attempted here. But the major political interests of Great Britain in world politics can be readily indicated along with the general policies which the British Government has adopted to protect and further those interests. If the purposes of British foreign policy could be summed up in a phrase, that phrase would be "Security for the Empire." When Great Britain has come into conflict with other States, the cause has been that those States have pursued policies and purposes which appear to Downing Street to menace some interest, actual or potential, of imperial defense. When Britain has entered into alliances and understandings with other States, it has been because her diplomats felt unable single-handed to repel some impending menace or achieve some objective necessary to imperial security. Here, as always, "security" has often required "aggression" as a weapon for in diplomacy, as in war, attack is often the best defense. Many minor States in the path of British imperial progress have felt the impact of British majesty and might. Great Powers which seem to threaten the Empire have been checkmated, turned aside from their course, or crushed by some superior combination engineered by British diplomats. With remarkably consistent success, Great Britain has expanded her imperial domain, rounded out and strengthened her vital lines of defense, destroyed weaker rivals and enemies, thwarted or deflected all combinations against her too strong to be destroyed, and made advantageous terms with States too powerful to be defied.

The most significant shift of British foreign policy in the two decades before 1914 was the abandonment of "splendid isolation" and the alignment of the Empire on the side of the Franco-Russian alliance against Germany. Ever since 1815 the British Government had felt able to play a lone hand and to avoid permanent entanglements with other Powers. Such entanglements were resorted to only when some overweening continental State threatened to upset the delicately poised balance of power and to achieve a hegemony prejudicial to British interests. Against the France of Louis XIV and the France of Napoleon I, Britain was prepared, in the interests of her own security, to build coalitions of weaker States to check the menace. After 1815 no continental State occupied any such threatening position. The British Government was content to keep its skirts clear of European diplomatic maneuvers and to rely for protection upon a fleet equal to that of any other two Powers. Only when imperial Germany rose like a young giant to a position of formidable economic and military power in Europe did doubts as to the wisdom of British aloofness begin to arise. And only when Bismarck's pacific *status quo* policy came to an end in 1890, and Germany gave evidences of desiring to add to her empire of commerce an empire of colonies and sea power, did these doubts take definite form.

A series of diplomatic difficulties in the eighties and nineties strengthened the conviction that isolation was no longer the way of security. British interests clashed more seriously with those of other Powers than with those of Germany—with France in the Sudan, Egypt, and Siam, with Russia in the middle East, with the United States in the Caribbean. Britain was prepared to abandon supremacy in the Caribbean to the United States without a struggle. But the French and Russian threats to British imperial aspirations were infinitely more serious. Britain seemed on the verge of war with France in 1893 and again in 1898. Anglo-Russian tension in Asia appeared chronic and incurable. By comparison, Anglo-German relations were friendly and even cordial. Projects of an alliance were broached at the end of the century, but without result because of Berlin's indifference. Except for German sympathy with the Boers in the South African war and a certain vague hostility in eastern Asia and the Near East, there was no basis for enmity between the two great commercial Powers. Only when a competitive race in naval armaments began did British policy assume a frankly anti-German orientation. This orientation, from a long-run point of view, was dictated by ancient balance-of-power considerations, for Germany was unquestionably emerging as the most powerful of the continental States. Further accretions to her power would place her in a position to menace the Low Countries, the mouth of the Scheldt, and the Channel coast, which points Great Britain has never permitted a powerful continental State to control. Germany, moreover, was apparently enlarging her sea forces to such a degree as to make possible the achievement of colonial conquests at British expense. Increasingly intense German competition in foreign markets was also a cause for uneasiness. These circumstances—and others of a less tangible nature—

disposed Downing Street, after the turn of the century, to seek protection by combinations with other States which promised to be less dangerous rivals than Germany.

The result was the Anglo-Japanese alliance of 1902, the Anglo-French entente of 1904, the Anglo-Russian settlement of 1907, and British participation in what had become the Triple Entente—the great counterpoise to the Triple Alliance. The Japanese alliance was directed more against Russia than against Germany. Since British sea power could not be exercised effectively in eastern Asia, British interests in this area could be better protected by a combination with Japan, the more so as Japanese aspirations jeopardized Russian and German, and possibly American, interests rather than British. The alliance specified that each party would remain neutral in the event of the other being attacked by an outside Power and would come to the other's defense in the event of an attack by two or more Powers. The Russo-Japanese war raised the danger of a British clash with Russia—"the bear that walks like a man"—now the enemy of the new Asiatic ally. But the crisis passed and the entente with France, Russia's European ally, was concluded before the war was well begun. The entente meant a common Anglo-French front against Germany in the Mediterranean and Africa, and British support to France in the event of any future German effort to overrun the Low Countries or the French Channel coast. This implied naval cooperation, and after 1906 plans were elaborated for military collaboration against Germany in Belgium and Flanders if the worst should come. An understanding with Russia regarding the respective interests of the two Powers in Asia was reached in 1907, though Britain had no enthusiasm for Russian designs on the Straits and Russian ambitions in the Balkans. In the face of Germany's growing battle fleet and the Franco-Russian naval convention of July, 1912, the Grey-Cambon letters were exchanged in November of the same year. They provided for consultation in the event of a threat to peace and implied British support of France in the event of war with Germany. Sir Edward Grey, the British Foreign Minister, insisted, even in the crucial days of early August, 1914, that Britain's hands were free. War with Germany was too dangerous and ruinous to contemplate frankly. But the commitments undertaken left Britain no honorable alternative save support of the Franco-Russian combination if war came. War would be less dangerous than the situation which would arise if Germany became military master of the Continent.

When the great crisis came the British Government, after some hesitation and reluctance, aligned itself with the anti-German forces. Grey strove desperately, if not always intelligently or sincerely, to keep the peace. He failed. "The lamps are going out all over Europe," he declared in despair. "I feel like a man who has wasted his life." The German invasion of Belgium to attack France removed all doubts and was made the *casus belli*. On August 4, 1914, Great Britain declared war on Germany— "just for a scrap of paper," the German Chancellor said bitterly, referring to the Belgian neutrality treaty. In reality Britain went to war to prevent German domination of Europe and to smash the power which had come to be regarded as a menace to the Empire. For this cause English soldiers died by the hundreds of thousands in Flanders mud, English sailors in the North Sea endeavored to starve Germany into submission by a blockade, and British colonial forces conquered the German colonies in Africa and the south Pacific, seized Mesopotamia and Palestine, and assaulted the Dardanelles. Once in the war, Britain agreed with her allies on September 5, 1914, to make only a joint peace. And when Germany was finally crushed the British Empire received the lion's share of the spoils: Iraq, Palestine, part of Togoland and the Cameroons, German East Africa, German Southwest Africa, German Samoa, Nauru, German New Guinea, and the other German Pacific islands south of the Equator. The German colonial empire was demolished. German sea power was destroyed. German foreign trade and investments were ruined. Germany was crippled economically and saddled with a huge reparations burden which Lloyd George, no less than Clemenceau, was determined to make as onerous as possible. Here indeed was victory and a Pax Britannica with a vengeance.

But the peace, no less than the war, brought its defeats, its humiliations, and its frustrations. The fruits of victory soon turned to the gall and wormwood of economic prostration and diplomatic futility. British economy, always dependent upon foreign trade and the income from investments and the merchant marine, found itself strangled in the economic paralysis which crept like a foul disease over the world in the wake of war. If Germany had been a competitor, she had also been England's best customer. She was now impoverished and burdened with an indemnity, the payment of which required that she curtail her imports sharply and enormously expand her exports. The great Russian market was lost in the revolutionary holocaust. The tremendous expansion of American industry during the war enabled American exporters to secure the edge on their British competitors in Latin American markets. Japanese export trade in Asia likewise cut into British profits. The loss of these foreign markets left British industry in a position of permanent depression, involving chronic unemployment for over a million workers at the very time when the huge burden of the war debt demanded heavier taxation than ever. The pound, once a world-wide symbol of financial stability and integrity, had depreciated and British financial power abroad was impaired. This weakening of the economic and financial structure of the British State necessarily diminished its political influence in world affairs and made Britain less able to achieve what was necessary for recovery: a permanent peace, a restoration of world trade and prosperity, security for the Empire and its customers, and a constructive solution of the manifold economic, financial, and political problems besetting post-war Europe.

Britain's war-time ally, France, loomed at once as the most serious obstacle in the way of the fulfillment of these purposes. Britain had checkmated a German bid for hegemony only to play into the hands of the Quai d'Orsay and to enable France to achieve a hegemony more complete than any Germany had ever exercised. France was neither a great sea Power nor a serious commercial competitor. But post-war France outstripped England in iron and steel production, and French diplomacy threatened British interests at many points. In the Turko-Greek war of 1921–1922 France favored the Turkish aspirations and Britain the Greek. The Turks won and British prestige in the Near East suffered correspondingly. In the Franco-German "war after the war" Great Britain opposed French efforts to use reparations to encompass Germany's economic ruin, once it was appreciated that Britain would suffer severely from any such disaster. The Entente was at an end, and the Liberal and Labor parties became openly anti-French in their attitudes. But British opposition to the Ruhr occupation availed nothing, and Germany was beaten to her knees. All British efforts to impose limits upon French supremacy have failed, and the Conservative party has favored coming to terms with Paris. Britain refused to play the game of French security in 1923–1924, but in 1925 felt obliged, in the Locarno pacts, to guarantee the French frontier. French air fleets and French submarine squadrons have given rise to tension and suspicion. The old balance of power is gone and Britain can neither act as an equipoise nor retire into isolation. Successive British Cabinets have sought alternately to check French preponderance and to yield to French demands in the hope of contributing to that peace and order in Europe without which a restoration of British prosperity is impossible.

As for other Powers, the situation is scarcely better from the British point of view. To the United States Britain has been obliged to pay a burdensome war debt and to concede naval parity. The Anglo-Japanese alliance was terminated in 1921. Anglo-Japanese relations remain cordial, but Britain's position in the Orient is less secure than it was before 1914. As for Russia, efforts to overthrow the Soviet régime in the intervention period failed. In 1921 trade relations were restored, and in 1924 *de jure* recognition was extended. But the old Anglo-Russian rivalry has re-emerged in a new form, and the new Russia is a more formidable rival than the old. Diplomatic relations with Russia were severed in 1927 but renewed in 1929. Whether Britain can check the march of Communism in Asia and the growing power of the U.S.S.R. remains to be seen. British efforts to encourage German rehabilitation have succeeded only at the price of concessions to France. British private loans in central Europe have become a source of weakness rather than of strength. In short, in the post-war epoch, Britannia no longer rules the waves, British products no longer dominate foreign markets, British capital no longer flows freely throughout the world, British diplomatic prestige is dimmed, and imperial defense is less secure than before.

The British Government has endeavored to meet this situation by a variety of expedients not directly connected with specific diplomatic problems. It has given whole-hearted support to the League of Nations and qualified support to the cause of disarmament, in the hope of promoting world peace. It restored the pound to its old value in 1925, *i.e.*, returned to the gold standard and balanced its budget by heroic sacrifices in the hope of restoring world confidence in British financial solvency and integrity. It has, at long last and after much Conservative pleading, abandoned free trade and resorted in 1931 to tariff protectionism. It has fostered closer intra-imperial relations, both political and economic. It has solved the ancient Irish problem, in part at least, by granting Dominion status to the Irish Free State in 1921. It has endeavored to work out a qualified form of self-government for India to allay nationalist unrest. It accorded "independence" to Egypt in 1922 and to Iraq in 1932. But Anglo-Irish friction goes on, ominous rumblings continue in India, and schemes of imperial federation have not restored prosperity or rescued England from her difficulties.

The weakness of Britain's position became clearly apparent in the Great Depression which began in 1929. British industry, commerce, and finance have been continually depressed since the war and were unusually hard hit in the general collapse of price levels, markets, and security values. Heavy gold withdrawals made it necessary for the Bank of England to borrow in Paris and in New York to save the pound. In spite of frenzied efforts to preserve it, the gold standard had to be abandoned once more in September of 1931, but the competitive advantage in foreign trade which this circumstance was expected to give British industry failed to manifest itself. The new tariff duties have diminished imports, without which England cannot live, but have not increased exports. British efforts to come to the economic rescue of Germany and Austria without meeting French political terms ended in disaster. Great Britain remains the mother of the largest of the world empires, but she is no longer the most prosperous and powerful of the Great Powers. The shifting of power relationships in the post-war period lends a certain credence to gloomy prognostications of the twilight of Britannia. But if the sun of Britain has passed its zenith, it is still high in the heavens and far from that horizon beyond which repose, in the darkness of the past, the shades of earlier empires.

5. JAPAN: ORIENTAL EMPIRE-BUILDER

The spirit of the Japanese nation is, by its nature, a thing that must be propagated over the seven seas and extended over the five continents. Anything that may hinder its progress must be abolished, even by force.—
GENERAL SADAO ARAKI, Minister of War, in *Kaikosha*, July, 1932.

The island Empire of the Rising Sun, lying off the eastern coast of the Asiatic continent, is the latest of the Great Powers to play a decisive rôle in international politics. Within the memory of people still alive, Japan emerged from the status of an ancient kingdom of feudal barons and cherry blossoms, shielded from the world by voluntary isolation, and became a great State of industrial magnates and battleships, holding the reins of power in the western Pacific. Prior to the middle of the nineteenth century, the realm of the Mikado was a mysterious and picturesque medieval empire, remote from the centers of western power and determined to safeguard itself from western contamination. But the dynamic impact of the industrialized west was not to be resisted. In 1853–1854 Commodore Perry led an American squadron into Tokyo bay and in accordance with his instructions from the American Government induced the Japanese authorities, partly by persuasion, partly by threats, to conclude a treaty with the United States opening the empire to American commerce. Other parties took advantage of the opportunity thus created to secure trading privileges for their own nationals. In 1867 the nobility, perceiving the wisdom of adopting western ways if Japan was to escape the fate already overtaking China, overthrew the Shogun or regent, restored full power to the young Emperor Mutsu Hito, and embarked upon a program of transforming the country into a State capable of coping with the western nations. All of the technological paraphernalia of the west was introduced: railways, telegraph lines, steamships, factories, and the western army and navy. This amazing metamorphosis, this swift adoption of western technology, has made Japan a Great Power and has enabled her to make a successful bid for hegemony in eastern Asia.

Once supplied with the technical prerequisites of power, Japan proceded to exert her new might to extend her influence over the mainland. In 1894 the Japanese Government sent troops into the "hermit kingdom" of Korea, a dependency of the Chinese Empire, earmarked for seizure by the forces of the Mikado. War with China followed, and in less than a year Japan had overrun Korea and south Manchuria and was threatening Peking. By the Peace of Shimonoseki, April 17, 1895, China was compelled to recognize the independence of Korea, pay an indemnity of $150,000,000, and cede to Japan Formosa, the Pescadores Islands, and the Liaotung peninsula, key to Manchuria and gateway to the Gulf of Pechili and the Chinese capital. At this point Russia, Germany, and France intervened and obliged Japan to give up the Liaotung peninsula in return for an increased indemnity. Japanese expansion was thus thwarted by rival western imperialisms. If Japanese power was to be extended over the Asiatic mainland, Japan must be prepared, not merely to participate in the dismemberment of an impotent and disorganized China, but also to defy the western Powers. Russia was the first great obstacle to be overcome. In 1902 Japan strengthened her position by concluding an alliance with Great Britain, Russia's hereditary enemy in Asia. In 1904, after appropriate preparation, Japan challenged the Muscovite giant to combat. The soldiers of Nippon captured Port Arthur and routed the Russian armies at Mukden, while the new Japanese fleet destroyed the Russian squadrons sent against it. By the Treaty of Portsmouth, September 5, 1905, Japan acquired southern Sakhalin as well as Russia's leaseholds to Port Arthur and the Liaotung peninsula, and Russian railway and coal-mining rights in south Manchuria.

The outcome of the Russo-Japanese War enabled Japan to achieve the status of a Great Power without qualification and to prepare the way for a further extension of her empire. The Anglo-Japanese alliance was renewed in 1905, and by agreements with France and Russia in 1907 Japan became practically a fourth member of the Triple Entente. Japan achieved a free hand in Korea and south Manchuria, and if an occasion presented itself in war between Germany and the Entente, she could displace Germany in Shantung as she had already displaced Russia further north. The United States had acquired the Philippine Islands in 1898, and America came across the Pacific out of the east as the champion of the Open Door and Chinese territorial integrity. Here was a possible new rival to Japan in the Orient. But in July, 1905, President Roosevelt, in a secret memorandum, agreed not to oppose Japan in Korea and to cooperate with Japan to maintain peace in the Far East in return for a Japanese disclaimer of any designs on the Philippine Islands. In the Root-Takahira agreement of November, 1908, the two Powers agreed to respect one another's possessions, maintain the *status quo* in the Pacific, and preserve the Open Door and the independence and integrity of China. In 1910 Japan annexed Korea. In 1913 Russia and Great Britain took advantage of the Chinese revolution to detach Outer Mongolia and Tibet from Chinese control. Further disintegration of China appeared imminent. Japan was already well along on the road to empire when the Great War broke out and provided an opportunity for further enhancement of Japanese power.

On August 15, 1914, Japan advised Germany to withdraw all her warships from the Far East and to deliver the Kiaochow leased territory to Japan "with a view to the eventual restoration of the same to China." In the absence of a reply, Japan declared war on Germany on August 23 and seized the area in question. On January 18, 1915, the Japanese minister presented to the President of China twenty-one demands embodying Chinese acceptance of any disposition Japan might make of Kiaochow and Shantung, the granting to Japan of a ninety-nine year lease on Port Arthur and Dalny, along with mining, railway, and financial concessions in south Manchuria and eastern or Inner Mongolia and participation in the Hanyehping Company, the great Chinese iron and steel concern on the Yangtse. China was also asked to agree "not to cede or lease to a third Power any harbor, bay, or island along the coast of China." Group V of the twenty-one demands provided for Japanese supervision of Chinese political, financial, and military affairs, a joint Sino-Japanese police force in important places in China, the purchase of at least half of China's munitions from Japan, and the granting to Japan of a sphere of influence in Fukien, opposite Formosa. Under threats of coercion, the Chinese Government yielded and the first sixteen of the demands were incorporated in treaties and notes on May 25, 1915. The preoccupation of the other Powers in the gigantic conflict in Europe enabled Japan to have her way. The Allies secretly agreed to support the Japanese claims at the Peace Conference, and even the United States, in the Lansing-Ishii agreement of November 2, 1917, recognized that "territorial propinquity" gave Japan "special interests" in China. In 1918 new concessions were wrested from China by the Japanese Government, despite the fact that China had entered the war on the Allied side.

At the close of the Great War, Japanese power in Asia reached its zenith. Tokyo had secured control of Shantung, Fukien, all of Manchuria, Inner Mongolia, and the German islands north of the Equator. Revolution and civil war in Russia enabled Japan to extend her conquests to the north. In cooperation with the Allies and the United States, Japan launched upon a program of military intervention in Russia in the summer of 1918. While the other intervening governments were interested primarily in aiding the counter-revolutionary White Armies and consummating the overthrow of the Soviet régime, Japan appeared to be concerned more with territorial acquisitions. Northern Sakhalin was occupied. Seventy thousand Japanese troops were poured into eastern Siberia, where they intrenched themselves with the apparent object of retaining permanent control of the Maritime Provinces, and perhaps of the whole vast area east of Lake Baikal. Friction developed between the American and Japanese forces in Siberia, and between Tokyo and Washington, but Japanese power was predominant in eastern Asia and the diplomatic representations of other States were unavailing.

Japan, however, had overreached herself in various directions and was subsequently obliged to abandon much of the territory which her troops had occupied. At the Peace Conference in 1919 she was persuaded, under

American pressure, to agree to retain only economic rights in Shantung, though the treaty transferred German rights in this province to Japan. The United States protested against the continued Japanese occupation of Siberia and denounced Japan's retention of Shantung. Anti-Japanese sentiment increased in the United States, in China, in Russia, and in Canada and Australia as well. The United States had embarked upon a naval program with which Japan could not hope to compete. The intervention in Russia had failed and Soviet troops were again east of Lake Baikal. At the Washington Conference of 1921–1922 the United States and Great Britain cooperated to bring Japan to terms. The Anglo-Japanese alliance was terminated. The Japanese Government found it expedient to compromise. By the Four Power Pacific Pact the United States, Great Britain, Japan, and France agreed "to respect their rights in relation to their insular possessions and insular dominions in the region of the Pacific Ocean" and to communicate with one another in the event of any threat of aggression. In the naval treaty of February 6, 1922, Japan was granted 315,000 tons of capital ships as against 525,000 tons each for Great Britain and the United States. The Powers agreed to maintain the *status quo* as regards naval bases and fortifications in the western Pacific.[1] At the London Naval Conference of 1930 Japan achieved the right to maintain a naval strength in cruisers and auxiliary vessels in the ratio of 7:10:10 as compared with Great Britain and the United States. Japan was thus recognized as the third greatest naval Power. The United States renounced all ambitions of establishing its naval supremacy in the western Pacific, and Japanese predominance in this area was assured. Japan was obliged to agree to the restoration of Shantung to China, however, and to sign the Nine Power Pact of 1922 for the preservation of the Open Door and of Chinese territorial integrity. She also gave informal assurances regarding Siberia, and in 1925 northern Sakhalin and the Maritime Provinces were restored to the Soviet Union. While the Japanese Government had surrendered much, it had achieved as much as the existing state of power relationships in the Far East permitted.

These developments constituted a postponement, rather than a final renunciation, of efforts to enhance Japanese power on the Asiatic mainland. Since 1925 the most serious threat to Japan's position has come not from other imperial Powers, but from the Nationalists in China, who are determined to oust foreign interests from the country and recover control of their own destinies. This determination, coupled with the chronic Chinese civil wars, has led to repeated "incidents" in Sino-Japanese relations. The process whereby Japan, in 1931–1932, occupied Manchuria, destroyed Chinese authority in this region, and set up the puppet State of

[1] See pp. 691–692 below.

Manchukuo has been reviewed above.[1] This action intensified Japanese-American diplomatic tension, created Soviet-Japanese friction because of Russian interests in north Manchuria, and led to alarm in the U.S.S.R. over a possible renewal of the Japanese assault on Outer Mongolia and Siberia. The Soviet Union is not prepared to challenge Japan by force in Manchuria and the United states is too remote to do so, even if it were so disposed. China is impotent to resist, and no other power in Asia is capable of thwarting Japanese designs. That Manchuria will fall completely under Japanese control is a foregone conclusion in view of these circumstances, whatever gestures of protest other Powers may make and whatever measure of condemnation is visited upon Tokyo by "world opinion." Whether this result will be followed by new efforts at Japanese expansion, leading perhaps to a clash with the Soviet Union or the United States, remains to be seen. Japanese imperialism has successfully despoiled China, checked Russia, eliminated Germany, and defied the United States and other Powers. That it has run its course is improbable.

A final word may be pertinent regarding the motives of this remarkable career of imperialistic aggrandizement. Japan, like all the other Great Powers in the Western State System, has sought to extend its domination over as wide an area as possible. Japan's theater of action in eastern Asia is remote from the centers of power of other great States. Japan—westernized and militarized—has found the huge disintegrating hulk of the Celestial Empire an easy prey. She has been able to dominate the western Pacific with her naval power and to dominate the Asiatic mainland with her army. The specific objectives of her quest for power have, as always, reflected the interests of her ruling classes: the new bourgeoisie, the old nobility, and the military, naval, and diplomatic bureaucracy. The goals have been the usual goals of imperialism everywhere in the age of competitive capitalism: markets for goods and investments, leaseholds, concessions, and other profit-making opportunities. "Surplus population" has been a plausible rationalization of expansionist ambitions, for Japan is densely populated and the United States and the British Dominions have closed their doors to Japanese immigration. While China furnishes no outlet for Japan's millions, Australia and New Zealand contain enormous expanses of empty land. But nothing is less likely than a Japanese descent upon these islands, for Great Britain is still able to defend them from her bases at Singapore and Hongkong. Japanese policy is directed more toward profitable economic opportunities for entrepreneurs and investors than toward land for peasants and workers. Japan's population problem could doubtless be solved by birth control and industrialization. Further industrialization will increase Japanese competition with Great Britain

[1] See pp. 415–419 above.

and the United States in Oriental markets and also will increase Japanese ability to dominate these markets, if need be, by military means. Barring some internal disaster, the rising sun on the flag of Nippon seems destined to shine over eastern Asia and the western Pacific with increased intensity and power. Those upon whom it sheds its fierce radiance will either scurry to shade or find themselves burned, for none are near enough or powerful enough to intercept its blistering heat at the source.

6. U. S. A.: AMERICAN COLOSSUS

Where is it written in the Book of Fate that the American Republic shall not spread her limits from the capes of the Chesapeake to Nootka Sound, from the Isthmus of Panama to Hudson Bay?—*The Nashville Clarion*, April 28, 1812.

The United States of North America shares with Japan the distinction of being the only Great Power not having its center of population and wealth on the European continent. But while Japan, from the beginning of its expansionist career, was in close proximity to the territories and interests of several other Great Powers, the United States occupied a position of relative isolation. After winning independence from Great Britain in 1783, the new republic of the western hemisphere—first non-European State to become a member of the Western State System—found itself too far from Europe to concern itself seriously with European quarrels or to be an object of serious concern on the part of European Powers. The United States could never hope to exercise its power effectively on the other side of the Atlantic. No European Power save Great Britain could hope to act effectively in the Americas. Spain's imposing empire disintegrated within four decades after the establishment of the United States and left only Cuba under the Spanish flag. The United States, within its own sphere of action, was confronted by only one Power, Great Britain, able to meet it on more or less equal terms. The American effort to conquer Canada in the War of 1812 failed miserably. The United States made its second peace with Great Britain in 1815 and has never since taken up arms against the mother country. The other American Powers—France, Spain, and Russia in Europe, and later the Latin American republics—were its political inferiors by virtue of their weakness or remoteness. The extension of American power westward and southward at the expense of weaker States led to successive territorial acquisitions. Louisiana was purchased from France in 1803, the Floridas acquired from Spain in 1819, Texas detached from Mexico in 1836, and the great southwest conquered from Mexico in 1848. American power was confronted with rival States to the south whose weakness facilitated territorial expansion and the assertion of American hegemony.

Out of these relationships of power, resting as they do upon the strategy of geography, have emerged the two great traditions of American foreign policy: isolationism and the Monroe Doctrine. The only formal alliance which the United States has ever concluded with a foreign Power was entered into during the struggle for independence. Once independence was won, the French alliance of 1778 became an embarrassment, particularly after the outbreak of the revolutionary wars in Europe in 1793. The intensity of partisan quarrels in American politics and the extent to which they were influenced by sympathies with or antipathies against Great Britain and France caused Washington, in his Farewell Address of 1796, to advise the nation to avoid permanent alliances and entanglements of its peace and prosperity in Europe. The French alliance was abrogated in 1798, amid mutual recriminations. Jefferson, in his inaugural address of 1802, likewise urged "honest friendship with all nations, entangling alliances with none." The precedent thus established has been followed ever since—not because the founding fathers were possessed of unusual virtue or wisdom, but because the United States, 3,000 miles from Europe and 7,000 miles from Asia, could not hope to play a successful diplomatic or military rôle in international politics outside of the American hemisphere.

The Monroe Doctrine, first enunciated by President Monroe in 1823, was a warning to the European Powers to keep out of the American hemisphere and, by implication and successive reinterpretations, an assertion of the hegemony of the United States over the American continents. The doctrine was inspired by rumors of European efforts to assist Spain to recover her Latin American colonies and by Russian encroachments on the northwest coast south of Alaska. This statement of American policy was approved by Great Britain, for reasons of commerce and imperial security. The European Powers were admonished to refrain from further efforts at colonization in the Americas, from interposition in American affairs, and from attempts to extend their political systems to the new world. These negative injunctions addressed to Europe—noncolonization, non-extension, non-interposition—implied American "protection" over the Latin American republics. Protection, here as always in international politics, implies, in greater or lesser degree, influence, control, domination.

These traditions were adequate as guides to action so long as the United States was occupied in westward expansion and in the agrarian imperialism of a land-hungry population. In their original form they ceased to correspond to realities as soon as the United States emerged out of its provincial preoccupations and became a world Power. This transition was foreshadowed in the purchase of Alaska from Russia in 1867, for here for the first time the United States had annexed non-contiguous

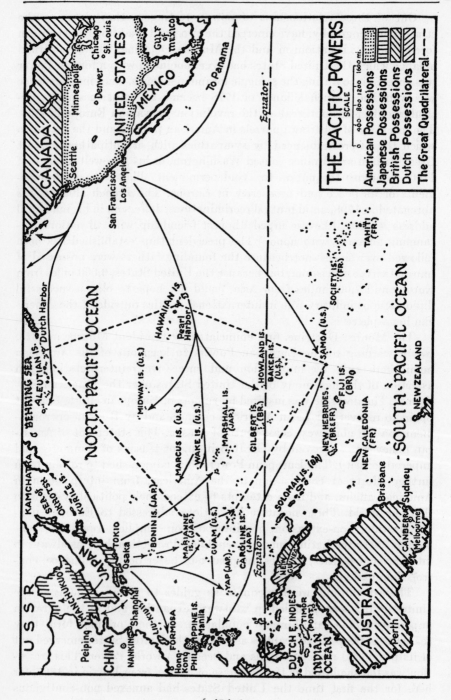

THE PACIFIC POWERS

SCALE
0   400   800   1200   1600 mi.

American Possessions
Japanese Possessions
British Possessions
Dutch Possessions
The Great Quadrilateral ----

territory. There followed American efforts to acquire Hawaii and Samoa in the Pacific, and Cuba, Santo Domingo, the Virgin Islands, and other points in the Caribbean. For three decades after the Civil War these efforts were unsuccessful, largely because of domestic opposition. But these decades were also a period of rapid industrialization, of a great accumulation of capital, of a vastly increased outflow of goods, of enormously enhanced economic power, and of the political ascendancy of the business classes. A modern navy was built to protect American commerce and investments abroad. The imperialism of population was replaced by the imperialism of dollars and goods. The power interests of the United States in international politics no longer reflected the yearning of an agrarian community for land, but the quest of an industrial society for opportunities for profitable trade and investment.

The decade between 1895 and 1905 was decisive in the inevitable reorientation of American foreign policy that followed these internal changes and the enhancement of American national power to which they led. In the Spanish-American war of 1898, Spain was ousted from the new world and from the southwestern Pacific. The United States annexed Porto Rico, liberated Cuba as an American protectorate, and took the Philippine Islands in the East Indies. The Hawaiian Islands were annexed at the same time, as was part of the Samoan group. The United States became a Pacific Power. The great quadrilateral—Dutch Harbor in the Aleutian Islands, Pearl Harbor in Hawaii, Pago-Pago in Samoa, and Guam in the Ladrones—opened up possibilities of naval dominance in the western ocean. The corresponding opportunities for hegemony in the Caribbean were at once utilized. Panama was taken from Colombia in 1903, converted into an American protectorate, and made the route for an interoceanic canal, completed in 1914. A financial protectorate was established over the Dominican Republic in 1904. American trade and investments were promoted in the entire Caribbean area by naval supremacy and military intervention. Great Britain yielded by withdrawing her Caribbean squadron, while the United States acquired and fortified all the seaways connecting the Caribbean with the Atlantic and the Pacific.

Under these circumstances the old Monroe Doctrine and the old isolationism no longer served American interests. The United States was a colonial power in Asia and Latin America. American commerce and capital moved throughout the world. Under Roosevelt's "police power" interpretation, the Monroe Doctrine ceased to be a negative admonition addressed to Europe and became an instrument of American imperialism. In 1895, to be sure, Britain was sharply warned to refrain from territorial acquisitions at the expense of Venezuela. And in 1912 Japan was informed that her corporations might not acquire land suitable for a naval base (Magdalena Bay) in Mexico. But in general the argument was advanced

that if the United States forbade non-American Powers to act in the
Americas to protect their interests, the United States must act for them,
even to the extent of preserving order and protecting foreign lives, property, and investments in disorderly States. Cuba and Panama were
already American protectorates. Haiti, the Dominican Republic, Nicaragua, and Costa Rica were likewise subjected to varying degrees of American political and financial control. In the eyes of Latin Americans, the
Monroe Doctrine became the symbol of the greed and rapacity of "the
Colossus of the North" and the Yankee Peril became an object of universal fear and detestation.

But the Monroe Doctrine was never reciprocal. If the United States
warned the world off of its own preserves, it did not regard itself as obligated to refrain from action in its own interests in Europe, Africa, or
Asia. The old isolationism persisted as a popular shibboleth but ceased to
be a guide to action in its original form. No alliances were concluded, but
a policy of aloof indifference to events outside of the western hemisphere
was no longer possible to a State whose merchants and bankers were
reaching out for profits all over the earth. A modified political isolationism
continued, for despite its enhanced economic power, the United States
could still not hope to meet the European Powers on equal terms in
Europe, nor Japan and other Powers on equal terms in Asia. Means must
be devised, however, for protecting American economic interests abroad
from the menace of exclusion or discrimination at the hands of monopolistic competitors, supported by their governments. These economic
interests became political interests, for the two are inseparable in the
days of imperialism and the empires of business. They became important
stakes of American diplomacy—more important, indeed, than domestic
security and Latin American hegemony, for these were already secured
and no longer contested by powerful rivals. The new stakes must somehow
be defended by methods not inconsistent with the isolationist tradition,
for this still represented the realities of relationships of power. But the
new methods must, if possible, be effective in achieving their purposes
within the limits of the tradition.

The American policies of the Open Door and Freedom of the Seas are
intelligible chiefly as devices to attain this goal. The American market in
Asia seemed to be menaced at the end of the century by the impending
partition of China, foreshadowed by the acquisition of foreign leaseholds
and concessions and by the creation of spheres of influence, within which
the controlling Powers proposed to give their own business men monopolistic advantages to the detriment of competing foreigners. During the
earlier period the United States had secured access to the Chinese market
on terms of equality with other States, through the conclusion of most-
favored-nation treaties obliging China to grant to Americans the same

privileges she extended to nationals of other States. After 1890 the doors to Chinese trade and investment were gradually closed by the other imperial Powers. To abandon American commercial interests in the Orient was impossible. To participate in the scramble for concessions and spheres was inexpedient, for the United States, despite its control of the Philippines, was too far away to engage in successful political and military rivalry with its commercial competitors. The solution arrived at by Secretary of State John Hay in 1899 was to urge upon the other Powers the acceptance of the principle of the Open Door (equality of economic opportunity for the citizens of all countries in China) and of the correlative principles of the preservation of the administrative entity and territorial integrity of China. This policy had the advantage of winning Chinese friendship, for it appeared to be a protective gesture. Somewhat reluctantly the other Powers were induced to acquiesce and the policy was incorporated in subsequent treaties, of which the Nine Power Pact of 1922 is the most recent and significant. In practice, the Open Door has been gradually pushed shut by the other imperialist governments—never so completely as to justify the charge that the policy has been deliberately violated, but sufficiently so to afford substantial advantages to favored nationals and to involve discrimination against outsiders. Chinese integrity was, after a fashion, preserved until the Japanese descent upon Manchuria. But the Open Door is no longer so wide open as it once was. It remains to be seen whether this American policy will protect American economic interests in the Far East as effectively in the future as in the past.

As for Europe, the protection of American interests appeared to require two policies: (1) insistence upon equal trading privileges with all States and (2) the prevention of the establishment of such a preponderance of power by any one State as might jeopardize American security. Neither of these policies required express formulation in peace time, for American commerce was not endangered and the balance of power kept each nation within limits without the United States throwing its weight to either side. The second policy never received clear formulation, even in war time, though the considerations lying behind it shaped American action. The outbreak of hostilities between the two European coalitions in 1914 caused the United States to proclaim its neutrality, as it had done in 1793 and in all subsequent European wars. An immensely profitable trade in munitions at once developed with the Allies. The effective Allied blockade of Germany prevented this trade from going to both sets of belligerents. But the continuation of this commerce was threatened by the efforts of the warring governments to injure one another economically by cutting off trade between the enemy and the outside world. The United States, in defending the liberty of its traders to do business of this kind, reverted to the principles of neutral rights and freedom of the seas, which it had evolved under comparable circumstances between 1793 and 1812. It protested the British contraband list, the British blockade, and the British interpretation of the doctrine of continuous voyage. It likewise protested the German submarine blockade of the Allies and was soon involved in acrimonious controversy with both sides.

In the sequel the United States leaned more and more toward the Allies, and this not for humanitarian or sentimental reasons expressed in war slogans, but for very tangible considerations connected with business and power politics. American capitalists made huge loans to the Allied governments, and American exporters sold, at great profit, huge quantities of goods to the borrowers. Allied defeat would probably mean Allied bankruptcy. American business had little to lose and everything to gain from Allied victory. A victory of the Central Powers would not only imperil these economic interests, but would completely upset the balance of power and give Germany such a position of overwhelming preponderance on the Continent and throughout the world that even American security might eventually be endangered. Circumstances permitted these economic and political interests to be presented on a high moral plane. Germany was an "autocracy" and the Allies and the United States were "democracies." The Allied cruiser blockade of Germany menaced American property and American legal rights, but the U-boat blockade of the Allies endangered American lives as well. Germany was ruthless, lawless, uncivilized. The Allies were considerate, law-abiding, and virtuous. When Germany announced the resumption of unrestricted submarine warfare, on February 1, 1917, President Wilson severed diplomatic relations. On April 6, 1917, the United States declared war on Germany. Other American States were induced to follow suit. The United States became an "Associate" of the Allies, not an "Ally." A large army was conscripted, trained, and sent to France. A strengthened American navy joined the Allied squadrons. Billions of dollars were raised and loaned to the Allied governments. The immense economic power of the United States more than overbalanced the defection of Russia, and its support was sufficient to turn the scales. As in 1812, neutrality had failed to protect American interests and isolation was abandoned in favor of active participation in the European contest. Victory came in 1918, and the United States shared in the glory thereof.

The disillusioning aftermath produced a violent popular reversion to extreme isolationism. Wilson went to the Paris Peace Conference, participated actively in the making of the treaty, took the initiative in the creation of the League of Nations, and committed the United States to cooperation with other Powers in preserving peace and dealing with post-war problems. On his return home he found himself a prophet without honor in his own land. The Treaty of Versailles was rejected by the Senate, with the Covenant of the League as the chief target of attack. Wilson and all his works were repudiated by Congress and the electorate. He retired from public life a defeated and broken man. In the election of 1920 the Democratic candidate, James Cox, was overwhelmed by the Republicans under Warren Gamaliel Harding, and the way was prepared for twelve continuous years of Republican rule. In foreign policy, Republican rule meant isolationism with a vengeance. A separate peace was made with Germany on August 25, 1921. The League was first ignored, then recognized as a stubbornly irreducible fact and later used, through its conferences and commissions, as an agency of cooperation— timidly at the outset and later with more confidence. American entrance into the World Court was pledged, but the pledge remained unfulfilled at the end of the Hoover administration. The ill-fated intervention in Russia of 1918–1920 was abandoned, but diplomatic recognition was sternly refused to the Soviet Government, even after all the other Great Powers had recognized it. High moral and legal principles were found to justify this attitude, but at bottom it reflected the deep hostility of the business men's government of the most capitalistic of modern States toward proletarian Communism. Immigration was cut off, and almost insurmountable tariff walls were erected, for isolationism and economic nationalism were opposite sides of the same coin. The Allies were required to sign on the dotted line for the repayment of their war debts. American dollar diplomacy in the Caribbean was continued in the best tradition, but Latin American sensibilities (which had a relationship to profitable trade) were soothed with assurances that the United States had no imperialistic designs and that the Monroe Doctrine was not what it seemed to be. The Open Door policy in Asia was reiterated. In short, the exclusive pursuit of American national interests was again couched in terms of long-established principles and policies.

These policies, however, were accompanied by various gestures in the direction of peace, disarmament, and international cooperation, for in the American mentality there runs an ineradicable strain of Puritan morality, ethical idealism, and political naiveté. The gestures themselves, moreover, could be made to serve American interests. Peace, disarmament, and international concord are, in a direct and immediate sense, politically and economically advantageous to the United States, for it is interested in profits, prosperity, trade, and investment. Prior to the Japanese occupation of Manchuria and the crises of debts and reparations during the Great Depression, the United States was pursuing no diplomatic objectives involving the clash of vital interests with other Powers. In 1921 the United States summoned the Washington Conference, where it secured naval parity with Great Britain in capital ships, in return for a general reduction of naval armaments. It likewise secured a new recognition of the Open Door principle and Japanese withdrawal from Shantung and Siberia, in return for the abandonment of its bid for naval supremacy in the Pacific. In 1927 it sought to promote further naval disarmament in the abortive Coolidge conference at Geneva. In 1928 it sponsored the Kellogg-Briand Pact for the Outlawry of War. In 1930 it participated in the five Power naval conference in London, where it acquired complete naval parity with Great Britain but no substantial reduction of naval armaments, because of Anglo-American differences regarding cruisers and Franco-Italian naval rivalry in the Mediterranean. In 1931 it cooperated with the Council of the League of Nations in the Manchurian crisis, though without tangible results. In 1932 the Hoover moratorium proposal for a one-year suspension of all reparation and debt payments was presented as a generous move toward world economic and financial rehabilitation. The United States likewise participated in the General Disarmament Conference of the League of Nations and eloquently urged armament reduction, without being willing to commit itself to consultation or cooperation with other Powers in the interests of peace. By all of these moves, national interests, moral principles, and humanitarian ideals were simultaneously served. And if none of them were served wisely or well in the long run, the cause lay in the refusal of Congress and the country either to implement patriotic power interests with Machiavellian diplomacy or to implement idealistic aspirations with concrete political arrangements contrary to past tradition.

In summary, the United States, in its efforts to protect its world interests, combines isolationism with sporadic cooperation in dealing with Europe; the Monroe Doctrine, economic penetration, and political hegemony with conciliatory gestures in dealing with Latin America; and championship of the Open Door, with pleading and consultation in dealing with Asia. American foreign policy continues to present these three faces to the world, and by these expedients seeks to promote national interests without becoming a partner in international organization and without sacrificing freedom of action in future situations. Thus far these policies have served the desires of their makers reasonably well. Whether they will continue to do so is more doubtful. The impact of the world depression on the United States may serve to discredit isolationism and economic nationalism sufficiently to bring about a modification of these policies. Hostility toward the U.S.S.R., increasing friction with Japan, and commercial and financial competition in many markets with Great Britain are three outstanding sources of possible future danger.

7. U.S.S.R.: PROLETARIAN REVOLUTION

Workers of the world, unite! You have nothing to lose but your chains.
—Communist Manifesto, 1848.

There remains to be considered the foreign policy of the largest and most populous of the Great Powers. The old Russian State, stretching in its immensity from the Arctic wastes to the tropic deserts of Turkestan, and from the Baltic and Black Seas across the steppes of Eurasia to the far Pacific, was created by a process of territorial conquest and accretion on the part of the Grand Duchy of Muscovy. Always bearing upon its face the imprint of the Tartar conquest, always half Asiatic and half European, the Russia of the Romanovs remained backward, primitive, isolated from the main currents of western culture, despite its efforts to secure "windows to the west" and to fashion itself after western models. In its political and economic institutions and its social life it was almost medieval. Its government was an arbitrary and unlimited autocracy until 1905, and the Duma or parliament which was the fruit of the first revolution was a debating society without authority. Its ruling class was a feudal, landowning aristocracy and a corrupt and irresponsible bureaucracy. The great mass of its population—the "dark people"— consisted of illiterate peasants steeped in ignorance and superstitious religiosity and living in a status of serfdom until 1863. The Industrial Revolution did not come to Russia until the seventies and eighties of the nineteenth century. The urban bourgeoisie which it brought in its wake pleaded for democracy and parliamentary government, but it was given little voice in public affairs. The urban proletariat, recruited from the peasantry, lived in misery under the pressure of ruthless exploitation and had no voice at all in government, except through terrorism and revolutionary violence. While the workers sought salvation in the western gospel of international Marxian Socialism and the bourgeoisie in the gospel of democratic and patriotic liberalism, the peasantry remained dumb and inert, moved only by blind land hunger and hatred of the landlords, and the Tsardom and the aristocracy were committed to reactionary obscurantism.

The foreign policy of this State reflected the interests and attitudes of a ruling class which was aristocratic, religious, and mystically loyal to Holy Russia and to the cult of racial patriotism known as Pan-Slavism. In its quest for power Tsarist Russia strove for diplomatic stakes, not expressed so much in terms of the profit motives of its merchants and industrialists as in terms of the demand for land on the part of its semi-feudal oligarchy of nobles. Some of its nobles were capitalists, and some of its non-noble capitalists were politically influential—and these groups had eyes open for concessions, leaseholds, and markets on the Asiatic fringes of the empire. But Russian economy imported capital and manufactured goods from abroad and exported grain and raw materials. Its imperialism was not a commercial and naval imperialism, but a military and agrarian imperialism of population. As early as the seventeenth century, it reached out across Siberia. In the eighteenth century it struck Sweden to the north, Poland to the west, Turkey to the south, and extended itself over large areas formerly controlled by these States. In the nineteenth century it penetrated central Asia, impinged upon Persia. Afghanistan, and China, and encountered the rival imperialisms of Great Britain and Japan. Friction with Britain led to the Crimean War of 1854–1856, in which the progress of the Russian steamroller toward Constantinople and the Straits was temporarily halted. Continued Anglo-Russian rivalry in Asia contributed to the decision to enter into the Dual Alliance with France in 1894. Conflict with Japan led to defeat in Manchuria in 1904–1905 and to internal revolution as the aftermath of defeat. In the years which followed, the continued drive toward the Straits and toward control of the Slavic States of the Balkans made Austria-Hungary and Germany the new enemies—and against these Powers an advantageous combination could be made with France, Great Britain, and even Japan.

The Great War of 1914 was precipitated by the Tsarist Government with the approval of the Quai d'Orsay. The Franco-Russian Alliance had already been "Balkanized" and French support of Russian Balkan policies was secured. Izvolsky, Russian Foreign Minister until 1910 and Russian Ambassador to Paris subsequently, smarted under the diplomatic defeat of 1908 arising out of the Austrian annexation of Bosnia and Herzegovina without compensation to Russia. He was spokesman for those at the Russian foreign office determined to acquire the Straits and to block the Teutonic *drang nach Osten*. In Poincaré he found a fitting helpmate for the realization of these ambitions. By 1914 Russian military preparations, financed from France, were sufficiently advanced to enable St. Petersburg to risk war over these issues. Russia accordingly championed Serbia in the Austro-Serbian conflict of July, 1914. It was the mobilization of the Russian army against Austria-Hungary and Germany on July 30 which made a general war inevitable, for it was understood in the Franco-Russian Alliance that "mobilization means war" and this was no less clear to Berlin and Vienna. Germany responded to this threat by an ultimatum which remained unanswered. A declaration of war followed on August 1. On September 5, 1914, Russia agreed with Great Britain and France not to conclude peace separately. The inter-Allied secret treaties of 1916 and 1917 promised to the Tsardom, in the prospective division on the spoils, all that it had been striving for and more besides.

But the terrific impact of the German military machine upon Russia brought overwhelming disaster to the entire economic, social, and political structure of the Romanov State. During 1915 and 1916 Galicia and Russian Poland were lost to the enemy, and the ill-equipped and badly led Russian army was driven back in defeat with enormous losses. The transport system collapsed. Food riots broke out in the cities. Mutiny raised its head at the front. "Dark forces" appeared at the court, favoring peace with Germany to save the autocracy. Their spokesman, the mad monk Rasputin, was assassinated by patriotic liberals, but the process of economic and social disintegration went on. The political authority of the reactionaries who surrounded the Tsar was reduced to a nullity as revolution spread throughout the country. In mid-March of 1917, following numerous strikes and revolts, Nicholas II was obliged to abdicate and give way to a "Provisional Government" composed of Duma members of a liberal bourgeois and mildly Socialistic persuasion. This government, under Kerensky's leadership, sought to continue the war and to pave the way for a constituent assembly which would solve all problems and make Russia a middle-class parliamentary democracy. While it deliberated and debated, however, peasants seized the estates of the nobles, workers occupied factories, and soldiers deserted from the front to share in the new freedom. Real power throughout the country passed to spontaneously organized councils or *soviets* of workers', soldiers', and peasants' deputies, who spoke for the war-weary masses and insisted upon an end of the imperialist war, the partition of the landed estates, and the socialization of industry.

There ensued the most revolutionary and far-reaching social upheaval of modern times, demolishing utterly the existing economic and social fabric of Russia and shaking all of western society to its foundations. Under the leadership of the revolutionary Bolshevik wing of the Social Democratic party, the trade unions demanded that the political revolution be transformed into a social revolution and that power be transferred to the soviets. The impotent Kerensky régime tottered to its doom, unable either to carry on the war or withdraw from it, helpless either to avert social revolution or to accept it. With their slogans of "All Power to the Soviets," and "Peace, Land, and Bread," the Bolshevik leaders secured ascendancy in the soviets and organized the new proletarian revolution. On November 7, 1917, the Provisional Government was overthrown by the armed workers of Petrograd, and the Second All-Russian Congress of Soviets approved the creation of a Council of People's Commissars, of which Lenin became president. The Soviet Government, thus established, proceded at once to expropriate the landlords and the bourgeoisie, to abolish private property in real estate and the means of industrial production, to distribute the land to the villages, to establish workers' control in the factories, mills, and mines, and to lay plans for a socialized economy. In 1918 the bolsheviki changed their name to the Communist party, in order to distinguish themselves from the Reformist Socialists. The former ruling classes were deprived of their wealth and power and replaced by the workers and peasants, under the leadership of the most class-conscious section of the urban proletariat, organized into the Communist party. This party brushed aside the constituent assembly, assumed a "monopoly of legality" in the Soviet Government, and ruled in the name of "the dictatorship of the proletariat" as a form of political authority intended to prepare the way for a Communistic social order and a classless State.

The foreign policy of the new workers' republic led to immediate friction with the bourgeois governments which were the allies of the old Russia. The Communists regarded their revolution as but a step toward a world revolution of the international proletariat, leading to the universal overthrow of capitalism, nationalism, and imperialism. The bourgeois governments regarded the Communists as a group of dangerous fanatics, whose subversive assault on the existing order must be met by ruthless suppression at the hands of the "sane" elements in Russia, *i.e.*, the expropriated classes, aided by the outside world. Quite apart from this class conflict across national frontiers, there were specific grievances which impelled the Allies and the United States to move against the proletarian dictatorship. The Soviet Government at once opened peace negotiations with the Central Powers. When the Allies refused to participate, the Communists published the secret treaties, in order to reveal to the masses the imperialistic war aims of the Entente. An armistice was concluded on the eastern front in December, 1917, and in March, 1918, the humiliating peace of Brest-Litovsk took Russia out of the war. The Soviet Government, moreover, repudiated the public debts contracted by the Tsarist and Kerensky régimes, including both the pre-war government bonds, held in enormous quantities by French and British investors, and the huge war loans extended by the Governments of Great Britain, France, and the United States. It likewise confiscated foreign property and private investments in Russia, along with the holdings of the Russian bourgeoisie. It summoned the workers of the world to revolt against the war and to overthrow the capitalistic governments which were directing it. The Central Powers seized upon the opportunity presented by the revolution to make an advantageous peace in the east. But between the Soviets and the Allies there could be no peace.

In August of 1918 Soviet Russia was subjected to an Allied blockade and to military intervention, participated in by Czechoslovakian, British, French, American, Japanese, and other Allied troops. The intervention coincided with counter-revolutionary uprisings within Russia, subsidized and supported by the Allied Governments, and with the beginning of the civil war. The moderate Socialist enemies of the Communist dictatorship played into the hands of the counter-revolution and were soon swept aside by Tsarist reactionaries or "Whites" who rallied to their cause the former landowners and business classes. Blockade, intervention, and revolt were supplemented by terrorism and sabotage, as weapons against the Soviets. In Finland the workers' government was drowned in blood by White terrorists, with German support. In the north, Allied and American troops seized Archangel and advanced southward toward Vologda and Moscow. In the Caucasus and the Ukraine, Denikin's White Army, with Allied financial and military support, prepared to invade central Russia. In Siberia, Kolchak's White Army, with Allied financial and military support, prepared to do likewise, while Japanese, American, and British troops occupied the Maritime Provinces. In Esthonia, Yudenitch's White Army, with Allied financial and military support, prepared to take Petrograd. The Soviet Government was assaulted on all sides from without and menaced by counter-revolutions from within. It met these threats to its existence by suppressing the opposition parties, by inaugurating the Red Terror as a reply to the White terrorism of its enemies, and by organizing the Red Army to defend the revolution. In March of 1919 the Communist or Third International was established, with its headquarters at Moscow, as an international federation of the revolutionary Communist parties throughout the world. It was designed to replace the bankrupt Amsterdam or Second International of the moderate Socialist parties and to serve as the general staff of the "world revolution" which would attack from the rear the bourgeois governments seeking to strangle the Russian proletarian dictatorship.

The civil strife which followed was long and bloody and characterized by unprecedented savagery and destructiveness, for it was not only an international conflict between Soviet Russia and the Allied and Associated Powers, but a class war between the Russian nobility and bourgeoisie on the one hand and the proletariat and peasantry on the other. The details of the campaigns need not be reviewed here. Suffice it to say that the Red Army, under the direction of Trotsky and his comrades, finally proved more than a match for its enemies, domestic and foreign. Kolchak's forces were driven back from Kazan in the spring of 1919. The Allied and American invaders from the north were finally stopped and later compelled to withdraw. In October of 1919—the darkest month of the revolution—Denikin's divisions approached Moscow from the south, while Yudenitch, with British support, attacked Petrograd. Both offensives were beaten back. Kolchak's army was crushed in central Siberia, and he was captured and executed in February of 1920. The other White Armies were similarly destroyed, despite desperate Allied attempts to save them. Peace seemed in sight in the spring of 1920, when the armies of the new Poland invaded the Ukraine in a mad imperialistic endeavor to restore the Polish frontiers of 1772. Kiev fell to the invaders, but in the summer of 1920 the Polish forces were pushed back and the Red Army approached the gates of Warsaw and threatened to carry revolution into central Europe. British and French assistance enabled the Poles to counter-attack successfully, and the war closed in October. Meanwhile, a new White leader, Baron Wrangel, had seized the Crimea, invaded the Ukraine, and secured diplomatic recognition and military and financial support from France. His troops were speedily dispersed by the Red Army in November, 1920, and the civil war came to a close with Soviet victory and the defeat of intervention and counter-revolution.

The year 1921 marked a definite turning point, both in the internal policies and in the foreign relations of the Soviet Government. The end of the assault from abroad left Russia economically prostrate as a result of six years of almost uninterrupted hostilities. Lenin executed a temporary "strategic retreat toward capitalism" in the New Economic Policy of March, 1921, which permitted a certain amount of individual trade for private profit. At the same time, Great Britain granted *de facto* recognition to the Soviet régime by concluding a trade agreement. The blockade was broken. The *cordon sanitaire* was at an end. A truce prevailed between the proletarian dictatorship and the bourgeois States, and the Communists could turn at last to the difficult task of laying the foundation of the new social order. The restoration of trade relations with the outside world was an integral part of the process, for economic rehabilitation required the importation of machinery, manufactures, and foreign technical skill to be paid for by the export of grain, oil, timber, and other Russian raw materials. At the Genoa Conference of 1922, Chicherin, Commissar for Foreign Affairs, met the representatives of the other European Powers in a general conference for the first time. They demanded payment of Russia's debt and compensation to expropriated investors as the price of recognition, credits, and trade relations. Their bill of 13 billions of dollars was met by a Soviet counter-claim of 60 billions for damage done during the intervention. Neither side would yield, and no general agreement was possible. But a bargain was struck with the new Germany in the Treaty of Rapallo, whereby all claims were canceled and mutually advantageous commercial relations were restored. Other States could not afford to ignore the Soviet market. Great Britain extended *de jure* recognition in February, 1924. France, Italy, Japan, and a dozen lesser States followed suit within the next eighteen months, with the United States alone among the Great Powers persisting in its refusal to restore diplomatic relations. The revolutionary outcast was received again into the community of nations, and a growing foreign commerce hastened the work of internal reconstruction.

Meanwhile the frontiers of the new Russia had been redefined and a territorial reorganization of the Soviet State effected. The Treaty of Brest-Litovsk was liquidated by the defeat of Germany in the Great War and by the express provisions of the Treaty of Versailles. During the intervention Great Britain and France sought to acquire spheres of influence in southern Russia, for reasons of strategy, oil, and high politics, while Japan seized eastern Siberia and Poland cast covetous eyes on the Ukraine. The United States opposed these territorial acquisitions by championing the integrity of Russia—of a capitalistic "national" Russia, which Washington hoped would emerge. But the Red Army ousted the invaders and Moscow pursued its own policies. In accordance with its principles of national self-determination, the Soviet Government was quite prepared to recognize the independence of Finland, Esthonia, Latvia, Lithuania, and Poland, with boundaries corresponding to the lines of language. The Baltic States became independent and their present boundaries were fixed in a series of treaties of 1920 and 1921. Poland and Rumania, however, were determined to seize Russian territory. Rumania occupied Bessarabia in 1918, with the approval of the Allied Powers, and has held it ever since in the face of the persistent refusal of Moscow to concede the legality of this action. The Polish invasion of 1920 was driven back, but the boundary drawn in the Treaty of Riga of March, 1921, was a compromise which transferred several million Ukrainians and White Russians to Polish rule. Still unsatisfied, Poland seized Vilna from Lithuania in October of 1920, but in this chronic quarrel between her western neighbors, Soviet Russia has not taken sides save for a certain moral support given to the Lithuanian claims. In the Caucasus the old boundaries were substantially restored by agreements with Turkey and Persia. On the Pacific coast the continued Japanese occupation was met by the creation of the "Far Eastern Republic," a semi-independent Soviet buffer State which was reabsorbed in 1922. In 1925 Japan extended full recognition to Moscow and evacuated all former Russian territory in return for oil and fishing concessions. The agreements with China of 1924 provided for joint ownership and management of the Chinese Eastern Railway across north Manchuria. Outer Mongolia is a Soviet dependency, and Chinese Turkestan has been penetrated by Soviet influence. Within Soviet jurisdiction, cultural autonomy was granted to the linguistic minorities, and under the constitution of 1923, creating the U.S.S.R., the Soviet State became a federation of seven units.

The power interests of the U.S.S.R. in international politics, like those of all other States, are intelligible by reference to the attitudes and values of its ruling class. While all other States are dominated

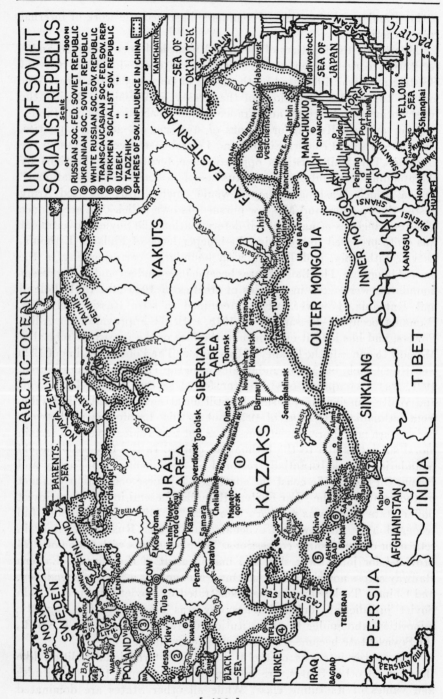

UNION OF SOVIET SOCIALIST REPUBLICS

Scale
0   900 M

① RUSSIAN SOC. FED. SOVIET REPUBLIC
② UKRAINIAN SOC. SOVIET REPUBLIC
③ WHITE RUSSIAN SOC. SOV. REPUBLIC
④ TRANSCAUCASIAN SOC. FED. SOV. REP.
⑤ TURKMEN SOCIALIST SOV. REPUBLIC
⑥ UZBEK   "   "   "
⑦ TADZHIK   "   "   "
SPHERES OF SOV. INFLUENCE IN CHINA

politically by nationalistic business men or land owners, moved by patriotism and by profit motives, these classes have been destroyed in Russia and replaced by the proletariat. The Russian proletariat, as represented by the Communist party, is anti-national, anti-capitalist, anti-imperialist. Social and political cohesion in Soviet society is not achieved through the symbols of national patriotism, but through those of the revolutionary international proletariat. For the Communists, lines of cleavage and conflict based on language, race, and nationality are effaced by the universal class war between the workers of the world and their exploiters. The Soviet State is composed of numerous linguistic and national groups. It is regarded by its builders, not as a national entity, but as the socialist fatherland, as the citadel of the world proletariat, as the precursor of that world federation of Soviet republics which will follow the world revolution. Its historic mission is the creation of a socialist society and the organization of the class-conscious workers of all countries for the revolutionary seizure of power on a world scale. Its foreign policy is necessarily dominated by the exigencies of this mission.

In view of the "temporary stabilization of capitalism" following the Great War, the U.S.S.R. has directed its energies toward building socialism on firm foundations in Russia, rather than toward working for an immediate world revolution. The view of 1917–1919 that a single socialist State could not survive in a hostile capitalistic world has been abandoned in favor of the view that political and economic relations with the bourgeois States can be advantageously employed to contribute toward the immediate task in Russia. The world revolution seemed imminent in 1919, with Soviet governments established in Bavaria and Hungary, with all of central Europe in turmoil, and with working-class unrest prevalent throughout the world. By 1921 these hopes had faded. Soviet support was given to the Kuomintang or revolutionary Nationalist party in China, but the party came to be dominated by bourgeois and militarist elements and expelled its Soviet advisers in 1927. The Communist movement in China was driven underground, but the seeds which had been sown flowered later in an indigenous Communism among Chinese peasants and workers, who have secured control of large areas of the central and southern provinces and successfully resisted the Kuomintang dictatorship. Lenin's disciple, Stalin, and his fellow rulers of the Soviet Union now hold that the final cataclysm of capitalism is in the future and that the world proletarian revolution will perhaps come only in the wake of the next great war. The Communist International and its national sections—the Communist parties of the various countries—continue to lay their plans in anticipation of this final event. But for the present, the greatest service to the international proletariat is the strengthening of socialist economy in the U.S.S.R.

This task has dominated Soviet domestic and foreign policy in recent years. Economic reconstruction was substantially completed by 1927. In 1928 the first Five Year Plan was launched, for the purpose of building socialism by collectivizing agriculture and industrializing the Union on a vast scale. The new economic order, which has been created in this way and which will be further developed in the second Five Year Plan (1933–1938), rests upon the abolition of private property and private profits in agriculture, industry, and commerce and upon large-scale economic planning in the interests of the urban working masses and the collectivized peasantry. Success requires peace and trade with the outside world. Security against renewed intervention is the prime objective of Soviet foreign policy. The means thereto have been the maintenance of the Red Army on a high level of efficiency, the granting of a certain amount of diplomatic support to the "revisionist" States of Europe against the dominant *status quo* bloc, in accordance with balance-of-power considerations, and the promotion of general disarmament. Moscow has also supported all international schemes and projects for the maintenance of peace, short of entrance into the League of Nations, which is still regarded as an association of hostile bourgeois Powers, either useless or dangerous from the point of view of Soviet interests. The U.S.S.R. was the first Great Power to ratify the Kellogg-Briand Pact of 1928. It has urged upon other Powers complete and general disarmament or, barring that, as much disarmament as possible. It has consistently urged the conclusion of non-aggression agreements with its neighbors, and it has sought peace, commerce, and normal diplomatic relations with all States.

Up to the time of writing, this foreign policy has been largely successful in accomplishing its purposes. Peace has been preserved and new interventionist attacks have been prevented, despite acute diplomatic friction with Great Britain between 1927 and 1929, with France in 1929 and 1930, and with other Powers at various other times. But the peace is a truce, and no Communist expects that it can continue indefinitely. The Soviet Union remains on the defensive and views with alarm every threat of war or intervention. The Japanese seizure of Manchuria in 1931 aroused lively apprehensions in Moscow. The U.S.S.R. will not fight to retain the Chinese Eastern Railway, to recover Bessarabia, or to further Soviet interests outside of its own frontiers. But it will resist to the death any invasion of its own territories and will call the Communist parties of the world to its defense in the event of war against it by the bourgeois governments. Time is doubtless on its side, for Soviet economy is self-contained and affected only indirectly by the crises of capitalism. The progress of industrialization, along with the rapid growth of population, promises to make the Soviet Union (already the greatest of the Powers in territory, population, and potential resources) the most powerful State of the world. Barring unforeseen misfortunes, it will then be easily capable of defeating all attacks upon it by any combination of Powers. It will perhaps also become capable, in the great conflict of the future which all Communists regard as inevitable, of spreading the new gospel by the sword throughout Europe and Asia, with the help of the revolutionary proletariat and the colonial subject peoples of other lands. But this is only one of several unpredictable future possibilities. In any case, a new heaven and a new earth are being built on the Eurasian steppes and the U.S.S.R. will assuredly play an increasingly important and perhaps vitally decisive role in the future of Great Power politics.

SUGGESTED READINGS

Adams, R. G.: *A History of the Foreign Policy of the United States*, New York, The Macmillan Company, 1924.

Bemis, S. F.: *The American Secretaries of State and Their Diplomacy* (10 vols.), New York, Alfred A. Knopf, 1927.

Blakeslee, G. H.: *The Recent Foreign Policy of the United States: Problems in American Cooperation with Other Powers*, New York, Abingdon Press, 1925.

Brown, A. J.: *Japan in the World Today*, New York, Fleming H. Revell & Company, 1928.

Chamberlin, W. H.: *Soviet Russia, A Living Record and a History*, Boston, Little, Brown & Company, 1930.

Cippico, A.: *Italy—The Central Problem of the Mediterranean*, New Haven, Yale University Press, 1926.

Fischer, L.: *The Soviets in World Affairs* (2 vols.), New York, Jonathan Cape & Harrison Smith, Inc., 1930.

Fish, C. R.: *American Diplomacy*, New York, Henry Holt & Company, 1923.

Grey, E.: *Twenty-Five Years* (2 vols.), New York, Frederick A. Stokes Company, 1925.

Hoetzsch, O.: *Germany's Domestic and Foreign Policies*, London, Oxford University Press, 1929.

Kawakami, K. K.: *Japan in World Politics*, New York, The Macmillan Company, 1917.

———: *Japan's Pacific Policy, Especially in Relation to China, the Far East and the Washington Conference*, New York, E. P. Dutton & Co., Inc., 1922.

Latané, J. H.: *A History of American Foreign Policy*, Garden City, New York, Doubleday, Doran & Company, Inc., 1927.

———: *The United States and Latin America*, New York, Doubleday, Doran & Company, Inc., 1921.

Lefebure, V.: *The Riddle of the Rhine*, New York, E. P. Dutton & Co., Inc., 1921.

Lutz, R. H.: *The Fall of the German Empire*, Palo Alto, Stanford University Press, 1932.

McGuire, C. E.: *Italy's International Economic Position*, New York, The Macmillan Company, 1926.

Moncado, H. C.: *America, the Philippines, and the Orient*, New York, Fleming H. Revell & Company, 1932.

Montgelas, M. M.: *British Foreign Policy under Sir Edward Grey*, New York, Alfred A. Knopf, 1928.

Moulton, H. G.: *Japan—An Economic and Financial Appraisal*, Washington, Brookings Institution, 1931.

Pooley, A. M.: *Japan's Foreign Policy*, London, Allen & Unwin, 1920.

Schuman, F. L.: *American Policy toward Russia since 1917*, New York, International, 1928.

Seton-Watson, R. W.: *The Balkans, Italy, and the Adriatic*, London, Nisbet, 1915.

Stuart, G. H.: *French Foreign Policy from Fashoda to Sarajevo*, New York, Century Company, 1921.

———: *Latin America and the United States*, New York, Century Company, 1922.

Treat, P. J.: *Japan and the United States, 1853–1921*, New York, Houghton Mifflin Company, 1921.

Trotsky, L.: *History of the Russian Revolution*, Simon & Shuster, Inc., New York, 1932.

Yakhontov, V. A.: *Russia and the Soviet Union in the Far East*, New York, Coward-McCann, Inc., 1931.

PUBLISHED DIPLOMATIC CORRESPONDENCE

Foreign Relations of the United States (Annual), Washington, Government Printing Office.

British Documents on the Origins of the War—1898–1914, London, British Foreign Office, 1926.

Documents Diplomatiques Français 1871–1914, Paris, Imprimerie nationale, 1929–

Die Grosse Politik der Europäischen Kabinette, 1871–1914, Berlin, 1922–1927.

CHAPTER XIII

THE POLITICS OF POWER

1. THE DYNAMICS OF FOREIGN POLICY

*But in the fear of admitting philosophers to power, because they are no longer to be had simple and earnest, but are made up of mixed elements; and in turning from them to passionate and less complex characters, who are by nature fitted for war rather than peace; and in the values set by them upon military strategems and contrivances, and in the waging of everlasting wars—this state will be for the most part peculiar.—*PLATO, *The Republic.*

ALL simplifications of political and social situations are misleading. The sketches of national foreign policy in the preceding chapter have necessarily been enormous oversimplifications of complex relationships between States and between political forces within States. It is perhaps legitimate to speak of "Great Britain," "France," "Germany," and other States as if they were individual persons with bodies and souls, muscles and minds, for national patriotism has brought about such a large degree of unity and cohesion in the national societies of the Western State System that these societies possess personalities and act toward one another like anthropomorphic monsters. But these States consist of millions of people, divided into innumerable sects, parties, classes, income groups, vocational associations, and the like. Their governments consist of thousands of individuals in ministries, legislatures, courts, and administrative services. It is easy to assume that there is a "popular will" which is expressed through representative organs and carried out by governments. It is easy to assume that governments are units which act consistently as organized intelligences for the attainment of preconceived objectives. Within limits and with qualifications, these things are true. And the patterns of State behavior within States and between States do exhibit sufficient uniformity and homogeneity to justify the type of simplification attempted above. The limits and qualifications remain to be noted, however, and the patterns remain to be described more clearly. These are the tasks of the present chapter, which will conclude this survey of the forces operating in contemporary international politics.

Foreign policies present the appearance of being formulated, at each given moment of time, by particular individuals occupying high executive posts in governments. The American Secretary of State, the British

Secretary of State for Foreign Affairs, the French, German, Italian, and Japanese Ministers of Foreign Affairs, the Peoples' Commissar for Foreign Affairs in the U.S.S.R.—these and their counterparts in the threescore sovereignties of the world are charged with the conduct of the foreign relations of their respective States. These foreign ministers occupy, in every case, a position of preeminence in their cabinets. In presidential governments, such as those prevailing in the United States and the Latin American republics, the secretary of state is appointed by a popularly elected president, by whom he may be removed. He succeeds to the presidency in the event of the death of the president and vice president. In parliamentary governments—Great Britain, France, Germany, etc.—the foreign minister is a popularly elected member of the legislature who is a leader of his party and who is picked by the prime minister in the name of the king or president. Sometimes the prime minister will himself take the portfolio of foreign affairs. In either case, the foreign minister is a leading member of a cabinet which is answerable to parliament. In the dictatorships the foreign minister is likewise appointed by those with executive power, unless the dictator himself assumes the post. In all forms of government the foreign minister works in close collaboration with the head of the cabinet and with the other ministers, particularly with the heads of the departments of war, navy, commerce, and colonies. To what degree he can impose his own views on his colleagues, and to what degree he is controlled by those with whom he works, depends largely on personal equations.

The relations, personal and political, between the foreign minister and the chief executive constitute only one factor influencing the determination of foreign policy. The minister is the head of the foreign office and of its field services. He is obliged to rely for information and advice upon the permanent civil servants under his direction. Theoretically, he gives orders to his subordinates. But the subordinates are experienced professional experts, while he is often a politician-amateur. In practice, therefore, the minister may easily become the slave of his servants, and the determination of policies may rest in the hands of professional bureaucrats who are answerable only to their consciences. For factual information about current political problems, the minister must rely upon diplomatic agents abroad and upon the geographical divisions of the foreign office. For knowledge of commercial and financial matters, he is dependent upon his economic adviser and upon consular agents abroad. Legal problems he must submit to the legal adviser of the foreign office. Problems of etiquette and ceremonial he refers to the division of protocol. Precedents, former policies, records of things past he derives from the historical adviser and the archives section. The experts in the foreign office are the custodians of the forms of international intercourse, and by these forms the foreign minister and his agents are rigidly bound. In these various ways the professional bureaucracy always exercises great influence over the nominal head of the ministry or department of foreign affairs. It is the custodian of tradition, the keeper of the seals, the preserver of the past. It resists innovation. It adheres to its habitual attitudes, purposes, and modes of behavior. It bends the foreign minister to its ancient ways more frequently than it is bent by him toward new departures. Here is an important cause of the stability and continuity of foreign policies in the face of changes in politicians and party alignment.

The foreign minister must likewise reckon with forces and influences outside of his own circle of superiors, colleagues, and subordinates, but still within the orbit of government machinery. The legislature must always be considered, for in every state it will have certain constitutional powers over foreign affairs and will endeavor to exercise a certain supervision over foreign policy. Almost all national parliaments are entrusted with decisions of peace and war and with the ratification of treaties. In the United States all treaties must be approved by two-thirds of the Senate. In most other governments, certain specified treaties must be approved by a majority of both branches of parliament. The legislature may also have a voice in diplomatic appointments, and it is always able to influence foreign affairs through its general powers of appropriating money and enacting laws. In parliamentary governments, where ministerial responsibility prevails, the legislature can turn out the cabinet on issues of foreign policy as readily as on questions of domestic import. In such governments the foreign minister will be a member of the legislature and will be always in intimate contact with it. But whether he is a member or not, he must at all times endeavor to secure legislative approval for such of his policies as cannot be executed without it. He must speak in explanation and defense before the chambers, or at least before their committees on foreign affairs. He must wangle the appropriations which his purposes require. He must treat legislative resolutions on foreign affairs with respect, even when he does not act upon them. He must secure support for such treaties as must receive parliamentary approval in order to be valid. The legislature is thus able to exercise an appreciable degree of influence upon foreign policy in most governments, despite the fact that initiative and control continue to rest with the executive.

The rôle of political parties is likewise not to be neglected. In many States foreign policy is supposed to be so stable, so continuous, so charged with the interests and welfare of the whole nation as to be above partisan politics. Even in this case, however, there may be a "right" foreign policy and a "left" foreign policy, with slight differences between them in methods and objectives. Foreign ministers are almost always party leaders. Issues of foreign policy are often grist for the mill of parliamentary debates and electoral contests. In most of the Great Powers, however, one is struck less by the differences in party programs on foreign affairs than by their similarity. Elections are seldom won or lost, candidates are seldom elected or defeated because of international questions. While there has everywhere been more popular interest in foreign affairs since the Great War than before, and while party politics in most States now has more significance for foreign policy than heretofore, it still remains true that these issues play a minor rôle in domestic political struggles and that changes in the partisan composition of government seldom lead to radical transformations of diplomatic purposes. This circumstance is due to many things: the continuity given to foreign policy by the permanent bureaucracy which administers it, the lack of popular interest in diplomatic problems as compared with domestic problems, the existence in each State of relatively fixed patterns of policy based upon the general power interests of the State in relation to other States, the propensity of patriots to view all criticism of foreign policy as "unpatriotic," etc. These considerations discourage innovation and keep foreign policy in its accustomed groove. Political expediency often dictates caution, circumspection, delay, and timidity. But it seldom dictates new departures.

If a foreign minister can, in many cases, hold himself aloof from party politics, he can never afford to ignore the daily press, either at home or abroad. In the twentieth century a "good press" is essential to diplomatic success in all ventures which cannot be conducted in secrecy. With the great metropolitan newspapers of the world's capitals influencing the thought and action of millions of readers, with "public opinion" and the moral imponderables spelling triumph or defeat for all far-reaching political schemes, it is of vital importance for foreign offices to gain the friendship of reporters, editors, and owners of the leading journals. Press conferences and press releases must be handled with extreme care. Foreign correspondence and foreign newspapers are particularly important, and various techniques of influencing them have been devised. Most foreign offices are granted secret funds to be used in shaping opinion abroad. For many years prior to 1914 the great majority of the newspapers of Paris were in the pay of the Russian Government. In return for bribes, they influenced French opinion favorably toward Russian bonds, toward the Dual Alliance, toward the prospects and purposes of the Tsardom, toward the necessity of close Franco-Russian diplomatic and military collaboration. This was not an isolated instance, for foreign offices everywhere resort to similar tactics for similar purposes. In a few cases, notably in France, it has even been alleged that such funds are utilized to bribe domestic newspapers. A free and independent press may often cause embarrassment to diplomats, either by jingoistic chauvinism or by attacks upon the power-and-profit motives of particular diplomatic enterprises. Foreign offices must therefore watch the world press constantly, and they must devise means of controlling those who have their price and of placating those whose influence is not for sale.

"Public opinion" is a vague, intangible force which must likewise be taken into account by foreign ministers and diplomatic representatives. Whether public opinion in the bourgeois democracies is reflected in the daily press, or is manufactured by the daily press, is an interesting subject of academic debate. For the foreign offices, it is enough to remember that newspapers print what editors and owners think people like to read and that people are likely to think in terms suggested to them by newspapers. The daily press is doubtless the most significant mirror of opinion and the most important force shaping that opinion. A thousand other forces play their rôles, and the skillful manipulator will finger them all like an organist at a huge keyboard. Every foreign office has need of such organists, for the state of the public mind may demand this diplomatic action and condemn that, it may overturn this government and support that, it may make success possible here and ensure failure there. This force operates through elections, through organized pressure groups and lobbies, and through the representative legislature. It is all-pervasive, insidious, fickle, changeable. In a dictatorship, all criticism of officialdom can be suppressed by censorship, by force, by election manipulation, and by other standardized techniques. A favorable opinion can similarly be created by rigid control of all the agencies which shape popular attitudes—the press, the schools, the churches, the political organizations, etc. In a democracy only certain of these means are available, and the foreign office which would insure popular support of its policies must resort to the more subtle devices of propaganda. By keeping its ear to the ground, by yielding or seeming to yield to pressure, by molding sentiments as it desires them, it can weave the shifting strands and threads into a pattern to its liking. By ignoring these duties it can readily involve itself in gnarls and tangles not of its own making. If it does not believe in the principle of *vox populi, vox dei*, it must at least appear to do so, for appearances are of the essence of politics and without an appropriate façade to present to the public nothing can be achieved.

This "public," however, is no homogeneous mass of like-minded individuals. It is no mythical, man-like monster possessed of a single will and of power to enforce that will. The great body of voters (and of non-voters) who constitute the public is divided into almost innumerable segments which join, separate, dissolve, coalesce, cooperate, and disintegrate in a dizzy waltz. Some lines of cleavage are relatively permanent, such as those arising out of economic class interests, religious affiliations, and sectional loyalties. Others are ephemeral and arise out of the whims and fancies and the particular problems of a given period of time. The public is a vast, complex aggregation of organized minorities of all kinds whose complex interactions account for the variability and the unpredictability of the final result. Some of these groups—prohibitionists, suffragettes, labor unionists, clerical reformers, farming organizations, many vocational associations—have little interest in foreign affairs. Others—professional patriots, peace societies, exporters' associations, militarists, foreign bond-holders' societies, linguistic minorities, etc.—are primarily concerned with foreign policy. All overlap and interpenetrate one another in unstable equilibrium, and all enter into the fabric of the political parties through which they present their demands. Counting noses and calculating numerical majorities is of much less practical utility than knowing which groups are influential and where the real sources of power lie in the electorate. Here is a political chess game more intricate and fascinating than the game of Great Power politics itself.

In analyzing the public from the point of view of the forces determining governmental policies and the elements with which the formulators of policies must reckon, the cleavages rising out of economic class distinction would seem to be of fundamental importance. Vocational groupings in themselves are politically significant, for in every national society there are butchers, bakers, candlestick-makers and a thousand other craftsmen, artisans, and professional people. But class groupings are broader than these. Rich men, poor men, beggar men, and thieves all feel a certain cameraderie with their fellows and all have political axes to grind. The modern societies of the western nation-states comprise four major economic groupings whose relations with one another vary greatly from country to country: a landed aristocracy surviving from the feudal nobility of the middle ages; an agrarian class of peasants or farmers descended from the medieval serfs; a bourgeois class of business men, shopkeepers, financiers, and industrialists, raised to immense power by the Industrial Revolution; and an urban wage-earning class slowly becoming aware of its interests and its potentialities. The nineteenth and twentieth centuries have been the epoch of private capitalism and the political ascendancy of the bourgeoisie. This class constitutes the ruling group in many lands. In Great Britain, in Germany, in pre-war Russia, in present-day Japan it shares power with the older landed gentry. In France only remnants of the old nobility have survived the revolution. In the United States no true landed aristocracy has existed since the end of slavery in the South. In all of these States and many others, peasants or farmers and industrial workers strive for political influence in competition with the predominant bourgeoisie, sometimes through political parties of their own, sometimes within the bourgeois parties. In Russia, where the old social order was demolished, bourgeoisie and nobility alike have been swept from power and destroyed, and the proletariat has become the ruling class. The process of politics in all nations is intelligible only in terms of the interests, attitudes, demands, and purposes of these socio-economic strata in the electorate. And governmental policies in foreign, no less than in domestic, affairs reflect at all times the prevailing political equilibrium between these forces.

But if modern bourgeois societies are complex, diversified, pluralistic in the confused heterogeneity of sections, cults, vocations, classes, and other types of groupings, they are at the same time unified and welded into some semblance of a single common will by national patriotism. Stockbrokers, coal heavers, psychiatrists, grocers, stenographers, and salesmen are all bound together in common loyalty to the fatherland. This common loyalty may break down and be replaced by sectional or class loyalties in times of crisis and social upheaval. But normally the nation is one and indivisible and all its citizens are good patriots, ready to sacrifice life or limb or wealth for purposes identified with the nation as a whole. Out of contacts, differences, controversies, and conflicts with other national communities, patriotic fervor is engendered and enhanced. The foreign office is the focal point in each nation at which the forces of patriotism are concentrated for dealing with other States. Foreign policy must reflect and enrich the personality of the national community in its relations with other national communities. No other agency of government is so charged with the responsibilities of patriotism. None is engaged in tasks which touch so intimately all that is dear to the patriot's heart, all that inspires him to pride, shame, anger, or fear. The worst accusation which can be hurled against a foreign minister is that his policies are "unpatriotic," that he has neglected the "national honor" and "vital interests" of the State, that he has ignored the prevalent conception of the needs of the fatherland. No foreign minister can survive such an accusation if his political enemies can find justification for it. Every foreign minister must be a patriot. An unpatriotic foreign policy is unthinkable. The all-pervasive power of national patriotism in each of the nation-states is at all times the most persistent and decisive force controlling foreign policy.

An adequate understanding of the foreign policy of any State would require a detailed analysis of the forces within the nation which have been suggested. These forces can scarcely be reduced to measurable terms. They are so numerous, so complex in themselves and in their interrelationships that all prediction regarding the future equilibrium between them is hazardous. But the determining factors in the total situation are fairly obvious. The dead hand of the past, moreover, always hangs heavy over the present and affords a stability and continuity which might otherwise be lacking. From the point of view of the formulation of foreign policy, these forces may be thought of as sources of pressures which beat in upon the foreign minister and drive him inevitably in a direction over which he has little personal control. Far from being a free agent, a foreign minister has most of his policies determined for him in advance by forces beyond his reach. Never can he escape from the principles of law, the institutional forms, the values, behavior patterns, and standardized procedures which make up the art and science of diplomacy in the Western State System. Never can he successfully defy the patriotic sentiments and traditions of the great mass of his fellow countrymen. Never can he pursue goals radically different from those dictated by the existing political equilibrium of social classes within the nation. He is often bound hand and foot by party politics, by legislative interference, by executive supervision, by the habits and opinions of the foreign-office staff and the diplomatic bureaucracy. He is bound by the diplomatic patterns and traditions inherited from the Baroque period of the dynasts and the aristocracies. A weak leader will be controlled completely by these pressures. A strong leader will know how to play them off against one another, how to gauge their potency with intuitive perception, how to enlarge somewhat the extremely narrow range of questions with regard to which he may exercise his personal judgment. The art of politics is the art of what is possible. The limits of what is possible for a foreign minister are closely defined by the juxtaposition of forces operating behind and around and within and through his own personality.

2. THE WILL-TO-POWER

It very rarely happens, or perhaps never occurs, that a person exalts himself from a humble station to great dignity without employing either force or fraud, unless indeed he attains it by gift or hereditary succession. I do not even conceive that force alone ever sufficed; but we shall find that cunning alone has sometimes succeeded.—MACHIAVELLI, *Reflections on Livy*.

Modern democratic theorists have generally assumed that in "popular" governments the mass of the citizenry, by a process of thorough study, orderly discussion, and reasonable compromise, arrive at a consensus of opinion regarding public policy and that this consensus, this "popular will," is carried out by representative lawmakers and administrators. It is contended that democracy in foreign affairs involves the rational formulation of a popular will as to how the nation's relations with other States should be conducted and the translation of this will into action by the elected servants of the people. These servants, it is argued, must act openly, honestly, frankly, in the full light of day, in order that the citizenry may at all times perceive whether its will is being carried out and may call to account those charged with this duty.

Secret diplomacy and selfish intrigue are viewed as relics of the pre-democratic age, to be discarded and rendered impossible of revival. This is to be achieved through the power of public opinion, as wielded by an enlightened electorate, and through popular and legislative control of foreign policy. Since the Great War there has been universal agitation for democratic control of international politics, general condemnation of the "old" diplomacy, and championship of the "new"—all on the assumption that democratic foreign policies will necessarily be enlightened, pacific, and constructive.

These assumptions demand critical examination before a successful effort can be made to depict in realistic terms the contemporary pattern of international politics. It is obvious that the assumptions, in their unqualified form, bear little relation to the facts. Foreign policies, even in the most democratic of countries, are not made in cafés, at firesides, in public forums, or anywhere else where the "popular will" is supposed to manifest itself. Neither are they made in electoral contests, nor in the deliberations of representative legislatures. They are made usually behind closed doors in cabinet meetings, foreign offices, and embassies by officials responding to the pressures put upon them. These pressures are either silent, steady, and traditional or they represent the demands of interested minorities seeking specific objectives. In no case does some vague and undefined "popular will" enter into the calculations of the policy makers, except as public sentiment is reflected in influential newspapers, in party politics, or in the gyrations of professional patriots capable of controlling votes or lobbies. The "public" is unorganized and inarticulate, except when aroused by patriotic jingoism. It responds, not rationally and deliberately to reason, but emotionally and impulsively to suggestion, to propaganda appeals, to hysteria—or it is inert, indifferent, and fails to respond at all. In considering every public question, it arrives in the middle of the third act, stays long enough to ascertain who the heroes and villains of the piece are, and departs to go about its private business.[1] In every case, the reins of effective power over foreign policy are not widely scattered and diffused throughout the entire electorate, but are concentrated in the hands of a few key officials and a small number of private organizations or interests with political influence.

Democracy and foreign policy can never mean control of decisions by the inarticulate, unorganized mass of voters, for this mass can exercise no control over anything. The exercise of political power requires concentration, organization, a clearly formulated purpose, and means to achieve that purpose. Special groups with specific interests to serve always tend to control the formulation of public policy. Democratic control can mean only that all interested groups shall have an equal opportunity to organize,

[1] See Walter Lippmann, *Public Opinion*, 1922, and *The Phantom Public*, 1925.

agitate, propagandize, lobby, and otherwise bring pressure to bear on behalf of their programs. These groups, whether they be based upon provincial loyalties, class allegiances, vocational interests or other common bonds, are ceaselessly engaged, inside and outside of political party struggles, in a competitive contest for power, in rival efforts to impress their wills upon the key officials who formulate policy. In an autocracy or dictatorship, certain groups occupy a position of legal privilege and monopolistic power and are able to discriminate against, or even destroy, rival groups. In a democracy all groups have at least a theoretically equal right to strive for influence and power. But the groups which will actually wield power will consist of interested persons with purposes of their own to serve. These purposes may be selfish or "disinterested," but they must exist, they must be verbalized and appreciated by the members of the group before it can act to influence policy.

In the formulation of foreign policy the best organized groups are within the governmental machine: the foreign-office staff and the diplomatic bureaucracy. These groups usually have their way, and since they naturally resent outside meddling they prefer to work in secrecy. Secrecy is desired, not merely to prevent interference by other groups, public or private, within the State, but also to accomplish those results in the arena of international politics itself which are impossible of achievement if purposes and methods are made known to the world press, to the public, to legislatures, and to other governments. Negotiations must be conducted in obscurity, if popular clamor is not to make advantageous compromises impossible. The results of negotiations, embodied in written agreements, are often kept secret for reasons of high policy. The exact terms and intentions of all the pre-war alliances and ententes were carefully guarded by the foreign offices, and no one can doubt but that similar secret commitments exist in the post-war world. Diplomatic correspondence in archives is often kept secret until it is of only historical or archæological significance. Since complete secrecy is impossible, partial publicity must be given to matters of general interest—coupled with misrepresentation, duplicity, and falsification when critical situations seem to demand such measures.[1]

[1] For example, the French Yellow Book of 1914 was deliberately falsified by the Quai d'Orsay to make it appear that Russian mobilization was ordered after, instead of before, general Austrian and German mobilization. The dispatch of Paléologue, French Ambassador in St. Petersburg, 10:45 A.M. July 31 (sent 16 hours after the event) declared "the mobilization of the Russian army has been ordered." The falsifiers in the French Foreign Office concocted the following statement in place of the dispatch. "As a result of the general mobilization of Austria and of the measures for mobilization taken secretly, but continuously, by Germany for the last six days, the order for the general mobilization of the Russian Army has been given, Russia not being able, without serious danger, to allow herself to be further outdistanced; really she is only taking military measures corresponding to those taken by Germany. For imperative reasons of strategy the Russian Government, knowing that Germany was arming, could no longer delay the conversion of her partial mobilization into a general mobilization." F.Y.B., 1914, No. 118.

Those who control directly the machinery of diplomacy are necessarily in the strongest position to use that machinery as they think best.

The democratization of foreign policy involves "meddling" and interference with the professional diplomatic bureaucracy on the part of outsiders. The professional bureaucracy is never insulated from the pressures of politically influential groups interested in foreign policy. At times it is the spokesman and servant of these groups. It uses for its own purposes, and is used by (for their purposes), journalists, merchants, investors, missionaries, industrialists, etc. People with axes to grind, people with special interests to serve, people who are high in the party in power and who occupy strategic economic positions in the ruling class will never be ignored by those who formulate foreign policy. Another step removed from the centers of power are the unofficial lobbies of pacifists, militarists, peace pleaders, preparedness advocates, professional patriots, internationalists, women's organizations, reformist groups, and other organized minorities of all kinds. These groups can seldom achieve results by working directly upon the foreign offices. Sometimes they can bring effective pressure to bear by influencing the legislature and public opinion. The "public" itself is not fully in the picture, except in crises when particular demands become almost universal. The task of those who would democratize foreign policy is to educate and organize the public, to induce it to take an interest in foreign affairs, to enable it to become vocal and to express its will to those who wield power at the center.

It is of fundamental importance, however, to bear in mind that the chief common bond which creates this "public," which gives cohesion and unity to the manifold interest groupings composing the electorates of the modern nation-states, is national patriotism. Except in the Soviet Union, where revolutionary proletarian internationalism has replaced bourgeois nationalism as the basis of political and social cohesion, the populations of all States have only such general and collective interests in foreign policy as emerge from a sense of common nationality, of identification with the nation, of loyalty to the fatherland. Democratic government on a national scale became possible only when sectional, group, and class loyalties were merged in common allegiance to the nation. The operation of democratic government strengthens this allegiance constantly. Democracy and nationalism have until recently been inseparable components in the political structure of the bourgeois nation-states. This can only mean that a democratic or popularly controlled foreign policy is a patriotic foreign policy—a policy reflecting the values, ideologies, symbols, and purposes of national patriots. To the degree to which national patriotism postulates international conflict, to the degree to which patriots are irrational, emotional, unreflective in their reactions, to that degree will a democratic foreign policy be bellivolent and unenlightened. To suppose that democratic control of foreign offices ensures pacific inclinations and informed altruism is to mistake the implications of patriotism and to overlook the relationship, in the political process, between democracy and nationalism. It would in fact be no exaggeration to say that a foreign policy which directly reflected popular patriotic passions would probably be more bellicose, less reasonable, more uncompromising, more exclusively devoted to the pursuit of selfish national interests than a foreign policy controlled by mature and experienced professional diplomats far removed from the tumult and the shouting of the market place.

That the foreign policies of all of the bourgeois nation-states are "patriotic," *i.e.*, are directed toward the pursuit of exclusive and competitive national interests, is a truism too obvious to require further demonstration. These nation-states of patriots, like the members of all state systems from time immemorial, are engaged with one another in a competitive struggle for power. The national wills-to-power are expressed in terms of patriotic symbols. The purposes and objectives of the foreign offices, in peace and war, spring from a desire to enhance the power, the prestige, the glory, the prosperity of the nation. This desire is the *sine qua non*, the alpha and omega of patriots everywhere. Patriots demand always a fuller, richer expression of the national personality, a more vigorous assertion of national rights and national interests. This demand is translated into action through foreign policy. If the foreign offices did not pursue policies aimed at national advancement, the patriotic citizenry would compel them to do so. When the foreign offices themselves secretly concoct grandiose and dangerous schemes for promoting the power-and-prestige interests of the State, they know that in the final test they can count upon the support of all good patriots. Democratically controlled and patriotically motivated foreign policies directed toward the promotion of national interests thus become the instruments of State action in that competitive struggle between rival sovereignties which is the essence of international politics in the Western State System.

All politics is a competitive struggle for power, but while power is sought in domestic politics as a means toward other ends, power is sought as an end in itself in international politics. "Power" means ability to impose one's will on others, capacity to dictate to those who are without power or who possess less power, opportunity to achieve the gains which power makes possible of attainment. In the political process within each of the nation-states a constant struggle for ascendancy goes on between political leaders, parties, factions, sections, classes, and other groups. Power means admission to public office, control of the machinery of law-making and administration, influence over the determination of public policy. Here, too, it sometimes seems to be sought for its own sake, *i.e.*, for the emotional satisfactions which accompany its exercise. But usually it is sought for the attainment of the ulterior purposes which can be served by its use. The politician desires patronage, profits, graft, honest or dishonest. The party desires to build up a machine which will afford jobs and profits to its members. The lobbyist desires to secure legislation and administrative favors, and the profits which go therewith. In international politics it is likewise true that power, diplomatic preponderance, political hegemony, military or naval supremacy serve ulterior purposes. But foreign offices and patriots often pursue these goals as things good in themselves. The great clashes of power interests between States frequently center about values which have no immediate relationship to tangible objectives. "National honor" is impugned when a State's power is challenged. A State's "prestige" must be respected by its rivals, for prestige is reputation for power and in power relationships reputations and appearances are as important as realities. "Vital interests" are as much related to power considerations as to material goals. These are the things for which men fight in the Western State System. These are the symbols and verbalizations of the universal quest for power in which the nation-states are engaged.

That international politics is a struggle for power is recognized in popular parlance more frequently than in the erudite tomes of jurists or in the idealistic pleas of pacifists. States are habitually spoken of as "Powers." This usage is based upon the assumption that the State is an embodiment of power and that its relations with other States are determined by power considerations. The most powerful States are Great Powers. Less powerful States are Secondary Powers. Still others are Third-class Powers or Minor Powers.[1] States with large war fleets are naval Powers. States with large armies are land Powers. The political equilibrium between States is the "balance of power" and the cooperative endeavors of States constitute the "concert of power." The State not merely strives for power. It *is* power, by the common usage of all western languages.

If power is sought as an end in itself, it is nevertheless true that the power interests of each State are expressed in terms of specific purposes which reflect the interests and attitudes of the politically dominant groups within the State. These purposes are formulated through the interaction of internal political forces. Once formulated, they are imposed upon the nation as a whole and become identified with the "national interests." The stakes of diplomacy arise from the interests of the ruling class in the State—or if there be no clearly defined ruling class, from the equilibrium of forces through which public policy is determined. These classes and forces grow out of social structures in which those with economic power are ultimately the rulers. An agrarian autocracy with a landed nobility

[1] See pp. 111–114 above.

as its ruling class, *e.g.*, pre-war Russia, will express its power interests in terms of land hunger and territorial aggrandizement. An agrarian democracy, *e.g.*, pre-Civil War United States, will similarly manifest a desire for territorial expansion in its foreign policy. A commercial State, *e.g.*, seventeenth century Holland or eighteenth century England, will be interested in commodity markets and sea power. An industrialized capitalistic State, *e.g.*, contemporary Great Britain, Germany, the United States, or Japan, will seek investment markets, concessions, opportunities for profit through trade and finance. An industrialized Communistic State, *e.g.*, U.S.S.R., will be interested in proletarian revolution, colonial emancipation, the creation of other Communistic States with which it may make common cause against capitalism. In every case, the economic and social structure of the State will determine the nature of the stakes of diplomacy which it pursues.

This is but another way of saying that the economically dominant classes within each State, which are likely to be politically preponderant because of their economic power, tend to dictate the specific purposes in terms of which the national interests of the State are expressed. In the contemporary period, the bourgeoisie is the economically dominant group in most western societies. It determines public policies, domestic and foreign, subject to pressures from landed nobles, farmers, and urban workers. National patriotism in itself is bourgeois in origin and is distinctly of the period of the political ascendancy of the bourgeoisie. The quest for power of the bourgeois States is couched in terms of bourgeois interests and objectives. Economic nationalism, imperialism, militarism, navalism, dollar diplomacy, and the like are unintelligible save in terms of the interests of the ruling bourgeois group. States in which agrarian groups predominate, or in which a dictatorship of the proletariat prevails, pursue correspondingly different objectives in their quest for power. In every instance, in all times and places, the power interests of politically competing States are comprehensible only in terms of the interests, values, and ideologies of the ruling group within each unit of the State System.

3. EQUILIBRIUM AND TENSION

Even though all high politics tries to be a substitution of more intellectual weapons for the sword and though it is the ambition of the statesman at the culminations of all the cultures to feel able to dispense with war, yet the primary relationship between diplomacy and the war-art endures. The character of battle is common to both, and the tactics and stratagems, and the necessity of material forces in the background to give weight to the operations. The aim too remains the same—namely, the growth of one's own life unit (class or nation) at the cost of the other's.—OSWALD SPENGLER, *The Decline of the West*, II.

> Plenty begets Pride; Pride, Envy, Envy, Warre,
> Warre, Poverty, Poverty humble Care;
> Humility breeds Peace, and Peace breeds Plenty;
> Thus round the World doth rowle alternately.
> —ROBERT HAYMAN, *The World's Whirlegigge*, 1631.

This universal quest for power goes on under the conditions imposed by the nature of the State System and by the technological differentials between its members. Each State left to itself tends to extend its power over as wide a sphere as possible. Its power flows outward from a central nucleus in all directions. It is directed toward control of territory and people. If the ruling class of the State is an agrarian aristocracy, as in most of the States of the ancient world, control over territory and people is sought in order that the agricultural resources of the territory may be utilized to the profit of the conquerors and the labor power of the people may be exploited through slavery or serfdom. If the ruling class is a commercial bourgeoisie, as in western Europe between the sixteenth and nineteenth centuries, conquests are sought in order that the import and export trade of the region conquered may be monopolized. If it is an industrial and financial bourgeoisie, as in the twentieth century western world, commodity and investment markets are sought—and they may be obtained by methods of control more subtle and indirect than open conquest and annexation. If the revolutionary proletariat is in power, as in the Soviet Union, it seeks conquests in order to extend the scope of the revolution and weaken the power of its enemies. These purposes are rationalized, disguised, modified, and supplemented by others, in accordance with the attitudes and sentiments of the ruling group. But the enhancement of State power is always the goal. The will-to-power necessarily expresses itself in economic terms, for control of territories and populations is sought for economic purposes and the methods of control depend upon the technical skill and the economic organization of conquerors and conquered.

In a State System in which the sovereign units are engaged in a constant competitive struggle, power is at all times a relative quantity. In a world of one State, power considerations would disappear unless that State were threatened by internal revolution or barbarian incursions. A State existing in complete isolation from all other States would have no "power interests," for such interests grow out of contact, competition, and conflict between States. The "power" of a State is a meaningless concept, except in relation to the power of other States. The power of each State, moreover, is significant only in relation to the other Powers with which it is in geographical proximity. The power of France is important as compared with the power of Germany, Italy, Spain, or Great Britain, but not of much importance as compared with the power of Japan, Bolivia, or Afghanistan, for normally French power will not come into contact with Powers so far away. The power of the United States is important in relation to the power of Cuba, Nicaragua, Mexico, and Great Britain, but not important ordinarily in relation to the Soviet Union, Nepal, or Abyssinia, for it cannot be exercised effectively in such remote places. The power of lesser States has meaning only in relation to their immediate neighbors. Czechoslovakia, for example, has no power in Asia, Africa, or the Americas, but only in central Europe. The power of a State is significant only with respect to other Powers with which it may conceivably engage in diplomatic or military conflict. There could be no conflict between Costa Rica and Liberia, between The Netherlands and Persia, between Finland and South Africa, or between Japan and Italy, for the spheres of power of these States do not touch at any point. Power has meaning only as against other Powers which can be reached by it.

In the extension of State power, natural barriers may constitute as important an obstacle as the power of neighboring rival States. The extent to which such barriers are obstacles to expansion depends largely on the technological devices available for overcoming them. Power is always local. Ability to exercise it at points remote from its center varies inversely with distance and directly with the level of technology. Waterways and sea channels, which are insuperable obstacles to people with small sailing vessels, become paths to empire for peoples with more effective modes of transportation. Deserts cease to be barriers and become sources of wealth for peoples acquainted with the science of irrigation. The tropical jungle which was an impassable wilderness in the sixteenth century is a rich source of rubber, woods, bananas, and other products in the twentieth, when railways, automobile roads, and steamships are available. Even arctic wastes and high mountain walls yield to the airplane. Machine technology facilitates the surmounting of such barriers and makes possible an extension of State power over distances once regarded as fantastic. The world empires of today are existing realities made administratively possible by the new technology. The world government of the future is already technologically possible, whatever may be the psychological and cultural difficulties in the way of its creation.

More serious obstacles to the extension of State power are encountered in the form of other States. These obstacles may also be overcome with ease if the technological differential between these States is sufficiently great. The people of the bow and arrow, the spear, the canoe, the sailing vessel must yield to the people of the machine gun, the battleship, and the bombing plane. Most of the peoples of the world not equipped with western technology have lost their independence to the western Powers. But the western Powers themselves, and the States of the non-European world which have adopted western ways, are on a parity of power so far as technology is concerned. Power relations between them are determined by size, population, man power, natural resources, armaments, shipping, commercial and industrial development, economic efficiency, organizing capacity, etc. These things are political objectives and stakes of diplomacy, because they are the measures of power and the means of power. Geographical and technological considerations are no less important in overcoming other States than in overcoming natural barriers. Control of topographical vantage points may be of vital significance, for the strategy of diplomacy rests at bottom upon the tactics of war. From the days when a handful of Spartans blocked the Persian hordes at the mountain pass of Thermopylae to the days when the hosts of von Hindenburg crushed the Russian invaders in the Masurian Lakes region of East Prussia and the French at Verdun hurled back the assaults of the foe, control of strategic areas has been an element of decisive significance in Power conflicts. Land power requires fortresses, mountain barriers, river boundaries, and forests as centers of defense and headquarters for attack. Sea power requires naval bases, fueling stations, domination of strategic waterways and of the great ocean channels. Many of the contests of Great Power politics are waged for control of points of strategic importance, though in prolonged combats between the Powers victory may depend less on tactics and strategy than on the economic organization and morale of whole populations.

The Western State System has developed in such fashion that no one of its members possesses at any time sufficient power to extend its control over all the others. In the interests of self-defense, the members tend to combine against any one which is a potential menace to all. Invariably the pretender to world power is repressed by a coalition of the prospective victims. Each Power thus retains its independence and the State System is preserved. Under these circumstances, an equilibrium or balance of power results. Any enhancement of the power of one State is a disturbance of the equilibrium and a potential threat to the others. At times this equilibrium is intangible, imponderable, and in the background of diplomatic action. At other times, and more frequently, it is clearly and sharply defined in alliances and coalitions. Each member of an alliance has an interest in forestalling any enhancement of the power of some member of the opposing alliance. The two coalitions or groupings of Powers are thus held together by common power interests, and conflicts for power become issues between the alliances as a whole. This pattern of power relationships has characterized the Western State System from its earliest beginnings.

The rôle of small States in this system of relationships is a peculiar one. The very minute States of Europe are historical curiosities and play no part in Power relationships. But such States as Portugal, Belgium, The Netherlands, Denmark, Switzerland, Albania, and the like are all adjacent to infinitely more powerful States which could easily impose their will upon them and extinguish their independence if granted a free hand. In a few cases this has happened: Ireland was conquered by England in the middle ages; Poland was partitioned among her three great neighbors at the end of the eighteenth century. But usually this result is rendered impossible by the conflicting power interests of the great States themselves. The small States, being impotent, have no power interests of their own save the preservation of their independence, and this they are able to protect, not by their own power, but by fitting themselves into the power relations of their mighty neighbors. The small States are often "buffers." They stand at the focal points of tension between the Great Powers, with the result that each Power prefers the maintenance of the independence of the small State to the extinction of that independence at the hands of a rival Power. Portugal was long a buffer of this kind between Spain and England. The Low Countries lie between England, France, and Germany. Each of these States opposes control by either of the others of this strategically vital area containing the mouths of the Rhine and the Scheldt. During the past two centuries England has successively fought Spain, Austria, France, and Germany when these States threatened to dominate this region. Belgium and The Netherlands are thus relatively secure in their independence, because of the power relations between their larger neighbors. Denmark is similarly a buffer between Germany and Great Britain, for the sea-power interests of the latter move the British Government to oppose control of Denmark by a powerful continental State as vigilantly as it opposes such control of The Netherlands, Belgium, or Portugal. Switzerland is most secure of all, for it is completely surrounded by Great Powers: France, Germany, Italy, and formerly Austria-Hungary. Albania, deliberately created as a buffer State in 1913, now lies between Jugoslavia and Italy, though it has largely fallen under the control of the latter. In every case the buffer State is dependent for its security in peace time upon the diplomatic rivalries of its neighbors. In a general war between the Powers it may be able to remain neutral (*e.g.*, Switzerland, The Netherlands, and the Scandinavian States, 1914–1918), unless it becomes a theater of battle between the belligerents (*e.g.*, Belgium in 1914). In the latter case it must align itself with that coalition which seems least likely to deprive it of independence in the event of victory.

Considerations of a similar character serve to explain the continued independence of small or weak native States in the areas of imperialistic rivalries between the Powers. The native States which lay directly athwart the path of expansion of a Great Power, unopposed by other Powers, have all succumbed. Those which survive are located at the tension points between rival imperialisms. Neither of the rival Powers wishes the other to enlarge its territory by annexing the intervening buffer State. The latter is enabled by this circumstance to play off the imperialists against one another. Abyssinia was thus the vortex of converging drives of British, French, and Italian expansionists. These drives neutralized one another and Abyssinia remained independent. Turkey has similarly profited by conflicts between Russia, Great Britain, France, Germany, and Austria-Hungary. Persia and Afghanistan have been buffer States between British and Russian imperialism. China has retained nominal control of Tibet, because neither Russia nor Great Britain could afford to permit the other to acquire it. China itself has thus far escaped complete partition for similar reasons. Siam lies at the focal point of British and French imperialism in southeastern Asia. The independence of the Latin American republics was originally championed by the United States to forestall European conquest. By the same token, the remaining colonial possessions of the Minor Powers are relatively secure against appropriation by the Great Powers, because none of the latter can permit any of the others to acquire them. The Portuguese colonies in Africa were long buffers between Great Britain and Germany. These two States agreed to a partition in 1908, but the bargain was not completed. With British power now supreme in the southern half of the African continent, Portugal's colonies would be less secure than formerly, save for the fact that Portugal itself is in a sense a British dependency. The Belgian Congo lies between British and French territory. Neither Great Britain nor France nor the United States nor Japan could permit either of the others to acquire the Dutch East Indies, for this would upset completely the established equilibrium in the southwestern Pacific.

As regards the complex plays and counter-plays of the Great Powers themselves in their constant efforts to maintain or upset the balance of power, it is useful to recall Bismarck's suggestive distinction between "satiated" and "unsatiated" States. At any given period of time, the existing equilibrium, the prevailing distribution of power, the established ratios of territories, populations, armies, navies, colonies, etc., will appear ideal to the States which are its beneficiaries and unendurable to the States which do not feel that they have received their just due. The satiated States, content with the *status quo*, will usually be those which have been victorious in the last armed conflict and have been able to create a *status quo* in accordance with their own interests. The unsatiated States, bent upon modifying the *status quo* to their own advantage, will normally be those defeated in the last war and deprived of power by the victors. Rival alliances and coalitions emerge out of these relationships, with the satiated States combining to protect what they have acquired and the unsatiated combining to acquire what they covet.

All States do not, of course, fall into these neat categories, for some have complex and contradictory interests which drive them in opposite directions. Great Britain and Italy are examples. But generally speaking, the broad currents of Great Power politics can be interpreted in these terms. Prior to 1870, France was a satiated State, determined to preserve the prevailing equilibrium. This equilibrium was upset by the unification of Italy and Germany. French efforts to thwart German unification ended in disaster, and after 1871 France became an unsatiated State, bent upon recovering what had been lost. Germany under Bismarck was content with the *status quo* and formed alliances with Italy and Austria-Hungary to preserve it. France sought allies as a counter-weight. Insatiable Tsarist Russia, driving toward the Straits and the Balkans, was a logical partner in the anti-German coalition. Great Britain was won over when German colonial, commercial, and naval ambitions caused Downing Street to regard Germany as a menace to the established distribution of sea power, markets, and imperial possessions. Britain was more interested in preserving the *status quo* than in upsetting it. Italy desired upsets both at the expense of Vienna and Paris. These two Powers were, therefore, not "loyal" members of the coalitions which they had joined. Britain joined the weaker side in 1914 only after considerable hesitation. Italy deserted her allies and followed suit in 1915. Since the Entente victory and the peace settlements of 1919, the new victors have become *status quo* States and the vanquished are now "revisionist," *i.e.*, *revancharde*, in their policies. The coalition of France, Belgium, Poland, and the Little Entente confronts a still inchoate coalition of Germany, Austria, Hungary, and Bulgaria, with the U.S.S.R. and Italy lending occasional support to the revisionist group and Great Britain tending to align itself with the *status quo* combination. The power interests of Japan and the United States lie outside of the European continent and they therefore take sides, as between the European coalitions, only when a complete upset of the balance of power is threatened. If American imperialism in the Caribbean and Japanese imperialism in Asia are taken to indicate a desire for a more satisfying place in the sun than these States now enjoy, they may be classified, with qualifications, as "unsatiated."

In this ceaseless and uneasy striving for power, distinctions between "defensive" and "aggressive" foreign policies are meaningless, save in relation to the pattern already suggested. States are seldom aggressive or defensive by virtue of the bellicose or pacific inclinations of their peoples or governments. States which benefit from the established *status quo* seek naturally to preserve that from which they benefit. States which feel humiliated, hampered, and oppressed by the *status quo* seek as naturally to modify it. Satiated States are therefore likely to appear to be "pacific." They are committed to peace. They demand "security," for they are content with the equilibrium which peace and security will perpetuate. Unsatiated States demand changes, rectifications of frontiers, a revision of treaties, a redistribution of territory and power. In so far as the fulfillment of these demands is resisted by *status quo* States, in so far as this resistance makes possible their realization only through coercion and conflict, such States appear to be "aggressive" and lacking in enthusiasm for peace. If such States have been reduced to impotence, as was the case with France from 1871 to 1894 and as is the case with post-war Germany, they must speak softly, conceal their aims, and refrain from challenges or provocations which would result only in further losses in the event of a test of force. The bellicose or pacific propensities of States are largely explicable in terms of their power in relation to rival States and in terms of the view which they take of the existing distribution of power.

Diplomatic friction between States arises from the fact that the existing equilibrium, at any given moment, is unstable because it rests upon a series of shifting tensions between the satiated and the unsatiated. The balance is unstable because it is seldom based upon a distribution of territory and power satisfactory to all the members of the State System. At the close of each great contest the rapacity of the victors and the weakness of the vanquished invite punitive settlements which are resented by their victims to such a degree as to ensure new conflict. Each peace contains the seeds of the next war. Each war results in a new peace. Even when great moderation is shown and mutual adjustments and compromises are achieved, the resulting equilibrium is only temporary, for uncontrollable and unforeseen factors are constantly upsetting the delicately poised balance and creating new tensions. These tensions usually center about territorial questions—for control of territory means land, population, resources, wealth, in short all the ingredients of power. Germany desires to recover the Polish corridor and Upper Silesia and to annex Austria. These acquisitions would enormously enhance German power. They are therefore staunchly resisted by Poland and her allies, for they would involve a corresponding diminution of the power of the *status quo* bloc to resist new German demands. Hungary desires to recover her lost provinces. The Little Entente stands armed and alert to prevent this. Bolivia and Paraguay dispute title to the Gran Chaco, a vast wilderness lying between them. Neither can afford to permit its occupation by the other. Japan seizes Manchuria and is assailed diplomatically by the United States. In such situations compromise is difficult, for power is relative and each State's gain is another State's loss. A constant struggle therefore goes on for control of the means of power: strategic centers, backward areas, markets, waterways, irredentas, and frontier provinces. In this unstable balancing of shifting forces there can be neither permanence nor peace.

4. THE RÔLE OF VIOLENCE

War is politics continued by other (*i.e.*, forcible) means.—CLAUSEWITZ, *On War*.

If you will only notice human proceedings, you may observe that all who attain great power and riches make use of either force or fraud; and what they have acquired either by deceit or violence, in order to conceal the disgraceful methods of attainment, they endeavor to sanctify with the false title of honest gains.—NICCOLO MACHIAVELLI, *History of Florence*.

That the assumption of violence lies behind all diplomacy is a truism which would be too obvious to dwell upon, were it not so frequently forgotten in contemporary discussions. Diplomatic bargaining and armed coercion are complementary weapons in the struggle for power between the nation-states. In the Western State System, as in all the state systems which have preceded it, military force has ever been the decisive means by which State power has been created, increased, reduced, or destroyed. The competitive struggle for hegemony and survival in which States have always engaged has been carried on from time immemorial through the clash of fighting soldiery and ships of war. The "Gallery of Battles" in the great palace at Versailles, depicting the combats by which the French nation was created and its power enhanced, could be duplicated for every sovereign State of the world. The world historical drama of international politics is a pageant of strife. Assyrians descend like the wolf on the fold. Hittite and Egyptian war chariots clash on the Mediterranean shore. Greek triremes ram Persian fighting ships at Salamis. Macedonian phalanxes conquer a world empire. The war elephants of Hannibal charge the legions of Rome. The hosts of the Caesars conquer a vast realm embracing all of classical civilization. Barbarian hordes overwhelm the Roman world State. Feudal knights and barons fight one another and battle the infidels. Mercenary armies of ambitious monarchs carve out nations. Popular armies of the nation-states engage in intermittent conflicts for power.

The mechanized war monsters of the machine age ride rough shod over Africa and Asia and cover with blood and destruction the fields of Flanders and Galicia, Picardy and Lombardy, Macedonia and Manchuria.

This universality of violence in international politics has been explained by numberless commentators in terms of original sin, the punishments of Providence, the machinations of the devil, the "fighting instinct" of man, the cry for bread, the periodical reversion of *homo sapiens* to savagery, etc. While certain of these explanations have suggestive value, the present study proceeds on the assumption that international politics is essentially a competitive struggle for power between sovereign members of State Systems. War is an incident of this struggle. Military violence is the ultimate means resorted to by States in their pursuit of power. The present problem is not that of explaining why men fight in general, but why States habitually resort to force in their differences with one another. All politics is a struggle for power, but in the domestic or national arenas recourse is had to violence only rarely. In international politics, on the contrary, violence or threatened violence is customary. War is to international politics what revolution is to national politics: a resort to physical coercion to achieve political objectives, *i.e.*, to preserve the power of the user against attack, to enhance that power at the expense of a rival, to upset an established equilibrium of power, or to prevent it from being upset. To be sure, national law forbids the use of force as a political weapon and international law does not. The League Covenant and the Kellogg-Briand Pact purport to make war in the legal sense unlawful, but they have not prevented recourse to force under other names. The question calling for answer is: Why is physical coercion more frequently resorted to by States in the struggle for power which constitutes international politics than by parties, factions, sections, and classes in the corresponding struggle within national frontiers which constitutes national politics?

The answer lies in the circumstance that States do not stand in the same relation to one another as do parties, factions, sections, and classes within States. These entities of national politics are normally bound together by a "constitutional consensus," by common interests, by a consciousness of being parts of a larger whole—the nation—to which all owe allegiance. This consciousness and these common interests furnish a frame of reference for the pacific settlement of particular differences. Special interests are subordinated to general interests and are couched in terms of general interests. Political leaders, trade-union officials, provincial spokesmen, and business men are not usually disposed to say, "My party right or wrong!" "My section right or wrong!" "My class right or wrong!" They are rather disposed to assert that the general interests will be served best by the promotion of their particular interests and by the acceptance of their particular demands. The assumption of violence is not ordinarily made. The assumption is rather that of discussion, compromise, acquiescence in the result of pacific processes of adjustment. Without this assumption, orderly government is impossible. When the assumption ceases to be accepted, when the constitutional consensus breaks down, when the parties in the struggle for power place particular interests above general interests, there is danger of a resort to violence, *i.e.*, of revolution, riots, coups d'état, and civil war. If the coercive power of the State, exercised in the name of the general interest, is insufficient to repress disorder, revolution breaks out. It is of the essence of revolution that particular interests are placed above general interests and that coercion is substituted for compromise. So long as the political process functions normally on the basis of the assumption suggested, violence is eschewed, a peaceable equilibrium of forces is maintained, and all acquiesce pacifically to the "general will."

Sovereign States do not deal with one another on the basis of these assumptions. They are not parts of a larger whole, except in a formal sense, for a State System is not comparable to a national society or a national government. It is an aggregation of separate entities, each of which pursues its own interests by self-help and keenly resents any suggestion that its interests are to be subordinated to the interests of other States or of the whole community of States. There is as yet no "international government" worthy of the name, despite the hopes of proponents of the League of Nations. There is no international "constitutional consensus." There is no international police force, no super-State monopolizing coercive authority, to be employed in the general interest. International law itself is only what States agree upon, and it is enforced by State action. Coercive power in international society resides not in central organs reflecting the general interests, but in particular States pursuing particular interests. "My country right or wrong!" is an accepted slogan of State behavior. Under these circumstances it is difficult to bring about the peaceable adjustment of inter-State differences through procedures and principles laid down by an inchoate international community on the basis of general interests which are largely nonexistent. Each State must rely upon its own strength. The struggle for power tends to involve coercion or threats of coercion, for States take what they can get and keep what they can hold. When coercion is threatened or openly resorted to, there is no effective international authority to repress the peace-breakers and preserve law and order. If anarchy involves the absence of government, the pursuit by each of his own ends, and the use of violence in the service of such ends, then the practice of international politics can indeed be described accurately as "international anarchy."

It is noteworthy that, by a singular paradox, the very force which makes for peace and unity within modern States makes for friction and conflict between them. That force is nationalism. A sense of common nationality, a consciousness of common national interests and of national solidarity disposes all pretenders to political power within each nation-state to place the nation above party, section, or class and to adjust differences on the basis of a common patriotism. Prior to the emergence of nationalism, armed conflict between feudal barons, free cities, provinces, and religious sects was frequent. Only when these lesser allegiances were merged in a national allegiance did local and neighborhood warfare come to an end. But, as Jean Jacques Rousseau once observed, "Men have suppressed little wars only to kindle greater ones." The nationalism which unites nations disunites the community of States of which each nation is a part. The national patriot exalts his own State and holds others in contempt. He vigorously opposes any subordination of national interests to international interests. He gives his support to those policies of national self-seeking which breed war. The power interests of States are couched in the language of nationalism, and nationalism leads to conflicts more gigantic and disastrous than any which were possible before the nation-states became unified.

Since the assumption of violence prevails in international politics, since physical coercion of State by State is an ever-present possibility, all States must keep swords sharp and powder dry to meet all eventualities. Each State must strive to have ready for instant use weapons of sufficient caliber, in sufficient numbers, to protect itself from attack and to promote its own interests by armed action whenever that appears necessary. Armaments are the spearpoints of foreign policy and the prime measure of power. As power is relative, the efficacy of armaments is also relative to the enemy armaments against which they may be pitted. "Preparedness" is never preparedness to fight some hypothetical State X or to fight the entire world, but to fight some specific State or States with which conflict seems likely. Each State arms against its neighbors, by land or by sea. Each State is the potential ally of its neighbor's neighbors and the potential enemy of its neighbor's friends. The increasing smallness of the world, resulting from modern techniques of transportation, communication, and warfare, greatly enlarges the number of a State's "neighbors" and requires ever heavier armaments to attain "security" and achieve national purposes. Not only must the number of soldiers, sailors, and aviators be increased, but their equipment must be as modern and effective as those of the prospective enemy. Man power is no longer decisive, for masses of men, however well trained and heroic, are mere cannon fodder and can readily be ground to bloody pulp by the machines of modern war. Soldiers must have rifles, machine guns, hand grenades, trench mortars, poison gas, gas masks, barbed wire, armored cars, tanks, and light and heavy artillery. Sailors must have dreadnaughts, cruisers, destroyers, submarines, and aircraft carriers. Aviators must have bombing planes, combat planes, pursuit planes, dirigibles, balloons, and all of the accompanying paraphernalia of defense and destruction. Without these devices, armed forces are helpless against mechanized enemy forces, as is clearly revealed by the whole history of imperialism, by the defeat of Russia in the Great War, by the military impotence of contemporary China. Man power and machinery are alike essential to effective modern armaments.

Competition in armaments is the inevitable corollary of competition for power. Armaments are the means of power and the measure thereof. An increase in the arms of one State automatically diminishes the power of its neighbors, unless they make a like increase. No State can permit its neighbors to enlarge their armaments to a point where they could feel certain of victory in war and could impose their will by the pressure of military superiority. Preparedness does not insure peace, but it may instil fear in other States, make them less likely to disturb the existing equilibrium and more disposed to yield to the demands of more heavily armed rivals. For precisely this reason, preparedness induces other States to strive for an equal or a superior measure of preparedness. Each State seeks preponderance over possible enemies. If it succeeds after a victorious war in disarming the enemy State, as the Allies disarmed Germany in 1919, it will be so much closer to preponderance. But even this security is unstable and transient when the disarmed State still has available the economic means, if not the legal right, of re-arming. No State can attain permanent preponderance. When all States endeavor to attain it, the result is a competitive race in armaments which may end in war, in bankruptcy, or in international agreements to limit or reduce arms. Each State must watch closely the armaments of all others and must attempt as best it can to prevent itself from falling too far behind in the race, for if this happens it will be exposed to diplomatic dictation and military attack.

Armaments are instruments of national policy, in peace no less than in war, for they largely determine the success of efforts to attain objectives through diplomacy. A diplomacy which is unsupported by potential fighting power is usually impotent. This fighting power need not be put to the test of war in order for it to count in the scales of diplomatic balances. A test of force is unnecessary when one disputant possesses an obvious superiority in armaments. The weaker party will yield without risking further losses through inevitable defeat in an open contest of strength. Mexico and the Caribbean States must yield to American diplomacy or be overwhelmed. War in resistance to American power is unthinkable, for the result is a foregone conclusion. China must yield to Japanese power for the same reason—or resort to non-military methods of resistance. France was obliged to yield to Germany in successive diplomatic crises between 1871 and 1914, because France and her allies were palpably inferior in fighting power to Germany and her allies. Germany since 1919 is obliged to yield to the French bloc, for she is disarmed and cannot defy the overwhelming preponderance of power arrayed against her. A test of force through war is necessary only when an apparent parity of strength exists and each side can hope to impose its will on the other. When one side knows that it is hopelessly inferior, it yields to diplomatic pressure and renders actual physical coercion unnecessary. It is for this reason that all States are reluctant to reduce their armaments, even when war seems remote, lest a reduction leave them at a disadvantage and expose them to diplomatic or military defeat. Diplomacy is war by another name. It differs from war, not in objectives, but only in methods.

Diplomacy and strategy must go hand in hand. Every Great Power must strive in peace time to prepare for war. It must maintain its armaments at a level which will secure recognition for the demands of its diplomats. It must strive, by persuasion or by force, to safeguard its power interests in areas of vital importance to it. Its diplomacy must be directed toward the control of strategic points which will enable it to exercise its power effectively. Power begets more power, and more power begets the demand for still more to protect what is already acquired. Great Britain must secure the Suez Canal, because she must defend India. To defend the Suez Canal she must control Egypt. To defend Egypt she must control the Sudan, Aden, Malta, Cyprus, and Gibraltar. To defend her vast empire she must maintain a navy second to none, control naval bases all over the world, and strive to dominate as many strategic waterways as possible. Japan must control Port Arthur and the Liaotung peninsula in order to protect Korea and dominate the Gulf of Pechili. To control Port Arthur she must control the railways of the Manchurian hinterland. To control these she must control Manchuria. To defend Manchuria she must dominate Mongolia. The United States must defend the Panama Canal. This requires American naval dominance in the Caribbean. This in turn demands the control of the passages of the Caribbean—Bahia Honda and Guantanamo in Cuba, Porto Rico, and the Virgin Islands. It likewise leads to the control of the Great Corn and Little Corn Islands off the east coast of Nicaragua and of Fonseca Bay on the west coast as strategic prerequisites to the defense of a possible Nicaraguan canal. France must acquire Tunis to defend Algeria, Madagascar to defend Reunion, and Annam to defend Cochin China. The diplomacy of strategy and the strategy of diplomacy are inseparable.

In a crisis, when a test of force appears imminent, control of policy passes from diplomats to strategists. When war is being waged, diplomacy is conducted directly by armies, navies, and air fleets. In the summer of 1914, in all of the belligerent States, a point in the crisis was sooner or later reached at which war became "inevitable." This was the point at which the general staffs and the army commanders insisted upon military measures which rendered further diplomatic conversations futile. These recommendations were at first refused by the diplomats, so long as a chance of peace remained, and then accepted after a decision for war had been reached. The pressure of the militarists in every instance influenced this decision. In Russia the foreign minister and the general staff agreed upon general mobilization on July 30. The Tsar hesitated but finally acquiesced in an action which made war unavoidable. In France General Joffre asked the Cabinet on July 31 for permission to move troops to the frontier. The Cabinet granted the request, with reservations (the ten-kilometer "withdrawal") dictated by diplomatic considerations. On August 1, Joffre demanded the mobilization of the French army and his demand was granted. Once the demands of the strategists were accepted, diplomatic maneuvers were replaced by military tactics. The same pattern was clearly revealed in Japanese policy toward China in 1931–1933. As soon as physical coercion is openly resorted to, the formulation of policy passes into the hands of the masters of force. War is diplomacy by another name and with a different technique.

In summary, military violence is the ultimate weapon of State power. So long as this is true, State power is necessarily directed toward increasing its opportunities for the effective exercise of military violence.[1] Power depends upon armaments. Armaments depend upon population, economic resources, and technology. In both diplomacy and war, attention is concentrated upon acquiring control of resources and strategic points which will enhance State power. The power interests of States are necessarily expressed in economic terms which reflect the interests of their ruling classes. These interests are defended and promoted by physical force, actual or potential. In diplomacy the apparent potentialities of the force of rival States determine the outcome of clashes of wills. In war the actual fighting power of the belligerents determines which will shall

[1] R. G. Hawtrey, in his *Economic Aspects of Sovereignty*, p. 107, puts the problem as follows. "When I say that the principal cause of war is war itself, I mean that the aim for which war is judged worth while is most often something which itself affects military power. Just as in military operations each side aims at getting anything which will give it a military advantage, so in diplomacy each side aims at getting anything which will enhance its power. Diplomacy is potential war. It is permeated by the struggle for power and, when potential breaks out into actual war, that is usually because irreconcilable claims have been made to some element of power, and neither side can claim such preponderance as to compel the other to give way to a mere threat."

prevail. In both cases the assumption of violence lies beneath the surface of politics. In a system of sovereign nation-states, armed conflict between the units is an inevitable incident in the competitive struggle for power in which they are engaged, so long as each pursues its own interests by self-help.

5. THE MEASURE OF POWER

For what are riches, empire, power,
But larger means to gratify the will?
—WILLIAM CONGREVE, *The Mourning Bride.*

Since the evolution of the Western State System has been shaped primarily by the relationships of power among its members and since there is no reason for assuming that its future will differ from its past in this respect, it should prove illuminating to conclude this survey of the politics of power with a brief consideration of the "power potential" of each of the great States at the present time. To the degree to which it is possible to gauge accurately the power of these States, it is possible to estimate the probable outcome of future clashes between them and thus to prognosticate, in a general way, the probable course of Great Power politics in the decades which lie ahead. Mathematical accuracy is unattainable in such an effort, for the imponderables of international politics are often decisive. But a rough measure of State power can be attempted. In view of the fact that power depends ultimately upon fighting capacity and upon the ability of the State to apply physical coercion successfully against its enemies, the problem is one of estimating the "war potential" of the Great Powers and of such Minor Powers as seem likely to play a rôle in Great Power politics.

The elements of national power, constituting the war potential of a State, are numerous, varied, and fluctuating. Only a few of them can be suggested here. Armaments on land, sea, and air are the most obvious and direct measures of power. But the efficacy of a State's armaments depends upon its geographical location and upon the human and material resources which make armaments possible. The most important of these resources are population[1] (or more specifically, military man power), merchant shipping, and iron and steel production. Without facilities for producing iron and steel in large quantities, no State can maintain modern armaments on an effective level, for iron and steel are the backbones of machine industry and of contemporary mechanized warfare. A State's foreign commerce is a measure of its economic productivity, though world trade may be a source of weakness rather than of strength for a State depending for its prosperity upon foreign markets which are

---

[1] The table shown at bottom of p. 520 is illuminating in this connection.

vulnerable and exposed to attack by enemies. If communications with foreign markets can be maintained in war time, however, these markets become a strategic asset of first importance. Other items could be utilized as criteria of power: foreign investments, gold reserves, national wealth and income, agrarian resources, total industrial production, productivity of chemical and other war industries, oil output, copper production, industrial and military efficiency, civilian morale, national unity or disunity, etc. These items will not be considered in the present survey, for while they are important and may even be decisive in a crisis, they are not susceptible of accurate measurement and comparison or, if measurable, are less constant and less revealing than the components of national power suggested above.

The accompanying charts are designed to indicate graphically the fluctuations in power of the great States during the past thirty years, as measured by population, standing armies, naval tonnage, merchant shipping, foreign trade, and production of iron and steel. The accuracy of some of the figures upon which these charts are based is, of course, open to question. The most carefully compiled statistics are subject to error, and comparisons are often misleading because of qualitative differences in the things measured and discrepancies between national methods of measurement. This is particularly true of naval armaments. But the charts at least afford a general picture of the varying war potentials of the Great Powers during the past three decades. By combining these and other figures into a single graph, an index of power could conceivably be worked out, but the results would be subject to so many qualifications that the effort is scarcely worth making. The charts themselves call for little comment. The preponderance of the United States and the constant rise in the power of the United States and Japan are noteworthy. The disappearance of Austria-Hungary and the great diminution of German power which followed the Great War are no less striking. The ascendancy of France over the European continent is not

RATES OF POPULATION GROWTH IN THE GREAT POWERS*

Country	Year	Birth rate	Death rate	Natural increase (per 1,000 people)
England and Wales	1926	17.8	11.6	6.2
France	1926	18.8	17.5	1.3
Germany	1926	19.5	11.7	7.8
Italy	1926	27.2	16.8	10.4
Japan	1925	34.9	20.3	14.7
United States	1926	20.6	12.2	8.4
U.S.S.R.	1927	43.8	20.8	23.0

* Encyclopedia Britannica.

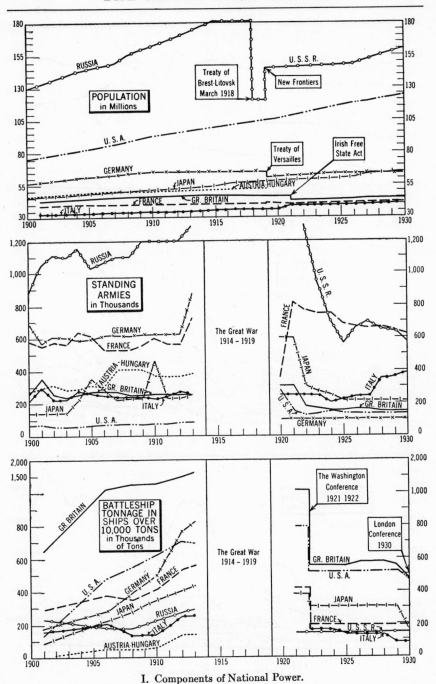

I. Components of National Power.

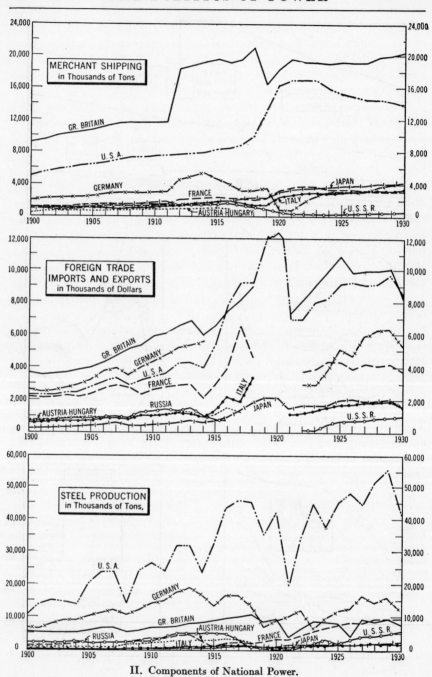

II. Components of National Power.

fully revealed, since there must be added to the power of France that of her eastern allies. The meteoric rise of revolutionary Russia is shown in the tables of population growth and iron and steel production. The effects of the Great War and of the Great Depression upon world productivity and commerce are likewise noticeable.

The larger chart which follows shows the relative positions of the Powers at the beginning of the fourth decade of the twentieth century, with respect to the same components of the war potential. A cursory glance at the figures is sufficient to indicate the ranking of the great States. The great land Powers, in order of rank, are France, the Soviet Union, Italy, and Japan. The great air Powers are France, the United States, Japan, Italy, Great Britain, and the Soviet Union. The great sea Powers are Great Britain, the United States, and Japan, with France and Italy next in order. In population the ranking of the Powers is as follows: the Soviet Union, the United States, Germany, Japan, Great Britain, France, and Italy. In iron and steel production, the order is: the United States, France, Germany, the Soviet Union, Great Britain, Japan, and Italy, though with the continued decline of metallurgical output in the western States during 1932 and 1933 the second place has been occupied by the U.S.S.R.[1] In merchant shipping Great Britain, the United States, Japan, and Germany lead the world, with France and Italy next and the Soviet Union far behind. The large merchant fleets of Norway, the Netherlands, Sweden, Greece, and Denmark are of great commercial importance but can scarcely be regarded as significant for the war potential of these States, since all of them for other reasons are Third-class Powers.[2] In foreign trade, Great Britain, the United States, and Germany lead the world, with France, Italy, Japan, and the Soviet Union next in order. The figures give only a partial picture of national

[1] Other leading iron- and steel-producing areas are:

Country	Year	Pig iron, tons	Steel, tons
Belgium	1930	3,394,000	3,390,000
Alsace-Lorraine (included in French figures on chart)	1930	3,526,000	2,839,000
Luxemburg	1930	2,474,000	2,270,000
Saar Valley	1930	1,912,000	1,935,000
Czechoslovakia	1929	1,643,000	2,145,000

[2] Other leading merchant marines are:

	Tons
Norway	4,065,506
The Netherlands	3,118,170
Sweden	1,704,669
Greece	1,397,782
Denmark	1,145,257

POWER QUOTIENTS OF THE GREAT POWERS

	Population	Armed forces	Naval tonnage	Air fleets	Iron and steel production (tons—1930)‡	Merchant marines (tonnage—1931)	Foreign trade (dollars 1930)‡
World totals	c. 1,800,000,000	Standing armies 7,388,500	5,178,000	18,000	Pig iron: 75,000,000 Steel: 80,500,000	65,641,035	Exports: 25,587,000,000 Imports: 28,191,400,000 Total: 53,778,400,000
France	41,840,000 Colonies: 60,000,000	617,750 Reserves: 6,327,500	628,603 9 capital ships 110 submarines 116 miscellaneous vessels	2,378	Pig iron: 10,106,000 Steel: 9,412,000	3,566,227	Exports: 1,678,900,000 Imports: 2,051,900,000 Total: 3,730,800,000
Great Britain	46,200,000 Colonies: 440,000,000	134,420 Reserves: 327,500	1,250,247 18 capital ships 64 submarines 223 miscellaneous	1,434	Pig iron: 6,197,000 Steel: 7,298,000	23,379,999	Exports: 3,199,900,000 Imports: 5,084,700,000 Total: 8,284,600,000
Germany	65,300,000 Colonies: None	100,500 Reserves: None	125,780 6 battle-ships* no submarines 32 miscellaneous	None	Pig iron: 9,694,000 Steel: 11,539,000	4,254,601	Exports: 2,870,500,000 Imports: 2,478,800,000 Total: 5,349,300,000

POWER QUOTIENTS OF THE GREAT POWERS.—*(Continued)*

	Population	Armed forces	Naval tonnage	Air fleets	Iron and steel production (ton—1930)‡	Merchant marines (tonnage—1931)	Foreign trade (dollars 1930)‡
Italy.........	41,500,000 Colonies: 2,200,000	414,850 Reserves: 5,560,750	404,005 4 capital ships 75 submarines 112 miscellaneous	1,507	Pig iron: 578,000 Steel: 1,774,000	3,335,673	Exports: 637,300,000 Imports: 911,300,000 Total: 1,548,600,000
Japan.........	66,000,000 Colonies: 27,300,000	259,300 Reserves: 1,900,000	850,328 10 capital ships 80 submarines 165 miscellaneous	1,639	Pig iron: 133,000 Steel: 2,037,000 (1929)	4,276,341	Exports: 726,000,000 Imports: 763,600,000 Total: 1,489,000,000
United States	126,000,000 Colonies: 14,670,000	139,950 Reserves: 289,180	1,144,110 15 capital ships 84 submarines 299 miscellaneous	1,752	Pig iron: 31,752,000 Steel: 40,699,000	13,642,183	Exports: 3,843,000,000 Imports: 3,060,900,000 Total: 6,903,900,000
U.S.S.R......	165,000,000 Colonies: None	562,000 Reserves: 4,528,000	166,247 4 capital ships 13 submarines 41 miscellaneous	1,000†	Pig iron: 4,969,000 Steel: 5,552,000	603,836	Exports: 533,700,000 Imports: 545,300,000 Total: 1,079,000,000

* Limited by the Treaty of Versailles to not more than 10,000 tons.
† This is only a rough estimate. The U.S.S.R. has not made public the size of its air fleet, but it has expanded it considerably in recent years.
‡ 1930 rather than 1931 or 1932 figures are given here since the effects of the Great Depression on production and trade give a false impression of national economic capacities. Army, navy, and air figures are taken from the League of Nations *Armaments Yearbook*, 1932. The figures for trained reserves are based upon United States War Department estimates as of October 1, 1931. Other figures are taken from the *World Almanac*, 1932.

power, however, for power is local and the only comparisons of political significance are those between States able to exert their power against one another in a particular theater of conflict in which each can bring its resources to bear effectively.

The hegemony of France over Europe, for example, cannot be fully appreciated without taking into consideration the power of France's allies. The French Republic, with 617,750 soldiers under arms and with a trained reserve of 6,327,000, maintains the largest land force of any of the Powers. France has a total man power of 9,474,000. France has 2,378 military aircraft. Since French power is directed primarily toward the maintenance of the *status quo* on the European continent and since France is in alliance with Belgium, Poland, and the Little Entente, French power is chiefly significant in relation to the power of those States which might conceivably upset the *status quo*. The overwhelming military preponderance of the French bloc is strikingly revealed by the following tables.

THE FRENCH BLOC

States	Standing armies*	Reserves†	Man power‡	Military aircraft
France	617,750	6,327,000	9,474,000	2,378
Belgium	86,384	495,000	2,015,000	195
Poland	265,980	1,645,000	5,967,000	700
Czechoslovakia	151,435	1,509,000	3,403,000	546
Jugoslavia	211,592	1,200,000	3,500,000	627
Rumania	240,501	1,485,000	4,500,000	799
Totals	1,573,642	12,661,000	28,859,000	5,245

* The figures in this table for standing armies and aircraft are taken from the League of Nations *Armaments Yearbook*, 1932.

† The figures for trained reserves are based upon estimates of the United States War Department as of October 1, 1931, *World Almanac*, 1932, p. 374.

‡ The figures for total man power include all males in the total population between the ages of fifteen and forty-nine. *Cf.* Table in League of Nations *Armaments Yearbook*, 1932, pp. 452–453.

THE "REVISIONIST" BLOC

States	Standing armies	Reserves	Man power	Military aircraft
Germany	100,500	None	16,741,000	None
Austria	21,463	None	1,421,000	None
Hungary	34,993	None	1,957,000	None
Bulgaria	18,552	None	1,361,000	None
Totals	175,508	None	21,480,000	None
Italy*	414,859	5,560,000	9,257,000	1,507
U.S.S.R.*	562,000	4,528,000	34,912,000	1,000

* Neither Italy nor the Soviet Union can be regarded as part of the "revisionist" bloc, though they have at times given diplomatic support to it. Italy, however, is the potential enemy of France in the Mediterranean and of Jugoslavia in the Adriatic, while the Soviet Union is the potential enemy of Poland and Rumania.

But French power is even greater than is revealed by these impressive figures. The defeated States are forbidden by the Peace Treaty to possess military aircraft, heavy artillery, and tanks—and without these weapons their 175,000 troops would, in a test of power, count for much less than one-tenth of the peace strength of the armies of the French bloc. The States of the French bloc, moreover, have 12,661,000 trained reserves, while the revisionist States are forbidden to possess any at all. The new French border fortresses are "impregnable."[1] In sea power France possesses a large margin in war vessels over her chief rival, Italy, and a slight margin in merchant shipping. France possesses, moreover, the largest submarine fleet of the world. In foreign trade France ranks next after Great Britain, the United States, and Germany, with Italy far behind. France has 60,000,000 colonial subjects inhabiting territories reasonably rich in resources. It is in iron and steel production, however, that French power is supreme. France itself now ranks second to the United States, having overtaken Germany and Great Britain. But to French production must be added that of the Saar valley, Belgium, and Czechoslovakia.[2] When these increments to French power are added to the total, it is clear that the French Government has available metal-lurgical facilities far greater than those of any of its neighbors and probably greater, in normal times, than the combined facilities of any two of the neighboring States. If these vast resources can be utilized effectively for war purposes in combination with land, air, and sea power, no coalition of enemy Powers can prevail against the French bloc in a test of strength.

The power of France, however, is relative to that of her great neighbor across the Rhine. Disarmed Germany is impotent on land, sea, and air. French "security" would be completely assured by this circumstance, save for certain other factors in Germany's situation which would place her on a parity of power with France if her resources could be utilized.

[1] The pre-war Belgian fortifications at Namur and Liège were also regarded as "impregnable" until they were battered to pieces by the new German heavy artillery in 1914.

[2] The combined iron and steel production available to France in 1930 can be indicated as follows:

States	Pig iron, metric tons	Steel, metric tons
France	10,106,000	9,412,000
Saar	1,912,000	1,935,000
French total	12,018,000	11,347,000
Belgium	3,394,000	3,390,000
Czechoslovakia	1,643,000 (1929)	2,145,000 (1929)
Grand total	17,055,000	16,882,000

There are twice as many Germans in Europe as Frenchmen. Germany possesses a potential man power far greater than that of France. Germany possesses the largest commercial air fleet in Europe, and commercial aircraft can readily be converted to military use. She possesses a much larger merchant marine than France. Her iron and steel industry is still formidable and larger in output than Great Britain's. Her foreign trade is much greater than that of France. And German scientific ingenuity and technical skill are undiminished, as shown by recent achievements in aviation and shipbuilding. The new North German Lloyd Liners, *Bremen* and *Europa*, hold the north Atlantic speed records. The German *DOX* is the largest flying boat thus far constructed. German dirigibles lead the world in safety and efficiency. The Treaty of Versailles forbids Germany to possess more than six large war vessels, and these must be not larger than 10,000 tons. But by new processes of electrical welding, new armor, and new guns, Germany has produced, in the battlec ruisers of the type of the *Deutschland*, fighting ships which are said to be powerful enough to destroy any vessel they cannot run away from and speedy enough to run away from any vessel they cannot destroy.

These things serve to explain continued French demands for security, for international sanctions, for an international police force. But considerations of geography enable the French general staff to calculate upon paralyzing German power at the very outset of a possible conflict, through the French air fleet and through swift offensives into the Rhineland and Bavaria from Alsace-Lorraine and Belgium, into Saxony from Czechoslovakia, and into the heart of Prussia from the Polish corridor. Only if the power of Poland and Czechoslovakia were immobilized by the Soviet Union and Hungary would this calculation miscarry. Even a fully re-armed Germany would probably be no match for the French combination, and without equality in armaments Germany is in a position of hopeless inferiority. It is a logical consequence of these relationships that equality in armaments should be a major objective of German foreign policy and should be vigorously opposed by the Quai d'Orsay. A re-armed Germany with Austria under her control could deal with France as a diplomatic equal. Because of the advantage of interior lines of communication and the possibilities of new offensive and defensive weapons so strikingly demonstrated in the Great War, Germany might even reckon with the possibility of crushing Poland and Czechoslovakia in the event of a combat and fighting a successful defensive war against France and Belgium, particularly if Russian, Hungarian, or Italian assistance were forthcoming. These calculations, however, are as yet among the pipe dreams of German super-patriots, plotting a future "war of liberation." For the present and the immediate future, Germany is helpless under the shadow of the successors of Louis XIV and Napoleon I.

Italy is in an even more feeble position, in spite of her large armaments. The Italian army is inferior in size to the French, both in permanent effectives and in trained reserves. In a future conflict Italy must
reckon with war on two fronts, for Jugoslavia is France's ally and Italian
military power is no match for such a combination. In sea power Italy
is in an even weaker position. She was granted parity with France in
capital ships at the Washington Conference, but France has consistently
refused to concede parity in other categories. For reasons of economy,
the Italian Government began the retirement of 130,000 tons of war
vessels from active service in August, 1932. The French fleet is larger
than the Italian, and Italy benefits little from the circumstance that
France must divide her squadrons between the Mediterranean, the
Atlantic, and the colonies. French and British sea power is dominant
in the Mediterranean, and even a successful naval attack upon the French
communications with north Africa would still leave Italy exposed to the
might of French arms by land. Italy is strategically weak because all
of her metropolitan territory and most of her colonies lie on the littoral
of an inland sea, the entrances of which are controlled by other States.
Italy, moreover, is poor in the resources which make for national power
in the machine age. She lacks coal and iron ore. She stands lowest among
the Powers in iron and steel production. Despite her teeming population,
she lacks the financial and economic resources to achieve that place
in the sun to which Fascist patriots aspire. Unless she can secure powerful
allies or take advantage of some future conflict between her neighbors,
she is doomed to chafe within her frontiers under the same shadow of
French hegemony which is cast over Germany.

Great Britain, having reduced to impotence her greatest rival, Germany, finds herself sorely afflicted by the common catastrophe involved
in that achievement. Her diplomats and strategists are obliged to reflect
painfully upon the economic consequences for British power of the long
post-war depression. Her merchant fleet is only slightly larger than it
was in 1913, while the United States has almost doubled its merchant
marine. Japan has almost tripled the number of her merchant vessels,
and Germany has all but recovered her pre-war position. British foreign
trade has increased since the war, but less rapidly than that of Germany
and the United States. The United States has steadily crept up on
Britain's supremacy in exports of goods and capital. In iron and steel
production Britain held third place before the war and now holds only
fifth place, having been outstripped by France and the Soviet Union.
She has been obliged to abandon the "two-Power standard" for her
navy and to concede naval parity to America. Her Government views
with apprehension the French air squadrons and the French submarine
fleet, for the Channel no longer affords protection. But despite these

darker aspects of the picture, Great Britain still has the largest navy, the largest merchant marine, and the largest volume of foreign trade and investments of any of the Powers. She is a member of an Empire which was already larger and richer in 1914 than all others combined and is now greatly expanded as a result of the war. She cannot exercise her power effectively on the European continent nor in the western hemisphere, nor in northeastern Asia, but everywhere else in the world British power is supreme. If she cannot aspire to that unchallenged world hegemony which the defeat of Germany seemed to promise, she is still far from that final disaster which her enemies have always predicted as her ultimate fate.

The power of the United States has risen to dazzling heights since 1914. Under the impetus of war demands and post-war prosperity, her industrial, commercial, agricultural, and financial facilities have expanded at an extraordinary rate until she dominates the world in all the leading branches of production. She produces almost one-half of the world's total output of steel and over two-fifths of its total iron output. She leads the world in railway mileage and in the production of petroleum, coal, corn, cotton, wheat, hogs, motor cars, machinery, and numberless other commodities. She has attained naval parity with Great Britain. She has a larger population and larger undeveloped resources than any other Power save the Soviet Union. If the United States does not play a rôle in world politics as significant as these circumstances would seem to make possible, the cause is to be found in her geographical remoteness from the centers of power of other great States and in her deliberate policy of isolation. American power is supreme on the American continent, in the western Atlantic, and in the eastern Pacific. But the United States cannot enforce its will on the European continent, nor in Africa, nor in the western Pacific, nor on the Asiatic mainland when that will is opposed by other Great Powers in these areas. To attain effective power in these regions the United States would require a navy not merely as large as the British navy, but larger than the British and Japanese navies combined and supported by naval bases and coaling stations all over the world. While it might be economically possible for the United States to achieve naval hegemony of this kind, it would be politically inexpedient and certain to lead to conflict. For the present, the United States is content to devote the bulk of her enormous resources to the tasks of peace and to remain mistress of the western hemisphere without seeking greater power abroad.

If the war potential of the United States is less than its economic power would make theoretically possible, the war potential of Japan is enormously greater than her economic resources would appear to warrant. This is due to the fact that Japan has devoted a relatively large proportion of her wealth to building up a powerful army and navy. It is due likewise to the circumstances of Japan's geographical position. Like the United States, Japan is far removed from the centers of power of other great States. Unlike the United States, she is within easy striking distance of important possessions of other Powers and she is next door to one of the great areas of imperialistic rivalry. To the west lies chaotic China, rich, populous, but impotent and torn by internal strife and by the ambitions of other States. To the north lies Soviet Siberia and to the south the Philippine Islands, the Dutch East Indies, and Britain's Asiatic and south Pacific Empire. Japan, with the third largest merchant marine in the world, is commercially dominant in most of this region. With the third largest army among the Great Powers, she is strategically dominant on the Asiatic mainland. With the third largest war fleet in the world, her sea power is supreme in the western Pacific and other Powers there cannot defy her will. These advantages more than overbalance the fact that Japan is poor in most of the essential resources of modern industry and ranks far down the list in iron and steel production. These deficiencies can be made up by the control and exploitation of the resources of Manchuria and possibly of other parts of China. Barring some unforeseen calamity, Japan bids fair to dominate the eastern hemisphere almost as completely as does the United States the western.

Finally, there is the greatest question mark in the future of power politics—the U.S.S.R. With its immense territories and its huge population (growing more rapidly than that of any of the other Great Powers), it bestrides Europe and Asia like a young giant and looks confidently to its future. If population, land, and resources were the sole measures of power, the Soviet Union would outweigh all the other Powers of Europe. But Russia is still agrarian rather than industrial. Her urban population numbers only about 20 per cent of the total. Her railway mileage is one-fifth that of the United States in an area two and one-half times as great. Her people are backward, unskilled, untrained in the ways of machine industry. She is of eastern Europe and the line between east and west is still a line between cleanliness, neatness, order, efficiency and slovenliness, squalor, waste, incompetence. The new Russia, however, is the world's first successful proletarian dictatorship and the world's first successful socialist economy. Her rulers and her people are fired with revolutionary enthusiasm and with a vision of a new social order and a new world State of workers' republics, the like of which has never before been seen. All prophecies regarding Russia fail of fulfillment if they leave out of account the implications of economic planning and of the wonder-working fervor which is building the new State. The Communist program of industrialization envisages the efficient exploitation of the fabulous natural wealth of Russia for the common benefit of Soviet society. In the midst of the economic paralysis which grips the bourgeois States, the

Soviet Union builds factories, mills, mines, and whole industrial cities almost overnight and increases its production each year at a rate never equaled elsewhere. She already stands second to the United States in iron, steel, and oil production and is first in grains, timber, furs, and other raw products. An effectively industrialized Russia would be the most powerful of the great States of the world.

The results of these achievements upon the Soviet Union's power potential are incalculable. For the present, Moscow is absorbed in internal construction and plays the game of power politics only to the extent necessary to protect its domestic interests and to achieve security from external attack. The Red Army is kept in readiness to resist all assaults. It is the second largest standing army of the world, but it is considerably smaller than the combined armies of the Soviet Union's most powerful neighbors—Japan, Poland, and Rumania. Its navy is negligible, its merchant marine is small, its foreign trade is still less than that of pre-war Russia. But the immensity of the Union makes it invulnerable. The great industrial establishments of the new era are for the most part located in the east, the south, and in central Siberia, where they will be completely secure from all attacks by land, sea, or air. Its location in relation to central Europe, the Near East, central Asia, and China gives it the possibility of future action in these regions on a scale not to be successfully resisted by other States. Its enormous military reserves and its new industries supply it with sinews of power not possessed by any other European or Asiatic nation. And in any future contest, it has strange weapons and strange allies at its disposal. The propaganda of international revolutionary Communism and the sympathetic support of millions of workers and peasants in Europe and Asia are imponderables, the effects of which cannot be gauged with any degree of accuracy. It is within the realm of possibility that before the middle of the twentieth century, the U.S.S.R. will have attained a position in which it will have greater power at its disposal than the combined power of all the States with which it may come into direct contact. How this power will be used and what its effects upon other Powers will be, remain to be seen.

SUGGESTED READINGS

Ballard, C. A.: *America and the Atlantic*, New York, E. P. Dutton & Co., Inc., 1923.
Bywater, H. C.: *Navies and Nations*, London, Archibald Constable & Co., Ltd., 1927.
———: *Sea-power in the Pacific, a Study of the American-Japanese Naval Problems*, Boston, Houghton Mifflin Company, 1921.
De Balla, V.: *The New Balance of Power in Europe*, Baltimore, Johns Hopkins Press, 1932.
Eckel, E. C.: *Coal, Iron, and War*, New York, Henry Holt & Company, 1920.
Fairgrieve, J.: *Geography and World Power*, New York, E. P. Dutton & Co., Inc., 1915.
Fleure, H. J.: *Human Geography in Western Europe*, London, Williams and Norgate, 1919.
Fullerton, W. M.: *Problems of Power*, New York, Charles Scribner's Sons, 1918.
Hawtrey, R. G.: *Economic Aspects of Sovereignty*, New York, Longmans, Green & Co., 1930.
Lippmann, W.: *The Stakes of Diplomacy*, New York, Henry Holt & Company, 1917.

Lowell, A. L.: *Public Opinion in Peace and War*, Cambridge, Harvard University Press, 1923.

Mahan, A. T.: *The Influence of Sea Power upon History*, 1660–1783, Boston, Little, Brown & Company, 1890.

Parmelee, M.: *Blockade and Sea Power*, New York, Thomas Y. Crowell Company, 1924.

Pavlovitch, M.: *Foundations of Imperialist Policy*, London, Labour, 1922.

Reinsch, P. S.: *Secret Diplomacy*, New York, Harcourt, Brace & Company, 1922.

——: *World Politics*, New York, The Macmillan Company, 1900.

BOOK FOUR
PROSPECTS

INTRODUCTION TO BOOK FOUR

The origins, forms, and forces of international politics in the Western State system have been outlined in the preceding books of this volume. There remains the final task of evaluating present tendencies and calculating future possibilities. This task is necessarily one of surveying contemporary efforts to devise and apply international remedies to the problems created by the conflicting policies of the nation-states. These problems are sufficiently grave to render credible the prognostications of pessimists who see in them the seeds of the destruction of the Western State System and the impending dissolution of western civilization. They are due to the political and economic consequences of nationalism, of imperialism, and of the competitive quest for wealth and power in which the nation-states have so long engaged. During the earlier centuries of local economies, of political provincialism, of nation-forging and empire-building, this struggle was fraught with no great peril for western culture as a whole. That culture was localized, fragmented, amorphous, secure in its totality against the separate misfortunes of its parts. Indeed, the great driving forces of power-seeking nationalism and of profit-seeking capitalism and imperialism contributed toward the enrichment of western civilization by unifying nations, promoting commerce and investment, and facilitating those cultural contacts requisite to a high development of the arts and sciences. But in the epoch of machine industry, mass production, and world economy these older behavior patterns and policies are fraught with danger for the future of the new world society which has willy-nilly been brought into being by the very forces now threatening its ruin.

The problem which has arisen out of this situation has assumed the proportions of a continuing and unresolved world crisis ever since the Great Powers unleashed the fury of war in the bloody summer of 1914. The security and prosperity which seemingly prevailed before that fatal year have been swept away in the backwash of international strife and revolution. The world society of the bourgeois nation-states has tottered on the brink of catastrophe during the ensuing two decades. That society, like all its predecessors, is a product of forces over which no organized human intelligence exercises control or direction. These forces threaten its dissolution if they cannot somehow, at long last, be subjected to guidance and redirection by informed social and political leadership. In one great human community—Russia—the old order has already collapsed beyond all hope of restoration, and out of its débris has emerged a new order committed to the annihilation of the *ancien régime* elsewhere. In the great national communities fronting on the Atlantic and its adjacent seas, the old order has after a fashion survived—but its survival is troubled, uncertain, and marked by dizzy alternations of hope and despair, of convalescence and relapse, of recovery and a recrudescence in malignant form of old maladies. In the turmoil of Asia's chaos, in the obscure stirrings beneath Africa's darkness, there is no peace and no promise of an ordered world. The governments of western Europe and of the Americas grapple confusedly with problems which they seem to be beyond their ability to solve. Under these circumstances, the mid-period of the twentieth century seems likely to mark a definite turning point in the history of western civilization and of the system of international politics which that civilization has developed. At the present time the vague and fluctuating lights on the horizons of the future can be viewed with equal plausibility as heralds of a new dawn or as precursors of a long twilight descending on western culture as it has in the fullness of time descended upon all the past civilizations of the world.

If western mankind is capable of making itself master of its destiny, of averting disaster, and of building a new and secure future, it must apply social intelligence to contemporary problems on a scale never before attempted. And that intelligence, if it is to be effective, must be applied not nationally, but internationally. No policies of national self-seeking or self-protection on the part of the nation-states can possibly cope with the world crisis, for such policies have produced the crisis and threaten to make it fatal. The dilemma can be resolved only if human welfare is envisaged in terms broader than national and imperial frontiers, only if national self-help is superseded by international collaboration, only if national interests are integrated with the interests of the world community as a whole. The salvation of a world society demands action on a world-wide scale and the subordination of old national allegiances and purposes to newer and broader allegiances and purposes as extensive as the planet itself. Neither in its political organization nor in its economic life can the western world return to the localisms, the provincialisms, the nationalisms of an epoch already dying, unless it is prepared to descend from a high plane of civilized life to a state of anarchic barbarism comparable to that prevailing in Europe during the "dark ages." Unless the old values and policies can be redefined and reintegrated into a course of action and a way of life adequate to the exigencies of the twentieth century, there can be little hope for the future of the Western State System or of the culture which gave it birth. And the task is no less than that of organizing the nation-states for international cooperative efforts in which each will cease to pursue its interests at the expense of its neighbors and all will collaborate to serve common ends.

In terms of materials of the present study, a consideration of this task will involve an examination of attempts to deal internationally with the problems created by the competitive strivings and conflicts of the nations. These problems are almost infinite in number and complexity. All of them, obviously, cannot be discussed within the limits of a single volume. But the future development of international politics seems destined to revolve about a few crucial problems upon which attention may profitably be concentrated. These are the problems arising out of the sickness of acquisitive capitalism; those resulting from the tension between the nation-states for control of backward areas and between the western peoples as a whole and the victims of their imperialisms; and those due to the vast suffering and destruction ensuing from the use of armed violence in the pursuit of national power. In short, it is proposed to survey the prospects of capitalism, the vistas stretching before the empire-builders, and the future of war in the contemporary world society. This will involve once more a consideration of the forms of the Western State System in so far as those forms offer procedures and institutions for effective remedial action. The present incomplete fabric of international government, woven at Geneva, must be weighed and examined with the object of studying in broad perspective the pattern of the cloth and of passing judgment upon the adequacy of the garment. Finally, on the basis of these estimates, certain suggestions may be offered regarding the future of the Western State System in its entirety.

This, it will be objected, is the work of the seer and prophet rather than of the objective and realistic political scientist. The objection is valid, for no one can undertake to foretell the future of a civilization so complex, confused, and variegated as our own. All that can be attempted is an estimate of the probable consequences for tomorrow of present tendencies as they are revealed by the facts and events of today. If the chapters which follow fulfill this function, they will have served their purpose and brought the entire study to a fitting conclusion.

CHAPTER XIV

THE ECONOMIC DILEMMA OF THE WORLD SOCIETY

1. THE CRISIS OF CAPITALISM

While men walk the streets and cannot find work to earn bread for their hungry families, the corn bins of the world are bursting with food that cannot be sold. Capital by countless millions is lying idle in banks waiting to be used. This vicious circle will not be broken by individual nations actuated by self-interest, but only when all countries unite and set aside every consideration of national interest and prestige.—ARTHUR HENDERSON.

ECONOMICS became known as "the dismal science" during the birth pangs of modern industrial society, when the new technology was transforming the green fields and sleepy towns of central England into an ugly wilderness of smoking factories and slum cities. The new monster of the machine sucked in men, women, and children and changed them from contented farmers and townsmen to miserable and sweated factory workers who were paid a pittance by profit-seeking employers and reduced to wage slavery and destitution. The new industry enormously increased productivity and profits, but in the period of laissez-faire individualism it brought almost incredible wretchedness to hundreds of thousands of hired producers. Western society appeared to be dividing itself into two great classes: a small and powerful bourgeoisie of capitalists, entrepreneurs, owners, and managers, growing ever richer on the profits of the new technology, and a large and helpless proletariat growing ever poorer as wages and living standards were pushed lower and lower. The new economics brought forth gloomy doctrines to explain this phenomenon. Ricardo propounded the "iron law of wages," according to which the income of workers would always tend to be pushed toward a bare subsistence level. Malthus postulated such a pressure of population upon resources that poverty and starvation seemed inevitable. Marx analyzed the functioning of capitalistic economy and argued the inevitability of its eventual collapse in social revolution.

Much of this early pessimism, however, was shown to be groundless as the new economic order developed. For many decades, markets for the fruits of the factory system seemed inexhaustible. Production and commerce increased steadily. Workers organized themselves into trade unions and by resorting to collective bargaining, implemented by the weapons of the strike and the boycott, were able to secure for labor a larger share of the proceeds of production than employers would otherwise have granted them. The gains of labor in the economic field were matched by gains in the political field. With the gradual attainment of universal suffrage in the western nations, labor could speak at the polls, albeit inarticulately and with many voices. Its power was sufficient to secure legalization of trade unions and to compel the enactment of laws regulating hours and conditions of work, safeguarding women and child workers, providing for various types of social insurance, and otherwise affording protection to wage-earners from the worst effects of their new status. The rich became richer as wealth and income became increasingly concentrated in the hands of the few. The poor became poorer in a relative sense, since the proletariat in general tended to receive a smaller and smaller proportion of the total wealth resulting from production. But production was growing so rapidly that the return to the workers, in an absolute sense, was constantly increasing. Real wages and living standards rose steadily despite an enormous increase in population. The average working-class family in the western industrialized nations found itself much better off in 1900 than in 1800—so much so that in periods of prosperity both economists and entrepreneurs could speak plausibly of a "new era" in which economic progress was continuous and uninterrupted and in which capitalists and wage-earners alike shared an ever-greater abundance of goods and services on a scale undreamed of in earlier ages.

These gains were achieved, however, as a result of economic processes involving human and material waste, painful maladjustments, alternating periods of prosperity and depression, and a large amount of suffering, social tension, and industrial conflict. Modern capitalism rests upon the ancient institution of private property and upon the equally ancient profit motive for economic activity. But in the era of industrialism, land is no longer the most socially significant form of private property. Factories, mills, mines, banks, stores, railroads, and steamship lines are the units of production and distribution in the new economic order and these are owned by private entrepreneurs and operated in the interests of the owners. The most significant forms of pecuniary gain from economic activities are no longer rents from farm lands and profits from small-scale trade, but income from industrial and commercial property, interest on capital investments, and profits derived from the difference between costs of production and prices in national and world markets. The modern economic order of western civilization operates through the new machine technology and the factory system, but it rests upon old social institutions and values. The fusion of the old and the new in the acquisitive society of the twentieth century has led to a ceaseless quest for the huge profits which the new technology and the new markets make possible, to world-wide competition between millions of uncoordinated producers and distributors, and to the allocation of land, labor, and capital among alternative enterprises in accordance with the dictates of profits as determined by costs and prices. These things have come to pass as a result of the unplanned private initiative of hosts of profit-seekers whose competing activities produce an anarchical state of affairs in which neither government nor business men possess any effective control over the larger trends of economic development.

This is not the place to examine in detail the effects of this situation. It is enough to note that the economic order of western civilization, like the international order, is as a whole less an order than a vast disorder, less a conscious organization of people for the promotion of common purposes than an unplanned system in which each pursues his own purposes and interests as best he can. If it is justifiable to describe the relations between sovereignties in the Western State System as "international anarchy" on the ground that each State acts for itself with no effective central agencies to integrate the parts into a greater whole, it is likewise justifiable to describe the relations between the parts of the economic order as "economic anarchy." Here, too, each part acts for itself, with no effective agencies to coordinate the units into a smoothly running organization. Each of the units, *i.e.*, industrial and commercial corporations, banks, labor unions, cooperatives, etc., is highly organized and specialized to achieve its own purposes. Within each unit of the economic order, as within each State of the international order, there is an unprecedented amount of cooperation, coordination, planning, and common efforts for common ends. But between the units there are competition and conflict, with each unit striving for a maximum of material gain as States strive with one another for a maximum of power and prestige.

The resulting pattern, to be sure, is not quite anarchy in either case. Just as the principles of international law, the practices of diplomacy, and the agencies of international cooperation and organization reflect the common interests of States and control their actions to an appreciable degree, so do business ethics, national legislation, and administrative regulations imposed by each State regulate and control economic activity within its borders. Prior to the middle of the nineteenth century, laissez-faire individualism reigned supreme in the economic realm, and the universal quest for profits went on with few restrictions on individual action in the common interest. During the same period, in the realm of international politics, States pursued their own interests by self-help and the universal struggle for power in which they engaged was seldom mitigated by common interests and cooperative action. During the past five or six decades, however, the freedom of entrepreneurs seeking profits and of States seeking power have both been limited in the interests of the whole community. In the first case, the effort to subject individual self-seeking to social purposes has taken the form of legislation by national governments attempting to conserve natural resources, to prevent waste, dishonesty, and unfair methods of competition, to check the formation (in the United States) of monopolistic trusts and combinations, to protect the weak and poor from the strong and rich, etc. In the second case, States have found it advantageous to subordinate exclusive national interests and unchecked national sovereignty to the common welfare of the whole community of States through the creation of "international government."

But in neither case has this process progressed far enough to modify the fundamentally competitive nature of the systems. The State System remains an aggregation of self-seeking national units whose cooperation is not yet sufficiently organized and sufficiently grounded in a general recognition of common interests to modify the basic patterns of international politics.[1] The economic system remains likewise an aggregation of uncoordinated units whose activities in most countries are not yet subjected to a sufficient degree of voluntary cooperation or governmental regulation to prevent the usual consequences of competitive profit-seeking by private entrepreneurs. These consequences are in part desirable, as measured by the promotion of material well-being and "the greatest good of the greatest number," for the competitive quest for profits has led to an enormous output of goods and services and to their wide distribution throughout the western world. The consequences are in part undesirable, as measured by the same criteria. Unemployment, poverty, economic exploitation, waste, strikes, lockouts, boycotts, cutthroat competition, dumping, bankruptcy, credit difficulties, monetary instability, and panics are also results of competitive profit-seeking. The undesirable consequences of economic anarchy have, in the past few decades, become so prevalent, so widespread, and so acute as to raise doubts in the minds of many as to whether the economic system of competitive private capitalism can continue to function in its traditional fashion. The alliance between the old and the new, between private property and profits on the one hand and the new technology on the other, must perhaps be terminated as the price of economic salvation. Numerous "left" critics have demanded the replacement of the old institutions and incentives by some form of collectivism as the only means of making the machine the slave, instead of the master, of men.

This "crisis of capitalism" has assumed its most acute form since the Great War. The "business cycle" has ever been a familiar phenomenon of modern capitalistic economy and indeed of earlier economies, for the alternation between famine and plenty, between "fat years" and "lean

[1] See pp. 823f. below and pp. 231f. above.

years" is an age-old feature of man's economic activity. But while periods of suffering in earlier agrarian economies were usually due to a shortage of goods, caused in turn by unfavorable climatic conditions, poor crops, and natural calamities, such periods in modern industrial economy are characterized by an overproduction of goods and services in relation to the buying power of consumers. For the first time in human history, mankind has at its disposal the technological means of supplying all human wants in abundance. These means are employed in such a way, however, as to lead to poverty in the midst of plenty, bankruptcy from superabundance, and unemployment at the very time when consumers are most in need of goods but lack the wherewithal to purchase them. Economists have long striven to explain these anomalies and to analyze the business cycle in terms of logical causes and results. Innumerable hypotheses have been advanced: overproduction, underconsumption, the fluctuating value of money, the expansion and contraction of credit, the disparity between saving and investment, overexpansion of productive facilities in "boom" periods, stringent contraction of credit and production in slack periods, etc. None of these efforts has been highly successful, for each places emphasis upon symptoms rather than causes and all seek to read into a competitive, disorderly, and anarchical economic system an order and logic which are nonexistent. Radical critics of capitalism have contended, on the other hand, that the business cycle is not a disease of the system but an inherent feature of it and that "crises" are destined to become more frequent, more severe, and more disorganizing, until the whole system crashes in catastrophic collapse.

The Great Depression which began in 1929 has indeed assumed worldwide and catastrophic proportions, and if it has not borne out all the gloomy predictions of pessimists, it has at least set at nought the efforts of economists, business men and statesmen to cope with it. It has been more severe and prolonged than any previous crisis and more nearly world-wide in its scope. It has exhibited in exaggerated form the general symptoms characteristic of all such depressions. Everywhere it grew out of the boom period of 1924–1928, marked by rising or stationary price levels, a great increase in almost all lines of production, high wages, huge profits, tremendous investments at home and abroad, credit expansion, and wild speculation in securities. Sales began declining in 1929 as markets became incapable of absorbing the flood of goods, even under the impetus of installment purchasing, long-term credits, and high-pressure advertising. Declining sales brought declining production and price cutting. The lofty structure of inflated credit and security values began to topple. The New York stock market panic of October–November, 1929, initiated a prolonged and progressive collapse of security prices which brought ruin to millions of speculating investors. Commodity prices and production began to decline rapidly. Factories closed, wages fell, unemployment increased, and purchasing power fell more swiftly than prices. In a desperate effort to save something of their vanishing markets, producers and distributors cut prices still more severely and deflation proceeded at an accelerated rate. All fixed obligations became increasingly difficult to meet. Banks closed, corporations became insolvent, tax revenues declined while millions of hungry unemployed clamored for relief. The collapse of the *Credit-Anstalt* of Vienna in the spring of 1931 presaged new disasters in Europe. The great industrialized nations—Germany, Great Britain, and the United States—were gripped by economic paralysis. Governmental deficits became enormous. Emergency measures were of no avail, and even the abandonment of the gold standard and the inflation of the currency in many countries were without effect. By the summer of 1932, the fall of price levels had apparently stopped for certain commodities, but countless millions were without work and wages, and recovery of production and trade was not in sight.

To the workers struggling along on a dole, or subject to the mercies of private and local charity, to the farmer whose mortgage is foreclosed because the prices of his crops net him no money with which to meet payments, to the business man forced into bankruptcy, and to the banker whose folly or indiscretion has led to the disappearance of depositors' money in worthless investments, it may appear a far cry from the depression to international politics. But to the exporter, the importer, the foreign investor, the diplomat, and the reflective observer of world affairs, the problems of the economic order and those of the political order, national and international, are inseparably linked together. The economic crisis is deserving of the careful consideration of the student of international politics, not merely because the power of States rests upon economic resources and productivity, but because the crisis is both a cause and a result of the policies of governments in their dealings with one another. Economic nationalism in all its aspects has played a large rôle in precipitating the crisis, and governments confronted with ruin have reacted defensively by becoming more nationalistic and mercantilistic than ever. In this fashion they have aggravated the conditions they have striven to ameliorate. The frenzied diplomacy of the depression period has centered about problems created by the crisis: vanishing gold reserves, the postponement or repudiation of public and private debts, barriers to trade, disappearing markets, dumping, social unrest and revolution. All national efforts to deal with the crisis have not only failed to achieve the expected results, but in many cases have actually worsened the situation. There has been general agreement that only international efforts can be effective. International efforts require cooperation between governments still primarily interested in national power and prestige and in the profits of their own nationals. Such cooperation is difficult to achieve and is often ineffective because of its halting and hesitant character.

It should, of course, be borne in mind that while the crisis of capitalism is international in scope, it is due no less to the malfunctioning of capitalistic economy within each State than to the effects of economic nationalism upon international trade and investment. If there existed anywhere in the world (as there does not) a land with a capitalistic economic system completely isolated and insulated from all contact with other countries, it is certain that that land would experience booms, depressions, panics, bankruptcies, unemployment, and most of the other ills to which capitalism is heir—for these ills are seemingly inherent features of an economy resting upon private property, private profits, and individual initiative. The same phenomena would doubtless appear in a genuine world capitalism in which nations and economic nationalism had been eliminated. The pattern of economic relations typified by Samuel Insull and Ivar Kreuger would appear in both so long as the institutions and incentives of capitalism remained what they are at present. Both of these situations are as hypothetical, however, as those with which classical and neo-classical economists habitually deal. There is no national capitalistic economy which is isolated from others, for every nation is more or less dependent upon its neighbors for goods, capital, or markets. There is no true world capitalism in twentieth century civilization, for that civilization is divided into sovereign States, each of which imposes obstacles to the free flow of goods and capital across frontiers, in the interests of national self-sufficiency and the profits of its own entrepreneurs. The crises of capitalism within each national society are aggravated by the increasing integration of the international economy and by the consequences for each State of power politics and profit economics on a world-wide scale. So long as the bourgeois governments are incapable of dealing successfully with the economic problems which arise within their own jurisdictions, it is not probable that they can deal effectively with international economic problems. But the most serious symptoms of capitalism's sickness arise from economic nationalism and from its international economic consequences— and governments must necessarily strive to cope with them as best they can.

This problem will persist, regardless of the outcome of the present crisis. It is the central problem of the world economy of the modern age. The survival of that economy hinges upon its solution. While it cannot here be analyzed in all its aspects, it will be profitable to deal with it as it relates to trade and tariffs and to debts and investments, public and private. In all of its phases, the problem is one of achieving a sufficient degree of collaboration between national governments to overcome the worst results of national economic self-seeking. International difficulties

[543]

permit only of international solutions. Whether the problem can be dealt with effectively by governments at all, so long as private capitalism persists in its present form, whether international solutions, if reached, will prove adequate to the exigencies of the crisis, are necessarily open questions. But the prospects cannot be estimated without some consideration of the national and international solutions which are being attempted.

2. TRADE AND TARIFFS

Each State acting alone has employed every means at its disposal to escape the effects of the crisis—constant increases in customs duties, surtaxes, prohibitions, quotas, and exchange control. It seems as if everywhere the aim has been to reduce imports, and the result has been an inevitable reduction in exports. The consequences of this policy of restriction have been fatal. . . . There is thus definite proof that no country can alter the course of economic evolution to its own advantage by the use of its own resources. Only concerted action and international solidarity can remedy the ills from which the world is suffering. It is time for solidarity to be shown otherwise than by words.—KING ALBERT of Belgium, June 19, 1932.

The origins of neo-mercantilism and the increasing prevalence throughout the world of prohibitive tariff policies have been considered above.[1] The economic result of these policies has likewise been suggested. If the entrepreneurs and merchants of each nation, with the support of patriots and politicians, induce their governments to bar out foreign goods to enhance producers' profits and promote national self-sufficiency, the exchange of goods across national frontiers becomes increasingly difficult. If protectionism is pushed to its logical limit, each State will exclude all imports from other States while it continues its efforts (obviously vain in such a situation) to market its own exports abroad. Under such circumstances, all international trade will be strangled and all the national economies will be left to suffocate within their closed compartments. In point of fact, this state of affairs has never quite been reached, though the western States seemed to be approaching it at the close of 1932. Normally, each government has a sufficient interest in keeping foreign markets open for its own nationals to induce it to keep open its own markets for foreigners, providing the requisite *quid pro quo* can be secured. Here is a basis for bargaining and a reciprocal exchange of favors. If in a particular case another State cannot be induced to grant tariff concessions, discriminatory or penalty duties may be resorted to. If the other State retaliates in kind, a "tariff war" results until one side or the other yields and strikes a bargain. As many such bargains and special arrangements can be entered into as there are States in the world and commodities entering into international trade.

[1] See pp. 350–360 above.

Many of the continental States of Europe, Germany and France among them, have regularly provided for two sets of tariff duties on each imported commodity, with the maximum duties charged against States failing to enter into special bargains and the minimum duties levied against other States. The American tariff system has for the most part been based upon a single set of duties, supplemented by reciprocity treaties with certain favored countries and by discriminatory duties against others refusing to afford favorable treatment to American commerce. Under the terms of the Elgin-Marcy Treaty of 1854, Canada and the United States entered into a special reciprocity bargain whereby each granted certain reductions in duties on goods imported from the other. This treaty was terminated in 1865 and was not renewed. The Canadian Government rejected the American reciprocity treaty of 1911. In 1875 the United States entered into a similar arrangement with the Hawaiian Islands (then independent), whereby Hawaiian sugar was admitted, duty free, to the United States. The treaty of 1902 with Cuba likewise admitted Cuban sugar at greatly reduced rates. The McKinley tariff of 1890 provided for penalty duties against countries discriminating against American commerce, but they were applied only to such small, weak States as Colombia, Venezuela, and Haiti. The Payne-Aldrich tariff of 1909 provided for maximum and minimum duties, but they were never applied. The tariff acts of 1922 and 1930 empowered the President to raise or lower duties in accordance with the recommendations of the tariff commission and to impose retaliatory duties. Tariff bargaining and discrimination of this kind have led to innumerable "tariff wars," such as those between Germany and Russia, 1893, Germany and Spain, 1894, Germany and Canada, 1897–1910, France and Italy, 1889–1899, France and Switzerland, 1893–1895, France and Great Britain, 1931, Great Britain and the Irish Free State, 1932, and the United States and the world since 1930. Such conflicts are costly and often disastrous to importers and exporters, and they breed diplomatic friction between the States engaging in them.

Out of this situation there emerged at an early period the "most-favored-nation" clause of commercial treaties, as a partial solution of the problem. Commercial treaties, *i.e.*, agreements setting forth the conditions of trade between the two signatory States, are of great antiquity. In the ancient State Systems and in the medieval and early modern period of the Western State System, they usually consisted of special bargains between the parties. As trade expanded, the resulting confusion of bilateral favors and discriminations became increasingly burdensome. State A might charge one rate of duties on a commodity coming from State B, another rate on the same commodity coming from State C, still a third rate on goods coming from State D, and so on, depending on the specific terms of its agreements with these States. It might also charge widely different rates of duties on different commodities. There was no uniformity in duties charged and no pretense of equity in tariff making. Each State made the most favorable bargains possible and discriminated against other States which would make no bargains or less favorable bargains. All States gradually recognized that this situation was advantageous to none and began incorporating into their commercial treaties reciprocal pledges whereby each signatory agreed to afford to the commerce of the other as favorable treatment as it granted to any "most favored" third State. The purpose of the most-favored-nation clause was to minimize special bargains and favors and to eliminate discrimination. To the degree to which States were bound by such clauses, general equality of commercial treatment was assured. Each State was bound to accord equal treatment in tariff duties and commercial regulations to the trade of all other States with which it had concluded such treaties. Some commercial treaties have gone beyond this and provided for "national treatment," *i.e.*, treatment of aliens as favorable as that granted to citizens. But national treatment has been limited for the most part to taxation and navigation rules and has little direct bearing on import or export duties.

During the nineteenth and early twentieth centuries, the American Government always adhered to the so-called "conditional" or "American" form of the most-favored-nation clause, in contrast to the "unconditional" or "European" form. The conditional form was incorporated into the first commercial treaty concluded by the United States—that with France of February 6, 1778—and was repeated, expressly or by implication, in all American commercial treaties prior to the Harding administration. Article 2 of the French treaty granted reciprocal most-favored-nation treatment, "in respect of commerce and navigation . . . freely, if the concession was freely made, or on allowing the same compensation if the concession was conditional." The American form of the most-favored-nation clause opened the door wide to extensive discriminations and to a large number of special bargains. Its meaning can be clarified by a hypothetical instance. If the United States should grant a reduction of tariff duties on wine imported from Spain, France might, under the terms of the treaty article quoted above, claim a similar reduction on French wines entering the United States. If the United States had freely granted the reduction to Spain, *i.e.*, without Spain paying a price in the form of some reciprocal reduction on imports coming from the United States, France would presumably be entitled to the same reduction, though even here the United States might, in its tariff legislation, distinguish between French and Spanish wines and refuse to regard them as the same commodity. But if Spain, let us say, had reduced its duties on

American raw cotton as the *quid pro quo* for more favorable American treatment of Spanish wine,'France would not be entitled to the same favor without paying the same price. The French Government would then be obliged to reduce its duties on American raw cotton in order to claim from the United States as favorable treatment as was being accorded to Spain.

The American State Department, however, always reserved the right to decide for itself what compensation was identical or equivalent. If it happened, in the hypothetical case suggested, that Spain imported large quantities of American raw cotton while France imported none, the American Government might refuse to regard a reduction of French cotton duties as equivalent to the Spanish reduction and it might refuse to reduce its duties on French wines until France made some other compensation in reduced duties on some commodity other than cotton. This interpretation of the most-favored-nation clause led to endless wrangling over "equivalence of compensation." The tariff history of the United States, and of other States adhering to the conditional interpretation, is filled with special bargains, inequalities of treatment, diplomatic protests and recriminations, and an amount of friction and misunderstanding out of all proportion to the advantages derived from this evasion of the fundamental purpose of most-favored-nation treatment.

In 1923 the United States abandoned the conditional form of the most-favored-nation clause in its new commercial treaties with Brazil and Germany. The American Government has subsequently adhered to the European or unconditional form. Under this form, which is now almost universal, each party agrees to levy against the commerce of the other "no higher or other duties, conditions, or prohibitions" than are imposed on the same commodity imported from or exported to any other foreign country. Any favor granted to a third State "shall simultaneously and unconditionally, without request and without compensation, be extended" to the same commodity of the other signatory party. These provisions are incorporated in the usual language in Article 7 of the German-American treaty, signed December 8, 1923, and proclaimed on October 14, 1925:

Each of the high contracting parties binds itself unconditionally to impose no higher or other duties or conditions and no prohibition on the importation of any article, the growth, produce, or manufacture, of the territories of the other than are or shall be imposed on the importation of any like article, the growth, produce, or manufacture of any other foreign country.

Each of the high contracting parties also binds itself unconditionally to impose no higher or other charges or other restrictions or prohibitions on goods exported to the territories of the other high contracting parties than are imposed on goods exported to any other foreign country.

Any advantage of whatsoever kind which either high contracting party may extend to any article, the growth, produce, or manufacture of any other foreign country shall simultaneously and unconditionally, without request and without compensation, be extended to the like article the growth, produce, or manufacture of the other high contracting party.[1]

It should be observed that the most-favored-nation clause is aimed at preventing discriminations and has no effect whatever upon the height of tariff walls. Under its provisions a State may levy as high duties on imports as it likes or prohibit them altogether, so long as the duties or prohibitions are applied equally to all States enjoying most-favored-nation treatment. The application of duties is dealt with in commercial treaties, but the level of duties is ordinarily a "domestic question" beyond the control of other States. The most-favored-nation clause has been only partially effective in achieving even the limited objective of equality of treatment. Neighboring States still find it advantageous to make special bargains with one another involving discrimination against third States. Such discriminations can be effected either by exceptions incorporated in treaties or by sundry legislative and administrative expedients. Minute classifications of commodities in tariff acts are sometimes resorted to. If Germany, for example, wishes to admit Austrian cattle duty free without according the same privilege to France, it may specify that white cattle with black spots shall be admitted free of duty while brown cattle with white spots shall be charged a tariff. The duties are in form general and non-discriminatory, but if Austrian cattle happen to fall into the first category and French into the second, Austria is granted a favor which is not extended to France. Or a State may impose quotas on imports or limit foreign-exchange operations to attain the same objective. Universal equality of treatment has never been achieved. Meanwhile tariff walls have risen steadily throughout the world.

The rising tide of protectionism is now threatening to engulf the most-favored-nation clause itself. Since the Great War, and particularly since the onset of the Great Depression, international commerce has been increasingly restricted by a variety of devices designed to bar out imports. These exaggerations of neo-mercantilism in periods of depression are a natural consequence of the purposes and motives which make for economic nationalism in times of prosperity. With prices falling, markets disappearing, and profits declining everywhere, entrepreneurs naturally seek to avert ruin by calling upon their governments for aid. To keep up prices at home they demand prohibitive restrictions on imported foreign products competing with their own wares. Competitive price cutting and "dumping," *i.e.*, selling in foreign markets at prices below the domestic

---

[1] This article makes the same arrangement for all advantages accorded by either party to the nationals, vessels, or goods of third States but excepts from these obligations purely border traffic within a ten-mile zone on either side of the customs frontiers and likewise excepts the commerce of the United States with Cuba, Panama, and other dependencies.

price or even below the cost of production, become universal. The commercial and industrial bourgeoisie of each of the nation-states strives to retain its profits, at least in its own domestic markets, by shutting out as many foreign goods as possible. Such measures lead to further price cutting by foreign competitors in an effort to surmount the new barriers, which are then in turn raised still higher. Other phenomena of depression and panic enter into the vicious circle. Governmental incomes are falling and higher import duties are imposed to raise revenue. Governmental budgets become unbalanced. The financial structure of national and international society becomes disorganized. International gold movements assume panic proportions. Each government and central banking system seeks to protect its gold reserves and to preserve the value of its currency on the international exchanges. Since imports in excess of exports must be paid for in gold—or, what is the same thing, in bills of exchange ultimately payable in gold—this apprehension over gold reserves leads to additional restrictions on imports through higher tariffs or limitations on foreign-exchange transactions.

If these efforts fail, as they did in Great Britain in September of 1931 and in a score of other States subsequently, the national currency is forced off the gold standard and specie payments are suspended. This in turn gives manufacturers and exporters in countries off the gold standard a competitive advantage in markets where prices are still quoted in gold, since domestic prices and costs usually rise less rapidly in such countries than the exchange value of their currencies abroad declines. Imports into the non-gold standard countries are discouraged and exports are encouraged. States still clinging to the gold standard raise new barriers to trade to protect themselves from these effects. Furthermore, States whose governments or bankers owe large sums abroad (for example, Germany and Great Britain in the 1929–1933 period) are obliged to default or to do all in their power to maintain an export surplus out of which the interest and principal on foreign loans can be paid without depressing the exchange rates and demoralizing the national currency. Inasmuch as they cannot expand exports because of foreign restrictions and declining markets, they are obliged to restrict imports. The net result of these policies is a pathological exaggeration of economic nationalism, paralyzing foreign trade and aggravating the very evils which it is designed to remedy.

The specific measures whereby these policies are carried out and the consequences flowing therefrom are too painfully familiar to require elaborate description. The United States set the pace for other States to follow by enacting the Smoot-Hawley Tariff Act of 1930. This act was followed by foreign retaliation and by a catastrophic decline in international trade. During the first six months of 1929 the United States exported goods to the value of $2,623,200,000. During the same period of 1932 American exports amounted to only $841,800,000. American exports thus fell 67.8 per cent in this period, while imports fell 62.1 per cent. During 1931 as compared with 1930, American exports fell 36.9 per cent, British exports 31.8 per cent, French 29.0 per cent, German 20.2 per cent, and Japanese 22.9 per cent. Creditor countries generally experienced a larger loss of exports than imports, while debtor countries curtailed their imports by a larger percentage than their exports declined. In the American revenue act of 1932 additional import duties were imposed on lumber, copper, coal, and oil. Great Britain resorted to "temporary" protectionism in the autumn of 1931 and on March 1, 1932, imposed a general 10 per cent ad valorem duty on imports, with other increases to follow as a result of the agreements considered at the Imperial Economic Conference at Ottawa during the summer. The French Government not only increased its import duties, but restricted imports by a system of quotas on a large variety of manufactured and semimanufactured articles. On September 6, 1932, Germany adopted a new scale of tariff duties, in many cases 100 per cent higher than those hitherto prevailing. Everywhere, among great and small Powers alike, similar prohibitions, quotas, licensing systems, foreign-exchange restrictions, and other insurmountable trade barriers were resorted to, all in the face of such a rapid rate of decline in international trade as to threaten its complete disappearance in the absence of a recovery of prices and markets.

This situation, which presents in exaggerated form the same tendencies operating in more normal times, has led to a frenzied quest for salvation through the same remedies (again in exaggerated form) attempted earlier. These remedies may be classified into three categories: (1) purely national remedies, consisting for the most part of carrying economic nationalism to its logical conclusion; (2) international remedies through bargains of various kinds between particular States or groups of States; and (3) international remedies through efforts at world-wide agreements between all States to deal with world-wide problems. The first type of remedy defeats its own purpose and cures the maladies of international trade by killing the patient. The second type of remedy has been widely resorted to, with only moderate success. On the whole it would seem to create more problems than it solves. The third type of remedy offers in the abstract the only promising way out of the dilemma, but the difficulties in the way of its application have thus far proved insuperable. Each of these efforts at recovery must be briefly considered if the prospects are to be evaluated with any degree of accuracy.

The forms and purposes of purely national action have already been suggested. Each national government strives to safeguard the domestic market for its producers by restricting imports. It may likewise grant favors or subsidies to exporters in the hope of retaining its foreign markets. But exports will vanish in proportion as imports are made impossible, for it is an axiom of international trade that he who does not buy, neither shall he sell. Retaliatory tariffs and restrictive measures on the part of other States will tend to destroy export markets. Each State is thus compelled to see its foreign trade approach the vanishing point and to have national economic self-sufficiency thrust upon it whether it will or no. In the period of the Great Depression the term "autarchy" has come into general use in Europe to describe such a self-contained national economy. It need scarcely be pointed out that this solution tends toward the abolition of international trade and is acceptable only to States which are prepared to forego the advantages of geographical specialization and to accept lower living standards for their populations. In the world economy of the twentieth century, no nation, however large and rich in resources, can sever its economic contacts with others without paying an enormous price. The United States is perhaps more nearly self-sufficient than any other country, but it is obliged to import tin, chromium, manganese, nickel, rubber, and dozens of other products not available in sufficient quantities in the United States to supply domestic needs. On the other hand, its economy is organized on the assumption that 20 per cent of its wheat crop, 40 per cent of its tobacco, 60 per cent of its cotton, and considerable proportions of other products will be sold in foreign markets. It has often been pointed out that less than 10 per cent of the total annual production of exportable commodities in the United States is sold abroad, but this margin is just sufficient to make the difference between prosperity and depression. The United States could not dispense with its foreign markets without disorganizing completely its whole economic structure and returning to a standard of life far below that now prevailing. Smaller and poorer States would obviously suffer even more severely from efforts at achieving autarchy. The uneven distribution of basic raw materials and the economic interdependence of nations renders this solution impossible. Those who advocate it preach a counsel of despair.

If national action is inadequate, international action must be resorted to. Tariff bargains between individual States have long been part of the established commercial policy of nations. In periods of crisis such bargains become more advantageous than ever, for when all States are raising barriers to trade, special arrangements between neighbors may be the means of economic survival. These arrangements, in their most limited form, consist of agreements for reciprocal reductions of duties or of mutually beneficial import quotas. The French quotas of 1932 were designed to afford more favorable treatment to States granting a *quid pro quo* to French export trade than to others. Great Britain, Germany,

Holland, and Belgium accordingly received more advantageous quotas than the United States. The German-Rumanian preferential tariff agreement of 1931 was motivated by similar considerations. The new German tariff duties of 1933 were especially high on goods imported chiefly from the United States. The new States of the Danube area have suffered severely from prohibitive tariff walls, since the area of old Austria-Hungary, within which trade moved freely, is now cut up into five nations, each bent upon autarchy for itself. Austria is especially hard hit, for its economic life was organized for a free-trade market of 54,000,000 people. Since the war Austria has been faced with the impossible task of readjusting its economy to a market of 6,000,000 people, for its trade with Hungary, Czechoslovakia, and Jugoslavia is seriously impeded by tariff barriers. The proposal for a Danubian customs federation has not yet been realized, though a plan for tariff preferences in this area was worked out of the Stresa Conference of September, 1932, subject to final approval at the proposed World Economic Conference of 1933.

Other customs unions have from time to time been established, with more or less satisfactory results. This is the most extreme form of bilateral arrangement for the reduction of trade barriers, for it involves the complete abolition of protective duties along the frontiers between the parties involved. Luxemburg maintained a customs union with Germany prior to the Great War and has since formed a similar union with Belgium. Leichtenstein maintained a customs union with Austria-Hungary prior to 1914 and has joined Switzerland in such an arrangement in the post-war period. Such unions have also existed between Italy and San Marino, and between France and Monaco. Other instances are to be found in the relations between Poland and Danzig, France and the Saar, the city of Geneva and the French districts of Gex and Savoy,[1] Syria and Palestine, and certain States of the Baltic region and of Latin America. At the Lausanne Conference of June, 1932, Belgium, The Netherlands, and Luxemburg signed a five-year convention for the limitation of trade barriers and for the progressive reduction of tariff duties by 10 per cent annually.

---

[1] This "free-zone" arrangement was established in 1815. An agreement of July, 1921, abolishing the zones, was rejected by a referendum vote of the Swiss electorate. The Governments at Paris and Berne differed as to whether Article 435 of the Treaty of Versailles, in stating that the zones were "no longer consistent with present conditions," had *ipso facto* abolished them. The zones were abolished by unilateral action of the French Government in 1923. The controversy was submitted to the Permanent Court of International Justice on October 31, 1924, and on June 7, 1932, following two preparatory decisions delivered on August 19, 1929, and December 6, 1930, the court held in its final opinion that France must, prior to January 1, 1934, withdraw its customs frontier and restore the zones to their 1815 status. See p. 892 below.

The greatest difficulty encountered in the formation of customs unions, apart from the objections of producers in each State, who fear lower profits as a result of free competition, arises out of considerations of political power. Customs unions are often preludes to the political fusion of the parties, as was the German Zollverein of 1833 and the Austro-Hungarian union of 1851. Post-war Austria has sought salvation in a customs union with Germany. The projected union announced in March, 1931[1] was assailed by France, Italy, Belgium, Czechoslovakia, and Jugoslavia, less for economic reasons than because it was regarded as a step toward Austro-German political union, which is forbidden by the Treaties of Versailles and St. Germain. Neither Italy nor the French bloc can permit such an *Anschluss*, for it would create a Germany of 70,000,000 people, completely surrounding western Czechoslovakia and stretching from the North and Baltic seas to the Tyrolean Alps and the Hungarian plain. The objecting States argued that the proposed arrangement was contrary to the Treaty of St. Germain and to the financial protocol of 1922,[2] forbidding Austria to alienate her economic independence. The controversy was carried before the Council of the League, which asked the Permanent Court for an advisory opinion. On September 5, 1931, the Court held by a vote of eight to seven that the project was unlawful under the terms of the protocol. Germany and Austria had already accepted defeat and abandoned the scheme under French financial and diplomatic pressure. In August of 1932 the Austrian Parliament reluctantly ratified a new financial protocol, providing for a League of Nations loan of $43,000,000 and forbidding all efforts at a customs union with Germany for twenty years. Austria's economic dilemma cannot be resolved in this fashion because of the power-and-prestige considerations of Great Power politics. Similar considerations have thus far blocked a Danubian customs union. Germany, Austria, and Hungary oppose any union which would place the whole Danube basin under the domination of France and the Little Entente. Italy, Poland, and Bulgaria all object for reasons of their own, while the Little Entente has no interest in a union which would not be dominated by the *status quo* bloc.

Even when schemes of customs unions and tariff preferences do not encounter such political obstacles, they are likely to be viewed with suspicion by other States left out in the cold. They frequently represent an enlargement of efforts at autarchy, rather than a diminution of such

---

[1] The proposed agreement, announced March 23, 1931, provided for the maintenance of the independence of the parties and for invitations to other States to enter into the arrangement (Article 1), for the elimination of import and export duties on traffic between the countries (Article 3), and for the abolition of import, export, and transit prohibitions (Article 7). Each State was to retain its own customs administration, however (Article 5), and the rights of third States were to be safeguarded (Articles 8, 9, 10).

[2] See pp. 125–126 above.

efforts. In almost every case they affect adversely the commerce of States not parties to the agreement. The British Imperial Economic Conference at Ottawa in the summer of 1932 affords an excellent example of such a situation. The self-governing Dominions of the British Commonwealth of Nations have long been autonomous in tariff matters, and so long as the mother country remained on a free-trade basis they imposed protective duties on goods from England as well as from other States. The adoption of protective duties by Great Britain in 1931 gave the British Government a bargaining weapon and paved the way for "imperial preference," long advocated by the Conservative party. The agreements signed at Ottawa on August 21, 1932, laid the basis for a five-year period of quotas and preferences designed to be mutually advantageous to the trade of the various parts of the Empire. The details of these arrangements are too complex to be reviewed here. Suffice it to say that the agreements—between the United Kingdom on the one hand and India, Canada, Newfoundland, Australia, New Zealand, and South Africa on the other, plus several agreements between the Dominions—represented a compromise between the economic nationalism of the Dominions and the desire of the "National Cabinet" in London to establish intra-imperial free trade. The complete attainment of this ideal, accompanied by the inevitable discriminations against trade outside the Empire, would have made the British Commonwealth a self-contained economic unit, to the great detriment of other States and probably to the detriment of the Empire itself. But the close economic ties between the Dominions and outside States (particularly between Canada and the United States), coupled with the desire of Dominion manufacturers to be protected in their domestic markets against all competitors, English as well as foreign, made an Empire customs union impossible of attainment. The limited and qualified preferences provided for are based upon agreements whereby the Dominions are to charge English manufactured goods lower duties than are charged outsiders, and Great Britain is to charge Dominion foodstuffs and raw materials less than foreigners will be obliged to pay.

Whether these arrangements will in fact promote the prosperity of imperial trade is not yet clear at the time of writing. Philip Snowden, Herbert Samuel, and other "free-trade Liberals" resigned from the National Cabinet in September, 1932, in protest against the provisions of the agreement obliging Great Britain to impose protective duties on imports from foreign States for a five-year period. It is reasonably clear that American and Argentine meats and breadstuffs, as well as Russian wheat and lumber, will be in part replaced in the English market by Australian and New Zealand meats and wheat and by Canadian wheat and lumber. American and German manufactures in the Dominions will be replaced by English manufactures, and a large variety of other foreign goods, formerly sold in the Empire, will now be discriminated against to the advantage of competing British products. It is equally clear that the Empire prices of these goods will be raised and that English and Dominion consumers will, as usual, pay the price of enhancing the profits of their protected producers. The agreements threaten not only higher prices for British consumers, but economic losses to the United States, the Soviet Union, Germany, Argentina, and other nations.

Such efforts as these to cope with the progressive paralysis of world trade resulting from economic nationalism appear likely in the long run to aggravate that paralysis and to endanger the future of the most-favored-nation clause as a device to insure equality of commercial treatment. The adverse effects of economic autarchy on international commerce are increased rather than diminished when the units striving for self-sufficiency are great blocs of States establishing preferences or customs unions between themselves, rather than individual sovereignties. It is, of course, arguable that if the blocs are sufficiently large and if trade barriers between their members are sufficiently reduced, all will gain, since large and diversified areas can conceivably become economically self-contained much more easily than single States. It is too early as yet to forecast the results of this tendency. The test to be applied is purely pragmatic. If the trade which is made possible within the customs union or preference area by the reduction of barriers is larger than the trade which is cut off by discrimination against outside States, the consequences can be adjudged advantageous. If the reverse is the case, as is not improbable in many instances, the opposite conclusion must be drawn.

In either case, the future of the most-favored-nation clause would appear to be extremely precarious. All schemes of tariff preferences, customs unions, and regional bargains, whether affecting two States as in the case of the Austro-German project, or a number of States as in the British program, or whole continents as in the "United States of Europe" proposal,[1] involve discrimination against the commerce of States not parties to the arrangement. Without such discrimination, preferences are pointless. Thus far, the most-favored-nation principle has been subtly evaded in the consummation of such schemes. In the future, commercial treaties may abandon the principle itself, unless these arrangements lead to a world-wide lowering of tariff barriers. There is already evident a tendency on the part of many States to make commercial treaties for only short periods of time and to refuse to accord most-favored-nation treatment to States maintaining prohibitive tariff walls. In the negotiations of August and September of 1932, for example,

[1] See pp. 843–844 below.

[555]

the French Government refused to sign a commercial treaty with the United States, granting unqualified most-favored-nation treatment to American commerce.[1] The emasculation of the most-favored-nation clause has already proceeded to a point which makes its final survival extremely doubtful.

There remain to be considered the efforts which have been made to deal with the problem on a world-wide scale, through established institutions and agencies of international cooperation. These efforts have necessarily centered at Geneva in the League of Nations. Since its establishment, the League has striven to facilitate trade by removing barriers and discriminations. It has championed economic interdependence, geographical specialization, capitalistic internationalism, and an unhindered flow of goods and services across national boundaries. It has opposed nationalistic parochialism, national self-sufficiency, and prohibitive tariffs and embargoes. These statements may seem paradoxical, since the League is little more than the sum of its part and its parts are national States which usually champion what the League opposes and obstruct what it proposes. But the "League" may here be taken to mean, not so much the sum of national governments as the international technical experts and economists, plus certain business men and diplomats who have adopted a new orientation. The small degree of success which these efforts have met with is in large part due to the reluctance of nationalistic governments and business men to sacrifice the immediate profits of economic nationalism for the less tangible benefits of international freedom of trade.

The early work of the League in this field was based upon what had already been done by the International Chamber of Commerce, organized in 1920. The first congress of this body was held in London in June, 1921.

---

[1] The French Commercial Federation, representing 450 syndicates and trade associations, addressed a letter to the French Government on September 5, 1932, opposing such treatment for American commerce. It declared in part: "It seems to us virtually useless to pursue negotiations with a country that does not intend to accord us any concession on its high protective tariff, while trying to obtain from us, for electoral campaigning purposes which do not interest us, the application to American products of our minimum tariff. The threat of applying to the products of our country Article 338 of the tariff act, which authorizes the President of the United States to increase the existing rates 50 per cent, does not deter us. Our answer is clear. The Americans wish an outlet for their merchandise. They need markets and France is a first-class client for them. The minute they apply Article 338 against us, our general tariff will be rigorously used against them. Should such action be necessary, you will have behind you the entire French industry and commerce. Our exports to America diminish every year and we have nothing to lose by being firm. . . . Any commercial treaty can only interest the parties involved if based on reciprocal concessions. If the Americans wish to obtain most-favored-nation treatment, they must grant us the possibility of increasing our exports to them. That is impossible until they agree to lower a certain number of clauses in their tariff which at present constitute a veritable prohibition."

The League Council, acting under Article 23 of the Covenant, had already established the Financial and Economic Committee of the League in October, 1920. In April of 1921 an international conference on communications and transit was held at Barcelona. In October–November, 1923, a conference for simplification of customs formalities was held at Geneva, and in December of the same year a second conference on communications and transit took place. Six international conventions[1] resulted from these early gatherings, but none of them touched the heart of the problem of tariff barriers. The first serious effort to grapple with the dilemma created by neo-mercantilism took the form of a World Economic Conference, held at Geneva May 4–May 27, 1927, under League auspices. At the Sixth Assembly of the League (September, 1925), M. Loucheur of France submitted a resolution calling for such a conference to investigate the obstacles to a revival of prosperity and to contribute toward the security of nations by ensuring economic peace. The Council chose a preparatory committee of thirty-five members in December, 1925, consisting of merchants, industrialists, financiers, economists, and representatives of workers' and consumers' organizations. This committee held two meetings in April and November, 1926, and prepared an agenda for the conference, largely modeled upon the agenda of the 1921 congress of the International Chamber of Commerce. The conference met in May, 1927, with 194 delegates and 226 experts from 50 States present. The United States, the Soviet Union and Turkey participated, though they were not members of the League.

The World Economic Conference worked through three committees: on commerce, on agriculture, and on industry. M. Jouhaux, representative of French labor, urged the creation of an international economic council to control world trade. M. Obolenski-Ossinsky of the Soviet Union argued that the crisis of capitalism was insoluble without a complete modification of the existing economic and social structure. M. Loucheur, whose views were shared by the conference as a whole, pointed out that the delegates could do no more than recommend the facilitation of trade and the removal of prohibitions on imports and exports. "Neither this conference nor any other body can override State sovereignty. This conference can only provide the means of economic disarmament, it cannot achieve it."[2] In the final report and resolutions of the conference, the delegates declared unanimously that "each nation's commerce is

---

[1] The General Convention on Freedom of Transit, April 20, 1921
The Convention on Régime of Navigation of Rivers, April 20, 1921
The Protocol for the Arbitral Settlement of Trade Disputes, September 24, 1923
The Convention for the Simplification of Customs Formalities, November 3, 1923
The Convention on International Régime of Railways, December 9, 1923
The Convention on Régime of Maritime Ports, December 9, 1923
[2] Proceedings of the World Economic Conference, I, p. 131.

today being hampered by barriers established by other nations, resulting in a situation, especially in Europe, that is highly detrimental to the general welfare." They further declared that "the time has come to put a stop to the growth of customs tariffs and to reverse the direction." They recommended adherence to various conventions already signed and participation in a conference for the abolition of import and export prohibitions, to be held in October, 1927. They urged stability and uniformity of tariff duties and condemned subsidies and dumping. They likewise urged national treatment of foreigners and of alien corporations. Their prescriptions were in every case merely recommendations, which were largely ignored by the governments of the participating States. In the hope of securing their adoption, the conference, acting through the League Council, enlarged the economic committee of the League and supplemented it with a consultative committee to follow up the execution of the task.

The subsequent history of League efforts in this direction is a tale of almost unrelieved failure. Thirty-six States, including the United States, participated in the conference of October, 1927. A carefully qualified convention, containing so many exceptions as to render it meaningless, was signed by 10 States on November 18, after heated controversy. A second Conference was held in July, 1928, where it was decided that ratification by 18 States would be necessary to give effect to the agreement. Twenty-six States signed the supplementary agreement to bring the convention into force, but only 17 ratified before the required date of September 30, 1929. Ten of these ratifications were conditional. A third conference met in Paris in December, 1929, where a protocol was drawn up (and signed by 16 States), permitting the convention to take effect between the parties which had ratified unconditionally. The convention was subsequently ratified by 20 States. The special conference on the abolition of import and export prohibitions on hides, skins, and bones held two sessions at Geneva in March and June, 1928 and drew up conventions ratified by 17 States, subject to Polish, Rumanian, and Jugoslav reservations, giving these States the right to levy export duties on all the items involved. A number of other conferences were called and certain additional conventions were drawn up, but most of the recommendations of the World Economic Conference remained pious hopes. In February–March, 1930, a Preliminary Conference with a View to Concerted Economic Action met at Geneva on the summons of the Council. Its original draft convention, calling for a cessation of tariff increases for one year, was rejected and on March 30, 18 States signed a commercial convention which did no more than provide for four months' delay in the denunciation of bilateral commercial treaties. In November, 1930, a second conference assembled in Geneva for the same purpose. In the interval the United States, Australia, India, New Zealand, Germany, Czechoslovakia, Poland, Jugoslavia, Rumania, Hungary, Italy, Greece, Sweden, and Lithuania had raised their tariff duties. Projects of a tariff truce failed of adoption and the conference broke up in disagreement. Neither was any success achieved in dealing with export subsidies and dumping. A third conference met in March, 1931, but accomplished nothing. In the face of this formidable and futile array of conferences, delegates, experts, draft conventions, recommendations, and endless documentation, the forces of neo-mercantilism went merrily on their way to accomplish the strangulation of world trade.

During 1932 efforts were initiated, in the various European chancellories, to summon a second World Economic Conference. It was clear from past experience, however, that nothing whatever could be achieved by the conference method if the conferees were unwilling to make concessions in the interests of an agreement on constructive measures. Since no general willingness to modify policies of economic nationalism was observable, the conference was repeatedly postponed. In July the United States agreed to participate, only on condition that there be no discussion of tariff, debts, and reparations—a demand which would make the conference resemble a wedding without the bride or, more appropriately, a funeral without the corpse. The conference was expected to meet in London in the late summer. It was then deferred to November, to January, and then to the summer of 1933. The British Government meanwhile committed itself by the Ottawa agreements to higher tariffs for a five-year period, an obligation which would prevent Great Britain from making any contribution toward the success of the conference. In the United States, the Republican party in the national election campaign stood firmly for prohibitive protectionism, in the face of Democratic criticism. The Democratic candidate, Franklin D. Roosevelt, who was elected to the presidency on November 8, was committed to a reduction of tariff barriers and his victory was interpreted as a repudiation of the Republican gospel. But the Democratic party had long since ceased to be a low-tariff party, and in any case the peculiar provisions of the American constitution made action by the new administration difficult before the end of 1933. Meanwhile, tariff walls elsewhere continued to be raised to ever-greater heights, and prohibitions and restrictions on international trade multiplied almost weekly. In the early months of 1933 the only hope which existed for the success of another World Economic Conference lay in the fact that economic nationalism was wreaking such havoc with the foreign trade of all countries that international agreements to resuscitate commerce seemed the only alternative to general ruin.

3. PRIVATE LOANS AND INVESTMENTS

Guess who is out here holding a convention? The bankers! The R.F.C. fixed 'em up so they could make the trip. They are likable rascals, and now that we are all wise to 'em, and it's been shown that they don't know any more about finances than the rest of us know about our businesses (which has proved to be nothing), why, they are getting just as human as the grocery man, the druggist, or the filling-station man. This panic has been a great equalizer, it's done away entirely with the smart man. So, the bankers are here having a good time. They don't feel that they have any position to uphold. They are just a lot of Elks.—WILL ROGERS, October 5, 1932.

The economic dilemma of the contemporary world is no less closely related to movements of capital across national frontiers than to movements of goods and services. International finance, like international commerce, has been blighted by the effects upon an interdependent and highly integrated world economy of the competitive quest for private profit and the exclusive pursuit of national interests. While trade is disorganized by national barriers and restrictions, finance is disorganized by national efforts to promote capital exports without proper safeguards to lenders and borrowers and by governmental attempts to collect huge sums from other governments without accepting any equivalent in commodities. Since the Great War an enormous debt burden, public and private, has hung like a millstone about the neck of western capitalism. The disorganization of finance in the period of the Great Depression has been more complete and more disastrous than the disorganization of trade, for the lending and borrowing of money are more frequently a speculative gamble than are the buying and selling of goods. Normally, goods must at least exist before they can become the objects of commercial transactions. But the values dealt with in financial transactions sometimes prove to be entirely imaginary. Bonds, stocks, and other certificates of indebtedness, public and private, are merely neatly engraved pieces of paper. Investors and speculators purchase them with real money, earned, borrowed, or stolen, only on the assumption that they represent tangible values resulting from the safe and productive use of the money lent. If the borrowers are dishonest, if they utilize investors' money unwisely, if they are engulfed in a world-wide economic collapse, repayment cannot be made and creditors and debtors alike are confronted with bankruptcy. The neatly engraved pieces of paper then become useful only for wall decorations. The structure of inflated credit collapses, great fortunes are wiped out, small investors are ruined, confidence is destroyed, and the necessary flow of liquid capital, both within and across national boundaries, comes to a standstill. This is, in brief, the situation which has confronted all of the western nations since 1929.

A detailed analysis of the financial aspects of the crisis is obviously beyond the scope of the present work and would not be germane to its major purposes. Attention must necessarily be limited to those problems which have a direct bearing on international politics now and in the future. Consideration must be given to those policies of national governments which have contributed to the crisis and to international efforts to deal with its results. In any such discussion it is indispensable to discuss separately the problems connected with private international debts and investments and the problems arising from intergovernmental loans and financial claims. The former problems center about the activities of private lenders across national frontiers: bankers, investors, stock promoters, financiers, and entrepreneurs of all kinds. They also arise out of loans extended to foreign governments by private financial interests in capital-exporting States. The latter problems arise out of the financial transactions between governments themselves. In the past decade the most important of these problems have centered about the repayment of the war loans between the Allied and Associated governments and about the Allied effort to collect reparations from the defeated States. These problems will be examined briefly in the next section, after the problem of private loans and investments has been sketched.

The general features of international movements of private capital and of governmental efforts to control such movements have already been considered.[1] The effects of the Great War in transforming the United States from the world's largest debtor nation to the second largest creditor nation has likewise been noted. Since 1924 Americans have invested money abroad on a larger scale than the citizens of any other capital-exporting State. Inasmuch as the American Government is the greatest creditor government in the world in terms of the sums owing to it by other governments, and in as much as Americans have loaned more private capital abroad in the post-war period than the people of any other State, the position of the United States is of paramount importance in any discussion of debts and investments. The precise amount of a State's private investments abroad is always difficult to estimate, since loans and investments are made in thousands of separate private transactions. Perhaps the best estimate of American private investments abroad at the time of their greatest volume was made by Doctor Max Winkler, of the Foreign Policy Association of New York, at the end of 1930.[2] His figures in thousands of dollars are shown at top of page 562.

[1] See pp. 360–372 above.

[2] In *Recent Economic Changes in the United States* (President's Conference on Unemployment), 1929, II, p. 727, the following estimates of American investments abroad at the end of each of the years indicated is given, in millions of dollars:

1922	8,522
1923	8,775
1924	9,589
1925	10,405
1926	11,195
1927	12,187

Region	January 1, 1914	January 1, 1930	January 1, 1931
Europe	350,000	5,107,495	5,607,332
Canada	750,000	4,389,000	4,436,011
South America	100,000	2,785,825	3,013,935
The Caribbean	1,200,000	2,936,510	2,985,135
Australasia	175,000	925,837	995,051
Miscellaneous	50,000	459,385	490,790
Totals	2,625,000	16,604,052	17,528,254

The relationship between exports of capital and exports of goods, as shown by American experience, is deserving of comment. In an earlier chapter it was laid down as a somewhat dogmatic proposition[1] that no nation can, in the long run, export more than it imports. This might seem to be contradicted by the fact that the United States has exported more commodities than it has imported for every single year since 1900. Since 1915 its "favorable" balance of trade has been enormous. The result has been an inflow of gold into the country, until almost half of the world's monetary gold was held in the United States in the post-war period. This gold served to raise American price levels, though not in proportion to its increased volume, since much of the gold did not enter into general circulation or furnish a basis for monetary or credit expansion. According to the classical theory of international trade, this movement of gold and prices should have checked exports and encouraged imports. The American tariff, however, made any large increase in imports impossible. Exports continued to increase between 1922 and 1929, and the United States had seemingly accomplished the mercantilist miracle of raising itself by its economic boot-straps through maintaining a permanent excess of exports over imports. In point of fact, however, nothing of the kind had occurred. For the United States as for all States, the debit and credit sides of the total balance of international payments are equal, whatever the balance of visible commodity imports and exports may be. The United States maintained a favorable balance of commodity trade and received (in addition to gold) war-debt payments, interest on American

---

(Estimates of Ray O. Hall, Assistant Chief of the Financial and Investment Division, Bureau of Foreign and Domestic Commerce, United States Department of Commerce.)

These figures are contrasted with an estimated total of $3,700,000,000 of American securities and properties held by foreigners, i.e., foreign capital investments in the United States at the end of 1927. Discrepancies in such estimates are due to the difficulty of securing the necessary data and to varying definitions of long-term and short-term loans. The volume of short-term credits is not included in these figures and cannot be estimated with any degree of accuracy.

[1] See pp. 352-353 above.

private investments abroad, and foreign-capital investments in the United States. But these items were balanced by others on the opposite side of the ledger, representing a compensatory outflow of wealth. These debit items included expenditures of American tourists abroad, which increased steadily between 1922 and 1929, remittances sent by immigrants in the United States to relatives abroad, and interest paid to foreigners on their investments here. The largest debit item, however, consisted of new long-term investments of American capital abroad, totaling hundreds of millions of dollars for each year of the period of pre-depression prosperity.

In reducing these relationships to simple terms, it might be said that the United States financed its export surplus of commodities by lending vast sums of money to foreigners, with which they were enabled to buy American goods and to pay their debts, public and private, to the United States. The United States could refuse to accept payment in goods (by restricting imports through tariff duties) only by exporting enormous quantities of capital. Payments of interest and principal, both on these private investments and on the intergovernmental war loans, could in turn be made in neither goods nor gold, since the tariff wall restricted the inflow of goods and the available quantities of gold were insufficient. These payments were made out of new borrowings in the New York money market. Whereas Great Britain, in her period of greatest commercial and financial prosperity before the war, exported goods and capital and received payment in the form of a steady excess of commodity imports over exports (made possible by her free-trade policy), American protectionism in the post-war period has rendered such an exchange impossible for the United States and has necessitated foreign payment for American goods and for old American loans out of new American loans. This result, it should be observed, was not due to any conscious purpose or plan on the part of any government or any group of individuals. It was rather the inevitable consequence of economic nationalism acting upon the commerce and finance of a capital-exporting and goods-exporting nation. The net result has changed the ancient arrangement of borrowing from Peter to pay Paul to one of borrowing from Paul to pay Paul. Europe has borrowed from the United States in order to pay the United States. Germany has borrowed huge sums of American capital to pay reparations. The Allied nations have borrowed to pay war debts. All have borrowed to pay for American goods. Under such circumstances, a fatal day of reckoning was inevitable, for this process could continue only so long as new loans were available. When they were no longer to be had, the whole investment and credit structure crashed catastrophically. American exports of capital ceased and exports of goods declined, while the loans already made became uncollectible.

Before considering the implications of the collapse which commenced in 1929, it will be well to notice again certain aspects of the efforts of governments to promote exports of private capital.[1] Many governments, as has been noted, have directed the flow of capital abroad to serve the purposes of diplomacy and to enhance the profits of privileged financial groups without regard to considerations of security and with little appreciation of the broader economic consequences of their policies. The American State Department, in the period of the largest American lending abroad, exercised no direct control over the process but continued the policy, inaugurated in 1921, of asking bankers to consult the department on the flotation of foreign issues. Approval was given or withheld, not on the basis of the economic wisdom of the loans, but only on the basis of diplomatic considerations.[2] In 1925, however, the Department did warn bankers against excess lending to German municipalities for nonproductive purposes and called attention to the fact that reparations were a first lien on German public revenues, but its warnings were not made public until 1932. The department has consistently opposed the flotation of Soviet bonds in the United States or the extension of long-term credits to finance Soviet-American trade. Regardless of avowed purposes and disclaimers, it was inevitable that the purchasers of foreign securities

---

[1] See pp. 364–367 above.

[2] In a public statement of January 7, 1932, the State Department defended its loan policy in the following terms: "The Department of State has not passed on the security or merits of foreign loans. The sole aim of the department has been in the interests of the citizens of the United States in connection with its foreign relations. These ideas have been repeatedly communicated to the public, and the public has been made to understand that the department's action carried no implication as to government approval of loans. In fact, it may be said that no foreign loan has ever been made which purported to have the approval of the American Government as to the intrinsic value of the loan. . . . The department has never assumed responsibility for the wisdom or worth of the loans of which it was informed. Its responses avoid all judgment of the matters of business risk involved and in no way represent measurement of the merit of any foreign loan as a business proposition, either for the bankers or investors. . . . In ordinary practice the form of words employed by the Department of State in acknowledging the advance notice of contemplated loan issues has been, with immaterial variations, as follows: 'In the light of the information before it, the Department of State offers no objection to the flotation of this issue in the American market.' Or, in the very infrequent instances where some reason led the department to the contrary judgment, the department, usually after explaining the reason therefor, employed in general merely the negative of this form: 'You will, therefore, appreciate that this department is not in a position to indicate that it perceives no objection to the financing to which you refer.' This form of reply was, after a first brief period, supplemented by the further paragraph: 'You of course appreciate that, as pointed out in the department's announcement of March 3, 1922, the Department of State does not pass upon the merits of foreign loans as business propositions nor assume any responsibility in connection with such transactions, also that no reference to the attitude of this Government should be made in any prospectus or otherwise.' Beginning August, 1929, it was decided to expedite the procedure of consultation with other departments of this Government and to simplify the forms used. Replies to bankers' letters were reduced merely to a brief paragraph of acknowledgment, followed by the sentence: 'In reply you are informed that the department is not interested in the proposed financing.'"

should regard State Department approval as constituting an official judgment upon the financial merits of the loan. In the case of Latin American issues, the department at times appears to have encouraged lending for political reasons, against the better judgment of the Department of Commerce.[1] There can be little question that the State Department's attitude exercised a significant, even if somewhat intangible, influence in encouraging the huge exports of American private capital in the boom period.

The history of American dollar diplomacy in the Caribbean suggests that the Department of State has been no less interested in the profits of the bankers handling foreign security issues than in the political implications of these transactions. The methods employed in marketing foreign bonds and stocks usually ensured the immediate payment of brokers' fees and commissions and left the purchasers holding the bag in the event of default. Enormous profits accrued from these transactions, since almost any piece of paper purporting to represent a lucrative foreign investment could be easily sold during the height of the speculative mania. The net profits to American bankers from German security flotations of a value of $1,280,000,000, marketed between 1924 and 1930, amounted to $50,000,000. The prices of many of these securities were artificially "pegged" on the New York Stock Exchange during the sale, in order to promote wider buying. The State Department's warnings were not concerned with profits or marketing methods and apparently had little effect in restraining the bankers' activities, since the department made no public objections to the proposed flotations.[2] In the case of Latin American flotations, the department not only failed to warn banking houses against excessive lending, but definitely encouraged the flotation of securities. Here again there existed a mutually advantageous combination of diplomats and private profit-seekers.

So long as the market for loans appeared inexhaustible, and so long as governments and private enterprises abroad could stave off the evil day of reckoning by new borrowing, all was well. The bankers were regarded as public benefactors, enabling small investors to amass fortunes without work, and the diplomats were viewed as useful aids of the bond salesmen. But when the crash took place and foreign security values

[1] In hearings before the Finance Committee of the Senate, Grosvenor M. Jones, chief of the financial and investment division of the Bureau of Foreign and Domestic Commerce, declared on January 6, 1932, that the State Department had overridden the objections of the Commerce Department in 1928 to a loan of $23,000,000 to Bolivia and a short-term credit of $20,000,000 to Colombia. Senator Carter Glass declared the State Department's apologia of January 7, 1932, a "wretched subterfuge" and asserted "it was well understood by the bankers issuing these loans that the failure of the State Department to object was tantamount to approval, and the foreign bonds were sold to investors of this country with the moral sanction of the Government."

[2] *Cf.* Robert R. Kuczynski, *Bankers' Profits from German Loans,* 1932.

descended dizzily toward the vanishing point, the "international bankers" forthwith became villains and the diplomats became fools or worse in the eyes of the millions of investors faced with ruin. Much of the criticism heaped upon the State Department and Wall Street in the United States —and upon other foreign offices and banking groups elsewhere—was unjustified in its implications. Bankers and diplomats are not gifted with omniscience or powers of prophecy to any greater degree than other mortals, nor do they possess any social purposes or any insight into the economic realities of modern finance proportionate to the power which they exercise. Those who lose through their activities are usually not victims of anything which can be regarded as dishonesty or misrepresentation by the standards of business ethics prevalent in a competitive economic order of advertisers and salesmen. But the sting is no less sharp. So long as gullible investors are fleeced by the results of the profit-and-power propensities of financiers and foreign offices, such resentment is inevitable, and the foundations of confidence and security upon which the credit structure of capitalism rests are endangered by the consequences.

The major features of the collapse of foreign investments since the onset of the Great Depression are well known. Under the impetus of the drive for profits, lenders besought borrowers to borrow more and still more, until an enormously inflated volume of long-term investments and short-term credits was created out of all proportion to the possibilities of productive use. When world price levels began to fall—slowly at first in 1929 and 1930, and then with great rapidity—all fixed obligations became increasingly burdensome on debtors. A debt of $1,000, whether incurred by a government, a corporation, or an individual, becomes equivalent to a debt of $1,500 if the prices of the goods and services exchangeable for money are cut in half and each dollar becomes $1.50 in terms of purchasing power. Profits disappear, wages decline, unemployment increases, and general bankruptcy impends. Governmental revenues fall off, while the burden of fixed public-debt charges becomes heavier owing to the falling price level. Emergency expenditures are required to relieve unemployment and budgetary deficits are incurred. Unless tax revenues are increased or expenditures are decreased or more money is borrowed (and governments find all of these measures increasingly difficult to execute in periods of deflation), gold is withdrawn from central banks and national currencies are endangered. Under such pressure, the final desperate expedient of abandoning the gold standard must sometimes be resorted to. The resulting devaluation of the currency amounts to a partial repudiation of all fixed obligations payable in paper money. Debtor nations become unable to pay their public and private debts, and the whole structure of international finance is disorganized.

All of these distressing phenomena took place in the Great Depression. The crash in central Europe made the repayment of loans impossible, and the British and American bankers who had invested heavily in public and private securities in this region were unable to collect on their loans. Under the pressure of gold withdrawals, Great Britain was forced off the gold standard in September, 1931, and was subsequently obliged to convert the public debt into bonds bearing lower interest rates. Many other States were caught in the same dilemma. Creditors were forced to extend new loans to safeguard themselves from complete loss on the old. Over a billion dollars' worth of American investments in Latin America were defaulted or repudiated. Many European loans were defaulted or tied up by "standstill agreements." Efforts were made by debtors to reduce interest payments and even principal on their obligations and creditors were reluctantly compelled to acquiesce. The private debts of Germany alone as of January 1, 1933, were estimated at $4,912,000,000, of which about 40 per cent was held in the United States. If the value of real property and stocks and bonds owned by foreigners in Germany is included in such an estimate, the total is $6,193,000,000. With the exclusion of these items from the estimate, it was calculated that the short-term credits amounted to $2,418,000,000, of which $1,702,000,000 was owed to foreign banks. The long-term credits were estimated at $2,494,000,000, of which $301,000,000 were held by foreign banks.[1] Payments were deferred on many of these obligations and no means of repayment in full were in sight at the close of 1932. It appears probable that a large proportion of the foreign investments of the United States and other capital-exporting States will be permanently lost before the process of deflation has run its course.

The general effects of this situation on international commerce have been disastrous, particularly for the exports of creditor countries with high tariff walls. Only seven States (the United States, Great Britain, France, Belgium, The Netherlands, Sweden, and Switzerland) are at present owed more abroad in public and private accounts than they themselves owe. During 1931 all of these States save Belgium experienced larger declines in exports than in imports, with the United States heading the list with a 36.9 per cent decline in exports as compared with a 31.7 per cent decline in imports. Almost all of the debtor States have restricted their imports to such a degree that they have declined more rapidly than have exports.[2] The United States, as the largest exporter of goods and

[1] Estimate of the National Industrial Conference Board, New York *Times*, October 2, 1932.

[2] The decline in the *volume* of imports and exports has of course been very much less than the decline in their monetary *value*, because of falling price levels. *Cf.* Charles Merz' "America's Foreign Trade," New York *Times*, July 31, 1932: "What has been happening is a fundamental readjustment in which the debtors—backed against the wall by circum-

capital, has suffered most severely from these circumstances. Its "favorable" balance of trade, financed by lending to foreign importers, can no longer be maintained in this fashion. The old loans are in default, new ones cannot be made, and foreign trade is greatly reduced because the American tariff wall makes impossible a redressing of the balance through payment in imports.

For the United States and for other countries in a similar position, there would appear to be only four ways out of this dilemma: (1) a resumption of large-scale lending abroad to finance new purchases of exports; (2) a complete abandonment of foreign markets in favor of autarchy and economic self-sufficiency; (3) a drastic reduction of tariff barriers on imports to make possible payment in goods for exports and for capital investments; or (4) the cancellation or drastic reduction of public and private foreign debts. The first solution appears to be a financial impossibility at present and for many years to come. The second would lead to a great reduction of living standards and possibly to permanent economic depression in the United States. The third would be advantageous in the long run, but would mean immediate losses to protected industries. The political obstacles in the way of its achievement are probably insuperable. The fourth would be even more painful and would be a confession of the bankruptcy of capitalistic economy. Which of these solutions, or what combination of solutions, will be adopted is not yet clear. The fourth is perhaps the most likely to be resorted to, with the second not beyond the realm of possibility.

stances, unable to obtain new loans, called upon to make large payments on old ones owed abroad, finding it increasingly difficult to pay in terms of goods because of higher tariffs, possessing little gold with which to pay and striving desperately to hold what small amounts of gold remain, in order to support their sagging currencies—have attempted to balance their national accounts by deliberate and drastic reduction in purchases from their creditors. As one of the largest creditors, the United States has felt the full force of this pressure in the loss of markets for its goods."

4. REPARATIONS AND INTERGOVERNMENTAL DEBTS

"Cheshire-Puss," Alice began. . . "would you tell me please which way I ought to go from here?" "That depends a good deal on where you want to go," said the Cat. "I don't much care where—" said Alice. "Then it doesn't matter much which way you go," said the Cat. "—so long as I get *somewhere*," Alice added as an explanation. "Oh, you're sure to do that," said the Cat, "if only you walk long enough. . . In *that* direction lives a Hatter; and in *that* direction lives a March Hare. Visit either you like: they're both mad." "But I don't want to go among mad people," Alice remarked. "Oh, you can't help that," said the Cat, "we're all mad here. I'm mad, you're mad." "How do you know I am mad?" said Alice. "You must be," said the Cat, "or you wouldn't have come here."—LEWIS CARROLL, *Alice in Wonderland*.

While these problems of private debts have been the subject of protracted negotiations, the intergovernmental obligations arising out of the Great War have been of more direct and immediate interest to the foreign offices. These obligations fall into two general categories: (1) loans between the Allied and Associated Governments for the purpose of prosecuting the war and (2) indemnity payments or "reparations" imposed upon Germany by the victors at the close of the conflict. In consequence of the war loans, the peace terms, and the debt-funding agreements, obligations from government to government of many billions of dollars were incurred. The total volume of these obligations was entirely unprecedented, and the economic and financial problems involved in their payment were of unparalleled magnitude and complexity. The story of fifteen years of negotiations and controversy over inter-Allied debts and reparations can be conveniently divided into five periods: (1) from the Peace Conference, 1919, to the Dawes Plan, 1924; (2) from the Dawes Plan to the Young Plan, 1929; (3) from the Young Plan to the Hoover moratorium, 1931; (4) from the Hoover moratorium to the Lausanne Conference, 1932; and (5) from the Lausanne Conference to the final collapse of the whole debt structure.

It is essential in the first instance to emphasize certain elementary economic facts regarding intergovernmental debt payments which were familiar enough to economists in 1919, but which were lost sight of by diplomats and politicians because of ignorance or the dictates of political expediency. If the government of State A is obliged to pay money to the government of State B, its first problem is that of raising the necessary funds within State A out of taxes or loans. State A's ability to accomplish this is obviously the primary measure of "capacity to pay." But the raising of the funds in State A does not of itself ensure payment. The funds will be in the currency of State A, while State B wishes payment in its own currency. If State B is willing to accept goods in payment, State A

may place the funds at its disposal for the purchase of such goods within *A*'s frontiers. They may then be transported to *B* and the obligation will be discharged by this transaction. In all probability, however, State *B* will refuse goods in any large quantity, for an inflow of goods will lower prices and cause State *B*'s producers to demand protection from such a catastrophe. State *B*'s consumers will usually have nothing to say in reaching this decision. At the same time, State *B*'s politicians and tax-payers will demand payment. State *A* must then pay in gold. But gold stocks are quite insufficient to meet payments of the magnitude of those in question. State *A* will in fact pay in bills of exchange, ultimately redeemable in gold, which is normally the only international medium and measure of value. With the funds it has raised in its own currency, the government of State *A* will purchase bills or drafts payable in *B*'s currency, or in the currency of some third State, and ultimately redeemable in gold. Such bills will be available for purchase in State *A* in proportion as State *A*'s exporters have sold abroad more than its importers have bought. Unless State *A* maintains a "favorable" balance of trade of sufficient magnitude to meet debt payments, its government cannot transfer funds to *B* by purchasing foreign exchange, without upsetting the exchange rates to its own disadvantage. If bills on *B* are not available in sufficient amount, the purchases by the government of *A* will increase their price, *i.e.*, will raise the value of *B*'s currency as measured in *A*'s currency on the international exchanges. *A*'s currency will decline in international exchange value and *A*'s whole monetary system will become demoralized, along with its commerce and industry. In the last analysis, payment can be made only in goods—if not in goods shipped to *B*, then in goods sold to outside States in excess of what is purchased. If international payments are not to prove disastrous to the payer, they must involve an export surplus. But an export surplus on the part of the payer is likely to be viewed with alarm by the payee, who erects tariff walls to keep out the payer's goods and resents any invasion of outside foreign markets by the payer in competition with his own exports. Here, in brief, is the riddle of international debts. By comparison, the old problem of eating one's cake and having it too is easy of solution.

The implications of this dilemma were scarcely appreciated at the Paris Peace Conference. During the war the Allied statesmen had promised their respective electorates that Germany would be compelled to pay the bill. The atmosphere of resentment, bitterness, and popular excitement prevailing in 1919 made it politically necessary to fulfill this pledge in the terms of the treaty, regardless of the economic consequences. Fantastic figures running into hundreds of billions of dollars were bandied about at the conference, but the absurdity of expecting Germany alone to pay for the colossal costs of the conflict were recognized, even by

Clemenceau and Lloyd George. It was accordingly decided to leave the exact amount to be fixed by "experts" and to impose only a blanket obligation on Germany in the treaty. The indemnity was to be disguised as "reparations," on the popular assumption that Germany, as the aggressor, had inflicted the war upon her innocent victims. Reparation payments were to include all civilian losses, destruction of non-military property, and military pensions. Germany was likewise required to make certain payments in kind and to pay 20 billion gold marks by May 1, 1921.[1]

Under the terms of these and related clauses of the treaty, an inter-Allied Reparation Commission was set up to fix a schedule of payments. At the Spa Conference of July, 1920, the Allied Governments agreed that France was to receive 52 per cent of the German payments, Great Britain 22 per cent, Italy 10 per cent, Belgium 8 per cent, and all the other participants the remaining 8 per cent. After much wrangling, accompanied by threats, ultimatums, declarations of default, and progressive reductions of the preliminary payments, the Reparation Commission fixed a total sum, in the London Schedule of May 5, 1921, which Germany accepted under duress. The Reich was to be charged with a burden of 132,000,000,000 gold marks (about $31,680,000,000), plus the entire Belgian war debt. The payments acknowledged to date were barely sufficient to pay the costs of the Allied armies of occupation in the Rhineland. Germany would pay annually 2,000,000,000 gold marks ($476,000,000), plus 26 per cent of the value of all German exports until the bonds to be issued should be redeemed. The German Government accepted these terms under threats of the military occupation of additional German territory. The preliminary payments were made out of foreign borrowing, while German currency depreciated within the country and on the foreign exchanges.

The London Schedule broke down by the end of 1922 and Germany was declared in voluntary default by the Reparation Commission on January 9, 1923, following a succession of futile conferences marked by growing Anglo-French dissension. The French Government, having already made huge expenditures for the reconstruction of its devastated regions, was determined to compel payment in the interests of military security and budgetary solvency, as well as for the promotion of the designs of the French metallurgists and coal producers. On January 11, 1923, French and Belgian troops occupied the Ruhr Valley—the most highly industrialized region of Germany—and attempted to coerce the Reich by seizing "productive guarantees" and taking possession of coal and iron mines and steel plants. The legality of this action was contested by the German and

---

[1] See footnote 1, p. 152, above, for the "war guilt" and reparations clauses of the treaty.

British Governments.[1] The British Government refused to cooperate. The United States withdrew its troops from the Rhineland. The German Government, unable to resist this invasion of its territory by force, resorted to passive resistance and the cessation of all reparation payments. Germany's economic life was disrupted and France failed to obtain either coal, money, or security. The franc fell from 14.98 to the dollar in January of 1923 to 22.64 in February of 1924. The German mark fell from 14,285 to the dollar in January, 1923 to 4,200,000,000,000 in December. In September, 1923, as Germany plunged toward national bankruptcy, the Stresemann Cabinet abandoned passive resistance. As early as December, 1922, Charles E. Hughes, American Secretary of State, had suggested the submission of the whole problem to an impartial committee of experts. The debacle of the Ruhr adventure disposed all parties to heed this advice. The Reparation Commission appointed a committee for the purpose, presided over by Charles G. Dawes of the United States, acting as a private citizen. This committee published its report in April, 1924, and on August 16, at a conference in London, it was accepted by all of the interested governments.

The so-called "Dawes Plan" was a stop-gap arrangement, designed to give Germany a breathing spell without offending French sensibilities. It did not reduce the total of Germany's obligations or fix the number of annual payments. It did provide for the evacuation of the Ruhr, for foreign control over German finances, and for a reduced schedule of annual installments. Germany was to pay 1,000,000,000 marks during the first year following the adoption of the plan, 1,220,000,000 the second and third years, 1,750,000,000 the fourth, and 2,500,000,000 the fifth and following years, plus an increment based on an index of prosperity. These sums were to be raised out of taxes, railway bonds, and industrial debentures. A transfer committee would supervise the actual payments in such fashion as to safeguard the exchange rate and the stability of German currency. This agreement temporarily removed the problem from the sphere of acute diplomatic controversy and paved the way for the

---

[1] Paragraphs 17 and 18 of Annex II of Part VIII of the treaty declared: "In case of default by Germany in the performance of any obligation under this part of the present treaty, the commission will forthwith give notice of such default to each of the interested Powers and may make such recommendations as to the action to be taken in consequence of such default as it may think necessary. The measures which the Allied and Associated Governments shall have the right to take, in case of voluntary default by Germany, and which Germany agrees not to regard as acts of war, may include economic and financial prohibitions and reprisals and in general such other measures as the respective Governments may determine to be necessary in the circumstances." The legal controversy centered about the phrase "such other measures as the respective Governments may determine to be necessary." The Quai d'Orsay contended that this authorized the occupation of additional German territory. Berlin and London argued that this was doubtful and that in any case the "respective Governments" had reached no agreement and that unilateral action on the part of France and Belgium was not permissible.

Briand-Stresemann period of Franco-German *rapprochement*, marked by the Locarno treaties of 1925, the admission of Germany to the League in 1926, the formation of the Franco-German steel cartel, and the final evacuation of the Rhineland in June of 1930.

Meanwhile there had been much friction over the inter-Allied debts, followed by the conclusion of a series of debt-funding agreements. During the first three years of the war, the British Government had loaned large sums of money to the French, Italian, and Russian Governments for war purposes. After American entrance into the conflict, the Liberty Loan Acts passed by Congress authorized the Secretary of the Treasury to make loans to the Allied Governments for the purchase of military and civilian supplies in the United States. At the conclusion of hostilities the nominal gross total of these intergovernmental obligations had reached the huge sum of 21½ billion dollars. Additional loans for various purposes were extended after the armistice, until the total reached 28 billions of dollars by 1923. The United States was owed roughly 11½ billions and Great Britain about the same amount. The British debt to the United States reduced Britain's net credit to 3¾ billions. France owed 3½ billions net, Italy 4⅓ billions, and Russia 4½ billions. The Soviet Government repudiated the Russian war debts on the ground, among others, that Russia had not shared in the fruits of victory, and the other debtor governments manifested no enthusiasm for meeting their obligations. No interest or principal was paid to the American Government until 1923. The Allied Governments in general, and the French Government in particular, took the view that the debts should be canceled, since the United States had entered the war belatedly, grown wealthy therefrom, and suffered negligible losses. The Allied taxpayers were persuaded of the injustice of repayment and, in the event that payment was demanded, were disposed to support policies to wrest the necessary sums from Germany. In 1922 Lord Balfour, the British Foreign Secretary, offered to reduce Britain's claims on Germany, France, and Italy to the amount demanded from Great Britain by the United States. The implication of this proposal was that general cancellation might be made possible by American generosity.

These and similar suggestions fell upon deaf ears in America. Payment in full was demanded by the new Republican administration. Secretary of State Hughes denied that any connection existed between the Allied debts to the United States and German reparation payments—a legal fiction, completely divorced from financial realities, to which the American Government has consistently attempted to adhere up to the present time. The Foreign Debt Funding Act, passed by Congress and approved February 9, 1922, created a debt commission of five members to refund or convert principal and interest into bonds "in such form . . . as shall be deemed for the best interest of the United States of America," provided that the maximum time of maturity should not exceed June 15, 1947, and the minimum rate of interest should be $4\frac{1}{2}$ per cent. These conditions proved unworkable and they were subsequently modified, with congressional approval. In 1921 pressure had been brought to bear upon the debtors by the State Department through a boycott on private loans to governments refusing to refund their obligations. Negotiations commenced first with Great Britain and were pursued with other debtors on the basis of "capacity to pay." The terms of the Liberty Loan Acts and of the Foreign Debt Funding Act were departed from. The principal sums were kept intact, but the reduction of interest rates and the spreading of the payments over a period of sixty-two years amounted to a cancellation of a substantial part of the original obligations. On a $4\frac{1}{2}$ per cent interest rate, the total indebtedness would have amounted to almost $33,000,000,000. Nearly $11,000,000,000 of this total was canceled, since the debt-funding agreement provided for total principal and interest payments of $22,188,484,000.

The various agreements were signed between 1923 and 1926, and during the same period the Allied Governments adjusted their debts to one another. The American Government signed a repayment agreement with Great Britain on June 19, 1923, with Italy on November 14, 1925, with France April 29, 1926, with Belgium August 18, 1925, with Poland November 14, 1924, and with Czechoslovakia October 13, 1925. The other eleven debtors owed the United States less than $100,000,000 apiece in principal. The total of the annual installments due the American Government varied from $204,333,750 in 1929 to $406,000,000 in 1983. While these terms appeared generous to many Americans, they were resented in Europe for a variety of reasons. The American tariff wall made payment in goods impossible and rendered difficult the attainment of favorable trade balances to furnish the economic means of payment. American insistence that there was no relationship between reparation payments and debts appeared to be the sheerest casuistry. What was perhaps most galling was the fact that the United States refused to deal with the debtors collectively and applied no consistent principles in negotiating the agreements, apart from the vague criterion of "capacity to pay." Great Britain, which was the first to offer to pay, was charged 3.3 per cent interest. France, which delayed longest, was charged 1.6 per cent interest. Italy, which likewise delayed negotiations, was charged only 0.4 per cent. Poland, Czechoslovakia, and Rumania paid 3.3 per cent, Belgium 1.7 per cent, and Jugoslavia 1 per cent. The figures for payments of principal and interest are shown on page 575.

No sooner were these agreements concluded than it became apparent that Germany could not meet the Dawes Plan annuities, even out of

Country	Funded debt	Principal plus interest
Austria...................	$ 24,614,885	$ 24,614,885
Belgium...................	417,780,000	727,830,500
Czechoslovakia...........	115,000,000	312,811,433
Esthonia.................	13,830,000	33,331,140
Finland..................	9,000,000	21,695,055
France...................	4,025,000,000	6,847,674,104
Great Britain............	4,600,000,000	11,105,965,000
Greece...................	18,125,000	20,330,000
Hungary..................	1,939,000	4,693,240
Italy....................	2,042,000,000	2,407,677,500
Latvia...................	5,775,000	13,958,635
Lithuania................	6,030,000	14,531,940
Poland...................	178,560,000	435,687,550
Rumania..................	44,590,000	122,506,260
Jugoslavia...............	62,850,000	95,177,635
Total....................	$11,565,093,885	$22,188,484,877

new American (private) loans. A new committee of experts, headed by Owen D. Young of the United States, was appointed, and after months of arduous and acrimonious negotiations, its report—the Young Plan—was accepted by the Powers on June 9, 1929. The plan was designed to be "complete and final." Total German indebtedness was scaled down to $26,500,000,000, with payments to run until 1988. With interest figured at 5½ per cent, the principal of the German debt would be about $8,800,-000,000 under this scheme. Germany was to pay variable annuities, ranging from 1,707,900,000 gold marks in 1930–1931 to 2,428,800,000 gold marks in 1965–1966. The payments were so adjusted that the sums owing to the United States by the Allies would equal 65 per cent of the annual German payment. The Reparation Commission was abolished and a Bank for International Settlements was created to handle reparation transactions. Germany recovered financial autonomy and was made responsible for transfers, with a right to postpone transfers or payments for a period not exceeding two years, subject to investigation by a special advisory committee. With slight modifications, the plan was approved at the conference at The Hague of August, 1929, and was incorporated into a final act, signed at The Hague on January 20, 1930. The annual schedule of intergovernmental payments, based on the Young Plan and the inter-Allied agreements, is indicated in the following diagram, with figures in millions of dollars and fractions thereof, as of 1931, when the whole structure broke down:

These "final" settlements proved to be no more final than their predecessors. Whether the payments could have been made had "pros-

perity" continued to prevail is an academic question. Germany borrowed
more in private loans from the United States between 1924 and 1930 than
she paid in reparations, and the whole process at bottom was one whereby
the American Government collected money paid to the Allies by Germany

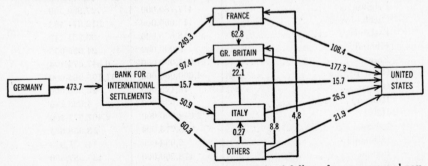

The stream of intergovernmental payments in millions of dollars of average annual payments under the Young Plan and the Interallied Debt Agreements. (*Adapted from Charles
Merz, "The War Debts Puzzle," New York Times, Nov. 1, 1931.*)

out of funds borrowed from American bankers and American purchasers
of foreign securities. The enormous sums involved represented no transfers of tangible goods and services across frontiers, but only the scribbling
of the mad bookkeepers of frenzied international finance. When this
process of paying debts by incurring still greater debts came to its
inevitable end in the crash of 1929–1931, the whole intergovernmental
debt structure collapsed, along with private credit.

American private lending to Germany came to an end in 1930. Symptoms of the depression appeared in Germany as early as the summer of
1928. The stream of American capital was already drying up as the result
of the diversion of funds for speculative purposes during the American
stock-market boom. The Wall Street debacle in the autumn of 1929 and
the onset of the Great Depression were followed by widespread bankruptcy
and unemployment. By the spring of 1931 it was clear that a gigantic
financial panic was impending in Germany and that all debts, public and
private, were jeopardized. Germany could borrow no more and her
foreign creditors were liquidating both short-term credits and long-term
investments. Further reparation payments were out of the question.
Allied debt payments to the United States likewise became impossible in
the face of budgetary deficits and disturbed exchange rates. The German
Government could apply for a moratorium under the Young Plan, but
an open confession of default at Berlin might have precipitated a financial
catastrophe. Early in June Chancellor Bruening and Foreign Minister
Curtius conferred with Ramsay MacDonald at Chequers—from which
Paris deduced that Berlin was seeking diplomatic aid from London
against France, Germany's chief creditor. Andrew Mellon, American
Secretary of the Treasury, was also in England at the time. French

irritation was increased by the fact that the Bank of England extended a temporary loan to the Austrian Government after the Quai d'Orsay had refused to permit French banks to participate in this project unless Austria definitely renounced her customs-union proposal. For Germany to seek aid from Great Britain or the United States was like the lame seeking guidance from the blind, for British and American banks were heavily involved in the impending insolvency of Germany. Of the German long-term foreign debt of $2,272,000,000, 55.2 per cent was held in the United States, 11.5 per cent in Great Britain, and only 5 per cent in France. Of the German short-term indebtedness of $2,450,000,000 (January 1, 1931), 37.1 per cent was held in the United States, 20.4 per cent in Great Britain, and only 6.5 per cent in France. The bankers and diplomats of London, New York, and Washington had a vital interest in maintaining German solvency. But the purse strings were now held by the Bank of France, which was relatively unscathed by the depression. The support of the French Government was essential to the success of any scheme of salvation.

In this critical situation, the Hoover moratorium proposal was announced on Saturday, June 20, 1931. The panic among Germany's creditors had reached such proportions that it seemed clear that most of the German banks would be unable to open on Monday morning, June 22. American bankers brought pressure to bear on Washington. After receipt of an appeal from President von Hindenburg and hurried consultations with financiers, officials, and congressmen, President Hoover announced his plan, probably with considerable reluctance in view of congressional and popular opposition in the United States to any reduction or cancellation of war debts. In his announcement he proposed "the postponement during one year of all payments on intergovernmental debts, reparations, and relief debts, both principal and interest, of course not including obligations of governments held by private parties. Subject to confirmation by Congress, the American Government will postpone all payment upon the debts of foreign governments to the American Government payable during the fiscal year beginning July 1 next, conditional on a like postponement for one year of all payments on intergovernmental debts owing the important creditor Powers." The announcement listed the Senators and Representatives who had sanctioned the plan, mentioned Messrs. Dawes and Young as having approved, and sought to soothe provincial opposition by presenting the scheme as a step toward the restoration of prosperity. The old formulas were reiterated once more:

The repayments of debts due to us from the Allies for the advances for war and reconstruction was settled upon a basis not contingent upon German reparations or related thereto. Therefore, reparations is necessarily wholly a European problem with which we have no relation.

I do not approve in any remote sense of the cancellation of the debts to us. World confidence would not be enhanced by such action. None of our debtor nations has ever suggested it. But as the basis of the settlement of these debts was the capacity under normal conditions of the debtor to pay, we should be consistent with our own policies and principles if we take into account the abnormal situation now existing in the world. I am sure the American people have no desire to attempt to extract any sum beyond the capacity of any debtor to pay, and it is our view that broad vision requires that our Government should recognize the situation as it exists.

This course of action is entirely consistent with the policy which we have hitherto pursued. We are not involved in the discussion of strictly European problems, of which the payment of German reparations is one. It represents our willingness to make a contribution to the early restoration of world prosperity in which our own people have so deep an interest.

I wish further to add that while this action has no bearing on the conference for limitation of land armaments to be held next February, in as much as the burden of competitive armaments has contributed to bring about this depression, we trust that by this evidence of our desire to assist we shall have contributed to the good will which is so necessary to the solution of this major question.

While the Hoover plan was hailed with enthusiasm in Germany, Austria, Great Britain, and Italy, it was resented by France and her allies. Next to the United States, France had most to lose by its acceptance and the French Government had not been consulted prior to its promulgation. The French reply of June 24 insisted that the Young Plan be kept intact and that Germany be required to pay into the Bank for International Settlements the non-postponable part of her reparation debt, to be used for improving general credit conditions in all countries of central Europe. There followed protracted and difficult Franco-American negotiations, ending in agreement on July 6. All intergovernmental payments were postponed from July 1, 1931, to June 30, 1932, and the German unconditional annuities were deposited in the Bank for investment in government-guaranteed German railway bonds, with the German railways passing the sums so received back to the German Government and thus relieving its budget. The shadow of the Young Plan was thus preserved, though its substance was already gone.

The immediate aftermath of the Hoover moratorium brought small comfort to those who had regarded it as the beginning of better days and of a more rational approach to the whole problem of intergovernmental obligations. A short-term credit of $100,000,000 was granted to Germany by the central banks on June 25. But the panic in Germany continued and the German Government refused to make political concessions to France as the price of French assistance, relying instead upon British and American support. Dr. Luther, president of the Reichsbank, sought loans at London and Paris, but without success. On July 14, by an ironic coincidence the French national holiday, all the banks in Germany were closed by government decree. The Reich surrendered the customs-union project with Austria in September, but too late to help the situation. The British Government meanwhile called a conference in London, July 20–23. Again Washington and London underestimated French power. Again France offered a large loan to Germany in return for political concessions. Again Germany refused to pay the price, and again the bankers and chancellories of Great Britain and the United States were helpless. The final agreement of July 23 merely recommended the renewal for three months of the $100,000,000 credit to the Reichsbank, the maintenance of existing short-term credits in Germany through "standstill" arrangements, and the convening of a committee by the Bank for International Settlements to study Germany's immediate credit needs and the possibility of converting a portion of the short-term credits into long-term credits. Withdrawals from Germany ceased and the German banks reopened. The committee met on August 8 at Basle. It was composed of ten representatives of central banks and presided over by Albert H. Wiggin, president of the governing board of the Chase National Bank and representative of the Federal Reserve Bank of New York. The "Wiggin committee" arranged for a six-months continuation of German short-term credits and urged a large long-term loan. It condemned as a "policy of obstruction" the attitude of governments which permitted the creation of huge international debts and erected high tariff walls to make payments impossible.

Not only has no progress been made toward the abandonment of the unworkable policies of economic nationalism which make the debt problem insoluble, but rising tariff walls have made the situation worse during the intervening months. The year of the Hoover moratorium witnessed an aggravation of the crisis and an intensification of the depression. Although Germany was relieved from reparation payments, she was still unable to meet her private obligations. The solvency of her creditors became questionable and the panic spread to London and New York. Heavy gold withdrawals from London began, and a joint credit of $250,000,000, extended to the Bank of England by the Bank of France and the American Federal Reserve Banks, did not suffice to save the situation. Britain's creditors became convinced that British solvency was dependent not merely on the balancing of the governmental budget, but upon the reduction of the operating costs of British industry through cuts in wages and in the "dole" or government subsidy to the unemployed. Under pressure from the bankers, MacDonald, Snowden, and Thomas in the British Labor Cabinet yielded to these demands in the name of saving the gold standard. This split the Labor party, which deposed MacDonald by a vote of 274 to 6. On August 24, 1931, the Cabinet resigned. MacDonald at once formed a new coalition "National

Ministry" composed of Conservatives, Liberals, and renegade Laborites, with the Labor rank and file going over to the opposition. A new Franco-American credit of $400,000,000 did not stay the "flight from the pound." Following a mutiny in the British fleet over pay cuts, gold withdrawals were enormously increased as foreign depositors scurried to safety. Between mid-July and mid-September $1,000,000,000 in gold was withdrawn from London. The new credits were exhausted. The Cabinet admitted defeat and abandoned the gold standard on September 20.

An international scramble for gold ensued. Gold hoarding in the United States and in Europe reached large proportions. Between September 20 and October 20 the United States lost $665,000,000 in gold to France, Holland, Switzerland, and Belgium. The "attack on the dollar" subsided in October and Premier Laval conferred with President Hoover in Washington October 23–25. France and the United States held three-quarters of the monetary gold stock of the world. The heads of their respective governments sought to put an end to American suspicions of French raids on the dollar and to French suspicions regarding the stability of the gold standard in the United States. They announced their intention of cooperating in maintaining their currencies on a gold basis. As for debts, they declared "we recognize that prior to the expiration of the Hoover year of postponement some agreement regarding them may be necessary covering the period of business depression, as to the terms and conditions of which the two governments make all reservations. The initiative in this matter should be taken at an early date by the European powers principally concerned within the framework of the agreements existing prior to July 1, 1931." This represented a return to the Young Plan and an admission by the American President that debts and reparations were inseparable. Signor Grandi, Italian Foreign Minister, likewise conferred with President Hoover in Washington November 16–20. The official statement issued was even more vague and meaningless than that following the Hoover-Laval conversations. It declared that "no particular arrangements" were reached. There had merely taken place "a frank and cordial exchange of views respecting the many problems of world importance in which the Governments of Italy and the United States are equally interested," including the financial crisis, debts, and armaments.

The period of the moratorium brought no modification of American debt policies. The winter and the spring brought no improvement in the financial and economic maladies gripping the world. The United States had already lost $747,000,000 in gold. Heavy gold withdrawals from New York were resumed in the spring of 1932, but the storm was weathered after an additional loss of $471,000,000. A score of States, including Japan, followed Great Britain in abandoning the gold standard. The process of deflation continued, with prices of all kinds continuing their rapid decline. In the British election of October 27, 1931, the National Government was returned to power, supported by an overwhelming Conservative majority (471 Tory members in a House of 615), with the ex-Laborite MacDonald retaining the premiership. The new coalition Cabinet abandoned free trade and adopted protective duties. As tariff walls rose higher throughout the world and commerce declined, the prospect for a resumption of payments on public and private debts became ever more dismal.

In December, 1931, the American Congress nevertheless refused to act upon President Hoover's recommendation that the World War Debt Funding Commission be reestablished. It ratified the moratorium but declared that it did not approve, in any remote sense, of the cancellation or reduction of the debts and that its action was not to be construed as foreshadowing any future modification of this policy. The Allied Governments were persuaded to sign agreements for the repayment of the postponed installments in annual sums at 4 per cent interest, to be remitted over a ten-year period—presumably in addition to the regular installments falling due under the debt-funding agreement. The Democratic platform of 1932 declared "we are opposed to the cancellation of debts owing to the United States by foreign countries," though Governor Roosevelt expressed his conviction that the American tariff must be lowered to make payment possible. The Republican platform made no mention of the future of the debts and the Hoover administration found it politically inexpedient to raise the issue. When the moratorium year expired on June 30, 1932, no new arrangements had been concluded, despite the fact that the debtors were even less able to pay than they had been a year previously.

German reparations, however, were at long last wiped out, albeit conditionally, by the Lausanne Conference of June–July, 1932. The European Governments were given to understand by Washington that any readjustment of the inter-Allied debts must be preceded by a solution of the reparations question. Such a readjustment must be brought about by the European Powers, and the United States refused to take any part in their deliberations. A conference at Lausanne for this purpose was scheduled for January, 1932, but was postponed because of disagreements between Paris, Berlin, and London. The meeting was finally scheduled for June and was preceded by extensive informal conversations. Even on the eve of the conference only one of the fourteen participating governments had formulated a clear-cut policy. The one in question was that of Germany, which declared early and repeatedly that reparation payments were at an end and that no more would be made. This attitude alarmed France and other creditor countries, the more so as the United States refused to participate and would give no assurances of any corresponding reductions of the Allied obligations. When the conference met on June 16, Great Britain, France, Italy, Belgium, and Japan agreed to "reserve" all reparation payments until a final settlement could be achieved. This suspension included inter-Allied European debt installments falling due in July. The Germany Chancellor, Franz von Papen, reiterated Germany's determination to pay no more reparations and unofficially suggested a moratorium on private debts as well. Great Britain expressed her willingness to cancel all intergovernmental obligations. For a time the French Premier, Herriot, resisted British and German pressure and suggested a new moratorium. Offers and counter-offers led to a deadlock, with the German representatives refusing to commit themselves to future payments and pleading for the abrogation of the "war-guilt" clause of the Treaty of Versailles (Article 231), which was the legal basis for reparations. This demand was finally dropped, and on July 8 an accord was signed in the form of five agreements.

The first "Agreement with Germany" (Annex 2 of the final act) abrogated the provisions of the Young Plan relating to reparations and provided that in lieu thereof Germany would deliver to the Bank for International Settlements 5 per cent bonds to the value of 3,000,000,000 marks ($714,000,000). These bonds were not to be negotiated by the banks for three years, and after fifteen years all bonds not marketed were to be canceled. None of the bonds was to be sold below 90. The second agreement, "Transitional Measures Relating to Germany" (Annex 3), provided for the prolongation of the moratorium until the coming into force of the new arrangement. The third agreement appointed a committee to consider non-German reparations and related questions. The fourth agreement, "Resolution Relating to Central and Eastern Europe" (Annex 4), appointed a committee to study the problem of suppressing exchange controls and restoring trade. The fifth agreement, "Resolution Relating to a World Economic and Financial Conference" (Annex 5), invited the League of Nations to convoke an international monetary and economic gathering and invited the United States to participate in the preparatory committee work. The German payments provided for were spoken of as a contribution toward a "European reconstruction fund." The Lausanne accords made no mention of the inter-Allied debts, but a supplementary "gentlemen's agreement" of July 7 provided that ratification should be contingent upon a satisfactory settlement with the United States.[1] This arrangement was apparently insisted upon by France.

[1] According to the contemporary published versions of this "secret" compact, its terms were as follows: "The Lausanne agreement will take effect only after ratification by the creditor Powers, as provided in the treaty. This ratification will not be effected until a satisfactory settlement has been reached between them and their own creditors. The creditor Powers will have an opportunity to explain the situation to their respective parliaments,

Herriot expressed his intention of not submitting the accords to Parliament for ratification until favorable trans-Atlantic developments should have occurred. "What must be clearly understood is that the link is now definitely established between the settlement of reparations and the solution of the debt problem with relation to the United States. Everything is now subordinated to an agreement with America."[1]

The American reaction to the Lausanne agreements did not at once offer promise of the fulfillment of European hopes. Despite American injunctions to settle the reparations problem first, the actual settlement was viewed with suspicion in Washington and throughout the country as foreshadowing a "united front" on the part of Europe to compel scaling down or cancellation of the war debts. This suspicion was increased by the so-called "Anglo-French entente" of June 13—an understanding between London and Paris to cooperate in dealing with disarmament and with economic, financial, and commercial problems. The State Department expressed its pleasure at the Lausanne accords, but declared that "on the question of war debts owing to the United States by the European Governments, there is no change in the attitude of the American Government" (Press Release of July 9, 1932). In a letter to Senator Borah, President Hoover declared on July 14: "While I do not assume it to be the purpose of any of these agreements to effect combined action of our debtors, if it shall be so interpreted, then I do not propose that the American people shall be pressed into any line of action or that our policies

---

but no reference to that must be made in the agreement with Germany. Consequently, if satisfactory settlements are reached concerning the debts, the creditor governments will ratify the Lausanne treaty and the agreement with Germany then will have its full effect. But if such agreements are not obtained, the agreement with Germany will not be ratified and a new situation will arise, and the interested governments will confer on what is to be done. In such an event the legal position will be that which existed before the Hoover moratorium. The German Government will be notified of this agreement." (The New York *Times*, July 11, 1932, copyrighted 1932 by the Chicago *Tribune*.) On July 14 the Associated Press made public a slightly different translation of the agreement, which was, however, the same in substance as that quoted, accompanied by a letter from Neville Chamberlain, British Chancellor of the Exchequer, to the French Government, declaring: "The government of the United Kingdom would have been very happy if it would have been possible to cancel the war debt of France in the general scheme of cancellation of war debts and reparations. In the present circumstance it regrets not to be able to take any definite measure modifying the agreement on war-debts funding or Franco-British war debts. However, it agrees that the suspension foreseen by the declaration of June 16 applies to the annuities owing under the terms of war-debts funding and under the terms of Annex 1 of the Hague agreement of August 31, 1929, until the coming into force of the Lausanne agreement, or until it has been decided not to ratify the latter agreement. In the eventuality of nonratification of the Lausanne agreement, the legal position of all interested governments in relation to one another would again become that which existed under the terms of the Hague agreement of January 20, 1930 and the accord on war-debts funding. In this case, the British and French Governments will have to examine the whole situation thus created."

[1] Herriot interview in *l'Intransigeant*, July 10, 1932.

shall be in any way influenced by such a combination, either open or implied." While many Senators and Representatives, with the support of a portion of the provincial press, professed to see a European "plot" in the German agreement and the Anglo-French understanding, Senator Borah declared himself in favor of a world conference to reduce or cancel all war obligations. Other public figures adopted a similar position, in some cases proposing that European disarmament be made the price of debt reduction.

But the administration adhered to its established policy, apparently out of fear of arousing the resentment of isolationists and irreconcilables seeking to make political capital out of opposition to debt reduction. That policy consisted of doing nothing prior to the presidential election of November 8, 1932, unless the European governments should solicit a reconsideration of the funding agreement. Each appeal would then be dealt with individually on its merits, on the basis of a revised estimate of "capacity to pay." And since the European governments, out of fear of upsetting confidence by confessing their inability to pay, were reluctant to make such appeals, months of drifting ensued, with the Lausanne agreements unratified and with no government daring to raise embarrassing issues. The zenith of futilitarianism was reached when the United States insisted on excluding these problems from the agenda of the proposed World Economic Conference as the price of its participation. Out of deference to the American view, the official invitation extended to the United States declared that "the questions of reparations, of debts, and of specific tariff rates (as distinguished from tariff policy) will be excluded from the scope of the conference."[1] The conference itself, as has been noted above, was repeatedly postponed, with nothing certain at the close of 1932 save that the Allied debts to the United States had become uncollectible and that the American Government found it politically inexpedient to take cognizance of this unpleasant fact.

On November 10, two days after the election of President Franklin D. Roosevelt, the British Ambassador presented to Secretary Stimson a note from his Government, asking for an exchange of views regarding the debts and proposing the suspension of the payments due on December 15 for the period of the suggested discussion. At the same time the French Government made an almost identical request. Similar requests were subsequently received from Poland and Czechoslovakia on November 21 and 22 respectively. On November 12 President Hoover invited President-elect Roosevelt to confer with him in Washington on the problems of policy raised by these notes. The conference took place on November 22,

[1] D. G. Osborne, Counselor of the British Embassy, to Secretary of State Stimson, July 28, 1932.

but resulted in a disagreement. Hoover reiterated his opposition to cancellation, declared that no facts had been presented which would justify postponement of the December 15 payments, and urged that negotiations "would proceed under more favorable circumstances" if these payments were made. He proposed that Congress should create a special agency for an exchange of views with the debtor governments on debts, economic recovery, and disarmament. Roosevelt took the view that the immediate question of the December 15 payments was the President's own responsibility. He agreed with Hoover that the loans had been made with the distinct understanding that they would be repaid and that the debts had no relation to reparations, but he declared that existing diplomatic channels were adequate for an exchange of views, without the necessity of setting up any new agency. Influential members of Congress hastened to express their opposition to the creation of such an agency, to any cancellation or reduction of the debts, and to any suspension of the expected payments.

Under these circumstances, Secretary Stimson, on November 23, answered the notes of the debtors by declaring that the President was prepared to recommend to Congress the establishment of a special agency to discuss the questions, but that no facts had been presented which would be likely to induce Congress to change its attitude. He asserted that payment of the December 15 installments would contribute to a satisfactory approach to the whole question. In response to this communication, the British Government on December 1 presented an elaborate and masterly analysis of the whole debt problem to the American State Department, buttressing its plea for the suspension of the December 15 payments and for a reexamination of the question with the arguments long familiar to economists everywhere. The French Government presented a similar note on the same day. In the subsequent correspondence, all of the parties reiterated the contentions already made and refused to modify the positions they had taken. Efforts to preserve a united Anglo-French front failed, because of the final decision of the British Cabinet to make the December 15 payment and the refusal of the French Parliament to support Premier Herriot in doing likewise. On December 14 Herriot was overthrown in the Chamber on the issue, and his successor, Joseph Paul-Boncour, was pledged to withhold further payments until the whole question was reexamined. The refusal of congressional and press opinion in the United States to accept postponement or reduction made it impossible for the administration at Washington to inaugurate any new policy. On December 15 the British Government paid the United States $95,550,000 in gold bars. Italy, Czechoslovakia, Lithuania, Latvia, and Finland also paid the smaller amounts due from them, while five debtor governments—France, Belgium, Poland, Hungary, and Esthonia—defaulted.[1]

The defaults of December 15, 1932, produced no change in the American attitude, apart from creating a popular outcry against the governments which failed to pay. The state of European opinion and the world economic and financial situation made it clear that no further payments under the old schedules would be made by any of the debtors. All assumed that the Lausanne agreement would be followed by a reduction of their debts to the United States. All expressed, unofficially, their determination to make no additional payments until the whole settlement should be revised. The next installments fell due in June of 1933. The international exchange value of the pound sterling had already declined sharply and it was obvious that a continuation of uncertainty would tend to bring about a further unsettling of financial confidence and an intensification of economic depression throughout the world. In the interests of all parties, it seemed imperative to reach an agreement as soon as possible. But President Hoover's efforts in this direction were rendered fruitless by the political situation in the United States. On December 17, he invited Roosevelt to join him in choosing a special delegation (which should include American delegates to the Disarmament Conference and to the projected World Economic Conference) to discuss the question with the European governments. On December 19, Roosevelt refused to cooperate on the terms suggested, expressed doubts of the wisdom of combining debt, disarmament, and economic negotiations, and suggested that no delegates to the economic conference be chosen until after March 4, 1933. In his rejoinder of December 20, Hoover asked Roosevelt to name Owen D. Young, Colonel House, or other leading Democrats to confer with the administration to see what steps could be taken to avoid delay in the examination of the debt problem. On the following day the President-elect reiterated his position and refused to accept any responsibility, either for policy determination or for exploratory fact-finding before the commencement of his administration. President Hoover's message to Congress of

[1] The amounts paid and defaulted are indicated in the following table:

Defaults		Paid	
France	$19,261,432.50	Great Britain	$95,550,000.00
Poland	3,302,980.00	Czechoslovakia	1,500,000.00
Belgium	2,125,000.00	Italy	1,245,437.50
Esthonia	266,370.00	Finland	186,235.00
Hungary	40,729.35	Latvia	111,852.12
		Lithuania	92,386.01
Total	$24,996,511.85		
		Total	$98,685,910.63

According to Treasury Department figures, these installments brought the total payments on the war debts owing to the American Government to $2,726,266,808.

December 19, proposing again the creation by congressional action of a special agency to consider the debt problem, also produced no results.

On January 20, however, a new White House Conference led to an agreement between Hoover and Roosevelt. Under its terms, Secretary of State Stimson, on behalf of the President-elect, invited the British Government to send representatives to Washington as soon as possible after March 4 to discuss the debts and the world economic situation with the new administration. This belated bid was accepted by Downing Street, though the Chancellor of the Exchequer, Neville Chamberlain, stated publicly that Great Britain would offer no concessions either as to tariffs or as to the gold standard, in return for debt reduction. Whether the British and American veiws could be reconciled appeared doubtful at the end of the Hoover Administration.

In summary, it may be said that German reparations have been definitely canceled, since there can now be no reasonable expectation of resumption of payments under any circumstances. The inter-Allied debts in Europe may also be regarded as at an end. That the Allied debts to the United States must be drastically reduced or canceled, either by agreement or by default, is likewise a foregone conclusion, however reluctant the American Government and American opinion may be to face this situation. The longer it is ignored the longer will be the period of uncertainty, confusion, friction, and recrimination. In short, the whole structure of intergovernmental debts resulting from the Great War has broken down completely under the impact of the Great Depression. The structure of international private debts is similarly imperiled, and many of the private investments and credits are already worthless. The fate of the remainder would seem to depend upon a recovery of price levels, of production, and of international trade. Such a recovery may come about as a result of forces beyond the control of governments. But the tariff and debt policies of governments would seem, at the time of writing, to constitute an almost insuperable obstacle to such recovery at a rapid rate and on a world-wide scale. The established order of anarchic, capitalistic profit-seeking and uncontrolled economic nationalism has not yet committed suicide, but it has inflicted such severe injuries upon itself that its illness has become chronic. Its full convalescence is rendered improbable by a continuation of the values, attitudes, and policies which have brought it to its present pass.

SUGGESTED READINGS

Baruch, B. M.: *The Making of the Reparation and Economic Sections of the Treaty,* New York, Harper & Brothers, 1920.
Bass, J. F., and H. G. Moulton: *America and the Balance Sheet of Europe,* New York, Ronald Press Company, 1921.
Bergmann, C.: *The History of Reparations,* London, Ernest Benn, Ltd., 1927.

Bonn, M J.: *The Crisis of Capitalism in America*, New York, John Day Company, Inc., 1932.

Culbertson, W. S.: *Commercial Policy in War Time and After*, New York, D. Appleton & Company, 1919.

————: *International Economic Policies: a Survey of the Economics of Diplomacy*, New York, D. Appleton & Company, 1925.

Delaisi, F.: *Political Myths and Economic Realities*, New York, Viking Press, Inc., 1927.

Delle-Donne, O.: *European Tariff Policies Since the World War*, New York, Adelphi Co., 1928.

Dexter, P. and J. Sedgwick: *The War Debts—an American View*, New York, The Macmillan Company, 1928.

Dunn, R. W.: *American Foreign Investments*, New York, Huebsch and Viking Press, Inc., 1926.

Gregory, T.: *Tariffs: a Study in Methods*, Philadelphia, J. B. Lippincott Company, 1921.

Hansen, A.: *Economic Stabilization in an Unbalanced World*, New York, Harcourt, Brace & Company, 1931.

Hobson, J. A.: *The Evolution of Modern Capitalism*, New York, Walter Scott, 1917.

Keynes, J. M.: *Economic Consequences of the Peace*, New York, Harcourt, Brace & Company, 1920.

————: *A Revision of the Treaty*, New York, Harcourt, Brace & Company, 1922.

Kuczynski, R. R.: *American Loans to Germany*, New York, The Macmillan Company, 1927.

Lippmann, W., and W. Scroggs: *The United States in World Affairs, an Account of American Foreign Relations*, 1931, New York, Harper & Brothers, 1932.

Long, R. E.: *The Mythology of Reparations*, London, Duckworth, 1928.

McClure, W. M.: *A New American Commercial Policy*, New York, Columbia University Press, 1924.

Moulton, H., and C. McGuire: *Germany's Capacity to Pay*, New York, McGraw-Hill Book Company, Inc., 1923.

Moulton, H., and L. Pasvolsky: *War Debts and World Prosperity*, New York, The Century Company, 1932.

Patterson, E. M.: *The World's Economic Dilemma*, New York, McGraw-Hill Book Company, Inc., 1930.

Rogers, J. H.: *America Weighs Her Gold*, New Haven, Yale University Press, 1931.

Salter, J. A.: *Recovery—the Second Effort*, New York, Century Company, 1932.

Sombart, W.: *The Quintessence of Capitalism*, New York, E. P. Dutton & Co., Inc., 1915.

Taussig, F. W.: *International Trade*, New York, The Macmillan Company, 1927.

————: *Tariff History of the United States*, New York, G. P. Putnam's Sons, 1922.

Tawney, R. H.: *The Acquisitive Society*, New York, Harcourt, Brace & Company, 1920.

Viner, J.: *Dumping: a Problem of International Trade*, Chicago, University of Chicago Press, 1923.

Walter, H. C.: *Foreign Exchange and Foreign Debts*, London, Methuen & Co., 1926

Webb, S. and B.: *The Decay of Capitalist Civilization*, New York, Harcourt, Brace & Company, 1923.

Weber, M.: *General Economic History*, New York, Greenberg, Publisher, Inc., 1927.

Williams, B. H.: *Economic Foreign Policy of the United States*, New York, McGraw-Hill Book Company, Inc., 1929.

Withers, H.: *The Case for Capitalism*, New York, E. P. Dutton & Co., Inc., 1920.

See also references at end of Chapter X, p. 373 above.

CHAPTER XV

THE WHITE MAN'S BURDEN

1. THE FRUITS OF IMPERIALISM

That "no man is good enough to be another's master" is also true of nations, and very specially true of those plutocrat-ridden Powers which have of late stumbled into an enormous increase of material wealth without having made any intelligent provision for its proper distribution and administration.—G. B. SHAW, Preface to *Major Barbara*.

THE political and economic consequences of empire-building constitute a phase of the world crisis of the twentieth century no less significant and no less fraught with weal or woe for western civilization than the results of economic nationalism and competitive profit-seeking. The effects of the latter are immediate and obvious. They are felt by millions of people in pay envelopes, jobs, sales, mortgages, and bank accounts. The effects of imperialism are less tangible to western peoples, for only indirectly and from afar do they seem to touch the everyday lives of the majority of Britishers, Frenchmen, Americans, and Italians. The historians of the future, however, in their efforts to analyze and explain the dynamic forces of the Western State System, will probably attach more permanent importance to the conquest, revolt, and possible emancipation of the non-European peoples of the world than to the ebb and flow of business activity within the western nations themselves. Contemporary signposts along the paths of empire deserve to be read with care by all who would penetrate the shadows of the international politics of the decades still to come.

The processes of imperialism have already been described above in some detail,[1] along with selected instances of empire-building. The suggestion was there advanced that these processes cannot be understood in terms of official apologias and rationalizations, emphasizing culture, Christianity, or capitalism. Neither can they be understood by reference to single sets of motives—whether they be proselyting fervor, humanitarian zeal, profit-seeking acquisitiveness, or hankerings after political domination. The conquest of the world by the western States has involved all of these elements and many more. If it is at all susceptible of any simple interpretation, that interpretation must be couched in terms of the patterns of power-and-prestige politics prevalent in the Western State

[1] See pp. 374–429 above.

System. These patterns and the values which underlie them have led to world imperialism in the period during which the technological and economic superiority of the European peoples enabled them to spread their power and their populations over Africa, Asia, the Americas, and the islands of the seas. Purposes and motives need not be discussed further at this point, since results and prospects are here the major objects of consideration. The present section will accordingly be devoted to an examination of the major effects of imperialism on its victims and its beneficiaries. This will be followed by an analysis of the specific ways in which the quest for empire has constituted a cause for war between the imperial States. Efforts to mitigate conflict and to remove the causes of friction will be considered as a preface to a discussion of the mandate system and of the endeavors of the subject peoples to throw off the western yoke.

From the point of view of backward peoples, the most obvious consequence of imperialism is the end of their political independence and the loss of their ability to control their own destinies for their own purposes. Political subjection has usually been accompanied by economic exploitation in one form or another. But even when the backward peoples have been benefited economically by western science and technology, they have none the less bemoaned the loss of the political patrimony of their ancestors. From the point of view of the present study, imperialism is significant only in so far as it affects the political relations between States and exercises an influence on the trends and tendencies of international politics. Judgments based upon moral or economic criteria are not directly relevant to this purpose. There are, moreover, no objective standards of morals and of material well-being which can be applied. Western civilization has imposed its own economic values and its own moral judgments upon the world as a whole. The western scholar who would weigh imperialism in the balance must either accept these standards as axiomatic or must devise others of broader scope. Whatever he does is likely to be of little political significance, for people's feelings and attitudes toward such questions are far more significant than the supposedly "objective" facts. Moral facts exist entirely in the eye of the observer. Economic facts can be reduced to statistical form. But in either case these facts will have different meanings for different people. The Briton and the Hindu, the American and the Filipino, the Frenchman and the Malgache, the Italian and the Berber are never likely to see eye-to-eye regarding them. Moral judgments and economic evaluations in the abstract are devoid of political significance. Only as they exist in the minds of empire-builders, colonial administrators, taxpayers, and native rebels do they influence political action and produce political consequence. Thus far, economic considerations and moral principles have almost always been subordinated ultimately to the verdict of force. There seems at present no reason for supposing that the subject peoples will not continue to resent bitterly the loss of political self-determination, regardless of any advantages of western morality and western technology which may be conferred upon them.

In view of the emphasis placed upon the "civilizing mission" of the imperial States, however, it will be well to examine the effects of the process upon its supposed beneficiaries. As for liquidating illiteracy and promoting education, the results in most colonies have been almost negligible, despite missionary efforts in these directions. Colonial budgets usually provide pitiably small appropriations for educational purposes, as compared with the appropriations for military purposes, administration, railway building, and economic development. In the United States 200 children attend school for every 1,000 inhabitants, as compared with 175 in the Hawaiian Islands, 120 in the Philippines, 40 in Madagascar and Uganda, 38 in the Dutch East Indies and British India, 37 in Haiti, 28 in Tunis, 26 in the Belgian Congo, 20 in Korea, 3 in French West Africa and French Cameroon, and 1 in Portuguese Angola.[1] In almost all the colonial dependencies it is clear that the masses are remaining illiterate. As for religious conversion of native population, the overwhelming majority of the inhabitants of Africa and Asia remain heathen. "While the missionary has been bringing the gospel to the natives, the traders too often have brought rum and guns, and traders and soldiers and officials have brought violence, fraud, and venereal disease."[2] In sanitation, road-building, and communication—all functions which facilitate economic development and contribute only indirectly to the cultural advancement of the population—more has been achieved. To overbalance these alleged gains are losses of a much more serious character. In much of Africa the native population has been robbed of its land by white concessionaires and profit-seekers aided and abetted by the colonial government. Beggary, starvation, and social disorganization have often ensued. In large areas of Africa and Asia the formerly indolent and carefree natives are compelled to labor for long hours at purely nominal wages for the benefit of their white taskmasters. If actual slavery is disappearing and compulsory labor is condemned, thousands of natives are nevertheless bound to work under collective contracts which they accept under duress and fulfill only under governmental coercion. Head taxes and hut taxes are imposed by governments, not to raise revenue but to compel the natives to toil for private employers in order to earn enough to pay them. To anyone not blinded by visions of imperial grandeur and by the specious claims of imperialism's defenders, it is abundantly clear that most of the backward peoples have obtained less of civilization and

[1] P. T. Moon, *Imperialism and World Politics*, pp. 559–561.
[2] *Ibid.*, p. 562.

enlightenment from the white man than of misery, impoverishment, and ruthless economic exploitation.

In any case, the assumption that western culture is an unmixed blessing to non-European peoples is being increasingly challenged by anthropologists, sociologists, and more enlightened colonial administrators. The "civilizing mission" of the white man, where it means anything at all, means the imposition of the white man's religion, language, moral standards, and social institutions upon the colored races. Native schools almost invariably teach, not the native language, but the tongue of the imperial State. Missions seek to replace paganism by Christianity. Humanitarians and moralists strive to substitute skirts and trousers for nakedness, monogamy for polygamy, "free" labor for slavery, western morality for native customs. These well-intentioned efforts have in many cases been disastrous, for they destroy the very bases of organized social life among the natives without substituting anything which is relevant to local conditions. The result more often than not is complete social chaos and demoralization. It is arguable that almost as many native tribes have been reduced to ruin and degradation by western missionaries and educators as by western rum merchants, gun runners, and syphilitics. In many of the South Sea Islands the whole native population is dead or dying. Elsewhere the natives have lost their own cult, their arts, their *mores* and folkways—all the elements of stability in the native cultures—and have become grotesque and debased caricatures of western white men. The agonizing process whereby China is sinking ever deeper into political anarchy and social collapse is directly traceable to the disorganizing effects upon the old culture of the Celestial Empire of western technology, western economics, and western politics. These calamities have been avoided elsewhere only to the extent to which "civilizing" efforts have been abandoned and replaced by efforts to conserve native life in its ancient ways. Such native leaders as Gandhi of India have proposed to turn their backs upon science, technology, machine industry, and all the other works of western culture. They would return to the simple and secure life of their ancestors. But what has been done cannot be undone. The return of the native to the ways of his fathers is probably impossible, whatever he may do to attain salvation by this path.

More significant for the immediate future of Great Power politics are the fruits of imperialism for the imperial States themselves. In an earlier chapter[1] it has been pointed out that most of the alleged purposes of empire-building have no relation to realities. Colonies are not acquired to Christianize the natives, or to do them good, or to provide outlets for surplus population, surplus goods, or surplus capital. These results, to be sure, do occur and missionaries, humanitarians, merchants, and capitalists

[1] See above, pp. 419–428.

[592]

may influence the determination of imperialist policy. In the long perspective of world history, however, modern imperialism is but a new expression of the will to power and the drive for conquest. It is due only to the cultural accidents of technology that the western nation-states have been able to extend their power over the non-European world. This power is necessarily directed toward the acquisition of the components of greater power: land, man power, natural resources, and markets. This power has been used, as State power is usually used, for the enrichment and glorification of the ruling classes of the conquering State—the investors, merchants, bankers, business men, journalists, and patriotic politicians of the western societies. These classes are a numerically small minority of the population of the imperial States. Frequently the economic beneficiaries of imperialism are but a minority of the whole bourgeoisie. These facts tend to obscure the consequences of imperialism for those who attempt to evaluate its results for the whole national community of the colonial Powers. The whole population has no interest in imperialism save in so far as popular patriotic pride is stimulated by conquest. The whole population is of no political significance. Policies are formulated by interested and politically effective minorities with economic power. The fruits of these policies are enjoyed by those who wield power within the State and are the beneficiaries of the State's exercise of its power in dealing with other States. The chief function of the mass of voters and taxpayers is to supply the soldiers and pay the bills. From this point of view, empire-building is a process whereby States extend their control over backward areas in response to the ambitions and pressures, the values and ideologies of their ruling classes, with resulting profits accruing, not to the national community, but to privileged and protected minorities.

If imperialism is viewed as a phase of the struggle for power between States, its results must be judged in terms of its rôle in power politics. The most obvious result of the competitive quest for empire is war—war, first between the imperial States and the backward peoples, and then war between the imperial States themselves. Whether investors use foreign offices to enhance profits or foreign offices use investors to extend State power, the diplomatic influence of the State is placed at the disposal of the empire-builders, and if diplomacy fails to attain the goal it is supported by coercion and military force. This force has been used on innumerable occasions against the native States which resist conquest. There is scarcely a single colony of any of the Great Powers which was not won through bloodshed. Such wars are often costly (*e.g.*, the Boer War and the Manchurian hostilities of 1931–1933); they are sometimes disastrous to conquerors and conquered alike (*e.g.*, Spain in Morocco, France in Mexico); they almost always involve atrocities, abuses, fierce resentment, and savage repression (*e.g.*, the United States in the Philippines and Haiti,

France in Madagascar and Syria, Germany in Southwest Africa, Great Britain in India, Egypt, the Sudan, China, and elsewhere). In general, however, colonial wars do not, in and of themselves, upset the balance of power or bring the conquerors to ruin. They tend rather to increase the power of the imperial States and to enhance the profits of their immediate beneficiaries. The situation is quite different when the imperial States engage in war with one another for mastery of tropical lands or oriental markets. Prior to the nineteenth century, even such wars normally had little effect upon the nation-states themselves, apart from changing titles to territories and bringing about redistributions of power and prestige. In the machine age, however, such conflicts have become enormously costly and destructive of life and property whenever Great Powers have been belligerents on opposite sides.[1] The fruits of empire-building, garnered by the war god, are destruction, death, bankruptcy, and national ruin. Yet these fruits are seldom weighed in the balances of those who tabulate profits and losses.

In the light of these results, the problem of imperialism in the twentieth century is a double one: that of protecting the subject peoples from the abuses of economic exploitation and political subjugation, and that of mitigating or minimizing the clash of force between the imperial Powers. The solution of these problems is obviously desirable from the point of view of humanitarianism, of international morality, of the social amelioration and economic welfare of conquerors and conquered alike. It is also dictated by practical political considerations, which are likely to influence foreign offices and diplomats more readily than humanitarian sentiment and philanthropic fervor. No argument is required to demonstrate that imperialist wars are costly, dangerous, and often disastrous. From the long-run point of view, even the pecuniary interests of exploiters, investors, concessionaires, and merchants will be better served by colonial populations living in a state of comfort and contentment on a high standard of living and possessing the purchasing power and the efficiency in labor which a high standard of living implies, than by misery, poverty, and degradation among the backward peoples. Similarly, from the point of view of governments controlling backward areas, the economy of colonial administration and even the preservation of their control depend upon the degree to which the population is satisfied with its lot. Resistance, revolt, and non-cooperation may be minimized by establishing disguised forms of control and by granting to the subject peoples as much of the shadow or substance of autonomy as is made possible by their own capacities and the purposes of the foreign ruler.

Here again, with regard to all these alternatives, the problem is one of choosing between or reconciling welfare values and profit, power, and

[1] See pp. 641f. below.

prestige values. The ruling classes of the imperial States are more than likely to pursue their own interests by objectives and methods not conducive to the welfare either of the subject peoples or of their own fellow citizens. It is not to be expected that empire-builders will cease to be moved by the motives which have driven them to action in the past. Business men seek markets; investors seek dividends; entrepreneurs seek cheap labor; strategists seek control of naval bases, waterways, mountain passes, and defensible frontiers; diplomats seek power and prestige and all the components thereof. These things are, have been, and will be so long as the values, attitudes, and institutions of western society remain fixed in their present mold. Those who urge the abandonment of imperialistic policies upon modern governments are ignorant of the great dynamic forces which have created the bourgeois nation-states and pushed them into courses of overseas expansion. Nothing short of a complete social, economic, and political revolution, national and international, can eradicate imperialism from the behavior patterns of the western nations. Only sincere revolutionists can logically argue for the cure of the evils of imperialism by the renunciation of the pattern itself.

"Practical" statesmen, reformers, critics, and scholars who accept the social and political *status quo* as fundamentally sound must therefore hope to deal with the undesirable consequences of imperialism, not through the use of the surgeon's knife, but through the application of soothing oils and ointments administered with appropriate incantations. These must be designed to ease tensions, remove frictions, and alleviate the worst symptoms of what has come to be recognized as one of the most menacing maladies afflicting contemporary world society. The cure requires a program, not of choosing one set of purposes and rejecting the other, but of reconciling profit, power, and prestige values with considerations of welfare. Those wielding political and economic authority must be persuaded to take a long-range point of view toward their own best interests. This savors of feeding the colonial cow more adequately and keeping her contented, in order that the imperial farmer will secure more and richer milk. That the farmer will continue to want to milk the cow goes without saying. That the cow will want to remain a cow—even a well-treated and contented cow—is by no means so certain. The final efficacy of the supposed remedies is consequently open to question. But the remedies themselves must be surveyed, if only to throw additional light on the nature of the problem.

With respect to the problems of imperialism, as with regard to those of trade, investment, and war, it is reasonably clear that solutions can be achieved, if at all, only through international action. This is no less true of problems of native protection and self-determination than of problems arising from competition and conflict between the imperial Powers. The

[595]

competitive quest for profits leads to a situation which is much the same for native labor in colonies as for domestic labor in national industries, save that the natives are usually unskilled, unorganized, and less able to defend themselves from exploitation and abuse. The colonial administration which permits the most ruthless, ambitious exploitation of its subjects will tend to drag down other colonial administrations to its own standards, particularly when the goods produced are sold in the world market in competition with similar goods exported from colonies of other States. Unless international standards and safeguards can be devised, it is improbable that abuses of this kind can be eliminated. No State, moreover, can afford to relinquish control over colonies, even if it is disposed to do so, so long as its rivals stand ready to take possession and thus increase their own power at the expense of their generous neighbors. Unless some scheme of international guarantee can be worked out, no imperial Power is likely to surrender colonial lands to the control of their inhabitants, particularly if the inhabitants are not adept at preserving order and protecting foreign vested interests—for disorder and insecurity will not only jeopardize the property and profits of the citizens of the former mother country, but will invite intervention and control by other outside States.

Demands for the protection of native populations have led to the development of the idea that colonies should be administered for the welfare of their inhabitants rather than for the profit of foreign investers and concessionaires.[1] All imperialists are disposed to issue mealy-mouthed and pious platitudes regarding their solicitude for native interests. Such statements must always be taken *cum grano salis* as rationalizations and justifications of policies of exploitation. It is nevertheless true that measurable progress has been made toward a policy of "trusteeship," even though grave abuses remain and the fundamental pattern of imperialism is for the most part unaltered. The new dispensation has reached its highest degree of development in the mandate system, to be considered below. Here attention may be called to certain specific problems which have in recent years been handled by some of the imperial governments with somewhat more consideration of the interests of the natives than has usually been displayed in the past.

[1] The British Colonial Office declared in 1923: "Primarily Kenya is an African territory, and His Majesty's Government think it necessary definitely to record their considered opinion that the interests of the African natives must be paramount, and that if, and when, those interests and the interests of the immigrant races should conflict, the former should prevail. . . . In the administration of Kenya His Majesty's Government regard themselves as exercising a trust on behalf of the African population, and they are unable to delegate or share this trust, the object of which may be defined as the protection and advancement of the native races. . . . There can be no room for doubt that it is the mission of Great Britain to work continuously for the training and education of the Africans toward a higher intellectual, moral, and economic level than that which they had reached when the crown assumed the responsibility for the administration of this territory. . . . " Cited from "Indians in Kenya," Cmd. 1922 (1923), in R. L. Buell, *International Relations*, 1929.

Land problems and labor problems are in the forefront of these efforts. Older colonial policies which facilitated the breakup of tribal lands into private allotments and encouraged the transfer of these allotments to white settlers and speculators have in some cases been modified so as to prevent this type of expropriation. Communal tribal ownership has been preserved in some of these instances and efforts have been made in others to render the transition to private property as gradual as possible. In the Dutch East Indies non-natives are forbidden to own land. In several of the British African colonies attempts have been made to safeguard native land titles by promoting the formation of individual farms on which the native works as a peasant, selling his produce to white middlemen, rather than as a slave or serf under white overseers. Sugar in the British West Indies, palm oil and cotton in Kenya, and cocoa on the British Gold Coast are now produced by native farmers working voluntarily on their own small estates. In many tropical colonies, however, large plantations and contract labor are still the rule. Indian and Chinese coolies are often imported for such purposes, with numerous attendant abuses such as starvation wages, inhuman treatment, and barbarous penalties for violations of labor contracts. A number of treaties have been entered into regulating the employment of coolie labor. The Sino-British agreements of 1860 and 1904, the Anglo-French New Hebrides agreement of 1906, and the Portuguese-Transvaal treaty of 1909 were of this character.

The treatment of natives was recognized to be a matter of international concern by the General Act of the Congress of Berlin of 1885, whereby the Powers bound themselves "to watch over the preservation of the native tribes and to care for the improvement of the conditions of their moral and material well-being." Belgium in the Congo and France in Equatorial Africa ignored this pledge with impunity by instituting atrocious systems of land exploitation and compulsory native labor. The slave trade became a matter of international action even earlier. By 1840 some two dozen bilateral treaties had been signed, granting rights to search suspected vessels off the west African coast. In 1841 the five Great Powers of Europe signed a general convention condemning the slave trade and providing for a reciprocal right of search. This treaty, however, was rejected by France. By the Anglo-French treaty of 1864, concerted naval action for the suppression of the traffic was provided for. The Anglo-American (Webster-Ashburton) treaty of 1842 likewise provided for naval cooperation, though the United States refused to concede the right of British war vessels to search its ships until 1862. In the General Act of Berlin of 1885 the Powers agreed to secure the complete suppression of slavery and the slave trade in Africa, though these aspirations were not entirely fulfilled. The Brussels convention of July 2, 1890, made elaborate provisions for the international suppression of the slave traffic in Africa, the Red Sea, and the Persian Gulf. In September, 1919, this act was abrogated and replaced by a new and almost equally vague obligation. Slavery and slave trading have continued in Abyssinia, Nigeria, and the Sudan. In 1926 a new slavery convention was signed at Geneva. It may be said that slavery and forced labor in colonial areas are now in process of reasonably rapid disappearance.

It is significant that these international efforts to cope with the social and economic abuses of imperialism have been applied not only to the colonies'of the imperial Powers, but to a few backward States which are still nominally sovereign and independent. When Abyssinia applied for admission to the League of Nations in 1923, the Swiss, Dutch, and British representatives at the Assembly doubted whether it could give effective guarantees of the abolition of slavery and the arms traffic. Abyssinia was admitted on condition of adhering to the September, 1919, convention. In 1930 an International Commission of Inquiry into the Existence of Slavery and Forced Labor visited Liberia and published a report which severely criticized the native government. In January, 1931, Liberia requested the League of Nations to tender assistance and advice concerning reforms. The League Council then established an "International Committee on Liberia," consisting of representatives of France, Germany, Great Britain, Italy, the United States, Liberia, Panama, Poland, and Spain. Three experts were sent by the Committee to investigate conditions in the summer of 1931. The dilatory attitude of the Liberian Government delayed consideration of their report until May, 1932, when the committee and the Council adopted a program of amelioration.

The United States has long exercised a quasi-protectorate over this Negro republic, founded by liberated slaves from America in the 1830's. Since the war American rubber interests, notably the Firestone company, have acquired concessions within its frontiers. On May 18, 1932, the United States submitted a memorandum to the Council, declaring that "the United States seeks no special advantage nor position in Liberia and desires only the welfare and development of the Liberian people and the proper protection of American nationals and their investments. In the opinion of the American Government, conditions in Liberia have now grown so chaotic and administration has become so demoralized that it is doubtful whether an effective government exists in the country." The United States dissented from the Council program, on the ground that it would not achieve the necessary reforms. On August 25, 1932, the United States reiterated its objections and insisted that Liberia must grant adequate authority to an official of an international agency. The American Government declared itself unable to approve the League plan or to consent to any diminution of the rights of the Finance Corporation of America on this basis. On October 12, 1932, the international committee made public at Geneva a revised text of the "General Principles of the Plan of Assistance," which provided for a chief adviser and three provincial commissioners for Liberia, to be named by the Council of the League and appointed by the Liberian President. This scheme (which has not yet been put into effect at the time of writing) contemplates international supervision of Liberian finances and administration, with the League agents working in collaboration with the Finance Corporation and the Firestone interests. Such arrangements are often motivated as much by "the proper protection of nationals and investments" as by solicitude for the natives, but at least they represent an effort to remedy abuses. International pressure of this kind is not, of course, ordinarily applied to the colonial Great Powers, but only to weak native States.[1]

2. COOPERATIVE EMPIRE-BUILDING

> Magnanimity in politics is not seldom the truest wisdom; and a great empire and little minds go ill together.—EDMUND BURKE, *On Conciliation with America*, March 22, 1775.

The other phase of the problem of imperialism—that of minimizing and mitigating conflicts between the imperial Powers themselves—has from the beginning demanded international action for its solution. The treatment which a colonial State accords to its subjects may be regarded as a "domestic question," though in practice the adequate protection of natives is seldom assured by exclusively national action. But if two rival States covet the same territory, the resulting tension can obviously be resolved only by cooperative action, for if each pursues its own purposes a clash of force will be inevitable. That such clashes have been relatively few in number[2] has been due less to the devotion of the Powers to peace and justice in the division of the backward areas among themselves than to the fact that mutually advantageous political bargains could be made so long as new lands remained to partition. The pacific parceling out of Africa and Asia among the Powers through treaties and international conferences has been discussed elsewhere.[3]

Since the process is now all but complete—save for the possibility of the future carving up of regions still undivided—the politics of partition is now primarily of historical interest, particularly in a period in which outright annexation has been superseded by other forms of control more subtle but no less effective. The satiated Powers have secured their share of the spoils and are now disposed to safeguard their gains through international guarantees and legal boycotts against new acquisitions by force. Imperialistic rivalries remain acute, however, at points of friction in such

[1] But see pp. 609–622 below on the mandate system.
[2] See pp. 102–103 above.
[3] See pp. 379–382 above.

"backward" States as China, Persia, Siam, Afghanistan, and Abyssinia, which are still nominally independent but are bones of contention between competing empire-builders. They are likewise acute in certain areas already under the domination of colonial States, but coveted by rival States: Manchuria, Mongolia, Tibet, Tunis, the Sudan, the Philippines, certain of the South Sea archipelagoes, and the former German colonies in Africa. These tensions will inevitably culminate in new conflicts unless they can be resolved by international action. The special problems with which such action must deal can be suggested by a resumé and evaluation of past efforts in this direction.[1]

These problems necessarily revolve about the stakes of imperialist diplomacy in undeveloped regions. In the twentieth century these stakes are couched in terms of commerce, industry, railroads, ports, strategic bases, raw materials, and markets for goods and for capital. Title to backward areas is seldom desired for its own sake in the era of competing nationalisms and capitalisms. It is desired for the opportunity which it offers for the aggrandizement of the power of the controlling State and for the enhancement of the profits of its entrepreneurs and investors. International friction in such regions develops over access to such opportunities. Capitalists and industrialists of rival nations seek concessions and franchises from native governments for the exclusive exploitation of certain resources or the construction and operation of certain industries or public utilities. Bankers seek exclusive rights of lending money to such governments at lucrative interest rates. Merchants seek access to markets on terms no less favorable (and if possible more favorable) than those granted to their competitors of other nationalities. Entrepreneurs seek contracts for the exploitation of cheap native labor. Steamship lines seek harbors and port facilities. Naval strategists seek advantageously located coaling stations and bases. Missionaries seek opportunities for the establishment of missions and schools. All of these empire-builders call upon their governments for support, assistance, and protection. In the ensuing scramble of rival governments, the rights of the natives are ruthlessly trampled underfoot, and the imperial Powers themselves may easily fall to bludgeoning one another fast and furiously.

One form of solution of this problem which has been attempted with little success is the international control of tension areas, with economic opportunities open on equal terms to the nationals of all States or partitioned by agreement in some mutually satisfactory fashion. The port of Tangier, commanding the western entrance to the Mediterranean, was long a focal point of international rivalries because of its strategic importance. Prior to the Great War, the city was governed by a council composed of representatives of the diplomatic corps. Plans were discussed

---

[1] On the problem of peace in general, see pp. 221f. above and pp. 672f. below.

from time to time for a true international government. France, mistress of adjacent Morocco, sought to secure exclusive control after the war, but was balked by Great Britain and Spain. The "Convention Regarding the Organization of the Statute of the Tangier Zone," signed December 18, 1923, left "sovereignty" in the hands of the Sultan of Morocco (controlled by France), but placed the government of the city in the hands of a committee of control and an international legislative assembly. The latter body is composed of twenty-six members, four each from France and Spain, three from Great Britain, others from the other participating States, and nine appointed representatives of the natives. The committee is composed of consular representatives and has the power to veto acts of the assembly. The administrator is French. He is aided by a British and a Spanish assistant, a Belgian commander of gendarmes, and a Moroccan customs collector. The zone is neutralized and demilitarized by the convention, which likewise provides for the Open Door. In 1928 the statute was revised to grant Italy three members of the assembly and certain administrative positions. In 1906 joint Anglo-French control was established over the New Hebrides, with a joint high commission, a joint court, and a joint naval commission. The Samoan Islands were under a joint Anglo-German-American condominium from 1889 to 1899, when they were partitioned. The Anglo-Egyptian Sudan is under the joint administration of Great Britain and Egypt. International control of this type is almost always unsatisfactory and is usually unsuccessful in the long run. Either one of the participating States secures a controlling voice in the administration, as at Tangier and in the mandates, or the checks and balances provided for lead to endless friction in which the interests of the natives are forgotten.

The Open Door represents an alternative solution which may be applied either to the possessions of colonial powers or to the regions of imperialist competition which are still independent. As an abstract principle, it means simply equality of economic opportunity in backward regions and equal treatment to nationals of all States without favors or discriminations. It is to trade and investment in colonial areas what most-favored-nation treatment is to the commerce between the western States. As a concrete policy, the Open Door has been championed most vigorously by States fearing the exclusion of their merchants and investors from some lucrative field of profit-making. In principle, it has been accepted by most States, since each State desires to prevent others from barring out its nationals from attractive preserves. In practice, it has been ignored by most States in certain areas where the profits of special privilege and discrimination are large. In theory it tends to minimize political friction arising out of economic rivalries for markets by keeping such markets open on a basis of equality to all—"open" here meaning that customs tariffs, port duties, taxes, railway, steamship, and telegraph rates, judicial procedure, and law enforcement shall afford equal privileges for, and impose equal burdens upon, the nationals of all countries. Markets will then be conquered by price and quality, rather than by the sword or by political and economic favors and discriminations. But the policy has been accepted less because of its theoretical advantages than because each State, in its quest for power and profits, has a tangible interest in keeping open trading opportunities in the colonies of other States and in preventing its rivals from converting independent areas into spheres of monopolistic exploitation.

In the vast regions which are already colonial possessions of the Great Powers, the governments in control are ordinarily free to maintain the Open Door or the "Closed Door" at their option, for this is a question of domestic policy. The type of policy adopted will usually depend upon whether the government feels that the advantages of increasing its power and promoting the profits of its nationals through excluding or discriminating against foreigners are less or greater than the advantages of securing free access for its nationals to the colonies of other Powers as a *quid pro quo* for the Open Door in its own. In tariff matters, only Belgium, The Netherlands, Great Britain, and Germany refrained in the pre-war period from discriminating in favor of their own merchants against the commerce between outside States and their colonies. Since the war Germany has lost her colonies, and in the "C" mandates there is no obligation upon the mandatories to maintain the Open Door. Britain's reversion to protectionism involves preferences and discriminations in the British colonies and Dominions. Protectionism everywhere usually involves to some degree a reversion to its corollary in the old mercantilism: monopoly of colonial trade for the merchants of the colonial Power. This may be achieved by preferential import or export duties, *i.e.*, different tariff duties in the colonies and the mother country, with favors granted to intra-imperial trade—or by tariff assimilation between the mother country and the colonies. Under the latter arrangement, followed by the United States, France, Japan, and various other States, a single tariff wall is drawn around the colonies and the mother country, with free trade between them. The Closed Door as applied to colonial shipping means that the carrying trade between the colonies and the home country is monopolized by the latter's vessels. The United States and Spain are among the few States still adhering to this mercantilistic policy. The Closed Door as applied to concessions, franchises, and investments in colonies means that foreigners are forbidden to participate in these profit-making ventures, which are reserved exclusively to the nationals of the home State. The whole purpose of the Closed Door is to strengthen the economic ties between the imperial States and their colonies and to exclude aliens from participation in the profits. An instance of the successful application of the Closed Door is represented by the Philippine Islands, whose trade with the United States increased from 13 per cent of the total foreign trade of the archipelago in 1894 to 61 per cent in 1921. Foreign States whose nationals are excluded from economic opportunities are certain to resent such arrangements. They may likewise be tempted to resort to force to seize the colonies of their rivals, in order that their business men may secure access to these markets.[1]

Various efforts have been made to insure by treaty the observance of the Open Door in colonies. The General Act of Berlin of 1885 provided for the maintenance of equality of economic opportunity in the Congo Basin. Originally no tariff duties whatever were permitted in this area. In 1890 a 10 per cent *ad valorem* tariff was permitted by international agreement. In 1919 all limitations on the height of tariff walls were removed, subject to the condition that duties must be applied equally and in a nondiscriminatory fashion. At the same time an effort was made to apply the Open Door to other parts of Africa, but without success. In 1885 Germany and Great Britain agreed to observe the Open Door in their possessions on the Gulf of Guinea, and in 1898 Great Britain and France made a similar agreement for West Africa. The Anglo-German agreement of 1886 guaranteed the Open Door in the Pacific possessions of the two Powers. The Anglo-German-American agreement of 1899 contained a like provision for Samoa. But such arrangements are frequently violated, either openly or through various subtle favors and discriminations contrary to the spirit of the Open Door. In British Nigeria, in the French and Belgian Congo, in Italian Somaliland, in the American Philippines, and in Japanese Korea the door has been effectively closed by discriminatory tariffs and by monopolistic privileges granted to the nationals of the Powers in control. Railways and other public utilities demand monopolistic franchises in colonies, no less than elsewhere, if capital is to be forthcoming for their construction.

[1] Buell aptly characterizes the result of the Closed Door policy as follows: "From the standpoint of the consumer, the Closed Door means high prices; from the standpoint of a native, it is but one more phase of the policy of exploitation; from the standpoint of the world at large, it means the perpetuation of the worst forms of nationalistic imperialism. Excluded from markets because they are under the political control of one power, a capitalist State, dependent on foreign markets for the essentials of existence, will attempt to annex colonies of its own. A hundred years ago, this might have been possible without provoking war, except with the natives, because of the great stretches of unappropriated territory in the world. Today, however, such a policy will lead to conflicts between the Powers already in possession and those which wish to enter such territory. . . . The continuance of this policy will eventually result in the destruction of colonial empires, just as the empires of the seventeenth and eighteenth centuries were destroyed by the mercantilist system of which the Closed Door is a lineal descendant. Only the adoption of the opposite policy of the Open Door throughout the world will destroy this cause of war and insure peace in the backward regions as far as capitalist powers are concerned." R. L. Buell, *International Relations*, 1929, p. 447.

In these instances, the Open Door may mean merely the continuation of costly cut-throat competition. Either the door must be closed, or international collaboration must be brought about to assure the bankers and investors of each interested Power a share in the profits. The Bagdad railway project, the Moroccan State bank, the Fez-Tangier railway, and the Six Power Chinese Consortium of 1920 are all examples of efforts to achieve such collaboration. In 1911 Secretary of State Knox proposed the "complete commercial neutralization of Manchuria" through international cooperation in railway construction and other investments, but Russian and Japanese opposition defeated the scheme. Such international arrangements are seldom applied to colonies, and when they are applied to independent backward States they often leave the native government at the mercy of a solid bloc of foreign bankers and diplomats. They frequently lead to friction among the participating States and to protests from States not parties to the arrangement. All things considered, the preservation of the Open Door in colonies and spheres of influence through treaties and international consortiums has not been conspicuously successful in insuring equality of opportunity and reducing economic and political tensions.

In the backward regions which are not colonies but are still held by native States, the scramble for markets and concessions has led to the setting up of "spheres of influence" by the imperial Powers, in order that their nationals may enjoy exclusive opportunities for profit-making in these areas. International agreements for the creation of such spheres usually contemplate the closing of the door to nationals of outside States. The Anglo-Russian compact of 1907 over Persia, the Franco-German agreement of 1914 relating to Turkey, the inter-Allied secret treaties of 1915–1917 dealing with the Near East, and sundry agreements concerning Africa and the Pacific were of this character. In 1925 the British and Italian Governments concluded an agreement for cooperation in the acquisition of certain waterway and railway concessions in Abyssinia—an arrangement which caused the latter State to protest to the League of Nations and to declare the agreement null and void. The pressure of outside States and the interests of the participating States have led, in some of these situations, to treaties for the preservation of the Open Door. The German-Russian agreement of 1910 pledged the parties to observe the Open Door in their respective spheres in Persia and Turkey. The Anglo-Franco-Italian agreement of 1906 over Abyssinia pledged equality of treatment in harbor and railway matters and cooperation in the acquisition of concessions. The Act of Algeciras of 1906 provided for "economic liberty without inequality" in Morocco. The United States was a party to this act. It has been the most consistent champion of the Open Door everywhere, save in the Caribbean and in its own possessions. The geographical position of the United States makes it difficult for the American Government to acquire exclusive spheres of interest for its nationals in Africa or Asia. In order to prevent their exclusion from the spheres of other Powers on these continents, it has striven to secure general recognition of the Open Door principle in treaties. These efforts, too, have been only moderately successful, since each Power is tempted to favor its own citizens in areas where it possesses influence and there is as yet no general agreement as to what does or does not constitute the Open Door in each concrete situation.

In recent decades the most acute diplomatic controversies over the Open Door have centered about China. It is here likewise that the United States has insisted most emphatically on the observance of the principle, that international agreements for its preservation have been concluded on the largest scale, and that the issues have been most clearly drawn. In the nineteenth century the problem was primarily one of trading privileges. When such privileges were forcibly wrested from China by the European Powers in the first and second Opium Wars (1839–1842 and 1858–1860), the United States secured the same favors for its own citizens by the simple device of concluding most-favored-nation commercial treaties with the Chinese Government, obliging it to grant to the United States as favorable treatment as had been granted, or might in the future be granted, to other States. American commerce in China was protected in this fashion by the Cushing Treaty of 1844[1] and the Burlingame Treaty of 1868. Later the outlying dependencies of the Empire—the Amur River provinces, the Liu-kiu Islands, Formosa, Hongkong, Korea, Annam, Tonkin, etc.—were detached and annexed by more powerful neighboring States. Following the Sino-Japanese War of 1894 there began that scramble for leaseholds and concessions which seemed to foreshadow the partitioning

[1] Caleb Cushing's instructions declared: "You will signify in decided terms and in a positive manner that the Government of the United States would find it impossible to remain on terms of friendship and regard with the Emperor if greater privileges or commercial facilities should be allowed to the subjects of any other government than should be granted to citizens of the United States." The Treaty of Wang-hsia of July 3, 1844 (Article 2), provided: "Citizens of the United States . . . shall in no case be subject to other or higher duties than are or shall be required of the people of any nation whatever. . . . And if conditional advantages or privileges, of whatever description, be conceded hereafter by China to any other nation, the United States and the citizens thereof shall be entitled thereupon to a complete, equal, and impartial participation in the same." Secretary of State Fish commented on the Burlingame Treaty of 1868: "The general principle which underlies the articles of July, 1868, is the recognition of the sovereign authority of the imperial Government at Peking over the people of the Chinese Empire and over their social, commercial, and political relations with the western Powers. . . . While it confirms the international jurisdiction conferred by former treaties upon European and American functionaries over the persons and properties of their countrymen, it recognizes at the same time the territorial integrity of China and prevents such a jurisdiction from being stretched beyond its original purpose."

of the entire country into colonial possessions or spheres of foreign influence. Within each of these a particular Power would monopolize opportunities for trade, investment, and railway construction for its own mercantile and financial groups.[1] Under these circumstances, the United States could hold itself aloof and thus lose its Chinese market, it could participate in the scramble—which would have been difficult in view of the inability of the United States to exercise its power effectively in the Far East—or it could seek to induce all the Powers to accept the Open Door principle. It chose the latter course for obvious reasons. In spite of her oriental possessions and spheres of influence, Great Britain had a similar interest in blocking French and Russian monopolistic designs on China. In 1898 the British Associated Chambers of Commerce dispatched a mission to China, headed by Lord Beresford, who subsequently championed the Open Door and the territorial integrity of China in his speeches in the United States. American commercial interests engaged in Chinese trade likewise brought pressure to bear upon the State Department.

On September 6, 1899, Secretary of State John Hay issued his famous circular letter, calling upon the Powers to subscribe to the principle that they would not interfere with Chinese tariff duties, harbor dues, or railway rates nor with treaty ports or vested interests in their spheres of influence in China. Great Britain agreed at once, with France, Italy, Germany, Japan, and finally Russia following suit. On March 20, 1900, Hay announced that the American Government would regard the acceptance of the principle as "final and definitive." On July 3, 1900, following the outbreak of the Boxer Rebellion, Hay despatched a second circular note to the Powers in which he urged action to "bring about permanent safety and peace to China, preserve Chinese territorial and administrative entity, protect all rights guaranteed to friendly Powers by treaty and international law, and safeguard for the world the principle of equal and impartial trade with all parts of the Chinese Empire." This championship of the territorial integrity and the administrative entity of China as a corollary of the Open Door has been a permanent feature of American policy in the Far East ever since. Friction developed with Russia and subsequently with Japan and other Powers as to the observance of the principle, but it was constantly reaffirmed and subscribed to by other Governments. In his inaugural address of March 4, 1909, President Taft intimated that in the future it might become necessary for the United States to use force in preserving the Open Door:

> In the international controversies that are likely to arise in the Orient, growing out of the question of the Open Door and other issues, the United States can maintain her interest intact and secure respect for her just demands. She will not be able to do so, however, if it is understood that she never intends to back

[1] See pp. 412–414 above.

up her assertion of right and her defense of interest by anything but mere verbal protest and diplomatic notes. For this reason the expenses of the army and navy and of coast defenses should always be considered as something which our Government must pay for, and they should not be cut off through mere considerations of economy.

Subsequent efforts on the part of the United States to insure equality of economic opportunity in China and the preservation of the territorial integrity of that country can only be sketched here. In the Root-Takahira Agreement of November 30, 1908, Japan and the United States agreed to maintain the *status quo* and to "preserve the common interest of all Powers in China by supporting by all pacific means at their disposal the independence and integrity of China and the principle of equal opportunity for commerce and industry of all nations in that Empire." American friction with Japan over these issues became acute during the Great War. The Lansing-Ishii Agreement of November 3, 1917, reiterated the principles already agreed upon, but the United States recognized that "territorial propinquity creates special relations between countries" and that "Japan has special interests in China, particularly in the part to which her possessions are contiguous." This admission was withdrawn in 1923, following the Washington Conference. Here the United States was successful in securing for the first time the incorporation of the Open Door doctrine into a general treaty to which China itself was a party. The Nine Power Pact of February 6, 1922, entered into by the United States, Japan, Great Britain, France, Italy, China, Belgium, Portugal, and The Netherlands, declared (Article I):

The contracting Powers, other than China, agree: (1) to respect the sovereignty, the independence, and the territorial and administrative integrity of China; (2) to provide the fullest and most unembarrassed opportunity to China to develop and maintain for herself an effective and stable government; (3) to use their influence for the purpose of effectually establishing and maintaining the principle of equal opportunity for the commerce and industry of all nations throughout the territory of China; (4) to refrain from taking advantage of conditions in China in order to seek special rights or privileges which would abridge the rights of subjects or citizens of friendly States, and from countenancing action inimical to the security of such States.

The Powers also agreed (Article III) not to support their nationals in seeking monopolies or preferences prejudicial to nationals of other Powers or "any general superiority of rights with respect to commercial or economic development in any designated region of China," or (Article IV) "any agreements . . . designed to create spheres of influence or to provide for the enjoyment of mutually exclusive opportunities in designated parts of Chinese territory." The Nine Power Treaty of the same date, relating to the Chinese customs tariff, likewise provided for equality of

[607]

treatment. The resolutions of the conference set up a board of reference to which questions arising out of these obligations might be submitted (third resolution) and provided for publicity of all treaties, agreements, and private contracts for concessions, franchises, and other privileges in China (tenth resolution). These agreements did not invalidate existing concessions and spheres nor pass judgment as to whether they were in conformity with the Open Door principle. The board of reference was to deal only with future concessions and contracts. The publicity provisions were ineffective, and general abstract principles were not translated into definite and specific engagements accompanied by adequate international machinery to insure observance of the Open Door.

At the present time it is abundantly clear that the future of the Open Door in China is by no means safeguarded by existing treaty arrangements and that the door is in process of being gradually pushed shut in the Japanese sphere and, to a lesser degree, in the British and French spheres. The Japanese seizure of Manchuria and the creation of the puppet State of Manchukuo[1] has been regarded at Washington and Geneva as a violation of the Nine Power Pact. It is an infringement upon Chinese territorial integrity, and it probably foreshadows special favors to Japanese interests in Manchuria, to the detriment of the nationals of other Powers. The Japanese Government has denied that it has violated any treaty obligations and has made it clear that it intends to hold Manchuria against all challengers. The Stimson doctrine of non-recognition of agreements, situations, or territorial gains achieved by force[2] is motivated as much by a desire to protect the American conception of the Open Door in China as by regard for the Kellogg-Briand Pact. The doctrine has to date been without visible effect upon Japanese policy. The only ultimate safeguard of the Open Door is China's own power to protect herself from aggression and to keep her territories open on equal terms to nationals of all States. But China has been progressively enfeebled by internal strife and is increasingly unable to defend herself, or even to avert complete chaos within her frontiers.

If a new scramble among the Powers for spheres and possessions takes place, the Open Door will perhaps cease to enjoy even the lip service of the imperial governments. The United States will then be obliged to decide whether it wishes to abandon the principle and the markets protected by it, or to resort to something stronger than treaties and diplomatic notes as protective devices. Japanese opinion is not sympathetic toward the view that Japan must observe the Open Door in Manchuria, while the United States, France, and Great Britain keep the door closed in their own Pacific possessions and mandates. Any effort on the part of the

[1] See pp. 412–419 above.
[2] See pp. 680–681 below.

United States to thwart Japanese designs in China would undoubtedly lead to a war in which the first blow would be the occupation of the Philippines by the Japanese fleet. The very fact that such a conflict is by no means "unthinkable" is enough to suggest that international efforts to reconcile competing imperialisms in the Far East through the Open Door principle are still very far from having fulfilled their purpose.

3. THE MANDATE SYSTEM

If there is an alternative to imperialism, there is far greater strength in anti-imperialistic public opinion. If there is nothing in the world but "each for himself," if there is no other way of dealing with the economic, the financial, the political, the military problems than the unguarded and the uncounciled will of each particular nation, then we cannot expect to find at home the necessary leverage for anti-imperialistic opinion to curb imperialistic opinion. But if there is a League of Nations, if it is fully developed, if it contains within itself all the political and judicial organizations capable of dealing with every possible problem in international life, then public opinion at home will be able to take up the point and will be able to conquer, because it will be on the side of reason and the future, against the side of animal impulses and the past.—SALVADOR DE MADARIAGA, February 4, 1928.

The Soviet Union is not a member of the League of Nations and does not participate in the League of Nations, first of all because it does not wish to assume responsibility for the imperialistic policy of the League, for the "mandates" which are issued by the League of Nations for the object of the exploitation and oppression of the colonial countries. The Soviet Union does not participate in the League of Nations, since it stands wholly and completely against imperialism.—JOSEPH STALIN, Moscow *Pravda*, November 13, 1927.

The most significant international effort which has thus far been made to deal effectively with the double problem of imperialism—that of protecting native interests and that of keeping the peace between the empire-builders—is to be found in the mandate system, devised at the Paris Peace Conference of 1919 and administered by the League of Nations. In spite of all its shortcomings and limitations, the mandate system represents the highest development thus far of the policy of trusteeship and the most complete subjection of colonial governments and backward peoples to international supervision. The system has been applied only to the spoils of the victors in the Great War. For reasons which will be noted, it is not likely to be applied elsewhere. It nevertheless constitutes an unusually interesting experiment in international administration, the results of which throw a flood of light upon the prospects of an adequate international solution of the problems which have been suggested.

Out of a complex background of "trusteeship," "self-determination," "rights of small nations," political expediency, and humanitarian sentiments, there emerged on the eve of the Peace Conference the ideas which were subsequently incorporated into Article 22 of the League Covenant and into the mandate agreements. On December 16, 1918, General Jan Smuts of South Africa published a scheme for the international control of certain regions formerly belonging to Austria-Hungary and Turkey. He had no expectation that his plan would be applied to the former German colonies in Africa, since it was contemplated that these would be annexed by the victors. President Wilson enlarged upon this plan in his second draft of the Covenant (January 10, 1919) and argued vigorously for its general application to the outlying possessions of the defeated Powers. In his Fourteen Points of January 8, 1918, Wilson had declared that "the interests of the populations concerned must have equal weight with the equitable claims of the government whose title is to be determined" (fifth point), and that "the nationalities which are now under Turkish rule should be assured an undoubted security of life and an absolutely unmolested opportunity of autonomous development" (twelfth point).

At the conference, however, these proposals encountered the annexationist aspirations which had been incorporated into the secret treaties negotiated during the war. Under the Sykes-Picot Agreement of 1916 and other inter-Allied commitments of the same period, the former Turkish possessions in the Near East were to be partitioned between Great Britain and France. These Powers had likewise agreed to the division of the German African colonies which their military forces had occupied, and Japan had secret treaties of February-March, 1917, with Great Britain, France, Italy, and Russia, whereby she was promised the German Pacific islands north of the Equator. But outright annexation was precluded by the pledges made during the war to certain native chieftains, notably in Arabia, and by the idealistic verbiage in which Allied war aims had been clothed. Complete independence for these regions was never seriously contemplated, and their restoration to Germany and Turkey was of course inconceivable. The distribution of the territories was already provided for in the secret treaties, and these would be followed in any case. The only question was the form in which the victors should take control. France desired to recruit black troops in the new African territories allotted to her. The British Dominions sought to close their new territories to foreign trade and immigration. Wilson secured general acceptance of the mandate principle only by yielding to the British Dominions on the Open Door, to France on the recruitment of native soldiers, and to all of the Allies on the maintenance of the territorial allocation provided for in the secret treaties.

Article 22 of the League Covenant in its final form[1] referred to the former enemy territories, "which are inhabited by peoples not yet able to

[1] See p. 903 below.

stand by themselves under the strenuous conditions of the modern world." To these territories was to be applied the principle "that the well-being and development of such peoples form a sacred trust of civilization and that securities for the performance of this trust should be embodied in this Covenant." The "tutelage" of such peoples was to be entrusted to the "advanced nations" best able to assume this responsibility and was to be "exercised by them as mandatories on behalf of the League." The independence of the Near Eastern peoples was to be "provisionally recognized, subject to the rendering of administrative advice and assistance by a mandatory until such time as they are able to stand alone. The wishes of these communities must be a principal consideration in the selection of the mandatory." The central African peoples were declared to be "at such a stage that the mandatory must be responsible for the administration of the territory under conditions which will guarantee freedom of conscience and religion, subject only to the maintenance of public order and morals, the prohibition of abuses such as the slave trade, the arms traffic, and the liquor traffic, and the prevention of the establishment of fortifications or military and naval bases and of military training of the natives for other than police purposes and the defense of territory, and will also secure equal opportunities for the trade and commerce of other members of the League." Southwest Africa and the South Pacific islands were said to be so situated that they "can be best administered under the laws of the mandatory as integral portions of its territory, subject to the safeguards above mentioned in the interests of the indigenous population." These distinctions furnished the basis for the later classification of the territories into A, B, and C mandates. The mandatories were obliged to render annual reports to the Council of the League which should define "the degree of authority, control, or administration to be exercised" by them, unless this should be previously agreed upon by the members of the League. The Council was likewise instructed to set up a permanent commission to advise it and to receive and examine the annual reports. The table at the top of page 612 indicates the regions affected by these provisions.

By Article 119 of the Treaty of Versailles, Germany was compelled to renounce her colonies to the principal Allied and Associated Powers. During the Peace Conference they were distributed with few departures from the terms of the secret treaties. On May 7, 1919, the Pacific islands were divided among Great Britain, Australia, New Zealand, and Japan, subject to an informal reservation by President Wilson regarding the Island of Yap, which he thought ought to be an internationalized cable center. German Southwest Africa was assigned to the Union of South Africa, German East Africa to Great Britain, while Togoland and Cameroon were partitioned between Great Britain and France. The French Government originally insisted upon full sovereignty, but finally con-

THE WHITE MAN'S BURDEN

Mandates	Area, square miles	Population	Mandatory
		Class A Mandates	
Iraq.....................	177,148	2,849,282 (1920) 1,146,685 Sunni Moslems 1,494,015 Shi'ah Moslems 87,488 Jews 78,792 Christians 42,302 Others	Great Britain
Palestine and Trans-Jordan.	70,000	1,295,154 (1931) 979,952 Moslems 175,006 Jews 120,607 Christians 19,589 Others	Great Britain
Syria and Lebanon.........	60,000	2,046,857 (1926) 1,185,818 Moslems 505,419 Christians 328,937 Druzes 16,526 Jews 10,157 Others	France
		Class B Mandates	
Tanganyika...............	373,494	4,363,438 (1921)	Great Britain
Ruanda-Urundi............	21,429	5,605,000 (1926)	Belgium
Togoland (British).........	13,240	275,968 (1931)	Great Britain
Togoland (French).........	21,893	730,504 (1931)	France
Cameroon (British)........	34,236	7,050 (1930)	Great Britain
Cameroon (French)........	166,489	1,900,000 (1928)	France
		Class C Mandates	
Southwest Africa..........	322,394	275,520 (1930)	South Africa
New Guinea...............	91,300	404,400 (1930)	Australia
North Pacific Islands.......	830	99,590 (1930)	Japan
Western Samoa............	1,133	44,535 (1931)	New Zealand
Nauru...................	9	2,692 (1931)	Great Britain

tented itself with annexing that portion of Cameroon ceded to Germany in 1911. France has insisted, however, upon her right to recruit troops in her African mandates for general war purposes, in spite of Article 22 of the Covenant. Belgium objected to the transfer of all of East Africa to Great Britain, and on May 30, 1919, was granted Ruanda-Urundi by the British Government. Portugal demanded a mandate but received merely recognition of her sovereignty over Kionga, a small territory adjacent to Mozambique which she had recognized as belonging to Germany in 1894.

The Turkish territory was distributed at San Remo on April 25, 1920. The British and French Governments failed to cooperate with Wilson in his efforts to ascertain the wishes of the inhabitants. He had sent the King-Crane Commission to the Near East in June-July, 1919. Its report revealed that Arab sentiment favored an independent united Syria, including Palestine, and strongly opposed the Zionist project, sponsored by Great Britain, to convert Palestine into a new Jewish homeland. If inde-

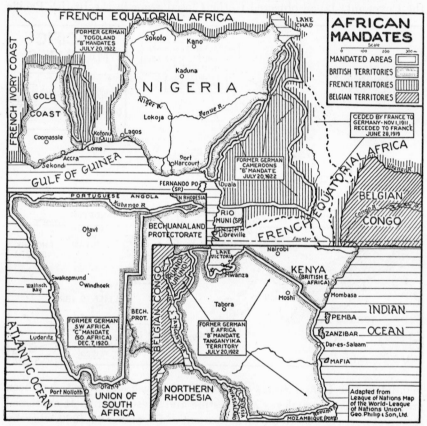

pendence could not be secured, the Arabs preferred the United States as mandatory, with Great Britain as second choice. This report was kept secret until 1922 and was ignored by the Allied Governments. France was assigned Syria and the Lebanon, and Great Britain received Palestine, Trans-Jordan, and Mesopotamia. The United States refused the proffer of a mandate over Armenia, which was subsequently divided between Turkey and the U.S.S.R. in defiance of the Allies. Under the abortive Treaty of Sèvres of 1920, Greece sought to annex the hinterland of Smyrna, while Italy and France had marked out Adalia and Cilicia respectively as annexations. But following the Turkish Nationalist victory over the Greeks, these regions were restored to Turkey by the Treaty of Lausanne of 1923.

The actual "mandates" in the legal sense were the agreements concluded between the Allied and Associated Powers under the direction of the Supreme Council. It was here that the A, B, and C classification was made, in conformity with the three categories mentioned in Article 22 of the Covenant. Japan objected to the Closed Door in the British Pacific

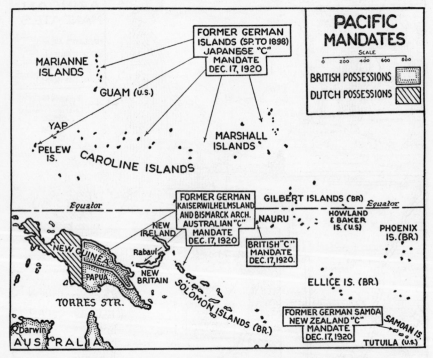

mandates. The United States objected that British oil interests had been granted exclusive privileges in Palestine and Mesopotamia. It expressed its regret over the San Remo oil agreement of December 23, 1920, whereby Great Britain granted France a 25 per cent share of the oil resources of Mesopotamia. The American Government reasserted the Open Door principle and declared that although it was not a member of the League it would not submit to the exclusion of its nationals from the benefits of equality of treatment. Lord Curzon agreed in principle to these contentions in February, 1921, but declared that American policy in the Philippines, Haiti, and Costa Rica was not consistent with the Open Door. In November, 1925, American oil interests (Rockefeller, Sinclair, and Doheny) were granted 25 per cent of the shares of the Turkish Petroleum

Company, which secured from Iraq an exclusive concession for the exploitation of the oil resources of the Bagdad and Mosul areas. The United States likewise objected to the omission of the Yap reservation in the Japanese mandate. The United States subsequently concluded treaties with Japan, France, Great Britain, and Belgium, safeguarding the rights of American nationals to equal treatment. These negotiations delayed final action on the mandate agreements. All of these instruments were subject to confirmation by the League Council. The C mandates

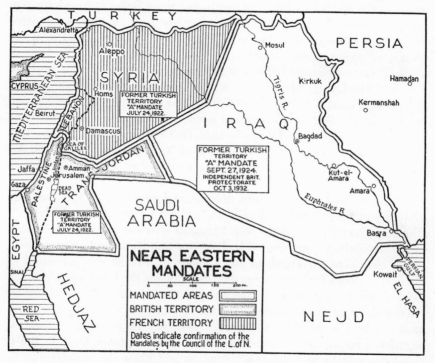

were confirmed by the Council on December 17, 1920. The B mandates were similarly confirmed on July 20, 1922.

Additional delays occurred before the A mandates were finally approved. The Palestine mandate was objected to by the Papacy, the Moslems, the Jews, and the British House of Lords—all for different and mutually incompatible reasons. Italy objected to confirmation of both the Palestine and Syrian mandates. These mandates were tentatively confirmed by the Council on July 22, 1922, and subsequently given full approval with the announcement of a Franco-Italian agreement on September 29, 1923. The Arabs of Mesopotamia revolted against the British mandate, with the result that Great Britain recognized the Kingdom of Iraq, with Feisal, son of King Hussein of the Hejaz, as its ruler. A

[615]

British-Iraq treaty of October 10, 1922, to be in effect for four years, defined British power in the new State and raised doubts as to whether Iraq was still a mandate or not. On September 27, 1924, the Council approved a document which made Iraq a British mandate but accepted the new treaty provisions, along with supplementary British pledges defining the mandatory's obligations. The boundary dispute over the Mosul district between Iraq and Turkey was submitted to the League Council by the Treaty of Lausanne of July 24, 1923. The Council award granting the district to Iraq was contingent upon Great Britain's remaining mandatory for twenty-five years, unless Iraq should be admitted earlier to the League. On March 11, 1926, the Council ratified the Mosul award, following a new British-Iraq treaty of January 13. On June 5, 1926, Turkey recognized the new boundary in return for the neutralization of the frontier and 10 per cent of the Iraq oil royalties. A third British-Iraq treaty of December 14, 1927, was not ratified, and on November 4, 1929, the British Government announced that it would recommend Iraq for admission to the League in 1932. On October 3, 1932, Iraq became the fifty-seventh member of the League of Nations by a vote of the Assembly, and thus began its career as an independent State under British protection.[1]

In these final arrangements, the original principle of the mandate system was "mutilated in details and sullied by the spirit of barter."[2] The essential purposes of the secret treaties were carried out. The wishes of the population were ignored in Palestine and Syria and not even consulted elsewhere. In Togoland and Cameroon, France was permitted to use native troops for general war purposes outside the territory. The Open Door, formerly maintained by Germany in the C mandates, was closed by the mandatories. It was protected in the A mandates neither by the Covenant nor by the mandate agreements, but only by subsequent treaties, negotiated largely at the insistence of the United States. Only in the B mandates was there a definite obligation laid upon the mandatories to maintain the Open Door. The Powers seemed to regard the mandates as annexations, as shown by the "compensations" granted to Italy in Jubaland (Kenya colony), in the Jarabud oasis, in Egypt, and in a strip of

[1] Nicholas Politis, President of the Assembly, characterized the admission as follows: "We see, with the consent and to the satisfaction of all, that a new State has come peacefully into existence, whereas in past centuries that State could probably only have come into existence by violent means. The League, therefore, once more has shown the error of those who think it merely exists to crystallize the present situation and prevent the normal development of the world. The admittance of Iraq shows that the League offers the possibility of carrying out peacefully what might otherwise have required revolution, and when, despite the difficulties and anxieties of the present time, we see a League of Nations doing its regular work so successfully, I think we realize that the crisis from which the League is supposed to be suffering is apparent rather than real." (Assembly meeting, October 3, 1932.)

[2] Q. Wright, *Mandates under the League of Nations*, 1930, p. 63.

eastern Tunis. For all practical purposes, the C mandates are treated as annexations and the B mandate administration is scarcely distinguishable from that which would have been provided for outright conquest. The A mandates are also under the effective control of the mandatories.

In all of these regions save Iraq, the aspirations of the inhabitants toward independence and self-determination have been crushed with the same ruthlessness which has characterized imperialism everywhere. When, in 1922, the Bondelzwart tribe in Southwest Africa resisted governmental measures designed to further the economic interests of the white settlers at the expense of the natives, South Africa replied with machine guns and bombing planes, which slaughtered scores of men, women, and children in the native villages. In Palestine the chronic friction between Arabs and Jews, engendered by British and Zionist efforts to create a Jewish settlement in what is preponderantly a Moslem country, has led to rioting and strife, with the British authorities (in the eyes of the Arab leaders) acting in accordance with the ancient principle of divide and rule. The Syrians were subjected to French control against their wishes, and they have indulged in insurrections almost annually until 1927. The Jebel Druze revolt of 1925 was repressed with the utmost severity by the French military forces, which attempted to terrorize the population into submission by destroying with artillery the whole central area of the ancient city of Damascus, with the loss of thousands of lives. Other disorders in Iraq, western Samoa, and elsewhere have likewise been dealt with by punitive expeditions and violent reprisals, as seems inevitable regardless of the form of administration, where white imperialists rule natives. Africans and Polynesians have been unable to distinguish the new modes of oppression and exploitation from the old. The Moslem leaders of the Near East have waxed indignant over the new dispensation. Imperialist diplomats have condemned the system as involving all of the obligations of annexation, with few of the advantages. Germans, Americans, Turks, Russians, and Arabs have jeered at the mandate principle as a hollow mockery. The mandatory governments have usually refused to spend any more money on the mandates than they collect in local revenue, and they have in many respects tended to treat the mandates as outright conquests. In the light of these circumstances, cynics and pessimists have concluded that the system is a hypocritical sham, designed to disguise old imperialistic wolves in new sheep's clothing.[1]

Regardless of these shortcomings, the mandate system represents a significant adventure in international supervision over backward areas. The legal position of the mandates and the mandatories does not permit this relationship to be described in terms of any well-established juridical

[1] See Q. Wright, op. cit., pp. 64–98, "The Reception of the System," for a résumé of favorable and unfavorable evaluations.

category. It is clear that the mandatories do not possess "sovereignty" in the mandated regions, and it is equally clear that sovereignty does not reside in the natives. The most satisfactory formula is that which holds that sovereignty resides in the League and is wielded by the mandatory with the consent of the Council.[1] The essence of the system is League supervision. The mandate system was not created by the League, but the Council confirmed the original mandate agreements, which provide that all subsequent modifications of their terms must meet with its approval. In accordance with this arrangement, the Council in 1923 approved the modification of the frontier between Ruanda-Urundi and Tanganyika, in order to protect the Ruanda tribesmen against an artificial division of their lands. The Council must also confirm any termination of a mandate, as in the case of Iraq, October, 1932. Its consent would likewise be necessary to transfer a mandate from one State to another, or to extend the system to areas not at present covered by it. The Council also accepts or rejects the recommendations of the Permanent Mandates Commission and transmits them, if accepted, to the mandatory Powers.

Most of the League functions are exercised by the Council, but the Assembly has never taken the view that it has no authority in mandate matters. At almost every Assembly, resolutions are passed relating to mandate affairs, addressed either to the Permanent Mandates Commission, to the Council, or to the mandatory Powers. The mandates section of the Secretariat handles petitions, correspondence, and publications and serves the Permanent Mandates Commission in a secretarial capacity. International disputes as to the interpretation or application of the mandate agreements are submitted to the Permanent Court of International Justice when they cannot be settled by negotiations.

The whole procedure of League supervision centers about the Permanent Mandates Commission. In accordance with the provisions of Article 22 of the Covenant, this body was established by the Council to advise it on mandate questions. It was originally composed of nine members, with a majority of nationals of non-mandatory Powers. In 1924 M. Rappard, formerly head of the mandates section of the Secretariat, was made an "extraordinary member" and provision was also made for an advisory member from the International Labor Office. In 1927 the number of regular members was increased to ten, in order to provide a place for a German national. The first Assembly recommended that one seat be always reserved for a woman member, and that no member be dismissed by the Council without the consent of a majority of the Assembly. The

[1] At the conclusion of an exhaustive discussion of the legal aspects of the mandates system, Quincy Wright concludes that "sovereignty of the areas is vested in the League, acting through the Covenant-amending process, and is exercised by the mandatory with consent of the Council for eventual transfer to the mandated communities themselves." *Op. cit.*, p. 530.

members are forbidden to hold any official post with their governments. All are appointed by the Council on the basis of personal merit and competence. They receive a fixed annual salary, plus traveling expenses. The commission usually meets once a year, ordinarily in private, with six members constituting a quorum. The mandatory Powers are required to submit annual reports to the Commission, which discusses them in the presence of a representative of the mandatory. Following his withdrawal, the Commission drafts its own observations for submission to the Council and the mandatory government.

The observations of the Permanent Mandates Commission are purely advisory, but in practice the Commission has become the agent of the Council, through which international supervision is exercised. The Commission receives its information from the annual reports, from questioning the representatives of the Mandatory Powers, and from petitions submitted by the inhabitants of the mandated regions. Such petitions, however, can be submitted only through the mandatory government, and the Commission refuses to consider petitions opposing the mandate itself. In March, 1927, the Council decided that petitioners should not be granted oral hearing. The Commission also receives information from other League bodies, but it never visits the mandated areas or dispatches investigators to them.

A survey of the Commission's proceedings leads to the conclusion that it is primarily dependent upon the mandatory Powers for information and that the native populations, in whose interest the whole system was presumably established, have little opportunity for the independent presentation of grievances or for a full and impartial hearing. Even when open rebellion is raging in a mandated area, as in Syria in 1925, the commission is disposed to hedge and hesitate and its dilatory criticisms are usually very mild—ordinarily taking the form merely of a request for further information from the mandatory government. Since the Council itself is dominated politically, if not numerically, by the mandatory Powers, it is scarcely strange that it should move with great circumspection in exercising its supervisory functions and that the Commission, its servant, should reflect this inevitable tendency. The Commission does serve to mobilize opinion and has, by its suggestions, influenced the conduct of the mandatories to some degree and made a beginning of establishing international standards of colonial administration. That imperial Powers should be obliged to report at all to an international body on the administration of the territories under their control is certainly a step in advance of the old imperialism. But it cannot be said that the Permanent Mandates Commission has thus far acted vigorously as a bold and independent agency determined to protect native interests, regardless of the prestige of the mandatories. Its procedure, its composition, and its relation to the Council make it improbable that it will play any such rôle in the future.

The mandate system must be evaluated in terms of its expressed purposes and its adequacy in solving the double problem of imperialism. Does it prevent or lessen international friction over the control of backward areas? Does it safeguard the interest of the natives and prepare them for self-government? These questions do not admit of easy and general answers, for the necessary information is not in all cases available and many imponderables must be weighed in the balance. Whether international friction in the backward regions is greater or less, whether the natives are better off or worse off than would have been the case under some alternative arrangement no one can say with any degree of certainty. Italy has resented the fact that she received no mandates and has cast longing glances in the direction of those held by Great Britain and France. The United States has had serious controversies with the mandatories over the Open Door. Germany has deplored the loss of her colonies. Many Germans hope for their restoration, or at least for a mandate for Germany —an arrangement which none of the mandatory Powers is likely to enter into voluntarily, since they have shown no enthusiasm for freeing the mandates from their control, much less transferring them to another State. The Soviet Union, and to a lesser degree the Moslem States, regard the whole arrangement with the utmost cynicism. That imperialistic tensions over these areas would have been greater had they been openly annexed is a proposition which it is impossible to prove or disprove. It is enough to notice that international tensions have continued. The system has made a concrete contribution to peace, in that it forbids the establishment of military bases or fortifications or the military training of the natives for other than police purposes and the defense of the territory. In practice, however, the exceptions allow a wide latitude for action, and France has reserved the right to herself to use Togoland and Cameroon Negroes for war purposes in Europe or elsewhere. From the point of view of the Open Door, which has been a fruitful cause of conflict between the Powers, the undoubted achievements of the system in the A and B areas are counterbalanced by the fact of definite retrogression in the C areas.

The second question is equally difficult to answer. It is probable that the interests of the natives are safeguarded more effectively than they might have been in the event of annexation. Article 22 of the Covenant obliges the mandatories to maintain freedom of conscience and religion and to prohibit the traffic in slaves, arms, and liquor. Article 23 of the Covenant requires all League members "to secure just treatment of the native inhabitants of the territories under their control." The mandate agreements provide for the prohibition of the slave trade, the eventual emancipation of slaves, the protection of natives against fraud in labor contracts, the prohibition of all forced labor except for essential public works, and the prohibition of land transfers from natives to non-natives without governmental consent. Some of these obligations have been well observed by some of the mandatories in some of the mandates. Others have been ignored. In a few instances the mandatories have done more in the interests of the natives than their legal obligations strictly require. But it is not to be imagined that the mandatory Powers which regard their own colonies as spheres of profit and exploitation for their nationals will adopt a fundamentally different view in the mandates. The available statistics of population growth, public health, land tenure, wages, education, civil security, capital investments, and the like[1] present conflicting and inconclusive evidence on most of these points. As for "preparation for self-government," only one mandated region—Iraq—has been granted its independence, and even here the new State is bound by treaty terms, making it as much a British protectorate as is Egypt. Hopes have been expressed that the other A mandates may soon receive their independence, but the time is not yet. There would seem to be no prospect of self-government for the B and C mandates in the visible future.

In its genesis, the mandate system was a weak compromise between Wilsonian idealism, self-determination, and the concept of trusteeship on the one hand, and annexationist ambitions, political subjugation, and economic exploitation on the other. Like all compromises, the system is unworthy either of the highest praises of its apologists or the most severe condemnations of its critics. It can only be characterized as a short step toward the protection of the backward races from the evils of imperialism through international supervision. The aspirations of its proponents are still greater than the achievements of its administrators. Its outstanding weakness is that it is narrowly limited in geographical scope and that imperial States have shown no disposition whatever to place their own colonies under this form of control. The mandated territories cover an area one-third the size of the United States, with a population one-sixth as large. A million and a quarter square miles and twenty million people are not negligible items in contemporary world affairs. But half of the world's total land surface, inhabited by six hundred million human beings, remains under the exclusive sovereignty of the imperial Powers. Apparently the only prospect of an extension of the system to other colonies is to be found in the possibility of a series of imperialist wars in which the colonies of the defeated States would successively be converted into mandates by the victors. This future remedy, however, would be worse than the present disease, and the League itself would expire in the process. The only proposals which have been put forward in official circles for the extension

[1] *Cf.* Quincy Wright, *op. cit.*, pp. 550–579.

of the system have related to backward States now independent. In the early 1920's Japan toyed with the idea, now completely abandoned, of converting Manchuria into a Japanese mandate. There has been some informal discussion of imposing a mandate on Liberia, but without results thus far. There remains the hope that the system will evolve high standards of colonial administration which will influence the policies of all the imperial States. But so long as the great driving forces of capitalism, nationalism, and imperialism persist and produce the same consequences in the future as in the past, the mandate system can scarcely become an ultimate solution of the problems of war and oppression created by the empire-builders.

4. THE REVOLT OF THE SUBJECT PEOPLES

> We demand the freedom of self-determination, *i.e.*, independence, *i.e.*, the freedom of separation for the oppressed nations, not because we dream of an economically atomized world, nor because we cherish the ideal of small States, but on the contrary because we are for large States and for a coming closer, even a fusion of nations, but on a truly democratic, truly internationalist basis, which is unthinkable without the freedom of separation.—NICOLAI LENIN, November, 1915.

In the last analysis, the essential nature of imperialism constitutes a stubborn and irreducible obstacle to the complete success of the efforts reviewed above. Imperialism is the imposition by force and violence of alien rule upon subject peoples, despite all moralizings and pretensions to the contrary. The empires of today are maintained by holding dissatisfied backward peoples in subjection. The empires of the future will be created by the same process. Force to the utmost has been and still is the final arbiter in disputes between subject peoples and imperial governments and between the imperial States themselves. Those who are ruled submit willingly to forcible control by rulers when they feel that the rulers represent themselves or symbolize certain common interests of the whole community, or are acting disinterestedly on behalf of the welfare of their subjects. They resent coercion and resist it when they have the means, in every situation in which the rulers are set apart from themselves by race, language, culture, or cleavages of economic interests.

In all of the empires, the gulf between rulers and ruled is impassable so long as the former pursue their own profit-and-power interests and the latter feel themselves to be the victims of foreign exploitation. Black men, brown men, and yellow men are usually far more willing to submit to oppression and misrule at the hands of people of their own color and kind than to the most benevolent dictation of the white man. This is incomprehensible to the western peoples, despite the paradoxical fact that no white community would for a moment regard the most enlightened and beneficent despotism of colored aliens as a desirable alternative to the blessings of liberty for themselves—even when these blessings involve graft, corruption, and the breakdown of democratic government and of all semblance of economic security. Political freedom for backward peoples may leave them infinitely worse off than they are under white rule, with the added disadvantage of having no one but themselves to blame for their troubles. But this freedom is no less highly cherished. The infection of the backward peoples with the cult of nationalism and the idea of self-determination is the inevitable result of cultural contact with the west. It is likewise a consequence of economic developments, fostered by the white man, which convert African and oriental nobles and peasants into bourgeois entrepreneurs and proletarians. And to the degree to which western bourgeois aspirations toward national independence and political democracy, and western proletarian aspirations toward economic independence and social democracy seize upon the imaginations of the subject races, to that degree will they be moved to cast off the foreign yoke.

The concept of "trusteeship" has seldom been extended to the point at which an imperial State is willing of its own volition to surrender sovereignty over colonial possessions into the hands of the natives. Indeed, political self-determination is incompatible with the very theory of trusteeship, for the latter assumes the necessity of alien control and guidance—if not for exploitation, then for uplift and perhaps for preparation for eventual self-government. Any voluntary relinquishment of control by the great imperial States is almost inconceivable, for power and profits are seldom surrendered except under duress. And such are the economic and cultural consequences of imperialism that its apologists can logically contend that their withdrawal would in many cases lead to disaster. The missionary, the merchant, the banker, the soldier, and the colonial administrator inevitably, even if unwittingly, disrupt and destroy the ancient modes of life of their subjects and then utilize the resulting chaos as an excuse for retaining control. If, on the other hand, the trusteeship principle is taken seriously and the natives are educated and made prosperous, the empire-builders usually find themselves confronted with demands for autonomy or independence, which are increased rather than diminished in intensity and insistence by alien efforts at native uplift. In dealing with such demands, imperial Powers customarily raise questions of native capacity for self-government and usually delay the grant of self-rule as long as possible.

Here are the seeds of inevitable rebellion. Bitterness against white domination will continue to grow among subject peoples, not in proportion as they are misgoverned and exploited, but in proportion as they become progressively imbued with the white man's own values and ideas. During the nineteenth century, the abuses of colonial administration were far greater than they are at the present time. But after initial resistance to foreign conquest was crushed, the African and Asiatic populations submitted docilely and dumbly. In the twentieth century the subject peoples are almost everywhere better off economically and enjoy more effective guarantees of their rights, more extensive protection of their interests, more voice in the determination of their own destinies. But in the epoch of trusteeship, humanitarianism, and the mandate system, the backward races are aflame with demands for independence and are disposed to resist their oppressors at every opportunity. Imperialism thus digs its own grave by educating its victims to accomplish its own destruction. Economic development, cultural interpenetration, and awakening political consciousness all render it unthinkable that hundreds of millions of colonial peoples should remain in subjection to the ten colonial Powers. The days of the empires are numbered, even though their decline will inevitably be slow and gradual. Whether it will be bloody and catastrophic or pacific and orderly is not yet clear. This attempt to weigh the white man's burden in the scales of the future may appropriately be brought to a conclusion with a consideration of the efforts of the imperial States to avert their doom, and the efforts of the backward peoples to emancipate themselves from the thralldom of foreign dominion.

The first and most elementary defense reaction on the part of the imperial governments in the face of resistance from their subjects is to crush such resistance by force and to adopt policies designed to enfeeble their victims and to destroy their identity. Such States have frequently, though seldom successfully, adopted the nationalistic policy of cultural assimilation. They have attempted by persuasion, education, or coercion to make the subject peoples good citizens of the empire. When the subjects are not too radically different in race, language, and cultural background from their conquerors, this policy has theoretically much to commend it, even though it has generally failed to fulfill its purposes when applied to minorities on the European continent. With qualifications, this is the policy of the United States in Hawaii, Porto Rico, and the Philippines, of Great Britain in many of the crown colonies, of France in Algeria, of Japan in Formosa and Korea.[1] It involves the government of the colony by officials appointed directly by the home authorities. It involves tariff assimilation, education in the language of the imperial State, and a

[1] A Japanese spokesman once declared: "The Korean peoples will be absorbed by the Japanese. They will talk our language, live our life, and will be an integral part of us. There are only two ways of colonial administration. One is to rule over the people as aliens. This you British have done in India, and therefore your Empire cannot endure. India must pass out of your rule. The second way is to absorb the people. This is what we will do. We will teach them our language, establish our institutions, and make them one with us." N. E. Buxton and T. P. Conwil-Evans, *Oppressed Peoples and the League of Nations*, 1922, p. 190.

variety of efforts to replace the language and culture of the natives by that of the conquerors. It may involve a pretense of colonial participation in the national government. In the French colonial empire, Algeria, Cochin China, Senegal, and the French possessions in India and North America are represented in the national Parliament at Paris. This avoids "taxation without representation"—the major grievance of the American colonial rebels of 1775—but colonials are usually more interested in abolishing taxation than in obtaining representation. Such representatives, whether elected or appointed, are always in a small minority in the central legislature. The whole arrangement is a substitute for self-determination rather than the attainment of it. It breeds resentment and resistance, and if the attempt to destroy native political institutions succeeds, no basis whatever remains for local self-government. In such a situation, the alternative to despotism is anarchy, as the British in India are in process of discovering.

The uniform failure of this policy has led to the development of various forms of autonomy, protection, and native participation in local government. Native rulers and native institutions are retained as the basis of foreign control. Decentralization is substituted for bureaucratic authority at the center. Legislation for the colonies is enacted by local assemblies, subject to various limitations and controls. Executive power is entrusted to an appointed governor who is given considerable discretion. Local courts are maintained, and military and fiscal affairs are handled in such a fashion as to encourage local participation and local responsibility. This system has been most extensively developed in the British Empire under the new colonial policy inaugurated after the American Revolution and the Canadian rebellion. In the native States of India and in Nigeria, Uganda, and Tanganyika, native princes or chieftains are used as agents of colonial government. In Morocco and Tunis, the French Government has maintained in operation the native monarchies, whose rulers are aided by French "advisers." In this fashion expenses are cut down, the necessary number of white administrators is reduced, and a more efficient and satisfactory régime usually results. Where the impact of western civilization has disintegrated native social and political institutions, this solution is of course unworkable. But in most of the colonial areas of Africa and Asia it is still quite feasible.

Colonial autonomy usually involves, not only native participation in administration, but native participation in lawmaking and taxation through local representative assemblies. Some two dozen colonial legislatures exist in the British crown colonies. The United States maintains local legislatures in the Philippines and Porto Rico. Other examples are to be found in the French, Dutch, Italian, and Japanese colonial empires. In most of these instances the franchise requirements and the structure of

[625]

the legislature are such that the natives are outnumbered by representatives of the nationals of the imperial Power. The native representatives, moreover, often speak, not for blocs of voters, but for various economic, religious, and racial groups. In almost all cases the principle of ministerial responsibility does not prevail, *i.e.*, the executive power is not controlled by the legislature, but by the home government. Deadlocks between the legislatures and executive branches of the colonial governments are avoided by limiting the powers of the legislature and authorizing the governor to ignore its decisions in certain instances. Or the legislature may be composed in part of members appointed by the executive and under his control. In India and Malta a system of "diarchy" prevails—in theory as a transition to complete local self-government—whereby the local legislature has no authority over certain "reserved" subjects and a dual executive exists, in which the native ministers are responsible to the legislature but have no powers which could be used to endanger foreign domination. The usual result in such cases is that the legislature becomes a forum of criticism and agitation, and friction between the two branches of the government becomes chronic.[1] Local participation in legislation and administration is not likely to alleviate native unrest, unless the native lawmakers and officials are given the full powers exercised by the foreign rulers—and since this would be equivalent to independence and the complete relinquishment of foreign control, it is seldom granted.

A third and more extreme policy is represented by the actual emancipation of colonial possessions or by the establishment of forms of control which are compatible with theoretical independence. The only significant instances in modern times of an imperial State definitely relinquishing power over its possessions without being compelled to do so by *force majeur* are to be found in the British Empire. The Dominions have become fully self-governing, with representative parliaments and responsible cabinets, and while they are still units of the British Commonwealth and acknowledge allegiance to the King and to the local governors-general of the crown, they are for all practical purposes independent. It is safe to say that they would all sooner or later have followed the example of the thirteen Atlantic seaboard colonies in 1776, had they not been granted self-government in this fashion. With the exception of South Africa, the Dominions are all inhabited by English immigrants, and in South Africa the native black majority is kept from political power by franchise restrictions giving the English and Dutch settlers effective control.

In February, 1922, Egypt, formerly a British protectorate in form as well as in fact, was granted its "independence," *i.e.*, became a British protectorate only in fact but not in form. Great Britain reserved control over security of com-

[1] For other examples, *cf.* Buell, *op. cit.*, pp. 378–387.

munication, defense, the protection of foreign interests and properties, and the Anglo-Egyptian Sudan. The British Government declared, moreover, that it would "regard as an unfriendly act any interference in the affairs of Egypt by another Power, and it will consider any aggression against the territory of Egypt as an act to be repelled with all the means at their command." British troops continued to be stationed in the country, and the Egyptian army remained under the command of Sir Lee Stack, Governor-general of the Sudan, much to the disgust of the Egyptian Nationalists and of Zaghlul Pasha, the native prime minister. When Sir Lee was murdered on November 9, 1924, the British Government dispatched a stiff ultimatum to Cairo and compelled Egypt to accede to its demands (including a $2,500,000 indemnity) by occupying the customs house at Alexandria. When Egypt appealed to the League of Nations, the British Government successfully sustained its contention that this was a "domestic question" beyond the purview of Geneva. The Egyptian constitution of April 19, 1924, does not expressly reserve British rights, but a British high commissioner and British civil and military advisers remain at the capitol. It is the purpose of the British Government to conclude an alliance with a "protected" Egypt which will safeguard British interests.

The A mandates of the Near East are in process of a similar evolution, though here the imperial Powers never formally established a protectorate or possessed sovereignty over these regions. The Anglo-Iraq alliance, incorporated in the treaty of October 10, 1922, the protocol of April 30, 1923, and the treaty of March 24, 1924, were made part of the mandate arrangement and continue in force at the present time, with Iraq independent.[1] British advisers were gradually withdrawn during the mandate period. The Iraq constitution provides for a legislature and a responsible executive, without participation by British officials. None has participated directly in the cabinet, save for one financial adviser who held a seat for six months in 1923. British influence was exercised through advisers in the various executive departments and through a staff of inspectors throughout the country, all paid by the Iraq Government. These arrangements have not as yet been terminated since Iraq's admission to the League. On January 29, 1931, the Iraq Parliament ratified a new treaty of alliance with Great Britain, providing for the maintenance of British military forces in the country and for two air bases for British air squadrons. In Palestine, independence would mean Arab control and the extinction of the hopes of the Zionists. This consideration has thus far prevented any serious steps toward emancipation. In Syria the French authorities permitted a constituent assembly

[1] "The aim which His Majesty's Government have set before themselves has been the establishment at the earliest possible date of a fully independent state of Iraq, inspired with the spirit of the League of Nations, animated by a sincere desire to observe its international obligations, and ready to accept not only the privileges, but also the responsibilities involved in accession to the Covenant. During the period under review, they have constantly kept in mind the principles embodied in Article 22 of the Covenant, that the well-being and development of the people of Iraq form a sacred trust of civilization, but they have never regarded the attainment of an ideal standard of administrative efficiency and stability as a necessary condition, either of the termination of the mandatory régime or of the admission of Iraq to membership in the League of Nations. Nor has it been their conception that Iraq should from the first be able to challenge comparison with the most highly developed and civilized nations of the modern world. What they have aimed at is the setting up within fixed frontiers of a self-governing State enjoying friendly relations with neighboring States and equipped with stable legislative, judicial, and administrative systems and all the working machinery of a civilized government." *Special Report to the Council of the League of Nations on the Progress of Iraq During the Period* 1920–1931, 1931.

to meet, but when it decided to establish a republic and to work toward the termination of the mandate, it was prorogued in February, 1929. Control remains in the hands of a French high commissioner, aided by French military forces.

It is probable, in view of recent developments, that the technique of imperialism in the future will be characterized less by outright annexation and direct administration than by various disguised forms of control. After the Spanish-American War, the United States "emancipated" Cuba as an independent State. The "Platt amendment" to the Army Appropriation Act of 1900, however, was incorporated into the Cuban constitution of 1903 and the Cuban-American treaty of the same year. It forbids Cuba to alienate its independence, limits the public debt, and reserves to the United States the right to acquire coaling stations and naval bases and to intervene to preserve order and protect Cuba's independence. The Hay-Bunauvarilla Treaty of November 18, 1903, with Panama similarly makes this State an American protectorate, without damaging its "sovereignty" save in the Canal Zone. American dollar diplomacy in the Caribbean has devised various schemes of financial advisers, customs collectors, and marine intervention which insure effective American control without destroying the fiction of independence. "Independent" Albania is likewise an Italian protectorate under the treaty of November, 1926. The Japanese Manchukuo treaty of September 15, 1932, provides that the two States shall cooperate in maintaining their security and that Japan shall station such troops in Manchukuo as are necessary to achieve this purpose.[1]

Where an independent native government is kept in power by foreign bayonets and foreign loans, such disguised forms of control will usually enable the imperial State to exercise authority in its protectorate without abandoning the pretense of independence and without provoking as much resistance as would be encountered in simple annexation. If the local government, however, represents native nationalism to any degree,

[1] The protocol signed at Changchun September 15, 1932, by General Nobuyoshi Muto, representing the Emperor of Japan, and Cheng Hsiao-hsu, Premier of Manchukuo, was as follows: "Whereas Japan has recognized the fact that Manchukuo, in accordance with the free will of its inhabitants, has organized and established itself as an independent State, and Whereas Manchukuo has declared its intention of abiding by all international engagements entered into by China in so far as they are applicable to Manchukuo; Now the Governments of Japan and Manchukuo, each respecting the territorial rights of the other, and also in order to secure the peace of the Far East, agreed as follows: (1) Manchukuo shall confirm and respect, in so far as no agreement to the contrary shall be made between Manchukuo and Japan in the future, all the rights and interests possessed by Japan or her subjects within the territory of Manchukuo by virtue of Sino-Japanese treaties, agreements or other arrangements, or through Sino-Japanese contracts, private as well as public. (2) Japan and Manchukuo, recognizing that any threat to the territory or peace and order of either of the high contracting parties constitutes, at the same time, a threat to the safety and existence of the other, agree to cooperate in the maintenance of their national security, it being understood that such Japanese forces as may be necessary for this purpose shall be stationed in Manchukuo."

friction is certain to develop. Local resentment against alien domination will be no less keen for the fact that the iron hand is hidden in a silken glove. Such resentment is endemic in the Caribbean protectorates of the United States. But so long as those who resist alien rule are weaker than the foreign conquerors, resistance merely intensifies foreign oppression and prolongs the dictatorial régime imposed from without. The rejection by the Haitian congress, for example, of the treaty with the United States signed September 3, 1932, will probably prolong rather than shorten the American marine occupation. The treaty provided for the evacuation by the end of 1934 of the American forces stationed in the black republic since 1915 and for the substitution of a fiscal representative and a deputy fiscal representative, appointed by Haiti on nomination of the American President, for the American receiver-general of customs and the financial adviser. These new officials were to safeguard the interest of American holders of Haitian bonds until 1942, when all the bonds would be retired. The Haitians took the justifiable view that these financial arrangements merely substituted one form of control for another. In rejecting the treaty they apparently calculated on the expiration in 1936 of the treaty of September 16, 1915, as provided by the terms. In such situations, however, imperial States seldom permit legal difficulties to stand in the way of the protection of their "interests." It is probable that long before 1936 Haiti will be obliged to accept either the 1932 treaty or some other arrangement equally unsatisfactory to native patriots.

The ultimate objective of nationalism is always complete political independence, and this is no less true of native nationalism in colonies or in semi-independent States than of western nationalism among the European peoples. The extent to which native leaders press their demands for complete emancipation will depend upon circumstances and considerations of political expediency. But nothing is more certain than final insistence upon complete independence and final repudiation of all half-measures short of this. This demand will be made regardless of the "capacity for self-government" of the subject races. This phrase is usually used by imperial States as an excuse for delaying or refusing the extension of political rights to their colonies. For thirty years the United States has been pledged to independence for the Philippine Islands, and for thirty years the grant of independence has been delayed on the ground that the Filipinos are not yet capable of standing alone. The same idea appears in Article 22 of the League Covenant, where it is applied to the mandated regions. States often hesitate to emancipate their colonies out of fear of their seizure by rival imperial Powers or of infringements upon the economic privileges of their nationals on the part of native rulers. These motives are rationalized into professed apprehensions over the prospective inability of the natives to manage their own affairs satisfactorily. In certain cases where western culture has undermined the bases of social cohesion and native initiative, there is no doubt but that the withdrawal of foreign troops and administrators would be followed by anarchy. In other cases it is clear that order is better preserved and economic welfare is more effectively promoted by colonial officials than would be the case under native régimes. But in many other cases there is no reason to suppose that native self-government would be any worse, from any point of view, than the government of some of the Latin American republics, of the Balkan States of Europe, or of certain municipalities in the United States. No objective standards of "capacity for self-government" exist, and no relation exists between this capacity, or the lack thereof, and the intensity of demands for self-rule—save that the social cohesion, civic consciousness, and political cooperation which are usually essential for effective agitation and rebellion likewise offer promise of the successful operation of native political institutions in the event of attainment of independence.

Space does not permit a detailed survey of the efforts of subject peoples to achieve control over their own destinies. Colonial revolts are too numerous, and the forms of native resistance are too varied, to make possible any complete account here of these contemporary phenomena. It will be sufficient to deal briefly and in general terms with the revolt of the subject peoples in Africa, in the Moslem world, in India, and in China. The course of recent events in these regions should offer a basis for prognosticating the probable success or failure of such efforts and for predicting to a certain degree the future of the empires.

A. Africa

The colored peoples of Africa have as a whole offered less effective resistance to imperialism than the people of other backward areas. The reasons are obvious: the native African peoples live for the most part in tribal societies on a preliterate cultural level. Their economic life and their technology are comparable to that prevailing in Europe in the late Stone Age or early Iron Age, or to that of the more primitive of the Amerindians at the time of Columbus. The Arab and Berber peoples of north Africa and Egypt have from time immemorial been aligned culturally and politically with the civilizations of the Mediterranean, rather than with those of the peoples across the desert. South of the Sahara sands is a broad strip of grasslands and forests inhabited by Sudanese, Senegalese, Guinea Negroes, and other black peoples skilled in primitive agriculture and handicraft. In the Congo wilds and in the lakes region of Equatorial Africa are various groups of Bantus and Negritoes (pigmies), living in a state of barbarism or savagery. In the south are other Bantus, Bushmen, and Hottentots, with the Polynesian Hovas from across the Indian Ocean inhabiting the island of Madagascar. Save for the Australian Bushmen and a few South Sea island peoples, these dark-skinned African tribesmen represent the most primitive groups with which the white man has come into contact in the course of imperial expansion. They possess no cultural unity, no sense of solidarity or common interests, no picture of the world outside of their jungles and plains. In many regions they have been so exploited and debauched by white adventurers and profit-seekers that they have lost all capacity for self-defense. Their numbers have probably declined since the advent of the white man, particularly in the Belgian Congo and in French West Africa. When forced labor, land robbery, and "Christian" atrocities have become intolerable, revolt has occurred—blind, sporadic, and doomed to swift futility. Hova resistance to the conquest of Madagascar was crushed by the French between 1896 and 1906. In South Africa the British were obliged to fight, not the Negroes, but the Boers for the privilege of ruling and exploiting the natives. The million and a half whites (Boer and British) have since joined hands to rob the six and a half million blacks of their ancestral estates. Here native resentment has begun to smolder. But throughout black Africa as a whole there are as yet few evidences of organized resistance to white rule, in spite of Marcus Garvey's somewhat fantastic Pan-African agitation of 1914–1924.

The situation is quite different in north Africa and throughout the whole Moslem world of which north Africa is a part. The ancient kingdom of Abyssinia, which has a Christian ruling class but a largely Mohammedan population, has preserved its independence in the face of the encroachments of the European Powers. The Arab followers of Mohammed Ahmed—the "Mahdi"—butchered Gordon in the Sudan in 1885 and defied Britain for thirteen years, until the dervishes were slaughtered by Kitchener at Omdurman in 1898. Egypt, Algiers, Tunis, Morocco, and Tripoli fell successively to the imperialists and have remained under the sovereignty or the effective control of the western Powers ever since. But the heirs of the ancient glories of Islam have never willingly accepted European rule. Rebellions have been frequent. Italy has expended vast quantities of blood and treasure to hold the deserts of Libya against the Arab tribesmen who claim them as their own. The incurable fever of native nationalism in Egypt compelled Great Britain to grant "independence" to the land of the Pharaohs. Unrest in Algeria and Tunis has often assumed alarming proportions. In Morocco the warlike native tribes almost succeeded in ousting their conquerors during and after the Great War. In the Spanish zone the Riffian warriors of Abd-el Krim inflicted such crushing defeats on the Spanish troops that Spanish authority was limited to the coastal areas, Spanish parliamentary government was discredited and replaced by the dictatorship of Primo de Rivera in 1923, and the Spanish monarchy itself was overthrown in 1931 as an aftermath. In 1925, following French encroachments on the valleys south of the Riff, Abd-el Krim's veteran forces invaded French Morocco and scored a series of victories over the French troops. Lyauty resigned as governor and by the end of the year the Riff war had cost France the lives of 11,419 troops and an expenditure of several hundred million francs. France and Spain joined forces and Marshal Petain finally drove Krim into the mountains and compelled him to surrender in 1926.

B. The Near East

This momentarily successful defiance of the armed might of the imperial States sent a thrill of joy throughout Islam. It was not entirely a coincidence that the Druze revolt in Syria broke out at the same time. It was drowned in blood after much loss of life and destruction of property. Successive rebellions of the Arabs of Palestine and Iraq have likewise availed nothing against European arms, though Iraq has attained an "independence" comparable to that of Egypt. In the Greco-Turk war of 1922–1923, the Turkish Nationalists of Mustapha Kemal defeated the Greeks and tore up the Treaty of Sèvres. Turkey reconquered the hinterland of Smyrna as well as Adalia, Cilicia, and part of Armenia, all earmarked for foreign seizure. Persia, Afghanistan, and the Hejaz-Nejd (renamed the Saudian Arabian Kingdom in October, 1932) have preserved a precarious independence, while the Moslems of India, once masters of that rich land in the days of the Mogul emperors, are under British rule. Of the 227,000,-000 Moslems in the world, almost half are under British control, 25,000,000 are subjects of France, and 30,000,000 live in the Dutch East Indies. Great Britain, for obvious reasons, has always been the *bête noire* of Islamic anti-imperialists.

In 1903 the Pan-Islam Society was established in London to unify the Moslem world. The Mohammedans were divided, however, into the orthodox Sunnis and the Shi'ahs, who refused to recognize the Caliphate at Constantinople. The Caliphate was abolished in 1924, with the separation of church and State in Turkey, but the Moslem world remains divided, ecclesiastically as well as politically. The anti-Turkish Pan-Arab Movement was supported by the Allies in the Great War. By the treaty of October 24, 1915, Emir Hussein of the Hejaz received a British pledge of support in establishing a Pan-Arabian State in return for entering the war against the Central Powers. The pledge was never fulfilled, for Iraq, Syria, and Palestine were detached as mandates and Arab revolts against the new order were put down. Schemes of Arab confederation have failed to bear fruit and Ibn-Saud, rival and successor of Hussein, has remained ruler of a truncated Arabian kingdom since 1924. If Pan-Islamism and Pan-Arabism have not achieved their goal, they remain forces to be reckoned with in the Near East. The ancient maxim of "divide and rule" has thus far been successfully applied by the imperial Powers in the Moslem world. But it is not improbable that the sword of Islam will again some day be unsheathed in the name of emancipation from Christian imperialism.

C. India

The native revolt against western imperialism in India constitutes one of the most fascinating chapters of contemporary history. Only its outlines can be sketched here. This ancient land covers 1,819,000 square miles, supporting 353,000,000 people—approximately one-sixth of the population of the globe. This population has for many centuries been sharply divided into social castes and hostile religious, racial, and linguistic groups. The Hindus number about 240,000,000, the Moslems of eastern Bengal, Punjab, and other regions 78,000,-000, the Buddhists probably 16,000,000, the Christians, mostly in Burma, 6,000,-000, and the Sikhs of the Punjab 4,500,000. Hindi is spoken by one-third of the population, Bengali by one-sixth, and dozens of other tongues by the remainder. In 1931 there were no less than 2,300 distinct castes, with the degraded "untouchables" comprising about one-third of the Hindu population. Racially the population is a complex blend of Aryans, Afghans, Arabs, Mongols, Persians, Dravidians, and lesser groups, some of them highly cultured and others on the primitive level. There remain, alongside of the British provinces proper, hundreds of native States comprising about one-third of the area and population of the country. Here native autocrats and their aristocracies are used as instruments of British domination. These internal cleavages facilitated the British conquest. They have rendered easy the continuation of British control and have been obstacles to effective and united Indian resistance against foreign rule.

On the other hand, it may be said that India has been united by common opposition to Great Britain—for here, as everywhere, nothing so readily unites a heterogeneous community as conflict with an alien group. The great Sepoy rebellion of 1857 was crushed by British military power. In the decades which followed, opposition to British rule increased with the growing national consciousness and political awareness of the upper classes. Demands for *swaraj* (self-government) were put forward with increasing frequency and energy. In 1885 the first Indian National Congress assembled as a gathering of upper-class Hindus to criticize British administration and to work for greater native participation in the government of the country. In 1912 the Moslem League was established with a similar purpose. In 1916 the two movements joined forces. Two years later they agreed upon a program of complete self-government, to be attained gradually during the next fifteen years. Aspirations for independence were nurtured by specific grievances, which became the symbols of the Nationalist movement. British rule was autocratic and arbitrary and was maintained, in the classic phrase, as a "system of outdoor relief" for the British upper classes which sent their sons to lucrative posts in the Indian civil service. British rule, moreover, was originally established and consistently maintained as a tool of commercial imperialism.

When unrest in Bengal assumed the form of bomb throwing and assassination of officials during the administration of the high-handed Viceroy, Lord Curzon, appointed in 1905, the British Government began to make concessions. The "Morley-Minto" constitution of 1909 made natives eligible to posts in the viceroy's executive council and in the councils of the provincial governors. It likewise enlarged the "legislative councils," but they remained undemocratic and purely advisory, with power to propose and criticize but no power to control the administration. The Montagu-Chelmsford report of 1918 declared that the 1909 arrangements had become obsolete and recommended changes, which were incorporated into the Government of India Act of 1919. This new charter established a central legislature, consisting of a council of state of 60 members and a legislative assembly of 144, with a majority of native representatives in both houses.

The 1919 constitution was regarded by the leaders of the independence movement as a miserable makeshift. Under the inspiration of Mohandas Gandhi, the demand for *swaraj* was intensified. In Gandhi's view, "the government established by law in British India is carried on for the exploitation of the masses. No sophistry, no jugglery in figures can explain away the evidence which the skeletons in many villages present to the naked eye. I have no doubt whatsoever that both England and the town dwellers of India will have to answer, if there is a God above, for this crime against humanity which is perhaps unequaled in history."[1] The 1919 arrangements gave voting rights to less than a million people, out of the 247,000,000 of the British provinces. Representation was on a class basis. Under the "diarchy" principle, certain "transferred subjects"—education, agriculture, public health, etc.—were placed under the control of officials responsible to the native councils, and certain "reserved subjects"—law, order, police, justice—were left in the hands of the appointed British governors, uncontrolled by the legislature. The Nationalists were not content to remain half slave and half free. Gandhi advocated non-violent noncooperation, passive nonresistance, civil disobedience, and economic boycott of British goods and a political boycott of the elections. His asceticism and his Tolstoyian doctrines

[1] M. Gandhi, *Speeches*, pp. 753–754, quoted in P. T. Moon, *Imperialism*, p. 290.

made him a Mahatma or holy man in the eyes of millions of Hindus. The prospect of tariff protectionism against British goods in an independent India caused Bombay manufacturers to give financial support to the movement. While Gandhi preached against violence, the British officials whose authority was defied by his followers necessarily resorted to force.

When several thousand unarmed natives assembled to hold a mass meeting at Amritsar on April 13, 1920, General Dyer ordered them mowed down with machine guns. This savage slaughter spurred the Nationalist movement to new efforts. Non-cooperation was intensified. British cloth was boycotted, while Gandhi urged a return to the spinning wheel, the hand loom, and cottage industry. The Moplah rebellion of the fanatical Moslems of Madras was crushed in 1921. Other disorders were followed by similar repressions. When the civil disobedience campaign was launched, Gandhi was arrested and sentenced to a six-year prison term in March, 1922. He was released two years later, with his influence temporarily diminished by factional differences between Hindus and Moslems, extremists and moderates, in the national congress. In April, 1926, Lord Irwin succeeded Lord Reading as Viceroy. Great Britain slowly began to yield before Nationalist pressure. In 1928 the Simon commission arrived to investigate the desirability of extending the principle of responsible government. Its report (1930) was cautiously conservative, but recommended greater independence for the local governments and the creation of a federal government for India as a whole. A "Council of Greater India" was contemplated, in which representatives of the native States would join with representatives of the British provinces in discussing matters of common concern.

In March, 1930, Gandhi commenced another civil disobedience campaign by marching with his followers from Ahmadabad to Dandi to make salt from sea water, thus defying the government monopoly and evading the salt tax. Riots and disturbances spread once more, as the British police clubbed the non-cooperationists with their lathis, and British troops battled border tribesmen on the northwest frontier. Gandhi and the other leaders of the congress executive committee were arrested once more. On November 12, 1930, the first Round Table Conference opened in London to prepare the new federal constitution, with some eighty Indians present, representing the more important races, religions, classes, and parties save the congress which boycotted the proceedings. The conference adjourned inconclusively on January 19, 1931, pending further discussions. On March 4, 1931, Lord Irwin and Gandhi (again released from prison) signed a truce providing for the discontinuance of civil disobedience and of the boycott in return for the withdrawal of repressive ordinances and the freeing of arrested Nationalists. Moslem-Hindu riots continued, however, and the British continued to use religious cleavages as an excuse for making haste slowly with constitutional reform. After much vacillation, Gandhi agreed to attend the second Round Table Conference which met in London September 14–December 1, 1931. There, amid imperial splendors, his gaunt figure, clad only in a loin cloth and a sheet, seemed to the west to be a grotesque symbol of futility and to the east to be an inspiration and an embodiment of the silent power of the oriental masses. The conference agreed on a federal structure, but Moslem-Hindu differences made an accord impossible on the question of minority representation in the legislatures.

Gandhi described the conference as a "complete failure." Terrorism and repression began once more in Bengal, and the holy man was again arrested. While more than 30,000 political prisoners languished in jail and while Hindu-

Moslem riots continued sporadically, the British authorities went forward with their plans for a federal State and an enlarged electorate, despite the failure of Gandhi's followers to cooperate. In October, 1932, Gandhi secured more favorable treatment of the "untouchables" by a sensational hunger strike. The new Viceroy, Lord Willingdon, and his colleagues, proceeded to make plans for a third Round Table Conference, despite continued Nationalist resistance. The third Round Table Conference opened in London on November 17, 1932. The Nationalists refused to cooperate in any way. On December 23 the conference closed with a report which was to be made the basis of a new constitution. The report contemplated the broadening of the Indian franchise and the administration of Indian finances by elected native officials, subject to certain British "safeguards" during the early years of the proposed federation. An Indian reserve bank would be established prior to the creation of the federation. Legislative seats would be allotted on the basis of a new plan of minority representation. No period of time was specified for the promulgation of the new constitution. In view of general economic and financial conditions, many Indians and some Britishers felt that the establishment of the reserve bank—the first step toward the constitution—would be delayed from five to ten years.

It seems probable that a new constitution for India will eventually emerge, though in all likelihood this will not be a development of the near future. It is equally probable that it will modify the forms of British control without modifying its substance. And it is certain that native opposition will continue with little abatement—either under Gandhi's guidance or under that of more extreme leaders, with a prospect of continued assassinations, repressions, lathi charges, imprisonments, and reprisals, until the Nationalist movement is either terrorized into impotence or British rule is undermined beyond all hope of restoration. Despite recent concessions, the key position of India in the British Empire makes it inconceivable that Great Britain will transfer effective control over the country into the hands of the natives. The universal psychology of nationalism makes it inconceivable that the natives will ultimately be satisfied with anything short of complete independence. In the long run there can be no halfway house for India's millions.

D. China

The rising flood of Asiatic nationalism in China has not beaten against a single foreign conqueror, but against the whole array of imperial Powers which have detached from China its outlying possessions, imposed upon it a status of political and juristic inferiority and subjected it to successive indignities and humiliations, leaving little of its theoretical sovereignty intact. China, like India, is a vast land of many peoples, with an area of 4,277,000 square miles and a population in excess of 450,000,000. China, like India, has undergone such a prolonged process of cultural and political disintegration under the impact of western civilization that it seems doubtful to many whether there is any alternative to complete foreign domination or anarchy. Unlike India, China has from time immemorial exhibited a large degree of cultural unity. Unlike India, China has never been subjected as a whole to any one of the western Powers. For countless millenniums China—the great human sea that salts all rivers flowing into it—has absorbed all her conquerors, for they were for the most part roving barbarian nomads swallowed up in a rich and ancient culture. The Mongol hordes of Genghis Khan overran the country in the thirteenth century, much as the Mongol Turkish conquerors later subdued India and created the Mogul Empire.

In the seventeenth century the Manchus imposed their power upon China and established the Manchu dynasty (1644–1911). In both cases the victors were largely assimilated by the vanquished. Only with the coming of the western white man and his machines did China become helpless. Her leaders now struggle in vain against western imperialism and internal chaos.

Soon after the Celestial Empire was first compelled to open its doors to the west,[1] anti-foreignism emerged out of traditional isolationism and aloofness. The great Taiping rebellion of 1850–1864 was directed more against the Manchu dynasty than against the alien. It was suppressed with foreign assistance. The partial dismemberment of China followed. In the Boxer Rebellion of 1899–1900 the government made common cause with the rebels in attempting to expel the westerners. The more farsighted spokesmen of the new Chinese nationalism soon perceived that China could resist the west only with the weapons of the west, and they began to advocate the adoption of western technology, western economics, western political ideas and institutions. Their pleas were entirely academic until economic and social changes increased the numbers of the Chinese business classes and urban working classes to a point where they furnished a fertile field for revolutionary agitation. Sun Yat Sen (1866–1924) became the spiritual father and the political organizer of the Chinese revolution. This nationalist revolutionary movement was at first directed against the corrupt and decrepit Manchu dynasty. It later aspired to the political and social regeneration of China as a means of resisting imperialistic aggression.

In 1911 the Manchus were overthrown—but the presidency of the new republic passed, not to Sun Yat Sen, who retired to Canton, but to the opportunist adventurer, Yuan Shih Kai, who aspired to become emperor. Followers of Sun, organized into the Kuomintang or National People's Party, were committed to a western bourgeois program of parliamentary democracy, tinctured with socialist elements. Yuan's subservience to foreign bankers, his surrender to Japan in 1915, and his assumption of royal honors in the following year led to a new revolution and to the commencement of an epoch of almost uninterrupted civil war which has continued down to the present day. This state of affairs is due to the impotence of the central government, the uncontrolled greed of the semi-independent provincial tuchuns or "war lords," the emergence of a mass of undisciplined mercenary soldiery, and the progressive disintegration of all the social and economic bases of political unity and cohesion.

Only the international aspects of these endless disorders can be outlined here. In June, 1916, Yuan Shih Kai died amid a ferment of revolutionary disturbances. There followed years of turmoil, marked by chronic struggles for the control of the central government among the war lords: Wu-Pei-fu of the Chihli clique, Chang Tso Lin of Manchuria, Feng Yu-hsiang, the "Christian general" of Shansi, and other lesser feudal chieftains. Chang's sphere of power was Manchuria and he was at all times dependent upon the whim of Japan for the continued rulership of his satrapy. Feng centered his power in Mongolia and looked toward Moscow. While the north was torn by these internecine conflicts, the Kuomintang followers of Sun Yat Sen remained in power at Canton and prepared themselves for the mission of unifying China on the basis of Sun's "three principles:" people's nationalism, people's democracy, people's livelihood. In 1921 Sun was "elected" president of the republic by a group of 1913 rump parliamentarians at Canton, but he encountered constant resistance from the militarists and led a most precarious existence. In his search for foreign aid,

[1] See pp. 605–606 above.

Sun received much sympathy from the anti-imperialist rulers of communist Russia.

In September, 1923, Michael Borodin arrived from Moscow to act as the chief adviser of the Kuomintang. His leadership, strengthened by a naval demonstration on the part of the western Powers against Sun's threat to seize the Canton customs receipts, initiated a four-year period of successful Soviet-Kuomintang cooperation. Russian military officers trained the new Nationalist army. The Kuomintang was reorganized on the model of the Russian Communist party as a rigidly disciplined brotherhood designed to assume dictatorial power and thus to achieve the purposes of the revolution. In 1924 the Chinese Communists, who were increasing in numbers, were admitted to the party. With this there began the internal struggle between the bourgeois elements and the peasant-proletarian elements, which was later to lead to disaster. For the moment, however, the movement was greatly strengthened by this alliance with Soviet advisers and native Communists. It launched upon a career which offered a brief hope of uniting the entire country under its rule.

Despite Sun's death in April, 1924, Chiang Kai-Shek, with the assistance of Borodin, assumed control in Canton after a period of disorder and continued the Communist-Kuomintang alliance. A political and military campaign was now launched to convert and conquer the entire nation. This campaign was directed as much against Chinese and foreign bourgeois interests as against the northern war lords. By March, 1927, the Yangtse valley and the Shanghai area had fallen to the southerners. But success brought the inevitable break between Chiang and Borodin, each of whom had sought to use the other for his own ends. While Chiang now summoned anti-Communist, bourgeois, and militarist elements to his aid, the Communistic left wing of the Kuomintang occupied Nanking and began a general assault upon foreign interests which led to the bombardment of part of the city by American and British war vessels. Chiang now allied himself with the merchants and bankers of Shanghai. In April, 1927, he purged Shanghai and Canton of Russians and Communists by wholesale arrests and executions. Feng Yu-hsiang, also supported by Moscow, now intervened and joined the right-wing Nationalists.

In July Borodin retired to Russia, after thousands of labor leaders, peasants, students, and radicals had been put to death by the now thoroughly bourgeois Kuomintang under Chiang's military domination. Borodin's Chinese followers, including Madame Sun Yat Sen, now denounced Chiang as a renegade and a betrayer of the social and agrarian revolution. Chiang himself retired in August, 1927, in the face of new rivalries and disorders. The "retirement" of Chinese leaders from public life is never to be taken seriously, however. Chiang has "retired" repeatedly, but he remains master of the "purified" and reactionary Kuomintang. He returned to power in January, 1928, and set up a personal dictatorship at Nanking, while the closing of Soviet consulates and the slaughter of Communists continued in the principal cities of the south. The Nationalist armies now moved on Peking, controlled by Chang Tso-lin, but they were delayed by an armed clash with Japanese troops at Tsinan. In June the Manchurian war lord, under Kuomintang pressure and on the advice of the Japanese minister, left Peking for Mukden. He was killed by a bomb explosion during the journey and was succeeded by his son, Chang Hsiao-liang.[1] At the same time Yen Hsi-Shan's troops occupied Peking in the name of the Kuomintang, and all

---

[1] See pp. 415–418 above.

of China was seemingly united under the Nationalist government of Chiang Kai-Shek at Nanking.

This unity, however, was entirely illusory and transitory. The party program of abrogating the unequal treaties, abolishing extraterritoriality, occupying the foreign concessions, and ousting foreign interests was soon paralyzed by new dissensions within the ranks and by the stubborn refusal of the innumerable war lords to be reformed. In October, 1928, an Organic Law of the National Government of the Republic of China was promulgated, providing for the indefinite perpetuation of the one-party dictatorship of the Kuomintang. But all efforts to demobilize the predatory armies of the tuchuns failed. In February, 1929, civil strife broke out in Shantung and Hunan. Chiang waged war on the Wuhan-Kwangsi faction and sent a punitive expedition against the now rebellious Feng, who "resigned" shortly afterward. In July, 1929, young Marshal Chang seized the Chinese Eastern Railway, with the result that Soviet forces under General Blücher, formerly Borodin's colleague and military adviser at Canton, entered Manchuria and compelled the war lord to observe established treaties. This incident led to the final rupture of diplomatic relations between Moscow and Nanking.

The unstable balance of power between independent war lords, self-seeking provincial governors, and rival Kuomintang factions could not long be maintained. Mutinies, riots, and coups d'états brought the Nanking government to the verge of destruction by the end of 1929. Early in 1930 a large-scale civil war broke out between Chiang on the one side and Feng and Yen Hsi-Shan on the other, allied in a new northern coalition. By October Chiang was again victorious, after tens of thousands of lives had been lost, much property destroyed, and the country reduced to bankruptcy. Chang Hsiao-liang cooperated with Chiang in crushing Feng and Yen, but he was removed from the scene by the Japanese occupation of Manchuria in 1931 and the setting up of the new State of Manchukuo in 1932 in what had formerly been his domain. The Sino-Japanese hostilities which accompanied these events brought no unity to the country. While Japanese trade was ruined by a nation-wide boycott, the Chinese Government was helpless against Japanese military power and Chiang was more interested in keeping himself in power than in organizing the nation for resistance. Diplomatic relations with the Soviet Union were resumed, but the days of Soviet-Kuomintang collaboration had long since passed. By the end of 1932, half a dozen new civil wars had broken out and the restoration of peace and order seemed as remote as ever.

Contemporary China presents a picture, not of successful resistance to western imperialism, but of a progressive descent into chaos, opening the door wide to foreign military action to protect life and property, and preparing the way for new alien aggressions. Popular boycotts against Great Britain and Japan have been more successful in disorganizing commerce than in bringing about any fundamental changes of policy on the part of the imperial Powers. Millions of peasants and workers have suffered disaster and death at the hands of the war lords, and of the arbitrary, corrupt despotism which the Kuomintang of Chiang Kai-Shek has established with the aid of the merchants, bankers, and landlords. Banditry is rampant throughout the country. Only in the large cities is there any semblance of security. In the central provinces the seeds sown by Borodin have borne fruit. New Communist leaders have arisen and have won over the peasantry, through the confiscation of mortgages and the partition of estates among the farmers. Some fifty million Chinese are living under indigenous Soviet rule, and the successive attempts of Chiang Kai-Shek to crush the Red Armies by military means have all ended in failure. In many cities Red rule is prevented only by wholesale execution of labor leaders, students, and intellectuals. Between the peasant-proletarian Communists and the bourgeois-militarist Kuomintang there can be no peace, but only implacable warfare until one or the other is exterminated. The Kuomintang would seem to offer no more hope of peace and order than the war lords and other bandits and brigands. In this situation, Communism perhaps offers China the only hope of unity and reconstruction. But Communists are radically anti-capitalist and anti-imperialist and their triumph in China, as in Russia, might easily be followed by foreign military intervention with international complications involving Japan, Great Britain, France, the United States, and the Soviet Union. It is not inconceivable that China may become the next focal point of a world combat between two social and economic systems which are irreconcilable. In any event, China is still very far from the goal of emancipating itself from western imperialism, and its political future involves issues of enormous portent for all the world, east and west.

These considerations suggest a fact of incalculable significance in the future relations between the subject peoples and their imperial oppressors. For the first time, one of the Great Powers is definitely aligned with the backward races and is the *agent provocateur* of colonial rebellion against imperialism and capitalism wherever it raises its head. This Power, moreover, is the citadel of a world-wide revolutionary movement which has won the allegiance of millions of workers, peasants, and colonial laborers. The Union of Soviet Socialist Republics is too occupied with its own problems to come to the actual assistance of Red revolution elsewhere— whether on the Yangtse, in Indo-China, in India, or in the western States themselves. But the Communist International lends its sympathy and support to all subversive agitation and all active resistance to the domination of the bourgeoisie, whether in the western world or in Africa and Asia. This relationship is of no immediate importance. The revolts of the subject peoples are still crushed with ease, even if at greater cost in lives and money than formerly. The strategy of the boycott, of passive resistance, and of non-cooperation has not yet achieved any noteworthy political results, save in India, in spite of their sometimes disastrous economic consequences for western merchants and investors. Until the subject peoples have adopted the technology and the industry of the west, they cannot fight the imperial Powers with their own weapons. But if there should develop a long period of colonial insurrection and of general conflict and disorder within the empires and throughout the western world, the potential alliance between the forces of native nationalist revolt and those of international revolutionary Communism may well prove to be the undoing of the empire-builders.

SUGGESTED READINGS

Andrews, F. F.: *The Holy Land under Mandate* (2 vols.); Boston, Houghton Mifflin Company, 1931.

Angelino, A. de Kat: *Colonial Policy*, Chicago, University of Chicago Press, 1931.

Balch, E. G.: *Occupied Haiti*, New York, Writers, 1927.

Banerjee, D. N.: *The Indian Constitution and Its Actual Working*, New York, Longmans, Green & Co., 1926.

Bau, M. J.: *The Open Door Doctrine in Relation to China*, New York, The Macmillan Company, 1923.

Beer, G. L.: *African Questions at the Paris Peace Conference*, Boston, World Peace Foundation, 1923.

Bukharin, N. I.: *Imperialism and World Economy*, New York, International, 1929.

Buell, R. L.: *The Native Problem in Africa* (2 vols.), New York, The Macmillan Company, 1928.

Carter, J. F.: *Conquest, America's Painless Imperialism*, New York, Harcourt, Brace & Company, 1928.

Dawson, W. H.: *The Future of Empire*, London, Williams and Norgate, 1930.

Dodwell, H.: *History of India 1858–1918*, New York, Longmans, Green & Co., 1926.

Gerig, B.: *The Open Door and the Mandates System*, London, Allen and Unwin, 1930.

Giddings, F. H.: *Democracy and Empire*, New York, The Macmillan Company, 1901.

Harris, J. H.: *Slavery or "Sacred Trust"?* London, Williams and Norgate, 1926.

Hocking, W. E.: *The Spirit of World Politics*, New York, The Macmillan Company, 1932.

Hornbeck, S. K.: *Contemporary Politics in the Far East*, New York, D. Appleton & Company, 1919.

Hsu, M. C.: *Railway Problems in China*, New York, Longmans, Green & Co., 1915.

Lugard, F. D.: *Dual Mandate in British Tropical Africa*, London, Blackwood, 1922.

MacDonald, A. J.: *Trade, Politics, and Christianity in Africa and the Far East*, New York, Longmans, Green & Co., 1916.

MacMurray, J. V.: *Treaties and Agreements With and Concerning China* (2 vols.), New York, Oxford University Press, 1921.

MacNair, H. F.: *China in Revolution*, Chicago, University of Chicago Press, 1931.

Monroe, P.: *China: a Nation in Evolution*, New York, The Macmillan Company, 1928.

Morel, E. D.: *The Black Man's Burden*, New York, Huebsch, 1920.

Nearing, S.: *Dollar Diplomacy, a Study in American Imperialism*, New York, Huebsch and Viking Press, Inc., 1926.

Norton, H. K.: *China and the Powers*, New York, Day, 1927.

Peffer, N.: *The White Man's Dilemma: Climax of the Age of Imperialism*, New York, John Day Company, Inc., 1927.

Powell, E. A.: *Struggle for Power in Moslem Asia*, New York, Century Company, 1923.

Rolland, R.: *Mahatma Gandhi*, New York, Century Company, 1924.

Schnee, H.: *German Colonization, Past and Future*, London, Allen and Unwin, 1926.

Stoddard, T. L.: *Revolt Against Civilization*, New York, Charles Scribner's Sons, 1922.

Willoughby, W. C.: *Race Problems in the New Africa*, New York, Oxford University Press, 1923.

Willoughby, W. W.: *Foreign Rights and Interests in China*, Baltimore, Johns Hopkins Press, 1920.

Wright, Quincy: *Mandates under the League of Nations*, Chicago, University of Chicago Press, 1930.

See also references at end of Chapter XI, p. 429, above.

Chapter XVI

WAR IN THE WORLD SOCIETY

1. International Conflict in the Machine Age

In so great a defeat (the battle of Anghiari, 1439), and in a battle which continued four hours, only one man died and he, not from wounds inflicted by hostile weapons or any honorable means, but, having fallen from his horse, was trampled to death. Combatants then engaged with little danger; being nearly all mounted, covered with armor, and preserved from death whenever they chose to surrender, there was no necessity for risking their lives; while fighting their armor defended them, and when they could resist no longer they yielded and were safe.—Niccolo Machiavelli, *The History of Florence.*

Bombardment, barrage, curtain fire, mines, gas, tanks, machine guns, hand-grenades—words, words, but they hold the horror of the world. . . . We see men living with their skulls blown open; we see soldiers run with their two feet cut off, they stagger on their splintered stumps into the next shell hole; a lance-corporal crawls a mile and a half on his hands, dragging his smashed knee after him; another goes to the dressing station and over his clasped hands bulge his intestines; we see men without mouths, without jaws, without faces; we find one man who has held the artery of his arm in his teeth for two hours in order not to bleed to death. The sun goes down, night comes, shells whine, life is at an end. Still the little piece of convulsed earth in which we lie is held. We have yielded no more than a few hundred yards of it as a prize to the enemy. But on every yard there lies a dead man.—Erich Maria Remarque, *All Quiet on the Western Front.*

DURING the years which have followed 1914, thousands of scholars, journalists, statesmen, and humanitarians in all lands have argued with an eloquence bred of fear and despair that war threatens western civilization with destruction. They have contended that a recurrence of armed combat between Great Powers will lead to disasters for the culture of the west comparable to those which overtook classical culture fifteen centuries ago. They have insisted that of all the problems confronting the contemporary world, that of preventing war and insuring peace is the most vital—for if war is permitted to break out once more between the nations, all of western society will be engulfed in irremediable catastrophe and common ruin. They have asserted that the problem of war and peace is *the* problem of international politics in the twentieth century, for unless civilization abolishes war, war will abolish civilization. Since these propositions are either injunctions to a particular line of action or are hypotheses, the validity of which can be demonstrated only experimentally, their truth or falsity cannot be passed upon here. It is nevertheless essential to examine certain features of modern warfare which lend color to these pleas and prognostications. Attention must be given to the more significant efforts to exorcise the demon of war from the body politic of the western world. The problems and prospects of capitalism and of imperialism have already been considered in the light of the fundamental political patterns of the Western State System. In the discussion which follows, an effort will be made to deal realistically with the problem of war in terms of these same patterns.

If war is to be discussed in terms of *realpolitik* rather than in terms of moral exhortation, it must be viewed as an incident in the competitive struggle for power between States. The Kellogg-Briand Pact to the contrary notwithstanding, war is not and has never been "an instrument of national policy"—if by "war" is meant the physical clash of armed public forces. State policy is never directed toward war as such or toward peace, but only toward objectives in the pursuit of which armed conflict may occur if the pursuit arouses resistance on the part of other States. In the grand strategy of diplomacy, war is neither an object nor, in the long run, a method, even though the precipitation of a combat may be tactically advantageous in a particular diplomatic conjuncture. The object of State action is power—and all the economic prerequisites thereof. The primary means by which power is sought are armaments, for the ability of a State to extend its power by imposing its will upon its rivals and enemies depends ultimately upon its ability to apply effective physical coercion against resistance. War is an incident or an accident which takes place when national wills-to-power clash and when armaments are utilized no longer as a force behind diplomacy but as a tool of direct diplomatic pressure. In every situation leading to war between nations, two elements are necessarily present: (1) the pursuit of conflicting diplomatic objectives by two States or groups of States which envisage their divergent power interests in such terms as to make surrender or compromise impossible save under superior pressure; and (2) an assumption on each side, simultaneously with an identical assumption on the other side, that it possesses a greater war potential than the other, so that each side believes victory to be possible in the event of a test of strength. If the contestants are willing to compromise, no war results. If one side obviously possesses such an overwhelming preponderance of power that the other cannot possibly hope for victory, no war results. War is never brought about by the action of a single State. It is a clash of forces between States. Mutual intransigeance in the pursuit of power and mutual faith in fighting superiority are the prerequisites of any open resort to violence in international politics.[1]

In the past history of the Western State System and of all the state systems which preceded it, war has ever been the decisive incident of the competitive struggle for power between sovereign entities. The contestants in the struggle have always engaged in peace time in the ancient game of diplomatic thrust and parry, with all its refinements of trickery and bargaining. But the great decisions have always been reached by resorts to physical coercion. Force has usually encountered resistance and war has been the consequence. From the point of view of international law, as well as from that of military science, the object of each belligerent is to break the resistance of the other and to restore peace as speedily as possible on advantageous terms. This is diplomacy in a new form and under new conditions. The art of war is the art of overcoming resistance and of imposing one's will upon rivals by actual coercion, instead of by threats and pacific pressures. Death and devastation are merely incidents and not objects in the practice of this art, just as war itself is an incident and not an object of the practice of international politics. Victory requires the disorganization of the armed forces of the enemy and the breaking of the enemy's powers of resistance. The killing of enemy nationals and the destruction of enemy property are means to this end and not ends in themselves. The State is power. The exercise and pursuit of power may require violence when resistance is encountered. But the violence itself is a method, not a goal. These propositions are elementary, but they have frequently been overlooked in the literature and the statesmanship of the seekers after peace. Their implications for the problem of peace will be considered below. They must also be borne in mind in any consideration, however brief, of the evolution of the technique of warfare.

If war has become a threat to the future of civilization, the cause is not to be found in the mere fact of war, but in the effects of the revolution in the art of war which has taken place in the recent period. Wars have occurred from time to time in all past state systems and with greater frequency than in the modern age. The dissolution of these civilizations was invariably accompanied by war. But their disappearance has in no case been attributed to war itself. If it is arguable that war threatens the destruction of western civilization in the twentieth century, this is due to the circumstance that war in the twentieth century is vastly different in its technique and in its economic and social consequences from what it has been in earlier epochs. The history of the art of war can scarcely be reviewed here. It may be pointed out, however, that the progress of military science during the past five hundred years has been more signifi-

[1] See pp. 512–519 above.

cant from the point of view of the effects of war upon society than all the changes in military technique which occurred between the Stone Age and the fifteenth century.

Primitive fighting among early men and other animals involved the use of teeth, claws, fists, and muscles. At some remote and unrecorded time men began supplementing these natural weapons with clubs, sticks, and stones. Warfare then became what it has remained ever since: the art of inflicting injury at a distance by hurling missiles through the air and the art of protecting oneself from such missiles. Hand-to-hand combat, to be sure, has persisted down to the present day—with fists, clubs, swords, daggers, bayonets, and other short-range weapons. But military science is primarily the science of producing effects at a distance by the use of projectiles, *i.e.*, the science of hurling objects through the air for the purpose of discomfiting the enemy and rendering him *hors de combat*. The whole history of warfare might almost be summarized in terms of (1) the types of projectiles used, (2) the motive force behind them, (3) the weapons employed in hurling them, and (4) the effects produced by their impact. The earliest projectiles were presumably stones hurled by hand or by slings and inflicting bruises or broken bones upon their targets. Larger stones in catapults were used to demolish fortifications in remote ages. At an equally early period, crude stones were supplemented by bits of sharpened rock or metal attached to wooden shafts as axes, arrows, or spears. These were hurled through the air with greater speed and accuracy, and with more telling effect, than could be achieved by earlier methods. The spear and bow and arrow are almost universal weapons of primitive peoples. They were already ancient in the first civilized societies known to historians and archeologists. The art of defense developed simultaneously with the art of attack. Shields, helmets, and armor are of equally incalculable antiquity. While these devices were supplemented by many others—horses, chariots, battering rams, fortresses, trenches, moats, movable attacking towers, and a variety of military formations—the sword, spear, and bow remained the basis of military science for countless centuries in many civilizations. From the perspective of the twentieth century, the war techniques employed by the Egyptians, the Babylonians, the Greeks, the Persians, the Romans, the barbarians, the Crusaders, and the condottieri were all much the same and all rested upon the same fundamental weapons.

The revolution in the technology of warfare effected by the peoples of western Europe began with the introduction of gunpowder in the early fourteenth century. This substance was apparently used in China for many centuries prior to its appearance in Europe. The heathen Chinese, however, not being blessed with the advantages of western enlightenment and Christianity, had used this for fireworks and festivities, without perceiving the possibilities of employing it to kill one another. This discovery is usually attributed to a German monk, Berthold Schwartz, in the year 1354, but it is known that powder and cannon were manufactured before his time—in Florence in 1326, in France in 1338, and in England in 1344. The great friar-scientist, Roger Bacon, described the explosive properties of a mixture of saltpeter, sulphur, and charcoal even earlier. In any case, however gunpowder came to be invented, discovered, or imported from the east, it was already being used during the Hundred Years' War to fire stone balls from crude cannon. Effective artillery did not come into general use until the fifteenth century. It spelled the doom of the medieval castles and was used by the national monarchs to crush the power of the feudal barons. Pistols and blunderbusses were also devised and soon superseded the bow and arrow, the spear, and the lance. The art of war was thus completely revolutionized by a mixture of chemicals which, when ignited at the closed end of a metal cylinder, would hurl a stone or metal sphere through the air with such power as to penetrate all existing armor at considerable distances. A new projectile, a new motive force, a new weapon, and a new effect rendered obsolete all the old methods of warfare and gave the Europeans an immense superiority over non-European peoples.

This technological revolution paved the way for an enormously more rapid and far-reaching transformation following the advent of machinery on a large scale. The changes in the art of war which have taken place since 1800 have overshadowed the changes of the earlier period as completely as these changes overshadowed earlier progress in the centuries before gunpowder. Between 1450 and 1650 the new firearms came into general use, and there was relatively little further development during the two hundred years which followed. The war of the American Revolution was fought with weapons and tactics not dissimilar to those employed in the Thirty Years' War. But at the end of the eighteenth century there began the application of science to technology and industry and the appearance of the great mechanical inventions which have continued to multiply at a constantly accelerated rate down to the present time. Within less than a hundred years the old projectiles—round shot and cannon balls—were replaced by cartridge bullets and shells of various types and sizes, filled with explosives, shrapnel, incendiary materials, or poison gas. The old motive force—crude powder—was replaced by powder of much greater refinement and efficiency and supplemented by nitroglycerin, dynamite, gun cotton, T.N.T., and numerous other new explosive combinations. The old weapons—the muzzle-loading cannon, the musket and pistol—were replaced by the breech-loading rifle, the revolver, the machine gun, the field gun, the trench mortar, the howitzer, and a variety of formidable heavy-artillery pieces. The old destructive effects—penetration of flesh by round shot or the shattering of fortifications by the sudden impact of heavy bits of metal—were outmoded by the enormously greater destruction wrought by rifle and machine-gun bullets, shrapnel slugs, jagged fragments of bursting shells, and heavy artillery projectiles filled with metal and high explosives capable of penetrating steel and concrete and demolishing completely the heaviest masonry. All the ingenuity and precision of the new science and the new industry were adapted to the development of new projectiles, new explosives, new weapons, and new destructive effects. The development of mass production through standardized machinery made possible an enormous output of the new tools of warfare in every industrialized State.

The industrial revolution in warfare was not limited to the various processes of hurling pieces of metal through the air at great distances. The new developments in chemistry, physics, mechanics, and engineering were applied to production, transportation, and communication. They led to the appearance of a bewildering variety of offensive and defensive devices not directly related to guns and projectiles. The steam engine led to the steamship as a vessel of war and peace. Wooden vessels were equipped with the new artillery and were armored with iron plates during the American Civil War. The Ironclad and the Monitor developed into the steel battleship, which soon evolved into the dreadnaught, heavily armored against shells and equipped with guns of large caliber and enormous range. The post-Jutland dreadnaughts of the type of the *Hood* and the *Nelson* of the British navy, with their frontal batteries of nine 16-inch guns, are the most formidable fighting monsters ever to take to the seas. In modern navies the capital ship is supplemented by auxiliary vessels undreamed of before the machine age—submarines, swift destroyers and cruisers, airplane carriers, balloons, hydroplanes, dirigibles, etc. The range and effectiveness of both vessels and guns have been increased to an extent unimaginable two centuries ago.

In land warfare the infantrymen now have not merely their rifles and bayonets, but employ hand-grenades, dugouts, machine guns, trenches, gas projectors, gas masks, flame throwers, barbed wire, wire cutters, and other devices. The new siege artillery bears little resemblance to the older cannon. During the Great War the German "Big Bertha" bombarded Paris from a distance of seventy miles. The internal combustion engine led to the appearance of the armored motorcar, the tank, and the airplane. Modern chemistry has adapted old and well-known compounds to war purposes and has devised a variety of new poisons—chlorine, arsenic mixtures, phosgene, mustard gas, etc. The mere listing of the items of technical equipment of modern armies, navies, and air forces would require many pages. Defense has kept pace with attack. The result, however, is not to diminish the destructiveness of the new weapons, but to produce the war of attrition, best exemplified by the western front between 1915 and 1918, with its intrenched armies wreaking vast slaughter and destruction upon one another without gaining any decisive advantage. In the twentieth century the god of the machine has placed in the hands of the god of war an inexhaustible array of weapons capable of spreading death and ruin on a scale so vast as to make the bloodiest devastation of Attila, Genghis Khan, or Tamerlane pale into insignificance.

Warfare has been transformed no less by the sociological and administrative revolution in armies than by the technological changes in the tools they employ. The essence of this revolution lies in the substitution of universal conscription and the nation-in-arms for the small professional standing army. Almost all ancient, medieval, and early modern armies consisted of relatively small numbers of paid professional fighting men. In war time the professional soldier might be aided by mercenaries and volunteers, but the burden of battle was borne by a select warrior caste. The nineteenth century changed these arrangements as completely as it revolutionized weapons and tactics. In July of 1793 the French Committee of Public Safety introduced national military conscription on a wholesale scale by summoning all the men, women, and children of France to resist the counter-revolution and the foreign invaders assisting its cause. This revolutionary *levée en masse* created a popular army of great size which hurled back the enemy and later, under Napoleon's leadership, almost achieved the conquest of Europe. Napoleon's enemies were compelled to fight fire with fire by resorting to the same system. After 1806 Prussia secretly trained successive contingents of 40,000 troops and prepared her forces for the War of Liberation. Universal male conscription became the basis of all continental armies, with each new generation of young men placed under compulsory military training for a number of months and subsequently required to undergo several weeks of training each year in the reserves. Great Britain at length followed suit in the Great War, despite traditional English opposition to conscription and to large armed forces. The United States likewise resorted to conscription in 1863 and again in 1917—in the earlier instance, in the face of popular protest, and in the latter one with no visible opposition.

In the twentieth century the "nation-in-arms" has come to mean not merely universal military conscription of the adult male population, but the mobilization of the entire material and moral resources of the State for war purposes. In the eighteenth century the operations of armies in distant theaters of hostilities were of little concern to the civilian population as a whole of the belligerent States. Taxes might be slightly increased and younger sons might encounter glory, adventure, and death. Otherwise life went on in the even tenor of its ways, little disturbed by war. In the twentieth century almost every civilian becomes a direct auxiliary of the soldier at the front. Stupendous sums of money must be raised. Enormous quantities of war supplies must be manufactured. The civilian must not merely "give till it hurts." He (or she) must put aside the ordinary pursuits of life and become a cog in a great industrial machine which has been regeared and redirected for the purpose of smashing the enemies of the nation. Each regiment at the front, with its weapons and supplies, represents the result of the intricately coordinated activities of a whole host of steel workers, shell makers, gun manufacturers, chemists, tailors, transport workers, doctors, farmers, miners, physicists, etc. In a prolonged international combat the issue will hang more upon the activities of those behind the front than upon the soldiers themselves. Railroad centers, mines, and factories become more important objects of attack than trenches and fortresses. Civilian morale becomes more decisive than the fighting spirit of troops. The old distinction between combatants and noncombatants breaks down, and war becomes a life and death grapple between whole peoples organized more efficiently for their mutual destruction than ever before in the life of the race.

These transformations in military science have made the mechanized armed forces of today enormously more effective instruments of State power than all earlier armies and navies. The non-European peoples, unequipped with European technology, can offer no resistance to this power, as the rapid conquest of the world by the imperial States attests. In contests between the western States themselves, those which are industrially backward and technically inefficient are doomed to defeat at the hands of effectively industrialized enemies, however great their potential resources and man power may be. In spite of the tactical stalemates sometimes resulting from an even balancing of defensive and offensive weapons, final defeat is likely to be more crushing and final victory more overwhelming than was possible in the ages preceding modern technology and modern economy. A State or coalition of States which triumphs in contemporary warfare can cripple the enemy more completely and come closer to effecting its political annihilation than was possible when the human and material resources of a State remained relatively unimpaired by war. With few exceptions, European wars of the sixteenth, seventeenth, and eighteenth centuries were drawn combats in which the weaker made concessions to the stronger at the peace conference, without suffering any overwhelming losses and without losing the means of speedy recuperation. Napoleon defeated Austria, Prussia, and Russia in 1804–1807, but within eight years they were able to bring about his overthrow. The allies crushed Napoleon and defeated France in 1813–1814, but France was again a Great Power within five years. When Prussia overwhelmed France in 1870–1871, however, the victor achieved a hegemony over Europe which endured for two decades and kept the vanquished in a condition of impotent isolation. When the Central Powers crushed Russia in 1916–1918, they achieved a disruption of the Russian State which might well have endured for generations had they won the war on the other fronts. When the Entente broke the power of the central coalition in 1918, it was able to consummate the complete political destruction of Austria-Hungary, the reduction of Germany to a position of military and diplomatic impotence, and the establishment over the Continent of the seemingly permanent hegemony of France and her new allies.

But it is precisely because modern warfare is capable of achieving these results that its continuation threatens the survival of civilization. The preponderance of the power of the victors is due only to the completeness of the defeat of the vanquished. This in turn is due to the enormous human and material losses involved in modern international conflict. These losses are shared by all belligerents alike. They may indeed be heavier for the victors than for the vanquished, as in the Great War. Their social and economic effects are likely to leave the defeated States completely at the mercy of the enemy. But the victors, too, are exhausted and "bled white" in a prolonged war of attrition under modern conditions. So appalling are the costs of modern warfare in money and in property and in lives that it is doubtful whether even societies as productive and prolific as those of the Western State System can long survive a succession of such disasters. The increasing destructiveness of war to human life is clearly revealed in the following table of wars between 1790 and 1914.

LOSS OF LIFE IN NINETEENTH CENTURY WARS[1]

Wars	Duration, days	Dead
Napoleonic, 1790–1815	9,000	2,100,000
Crimean, 1854–1856	730	785,000
Prussian-Danish, 1864	135	3,500
Prussian-Austrian, 1866	40	45,000
American Civil, 1861–1865	1,350	700,000
Franco-Prussian, 1870–1871	210	184,000
English-Boer, 1899–1902	995	9,800
Russian-Japanese, 1904–1905	548	160,000
Balkan, 1912–1913	238	462,000
Total Loss of Nineteenth Century		4,449,300

[1] E. L. Bogart, *Direct and Indirect Costs of the Great World War*, 1919, p. 270.

These figures may be compared with the estimates of loss of life in the Great War:

CASUALTIES OF ALL BELLIGERENTS IN THE WORLD WAR[1]
(Compiled by United States War Department; checked on February 25, 1924; corrected June 30, 1928.)

	Total mobilized forces	Killed and died	Wounded casualties	Prisoners and missing	Total casualties	Per-cent-age
Allies						
Russia...............	12,000,000	1,700,000	4,950,000	2,500,000	9,150,000	76.3
France..............	8,410,000	1,363,000	4,266,000	537,000	6,160,800	73.3
British Empire.......	8,904,467	908,371	2,090,212	191,652	3,190,235	35.8
Italy................	5,615,000	650,000	947,000	600,000	2,197,000	39.1
United States........	4,355,000	126,000	234,300	4,500	350,300	8.0
Japan...............	800,000	300	907	3	1,210	0.2
Rumania............	750,000	335,706	120,000	80,000	535,706	71.4
Serbia..............	707,343	45,000	133,148	152,958	331,106	46.8
Belgium.............	267,000	13,716	44,686	34,659	93,061	34.9
Greece..............	230,000	5,000	21,000	1,000	27,000	11.7
Portugal............	100,000	7,222	13,751	12,318	33,291	33.3
Montenegro.........	50,000	3,000	10,000	7,000	20,000	40.0
Total..............	42,188,810	5,157,315	12,831,004	4,121,090	22,089,709	52.3
Central Powers						
Germany............	11,000,000	1,773,700	4,216,058	1,152,800	7,142,558	64.9
Austria-Hungary.....	7,800,000	1,200,000	3,620,000	2,200,000	7,020,000	90.0
Turkey..............	2,850,000	325,000	400,000	250,000	975,000	34.2
Bulgaria............	1,200,000	87,500	152,390	27,029	266,919	22.2
Total..............	22,850,000	3,386,200	8,388,448	3,629,829	15,404,477	67.4
Grand totals.....	65,038,810	8,543,515	21,219,452	7,750,919	37,499,386	57.6

Killed and died includes deaths from all causes; German and French figures official.

Figures for the United States include marines serving with the army. Wounded casualties include, for the United States, those who died of wounds, numbering 14,500.

Excluding members of the United States Marine Corps who served with the Army in France, the United States Army casualties were as follows—

Total mobilized forces, 4,057,101; killed and died, 119,956; wounded casualties, 193,663 (representing 182,674 individuals, but not including 12,942 who died of wounds); prisoners and missing, 4,423 (representing prisoners only, all missing cases cleared up); total casualties, 318,042; percentage, 7.0.

[1] *World Almanac.*

These enormous losses were due not only to the unprecedented number of troops which were hurled into the struggle, but to the fact that of the troops actively engaged in hostilities, a higher proportion were slain or died of wounds than in most earlier combats—and this in spite of elaborate protective devices, preventive medicine, and aseptic surgery. Over half of all the troops mobilized were casualties of one kind or another, with the Austro-Hungarian, Russian, French, and German armies suffering casualties respectively of 90 per cent, 76 per cent, 73 per cent, and 65 per cent.

The murderous effects of the machine gun, the shrapnel shell, the hand-grenade, and the artillery barrage are shown in the fact that approximately one-sixth of the French, Russian, Austro-Hungarian, and German troops mobilized were killed. Out of every seven soldiers in the warring armies, one was killed, one was captured, two were wounded, and only three escaped unscathed. For the first time, deaths in battle in most of the armies were more numerous than deaths from disease. Of the total Allied forces of 42,188,810 (not including the Latin American armies), 5,157,315 were slain. Of the total forces of the Central Powers—22,850,000—over 3,300,000 perished, despite the greater efficiency of Germany and her allies in protecting their own troops and wreaking death and destruction on the enemy.[1] In addition to the deaths in the armed forces, it is estimated that the total loss of civilian life, including deaths directly due to hostilities as well as those caused by famine, pestilence, increased mortality rates and decreased birth rates, was in excess of 10,000,000.

Figures for expenditure of money and destruction of property are perhaps less impressive, because they reach such astronomical proportions as to render them almost meaningless. Even approximate estimates are difficult to arrive at, because of the innumerable items of cost involved. It would appear, however, that direct expenditures for war purposes reached $10,000,000 per hour in 1918 and that the total direct expenditures of the belligerent governments between 1914 and 1918 were in the neighborhood of $200,000,000,000. The number of human lives snuffed out by the Great War reaches the staggering total of almost twenty millions. Bogart estimates the capitalized value of the lives lost as $33,000,000,000. Property losses were appalling. In France alone, 250,000 buildings were completely destroyed and another 250,000 damaged. In the course of hostilities, 15,398,000 tons of merchant shipping were sunk, with a money loss of vessels and cargo estimated at $6,800,000,000. Property losses on land were about $30,000,000,000. Bogart adds to these items the losses of production, the losses to neutrals, and the costs of war relief. He arrives at a grand total in excess of $337,946,000,000.[2] This figure is obviously incomprehensible, save to astronomers accustomed to dealing with interplanetary and interstellar distances. It is literally true that the costs of modern war are so enormous as to be incalculable.

If the losses involved in modern war are put, not in absolute figures, but in terms of comparisons and analogies, they perhaps appear more real. It has been estimated that if the British dead in the Great War began marching down Fifth Avenue, New York, twenty abreast, from dawn

[1] The 22,850,000 soldiers of the Central Powers inflicted 22,094,900 casualties on the Allies, while the Allied forces of 42,188,810 inflicted only 15,404,477 casualties on the enemy.

[2] *Op. cit.*, p. 299.

to dusk, the ghostly parade would require ten days to pass a given point. The total war dead would require four months to pass in review. Early in 1917 it was calculated that the money expenditures of three days of war would be equivalent to the entire cost of the Panama Canal. Eight days of war would rebuild the entire city of Boston. Ten months' wages of all the workers in the United States would run the war only two weeks. All the deposits in American savings banks would run the war only one month. The cost of all public schools in the United States in 1913 would pay war expenses for only one week. With nine exceptions, there is no college or university in the United States which cost as much to build as a single modern cruiser.[1] The post-war developments of military science in aircraft, artillery, tanks, lethal gases, and naval architecture make it certain that the next war between Great Powers will be accompanied by destruction and death on a scale which will make the losses of the last great combat appear almost negligible by comparison.

Wholesale death and ruin, however, are not the most serious menace of modern warfare to civilization. Western society, with its great capacity for production and reconstruction, can repair or replace the physical wreckage caused by war with comparative ease, despite the retardation of economic development occasioned by the destruction of capital on so vast a scale. Until recently, western birth rates offered promise of overcoming the appalling human costs of war within a few generations. Such losses, or even greater ones in the future, do not of themselves threaten western culture with irreparable disaster. The threat lies rather in the fact that the whole process of warfare in the machine age leads to an inevitable aftermath of economic breakdown, social dissolution, and political upheaval, rocking the established order of private capitalism and bourgeois nationalism to its foundations and toppling the whole structure of civilized living into a chaos of anarchy and revolution. These demoralizing and disintegrating consequences will doubtless become more pronounced as war becomes more mechanized, more destructive, more and more a death struggle between whole peoples, with no lines drawn between combatants and noncombatants and quarter neither asked nor given.

The probable social and political results of the next general war may be calculated by observing the consequences of the last one and multiplying them by an unknown quantity. The state of the world in 1919 is indicative of the immediate effects. One great belligerent, Tsarist Russia, had been completely overwhelmed. In the agony of defeat, its entire political, economic, and social organization had dissolved into violent revolution and civil war, accompanied by terrorism, famine, pestilence, and an economic collapse of unprecedented proportions. Out of this chaos

[1] Devere Allen, *The Fight for Peace*, 1930, *passim*.

there emerged a dictatorial régime with a program of salvation based upon the abolition of private property, the expropriation and destruction of the old ruling classes, and relentless hostility toward the whole established order of capitalism, nationalism, and bourgeois democracy. Central Europe escaped a similar fate only by the narrowest of margins. Austria-Hungary was entirely demolished as a political entity. The specters of hunger, disease, and social revolution haunted the survivors clinging to the wreckage. In Hungary and Bavaria, Bolshevist dictatorships were set up and subsequently crushed by military force, accompanied by a White Terrorism more horrible than the Red. Throughout Germany there were rioting, bloodshed, and threats of anarchy which even the Teutonic passion for *Ordnung* seemed incapable of resisting. Among the "victors," Italy was already in the state of political and social paralysis which preceded the breakdown of parliamentary government and the establishment of the Fascist dictatorship. France, for all the glory of her new hegemony, was confronted with economic ruin and financial collapse. Great Britain was under a shadow of despair which has never lifted. The state of the world in 1932–1933 is indicative of the more remote effects of modern warfare: world-wide economic collapse; unemployment, poverty, and hunger afflicting belligerents and neutrals alike and affecting most severely the United States and Japan, which seemed unharmed in 1919; a staggering burden of public and private debts accruing from the war and the illusory post-war recovery—threatening further economic collapse if the burden is not lifted and threatening the demoralization of capitalism if it is repudiated; a paralysis of commerce, due to the breakdown of money and credit, the debacle of prices, the slump in production, and the political obstacles in the way of an interchange of goods and services; a collapse of the established political order in many countries, under the pressure of suffering and social tension; diplomatic friction and armed conflict between States; insecurity, unrest, dictatorship, terrorism, revolution—and finally more war to recommence the cycle.

To raise the question as to whether western civilization can survive the next great international combat at a time when it is by no means clear as yet that it is going to survive the effects of the last struggle is doubtless premature. But if past and present experience is any guide to future probabilities, it may be predicted with a reasonable degree of certainty that any recrudescence of general armed conflict between the Powers in the twentieth century will have an effect upon the world society of the Western State System not dissimilar to that of the barbarian invasions upon the Mediterranean society of classical civilization.

2. THE CRY FOR PEACE

> The victories of the ancient and well-organized republics enabled them
> to fill their treasuries with gold and silver won from their enemies, to dis-
> tribute gratuities to the people, reduce taxation, and by games and solemn
> festivals disseminate universal joy. But the victories obtained in the times
> of which we speak, first empty the treasury, and then impoverish the
> people, without giving the victorious party security from the enemy. This
> arose entirely from the disorders inherent in their mode of warfare.—
> NICCOLO MACHIAVELLI, *History of Florence*.

That peace in the abstract is preferable to war in the abstract has
probably been the general conviction of the majority of men and women
everywhere since the dawn of civilized social living—and this in spite of
the fact that each particular war seemed to its participants to be preferable to peace. This paradox helps to explain much of the futility of the
"peace movement." The movement itself deserves examination, for it has,
directly or indirectly, produced the various panaceas for war which are
still in process of being tested. It is usually assumed that the future of
peace depends upon the success of these or other panaceas still to be
devised. This assumption is perhaps questionable, but questioning may
be deferred until the panaceas themselves and the movements which
produce them have been examined.

The general motives and purposes of peace seekers and war makers
may first be suggested. "Arguments" for peace are as numerous as
theories of the causes of war. Thousands of gallons of ink and millions of
pounds of paper have been consumed in efforts to explain why wars occur,
to depict their horrible and destructive effects, and to convince mankind
of the desirability of avoiding them. This enormous literature, equally
voluminous in almost all languages, cannot be reviewed here, nor would
the results of such a review add very much to existing knowledge of the
problem. That literature is primarily polemical, emotional, and persuasive
rather than scientifically realistic. It is possible, however, to reduce the
problem to reasonably simple and universal terms.

All civilized societies require for their perpetuation the general
prevalence of certain familiar values, attitudes, and patterns of behavior
which are the direct antithesis of the values and patterns of war. These
prerequisites of civilized life are suggested in the terms: cooperation,
toleration, interdependence, mutual forbearance, charity, fellowship, a
sense of unity and devotion to certain symbolic ideals of a moral and
quasi-religious character, giving cohesion and solidarity to the social
group. With minor variations of time and place, these are the virtues
and ideals of social living everywhere. In the interest of cooperative community life, the "anti-social" propensities of human beings are everywhere

curbed, repressed, sublimated, or conditioned to socially acceptable modes of expression. Murder, incest, and suicide are frowned upon and all acts which are assumed to be socially destructive and disruptive are labeled "sins" or "crimes." War involves the performance of such acts on a colossal scale and in organized fashion. It normally leads to the commission of all the crimes and sins condemned by the religious precepts, the moral doctrines, and the penal legislation of all modern States: murder, arson, suicide, mayhem, rape, petty and grand larceny, and savagery of all varieties. All the moral, religious, and economic propensities of mankind revolt against it (in the abstract) as the quintessence of all that is anti-social, hideous, and bestial. Moral, economic, and religious "arguments against war" are almost as old as war itself. They have been restated in every age, with a thousand variations and accompaniments. In the modern period, humanitarian sentiments have become universal, the grosser forms of cruelty and torture have been abandoned within the western nations, and Calvinism and capitalism have placed greater emphasis than ever before on thrift and the conservation of wealth. At the same time, war has become progressively more frightful, more bloody, more wasteful and destructive. It is therefore natural that organized pacifism should become a world-wide movement, denouncing war and pleading for peace more eloquently and persuasively than ever before.

If the peace movement has been inspired by humanitarianism, morality, religion, and economics, the war habit has been perpetuated by the very fact that war affords a release from the restrictions and repressions of morality and religion on elementary emotional drives. Without raising again the moot question of "instinct," it may be pointed out that every human personality is in a state of more or less unstable equilibrium, poised between forms of behavior which are "anti-social" and destructive and those which are socially acceptable and "constructive." The former drives to action are kept in check by the latter. In the psychiatrist's terminology, the primitive inherited impulses of the "id," which are socially disruptive in their simpler expressions, are repressed and redirected by the socially acquired patterns of the "super ego"—with the "ego" or conscious personality a synthesis of these two elements, coupled with conscious mind and emotion. War breaks down the checks of the super ego. It renders heroic and makes socially acceptable the most elemental expressions of id impulses. All the long subdued propensities of the Old Adam are released. Man is enabled to become again a carnivorous beast of prey. He is permitted to utilize all the skill of science, the better to satiate his atavistic hunger for destruction and his animalistic thirst for blood. Drama, excitement, danger, tragedy, the sweetness of life in the face of death are experienced for the first time by stolid farmers, prosaic bookkeepers, routinized factory hands, and twelve-dollar-a-week shoe clerks. Forbidden pleasures are permitted freely in war time—directly by the soldier at the front and vicariously by the civilians behind the lines. The savage satisfactions of battle are the more keenly relished because they are precisely the joys in which one may not indulge during the humdrum times of peace.

From the point of view of the psychology of war and peace (if use may be made of a sadly abused term), the most significant aspect of the innate impulses satisfied by fighting is that their normal expression, so largely repressed in peace, becomes not merely permissible but honorable and laudable in war. No useful purpose is to be served by setting "social instincts" over against "anti-social instincts," by assuming that the former make for peace and the latter for war and by concluding that the former ought to be encouraged and the latter discouraged. The same elemental drives underlie human motives and behavior in peace-time and war-time activities. The more primitive expressions of these drives are regarded as anti-social. They are repressed in peace and released in war. In the heat of combat original sin becomes respectable. Sadism, masochism, and all varieties of bestiality are praised in the name of patriotic devotion. State and church unite in singing hymns to the heroes of slaughter and destruction. And—what is most important—these activities become not merely socially acceptable but identified with the highest interests of the community. The intimate relationship between national patriotism and war has been commented on above. Fighting a common enemy unifies the national group as does no other shared experience. The dominant institutions and patterns of political behavior in the Western State System—nationalism, imperialism, militarism—involve the promotion of social cohesion through conflict and the sanctification of the fatherland through the sacraments of Mars.

These considerations suggest that the problem of the peace seekers is not to be solved by argument, by moral exhortation, by emphasis upon the horror and waste of war, or by condemnation of man's murderous and destructive propensities. The solution must rather be sought by attempting to modify the dominant institutions and patterns of political behavior. Its solution requires that recognition be granted to the deep-seated drives to action which are given free play in war. The tensions generated by their repression in peace time must be lessened. Socially acceptable forms of expression other than war must be provided. William James' "moral equivalent for war" took cognizance of this need, though it cannot be said that any satisfactory moral equivalent has yet been devised, despite pugilism, football, stock speculation, and other forms of conflict and competition. The problem of the moral equivalent is not merely a problem of substitution and sublimation. It is a problem of political psychology.

It is a problem of reorienting political allegiances, of reorganizing political entities, of recasting the prevalent power-and-prestige ideology and symbolism of the sovereign units of the Western State System into a mold in which tensions are minimized, conflicts are prevented, and differences are pacifically reconciled on the basis of common interests. It is a problem not of the id, but of the super ego. It is indeed a problem of "changing human nature," but not one of modifying men's biological impulses and instincts. It is a problem rather of modifying the political patterns of western culture through which these receive expression. It is, in short, less a matter of reforming men's hearts and minds by a direct assault upon them than a matter of politico-social engineering. "Good" institutions and policies are not the product of "good" men. "Good" men are rather the product of "good" institutions and policies. Man does not create society in his own image. Society molds men into the patterns inherited from the past. The peace seekers who would hope for success in their quest must change nature by a process of indirection and they must begin their labors by examining those elements in the political constitution of the world society which breed international conflict.

If this orientation toward the problem be tentatively accepted for the purpose of evaluating the peace movement, it leads at once to the obvious comment that the pacifists until recently have had the cart before the horse. They have been approaching the problem from the wrong end. Most peace seekers have sought to attain their goal by depicting the horrors of war in sermons, peace pamphlets, novels, and motion pictures, by dwelling upon the frightful wastage of life and goods, and by painting word pictures of putrifying corpses, of hideous mangled men, of death and devastation in a thousand horrid guises. Religious pacifists and clergymen have been particularly active in this type of peace propaganda—the same clergymen who in war time have often blessed the departing troops, intoned hymns of hate against the foe, and canonized mass murderers in the name of the fatherland and the Prince of Peace. These horrors exercise a terrible fascination over human imagination. They perhaps feed the very impulses they are designed to frighten away. "The effect, especially in a rather effete civilization, is not entirely unlike that achieved by a window made opaque except for one round transparent hole labeled 'don't look in here.'"[1] Even less effective are moral and religious denunciations of the war spirit, for they rest upon repression as a panacea. Impulses which are repressed usually break out in their most undesirable manifestations at the first favorable opportunity. Pleas for peace and brotherhood are vague abstractions. Men seek peace with honor in victory and they know no brotherhood which is warmer than the brotherhood of comrades in arms. The task of changing human nature without changing the political,

[1] Devere Allen, *The Fight for Peace*, p. 214.

[657]

social, and economic mold into which human nature is poured is fore-doomed to failure. Only since 1850 have peace seekers directed their attention seriously to the politics and economics of war, and only since 1914 have they put forward any serious proposals having some relation to the political and economic realities of the problem.

A brief résumé of the peace movement will substantiate these general-izations. Leaving out of account the medieval and early modern schemes for the preservation of peace, it may be said that the contemporary movement dates back to the "peace societies" of the period following the Napoleonic wars. Three such societies existed in the United States by 1815. The British "Society for the Promotion of Permanent and Universal Peace" was established in 1816. Religious leaders, particularly Quakers, played a prominent rôle in the early movement. War was held to be incompatible with Christianity, and non-resistance was advocated as a remedy. Propagandist journals were launched. A New Hampshire sea captain, William Ladd, served to bring together the British and American societies between 1823 and 1840. The three American societies fused into the "American Peace Society" in 1828. All emphasis was not placed upon the virtues of peace and the vices of war, for the American groups pleaded for arbitration and a congress of nations almost from the beginning. But the movement was essentially religious and moral, despite the valuable aid received from the free-trade economists and pamphleteers. Other groups appeared in Holland, France, and Switzerland.

In 1837 Ladd's proposal for a "Court of Nations" for the arbitration of all disputes was accepted by the American Congress, but the President failed to act on the congressional resolution. William Lloyd Garrison and Henry Clarke Wright founded the New England Non-resistance Society in 1838 as a secessionist movement from the American Peace Society. Various international prize-essay contests were held in the 1830's. Ladd's *Essay on a Congress of Nations* was not lacking in political ingenuity. The move-ment organized itself internationally in the First General Peace Conven-tion, held in London in 1843. Elihu Burritt's *Christian Citizen* became the leading pacifist journal in America in the 1840's. A second great peace congress was held in Paris in 1849, with others following at Frankfort, 1850, London, 1851, and Manchester and Edinburgh, 1853. The series of congresses then came to an end, and the first phase of the modern peace movement fell upon sorry days during the mid-century wars in Europe and the United States. Governments and publics were unmoved by arguments and exhortations.

The second phase of the movement may be dated roughly from 1867, when the Ligue de la Paix was founded in Paris. New peace societies were established and old ones were reorganized. New strength was derived from socialist and humanitarian groups, and the whole movement became less dominantly ecclesiastical. Moral exhortation and the idea of a congress of nations were supplemented by new attention to disarmament and to the project of a United States of Europe, sponsored by the Geneva League for Peace and Liberty. The Franco-Prussian War multiplied the number of peace organizations and led to new demands for the arbitration of international disputes. International congresses were resumed, and the movement became firmly established and world-wide in scope, with little active support from the churches. In 1889 the Interparliamentary Union was established and the universal peace congresses, representing the movement in many lands, began their annual meetings. Heterogeneous elements were thus brought together, with a variety of programs and panaceas. The spirit of this phase of the movement is well represented by the words of W. E. Darby at the universal peace congress held in Chicago in 1893:

> Our work is to provide principles, not policies, for governments, taking care, of course, to show the bearing of our principles on policies. The presentation of right principles will, if it be judicious, appeal to the reason and conscience of rulers and will be really effective even where it may seem to be unheeded. The attempt to furnish policies will surely be resented as an interference with the prerogative of government and expose us to the charge of arrogant meddlesomeness.[1]

Between 1889, the year of the publication of Bertha von Suttner's *Die Waffen Nieder*, a peace novel which attained wide circulation and influence, and 1899, the year of the first Hague Conference, the movement was further enlarged and strengthened, and the churches were once more enlisted in the cause. The invitation of the Tsar to the Powers to attend a conference on disarmament was hailed with enthusiasm. While the innocuous disarmament resolutions of The Hague were a bitter disappointment to pacifists, the establishment of the Permanent Court of Arbitration was hailed as no small victory. The peace movement had now become sufficiently widespread to influence governmental policies. Numerous arbitration treaties were being signed, despite the failure of the Anglo-American treaty of 1897. The Nobel Peace Prize was established in the same year. Arbitration made rapid progress after 1900. Jurists worked actively for arbitration and adjudication, and diplomats paid lip service to peace. More attention was paid by the peace seekers to political questions. The national movements passed through various vicissitudes, but the cause of peace everywhere seemed in the ascendancy. The second Hague Conference (1907) aroused new interest, in spite of its rather negligible achievements. In 1910 Andrew Carnegie founded the Carnegie Endowment for International Peace. In 1914 the World Alliance for International Fellowship Through the Churches was established. By this time there were 130 organizations in 26 States. Much had been achieved. But

---

[1] A. C. F. Beales, *The History of Peace*, 1931, pp. 196–197.

that much was too little to exercise any appreciable influence on the foreign policies of the Powers. When those policies precipitated the Great War, the peace movement was shattered and disorganized. Its national units split, disintegrated, or were suppressed, and all of them passed into the shadow of a great darkness.

The post-war resurrection of the peace movement was due to the appalling character of the combat in Europe and to the fact that peoples and governments everywhere, particularly in the Allied States, were committed by the end of the struggle to a political reorganization of the world to prevent a recurrence of the catastrophe. The League of Nations and the World Court were the fruits of a new determination to preserve peace. New interest developed in arbitration, security, and disarmament. Many of the earlier aspirations of the movement were realized, and the cause was reorganized on an international scale. The International Federation of League of Nations Societies, the revived interparliamentary conferences and universal peace congresses, the Federal Council of Churches in the United States, and corresponding organizations in other countries all worked actively for disarmament. The American idea of the "outlawry of war" received wide support. International organization, *i.e.*, a return to Ladd's project of a congress of nations, became the new watchword. Innumerable peace organizations, with a bewildering multiplicity of panaceas, sprang up everywhere in the post-war period. Nowhere were they more numerous than in the United States, which, paradoxically, refused to join the League or the World Court. The peace movement became truly universal and its advocates attained complete respectability everywhere, save among the most ardent superpatriots and militarists. It now supplemented moral exhortations and object lessons in war horrors with an active consideration of the politics of peace. Successive failures and disappointments and the growth of international friction and armaments only spurred the pacifists to greater efforts. If peace could be secured by enthusiasm, propaganda, emotional fervor, and lobbying activities, it would already be assured beyond all danger of disturbance.

If this happy state of affairs has not yet been achieved, the reasons are not difficult to discover. The pacifist movement is nowhere grounded in any single social class or sect in any nation. Its recruits are farmers, workers, business men, Catholics, Protestants, Jews, preachers, mechanics, and philanthropists. This might be a source of strength if the peace workers numbered a significant proportion of these various groups, but since they do not, it is a source of weakness. The active apostles are few in number; they are divided in their views; they are supported by a large mass of peace-loving opinion, but the support is feeble and unorganized. Patriotism is still stronger than pacifism, even among the pacifists themselves—not because they love peace less, but because they love their country more. The most energetic pacifists are likely to be those who still deal with the problem in terms of moral exhortation and religious conversion, rather than in terms of political realities. The effective political pressure which the movement can bring to bear depends upon its ability to control votes. But elections seldom turn upon the issues in which pacifists are interested. The political remedies which they propose, moreover, are seldom based upon clear and incisive thinking about the fundamental nature of the problem. The remedies are likely to be too simple, too naive to touch the heart of the difficulty.

The panaceas are too numerous to be reviewed here, for they range all the way from conscientious objection, non-resistance, and the general strike, to the creation of international federations and superstates. Only those which are of contemporary political significance and have a direct bearing on national policies need be dealt with. These comprise: (1) disarmament, (2) arbitration and other pacific means of settlement, (3) security pacts, (4) the "Outlawry of War," and (5) international government. These proposals will be evaluated in the following section as abstract propositions, with the succeeding chapter devoted to a survey of the actual efforts of governments to prevent war by adapting these panaceas to the exigencies of practical politics.

3. PACIFIST PANACEAS

> From whence come wars and fightings among you? Come they not
> hence, even of your lusts that war in your members?—Epistle of James,
> IV, 1.

The peace advocates, official and unofficial, who urge disarmament as the ultimate solution of the war problem usually argue that armament, and particularly competition in armament building, is the primary cause of war. They emphasize the enormous financial cost and the immense economic waste of armaments. They point out that the world spends annually for the maintenance of soldiers and sailors and the construction of war equipment over four billions of dollars and that these nonproductive expenditures increased steadily between 1925 and 1930, the years of Locarno, the Kellogg Pact, new arbitration treaties, and the strengthening of the League. In 1925 $3,497,000,000 was spent on armaments; in 1926, $3,557,000,000; in 1927, $3,873,000,000; in 1928, $3,950,000,000; in 1929, $4,107,000,000; and in 1930, $4,128,000,000.[1] Proponents of disarmament recall that armament rivalry between the Powers played a large rôle in the

---

[1] League of Nations, *Armaments Year-book*, 1932, p. 454. It is noteworthy that about one-fifth of this total represents expenditures by the United States alone. The American Government not only spends more on armaments than any other State, but its expenditures represent approximately 20 per cent of the total expenditures of all the sixty odd sovereign States of the world.

promotion of the international fears and suspicions which made 1914 possible. They insist that contemporary armament competition will have the same consequences in the future as in the past. They argue that if competitive armament building can be stopped by international limitations, one of the major causes of international conflict will be eliminated. They argue further that if armaments are reduced, war will become less possible and therefore less probable. The complete abolition of arms is the eventual goal to be aimed at. When it is achieved, peace will be secured by virtue of the fact that peace breakers will have no means at their disposal for waging war.

This line of logic deserves critical examination because of its widespread prevalence among peoples and governments. In its simplest form it is based upon a fundamental fallacy which renders the whole sequence of reasoning invalid. The fallacy lies in the assumption that armaments cause wars. The preceding discussion of the rôle of armaments in Great Power politics[1] has already suggested the error of this view. The opposite view—that wars cause armaments—would be more nearly correct. Wars arise out of irreconcilable conflicts of interests and policies between sovereign States engaged in a competitive struggle for power, profits, and prestige. The fighting potential of a State is the ultimate measure of its influence and power in war and peace. Wars seldom occur merely because those possessing bright shiny weapons are tempted to use them. States possess weapons because armaments are a test of power and because combats for power between States are fought with armaments.

If by some miracle all weapons were abolished tomorrow, no change whatever would thereby be effected in the pattern of Great Power politics into which war is so closely woven. Power contests between States would be conducted with brickbats and rowboats until the scientists, engineers, and manufacturers had time to produce modern weapons once more. States will not consent to the abolition of armaments so long as they continue to engage in diplomatic contests for power and prestige and so long as armaments continue to be the primary weapons of such contests, whether they are used in war as instruments of coercion or maintained in peace to intimidate prospective enemies and insure "respect for national interests." States will not consent to reduce armaments unless each perceives some advantage to itself, from the point of view of power relationships, in diminishing the strength of possible rivals in return for a reduction in its own strength. States will not consent even to the limitation of future armaments unless they similarly perceive some advantage to themselves in checking competition. The task of insuring peace through disarmament is an impossible one so long as war remains a possibility, for States necessarily feel bound to be prepared for all eventualities. And to

[1] See pp. 512–519 above.

the degree to which they are prepared the possibilities become probabilities. The advocates of disarmament—in pulpits, on lecture platforms, in the press, and in the foreign offices—have not yet succeeded in breaking through this circle, nor does it seem likely that they can do so.

Some advocates of disarmament, to be sure, recognize the relevancy of these considerations and propose to achieve disarmament by indirection through "organizing peace." This phrase symbolizes the disarmament thesis of France and her eastern allies. They have insisted that disarmament is possible only to the degree to which peace, *i.e.*, "security," is guaranteed. Security can be attained only by definite commitments of international cooperation in resisting an aggressor. This view is logically defensible, despite the ambiguity of the concepts of "security" and "aggression" and despite the special interests of the French bloc which are served by this line of argument.[1] The French thesis of indirect disarmament via security is opposed to the American and British theses of security via direct disarmament. Neither thesis can achieve the goal because it is inacceptable to the proponents of the other. It is as if a committee on law and order, in a riotous American frontier town of the last century, were discussing the best means of putting an end to shooting frays between the citizens. The United States argues that all citizens must be persuaded to throw away their firearms, for without firearms there can obviously be no shooting. The French representative says, "Quite true, but I have dangerous and untrustworthy neighbors. I cannot throw away my revolvers and bullet belt until I am assured of some alternative protection. Let us appoint a sheriff and organize a police force to which we will turn over all our weapons and to which we will entrust the task of keeping peace." The United States replies, "No, I do not believe in sheriffs and police forces. I have no dangerous nearby neighbors. I cannot agree to protect you against your neighbors. Shooting cannot be done away with by more shooting. If all guns are scrapped, the problem will be solved." The Frenchman rejoins, "Sorry, but I cannot surrender my only protection unless you join me in supplying an alternative." The discussion gets nowhere. Despite the logic in each position, the other cannot accept it and neither disarmament nor security is achieved. This analogy, as will be pointed out below, is in some respects misleading, but it reflects the spirit in which recent disarmament discussions between the Powers have been carried on.

Almost equally barren of constructive results are the proposals for arbitration, adjudication, conciliation, and other procedures for the pacific settlement of disputes. The utility of these procedures in modern diplomacy is not to be disparaged.[2] But to assume that their further

[1] See pp. 435–439 above and 716f. below.
[2] See pp. 198–229 above.

elaboration, unaccompanied by changes in attitudes and values, would prevent war is to overlook the obvious fact that the conflicts of power and honor which lead to war are precisely the conflicts which are non-justiciable. The only wars prevented by procedures of pacific settlement are those which would never be fought, for they concern issues not directly relevant to the "vital interests" and "national honor" of States. Such issues are not likely to be made occasions for armed trials of strength. It is of course quite true that the creation and utilization of peaceable means of adjusting controversies may in course of time modify the prevalent conceptions of power interests, sovereignty, and national honor. They may cause States in the future to view controversies as justiciable which are now regarded as not susceptible of any type of pacific settlement. But it is assuredly not true that States fight because they have no alternative means of settling controversies. Japan and China in 1931, Bolivia and Paraguay in 1932 had ample means of pacific settlement at their disposal, but they nevertheless resorted to force. Dueling between individuals did not disappear because courts were created. It disappeared when personal "honor" was no longer envisaged in terms which required bloodshed for its vindication. States fight for power, prestige, and profits and they are still unwilling to submit to the judgment of courts, councils, and tribunals such controversies as touch directly upon these stakes of diplomacy. War will disappear when States no longer adhere to this view—when they pursue different objectives or when they are prepared to pursue these goals by non-violent methods. The development of agencies of pacific settlement may contribute to this moral and mental transformation. The procedures themselves are not alternatives to war and will not diminish appreciably the likelihood of war.

Proposals for security pacts, general defensive alliances, and international collaboration to repress peace breakers have been much discussed by pacifists and diplomats in the post-war period. The concrete political results of these discussions will be examined in the next chapter. Here certain general considerations may be advanced by way of suggesting a basis for evaluating such proposals. It is somewhat singular that the very arrangement—the "defensive" military alliance or the security pact—which has played such a large rôle in all the general wars of the past should now be urged as a means to peace. It is argued, however, that past alliances promoted war because they were limited in scope and were directed against particular States. If a world-wide defensive alliance could be concluded, whereby all States agreed to oppose by force any single State breaking the peace, war would become impossible, for no State, it is argued, could resist the world. Or, barring this, a general continental alliance in Europe and similar regional alliances elsewhere might achieve the same purpose.

The contention again overlooks the rôle of alliances in relationships of power. All alliances with any vitality and durability—in the past, the present, and, it may be predicted, in the future—are based upon a set of common power interests shared by the allies *vis-à-vis* potential common enemies. An alliance not based upon such interests is necessarily a scrap a paper, a meaningless gesture, and a shadowy pledge without substance. Since power is relative and power interests are competitive, the organization of all States of the world into an alliance is not within the realm of present political possibilities unless one should postulate some common enemy of all States menacing the world from a base of operation in the moon or the planet Mars. A hypothetical peace-breaking State is not such a common enemy. Other States will not make sacrifices of blood and treasure to coerce such a State if they have nothing more tangible at stake in the situation than an abstract devotion to peace.

It is questionable, moreover, whether peace can be preserved by force in a community of unequal sovereignties, some of which possess immense power within their own spheres of interest. Nicaragua, Liberia, or Luxemburg could readily be brought to terms by the organization of an international force against them. But the efficacy of such a force as a means of coercion would be doubtful if it were directed against such States as France, Germany, or Italy. The insufficiency of any possible mobilization of forces would be at once apparent if it were directed against the United States, the Soviet Union, or Japan. Power is local. Each of these States has at its disposal, within its own sphere, sufficient means of resistance to defy the entire world if necessary. No combination of Powers could succeed in coercing the Soviet Union if it were determined to resist. No combination of Powers could act effectively against Japan in the western Pacific and eastern Asia. Neither could any combination of Powers bring to bear in the western hemisphere sufficient pressure upon the United States to modify its course of action. Such pressure would be more likely to have precisely the opposite result from that desired. Here is the fatal flaw in the whole theory of sanctions, security pacts, and international police forces.

The outlawry-of-war idea is even more naive and irrelevant if it is evaluated in terms of the realities of Great Power politics. This panacea is based upon the assumption that war can be abolished by international engagements whereby States commit themselves not to resort to war. Such engagements, far from being new or modern, are of great antiquity, dating back to the earliest treaties. Until recently all treaties contained pledges of eternal peace and friendship between the parties. No historical instance is recorded of a powerful State refraining from using force to protect its interests because of such pledges. Their obvious futility led to their abandonment in modern treaties. They have been revived in a new form in the Kellogg-Briand Pact of 1928,[1] a world-wide multilateral convention in which the signatories pledge themselves to renounce war as an instrument of national policy and to resort only to pacific means of settlement. This gesture of the foreign offices followed an extensive publicity campaign in the United States and other countries on the part of earnest American advocates of this method of solving the peace problem. These peace seekers, including among their numbers Clayton Morrison, Salmon O. Levinson, Senator William E. Borah, and Nicholas Murray Butler, contended that all efforts to abolish war through disarmament, arbitration, security pacts, and sanctions were foredoomed to failure and that the way to abolish war was to abolish war—by international agreement. If all States will solemnly pledge their word to renounce war, and if all States will abide by their pledges, the problem will forthwith be solved. With war "outlawed," States will be willing to disarm, for there will be no point in maintaining weapons which will never again be used; security will be assured, for no State can attack another without violating its solemn obligation; diplomacy, arbitration, and adjudication will then be resorted to for the settlement of all disputes.

The engaging simplicity of this logic accounts for its wide acceptance prior to the signature of the Kellogg Pact and suggests its inadequacy. The solution postulates written international engagements between States. Written engagements are drawn up by diplomats skilled in the art of using language to conceal meaning and adept in the science of reservations and interpretations designed to safeguard freedom of action without destroying the appearance of solemn commitments. Apart from this difficulty, the adequacy of the solution depends upon the application of these engagements to specific situations threatening war. When powerful States find their "national interests" jeopardized in such situations, they will not be deterred from acting in their customary fashion by scraps of paper. Open repudiation will be unnecessary, for interpretations and reservations will already have opened the way for graceful disclaimers of responsibility. Only "aggressive" war will be outlawed, since no sovereign State will surrender the right of self-defense. In fact, however, all modern wars are regarded as "defensive" on both sides. The competitive quest for power between sovereign entities composed of patriots bent upon promoting national interests is not touched upon in any way by these proposed solutions. No solution which ignores the causes of war can insure peace.

All of these difficulties are inherent in the Kellogg-Briand Pact. Its very phraseology is based upon misconception. War is not, and never has been, an "instrument of national policy," unless the formal act of a declaration of war be regarded in this light. The use of arms for coercive

[1] See pp. 677–685 below and also pp. 224–225 above.

purposes may be an instrument of national policy, but their use leads to war only when they encounter armed resistance. There then takes place a physical clash of forces, accompanied by a new legal status—"war"—designed to indicate the rules and principles to be followed in the conflict. The Kellogg Pact makes States reluctant to admit the existence of this legal status. But in its present meaning, it does not forbid the use of arms by States to protect their interests. The same President Coolidge who championed the Pact and the same President Hoover who proclaimed it in effect were most emphatic in their insistence on the right of the United States to protect the lives and property of its nationals everywhere. Neither does the outlawry of war offer any guarantee that resistance will not be encountered or that physical conflict will not take place. At most, it denies the benefits of the legal status of "belligerents" to the contestants and, in its most recent form, it denies the validity of agreements entered into under the pressure of armed coercion. The adequacy of these measures as a means of preventing conflict between nations is extremely doubtful, quite apart from their questionable desirability.

During the five years in which the Kellogg Pact has been in operation, no legal state of war has been acknowledged anywhere in the world by States fighting one another. But States have fought as of yore, and the frequency of physical combats between nations has not been demonstrably diminished by the engagements of 1928. There seems no reason for supposing that any other engagements of a similar character could achieve any more than this in the future. "Outlawry of war" has a symbolic, moral, educational, and propagandist value in so far as it mobilizes opinion against war and puts governments on record as opposing it. This value may in the long run be very considerable, if governments and peoples are gradually brought around to the view that armed force should never be used in international controversies under any circumstances. This view will become prevalent only when current conceptions of the State and of "national interests" are radically modified. Meanwhile, "outlawry of war" comes no nearer to achieving an immediate solution of the problem than the other panaceas.

Finally, there remains to be considered the proposals of "international government," "international organization," or "world federation" as the road to peace. These proposals are also of great antiquity. All medieval and modern thinkers who have dealt seriously with war and peace as a political problem have been unanimous as to the necessity of bringing States of the world together into some semblance of political unity. The schemes of Crucé, Sully, William Penn, St. Pierre, Rousseau, Kant, and others have been discussed elsewhere.[1] William Ladd, the founder of the modern peace movement in the United States, was no less insistent upon

[1] See pp. 233–238 above.

the need of a "Congress of Nations." Apart from the Holy Alliance and the "Concert of Europe," such proposals never achieved practical realization prior to the Paris Peace Conference of 1919. There, at the initiative of peace seekers who possessed political vision and authority as well as idealistic enthusiasm, these aspirations were translated into reality in the creation of the League of Nations, whose organization has been described above and whose achievements will be evaluated in a separate chapter.

Pending such an evaluation, the necessary criteria of judgment may be suggested at this point. Almost all proposals for international government have, to a certain degree, been grounded in the political realities of the Western State System. They have therefore been less naive and simpleminded than the panaceas of disarmament, arbitration, security pacts, and outlawry of war, though almost all of them have contemplated the incorporation of these devices, in one form or another, into the general scheme. Almost all plans for international government, in the political as distinct from the administrative sphere, have been inspired by a desire to discourage war and insure peace. All of them have recognized the essential nature of the problem, though their proponents have sometimes perceived reality confusedly and as through a glass darkly. They have for the most part recognized that wars result from competition and conflict between States pursuing irreconcilable political interests in an uncompromising fashion.

"Government" is a method of insuring peace within the community over which it has jurisdiction. It consists of a set of procedures whereby political entities—parties, factions, sections, classes, or nations—can strive for power with one another by pacific means through fixed legal and constitutional patterns of action. Discussion and compromise are substituted for coercion within the limits of the common interests and values of the participants. If the nation-states of the world can somehow be organized into a "world government" which will perform the same political functions in the world society as national governments perform within national societies, the hazard of international war will be reduced to the level of the present hazard of revolution or civil war within well-organized States. Armaments will then be used internationally as police forces are used within States—to protect government, to preserve the established distribution of wealth and power, and to suppress criminals and lawbreakers. Within the limits of common interests and purposes, controversies and differences of interests will be dealt with administratively and judicially, with the whole power of the world community available to enforce decisions and awards. Such disputes as are non-justiciable and non-arbitrable will be dealt with politically through debate and compromise between appointed or elected representatives. Disarmament, arbitration, and the genuine "outlawry of war" will be attained and "security" for all will be available within the general structure. These "solutions," futile in themselves as panaceas for war, will then become part of an established fabric of peaceful collaboration between States.

The implications of this argument for the problem of war deserve close examination and analysis, for it is the conviction of the great majority of thoughtful students of the whole question that an effective scheme of international government offers the only ultimate guarantee of peace between nations. These implications may be conveniently presented in the form of a review of the rôle of violence in the political process on all levels. Social groups pursuing political objectives, *i.e.*, seeking power as an end in itself or as a means of furthering ulterior interests, seek to overcome rival groups by violent coercion only when neither side will yield and there is no disposition to compromise. If the groups involved are bound together by broad common interests and feel themselves a part of a larger whole to which all acknowledge allegiance, there will be no violence. Each will couch particular interests in terms of the general interest, on the basis of the prevailing "constitutional consensus" and all will accept the verdict of a political process involving debate, discussion, voting, and a mutual give-and-take. This is the situation normally existing within every civilized State. But if each group pursues its own ends as supreme goods which cannot be compromised, then each contestant is irreconcilable and threats and appeals to force become inevitable. Here there is no consensus. There is an insufficiency of common interests in terms of which particular divergencies can be reconciled. Might makes right, for there is no general conception of right which disputants acknowledge to be superior to their special interests. This is the situation normally existing in international society. The problem of peace is a problem of creating a genuine international community of interests and attitudes, of inducing sovereign States to subordinate their national interests to the world society, of integrating the particular and conflicting interests into a general consensus.

If the problem be envisaged in these terms, its solution does not involve an attitude of naive oblivion toward the fact that States compete with one another for power and prestige. All politics is a struggle for power, and any political reorganization of the Western State System designed to insure peace must take cognizance of this circumstance. What is required is not that States cease to be political entities or cease to have political relations with one another, but that they envisage their power interests in terms fundamentally different from those prevailing hitherto. This requires a revolution in attitudes, ideologies, values, and in all of the established modes of feeling and thinking and living. It involves specifically a transformation of the accepted concepts of sovereignty, patriotism, national honor, national interests, and national prestige. This

[669]

transformation is by no means a psychological impossibility, for something comparable to it has already taken place in the formation of every national society. In this process sections, provinces, classes, castes, parties, etc.—all of which formerly pursued political power by violence—were induced to modify their attitudes toward one another in such fashion as to permit them to pursue political power by pacific means on the basis of a new conception of the general interests. Violence will be eliminated in the political relations of the States of the world if and when they undergo a similar transvaluation of values. The obstacles to this process in the building of an international community are infinitely greater than the corresponding obstacles which were overcome in the creation of the present national communities. Whether they are insuperable remains to be seen. Until they are overcome there can be no assurance of permanent peace.

The nature of these obstacles and the degree of success or failure thus far achieved in overcoming them may be considered more appropriately in an evaluation of the Geneva League, after the endeavors of government to insure peace through disarmament and security schemes have been surveyed. Here only two general criticisms need be offered of the position of most of the advocates and practitioners of international government. The first is that they have emphasized machinery instead of attitudes and values. No government, national or international, can function without formal institutions, agencies, departments, bureaus, councils, cabinets, deliberative assemblies, and the like. But the structural paraphernalia is worthless if the will to make it function is lacking. The existence of the machinery may help to create the will by encouraging the formation of attitudes, interests, and values which will insure its successful operation. The machinery alone, however, cannot attain the goal. The literature and the politics of international government have thus far been concerned almost exclusively with forms rather than forces and have neglected all that is most essential to breathe into the dead forms the breath of life.

The second general criticism to be offered is that even those who have conceded the necessity of a transformation of national values have often failed to perceive the imperative necessity of applying the new machinery and the new attitudes to concrete problems of power relationships between rival sovereign entities. Good intentions, pious aspirations, and soothing platitudes will not attain this end. The new international order will be securely established only when it becomes capable of dealing directly and effectively, not merely with the problems upon which States have reached agreement, but also with those upon which States still disagree fundamentally. The most important of these problems relate to territory, frontiers, armaments, economic opportunities, and other aspects of the values of power, profits, and prestige which will, in any case, disappear only very gradually. Here are the seeds of war. Here are the problems which must be dealt with successfully by international government if it is to fulfill its major purpose of preserving peace.

SUGGESTED READINGS

Allen, D.: *The Fight for Peace*, New York, The Macmillan Company, 1930.

Angell, N.: *The Fruits of Victory*, New York, Century Company, 1921.

———: *The Great Illusion*, New York, G. P. Putnam's Sons, 1913.

Bodart, G.: *Losses of Life in Modern Wars: Austria-Hungary, France*, New York, Milford, 1916.

Bogart, E. L.: *Direct and Indirect Costs of the Great World War*, New York, Oxford University Press, 1919.

Brailsford, H. N.: *War of Steel and Gold*, New York, The Macmillan Company, 1915.

Bratt, K. A.: *That Next War?* New York, Harcourt, Brace & Company, 1931

Carter, J.: *Man Is War*, Indianapolis, Bobbs-Merrill Company, 1926.

Clark, J. M.: *The Costs of the World War to the American People*, New Haven, Yale University Press, 1932.

Curti, M. E.: *The American Peace Crusade*, Durham, N. C., Duke University Press, 1929.

De Bloch, J.: *The Future of War*, Boston, Ginn & Company, 1899.

Dickinson, G. L.: *War: Its Nature, Cause, and Cure*, New York, The Macmillan Company, 1923.

Dumas, S., and Vedel-Petersen: *Losses of Life Caused by War*, New York, Oxford University Press, 1923.

Kenworthy, J. M.: *Peace or War?*, New York, Boni & Liveright, 1927.

Ladd, W.: *An Essay on a Congress of Nations*, New York, Oxford University Press, 1916.

Lasswell, H. D.: *Propaganda Technique in the World War*, New York, Alfred A. Knopf, 1927.

———: *Psychopathology and Politics*, Chicago, University of Chicago Press, 1930.

Morrison, C. C.: *The Outlawry of War: a Constructive Policy for World Peace*, Chicago, Willet Clark, 1927.

Nicolai, G. F.: *The Biology of War*, New York, Century Company, 1918.

Novicow, J.: *War and Its Alleged Benefits*, New York, Henry Holt & Company, 1911.

Page, K.: *War: Its Causes and Cure*, New York, Doubleday, Doran & Company, 1923.

———: *National Defense, a Study of the Origins, Results, and Prevention of War*, New York, Farrar & Rinehart, Inc., 1931.

Salter, A., *et al.*: *The Causes of War*, New York, The Macmillan Company, 1932.

Trotter, W.: *Instincts of the Herd in Peace and War*, New York, The Macmillan Company, 1917.

Veblen, T. B.: *An Inquiry into the Nature of Peace and the Terms of its Perpetuation*, New York, The Macmillan Company, 1917.

CHAPTER XVII

THE POLITICS OF PEACE

IN TURNING from theoretical considerations to the practical efforts of governments to cope with the problem of abolishing war, one is confronted with what appears on the surface to be a vast, futile confusion, occasionally relieved by limited achievements in the desired direction. The futility can be explained by reference to the criteria suggested in the preceding chapter. The confusion is due in large part to simultaneous efforts on the part of dozens of governments to attain the goal of permanent peace by a bewildering variety of expedients and policies which appear to the layman to be uncoordinated and unrelated. It is difficult at times to discover very much logic or consistency in the policies of a single government. When all are striving together, at Geneva or elsewhere, there is necessarily much working at cross purposes and a tendency for the various solutions to revolve about one another in vain gyrations, with progress achieved by one step forward, two backward, and half a dozen to either side. Many volumes have been devoted to these efforts, and in the resulting babel of tongues the confusion is worse confounded. In the present chapter an attempt will be made to reduce the story to comprehensible terms by surveying first the progress of efforts at the renunciation of war, then the steps taken toward disarmament, and finally the corresponding efforts to achieve peace and security through alternative methods. This distinction is artificial, for the three lines of endeavor are inextricably interwoven, as will be seen. But it will nevertheless serve as a basis for discussion and analysis.

1. THE RENUNCIATION OF WAR

> History is full of invasions, full of wars and of aggressions and there have always been pacts, always military guarantees, and always military security. The history of the world is a history which shows the nations always ready for war and always at war, and the one is absolutely essentially and organically connected with the other. History is full of the doom of nations which have trusted that false security.—RAMSAY MACDONALD at Geneva, September, 1924.

The solution of the problem of peace through international agreements, wherein the signatories pledge themselves to refrain from war, is not distinctive of the post-Versailles period, though this device has been greatly extended and given new form. Early treaties pledging eternal peace and friendship between the parties constituted, by implication, a renunciation of war, as do all treaties providing for the pacific settlement of disputes. General positive obligations requiring the signatories to preserve peace were in course of time replaced by specific positive obligations to settle disputes by pacific means—arbitration, adjudication, conciliation, etc., subject to such exceptions and reservations as the parties might make. These positive obligations have more recently been buttressed by negative obligations to refrain from "aggression" and to observe neutrality, with the two kinds of obligations incorporated, again in general terms and in negative form, in the Kellogg-Briand Pact. The positive obligations have been reviewed elsewhere.[1] Here attention may be given first to the specific negative obligations incorporated in bilateral or multilateral treaties, after which the League of Nations Covenant and the Kellogg-Briand Pact will be examined once more from the point of view of their efficacy as general multilateral arrangements for the renunciation of war.

The Locarno treaties, signed December 1, 1925, constituted a special and regional multilateral agreement for the renunciation of war in western Europe, in accordance with Sir Austen Chamberlain's dictum, "special agreements to meet special needs." They likewise contained provisions for security, arbitration, and mutual guarantees. In the Treaty of Mutual Guarantee (the "Rhine Pact") Germany and Belgium, and likewise Germany and France, agree "in no case to attack or invade each other or to resort to war against each other" except (1) in self-defense, which includes resistance to a flagrant breach of the articles of the Treaty of Versailles demilitarizing the Rhineland, (2) in the course of action under Article 16 of the League Covenant, and (3) in action resulting from a decision of the Council or Assembly of the League of Nations. The four Treaties of Conciliation, Arbitration, and Compulsory Adjudication (Germany-Belgium, Germany-Czechoslovakia, Germany-France, and Germany-Poland) provide unqualifiedly that "all disputes of every kind between Germany and (the other signatories) with regard to which the parties are in conflict as to their respective rights, and which it may not be possible to settle amicably by the normal methods of diplomacy, shall be submitted for decision either to an arbitral tribunal or to the Permanent Court of International Justice as laid down hereafter. It is agreed that the disputes referred to above include in particular those mentioned in Article 13 of the Covenant of the League of Nations" (Article 1). A permanent conciliation commission is established by each of the treaties. To this body all disputes not settled by adjudication or arbitration are to be submitted, with the right of appeal to the Council of the League. All the parties are thus bound to resort to pacific means of settlement. This *implies* a nega-

[1] See pp. 221-229 above.

[673]

tive obligation not to resort to force, but does not expressly say as much, save for the Treaty of Mutual Guarantee applying to Germany's western frontiers. The latter instrument is a definite renunciation of war, subject to the broad and somewhat ambiguous exceptions noted. The other treaties renounce the use of force only by implication. Germany was unwilling to accept her eastern frontiers as definitive, and Great Britain and Italy were unwilling to guarantee them. Germany has agreed not to attack or invade France and Belgium, and they have accepted the same obligation toward Germany. But with regard to Poland and Czechoslovakia, the German Government has merely agreed to settle all disputes by pacific means.

The conclusion of the Locarno Pacts was followed by negotiations, initiated by the Soviet Union, for similar pacts in eastern Europe. From the Soviet point of view, Locarno represented, in the words of Karl Radek, "Germany's subordination under the League of Nations" and "a step on the road to the creation of an alliance of capitalistic Powers which is directed against the Soviet Union." To counterbalance Locarno and to insure peace in eastern Europe, the Union of Soviet Socialist Republics devised a system of neutrality and non-aggression treaties with its neighbors. This system involved no pledges of mutual guarantee, but embodied simply a negative renunciation of war and pledges of benevolent neutrality. On December 17, 1925, the first of these treaties was concluded at the Soviet embassy in Paris between the Union of Soviet Socialist Republics and Turkey. Article 1 provides for the neutrality of each party in the event of the other party being attacked by any third party or parties. In Article 2 each party undertakes not to attack the other and not to participate in hostile acts or agreements with third parties directed against the other, including financial and economic boycotts. The appended protocols provide for pacific means of settlement. The original agreement was to run for three years, but it was renewed with an indefinite duration December 17, 1929. "The best proof of the peaceable intentions of the agreement," declared Litvinov, "is the fact that the Soviet Government is ready to conclude an analogous agreement with all countries with which it has normal relations."

Moscow, still hoping either to win Germany away from the western Powers or at least to counteract Locarno with comparable arrangements for her own protection, found its opportunity in German resentment at the failure of the March (1926) Assembly to admit Germany to the League. The renewal in the same month of the Polish-Rumanian alliance of March 3, 1921, likewise influenced Berlin's attitude. Foreign Minister Stresemann and Ambassador Krestinsky signed a Soviet-German treaty in Berlin, modeled upon the Turkish agreement, on April 24, 1926 (renewed June 24, 1931). Stresemann pointed out that this arrangement was not incompatible with Germany's obligations under either the Locarno treaties or the Covenant of the League, since it provided for neutrality only when one of the parties should be a victim of unprovoked aggression. On September 28, 1926, a Soviet-Lithuanian treaty containing similar provisions, as well as Soviet recognition of Lithuanian title to Vilna, was signed at Moscow. Agreements for the pacific settlement of frontier disputes were signed with Poland, August 3, 1925, with Latvia July 19, 1926, and with Esthonia on August 8, 1927. On August 31, 1926, a Soviet Treaty of Neutrality and Non-aggression was concluded with Afghanistan. It was renewed June 24, 1931. On October 1, 1927, a Soviet-Persian Pact of Guarantee, Neutrality, and Non-aggression was signed. Turkish-Persian, Persian-Afghanistan, and Afghanistan-Turkish neutrality agreements completed the system in the Near East. All provide for non-aggression and non-participation in hostile agreements. Unlike the League Covenant, their purpose is to localize conflict. The Italian-Spanish treaty of August 7, 1926, the Greek-Rumanian treaty of March 12, 1928, the Italian-Turkish treaty of May 30, 1928, and the Italian-Greek treaty of September 23, 1928 indicate partial acceptance by these States of the same plan, which was incorporated, with qualifications, into the draft treaties prepared by the security committee of the League and approved by the Ninth Assembly (1928). Soviet efforts to conclude neutrality and non-aggression pacts with Poland and Rumania have thus far been unsuccessful, because of Bukharest's insistence on Moscow's recognition of Rumanian title to Bessarabia. In view of events in Germany, however, Poland signed such a pact in the summer of 1932. At the time of writing the protracted negotiations for non-aggression agreements between the Soviet Union on the one hand and Poland, Rumania, and France on the other are still going on, with the Polish pact still unratified. Japan, Finland, Latvia, and Esthonia have thus far refused to enter into such pacts with the Union of Soviet Socialist Republics.

These agreements and various others to be noticed below are all regional in character and provide for the renunciation of war by bilateral or (as in the case of the Rhine Pact) multilateral agreements. The Covenant of the League of Nations, on the contrary, is a general renunciation of war by world-wide agreement.[1] Article 11 of the Covenant makes any war or threat of war a matter of concern to all members of the League. Article 12 obliges all members to submit disputes to arbitration, adjudication, or inquiry by the Council. "They agree in no case to resort to war until three months after the award by the arbitrators, or the judicial decision, or the report by the Council." The members further agree (Article 13) "that they will not resort to war against a member of the League which complies" with any award or decision or (Article 15) with

[1] See pp. 222–225 above.

the Council's recommendations. Under the Covenant, war is still possible three months after an award, decision, or Council report, in the event of the rejection of the settlement by one or both parties. It is likewise permissible, if the Council fails to make a unanimous recommendation, if there is unreasonable delay in arriving at an award, decision, or recommendation, if a dispute is found to be "domestic," if the dispute is between non-member States, and if sanctions are applied against a Covenant-breaking State. These obligations, therefore, constitute a renunciation of war which is partial and incomplete, with many loopholes remaining open.

Following the establishment of the League, a long series of efforts was embarked upon to plug up the loopholes in the Covenant and to render more specific and effective the obligations not to resort to war. The first of these was embodied in the Cecil-Requin Draft Treaty of Mutual Assistance of 1923, which declared (Article 1) that "aggressive war is an international crime and (the contracting parties) severally undertake that no one of them will be guilty of its commission." The knotty problem of defining aggression was to be left to the League Council, which would designate the State which was the victim of aggression in a particular conflict and therefore entitled to assistance from the other signatories. After the rejection of this arrangement, the Geneva Protocol of 1924 appeared.[1] Its preamble asserted that "a war of aggression constitutes a violation of [the solidarity of the members of the international community] and an international crime." It contemplated the amendment of the Covenant and provided that the signatory States would agree "in no case to resort to war," except in resistance to aggression or with the consent of the Council or Assembly. The signatories also agreed to "abstain from any act which might constitute a threat of aggression against another State." An aggressor State was defined as one going to war after refusing to accept the procedures for pacific settlement provided for, or rejecting a decision. In doubtful cases the Council would designate the aggressor and apply sanctions. The British Government failed to ratify the Protocol and it was abandoned. The Locarno pacts followed as a regional substitute for general agreement.

When certain delegations attempted to revive the Geneva Protocol, the Assembly, on September 24, 1927, resolved that "all wars of aggression are and shall always be prohibited" and that "every pacific means must be employed to settle disputes of every description which may arise between States." The Sixth Pan-American Conference at Havana (January-February, 1928) provided for a Pan-American Arbitration and Conciliation Conference which met in Washington and drew up, on January 5, 1929, a General Convention of Inter-American Conciliation, a General

[1] See p. 225 above.

Treaty of Inter-American Arbitration, and a Protocol of Progressive Arbitration.[1] These agreements have been described (somewhat optimistically in view of their provisions and the reservations attached to them) as "the first pact for the outlawry of war which was consummated by the setting up of machinery for the pacific settlements of international disputes."[2]

Meanwhile the Kellogg-Briand Pact (the General Treaty for the Renunciation of War) had intervened. The negotiations preceding it had been initiated in June, 1927, by a proposal from M. Briand to Secretary of State Kellogg for a bilateral Franco-American treaty solemnly renouncing war as an instrument of national policy. Mr. Kellogg, with the support of peace seekers everywhere, proposed making the treaty multilateral and general. Briand agreed, providing that it should be restricted to "wars of aggression." Kellogg dissented and the French Government finally agreed to general renunciation on the following conditions: universal adherence; retention by each signatory of a right of self-defense; nonapplication of the Pact to prior obligations under the Covenant, the Locarno Treaties, and neutrality agreements; and an automatic release of all signatories from the new obligation in case any one signatory violated the pledge. On this understanding the Franco-American proposals were transmitted to Great Britain, Germany, Italy, Japan, Belgium, Czechoslovakia, Poland, India, and the British Dominions. Great Britain agreed to become a party on condition of reserving its liberty of action in "certain [undefined] regions of the world, the welfare and integrity of which constitute a special and vital interest for our peace and safety."[3] This British "Monroe Doctrine" was accepted, though the Canadian and Irish Governments, and subsequently the Egyptian, Turkish, and Persian Governments declared themselves not bound by it. The Pact was signed at the Quai d'Orsay on August 27, 1928, by representatives of fifteen States. By the close of 1930 it had been adhered to by sixty-one States, Argentina and Brazil being the only important abstentions. After considerable wrangling over ratification and some subsequent interpretations and understand-

[1] See p. 227 above.

[2] J. W. Wheeler-Bennett, *Disarmament and Security Since Locarno*, 1932, p. 244.

[3] "There are certain regions of the world the welfare and integrity of which constitute a special and vital interest for our peace and safety. His Majesty's Government have been at pains to make it clear in the past that interference in these regions cannot be suffered. Their protection against attack is to the British Empire a measure of self-defense. It must be clearly understood that His Majesty's Government in Great Britain accept the new treaty upon the distinct understanding that it does not prejudice their freedom of action in this respect. The Government of the United States have comparable interests any disregard of which by a foreign Power they have declared that they would regard as an unfriendly act. His Majesty's Government believe, therefore, that in defining their position they are expressing the intention and meaning of the United States." (Cited in Wheeler-Bennett, *op. cit.*, p. 247.)

ings, President Hoover proclaimed the Pact in force on July 24, 1929. Its text follows:

. . . Deeply sensible of their solemn duty to promote the welfare of mankind;

Persuaded that the time has come when a frank renunciation of war as an instrument of national policy should be made to the end that the peaceful and friendly relations now existing between their peoples may be perpetuated;

Convinced that all changes in their relations with one another should be sought only by pacific means and be the result of a peaceful and orderly process, and that any signatory Power which hereafter seeks to promote its national interests by resort to war should be denied the benefits furnished by this treaty;

Hopeful that, encouraged by their example, all the other nations of the world will join in this humane endeavor and by adhering to the present treaty as soon as it comes into force bring their peoples within the scope of its beneficent provisions, thus uniting the civilized nations of the world in a common renunciation of war as an instrument of their national policy; [the high contracting parties]

Have decided to conclude a treaty and for that purpose have appointed as their respective plenipotentiaries. . . .

Article 1

The high contracting parties solemnly declare in the names of their respective peoples that they condemn recourse to war for the solution of international controversies, and renounce it as an instrument of national policy in their relations with one another.

Article 2

The high contracting parties agree that the settlement or solution of all disputes or conflicts of whatever nature or of whatever origin they may be, which may arise among them, shall never be sought except by pacific means.

Article 3

The present treaty shall be ratified by the high contracting parties named in the preamble in accordance with their respective constitutional requirements, and shall take effect as between them as soon as all their several instruments of ratification shall have been deposited at Washington.

This treaty shall, when it has come into effect as prescribed in the preceding paragraph, remain open as long as may be necessary for adherence by all the other Powers of the world. Every instrument evidencing the adherence of a Power shall be deposited at Washington and the treaty shall immediately upon such deposit become effective as between the Power thus adhering and the other Powers parties hereto.

It shall be the duty of the Government of the United States to furnish each Government named in the preamble and every Government subsequently adhering to this treaty with a certified copy of the treaty and of every instrument of ratification or adherence. It shall also be the duty of the Government of the United States telegraphically to notify such Governments immediately upon the deposit with it of each instrument of ratification or adherence. . . .

This sweeping and general renunciation of war was followed by various supplementary efforts to give it full effect. The Soviet Union was the first State to ratify it, despite the fact that it was denounced in Moscow for its indefiniteness and irrelevance. On December 29, 1928, the Soviet minister in Warsaw proposed that the two Powers, along with Lithuania, should sign a protocol (the "Litvinov Protocol") making the pact effective between them at once without waiting for the general exchange of ratifications. The Soviet note deplored Poland's earlier refusal to sign a non-aggression and neutrality agreement. The Polish Government accepted in principle but made formal objections and counter-proposals for the inclusion of Rumania and all of the Baltic States. Litvinov accepted these suggestions at once. Lithuania had already accepted the Soviet proposal on January 3, 1929, and suggested to Latvia and Esthonia that they should adhere to the protocol. On February 9, 1929, the protocol was signed at Moscow by representatives of the U.S.S.R., Poland, Latvia, Esthonia, and Rumania. Lithuania and Turkey adhered on April 1, Danzig on April 30, and Persia on July 4. Simultaneous efforts to "close the gap in the Covenant" by incorporating the Kellogg Pact into amendments failed for reasons noted elsewhere.[1] No agreement had been reached regarding this problem by 1933.

Quite apart from the question of the exact nature of the obligations incurred by the Kellogg Pact, which is by no means what it appears to be, it was at once pointed out that the Pact was purely negative and contained no provisions for its enforcement. What were the "pacific means" of settlement which the signatories were to utilize? What in particular would the attitude of the United States be in the event of a violation of the Pact? Resolutions were introduced in the American Congress, suggesting that American aid be refused to aggressor States, but none of these was passed or acted upon. In the summer and autumn of 1929, in the course of Sino-Soviet hostilities in northern Manchuria, Secretary of State Stimson consulted with the other signatories as to what should be done. After much discussion, identic notes were despatched to Moscow and Nanking by the United States, Great Britain, France, and Italy in December, 1929. They arrived when the hostilities had ended and a new agreement had been signed. Litvinov failed to comprehend how the American Government, which refused to recognize the U.S.S.R., could undertake to advise it on the conduct of its foreign affairs. The lack of established procedures of consultation which was partly responsible for this embarrassing situation led Mr. Stimson to suggest to M. Claudel, French Ambassador in Washington, that machinery be set up in the form of an impartial conciliation commission for consultation and for the mobilization of public opinion against an aggressor State. At the London Naval Conference of 1930 the question was again raised, since France refused to reduce her armaments without assurances of international support against an aggressor State. Mr.

[1] See pp. 224–225 above.

Stimson tentatively considered the conclusion of a "consultative pact," but a great hue and cry was at once raised in the American hinterland against this "foreign entanglement" and the proposal was dropped, like the proverbial hot potato. No agreement could be reached on guarantees of security, and France and Italy refused to become parties to the whole of the naval treaty. On November 11, 1930, President Hoover spoke of the desirability of "strengthening and buttressing" the Pact by agreements for negotiation, conciliation, and arbitration. Later in the month, however, the State Department, again bowing to American isolationist sentiment, denied that any negotiations to this effect had been opened. Periodical denials of this kind have been issued from time to time subsequently.

The Sino-Japanese crisis of 1931–1932 produced a new emergency and led to a definite crystallization of opinion in the United States and at Geneva as to the means by which the Pact was to be enforced. On October 9, and again on October 12, 1931, Secretary Stimson urged the League of Nations to do all in its power to settle the dispute and insure observance of obligations not to resort to war on the part of the contestants. The United States subsequently recalled the obligations of the Pact to both Japan and China. On October 16 Mr. Prentiss Gilbert, American Consul General at Geneva, took a seat at the Council table with instructions from Washington "to take part in the discussions when they relate to the possible application of the Kellogg-Briand Pact." A month later Ambassador Dawes was instructed to hover in the vicinity of the Council meeting in Paris for the same purpose, though he was ordered not to sit in on the sessions. This informal procedure of consultation did not produce any visible effect on the course of events in Manchuria.[1] On January 7, 1932, in identic notes to Japan and China, the American Government formulated the "Stimson Doctrine" as a statement of the means to be employed in insuring observance of the Kellogg Pact:

In view of the present situation and of its own rights and obligations therein, the American Government deems it to be its duty to notify both the Government of the Chinese Republic and the imperial Japanese Government that it cannot admit the legality of any situation *de facto* nor does it intend to recognize any treaty or agreement entered into between these Governments, or agents thereof, which may impair the treaty rights of the United States or its citizens in China, including those which relate to the sovereignty, the independence, or the territorial and administrative integrity of the Republic of China, or to the international policy relative to China, commonly known as the Open Door policy; and that it does not intend to recognize any situation, treaty, or agreement which may be brought about by means contrary to the covenants and obligations of the Pact of Paris of August 27, 1928, to which treaty both China and Japan, as well as the United States, are parties.

[1] See pp. 415–419 above.

In a letter to Senator Borah of February 24, 1932, Mr. Stimson expressed the hope that a similar decision would be reached by the other governments of the world, in order that "a caveat will be placed upon such action which, we believe, will effectively bar the legality hereafter of any title or right sought to be obtained by pressure or treaty violation, and which, as has been shown by history in the past, will eventually lead to the restoration to China of rights and titles of which she may have been deprived." On March 11, 1932, the League Assembly accepted this means of enforcement in a resolution:

The Assembly . . . declares that it is incumbent upon the members of the League of Nations not to recognize any situation, treaty, or agreement which may be brought about by means contrary to the Covenant of the League of Nations or to the Pact of Paris.

In an address of August 8, 1932, Secretary Stimson completed the formulation of the new policy by declaring that the Pact implied consultation, thus rendering a separate consultative agreement unnecessary. The Pact, moreover, rests for its enforcement upon public opinion and not upon coercion or international sanctions, according to the Stimson interpretation:

Consultation between the signatories of the Pact, when faced with a threat of its violation, becomes inevitable. Any effective invocation of the power of world opinion postulates discussion and consultation. As long as the signatories of the Pact support the policy which the American Government has endeavored to establish during the past three years of arousing a united and living spirit of public opinion as a sanction of the Pact, as long as this course is adopted and endorsed by the great nations of the world who are signatories of that treaty, consultations will take place as an incident to the unification of that opinion. . . . The Briand-Kellogg Pact provides for no sanctions of force. It does not require any signatory to intervene with measures of force in case that Pact is violated. Instead it rests upon the sanction of public opinion, which can be made one of the most potent sanctions of the world. Any other course, through the possibilities of entangling the signatories in international politics, would have confused the broad, simple aim of the treaty and prevented the development of that public opinion upon which it most surely relies. Its efficacy depends upon the will of the people of the world to make it effective.

In summary, then, the States of the world have renounced war and have agreed to enforce this renunciation by refusing to recognize any advantage, territorial or otherwise, achieved by one State through warlike coercion of another. Why, then, is peace not assured? Why do peoples and governments everywhere live in continued fear of war? Why is this fear more terrifying, more disheartening, than ever before? Why have world expenditures on armaments increased steadily since the signature of the Pact? And why have States continued to use military force to achieve diplomatic objectives—in Nicaragua, in Manchuria, at Shanghai, in the Gran Chaco, and elsewhere?

These questions are not difficult to answer. The Kellogg Pact, despite its appearance, is not a renunciation of the use of military force by the signatory States for any purpose for which States have resorted to force in the recent past. It is a moral symbol and a diplomatic gesture. It is perhaps an "outlawry of war" in a narrowly legal sense. But it is not a pledge on the part of any State to refrain from military violence in the pursuit of diplomatic objectives, nor does it offer any assurance that such violence will not encounter resistance, with armed conflict resulting. It does not require any particular State to submit any particular controversy to any particular mode of pacific settlement. It does not even require consultation, except by Mr. Stimson's implication. To a much greater degree than is true of most treaties, it is a scrap of paper binding no one to anything. It is capable of becoming something more than an idle gesture only when governments and peoples modify fundamentally the traditional attitudes and values which have bred war in the past and will breed war (by another name) in the future.

The explanation of this paradox is to be found in the meaning attached to the Pact in the interpretative notes and understandings which preceded its ratification. No technical "reservations" were made. In form, the signatory States agreed to "condemn recourse to war for the solution of international controversies" and to "renounce it as an instrument of national policy in their relations with one another." They also agreed never to seek the solution of disputes and conflicts "except by pacific means." In fact, the real meaning of the Pact is not to be found in these phrases, but in definitions attached to them by the leading signatories during the negotiations. At French insistence the Pact was expressly understood not to apply to wars of self-defense or to obligations under existing military alliances. At British insistence the Pact was understood not to interfere with a State's liberty of action in areas vital to its interests—and these areas were purposely left undefined in the British "Monroe Doctrine." In the United States it was understood (at least by the State Department) that the Pact in no way interfered with the right of the United States to enforce the American Monroe Doctrine—likewise undefined—in the name of self-defense. During the negotiation of the Pact, representatives of the United States at Havana strongly opposed the non-intervention resolution sponsored by the Latin Americans. It was agreed by all parties that the Pact forbade only "wars of aggression" and did not apply to defensive hostilities, to hostilities against a State violating its obligations under the agreement, or to hostilities required by the League Covenant, the Locarno treaties, or other engagements of alliance or neutrality.

It follows logically and legitimately from these considerations that the only kinds of wars which the Pact forbids are those which would never occur under twentieth century conditions. "Wars of aggression" are non-existent, for no State undertakes to apply military force against another without insisting loudly and eloquently that its action is required for its own defense. The signatories of the Pact, being free to fight in self-defense, are free to define for themselves what constitutes self-defense and to take whatever action they think is demanded by their "interests." Austria-Hungary waged war on Serbia in 1914 in the name of self-defense. Russia waged war on Austria-Hungary and Germany in the name of defending Serbia and protecting vital Russian interests in the Balkans. Germany invaded Belgium and France in the name of self-defense. Great Britain declared war on Germany on the same grounds. The United States fol-lowed suit in 1917 for similar reasons. Both sets of belligerent govern-ments convinced their peoples and themselves that they were fighting a defensive war against enemy aggressors. Questions of "guilt" and of "responsibility for aggression" are pointless. The stakes of modern diplo-macy, in the pursuit of which States resort to force, are always couched in terms of protecting or defending rights and interests. And it is likewise pointless to contend that military action in self-defense must stop at national frontiers. All of the imperial Powers have vital interests the defense of which constantly demands action outside of their frontiers. All the foreign wars of the United States have been "defensive" in the eyes of the American nation. All of them have been fought on the territories of other States. In many situations the best "defense" is attack, as the veriest novice in military science knows. Japan detached Manchuria from China and conducted military operations on Chinese soil in 1931–1933 in the name of defending Japanese interests. These interests are exactly comparable to American interests in the Caribbean, British interests in Egypt, Iraq, Afghanistan, and Persia, French interests in Siam, south China, north Africa, etc. In a State System in which power is pursued competitively and by force, "aggression" and "self-defense" are meaning-less concepts, and a pact for the renunciation of war which permits "defensive" wars is likewise meaningless.

Apart from this difficulty, the Pact lacks any effective means of enforcement. Waiving the question as to whether obligations which are so indefinite as to be meaningless can ever be enforced, it remains true that no procedure has been devised for enforcing these obligations, how-ever they may be defined. It is understood that if one signatory violates the Pact, the others are released from it. The Pact is no stronger than its weakest link. But a State resorting to force to protect or promote its interests can always argue, with much show of reason, that the Pact does not apply, since it is acting in "self-defense." It can also argue, with equal reason, that all measures of "settlement" unaccompanied by a declaration of war are "pacific," as indeed they are in a technical, legal sense. Other States may dissent and "world opinion" (if one admits its possibility in a world of multitudinous diversity and discord) may condemn. But a State which is strong and determined will not be restrained by verbal censure. It will be restrained only by superior force. The application of superior force, however, will provoke resistance and produce conflict—precisely what the Pact is intended to prevent.

The efficacy of the Stimson Doctrine as a restraining influence remains to be demonstrated. The foreign office at Tokyo, in its note to the United States of January 16, 1932, commented dryly:

> The Government of Japan takes note of the statement by the Government of the United States that the latter cannot admit the legality of matters which might impair the treaty rights of the United States or its citizens or which might be brought about by means contrary to the treaty of August 27, 1928. It might be the subject of an academic doubt, whether in a given case the impropriety of means necessarily and always voids the ends secured, but as Japan has no intention of adopting improper means, that question does not practically arise.

Even a world-wide legal boycott will be without effect on a Great Power. No one supposes that Japanese policy in Manchuria will be modified by the Stimson Doctrine. If it is modified, it will be as a result of Japanese inability to coerce China and Manchuria into accepting it. No one can suppose that the United States would have been restrained from "taking Panama" in 1903 by the attitude of the outside world. No significant instance of territorial annexation or intervention by a Great Power can be suggested in which it could be supposed that a world-wide legal boycott would have changed the result in any way. All the States of the world boycotted Soviet Russia, legally and economically, between 1918 and 1921, with no result save war and suffering on a large scale. A universal boycott of a *fait accompli* is difficult to maintain, moreover, for governments are obliged to deal with facts, not with fiction. The Kellogg Pact and Article 10 of the League Covenant can be regarded as invalidating conquest as the basis of title to territory only on the supposition that all other States will permanently refuse to take cognizance of future conquests and other infringements upon territorial integrity, and that the would-be conquerors will thereby be chastened and persuaded to abandon their designs. This supposition is highly questionable. Sooner or later, for political and economic reasons, "Manchukuo" will be recognized as a State by other Powers, and the universality of the boycott will disappear. A boycott which is less than universal will inevitably fail to achieve its purposes. The United States has maintained a legal and diplomatic boycott against the Soviet Union for sixteen years without producing the slightest effect on Soviet policies. The underlying assumption of the Stimson Doctrine is as naive and as far removed from the realities of international politics as is the whole theory of the outlawry of war itself.

The Kellogg Pact and other agreements for the renunciation of war, however, have had one legal effect of considerable significance. They render it expedient for States to refrain from formal declarations of war or from the expression of any intention to inaugurate a state of war in the legal sense. Since 1928—and indeed since 1920—there have been no declarations of war and therefore no "wars" from the legal point of view. There have been numerous armed combats between the military forces of contending States, with all the incidents of war as a physical fact. But according to the new dispensation, undisturbed "peace" has prevailed and pacifists have taken comfort in the serene assumption that a skunk-cabbage by some other name smells like a rose. States using military coercion against other States have preferred to designate their action as "intervention," "reprisal," "retaliation," and the like and have argued that all coercive measures not accompanied by an intention to inaugurate war in a legal sense are "pacific." Whether this interesting legal fiction will continue to prevail in the future is uncertain, for in conflicts between naval Powers the rights of capture and blockade cannot be enforced against "neutrals" without a legal state of war. In such an eventuality the contestants may conceivably decide that the material advantages of declaring war are greater than the moral advantages of adhering to the fiction that war is "outlawed." This would automatically release all of the other signatories of the Kellogg Pact from their obligation. They will then be confronted with the alternative of abandoning the Pact and declaring their neutrality, or of acting on the assumption, implied in the Pact and expressed in Article 16 of the League Covenant, that neutrality is no longer a recognized legal status and that the warring States are at war with all others. In the latter case, the war would immediately become a general conflagration. This suggests that the new fiction is of doubtful value. It also opens up the possibility of the progressive disappearance of the international law of war, with armed combats in the future waged with that unprincipled ferocity and lack of restraint which brought grief to Grotius in the early seventeenth century. That this would represent a gain no one in his senses would contend. But for the present, the States of the world, while reserving their right to use military force in defense of their interests, are committed to the legalistic myth that war is no more.

2. DISARMAMENT: THE NAVAL POWERS

Heat not a furnace for your foe so hot
That it do singe yourself.—WILLIAM SHAKESPEARE, *Henry VIII.*

Attention may now be given to efforts to achieve peace through disarmament. Such efforts must, by their nature, be "international," *i.e.*, based upon agreements between States, for no State can safely discard or reduce its armaments while its rivals and potential enemies remain armed. A few small and weak States, notably Denmark, have taken such steps because of the realization that their armaments are in any case useless against powerful neighbors. But the Great Powers and the Secondary Powers cannot act in this fashion. They can disarm only together or not at all—and even simultaneous and proportionate disarmament is accompanied by innumerable difficulties, as will be seen. The story of international efforts at disarmament is one of occasional limited success and of more frequent unmitigated failure. The intricate technical involvements need not be discussed here, for they are scarcely pertinent to the main question. The nature of the problem can be readily revealed by a brief survey of post-war efforts, at Geneva and elsewhere, to achieve reduction or limitation.

All efforts at disarmament genuinely motivated by a desire to promote peace are obviously based upon the repudiation of the familiar Roman adage: *Si vis pacem, para bellum* ("If you wish peace, prepare for war"). This slogan is still utilized everywhere to justify the maintenance of powerful military and naval forces. Preparedness and militarism are seldom regarded as respectable if they are presented as instruments of aggression and conquest. They are invariably presented, therefore, as means toward preserving peace—in the period since the Covenant and the Pact no less than in the period before Sarajevo.[1] The fallacy of this argument is too patent to deserve extended refutation. The armaments of a nation insure peace only when the nation in question possesses such an overwhelming preponderance of force over all others that a test of strength is unnecessary and impossible. If one State can conquer all others

[1] Ralph T. O'Neil of Topeka, Kansas, then National Commander of the American Legion, declared before the Hamilton Club of Chicago on Memorial Day, 1930: "Permanent peace can best be achieved through adequate defensive preparedness. It is necessary for us to take the lead for world peace, but we cannot do this until we have standing and prestige among the nations. And to achieve this standing we should have an army and navy equal to those of any other nation."

Rear Admiral W. A. Moffett, Chief of the United States Navy Bureau of Aeronautics, asserted in a Memorial Day address (1930) in Passaic, New Jersey: "The best way to prevent war is to have sufficient force to prevent it. Had we had the army and navy, and air forces commensurate with the population and resources of America, there probably would not have been any World War."

Rear Admiral William V. Pratt, Chief of the Bureau of Operations of the Navy Department, declared on the same day, in Newport, Rhode Island: "There is an element in

and create an enduring world empire, peace will indeed be assured through arms. Imperial Rome achieved this goal in the ancient world. In the modern State System no single State seems capable of achieving it, for the distribution of population, resources, and power between the threescore sovereignties of the world is such that no one of them can impose its power upon the others. If each seeks security through preponderance in arms, a competitive armament race takes place. Crushing financial burdens are imposed upon the taxpayers, and when war comes it is appallingly murderous and destructive. So obvious has this become in recent decades that no one adheres any longer to the view that armaments insure peace, save a few French, Polish, and Little Entente diplomats who hope to perpetuate the *status quo* by maintaining an enormous military preponderance over possible disturbers, and a few generals, admirals, and munition makers in every country who feel obliged to disguise their trade in the white robes of peace.

Prior to 1914 attempts at disarmament by international agreement were few in number and limited in application. The Anglo-American Rush-Bagot Agreement of 1817 provided for the limitation of armaments on the Great Lakes to three vessels for each Power, not over 100 tons burden and possessing no weapons larger than one 18-pound cannon apiece. Though these limits have been departed from subsequently, the agreement laid the basis for the effective demilitarization of the Great Lakes and of the entire 3,000-mile frontier between Canada and the United States. In 1856 Russia and Turkey agreed to limit the number of their war vessels in the Black Sea to 10 apiece, but the agreement was later abrogated. In 1902 Argentina and Chile bound themselves not to increase their naval armaments, and in the following year they agreed to reduce their navies. Brazilian naval construction later led to the non-renewal of this agreement. In 1899 the first Hague Conference met for the purpose of limiting armies, navies, and war budgets. Most of the participants had no intention whatever of even contemplating any such limitation, and the conference merely expressed its conviction that "reduction of military charges, which are at present a heavy burden on the world, is extremely desirable for the increase of the material and moral welfare of mankind." The assembled diplomats expressed the pious hope that governments would consider "the possibility of an agreement." This convenient procedure was repeated at the second Hague Conference

---

the service that believes that limitation of armaments would be destructive. I do not believe this. I feel that a certain amount of limitation of destructive armaments would put our country in a favorable position. Great Britain may have the balance of power on the Continent, but the United States stands in the position of being the balance of power in the world, whether in peace or at war. We should be prepared. Paper navies mean nothing. It is only when you are prepared that you feel secure."

of 1907. In 1911 Great Britain sought a cessation of Anglo-German naval competition through a naval holiday on a 16:10 basis, but no agreement could be reached. Other efforts were equally fruitless. Armies and navies continued to increase, and competition in armaments between the Powers played a large rôle in producing the rivalries and tensions culminating in the Great War.

At the Paris Peace Conference of 1919, lip service was paid to disarmament as one of the major "war aims" of the Allies. The Allied statesmen incorporated into the treaty provisions for the disarmament of the defeated States. The forcible disarmament of vanquished by victors was not new (in 1808 Napoleon compelled Prussia to limit her armies to 42,000 men for ten years), but it was carried out more completely in the peace treaties concluding the Great War than ever before. The German general staff was abolished, military conscription in Germany was forbidden, and the German army was limited to 100,000 men. These soldiers must be enlisted for twelve consecutive years, and not more than 5 per cent of the total effectives may be discharged in any one year— a device designed to prevent a repetition of the Prussian tactics of the Napoleonic period, whereby a large trained reserve was built up by successive installments. Tanks, poison gas, heavy artillery, and aircraft were forbidden to the German army. Munition plants were dismantled or converted to peace purposes, and Germany was subjected to the supervision of inter-Allied military, naval, and aeronautical commissions to insure observance of these terms. The Rhineland was demilitarized and Germany was forbidden to maintain forts or garrisons within a 50-kilometer zone east of the Rhine. For 15 years the Rhineland and the Rhine bridge-heads were to be subjected to Allied military occupation, though the last of the occupying forces were in fact withdrawn in 1930. The imperial German navy was surrendered—and sunk by order of its officers in defiance of the Allies. For the future the German navy was limited to 6 battleships not to exceed 10,000 tons, 6 light cruisers, and 12 destroyers. Germany was denied the right to construct or use submarines or military and naval airplanes (Articles 173 to 210 of the Treaty of Versailles). The supervisory commissions were later dissolved, but, by Article 213 of the Treaty, "Germany undertakes to give every facility for any investigation which the Council of the League of Nations, acting if need be by majority vote, may consider necessary." Austria was limited to an army of 30,000, Hungary 35,000, and Bulgaria 33,000. Similar efforts to disarm Turkey were frustrated by the repudiation of the Treaty of Sèvres, but by the Straits Convention of 1923 the Turkish garrison at Constantinople is limited to 12,000 men, the Bosphorus and the Dardanelles are demilitarized, and the number and size of war vessels to be admitted to the Black Sea are limited.

The Allied Powers felt obliged, by their war-aims declarations, to specify that the disarmament of the defeated States was not to be permanently one-sided but was to be a step toward general disarmament. Article 8 of the League Covenant declared, "the members of the League recognize that the maintenance of peace requires reduction of national armaments to the lowest point consistent with national safety and the enforcement by common action of international obligations." The Treaty of Versailles asserted: "In order to render possible the initiation of a general limitation of the armaments of all nations, Germany undertakes strictly to observe the military, naval, and air clauses which follow." A note of the Allied and Associated Powers, in reply to the observations of the German delegates, was handed by M. Clemenceau to Count Brockdorff-Rantzau on June 16, 1919. It declared in part:

I. The Allied and Associated Powers wish to make it clear that their requirements in regard to German armaments were not made solely with the object of rendering it impossible for Germany to resume her policy of military aggression. They are also the first steps towards that general reduction and limitation of armaments which they seek to bring about as one of the most fruitful preventives of war, and which it will be one of the first duties of the League of Nations to promote.

II. They must point out, however, that the colossal growth in armaments of the last few decades was forced upon the nations of Europe by Germany. As Germany increased her power, her neighbors had to follow suit unless they were to become impotent to resist German dictation or the German sword. It is therefore right, as it is necessary, that the process of limitation of armaments should begin with the nation which has been responsible for their expansion. It is not until the aggressor has led the way that the attacked can safely afford to follow suit.

III. . . . . Germany must consent unconditionally to disarm in advance of the Allied and Associated Powers. . . . No deviation from the organization in armament laid down in the present treaty can be permitted until Germany is admitted to the League of Nations, which may then agree to such modifications as may seem desirable. . . .

Pending the realization of the general disarmament which was thus anticipated in the peace settlement, the naval Powers began considering the possibility of putting an end to the new armaments race which had already begun. The German navy was gone—surrendered to the Allies and scuttled by its crews at Scapa Flow on June 27, 1919. But the British Government was disturbed at the rapid development of American and Japanese naval power during and after the war. In 1914 the American navy ranked third after that of Great Britain and Germany. In 1916 Congress enacted a program for the construction of 10 battleships with twelve 16-inch guns apiece, 6 battle cruisers with eight 16-inch guns, 10 scout cruisers, and over a hundred smaller auxiliary vessels. The completion of this program would have given the United States an easy preponderance over Great Britain, despite the fact that the British navy, at the close of the war, had more capital ships than all other navies combined. The Admiralty therefore laid plans for superdreadnaughts of 45,000 to 50,000 tons, with 18- or 20-inch guns. In Japan the American program produced even more apprehension. In 1920 the Japanese Government prepared a program for the construction of 48 battleships and battle cruisers. This new rivalry boded ill for peace and threatened Great Britain and Japan with a crushing financial burden. From the American point of view, the completion of the specified program was certain to lead to resentment and retaliation on the part of the other naval Powers. Under these circumstances, Senator Borah's amendment to the naval appropriation bill of 1921 was passed, recommending a conference for the reduction of naval expenditures and building programs. President Harding invited the other naval Powers—Great Britain, Japan, France, and Italy—to attend such a conference, which was broadened to include China, The Netherlands, Belgium, and Portugal, for the discussion of Pacific and Far Eastern problems.

The measure of success achieved by the Washington Conference, which met on November 12, 1921, has never been equaled by any succeeding disarmament conference. Its success was due to the fact that none of the participants had any political purposes to serve by establishing its naval superiority over any of the others and that all of them had both a political and a financial interest in stabilizing armaments at the existing levels. If naval armaments were limited or reduced proportionately for all, the "security" and the fighting potential of each would be unaffected. All the participating governments, moreover, had become somewhat skeptical of the strategic value of the great capital ship which was, as it turned out, the only type of vessel in which competitive building was limited. The wide geographical separation between the three great naval Powers also contributed to success, for neither the British, American, nor Japanese navies could hope to operate effectively against either of the other two in the home waters of the prospective enemy and each Government was content to accept defensive supremacy within its own sphere. In the opening address of the conference, Charles Evans Hughes, the American Secretary of State, offered to abandon the American building program in return for concessions from Great Britain and Japan. He proposed limitation and reduction on the basis of the *status quo*, through the scrapping of certain ships and the abandonment of building plans.

This bold proposal was at length accepted and Great Britain, the United States, and Japan agreed on a 5:5:3 ratio in capital ships, *i.e.*, battleships and battle cruisers. France and Italy later accepted a ratio of 1.67 each. The five Power Treaty Limiting Naval Armament, signed February 6, 1922, provided for the scrapping of 68 ships, built or planned.

The United States was left with 18 capital ships of 525,850 tons, Great Britain with 20 ships (most of them smaller and older than the American) of 558,950 tons, Japan with 10 of 301,320 tons, France with 10 of 221,170 tons, and Italy with 10 of 182,800 tons. The revised figures of December 31, 1929, based on the standard ton of 2,240 pounds, showed that the United States had 532,400 tons of capital ships to Great Britain's 608,650 tons. The replacement program provided for, however, would give Great Britain and the United States 525,000 tons each by 1942, with 315,000 for Japan and 175,000 each for France and Italy. The treaty likewise limited aircraft carriers to a total of 135,000 tons each for Great Britain and the United States, 81,000 for Japan, and 60,000 each for France and Italy. No agreement could be reached on other types of vessels. Great Britain urged the abolition of submarines, but the other Powers refused to consider this. The French Government announced its intention of constructing 90,000 tons of submarines.[1] The British then refused to consider any limitation of destroyers, which in turn made cruiser limitation impossible. A draft treaty forbidding the employment of submarines as commerce destroyers was signed, but it failed of adoption because of French refusal to ratify it. No agreements were reached regarding aircraft and land forces.

The Washington Conference likewise formulated a number of agreements relating to the Far East and the Pacific. The prospective increase of American fortifications in Guam and the Philippine Islands had been viewed with the greatest apprehension by Japan, since these bases constituted a direct threat to Japanese naval ascendancy in the western Pacific. Persistence on the part of the United States in a policy of establishing its naval hegemony west of Hawaii would probably have led to war as certainly as would Japanese efforts to acquire and fortify bases in the eastern Pacific. The Japanese Government demanded the limitation of Pacific fortifications as the price of agreeing to the 5:5:3 ratio and of relinquishing the Anglo-Japanese alliance. Despite opposition from American naval officers, Secretary of State Hughes accepted this bargain. Article 19 of the Naval Treaty provided that the United States, Great Britain, and Japan "agree that the *status quo* at the time of the signing of the present treaty, with regard to fortifications and naval bases, shall be maintained in their respective territories and possessions specified hereunder." The United States agreed to maintain the *status quo* in all its Pacific possessions save Hawaii and the islands adjacent to the coast of

---

[1] The French Government likewise resented the implication of naval parity with Italy and declared in July, 1923, when it ratified the treaty: "The French Government considers, and always has considered, that the ratios of total tonnage in capital ships and aircraft carriers allowed to the several contracting Powers do not represent the respective importance of the maritime interests of those Powers and cannot be extended to the categories of vessels other than those for which they were expressly stipulated."

the United States, Alaska, and the Panama Canal zone; Great Britain accepted the same obligations for its possessions east of 110° longitude (just east of Singapore, the site of an important projected naval base) save for Australia, New Zealand, and the coasts of Canada; Japan agreed not to change the *status quo* of its fortifications in the Kurile Islands, the Bonin Islands, Amami-Oshima, the Liu-Kiu Islands, Formosa, and the Pescadores

The Four Power Pact, concluded at the same time between the United States, Great Britain, France, and Japan, specified that "with a view to the preservation of the general peace and the maintenance of their rights in relation to their insular possessions and insular dominions in the region of the Pacific Ocean" the parties "agree as between themselves to respect their rights" in these possessions. It further stipulated that any future controversies between the signatories over these territories would be submitted to a conference, while in case of any outside threat the parties would communicate with each other "in order to arrive at an understanding as to the most efficient measures to be taken, jointly or separately, to meet the situation."[1] The Nine Power Treaty of February 6, 1922, relating to principles and policies in matters concerning China, reiterated the principle of the Open Door and bound the signatories to respect the sovereignty, the independence, and the territorial and administrative integrity of China as well as to use their influence to maintain equality of economic opportunity. The other conference agreements and resolutions also related to Chinese problems.

If the Washington Conference had reduced the number of capital ships and terminated competition in their construction, it left the Powers quite free to construct whatever other types of vessels they desired. Naval competition shifted to cruisers and submarines. In 1922 Japan laid down keels for 5 cruisers and France for 3. In 1924 Great Britain and France laid down 5 cruisers each and Japan 2. Between February 6, 1922, and

---

[1] The broader political and strategic significance of these arrangements is accurately summarized by R. L. Buell, in *The Washington Conference*, p. 200, as follows: "As a result of the Naval Treaty, adopting the 5:5:3 ratio and the nonfortification agreement, it is now impossible for any Power to intervene successfully in the Orient by force, if acting alone. By the Four Power Treaty, it is now impossible for Great Britain and the United States to combine their fleets in order to intervene jointly. Moreover, by the Four Power Treaty the freedom of the United States and Great Britain to bring diplomatic pressure against Japan is also probably limited. Consequently, as long as these treaties are adhered to, Japan is absolutely supreme in the eastern Pacific and over Asia.

"At the same time, the Naval Treaty has made a successful Japanese attack on the Pacific Coast impossible, because Japan, as far as capital ships are concerned, will have a fleet 40 per cent inferior to the American fleet; because Japan has no real bases or fortifications in the Pacific this side of the Bonins; and because the United States retains the right to increase the fortifications in Hawaii. As a result of this treaty, it has become a physical impossibility for the United States successfully to attack Japan and Japan to attack the United States."

October 1, 1928, the United States began construction of 8 cruisers, Great Britain 15, Japan 15, France 8, and Italy 6. This competition led to new alarm, especially in the United States, which was being outstripped in cruisers by Great Britain and Japan. On February 10, 1927, President Coolidge invited Great Britain, Japan, France, and Italy to participate in a conference with the United States to limit construction of the types of vessels not covered by the Washington agreement. Great Britain and Japan accepted, while France and Italy refused, the former on the ground that outside conferences would hinder the disarmament work of the League of Nations, the latter on the ground that Italy's geographical situation made further limitation unwise.

The Geneva or Coolidge Conference which met on June 20 was, therefore, a three Power conference, with the participants represented by their delegations to the League of Nations Preparatory Commission for the Disarmament Conference. These gentlemen were largely admirals and naval experts with no great enthusiasm for abolishing their own jobs. The problems to be dealt with were highly complex. Great Britain objected to the American proposals for a global limitation on cruiser tonnage, contending that the proposed tonnage was too low for British needs and that 8-inch gun cruisers and 6-inch gun cruisers should be limited separately and not lumped together. The British Government desired a large number of small cruisers, for it had naval bases scattered over the world and was perhaps reluctant, in any case, to concede cruiser parity to the United States. The American Government, lacking such bases, championed large cruisers, insisted on parity, and viewed with skepticism the British notion of "absolute" naval needs unrelated to the naval strength of other Powers. Great Britain insisted that she needed seventy cruisers to protect her sea routes. On this basis, parity would require the United States to build thirty new cruisers at a cost of $450,-000,000. During the discussion of these differences of views, an American lobbyist, William B. Shearer, generously paid by three large shipbuilding firms, did his patriotic bit to wreck the conference by dispensing unfavorable publicity. On August 4 the conference broke up in failure.

There followed a period of more or less obscure bilateral negotiations between Great Britain and France in the interests of paving the way for an agreement which would facilitate the progress of the League of Nations disarmament efforts. London proposed to abandon its opposition to the French policy toward trained army reserves, in return for French concessions on cruisers and submarines. These discussions began in March, 1928, and continued simultaneously with the Kellogg Pact negotiations. In making counter-suggestions, Briand's note of July 20 declared: "The Government of the Republic are convinced that the concerted action of France and Great Britain will enable the two Governments to obtain the approval of the naval Powers concerned." But should this hope prove illusory, "the two Governments would, none the less, be under the urgent obligation (*l'impérieux devoir*) to concert either to insure success by other means, or to adopt a common policy so as to deal with the difficulties which would inevitably arise from a check to the work of the Preparatory Commission." A tentative compromise was worked out and announced in vague terms. In Washington it was at once assumed that the secret Anglo-French bargain was directed against the United States. It was, in fact, based upon a formula already rejected by the American Government. In Berlin it was viewed with similar apprehension (which subsequent events showed to be entirely justified) as foreshadowing the abandonment of British opposition to the exclusion of trained reserves from the Draft Disarmament Convention. The British Foreign Office admitted the correctness of this interpretation and, while explanations and apologies were forthcoming, neither London nor Paris seemed anxious to allay suspicion by publishing the text of the agreement.

At this juncture the Paris representatives of the Hearst newspaper chain in the United States secured the text by methods familiar to newspaper men. It was published on September 21, 1928, in the New York *American*, with the customary sensational trimmings. The French Government arrested and deported the Hearst reporters in Paris, suspended two subordinate officials at the Quai d'Orsay, and in 1930 deported Mr. Hearst himself as "an enemy of the Republic." A terrific storm ensued. The French Government became alarmed and forced the British hand by publishing the full correspondence. The American Government, in its note to Great Britain of September 28, unqualifiedly rejected the compromise on the ground that it provided only for limitations of 10,000 ton 8-inch gun cruisers, which were peculiarly suited to the needs of the United States. The compromise was further objected to on the ground that it provided no limitation of 6-inch gun cruisers or submarines. The United States could not "consent to proposals which would still allow the unlimited building of certain types of highly efficient fighting ships while imposing restrictions on types peculiarly suitable to American needs." Italy likewise rejected the compromise on October 6 and declared that all armaments must be considered together. Italy, for its part, was prepared to accept any figures, however low, provided that they were not exceeded by those of any other continental Power. The compromise was dead, and the manner of its birth and death led to suspicion and resentment. On February 13, 1929 the American Congress authorized the President to construct fifteen 10,000-ton cruisers and one aircraft carrier at a cost of $274,000,000.

On April 22, 1929, Mr. Hugh Gibson, at the Preparatory Commission for the Disarmament Conference, took the first step toward allaying the new friction by declaring that the United States was prepared to consider further limitation and reduction on the basis of the French thesis: global limitation by tonnage and division of total tonnage for each State into the four categories of capital ships, aircraft carriers, surface vessels below 10,000 tons, and submarines, with maximums fixed for each category. On May 30 President Hoover reiterated the desire of the American Government to cooperate in finding a new yardstick for naval limitation and reduction. The new American Ambassador, Charles Dawes, conferred with the new British Prime Minister, Ramsay MacDonald. Conversations went on throughout the summer. On July 23 President Hoover declared that American "current expenditure on strictly military activities constitutes the largest military budget of any nation in the world today." He cited the Kellogg Pact as reason for efforts to reduce this outlay. On the following day, MacDonald announced suspension of work on several warships under construction. President Hoover followed this example by a like move, though insisting on parity with Great Britain. The way was gradually prepared for a new agreement. The British Government, in view of the Kellogg Pact, decided to reduce its cruiser demands from seventy to fifty units. On October 4 MacDonald arrived in New York on a good-will tour, and on October 8 invitations to a new naval conference were dispatched by the British Government to the United States, Japan, France, and Italy after the Prime Minister had spent a week-end with Hoover at Rapidan.

The London Naval Conference opened on January 21, 1930. The British representatives expressed their desire to bring down to the lowest possible level the building programs of all the participants and to prevent future competition in the building of all types of vessels, as the Washington Treaty had done for capital ships. The United States concurred in this aspiration, but insisted on parity with Great Britain. Japan demanded a 70 per cent ratio in large cruisers, as compared with Great Britain and the United States, and the retention of her existing strength in submarines. The French delegation dwelt on the absolute naval needs of France in defending her colonial empire and proposed global limitation once more as a solution which would permit each State to specialize in whatever types of vessels it required. The French delegation later accepted a compromise, involving limitation by six categories of ships, with the possibility of transferring tonnage from one category to another. The Italian Government repeated its willingness to reduce its naval armaments to any level, providing it was granted parity with other continental Powers, *i.e.*, France. The United States supported Great Britain in advocating the abolition of the submarine, but France and Japan refused to agree.

Involved bargaining went on for many weeks, with little result. The chief obstacle to an agreement was the large tonnage demand of France and French refusal to admit parity with Italy. On the first point, France refused to reduce her figures except in return for political guarantees which neither Great Britain nor the United States was prepared to give. On the second point, Italy refused to be a party to any agreement which did not grant her equality in naval armaments with any other continental Power—an arrangement wholly unacceptable to France, since it would give Italy a preponderance over France in the Mediterranean. On March 25 Mr. Stimson, as head of the American delegation, announced from London that while the United States could give no political or military guarantees, it "had no objection to entering a consultative pact as such" —a statement which created the usual furore among the isolationists in the American hinterland and necessitated reassuring statements from President Hoover, followed by a final denial of any such intention on the part of the American delegation. Discussion of the sanctions of Article 16 of the Covenant followed between British, French, and Italian representatives, but no agreement could be reached as to whether the article could be interpreted to mean that military collaboration was obligatory, as the French desired, or was discretionary, as the British insisted. Further difficulties arose over the Japanese demands. The Franco-Italian differences proved insuperable, and the treaty as finally signed left much to be desired.

The London Naval Treaty of April 22, 1930, was divided into five parts, of which Part III—the essence of the agreement—was not signed by either France or Italy. According to Part I, all five signatories agreed not to exercise their rights under the Washington Treaty of 1922 to lay down the keels of capital ship replacement tonnage during 1931–1936. Great Britain agreed to scrap 5 capital ships, the United States 3, and Japan 1. Armaments on aircraft carriers were limited to 6.1-inch guns. Submarines in the future were to be limited to 2,000 tons, with 5.1-inch guns, though each signatory retained the right to not more than 3 submarines of 2,800 tons, with 6.1-inch guns. The limitation on cruisers and destroyers (binding only on Great Britain, the United States, and Japan) divided cruisers into two categories: those carrying guns above 6.1-inch caliber and those carrying guns of less than 6.1-inch caliber. As for the first category, the United States was allotted 18 totaling 180,000 tons, the British Empire 15 of 146,800 tons, and Japan 12 of 108,400 tons. As for the second category, the United States received 143,500 tons, the British Empire 192,200 tons, and Japan 100,450 tons. The United States and the British Empire were each granted 150,000 tons of destroyers, as compared with Japan's 105,000, and all three Powers were granted 52,700 tons of submarines each. Limited transfers of tonnage from one category to another were permitted. In view of French and Italian abstention and the resulting danger to Great Britain from growing continental navies, a "safeguarding clause" was inserted whereby these limits might be exceeded if necessary.[1] Part IV of the treaty required submarines operating against merchant ships to place passengers and crews in a place of safety before sinking the vessel. Part V specified that the treaty would endure until December 31, 1936, except for Part IV, which was given an indefinite duration. A new conference in 1935 was provided for.

Whether this extremely modest achievement, attained after so much travail, can be regarded as a triumph for disarmament is still a matter of controversy among naval technicians. The treaty was ratified by the signatories, though it encountered strong opposition from naval circles in Japan. The safeguarding or escalator clause made the whole arrangement conditional. It was necessitated by the fact that Great Britain was determined to maintain a fleet at least as powerful as the two largest continental fleets combined. The British Government has accepted parity with the United States, but adhered to the "two Power standard" as regards Europe. The projected French navy, together with the Italian demand for parity with France, would result in Great Britain's requiring a much larger fleet than was contemplated by the treaty. This in turn would upset the British ratio with the United States and Japan and necessitate an upward revision of the whole schedule. Even should this contingency not arise, the treaty is one of limitation on future building, rather than of reduction of existing strength. If the United States is to achieve a navy by 1936 equal to the treaty specifications, it must increase its tonnage over the 1930 level rather than decrease it, thus achieving the paradox of "reduction" *upward*. Up to the time of writing, all efforts to reconcile the Franco-Italian differences and to secure the adherence of these Powers to Part III of the treaty have been in vain. On April 28, 1930, the Italian Cabinet authorized 42,900 tons of new naval construction, and on May 17 Mussolini declared at Milan that while words were beautiful, guns and airplanes were more beautiful. American and British efforts to effect an agreement led to the announcement of a satisfactory compromise on March 1, 1931, but the question of French replacement rights was a new bone of contention and by September the proposed arrangement was conceded to be defunct. Italy was willing to abandon parity in fact, if

---

[1] Article 21: "If, during the term of the present treaty, the requirements of the national security of any high contracting party in respect of vessels of war limited by Part III of the present treaty are in the opinion of that party materially affected by new construction of any Power other than those who have joined in Part III of this treaty, that high contracting party will notify the other parties to Part III as to the increase required to be made in its own tonnages within one or more of the categories of such vessels of war, specifying particularly the proposed increases and the reasons therefor, and shall be entitled to make such increase. Thereupon the other parties to Part III of this treaty shall be entitled to make a proportionate increase in the category or categories specified; and the said other parties shall promptly advise with each other through diplomatic channels as to the situation thus presented."

not in form, but France adhered to her original position that general disarmament must be preceded by a political agreement guaranteeing "security."

3. DISARMAMENT: THE LEAGUE OF NATIONS

In the investigation of the motives for disarmament we may find higher necessities still and higher aims than the mere discarding of destructive weapons. The existence of armaments in the world is a formidable loss and a formidable danger.—SALVADOR DE MADARIAGA, *Disarmament.*

"Security," in the last analysis, is the rock upon which League of Nations efforts to promote general land disarmament have likewise been wrecked. The painful story of these efforts begins with the appointment by the Council in 1920 of a body known subsequently as the Permanent Advisory Commission, composed of a naval, a military, and an air representative of each State on the Council. This group of technical experts was ill adapted to its purpose[1] and in November, 1920, the Assembly decided to supplement it with a Temporary Mixed Commission, appointed by the Council and consisting of six civilians of recognized authority in political, social, and economic matters, as well as representatives of the Permanent Advisory Commission, the economic and financial committees, and the governing body of the International Labor Organization. In September, 1921, the Second Assembly requested the Temporary Mixed Commission to prepare a draft treaty for disarmament. Between February and September of 1922 the Temporary Mixed Commission considered a plan for general disarmament submitted by Lord Esher, based upon the limitation of peace-time standing armies by ratios in units of 30,000 men, excluding reserves and overseas colonial forces and likewise excluding all consideration of weapons. In September, 1922, the commission reported that no agreement had been reached and that the problem of disarmament was not to be solved directly by international limitation, but only indirectly by providing that security without which States were unwilling to disarm.

The 1922 Assembly accepted this view in Resolution XIV, which asserted that "in the present state of the world, many governments would be unable to accept the responsibility for a serious reduction of armaments unless they received in exchange a satisfactory guarantee of the safety of their country." The subsequent League efforts to promote disarmament have all been based upon this assumption. They have therefore been

[1] "It was as foolish to expect a disarmament convention from such a commission as a declaration of atheism from a commission of clergymen. . . . The military profession cannot recognize any duty above that which constitutes its very essence: the insuring the safety of its country. A military delegation sent to discuss disarmament problems cannot and should not envisage them—as it is implicitly requested to do—in a somewhat general and abstract light." S. de Madariaga, *Disarmament,* 1929, p. 91.

directed toward providing security. When this endeavor failed, the General Disarmament Conference of 1932–1933, representing the culmination of League efforts, returned to the method of direct limitation and failed once more to accomplish anything thereby. The effort to achieve security will be discussed in the next section. Here it will be considered only in so far as it bears upon the disarmament problem.

The Temporary Mixed Commission sought to achieve security as a step toward disarmament by implementing Articles 10 and 16 of the Covenant. The first fruit of its labors was the adoption by the Fourth Assembly (1923) of a Draft Treaty of Mutual Assistance for international aid to victims of aggression. Following the failure of this instrument to win general favor, the element of arbitration was introduced as a substitute for war and a test of aggression. The formula had been "Disarmament → Security → Arbitration." The formula now became "Arbitration → Security → Disarmament." The Fifth Assembly (1924) unanimously adopted the Geneva Protocol for the Pacific Settlement of International Disputes and laid plans for a General Disarmament Conference to meet on June 15, 1925. But the Geneva Protocol failed of adoption, just as the Draft Treaty had failed, because certain States, notably Great Britain, were unwilling to accept general and indefinite obligations to come to the defense of other States in controversies in which they had no immediate interests. General solutions having failed, special ones were attempted and the Locarno treaties of 1925 resulted. The Sixth Assembly (1925) resolved: "In conformity with Article 8 of the Covenant [the Assembly] requests the Council to make a preparatory study with a view to a Conference for the Reduction and Limitation of Armaments, in order that, as soon as satisfactory conditions have been assured from the point of view of Resolution XIV of the Third Assembly, the said conference may be convened and a general reduction and limitation of armaments may be realized." The Council accordingly abolished the Temporary Mixed Commission and replaced it by the "Preparatory Commission for the Disarmament Conference," composed of representatives of States on the Council, plus certain other League members, and the U.S.S.R., the United States, and Germany from among the non-League States. Argentina and Chile were invited to become members in 1926, Greece in 1927, and Turkey in 1928. Representatives from the Soviet Union did not attend the sessions until 1927, after the Swiss Government had made appropriate reparation and apologies for the assassination of Vorovsky, Soviet delegate to the Lausanne Conference of 1923. The other non-League Powers, including the United States, accepted membership at once.

The seven sessions of the Preparatory Commission for the Disarmament Conference revealed clearly the difficulties of its task and foreshadowed the obstacles encountered later by the conference itself. The first session met on May 18, 1926, and considered an elaborate questionnaire, already prepared by the Council. The questions were referred to Subcommittee A on military, naval, and air questions and to Subcommittee B on non-military matters. Pending reports from these subcommittees, the Commission as a whole relapsed into a state of suspended animation, much to the disappointment of the third committee of the Seventh Assembly of September, 1926. On September 24 the Assembly passed a resolution requesting "the Council to call upon the Preparatory Commission to take steps to hasten the completion of the technical work and thus be able to draw up, at the beginning of the next year, the program for a conference on the limitation and reduction of armaments corresponding to existing conditions in regard to regional and general security, and it asks the Council to convene this conference before the Eighth Ordinary Session of the Assembly unless material difficulties render this impossible." Germany was now a member of the League, and her representative, Dr. von Schubert, anticipated the later German position by declaring, in reply to French contentions, that Germany could not regard any mere fixing of the armament *status quo* by the proposed conference as an advance, since its final object must be "to reduce the existing disproportion between the armaments" of the League members. The second session of the Preparatory Commission was held September 22–27, 1926. It induced the subcommittees to submit voluminous reports, which were published and circulated. On December 8, 1926, the Council directed the Preparatory Commission to make suggestions for the date of the General Disarmament Conference and to draw up an agenda as the basis of its work.

The later sessions of the Preparatory Commission were devoted to the elaboration of a draft convention to serve as the framework upon which the General Disarmament Conference would hang its achievements. At the third session, which met March 21, 1927, Lord Cecil of Great Britain and Paul-Boncour of France submitted proposed draft conventions, reflecting the views of their Governments. Count von Bernstorff of Germany declared that "the States which have been disarmed by international treaties . . . are perfectly entitled to demand that general disarmament should be achieved. The disarmament of the country which I have the honor to represent is complete. You are well aware that, according to the Treaty of Versailles, this disarmament should only be a prelude to general disarmament." The British and French drafts differed in almost everything, except that they were agreed that the conference should aim at limitation, and not reduction, of armaments. The British draft proposed to limit military, naval, and air forces to figures agreed upon, with provision for reports to the Secretary-General of the League on budgetary expenditures. Land armaments would be limited by number of effectives, air armaments by number of aircraft, and naval armaments by tonnages and categories of ships. The French proposal contemplated the treatment of land, sea, and air armaments as interdependent. Naval armaments would be limited by total tonnage only, and not by categories. There would be no limitation of military reserves and the "war potentials" of States, apart from armaments, would be weighed in the balance. Budgetary expenditures would be used as a basis of comparison, and machinery would be set up for international supervision of the execution of whatever scheme might be agreed upon.

These and other divergencies of views were debated, with little result, at the fourth and fifth sessions of the Preparatory Commission. As for land armaments, the most knotty problem was how to estimate the number of effectives, Great Britain arguing for inclusion of trained reserves in such estimates and the French bloc arguing against this. It was finally agreed that reserves should not be counted, but that a limit should be placed on the period of service in conscriptionist countries. Germany, the United States, and Great Britain made reservations to this solution. No agreement was reached on the issue of naval limitation by category *versus* limitation by global tonnage. Neither was any agreement reached on international supervision, nor upon the technique of budgetary limitations. The preliminary draft convention, drawn up and approved on April 26, 1927, was little more than a record of these disagreements.[1]

Meanwhile, the Soviet delegates had appeared and had thrown the commission into consternation by suggesting that the way to disarm was to disarm. On November 30, 1927, Litvinov proposed the complete abolition of all land, sea, and air armaments within one year, the abolition of conscription, of general staffs, and of war ministries, and the suppression of all war appropriations. Consideration of this proposal was deferred, and at the fifth session, on March 15, 1928, Litvinov presented a draft convention of sixty-three articles, embodying the Soviet project for immediate and complete disarmament. For the first time, the other members of the commission were almost unanimous. They rejected the Soviet proposal. Only the German and Turkish delegates supported it. Litvinov then produced a second draft convention for partial and gradual disarmament, based upon the disarmament of the defeated States in the peace treaties. This was likewise rejected. The president of the Commis-

---

[1] The Belgian delegate, M. de Brouckere, characterized this outcome as follows: "We began with that celebrated trilogy which has aroused such enthusiasm: Arbitration, Security, and Disarmament. We then said: 'We are not concerned with disarmament but with reduction.' Then in a subsequent stage of our work it was pointed out that it would perhaps be too ambitious to attempt reduction, and that we should have to content ourselves with limitation. Well, we have now reached a point when we may even have to erase this last word."

sion, M. Loudin, called upon the Soviet delegates on March 24 "in all seriousness to attend our next and any ensuing meetings in a constructive spirit, and not with the idea of destroying the work we have already done." While the Commission had formerly held that the progress of its work was impeded by the absence of Soviet representatives, it now held, in effect, that it was impeded by their presence. Litvinov astutely used the occasion to embarrass the Commission, since it had done nothing as an alternative to the Soviet plan, with the result that the Commission, at its sixth session, hesitated to reject the proposal outright. On April 19, 1929, the commission finally decided (with Turkey abstaining, and China and the U.S.S.R. voting in the negative) that it could not accept the Soviet plan, but that the Disarmament Conference itself might consider its principles.

Over a year elapsed between the fifth and sixth sessions of the Preparatory Commission. In April of 1929 the prospects were more dismal than ever. The Commission proceeded to a second reading of the slowly emerging Draft Convention. On April 22 Hugh Gibson of the United States pleaded for reduction, not merely limitation, and offered to make concessions to the French position on limitation of naval armaments. Both the British and American delegates then reversed their earlier attitudes in the interests of achieving an agreement and offered to accept the French view that trained reserves should not be included in any limitation scheme. This view was adopted, despite protests from the German, Soviet, and other delegations. The commission next considered the problem of limitation of war materials. Germany, with Soviet, Swedish, and Dutch support, argued for direct limitation of the type provided for in the Treaty of Versailles. France, with Japanese, Italian, and Little Entente support, argued for indirect and elastic limitation based on budgetary expenditures, on the ground that direct limitation was feasible only with international supervision, which the United States opposed. Gibson declared that the United States could not accept any form of budgetary limitation, and the Commission, by a vote of twenty-two to two (China and the U.S.S.R. in the negative), adopted his innocuous compromise suggestion which provided merely for giving publicity to budgetary expenditures. Bernstorff expressed Germany's dissatisfaction and impatience with "agreements" which achieved nothing toward armament reduction. The commission adjourned on May 6 to allow time for further study of the naval question. Nothing had been achieved toward disarmament save the reopening of naval negotiations and an agreement to renounce chemical and bacteriological warfare. The surrender of Great Britain and the United States to the French view on trained reserves and budgetary limitations alienated Germany and promised to make the draft worthless. At the Tenth

Assembly Lord Cecil denounced these arrangements as "profoundly unsatisfactory" and declared, "it is easy to agree to nothing." He moved a critical resolution, calling upon the Preparatory Commission to hasten its work. The French press replied with a storm of protest. The resolution was modified and passed in innocuous form.

The seventh and final session of the Preparatory Commission met on November 6, 1930. Technically it was the second part of the sixth session. The death of Gustav Stresemann on October 3, 1929, led to increasing disgust in Germany for the League of Nations and an increasing spirit of hostility toward the Stresemann policy of treaty fulfillment. Hitler's Nazis rose to political ascendancy on a wave of Nationalist and revisionist sentiment. The failure of the London Naval Conference to reach a five Power agreement was likewise an unfavorable omen. Briand's United States of Europe proposal of May, 1930, served to align Italy, Germany, Austria, Hungary, Bulgaria, Turkey, Greece, Albania, and the Soviet Union against the French bloc. In the German election of September 14, 1930, the Nazis increased their representation in the Reichstag from 12 to 107. At the Eleventh League Assembly Bernstorff condemned the endless delays in achieving general disarmament and proposed that the General Conference be called before the end of 1931. Lord Cecil deprecated undue haste as likely to lead to the failure of the conference, and the Assembly refused to set any definite date. While the Nationalist opposition to Briand in the French Parliament denounced further concessions to Germany and denied that the Treaty of Versailles obligated the Allies to disarm as a sequel to German disarmament, Curtius and the German press insisted that general disarmament was the only alternative to the granting to Germany of a right to re-arm. Under Nazi pressure at home, Bernstorff, at the November meeting of the Preparatory Commission, was obliged to adopt an even less conciliatory attitude than heretofore. He made an effort to reopen the question of trained reserves, but without success. He likewise failed to secure direct limitation of war materials, in spite of Italian, Turkish, Soviet, and American support. The United States objected to budgetary limitation for either land or naval armaments, though this was combined in the draft with limitation by tonnage and categories, on the model of the London Treaty. Italy declared that she could not agree to any specific method of naval limitation before "all the Powers had agreed on the proportions and levels of maximum tonnage." Budgetary limitation on air armaments was voted down in favor of direct limitation by number of aircraft and horse power, with no limitation of reserve stock or of commercial aircraft. The method of budgetary limitation was applied to total armament expenditures, in the face of German and American objections. The provision for publicity of armaments was so emasculated as to provoke Italian, German, and

Dutch protests. As for international supervision, it was agreed that a Permanent Disarmament Commission should be established at Geneva, with members appointed by governments but not representing them to collect information and make annual reports to the Council. Article 53 of the convention specified that "the present convention shall not affect the provisions of previous treaties under which certain of the high contracting parties have agreed to limit their land, sea, or air armaments and have thus fixed in relation to one another their respective rights and obligations in this connection . . . the maintenance of such obligations being . . . an essential condition for the observance of the present convention." The French Government insisted on this reaffirmation of Germany's disarmament obligations as the price of its participation in the conference. This and the other provisions of the draft convention led Count von Bernstorff to declare:

In the draft in its present form, the idea of genuine disarmament, as regards land armaments, only survives in the title. If the majority of the commission would only realize this deplorable result of its five years' work, they would avoid placing this artificial work in relationship with the earlier treaties. . . . It may be that some delegates here are under the impression that my Government might be induced to accede to a convention which, instead of leading to genuine disarmament, would merely serve as a cloak for the actual state of the world's land armaments, or—even worse—would make it possible to increase these armaments. That in my opinion would be tantamount to renewing the German signature to the disarmament clause of the Treaty of Versailles. I beg you, gentlemen, to renounce any such illusions . . . you are well acquainted with the conditions which the German Government consider essential if this convention is to be regarded as discharging the obligations incurred by other nations towards disarmed Germany. . . . We consider that Germany cannot recognize anything as a first Disarmament Convention unless the solution which it provides is just and equitable and pays regard to the security of all States.

The Preparatory Commission closed its work on December 9, 1930. Germany made a formal reservation to Article 53 and failed in her efforts to persuade the commission to set a date for the General Disarmament Conference. In January the League Council fixed the opening date for February 2, 1932, despite German pleas for November, 1931. In May the Council appointed Arthur Henderson, then British Foreign Secretary, president of the conference. The Draft Convention—incomplete, emasculated, and devoid of any assurance of armament reduction—was a document of sixty articles, accompanied by blank tables of ratios and quotas, to be filled in by the conference. It provided for budgetary limitation, limitation of the period of military service, limitation of effectives of land, sea, and air forces, the London Treaty method of naval limitation, and the creation of a Permanent Disarmament Commission. This skeleton could be clothed with flesh and blood and made the basis for a genuine reduction of armaments if agreements could be reached at the conference. But the chronic disagreements in the Preparatory Commission offered little hope of concrete achievement. Owing to these disagreements, the convention contained no provision for limiting trained reserves, none for direct limitation of war materials of armies and navies, and none for the limitation of the cost of materials of air forces.

The pessimism aroused by these *lacunae* was enhanced by the financial panics of 1931, the increase of Franco-German tension, the continued inability of France and Italy to agree on naval armaments, the customs-union imbroglio, Franco-American friction over the Hoover moratorium, the conflict in the Far East, the controversies between the United States and Japan, and similar events not calculated to promote international concord. On May 19, 1931, the new German "pocket battleship," the *Deutschland*, was launched at Kiel—a marvel of German ingenuity and the most efficient fighting craft of its size afloat. As Chancellor Bruening, in the christening ceremonies, reached the portion of his address dealing with the League of Nations and disarmament, the warship slipped inadvertently into the water, unchristened—like Germany, "tired of phrases," as one onlooker remarked.[1] The French Government forthwith authorized the construction of a 23,000-ton battleship and speeded up work on its eastern frontier fortifications. France was more predominant, diplomatically and financially, than ever before, and French efforts to wrest political concessions from Germany, as the price of financial aid, led to increased bitterness.

On July 21, 1931, the French Government published an armament memorandum in which it again denounced the German thesis and declared itself unable to reduce its armaments further without some international provision for security.[2] France could make no contributions to disarmament unless international guarantees of security replaced armaments as a safeguard. Meanwhile, Germany's status of inequality must remain permanent. The first proposal was utterly unacceptable to Great Britain, the United States, and many other governments. The second was utterly unacceptable to Germany, which had no interest in the conference except

---

[1] Wheeler-Bennett, *op. cit.*, p. 336.

[2] The French memorandum insisted that "reduction of armaments implies confidence. Can that confidence be expected to prevail, so long as the feeling is abroad that, in the eyes of many, the problem is not so much one of organizing peace for the benefit of all, as of modifying the existing order for the benefit of a few and so long as it is possible for some States to feel that the very existence conferred upon them by the treaties is threatened? The decision of the conference must be based upon respect for the treaties.

"Should an attempt be made, for instance, in the name of a theoretical principle of equality, to modify the relative situation created by the provisions of Part V of the peace treaties, it would prove impossible to maintain the reductions already accomplished and still less practicable would become the general limitation of armaments. . . .

" . . . It by no means follows, however, that the member States of the League, whose standards of forces have not been expressly defined by the treaties, are under the obligation to secure equality in armaments and a "parity of security." In view of this development and in view of the further fact that the fall of the Labor Government and the split of the Labor party left Mr. Henderson as leader of the opposition in the British Parliament, unofficial proposals for a postponement of the General Disarmament Conference were broached. But no Government dared to sponsor the suggestion, because of the twelve years of futility which had already gone by. The Twelfth Assembly of the League secured the general adoption of an armaments truce for twelve months, on the proposal of the Italian representative, but the year closed with no prospects of the conference achieving success. France held the key to disarmament. France refused to disarm without an international guarantee of security and the perpetuation of Germany's inferior status. The first condition was regarded as impossible at Washington and London, and the second was viewed in the same light at Berlin and Rome. Tokyo was too occupied in seizing Manchuria to be directly interested, and Moscow eyed the whole situation with sneering cynicism.

The General Disarmament Conference of the League of Nations—the culmination of a decade of international efforts to attain disarmament and insure peace—met at Geneva on February 3, 1932, with Arthur Henderson presiding over 232 delegates, representing 57 States. By an ironic coincidence, open warfare was going on at Shanghai while the delegates deliberated at Geneva. Five main committees were created to deal with budgetary limitation, political problems, and land, air, and naval armaments. The delegates brought with them no less than 337 separate proposals. On February 5 André Tardieu, head of the French delegation and, perhaps not inappropriately, Minister of War, presented a sensational scheme for the creation of a "preventive and punitive international police force" through action by the various States to place at the disposal of the League of Nations civil aircraft over a specified tonnage, bombing planes, and all other "offensive" weapons such as capital ships, batteries of long-range artillery, submarines, etc. This scheme was to be accompanied by compulsory arbitration and a new definition of aggression. The proposal at once encountered strong American, British, and German opposition.[1] The British proposal, presented by Sir John

of adopting either the methods or the figures laid down in Part V of the treaties as regards the general limitation of armaments. When the treaties were framed, at no time and no place was the agreement advanced, either in speech or in writing, that other States should in their turn place their armaments on the level prescribed for certain States. . . . Were it to be admitted that the standards prescribed in Part V of the treaties for certain States should apply in an equal and uniform manner to other States, Article VIII of the League Covenant would clearly be bereft of all value and all significance."

[1] Senator Borah, chairman of the Foreign Relations Committee of the United States Senate, declared: "An international police force to guarantee the security of the world . . . is a perfectly logical product of the Versailles Treaty. A treaty which has neither honor nor

Simon, attacked Tardieu's plan and declared armaments useless as instruments of peace. It proposed a general limitation of armaments on the basis of the Draft Convention, the abolition of submarines and chemical warfare, and the acceptance of the results of the London Conference. Chancellor Bruening, in his address of February 9, declared that Germany expected general disarmament to follow her own disarmament, with an equal measure of security for all nations. He regarded the Draft Convention as inadequate to achieve this result, however, and reserved the right to propose amendments to it later. The French conception, he declared, would only insure the failure of the conference and the perpetuation of an armed peace based on unequal rights. Hugh Gibson for the United States presented a nine-point American program involving use of the Draft Convention as a basis of discussion, prolongation of the Washington and London naval treaties, with the adherence of France and Italy, proportional naval reductions, the abolition of submarines, lethal gases, and bacteriological warfare, protection of civilians against aerial bombing, computation of armed forces on the basis of the absolute effectives necessary to maintain internal order, plus a relative contingent for defense, special restrictions on tanks and mobile heavy guns as weapons of a peculiarly offensive character, and budgetary limitation on materials as a complement to direct limitation. An Italian memorandum advocated abolition of battleships, heavy artillery, tanks, submarines, aircraft carriers, bombing planes, and chemical and bacteriological warfare, i.e., abolition of "offensive" weapons. The Soviet delegation once more proposed immediate and complete disarmament.

On April 11 the conference reassembled, following an Easter recess. Briand had died on March 7—and to many who viewed the work at Geneva, his passing symbolized the end of hope. Since no progress toward an agreement had been achieved, Gibson suggested that a beginning be made by an agreement for the abolition of offensive weapons, in order to lessen fear of aggression and restore the supremacy of defense. President Motta of Switzerland and Sir John Simon of Great Britain approved this suggestion, but Count Nadolny of Germany criticized it as failing to insure equality, while Tardieu pointed out that such suppression would be ineffective without a system of international controls and penalties. In any case, he asserted, a peace-loving nation has as much need for offensive weapons as an aggressor, for counter-attack is the best defense against invasion. On April 16 Secretary of State Stimson arrived in Geneva and conferred, without visible results, with Sir Eric Drummond,

---

justice as its foundation can, of course, be maintained and preserved by force and in no other way. The theory back of such a proposition is that, regardless of the right of peoples to grow and develop, the *status quo* must be maintained."

Tardieu, MacDonald, Bruening, and Grandi. On April 22 two resolutions were adopted. The first declared in favor of qualitative disarmament, *i.e.*, the selection of certain classes of weapons for general prohibition or internationalization. The second called upon the special commissions to examine land, sea, and air armaments with a view toward deciding which weapons were offensive and which defensive. This effort was doomed to failure almost from the outset, since it is obvious even to the merest amateur in the art of war that the offensive or defensive character of weapons in the machine age depends less upon the nature of the weapons than upon the use to which they are put. In the subsequent discussions, each State tended to regard its favorite weapons as defensive and weapons which it feared in the hands of others as offensive. The United States and Great Britain held battleships to be defensive and submarines offensive, while the French held the reverse to be true. The German delegates dryly reminded their colleagues that all important weapons had been regarded as offensive in 1919, when they were forbidden to Germany. No agreement could be reached. The French elections, coupled with the illness of MacDonald, furnished a convenient pretext for delay. On May 10 two new technical commissions were created—one to deal with comparable bases for limiting effectives and the other with gas and bacteriological warfare. The conference suspended work pending their report.

During June, with the delegations stalemated, private discussions went on at considerable length. The victory of the Left in the French elections and the assumption of power by Edouard Herriot brought no change of French policy, save an admission that there was little prospect of general acceptance of the French plan for an international police force. On June 22, 1932, President Hoover, in an effort to revive the moribund conference, presented a drastic and dramatic proposal for a general one-third cut in all arms.[1] This plan also sought to increase the power of defensive weapons as against offensive. It proposed the abolition of tanks, large mobile guns, chemical warfare, bombing planes, and all bombing from the air; a one-third reduction in all land armies over and above a "police component" which should be calculated on the basis applied to Germany in the Treaty of Versailles, *i.e.*, 100,000 troops for 65,000,000 people; a one-third reduction in battleships; a one-fourth reduction in aircraft carriers, cruisers, and destroyers; and a one-third reduction in

[1] The general principles of this proposal, as set forth in the original statement, were as follows: "The time has come when we should cut through the brush and adopt some broad and definite methods of reducing the overwhelming burden of armament which now lies upon the toilers of the world.

"This would be the most important world step that could be taken to expedite economic recovery. We must make headway against the mutual fear and friction arising out of war armament, which kill human confidence throughout the world. We can still remain practical in maintaining an adequate self-defense among all nations; we can add to

submarines, with no nation retaining a greater submarine tonnage than 35,000 and with French and Italian cruiser and destroyer strength to be "calculated as though they had joined in the Treaty of London, on a basis approximating the so-called Accord of March 1, 1931." "These proposals are simple and direct. They call upon all nations to contribute something. The contribution here proposed will be relative and mutual. I know of nothing that would give more hope for humanity today than the acceptance of such a program, with such minor changes as might be necessary. It is folly for the world to go on breaking its back over military expenditure, and the United States is willing to take its share of responsibility by making definite proposals that will relieve the world."

This surprise proposal[1] created a sensation and was received so favorably by large sections of public opinion that almost all of the delegations at Geneva were obliged to express their sympathy with it. Only Italy declared her willingness to accept it unqualifiedly, however. Liberal and radical opinion in many countries hailed the plan with enthusiasm, but the conservative and nationalist press was skeptical. Premier Herriot, having failed in his efforts to forestall the presentation of the proposal, declared it unacceptable to France. "We French always have demanded, and still demand, international organization and control." The French formula remained the same: no disarmament without security and no security without international guarantees and sanctions. At Washington it was intimated that under no circumstances would the United States consider a security pact with France. The tentative proposals of the new German Chancellor, Franz von Papen, for a Franco-German military alliance to give France security came to nothing. The Hoover plan was rejected in Tokyo because of Japanese-American tension over Manchuria

---

the assurance of peace and yet save the people of the world from ten to fifteen billions of wasted dollars during the next ten years.

"I propose that the following principles should be our guide:

"First, the Kellogg-Briand Pact, to which we are all signatories, can only mean that the nations of the world have agreed that they will use their arms solely for defense.

"Second, this reduction should be carried out, not only by broad general cuts in armaments, but by increasing the comparative power of defense through decreases in the power of the attack.

"Third, the armaments of the world have grown up in general mutual relation to each other and, speaking generally, such relativity should be preserved in making reductions.

"Fourth, the reductions must be real and positive. They must effect economic relief.

"Fifth, there are three problems to deal with—land forces, air forces, and naval forces. They are all interconnected. No part of the proposals . . . can be disassociated one from the other.

"Based on these principles, I propose that the arms of the world should be reduced by nearly one-third."

[1] A White House statement of June 22 denied that the proposal had any relation, direct or indirect, to war debts, thus silencing rumors that European acceptance of the plan was to be a *quid pro quo* for reduction of debts.

and because of Japan's refusal either to reduce her fleet further or to accept as permanent the London ratios. It was regarded as unacceptable by the British Government, because it involved a reduction of cruiser strength below the minimum regarded as irreducible. Sir John Simon suggested another five Power naval parley to discuss the application of the Hoover plan to naval forces—a proposal which was resisted by the American representatives as a means of defeating the plan by dealing with it piecemeal or by permitting Japan to veto it forthwith. At this critical juncture the conference began casting about for some way of adjourning as gracefully as possible, on the pretext of allowing time for a further study of the Hoover plan. This decision was apparently approved by the British, French, and Japanese delegates as an easy way of shelving the plan and by the American representatives as a means of forestalling its open rejection. On July 7 the British Government offered a counter-plan which accepted the Hoover proposals for abolishing air bombing, gas warfare, and mobile land guns and accepted (in principle) a one-third naval cut. But instead of agreeing to a one-third cut in the number and total tonnage of ships, Great Britain proposed a one-third reduction in tonnage and gun caliber of all categories of vessels, leaving the size of navies in number of ships intact. Japan received this proposal sympathetically. The United States was seemingly unimpressed. Endless "conversations" got nowhere. The Hoover plan was buried. The conference itself seemed on its death-bed.

On July 23, 1932, the Disarmament Conference adjourned, subject to reconvocation by its bureau before January 21, 1933. It extended the arms truce until January and adopted a resolution designed to sum up the "progress achieved" in its first phase. In reality the resolution confessed the failure of the conference to achieve any limitation or reduction of armaments. This declaration, called the Benês Resolution, after Edouard Benês, Foreign Minister of Czechoslovakia, and rapporteur of the general commission, contained a wordy and vaporous preamble paying lip service to the Hoover proposal and to the principles of "substantial reduction of world armaments" and of limitation or prohibition of offensive weapons. It then stated that the conference was agreed on the prohibition of air attacks on civilian populations and on the principle of abolishing all bombardment from the air through "limitation by number and restriction by characteristics of military aircraft" and through "regulation and full publicity" of civil aircraft. No agreement was recorded on the means of abolishing aerial bombardment or on the numbers and characteristics of aircraft to be limited or restricted. Heavy land artillery should be limited as to caliber and as to numbers. No agreement was recorded as to the calibers or numbers involved. "The maximum unit tonnage of tanks shall be limited." No agreement was recorded as to the maximum. "Chemical, bacteriological, and incendiary warfare shall be prohibited," and a Permanent Disarmament Commission shall be set up. No agreement was recorded as to its functions. The bureau of the conference was instructed to frame draft texts on the questions on which agreement had been reached. The bureau should examine the problem of limiting and reducing military effectives. It should draw up a plan for budgetary limitation on the basis of the future report of the committee on national defense expenditure. It should likewise examine the problem of regulating private production and exchange of war materials. The parties to the Washington and London treaties were invited to "confer together and report to the general commission, if possible before the resumption of its work, as to further measures of naval reduction which might be feasible as part of the general program of disarmament."

This resolution was not entirely futile, for it represented agreement on a number of points. But it committed the participating States to very little which was specific and it left the conference at the impasse where it had begun. "Security" was not assured, and without security the French bloc would not disarm. The conference adjourned in an atmosphere of dissatisfaction and recrimination. Gibson supported the resolution and Litvinov's effort to get the Hoover plan written into it was rejected, thirty to five, with sixteen abstentions. In view of the anti-Soviet orientation of the von Papen Cabinet, Litvinov declared that the U.S.S.R. would under no circumstances support Germany's claim to re-armament. The Italian Government characterized the resolution as a vain effort and "entirely inadequate when compared to the hopes and wishes of the world." In the final vote Germany and the Soviet Union voted against the resolution and Afghanistan, Albania, Austria, Bulgaria, China, Hungary, Italy, and Turkey abstained from voting. The German delegation announced its intention of refraining from further participation in the work of the conference in 1933, unless the principle of equality should be conceded in the interval.

Developments during the period between the conference's adjournment and its reconvocation were discouraging in the extreme and foreshadowed the final failure of the whole enterprise. During August Lieutenant-general Kurt von Schleicher, German Minister of Defense, reiterated Germany's demand for equality and her conviction that neither the Draft Convention nor the Benês Resolution offered any hope of fulfilling this demand. On August 29, 1932, Berlin dispatched a memorandum to Paris, suggesting Franco-German conversations of a confidential character looking toward the substitution for Part V of the Treaty of Versailles of a general disarmament convention, involving the concession to Germany of the principle of equality. The memorandum also suggested desired changes in German military organization, including a reduction of the training period of the Reichswehr and the granting to Germany of the permission to employ experimentally certain forbidden weapons. MacDonald proposed consultation between Great Britain, France, Italy, and Poland on the German position. On September 12 the French Government replied, denying Germany's right to claim release from Part V of the Treaty by any general agreement. France would promote disarmament in proportion to the attainment of security through the general organization of peace. The German demand for re-armament was declared inadmissible. This demand would affect the armaments and the treaty rights of all the Powers, including the United States. It could not, therefore, be made a subject of Franco-German conversations, but must be made a matter of general negotiations. Only the Council of the League could consider the request. Germany must appeal to Geneva, not to Paris. On September 14 Baron von Neurath, German Foreign Minister, dispatched a communication to Arthur Henderson, informing him of Germany's inability to participate further in the Geneva discussions and of her refusal to accept the invitation to attend the meeting of the bureau on September 21.[1] The German Government subsequently sought to enlist British sympathy, but was severely rebuffed in Sir John Simon's note of September 18, which declared, on the basis of involved legal reasoning, that "it could not be maintained, as the correct legal construction of the Treaty of Versailles and connected correspondence, that Germany is legally entitled to abrogate Part V of the Treaty of Versailles by any disarmament convention to be concluded or by the failure to conclude any convention at all."

This refusal of Germany's claim to equality of rights merely confirmed the German Government in its refusal to participate in further disarmament discussions and encouraged the Junkers and military leaders who dominated the von Papen Cabinet to look forward to re-armament and

---

[1] Von Neurath's note declared: "In the German Government's view, only one solution can be considered, namely: that all States should be subject to the same rules and principles in respect to disarmament, and that no discriminatory exceptional system should exist in the case of any one of them. Germany cannot be expected to take part in negotiations with regard to measures of disarmament to be laid down in the convention, until it is established that the solutions which may be found are also to apply to Germany.

"With a view to the earliest possible realization of the condition for the future cooperation of Germany with the conference, the German Government has in the interval endeavored to clear up the question of equality of rights through diplomatic channels. Unfortunately, it must be stated that the German efforts have not hitherto led to any satisfactory result. I am compelled to inform you that the German Government is unable to avail itself of the invitation to the session of the bureau of the conference, beginning September 21.

"The German Government is now, as ever, convinced that thoroughgoing general disarmament is urgently necessary for the purpose of insuring peace. It will follow the labors of the conference with interest and determine its further attitude by the course they may take."

the open repudiation of the Treaty. Ominous rumors of the French reoccupation of the Rhineland began to circulate. A resumption of the conference with Germany absent would be pointless. A disarmament treaty which Germany would not sign would be a mockery. MacDonald cast about for ways and means of insuring a prospect of sufficient disarmament to coax Germany back into the conference. He proposed a four Power conference to discuss this possibility. Herriot conferred with the British Prime Minister in England in mid-October on the possibility of calling a conference to persuade Germany to attend the bureau meeting, which would prepare the way for a resumption of the general conference. His own plans for disarmament plus security were opposed by the French general staff. He suggested a conference in Geneva. Germany refused to attend. He suggested a conference at Lausanne, with Polish and Czechoslovakian representatives participating. Germany refused to attend. The old deadlock remained unbroken. For France there could be no further disarmament without security, and no security without international sanctions and guarantees. For Great Britain and the United States, sanctions and guarantees were as unthinkable as ever. For Germany there could be no participation in a conference which was pledged to perpetuate her inferior status.

The events of November and December, however, created an impression—largely illusory—that these difficulties were being overcome. On November 14 the French Government issued a "new" memorandum in which the inseparability of disarmament and security was expounded once more. The new proposals, presented as "an indivisible whole," constituted a synthesis of much that was old with a few new suggestions designed to placate Berlin. The Powers at the Disarmament Conference were called upon to implement the Pact of Paris by agreeing to consult with one another over any breach or threatened breach of the Pact, to prohibit "direct or indirect economic or financial relations with the aggressor country," and to "declare their determination not to recognize any *de facto* situation brought about in consequence of the violation of an international undertaking." "France considers the effective and loyal application of Article 16 of the Covenant as an essential element of the plan she has worked out." Aggression in Europe would be defined in such fashion that a State attacked or invaded by foreign forces would be entitled to general assistance. The League Council, by majority vote, would order such assistance on ascertaining that an attack or invasion had taken place. Land forces of all States of continental Europe (*i.e.*, exclusive of colonial forces) would be reduced to "a uniform general type—that of a national short-service army with limited effectives." Security would be assured by strengthening the defense and limiting offensive weapons, and by having each State place at the disposal of the

League of Nations, for common action against an aggressor, certain specialized units equipped with the powerful weapons forbidden to the national armies. War materials would be made uniform, and their manufacture would be "internationally supervised and organized." Naval and overseas forces would be dealt with separately. Aerial bombardment would be prohibited, and European civil aviation would be internationalized. An international military air force would be maintained by the League. Here was simply a modified version of Tardieu's scheme of the preceding spring for an international police force.

This plan was a gesture to induce Germany to return to the conference by holding out the hope of equality. But equality would be granted within a framework of sanctions and safeguards designed, as of old, to perpetuate a political *status quo* regarded as intolerable by the revisionist States. The "new" British proposal of November 17, presented by Sir John Simon, resembled Herriot's scheme in that it was designed more to soothe Berlin and to serve the political interests of the proposer than to serve the cause of general disarmament. Germany would be granted "equality" in naval armaments by being permitted to construct battleships over 10,000 tons, provided she did not increase her total tonnage in any category beyond the limits fixed in 1919. Submarines should be abolished. Large "offensive" tanks should also be abolished, and Germany might be permitted to have a limited number of such light tanks as might be agreed upon. Large mobile land guns, already forbidden to Germany, should be generally abolished. Other Powers should reduce their air forces to the level of those of Great Britain, following which all air forces should be cut one-third. International control of civil aviation should be established, and air bombing should be forbidden, except "for police purposes in outlying places." Meanwhile, Germany should "refrain from making any claim to possess military and naval aircraft." The principle of quantitative disarmament and qualitative equality must be applied to Germany in such fashion as to involve no increase in her "powers of military aggression."

Involved negotiations followed these gestures. On December 6, 1932, an "equality formula" was worked out at a five Power parley in Geneva and was offered to the new German Cabinet, now headed by Chancellor Kurt von Schleicher. On December 11 the German Government accepted and agreed to return to the Disarmament Conference. The "formula" was incorporated in a five Power declaration, whereby the Powers agreed "in principle" to grant Germany "equality of rights in a system which would provide security for all nations." They likewise expressed their willingness to join in a declaration by all European States that they would not resort to force in the settlement of any dispute.[1] This successful effort to bring

[1] The text of the five Power declarations are shown at the bottom of p. 715.

Germany back to the conference brought comfort only to those who mistook words for reality. In Poland and Czechoslovakia the accord was viewed with apprehension as foreshadowing an enhancement of German military power which would be dangerous to their own "security." Without an "Eastern Locarno" there could be no acceptance by Warsaw or Prague of German equality in armaments. The accord itself, however, was merely an agreement "in principle." Barring an entirely improbable modification of German policy, Germany would continue to insist on actual equality as an indispensable prerequisite to the successful pursuit of her program of treaty revision. Barring an entirely improbable modification of French policy, France and her allies would continue to resist this claim unless they were assured of "security," *i.e.*, the perpetuation of the *status quo* by international political and military action. Here there was no possible basis of agreement. Herriot's plan of November 14 was as unacceptable to the other Powers as all its predecessors. "Security," "aggression," "equality" remained undefined words, bandied about to conceal underlying political objectives. The conference remained at an impasse which no amount of verbal circumlocution could disguise.

When the conference reassembled in 1933, nothing was certain save that it was foredoomed to failure. That pious resolutions would be passed, that some kind of treaty would be signed, that plans would be made for a new conference went without saying. But no significant reduction of armaments could be achieved and no amount of postponement, evasion, or rationalization could conceal this tragic fact. The reasons for failure are clear from the preceding narrative and from the whole analysis of Great Power politics attempted in the present study. In the contemporary struggle for power the interests of the satiated *status quo* States and of the

---

1. The Governments of the United Kingdom, France, and Italy have declared one of the principles that should guide the conference on disarmament should be the grant to Germany, and to the other disarmed Powers, of equality of rights in a system which would provide security for all nations, and that this principle should find itself embodied in the convention containing the conclusions of the Disarmament Conference.

This declaration implies that the respective limitations of the armaments of all States should be included in the proposed disarmament convention. It is clearly understood that the methods of application of such equality of rights will be discussed by the conference.

2. On the basis of this declaration Germany has signified its willingness to resume its place at the Disarmament Conference.

3. The Governments of the United Kingdon, France, Germany, and Italy are ready to join in a solemn reaffirmation to be made by all European States that they will not in any circumstances attempt to resolve any present or future differences between the signatories by resort to force. This shall be done without prejudice to fuller discussions on the question of security.

4. The five Governments of the United States, the United Kingdom, France, Italy, and Germany declare that they are resolved to cooperate in the conference with the other States there represented, seeking without delay to work out a convention which shall effect a substantial reduction and a limitation of armaments with provision for future revision with a view to further reduction.

[715]

unsatiated revisionist States are irreconcilably opposed at all points. Unless she is completely crushed by a new French "war of defense" in the near future, Germany will inevitably recover a parity of power with her encircling potential enemies—either by general disarmament, which will leave the French bloc in a much weaker position than that which it now occupies, or by German re-armament. The attitude of the United States and Great Britain toward "security," *i.e.*, the perpetuation of French hegemony, makes it impossible for the French bloc to accept general disarmament. In all probability, the gradual re-armament of Germany cannot be prevented by British and American admonitions, nor yet by any French pressure short of an actual invasion of German territory, which would have incalculably disastrous consequences. Given the present objectives of German foreign policy and the inevitably continuing tension between the Reich and its neighbors, the re-armament of Germany means an eventual "war of liberation." By no stretch of the imagination can it be regarded as conceivable that the western European social order of private capitalism, political democracy, and bourgeois nationalism could survive the shock of such a conflict. The letters of FAILURE, writ large over the doors of the Geneva Disarmament Conference, may well become letters of doom for the western world.

4. SECURITY AND SANCTIONS

> Justice without might is impotent. Might without justice is tyranny. Justice without might is unavailing, for the wicked are ever with us. Might without justice stands condemned. We must therefore mate justice with might and to that end we must insure that what is just is mighty and that what is mighty is just.—PASCAL, cited by Edouard Herriot, Geneva, 1924.

It is clear from the preceding discussion that peace has not been, and probably cannot be, assured through the renunciation of war or through efforts at disarmament. The renunciation of war is an idle gesture which imposes no effective limitation upon the right of sovereign States to employ military violence against one another, so long as they refrain from making "war" in the legal sense and so long as they insist, as all States do, that they are acting in "self-defense." Efforts at disarmament have reached a blind alley. Limitation of naval armaments has been achieved. Limitation and reduction of land armaments on any large scale seem impossible, so long as France and her allies insist upon security through the organization of peace as the price of concessions. The problem of peace has therefore become the problem of security. In the abstract, this problem is a general one of interest to all States, however "security" may be defined. Practically, it is a problem of peculiar interest to the French bloc in Europe, which possesses supremacy on the Continent and holds within its hands the keys to the future of the politics of peace.

If efforts at disarmament are ineffective and if the renunciation of war has not achieved its purpose, the cause lies in the fact that the French Government and the Governments of the States allied to France do not feel that security can be attained by such measures. This feeling is due to the fact that the revisionist States in general, and Germany in particular, are bent upon upsetting the existing distribution of power. The French bloc is prepared to make any sacrifices to prevent this. It will make no sacrifices which threaten to open the door to this menace to its interests. At Paris, Brussels, Warsaw, Prague, Belgrade, and Bucharest there is confidence neither in the renunciation of war nor in the elaboration of procedures of pacific settlement. There is confidence only in military alliances and in the overwhelming military preponderance which these States enjoy. These alliances and this preponderance must be preserved at all costs as the bulwarks of "peace," *i.e.*, the perpetuation of a hegemony which will inevitably be upset unless it is guarded with unceasing vigilance. These bulwarks cannot be abandoned unless the entire world is so organized for "peace" that the beneficiaries of the existing hegemony can rely upon world support against any revisionist effort to disturb the *status quo*. Security thus becomes a problem of international guarantees and sanctions on a world-wide scale, to replace national armaments and military alliances.

The problem of sanctions thus lies at the very heart of all international efforts to prevent war. The problem is not new, although it has been dealt with seriously by governments only since 1919. It has already been pointed out that international law differs from national law in that there is no collectively organized, coercive authority in the existing structure of international government to restrain lawbreakers and preserve order.[1] The "sanctions" or methods of enforcement of international law were described as habit, expediency, good faith, and organized force. The first three of these involve individual action by separate States—with each State protecting its rights by self-help, holding others responsible for violations of its rights, and observing the rights of others to the degree dictated by custom, honor, or fear of reprisals and retaliations. These national sanctions rely ultimately upon national power or upon force exercised by a State or a group of States with common power interests. The application of physical coercion becomes the ultimate means of preserving peace, with the paradoxical result that the means often defeat their own end by producing war.[2] Almost all observers, save the most

[1] See pp. 126–127 above.

[2] "It is impossible to agree with those publicists who hold that war is the real or main sanction of the law of nations; for the attempt to characterize war as a guarantee of law or as a means of justice in ordinary cases must be considered harmful as well as vain unless concurred in by practically the whole or main body of the international community." A. S. Hershey, *Essentials of International Public Law and Organization*, 1927, pp. 10–11.

ardent advocates of military preparedness, have agreed in the post-Versailles period that purely *national* sanctions of a coercive character offer no hope of preventing war in the future. They have differed fundamentally, however, regarding the deductions to be drawn from this conclusion.

Some peace seekers have argued that no sound analogy can be drawn between police forces within States and the instruments of physical coercion in the relation between States; that peace can never be preserved by force; and that the whole effort to insure peace through war or threats of war is doomed to failure. Those who accept this view seek to provide non-coercive sanctions: "public opinion," a sense of duty, reciprocal respect for rights, moral obligations, etc.[1] Others—including the Governments of the French bloc—have contended that coercion is undesirable as a sanction only when it is applied nationally by single States or groups of States against other States. They have argued that the sanction of general *international* organized force offers the only hope of preserving peace. In this way war makers will be restrained through the application of coercion against them on the part of the whole community of States. All the States of the world must therefore be organized to preserve peace by force—and since no single State could defy the entire world, acts of aggression will become so inexpedient as to compel their abandonment.

This cleavage between the advocates and the opponents of collective international coercion underlies all post-war efforts to achieve security. At the Paris Peace Conference the view prevailed that peace could be assured only by organized force on a world-wide scale. This notion had been developed by the American "League to Enforce Peace," the British League of Nations Society, and other groups of peace seekers interested in the problem of international political organization. It had been accepted by Wilson, Lloyd George, Clemenceau, and the Allied Governments generally. Pre-war experience was rich in instances of the successful application of international force by the Powers against small weak States. As early as 1904 Theodore Roosevelt had spoken of the necessity of an international police force, and in 1910 he declared that the weakness of the Hague peace machinery "arises from the lack of any executive power, of any police power to enforce the decrees of the court."[2] An American congressional resolution of the same year (Resolution 43, June 25, 1910) proposed the combining of the navies of the world into "an

---

[1] Lord Parmoor has aptly expressed this idea: "The ordinary citizen is law-abiding, and complies with legal obligations, because these obligations accord with nis sense of moral duty, and are accepted as regulations beneficial to the peaceful conduct of mutual intercourse with other members of the same community. In the ultimate analysis, the obligations of nations, and individuals, towards one another stand on not dissimilar principles." Cited in E. C. Mower, *International Government*, 1931, p. 233.

[2] Nobel Prize speech of May 5, 1910.

international force for the preservation of universal peace." In 1916 Senator Henry Cabot Lodge had declared that force must be placed behind international peace.[1] In view of these developments, it was natural that the framers of the Covenant of the League of Nations should have incorporated into that document provisions for the application of international force against Covenant-breaking States.

Article 16 of the Covenant provides for sanctions of pacific settlement:

1. Should any member of the League resort to war in disregard of its covenants under Articles 12, 13, or 15, it shall *ipso facto* be deemed to have committed an act of war against all other members of the League, which hereby undertake immediately to subject it to the severance of all trade or financial relations, the prohibition of all intercourse between their nationals and the nationals of the Covenant-breaking State, and the prevention of all financial, commercial, or personal intercourse between the nationals of the Covenant-breaking State and the nationals of any other State, whether a member of the League or not.

2. It shall be the duty of the Council in such case to recommend to the several Governments concerned what effective military, naval, or air force the members of the League shall severally contribute to the armed forces to be used to protect the covenants of the League.

3. The members of the League agree, further, that they will mutually support one another in the financial and economic measures which are taken under this article, in order to minimize the loss and inconvenience resulting from the above measures, and that they will mutually support one another in resisting any special measures aimed at one of their number by the Covenant-breaking State, and that they will take the necessary steps to afford passage through their territory to the forces of any of the members of the League which are cooperating to protect the covenants of the League.

4. Any member of the League which has violated any covenant of the League may be declared to be no longer a member of the League by a vote of the Council concurred in by the representatives of all the other members of the League represented thereon.

This arrangement obviously contemplates the application of international economic pressure and military force against peace breakers, under the direction of the League Council. Non-member States which resort to war against League members may be proceeded against in the same fashion as members (Article 17 §3). These provisions were at once criticized by the advocates of international sanctions as being too weak and by its opponents as being too strong. At the Peace Conference the French Government made a much more far-reaching proposal for an international police force under an international general staff, with the Council empowered to entrust enforcement of League decisions to particular States. This plan, which amounted to a revival of the procedure of the Holy Alliance, was rejected by the other Allies. The sanctions article as written into the Covenant was further weakened by the interpretations attached to it. It was discussed in connection with Article 10,

---

[1] See p. 252 above.

guaranteeing the League members against external aggression and authorizing the Council to "advise upon the means by which this obligation shall be fulfilled." At the Fourth Assembly (1923) an interpretative resolution was introduced, declaring that the Council, in recommending the application of military measures, "shall be bound to take account, more particularly, of the geographic situation and of the special conditions of each State. It is for the constitutional authorities of each member to decide, in reference to the obligations of preserving the independence and the integrity of the territory of members, in what degree the member is bound to assure the execution of this obligation by employment of its military forces." Each State would thus determine for itself whether it would cooperate in the application of sanctions. In the vote on the resolution, twenty-nine States approved, thirteen abstained, and one (Persia) disapproved.

The interpretation given to Article 16 itself led in the same direction. In 1921 the Second Assembly adopted a resolution making the application of an economic boycott against a Covenant-breaking State optional and discretionary, rather than obligatory and automatic, on the part of other members. "The unilateral act of the defaulting State cannot create a state of war; it merely entitles the other members of the League to resort to actual war or to declare themselves in a state of war with the Covenant-breaking State; but it is in accordance with the spirit of the Covenant that the League of Nations should attempt, at least at the outset, to avoid war, and restore peace by economic pressure." Moreover, "it is the duty of each member of the League to decide for itself whether a breach of the Covenant has been committed." The Council was further authorized to "postpone the coming into force of any of these measures for a specified period where it is satisfied that such postponement will facilitate the attainment of the object of the measures . . . or that it is necessary to minimize the loss and inconvenience which will be caused to such members." This resolution was unanimously adopted and incorporated into a proposed amendment to Article 16, which, however, has never been approved. It was clear that in the view of the League members the Council could merely "advise" (Article 10) or "recommend" the application of sanctions, military or economic. It could not mobilize the sanctions and command States to apply them, since each State would decide its obligations for itself.

This was, in effect, a recognition of a fact which has subsequently become obvious: that the whole sanctions system, as incorporated in the Covenant, is unworkable. States are still moved by self-interest. States which are far removed from a particular conflict in which they have nothing tangible or immediate at stake will not sacrifice blood and treasure to restrain an "aggressor," nor will they submit to the economic losses involved in a boycott—and this despite the fact that the Covenant seeks to make such conflicts "everybody's business," in Wilson's phrase. Neither are States prepared to authorize any international body to control their policies or to order them to proceed against a Covenant-breaking State. A universal boycott cannot be achieved in this fashion, so long as State action is motivated by the power, prestige, and profit interests of national diplomats, patriots, and entrepreneurs. A universal application of military force against a State breaking the peace cannot be achieved so long as States use force to protect and promote their own interests, rather than those of their neighbors or of the world community. And any boycott which is less than universal, any application of force which is not world-wide, will necessarily be ineffective, since it can be resisted successfully in almost any conceivable situation in which a Great Power is being proceeded against. The result will then be war, rather than the preservation of peace. Article 16 of the Covenant has never, in fact, been applied in any international conflict since the establishment of the League. For all practical purposes it may be regarded as a dead letter.

The circumstances which led to this result have likewise frustrated all succeeding efforts to assure security through international sanctions on a world-wide scale. When it was perceived that the Covenant was inadequate in this regard and that disarmament was impossible because of the insistence of the French bloc on security through some alternative arrangement, efforts were launched to supplement the Covenant with other instruments. The Draft Treaty of Mutual Assistance, considered by the Fourth Assembly in 1923, proposed to give the Council definite authority to designate the "aggressor" State in each conflict and to decide what military forces each State should be required to place at the disposal of the victim of aggression. This proposal proved quite unacceptable to the States outside of the French bloc, as had its predecessors. The Geneva Protocol of 1924 laid greater emphasis upon compulsory arbitration, adjudication, or decision by the Council. States refusing to resort to this procedure, or violating such decisions as might be reached, would be presumed to be aggressors unless the Council unanimously held otherwise. In cases not covered by this presumption, the Council would determine the fact of aggression. The Council could not mobilize sanctions, but, declared the protocol, "these obligations shall be interpreted as obliging each of the signatory States to cooperate loyally and effectively in support of the Covenant of the League of Nations and in resistance to any act of aggression, in the degree which its geographical position and its particular situation as regards armaments allow." Each State would determine for itself what constituted "loyal and effective" cooperation, but once the Council had decided which State was the aggressor, the other signatories of the protocol would be bound forthwith to apply the sanctions. The protocol failed of adoption. Despite the fact that it conferred less authority upon the Council than the Draft Treaty, it was nevertheless regarded as limiting freedom of State action too rigidly and as involving States in conflicts in which they had no direct interest. This view was taken by the British Government, which urged special and regional agreements in place of such general arrangements.

Subsequent efforts at Geneva to increase security by general arrangements have been based upon a practical abandonment of schemes to define aggression and mobilize sanctions. They have instead devoted greater attention to the procedures of pacific settlement. After Locarno, it was assumed erroneously that the security problem had been solved. In setting up the Preparatory Commission for the Disarmament Conference, no provision was made for a reconsideration of the question. The Preparatory Commission reached a complete deadlock on this point in 1927, as did the Disarmament Conference itself five years later. In the 1927 Assembly France sought unsuccessfully to revive the Geneva Protocol. The Assembly adopted a Polish proposal outlawing aggression. This Assembly resolution of 1927 was of only moral value, however, and provided neither for sanctions nor for additional procedures of pacific settlement. The Assembly further requested the Council to instruct the Preparatory Commission to appoint a committee "to consider . . . the measures capable of giving all States the guarantees of arbitration and security necessary to enable them to fix the level of their armaments at the lowest possible figures in an international disarmament agreement."

The Security and Arbitration Committee was set up at the fourth session of the Preparatory Commission in November, 1927. The United States and the Soviet Union declined to be represented. The committee circulated a questionnaire to secure additional light on the problem of the interpretation of Articles 10, 11, and 16 of the Covenant. The British reply declared that "an arbitration treaty which goes beyond what the public opinion of a country can be counted upon to support, when the interests of that country are in question, and when a decision unfavorable to those interests is pronounced, is a treaty which is useless." It proposed, therefore, "knitting together the nations most immediately concerned, and whose differences might lead to a renewal of strife, by means of treaties framed with the sole object of maintaining, as between themselves, an unbroken peace." The Committee ultmately proposed the drawing up of models of general and bilateral arbitration treaties. Within six months, ten draft treaties were prepared and submitted to the Ninth Assembly in 1928. In the face of British and Japanese objections, the Assembly combined the three collective treaties for arbitration and conciliation into one General Act for the Pacific Settlement of International Disputes.[1]

[1] See pp. 226–227 above.

The Act may be adopted in whole or in part by States at their option, as may the model bilateral conventions which accompanied it.

In 1930 the Assembly approved the Convention for Financial Assistance, providing for international loans to victims of aggression. The operation of this convention was made contingent upon a successful outcome of the General Disarmament Conference. This arrangement was a reversal of the principle of the Kellogg Pact—*si vis pacem, para pacem*—since it undertook to promote peace by financing war. It raised again the insoluble problem of defining aggression and provided that aid should be extended only by unanimous vote of the Council. The 1930 Assembly also considered a Draft General Convention to Strengthen the Means of Preventing War, adopted by the Twelfth Assembly in 1931. This Draft Convention provides that the signatories will carry out such military or non-military measures as the Council may recommend to keep the peace, in the event of a threat of war. All of these conventions are purely optional and have not yet received general ratification. The events of 1931–1932 have made it abundantly clear that these arrangements, for all their ingenuity and complexity, have not ensured security in the eyes of the governments which are most insistent upon its attainment.

The failure of these general international efforts to achieve security has stimulated the search for security through special and regional arrangements. Such arrangements also reveal a bewildering variety of expedients. There are, in the first place, bilateral and multilateral agreements of various types for the pacific settlement of international disputes.[1] There are, in the second place, a number of neutralization agreements for particular States, areas, ports, waterways, etc. Thirdly, there are agreements to respect the "territorial integrity" of certain States—an obligation imposed, in any case, by general international law but made specific in certain instances for States whose integrity appears to be jeopardized, such as China, Tibet, Persia, and Abyssinia. Such arrangements are sometimes accompanied by national or international guarantees of sovereignty and independence, as in the case of most protectorates. Agreements of this type frequently constitute perfect examples of the use of words to conceal meanings, for they are often followed by the partition or annexation of the supposed beneficiaries, *e.g.*, Korea, Colombia, Annam, Turkey, etc. Fourthly, there are non-aggression pacts and agreements to remain neutral in the event of war in designated contingencies. Finally, there are military alliances for common defense and for the guarantee by mutual support of specified frontiers or of the independence and integrity of the parties.

Military alliances of the pre-war type now prevail between France and her allies. There are similar agreements between the Baltic States and the members of the Little Entente. It is possible that there are secret com-

[1] See pp. 221–229 above.

mitments between other States which are still unknown. The post-war French alliances are less secret than those of the old model, since they are registered with the League of Nations. The technical understandings between the general staffs, however, are neither registered nor published and these are the most significant documents in all such arrangements. The French system of alliances began with a Franco-Belgian military agreement of September 7, 1920, and a defensive alliance with Poland of February 19, 1921. On August 4, 1920, Czechoslovakia and Rumania concluded a military alliance. This arrangement was superseded by new agreements of April 21, 1921, and buttressed by an alliance between Rumania and Jugoslavia signed on June 7, 1921. The "Little Entente" was thus created. It was strengthened and institutionalized by the agreement of February 15, 1933. On November 11, 1927, Jugoslavia became an ally of France. France and Czechoslovakia concluded an alliance on January 25, 1924, following a preliminary agreement of August 31, 1922. Czechoslovakia in turn is allied with Rumania, and Rumania with Jugoslavia and Poland. It is safe to assume that the general staffs of all these States have worked out detailed plans for military cooperation against Germany, Austria, Hungary, Bulgaria, Italy, and the U.S.S.R. in the event of war. At the Peace Conference France secured an Anglo-American guarantee against future German aggression, but both the British and American Governments failed to ratify it. The Quai d'Orsay sought to replace these defunct agreements by an Anglo-French treaty of guarantee. A draft treaty was proposed at Cannes in January, 1922, but Great Britain refused to guarantee the frontiers of Poland and Czechoslovakia and the project was abandoned.

These pacts resemble the Triple Alliance and Triple Entente arrangements of the period prior to 1914, in that they represent a community of power interests and aspirations on the part of the signatories. The Locarno Treaty of Mutual Guarantee, applying to Germany's western frontiers, on the other hand, represented a new type of "alliance" cutting across the natural lines of power interests. Unlike the older types of agreement, this constituted not an alignment of States against a prospective enemy (despite the apprehensions of the Soviet Union), but an arrangement of mutual guarantee. It is an alliance, however, in the sense that Great Britain and Italy bind themselves to come at once to the military assistance of either France or Germany if either is the victim of unprovoked aggression at the hands of the other. In the eastern pacts, France on the one hand and Poland and Czechoslovakia on the other agreed to come to one another's assistance in the event of German aggression. If Germany attacks France, she will presumably find herself at war with Great Britain, Belgium, Italy, Poland, and Czechoslovakia. If France attacks Germany, she will be at war with Great Britain and Italy, but not with

Poland and Czechoslovakia. If Germany attacks Poland or Czechoslovakia, France alone is bound to come to their aid. Here was the regional security pact which logically followed the failure of the general guarantees attempted in the Draft Treaty and the Geneva Protocol.

The answer to the question as to why these special and regional arrangements have likewise failed to afford security to their signatories has already been suggested. No confidence is placed in procedures of pacific settlement, however general and all-inclusive, for wars result precisely from the controversies which States are unwilling to submit to arbitration, adjudication, or conciliation—and the exceptions to such general arrangements can always be interpreted to exclude a particular case from their application, if the parties desire to do so. Neutralization agreements and non-aggression pacts have frequently been "scraps of paper." Agreements to respect or even to guarantee frontiers offer no permanent assurance that they will be observed if national self-interest dictates non-observance in a crisis. Regional guarantees and alliances, like the Locarno pacts which cut across natural lines of power interests, are untrustworthy for precisely this reason. No one, for example, supposes, treaties to the contrary notwithstanding, that Italy would feel herself obliged to go to the defense of France in a new Franco-German war, no matter how eloquently France insisted that she was a victim of "unprovoked aggression." This phrase, like all pretended distinctions between defensive and offensive war, is meaningless. It describes no situation which has reality in twentieth century international politics. There remain military alliances of the old type, reflecting the common purposes of States aligned against common prospective enemies. But here too there is no security—not even when such an overwhelming preponderance of power prevails as the French bloc enjoys—for coalitions directed against other States breed counter-coalitions, and out of this new competition for power comes war on the greatest scale.

There is, then, no security. There is apparently no way of attaining security, so long as present national attitudes and policies prevail. The attempt to organize general international sanctions has ended in failure. The quest for security through regional pacts has ended in failure. From this it follows that verbal renunciations of war are futile and that further disarmament is highly improbable. The deeper reasons for this impasse are to be found in the implications for power politics of the prevalent conceptions of "security" and "sanctions," which will be examined in the next section.

5. THE DILEMMA OF THE PEACE SEEKERS

We have war because we are not sufficiently heroic for a life which does not need war.—BARTOLOMEO VANZETTI.

The loud little handful—as usual—will shout for the war. The pulpit will—warily and cautiously—object—at first; the great big dull bulk of the nation will rub its sleepy eyes and try to make out why there should be a war, and will say, earnestly and indignantly, "It's unjust and dishonorable and there is no necessity for it." Then the handful will shout louder. . . . And now the whole nation—pulpit and all—will take up the war cry, and shout itself hoarse, and mob any honest man who ventures to open his mouth; and presently such mouths will cease to open. Next, the statesmen will invent cheap lies, putting the blame on the nation that is attacked, and every man will be glad of those conscience-soothing falsities, and will diligently study them, and refuse to examine any refutations of them; and thus he will by and by convince himself that the war is just, and will thank God for the better sleep he enjoys after this process of grotesque self-deception.—MARK TWAIN, *The Mysterious Stranger*, 1898.

Whether the search for permanent peace has been as fruitless as it appears to be from the bare recital or the post-war story of disarmament, security, and the renunciation of war cannot well be determined until the world's peace machinery is put to a more severe test than any which has been applied hitherto. It is possible that the more subtle and less tangible results of these seemingly barren efforts are working on opinion in many lands and molding a new will to peace. But the efforts themselves have clearly not fulfilled the expectations of those who anticipated that the demon of war would be exorcised by benevolent intentions, world conferences, bureaus, commissions, draft treaties, and international agreements to settle disputes pacifically. "Peace, peace," has been cried from the house tops, from the chancellories, from the conference rooms—and after fifteen years there is no peace. Treaties have been drawn up, amended and multiplied in confusing complexity. The governments of the world have entered into scores of pacts, conventions, protocols, and covenants—to outlaw war, to reduce armaments, to settle disputes, to respect frontiers, to guarantee independence and integrity, to ensure neutrality, to come to one another's assistance against attack, to renounce aggression, to tie down the dogs of war by a thousand chains. But the chains are of paper and from under the seemingly crushing weight of documents issue ominous growlings as disturbing to the peace seekers as the muffled thunder of the decade before 1914. War is unthinkable, argue pacifists, for it would be the suicide of civilization. But other civilizations have also died. War is impossible, argue jurists, for it has been outlawed. But law is feeble indeed when it is supported neither by force nor by public sentiment.

The prevailing state of insecurity and the current lack of confidence in the established peace machinery is indicated by the fact that all governments continue to prepare feverishly for war on an unprecedented scale. These preparations, considered collectively, are madness—but in war, as in financial panics, what is collective insanity may be individual wisdom. Elementary considerations of defense dictate military preparedness everywhere, for war goes on in physical fact, if not in legal theory, in spite of all pacts and covenants to the contrary. Since 1928 armies have fought, killed, and destroyed on the plains of Manchuria, in the swamps around Shanghai, in the jungles of Nicaragua, in the wilderness of the Gran Chaco—and all this in addition to the numerous revolutions and civil wars which have followed in the wake of the Great Depression. None knows when ruin and death may again descend on the Rhine, the Vistula, the Dneister, or the Danube or when the fighting fleets may again deal destruction to one another on the great seaways. The great metropolitan centers of western culture which lie within striking distance of enemy air squadrons are ever under the shadow of the terror from the skies. Never was "preparedness" in greater demand. Never was militant Fascist nationalism more widespread. Never were governmental policies and popular attitudes more definitely oriented in the direction of conflict. If progress toward peace is to be measured by these things rather than by documents and gestures, it is clear that the western world in the third decade of the twentieth century is very far indeed from taking a farewell to arms.

The causes of this paradox of a world professing peace and everywhere planning for war have already been indicated. They may here be made more explicit, with the whole problem of the politics of peace formulated as precisely as possible. The concept of "security" first deserves examination, for the demand for security obviously constitutes the greatest single obstacle in the way of disarmament and of international organization against war. If this concept had any exact meaning, or if there existed any yardstick whereby the relative security of States could be measured, the discussion would be simplified. But such is not the case. In its simplest form, security might be taken to mean assurance against invasion. If each State felt itself to be in no danger of an incursion of enemy armies over its frontiers, security in this sense might be assured. Not only do few States have such an assurance, despite covenants and pacts, but for the Great Powers security does *not* mean merely protection of home territory.

Security means protection of allies, of colonies, of dependencies, of sea routes, of markets, of all the stakes of contemporary diplomacy. Since Versailles and Locarno, France has been in no danger of invasion from any quarter. But French security does not end at the line of the Alps. French security demands the protection of Poland, Czechoslovakia, Rumania, and Jugoslavia. France's frontiers for purposes of security extend to the Polish corridor, Vilna, Bessarabia, the Hungarian plain, and the Adriatic. They likewise extend to Arabia, the Sahara, central Africa, the Indian Ocean, Siam, and the southern Pacific. British security no longer means insular isolation. Not the Channel, but the Rhine is the frontier which Britain is pledged to maintain since 1925. The road to Mandalay and the seaways east and west of Suez are Britain's vital lines of defense. American security demands defense of the Caribbean, the Panama Canal, the Hawaiian Islands, the Philippines, and Alaska. Japanese security demands the protection of Japanese interests on the Amur, in Mongolia, in Fukien, on the Yangtse, in the Pacific islands.[1] Security clearly does not call simply for the integrity of "national" frontiers, but rather for the defense of power interests throughout the world.

There can be no statistical or political measure of such security in either an absolute or a relative sense, for the future of power interests hinges upon all of the imponderables making up the "war potential" of all States. In short, security means—for satiated States—the perpetuation of the *status quo* and of the existing distribution of territory and power; and for unsatiated States it means a redistribution of territory and power. This proposed revision of existing settlements is precisely what is most menacing to the "security" of the beneficiaries of the *status quo*, precisely what is interpreted as "aggression," and precisely what must be resisted at all costs. The satiated States (France and her allies in Europe) are most concerned with security, most eloquent in demanding peace, most insistent on guarantees and sanctions, for they have most to lose from change and they are prepared to fight to resist it. The tragic madness of the peace seeker's paradox is shown by the fact that such States would "fight for peace"—*i.e.*, for the pacific and undisturbed perpetuation of the *status quo* from which they benefit. But in fighting there is no security, even for States with a great preponderance of power, for the accidents of war are unpredictable and all may be ruined in a common catastrophe. The possibility of fighting must therefore be minimized. The revisionist States

[1] Jules Cambon, pre-war French Ambassador at Berlin, puts the matter as follows: "When I have said that security has always been the cardinal aim of France, that term must be understood in its fullest sense. There is a France outside our own frontiers. Just as England cannot permit her communications with India to be menaced in Egypt, and just as the United States considers that one of her elementary interests is to safeguard the Panama Canal, just so France must guard her communications with her possessions in north Africa and preserve her freedom of action in the Mediterranean. Here we touch the problem of the relations of States at its most delicate point. For it is when States come into direct contact that practical accommodations become imperative.

"Security! The term signifies more, indeed, than the maintenance of a people's homeland, or even of their territories beyond the seas. It also means the maintenance of the world's respect for them, the maintenance of their economic interests, everything, in a word, which goes to make up the grandeur, the life itself, of the nation." *Permanent Bases of Foreign Policy*, 1931, p. 25.

which might conceivably be disposed to fight if they are unable to obtain their objectives peaceably, must be deterred from fighting. This in turn can best be accomplished by keeping them impotent and incapable of fighting, *i.e.*, by insisting unyieldingly upon the perpetuation of the *status quo*. But the maintenance of the *status quo* is intolerable to its victims and predisposes to war more effectively than any other procedure. Here is the ultimate *reductio ad absurdum* of the cry for security and of the values and assumptions of power-and-prestige politics itself.

The problem of sanctions is intelligible only in terms of these relationships of power. The satiated States seek security not only by keeping the "enemy" helpless, but by enlisting the political and military support of as many other States as possible to maintain the *status quo*. France and her satellites were interested in the League of Nations chiefly as a device to enlist world aid in maintaining French hegemony over the Continent. They are interested in security pacts, consultative agreements, and implementations of the outlawry of war for the same reason. But no effective guarantees, no assurance of international sanctions are forthcoming, because all States act to defend and promote their own power interests and not those of their neighbors and rivals. The *status quo* bloc cannot possibly induce outside States having no direct interest in the preservation of the *status quo* to commit themselves to the application of economic and military force in its behalf. France can persuade Great Britain and Italy to defend the *status quo* only within narrow limits. Germany has accepted the existing frontiers in the west, but will never commit herself to accept those in the east as fixed for all time. The U.S.S.R. and the United States will offer no guarantees whatever and will participate in no sanctions. Neither will Japan, which is too remote to act in Europe in any case. In the absence of international guarantees and sanctions, the *status quo* bloc must rely on its military alliances and on its preponderance in armaments. Disarmament is impossible and the revisionist group sees no hope of redress, save in re-arming up to the level of its adversaries, in order that it may achieve its objectives by coercion. The vicious circle is unbroken and the wheels of war grind slowly toward another clash of armed forces.

The essence of the problem lies in the lack of any effective procedure whereby conflicting power interests can be reconciled and pacific adjustments of power relations can be brought about.[1] If the *status quo* bloc insists, as it has done thus far, on maintaining intact the existing allocation of power and territory and if the revisionist bloc insists, as it does with increasing determination, that this distribution must be altered, war is inevitable in the absence of any machinery to reconcile these conflicting aspirations. They cannot be reconciled without concessions on both sides,

[1] See pp. 799—801 below on Article 19 of the Covenant.

in a spirit of give and take. Reconciliation implies a willingness to subordinate particular and special interests to broader, general interests. It also requires mechanisms and agencies through which frontiers can be modified and opposed policies can be adjusted. The will to peace is lacking so long as patriotism and the national quest for power and profits preclude acquiescence in changes of the *status quo* on the part of its beneficiaries. The mechanisms and agencies are lacking so long as the existing procedures of pacific settlement rest solidly upon a system of treaties and public law which envisages the perpetuation of a particular and temporary distribution of territory and power. The Covenant of the League is part of the peace treaties. All treaties for arbitration, adjudication, conciliation, non-aggression, etc., postulate the maintenance of the *status quo* as incorporated into existing settlements. All efforts at disarmament assume the sanctity of existing obligations. Law must always rest upon established law, and the established system of international public law is so rigid and inflexible as to render almost impossible any peaceable modification, any pacific readjustment of power relationships, even when these cease to correspond to changing realities. But life cannot be restrained forever by law. The great forces making for change cannot be forever confined within a rigid legal framework. Change is the law of all life and of all politics, and it is inevitable by one means or another. If no disposition exists to render the international *status quo* flexible and adaptable to changing conditions, if no procedures are devised to accomplish changes in a pacific and orderly fashion, then changes will be ultimately achieved, as they have always been achieved in the past—by force.

It is useful to recall again at this point certain analogies between the political process as it operates within national States and as it operates internationally within the Western State System as a whole. It has repeatedly been argued in the course of the present volume that the process of politics on all levels is a competitive struggle for power. This struggle involves constant shifts and changes in relationships of power between political groups, whether they be classes, parties, factions, sections, provinces, or States themselves. These changes take place through a process of compromise, adjustment, reconciliation, acquiescence, when all the parties are prepared to compose their differences pacifically and when constitutional or statutory procedures have been established for representation, deliberation, and policy formulation. All law-making involves the accommodation of competing interests with conflicting demands by means of formulas, symbols, and programs acceptable to all. It involves the continuous pacific adjustment of relationships of power. Law enforcement involves the protection of common interests, the execution of the policies which have been agreed upon as reflections of these common interests, and the application, if need be, of the police force of the State to preserve

[730]

peace and order and subdue criminals and transgressors. This orderly procedure breaks down in revolution, *i.e.*, in a resort to violent coercion in the pursuit or defense of power, only when conflicting demands become wholly irreconcilable and the constitutional consensus of common in-' terests and values disappears.

The international community is composed of competing sovereignties which traditionally pursue their own purposes and are bound together by no effective sense of common interests and values. Competing demands are traditionally presented in irreconcilable form, with no common denominator to solve the equation. Within a State, the political equation is: Party *A versus* Party *B* equals government by Party *A* or by Party *B*, with the other acquiescing, or perhaps a coalition government of both. Between States, the equation is: State *X versus* State *Y*, with threats of coercion or war resulting and the weaker yielding to the stronger under forcible pressure. The assumption of violence is made because of the irreconcilability of the demands and because of the absence of any constitutional consensus of common interests within the framework of which an adjustment may be reached. Phrases to the contrary notwithstanding, there is in the Western State System no true process of international legislation comparable to the law-making process within States. The Assembly of the League of Nations notwithstanding, there is no international legislature in which pacific changes and readjustments of power relationships can take place. The entities involved are sovereign States, and changes in power relations between States usually involve changes in frontiers, in the distribution of territory, in the level of armaments, in the alignment of alliances, in the availability of economic opportunities, etc. States do not ordinarily yield on such issues, except under coercive pressure. Existing frontiers, levels of armaments, and political alignments are incorporated in treaties which are usually the result of coercion applied by victors to vanquished in the last armed combat. The beneficiaries of such treaties inevitably resist their modification, by force if necessary, and no procedure has as yet been devised for bringing about fundamental changes in power relationships except greater force applied by the States bent upon revising the *status quo*.

If the problem of international sanctions be viewed in the light of this analysis, it is at once apparent that the preservation of international peace by the organized force of cooperating States is a process quite different from that of the preservation of law and order within States by police and militia. There is, to be sure, a superficial resemblance. The State as a social institution may be viewed as an embodiment of coercive power whereby a ruling class or an *élite* preserves an established distribution of wealth and of social prestige and political influence beneficial to itself. This coercive power need not be applied to any save isolated criminals and law-breakers, except when a fundamental alteration of the established order is threatened by a breakdown of the prevalent patterns of prestige and deference. When the menace of social revolution raises its head, the coercive authority of the State is employed against those who would upset the *status quo*, unless the constitutional structure is sufficiently adaptable to permit such changes to take place peaceably. In the international order, coercive authority may similarly be applied by the dominant States against States bent upon upsetting the existing distribution of power. Almost never is the international constitutional order sufficiently flexible to permit significant changes without coercion. But the application of force by State against State is vastly different from the application of force by class against class within a State. In international society there are satiated States and unsatiated States, but there is no clear division throughout the world as a whole between "ruling" States and "oppressed" States. The States of the world will not cooperate to preserve by force the hegemony of a particular group of States in a particular area.

Power is local, moreover, and the whole theory of sanctions breaks down if it is examined in the light of this fact. Even if it were possible to organize the forces of all the States of the world against a peace breaker, that power could not be concentrated effectively at the proper place at the proper time. Each of the Great Powers can defy the entire world within its own sphere of action. China cannot be protected against Japan by assistance from other States, even were they willing to grant it (and they are not)—for Japanese power is supreme in eastern Asia. Nicaragua cannot be protected against the United States by any conceivable mobilization of international sanctions by outside States. It is even doubtful whether Poland could be successfully defended against the Soviet Union, or Czechoslovakia against Germany, in this fashion. States will put their wealth and man power at the disposal of other States not to preserve "peace" in the abstract, but only to promote their own power interests. An organization of international force will be effective only within a particular sphere, against a particular State, in a particular set of circumstances. It cannot afford security to all States in all circumstances. Each State must therefore rely upon its own power and upon that of its allies. International sanctions have never been applied on a world-wide scale against peace-breaking States. If the analysis of international politics underlying the present study is correct, sanctions of this type never will be applied. They cannot be successfully invoked against any of the Great Powers, so long as the Western State System retains the fundamental characteristics which its past history has given to it.

The problem of peace at bottom is not the problem of security, of sanctions, of guarantees, of the renunciation of war, of pacts and covenants and procedures of pacific settlement. It is the problem of making possible the peaceable and orderly readjustment of power relationships between States. This in turn is not a problem of mechanisms, but a problem of values, attitudes, ideologies, sentiments, emotions, loyalties, and allegiances. It is insoluble so long as the prevalent cult of the nation-state exalts national power to the skies as the alpha and omega of political action. This cult is woven into the very warp and woof of contemporary western civilization. Not "war," but the quest for power, the search for profits, the demand for empire must be renounced if peace is to be assured. It is doubtful whether the present propaganda techniques and political panaceas of peace seekers will contribute toward this end. It may be argued that pacts, covenants, procedures and agencies of pacific collaboration, coupled with portrayals of the horrors and wastes of war, will in time create an international community and lead to the necessary transformation of attitudes and values. But it is equally arguable that they may have precisely the opposite effect. What is forbidden is always more fascinating than what is permitted. Renunciations of sin, confessions of guilt, pledges of good behavior often lead not to sublimation, but to repression of the impulses producing behavior which is outlawed. Repression leads to explosion. Emphasis upon war horrors stimulates all the latent sadistic and masochistic tendencies making for conflict. Disarmament conferences unconsciously concentrate attention on armaments and on the conflicting power interests of States which breed armaments and war. There is perhaps a tragic psychological fallacy in all that has hitherto been said and done to ensure peace. But whether this is so or not, there can be no assurance of permanent peace until the ruling classes of the western nation-states have revolutionized their political values and attitudes and arrived at a fundamentally new orientation toward themselves and their relation with one another.

Such a revolution is stoutly resisted by all the dominant interests and forces in the bourgeois societies, not because these interests desire war or are insensible to the benefits of peace, but because the thoughts, emotions, and behavior patterns of people everywhere are organized around symbols and attitudes which breed international conflict. The cult of national patriotism is foremost among these. The western peoples have yet to develop a patriotism which is not characterized by belligerency, national braggadocio, swashbuckling self-assertiveness, and all the attributes of primitive, ethnocentric tribalism. In every national society the widespread prevalence of these attitudes makes it impossible for statesmen and diplomats to pursue foreign policies which are other than "patriotic," *i.e.*, devoted to the exclusive pursuit of national interests, envisaged in terms of the in-group versus the out-group. These attitudes likewise make it easier for self-interested minorities to wrap themselves in the flag and to serve their special interests by identifying them with the symbols of the

[733]

national community. Professional patriotic societies, protected manufacturers, armament firms, military and naval officers, jingo journalists, and political demagogues have all learned only too well how to profit from appeals to patriotic emotionalism and nationalistic irrationality. These appeals strengthen and confirm the very attitudes upon which they rely for success. State and church, school and home, press and lecture platform, radio and cinema all collaborate in inculcating these attitudes in each new generation and in manufacturing patriots by mass production. Distinctions between "good" and "bad" patriotism, between "defensive" and "aggressive" nationalism are pointless, for all national patriotism in its contemporary form involves sanctification and exaltation of the nation-state in competition and conflict with other States.

The quest for profits is an obstacle to the transformation of values which is the prerequisite of peace, no less than is the cult of the nation-state. Private profit is not in itself a motive which drives whole national communities to war, for civilized peoples no longer fight one another for cattle, slaves, women, and booty. And it is naive to explain modern wars in terms of conspiracies of capitalists, "international bankers," and entrepreneurs, eminent authorities to the contrary notwithstanding.[1] Economic competition within national societies does not involve physical violence, except when class conflicts become acute. If the quest for profits plays a rôle in promoting violence in international society, it is because the protected and subsidized profit-seekers of each national community act in cooperation with patriots and diplomats to achieve national self-sufficiency and to conquer foreign markets. Profit-making opportunities become stakes of diplomacy in the rivalries of the Powers, for political goals inevitably reflect the economic interests of ruling classes and power can be expressed only in economic terms. The profits of war itself for small groups of entrepreneurs are enormous, despite the general misery and ruin—and occasionally an entire nation can promote its own prosperity, at least temporarily, by supplying the needs of belligerents or by engaging in war itself. Such was the situation of the United States between 1793 and 1814, and again between 1914 and 1918. Even in these cases it is not arguable that the nation as a whole benefited economically from war, if the post-war depressions are taken into consideration. But small and influential groups of profiteers do reap a rich harvest from war, for war involves the purchase by governments out of public funds of huge quantities of goods at high prices and the subsidizing by governments of such

---

[1] Thus Woodrow Wilson: "Why, my fellow citizens, is there any man here, or any woman—let me say, is there any child here—who does not know that the seed of war in the modern world is industrial and commercial rivalry? . . . This war in its inception was a commercial and industrial war. It was not a political war." Address at St. Louis, September 5, 1919.

industries as are essential for war purposes. Bankers and financiers always secure a large share of the resulting profits. Stock brokers, industrialists, railway corporations, shipping companies, and merchants generally likewise make substantial gains from government orders and from the rising prices which usually accompany war. Various schemes for "taking the profits out of war" or for "conscripting capital as well as men" are not likely to change this situation. War in modern capitalistic society requires production on a vast scale to consummate the work of vast destruction, and in that society productivity can be stimulated only by profit. These considerations do not justify the conclusion that modern wars are invariably engineered by profiteers. They do explain why profit-seekers are not averse to war, are usually ready to support patriots and diplomats in policies likely to lead to war, and are always ready to supply the sinews of war (at a price) to all war makers.

The economic consequences of the Great War in the United States offer an interesting illustration of these relationships. By the end of 1916, American bankers had loaned some two billions of dollars of American private capital to the Entente Governments at high interest rates and with fat commissions. The banking community profited from a prolongation of the war and stood to profit more from American participation.[1] The metallurgical interests of the country were particularly anxious for war and well satisfied with the results thereof.[2] Exporters and manufacturers profited no less handsomely. Between August 1, 1914, and February 1, 1917, American foreign trade reached unprecedented proportions and $10,500,000,000 worth of goods were exported from America to Europe. As American entrance into the war approached, prices of stocks and foodstuffs soared. In 1916 the United States Steel Corporation earned $330,574,178, and in 1917 $528,757,615. According to reports of the Federal Trade Commission, ten other leading steel concerns made profits in 1917 ranging from 52 per cent to 109 per cent on their investments. The war created 21,000 new American millionaires and distributed among 69,000 people three billions of dollars over and above their normal income.[3] These were the profits of a war initiated by an idealistic President and supported by a patriotic populace to crush German militarism and

[1] The Philadelphia *Public Ledger* of March 22, 1917, declared quite accurately: "Wall Street believes that war is just one month ahead. And Wall Street is glad that it is so. The financial district here is unqualifiedly for war as soon as it can be declared."

[2] On October 3, 1917, Judge Gary of the United States Steel Corporation was quoted in the press as saying: "We have no reason to complain of the action and attitude of the Government. To win the war the Government must have steel and more steel. There is no room for disloyalty in America."

[3] In a public address of August 29, 1921, President Harding asserted: "Our Government . . . expended between five and six billion dollars for the manufacture of aircraft, artillery, and artillery amunition. To show for this expenditure it has been officially testified that less than 200 American-made airplanes or 200 American-made cannon ever went into

"make the world safe for democracy." The national honor symbols in the name of which the United States went to war were "neutral rights," "freedom of the seas," "democracy," "self-determination," "rights of humanity," and the "war to end war." But the most significant results of the conflict were measured by the vast fortunes accruing to those who supplied the weapons of battle.[1]

The peculiar rôle occupied by armament manufacturers, chemical industries, and iron and steel producers deserves special attention in this connection. Modern war requires an enormous expenditure of munitions and other chemical and metallurgical products. In England alone, in July, August, and September of 1918, almost 16,000,000 shells were produced. During the entire war the British army and navy fired almost 200,000,000 shells. The British army in France consumed weekly 2,000 tons of shells at the end of 1915 and 100,000 tons in the later months of 1918.[2] Victory in modern warfare is achieved by raining a veritable deluge of steel and explosives upon the enemy forces. This procedure—and peace-time preparations for this procedure—spells huge profits to munition makers and steel companies—and these entrepreneurs are invariably "internationally minded" in that they are willing to sell their goods to any government willing to pay the right price. Before the war the European metal industry was symbolized by Sir Basil Zaharoff, a curious cosmopolite with interests in many lands. The Nobel group controlled explosive factories and chemical plants in various countries. Armor-plate and artillery manufacturers were no less international in their activities and cooperated with one another in an easy and profitable liaison. The English Vickers concern bought up the Italian Terni interests. In the Balkan Wars, Vickers sold battleships to Turkey and Armstrong (also English) sold submarines and destroyers to Greece. In 1913 Vickers and Armstrong built up the Turkish fleet, while the French Schneider-Creuzot interests equipped the Russian naval base at Nikolaev on the Black Sea. In 1912 Krupp (Ger-

---

action on the fighting front of the war, while not more than 1 per cent of the ammunition expended by American artillery was, according to the same testimony, of American manufacture. Approximately $3,500,000,000 has been poured out by the Shipping Board, yet I have from the War Department the curious bit of information that only one vessel built by the Shipping Board ever carried any American troops to fight in Europe."

[1] J. K. Turner, in *Shall It Be Again?* (1922), has worked out a persuasive economic interpretation of American entrance into the Great War on the basis of these facts. He concludes (pp. 363–370): "Wall Street's heart was with the Entente. And Wilson's heart was with Wall Street. A day came when it was evident that the Entente could never score a decisive victory without the full assistance of America as a belligerent. The tightening of the submarine blockade furnished the pretext. So, guided by Wilson, America rushed into the war in a blaze of superpatriotism and profit-taking. . . . The theories of a war for defense, a war for international law, a war for democracy, a war for permanent peace all break down before examination. The theory of a war for business alone harmonizes with the facts."

[2] Victor Lefebure, *Scientific Disarmament*, 1931, p. 68.

man), Schneider (French), and Bohm and Voss (German) secured control of the Russian Putilov works after an agreement with Vickers and Armstrong. Krupp and Creuzot later agreed not to compete with one another. In all the foreign offices and war ministries there were spokesmen for the armament firms.

During the war profits were multiplied manyfold. Basil Zaharoff was made an English Baronet and awarded the Grand Cross of the Legion of Honor for his patriotic services to the Entente. After the war he became a leading figure in the Anglo-Russian Oil Company. Schneider and Vickers acquired control of the Polish armament industry. Schneider took over the former Skoda works in Czechoslovakia. The manufacture of chemicals and explosives in Europe is dominated by the Nobel Dynamite Trust, Ltd.[1] In these lucrative activities, manufacturers, banks, diplomats, and general staffs all cooperate. Cynics and psychiatrists find interesting food for thought in the fact that dynamite makers and steel manufacturers are often the most ardent apostles of peace, e.g., the Nobel Peace Prize and the Carnegie Endowment for International Peace.[2] In every clash of arms between States or within States, armament makers earn large profits, along with bankers, newspapers, manufacturers, shippers, and other capitalistic entrepreneurs. During the Sino-Japanese hostilities of 1931–1933, large orders for war supplies were placed by both Governments in the United States, Great Britain, and other countries. During 1930–1932 the Government of Bolivia purchased $15,000,000 worth of armaments in Great Britain, while Paraguay purchased $5,000,000 worth in the United States with money borrowed in New York, with the approval of the American State Department—all this while the dispute between the two States over the Grand Chaco was pending before the League Council and the Pan-American Commission, and all in preparation for the open hostilities which broke out in the summer of 1932. Bolivia also purchased arms from Czechoslovakia and Chile and took one-third of the total arms exports of Switzerland in 1931. Paraguay purchased from France, Belgium, and Czechoslovakia as well as from the United States. In 1929 American firms sold $49,000 worth of powder to Bolivia and $24,000 worth

[1] See K. A. Bratt, *That Next War?* 1931, pp. 152–156.

[2] In his letter of December 14, 1910 (quoted in J. E. Harley, *International Understanding,* 1931, p. 354), Andrew Carnegie declared to the trustees of the new endowment: "I have transferred to you as trustees of the Carnegie Peace Fund, ten million dollars of 5 Per Cent first-mortgage bonds, the revenue of which is to be administered by you to hasten the abolition of international war, the foulest blot upon our civilization. Although we no longer eat our fellow men nor torture prisoners, nor sack cities killing their inhabitants, we still kill each other in war like barbarians. Only wild beasts are excusable for doing that in this, the twentieth century of the Christian era, for the crime of war is inherent, since it decides not in favor of the right, but always of the strong. The nation is criminal which refuses arbitration and drives its adversary to a tribunal which knows nothing of righteous judgment. . . . "

[737]

of machine guns to Paraguay.[1] International efforts at Geneva and else-where to regulate the private trade in war supplies have been even less successful than efforts to promote limitation and reduction of armaments.

The cult of the nation-state, as it expresses itself in the patterns of conflicting nationalisms and rival imperialisms, and the search for profits reflected in competing capitalisms, obviously lie at the bottom of that competitive quest for power and prestige which is the essence of inter-national politics and the fundamental cause of war. This quest is not the work of scheming diplomats, secret conspirators, and unscrupulous profiteers who plunge nations into seas of tears and blood for their own advantage. Diplomats and profit-seekers do indeed scheme and conspire, and peoples often find themselves at war under circumstances requiring that they find reasons for fighting after hostilities have broken out rather than before. This was the situation in which almost all the European peoples found themselves in 1914. Each war crisis, however, has a long train of antecedents in conflicting governmental policies which are sup-ported by patriots. In the quest for power, diplomats and entrepreneurs are the tools rather than the masters of the great forces moving States to action. Questions of "war guilt" and of responsibility for "aggression" are quite irrelevant. The roots of power politics and the seeds of war are deep in the soil of western civilization—and only optimistic idealists can delude themselves into believing that the trimming of the twigs and the disguising of the flowers which have gone on since 1919 have killed the plant. It would be more reasonable to hope for an earthquake or a plague which would destroy the soil itself or render it barren. To poison the soil will kill the tree—but nothing else will grow in its place. To permit the tree to grow will accomplish the same ultimate result. In the face of this dilemma, peace seekers must either despair or else develop a more effective technique for uprooting the seeds of war than any which has appeared hitherto.

SUGGESTED READINGS

Bakeless, J. E.: *The Economic Causes of Modern War*, New York, Dodd, Mead & Company, Inc., 1921.
Baker, P. J.: *Disarmament*, London, Hogarth Press, 1927.
————: *The Geneva Protocol for the Pacific Settlement of International Disputes*, London, King, 1925.
Barbusse, H.: *The Soviet Union and Peace*, New York, International Publishers, 1929.
Beales, A. C.: *The History of Peace*, New York, Dial Press, 1931.
Buell, R. L.: *The Washington Conference*, New York, D. Appleton & Company, 1922.
Kellor, F. A., and A. Hatvany: *Security Against War*, New York, The Macmillan Company, 1924.
Lefebure, V.: *Scientific Disarmament*, New York, The Macmillan Company, 1931.
Madariaga, S. de: *Disarmament*, New York, Coward-McCann, Inc., 1929.
Miller, D. H.: *The Geneva Protocol*, New York, The Macmillan Company, 1925.

[1] New York *Times*, September 15, 1932, citing League of Nations officials.

————: *The Peace Pact of Paris*, New York, G. P. Putnam's Sons, 1928.

Mitrany, D.: *The Problem of International Sanctions*, London, Oxford University Press, 1925.

Moore, J. B.: *International Law and Some Current Illusions*, New York, The Macmillan Company, 1924.

Page, K.: *Dollars and World Peace*, New York, Doubleday, Doran & Company, Inc., 1927.

Poliakoff, V.: *Peace in Europe*, London, Selwyn and Blount, 1927.

Quigley, H. S.: *From Versailles to Locarno*, Minneapolis, University of Minnesota Press, 1927.

Scott, J. B.: *Treaties for the Advancement of Peace*, New York, Oxford University Press, 1920.

Shotwell, J. T.: *War as an Instrument of National Policy and Its Renunciation in the Pact of Paris*, New York, Harcourt, Brace & Company, 1929.

Turner, J. K.: *Shall It Be Again?*, New York, Huebsch, 1922.

Vestal, S. C.: *The Maintenance of Peace*, New York, G. P. Putnam's Sons, 1920.

Wheeler-Bennett, J. W.: *Disarmament and Security since Locarno, 1925–1931*, New York, The Macmillan Company, 1932.

————: *Information on the Renunciation of War* (1927–1928), London, Allen and Unwin, 1928.

Williams, B. H.: *The United States and Disarmament*, New York, McGraw-Hill Book Company, Inc., 1931.

League of Nations, *Armament Year-book*, 1932, Geneva.

CHAPTER XVIII

THE TESTING OF THE LEAGUE

1. THE ENFORCEMENT OF THE PEACE TREATIES

When drums speak laws are dumb (*silent enim leges inter arma*).—CICERO.
For what can war but endless war still breed?—JOHN MILTON to LORD
FAIRFAX.

IF THE preceding chapters of this volume point to any single conclusion which is more significant than any other for the reflective
student of international relations, it is that the contemporary crisis
of the world society cannot be resolved by the independent and uncoordinated action of national governments. This survey of the consequences
of economic nationalism, imperialism, militarism, and war has not been
designed to point "lessons" or to furnish material for moralizing. These
consequences will be adjudged "bad" by most observers who apply to
them the criteria of human welfare and the hope of a richer life for all
peoples in an organized world society. To the realistic political scientist,
judgments of this kind are of minor significance, except as they influence
political behavior. What is important is that the results of competitive
self-seeking among the nation-states threaten to undermine the economic
and social foundations of western culture. These results cannot be
modified by exclusively national action. Whether they can be changed
by international action and by international organizations in a world of
rival sovereignties, competing capitalisms, and conflicting imperialisms
is not yet clear. But it is perfectly clear that if any method can be devised
for averting catastrophe, that method will require international action
and "international government." Ever since the Paris Peace Conference
of 1919, which launched upon the world in one document the Treaty of
Versailles and the Covenant of the League of Nations, the hopes, aspirations, and achievements of a war-weary world struggling toward peace
have centered in Geneva.

The choice of Geneva as the seat of the League is not without its own
significance. Switzerland, as a neutralized State relatively aloof from the
cross currents of continental politics, has long been a favorite meeting
place for international conferences, congresses, and bureaus. Geneva is its
westernmost city. It is situated on the plain north of Mont Blanc at the
southwestern tip of Lake Leman, whose blue waters there converge around
Rousseau's island in the heart of the city itself to form the river Rhone,

[740]

flowing through France into the Mediterranean. Geneva is French speaking. It is part of French Switzerland and, save for the lake, it is surrounded by French territory. A French atmosphere is appropriate for an organization created by the peace settlement which restored French hegemony over Europe. But cosmopolitanism, pacifism, reformism, internationalism are also a part of the flavor of Geneva. Here was one of the great centers of the Protestant Reformation. Here the stern and austere John Calvin preached predestination, founded his theosophy, and burned heretics for the greater glory of God. Calvinism and its offshoot, Puritanism, have given Geneva a legacy of bourgeois propriety, religiosity, uplift, and moral exaltation. Later, as a kind of antidote to Calvin, Geneva produced Jean Jacques Rousseau—vagabond iconoclast and revolutionary preacher of international peace, social justice, and intellectual enlightenment. Peace societies flourished in Geneva during the nineteenth century and the city became the seat of early efforts at international organization. Here the International Red Cross was established and here the United States and Great Britain arbitrated their famous dispute over the "Alabama claims." This background furnished a perfect setting for the League. The League of Nations Commission of the Peace Conference, rejecting French pleas for the selection of Brussels, chose Geneva as the most appropriate site of the new organization. To Geneva Sir Eric Drummond proceeded from London with his preliminary staff, to organize the Secretariat. A large mansion on the north side of the lake, along the Quai Wilson, became the "Palace of the League of Nations," housing the Secretariat, the library, the Council chamber, and various technical bodies. To the north of it was built the headquarters of the International Labor Organization. The "Hall of the Reformation," a ramshackle barn-like structure on the south side of the city, became the meeting hall of the Assembly. On September 7, 1929, the cornerstone was laid for an imposing group of buildings in Ariana Park, overlooking the city and the lake. These structures, when completed, will house permanently all of the League agencies.

The structure of the League itself has been described elsewhere in this study as a phase of the forms of the Western State System.[1] The admission of Iraq by the Thirteenth Assembly in 1932 made it an organization of fifty-seven members. As has been pointed out above, it is not a confederation, still less a super-State, but a true international organization of States, each of which retains its "sovereignty." It is a "League" or a "Society" (French: *société des nations*) or a "Union" (German: *Völkerbund*), composed of the nation-states of the world. It acts by States, on States, and through States and the government of each State is represented by special diplomatic agents. The Council is a body of delegates

[1] See pp. 258–273 above.

of fourteen States. The Assembly represents all of the fifty-seven members. The League Civil Service (the Secretariat), its judicial agency (the Permanent Court), and many of its technical advisory commissions are truly international in the sense that the individuals who compose them are not representatives of national governments, but are international officials answerable to international agencies. The whole organization may eventually evolve into a world super-State transcending national frontiers. But for the present it is a halfway house whose masonry is no stronger than the States which support it. More accurately, it is a method of institutionalized cooperation between States. The abstention of the United States and the despairing cynicism which surrounded its establishment made its original watchword the facetious slogan: "Half a league onward." But by 1933 only a few States were outside of the fold: the United States, the U.S.S.R., Brazil, Costa Rica, Ecuador, Arabia, Afghanistan, Iceland, Nepal, Oman, and Egypt. With these exceptions, it has become a genuine world organization.

The purpose of the present chapter will be to survey the actual functioning of the League with regard to problems not already discussed in other connections and to attempt an evaluation of its present international significance in terms of its adequacy to fulfill its functions. These tasks can be undertaken most conveniently in the light of M. Rappard's suggestive description of the League as "three Leagues in one": (1) the League for the enforcement of the peace treaties; (2) the League for the promotion of international cooperation; and (3) the League for the prevention of war.[1] These general categories indicate the broad functions assigned to the League by the Covenant and by other international engagements, as well as those which it has in practice assumed. They also suggest the hopes of its founders and the criteria which must be applied in passing judgment upon its achievements.

From its inception and throughout its career, the League has been inseparably connected with the peace settlement following the Great War. The Covenant constituted the first twenty-six articles of the treaties of Versailles, St. Germain, Trianon, and Neuilly. It was written into the treaties largely at Wilson's insistence, on the assumption that this would make it impossible for the Allies to sidetrack the project and on the further assumption (a mistaken one in this case) that the "irreconcilables" in the American Senate who were against the League *per se* might accept it as part of the general peace treaty. The intimate association between Geneva and Versailles has caused liberals, radicals, and "revisionists" throughout the world to view the League as a mere façade to a conquerors' peace which they regard as certain to provoke new wars. The Peace of Paris was not a "peace without victory," but was inevitably, in view of the

[1] See W. E. Rappard, *International Relations as Viewed from Geneva*, 1925.

military and political relationships between victors and vanquished in 1919, a vindictive, punitive settlement designed to cripple the defeated States in every possible way. In all of the Allied countries, the League was envisaged as an international agency to insure the enforcement and perpetuation of the new *status quo* which they had established. Neither the defeated enemy—Germany—nor the undefeated enemy—Soviet Russia—would be permitted to join. The triumphant Allies, with the aid of all the neutrals, would create a world organization to make forever impossible any resumption of "German aggression." The League would help to enforce the treaties and would thereby aid in keeping Germany, Austria, Hungary, and Bulgaria in a position of impotence and inferiority. In France interest in the League was proportionate to the prospect of making it serve as an international agency to insure French "security" and the indefinite perpetuation of French hegemony. Wilson, it is true, looked upon the League as a future corrective to the manifest iniquities and stupidities of the peace.[1] But he was repudiated by his own people. The governments which actually established the League unquestionably looked upon it as a bulwark against all efforts to upset an equilibrium which left them the spoils of war and with which they were reasonably content.

Despite the broadening functions of the League and the admission of Germany in 1926, the Geneva organization has in many respects retained its original character of a new "Holy Alliance" designed to render impossible any modification, peaceable or otherwise, of the established distribution of power. It necessarily rests upon the sanctity of treaties and particularly of the peace treaties of which its Covenant is an integral part. Article 10 of the Covenant was designed to safeguard for all time to come the existing frontiers and existing power interests of the members, by guaranteeing their political independence and territorial integrity. Article 16 was designed to mobilize the economic and military power of the entire world against any State which might attempt by force to upset the equilibrium. The victors had taken the spoils and were satiated. All other States were henceforth to be forbidden, under threats of international sanction, to wage war, to modify frontiers by force, to change levels of armaments, or to violate treaties. The new distribution of power was written into the new public law of the world, and the League was appointed its guardian to forbid all modifications of it save those to which its beneficiaries would consent. This meant that in all things affecting fundamental relationships of power the *status quo* could not be changed at all.

This essentially impossible function has limited the efficacy of the League in countless ways and may eventually prove its undoing. The

[1] See pp. 255–257 above and the discussion below (pp. 799–801) of Article 19 of the Covenant.

implications of this situation will be discussed below. Here it is enough to note the futility of the assumptions upon which this function rests and to survey the specific tasks of the League machinery in this connection. The folly of postulating that any international body can perpetuate an existing distribution of power at any given moment of time calls for no extended demonstration for those who have read the preceding pages.[1] This assumption underlies Articles 10 and 16 of the Covenant of 1919 and likewise is the basis of the "Stimson Doctrine" of 1932. The whole history of the Western State System, and indeed of all human civilization, is a complete and final refutation of the idea that power relationships can be crystallized into an unchanging mold. Nothing is permanent in these relationships save the certainty of change. In an unstable equilibrium of shifting forces, no distribution of territory, armaments, economic opportunities, and other power interests of States, however just, equitable, and generally satisfactory, can be fixed for very long. Each general peace settlement in European diplomacy has bred the tensions, dissatisfaction, and changes of forces which sooner or later consummated its own destruction. A settlement like that of 1919, which is harsh, revengeful, and directly conducive to hot anger and undying resentment on the part of its victims, can by no stretch of the imagination be regarded as "permanent" for all time to come.

The creation of the League did not modify the fundamental patterns of power relationships nor bring under organized control and direction the dynamic forces which invariably upset each settlement. If it be argued that the League system does not forbid change but only forbids forcible change, the answer is that fundamental changes of power relations, now as in the past, cannot be brought about by pacific means so long as the beneficiaries of an existing equilibrium refuse to yield to any considerations save *force majeur*. If the League does not serve to uphold the existing *status quo* by enforcing the peace treaties, it will become worthless to its founders, who will proceed to abandon it. If it does seek to perpetuate that *status quo*, it will be worthless to all the revisionist States of the world, which will sooner or later resort to force and destroy the League in the process. Unless the dilemma can somehow be resolved, there can be no hope of peace through Geneva.

Meanwhile, the League at its inception was utilized by its members as a convenient agency to perform certain necessary functions connected with the peace settlement. These functions were largely limited to routine administrative matters, for the League did not then possess sufficient prestige to permit the Allied Governments to contemplate the submission to it of decisions on matters of grave importance. The great international crises of the years immediately following 1919 were not even discussed

[1] See especially pp. 67–109 above.

at Geneva, much less acted upon. The Allied Supreme Council (successor to the Council of Four at the Peace Conference), the Conference of Ambassadors, and numerous special commissions continued to meet for the discussion of such questions. The list of post-war international problems connected directly or indirectly with the peace treaties which were not permitted to come within the purview of League agencies is impressive: the Allied blockade and military intervention in Russia, the Soviet-Polish War of 1920, the dispute over Bessarabia, the Turko-Greek War of 1921–1922, the dismemberment of Hungary, the allocation of the former German colonies, the *Anschluss* question in its initial stages, the reparations controversy, the Franco-Belgian occupation of the Ruhr, naval disarmament, etc. Even with regard to problems submitted to League agencies, the important decisions had already been reached through regular diplomatic channels and it fell to the League simply to carry out commands not formulated through its own machinery. All of the peace treaties, including the Treaty of Lausanne with Turkey of 1923 and a number of other international agreements, conferred certain executive and administrative functions upon Geneva. This served to make the League unpopular in the defeated States. But these functions would have been performed, in any case, and it is probable that they were performed with more intelligence and impartiality by an international body than would have been the case had they been entrusted to agencies of the Allied Governments.

Some of these functions have already been discussed above. The tasks of the League connected with the minority treaties and with the post-war plebiscites have been considered in relation to the general problem of national self-determination.[1] The confirmation by the Council of the mandates agreements and the forms of League supervision over the mandates have likewise been dealt with.[2] Notice has also been taken of the authority conferred upon the Council to supervise Germany's execution of her disarmament obligations.[3] The only other important League functions growing out of the peace settlement relate to the status of the Saar valley, the Free City of Danzig, and the district of Memel. These constitute interesting examples of international administration which are worthy of careful attention.

The Saar valley lies in the western Rhineland northeast of Alsace, southeast of Luxemburg, and roughly in the center of a triangle drawn between Metz, Treves, and Speyer.[4] It covers about 700 square miles, inhabited by a solidly German population of 700,000. Only 100 French-

[1] See pp. 312–319 above.
[2] See pp. 610–622 above.
[3] See p. 688 above.
[4] See map, p. 437 above.

[745]

men lived in the area in 1918, though it was under French control for sixty-eight years under Louis XIV and was again French under Napoleon I. Its coal reserves are estimated at eleven billion tons. Its towns and cities are clustered about mines, coke ovens, and steel foundries. Six of the nine railways connecting France and Germany pass through the district. When the French delegation of the Peace Conference failed to secure the annexation of the Rhineland, Clemenceau insisted at least on control of the Saar coal resources to compensate France for the destruction by the Germans of the Lens and Pas de Calais coal mines during the war. This demand was granted by Lloyd George and Wilson, and a Saar district was carved out, consisting not only of the coal region but of the adjacent industrial areas and forests. By the Saar Annex to the Treaty of Versailles, the district was included in the French tariff wall and thus forms a customs union with France. The French Government was given complete control and an unrestricted right of exploitation of the coal mines for fifteen years.

Germany renounced her right to govern the territory, and the League of Nations became "trustee" with authority to decide the ultimate sovereignty in 1935, in accordance with a plebiscite in which the inhabitants will choose between union with Germany, union with France, or a continuation of the international status under League supervision. In this plebiscite all Saarois twenty years of age or over, residing in the territory on January 10, 1920, may vote. Voting lists were compiled in 1921. If the basin is returned to Germany, she may repurchase the mines at a price fixed by experts and payable in gold within six months.[1] Meanwhile, the coal deposits are "the complete and absolute property of the French State," with all the accessories and subsidiaries of the mines. Government of the territory was intrusted to a commission representing the League and consisting of five members chosen by the Council: one Frenchman, one Saarois, and three nationals of countries other than France or Germany. The Council appoints the chairman from among the members. The commission has all powers of government formerly exercised by the Reich, Prussia, and Bavaria.[2]

On February 26, 1920, the commission took up the reins of government in the Saar. The first chairman was M. Rault, who spoke no German and who, as a political partisan of Poincaré, had formerly advocated French annexation of the basin. The Belgian member, Major Lambert, was

[1] See Articles 45–50 of the Treaty of Versailles and its Saar Annex.

[2] See Articles 16–33 of the Saar Annex. Article 35 reads as follows: "The League of Nations shall decide on the sovereignty under which the territory is to be placed, taking into account the wishes of the inhabitants as expressed by the voting; (1) if, for the whole or part of the territory, the League of Nations decides in favor of the maintenance of the régime established by the present treaty and this annex, Germany hereby agrees to make such renunciations of her sovereignty in favor of the League of Nations as the latter shall

definitely French in his outlook, and a Danish member, Count Moltke-Huitfeld, had resided for sixteen years in Paris. Aside from Herr von Boch, the Saar representative, the only member who could be suspected of impartiality was R. D. Waugh, a Britisher. This commission made a bad beginning of its administration and was invoking courts-martial and press censorship against its critics by April. The Saar was cut off from the fatherland diplomatically, fiscally, judicially, economically, educationally. The French schools which were established appeared to the inhabitants to be designed to spread French propaganda. Numerous Germans lost their positions to Frenchmen, and within five years the French population grew from 100 to 12,000. A strike of railway workers in October, 1920, caused M. Rault to declare a state of siege, put military forces in command, and call into action a field railway company from the French army on the Rhine. Strike leaders were expelled and public meetings prohibited. There followed a 24-hour general strike of all workers against the Commission. German complaints to the League were met by a ruling that all petitions must be presented first to the commission, which would decide whether they should be submitted to the Council. The locally elected advisory council was largely ignored by the commission. A strike of Saar miners in January, 1922, led to new and severe repressive measures. A delegate sent by the League Council to Saarbrücken refused to see complainants and made his investigation through the commission, with which he was housed. The Council ignored abuses and indicated that the members of the commission would be reappointed for another two years. Another investigation in 1924 revealed that the chairman ruled in a purely arbitrary and oppressive manner and regarded himself as a representative of the French Government rather than of the League. The first period of League administration was assuredly not calculated to enhance the prestige of Geneva in particular or of international administration in general, either in the eyes of the Saarois or of the world at large.

Since 1926 the Saar Governing Commission has tended to conduct itself more in accordance with the spirit of its supposed functions. On April 1, 1926, M. Rault was replaced by M. Morize and Mr. Stephens of Canada became president. In June, 1927, the chairmanship passed to Sir Ernest Wilton of Great Britain, who was in turn succeeded by another Britisher, Mr. Knox, in 1932. High-handed decrees dictated by

deem necessary. It will be the duty of the League of Nations to take appropriate steps to adapt the régime definitively adopted to the permanent welfare of the territory and the general interests; (2) if, for the whole or part of the territory, the League of Nations decides in favor of union with France, Germany hereby agrees to cede to France in accordance with the decision of the League of Nations all rights and title over the territory specified by the League; (3) if, for the whole or part of the territory, the League of Nations decides in favor of union with Germany, it will be the duty of the League of Nations to cause the German Government to be reestablished in the government of the territory specified by the League."

French interests became less frequent, and the advisory council was permitted, within limits, to advise. The commission's alleged efforts to promote French schools and French language have continued to be a source of grievances. The reorganized school system gave French precedence in each grade. In February, 1929, all political parties save the Communists signed a manifesto warning parents against sending their children to the French mine schools. The continued presence of French troops in the basin likewise bred resentment. With Germany in the League, Stresemann brought pressure to bear for reform, and in March, 1927, the Council agreed to a plan for the withdrawal of troops and the substitution of a Railway Defense Corps of 800, of which 600 were French troops, 100 British, and 68 Belgian. Franco-German negotiations over the Saar, initiated by Briand and Stresemann at Thoiry in 1926, have gone on intermittently ever since. In December, 1930, the last of the troops were withdrawn and the Railway Defense Corps was replaced by a special local organization. Practically all Germans in the Saar and in Germany look forward to the recovery of German control in 1935. Pending that happy event, they are prepared to accept League control as a lesser evil than French rule.

The interesting legal question as to whether the League possesses "sovereignty" over the Saar during the 15-year period has led to some differences of opinion among jurists, but it has usually been answered in the affirmative. In any case, Germany's sovereignty, if any, has been suspended. The local administration represents the only clear instance of the actual government of a territory by an agency of the League of Nations. If that government has been unsatisfactory, the fault lies less in the League than in the clash of French and German nationalism in the area itself. French efforts to "Frenchify" the population have, as usual, failed miserably. All observers agree that the plebiscite of 1935 will result in an overwhelming vote for the complete return of the region to Germany. Unofficial French suggestions that the basin be permanently internationalized, or converted into a buffer State, or made the seat of the League[1] seem unlikely to change the final result. Controversy will doubtless arise regarding the repurchase price of the mines, since most Germans will regard this payment as having no more justification than reparations. Meanwhile, the League carries on.

The problem of Danzig has given rise to similar difficulties. This old German trading city at the mouth of the Vistula was detached from Germany by the peace settlement, in order to afford Poland a port on the Baltic. The fact that its population of 200,000 is almost purely German made annexation to Poland seem undesirable, and the Treaty of Versailles therefore provided (Article 102) that "the principal Allied and Associated

[1] See *le Temps*, November 16, 1931.

Powers undertake to establish the town of Danzig . . . as a Free City. It will be placed under the protection of the League of Nations." Germany was required to renounce sovereignty (Article 100), and it was provided that a constitution should be drawn up by representatives of the Free City and a League High Commissioner. The constitution would be under the protection of the League, and disputes between Poland and Danzig would be settled by the high commissioner (Article 103). Germans in the territory were given the option of leaving within twelve months or of renouncing their German citizenship in favor of Danzig citizenship (Articles 105, 106). Sir Reginald Tower was appointed temporary administrator by the Allied Governments in October, 1919, and a Polish-Danzig treaty of forty articles was signed November 9, 1920. By its terms Poland is given control over Danzig's foreign relations, though the League high commissioner is empowered to veto any international arrangement he regards as inconsistent with the treaty or with the status of the Free City. Danzig is included in the Polish customs frontier. The "free zone" of the port is placed under the jurisdiction of the Danzig Port and Waterways Board, with five Danzig and five Polish members and an impartial chairman appointed by the Council, with appeals from its decisions to the League high commissioner. Railways outside of the free zone, with the exception of the municipal tramways, are administered by Poland. Minorities are given the usual protection. All disputes between Poland and Danzig are submitted to the high commissioner, with an appeal to the League Council. The Council assumed the guarantee of the constitution on November 17, 1920, the date of the definite establishment of the Free City by the Allies. Another Danzig-Polish agreement of October 24, 1921 (244 articles), dealt with naturalization, frontier permits, legal questions, communication, etc. An elected constituent assembly of 120 members drew up a draft constitution which was finally approved by the Council in May, 1922. It provides for a popular assembly and a senate. All amendments must be approved by the League Council.

Danzig is thus a kind of protectorate, with Poland and the League sharing the protective function. The League high commissioner, unlike the Saar governing commission, is not an actual administrator, but a kind of umpire or referee between the Free City and the Polish Government. The president of the Port and Waterways Board, however, who is also named by the Council, does have administrative functions.[1] Both parties may appeal from the decisions of these League officials to the Council, whose word is final. In July, 1923, Poland proposed to have all disputes

---

[1] Article 39 of the Danzig-Polish Treaty of November, 1920, specifies: "Any differences arising between Poland and the Free City in regard to the present treaty or any other subsequent agreements, arrangements, or conventions, or to any matter affecting their relations, shall be submitted by one or the other party to the decision of the high com-

brought directly to the Council, but this was refused for obvious reasons. In September, 1929, the Council approved new rules regarding the exercise of the high commissioner's right of vetoing treaties affecting Danzig. Such treaties are discussed by the Council only if the high commissioner considers them inconsistent with existing obligations or if a member of the Council requests their examination. All appeals from decisions of the high commissioner must be sent to him in writing within forty days after decisions are notified to the representatives of both parties at Danzig. He may receive petitions from Danzig citizens, but only for his information. The first high commissioner of the League was General Sir Richard Haking (British), 1920–1922. The post has subsequently been held by Mr. M. S. MacDonnell (Irish), 1923–1925, M. Van Hamel (Dutch), 1926–1929, and Count Manfredi Gravina (Italian), 1929–1932. Count Gravina's successor is Mr. Helmer Rosting. The high commissioner has been obliged to deal with a staggering number of disputes between the Free City and the Polish Government—over questions of domicile and residence, citizenship rights, the legal position of Polish officials, property and ships in Danzig, expulsions of Polish citizens, foreign relations, judicial relations between Danzig and Germany, post boxes, customs dues, admission of Polish war vessels to the harbor, transportation of Polish war materials, etc. The expenses and salaries of the high commissioner and of the president of the board are borne by Poland and Danzig on a fifty-fifty basis. The Council refused Danzig's request in 1927 that these expenses be borne by the League. Many appeals from the decisions of the League officials have been taken to the Council by both parties.

The nearby port of Memel on the Baltic and the adjacent area north of the river Niemen are likewise subject to League supervision. Here, even more obviously than in the other cases, the League appeared on the scene only to accept the results of a political *fait accompli*. This German town of 145,000 population lies between Lithuania and East Prussia. In the name of giving Lithuania access to the sea, Germany was required by the Treaty of Versailles to renounce title to the district in favor of the

---

missioner who shall, if he deems it necessary, refer the matter to the Council of the League of Nations. The two parties retain the right of appeal to the Council."

The Council's report to the Fourth Assembly declared: "The main task of the League, as far as Danzig questions are concerned, since the laying down of the foundation for the status of the Free City, has consisted in the working out of a great many questions of detail, on subjects either not specially foreseen in the acts constituting the Free City or deferred by these acts for further discussion and settlement. Formally, most of the Danzig questions before the Council have had the character of disputes between Poland and the Free City, but it should be understood that a great number of such disputes is due to a practical desire to obtain closer definition of many of the treaty stipulations. In other words, the settlement of a great many of the Danzig-Poland differences is of a constructive character, aiming at the laying down of the foundation of stable conditions in the future."

Allied and Associated Powers. Some type of internationalization was contemplated and the Conference of Ambassadors continued to exercise jurisdiction. The Lithuanian Government, however, learned something of the art of politics from the Polish seizure of its own capital, Vilna, in October, 1920, and from the French occupation of the Ruhr. Early in 1923 Lithuanian irregulars took possession of Memel by a sudden *coup* and defied the Conference of Ambassadors to say them nay. The calculation upon which this act was based was correct. On February 16, 1923, Lithuanian sovereignty over Memel was acknowledged. The Conference of Ambassadors, glad to be rid of a thankless task, referred the final disposition of the territory to the Council of the League, which accepted the Lithuanian occupation. It appointed a commission, headed by an American, Norman H. Davis, which drew up a convention providing for the transfer of the territory to Lithuania.

The "Statute of the Memel Territory," ratified May 17, 1924, provides for local autonomy, with a directorate of five Memel citizens responsible to a locally elected chamber of representatives. The governor is appointed by the president of Lithuania and may veto the acts of the chamber which he regards as contrary to existing international obligations. Memel was declared to be a port of international concern. The harbor board manages the port, subject to the supervision of an economic advisory committee consisting of three members appointed respectively by the Memel, the Lithuanian, and the Polish Governments. Memel undertook to lease to Poland for ninety-nine years a "free zone" necessary for Polish shipping needs. The League exercises supervision only in the sense that appeals may be taken to the Council in the event of disputes over the recommendations of the economic advisory committee. In the 1925 election the parties favoring a plebiscite to determine the sovereignty of the territory polled 47,466 votes and won 29 seats in the chamber, as compared with 3,677 votes for the pro-Lithuanians. Friction between the Lithuanian Government and the German population has been chronic ever since. No scheme of international supervision seems likely to ameliorate the situation in the near future.

Here, as in the Saar and in the mandates, the abstract merits of international administration through the League are completely overshadowed by political considerations having nothing to do with the international administration but growing out of deep currents of national interests and policies running counter to one another. In Danzig and throughout Germany the status of the Free City is no less hotly resented than the transfer of the "corridor" to Poland and the loss to the Reich of Memel and the Saar. These instances of international administration by the League all involve the perpetuation of treaty terms which appear utterly iniquitous to all patriotic Germans. The loss of the Saar, though temporary, is the more bitterly resented because of the other provisions of the treaty requiring German coal deliveries and pecuniary reparations for France, involving, in German eyes, more than adequate compensation for the destruction of the French mines. The League administration is viewed as a thin disguise for predatory French imperialism. Similarly, the loss of Danzig is the more keenly felt because the Polish corridor already affords Poland access to the Baltic without Danzig. The city itself has prospered as a Polish port of entry, but the construction of the Polish harbor and naval base of Gdynia in the adjacent corridor is viewed with alarm. No settlement of these issues through treaty modification of a nature satisfactory to German opinion would be acceptable to Polish nationalists. And the perpetuation of the *status quo* is equally unacceptable to German nationalists. The League here falls between two stools. The dilemma with which it is confronted appears extremely difficult of solution. The League is expressly committed to the perpetuation of the hegemony of France and her allies, as incorporated into the 1919 peace settlement. There is no danger to the League in this situation, so long as this hegemony is effectively maintained, for the League must rest upon the realities of power politics. But if the supremacy of the French bloc should be undermined by unexpected accretions to the power of the revisionist bloc, the crucial question will arise as to whether the League can be utilized to bring about pacific readjustments. Upon the future answer to this question hinges the future of the League itself as an agency of treaty enforcement and international administration.

2. THE PROMOTION OF INTERNATIONAL COOPERATION

The League is submerged in immensities, haunted by the shades of ancient timorousness, entangled in its own complexities. It is prolific in figures, commissions, statistics, preliminary to nothing. It travails like a mountain and brings forth—a blank report. Its discussions, its oratory have their aspects of façade, futility, waste. Yet there are achievements both valuable and inconceivable without this particular agency. This is enough to save it. It is kept to its work, as is every honest institution, by the unremitting spur of its original motive. That motive is in no sense a *beau geste*, nor a grandiloquent phrase, nor a dreamy sentiment, but an item of suffering or despair in some corner of an ill-connected world. All this paper work, bureau business, committee vaporing stand for the destinies of unique lives which will be either known about, talked about, and eventually helped or else silenced, crushed without recourse because some one of those interests we call political, unconscious if only by its magnitude, sweeps ignorantly over their heads.—WILLIAM E. HOCKING, *The Spirit of World Politics.*

The "second League"—that for the promotion of general international cooperation in dealing with technical and social problems—has in practice been the most significant of the three Leagues thus far and it is in this field that the most solid achievements are to be counted to Geneva's credit. Attention has already been called to the rapid expansion of the field of international relations to cover more and more matters formerly of only domestic concern.[1] The enormous multiplication of international contacts and the rapid growth in the economic, technical, and cultural interdependence of nations have, to an ever greater degree, made purely national action inadequate in dealing with a great variety of public problems. Some of these problems arise out of the necessity of facilitating international communication and transportation by land, sea, and air. Others, such as problems of health and sanitation, labor legislation, the trade in opium, the traffic in women and children, intellectual cooperation, commerce and finance, arise out of the obvious inefficacy of national action in dealing with problems which have become international in scope. Successful international action in dealing with any problem requires, in the first place, a willingness among nations to cooperate and, in the second place, the creation of effective agencies to achieve cooperation. Without common goals and purposes a will to cooperate is lacking. Without machinery and procedures of common action the will remains unimplemented and futile. The creation of the will to cooperate, *i.e.*, the reconciliation of conflicting interests and the formulation of common policies and programs, is a task of international politics. The implementation of the will, *i.e.*, the execution of policies and programs already agreed upon, is the task of international administration. The efficacy of international administrative agencies is dependent not only on their technical adequacy from the viewpoint of function and structure, but also, and more significantly, upon the scope of interests with regard to which States are willing to cooperate.

The League of Nations was at the outset designed to promote such cooperation and to perfect international administration by coordinating the activities of existing agencies and by creating new agencies to deal with new problems.[2] The rise and organization of the public international unions have been discussed above in terms of the analysis already suggested. It was hoped at the beginning that all the existing international

[1] See pp. 241–243 above.
[2] Article 24 of the League Covenant is as follows: "(1) There shall be placed under the direction of the League all international bureaus already established by general treaties if the parties to such treaties consent. All such international bureaus and all commissions for the regulation of matters of international interest hereafter constituted shall be placed under the direction of the League. (2) In all matters of international interest which are regulated by general conventions but which are not placed under the control of international bureaus or commissions, the Secretariat of the League shall, subject to the consent of the Council and if desired by the parties, collect and distribute all relevant information and shall render any other assistance which may be necessary or desirable. (3) The Council may include as part of the expenses of the Secretariat the expenses of any bureau or commission which is placed under the direction of the League."

unions would be placed "under the direction of the League." In this fashion, private interests and administrative officials would be brought into direct and fruitful contact at Geneva for purposes of consultation and coordination. In the pursuit of this objective, the signatory States which had by convention established various international organizations agreed to League direction of their activities, as contemplated in Article 24 of the Covenant. The organizations which have from time to time availed themselves of this opportunity include the International Hydrographic Bureau, the International Association for the Promotion of Child Welfare, the International Commission for Air Navigation, the Central International Office for the Control of the Liquor Traffic in Africa, the International Bureau for Information and Inquiries regarding Relief for Foreigners, the International Educational Cinematographic Institute, the International Institute of Intellectual Cooperation, the International Institute for the Unification of Private Law, and the International Institute of Agriculture. In other cases the abstention from the League of the United States and certain other States created a difficulty which has not yet been resolved. States not members of the League but signatories of conventions establishing international unions and bureaus have for the most part been unwilling to agree to the direction of these organizations from Geneva. Most of the public international unions accordingly remain outside of the fold. Despite this unfortunate limitation, the League Secretariat and the various technical organizations at Geneva have greatly increased the efficiency of the organizations which have joined in the new arrangement and have likewise contributed appreciably, through close informal cooperation, to that of the organizations still outside.

The practical efficacy of such cooperation depends upon the willingness of States to subordinate national interests to general interests and to act jointly in the execution of a joint program. With respect to certain problems, *e.g.*, public health, the common interests of all States are so obvious that the general will to cooperate is ever present and the problem can be dealt with on an administrative level. With respect to others, *e.g.*, armaments, the divergencies of national interests are so great that cooperation is almost impossible to achieve and the problems remain "political" problems within the realm of competitive power politics and therefore not susceptible of administrative treatment. Space does not permit an adequate treatment of all the problems of international cooperation which fall within the purview of Geneva. The major problems may be reviewed, however, in the order of the relative difficulty of cooperation. This order involves a rough ranking of the problems in terms of the degree to which States have become aware of common interests and have manifested a disposition to act together in the promotion of such interests.

A survey will accordingly be attempted of international efforts to deal, through the League machinery, with problems of health, communications and transit, codification of international law, intellectual cooperation, protection of women and children, control of the drug traffic, and commerce and finance.

The health organization of the League was anticipated in Article 23 of the Covenant, which stated that the members of the League "will endeavor to take steps in matters of international concern for the prevention and control of disease." In February, 1920, the Council summoned an International Conference of Health Experts to draw up a plan. A temporary epidemics commission was set up to cooperate with the governments of eastern Europe in coping with post-war pestilences. A provisional health committee was set up meanwhile in Geneva. The scheme of organization which it drew up in May, 1923, in cooperation with the Permanent Committee of the International Office of Public Hygiene, was adopted by the Fourth Assembly. The health organization was set up in the form of three agencies: the health committee, a nonpolitical and nongovernmental body of twenty medical specialists and public health officials, meeting twice a year to draw up programs and give expert advice; the advisory council, appointed by the Permanent Committee of the International Office of Public Hygiene; and the health section, which is the executive agency of the organization and an integral part of the League Secretariat. Through these organs and various subsidiary bodies, expert information is gathered and circularized from a central point, administrative officials are brought into constant contact with one another, and national public health services are coordinated and geared together into an effectively integrated international system. This system has performed numerous useful functions which could be performed by no other type of agency. It has established the Epidemiological Intelligence Service to publish reports on health conditions in eastern Europe and Russia in monthly and annual bulletins. An auxiliary agency—the Eastern Epidemiological Intelligence Center—was established at Singapore in 1925. The information which it supplies and the results of its research are invaluable in checking epidemics by timely quarantine measures at the proper point. The health organization has likewise made useful contributions to the standardization of morbidity and mortality statistics. Study tours, research centers, special investigations, education in hygiene, technical work in preventive medicine, standardization of serums, and cooperation with insurance organizations have all constituted a part of these international activities.

With regard to international problems of communication and transit, as with regard to public health, all States have certain general common interests which facilitate collaboration. By Article 23 of the Covenant, the League members agreed to "make provision to secure and maintain freedom of communications and transit." Other portions of the peace treaties likewise conferred special functions on the League in this field. A number of conferences during the year 1920 paved the way for the creation of the Communications and Transit Organization of the League by the first General Conference, held at Barcelona in March and April, 1921. The conference became the chief agency of the organization. It consists of governmental representatives and meets every four years at the call of the League Council, to draw up recommendations, conventions, and resolutions. The advisory and technical committee is a smaller body of experts which meets twice a year. It directs the work of the organization, prepares the agenda of the conferences, supervises the execution of the conference resolutions, and settles disputes over transit matters on its own initiative or in cooperation with the Permanent Court. The secretariat of the organization is the transit and communications section of the Secretariat of the League. Here again one of the prime functions of the organization is the coordination of the activities of existing agencies and services, national and international. The second general conference was held in Geneva November–December, 1923, the third in August, 1927, and the fourth in October, 1931, with numerous lesser meetings during the intervals between conferences. Several general conventions, dealing with various aspects of international communications, have been signed and generally ratified. The political obstacles in the way of effective cooperation have been relatively few. The scope of these activities may be suggested by the following enumeration of problems with regard to which international action of one kind or another has been taken: passports, road transit, commercial motor traffic, air traffic, sleeping-car services, competition between railways and waterways, distribution of hydroelectric power, long-distance telephone communication, telegraphy and radio, inland navigation, registration of vessels, unification of river law, smuggling, buoys and lighthouses, double taxation on sea-borne trade, tonnage measurements of ocean ships, uniform nomenclature of goods, transport of periodicals and newspapers, and calendar reform.

Comparable progress has been achieved in the promotion of international intellectual cooperation, though work in this field has been largely experimental and its results can scarcely be measured by such definite standards as are available with regard to public health and communication. In 1921 the Council, on the motion of M. Leon Bourgeois, proposed the appointment of a committee "to deal with questions of intellectual cooperation and education." The Second Assembly dropped the reference to education, and the Committee on Intellectual Cooperation was established in 1922. It consists of eminent scholars in various fields of intellectual interest. Such pre-war organizations as the International Association of Academies and the International Research Council had been shattered, and it was not until 1926 that a genuine international organization was again created in any one field of learning, with the establishment of the International Committee on Historical Studies. This general lack of organization rendered the new committee's task difficult. In 1924 the committee issued an appeal for financial aid from outside sources. M. Bergson, the French philosopher and first chairman of the committee, declared in his plea: "In thus coming to the assistance of nations whose intellectual life is endangered, you will be strengthening the sense of professional brotherhood . . . you will be taking effective and practical action to promote intellectual cooperation, and above all you will be helping to support civilization in the struggle against deadly perils which threaten."

In response to this appeal, the French Government offered the committee an annual stipend and quarters for an international institute. This proposal was accepted by the committee and by the League Council and Assembly, and in November, 1925, the International Institute of Intellectual Cooperation began its work in Paris. Its governing body is the Committee on Intellectual Cooperation, with a French chairman. In one sense this arrangement represented a phase of the French Government's program of cultural propaganda throughout the world. The Italian Government made similar arrangements in establishing at Rome the International Institute for the Unification of Private Law in 1928 and the International Educational Cinematographic Institute in 1929. Some thirty-five national committees on intellectual cooperation have been established. The institute has dealt with such problems as an international language, publicity of chemical discoveries applicable to warfare, status of foreign students, financial aid for intellectuals, promotion of scientific publications, the unification of archaeological and scientific nomenclatures, international coordination of libraries and museums, encouragement of international studies, popular arts, bibliography, protection of literary and scientific property, translations of literary works, and international equivalents of academic degrees. Apart from these activities the League has sought to encourage the instruction of youth in its own aims. Difficulties have resulted from differences in national attitudes and institutions, but much has been achieved in this direction. This much has been little, however, compared with the inculcation into youth everywhere of the ideology of militant nationalism.[1]

The international protection of women and children has also been a significant League function almost from the beginning. By Article 23 the League members agreed to "entrust the League with the general super-

[1] "No doubt this task of adjustment, with all its accompanying psychological difficulties, is one of great delicacy—more delicate, perhaps, in its own sphere than political

vision over the execution of agreements with regard to the traffic in women and children." Efforts to suppress prostitution and the "white-slave traffic" were well under way in the second half of the nineteenth century. They centered at first about governmental efforts to prevent the spread of venereal disease. In 1904, following a private international congress of 1899, a public international conference was held to facilitate the exchange of information between governments regarding "the pro-curation of women or girls with a view to their debauchery in a foreign country." In 1910, at another public conference, recommendations were made for the punishment of procurers and their extradition. By 1920 only sixteen States were parties to the 1904 agreement and nine to the 1910 convention. In June–July, 1921, an International Conference on the White Slave Traffic was held at Geneva. At the Second Assembly its recom-mendations were embodied in a convention which, by 1929, had been ratified by thirty-four States. Various suggestions for the regulation and restriction of prostitution were made to the Council, which, in January, 1922, organized the Advisory Committee on the Traffic in Women and Children. In 1924 this agency was reorganized as the Advisory Commis-sion for Protection of Children and Young People, with two committees, one on child welfare and the other on the traffic in women. The com-mittees are composed of governmental representatives and of advisory members from private organizations. Annual reports from governments are considered at the yearly meetings. With the aid of $75,000 donated by the American Social Hygiene Bureau, an inquiry was launched into the extent of the commercialized traffic in prostitutes in Europe, the Mediterranean, and America. Much interesting information was gathered in this fashion and the inquiry was extended to the Far East in 1930, with the aid of another gift of $125,000 from the same source. On the basis of such information, numerous recommendations have been made. The committees have urged the abolition of licensed houses as one means of combating the international traffic. In September, 1923, a conference was held in Geneva on the traffic in obscene publications. It drew up a conven-tion for the suppression of this traffic, which was ratified by thirty-five States by 1929. No agreement was reached on birth-control propaganda, which some delegates wished to have suppressed. Differences of national *mores* and in governmental policies have been obstacles to the success of these efforts, but it is generally agreed that more has been accomplished

adjustment dealt with under Article 11 or 15 of the Covenant. Happily, however, it is taking place under conditions which allow time for growth and harmonization. It is perhaps not too much to say that it involves the severest test to which the method of cooperation is being subjected during these early years. Upon its success or failure largely depends the fulfillment of the promise held out in the Covenant of the permanent elimination of war from human affairs." League of Nations, *Ten Years of World Cooperation*, 1930, pp. 328–329.

in a single decade under League auspices than in the preceding century.

League efforts to regulate or suppress the traffic in opium and other dangerous drugs have encountered similar difficulties, but have met with a considerable measure of success. The Hague Opium Convention of 1912 bound its signatories to control the production and distribution of raw opium and to suppress, by gradual stages, the use of smoking opium. This convention failed to secure general ratification, but its ratification by the signatories of the peace treaties was provided for through a clause to this effect. Article 23 of the Covenant specifies that the League members "will entrust the League with the general supervision over the execution to agreements with regard to . . . the traffic in opium and other dangerous drugs." The impotence of the central government in war-torn China has led to an expansion of poppy growing in many provinces. Throughout the world the whole problem has become more serious than it was before 1914. In accordance with a resolution of the First Assembly, an Advisory Committee on the Traffic in Opium and other Dangerous Drugs was set up to assist League members in discharging their obligations. It now consists of representatives of twenty governments. Opium Conferences were held in Geneva in 1924 and 1925 and drew up an agreement and convention. The American and Chinese representatives withdrew, however, because no definite date was fixed for the prohibition of opium smoking in the Far East and no effective provisions were made for the necessary drastic reduction in the manufacture of opium and other drugs which were being produced throughout the world in a quantity roughly ten times that required for scientific and medical use. The signatories of the convention—the British Empire, France, India, Japan, Portugal, The Netherlands, and Siam—agreed to suppress smuggling within five years and to suppress smoking within fifteen years if sufficient progress had been made to permit this. The Indian Government refused to forbid poppy cultivation. A Central Opium Board was established to gather information through quarterly reports from governments. By 1930 the Geneva convention had been ratified by thirty-seven States. Later efforts have been made to limit production by a system of quotas. Investigations have been made in Persia and in China. A large volume of illicit traffic in narcotics continues, however, and League efforts have not yet been effective in dealing with this social evil, because of the absence of any general international agreements on adequate measures of suppression.

The systematic codification of international law has likewise been an important League function, though serious difficulties have also been encountered in this field. The Fifth Assembly, on September 22, 1924, requested the Council to convene a committee of experts "representing the main forms of civilization and the principal legal systems of the world" to prepare a provisional list of subjects suitable for codification, to solicit comments from governments, and to report to the Council on the procedures to be followed. A committee of distinguished jurists was chosen. It met in Geneva in April, 1925, and again in January, 1926, and March, 1927. It selected seven subjects as suitable for international action: (1) nationality, (2) territorial waters, (3) diplomatic privileges and immunities, (4) responsibility of States for damage to persons or property of foreigners, (5) procedure of international conferences and procedure for the drafting and conclusion of treaties, (6) piracy, and (7) exploitation of sea products. International codification conferences were recommended for all of these, save (5) and (7), which were referred to special investigators. The Council recommended omission of (3) and (6). The Assembly, in September, 1927, approved action on (1), (2), and (4). Questionnaires were despatched to governments by the Secretary-general. The Eighth Assembly likewise discussed the problems involved. After further preparation, the first meeting of a general conference on codification was held at The Hague in March, 1930, with forty-eight States represented. There was much controversy and little agreement in the subcommittees. The drafts reported out were inevitably compromises between divergent views. Two draft conventions on nationality and territorial waters were embodied in the final act of April 12, 1930. The convention on nationality sought to abolish Statelessness and double nationality and to achieve uniform rules regarding expatriation and nationality of married women and of children. The convention on territorial waters dealt with the limits of maritime jurisdiction, bays, roadsteads, ports, islands, straits, rivers, and passage of warships. On the whole, the results of the first codification conference were disappointing, since agreements were reached on only a few relatively unimportant subjects and many delays have taken place in ratification. Codification is necessarily a slow process, because of differing national interests and interpretations. Its wisdom is doubted by some authorities. But it is probable that most future progress in this direction will be achieved through the League.

The obstacles to successful international cooperation have been even more apparent in the financial and economic activities of the League. In so far as these have been of a humanitarian nature, they have been reasonably effective. Funds have been raised and expended under League auspices for famine relief, repatriation of war prisoners, rehabilitation of revolutionary and war refugees, and general international relief work in various parts of the world. Useful work has likewise been done at Geneva in arranging international loans for needy States. In March, 1921, the financial committee of the League was entrusted with the seemingly endless and impossible task of achieving the financial reconstruction of Austria, but it was unable to accomplish anything, largely because of the refusal of the American Government to release liens on loans already made. Following further disintegration of Austrian economy and finance, the problem was again referred to the League in 1922 and a Financial Protocol was drawn up, whereby Austria was obliged to accept certain international controls and limitations upon her freedom of action in return for a League of Nations loan of £26,000,000, guaranteed by ten States. This arrangement accomplished its immediate purpose and was applied, with slight modification, to Hungary, which received a £10,000,-000 loan in 1923, to the Greek Refugee Settlement scheme, for which a loan of £9,700,000 was raised, and to the Bulgarian Refugee scheme. These and other League loans, totaling £83,000,000, were all defaulted in the Great Depression (with the exception of the obligations of Danzig and Esthonia), with resulting losses to investors and damage to the prestige of the League. The efforts of the League, through its financial and economic committees, to deal with general international problems of currency, tariffs, and trade barriers have been reviewed elsewhere.[1] These efforts have been singularly unsuccessful, not because of any defect in League methods or machinery, but because of irreconcilable differences of national interests and policies.

To sum up, the whole League system, with its commissions, institutes, and technical organizations, has proved enormously valuable as an agency of international cooperation and administration with regard to those problems concerning which States are aware of their common interests and are disposed to act together to serve common purposes. Obstacles have been encountered in the form of the limitations of national machinery for dealing with many problems, for without effective national administration there can be no effectively coordinated international administration. In a world of individualistic, bourgeois societies, the scope of effective governmental action in dealing with social and economic problems is definitely limited. Differing methods of national control are also a difficulty. But, more significantly, success in these various enterprises has been limited by the circumstance that States have no awareness of common interests and no disposition to cooperate with regard to many serious problems. In these fields they are aware only of exclusive national interests, and they are disposed to deal with one another in accordance with the traditional symbols and patterns of competitive power politics. The problems of international politics, in the narrowest sense, *i.e.*, the problems dealt with in terms of national power, prestige, and profit values, are precisely the problems which most urgently demand solution. These are the problems of territorial rivalry, armament ambitions,

[1] See pp. 556–559 above.

economic and political nationalism, and competing capitalisms and imperialisms. Here are the seeds of war and of world disaster. These problems cannot be dealt with administratively by the use of the League technique, because there is no adequate consensus of common values to serve as a basis for cooperative action. Bureaus, conferences, commissions, and other pieces of administrative machinery, however cleverly devised, are useless when the will to use them is lacking. The willingness or unwillingness of States to utilize the machinery at Geneva for the solution of these problems will determine the ultimate place of the League in contemporary international relations.

3. THE PREVENTION OF WAR

The final cause, end, or design of men, who naturally love liberty, and dominion over others, in the introduction of that restraint upon themselves, in which we see them live in commonwealths, is the foresight of their own preservation, and of a more contented life thereby; that is to say, of getting themselves out from that miserable condition of war, which is necessarily consequent to the natural passions of men, when there is no visible power to keep them in awe, and tie them by fear of punishment to the performance of their covenants.—THOMAS HOBBES, *Leviathan*.

. . . the League must either develop further or be destroyed. It can only develop by the continuous restriction of the rights of individual States. What in fact is involved in its successful evolution is its expression of a power, within an increasingly wider field, to limit the subject matter upon which States are entitled to legislate upon their own initiative. It must assume authority to lay down ways of behavior for States in all matters of common concern to international society.—HAROLD LASKI, *Politics*.

The third League—that which is dedicated to the preservation of peace between States—is rightly regarded in lay circles as the most important of the three. The accomplishments attained through the Geneva machinery in the fields of treaty enforcement and general international cooperation have thus far been of major significance if the League is evaluated in terms of its concrete contributions toward serving the common purposes of nations. But in the long perspective of the future, the League will stand or fall not by what it does to discourage opium smoking and prostitution, to protect minorities, to supervise mandates, to promote higher standards of public health, etc., but by what it does or fails to do toward ending war between States. In the past the rents torn by war in the fabric of international collaboration have been repaired and the fabric itself has been constantly strengthened. Even under modern conditions it can still survive minor wars or hostilities between minor States called by some other name. But in the future the whole fabric itself will be torn to shreds if war occurs again between Great Powers. It is conceivable that the League might be reconstituted and might continue to perform its indispensable administrative functions after another world catastrophe of the magnitude of 1914–1918. A new general war between Great Powers, however, would be enormously more destructive and disruptive than was the last conflict. Its occurrence would reduce the whole theory of the League to a mockery in the eyes of those who have pinned their hopes upon it. Its consequences would be so catastrophic that the League itself would probably collapse in the general wreckage, as that other and far more powerful symbol of world unity—the Roman Empire—collapsed in the wreckage of classical civilization. Unless the League can prevent war, it can have no enduring future.

At the outset of any consideration of this most crucial of the League's functions, it cannot be too strongly emphasized that the League itself is little more than the sum of the States which compose it. It is not a super-State or an entity which has reality apart from the sovereignties which have created it. All its organs and all its activities rest upon agreements between States. The Secretariat, the technical organizations, and the Permanent Court may appear to exist independently of States, but they have only such functions as the States of the world are willing that they should perform. This obvious characteristic of the League system is often forgotten by those who criticize "the League" for its failures and shortcomings. "The League" is nothing more than a method of cooperation between States. If the cooperation is unsuccessful, the fault usually lies not in any defects of the method or the machinery, but in the unwillingness of States to subordinate their competitive wills-to-power to the service of common interests. In treaty enforcement and in efforts to deal with social and humanitarian problems, States have been willing to yield up a large portion of their "sovereignty," *i.e.*, their freedom to act independently by self-help, each in its own interests, in order to make possible mutually advantageous collaboration through the League organs. In the realm of political and economic questions they have been much less willing to do this. If the League is tested in the balance and ultimately found wanting, responsibility will lie not with the conscientious officials of the Secretariat nor with the statesmen who have sought to use the League, nor yet with the League's own agencies, but with the peoples and governments and ruling classes of the nation-states who place national interests above the cause of peace and above the interests of the still inchoate world community which is striving to be born.

The general principles and procedures for preventing war which are incorporated in the League system have already been discussed in other connections. Here it will suffice merely to enumerate them once more and to examine in some detail their functioning in concrete situations, with a view toward forming an estimate of what has been accomplished and what is likely to be accomplished in the future. The League system for the preservation of peace is a synthesis of almost all available solutions and procedures. It embodies (Articles 12–13) solemn international engagements for the renunciation of war, though the "gap in the Covenant" is not yet closed and the member States are still free, so far as the Covenant is concerned, to resort to war in certain contingencies.[1] It embodies (Articles 11, 13–15, 17) utilization of the established modes of pacific settlement—arbitration, adjudication, conciliation—through the Council and the Permanent Court.[2] It involves (Article 10) an international guarantee of the independence and integrity of the members.[3] It involves, in addition (Article 16), the mobilization of international economic and military sanctions against peace-breaking States.[4] It likewise involves efforts to promote disarmament (Article 8), to insure open diplomacy by registration and publication of treaties (Article 18), to bring about the reconsideration of treaties which have become inapplicable (Article 19), and to promote in general the pacific cooperation of States through the Council and the Assembly in the settlement of their controversies and the solution of their common problems.

The actual procedures which have developed in the application of these principles to concrete diplomatic crises likely to lead to war can best be described by a survey of a few of the more important and typical disputes which have been dealt with through this machinery. A review of all the controversies of which the League has taken cognizance since 1920 would require more space than can here be given to the subject. A few representative cases—some dealt with successfully and others unsuccessfully—will reveal the League at work and will indicate the advantages and limitations of its procedure. The development through the League of the well-established practices of arbitration and adjudication for dealing with "justiciable" or "nonpolitical" controversies may first be reviewed. Consideration may then be given to the more difficult question of "political" disputes and to the procedures of investigation, conciliation, and international action which have been developed at Geneva to deal with such problems.

As regards arbitration, the League machinery has been instrumental in promoting the conclusion of bilateral arbitration treaties which, in some respects, represent an advance on pre-war practices. The General Act of 1928 and the draft arbitration treaties prepared at Geneva are especially noteworthy in this connection, despite their limited acceptance thus far. The League machinery itself, however, does not include new arbitral agencies. The Hague tribunal remains available, and States remain free

[1] See pp. 675–676 above.
[2] See pp. 219–224 above.
[3] See pp. 719–720 above.
[4] See pp. 718f. above.

to set up special arbitral tribunals for the settlement of particular controversies. There are few disputes, moreover, which are suitable for arbitration and not suitable for adjudication. The latter procedure is tending more and more to replace the former, and it is unlikely that the cause of peace will be furthered by any new developments in the field of arbitration proper.[1]

In the field of adjudication, it may truly be said that the League has achieved more in a decade than was achieved in all previous time. Prior to 1914, international adjudication was limited to the Central American Court of Justice and to the unrealized projects of world courts, sponsored from time to time by numerous peace organizations, by the American Government, by the second Hague Conference, and by the London Naval Conference of 1909. With the creation of the Permanent Court of International Justice at The Hague in 1922, there was brought into being for the first time a genuinely international judicial tribunal of world-wide scope, capable of adjudicating such controversies as States might be willing to submit to it. The establishment of this tribunal was contemplated in Article 14 of the Covenant and its Statute was drawn up by a committee of jurists appointed by the League Council. While it exists independently of the League, it is in a real sense the judicial branch of the League system, as has been indicated in the earlier account of its structure.[2] It is entrusted with the making of decisions in controversies which States submit to it and with the handing down of advisory opinion requested by the Council and Assembly of the League. Its place in the whole League scheme can be indicated by a survey of its jurisdiction and by summaries of a few representative cases which have come before it.

The original proposal of the jurists that the Permanent Court be given "compulsory" or obligatory jurisdiction was rejected by the Council and Assembly. The Statute, in its final form, gives the court "voluntary" jurisdiction. It can hear only such cases as States are willing to submit to it. It has no authority to compel States to submit controversies if they are unwilling to do so, and the Statute itself does not obligate its signatories to submit any particular dispute, or disputes in any specified category, to adjudication. By Article 36, however—the "optional clause"—States may at their discretion commit themselves, definitely and in advance, to adjudicate certain types of controversies with States accepting a like obligation.[3] The types of disputes covered by

[1] On the distinction between arbitration and adjudication, see pp. 216–218 above.

[2] See pp. 219–221 above.

[3] Article 36 of the statute: "The jurisdiction of the court comprises all cases which the parties refer to it and all matters specially provided for in treaties and conventions in force.

"The members of the League of Nations and the States mentioned in the annex to the convention may, either when signing or ratifying the protocol to which the present

the optional clause are those relating to treaty interpretation, international law, breaches of international obligation, measures of reparation for such breaches, and interpretations of the court's own judgments. Almost fifty States have signed the optional clause and over thirty have ratified it. These States have bound themselves to submit their disputes with one another, falling within the specified categories, to the jurisdiction of the court. If one signatory party claims that a particular dispute is covered by the clause and the other dissents, the court itself decides whether it has jurisdiction. Unfortunately, however, this broad commitment has been qualified by various interpretations and reservations attached by some of the signatories, which leave the way open, as do so many arbitration treaties, to the contention that a particular dispute does not, after all, fall within the category of justiciable controversies as defined by Article 36 of the statute. Apart from the optional clause, the court, like the League machinery as a whole, simply affords States an opportunity for pacific cooperation. It does not in any way compel them to accept its jurisdiction in particular instances, except in so far as they pledge themselves to do so in treaty engagements. All of the peace treaties contain pledges to submit to the court certain kinds of disputes arising out of their terms, as do the minority treaties, the League mandates, certain bilateral arbitration and conciliation treaties, and a large number of multilateral conventions.

The procedure of the court is much the same whether it is reaching a decision or preparing an advisory opinion. Decisions are the outcome of litigation initiated by disputing States. Opinions are delivered only at the request of the Council or Assembly of the League. In both cases the court applies international law, based upon agreements, custom, reason, and authority, to the conflicting claims of rights before it. Proceedings are public, on the basis of written and oral arguments, and judgments are handed down by a majority vote of the fifteen members of the court, with dissenters free to submit minority opinions. Decisions are binding upon the litigants and dispose definitively of the cases submitted. Opinions are purely advisory and have no legally binding effect, though they will necessarily loom large in the deliberations of the Council and Assembly.

statute is adjoined, or at a later moment, declare that they recognize as compulsory *ipso facto* and without special agreement, in relation to any other member or State accepting the same obligation, the jurisdiction of the court in all or any of the classes of legal disputes concerning: (1) the interpretation of a treaty, (2) any question of international law, (3) the existence of any fact which, if established, would constitute a breach of an international obligation, (4) the nature or extent of the reparation to be made for the breach of an international obligation.

"The declaration referred to above may be made unconditionally or on condition of reciprocity on the part of several or certain members or States, or for a certain time.

"In the event of a dispute as to whether the court has jurisdiction, the matter shall be settled by the decision of the court."

Neither type of judgment is a precedent for future judgments, but the court is nevertheless building up a solid body of consistent case law in international jurisprudence which in time should minimize appreciably the moot points and the unexplored areas in this branch of legal science.

Up to the close of 1932 the court had handed down some fifty decisions and advisory opinions.[1] A few representative instances of each will indicate the types of controversies which the court is called upon to consider and the types of judgments which it arrives at. The four following decisions involve respectively the interpretation of a peace treaty, a question of general international law and treaty interpretation, the application of a minority treaty, and the definition of the jurisdiction of an international commission. The court, like most judicial bodies, seldom has difficulty in arriving at conclusions, though it often has considerable difficulty in agreeing upon the reasons to be given therefor. Its decisions and opinions are always reasoned documents, citing authorities and precedents for its conclusions and often accompanied by opinions, dissenting either from the conclusions or from the reasons given for them by the majority of the judges.

The first case submitted to the court for a decision was that of the steamship *Wimbledon*. This vessel, of English registry but temporarily chartered by a French company, took on 4,200 tons of munitions at Salonica, consigned to the Polish naval base at Danzig. On March 21, 1921, it was refused passage through the Kiel Canal, on the ground that the neutrality orders of the German Government issued in connection with the Russo-Polish War of 1920 forbade the shipment of war supplies through Germany for either of the belligerents. Since the Treaty of Riga had not then been ratified, Russia and Poland were still technically in a state of war. The French Government protested against the German action, on the ground that Article 380 of the Treaty of Versailles required Germany to maintain the canal "free and open to the vessels of commerce and war of all nations at peace with Germany on terms of entire equality." The *Wimbledon* was obliged to proceed through the Danish Straits and was delayed eleven days on its voyage to Danzig. On January 16, 1923, Governments of Great Britain, France, Italy, and Japan, with Poland subsequently joining in the plea, applied to the court under the Treaty of Versailles to pass upon claims for damages against Germany of 174,082 francs for the wrongful detention of the steamer. The German Government, as required by the treaty, accepted the court's jurisdiction and named Herr Schucking as a German national judge to sit with the court, as it was entitled to do. With two judges and Herr Schucking dissenting, the court held that Germany was not entitled to apply her neutrality regulations to the Kiel Canal and that she must pay the French Government, within three months, 140,749 francs and 35 centimes, with 6 per cent interest from the day of judgment.

The case of the denunciation of the treaty of November 2, 1865, between China and Belgium was initiated by the Belgian Government to determine the legality of the action of the Chinese Government on April 16, 1926, in informing

[1] All of the decisions and advisory opinions are listed and summarized in brief form, with documentary references, in Appendix V, pp. 890–896 below.

Belgium that it would regard the Belgian extraterritoriality treaty as non-operative after October 27, 1926. The treaty in question specified (Article 46) that the Belgian Government, but not the Chinese Government, might after ten years give six months' notice of modifications in its terms, failing which the treaty would continue for successive 10-year periods. Belgium contended that China had no right to denounce this engagement unilaterally. China objected to submitting the question to the court, but since both parties had ratified Article 36 of the statute the court took jurisdiction and handed down a provisional "Order" on January 8, 1927, upholding the Belgian contention and safeguarding the treaty rights of Belgian nationals in China. China failed to respond to the court's plea to file its counter-case, despite five successive extensions of time. The matter was finally settled by a new Sino-Belgian treaty, signed at Nanking November 22, 1928. Following its ratification, the Belgian Government withdrew its original action. This incompleted case raises the interesting and still unanswered question as to what action the court might take with regard to a signatory of the optional clause, when such a signatory refuses to accept the court's jurisdiction and ignores its orders.

The Upper Silesian minorities case was initiated by a suit of the German Government on January 2, 1928, claiming that the Polish Government, under the convention of May 15, 1922, had no right to interfere with minority schools in Upper Silesia by striking off children's names from the registers and by bringing pressure to bear on parents to send their children to Polish schools. Prior to the initiation of the suit, the problem had been considered by the League Council, with results unsatisfactory to the Reich. The Polish counter-case asked the dismissal of the German claim, and the Polish rejoinder asked the court to decline jurisdiction. On April 26, 1928, the court asserted its jurisdiction and by a vote of eight to four held that the convention bestowed "upon every national the right freely to declare according to his conscience, and on his personal responsibility, that he does or does not belong to a racial, linguistic, or religious minority and to declare what is the language of a pupil or child for whose education he is legally responsible." The court further held that "the question whether a person does or does not belong to a . . . minority [is] subject to no verification, dispute, pressure, or hindrance whatever on the part of the authorities." The court, however, was not called upon to pass on any particular measures alleged to be discriminatory, but only upon the general principle. Its decision appears to have been instrumental in bringing about the partial modification of the Polish policy of which the German Government complained.

The case relating to the territorial jurisdiction of the International Commission of the River Oder arose out of Article 341 of the Treaty of Versailles, which placed the Oder under the administration of a commission composed of Polish, Prussian, Czech, British, French, Danish, and Swedish representatives. The commission was authorized to define the section of the river and its tributaries to which the international régime was to apply. In the performance of this task, the Polish delegate insisted that two tributaries of the Oder—the Warthe and the Netze—should be internationalized up to the Polish frontier. The Prussian delegate, with the support of all his colleagues save the Pole, argued that if tributaries were to be internationalized the portions of them in Polish territory should not be excluded. A suggested solution, transmitted on the application of the British Government by the League's Advisory and Technical Committee for Communications and Transit, was rejected by the Polish Government. On October 30, 1928, all the Governments concerned agreed to ask the Permanent

Court whether the jurisdiction of the commission extended to the portion of the Warthe (Warta) and Netze (Notec) within the Polish frontiers. The Polish Government denied this, while the six other Governments affirmed it. The court based its decision upon the treaty and held by a vote of nine to three that the Polish Government's contention was unfounded and that the commission had jurisdiction over the rivers in question.

Representative instances of advisory opinions are presented by the International Labor Conference case, the Eastern Karelia case, the Mosul case, and the Danzig court case.[1]

The first of these involved the nomination by the Government of The Netherlands of the workers' delegate to the third session of the International Labor Conference. The nomination was made in agreement with the Confederation of Catholic Unions, the Confederation of Christian Trade Unions, and the Netherlands General Confederation of Trade Unions, but not in agreement with the Netherlands Confederation of Trade Unions. The last was the largest single labor organization in the country but possessed a smaller membership than the other three combined. It protested that the action of the Dutch Government was a violation of Article 389 of the Treaty of Versailles, requiring that delegates be chosen in agreement with the most representative organizations of employers or work people. In spite of this protest, the International Labor Conference admitted the Dutch delegates, but passed a resolution inviting the Governing Body of the International Labor Organization to request the League Council to obtain an opinion from the court as to the proper interpretation of Article 389. On May 12, 1922, the Council adopted a resolution asking the court whether the Dutch workers' delegate had been chosen in accordance with the treaty provisions. On July 31, 1922, the court delivered it as its unanimous opinion that the delegate had been properly selected and seated; it held that governments might consider any or all labor organizations in deciding which was "most representative," without being obliged to consult the largest single organization. This view has since been accepted as authority.

The Eastern Karelia case involved more important issues, both in regard to the political aspects of the controversy and to the jurisdiction and procedure of the court itself, despite the fact that the court's opinion, somewhat paradoxically, was a refusal to give an opinion. On October 14, 1920, Soviet Russia and Finland signed a peace treaty at Dorpat to which was annexed a declaration by the Russian delegates, promising autonomy to Eastern Karelia—the region between the Finnish frontier and the White Sea, in part inhabited by Finns. The Finnish Government regarded this declaration as a condition of its own acceptance of the present boundary. It subsequently complained of Soviet nonfulfillment of the condition and carried its complaint before the League Council in 1921. On April 21, 1923, the Council asked the court for an opinion as to whether Articles 10 and 11 of the treaty, coupled with the annexed declaration, constituted engagements of an international character, placing Russia under an obligation to Finland to carry out their provisions. Since the U.S.S.R. was not a member of the League and refused emphatically to accept the League's jurisdiction, it is difficult to see what the Council could have done about the situation in any case. On June 22 and 26 the court heard the Finnish case. The Soviet Government refused to take any part in the pro-

---

[1] On the Austro-German customs-union case of 1931, see p. 553 above.

ceedings, holding that the declaration given was merely for information, that there was no contractual obligation involved, and that the question was therefore a domestic one. On July 23, 1923, by a vote of seven to four, the court refused to give an opinion, on the ground that action by the court "presupposed the consent and the cooperation of both parties" and on the further ground that the question was not one of abstract law, but "concerned directly the main point of the controversy between the two States, which could be decided only by an investigation into the facts of the case." The court asserted, moreover, that "the refusal which Russia had already opposed to the steps suggested by the Counc'l have been renewed upon the receipt by it of the notification of the request for an advisory opinion. The court therefore finds it impossible to give its opinion on a dispute of this kind."

The Mosul case involved equally interesting procedural questions. It arose out of the boundary controversy over the Mosul area between Turkey on the one hand and Great Britain, as mandatory of Iraq, on the other. The case represents the type of situation in which certain functions are conferred upon the League Council, not by the Covenant, but by a separate treaty, one of the parties to which is not a member of the League. Article 3 of the Treaty of Lausanne of July 24, 1923, provided for the submission of the dispute to the League Council. Differences of opinion developed, however, as to the nature of the Council's function. Great Britain held that the Council was authorized to act as an arbitral body capable of rendering a binding decision by a majority vote. Turkey held that the Council could merely act as mediator under Article 15 of the Covenant and that it could, therefore, reach a conclusion only by unanimity. Since Turkey was a member of the Council for the purpose of the dispute, it could thus block an unsatisfactory settlement by its single vote. The Council appointed a non-partisan commission of inquiry, which proceeded to Mosul and made its report in July, 1925. It advised against a plebiscite and recommended acceptance of the provisional boundary, giving Mosul to Iraq, on condition that Great Britain retain the mandate for twenty-five years and give cultural autonomy to the Kurds. Inasmuch as the questions of how the Council should act and whether the Council's action under the treaty was to be regarded as an arbitral award or merely as a recommendation were not questions of fact but legal questions of treaty interpretation, the Council, on September 19, 1925, asked the court for an advisory opinion. Two questions were put to the judges: Was the Council's action under the treaty to be an arbitral award, a recommendation, or a simple mediation? May the representatives of the interested parties take part in the vote?

The court held that the intention of the Treaty of Lausanne was to empower the Council to reach a definitive and binding settlement. But the Council could not be regarded simply as a tribunal of arbitrators. It must follow its normal procedure under Article 15 of the Covenant, since no express departures from that procedure had been provided for. The rule of unanimity in Article 5 of the Covenant could not be set aside by specific agreements to the contrary, and in any event there had been no such agreements here. The Council must therefore follow the rule of unanimity, but it must interpret the rule in accordance with Article 15 and with the well-known principle that no one can be judge in his own suit. The votes of the litigating parties could not be counted in ascertaining whether there was unanimity. This opinion was regarded as establishing the principle that the Council might both request and accept an advisory opinion from the court by less than a unanimous vote, but whether this meant a simple majority or unanimity minus the litigating parties is not yet entirely clear.[1] In November and December, 1925, the Council examined and accepted the court's opinion. It then handed down a binding decision, awarding Mosul to Iraq. The Turkish representative voted in the negative, but his vote was not counted and the vote was therefore technically "unanimous." Turkey at length accepted this settlement as final.

The Danzig court case centered about the question of whether railway officials and workers could bring suit, as individuals, in the courts of the Free City on the basis of alleged rights to salaries, pensions, etc., involved in the Polish-Danzig Agreement of October 22, 1921. By Article 104 of the Treaty of Versailles, Poland was given control over the Danzig railways. When German workers brought suit against the Polish railways administration, the Polish Government denied the jurisdiction of the Danzig court. The League high commissioner upheld the Polish contention on April 3, 1927. Danzig then requested the Council to ask the court for an advisory opinion on this point. The Council acted upon this request and on March 3, 1928, the court advised it that the high commissioner's decision was not well founded in law. The judges contended that since the agreement had created a special legal régime governing the relations between the Polish railways administration and the employees, the latter were entitled to sue, on the basis of this agreement, in the courts of Danzig.

In turning from justiciable to non-justiciable or "political" controversies dealt with by the League machinery, a similar resumé of a few important instances will reveal the League procedure in practical operation. For this purpose attention will be directed toward the Aaland Islands controversy, the Tacna-Arica dispute, the Vilna dispute, the Corfu incident the Greek-Bulgarian frontier case, the Gran Chaco conflict, and the Far Eastern hostilities of 1931–1932.

The Aaland Islands controversy involved the status of a group of islands in the Baltic Sea, inhabited by some 16,000 Swedish-speaking people. Prior to 1809 they were part of the Kingdom of Sweden. Between 1809 and 1917 they were under Russian sovereignty. In 1918 and 1919 the islanders, by plebiscite, voted in favor of reunion with Sweden. The Swedish Government supported this claim, but its efforts to negotiate a settlement were repulsed by Finland, which insisted upon its title to the archipelago. When relations between the two States became strained, Great Britain, on June 19, 1920, drew the attention of the Council to the dispute under Article 11, which makes any war or threat of war a matter of concern to the whole League and reserves the friendly right of each member to bring to the attention of the Assembly or the Council any circumstance threatening to disturb the good understanding between nations. Finland, not then a member of the League, contended that the case was a "domestic question" and therefore not subject to the Council's jurisdiction. Since the Permanent Court was not yet in existence, the Council appointed a committee of jurists, consisting of a Frenchman, a Dutchman, and a

---

[1] See pp. 807–809 below.

Swiss, to pass upon this delicate point. The jurists held that "the transition from a *de facto* situation to a normal situation *de jure* cannot be considered as one confined entirely within the domestic jurisdiction of a State. . . . This transition interests the community of States very deeply, both from political and legal standpoints." They concluded, therefore, that the Council could properly investigate the matter. The Council accordingly held the question to be not "domestic," but to be one of international concern. It appointed a committee of inquiry of one Belgian, one American, and one Swiss to make a recommendation. This committee made an exhaustive investigation, visited the Aaland archipelago, took testimony, and recommended that the islands be left under Finnish sovereignty subject to minority guarantees, neutralization, and demilitarization. The solution was accepted, though not without some grumbling from the Swedish representatives, and the disputing States have since acquiesced in the settlement.

League efforts to deal with the dispute between Chile on the one hand and Bolivia and Peru on the other over Tacna-Arica were less successful. The provinces in question lie in the desert waste of Atacama, on the western coast of South America. They were uninhabited and of no concern to the adjacent States until valuable nitrate deposits were discovered in the region. The resulting scramble led to the "War of the Pacific" (1879–1884), declared by Chile against Bolivia and Bolivia's ally, Peru. Chile was an easy victor. By the treaty of Ancon of 1884, Tacna and Arica were to remain under Chilean control for ten years, after which a local plebiscite would determine whether they were to remain with Chile or go to Peru. The State retaining the territory would pay the other ten million pesos. When 1894 came the Chilean Government refused to hold the plebiscite and continued to postpone action year after year. Various efforts on the part of the United States to adjust the resulting dispute by mediation failed to achieve a settlement. On November 1, 1920, Bolivia appealed to the League, under Article 19 of the Covenant, which authorizes the Assembly to advise the reconsideration of treaties which have become inapplicable. Bolivia desired a sea port and contended that the treaty of 1904, whereby her claims to Tacna-Arica were finally extinguished, should be revised. Peru sought League assistance on similar grounds. Chile contended that the League was incompetent to act, since she was unwilling to consider the treaties and the League could under no circumstances advise the reconsideration of treaties against the will of one of the parties.

On January 18, 1922, President Harding invited the States immediately concerned to conduct their negotiations in Washington. Secretary of State Hughes apparently sought to boycott the League by insisting on a settlement through American agencies. When negotiations got nowhere,

Hughes suggested arbitration. This was agreed to, but Bolivia's case was ruled out and the arbitration was limited to a textual interpretation of the treaty of Ancon. Since the provinces had been Chileanized, Chile now declared her willingness to hold the plebiscite. President Coolidge's arbitral award of March 4, 1925, recommended that a plebiscite be held. The inadequacy of this solution became manifest when the Plebiscitory Commission, headed by General Pershing, who was succeeded in 1926 by General Lassiter, found it impossible to carry out the proposal. The commission was forced to the conclusion by the Chilean tactics that "a free and fair plebiscite, as required by the award, is impracticable of accomplishment." Recourse was now had once more to direct negotiation, with Secretary Kellogg acting as mediator. Many delays took place, but on July 28, 1929, the Treaty of Santiago was signed, whereby Tacna was granted to Peru and Arica to Chile and the latter State agreed to pay six million pesos to the former. As in the past, Bolivian interests were ignored. Here, as in other instances, League efforts to deal with an American dispute were blocked by the attitude of the United States.

In the Vilna dispute, the uncompromising attitude of the parties made any satisfactory settlement impossible. The controversy represents an outstanding instance of the refusal of States to utilize the League machinery for the orderly settlement of their differences. Vilna is the ancient capital of Lithuania. It was ceded by Russia to Lithuania in 1920. The city has a mixed population, while the surrounding countryside is largely Polish. The Polish Government cast covetous eyes on the district, following the defeat of the Red Army before Warsaw in August of 1920. The Council took cognizance of the situation and recommended a boundary giving Vilna to Lithuania. An armistice agreement was signed at Suwalki, but on October 8, 1920, a division of Polish troops under General Zeligowski seized the city and set up an administration of rebel patriots. The Polish Government disavowed this act of violence, but acquiesced most willingly in its results. The Council made plans for a plebiscite under the supervision of a police force composed of French, British, Belgian, and Spanish troops, with possible Danish, Dutch, Norwegian, and Swedish contingents—all of these States to be reimbursed later for their expenses by Poland and Lithuania. This proposal represents the nearest point to which the Council has ever come to organizing any type of international police force. Switzerland declined to permit the passage of troops through her territory, because of her neutralized position. But the Polish Government refused to oust Zeligowski or to permit an international force to supervise the plebiscite. All the efforts of the League Council to mitigate the ambitions of the Polish annexationists were in vain. Poland confronted the world with a *fait accompli* and refused to budge, despite protests from Lithuania and admonitions from Geneva.

Poland has since made good her title to Vilna. In March, 1922, the Polish Government proclaimed the annexation of the district, and in the following year the Allied Governments recognized her title. This action, like the Allied recognition in 1920 of Rumanian title to Bessarabia, was of doubtful legality. But Lithuania, as a small, weak State without allies, was in no position to resist this spoliation of her territory by force. Her Government continued to protest at Geneva and refused to enter into diplomatic relations with Poland. Between 1922 and 1927 an unofficial state of "war" prevailed between the two countries. League efforts to secure Polish evacuation were unsuccessful. The French bloc stood behind Poland and dominated the Council. League efforts to secure Lithuanian acquiescence in the Polish conquest likewise failed. Not only the Allied Governments, but the Vatican as well, accepted the situation, for in 1925 the Roman Church created a special diocese for Poland, with Vilna as its center. Reprisals, repressions, and border incidents were chronic along the closed frontiers. At Geneva the fiery President Waldemaras of Lithuania and the obdurate Polish Foreign Minister, Zaleski, periodically exchanged veiled insults. In 1929, after the Council had repeatedly pointed out that a state of war between two League members was incompatible with the Covenant, pacific relations of a kind were restored, but the continued Polish control of Vilna remained a rankling injustice in Lithuanian eyes. "Peace" was thus preserved by League efforts. It would have been preserved in any case, however, because of the disparity in power between the contestants. Article 10 failed to protect Lithuania, although on narrow technical grounds she was, of course, not entitled to its protection, since she was not a member of the League in 1920. The sanctions of Article 16 were not invoked against Poland, despite her defiance of Council injunctions. In this instance the League machinery was clearly incapable of transcending the limits imposed upon it by the hegemony of a group of States which viewed the aggrandizement of one of its members with approval and by the indifference to the whole situation of other States which might have been capable of acting.

The limitations of the League method were also apparent in the Corfu incident. This imbroglio arose out of the activities of the commission appointed by the Conference of Ambassadors to fix the frontiers between Albania and Greece. The commission was headed by an Italian, General Tellini, who was accused by the Greeks of deciding all disputed points in Albania's favor. On the morning of August 27, 1923, Tellini, his chauffeur, and some other Italians riding with him were murdered near the village of Janina on Greek territory. The Greek Government expressed its profound regret to the Italian Minister in Athens and pledged itself to do all in its power to apprehend and punish the culprits. Patriotic indignation in Italy reached white heat. Here was an opportunity for the new

Fascist régime, not yet a year old, to play a strong hand by proceeding from sword rattling to action. On August 29 Mussolini sent an ultimatum to the Greek Government, demanding (1) an unreserved official apology, (2) a solemn memorial service for the victims, to be held in Athens and attended by all members of the Greek Government, (3) honors to the Italian flag and to an Italian squadron by the Greek fleet at Piraeus, (4) an official Greek inquiry within five days at the scene of the murders, in the presence of the royal Italian military attaché, (5) capital punishment for all the authors of the crime, (6) the payment of a fifty million lira indemnity within five days, and (7) military honors to the bodies of the dead. The Greek Government declared itself prepared to make apologies and reparations, but asserted that demands (4), (5), and (6) were "an infringment on Greek sovereignty and injury to the honor of Greece." At the same time the Greek Government addressed an appeal to the Secretary-general of the League to bring the matter before the Council under Articles 12 and 15. Meanwhile the Italian Government had rejected the reply as unsatisfactory and had ordered its naval forces to occupy the Greek island of Corfu, near the mouth of the Adriatic. The occupation was completed after a bombardment in which a number of Greek and Armenian refugee children on the island were killed or wounded by exploding shells. Italy's "honor" was thus happily vindicated.

The first Greek appeal to the Council had been made before the news of the Corfu occupation was known. M. Politis, representing Greece on the Council, now declared (September 1) that Greece was ready to accept and execute in good faith any proposals the Council might make to give Italy full satisfaction. Salandra, the Italian representative on the Council, assumed an attitude of irritated aloofness, said he had no instructions from his Government, and expressed doubt as to whether the matter was within the Council's competence. When Politis spoke of applying Article 16 he declared: "Article 16 cannot be applied to Italy. As appears from the official declarations of the Italian Government, Italy did not intend to commit an act of war. No Power, under these circumstances, would tolerate the application of Article 16." Lord Cecil, representing Great Britain, declared, with the support of the Swedish delegate, that the Council, under Articles 12 and 15, had clear and unmistakable jurisdiction over the dispute. Cecil asserted:

It seems to me very difficult to understand how the occupation of a portion of territory of another State by armed forces, accompanied . . . by a bombardment which killed fifteen individuals and wounded others, can be regarded as a pacific measure. I feel great difficulty in understanding how that can be differentiated from an act of war.

Discussion was adjourned until Salandra could secure instructions from Rome. For the first time the Council was confronted with a controversy in which a Great Power was disposed to challenge the League and to insist that the dispute concerned only the two parties directly involved.

On September 5 Salandra sought to turn the discussion away from the Corfu occupation to the original assassination. He asked that the Council take no action on the Greek request. Politis at once denied Greek responsibility for the murder. Cecil asked for the reading of Articles 10, 12, and 15 and said that inasmuch as they were incorporated into all the peace treaties, any disregard of them by the Council would shake the whole European *status quo*. In the Assembly, meeting simultaneously, general resentment at the Italian attitude was apparent. In the Council meeting of September 6 Salandra objected to a Spanish resolution looking toward a settlement and also sought to block the communication of the resolution to the Conference of Ambassadors. The matter was nevertheless referred to this body, whose recommendations for a settlement, transmitted on September 7, were at once accepted by the Greek and Italian Governments. The settlement specified that the Greek naval salute was to be given to British, French, and Italian squadrons. It made no mention of capital punishment, provided for an investigation of the Janina murders by an international commission, and specified that Greece should deposit fifty million lira in the Swiss National Bank, subject to a determination by the Permanent Court of the proper amount of the indemnity. This latter provision was later withdrawn and Greece was ordered by the Conference of Ambassadors to pay the entire amount to Italy. Greece received no indemnity for the loss of life and destruction of property at Corfu, but the Italians discontinued their preparations for an indefinite occupation and evacuated the island.

"Peace" had been preserved and territorial conquests averted. But Greece was obliged to bow to superior force, and the Conference of Ambassadors acceded to practically all of the Italian demands. The whole settlement, moreover, had been taken out of the hands of the League Council. The Council later referred to a commission of jurists the question as to whether it was obliged to suspend its inquiry into a dispute when the settlement was being sought through some other channel. This question, along with that of the right of a State, under Article 10, to occupy another State's territory as a measure of reprisal, would have been referred to the Permanent Court save for Italian opposition. The commission of jurists reported in the spring of 1924 to the effect that coercive measures are not barred under Article 10, but that the League has a right to decide at once whether they should be maintained or withdrawn. On the other point the jurists held that "where, contrary to the terms of Article 15, paragraph 1, a dispute is submitted to the Council on the application of one of the parties, where such a dispute already forms the subject of arbitration or of judicial proceedings, the Council must refuse to consider the application. . . . It is in conformity with the general principles of law that it should be possible for a reference back to such jurisdiction to be asked for and ordered."[1] These statements of principle were not calculated to increase the Council's prestige nor to cause small States to regard the Covenant as an adequate protection of their rights.

The Council has usually achieved more satisfactory results in dealing with disputes and threats of hostilities not involving Great Powers. Its procedure was revealed at its best in the Greek-Bulgarian frontier case of 1925. A Greek soldier had crossed the boundary and fired on a Bulgarian sentry, who replied by killing the Greek. General firing ensued and the Greek Government, alleging fear of a Bulgarian invasion, ordered its troops to occupy the Struma Valley in Bulgaria on October 22. They were ordered to launch a general offensive on October 24. On October 23 the Bulgarian Government telegraphed to the Secretary-general, invoking Articles 10 and 11 of the Covenant. The Council was hurriedly summoned to meet in Paris. Before it convened, its President, Briand, telegraphed to both Governments, reminding them of their obligations under Article 12 and asking them to withdraw their troops behind the frontiers. Both Governments agreed to this, and the threatened Greek offensive was called off two and one-half hours before it was scheduled to begin. The Council met two days later and approved Briand's action, confirming it by asking notification from both States within twenty-four hours that all troops had been ordered withdrawn and notification within sixty hours that hostilities had ceased and that all forces had retired behind the frontiers. French, British, and Italian officers were ordered to the scene to report to the Council as soon as withdrawal should have been effected. This is the classic example of the Council's "stop-fight" resolution, accompanied by inquiry at the point of hostilities. By October 28 all Greek soldiers had been retired into Greek territory. Once the danger of fighting was averted, the Council proceeded to look into the merits of the dispute. A commission of inquiry was sent to the theater of conflict. On the basis of its report the Council held that Greece had violated Bulgarian territory without sufficient cause. Greece was obliged to pay an indemnity to Bulgaria of 30,000,000 livas or about $210,000. The commission recommended that neutral officers be appointed to take charge of Greek and Bulgarian frontier forces and that steps be taken to deal with political problems created by dissatisfied minorities and by the "Comitadjis" or armed irregulars in Macedonia. Briand declared that it would be "extremely dangerous" for members of the League to decide for themselves what constituted legitimate defense. In this instance the Greek decision on this matter was in effect reviewed and overruled by the Council.

[1] *Official Journal*, April, 1924, p. 525.

Even in dealing with Third-class Powers, however, the Council is sometimes unsuccessful in preventing hostilities. This is more likely to be true when the States in question are far removed from the spheres of action of the Great Powers in the League. In the Bolivia-Paraguay controversy the situation was further complicated by the traditional attitude of the United States toward international disputes in the western hemisphere. Here the League machinery broke down almost completely, because of the attitude of the contestants and their remoteness from the sources of effective League pressure. The two South American States have long been engaged in a chronic quarrel over their respective claims in the Chaco Boreal, that portion of the Gran Chaco which lies between Bolivia to the north, Paraguay to the southeast, Brazil to the east, and Argentina to the south. This region is about the size of Great Britain and is covered with jungle and swampy plains. Bolivia, having lost her outlet to the Pacific in the war with Chile (1879–1884), has directed her energies toward securing an outlet to the Atlantic through the Paraguay River, which borders the Chaco on the east. The original Paraguayan claim to this area, inherited from Spain, rested upon the now outmoded contention that a State discovering the mouth of the river secures title to all territory drained by it. The Bolivian claim rests upon the alleged boundaries of the Spanish viceroyalties, captaincies-general, and audiencias as of 1810. Three boundary treaties between the disputants were negotiated—in 1879, 1887, and 1894—but none was ratified. In 1907 it was agreed to submit the question to the arbitration of the President of Argentina, but he failed to act. New protocols were signed in 1913 and 1927, but without results. Following the failure of negotiation, Paraguayan troops launched a successful attack upon the Bolivian stronghold of Fort Vanguardia on December 5, 1928.

The fifty-third session of the League Council met at Lugano, Switzerland, on December 10. On the same day the Pan-American Conference on Conciliation and Arbitration met in Washington to adopt a general treaty for the pacific settlement of disputes. Chile was a member of the Council, but Brazil had quit the League and neither Bolivia, Paraguay, Argentina, nor Peru was an active member. None of these States brought the matter before the Council, nor did any outside State. Nevertheless, on December 11, 1928 the, Council unanimously requested its president to send a cable to both contestants. Briand accordingly reminded Bolivia and Paraguay of their obligations under the Covenant and expressed the hope that pacific methods of settlement would be resorted to. On December 12, before the Council's message was received, the Bolivian minister in Paris sent a 2,000-word telegram to Lugano, condemning the Paraguayan attack and stating Bolivia's intention of severing diplomatic relations with Paraguay until reparations should be paid. On December 11 the

Paraguayan *chargé d'affaires* had informed the Secretary-general that Bolivian troops had attacked the Paraguayans and had been repulsed, and that Bolivia had refused to submit the controversy to the international commission of inquiry at Montevideo, as provided for by the Gondra Pact of 1923. The Paraguayan reply to the Council's communication was received December 12 and found to be conciliatory in tone. The Bolivian reply, received December 14, denounced Paraguay for an act of aggression contrary to Articles 10 and 13 of the Covenant. Bolivia, not having ratified the Gondra Pact, declined to be bound by its terms. Meanwhile preparations for further hostilities continued.

On December 18, 1928, Briand, as acting president of the Council, dispatched an *aide-mémoire* to the Governments of Argentina and the United States, asking for information regarding the action initiated by Argentina and by the Pan-American Arbitration Conference to preserve peace. On December 13 a special committee of five, appointed by the conference, had met and on the following day the conference had extended its good offices to the Bolivian and Paraguayan Governments, both of which accepted. This action was approved by the League Council, which thus permitted the dispute to be dealt with by American agencies, partly out of deference to the United States. At the end of the month the special committee drew up a protocol, signed January 3, 1929, providing for a nine-member international Commission of Investigation and Conciliation. This body, which met in Washington March 13, 1929, and elected Brigadier-general Frank R. McCoy of the United States as president, arranged an exchange of prisoners and got both Governments to pledge themselves to precautions designed to present further outbreaks. On July 1 Bolivia and Paraguay agreed that the commission might take up the boundary dispute, though this was outside the original scope of its authority. On January 3 Bolivia had suggested to Briand that the frontier question be submitted to the Permanent Court. On January 17 the Secretary-general had cabled La Paz that Paraguay had accepted this proposal, but the suggestion was never pursued. Since there seemed to be no danger of further hostilities, the Council was content to permit the Pan-American Commission to continue its work. The commission, however, could arrive at no formula acceptable to both disputants and the long delay which was permitted to occur finally proved fatal to all prospects of a pacific settlement. Except for minor incidents, no further fighting took place in the Chaco between 1929 and 1932, but both States armed themselves for war.

By the spring of 1932 the commission, which was still sitting in Washington, had drawn up a plan for a Bolivia-Paraguay non-aggression pact providing for a three-mile neutral zone, investigation of any further fighting by a commission of five to sit in Buenos Aires, a resumption of diplomatic relations and the commencement of direct negotiations. This proposal proved unsatisfactory, however, and Paraguay withdrew from the negotiations, alleging Bolivian acts of aggression. On June 15 the Bolivians captured Fort Carlos Antonio Lopez, which the Paraguayans retook in mid-July. *El Dario*, organ of the Bolivian Liberal party, then declared that Bolivia must "either show itself to be the ideal country of ultra-Christian peacefulness or give back to the Bolivian soul all the vigor of its masculine grandeur."[1] While the commission in Washington (now a "Committee of Neutrals" presided over by Secretary of State Stimson) sought in vain to persuade the Paraguay delegates to return, each State prepared to "defend its interests" against alleged attack from the other. On July 21 Bolivia instructed its spokesmen in Washington to discontinue negotiations. The Paraguay delegates now returned to the parley, but Bolivia refused to follow suit.

At the end of July large-scale hostilities opened with a Bolivian attack on the Paraguayan positions in the Chaco. Forts Boqueron and Toledo fell, while Paraguay declared a state of siege and ordered general mobilization. On August 1 the Paraguayan Government appealed to the League under Articles 10 and 11 of the Covenant, following receipt of a note from the Council expressing hopes for peace. While the Committee of Neutrals called on all American Governments to cooperate in efforts at mediation, the League Council took no effective action, preferring again to await the outcome of the Pan-American efforts. On August 2 the Committee of Neutrals asked Bolivia to suspend hostilities and agree to negotiation. On the same day the president of the League Council recalled the obligations of the Covenant to both contestants. On August 3, presumably at the initiative of the United States, the Stimson Doctrine was applied to the situation. Nineteen American Governments joined in an identic note to Bolivia and Paraguay (signed in the Washington office of Francis White, Assistant Secretary of State), declaring that "they will not recognize any territorial arrangement of this controversy which has not been obtained by peaceful means, nor the validity of territorial acquisitions which may be obtained through occupation or conquest by force of arms." Simultaneously the League Secretariat announced that Paraguay had agreed to arbitrate, the Bolivian Government, in reply to the League notes, declared that it did not reject pacific means of settlement, and the British Government announced its support of the peace efforts at Geneva and Washington.

Even this impressive combination of pressures was without result. Bolivia agreed to arbitrate on the basis of the new military position. The Committee of Neutrals rejected this as a basis for a settlement, insisting instead on the *status quo* of June 1. Bolivia refused to surrender the three

[1] Quoted in New York *Times*, July 14, 1932.

forts recently taken and held that the new doctrine could not be applied retroactively. On August 29 the committee proposed a 60-day truce, to begin September 1, on the basis of the new *status quo*. Paraguay rejected this proposal and contended that her security required Bolivian evacuation of the recently occupied territory. On September 10 the committee proposed immediate suspension of hostilities, to be followed by a three-month period for negotiation, beginning October 1. It also suggested the eventual submission of the controversy to the Pan-American Conference, to meet in Montevideo in 1933, or to the Permanent Court at The Hague. These and other proposals produced no change in the situation. The Paraguayan forces now launched a counter-attack on Fort Boqueron and heavy fighting developed between the opposing armies. At the same time an inquiry came from Geneva to Washington (apparently one of a series of similar requests), asking whether the United States would object to vigorous action by the League Council to uphold the Covenant. The American Government again replied that it hoped the efforts of the Committee of Neutrals would soon meet with success. Paraguay agreed to a truce, on condition of Bolivian retirement, and Bolivia rejected the condition. All these efforts were fruitless—the more so as prospects developed of a new unofficial "war" between Peru and Colombia over the former's seizure on September 1 of the town of Leticia, on the Amazon River, ceded by Peru to Colombia in a treaty of 1922. In the Chaco the disputing States rushed new troops into battle. The fortunes of war now began to favor Paraguay, whose forces took Fort Falcon and began a general advance, after heavy fighting with numerous casualties. On September 23 the sixty-eighth session of the League Council opened in Geneva. Senor de Madariaga of Spain pointed out that inasmuch as Bolivia had not ratified the Kellogg-Briand Pact, the League Covenant was the only treaty binding the contestants to settle their disputes pacifically. The Council limited itself, however, to appointing a committee to follow the efforts of the Committee of Neutrals.

Meanwhile, thousands of soldiers fought, killed, and destroyed in the Chaco, as the Paraguayans recaptured Forts Boqueron and Toledo and finally took Fort Arce, Bolivian general headquarters. On September 27 the League Council once more reminded Bolivia and Paraguay of their obligations under the Covenant and earnestly requested them to accept the proposals of the other American republics and to "put an immediate stop to military action and preparation." A committee, consisting of Council President Eamon de Valera, former President José Matos of Guatemala, and Salvador de Madariaga, was appointed to follow developments. The Paraguayan delegate in the Assembly approved this action and spoke of invoking the Covenant against Bolivia if peace efforts failed. On October 14 Paraguay declared her willingness to open negotiations. On

October 26 Bolivia followed suit and negotiations began in Washington. This tardy resort to diplomacy, however, was no victory for "peace" but was a result of war, albeit undeclared. The Paraguayan armies had captured a dozen forts from the enemy, and in the humiliation of defeat two Bolivian Governments were overturned within a week. The resumption of peace negotiations was a consequence of the verdict of force. Neither the League Council nor the Committee of Neutrals had succeeded in promoting a settlement uninfluenced by military coercion. A final solution of the problem has not yet been reached at the time of writing. If and when it is reached, it will probably reflect the outcome of the 1932 hostilities or of later fighting, the League Covenant and the Stimson Doctrine to the contrary notwithstanding.

The most complete and tragic breakdown of the League's peace machinery occurred in the Sino-Japanese conflict of 1931–1932 over Manchuria. The causes of this crisis and its general course have been reviewed above.[1] Here it will suffice to survey the unsuccessful efforts of the League to keep the peace and protect the integrity of China. This instance differs from the Bolivia-Paraguay case in that League action was supported by the United States, rather than being inhibited through fear of offending American sensibilities. But the object of pressure here was a Great Power whose government and people were determined to brook no outside interference with their own conception of their interests. League pressure failed to protect China's integrity and to avert widespread fighting, accompanied by heavy loss of life and wholesale destruction of property.

Following the initial Japanese occupation of Mukden and other points in Manchuria, the Chinese Government, through Dr. Alfred Sze, chief Chinese delegate in Geneva, invoked Article 11 of the Covenant on September 21, 1931. It asked the Council to take immediate steps "to prevent the further development of a situation endangering the peace of nations, to reestablish the *status quo ante*, and to determine the amounts and character of such reparations as may be due to the Republic of China." In the ensuing Council discussions, M. Yoshizawa, for Japan, declared that the Japanese military action was required by self-defense and that Japan would welcome a proposal for direct negotiation. Dr. Sze asserted that China would never consent to direct negotiation under pressure of foreign military occupation of her territory. Lord Cecil recalled the Council's first action in the Greek-Bulgarian dispute of 1925. After further discussion the Council, on the same evening (September 21), dispatched an identic cable to Nanking and Tokyo, appealing to them to refrain from any action which might aggravate the situation and asking

[1] See pp. 412–419 above.

them to find means to withdraw their troops immediately. Secretary of State Stimson expressed his approval of this action in a note of September 23, addressed to the President of the Council, then M. Lerroux of Spain. On September 29, at the end of the Assembly meeting, Lerroux assured the larger League body that the outlook for a peaceable settlement was favorable. The Chinese reply of September 24 had accepted the Council resolution, but the Japanese reply of September 25 merely stated that troops would be withdrawn "in proportion as the situation improved." On the twenty-sixth Yoshizawa again solicited direct negotiations, with the same result as before. The Japanese Government disclaimed any territorial designs in Manchuria. On September 30 the Council adjourned until October 14, after unanimously adopting a resolution requesting both parties to hasten the restoration of normal relations and to furnish information to the Council at frequent intervals. China at least fulfilled the latter part of this injunction by sending ninety-three separate telegrams to Geneva between September 19 and October 24.

The Council met again on October 13, 1931, in response to a Chinese request. Fighting had spread over southern Manchuria, and Chinchow had twice been bombed by Japanese planes. In this instance the "stop-fight" resolution was ineffective. On October 12 Tokyo indicated that the Japanese forces could be withdrawn only if China agreed to certain "fundamental points." In the Council meeting the Japanese delegate rested his case on Chinese infringements of Japanese treaty rights. Dr. Sze again refused direct negotiations and declared that China placed her faith in the League. The United States had already declared, on October 9, that it would "endeavor to reenforce what the League does." Prentiss B. Gilbert, American Consul-general in Geneva, was authorized to participate in the Council discussions relating to the Kellogg-Briand Pact. Yoshizawa objected to American participation, but on October 15 the United States was invited to attend by a thirteen to one vote, with Japan in the negative. Briand, who had replaced Lerroux as Council President, delicately invited the United States to associate itself with the League's efforts. On October 16 Mr. Gilbert took his seat at the Council table. On the following day the Council invoked the Pact of Paris and Briand dispatched a formal cable, calling the attention of the parties to their obligations under Article 2 of that instrument. The United States, acting independently, did likewise on October 20.

Briand now suggested that Japan withdraw her troops into the railway zone and that China agree to respect all her treaty obligations. But no agreement could be reached as to what these obligations were, in view of Japanese references to the "parallel railway protocols" and the 1915 demands, the validity of which China denied. Tokyo argued that governmental support of the anti-Japanese boycott in China was not in harmony with the letter or spirit of the Pact of Paris. Lord Cecil argued that evacuation must precede negotiation and that all questions of treaty obligations should be submitted to the Permanent Court. On October 24 the Council, by a thirteen to one vote, with Japan in the negative, adopted a resolution calling upon Japan to withdraw all troops before November 16 and asking China to assume responsibility for the safety of Japanese subjects. China would take over the evacuated territory and direct negotiations would be begun as soon as evacuation should be completed. The Council then adjourned until November 16. Since the resolution was not passed unanimously, it had only "moral" force, though the distinction between the moral and legal effects of the Council's action is difficult to draw in this case, since in fact the Council's resolutions had no force at all.

Private conferences and negotiations ensued. On October 26 the Japanese Government proposed an agreement with China on five basic principles: (1) mutual repudiation of aggressive policies and conduct; (2) respect for China's territorial sovereignty; (3) complete suppression of all organized movements interfering with trade and stirring up international hatred; (4) effective protection throughout Manchuria of peaceful pursuits undertaken by Japanese subjects; and (5) respect for Japanese treaty rights in Manchuria. Briand replied that China had already given the necessary pledges, but Tokyo did not regard them as sufficiently explicit and comprehensive. Following further hostilities and the extension of the area of Japanese occupation, Briand on November 6 asked both Governments to instruct their commanders to "remove all possibility of sanguinary engagements." China charged Japan with repudiating her own promises, ignoring the Council's resolutions, and violating Article 10 of the Covenant and Article 1 of the Nine Power Treaty. On November 11 Briand sent another ineffective plea to both Governments.

On the afternoon of November 16 the Council met in Paris. Not only had the Japanese forces not been withdrawn, but they were fighting their way into North Manchuria. While the Council deliberated, new battles were fought and the Japanese captured Tsitsihar on November 19. The United States was not represented in the Council meetings at the Quai d'Orsay, though Ambassador Dawes was sent from London to confer informally with the Council members. Inasmuch as the Council had failed to secure evacuation prior to negotiation, it now sought, over Chinese protests, to secure provisional acceptance of the *status quo* and to dispatch a neutral commission of inquiry to Manchuria. The appointment of such a commission would normally have been the immediate sequel to the "stop-fight" resolution, but the Council had hesitated to act because of Japanese opposition and American indifference. Now, on November 21, Yoshizawa himself suggested such a commission and solemnly reiterated his Government's "sincere desire to withdraw its troops as quickly as possible within the railway zone" in pursuance of the resolution of September 30. Dr. Sze objected to an inquiry unaccompanied by immediate cessation of hostilities and Japanese evacuation. The United States supported the commission proposal.

Many days of secret Council deliberations failed to achieve unanimity. Finally, however, on December 10, two and one-half months after the beginning of hostilities, the Council unanimously adopted a resolution reaffirming the resolution of September 30 and appointing a commission of five members which should "study on the spot and report to the Council on any circumstance which, affecting international relations, threatens to disturb peace between China and Japan or the good understanding between them on which peace depends." The commission was to have no authority to interfere with the military arrangements of either party, nor to take part in any negotiations which might be initiated. In accepting this proposal, China reserved its sovereignty over Manchuria and its claims for reparations, and Japan reserved its right to protect Japanese lives and property "against the activities of bandits and lawless elements." The United States strongly supported the resolution and warned against the use of "military pressure" to obtain "the ultimate solution of the Manchurian problem." The Council adjourned until January 25, 1932. Early in January the commission was set up, with Lord Lytton of Great Britain as chairman, and with the four other places assigned to General Henri Claudel of France, General Frank R. McCoy of the United States, Dr. Heinrich Schnee of Germany, and Count Luigi Marescotti of Italy.

The situation in the Far East, instead of ameliorating as a result of the Council's action, grew steadily worse and reached the proportions of a major war in January. On the second of the month Japanese troops occupied Chinchow, the last stronghold in Manchuria still held by Chinese forces. On January 7 the American Secretary of State formulated the "Stimson Doctrine." The Commission of Inquiry organized itself at Geneva, but it did not sail from France until February 3 and did not reach the Orient until the end of the month. Meanwhile, the Council reassembled on January 25. Dr. Sze had been succeeded by Dr. W. W. Yen and M. Yoshizawa (now Japanese Foreign Minister) by Naotake Sato. Dr. Yen at once assailed Japanese policy as "cynical and ruthless" and threatened to invoke other articles of the Covenant. On January 29 came news of a Japanese attack on Shanghai. Dr. Yen at once invoked Articles 10 and 15. M. Sato immediately challenged the competence of the Council to take action simultaneously under more than one article of the Covenant, but he was overruled. The Secretary-General appointed a consular committee at Shanghai for purposes of investigation. On February

12 this committee reported that "since the third of February a state of open war has existed, any pretense of a truce being abandoned. . . . The offensive is entirely in the hands of the Japanese, whose declared object is to capture the Woosung forts and drive all Chinese troops a considerable distance from Shanghai."

On the same day the Chinese Government gave up hope of protection from the Council and referred the whole dispute to the Assembly. On February 19 the Council summoned an extraordinary session of the Assembly to convene on March 3, 1932. On February 16, however, the twelve neutral members of the Council warned Japan that "no infringement of the territorial integrity and no change in the political independence of any member of the League brought about in disregard of this article [10] ought to be recognized as valid and effectual by the members of the League of Nations." On February 23 the Japanese Government replied to this declaration with a denial that China was an "organized people" entitled to treatment as such. Stimson's letter to Senator Borah of the same date invited the League to subscribe to the Stimson Doctrine and threatened modifications of the military agreements in the Pacific if Japan persisted in ignoring the Nine Power Pact. All of these gestures were without result. After destructive fighting, Chinese defenders of Shanghai were beaten back by the invaders in the early days of March, and on March 9 Henry Pu Yi was proclaimed regent of "Manchukuo" at Changchun.

On March 3 the Extraordinary Assembly met at Geneva. This was the first instance in which an international dispute had been referred by the smaller League body to the larger one. Here the small Powers were predominant and their delegates at once indicated their unfriendly attitude toward the course which Japan had embarked upon. On March 4 the Assembly unanimously adopted a resolution calling for the cessation of hostilities and the withdrawal of Japanese forces at Shanghai. On March 11 the Assembly subscribed to the Stimson Doctrine.[1] At the same time the Assembly created a Committee of Nineteen to report on the cessation of hostilities and Japanese withdrawal, to follow the execution of the Council resolutions of September 30 and December 10, and to prepare a settlement of the dispute in agreement with the parties. The committee was to consist of the members of the Council other than the parties to the dispute and six other members to be elected by the Assembly by secret ballot. The Assembly then elected Switzerland, Czechoslovakia, Colombia, Portugal, Hungary, and Sweden to these posts and adjourned. The Committee of Nineteen continued in session. On May 5 an armistice was signed at Shanghai and the Japanese retired. This was widely interpreted

[1] See pp. 680–681 above.

to mean that the Assembly had been more successful than the Council in its efforts to terminate the conflict. The world-wide condemnation visited upon Japan and the focusing of this disapproval through the League Assembly undoubtedly influenced the decision of the Japanese Government to abandon a sorry and costly enterprise. But the Shanghai incident was in any case only an interlude, albeit a strange and tragic one, in the drama of empire-building in Manchuria. And here the Assembly was no more successful than the Council. Neither the Assembly nor its Committee of Nineteen made any serious effort to grapple with this problem. The long delay in the submission of the report of the Lytton Commission furnished a convenient pretext for postponement. Until the commission reported, there was obviously no point in further action at Geneva.

Between May and October, 1932, no significant changes in the situation took place in the Far East, save for Japanese recognition of Manchukuo on September 15. China relapsed into anarchic political dissension and civil war. The Japanese and Manchukuo forces in the north were confronted with sporadic outbreaks of rebellion and banditry. The tension between Tokyo and Moscow eased somewhat, but Japanese resentment at the attitude of the American Government continued unabated. The Lytton Commission made a leisurely visit to China, Japan, and Manchuria and gathered tons of documents and notes. On October 2, 1932, its voluminous report (100,000 words) was released for publication simultaneously at Washington and Geneva. This elaborate statement—perhaps the most remarkable and complete of any ever prepared by a League commission of inquiry—consisted of ten chapters, which may be briefly summarized as follows.

The first chapter described China's affliction—war lords, banditry, and Communism—and observed that Japan "has suffered more than any other Power from the lawless conditions" depicted. Chapter II dealt with Manchuria, where the commission concluded that Chinese rule had been accompanied by "nepotism, corruption, and maladministration," but not to any greater degree than elsewhere in China. Japan's fear of an alliance between Communist Russia and the anti-Japanese Kuomintang was mentioned as a motive for her desire to create a Manchuria which should be free from the control of either. Chapter III analyzed the conflicting interests of Japan and China in the Manchurian imbroglio. "Each side had legitimate grievances against the other." As for the events of September 18–19, 1931, the commission found that the Chinese had no plan of attack on the Japanese and that the "bomb explosion" on the South Manchurian railway tracks near Mukden "was not in itself sufficient to justify military action. The operations of the Japanese troops during this night cannot be regarded as measures of legitimate self-defense." Chapter V summarized the events at Shanghai. Chapter VI dealt with "Manchukuo," which the commission found to be "made in Japan." The independence movement which led to the creation of this State "was made possible only by the presence of the Japanese troops," and was not the result of any genuine and spontaneous local sentiment. The constant presence of Japanese officials and advisers, able to exert "irresistible pressure" on the new government, was emphasized, and the conclusion was reached that the new régime could not carry through desired reforms "in the conditions of insecurity and disturbance which existed in 1932." Chapter VII dealt with the economic boycott as a Chinese weapon, but declined to pass upon the international law aspects of boycott activities. Chapter VIII described the economic interests in Manchuria. "It is as necessary for China to satisfy the economic interests of Japan in this territory as for Japan to recognize the unalterably Chinese character of its population. . . . The maintenance of a real Open Door, manifested by free competition in the field of trade, investment, and finance, would be in the interests of both Japan and China."

Chapter IX, "Principles and Conditions of Settlement," rejected as equally unsatisfactory the restoration of the *status quo ante*, "which would . . . merely invite repetition of the trouble," or the maintenance of Manchukuo, which the commission did not regard as "compatible with the fundamental principles of existing international obligations, nor with the good understanding between the two countries upon which peace in the Far East depends." As to the latter solution, the commission asserted: "It is opposed to the interests of China. It disregards the wishes of the people of Manchuria, and it is at least questionable whether it would ultimately serve the permanent interests of Japan. . . . To cut off these provinces from the rest of China, either legally or actually, would be to create for the future a serious irredentist problem, which would endanger peace by keeping alive the hostility of China and rendering probable the continued boycott of Japanese goods." Any solution of the problem which ignored the interests of other Powers, including the U.S.S.R., would endanger peace. Ten conclusions looking toward a settlement were enumerated: (1) Japanese and Chinese interests must be equally protected; (2) the interests of the U.S.S.R. must be safeguarded; (3) any solution reached must conform to the provisions of the Covenant, the Kellogg Pact, and the Nine Power Treaty; (4) Japanese rights and interests in Manchuria must be recognized; (5) the rights and interests of both Japan and China should be restated in new treaties; (6) effective provisions must be made for facilitating the prompt settlement of disputes as they might arise in the future; (7) Manchuria must be granted good government and a large measure of autonomy consistent with the sovereignty and administrative integrity of China; (8) internal order must be preserved by an effective local gendarmerie; and "security against external aggression should be provided by the withdrawal of all armed forces other than the gendarmerie and by the conclusion of a treaty of nonaggression between the countries interested"; (9) a new Sino-Japanese commercial treaty should be concluded to facilitate an economic *rapprochement;* (10) in the interests of general peace and of a strong central government in China "the final requisite for a satisfactory solution is temporary international cooperation in the internal reconstruction of China, as suggested by the late Dr. Sun Yat Sen." Chapter X, "Considerations and Suggestions to the Council," recommended that the Council should invite China and Japan to discuss a solution along the lines suggested. If this invitation should be accepted, an advisory conference should be called to recommend a special régime for Manchuria, to be followed by a Chinese declaration constituting a special administration for the three Eastern Provinces, a Sino-Japanese treaty dealing with Japanese interests, a Sino-Japanese Treaty of Conciliation and Arbitration, Nonaggression, and Mutual Assistance, and a Sino-Japanese commercial treaty. The balance of the report consisted of suggestions regarding the details of these proposed arrangements.

This report—so realistic and yet so unreal—was received in Japan and China with mixed feelings and was regarded by most commentators throughout the world as an extremely able document which was unlikely to be accepted. The formula of Japanese evacuation prior to the initiation of Sino-Japanese negotiations was abandoned, and this much was a concession to the realities of power politics in the Far East. The report as a whole, however, consisted of a nice balancing of Chinese and Japanese sensibilities in the hope of achieving a settlement. Since China would prefer continued passive resistance and guerrilla obstructionism to any solution involving the perpetuation of Manchukuo, the dissolution of this puppet State was proposed, though there was little likelihood that Japan would thus disown her new-born child. Since Japan would accept no solution not involving adequate protection to Japanese interests, the proposed solution forbade a return to the *status quo ante*, though there was little likelihood that China could be induced to accept any alternative. For the rest, the report refrained from passing direct judgment on whether Japan had violated existing treaties or whether China had received the protection from the other League Powers to which she was entitled. The new régime was to conform to existing engagements and to be buttressed by new engagements. Whether past engagements had been violated on either side was not indicated.

Probably no set of recommendations could have come closer to harmonizing the conflicting interests involved, fulfilling the several divergent purposes of the commission, and preparing the way for a pacific settlement. Had the Lytton report appeared in October, 1931, instead of October, 1932, it would probably have been accepted by Japan, though its chances of acceptance by China would have been less. But it came a year too late. It necessarily envisaged compromise on the basis of common interests. But common interests had been destroyed by a year of bitter conflict, and compromise was impossible between a resentful and impotent China, incensed at its own feebleness and at the world's betrayal of faith, and a victorious and militant Japan, powerful and proud in its mastery of Manchukuo. Japan had wrought her will on China by force. Power begets more power, and Japanese power was now too great for Tokyo to contemplate a weak surrender. Since the Lytton Commission aimed at peace rather than war, it recommended no sanctions, no coercion, no application against Japan of an equivalence of power. Without this, however, the solution contemplated was unworkable, since it postulated on the part of Japan a type of diplomatic and military about-face which no Great Power ever accepts, save under irresistible pressure. Here, in essence, were the tragedy and the futility of the whole proceeding and the ineffectiveness of the League method in general.

On November 21, 1932, the League Council commenced its consideration of the Lytton Report. The Japanese Government refused to accept the report as a basis for a settlement and insisted on the independence of Manchukuo, a condition which China continued to regard as wholly unacceptable. The problem was again referred to a special session of the Assembly, which met on December 6. The small Powers condemned Japan and demanded action, but the Great Powers remained noncommital. The Japanese spokesmen indicated that Tokyo's position would be adhered to, regardless of consequences, and made threats of Japanese withdrawal from the League in the event of the Assembly accepting the resolution proposed by the small Powers. On December 9 the Assembly evaded its embarrassments by referring the issue once more to the Committee of Nineteen, with instructions "to study the report of the commission of inquiry, the observations of the parties, and the opinions and suggestions expressed in the Assembly," and to submit to the Assembly as soon as possible proposals for a settlement. On December 15 the Committee of Nineteen proposed the transference of the question to a conciliatory body, composed of its own members and representatives of the United States and the U.S.S.R. Japan rejected this suggestion, objecting particularly to the competence of the proposed body and to the inclusion of American and Soviet representatives. On December 20 the Committee of Nineteen adjourned until January 16, 1933, hoping in the interim to persuade Tokyo to accept its plan. This hope proved vain. When the Committee reassembled, new fighting was going on in Jehol and the dispute was as far from a settlement as ever.

Under these circumstances further efforts at conciliation were abandoned and the League machinery moved at last toward a conclusion on the merits of the issue. On February 17, 1933, the Committee of Nineteen issued a report reviewing the course of the conflict from the beginning and recommending a settlement along the lines suggested by the Lytton Commission. On February 24 the report was unanimously accepted by the Assembly. The vote was 42 to 1, with the sole negative vote of the Japanese delegation not counted in ascertaining unanimity. Thirteen delegations were absent. Of those present only the Siamese delegation refrained from voting. In this fashion the League States condemned Japan, upheld Chinese sovereignty over Manchuria, and committed themselves to non-recognition of Manchukuo. In the face of this public censure Yosuke Matsuoka and the other Japanese representatives in the Assembly withdrew from Geneva, while the Japanese Cabinet considered formal withdrawal from the League. The controversy had gone from Council to Assembly, from Assembly to committee, from committee to commission, from commission to Council, from Council to Assembly, from Assembly to committee, from committee to Assembly. The end was not yet. But after seventeen months of "passing the buck" the League States had acted and condemned Japan in a legally binding Assembly resolution—which Japan proposed to ignore, even at the cost of defying the world. The application of sanctions was not in prospect, as it would obviously lead to war. The League method had failed. It will remain unworkable as long as the Great Powers are moved only by their own national interests.

4. THE RIDDLE OF GENEVA

"Now! Now!" cried the Queen. "Faster! Faster!" And they went so fast that at last they seemed to skim through the air, hardly touching the ground with their feet, till suddenly, just as Alice was getting quite exhausted, they stopped, and she found herself sitting on the ground breathless and giddy.

The Queen propped her up against a tree, and said kindly, "You may rest a little now."

Alice looked around her in great surprise. "Why, I do believe we've been under this tree the whole time! Everything's just as it was!"

"Of course it is," said the Queen: "what would you have it?"

"Well, in *our* country," said Alice, still panting a little, "you'd generally get to somewhere else—if you ran very fast for a long time, as we've been doing."

"A slow sort of country!" said the Queen. "Now, *here*, you see, it takes all the running you can do, to keep in the same place. If you want to get somewhere else, you must run at least twice as fast as that!"—LEWIS CARROLL, *Through the Looking-Glass.*

In attempting to evaluate the varied results of League efforts to keep the peace between States, one is confronted at the outset by the absence of any generally recognized criteria which might be used as a basis for judgment. Uncritical League enthusiasts point out that none of the League members has ever gone to "war" with another in the technical sense and that "peace" has therefore been preserved, despite the failure of the League machinery in some instances to achieve a satisfactory settlement. Scoffing cynics point out that all this is a sham and a mockery and that it makes no difference whatever, in terms of human values, whether conquest, bombardment, and butchery are called "war" or are given another name. Both of these characterizations are perfectly accurate, and yet neither furnishes any frame of reference within which the achievements and shortcomings of the League method can be weighed. Neither the League agencies themselves nor any of the innumerable critics, advocates, observers, and chroniclers have offered any criteria worthy of the attention of the reflective student of international politics. Loose analogies have, to be sure, been drawn between certain international crises dealt with at Geneva and the crisis of 1914. There have been assumptions made

[791]

as to what would have happened in 1914 if the League had existed, or what would have happened in 1923 or 1928 had the League not existed. All of this is as much beside the point as is the interminable discussion of "war guilt." No League existed in 1914, because none could have existed in the then state of national attitudes and policies. The League exists now because the modifications of these attitudes and policies, produced by the aftermath of 1914, have made it possible. It is part of the established fabric of international life in the here and now. Speculation of the "might-have-been" or "would-have-been" variety is quite fruitless. It furnishes no basis for passing judgment upon the present and future significance of the League peace machinery.

The analysis of the politics of power attempted in the present study may be used as a point of departure for suggesting the type of criteria which must be applied to this problem. "Peace" is a negative concept which by itself means nothing save the absence of war. "War," in fact rather than in law, is the physical clash of rival wills to power in the pursuit of irreconcilable objectives. The League machinery has not prevented war in this sense. If war is to be prevented, States must either be deterred from pursuing competitive power interests (and this is an impossibility in any predictable future) or they must be induced to pursue these interests by means other than those of military coercion. The assumption of violence must be superseded by the assumption of discussion, compromise, and conciliation on the basis of common interests. There can be no assurance of peace without such a modification of basic postulates and methods in the pursuit of diplomatic objectives by the members of the Western State System. If, in a particular conflict of interests and policies, a result is arrived at which represents the successful application of physical coercion by one disputant against another (e.g., the Vilna dispute, the Corfu incident) or a situation of deadlock, reflecting a stalemate in reciprocal efforts at coercion (e.g., the Gran Chaco and Manchurian conflicts), then it cannot be said that common interests have prevailed over special interests or that the assumption of violence has not been made. The nature of this result is the same, regardless of whether war has been declared or hostilities have broken out or mere threats have sufficed to impose the will of the stronger on the weaker party. Only a sophist could call such a settlement "pacific." If, on the other hand, a conflict between rival wills-to-power is resolved, not by coercion, open or concealed, but by mutual accommodation on the basis of interests and values broader than those immediately involved—and if this accommodation does not constitute in any sense the imposition of the will of the strong upon the weak—then it may reasonably be said not only that "peace" (i.e., the absence of coercion) has been maintained, but that "justice" (the prerequisite of peace) has been secured.

It may, of course, be objected that there is often no such sharp line in the political process between coercion and the absence of coercion. It may be argued that the threat of an ultimate resort to force is always in the background in all rivalries for power, whether between parties, classes, or States. This is quite true. Each particular configuration of power relationships, however, must be analyzed in terms of the way in which the parties envisage their particular interests in that particular context. Parties within a State may resort to force if one proposes to overthrow the constitution and the other proposes to preserve it. But if one proposes to interpret the constitution in this way and the other in that way, and both are agreed as to the desirability of its preservation, there will probably be no coercion, but only compromise and acquiescence on the basis of the prevailing consensus. Social classes may fight over the fundamental distribution of power within the State. They will not fight over the detailed implications of a particular distribution which all accept. States may fight over their major power interests. They will not fight if all accept a particular *status quo* or a particular procedure of modifying their power relations and differ only as to concrete application and immediate problems of detail. There is an infinite series of gradations in the interests over which political entities quarrel and in the way in which these interests are envisaged. The fact that they may resort to force and coercion on one level is not directly relevant in a consideration of what they may do on another level. International peace merely requires that States deal with those conflicting interests which breed war on a level at which their conception of these interests does not predispose disputants to coercion.

Another objection may be anticipated. That is the contention that the presence or absence of coercion is less important for the problem of peace than the question of whether coercion is violent or non-violent. If in a particular controversy one State coerces another into accepting a settlement favorable to itself and the coercion is achieved without bloodshed or destruction of property, then it may be said "peace" has been maintained. From a short-run point of view this is likewise true. The difficulty with this argument lies in the fact that such settlements, unless they entirely destroy one party to the dispute, are likely to increase resentments and tensions rather than diminish them, even if the weaker party is perforce obliged to acquiesce in the result for a long period of time. Here there is no "justice," for the concept of justice implies the settlement of controversies on the basis of general principles and common interests, unaccompanied by coercion, open or veiled, violent or non-violent. There can be no guarantee of peace in settlements which are regarded as "unjust" by the victim, nor in modes of settlement which permit such "injustices." Power relations are constantly shifting. The weak State of today may become the strong State of tomorrow, either by its own efforts or by the aid of powerful allies. When weak States whose peoples and governments are obsessed with a consciousness of unjust treatment become strong, they will "demand" justice, even at the cost of obtaining it by force. The ultimate result is not peace, but war. Non-violent coercive settlements may indeed present greater dangers of future hostilities than do violent settlements themselves, for the latter usually cripple the victim's powers of future reprisal while the former may leave them relatively unimpaired. There can be no assurance of permanent peace in coercive settlements of any kind.

From these considerations it follows that a relatively simple criterion can be applied in testing the League's adequacy as an instrumentality for preserving peace: to what degree has it prevented coercive settlements of international disputes and substituted for them settlements based upon "justice" and community interests? Or, stated differently, to what degree has it led to the disappearance of the assumption of violence and predisposed States to settle disputes on the assumption of a consensus of common values, making possible compromise, conciliation, and orderly readjustments?

With respect to disputes submitted to arbitration of adjudication, it is clear that the settlements achieved involve neither violence nor threats of violence. It is of the essence of these procedures that the disputants expressly disclaim all intention of resorting to self-help and agree in advance to submit to the outcome of litigation. General principles of law are applied to the facts in hand, and an award or decision is arrived at which all parties accept in good faith. The pertinent question here is whether or not the League method has been instrumental in inducing States to renounce coercion and to resort to arbitration or adjudication more frequently than heretofore. Have the members of the League modified their conceptions of their interests sufficiently to bring about an actual expansion of the field of disputes which are regarded as arbitrable or justiciable? An examination of post-war arbitration treaties and of the ratifications of Article 36 of the Statute of the Permanent Court leads to an affirmative answer to this question. Undoubtedly the States of the world are more deeply committed to the arbitration or adjudication of more types of disputes than has ever been the case before.

There are still numerous loopholes in such agreements, however, as experience has abundantly demonstrated, and the time is not yet when hopes for peace can be based upon the possibility of transferring all international controversies from a "political" to a "legal" or justiciable level. By no possible juggling of statistics can be it proved or disproved that a larger percentage of disputes likely to lead to war are now being arbitrated or adjudicated than in times past. Whether a particular dispute is likely to lead to coercion, *i.e.*, to be dealt with as a political question of power relations, or to be arbitrated or adjudicated, *i.e.*, to be dealt with as a legal question, depends less upon the subject matter of the controversy than upon the attitudes of the parties toward that subject matter. Disputes over financial claims and commercial opportunities are more frequently submitted to tribunals or courts than disputes over territory. But the earliest treaty of which any record remains was an agreement for the arbitration of a boundary dispute. And, if the professions of the contestants are to be believed, the most recent large-scale hostilities between States (the Sino-Japanese conflict) centered not about territory, but about financial and commercial opportunities. Disputes can be litigated, whether they be between individuals, corporations, or States, only when the parties are prepared to acquiesce in those fixed principles and permanent relationships of power incorporated into "law." There will always be disputes not susceptible of settlement by law. However wide the scope of the law and however extensive the jurisdiction of courts, the realm of politics will remain. It will consist of that field of controversies which involve temporary interests and changing relationships of power not capable of being dealt with by the judicial technique. However wide the scope of arbitration and adjudication, there will persist a wide field of international political disputes sown, as always, with the dragon's teeth. So long as this is true, the hope of eliminating the element of coercion from the settlement of disputes does not lie in the remote prospects of States so far abandoning their traditional power, profit, and prestige values that they will be willing to deal with all disputes judicially. It lies rather in the possibility of dealing by noncoercive methods with controversies which are frankly political.

This suggests a general distinction which it is useful to recall at this point before evaluating the League method of dealing with political disputes. Jurists are sometimes disposed to hold that all disputes not capable of being settled by international law are domestic questions.[1] The distinction between "international" questions and "domestic" questions is a valid one in law and is recognized in the League Covenant. International agencies, by their nature, cannot deal with domestic questions, even if the effects of domestic legislation, *e.g.*, on tariff matters or immigration, breed international friction. Many questions formerly regarded as domestic have been "internationalized" by virtue of the fact that States have concluded agreements regarding them. But within each of these realms—domestic and international—there is another and equally significant distinction, cutting across this line of division: the distinction between political questions and legal questions. Domestic disputes may involve questions of domestic politics, to be dealt with by party conventions,

[1] This was substantially the view taken by the Permanent Court in the Tunisian nationality case. See Appendix V, below, p. 893.

elections, and national legislative assemblies. Similarly, international disputes may involve questions of international law, to be dealt with by arbitrators and judges, or they may involve questions of international politics, to be dealt with by diplomats and soldiers. For the latter type of dispute, international law can only provide procedures to be followed in achieving a solution, and symbols and phrases in terms of which interests ("rights") may be verbalized. International law cannot itself supply solutions. Law is static and politics is dynamic. Political disputes can be settled only by readjustments of relationships of power.

One great merit of the League method is that it makes a clear distinction of this kind and enables legal disputes to be dealt with in one way and political disputes in another. This distinction is expressly stated in the Covenant and is implicit in all that is done through the League agencies. Arbitration and adjudication are provided for to deal with legal controversies. Conciliation through the Council is provided for to deal with political controversies. The first question which arises in every crisis is whether the questions involved are domestic or international. Formerly each disputant determined this for himself. For disputes which come before the League Council, this question is now determined judicially. The Council, in such situations, will ask the Permanent Court for an advisory opinion as to whether the dispute is "international," *i.e.*, whether the Council is competent to consider it. If the dispute is found to be international, the second question arises: is it a political or a legal controversy? This question is of necessity answered politically. Whether a particular controversy falls within one category or the other depends on the attitudes of the parties toward it. These attitudes often reflect the relative power of the disputants. Weak States frequently have difficulty in persuading strong States to deal with differences by arbitration or adjudication, rather than by diplomacy supported by force. When strong States regard it as advantageous to do so, they can often compel weak States to accept judicial treatment of a dispute, rather than political treatment, though the result is less a "settlement" than a submission induced by coercion. Germany and Austria were thus compelled by irresistible diplomatic pressure to submit the customs-union controversy to the Permanent Court for an advisory opinion. In spite of the obvious defects of a procedure which permits the distinction between legal and political questions to be made politically under pressure, the League method does nevertheless make possible a reasonably clear distinction of this kind. It has thus proved helpful in clarifying earlier confusion.

What this means in practice can be suggested by a résumé of the normal procedure of the Council in handling disputes which come before it. Such disputes are necessarily "political" or they would not come before the Council at all, but be submitted to arbitration or adjudication by the parties. They are, moreover, political disputes of an exceptionally difficult character, or they would have been settled by direct diplomatic negotiations without appeal to the Council. All such disputes will necessarily have both legal and political aspects. One advantage of the Council procedure is that it enables these aspects to be disentangled and dealt with separately. If the Council assumes jurisdiction as an agency of conciliation, it moves first of all to obviate the danger of hostilities by a "stop-fight" resolution, reminding the disputants of their obligations and requesting them to call off the dogs of war. The Council next seeks to ascertain the facts through an impartial commission of inquiry sent to the scene of the difficulty. With the facts before it, the Council then endeavors to arrive at a solution acceptable to the contestants. This will usually involve both redefinitions of legal rights and readjustments of power relations. The former function the Council does not itself undertake, but refers to the Permanent Court. When the court, by an advisory opinion, has defined the legal rights of the parties, the Council strives to bring about the necessary readjustments on the basis of the facts and the law, as ascertained by impartial agencies, and on the basis of the policies of the disputants, as expounded by their own representatives.

If this method fails to achieve a non-coercive settlement, as has frequently been the case, the fault lies less in the method, which is admirable and far in advance of any earlier procedure, than in the unwillingness of States to submit to the method. This unwillingness is a product of the prevalent attitudes, values, and behavior patterns in international politics, which it has been the major purpose of this volume to describe. This ancient unwillingness to "listen to reason" has not had the result merely of causing the failure from time to time of the League method. It has also gotten itself into the Covenant and into the League method as such. There are inherent and internal weaknesses in this procedure which reflect the unwillingness of States to yield up their traditional prerogatives at the time the Covenant was framed. The rule of unanimity comes to mind at once as a serious limitation on the efficacy of the Council's action—and this in spite of the fact that in practice it has been widely departed from through the exclusion of the litigating parties from a count of votes, through the practice of regarding many questions as "procedural" and therefore susceptible of decision by a majority vote, and through the constant and effective pressure of majorities on obstructive minorities.[1] This age-old embodiment of the pride of sovereignty and power is only one of a number of features of League procedure which casts doubt upon the ultimate efficacy of the Covenant method as a means of keeping the

[1] See p. 265 above. In the Assembly action usually takes the form not of "decisions" requiring unanimity, but of "voeux" (wishes or recommendations) requiring only a majority vote. This practice, however, has not developed in the Council.

peace. The sanctions idea, incorporated into Article 16 and the meaningless verbiage of Article 19, which touches upon a problem of transcendant importance for the whole League structure, must likewise be considered in any effort to unravel the problem of peace as it presents itself at Geneva.

Article 16 has already been discussed in connection with the general problem of security.[1] Its incorporation into the Covenant may be regarded as a result of the stubborn and unshakable persistence of the assumption of violence in international relations. The underlying concept of the sanctions Article is: "peace and security by coercion"—the theory that if only a sufficient force can be mobilized to repress the peace breaker, then peace will be secured. This notion is based upon a fundamental and fatal inconsistency of ideas. It is as true today as it was when Edmund Burke uttered the words, that there is no way of indicting a whole people. Nation-states are not criminals, to be dealt with by an international police. They are sovereignties struggling with one another for power. This struggle can be rendered pacific when its coercive elements are reduced to a minimum. By no stretch of the imagination can it be rendered pacific by making coercion universal. For reasons stated elsewhere,[2] it is physically and psychologically impossible for any conceivable combination of States to coerce a Great Power by economic or military means, if that Power is determined to meet coercion by resistance and counter-coercion. The result of such an effort would be war on the greatest scale. Weak States can usually be brought to terms by powerful neighbors, if the latter are interested in keeping the peace. Strong States, bent upon pursuing their own interests and purposes, cannot be brought to terms by any amount of coercion except at the cost of a world conflict.

In point of fact, the sanctions have never been applied, to either great States or small ones, nor has any statesman in his right mind, either at Geneva or elsewhere, ever seriously proposed that they should be applied—the French bloc always excepted.

The preoccupation of the Governments of the French bloc with international coercion and sanctions flows not at all from any abstract consideration of the merits or workability of the sanctions idea. It flows from specific power interests of an obvious variety which could be served in this fashion, if other States would consent to serve them. But other States have not consented to serve them, nor are they likely to do so. Article 16 of the Covenant remains a dead letter. It is utterly improbable that any amount of diplomatic legerdemain can breathe into it any life, for it rests upon impossibly unreal assumptions regarding the nature of international politics. If the sanctions were ever to have been applied, they would have been applied against Japan in 1931–1932. They were not applied, and no

[1] See pp. 719–720 above.
[2] See pp. 730–732 above.

government suggested that they should be. Nevertheless, Article 16 remains in the Covenant and it continues to fascinate the imaginations of those States which hope that they can somehow make it work at some future time to suppress all efforts to change the *status quo*. Here is a serious incongruity and a source of confusion in the League machinery. Article 16 renders the League ridiculous so long as it remains in the Covenant and is never acted upon, even in the fact of the most flagrant provocation. If it ever should be acted upon, it would make an agency for the preservation of peace an instrument of universal war.

More serious are the problems raised by Article 19.[1] This article was designed to meet the criticism that the League was simply another Holy Alliance dedicated to the eternal perpetuation of the 1919 *status quo*. In Wilson's mind, Article 19 was designed to complement Article 10. The League was not to guarantee for all time the territorial integrity and existing political independence of its members without providing some method of pacific and orderly change. Article 19 does not rest upon the legal doctrine of *rebus sic stantibus*, since it does not designate any circumstances under which it might be contended that treaty obligations were no longer binding. The Assembly may merely "advise" (in the French text, "*inviter*") the reconsideration of treaties which have become inapplicable. The parties themselves will judge of the inapplicability and of the wisdom of the advice. In point of fact, no such advice has ever been given, and no action whatever has been taken under Article 19. When Bolivia sought to initiate a consideration of the treaty of 1904, the Chilean delegate, in September, 1921, declared the League incompetent to revise treaties. The question of competence was referred to a commission of jurists, who declared in their report that "the Assembly . . . cannot of itself modify any treaty, the modification of treaties lying solely within the competence of contracting States." The matter was then dropped. Peru's simultaneous effort to secure a reconsideration of the Treaty of Ancon led to the same result. In 1925 the Chinese delegate called attention to the possible application of Article 19 to China's efforts to secure revision of the "unequal" treaties. In 1929 China asked for the appointment of a commission to study the application of the article. This proposal was warmly supported by the German, Austrian, and Hungarian delegates, but was voted down. The Assembly merely passed a meaningless resolution (September 25, 1929) reaffirming the principle of Article 19. The article itself, like Article 16, is thus far a dead letter. If it should ever be acted upon, the advice given by the Assembly would have no legal effect whatever, in any case.

[1] Article 19 reads as follows: "The Assembly may from time to time advise the reconsideration by members of the League of treaties which have become inapplicable and the consideration of international conditions whose continuance might endanger the peace of the world."

This circumstance is of vastly greater import than a simple lapse of certain articles of the Covenant. The issues raised by Articles 10 and 16 on the one hand, and by Article 19 on the other, touch the heart of the whole problem of the League's efficacy as an agency of peace. That problem, put in its simplest terms, is the problem of reconciling the first League with the third League—of rendering an agency already adequate for enforcing the peace treaties, *i.e.*, for perpetuating a particular distribution of power, equally adequate for revising treaty arrangements, *i.e.*, for bringing about pacific and non-coercive modifications of power relationships.

As has been repeatedly pointed out in the present study, the problem of peace rests at bottom upon the possibility of bringing about non-violent modification of relationships of power between States. Every war which has ever been fought has been fought because the ruling classes of rival States have struggled for some component of power, some element of prestige, some opportunity for profit and have been unwilling and unable to fit their conflicting interests into any frame of reference in terms of which they could reconcile their differences. The interests at stake have been glorified into principles, symbols, and myths, and millions of tax-payers, artisans, and farmers have slaughtered one another in the name of truth, justice, and rectitude. No procedures of pacific settlement are of the slightest avail if States pursue incompatible interests in an irreconcilable spirit. But the incompatibility of interests depends upon how States envisage their objectives. Where there is a will to compromise and to reconcile differences in terms of general values, procedures must be available for the pacific functioning of the political process and for the non-coercive readjustment of power relationships.

The League will ultimately stand or fall by this test. If the States of the world are prepared to use it to accommodate their conflicting interests and to bring about by pacific means those revisions of treaty terms and those readjustments of power relations which are inevitable in a changing world, the problem of peace will be solved. If they are prepared to use it only to buttress an established equilibrium and to support a temporary and static distribution of power, eventual conflict is inevitable. No settlement can ever be permanent in international politics, and unless change can be achieved pacifically it will be achieved by violence. In the resulting clash of forces, the League itself will inevitably be destroyed. Thus far the League has been dominated by the satiated *status quo* States of the French bloc—and they have sought to use it to prevent change and to perpetuate the settlement of which they are the beneficiaries. Security and sanctions are fixed ideas in the minds of the political leaders of these States, for they sense the bitter resentment of the victims of their hegemony and they anticipate the eventual undoing of their handiwork. They refuse to reduce their armaments without alternative bulwarks to their supremacy.

These bulwarks they seek by sanctions, by implementing Article 16 and Article 10, by military alliances, by defensive pacts, by organized coercion, by every international scheme and device which they think can be utilized to render permanent and unchangeable the distribution of power which they have established. This distribution, like all its predecessors, is doomed to ultimate modification by the very nature of international politics itself in the Western State System. The League, as it deals with political disputes, has thus far acted as the tail to the French kite, as an agency for perpetuating French hegemony over Europe. If it continues to be limited to this function, it will survive as long as French hegemony survives and no longer.

The alternative, obviously, is for the League to become a means of preventing the ultimate clash of forces which is inevitable if the ancient game of diplomacy is played in the ancient way. This can be achieved only by affording an opportunity for pacific modifications of the *status quo*. It cannot be achieved by organizing coercion to maintain the *status quo*. If the League States fail to afford this opportunity, the nations which insistently demand revisions of existing settlements will one by one drop away from the Geneva organization. Veiled threats of withdrawal—in Japan, in Germany, in Italy, and elsewhere—foreshadow a future development which is unavoidable unless revision can be accomplished through the practical implementation of Article 19. The French bloc has thus far opposed all efforts in this direction. The revisionist bloc will in the future disrupt the League, unless its aspirations can be realized, at least in part. The third League cannot fulfill its functions because the first League functions too well. And if the third League fails to function, the first and second Leagues are bound sooner or later to be swept away when the French bloc is overwhelmed in common catastrophe. The Geneva vessel rides stormy waters between a forbidding Scylla and a menacing Charybdis. Only the most skillful navigation, the most perfect cooperation, the most extraordinary efforts and sacrifices in the common interests can prevent eventual shipwreck. The lines of decision flow away from Geneva to Paris, Brussels, Prague, Warsaw, Bucharest, and Belgrade—and in these centers of French power there is as yet no disposition to sacrifice or to cooperate for any purpose other than the perpetuation of the peace settlement of Versailles. The League will have taken its first great step toward eventual success on the road to peace when its members permit it to be used to bring about changes of treaty terms, of frontiers, of armament levels, of economic opportunities whereby Great Powers, unthreatened and uncoerced, yield up a portion of their power to other States in the interests of general peace and the common welfare. That day is not yet—and the disastrous alternative draws ever nearer.

Here again the problems, in its fundamentals, is not a problem of the defects of the League machinery, but of defects in the wills and purposes of those who use or fail to use that machinery. It is, in short, a problem of modifying the attitudes, values, ideologies, symbolisms, and myth-ologies of the ruling classes of the nation-states. It is a problem of trans-formation, of transvaluation, of revolution. In the light of this diagnosis, it should prove helpful to conclude this survey with a consideration of the effects of the policies pursued by that Great Power in which the traditional attitudes are most firmly fixed: the United States. So far as the immediate future of power politics is concerned, salvation and peace rest with France and with the States of Europe allied to France. But the immense power of the United States and the peculiar ideology of the American nation in international affairs give to the American attitude a greater long-run significance and render a consideration of the American rôle peculiarly illuminating as regards the whole dilemma.

5. THE UNITED STATES AND THE NEW WORLD ORDER

It is therefore very difficult to ascertain, at present, what degree of sagacity the American democracy will display in the conduct of the foreign policy of the country; and upon this point its adversaries, as well as its advocates, must suspend their judgment.—ALEXIS DE TOCQUEVILLE, *Democracy in America*, 1839.

Unhappily, the policies as to international affairs—or perhaps the lack of policies—that have been pursued by our Government since the Armis-tice, have made this nation of ours a dangerous derelict adrift on the high seas of international intercourse, and lying straight across the path of every ship that sails laden with the precious cargo of international friend-ship and concord.—NICHOLAS MURRAY BUTLER, *The Path to Peace*.

Along the vine-covered balustrade which separates the Quai Wilson from the gardens of the palace housing the League Secretariat, the municipal authorities of Geneva have placed a tablet: "To the memory of Woodrow Wilson, President of the United States and Founder of the League of Nations." As has been pointed out above, the American war President played a major rôle in the creation of the League. The establish-ment of the Permanent Court of International Justice was urged by the American State Department and by innumerable distinguished citizens of the United States for many years prior to 1914. One of the most singular paradoxes of the contemporary world scene is presented by the refusal of the American Government to join either of these organizations. The League of Nations it would have none of. The Court it proposes to join on terms unacceptable to the other mem-bers. The only other Great Power which holds itself aloof from these efforts at institutionalized international cooperation is the U.S.S.R.—

precisely the Power which the United States refuses to recognize. That the Communist rulers of Russia should view the League and all its works as a futile aggregation of bourgeois capitalisms and imperialisms is a natural result of the revolutionary ideology of Communism everywhere. The reasons for the American attitude do not lie in any fundamental disharmony of social and economic philosophies between the United States and the League members. They lie rather in the persistence in the United States of a peculiar type of isolationist nationalism which will not permit the American Government to pledge itself to regularized collaboration with other States. The effects of this popular attitude on American policy and the effects of this policy upon the Geneva system are worthy of the careful consideration of all who would understand the problem of peace and the place of international organization in the contemporary Western State System.

The contributions of President Wilson to the drafting of the Covenant have already been reviewed.[1] Many provisions of the Covenant reflect his views, and some of them—notably Article 21—were deliberately devised to meet American objections. The President returned to the United States at the close of the Paris Peace Conference and personally submitted the treaty to the Senate on July 10, 1919, with an appeal for prompt ratification. The Senate Committee on Foreign Relations proceeded with great deliberation and held public hearings lasting until September 12. There was little discussion of the terms of the Treaty of Versailles beyond the first twenty-six articles, i.e., the League Covenant. Three factors in the American political situation contributed to the final rejection of Wilson's work. The first was the popular recrudescence of extreme isolationist sentiment, due to the relaxation of the tensions of the war period, the reaction of disillusionment against the emotional appeals of the great crusade, and a general "morning-after-the-night-before" feeling which gave everything associated with the war and the peace a bitter taste in the public mouth. The second was the intense rivalry between the Democratic and Republican parties in Congress. The Republican leaders, thirsting for power after eight years out of office, were determined to make political capital out of every possible attack upon the Wilson administration. The Covenant of the League furnished a suitable target, and during the latter part of 1919 the struggle between the parties centered entirely around the question of the ratification of the treaty. The third element was the personal enmity which had developed between Wilson and Senator Henry Cabot Lodge, one of the spokesmen of the Senate "irreconcilables." In 1916 the Massachusetts senator was more enthusiastic than Wilson for "compulsory arbitration" and international organization to keep the peace. In 1919 he could find no word of abuse

[1] See pp. 251–257 above.

severe enough to heap upon Wilson and the League, though many of his fellow Republicans, including Taft and Root, regarded it as a satisfactory realization of their aspirations in the period of neutrality. In the late summer of 1919 President Wilson, realizing the extent of Senate opposition to the treaty, toured the country in an appeal to the electorate. He was trailed by Senator Hiram Johnson of California, another prominent irreconcilable. The President's health broke down in the course of his journey and he was obliged to abandon active participation in the struggle for ratification.

In the course of the Senate debates, the "irreconcilables," led by Lodge, Johnson, Borah, Sherman, Reed, and Poindexter, assailed the Covenant as a dangerous instrument and presented American participation in the League as an outrageous violation of traditional American policies. Article 10 was condemned as committing the United States to armed defense of Europe's new frontiers. Article 16 was viewed with even greater alarm as foreshadowing the conscription of American men and money "to fight Europe's wars." The bitter-end irreconcilables opposed the treaty in any form. Another group favored acceptance with reservations which would "safeguard" American liberty of action. A third group favored mild reservations of an interpretative character. The number favoring unqualified ratification was far less than the necessary two-thirds. On September 10 the Committee on Foreign Relations reported the treaty back to the Senate, with a long list of amendments, to all of which the minority, favoring outright repudiation of the Covenant, objected vigorously. The reservations and amendments dealt with "sovereignty," "independence," "domestic questions," "neutrality," "avoidance of foreign entanglements," and the "Monroe Doctrine." For two months the treaty was debated in the Senate. The amendments were all rejected by substantial majorities, made up of those who opposed the Covenant in any form and those who approved it without qualifications. Lodge finally submitted 14 new reservations, which Wilson indicated that he would not accept.

On November 19 the Senate voted on the treaty, with the reservations. In this form it was rejected by 39 votes for and 55 against. A motion to reconsider was at once adopted. Senator Hitchcock, the Democratic leader, proposed five mild reservations which were rejected 52 to 41. The Lodge reservations were also rejected 51 to 41. Senator Underwood's resolution to ratify the treaty without reservations was rejected 53 to 38. At the end of January, 1920, Wilson announced that he would accept the Hitchcock reservations, but Lodge refused to compromise. On February 9 the Senate again referred the Treaty to the Committee, which added a fifteenth reservation expressing sympathy for Ireland. The new Senate (Republican by two votes) was organized in March, with Lodge as chairman of the Committee on Foreign Relations. On March 19, 1920, the final vote on the ratifying resolution was taken. The vote was 58 for and 22 against. The Covenant thus fell short by 7 votes of securing the necessary two-thirds.

The overwhelming victory of the Republican ticket, headed by Harding and Coolidge, in the election of November, 1920, was widely interpreted as a popular repudiation of the League, though this was scarcely an issue in the eastern part of the country and the Republican candidate declared himself in favor of *a* League of Nations, rather than *the* League of Nations. In his first message to Congress, President Harding stated that "in the existing League of Nations, with its superpowers, this Republic will have no part." On June 21, 1923, he declared at St. Louis: "In the face of the overwhelming verdict of 1920, the issue of the League is as dead as slavery." Secretary of State Hughes was left considerable discretion by the President in the formulation of foreign policy, and in accordance with the spirit of the new dispensation he completely ignored the very existence of the League for a period of six months, refusing even to acknowledge communications from the Secretariat. A more polite attitude was subsequently adopted, but the League had become a phobia in certain parts of the country, particularly the midwestern hinterland. In deference to this obsession, the State Department refused to cooperate in any official way with League activities. Colonel George Harvey, new American Ambassador to Great Britain, declared in the presence of Lloyd George, on May 28, 1921, that "our present Government will have nothing to do with it (the League) or any commission or committee appointed by it, or responsible to it, direct or indirectly, open or furtively." A separate peace treaty was signed with Germany on August 25, 1921. Isolationism was triumphant.

This early attitude of complete aloofness was gradually softened into one of tentative cooperation, which in turn merged into active participation in many League activities. By the close of the twelve-year period of Republican rule (1921–1933), the American Government was cooperating closely with the League in many respects. In 1923 the State Department began sending "unofficial observers" to various League conferences. The American consul at Geneva participated in a "consultative" capacity at the second General Conference on Communications and Transit in November-December, 1923. Observers were likewise sent to a considerable number of other League gatherings dealing with technical and administrative problems. At the second Opium Conference (November, 1924, to February, 1925) the United States was represented by an official plenipotentiary. Official representatives were later sent to other League conferences of a "non-political" character, dealing with drugs, arms traffic, communications, codification of international law, etc. At the first session of the Preparatory Commission for the Disarmament Conference, the United States was represented for the first time by a minister—Hugh Gibson, American Minister to Switzerland. Delegates were likewise sent to the World Economic Conference of 1927. By the end of 1930 the United States had signed a dozen international conventions drafted by League conferences. The American Government likewise made financial contributions to the expenses of League gatherings attended by its representatives. More than a score of Americans have at one time or another held official positions in the League Secretariat. Millions of dollars have been donated from private American sources to aid various League activities. The United States has been represented at several conferences of the International Labor Organization, and many Americans have served in the International Labor Office, though the United States is not a member of this body. In the autumn of 1931 the United States co-operated with the League for the first time in dealing with political questions, by appointing a representative to sit with the Council in considering the Far Eastern crisis.[1] Throughout the entire Sino-Japanese conflict Secretary Stimson sought to support League efforts in every possible way short of actual membership. The American tourists who thronged the galleries at the Assembly meetings, however, have always looked in vain for the American delegation.

The story of American relations with the Permanent Court is even more illuminating for the light which it throws upon isolationist psychology and upon the inability of the executive to persuade the legislature to take a more generous view of international cooperation. Elihu Root was a member of the commission of jurists which framed the statute. An American judge has been a member of the court from the beginning—first, John Bassett Moore (1921–1928), then Charles Evans Hughes (1928–1930), and Frank B. Kellogg since 1930. This list, it will be noted, includes two former Secretaries of State and the present Chief Justice of the Supreme Court. These gentlemen were, of course, nominated not by the American Government but by the various national groups on the Hague tribunal, and elected by the Council and the Assembly without American governmental participation. At no time has the United States, as a Government, officially been a member of the court. This has not been due to any disapproval of American membership on the part of the three Republican administrations, but to the attitude of the Senate. All of the Republican Presidents and Secretaries of State since 1920 have favored American membership, but up to the time of writing the Senate's policy has made the fulfillment of this purpose impossible. On February 24, 1923, President Harding transmitted to the Senate a message urging American

[1] See pp. 783–784 above.

adherence to the Protocol of Signature of December 16, 1920, accepting the Statute. This message was accompanied by a letter of February 17, 1923, from Secretary of State Hughes, emphasizing the important rôle of the United States in sponsoring international adjudication in the pre-war period and urging adherence on four conditions, necessitated by American non-membership in the League. These conditions, with minor changes of phraseology, were incorporated later into the Senate reservations.

Almost three years elapsed before this recommendation was acted upon. On March 3, 1925, by a vote of 303 to 28, the House of Representatives urged adherence. On January 27, 1926, by a vote of 76 to 17, the Senate approved ratification of the protocol, subject to the Hughes conditions plus a fifth reservation which the Senators in their wisdom saw fit to add to the four suggested by the Secretary of State. The five Senate reservations follow:

1. That such adherence shall not be taken to involve any legal relation on the part of the United States to the League of Nations or the assumption of any obligations by the United States under the Treaty of Versailles.

2. That the United States shall be permitted to participate through representatives designated for the purpose and upon an equality with the other States, members, respectively, of the Council and Assembly of the League of Nations, in any and all proceedings of either the Council or the Assembly for the election of judges or deputy judges of the Permanent Court of International Justice or for the filling of vacancies.

3. That the United States will pay a fair share of the expenses of the court as determined and appropriated from time to time by the Congress of the United States.

4. That the United States may at any time withdraw its adherence to the said protocol and that the statute for the Permanent Court of International Justice adjoined to the protocol shall not be amended without the consent of the United States.

5. That the court shall not render any advisory opinion except publicly after due notice to all States adhering to the court and to all interested States and after public hearing or opportunity for hearing given to any State concerned; nor shall it, without the consent of the United States, entertain any request for an advisory opinion touching any dispute or question in which the United States has or claims an interest.

The first four of these reservations and the first part of the fifth gave rise to no important difficulties. They merely gave the United States the same privileges and responsibilities enjoyed by the other signatories of the protocol. All of them were acceptable to the other signatories. The second part of the fifth reservation, however, presented a serious problem. The court was to be forbidden to "entertain any request for an advisory opinion, touching any dispute or question in which the United States has or claims an interest." In practice, advisory opinions are requested by the League Council, though the Assembly also has this right. In so far as the Senators who framed the fifth reservation did not design it for purely obstructionist purposes, they were acting in the interest of placing the United States in a position of equality with the members of the League Council in regard to this particular function of the court. But the reservation was based upon the supposition that all requests for an advisory opinion require unanimity in the Council. It was assumed that each member of the Council, by its single vote, could block a request for an advisory opinion. The United States was to be given this same right. It was to be granted the privilege of blocking advisory opinions, not merely in disputes in which it had an interest, but in those in which it *claimed* an interest.

The ideas behind this reservation are obvious. They are in line with the Senate's traditional attitude. The Senate has always held that, so far as possible, the United States ought not to cooperate at all with other nations in the preservation of peace and that, if it must cooperate, it should do so on terms which reserve its complete liberty not merely to refrain from submitting to procedures of pacific settlement, but likewise to prevent other States from doing so if the matter in hand has any connection, however remote, with American "national interests." In the present instance the Senate, in effect, said: we recognize that advisory opinions are purely advisory and have no legally binding results. But they have moral weight. A situation may arise in the League Council touching some national interest of the United States. The American Government will not submit such questions to any international body, even for discussion. It must consequently reserve to itself the right to prevent the Court, not only from delivering an advisory opinion which might be unfavorable to the United States, but even from considering a request for such an opinion. The Court must therefore be forbidden to consider such requests whenever the United States chooses to forbid it.

This reservation might have had some justification if the members of the League Council had possessed a similar veto power over such requests. In fact, however, it is by no means clear that this is the case. Whether a request from the Council for an advisory opinion is a "decision" requiring unanimity or an action requiring unanimity with the exception of the States directly concerned, or merely a procedural matter requiring only a majority vote has never been authoritatively determined. Such requests, in practice, have been made by a unanimous vote of the Council, but it has never been established that a single State on the Council could forbid such a request. In view of the great utility of advisory opinions, moreover, it was not to be expected that League members would act in such a fashion. A non-League State, however, might adopt a different attitude. Apart from this consideration, the Court itself had laid it down as a principle in the Eastern Karelia case[1] that it would not deliver an advisory opinion if one of the States affected by it objected to its taking jurisdiction. The fears of the Senate on this score were groundless. But the reservation opened up the possibility that the United States, through the privilege of a special veto which general acceptance of the fifth reservation would accord it, might, at its own discretion or caprice, interfere seriously with the whole institution of advisory opinions by "claiming" an interest in all sorts of disputes in which an opinion from the Court would be extremely helpful to the Council.

Under these circumstances, the other members of the Court found it impossible to accept the fifth reservation without some further interpretation of its meaning. At the March, 1926, meeting of the Council Sir Austen Chamberlain pointed out that the wording of Part II of the fifth reservation was capable of an interpretation which might "hamper the work of the Council and prejudice the rights of the members of the League, but it is not clear that it was intended to bear any such meaning. The correct interpretation of this paragraph of the resolution should be the subject of discussion and agreement with the United States Government." A conference was therefore called to meet at Geneva on September 1, 1926, to discuss the meaning of the fifth reservation and to consider the possible changes in the Statute necessitated by its terms. The United States was invited to attend. By this time, however, the administration in Washington had become alarmed by certain domestic political developments. Isolationism continued to furnish emotional slogans and irrelevant catchwords with which demagogues could easily ensnare the votes of the yokelry. The fact that the Senate should accept the Court at all, in any form, furnished a new opportunity for political quackery of the cheapest type. William Randolph Hearst and his chain of newspapers launched a furious assault upon the Court. Johnson, Borah, and other irreconcilables began once more to thunder their fulminations. "Big Bill" Thompson, with the support of Len Small and other worthies in the Illinois Republican party, won the Chicago mayoralty primary (and subsequently the election) on a platform of "America First," "Biff King George on the Snoot," and "No World Court."

In view of these discouraging manifestations of the democratic process, the administration beat a nervous retreat from a position which might make it a target of new shafts cast by the isolationists. Secretary Kellogg refused the invitation extended to the United States to attend the September conference. He declared that the meaning of the reservation was "clear and unequivocal," which was manifestly absurd. Out of fear of giving the appearance of any cooperation whatever with the League Council, he further made the fantastic suggestion that any discussion should be

[1] See pp. 769–770 above.

[809]

handled, not by a conference but by individual exchanges of notes between the United States and the fifty other members of the Court.

The representatives of the members of the Court thus met in Geneva in September, 1926, to consider the American reservations, with no cooperation from the American Government. They accepted the first four reservations unconditionally, except for the first part of the fourth, relating to the American right of withdrawal. This they likewise accepted, along with the ambiguous fifth reservation, on the condition that if the results proved unsatisfactory the acceptance might be withdrawn by a two-thirds vote of the signatories. The conference agreed that the Court could not give any advisory opinion in a dispute to which the United States was a party, if the American Government objected. With respect to disputes in which the United States merely claimed an interest, it should be given a position of equality with the Council members—"that is to say, in any case where a State represented on the Council or in the Assembly could possess the right of preventing, by opposition in either of these bodies, the adoption of a proposal to request an advisory opinion from the Court, the United States shall enjoy an equivalent right." The conference, in its final act of September 23, proposed a special protocol to put the American reservations into effect. Twenty-four States sent individual replies to the American Government regarding the whole question, but the State Department took no cognizance whatever of any of the replies or of the conference. Fear of offending the isolationists again blocked all progress toward international agreement.

Two more years now went by, with no further action taken at Washington to make the United States a member of the Court. On February 6, 1928, Senator Gillett of Massachusetts introduced a resolution recalling that the signatories had requested a further exchange of views and suggesting that the exchange be entered into "in order to establish whether the differences between the United States and the signatory States can be satisfactorily adjusted." At the end of May the Senate Committee on Foreign Relations agreed to act on the resolution in December. On November 24, 1928, President Coolidge announced his desire for a further exchange of views. On February 19, 1929, Secretary Kellogg sent a note to the Secretary-General of the League, informing him that he was simultaneously despatching a note to all the signatories of the original protocol, expressing the desire of the American Government to accept the suggestions in the final act of the 1926 conference, but declaring that these suggestions "would not afford adequate protection to the United States," since the League Covenant and the rules of the Court could be amended at any time without American consent. It was therefore urged that new exchanges of views take place, as a means of arriving at some alternative formula. There followed the elaboration of the so-called "Root formula."

The Council had already appointed a committee of fifteen jurists, with Elihu Root among them, to suggest needed amendments in the Statute. The Council now asked the committee to consider also the question of the accession of the United States to the Court. On March 18, 1929, the committee recommended certain changes in the Statute and approved a draft protocol, superseding the 1926 proposal and accepting the Senate reservations *in toto* on the basis of Mr. Root's suggestion. The Council unanimously approved both reports of the committee. In September, 1929, both of the new protocols were open to signature, after meeting with the approval of the League Assembly and of a special conference of Court members.

The Root formula, as embodied in the Protocol of Accession of March 18, 1929, constituted an ingenious settlement of the tangle. The reservations were accepted and reference was made to Articles 73 and 74 of the revised rules of the Court, relating to advisory opinions. Article 5 of the protocol dealt with the vexatious fifth reservation. It proposed that in every case in which the Council or Assembly might request an advisory opinion, the Secretary-General of the League should inform the United States and should, if asked to do so, initiate an exchange of views between the Council or Assembly and the United States "as to whether an interest of the United States is affected." The registrar of the Court should also inform the United States of all requests, and the Court proceedings should be stayed for a period sufficient to enable such an exchange of views to take place. The article continued:

With regard to requesting an advisory opinion of the court in any case covered by the preceding paragraphs, there shall be attributed to an objection of the United States the same force and effect as attaches to a vote against asking for the opinion given by a member of the League of Nations in the Council or in the Assembly.

If, after the exchange of views provided for in paragraphs 1 and 2 of this Article, it shall appear that no agreement can be reached and the United States is not prepared to forego its objection, the exercise of the powers of withdrawal provided for in Article 8 hereof will follow naturally without any imputation of unfriendliness or unwillingness to cooperate generally for peace and good will.

On September 5, 1929, Secretary Stimson expressed his approval of the new Protocol of Accession. On November 18 he recommended to the President signature of the three Court Protocols: Protocol of Signature of the Statute, December 16, 1920; Protocol of Revision of the Statute, September 14, 1929; and Protocol of Accession of the United States of America to the Protocol of Signature of the Statute, September 14, 1929. On November 26 the President authorized signature. American signatures were attached to all three instruments on December 9, and a year later, December 10, 1930, the President transmitted them to the Senate and requested consent for ratification. At last the way seemed clear for action. But again the Senate moved in mysterious ways its wonders to perform. On December 17, 1930, the Foreign Relations Committee voted ten to nine to postpone further consideration until December, 1931. On January 21, 1931, Mr. Root explained the formula to the Committee. On February 11 Senator Walsh of Montana moved to reconsider the decision of December 17, but it was reaffirmed ten to eight. Senator Borah, chairman of the committee, now led a new fight against ratification. The weapons of the irreconcilables were, as in the past, interminable delay, verbal hair splitting, and the injection of as much confusion as possible into the discussion. The Austro-German customs-union opinion of September 5, 1931, was made a new target of attack. The Senate failed to act in December, 1931. The Protocols remained pigeonholed in the committee. On March 2, 1932, Senator Walsh moved that they be reported out. On the same day the Foreign Relations Committee, by a vote of eleven to nine, rejected a proposal to defer all action until April 15, with Borah, Johnson, Moses, LaFollette, Vandenberg, Robinson, Cutting (all Republicans), Lewis (Democrat), and Shipstead (Farmer-Labor) voting for postponement. The Foreign Relations Committee now adopted a resolution, proposed by Senator Reed of Pennsylvania, declaring "said protocol is ratified with the clear understanding that the Permanent Court of International Justice shall not, without the consent of the United States, entertain any request for an advisory opinion touching any dispute or question in which the United States has or claims an interest."

This was a reiteration of the fifth reservation and an "interpretation" of the Root Formula, which left the confusion worse confounded. Was this another "reservation," requiring the consent of the other signatories, or was it merely an "explanation"? Bitter wrangles followed in the committee, to the great glee of the irreconcilables. On March 16 Senators Pittman and Lewis offered resolutions designed to add to the confusion and delay. On March 23 Secretary Stimson transmitted a letter to the committee, declaring that the fifth reservation had already been "accepted in its entirety by the pending protocol." Senator Borah declared this to be "unsatisfactory." He and his fellow obstructionists professed to see inconsistencies between the Stimson letter and Root's own explanation. On May 12, by a vote of eleven to nine, the committee ordered the resolution reported to the Senate, with the recommendation that ratification be approved only on condition that the other signatories, in separate written notes, expressly accept the fifth reservation. When asked when he thought the report would come up for debate on the Senate floor, Senator Borah, who voted against it, declared: "So far as I am concerned, never."[1] The Senate ended its session without taking action. Neither was any action

[1] New York *Times*, May 13, 1932.

taken in the December, 1932–March, 1933 session of Congress. By the close of the year 1932, three years had elapsed since the Root formula was devised. Six years had elapsed since the signatories had expressed their views on the Senate reservations. Almost ten years had elapsed since President Harding first recommended adherence to the Court. The United States was still not a member and was apparently not likely to become one in the near future.

This extraordinary tale of delay, frustration, demagoguery, and unscrupulous skullduggery merits telling in such detail not because of the intrinsic importance of its subject matter (American membership in the Court would at best be only a short step toward effective international cooperation), but because it serves to explain many aspects of American foreign policy otherwise incomprehensible. It reveals the Senate and the State Department working at cross purposes, with the latter seeking to promote cooperation and the former standing staunchly as a citadel of obstruction and isolation. It reveals the reasons for European incredulity and resentment at the position of the United States. It reveals the emotional mysticism, the unshakable irrationality, the almost unbelievable stupidity and provincialism of a large section of the American electorate. It reveals the effects of these things on the conduct of elected representatives in a democratic government. It reveals finally the isolationist tradition as a phase of popular patriotic mythology, functioning at its best. The implications of this tradition for the whole problem of peace through international organization may now be examined briefly in terms of the influence of ancient symbols and stereotyped formulas upon the conduct of policy, and in terms of the results of this policy in limiting the efficacy of the Geneva League.

The isolation doctrine itself originated at the end of the eighteenth century, when the feebleness of the young republic, coupled with the embarrassments in which the American Government found itself in consequence of the French alliance and the European wars, made the doctrine a reasonable formulation of the interests of the United States in the contemporary pattern of power relationships. In his Farewell Address of 1796, Washington urged the avoidance of "entanglements of our peace and prosperity." In his Inaugural Address of 1801, Jefferson urged "peace, commerce, and honest friendship with all nations, entangling alliances with none." These phrases were later sanctified and invested with magic properties. They were repeatedly referred to during the nineteenth century to justify the foreign policies of each administration. They were used by the isolationists a century and a quarter later for purposes of self-hypnosis and the bamboozlement of the hinterland provinces. In so far as the isolation doctrine is susceptible of any precise definition, it may be taken to mean that the United States should refrain

[813]

from entering into alliances with foreign States, should remain neutral in foreign wars, should resist foreign encroachments in the western hemisphere, and should avoid commitments in other parts of the world. The doctrine is still a not inaccurate statement of the inevitable position of the United States in Great Power politics, since the American nation, by its geographical position, cannot exert its power effectively in Europe or Asia and must make the new world its sphere of political activity. Not even the conquests of time and space made possible by machine technology have wrought any fundamental change in this situation.

The incongruity of isolationism in the twentieth century arises from the fact that the United States, with its enormously valuable markets for trade and investment scattered over the globe, can no longer protect the diplomatic interests which these economic contacts have created through holding itself sublimely aloof from the existing structure of international cooperation. In 1919 the League Covenant was condemned as an entangling alliance, but its proponents pointed out that Washington had advised only against entanglements "with any portion of the foreign world," and not with the world as a whole. The obsolescence of Articles 10 and 16 has made it clear, in any case, that the League is neither a super-State nor an alliance. It is a method of cooperation for the maintenance of peace and for the promotion of the common interests of the nation-states. The United States has a larger economic stake in peace throughout the world than any other Power. That stake cannot be defended by the single-handed action of the American Government, nor can it be protected by isolationism, for it is impossible for the United States to avoid being drawn into combats between other Powers which threaten any fundamental upset of the existing equilibrium. Popular attitudes and the policies influenced by them, however, are molded not by facts, but by myths and symbols whose antiquity and irrelevancy render them more, rather than less, efficacious as devices for stirring mass emotions. Isolationism is associated with "sovereignty," "independence," "vital interests," "national honor," and other antique shibboleths. The concrete result of the prevalence of these myths is the pursuit of a policy designed to reduce to a minimum American cooperation with other States. Far from protecting American interests, this policy exposes them to a peculiar degree to the inevitable dangers attending the exclusive and isolated pursuit of national interests in an integrated and interdependent world. In such a world the interests of each State can be safeguarded only by the type of international collaboration which the League of Nations makes possible. And to the degree to which the efficacy of the League is limited by the absence from its membership of the greatest of the Great Powers, to that degree are the interests of all States, including the United States, jeopardized by the inevitable results of continuing international anarchy.

But since this consideration is a logical deduction from observable facts rather than an irrational verbalization of traditionalized and emotionalized catchwords, it is without appreciable influence on attitudes and policies.

The Monroe Doctrine is another ancestral symbol of national ethnocentrism which stands in the way of international cooperation. Its meaning is even less precise than that of isolationism.[1] It has been said that there have been almost as many Monroe Doctrines as Secretaries of State. This statement of policy has been aptly defined as that doctrine for which all Americans are prepared to fight, but which no American understands. As a corollary of isolationism and of the "two spheres doctrine" of John Quincy Adams, however, the Monroe Doctrine may be taken to mean that the United States will resist all efforts on the part of outside States to extend their power to the western hemisphere and will regard this area as its own exclusive arena of expansion. The doctrine has never been reciprocal, for the United States has always reserved its right to extend its own power to other continents. Since 1900 the Doctrine has been regarded in Latin America as an excuse for North American imperialism. In terms of power relationships, it may be taken to mean that the United States should refrain from international commitments hampering its liberty of action on the American continent. Recently it has been presented once more as an injunction addressed to Europe, and not to Latin America,[2] though Latin Americans take this *cum grano salis.*

[1] "In one sense the Monroe Doctrine symbolizes a sentiment with no precise meaning at all. It is a shibboleth which, from the standpoint of arousing the American people, is certainly not obsolete. In this sense it has the same relation to international law as the flag, the highly colored newspaper, the political orator, and other stimuli of emotions. Foreign nations have learned to take cognizance of the fact that in the United States the Monroe Doctrine is associated with highly charged emotional dispositions which, if aroused, may lead the United States to action, wholly regardless of law." Quincy Wright in *Proceedings of the American Society of International Law,* 1924, p. 64.

[2] On February 6, 1931, Secretary of State Stimson announced before the Council of Foreign Relations in New York City: "The Monroe Doctrine was a declaration of the United States *versus* Europe, not of the United States *versus* Latin America." This view was more fully expressed in a memorandum submitted to the Secretary of State on December 17, 1928, by the then Under-secretary, J. Reuben Clark, later appointed Ambassador to Mexico. The Clark memorandum asserted: "The doctrine does not concern itself with purely inter-American relations; it has nothing to do with the relationship between the United States and other American nations, except where other American nations shall become involved with European governments in arrangements which threaten the security of the United States, and even in such cases the doctrine runs against the European country, not the American nation, and the United States would primarily deal thereunder with the European country and not with the American nation concerned. . . . So far as Latin America is concerned, the doctrine is now, and has always been, not an instrument of violence and oppression, but an unbought, freely bestowed, and wholly effective guarantee of their freedom, independence, and territorial integrity against the imperialistic designs of Europe." *Senate Document* 114, 71st Congress, 2d Session, pp. xxiv to xxv.

During the war President Wilson developed an interpretation of the doctrine which would make it a statement of a general principle forbidding territorial conquest anywhere. On January 22, 1917, he declared in the Senate: "I am proposing, as it were, that the nations should with one accord adopt the doctrine of President Monroe as the doctrine of the world; that no nation should seek to extend its polity over any other nation or people, but that every people should be left free to determine its own polity, its own way of development, unhindered, unthreatened, unafraid, the little along with the great and powerful. I am proposing that all nations henceforth avoid entangling alliances which would drag them into competitions of power, catch them in a net of intrigue and selfish rivalry, and disturb their own affairs with influences intruded from without. There is no entangling alliance in a concert of power." Wilson regarded Article 10 of the Covenant as a logical extension of the doctrine, and he consented to the inclusion of Article 21[1] to meet possible Senate criticism. Senator Borah had already argued, in December, 1918, that American membership in the League would abrogate the Monroe Doctrine. In the discussion of Article 21, several foreign governments objected to any mention of the Monroe Doctrine without a definition of it. The article was accepted, however, in a form which referred to it as "a regional understanding . . . for the maintenance of peace." It was not, and has never been, an "understanding," except by tacit consent, for it is a unilateral policy of the United States. Whether it has contributed to the maintenance of peace is at least open to question. Nevertheless, the other Powers accepted this vague and ambiguous statement and Wilson hoped that it would prove acceptable to the Senate. This hope was vain. Senate Reservation 4 declared " . . . said doctrine is to be interpreted by the United States alone and is hereby declared to be wholly outside the jurisdiction of said League of Nations and entirely unaffected by any provision contained in the said Treaty of Peace with Germany."

The proponents of the Covenant argued that the Monroe Doctrine was sanctioned by international law in Article 21 and was thus, for the first time, expressly accepted by other States. The irreconcilables insisted that it was threatened with destruction, in so far as its definition and interpretation would now be in the hands of the League. Senator Lodge spoke of it as a protective fence around the United States. Wilson asserted that Article 10 of the Covenant extended this protection to all States of the world. Lodge expressed his inability to understand how a fence could be maintained by tearing it down. Some Senators argued that Article 10 would prevent the United States from extending the beneficent

---

[1] Article 21 of the Covenant reads as follows: "Nothing in this Covenant shall be deemed to affect the validity of international engagements, such as treaties of arbitration or regional understandings like the Monroe Doctrine, for securing the maintenance of peace."

influence of its civilization throughout Latin America. A number of Latin American States subsequently objected to Article 21 and made reservations regarding it on joining the League. In the defeat of the Covenant in the United States, the doctrine played a significant rôle in arousing patriotic emotionalism and in contributing to the impression that the Covenant was incompatible with American national interests.

The type of American policy symbolized by the Monroe Doctrine has visibly diminished the utility of the League to the Latin American States and has inhibited action at Geneva designed to preserve peace between the American republics. In the case of Bolivia and Peru *versus* Chile, the Monroe Doctrine was not expressly mentioned and the Assembly would, in any case, have taken no action under Article 19 against Chile's objection. But the traditional insistence of the United States that American disputes must be dealt with by American agencies was one of the imponderables in the background of the discussion which made the League Powers reluctant to do anything to which the United States might object. In the Costa Rica-Panama boundary conflict of 1921, the League Council welcomed American mediation and in effect washed its hands of responsibility. The summary of the Gran Chaco conflict which has already been presented[1] makes it clear that League action was obstructed by the United States. It does not follow that the League method would have proved successful in these instances, had the American Government not stood in the way of its vigorous application. It is obvious, however, that the Monroe Doctrine, as an assertion of the hegemony of the United States over the American continent, renders the League's task extremely difficult on the western side of the Atlantic. All of the Latin American republics save Brazil, Ecuador, and Costa Rica are now members of the League. The non-membership of the United States, coupled with the Monroe Doctrine, has appreciably reduced the benefits of this membership.

The American policies symbolized by "neutrality" and "freedom of the seas" have been widely regarded as even more serious obstacles to the effective operation of the League machinery. The American neutrality policy has meant that in conflicts between other States not directly affecting American interests, the United States will observe the obligations of a neutral and insist upon respect for its rights as a neutral. Neutral obligations offer no difficulty, from the point of view of the League Covenant. But "neutral rights" and "freedom of the seas," as interpreted by the United States, mean that the profitable activities of American citizens in selling goods to belligerents are not to be unduly interfered with by other belligerents. The freedom in question is freedom to make money by supplying the sinews of war to the combatants. If the Covenant is interpreted literally, the status of neutrality is abolished for League

[1] See pp. 778–782 above.

[817]

members in relation to a Covenant-breaking State, since members resorting to war in disregard of Articles 12, 13, or 15 "shall *ipso facto* be deemed to have committed an act of war against all other members of the League" (Article 16), who undertake to apply military and economic sanctions against such a State. The United States rejected the Covenant in part because of the sanctions article, and the American Government has subsequently expressed its dissent from the whole theory of sanctions at every possible opportunity.[1] It has been contended in certain quarters that the chief reason for the nonapplication of sanctions has been fear on the part of the League States that the United States would insist on protecting the right of its citizens to trade with the victims. If such trade were permitted, the sanctions would be useless. If it were interfered with by the League States enforcing the sanctions, diplomatic friction with the United States would result. Twice in its history—in 1812 and 1917—the United States has gone to war with States interfering with its neutral trading rights. On July 30, 1928, Sir Austen Chamberlain asserted in the House of Commons that the practical effects of the Kellogg Pact would depend upon "how the rest of the world thought the United States was going to judge the action of the aggressor and whether they would help or hinder him in his aggression."

This danger, which has helped to hamstring the whole sanctions arrangement, could be removed only if the American Government would disclaim any intention of protecting its citizens engaged in trade with Covenant-breaking or Pact-breaking States. A number of resolutions have from time to time been introduced in Congress since the ratification of the Kellogg Pact, looking toward a modification of the traditional American policy in such situations. It has been contended that American signature of the Pact makes the concept of neutrality as obsolete for the United States as if it had signed the Covenant. The Capper resolution of February 11, 1929, demands "that whenever the President determines,

[1] William R. Castle, Acting Secretary of State, accurately expressed the established American attitude on May 4, 1932, in an address before the American Conference on International Justice: "The borderline between aggression and self-defense is seldom clearly defined, yet if we are going to fight to keep the peace the question must be instantly decided. The Council of the League or the World Court is most often mentioned as the body to make the decision as to whether the United States, among other nations, shall fight for peace. But surely this is not in accord with the American tradition. We never have, and please God we never shall, put into the hands of any alien body the right to decide whether our young American manhood shall be sent out to die in battle.

"This plan to prevent war by war, to place in the custody of others the right to send our citizens into the trenches, has never been seriously considered by the American Government. It is the one point, I think, on which we most fundamentally differ from the League of Nations, and granting all the virtues of the League, I cannot foresee any possibility that America will join that organization while the possibility of war to prevent war, with the concurrent necessity to send out our young men to fight at the behest of other governments than our own, remains in the Covenant."

and by proclamation declares, that any country has violated the Multi-lateral Treaty for the Renunciation of War, it shall be unlawful, unless otherwise provided by act of Congress or by proclamation of the President, to export to such country arms, implements of war, or other articles for use in war until the President shall by proclamation declare that such violation no longer continues."

This arrangement seeks to outlaw not all trade with States violating the Pact (such States would presumably also be violating the Covenant), but only trade in war supplies. The President would determine the fact of violation. If his determination happened to coincide with that of the League Council, the way would be clear for the application of League sanctions in so far as they would involve an embargo on trade in war materials. Various private groups in the United States have sought to secure American cooperation in the prospective application of sanctions. None of the congressional resolutions has been passed, however, and the American Government has never committed itself to any general policy of forbidding trade with Pact-breaking or Covenant-breaking States. Many peace seekers have argued that until it does so the League members will never apply sanctions against an aggressor, and without sanctions, so the argument runs, there can be no assurance of peace.

That this view has very little foundation in the realities of international politics has already been suggested in the course of the present study. It is the writer's opinion that sanctions will never be successfully applied as a means of preventing war, regardless of the attitude of the United States toward neutral rights and freedom of the seas. In the post-war period States have avoided this possibility by refraining from waging "war" when they resort to military coercion to promote their interests. The use of coercion itself is not forbidden by the Covenant or the Pact, except in so far as it involves a violation of obligations to keep the peace. The question of whether a resort to force does or does not involve such a violation must be answered authoritatively before sanctions can be applied. An answer requires that some method be devised to designate the Covenant-breaking or Pact-breaking State which is to be indicted and proceeded against as an "aggressor." But it is impossible, in most diplomatic crises, to make any clear distinction between aggressive and defensive war, because both sides act in "self-defense" and the assumed distinction has no application to events taking place in the world of reality. Even if this difficulty could be overcome (as it has never, in fact, been overcome), the difficulty would remain that sanctions are unnecessary in dealing with small States and are unworkable in dealing with Great Powers.

No possible mobilization of force, whether supported by the United States or not, can coerce a Great Power without precipitating large-scale hostilities. In 1931–1932 it was intimated in Japan that any application of sanctions, economic or military, would be regarded as an act of war and would be followed by armed resistance, accompanied by immediate Japanese withdrawal from the League. No such application was attempted or even seriously suggested, though it is possible that some still unpublished notes were exchanged on the subject between the League Powers and the United States. In any comparable crisis, every other Great Power would adopt a position identical with that of Japan. If coercive sanctions could be mobilized, they would lead, not to the maintenance of peace, but to general conflict. For these reasons, and not because of American policy, the sanctions theory is an impossible one. The most that can be said is that the *threat* of sanctions might, in certain circumstances, suffice to prevent fighting and that the League Council cannot safely make such a threat, in view of the American attitude. But in view of the record of the past twelve years, there is very little likelihood of the Council even threatening sanctions, much less trying to apply them.

Apart from the artificiality of current discussions of sanctions, it remains true that the traditional policies of the United States do constitute an obstacle to the successful functioning of the League peace machinery. American non-membership in the League, American non-membership in the Permanent Court, American refusal to implement the Kellogg Pact, American adherence to old conceptions of isolationism, neutrality, freedom of the seas, and the Monroe Doctrine are genuine barriers in the way of effective international cooperation to prevent war and promote the common purposes of the States of the world. The United States, to be sure, has made certain compensatory gestures designed to contribute to these purposes without violating the sacred traditions and arousing the ire of the isolationists. During the twelve years of Republican rule, the State Department has championed disarmament, sponsored the Kellogg Pact, engaged in "independent cooperation" with the League, and presented the world with the Stimson Doctrine. These policies will doubtless be continued, with minor variations, during the Roosevelt administration. None of them is an adequate substitute for full membership in the League, nor are all of them taken together likely to produce the results which might reasonably be expected to follow full American participation in the existing framework of international government. This is probably appreciated by all recent American Presidents and Secretaries of State. But the attitude of the Senate and the temper of the public mind forbid any action beyond half measures. It is conceivable that a campaign of education and propaganda, vigorously pushed by the present Democratic administration, with the support of leading figures of both parties who have perceived the futility of the ancient modes of thought, might produce a change of sentiment and make possible American entrance into the Court and the League. But this is still a remote possibility.

The significance of the traditional American myths and symbols which keep the United States away from Geneva is broader than any question of American foreign policy or any question of the effects of that policy upon the League. These attitudes are not limited to the United States. They appear most clearly in America only because they have kept the United States in the position of the only one of the bourgeois Great Powers which is outside the League. They are prevalent over the world, however, within the League and without. Great Britain is no more willing to participate in sanctions or to implement the Kellogg Pact than is the United States. English isolationism has repeatedly paralyzed action at Geneva quite as effectively as has the isolationism of the United States. Great Britain and Japan are no less insistent upon their own "Monroe Doctrines" in their particular spheres of interest than is the United States. France and her allies have sought to use the League to bolster up their hegemony over Europe. The revisionist bloc has sought to use it to realize its hopes of modifying the *status quo*. Everywhere traditional ideas, "sovereignty," "independence," "national honor," and "vital interests," have dominated governmental action and have inhibited international cooperation. Everywhere all States, as of yore, have pursued their own power interests, whether within or without the framework of the new order. Everywhere this pursuit, as always, has bred tension, animosity, conflict, and the frustration of efforts at collaboration between States. The attitude of the United States toward such collaboration is merely "Exhibit *A*" in the living museum of political symbolisms and mythologies. Every other State has its own exhibit and the traditional values, myths, and symbols on display are world-wide barriers lying across the path to peace.

Here is the ultimate reason why the testing of the League leads to skepticism regarding the future utility of the Geneva experiment. It is not lacking in high purposes, good intentions, ingenious procedures, and clever devices. It is lacking only in the disposition of States to avail themselves of a new opportunity to replace national interests and symbols with international interests and symbols adequate to achieve that political unity of the world without which the great society of the machine age cannot survive. Here is the final source of that pessimism with which many thoughtful observers of the international drama view the prospects of the League of Nations. And here, in the last analysis, is the supreme dilemma of the Western State System in the twentieth century.

SUGGESTED READINGS

Buell, R. L.: *The International Opium Conference*, Boston, World Peace Foundation, 1925.
Churchill, W. S.: *The Aftermath: 1918–1928*, New York, Charles Scribner's Sons, 1929.

Coolidge, A. C.: *Ten Years of War and Peace*, Cambridge, Harvard University Press, 1927·

Dangerfield, R. D.: *In Defense of the Senate*, Norman, Okla., University of Oklahoma Press, 1933.

Fanshawe, M.: *Reconstruction*, London, Allen and Unwin, 1925.

Fleming, D. F.: *The United States and the League of Nations*, 1918–1920, London, Putnam, 1932.

Hart, A. B.: *The Monroe Doctrine—An Interpretation*, Boston, Little, Brown & Company, 1916.

Jackson, J., and King-Hall, S.: *The League Year-book, 1932*, New York, The Macmillan Company, 1932.

Kellor, F. A.: *The United States and the International Court*, New York, Albert & Charles Boni, 1925.

Morley, F.: *The Society of Nations*, Washington, D. C., Brookings Institution, 1932.

Myer, D. P.: *Handbook of the League of Nations* (1930), Boston, World Peace Foundation.

Osborne, S.: *The Saar Question: a Disease Spot in Europe*, London, Allen and Unwin, 1923.

Quigley, H. S.: *From Versailles to Locarno*, Minneapolis, University of Minnesota Press, 1927.

Simonds, F. H.: *How Europe Made Peace without America*, Garden City, N. Y., Doubleday, Doran & Company, Inc., 1927.

Thomas, D. Y.: *One Hundred Years of the Monroe Doctrine*, 1823–1923, New York, The Macmillan Company, 1923.

Williams, B.: *State Security and the League of Nations*, Baltimore, Johns Hopkins Press, 1927.

Williams, J. F.: *International Change and International Peace*, New York, Oxford University Press, 1932.

Zimmern, A.: *America and Europe and other Essays*, New York, Oxford University Press, 1929.

League of Nations, *Ten Years of World Cooperation*, Geneva, 1930.

See also references at end of Chapter VII, p. 274 above.

Periodical Sources on League Activities

Official Journal of the League of Nations.

Reports of the Permanent Court of International Justice.

Monthly Summary of the League of Nations, Boston, World Peace Foundation.

Monthly Summary of the International Labor Organization, Boston, World Peace Foundation.

Chapter XIX

THE FUTURE OF THE WESTERN STATE SYSTEM

1. THE QUEST FOR WORLD UNITY

> The attaining to sovereign power is by two ways. One, by natural force; as when a man maketh his children to submit themselves, and their children, to his government, as being able to destroy them if they refuse; or by war subdueth his enemies to his will, giving them their lives on that condition. The other is, when men agree amongst themselves to submit to some man, or assembly of men, voluntarily, on confidence to be protected by him against all others. This latter may be called a political commonwealth.—THOMAS HOBBES, *Leviathan*.

> When we say that we face a race between chaos and education, we mean that the capacity to change our ideas is not keeping pace with our capacity to produce by mechanical means changes which, if they are not to destroy us, *must* be accompanied by a change of ideas.—NORMAN ANGELL, *The Unseen Assassins*.

THE rôle of the prophet is given only to those who control the behavior of men—to mystics who find wisdom within the soul and who convert men to new visions of salvation in heaven, or to statesmen who wield power wisely and work for the creation of a new order on earth. The observer who stands on the sidelines of life, watching, studying, comparing, can neither prophesy nor control, for he is too obsessed with the confused and multitudinous complexity of the world to attempt either task. The assurance born of a simple and unreflective will-to-action is lacking to him. And if he is one of the fraternity of so-called "social scientists," he will in all likelihood be content to watch and to study and to depict the slowly unraveling destiny of mankind, without seeking to control, or even predict, its future course. The present inquiry has been largely limited to describing the origins, forms, and forces of those patterns of western culture known collectively as "international politics." To add to the work of description and analysis the work of prognostication is a thankless and doubtless dangerous enterprise —for the world knows full well that no man can read the future and that facts and events are forever upsetting the prophecies of seers. In spite of all these deterrents, it seems not entirely profitless to venture certain suggestions regarding future possibilities—not in the hope that they will influence the choice of alternatives before western civilization, but rather

[823]

in the hope that they will furnish perspectives through which future events may be more intelligently evaluated.

The Western State System and the civilization out of which it has grown no longer appear young when they are compared with the life cycles of earlier cultures. The city-state systems of the ancient Near East doubtless existed some centuries before they became known by written records. At some remote and half-forgotten time, the independent communities of the Nile Valley were merged into a unified kingdom. The successive cultures of the land of the two rivers north of the Persian Gulf retained a fairly uniform political configuration for a millennium before they also manifested the pattern of political unification. The larger State System of which Egypt, Assyria, the Kingdom of the Hittites, and lesser States were the units endured for a shorter period. For some seven centuries these States struggled with one another for ascendancy. Assyria then conquered the rest and was in turn conquered by Persia. The Greek city-state System lasted for only two bright centuries before its members destroyed their own power by incessant feuds and thus opened the gates to the Macedonians. The Alexandrine Empire gave temporary political unity to the civilizations of the Near East and then dissolved into a new chaos of warring States, out of which emerged in turn the State System of the Hellenistic age. This was a part of the larger Mediterranean State System which endured for barely two hundred years. One by one its units were subjugated by Rome. By the time Christianity had prevailed over the other cults which came out of the East, the civilizations of the west were already ruled by a world State. For four centuries and more the Imperium of the Caesars gave political unity to the western world before its waning power crumbled and collapsed under the impact of the barbarians. Classical culture then entered into the shadows from which it never more emerged during the dark confusion of the five hundred years which ensued.

These time intervals are relatively short compared with the period during which western civilization and the Western State System have endured. The magic year 1500—taken by numberless historians to divide "medieval" from "modern" times—is, of course, meaningless to those who view western culture as an uninterrupted continuum. The year 1000 A.D. is more significant, at least to Spenglerians, in the chronology of that culture, for it was in this general period that the western societies clearly emerged out of the turbulent centuries which had gone before. Their early forms were by then crystallized: the universal Church, the Empire, the feudal hierarchy, and the feudal State. Relatively stable communities had by then appeared in western Europe, with well-defined castes and classes, with rulers, priests, and ruled, with landowners, merchants, artisans, and peasants. By then the economic, social, political, and aesthetic patterns of the first great phase of western culture were taking definite shape. Political unity, even in areas which seem small by present standards, was precluded by the inescapable diversity of the European scene and by the fragmentation of power among princes, dukes, barons, and knights. But a large measure of cultural unity had been achieved through cultural diffusion, through the common Germanic origins of the western peoples, and through the great legacies of the classical age. This unity was reflected spiritually in the common Catholic faith of all the western communities, and it was symbolized politically in the myth of the Holy Roman Empire. The generations which followed grew and garnered the richest fruits of the "medieval" phase of this new civilization: Gothic architecture, systematic theology, scholasticism, the universities, oil painting, a new music, the erudition and artistry of the so-called "Renaissance," the institutions of the national monarchies, the patterns of trade, industry, and economic life, and the forms of statesman-ship, diplomacy, international law, and international practice which were slowly woven into a new State System. The forms of that State System became fixed in the sixteenth and seventeenth centuries, but their roots lay far behind in the high middle age. The development of that State System has been uninterrupted and continuous from 1300 to 1933. In another seven decades it will have lasted for seven centuries, and the civilization which brought it forth will have endured—if it endures so long—for a thousand years. No earlier civilization, and no earlier State System outside of Asia, has had so long a life span.

The Western State System, in the course of its evolution, has in-evitably reflected the major phases of the civilization which gave it birth. Throughout its history it has exhibited, to a greater extent than its predecessors, a large degree of linguistic diversity among the peoples which compose it, an unusual aptitude in technology, an unparalleled pro-ductivity of wealth, and an unprecedented drive for power and greater power on the part of its successive ruling classes. But within the frame-work of these relatively uniform and constant characteristics, it has passed through several well-defined periods. The first was the feudal age, with its feudal State forms and its local and scattered polities, whose relations with one another were scarcely close enough to constitute a true State System. The second period was that of the national monarchies, the absolute kings, and the agrarian aristocracies, heirs of the feudal baronage. Here well-defined territorial States emerged, and out of their relations developed the concept of sovereignty, the principle of the balance of power, the rules of the law of nations, and the procedures of power-and-prestige diplomacy.

The third epoch was marked by the rise to political ascendancy of the bourgeoisie. Aristocratic absolutism was superseded by bourgeois

[825]

democracy. Agriculture was superseded by industry and commerce on a vast scale, with population expanding rapidly, with the new engines of production turning out goods in abundance, with the ships of trade and of war going to the ends of the earth in quest of markets and conquests. The forms of the State System became fixed in the established mold. The cult of the nation-state became the new religion of the west. Overseas imperialism reflected the enormous power which was now wielded by the new rulers of the western nations. The fourth and present period, which is only well begun, finds the bourgeoisie challenged by the proletariat and by the complex problems of an age which has outgrown its past but is unable to emancipate itself from the domination of its ancestors. The power of landed wealth is completely overshadowed by the power of commercial and financial capital. Democracy passes into dictatorship. Imperialism is practised on a vast scale, until all the world is conquered. The imperial Powers engage in suicidal combats for supremacy. The new world economy first attains enormous productivity and then faces disruption at the hands of the forces surviving from the preceding age. The States of the entire world knit themselves together into a fabric of international organization through which they strive, none too successfully, to grapple with the mighty problems which seem to threaten them with disaster. In the eyes of the sophisticated and cynical cosmopolites who throng the chambers of learning in the great cities of the West, these problems seem to foreshadow the impending doom of the State System and of the civilization which brought it forth.

The most significant feature of the Western State System, as it has developed through these various stages, is its failure to evolve in the direction of the political unification of its members. All earlier State Systems developed from city-states to kingdoms, from kingdoms to empires, from empires to world States, embracing the whole area of their cultures within the confines of a single power. For the political scientist to postulate a "law" of the evolution of State Systems on the basis of this seemingly universal tendency would be rash, for social and political phenomena have not yet been studied and analyzed with sufficient precision to admit of the formulation of universal "laws." To a large extent each culture develops in accordance with its own "laws" and its own inner compulsions. It nevertheless appears to be true that as political power is increased and becomes concentrated with the development of a civilization, as differences are merged into uniformities through cultural diffusion, the process of empire-building leads to the conquest of weaker States by stronger rivals and to the fusion of strong States, usually through war, into great imperiums giving political unity to the whole civilization. This development occurred not only in the early State Systems of western Asia and of Europe, but also in the State Systems of ancient India and China and in the governmental forms of the Aztecs and the Incas in pre-Columbian America. It has not yet occurred in the world State System of contemporary western civilization. The ghost of unity, symbolized by the Holy Roman Empire, soon vanished in the dawn of the territorial sovereignties, and it has never been recaptured. No State or group of States has as yet succeeded in imposing its will upon Europe or upon the world. So perfectly has the balance-of-power principle operated that each contender for supremacy—Charles V, Louis XIV, Napoleon I, and imperial Germany—has been eventually thwarted and crushed by armed and alert enemies. The Western State System of the twentieth century remains a system of irreducible political diversity, composed of some three-score sovereignties, none of which can impose unity upon the remainder.

The fact that this situation has persisted for so many centuries has inevitably produced permanent effects not merely upon the legal and institutional forms of the Western State System, but likewise upon the configuration of western culture as a whole. That culture has lost what homogeneity it possessed in the medieval period and has become "nationalized." To most observers it appears more natural to speak of French culture or German culture or British culture or Italian culture than of "western" culture as a totality. From the point of view of the political organization of western civilization, this circumstance has obviously meant that political attitudes and public behavior patterns have centered, to an ever increasing degree, about the nation-states rather than about urban or provincial or continental divisions. Western peoples have become aware of themselves politically as members of national communities. They have identified themselves with the fatherland. They have integrated themselves politically about the symbols of the nation. The myths, traditions, values, attitudes, and opinions which furnish the bases of social cohesion and political action for the western peoples are all associated with the national State. The populations of these entities necessarily feel, act, and think in terms of the values and ideologies of nationalism. Their loyalties and allegiances are no longer in a state of easy flux but are definitely crystallized into a pattern which is already so old and well established that it is scarcely susceptible of any fundamental modification. If the pattern can be modified at all, the change must be very gradual. Almost irresistible pressure is required to effect such changes, for the inertia of the past is not to be moved by small and sudden efforts.

Almost from the beginning of the Western State System, appeals for unity have been made by enlightened and socially minded commentators who deplored the anarchical confusion resulting from the unbridled rivalry of competing sovereignties. The world society has come to such a pass in the twentieth century that the achievement of political unity on a world-wide scale may well be regarded as the only alternative to catastrophe. It is the assumption of the concluding chapter of this volume that the central problem of western civilization in the present generation is the political unification of the world. This assumption does not flow from any *a priori* hypothesis of the inevitable unification of all State Systems, nor from the pleas of idealists and peace seekers, nor yet, it is hoped, from any abstract and unconscious predilection for monism, for systematization, for order and organization on the part of the present writer. It flows rather from the whole analysis of power politics and of the contemporary dilemma of the world society attempted in the preceding pages. That analysis need not be restated here. It is sufficient to observe that any objective examination of the forces of international politics and of the efforts of governments to cope with the problems created by these forces can lead to but one conclusion: that the States of the modern world must either stand united to deal with the perils which threaten them, or fall divided in a chaotic welter of competition and conflict. The conclusion is the same whether one examines the effects of those behavior patterns and policies suggested by the terms nationalism, imperialism, militarism, and capitalism or studies the unhappy story of international efforts to cope with the consequences of these policies. The ultimate alternatives are unity or chaos. And these alternatives are not choices of the remote future. Western civilization is already old. It may already have run its course and be headed toward a long twilight of decline. In any case, its problems are immediate, pressing, threatening. They will be solved within the next few decades, or they will not be solved at all.

The nature of the alternatives deserves closer examination before any effort is made to suggest which road is likely to be taken. If the alternative to "unity" is not merely a continuation of the disunity and diversity of the past but "chaos," the characteristics of this alternative ought to be clearly perceived. By "chaos" is meant a continuation of the international anarchy of the past, with prospective results which are readily predictable on the basis of evidence already available. The "international anarchy" is a consequence of armed and militant nationalism, of "my country, right or wrong," of the uncontrolled militarism and imperialism of the machine age. The patriot's pride of power, the diplomat's penchant for prestige, the empire-builder's lust for conquest, the soldier's thirst for glory, the entrepreneur's quest for profits have set nation against nation and people against people. The results are only too painfully apparent twenty years after Sarajevo. The observable consequences are bloodshed and destruction on an appalling scale, the breakdown of the intricate structure of credit, production, and trade, universal bankruptcy, widespread unemployment and destitution, social unrest, the collapse of governments and societies in revolution, and a colossal and incalculable quantity of human suffering and misery.

These results, bad in themselves, are the more serious in that they threaten for the future a gradual lowering of standards of civilized life, a slow dissolution of the existing bonds of political cohesion, and an ultimate disintegration of the economic and social foundations of western civilization. These future results are not yet clearly perceptible in all parts of the world, though in particular localities, once centers of a thriving and prosperous community life, they are so obvious as to be apparent to even the dullest onlooker, however unaware he may be of their causes. Casual passersby are still free to assume, if they choose to think at all about causes, that the present difficulties of the world society are of a temporary and fortuitous character, that they were caused by an "accidental" war or by the visitations of an unkind Providence, that they will pass away of themselves with a lapse of time. They are too near, too immediate to admit of fully objective description and analysis. But no great perspicacity is required to see that their roots are not in the present but in the remote past and that they are the products of deep-seated forces and tensions inherent in the fundamental structure of western civilization. These forces are operating in the present much as they have operated in the past. They will of necessity produce the same results in the future as they are producing in the present—save that the results are cumulative and the future will therefore be worse than the present, unless the forces themselves are brought under control. This conclusion regarding tomorrow admits of no doubt in the minds of the great majority of thoughtful observers of the chaos of today.

In saying that salvation lies in "unity," one is attempting to say in a word what many words are needed to express adequately. There is little mystery about what is requisite to ward off worse disasters than those which have already befallen. The mystery lies only in devising means for applying to an irrational world the solutions which sober reason suggests. What is required is that the tensions and conflicts which beset the world society be reduced to a minimum and that the social intelligence of mankind be organized on a world-wide scale to cope effectively with economic and social problems which will remain insoluble so long as they are dealt with in the old ways. Divergent interests must somehow be reconciled. Common values and community welfare must somehow be substituted for exclusive and competitive self-seeking. The emotionalized unreason of ethnocentric tribalism must be leavened with an appreciation of economic realities. The single-minded acquisitiveness of the great captains of capitalism must be replaced by obligations and social responsibilities commensurate with economic power. The intrigues of diplomats and war makers, bent upon prestige and glory, must give way to new motives and new behavior, inspired by a vision of an ordered world. The destructive impact of empire-builders upon subject peoples, with its exploitation, degradation, rebellion, and repression, must be superseded by new values and attitudes in the relations between the races. The eighteenth century symbols and mythologies of the western world must be replaced by myths and symbols compatible with twentieth century realities, if, as is more than likely, they cannot be superseded by the "rationalism" in which the eighteenth century mistakenly placed its faith. If and when all this is done, when common interests and orderly compromise have replaced self-seeking and conflict, then the political machinery and the administrations of the world society must be so integrated and interlocked as to render them adequate to achieve and execute world solutions for world problems.

The political unification of the Western State System appears to be a prerequisite to salvation from chaos, because the concrete situations which must be dealt with cannot be dealt with effectively by any human agencies possessed of less authority than the governments of States. It is easy to exaggerate the scope of possible governmental action in the western nations. Governments are hedged about and limited in numerous ways by the social and economic configuration of the communities which they govern. In an age which is still democratic (in part), they are pulled and pushed hither, thither, and yon by unreasoning opinion, by the greeds and follies of demagogues and grafters, by the incurable emotionalism and irrational suggestibility of the mob mind. The transformations of social values and attitudes which the problems of the century so urgently call for cannot be consummated directly by governments. They hinge upon the press, the school, the pulpit, the radio, the cinema, and all the other agencies of public education and social control. It is nevertheless true that the most pressing problems of the present and future are "political" problems. They involve relationships of power and they require the services of statesmen and administrators for their solution. If governments cannot cope with these problems, they cannot be solved. A single world government of a single world State, to which the citizens of a world society acknowledge allegiance, would be in a vastly better position to cope with them than are the sixty governments of sixty States, claiming the allegiance of sixty groups of citizens and all working at cross purposes. In the absence of such a world State, the governments of the existing States encounter innumerable obstacles in the way of cooperation and find it impossible even to deal effectively with their own "domestic" problems, for most of these problems are already international in scope. If political unity cannot be achieved through a world State (and this is clearly impossible in any visible future), it must be achieved by institutionalized collaboration between States, by the gradual strengthening of the bonds of an "international government" resting upon States and gradually welding them together into a world-wide political community of interests. Only through "unity" of this type can chaos be resolved into order.

The difficulties in the way of such a development are almost too many and too complicated to enumerate. Most of them have been suggested in earlier chapters. They are inherent in the whole past of western culture and in the very fabric of the Western State System itself. Only two obstacles of a general nature need be noticed here. One is the conception of government and of the whole political process which is prevalent in western civilization. All government is an institutionalization of relationships of power, of patterns of social deference and domination. The State is power. It is the symbol and embodiment of the will-to-power of the national community as it deals with other national communities. Within each community the institutions of government represent particular configurations of power relations between sections and classes. They are devices whereby ruling classes maintain their rule. This rule is made possible by popular acquiescence, by a popular consensus of values, by popular myths, legends, loyalties, and habits of deference and obedience. Ultimately this power rests upon force and upon the ability of the ruling classes to maintain their rule without giving too obvious an appearance of oppressing or exploiting the ruled.

If there were a world ruling class in the world society, the problem of political unification would be considerably simplified. But there is no such élite with a consciousness of its solidarity on a world-wide scale. The dominant bourgeoisie is sharply divided into competing and conflicting national groups. There can, moreover, be no world-wide concert of power among these ruling classes, for "power" itself is relative and postulates not a community of interests but a divergency of interests. The bourgeois ruling groups of the nation-states might conceivably be hammered into unity on the anvil of a world-wide revolutionary movement of the proletariat, threatening their domination everywhere. But this is not yet in prospect. States and governments, as embodiments of power, can function only *vis-à-vis* other and potentially hostile embodiments of power. They cannot function in the abstract on a world-wide scale. The ability of international government to arrive at solutions of problems and to formulate and execute programs is limited by the conflicting power interests of its component parts. Unless these can be reconciled, no solutions or programs can be formulated. International government must concern itself with this task. But in western civilization, government functions nationally, not internationally. It rests upon power relations within States and between States, not upon common power interests of all States *vis-à-vis* some extramundane and nonexistent entity. If a community of interests

[831]

can be achieved, if government can become simply a service agency, if the State can be made simply a planning and administrative mechanism, then political institutions can function equally well in jurisdictions of any size, whether they be city wards or the entire planet. States and governments, however, do not yet exhibit these characteristics. Here is a difficulty in the way of the political unity of the world inherent in the whole conception and function of government in western civilization.

The other general difficulty is closely related to these considerations. All government rests both upon force and upon those social values, attitudes, and ideologies which make for social cohesion, consensus, and like-mindedness. These elements of cohesion consist primarily of emotionalized and traditionalized symbols, myths, associations, identifications, folkways, *mores*, and stereotyped patterns of feeling, action, and thought. These phenomena are essentially "religious" or mystical in nature. Early governments required priesthoods to inculcate obedience and acquiescence and to furnish the necessary mysteries and metaphysical miracles to induce deference. Modern government similarly rests upon a "religious" basis. But the religion in question is non-ecclesiastical. It is the cult of national patriotism. Its symbols and myths are those of the nation-states. They furnish the necessary devices whereby peoples are welded into that national unity of purposes and attitudes without which national government would be impossible. As has been suggested above, these myths and symbols are so ancient and so firmly fixed in all the national societies that they are seemingly ineradicable, so long as these societies endure. The problem of attaining world unity is not simply a problem of "international government" in the mechanical and structural sense. Neither is it a problem of force or of international sanctions. It is a problem of substituting world citizenship for national citizenship, of replacing national shibboleths, slogans, and mysteries with their international or world equivalents. A new world religion is needed to achieve this, or at least a new political cult, world-wide in scope, which will transfer loyalties and allegiances from the nation-state to the whole society of nations. Here, indeed, is the most fundamental difficulty, and all the inertia of the past, all the weight of tradition, all the immobility of time-worn custom and habit stand in the way of overcoming it.

2. LEFT AND RIGHT EXITS FROM CHAOS

> You ought to speak of other States in the plural number; none of them
> is a city, but many cities. . . . For indeed any city, however small, is in
> fact divided into two, one the city of the poor, the other of the rich; these
> are at war with one another; and in either there are many smaller divisions,
> and you would be altogether beside the mark if you treated them all as a
> single State.—PLATO, *The Republic*.

From the point of view of the future of the Western State System, the
most significant cleavage of views and values throughout the world is
between those who are striving, in one way or another, to promote the
political unification of the world society and those who are opposed to
such efforts and are content with the present political configuration of
western civilization. In the former category one finds a heterogeneous
collection of groups, presenting a wide variety of panaceas and suggestions
as to how unity might best be achieved: "internationalists," Socialists,
Communists, pacifists, sundry brands of liberals, many churchmen,
international financiers, some business men, many labor leaders, numerous scientists and intellectual workers, many who are at odds with the
status quo and who welcome all bold proposals for change, and all whose
political emotions and ideas are organized about myths and symbols
transcending national frontiers. In the latter category an equally heterogeneous aggregation of interests, causes, and organizations is to be found:
professional patriots in all lands, the military and diplomatic bureaucracy
of most governments, apologists and beneficiaries of militarism and
imperialism, protected manufacturers, favored merchants, jingo journalists, demagogue-politicians, most social and economic conservatives, all
timid souls fearful of new departures, all who benefit materially or psy-
chically from the prevailing international disorder, and all whose political
emotions and ideas are organized about the myths and symbols of the
nation-state. Between these two schools an incessant and still indecisive
struggle goes on for the control of popular attitudes and public policies.
And within each school an even more bitter battle is waged between the
proponents of the various panaceas. The description of these divergencies
is no part of the present task. It is important, however, to inquire into
the implications for the future of international politics of the possible
triumph on a world-wide scale of one or the other of these two great
schools of thought. It is equally important to suggest the alternatives
presented by the most significant subgroups within each school.

On the threshold of such a discussion it should be pointed out that
one of the two great groups mentioned is obviously committed to the
maintenance of the world as it is. By the same token it is opposed to any
fundamental modification of the established patterns of the Western State

[833]

System. In considering possible changes in the political configuration of the world society, the program of this group calls for no extended commentary, for if it prevails there will presumably be no significant changes. It is important primarily as a dead weight, as an obstacle, as an inert mass which resists the efforts of the opposing group to build a unified and ordered world. There will be no changes in the political structure of the world as a whole brought about by the conscious purpose of this school of thought. Change there will be—for nothing is changeless save change itself, in the ebb and flow of cultures on the planet. But the changes which occur will not reflect any world-wide will and purpose on the part of the forces of conservatism or reaction. These forces are by their nature nationally minded, not internationally minded. Such changes as they seek in the international order, they seek not in the interests of the world society—for they acknowledge no allegiance to any such society, and they may indeed deny its existence—but in the interests of the particular national tribe to which they happen to belong. Patriots, militarists, and imperialists are not concerned with international order or international anarchy. They are concerned with enhancing the power and prestige of their own particular nation-states at the expense of rivals. The foreign policies sponsored by such groups are the ancient and traditional policies of national self-seeking, directed toward the traditional goals of the diplomacy of power, profits, and prestige.

It follows that such pressure as these groups exert (and that pressure is thus far enormously more potent than that of the opposing group) leads in the direction of a perpetuation of the political division of the world into jealous and independent territorial sovereignties, each pursuing its own interests, with the devil taking the stragglers. The only form of world-wide political unification which such groups would approve would be one similar to that envisaged by the patriots of ancient Rome, *i.e.*, the conquest of all other States by the particular State to which the patriots acknowledge allegiance. Such a development is a palpable impossibility. Unity in any other form, involving the subordination of national interests to world interests, is anathema to the superpatriots of all lands. The practical effect of their efforts, therefore, is an indefinite maintenance of the political fragmentation of the world society into nation-states and an uncontrolled continuation of the competitive struggle for power between these States. According to this dispensation, patriots will continue to preach and practice "my country, right or wrong"; profit-seekers will continue to seek profits abroad, with the support and protection of their national governments; empire-builders will continue to cultivate the art of subverting the independence of defenseless communities and the science of annexing and exploiting them for the benefit of the ruling classes of the imperial States; diplomats will continue to intrigue and conspire to secure advantages for their States by driving hard bargains and enhancing their power and prestige at every opportunity; soldiers will continue to prepare for war and to hold the threat of the sword over the heads of national rivals and enemies. Here is the antithesis of world unity and the apotheosis of international anarchy and conflict.

Such changes in the political complexion of the world society as the pursuit of these policies brings about will be accidental and unpredictable. They will result from the clash of competing national forces beyond the control of any man or group of men. They will be comparable to the great shifts of power relationships between the nation-states which have taken place in the past under the rule of force and the law of the jungle. But they will, in all probability, produce economic and social consequences in the twentieth century vastly different from those produced in the past, when each national society lived simply and self-sufficiently in relative security. The *leit-motif* of the last book of this volume has been the threat of disaster which hangs over the world society as a result of the competitive pursuit of power by national sovereignties. That society has already become an integrated and interdependent community, however ill coordinated the strivings of its parts may be, however inchoate may be the values and symbols which give it spiritual unity and cohesion. Its richness and colorfulness and productiveness cannot much longer survive the disrupting disturbance to its economic and social foundations produced by economic nationalism, imperialist rivalries, power politics, and war. The world society is already in process of incipient dissolution as a result of the shock of the Great War and the Great Depression which followed in its wake. If that dissolution continues unchecked, to the accompaniment of new conflicts, all the established standards of civilized life will progressively decline and the bourgeois nation-states themselves, with their patriots, profiteers, and power-and-prestige diplomats, will be swept into common ruin. This will indeed spell change of the most radical character in the political patterns of the Western State System, but not change of a type desired or planned for by anyone.

The only prospect for intelligently directed change is to be found, then, in the programs and panaceas of those who oppose the continuation of the established behavior patterns of international politics and who urge world unity in one guise or another. These advocates of the political unification of the world society may, for purposes of the present discussion, be divided into two general groups, one of which is bourgeois in its origins and orientation and the other of which is proletarian. It is not strange that the two great social classes, whose conflicts and divergencies of interests are reflected in the politics of all modern States, should produce two different sets of programs, symbols, values, and ideas in the realm of international affairs. This is not meant to imply that all the competing proposals for a new international order can be neatly pigeonholed into class categories. But it is clear that if such a new order is brought into being, its creation will be the work either of political and economic groups which are part of the ruling classes of the nation-states, *i.e.*, financiers, entrepreneurs, and leaders of industry and commerce, or of groups which are a part of the class of politically conscious industrial workers and wage-earners. If the unification of the world is to be achieved, it will be achieved not by peasants or aristocrats, but by business men or by workers. For many years past these two dominant groups have presented conflicting programs of international reconstruction and have pointed to alternative paths for the attainment of world unity.

These alternatives may be designated by the adjectives "left" and "right," in conformity to current political phraseology, based upon the seating arrangements of parties in continental parliaments. Generally speaking, bourgeois party groups, conservative or liberal, are politically "right" or "center," while proletarian groups are radical or revolutionary and are politically "left-center" or "left." In this political spectrum, the extreme right would of course be represented by the ultra-nationalist and Fascist forces, which need not be considered here, since their programs repudiate world unity and look forward to continued competition and conflict between the nations. The right road to unity is the road taken by the conservative or liberal bourgeois elements in each national society. The left road is that pointed to by the proletarian parties. The destination to which each of these roads leads is necessarily envisaged in terms reflecting the economic interests and political ideologies of the classes in question. If either of the alternative destinations is ever reached, the arrival will take place in a future which is still somewhat remote. But the proposed destinations are already sufficiently clear to render possible a brief account of each of the projected excursions and a description of the widely separated end-stations looming dimly through the dust of the journey.

Those who propose to take the left road are convinced that the right road leads into a blind alley and that the ruling classes of the bourgeois societies will either not take it at all (and descend forthwith into chaos) or will find that it leads into a wilderness, with ultimate chaos beyond the horizon. The advocates of the left road are for the most part Marxian radicals and leaders and spokesmen of labor in the economic or political fields. They are inseparably associated with trade unions, with Marxist political parties, with the Marxist conception of the class struggle, with the Marxist myths and symbols of proletarian unity and social revolution. The Communist Manifesto of 1848, issued by Karl Marx and Friederich Engels, concluded its appeal with the memorable battle cry: "Workers of the world, unite; you have nothing to lose but your chains!" Those who respond to this appeal have ever contended that the common class interests of the proletariat transcend national frontiers. The proletarian revolutionary movement, inspired and led by Marx and his disciples, has from the beginning been world-wide and international in scope and emphasis. It has endeavored to promote the political and economic solidarity of the working classes in all lands and to create a truly world-wide organization of wage-earners who would eventually overthrow the established order and inaugurate a cooperative commonwealth under a workers' government—not merely within each State, but in all States and throughout the world. The revolutionary program of the proletarian radicals is of necessity directed against all the values and ideologies of the enemy class, not merely in the national realm but in the international realm as well. Nationalism, imperialism, and the diplomacy of power and prestige are targets of attack, no less than capitalism, private property in the means of production, the profit system, and traditional religion. This program, as it concerns the future political pattern of the world society, contemplates the eventual creation of a world federation of workers' republics, in which peace and security for all will presumably be assured by virtue of the liquidation of the forces which are assumed to be responsible for war and disorder.

Prior to 1914 this movement had attained a semblance of world-wide unity through the international trade unions of Europe and through the so-called "Second International"—the federation of Socialist parties, which maintained its headquarters at Amsterdam and endeavored, through periodical congresses, to promote the common purposes of Marxists in all countries. In the aftermath of Sarajevo, however, the allegiance of the workers of the world to the myths and symbols of bourgeois nationalism proved more powerful than their allegiance to proletarian internationalism. They quickly forgot the international solidarity which was to keep the peace and the general strike which was to paralyze the efforts of the war makers. They willingly fell to slaughtering one another in the name of defending their respective fatherlands from the foreign foe. The Second International was disrupted. With few exceptions, the Socialists in each country supported the war as loyal patriots and sang hymns of hate as lustily as the most nationalistic of the bourgeoisie. The exceptional Socialists, however, were by no means insignificant, and they denounced their colleagues as cowards, scoundrels, "social-patriots," and traitors to the toiling masses and to the cause of world revolution. In the wake of war came economic collapse and social disintegration. Throughout central and eastern Europe the moderate or revisionist Socialist parties found an opportunity to seize power. But they were divided, impotent, enfeebled by decades of pacific parliamentarianism. In Russia they supported the war and strove to establish a bourgeois democracy upon the ruins of the Tsardom, until they were swept into oblivion by the Bolshevik uprising. In

Germany, Austria, and Hungary they had power thrust upon them. They used that power to bolster up the tottering structure of capitalism and to enable the bourgeoisie to wreak bloody vengeance upon their more revolutionary comrades. In Italy they debated until they were suppressed by the Fascists. The golden moment came and passed. Outside of Russia the proletarian revolution was nowhere achieved.

These events, coupled with developments in Russia, led to an open split between the moderate and revolutionary Marxists. This cleavage had appeared long before the war in the congresses of the Second International, but it did not become an irreparable breach until the close of the great conflict. In all the national parties the bases of cleavage were much the same. The moderate revisionist Marxists were content with electoral and parliamentary tactics and contemplated "peaceful revolution" through the attainment of legislative majorities. The orthodox revolutionary Marxists insisted upon the inevitability of forcible bourgeois resistance to expropriation and upon the resulting necessity of revolutionary violence. In the Russian party the moderate minority (Menshevik) faction was at war with the revolutionary majority (Bolshevik) faction. In Germany the radical Independent Socialists separated themselves from the Social-Democrats and gave birth in turn in 1918 to the ultra-revolutionary Spartacists, forerunners of the present German Communist party. Similar splits took place elsewhere. Meanwhile the Russian Bolsheviks, under Lenin's leadership, seized power, expropriated the nobility and the bourgeoisie, and established a proletarian dictatorship. Soviet governments were likewise set up in Hungary and Bavaria in the spring of 1919, but they were quickly suppressed by military force and reactionary terrorism. In Russia the Bolsheviks—or "Communists," as they dubbed themselves in 1918—succeeded in destroying the enemy classes and parties and in beating off a world attack upon their régime. In March of 1919 they called their sympathizers in other countries into conference and established the Communist or Third International, with its headquarters at Moscow. This was an international federation of the Communist parties of the world, dedicated to the repudiation of bourgeois democracy and to the violent seizure of power by the world proletariat. The Second or Amsterdam International was reconstituted by the German Social Democrats, the British Laborites, the French Unified Socialists, and other revisionist groups elsewhere. Between the two Internationals a bitter and implacable feud has raged for over a decade, with each seeking to win the workers over to its banner and with the Communists making slow but steady inroads upon the Socialists in most of the continental countries.

These developments mean that the left road to world unity has now become two roads—one via Amsterdam and the other via Moscow. The doctrinal debates, the ideological hair-splitting, and the rude skull-cracking in which the Socialists and Communists have engaged need not here be reviewed. Suffice it to say that the events of the past ten years have made it abundantly clear to most observers that the Socialist parties are inherently incapable of achieving the social revolution in particular countries or of arriving at the eventual goal of world federation. The ex-rebels and renegades who have assumed the leadership of these parties— Ramsay MacDonald, Philip Snowden, Fritz Ebert, Philip Scheidemann, Gustav Noske, Otto Braun, Leon Blum, Morris Hillquit, Norman Thomas, etc.—have in most cases continued to pay lip service to revolution, though in Germany (1919) they drowned working-class uprisings in blood and in Great Britain (1931) they deserted the party to become ministers in a high Tory, ultra-bourgeois, and aristocratic "National Cabinet." Such leaders, by virtue of long preoccupation with the rituals and ceremonies of bourgeois democracy, have become interested exclusively in oratory, in electoral majorities, in the pride and perquisites of public office. Political power has become for them an end in itself and not a means of revolution-izing society. Not only are they inhibited from all revolutionary action, but they are committed to opposing revolution wherever it raises its head. In theory they strive to attain reforms and to build a new social order, national and international, by parliamentary methods. In practice they leave the foundations of bourgeois civilization intact and serve as bul-warks for the established order. The most they can accomplish toward the political unification of the world is to put a brake upon the more belliger-ent manifestations of bourgeois nationalism and militarism in govern-ments where they possess effective influence. For them today's task is to fight Communism and tomorrow promises futility and the end of a dream doomed to perpetual frustration.

International Communism is thus left in the vanguard of the revolu-tionary movement of the world proletariat. It has been in power in Russia for over fifteen years, and its bid for power elsewhere—in China, in Ger-many, in the Balkans—becomes menacing to the established order in proportion as the misery and suffering of the victims of the present chaos dispose them to revolutionary action. The high hopes for immediate world revolution entertained in 1918 and 1919 have faded with the "temporary stabilization of capitalism." Most Communists, from Stalin downward, now adhere to the view that the world revolutionary situation which will make possible the universal overthrow of the bourgeoisie will appear in the wake of the next general war. That war they regard as inevitable, and the revolution itself they see written in the stars. The inconsistencies and contradictions of the world of capitalism can, in their opinion, have only one outcome. Economic competition, imperialist rivalries, and militaristic ambitions will breed inescapable armed combat between the contending ruling classes of the nation-states. This conflict will be progressive, cumulative, and terrible. Armies and fleets will slaughter and destroy on an unprecedented scale. Millions will perish in the wreckage of a civilization. Capitalism will commit suicide. Bankruptcy and economic collapse will breed widespread disorder. Dictatorship and terrorism will become the order of the day. At the right moment the various Communist parties will attack and will lead the vanguard of the proletariat to victory, as the only hope of peace and salvation. A mighty life-and-death grapple will be inaugurated, under the direction of the Communist International, between the world bourgeoisie and the world proletariat. The international war will be converted into a civil war of classes, and the class struggle in turn will be fought throughout the international arena. The U.S.S.R. will throw its power into the contest. The citadels of capitalism, nationalism, and imperialism will fall, one by one, to the Red Armies of the triumphant proletariat. Out of the wreckage will emerge the world federation of Soviet republics, committed to eternal peace, brotherhood, and fraternal reconstruction of a shattered world.

This is obviously a road to world unity which leads to the goal through oceans of tears and blood. It postulates the inevitability of complete chaos and irremediable catastrophe before chaos can be replaced by a new order. The prognostications upon which this vision is based, however, are not entirely fantastic or unreal, despite the fact that the vision itself is part of a new Red mythology characterized, like all mythologies, by much wish-fulfillment thinking. There can be little doubt that the myths and symbols of revolutionary proletarian class consciousness are quite capable of furnishing the psychological foundations of social integration and political organization in a new world society, as they are already doing in the Soviet Union—if and when the world revolution is achieved. But the "if" is the great riddle. Almost anything is rather more than likely to happen in the coming chaos, as the Communists picture it. Whether enough material wealth and enough human lives to permit reconstruction would survive a universal war, followed by a universal revolution, is at least open to question. The world revolution might see most of the western societies reduced to ashes and wreckage. In so immense a catastrophe the débris might prove insufficient for reconstruction, even in the event of speedy Communist victory. In the absence of victory, or in the event of victory after a long combat of mutual exhaustion and destruction, the triumphant comrades might find the world a charnel house of smoldering ruin—scarcely a fit scene of social and economic experimentation.

This unhappy prospect, so far as Europe is concerned, could be averted only by rapid military conquest of the western States by the Red Army. This possibility, in turn, would depend upon the level of technological efficiency attained by the U.S.S.R. by the time of the crisis, upon the extent of the disintegration and paralysis of the bourgeois Powers, and upon successful proletarian uprisings behind the lines of battle. The U.S.S.R,, with its immense population and resources, may eventually become efficiently industrialized. Its power extends into Europe, into the Near East, into India, and into the Far East. It is the only Great Power which possesses even a remote possibility of conquering Europe, Asia, and Africa. This possibility hinges upon properly timed and successful colonial rebellions among the backward peoples and upon victorious proletarian revolts in the western nations. The Communist International, as the "General Staff of the World Revolution," is already preparing the blueprints of this open conspiracy against the established order. If the sequence of events unfolds as the Communists anticipate, and if their plans are eventually carried into successful execution, the world, or most of the world, will indeed attain political unity before the close of the present century. But it will be a world over which the four horsemen of the Apocalypse have ridden roughshod on hoofs of steel. It will be a world so broken, so gutted, so bloodstained and weary and hungry that the survivors may easily become more interested in merely keeping alive than in the splendid vision of the future cooperative commonwealth of the world proletariat. This road lies through the valley of the shadow, and none who still hope for peace and the triumph of reason can willingly accept it.

The alternative is the right road to world unity. This is the road proposed by internationally minded conservatives, by reasonable and reasoning liberals, by the Socialists, and by the more advanced of the other bourgeois party groups. These prophets of world peace and unity conceive of the possibility of attaining their goals directly and gradually by discussion, by education, by reform, by the slow inculcation of new values and attitudes to replace the old. They recoil from the prospect of years of conflict and destruction, of decades of war and revolution. They prefer to believe that existing institutions and living men and women can be remodeled sufficiently by a pacific process of compromise to render feasible the unification of the world, without the necessity of sweeping away completely the old order in a universal conflagration. The bourgeois liberals would agree with the proletarian revolutionaries that disaster is threatened by the unmitigated pursuit of national power, prestige, and profits, by the belligerent manifestations of nationalism and imperialism, by international tension and conflict engendered by the competitive struggle for the traditional stakes of diplomacy. But they would seek to reform, to persuade, to educate, rather than to demolish. More specifically, their program is based upon the hope of substituting for the values, myths, and symbols of nationalism a new set of values, myths, and symbols of "internationalism."

This new "internationalism" would rest not upon the revolutionary class consciousness of a militant proletariat, but upon the established foundations of international collaboration between the nation-states. The loyalties and allegiances of people everywhere to their tribal gods and to the emblems and shibboleths of the nations would gradually be merged and reoriented about a new series of emblems and shibboleths, representing the world community and bespeaking a world citizenship, broader than national citizenship but not inconsistent with it. Tensions would be prevented by appropriate remedial action rather than stimulated to the point of open conflict. This program contemplates no fundamental alteration of the existing distribution of wealth and power within the nation-states, nor any immediate modification of the pattern of relations between them. The existing national societies would be integrated, coordinated, woven together into a solid structure of pacific cooperation out of which would finally emerge the parliament of man and the federation of the world.

The League of Nations is necessarily the center of attention in all efforts in this direction. Geneva is already the new world capital, and the League is already in embryo a world confederation of sovereignties. Its agencies are already being utilized by States for the performance of a variety of indispensable functions. It is already—with certain important qualifications—a world government. It has its deliberative Assembly, its executive Council, its Secretariat, administrative services and technical bodies. It has its own flag. Despite its youth, it has its traditions, its myths, symbols, and ideologies, and its saints, heroes, and martyrs. All of these are in flux, still formless and uncrystallized. It has no territory, no citizens, no authority beyond that given to it by its sovereign members. It has no international anthem capable of arousing emotional responses comparable to those evoked by the anthems of the nation-states. It has no army, no navy, no police. Outside of its own officialdom, it has no authority whatever over individuals and no claim upon their services. It cannot apply coercion against those who defy its will, for its sanctions are impotent. It has no force at its command to impose unity upon the recalcitrant States of the world society. It can only admonish, warn, advise, and persuade. It is weakest where it should be strongest and incapable of acting where it should act most vigorously. As a "government" it has less power and prestige than the old Kingdom of Poland or the Government of the United States under the Articles of Confederation. But it exists and it functions—after a fashion. It is increasingly useful to its members, and if the next great international conflict can be deterred long enough to give it time to grow and become strong and secure, it may yet fulfill the hopes of its founders.

The fundamental difficulty in the way of this type of evolutionary development is that life is short and time is fleeting, and the necessary psychological foundations of the new world order can scarcely be fabricated in a brief decade or in a generation. The deep-seated allegiances of the western peoples to their sense of nationhood is a product of centuries of growth. Within each national community like-mindedness emerged very slowly, and only slowly did the symbols and representations of the nation take hold of men's emotions and imaginations. Only gradually were French, British, American, German, and Italian nationalisms firmly established among the peoples of these communities. In each case cultural homogeneity and economic collaboration paved the way for political unification. In each case force was used generously and repeatedly to suppress dissent, to impose the dominant national ideology and mythology on the whole population, and to put down such loyalties to class, caste, section, or province as were incompatible with national allegiance. The new international order has not as yet evoked reactions of deference and loyalty on a world-wide scale. Except for a few pacifists, idealists, and professional reformers, it arouses no heart-warming enthusiasms, no inspiring sense of oneness in a world community. The attention-value of its slogans and symbols is immeasurably less than that of the competing stimuli of national patriotism and of revolutionary class conflict. It is confronted with a vast, confused heterogeneity of purposes, a babel of discordant voices, and a chaos of conflicting national interests. Its problem is one requiring a prolonged process of slow education. In the words of H. G. Wells, history has become a race between education and catastrophe. But a new generation of world citizens is not to be raised up within a few years in a world dominated by the cult of the nation-state. And without a sense of world citizenship, without a universal allegiance, without a disposition everywhere to uphold the League as a symbol of world unity—not out of consideration of reason, interest, or expediency, but because of warm emotional attachment—it is doubtful whether the experiment can succeed in time to avert disaster. If catastrophe to the Western State System is to be prevented, the League of Nations must fulfill its mission within the visible future. It does not have centuries in which to accomplish its task. It must bring international order out of chaos within a few brief decades or go down to final defeat.

These same observations apply to all regional efforts at political unification which cut across established lines of language, culture, and power. The feebleness of Pan-Americanism calls for no comments. Its proponents have never achieved appreciable success in welding into unity the mechanized, speed-mad, power-hungry Colossus of the Anglo-Saxon North and the weak, leisurely, agrarian republics of the Latin South. Pan-Africanism and Pan-Asianism encounter comparable obstacles. The interesting scheme of "Pan-Europa," propounded so energetically by Count Coudenhove-Kalergi and subsequently taken up by Briand, has encountered the same difficulty. The Hungarian publicist contemplated the division of the world into five great units: the British Empire, the Soviet Union, Eastern Asia, Pan-America, and Pan-Europe. Pan-Europeanism has been sponsored by industrialists, economists, and statesmen, as well as by propagandists and idealists. M. Loucheur, Caillaux, and Herriot have been no less interested in the project than was Briand. As subject matter for practical (or impractical) politics, the scheme has been sponsored most warmly by the French Government. Briand advocated European union before the Tenth Assembly of the League in 1925.[1] In the same year the "Minister of Peace" told the French deputies: "It is my greatest wish to see the realization of the United States of Europe. And if I have devoted my energies . . . to the League of Nations, I have done so because in that great institution I have seen a rough draft of the United States of Europe."

On September 9, 1929, Briand discussed the project at Geneva with representatives of other European governments, and on May 17, 1930, the Quai d'Orsay dispatched to the twenty-six European members of the League a "Memorandum on the Organization of a System of European Federal Union." It proposed a "regional entente within the terms of Article 21 of the Covenant and its self-functioning within the League." A European conference was suggested and measures of economic collaboration were proposed. The replies were not unfavorable, though Great Britain and other States made reservations. The revisionist bloc insisted upon equality of rights and looked askance at the whole scheme as a new device to perpetuate French hegemony. In September, 1930, the League Assembly passed a resolution providing for a Commission of Inquiry of European Union, which convened in January, 1931. It decided to limit the project to economic cooperation and to invite Iceland, Turkey, and the U.S.S.R. to join in the enterprise. Various subcommissions were appointed, and the commission continued to meet periodically. The Austro-German customs-union quarrel and the other disturbing events of 1931 and 1932, however, were sadly out of harmony with the spirit of union, and the commission has thus far accomplished nothing of political significance.

The Pan-Europa idea, like the idea of the League itself, anticipates the integration of national interests into international interests and the setting up of a new political framework for the protection and promotion of such interests. But the idea cuts across the lines of language, of economic interests, and of power politics. The common interests, values,

[1] "I think that between peoples constituting geographical groups, like the peoples of Europe, there should be some kind of federal bond; it should be possible for them to get into touch at any time to confer about their interests, to agree on joint resolutions, and to establish among themselves a bond of solidarity which will enable them, if need be, to meet any grave emergency that may arise." Cited in Edouard Herriot, *The United States of Europe*, 1930, p. 51.

attitudes, and ideologies which are the prerequisites of successful union are nonexistent—or are existent in insufficient degree to move men to effective action. Frameworks, commissions, mechanisms remain fruitless under these circumstances. There is as yet no adequate social and psychological basis for successful organization. There are only disharmony, tension, discord, and competitive striving for national goals and purposes which are still very far from being coordinated into a single consistent and harmonious whole. The process of coordination requires time, effort, much thinking and acting together, a variety of shared experiences, perhaps some coercion, and the gradual emergence of the spiritual values and emotionalized symbols of the new order. But increasing tensions and conflicts threaten disaster before this can be achieved and they render its achievement increasingly difficult. The verdict of history on these efforts at unity may be: "Too late!" The efforts go on, however, and the end is not yet. The "far-off divine event" may perhaps not be so far off, so remote, so unreal, so tragically belated as pessimists assume it to be. But no realistic observer can afford to be optimistic over the prospects.

3. THE PASSING OF POWER POLITICS

Ours is essentially a tragic age, so we refuse to take it tragically. The cataclysm has happened, we are among the ruins, we start to build up new little habitats, to have new little hopes. It is rather hard work: there is now no smooth road into the future: but we go round, or scramble over the obstacles. We've got to live, no matter how many skies have fallen.—D. H. LAWRENCE.

A twofold reason may be assigned why we cannot change our opinions and sentiments so frequently as the times vary; first, because we cannot easily oppose ourselves to what we have been accustomed to desire; secondly, that, having repeatedly been prosperous in one way, we cannot easily persuade ourselves that we shall be equally so in another.—MACHIAVELLI, *Reflections on Livy.*

Before the middle of the twentieth century, western civilization and the Western State System will in all probability have embarked definitely and irrevocably on a course of development which will be peculiarly decisive for the destinies of the world society for many centuries to come. Every age is an age of change, since the stream of history is continuous and unbroken. Adam is reputed to have said to Eve, as the angel with the flaming sword drove them from Eden: "My dear, we live in an age of transition." Every historical epoch is necessarily a transition between an age which is past and an age which lies ahead. But in retrospect the events of certain periods appear especially significant for their effect upon developments for many generations beyond them. Some events which loom large to the actors and to contemporary observers are soon forgotten by posterity. Others cast long shadows down the endless aisles of time—shadows which lengthen as each successive milestone is passed. Such were the events of the fifth century B.C., when the hordes of Persia were beaten back and Greek civilization was preserved from barbarian conquest and permitted to blossom and bear its rich fruit in later ages. Such were the events of the period between 400 and 450 A.D., which spelled the doom of the Roman world State and of classical culture. The happenings of the century between 662 and 732 A.D. were similarly decisive, for they imposed the power of Islam on much of the western world for many centuries to come and they prevented the Moslem conquest of the barbarian Christian kingdoms of western Europe. In the same category are the literally "epoch-making events" of 1050 to 1100, 1475 to 1525, 1608 to 1648, 1789 to 1815, 1914 to 1919. The middle decades of the present century, 1935 to 1955, are likely, in the eyes of later ages, to assume an equally momentous significance, though evaluation in prospect is obviously much more difficult than evaluation in retrospect.

The reasons which support this prophecy have been suggested repeatedly in the preceding pages. The Western State System, already hoary with the frosts of centuries and now strangely transfigured, energized, and confounded by the magic of machine technology, finds itself confronted with a vast phenomenon of cultural lag which offers it the alternatives of destruction or of radical reformation. Its capitalists, entrepreneurs, merchants, and toilers, each working in his own interests with no vision of an integrated and coordinated world, have unwittingly contrived to construct a huge and intricate economy which has spread itself over the earth and wrought astonishing social transformations in every community touched by the new dispensation. Great metropolitan centers have sprung up like mushrooms in the course of a single century at all the crossroads of commerce. Steamship lines have penetrated the remotest seas. Railways and air routes cross mountains, deserts, plains, and jungles where recently was an untrodden wilderness. A complicated interchange of goods and services between all parts of the planet has been brought into being through intricate mechanisms of trade and credit. Vast populations have arisen on the basis of the new technology and the new economy. All these economic and social changes have gone forward without plan, without design, with no conscious world purpose behind them. They have transcended political frontiers, political ideas, political institutions. They have created a great world community whose peoples are for the most part politically unprepared to face the problems produced by these developments.

The political myths and symbols of the pre-industrial age have persisted with little change into the twentieth century: "sovereignty," "national independence," the balance of power, mercantilism, the diplomacy of power and prestige, tribal gods, ethnocentric provincialism, and a great variety of other antiquated and obsolete doctrines, ideas, and values. These patterns of thought and action among the peoples and ruling classes of the nation-states are irrelevant in an economically integrated world community. The members of that community have permitted the scientific, technological, and economic phases of western culture to advance so much more rapidly than their social, political, and legal legacies that a condition of dangerous disharmony and disequilibrium has been brought into being. A Fiji islander, attempting to manipulate a linotype press, would scarcely run more danger to himself and to the machine than does western mankind, with its petit bourgeois political philosophy and the aristocratic diplomatic patterns of the French "enlightenment," in its efforts to operate the world economy of the modern age.

Two great sources of friction and conflict confront contemporary civilization with problems which are as yet unsolved. On the one hand, the divergent and seemingly irreconcilable interests of those who own wealth, manage industry, and reap the profits of business, and of those who own nothing but labor power and who work for wages, breed class conflict, social unrest, political disorder, and threats of proletarian revolt and bourgeois dictatorship. On the other hand, the competitive struggles for power between the ruling classes of the great nation-states breed militaristic nationalism, imperialism, and war. Class conflict threatens the disruption of the social foundations of capitalism. International conflict threatens the dissolution of the world economy. One set of conflicts reacts upon the other. Social unrest in the great national societies is alleviated by more assiduous inculcation of nationalism, by the intensification of the appeal of the nation as an entity which commands an allegiance higher than the allegiance of class, by the pursuit of policies of aggrandizement designed to acquire new markets for surplus goods, new fields of investment for surplus capital, new sources of wealth for the ruling classes. The successful pursuit of such policies tends to alleviate social unrest. But their pursuit leads to war on a vast and unprecedentedly destructive scale. War has already disrupted the world economy, with disastrous effects upon the laboring masses everywhere. Labor unrest and threats of revolt give rise in turn to Fascist nationalism, dictatorship, and terrorism. International tensions are further increased thereby. Unless this cycle is broken, it can lead only to irremediable disaster for the whole social and political structure of the world society.

The dilemma confronting the Western State System began to manifest itself before the turn of the century. It has become peculiarly critical and acute in the present generation. Any solution of the dilemma postulates the organized application of social intelligence on a world-wide scale for the purpose of easing tensions, preventing conflict, and integrating divergent class and national interests into a new synthesis of values adequate as a basis for the political reformation of the world society. But the ruling classes of the nation-states are like all ruling classes of the past in that they are concerned primarily with their own immediate interests, in relation to other classes in their own communities, and in relation to rival ruling classes in other States. They are limited by the values and ideologies inherited from earlier generations, emotionalized into the symbols and myths of the present, perpetuated for the future by the weight of inertia and by the dead hands of yesterday. In the bourgeois economic order, conscious social planning and the intelligent direction of economic activity are rendered difficult by the individualistic and competitive character of an economy resting upon private property, great inequalities of wealth, and the private-profit motive. In the bourgeois political order, the State, despite its new service functions, remains an institutionalization of power relationships and an embodiment of coercive authority to serve the interests of the classes which control it. In the international order, each State, as of yore, envisages its own interests in exclusive and competitive terms and pursues these interests by self-help and violence. The mass of the population in the national societies frequently exhibits the political behavior patterns of an unorganized mob, dominated by ancient superstitions, frightened by bogies and phobias, excited by obsolete shibboleths, and swept helplessly along in the torrent by old and stereotyped emotions which it can neither comprehend nor control.

"Economic planning" and "international government" are phrases which suggest the requisite roads to salvation whereby the dilemma may be resolved and further conflict and dissolution may be averted. Both imply the organization of technical knowledge and socially directed intelligence for the rational solution of the problems which press in upon a harried world from all sides. Both postulate a substitution of the rule of reason for the rule of emotion, superstition, and blind faith in outworn formulas. But reason can operate only within the limits imposed by prevalent superstitions and mythologies. Unless a genuine sense of common interests can be made to prevail over selfish class loyalties and ancient tribal allegiances, reason cannot function. Problems of social relationships can be dealt with scientifically and administratively only after they have been resolved politically and common goals and purposes have been formulated. The established institutions and behavior patterns of individualistic capitalism encourage private acquisitiveness and render a genuine and effective consensus of interests extraordinarily difficult to attain, either between competing entrepreneurs or between the bourgeoisie as a whole and other groups in industrial society. The established institutions and behavior patterns of Great Power politics similarly stand

[848]

as formidable obstacles in the way of the building of a true world community. The social and psychological bases of cooperation and coordination are lacking. Failure to recognize this fact explains much of the futility and frustration of current thought and action designed to promote economic planning and international government. Whether these bases can be fabricated by taking thought, whether a transformation of established patterns and institutions can be achieved by consciously directed effort is not yet clear. What is clear is that the crisis of the world society is rapidly reaching high tide and that solutions must be devised soon, or they will be useless.

Put more simply, the central problem of the twentieth century is this: can the individualistic societies and the bourgeois governments of the western nation-states renounce uncontrolled acquisitive capitalism and the diplomacy of power, profits, and prestige to a sufficient degree to prevent the dissolution of the world in which they live? Can they achieve world unity and the social direction of economic activity before they are overwhelmed by the forces which have created the present order and which now threaten that order with destruction? These questions call urgently for answer in the immediate future. Upon the answer hinges the whole future of western civilization and the Western State System. And a negative answer, in all probability, does not mean a mere tedious continuation into the indefinite future of the present muddling and fumbling and befuddled confusion. It means rather a progressive and accelerated disintegration of the world economy and a relapse of the western world into international anarchy, war, and suicidal combat between the imperial Powers. In the course of such a new Armageddon the Powers will deal themselves a *coup de grâce* as deadly as that dealt to the decadent world of Rome by the migrating barbarians. Out of chaos may emerge universal social revolution, universal destruction of the old ways of life by a world rebellion of the industrial proletariat and the colonial subject peoples. And out of the wreckage may emerge economic planning and international government along the lines already foreshadowed in the U.S.S.R. Eventually life in the western world may be resumed at something like its old level, with a new ideology, a new mythology, a new set of social relationships, economic patterns, and political institutions adequate to the exigencies of a mechanized world community. Or—and the alternative is quite as probable—western mankind may slip down into a long and bloody decline at the end of which the whole fabric of the world economy will have been shattered and those who survive will be reduced to ruder and more primitive modes of living which will seem barbarous and brutish by comparison with the vanished golden age of capitalism and nationalism. In either case, the old order will be doomed.

The sequence of events which may lead to this result can almost be predicted in detail on the basis of an analysis of the present forces and tensions operating in the international arena. If disarmament fails, if the League of Nations fails, if all efforts to build world unity and peace are frustrated, the nation-states will return to the old ways which they have never in reality abandoned, and peoples and governments everywhere will turn their backs upon the vision of a pacific and ordered world. Each will pursue its own interests by force as in the past, and each will seek to protect itself from the immediate consequences of economic anarchy by exaggerated policies of political and economic nationalism. In Asia the disintegrating hulk of China will become a prey of the great States which, in despair of protecting their markets by cooperative efforts, will descend like vultures upon the carcass. They will rend and tear their victim and fall afoul of one another in the process. The long-deferred struggle for mastery of eastern Asia and the Pacific will assume violent form. In this contest Japan will possess the strategic advantages inherent in her geographical position. If her predominance is challenged by other Powers, as it will be, her armies will descend upon the Asiatic mainland and her naval forces will wrest the Philippine Islands from the United States and perhaps in the sequel attack the Dutch and Portuguese East Indies and Australia and New Zealand as well. Neither the United States nor Great Britain will be able to bring its enormous power to bear effectively in this sphere of action and they will perhaps be obliged to accept the loss of portions of their Pacific empires. The struggle of the imperial States in China, which may eventually assume the form of international intervention to suppress Chinese Communism, may well lead to war between the interventionists and the Soviet Union, with the latter supporting a Red China against western imperialism.

In Europe the revisionist bloc of unsatiated States will align itself against the French *status quo* bloc. It will inevitably re-arm and challenge by force the hegemony of France, Belgium, Poland, and the Little Entente. The States committed to a perpetuation of the 1919 peace settlement will be confronted by a formidable alliance of Germany, Italy, Austria, Hungary, Bulgaria, Albania, Lithuania, and possibly other States. Hostilities will be begun by some spark, some local conflagration at Danzig, at Vilna, in the Adriatic, in the Saar, in Transylvania, or at some other of the innumerable areas of tension. No war will be declared, for war has been outlawed. If the revisionist States have not already withdrawn from the League, the Council will pass resolutions and appoint commission of inquiry. The *status quo* bloc will seek to use the League as an agency to keep the peace. Great Britain and the United States will bring pressure to bear to avert fighting. But while the diplomats debate at Geneva, the patriotic crowds in Rome, in Budapest, in Vienna, in Munich, in Berlin will howl for action in the new "war of liberation." The strategists and the general staffs on each side will seek to paralyze the power of the other through swift blows by land, sea, and air. The Italian fleet will seek to cut communications between France and north Africa, while the French squadrons attack the Italian coast. The Italian army will fight Jugoslav and French divisions in Istria and Savoy, as Italian air fleets seek to bombard Toulon and Marseilles. French and Czechoslovak forces will endeavor to converge upon Bavaria, while German forces seize the Polish corridor and invade Bohemia. Death from the skies will rain down upon the great industrial centers. A savagely destructive war of movement will be initiated, not in predominantly agrarian regions as in the Great War, but in the thickly settled industrial centers of mid-Europe. Great Britain, the United States, and the U.S.S.R. will maintain a precarious neutrality which they will find it impossible to maintain if the struggle is prolonged.

The United States may conceivably find itself at war with Japan or with Great Britain or with both. Central Europe will be devastated on a scale unknown since the Thirty Years' War. Victors and vanquished alike will be brought to ruin, and out of the wreckage Red revolution will inevitably raise its head. If the Soviet Union succeeds in holding itself aloof from the earlier phases of the combat, it will intervene as soon as the prospects of proletarian revolt in the west appear to be promising. Its armies will crush Poland and Rumania and carry the Red flag on the tips of a million bayonets into Germany and Hungary. A gigantic struggle between two conflicting classes and two irreconcilable social systems will then ensue, with the bourgeois governments uniting belatedly in a great crusade to make the world safe for capitalism. The crusade will probably fail, for the U.S.S.R. will have become impregnable and the anarchy in central Europe will leave Communism as the sole hope of any semblance of order. The scourge of war and revolution will spread into France, Italy, the Baltic States, the Near East, and over the great seaways. The empires will disintegrate as the Communist International summons the subject peoples to revolt and sends the Red Armies to their assistance in Persia, in India, and in China. In the fullness of time a peace of exhaustion will descend like a pall upon the ruined contestants. Regardless of the verdict of the god of battles, the western societies will have been shattered beyond all hope of early restoration. Weary decades of disorder and disintegration will follow. The Western State System and the great culture which produced it will descend into the shades. The great world economy will have been destroyed by the very weapons which it forged. Silence will fall over the empty ruins of bomb-battered cities. A bedraggled peasantry will survive to eke out a miserable existence on shell-scarred fields strewn with the bones of millions of dead. Fire, famine, and disease will all but wipe out the great industrial and commercial metropolitan centers of the western world. The decline of the west will have reached its inevitable end, and some millenniums hence the archaeologists of other cultures of the remote future will return to the scenes of desolation to rewrite the history of the catastrophe.

This is not a horrendous and apocryphal fantasy conjured up out of the morbid imaginings of despair. It is rather the inevitable sequel to the failure of the present generation to cope with the problems presented by the contemporary dilemma of the world society. The forces of destruction which are at present operating in the international arena to produce new conflicts will work these results in the next great war. The social and economic consequences of such a combat are plainly discernible and clearly predictable. Such a contest will be final and conclusive, for it will be the death agony of a civilization. The wreckage which it will strew over the western world will be far too vast and too appalling to permit of early reconstruction, regardless of whether revolutionary Communism or Fascist capitalism prevails in the struggle. A world will have ended, and the survivors will perhaps be hardly more aware of what has overtaken them than were the Romans in the days of Alaric and Attila.

The alternative to such a future has been repeatedly suggested in these pages. If this imminent catastrophe to western culture is to be warded off, the Western State System must definitely choose the right road to world unity before disunity and conflict produce the chaos which advocates of the left road regard as inevitable. The politics of power must be renounced in the dealings of the nation-states with one another—or, if not renounced, must be so modified as to make possible the pacific readjustment of power relationships in accordance with changing conditions. The exclusive pursuit of national interests through coercion must be replaced by the integration of those interests into a new conception of a world community. For their own preservation, the ruling classes of the great national societies must somehow contrive to afford a greater measure of security and comfort to the masses of wage-earners than they enjoy in a world afflicted by financial panics, wholesale bankruptcies, and widespread unemployment and privation. Only in this fashion can the revolutionary preachers of desperation be deprived of the possibility of an effective appeal to the "fourth estate." Economic security and the easing of social tensions demand not national action, but international action, for the world economy can be saved from disintegration only by remedies which are world-wide in scope. The competitive quest for private profits through tariff protectionism, "autarchy," dollar diplomacy, and financial imperialism must give way to cooperative efforts designed to promote the general welfare of all nations in a world society. Territorial ambitions, irredentist aspirations, revisionist designs can scarcely be renounced by the States adversely affected by the present distribution of power. But armed violence as a means of realizing these hopes must be renounced. It will be renounced only if the dominant States are willing to make necessary concessions and to provide opportunities for peaceable modifications of the *status quo*. Finally, a new internationalism must be brought into being to furnish the necessary emotional bases for world citizenship and world federation. Only in this fashion can a true "international government" be solidly established and rendered capable of dealing with contemporary problems. The "irrepressible" conflict between capitalism and Communism, both as a class struggle between the bourgeoisie and the proletariat and as an international struggle between the U.S.S.R. and the western States, must be averted by mutual toleration and collaboration. Only in this fashion can the road to Geneva be made an adequate alternative to the road to Moscow.

No observer can say as yet that these developments are politically and psychologically impossible. The whole weight of the past, the whole force of habit and tradition stand in the way of the transformation. It involves concessions and adjustments which ruling classes and ruling States have seldom been willing to make, except under coercion. It may well be that those who wield power cannot emancipate themselves from their inherited values and ideologies and cannot attain the necessary breadth of view, the enlightenment of vision, and the requisite disposition to yield and to renounce. But the very urgency of the world crisis supplies a powerful incentive to concession and compromise. If those in authority fail to achieve a new orientation, they will not merely be endangering their own positions in western society, but they will be jeopardizing the very survival of western culture. This responsibility is overwhelming in its implications. These implications will be appreciated and will be acted upon within the next decade, or catastrophe will become inevitable. With this formulation of the alternatives facing the western world on the horizons of tomorrow, this effort at prognostication may be brought to a close.

SUGGESTED READINGS

Angell, N.: *The Unseen Assassins*, New York, Harper & Brothers, 1932.
Burns, C. D.: *Modern Civilization on Trial*, New York, The Macmillan Company, 1931.
Bury, J. B.: *The Idea of Progress*, London, Macmillan & Co., Ltd., 1921.
Cole, G. D. H.: *A Guide Through World Chaos*, New York, Alfred A. Knopf, 1932.
Conklin, E. G.: *The Direction of Human Evolution*, New York, Charles Scribner's Sons, 1921, 1922.
Coudenhove-Kalergi, R. N.,: *Pan-Europe*, New York, Alfred A. Knopf, 1928.
Cunningham, W.: *An Essay on Western Civilization in Its Economic Aspects*, Cambridge, Cambridge University Press, 1924.
Ferrero, G.: *The Unity of the World*, New York, Boni & Liveright, 1931.
Friedell, E.: *A Cultural History of the Modern Age* (3 vols.), New York, Alfred A. Knopf, 1931–1932.
Herriot, E.: *United States of Europe*, New York, Viking Press, Inc., 1930.

[853]

Huntington, E.: *World Power and Evolution*, New Haven, Yale University Press, 1919.

Marvin, F. S.: *The Unity of Western Civilization*, New York, Milford, 1915.

Muir, R.: *Nationalism and Internationalism*, Boston, Houghton Mifflin Company, 1917.

Nitti, F.: *The Decadence of Europe*, New York, Henry Holt & Company, 1923.

Nomad, M.: *Rebels and Renegades*, New York, The Macmillan Company, 1932.

Playne, C. E.: *The Neuroses of the Nations*, New York, Albert & Charles Boni, 1925.

Rappard, W. E.: *Uniting Europe*, New Haven, Yale University Press, 1930.

Scott, J. B.: *The United States of America: A Study in International Organization*, New York, Oxford University Press, 1920.

Strachey, John, *The Coming Struggle for Power*, New York, Covici-Friede, 1933.

Spengler, O.:*The Decline of the West* (2 vols.), New York, Alfred A. Knopf, 1928.

Wallas, G.: *Human Nature in Politics*, New York, Alfred A. Knopf, 1921.

———: *Our Social Heritage*, New Haven, Yale University Press, 1921.

Wells, H. G.: *The Work, Wealth, and Happiness of Mankind*, Garden City, Doubleday, Doran & Company, 1931.

APPENDICES

TREATY SERIES, No. 831

ARBITRATION

TREATY

BETWEEN

THE UNITED STATES OF AMERICA
AND ITALY

Signed at Washington, April 19, 1928.
Ratification advised by the Senate of the United States, May 10, 1928 (legislative day of May 3, 1928).
Ratified by the President of the United States, May 15, 1928.
Ratified by Italy, November 27, 1930.
Ratifications exchanged at Washington, January 20, 1931
Proclaimed by the President of the United States, January 21, 1931.

UNITED STATES
GOVERNMENT PRINTING OFFICE
WASHINGTON : 1931

A PROCLAMATION

WHEREAS a Treaty of Arbitration between the United States of America and Italy was concluded and signed by their respective Plenipotentiaries at Washington on the nineteenth day of April, one thousand nine hundred and twenty-eight, the original of which Treaty, being in the English and Italian languages, is word for word as follows:

The President of the United States of America and His Majesty the King of Italy

Determined to prevent so far as in their power lies any interruption in the peaceful relations that happily have always existed between the two nations;

Desirous of reaffirming their adherence to the policy of submitting to impartial decision all justiciable controversies that may arise between them; and

Eager by their example not only to demonstrate their condemnation of war as an instrument of national policy in their mutual relations, but also to hasten the time when the perfection of international arrangements for the pacific settlement of international disputes shall have eliminated forever the possibility of war among any of the Powers of the world;

Have decided to conclude a new treaty of arbitration enlarging the scope and obligations of the arbitration convention signed at Washington on March 28, 1908, which expired by limitation on January 22, 1924, and for that purpose they have appointed as their respective Plenipotentiaries

The President of the United States of America, Frank B. Kellogg, Secretary of State of the United States, and

His Majesty the King of Italy, Nobile Giacomo de Martino, Ambassador Extraordinary and Plenipotentiary to the United States,

who, having communicated to one another their full powers found in good and due form, have agreed upon the following articles:

Il Presidente degli Stati Uniti dell'America del Nord e Sua Maestà il Re d'Italia,

decisi a prevenire, per quanto è in loro potere, qualunque interruzione delle relazioni pacifiche che sono sempre felicemente esistite fra le due Nazioni;

desiderosi di riaffermare la loro adesione al sistema di sottomettere ad una decisione imparziale tutte le controversie suscettibili di una soluzione giuridica che possano sorgere fra essi; e

intendendo con il loro esempio non solo di dimostrare che essi condannano la guerra come mezzo di politica nazionale nelle loro mutue relazioni, ma anche di affrettare il momento che il perfezionamento degli accordi internazionali per il regolamento pacifico delle controversie internazionali avrà eliminato per sempre la possibilità di guerre fra le Potenze del mondo;

hanno deciso di concludere un nuovo Trattato di Arbitrato che allarghi lo scopo e le obbligazioni della Convenzione di Arbitrato firmata a Washington il 28 marzo 1908 e spirata il 22 gennaio 1924, e a questo fine hanno nominato come loro Plenipotenziarii rispettivamente

Il Presidente degli Stati Uniti dell'America del Nord, Frank B. Kellogg, Segretario di Stato degli Stati Uniti, e

Sua Maestà il Re d'Italia, il Nobile Giacomo de Martino, Suo Ambasciatore Straordinario e Plenipotenziario agli Stati Uniti,

i quali, essendosi comunicati i loro pieni poteri e avendoli trovati in buona e debita forma, hanno concordato i seguenti articoli:

[858]

APPENDIX I

ARTICLE I

All differences relating to international matters in which the High Contracting Parties are concerned by virtue of a claim of right made by one against the other under treaty, or otherwise, which it has not been possible to adjust by diplomacy, which have not been adjusted as a result of reference to the Permanent International Commission constituted pursuant to the treaty signed at Washington May 5, 1914, between Italy and the United States and still in force, and which are justiciable in their nature by reason of being susceptible of decision by the application of the principles of law or equity, shall be submitted to the Permanent Court of Arbitration established at The Hague by the Convention of October 18, 1907, or to some other competent tribunal, as shall be decided in each case by special agreement, which special agreement shall provide for the organization of such tribunal if necessary, define its powers, state the question or questions at issue, and settle the terms of reference.

The special agreement in each case shall be made on the part of the United States of America by the President of the United States of America by and with the advice and consent of the Senate thereof, and on the part of the Kingdom of Italy in accordance with the constitutional laws of that Kingdom.

ARTICLE II

The provisions of this treaty shall not be invoked in respect of any dispute the subject matter of which

(a) is within the domestic jurisdiction of either of the High Contracting Parties;

(b) involves the interests of third Parties;

(c) depends upon or involves the maintenance of the traditional attitude of the United States concerning American questions, commonly described as the Monroe Doctrine;

ARTICOLO I

Tutte le controversie relative ad affari internazionali nelle quali le Alte Parti Contraenti siano impegnate in seguito a una pretesa giuridica avanzata da una Parte contro l'altra, e fondata o sopra un trattato o altrimenti, le quali non sia stato possibile comporre in via diplomatica, le quali non siano state risolte in seguito a ricorso alla Commissione Permanente Internazionale, costituita in base al trattato firmato a Washington il 5 maggio 1914 tra l'Italia e gli Stati Uniti dell'America del Nord e attualmente in vigore, e le quali siano di loro natura suscettibili di una soluzione giuridica, in quanto suscettibili di una decisione derivata dalla applicazione dei principii del diritto o dell'equità, saranno sottomesse alla Corte Permanente di Arbitrato stabilita all'Aja dalla Convenzione del 18 ottobre 1907 o ad altro tribunale competente, secondo quanto sarà stabilito in ogni singolo caso con un accordo speciale; il quale accordo speciale regolerà l'organizzazione di tale tribunale, se necessario, definirà i suoi poteri, esporrà la questione o le questioni di cui si tratta e ne fisserà i termini.

L'accordo speciale in ogni singolo caso sarà concluso da parte degli Stati Uniti dell'America del Nord dal loro Presidente con l'avviso e il consenso del Senato, e da parte del Regno d'Italia secondo le sue leggi costituzionali.

ARTICOLO II

Le disposizioni del presente Trattato non saranno invocate per qualunque controversia il cui contenuto:

(a) si riferisca alla giurisdizione interna di una delle Alte Parti Contraenti;

(b) implichi gli interessi di terzi Stati;

(c) derivi dall'atteggiamento tradizionale degli Stati Uniti dell'America del Nord verso le questioni americane che è comunemente indicato come dottrina di Monroe, o ne riguardi il mantenimento;

APPENDIX I

(d) depends upon or involves the observance of the obligations of Italy in accordance with the Covenant of the League of Nations.

Article III

The present treaty shall be ratified by the President of the United States of America by and with the advice and consent of the Senate thereof and by the Kingdom of Italy in accordance with its constitutional laws.

The ratifications shall be exchanged at Washington as soon as possible, and the treaty shall take effect on the date of the exchange of the ratifications. It shall thereafter remain in force continuously unless and until terminated by one year's written notice given by either High Contracting Party to the other.

In faith whereof the respective Plenipotentiaries have signed this treaty in duplicate in the English and Italian languages, both texts having equal force, and hereunto affix their seals.

Done at Washington the nineteenth day of April in the year of our Lord one thousand nine hundred and twenty-eight.

(d) derivi dalle obbligazioni dell'Italia in conformità al Patto della Società delle Nazioni, o ne riguardi l'osservanza.

Articolo III

Il presente Trattato sarà ratificato dal Presidente degli Stati Uniti dell'America del Nord con l'avviso e il consenso del Senato e dal Regno d'Italia secondo le sue leggi constituzionali.

Le ratifiche saranno scambiate a Washington appena possibile e il Trattato entrerà in vigore al momento dello scambio delle ratifiche. Esso resterà quindi continuativamente in vigore, a meno che e fino a quando esso non sia denunciato con una comunicazione scritta, a un anno di anticipo, di una delle Alte Parti Contraenti all'altra.

In fede di che i rispettivi Plenipotenziarii hanno firmato il presente Trattato in duplice esemplare in inglese e in italiano, facendo ambedue i testi ugualmente fede, e vi hanno apposto i loro suggelli.

Fatto a Washington il diciannove aprile dell'anno di Nostro Signore millenovecentoventotto.

FRANK B KELLOGG [SEAL]
GIACOMO DE MARTINO [SEAL]

AND WHEREAS the said Treaty has been duly ratified on both parts, and the ratifications of the two Governments were exchanged in the city of Washington on the twentieth day of January, one thousand nine hundred and thirty-one;

NOW, THEREFORE, BE IT KNOWN THAT I, HERBERT HOOVER, President of the United States of America, have caused the said Treaty to be made public, to the end that the same and every article and clause thereof may be observed and fulfilled with good faith by the United States of America and the citizens thereof.

IN TESTIMONY WHEREOF, I have hereunto set my hand and caused the seal of the United States of America to be affixed.

DONE at the city of Washington this twenty-first day of January in the year of our Lord one thousand nine hundred and thirty-one, and of the Independence of the [SEAL] United States of America the one hundred and fifty-fifth.

HERBERT HOOVER

By the President:
HENRY L STIMSON
Secretary of State.

AN ARBITRAL *COMPROMIS*

ARBITRATION OF CLAIMS
GROWING OUT OF THE ALLEGED DETENTION
OF THE MOTORSHIPS
"KRONPRINS GUSTAF ADOLF" AND "PACIFIC"

———

SPECIAL AGREEMENT
BETWEEN THE UNITED STATES OF AMERICA
AND SWEDEN
(U. S. Treaty Series, No. 841)

———

Signed at Washington, December 17, 1930.
Ratification advised by the Senate of the United States, February 14, 1931
   (legislative day of January 26, 1931).
Ratified by the President of the United States, April 17, 1931.
Ratified by Sweden, January 3, 1931.
Ratifications exchanged at Washington, October 1, 1931.
Proclaimed by the President of the United States, October 2, 1931.

By the President of the United States of America

A PROCLAMATION

WHEREAS an agreement between the United States of America and Sweden for the arbitration of certain claims of the Rederiaktiebolaget Nordstjernan, a Swedish corporation, growing out of the alleged detention in ports of the United States of America of the motor-ships KRONPRINS GUSTAF ADOLF and PACIFIC, belonging to the said Swedish corporation, was concluded and signed by their respective Plenipotentiaries at Washington on the seventeenth day of December, one thousand nine hundred and thirty, the original of which agreement, being in the English language, is word for word as follows:

WHEREAS, the Government of Sweden has presented to the Government of the United States of America certain claims on behalf of Rederiaktiebolaget Nordstjernan, a Swedish corporation, for losses said to have been incurred as a result of the alleged detention in ports of the United States of America, in contravention of provisions of treaties in force between the United States of America and Sweden, of the motorship KRONPRINS GUSTAF ADOLF and the motorship PACIFIC belonging to said Swedish corporation; and

WHEREAS, the Government of the United States of America has disclaimed any liability to indemnify the Government of Sweden in behalf of the owners of the said motorships, therefore:

The President of the United States of America and His Majesty the King of Sweden being desirous that this matter of difference between their two Governments should be submitted to adjudication by a competent and impartial Tribunal have named as their respective plenipotentiaries, that is to say:

The President of the United States of America,

Henry L. Stimson, Secretary of State of the United States of America; and

His Majesty the King of Sweden,

W. Boström, Envoy Extraordinary and Minister Plenipotentiary at Washington;

Who, after having communicated to each other their respective full powers found in good and due form, have agreed upon the following articles:

ARTICLE I

There shall be submitted to arbitration pursuant to the Convention for the Pacific Settlement of International Disputes, signed at The Hague, October 18, 1907, and the Arbitration Convention between the United States of America and Sweden, signed at Washington, October 27, 1928, the following questions:

First, Whether the Government of the United States of America detained the Swedish motorship KRONPRINS GUSTAF ADOLF between June 23, 1917 and July 12, 1918, and the Swedish motorship PACIFIC between July 1, 1917 and July 19, 1918, in contravention of the Swedish-American Treaties of April 3, 1783 and July 4, 1827.

Second, Whether, if the first question be decided in the affirmative, the Government of the United States of America is liable to the Government of Sweden in behalf of the owners of the motorships for damages resulting from such unlawful detention; and,

Third, Should the reply be in the affirmative what pecuniary reparation is due to the Government of Sweden on behalf of the owners of the motorships above mentioned.

[862]

APPENDIX II

ARTICLE II

The questions stated in Article I shall be submitted for a decision to a sole arbitrator who shall not be a national of either the United States of America or Sweden. In the event that the two Governments shall be unable to agree upon the selection of a sole arbitrator within two months from the date of the coming into force of this Agreement they shall proceed to the establishment of a Tribunal consisting of three members, one designated by the President of the United States of America, one by His Majesty the King of Sweden, and the third, who shall preside over the Tribunal, selected by mutual agreement of the two Governments. None of the members of the Tribunal shall be a national of the United States of America or of Sweden.

ARTICLE III

The precedure in the arbitration shall be as follows:

(1) Within ninety days from the date of the exchange of ratifications of this Agreement, the agent for the Government of Sweden shall present to the Agent for the Government of the United States of America a statement of the facts on which the Government of Sweden rests the claim against the United States of America, and the demand for indemnity. This statement shall be accompanied by the evidence in support of the allegations and of the demand made;

(2) Within a like period of ninety days from the date on which this Agreement becomes effective, as aforesaid, the Agent for the Government of the United States of America shall present to the Agent for the Government of Sweden at Washington a statement of facts relied upon by the Government of the United States of America together with evidence in support.

(3) Within sixty days from the date on which the exchange of statements provided for in paragraphs (1) and (2) of this Article is completed each Agent shall present in the manner prescribed by paragraphs (1) and (2) an answer to the statement of the other together with any additional evidence and such argument as they desire to submit.

ARTICLE IV

When the development of the record is completed in accordance with Article III hereof, the Government of the United States of America and the Government of Sweden shall forthwith cause to be forwarded to the International Bureau at The Hague, for transmission to the Arbitrator or Arbitrators, as the case may be, three complete sets of the statements, answers, evidence and arguments presented by their respective Agents to each other.

ARTICLE V

Within thirty days from the delivery of the record to the Arbitrator or Arbitrators in accordance with Article IV, the Tribunal shall convene at Washington for the purpose of hearing oral arguments by Agents or Counsel, or both, for each Government.

ARTICLE VI

When the Agent for either Government has reason to believe that the other Government possesses or could obtain any document or documents which are relevant to the claim but which have not been incorporated in the record such document or documents shall be submitted to the Tribunal at the request of the Agent for the other Government and shall be available for inspection by the demanding Agent. In agreeing to arbitrate the claim of the Kingdom of Sweden in behalf of Rederiaktiebolaget Nordstjernan the Government of the United States of America does not waive any defense which was available prior to the concluding of the Agreement.

[863]

APPENDIX II

ARTICLE VII

The decision of the Tribunal shall be made within two months from the date on which the arguments close, unless on the request of the Tribunal the Parties shall agree to extend the period. The decision shall be in writing.

The decision of the majority of the members of the Tribunal, in case a sole arbitrator is not agreed upon, shall be the decision of the Tribunal.

The language in which the proceedings shall be conducted shall be English.

The decision shall be accepted as final and binding upon the two Governments.

ARTICLE VIII

Each Government shall pay the expenses of the presentation and conduct of its case before the Tribunal; all other expenses which by their nature are a charge on both Governments, including the honorarium for the Arbitrator or Arbitrators, shall be borne by the two Governments in equal moieties.

ARTICLE IX

This Special Agreement shall be ratified in accordance with the constitutional forms of the Contracting Parties and shall take effect immediately upon the exchange of ratifications, which shall take place at Washington as soon as possible.

In witness whereof, the respective plenipotentiaries have signed this Special Agreement and have hereunto affixed their seals.

Done in duplicate at Washington this seventeenth day of December, nineteen hundred and thirty.

HENRY L STIMSON [SEAL]

W. BOSTRÖM [SEAL]

AND WHEREAS the said agreement has been duly ratified on both parts, and the ratifications of the two Governments were exchanged in the city of Washington on the first day of October, one thousand nine hundred and thirty-one;

Now, THEREFORE, be it known that I, Herbert Hoover, President of the United States of America, have caused the said agreement to be made public to the end that the same and every article and clause thereof may be observed and fulfilled with good faith by the United States of America and the citizens thereof.

IN TESTIMONY WHEREOF, I have hereunto set my hand and caused the seal of the United States of America to be affixed.

DONE at the city of Washington this second day of October in the year of our Lord one thousand nine hundred and thirty-one, and of the Independence of the United [SEAL] States of America the one hundred and fifty-sixth.

HERBERT HOOVER

By the President:
HENRY L STIMSON
Secretary of State.

[864]

APPENDIX III

AN EXTRADITION TREATY

EXTRADITION

TREATY
BETWEEN THE UNITED STATES OF AMERICA
AND GREAT BRITAIN
(U. S. Treaty Series, No. 849)

Signed at London, December 22, 1931.

Ratification advised by the Senate of the United States, February 19, 1932 (legislative day of February 17, 1932).

Ratified by the President of the United States, March 3, 1932.

Ratified by Great Britain, July 29, 1932.

Ratifications exchanged at London, August 4, 1932.

Proclaimed by the President of the United States, August 9, 1932.

AND

EXCHANGES OF NOTES EXTENDING THE APPLICABILITY
OF THE TREATY TO PALESTINE AND
TRANS-JORDAN

By the President of the United States of America

A PROCLAMATION

Whereas an extradition treaty between the United States of America and Great Britain was concluded and signed by their respective Plenipotentiaries at London on December 22, 1931, the original of which treaty is word for word as follows:

The President of the United States of America,

And His Majesty the King of Great Britain, Ireland and the British Dominions beyond the Seas, Emperor of India;

Desiring to make more adequate provision for the reciprocal extradition of criminals,

Have resolved to conclude a Treaty for that purpose, and to that end have appointed as their plenipotentiaries:

The President of the United States of America:

General Charles G. Dawes, Ambassador Extraordinary and Plenipotentiary of the United States of America at the Court of St. James;

And His Majesty the King of Great Britain, Ireland and the British Dominions beyond the Seas, Emperor of India:

for Great Britain and Northern Ireland:

The Right Honourable Sir John Simon, G.C.S.I., M.P., His Principal Secretary of State for Foreign Affairs;

who, having communicated their full powers, found in good and due form, have agreed as follows:—

ARTICLE 1

The High Contracting Parties engage to deliver up to each other, under certain circumstances and conditions stated in the present Treaty, those persons who, being accused or convicted of any of the crimes or offences enumerated in Article 3, committed within the jurisdiction of the one Party, shall be found within the territory of the other Party.

ARTICLE 2

For the purposes of the present Treaty the territory of His Britannic Majesty shall be deemed to be Great Britain and Northern Ireland, the Channel Islands and the Isle of Man, and all parts of His Britannic Majesty's dominions overseas other than those enumerated in Article 14, together with the territories enumerated in Article 16 and any territories to which it may be extended under Article 17. It is understood that in respect of all territory of His Britannic Majesty as above defined other than Great Britain and Northern Ireland, the Channel Islands, and the Isle of Man, the present Treaty shall be applied so far as the laws permit.

For the purposes of the present Treaty the territory of the United States shall be deemed to be all territory wherever situated belonging to the United States, including its dependencies and all other territories under its exclusive administration or control.

[866]

APPENDIX III

ARTICLE 3

Extradition shall be reciprocally granted for the following crimes or offences:—

1. Murder (including assassination, parricide, infanticide, poisoning), or attempt or conspiracy to murder.
2. Manslaughter.
3. Administering drugs or using instruments with intent to procure the miscarriage of women.
4. Rape.
5. Unlawful carnal knowledge, or any attempt to have unlawful carnal knowledge, of a girl under 16 years of age.
6. Indecent assault if such crime or offence be indictable in the place where the accused or convicted person is apprehended.
7. Kidnapping or false imprisonment.
8. Child stealing, including abandoning, exposing or unlawfully detaining.
9. Abduction.
10. Procuration: that is to say the procuring or transporting of a woman or girl under age, even with her consent, for immoral purposes, or of a woman or girl over age, by fraud, threats, or compulsion, for such purposes with a view in either case to gratifying the passions of another person provided that such crime or offence is punishable by imprisonment for at least one year or by more severe punishment.
11. Bigamy.
12. Maliciously wounding or inflicting grievous bodily harm.
13. Threats, by letter or otherwise, with intent to extort money or other things of value.
14. Perjury, or subornation of perjury.
15. Arson.
16. Burglary or housebreaking, robbery with violence, larceny or embezzlement.
17. Fraud by a bailee, banker, agent, factor, trustee, director, member, or public officer of any company, or fraudulent conversion.
18. Obtaining money, valuable security, or goods, by false pretences receiving any money, valuable security, or other property, knowing the same to have been stolen or unlawfully obtained.
19.—(a) Counterfeiting or altering money, or bringing into circulation counterfeited or altered money.
    (b) Knowingly and without lawful authority making or having in possession any instrument, tool, or engine adapted and intended for the counterfeiting of coin.
20. Forgery, or uttering what is forged.
21. Crimes or offences against bankruptcy law.
22. Bribery, defined to be the offering, giving or receiving of bribes.
23. Any malicious act done with intent to endanger the safety of any persons travelling or being upon a railway.
24. Crimes or offences or attempted crimes or offences in connection with the traffic in dangerous drugs.
25. Malicious injury to property, if such crime or offence be indictable.
26.—(a) Piracy by the law of nations.
    (b) Revolt, or conspiracy to revolt, by two or more persons on board a ship on the high seas against the authority of the master; wrongfully sinking or destroying a vessel at sea, or attempting to do so; assaults on board a ship on the high seas, with intent to do grievous bodily harm.
27. Dealing in slaves.

[867]

APPENDIX III

Extradition is also to be granted for participation in any of the aforesaid crimes or offences, provided that such participation be punishable by the laws of both High Contracting Parties.

ARTICLE 4

The extradition shall not take place if the person claimed has already been tried and discharged or punished, or is still under trial in the territories of the High Contracting Party applied to, for the crime or offence for which his extradition is demanded.

If the person claimed should be under examination or under punishment in the territories of the High Contracting Party applied to for any other crime or offence, his extradition shall be deferred until the conclusion of the trial and the full execution of any punishment awarded to him.

ARTICLE 5

The extradition shall not take place if, subsequently to the commission of the crime or offence or the institution of the penal prosecution or the conviction thereon, exemption from prosecution or punishment has been acquired by lapse of time, according to the laws of the High Contracting Party applying or applied to.

ARTICLE 6

A fugitive criminal shall not be surrendered if the crime or offence in respect of which his surrender is demanded is one of a political character, or if he proves that the requisition for his surrender has, in fact, been made with a view to try or punish him for a crime or offence of a political character.

ARTICLE 7

A person surrendered can in no case be kept in custody or be brought to trial in the territories of the High Contracting Party to whom the surrender has been made for any other crime or offence, or on account of any other matters, than those for which the extradition shall have taken place, until he has been restored, or has had an opportunity of returning, to the territories of the High Contracting Party by whom he has been surrendered.

This stipulation does not apply to crimes or offences committed after the extradition.

ARTICLE 8

The extradition of fugitive criminals under the provisions of this Treaty shall be carried out in the United States and in the territory of His Britannic Majesty respectively, in conformity with the laws regulating extradition for the time being in force in the territory from which the surrender of the fugitive criminal is claimed.

ARTICLE 9

The extradition shall take place only if the evidence be found sufficient, according to the laws of the High Contracting Party applied to, either to justify the committal of the prisoner for trial, in case the crime or offence had been committed in the territory of such High Contracting Party, or to prove that the prisoner is the identical person convicted by the courts of the High Contracting Party who makes the requisition, and that the crime or offence of which he has been convicted is one in respect of which extradition could, at the time of such conviction, have been granted by the High Contracting Party applied to.

ARTICLE 10

If the individual claimed by one of the High Contracting Parties in pursuance of the present Treaty should be also claimed by one or several other Powers on account of other crimes or offences committed within their respective jurisdictions, his extradition shall be granted to the Power whose claim is earliest in date, unless such claim is waived.

ARTICLE 11

If sufficient evidence for the extradition be not produced within two months from the date of the apprehension of the fugitive, or within such further time as the High Contracting Party applied to, or the proper tribunal of such High Contracting Party, shall direct, the fugitive shall be set at liberty.

ARTICLE 12

All articles seized which were in the possession of the person to be surrendered at the time of his apprehension, and any articles that may serve as a proof of the crime or offence shall be given up when the extradition takes place, in so far as this may be permitted by the law of the High Contracting Party granting the extradition.

ARTICLE 13

All expenses connected with the extradition shall be borne by the High Contracting Party making the application.

ARTICLE 14

His Britannic Majesty may accede to the present Treaty on behalf of any of his Dominions hereafter named—that is to say, the Dominion of Canada, the Commonwealth of Australia (including for this purpose Papua and Norfolk Island), the Dominion of New Zealand, the Union of South Africa, the Irish Free State, and Newfoundland—and India. Such accession shall be effected by a notice to that effect given by the appropriate diplomatic representative of His Majesty at Washington which shall specify the authority to which the requisition for the surrender of a fugitive criminal who has taken refuge in the Dominion concerned, or India, as the case may be, shall be addressed. From the date when such notice comes into effect the territory of the Dominion concerned or of India shall be deemed to be territory of His Britannic Majesty for the purposes of the present Treaty.

The requisition for the surrender of a fugitive criminal who has taken refuge in any of the above-mentioned Dominions or India, on behalf of which His Britannic Majesty has acceded, shall be made by the appropriate diplomatic or consular officer of the United States of America.

Either High Contracting Party may terminate this Treaty separately in respect of any of the above-mentioned Dominions or India. Such termination shall be effected by a notice given in accordance with the provisions of Article 18.

Any notice given under the first paragraph of this Article in respect of one of His Britannic Majesty's Dominions may include any territory in respect of which a mandate on behalf of the League of Nations has been accepted by His Britannic Majesty, and which is being administered by the Government of the Dominion concerned; such territory shall, if so included, be deemed to be territory of His Britannic Majesty for the purposes of the present Treaty. Any notice given under the third paragraph of this Article shall be applicable to such mandated territory.

ARTICLE 15

The requisition for the surrender of a fugitive criminal who has taken refuge in any territory of His Britannic Majesty other than Great Britain and Northern Ireland, the Channel Islands, or the Isle of Man, or the Dominions or India mentioned in Article 14, shall be made to the Governor, or chief authority, of such territory by the appropriate consular officer of the United States of America.

Such requisition shall be dealt with by the competent authorities of such territory: provided, nevertheless, that if an order for the committal of the fugitive criminal to prison to await surrender shall be made, the said Governor or chief authority may, instead of issuing a warrant for the surrender of such fugitive, refer the matter to His Majesty's Government in the United Kingdom of Great Britain and Northern Ireland.

ARTICLE 16

This Treaty shall apply in the same manner as if they were Possessions of His Britannic Majesty to the following British Protectorates, that is to say, the Bechuanaland Protectorate, Gambia Protectorate, Kenya Protectorate, Nigeria Protectorate, Northern Rhodesia, Northern Territories of the Gold Coast, Nyasaland, Sierra Leone Protectorate, Solomon Islands Protectorate, Somaliland Protectorate, Swaziland, Uganda Protectorate and Zanzibar, and to the following territories in respect of which a mandate on behalf of the League of Nations has been accepted by His Britannic Majesty, that is to say, Cameroons under British mandate, Togoland under British mandate, and the Tanganyika Territory.

ARTICLE 17

If after the signature of the present Treaty it is considered advisable to extend its provisions to any British Protectorates other than those mentioned in the preceding Article or to any British-protected State, or to any territory in respect of which a mandate on behalf of the League of Nations has been accepted by His Britannic Majesty, other than those mandated territories mentioned in Articles 14 and 16, the stipulations of Articles 14 and 15 shall be deemed to apply to such Protectorates or States or mandated territories from the date and in the manner prescribed in the notes to be exchanged for the purpose of effecting such extension.

ARTICLE 18

The present Treaty shall come into force ten days after its publication, in conformity with the forms prescribed by the laws of the High Contracting Parties. It may be terminated by either of the High Contracting Parties by a notice not exceeding one year and not less than six months.

In the absence of an express provision to that effect, a notice given under the first paragraph of this Article shall not affect the operation of the Treaty as between the United States of America and any territory in respect of which notice of accession has been given under Article 14.

The present Treaty shall be ratified, and the ratifications shall be exchanged at London as soon as possible.

On the coming into force of the present treaty the provisions of Article 10 of the treaty of the 9th August, 1842, of the Convention of the 12th July, 1889, of the supplementary Convention of the 13th December, 1900, and of the supplementary Convention of the 12th April, 1905, relative to extradition, shall cease to have effect, save that in the case of each of the Dominions and India, mentioned in Article 14, those provisions shall remain in force until such Dominion or India shall have acceded to the present treaty in accordance with Article 14 or until replaced by other treaty arrangements.

In faith whereof the above-named plenipotentiaries have signed the present Treaty and have affixed thereto their seals.

Done in duplicate at London this twenty-second day of December, 1931.

[SEAL]   CHARLES G DAWES

[SEAL]   JOHN SIMON

AND WHEREAS, the said treaty has been duly ratified on both parts, and the ratifications of the two Governments were exchanged at London on the fourth day of August, one thousand nine hundred and thirty-two;

Now, THEREFORE, be it known that I, Herbert Hoover, President of the United States of America, have caused the said treaty to be made public, to the end that the same and every article and clause thereof may be observed and fulfilled with good faith by the United States of America and the citizens thereof.

IN TESTIMONY WHEREOF, I have hereunto set my hand and caused the seal of the United States of America to be affixed.

DONE at the city of Washington this ninth day of August in the year of our Lord one thousand nine hundred and thirty-two, and of the Independence of the United [SEAL] States of America the one hundred and fifty-seventh.

HERBERT HOOVER

By the President:
HENRY L STIMSON
Secretary of State.

NOTES EXCHANGED CONCERNING THE EXTENSION TO PALESTINE AND TRANS-JORDAN OF THE EXTRADITION TREATY BETWEEN THE UNITED STATES OF AMERICA AND GREAT BRITAIN

The British Secretary of State for Foreign Affairs (Simon) to the American Ambassador (Dawes)

No. T 15523/46/374.

FOREIGN OFFICE, S.W. 1.
22nd December, 1931.

YOUR EXCELLENCY,

With reference to Article 17 of the Extradition Treaty between His Majesty The King of Great Britain, Ireland and the British Dominions beyond the Seas and the President of the United States of America, signed this day at London, I have the honour to inform Your Excellency that His Majesty's Government in the United Kingdom desire that the provisions of the above mentioned Treaty shall, as from the date of its entry into force, be applicable to Palestine (excluding Transjordan).

2. I have accordingly the honour to enquire whether the United States Government agree with this proposal. In this event the present note and Your Excellency's reply to that effect will be regarded as placing on record the agreement arrived at in the matter.

I have the honour to be, with the highest consideration,

Your Excellency's obedient Servant,

JOHN SIMON

HIS EXCELLENCY
GENERAL CHARLES G. DAWES, C.B.,
etc., etc., etc.

The American Ambassador (Dawes) to the British Secretary of State for Foreign Affairs (Simon)

No. 1582.

EMBASSY OF THE UNITED STATES OF AMERICA
LONDON, *December 22, 1931.*

SIR:

With reference to Article 17 of the Extradition Treaty between the President of the United States of America and His Majesty The King of Great Britain, Ireland and the British Dominions beyond the Seas, signed this day at London, I have the honor to inform you that the Government of the United States of America is agreeable to the proposal of His Majesty's Government in the United Kingdom that the provisions of the above mentioned Treaty shall, as from the date of its entry into force, be applicable to Palestine (excluding Transjordan).

I have the honor to be, with the highest consideration, Sir,

Your most obedient, humble Servant,

CHARLES G. DAWES.

THE RIGHT HON^BLE.
SIR JOHN SIMON, G.C.S.I., etc., etc., etc.,
Foreign Office, S.W. 1.

APPENDIX III

The British Secretary of State for Foreign Affairs (Simon) to the American Ambassador (Dawes)

No. T 15523/46/374.

FOREIGN OFFICE, S.W. 1.
22nd December, 1931.

YOUR EXCELLENCY,

With reference to Article 17 of the Extradition Treaty between His Majesty The King of Great Britain, Ireland and the British Dominions beyond the Seas and the President of the United States of America, signed this day at London, I have the honour to inform Your Excellency that His Majesty's Government in the United Kingdom desire that the provisions of the above mentioned Treaty shall, as from the date of its entry into force, be applicable to Transjordan.

2. I have accordingly the honour to enquire whether the United States Government agree with this proposal. In this event the present note and Your Excellency's reply to that effect will be regarded as placing on record the agreement arrived at in the matter.

I have the honour to be, with the highest consideration,

Your Excellency's obedient Servant,

JOHN SIMON

HIS EXCELLENCY
GENERAL CHARLES G. DAWES, C.B.,
etc., etc., etc.

The American Ambassador (Dawes) to the British Secretary of State for Foreign Affairs (Simon)

No. 1583.

EMBASSY OF THE UNITED STATES OF AMERICA
LONDON, *December 22, 1931.*

SIR:

With reference to Article 17 of the Extradition Treaty between the President of the United States of America and His Majesty The King of Great Britain, Ireland and the British Dominions beyond the Seas, signed this day at London, I have the honor to inform you that the Government of the United States of America is agreeable to the proposal of His Majesty's Government in the United Kingdom that the provisions of the above mentioned Treaty shall, as from the date of its entry into force, be applicable to Transjordan.

I have the honor to be, with the highest consideration, Sir,

Your most obedient, humble Servant,

CHARLES G. DAWES.

THE RIGHT HON^BLE.
SIR JOHN SIMON, G.C.S.I., etc., etc., etc.,
Foreign Office, S.W. 1.

Appendix IV

A COMMERCIAL TREATY

FRIENDSHIP, COMMERCE AND
CONSULAR RIGHTS

———

TREATY
BETWEEN THE UNITED STATES OF AMERICA
AND AUSTRIA
(U. S. Treaty Series, No. 838)

———

Signed at Vienna, June 19, 1928.
Ratification advised by the Senate of the United States, with
reservation and understanding, February 11, 1929.
Ratified by the President of the United States, April 29, 1931.
Ratified by Austria, January 17, 1929.
Ratifications exchanged at Vienna, May 27, 1931.
Proclaimed by the President of the United States, May 28, 1931.

A PROCLAMATION

WHEREAS a Treaty of Friendship, Commerce and Consular Rights between the United States of America and the Republic of Austria was concluded and signed by their respective Plenipotentiaries at Vienna on the nineteenth day of June, one thousand nine hundred and twenty-eight, the original of which treaty, being in the English and German languages, is word for word as follows:

Treaty of Friendship, Commerce and Consular Rights

between the United States of America and the Republic of Austria

The United States of America and the Republic of Austria, desirous of strengthening the bond of peace which happily prevails between them, by arrangements designed to promote friendly intercourse between their respective territories through provisions responsive to the spiritual, cultural, economic and commercial aspirations of the peoples thereof, have resolved to conclude a Treaty of Friendship, Commerce and Consular Rights and for that purpose have appointed as their plenipotentiaries:

The President of the United States of America,

Mr. Albert Henry Washburn, Envoy Extraordinary and Minister Plenipotentiary of the

United States of America to Austria,
and

The Federal President of the Republic of Austria,

Monsignore Ignatius Seipel, Doctor of Theology, Federal Chancellor,

Who, having communicated to each other their full powers found to be in due form, have agreed upon the following articles:

ARTICLE I. The nationals of each of the High Contracting Parties shall be permitted to enter, travel and reside in the territories of the other; to exercise liberty of conscience and freedom of worship; to engage in professional, scientific, religious, philanthropic, manufacturing and commercial work of every kind without interference; to carry on every form of commercial activity which is not forbidden by the local law; to employ agents of their choice, and generally to do anything incidental to or necessary for the enjoyment of any of the foregoing privileges upon the same terms as nationals of the state of residence or as nationals of the nation hereafter to be most favored by it, submitting themselves to all local laws and regulations duly established.

The nationals of each of the High contracting Parties within the territories of the other shall be permitted to own, erect or lease and occupy appropriate buildings and to lease lands for residential, scientific, religious, philanthropic, manufacturing, commercial and mortuary purposes upon the same terms as nationals of the country.

As regards the acquisition, possession, and disposition of immovable property, except as regards the leasing of lands for specified purposes provided for in the foregoing paragraph, the nationals of each of the High Contracting Parties shall enjoy in the territory of the other, subject to reciprocity, the treatment generally accorded to foreigners by the laws of the place where the property is situated.

The nationals of either High Contracting Party within the territories of the other shall not be subjected to the payment of any internal charges or taxes other or higher than those that are exacted of and paid by its nationals.

The nationals of each High Contracting Party shall enjoy freedom of access to the courts of justice of the other on conforming to the local laws, as well for the prosecution as for the defense of their rights, and in all degrees of jurisdiction established by law.

The nationals of each High Contracting Party shall receive within the territories of the other, upon submitting to conditions imposed upon its nationals, the most constant protection and security for their persons and property, and shall enjoy in this respect that degree of protection that is required by international law. Their property shall not be taken without due process of law and without payment of just compensation.

Nothing contained in this Treaty shall be construed to affect existing statutes of either of the High Contracting Parties in relation to the immigration of aliens or the right of either of the High Contracting Parties to enact such statutes.

ARTICLE II. With respect to that form of protection granted by National, State or Provincial laws establishing civil liability for injuries or for death, and giving to relatives or heirs or dependents of an injured party a right of action or a pecuniary benefit, such relatives or heirs or dependents of the injured party, himself a national of either of the High Contracting Parties and within any of the territories of the other, shall regardless of their alienage or residence outside of the territory where the injury occurred, enjoy the same rights and privileges as are or may be granted to nationals, and under like conditions.

ARTICLE III. The dwellings, warehouses, manufactures, shops and other places of business, and all premises thereto appertaining of the nationals of each of the High Contracting Parties in the territories of the other, used for any purposes set forth in Article I, shall be respected. It shall not be allowable to make a domiciliary visit to, or search of any such buildings and premises, or there to examine and inspect books, papers or accounts, except under the conditions and in conformity with the forms prescribed by the laws, ordinances and regulations for nationals.

ARTICLE IV. Where, on the death of any person holding real or other immovable property or interests therein within the territories of one High Contracting Party, such property or interests therein would, by the laws of the country or by a testamentary disposition, descend or pass to a national of the other High Contracting Party, whether resident or non-resident, were he not disqualified by the laws of the country where such property or interests therein is or are situated, such national shall be allowed a term of three years in which to sell the same, this term to be reasonably prolonged if circumstances render it necessary, and withdraw the proceeds thereof, without restraint or interference, and exempt from any succession, probate or administrative duties or charges other than those which may be imposed in like cases upon the nationals of the country from which such proceeds may be drawn.

Nationals of either High Contracting Party may have full power to dispose of their personal property of every kind within the territories of the other, by testament, donation, or otherwise, and their heirs, legatees and donees, of whatsoever nationality, whether resident or non-resident, shall succeed to such personal property, and may take possession thereof, either by themselves or by others acting for them, and retain or dispose of the same at their pleasure subject to the payment of such duties or charges only as the nationals of the High Contracting Party within whose territories such property may be or belong shall be liable to pay in like cases.

ARTICLE V. The nationals of each of the High Contracting Parties in the exercise of the right of freedom of worship, within the territories of the other, as hereinabove provided, may, without annoyance or molestation of any kind by reason of their religious belief or otherwise, conduct services either within their own houses or within any appropriate buildings which they may be at liberty to erect and maintain in convenient situations, provided their teachings and practices are not inconsistent with public order or public morals and provided further they conform to all laws and regulations duly established in these territories; and they may also be permitted to bury their dead according to their religious customs in suitable and convenient places established and maintained for the purpose, subject to the established mortuary and sanitary laws and regulations of the place of burial.

ARTICLE VI. In the event of war between either High Contracting Party and a third State, such Party may draft for compulsory military service nationals of the other having a permanent residence within its territories and who have formally, according to its laws, declared an intention to adopt its nationality by naturalization, unless such individuals depart from the territories of said belligerent Party within sixty days after a declaration of war.

ARTICLE VII. Between the territories of the High Contracting Parties there shall be freedom of commerce and navigation. The nationals of each of the High Contracting Parties equally with those of the most favored nation, shall have liberty freely to come with their vessels and cargoes to all places, ports and waters of every kind within the territorial limits of the other which are or may be open to foreign commerce and navigation. Nothing in this Treaty shall be construed to restrict the right of either High Contracting Party to impose, on such terms as it may see fit, prohibitions or restrictions of a sanitary character designed to protect human, animal or plant life, or regulations for the enforcement of police or revenue laws.

Each of the High Contracting Parties binds itself unconditionally to impose no higher or other duties or charges, and no conditions, prohibitions or restrictions, on the importation of any article, the growth, produce or manufacture of the territories of the other Party, from whatever place arriving, than are or shall be imposed on the importation of any like article, the growth, produce or manufacture of any other foreign country; nor shall any such duties, charges, conditions, prohibitions, or restrictions on importations be made effective retroactively.

Each of the High Contracting Parties also binds itself unconditionally to impose no higher or other charges or other restrictions or prohibitions on goods exported to the territories of the other High Contracting Party than are imposed on goods exported to any other foreign country.

In the event of licenses being issued by either of the High Contracting Parties for the importation into or exportation from its territories of articles the importation or exportation of which is restricted or prohibited, the conditions under which such licenses may be obtained shall be publicly announced and clearly stated in such a manner as to enable traders interested to become acquainted with them; the method of licensing shall be as simple and unvarying as possible and applications for licenses shall be dealt with as speedily as possible. Moreover, the conditions under which such licenses are issued by either of the High Contracting Parties for goods imported from or exported to the territories of the other Party shall be as favorable as the conditions under which licenses are issued in respect of any other foreign country. In the event of rations or quotas being established for the importation or exportation of articles restricted or prohibited, each of the High Contracting Parties agrees to grant for the importation from or exportation to the territories of the other Party an equitable share in the allocation of the quantity of restricted goods which may be authorized for importation or exportation. In the application of the provisions of this paragraph no distinction shall be made between direct and indirect shipments. It is agreed, moreover, that in the event either High Contracting Party shall be engaged in war, it may enforce such import or export restrictions as may be required by the national interest.

Any advantage of whatsoever kind which either High Contracting Party may extend, by treaty, law, decree, regulation, practice or otherwise, to any article, the growth, produce or manufacture of any other foreign country shall simultaneously and unconditionally, without request and without compensation, be extended to the like article, the growth, produce or manufacture of the other High Contracting Party.

All articles which are or may be legally imported from foreign countries into ports of the United States or are or may be legally exported therefrom in vessels of the United States may likewise be imported into those ports or exported therefrom in Austrian vessels without being liable to any other or higher duties or charges whatsoever than if such articles were imported or exported in vessels of the United States; and, reciprocally, all articles which are or may be legally imported from foreign countries into the ports of Austria or are or may be legally exported therefrom in Austrian vessels may likewise be imported into those ports or exported therefrom in vessels of the United States without being liable to any other or higher duties or charges whatsoever than if such articles were imported or exported in Austrian vessels.

With respect to the amount and collection of duties on imports and exports of every kind, each of the two High Contracting Parties binds itself to give to the nationals, vessels and goods of the other the advantage of every favor, privilege or immunity which it shall have accorded to the nationals, vessels and goods of a third State, whether such favored State shall have been accorded such treatment gratuitously or in return for reciprocal compensatory treatment. Every such favor, privilege or immunity which shall hereafter be granted the nationals, vessels or goods of a third State shall simultaneously and unconditionally, without request and without compensation, be extended to the other High Contracting Party, for the benefit of itself, its nationals, vessels and goods.

The stipulations of this Article shall not extend to the treatment which either Contracting Party shall accord to purely border traffic within a zone not exceeding ten miles (15 kilometres) wide on either side of its customs frontier, or to the treatment which is accorded by the United States to the commerce of Cuba under the provisions of the Commercial Convention concluded by the United States and Cuba on December 11, 1902, or any other commercial convention which hereafter may be concluded by the United States with Cuba, or to the commerce of the United States with any of its dependencies and the Panama Canal Zone under existing or future laws.

Article VIII. The nationals and merchandise of each High Contracting Party within the territories of the other shall receive the same treatment as nationals and merchandise of the country with regard to internal taxes, transit duties, charges in respect to warehousing and other facilities and the amount of drawbacks and bounties.

Article IX. Limited liability and other corporations and associations, whether or not for pecuniary profit, which have been or may hereafter be organized in accordance with and under the laws, National, State or Provincial, of either High Contracting Party and maintain a central office within the territories thereof, shall have their juridical status recognized by the other High Contracting Party provided that they pursue no aims within its territories contrary to its laws. They shall enjoy free access to the courts of law and equity, on conforming to the laws regulating the matter, as well for the prosecution as for the defense of rights in all the degrees of jurisdiction established by law.

The right of such corporations and associations of either High Contracting Party so recognized by the other to establish themselves within its territories, establish branch offices and fulfill their functions therein shall depend upon, and be governed solely by, the consent of such Party as expressed in its National, State or Provincial laws.

ARTICLE X. The nationals of either High Contracting Party shall enjoy within the territories of the other, reciprocally and upon compliance with the conditions there imposed, such rights and privileges as have been or may hereafter be accorded the nationals of any other State with respect to the organization of and participation in limited liability and other corporations and associations, for pecuniary profit or otherwise, including the rights of promotion, incorporation, purchase and ownership and sale of shares and the holding of executive or official positions therein. In the exercise of the foregoing rights and with respect to the regulation or procedure concerning the organization or conduct of such corporations or associations, such nationals shall be subjected to no conditions less favorable than those which have been or may hereafter be imposed upon the nationals of the most favored nation. The rights of any of such corporations or associations as may be organized or controlled or participated in by the nationals of either High Contracting Party within the territories of the other to exercise any of their functions therein, shall be governed by the laws and regulations, national, state or provincial, which are in force or may hereafter be established within the territories of the Party wherein they propose to engage in business. The foregoing stipulations do not apply to the organization of and participation in political associations.

The nationals of either High Contracting Party shall, moreover, enjoy within the territories of the other, reciprocally and upon compliance with the conditions there imposed, such rights and privileges as have been or may hereafter be accorded the nationals of any other State with respect to the mining of coal, phosphate, oil, oil shale, gas, and sodium on the public domain of the other.

ARTICLE XI. Commercial travellers representing manufacturers, merchants and traders domiciled in the territories of either High Contracting Party shall on their entry into and sojourn in the territories of the other Party and on their departure therefrom be accorded the most favored nation treatment in respect of customs and other privileges and of all charges and taxes of whatever denomination applicable to them or to their samples.

If either High Contracting Party require the presentation of an authentic document establishing the identity and authority of a commercial traveller, a certificate issued by any of the following in the country of his departure shall be accepted as satisfactory:

a) the authority designated for the purpose;
b) a chamber of commerce;
c) any trade or commercial association recognized for the purpose by the diplomatic representative of the Contracting Party requiring such certificates.

ARTICLE XII. There shall be complete freedom of transit through the territories including territorial waters of each High Contracting Party on the routes most convenient for international transit, by rail, navigable waterway, and canal, other than the Panama Canal and waterways and canals which constitute international boundaries of the United States, to persons and goods coming from or going through the territories of the other High Contracting Party, except such persons as may be forbidden admission into its territories or goods of which the importation may be prohibited by law. Persons and goods in transit shall not be subjected to any transit duty, or to any unnecessary delays or restrictions, and shall be given national treatment as regards charges, facilities, and all other matters.

Goods in transit must be entered at the proper customhouse, but they shall be exempt from all customs or other similar duties.

All charges imposed on transport in transit shall be reasonable, having regard to the conditions of the traffic.

ARTICLE XIII. Each of the High Contracting Parties agrees to receive from the other, consular officers in those of its ports, places and cities, where it may be convenient and which are open to consular representatives of any foreign country.

Consular officers of each of the High Contracting Parties shall, after entering upon their duties, enjoy reciprocally in the territories of the other all the rights, privileges, exemptions and immunities which are enjoyed by officers of the same grade of the most favored nation. As official agents, such officers shall be entitled to the high consideration of all officials, national or local, with whom they have official intercourse in the state which receives them.

The Government of each of the High Contracting Parties shall furnish free of charge the necessary exequatur of such consular officers of the other as present a regular commission signed by the chief executive of the appointing state and under its great seal; and it shall issue to a subordinate or substitute consular officer duly appointed by an accepted superior consular officer with the approbation of his Government, or by any other competent officer of that Government, such documents as according to the laws of the respective countries shall be requisite for the exercise by the appointee of the consular function. On the exhibition of an exequatur, or other document issued in lieu thereof to such subordinate, such consular officer shall be permitted to enter upon his duties and to enjoy the rights, privileges and immunities granted by this Treaty.

ARTICLE XIV. Consular officers, nationals of the state by which they are appointed, shall be exempt from arrest except when charged with the commission of offenses locally designated as crimes other than misdemeanors and subjecting the individual guilty thereof to punishment. Such officers shall be exempt from military billetings, and from service of any military or naval, administrative or police character whatsoever.

In criminal cases the attendance at the trial by a consular officer as a witness may be demanded by the prosecution or defense. The demand shall be made with all possible regard for the consular dignity and the duties of the office; and there shall be compliance on the part of the consular officer.

Consular officers shall be subject to the jurisdiction of the courts in the state which receives them in civil cases, subject to the proviso, however, that when the officer is a national of the state which appoints him and is engaged in no private occupation for gain, his testimony shall be taken orally or in writing at his residence or office and with due regard for his convenience. The officer should, however, voluntarily give his testimony at the trial whenever it is possible to do so without serious interference with his official duties.

ARTICLE XV. Consular officers, including employees in a consulate, nationals of the State by which they are appointed other than those engaged in private occupations for gain within the State where they exercise their functions shall be exempt from all taxes, National, State, Provincial, and Municipal, levied upon their persons or upon their property, except taxes levied on account of the possession or ownership of immovable property situated in, or income derived from sources within the territories of the State within which they exercise their functions. All consular officers and employees, nationals of the State appointing them, shall be exempt from the payment of taxes on the salary, fees or wages received by them in compensation for their consular services.

Lands and buildings situated in the territories of either High Contracting Party, of which the other High Contracting Party is the legal or equitable owner and which are used exclusively for diplomatic or consular purposes by that owner, shall be exempt from taxation of every kind, National, State, Provincial and Municipal, other than assessments levied for services or local public improvements by which the premises are benefited.

ARTICLE XVI. Consular officers may place over the outer door of their respective offices the arms of their State with an appropriate inscription designating the official office. Such officers may also hoist the flag of their country on their offices including those situated in the capitals of the two countries. They may likewise hoist such flag over any boat or vessel employed in the exercise of the consular function.

The consular offices and archives shall at all times be inviolable. They shall under no circumstances be subject to invasion by any authorities of any character within the country where such offices are located. Nor shall the authorities under any pretext make any examination or seizure of papers or other property deposited within a consular office. Consular offices shall not be used as places of asylum. No consular officer shall be required to produce official archives in court or testify as to their contents.

Upon the death, incapacity, or absence of a consular officer having no subordinate consular officer at his post, secretaries or chancellors, whose official character may have previously been made known to the government of the State where the consular function was exercised, may temporarily exercise the consular function of the deceased or incapacitated or absent consular officer; and while so acting shall enjoy all the rights, prerogatives and immunities granted to the incumbent.

ARTICLE XVII. Consular officers, nationals of the State by which they are appointed, may, within their respective consular districts, address the authorities, National, State, Provincial or Municipal, for the purpose of protecting their countrymen in the enjoyment of their rights accruing by treaty or otherwise. Complaint may be made for the infraction of those rights. Failure upon the part of the proper authorities to grant redress or to accord protection may justify interposition through the diplomatic channel, and in the absence of a diplomatic representative, a consul general or the consular officer stationed at the capital may apply directly to the government of the country.

ARTICLE XVIII. Consular officers may, in pursuance of the laws of their own country, take, at any appropriate place within their respective districts, the depositions of any occupants of vessels of their own country, or of any national of, or of any person having permanent residence within the territories of, their own country. Such officers may draw up, attest, certify and authenticate unilateral acts, deeds, and testamentary dispositions of their countrymen, and also contracts to which a countryman is a party. They may draw up, attest, certify and authenticate written instruments of any kind purporting to express or embody the conveyance or encumbrance of property of any kind within the territory of the State by which such officers are appointed, and unilateral acts, deeds, testamentary dispositions and contracts relating to property situated, or business to be transacted, within the territories of the State by which they are appointed, embracing unilateral acts, deeds, testamentary dispositions or agreements executed solely by nationals of the State within which such officers exercise their functions.

Instruments and documents thus executed and copies and translations thereof, when duly authenticated under his official seal by the consular officer, shall be received as evidence in the territories of the contracting parties as original documents or authenticated copies, as the case may be, and shall have the same force and effect as if drawn by and executed before a notary or other public officer duly authorized in the country by which the consular officer was appointed; provided, always that such documents shall have been drawn and executed in conformity to the laws and regulations of the country where they are designed to take effect.

ARTICLE XIX. In case of the death of a national of either High Contracting Party in the territory of the other without having in the territory of his decease any known heirs or testamentary executors by him appointed, the competent local authorities shall at once inform the nearest consular officer of the State of which the deceased was a national of the fact of his death, in order that necessary information may be forwarded to the parties interested.

In case of the death of a national of either of the High Contracting Parties without will or testament, in the territory of the other High Contracting Party, the consular officer of the State of which the deceased was a national and within whose district the deceased made his home at the time of death, shall, so far as the laws of the country permit and pending the appointment of an administrator and until letters of administration have been granted, be deemed qualified to take charge of the property left by the decedent for the preservation and protection of the same. Such consular officer shall have the right to be appointed as administrator within the discretion of a tribunal or other agency controlling the administration of estates provided the laws of the place where the estate is administered so permit.

Whenever a consular officer accepts the office of administrator of the estate of a deceased countryman, he subjects himself as such to the jurisdiction of the tribunal or other agency making the appointment for all necessary purposes to the same extent as a national of the country where he was appointed.

ARTICLE XX. A consular officer of either High Contracting Party may in behalf of his non-resident countrymen collect and receipt for their distributive shares derived from estates in process of probate or accruing under the provisions of so-called Workmen's Compensation Laws or other like statutes, for transmission through channels prescribed by his Government to the proper distributees.

ARTICLE XXI. Each of the High Contracting Parties agrees to permit the entry free of all duty and without examination of any kind, of all furniture, equipment and supplies intended for official use in the consular offices of the other, and to extend to such consular officers of the other and their families and suites as are its nationals, the privilege of entry free of duty of their personal or household effects actually in use which accompany such consular officers, their families or suites, or which arrive shortly thereafter, provided, nevertheless, that no article, the importation of which is prohibited by the law of either of the High Contracting Parties, may be brought into its territories.

It is understood, however, that this privilege shall not be extended to consular officers who are engaged in any private occupation for gain in the countries to which they are accredited, save with respect to governmental supplies.

ARTICLE XXII. Subject to any limitation or exception hereinabove set forth, or hereafter to be agreed upon, the territories of the High Contracting Parties to which the provisions of this Treaty extend shall be understood to comprise all areas of land, water, and air over which the Parties claim and exercise dominion as sovereign thereof, except the Panama Canal Zone.

ARTICLE XXIII. Nothing in the present Treaty shall be construed to limit or restrict in any way the rights, privileges and advantages accorded to the United States or its nationals or to Austria or its nationals by the Treaty between the United States and Austria establishing friendly relations, concluded on August 24, 1921.

ARTICLE XXIV. The present Treaty shall remain in full force for the term of six years from the date of the exchange of ratifications, on which date it shall begin to take effect in all of its provisions.

If within one year before the expiration of the aforesaid period of six years neither High Contracting Party notifies to the other an intention of modifying, by change or omission, any of the provisions of any of the articles in this Treaty or of terminating it upon the expiration of the aforesaid period, the Treaty shall remain in full force and effect after the aforesaid period and until one year from such a time as either of the High Contracting Parties shall have notified to the other an intention of modifying or terminating the Treaty.

APPENDIX IV

ARTICLE XXV. The present Treaty shall be ratified, and the ratifications thereof shall be exchanged at Vienna as soon as possible.

IN WITNESS WHEREOF the respective Plenipotentiaries have signed the same and have affixed their seals hereto.

DONE in duplicate in the English and German languages at Vienna, this 19th day of June 1928.

ALBERT HENRY WASHBURN.

[SEAL]

SEIPEL

[SEAL]

AND WHEREAS, the Senate of the United States of America did advise and consent to the ratification of the said treaty subject to the following reservation and understanding to be set forth in an exchange of notes between the High Contracting Parties so as to make it plain that this condition is understood and accepted by each of them:

"That the sixth paragraph of Article VII shall remain in force for twelve months from the date of exchange of ratifications, and if not then terminated on ninety days' previous notice shall remain in force until either of the high contracting parties shall enact legislation inconsistent therewith when the same shall automatically lapse at the end of sixty days from such enactment, and on such lapse each high contracting party shall enjoy all the rights which it would have possessed had such paragraph not been embraced in this treaty.";

AND WHEREAS, the said reservation and understanding was accepted by the two Governments in an exchange of notes dated January 20, 1931, between the Envoy Extraordinary and Minister Plenipotentiary of the United States of America at Vienna, and the Vice Chancellor and Federal Minister for Foreign Affairs of the Republic of Austria, subject on the part of the Republic of Austria to ratification;

AND WHEREAS, the said treaty and the said reservation and understanding have been duly ratified on both parts and the ratifications of the two governments were exchanged at Vienna on the twenty-seventh day of May, one thousand nine hundred and thirty-one;

NOW, THEREFORE, BE IT KNOWN THAT I, HERBERT HOOVER, President of the United States of America, have caused the said treaty to be made public to the end that the same and every article and clause thereof may be observed and fulfilled with good faith by the United States of America and the citizens thereof, subject to the reservation and understanding aforesaid.

IN TESTIMONY WHEREOF, I have hereunto set my hand and caused the seal of the United States of America to be affixed.

DONE at the city of Washington this twenty-eighth day of May in the year of our Lord [SEAL] one thousand nine hundred and thirty-one, and of the Independence of the United States of America the one hundred and fifty-fifth.

HERBERT HOOVER

By the President:

HENRY L STIMSON
Secretary of State.

SENATE RESOLUTION ADVISING AND CONSENTING TO RATIFICATION

In Executive Session, Senate of the United States.

Monday, February 11, 1929.

Resolved (Two-thirds of the Senators present concurring therein), That the Senate advise and consent to the ratification of Executive B, 70th Congress, 2nd Session, a treaty of friendship, commerce and consular rights with Austria, signed at Vienna on June 19, 1928, subject to the following reservation and understanding to be set forth in an exchange of notes between the high contracting parties so as to make it plain that this condition is understood and accepted by each of them:

That the sixth paragraph of Article VII shall remain in force for twelve months from the date of exchange of ratification, and if not then terminated on ninety days' previous notice shall remain in force until either of the high contracting parties shall enact legislation inconsistent therewith when the same shall automatically lapse at the end of sixty days from such enactment, and on such lapse each high contracting party shall enjoy all the rights which it would have possessed had such paragraph not been embraced in this treaty.

Attest:

EDWIN P. THAYER
Secretary.

[RATIFICATION]

HERBERT HOOVER,

President of the United States of America,

TO ALL TO WHOM THESE PRESENTS SHALL COME, GREETING:

KNOW YE, That whereas a Treaty of Friendship, Commerce and Consular Rights between the United States of America and the Republic of Austria was concluded and signed by their respective Plenipotentiaries at Vienna on the nineteenth day of June, one thousand nine hundred and twenty-eight, the original of which Treaty is hereto annexed:

AND WHEREAS, the Senate of the United States of America by their resolution of February 11, 1929, (two-thirds of the Senators present concurring therein) did advise and consent to the ratification of the said Treaty subject to the following reservation and understanding to be set forth in an exchange of notes between the High Contracting Parties so as to make it plain that this condition is understood and accepted by each of them:

"That the sixth paragraph of Article VII shall remain in force for twelve months from the date of exchange of ratifications, and if not then terminated on ninety days' previous notice shall remain in force until either of the high contracting parties shall enact legislation inconsistent therewith when the same shall automatically lapse at the end of sixty days from such enactment, and on such lapse each high contracting party shall enjoy all the rights which it would have possessed had such paragraph not been embraced in this treaty.";

AND WHEREAS, the said reservation and understanding was accepted by the two Governments in an exchange of notes dated January 20, 1931, between the Envoy Extraordinary and Minister Plenipotentiary of the United States of America at Vienna and the Vice-

Chancellor and Federal Minister for Foreign Affairs of the Republic of Austria, subject on the part of the Republic of Austria to ratification, the originals of which notes are word for word as follows:

"EXCELLENCY:

"Referring to the Treaty of Friendship, Commerce and Consular Rights signed by the United States and Austria on June 19, 1928, I have the honor to inform you that the United States Senate on February 11, 1929, gave its advice and consent to the ratification of the said Treaty in a resolution, as follows:

'*Resolved* (*two-thirds of the Senators present concurring therein*), That the Senate advise and consent to the ratification of Executive B, Seventieth Congress, second session, a treaty of friendship, commerce, and consular rights with Austria, signed at Vienna on June 19, 1928, subject to the following reservation and understanding to be set forth in an exchange of notes between the high contracting parties so as to make it plain that this condition is understood and accepted by each of them:

That the sixth paragraph of Article VII shall remain in force for twelve months from the date of exchange of ratifications, and, if not then terminated on ninety days' previous notice, shall remain in force until either of the high contracting parties shall enact legislation inconsistent therewith, when the same shall automatically lapse at the end of sixty days from such enactment, and on such lapse each high contracting party shall enjoy all the rights which it would have possessed had such paragraph not been embraced in this treaty.'

"It will be observed that by this resolution the advice and consent of the Senate to the ratification of the Treaty are given subject to a certain reservation and understanding.

"I shall be glad if when bringing the foregoing resolution to the attention of your Government, Your Excellency will state that my Government hopes that the Austrian Government will find acceptable the reservation and understanding which the Senate has made a condition of its advice and consent to the ratification of the Treaty. You may regard this note as sufficient acceptance by the Government of the United States of this reservation and understanding. An acknowledgment of this note on the occasion of the exchange of ratifications, accepting by direction and on behalf of your Government the said reservation and understanding, will be considered as completing the required exchange of notes and the acceptance by both governments of the reservation and understanding.

"Accept, Excellency, the renewed assurance of my highest consideration.

G. B. STOCKTON

HIS EXCELLENCY
   DR. JOHANN SCHOBER,
      Vice-Chancellor and Federal Minister
         for Foreign Affairs,
            Vienna."

AND WHEREAS, the said reservation and understanding has been ratified by the Republic of Austria;

NOW, THEREFORE, BE IT KNOWN THAT I, HERBERT HOOVER, President of the United States of America, having seen and considered the said Treaty, do hereby in pursuance of the aforesaid advice and consent of the Senate, ratify and confirm the same and every article and clause thereof, subject to the reservation and understanding aforesaid.

IN TESTIMONY WHEREOF, I have hereunto set my hand and caused the seal of the United States of America to be affixed.

[885]

APPENDIX IV

Done at the city of Washington this twenty-ninth day of April in the year of our Lord [SEAL] one thousand nine hundred and thirty-one, and of the Independence of the United States of America the one hundred and fifty-fifth.

HERBERT HOOVER

By the President:
    HENRY L. STIMSON
        Secretary of State.

SUPPLEMENTARY AGREEMENT TO THE TREATY OF JUNE 19, 1928,
BETWEEN THE UNITED STATES OF AMERICA AND AUSTRIA
(U. S. Treaty Series, No. 839)

Signed at Vienna, January 20, 1931.
Ratification advised by the Senate of the United States, February
20, 1931 (legislative day of February 17, 1931).
Ratified by the President of the United States, April 29, 1931.
Ratified by Austria, March 28, 1931.
Ratifications exchanged at Vienna, May 27, 1931.
Proclaimed by the President of the United States, May 28, 1931.

By the President of the United States of America

A PROCLAMATION

Whereas a Supplementary Agreement to the Treaty of Friendship, Commerce and Consular Rights between the United States of America and the Republic of Austria, concluded and signed on the nineteenth day of June, one thousand nine hundred and twenty-eight, was concluded and signed by their respective Plenipotentiaries at Vienna on the twentieth day of January, one thousand nine hundred and thirty-one, the original of which Supplementary Agreement, being in the English and German languages, is word for word as follows:

SUPPLEMENTARY AGREEMENT

TO THE TREATY OF FRIENDSHIP, COMMERCE AND CONSULAR RIGHTS BETWEEN THE UNITED STATES OF AMERICA AND THE REPUBLIC OF AUSTRIA, SIGNED ON JUNE 19, 1928.

The United States of America and the Republic of Austria, by the undersigned Mr. Gilchrist Baker Stockton, Envoy Extraordinary and Minister Plenipoteniary of the United States of America at Vienna, and Dr. Johann Schober, Vice-Chancellor and Federal Minister for Foreign Affairs of the Republic of Austria, their duly empowered plenipotentiaries, agree, as follows:

Notwithstanding the provisions of the first paragraph of Article XXIV of the Treaty of Friendship, Commerce and Consular Rights, between the United States of America and the Republic of Austria, signed June 19, 1928, to the effect that the said Treaty shall remain in force for the term of six years from the date of the exchange of ratifications, it is agreed that the said Treaty may be terminated on February 11, 1935, or on any date thereafter, by notice given by either high contracting party to the other party one year before the date on which it is desired that such termination shall become effective.

Done in duplicate, in the English and German languages, at Vienna, this 20th day of January One Thousand Nine Hundred and Thirty-one.

G. B. Stockton
Schober

[SEAL]
[SEAL]

And Whereas, the said Supplementary Agreement has been duly ratified on both parts and the ratifications of the two governments were exchanged at Vienna on the twenty-seventh day of May, one thousand nine hundred and thirty-one;

Now, therefore, be it known that I, Herbert Hoover, President of the United States of America, have caused the said supplementary agreement to be made public to the end that the same and every article and clause thereof may be observed and fulfilled with good faith by the United States of America and the citizens thereof.

In testimony whereof, I have hereunto set my hand and caused the seal of the United States of America to be affixed.

[888]

APPENDIX IV

D ONE at the city of Washington this twenty-eighth day of May in the year of our Lord
        one thousand nine hundred and thirty-one, and of the Independence of the
[SEAL]   United States of America the one hundred and fifty-fifth.

                                                        HERBERT HOOVER
By the President:
    HENRY L. STIMSON
        Secretary of State.

SUMMARY OF CONTROVERSIES DEALT WITH BY THE PERMANENT COURT OF INTERNATIONAL JUSTICE TO JULY, 1932[1]

(Citations refer to the Publications of the Court)

A. JUDGMENTS

1. S. S. WIMBLEDON, judgment rendered August 17, 1923 (Series A, No. 1)
   France, Great Britain, Japan, and Italy *vs.* Germany

Question: Was the German Government justified as a neutral in the Russo-Polish War of 1920 in refusing passage through the Kiel Canal to the S.S. "Wimbledon" (a vessel time-chartered by a French company, loaded with munitions, and bound for the Polish naval base at Danzig) in view of the fact that the Canal, under Article 380 of the Treaty of Versailles, has ceased to be an internal waterway?

Decision: Under the Treaty the German Government has no right to refuse passage to a vessel flying the flag of a State not at war with Germany. Germany must pay for the loss resulting from the delay.

2. THE MAVROMMATTIS CONCESSION, August 30, 1924 (Series A, No. 2)
   Greece *vs.* Great Britain

Question: Would the granting of concessions to a private individual overlapping concessions granted before the war to a Greek subject of the Ottoman Empire constitute a breach of the Palestine Mandate (ratified after the granting of the concession) and would such a breach fall within the jurisdiction of the Court?

Decision: The granting of the concession in question, contrary to the rights of a concessionaire under the Ottoman Empire, would constitute a breach of Article 11 of the Palestine Mandate, which holds that such expropriation is permissible only when the ownership is passing from a private to a public interest. The Court has jurisdiction.

SAME, March 26, 1925 (Series A, No. 5)

Question: Would the erroneous description of M. Mavrommattis as an Ottoman subject in the draft of the Ottoman concessions render them invalid and entitle M. Rutenberg to appropriate the rights in question under the terms of the overlapping concession granted him by the British High Commissioner?

Decision: Since the nationality of M. Mavrommattis was not a condition of the contract, the error would have no effect upon its validity. The grant of the overlapping concession to M. Rutenberg was "contrary to the obligations entered into by the Mandatory."

[1] The following summaries are not intended to present an adequate picture of the questions of law and fact considered by the Court in each case, but merely to suggest the types of controversies which come before the Court. The summaries are arranged in chronological order of disputes, rather than by the numbers of the judgments and opinions of the Court. Readers interested in the details of cases are referred to the Publications of the Court, Series A and B, as cited under each controversy.

[890]

SAME, October 10, 1927 (Series A, No. 11)

Question: Does Greece, on behalf of M. Mavrommattis, have a right of further appeal to the Court for reparation because of delay on the part of the British High Commissioner in granting approval to the new contract of M. Mavrommattis?

Decision: This question is merely one of non-fulfillment of a contract and as such must be dealt with by the Palestinian or British courts.

3. THE TREATY OF NEUILLY (ANNEX), September 12, 1924 (Series A, No. 3)
   Greece *vs.* Bulgaria

Question: Was the arbitrator appointed under the Treaty of Neuilly competent to hear personal claims for damages for acts committed by Bulgaria outside of Bulgarian territory prior to the entrance of Greece into the war and do such claims, if valid, require payment above and beyond the reparations fixed in Part VII of the Treaty?

Decision: The arbitrator is competent to hear such claims but any indemnities due on this ground are included in reparations.

SAME, March 26, 1925 (Series A, No. 4)
Question: Request for interpretation of above judgment.

Decision: Request refused on the ground that, as put, it involved the making of a new decision on a new question rather than a mere interpretation of a judgment already rendered.

4. GERMAN INDUSTRIAL PROPERTIES IN UPPER SILESIA, August 25, 1925 (Series A, No. 6)
   Germany *vs.* Poland

Question: What articles of the German-Polish convention of 1922 apply to Polish expropriation of German industrial estates in Upper Silesia? Is the jurisdiction of the Court precluded by the fact that the controversies involved have already been submitted to the Polish-German mixed arbitral tribunal at Paris and to the Polish civil court at Kattowitz?

Decision: Articles 6 to 22 of convention held applicable. Jurisdiction of Court not precluded, since question of interpretation of Convention is not same as question submitted to arbitral tribunal and Polish court.

SAME, May 25, 1926 (Series A, No. 7)
Question: Are certain specific expropriations legal under convention?

Decision: Held not legal.

SAME, July 26, 1926 (Series A, No. 8)
Question: (several specific questions as to extent of Court's jurisdiction in such cases)

Decision: The Court has jurisdiction and reserves suit for judgment on its merits.

SAME, December 16, 1927 (Series A, No. 9)
(Question of interpretation of Judgment No. 7)

SAME, September 13, 1928 (Series A, No. 17)
(Question of reparation by Poland to Germany for Polish violations of Convention of 1922)

Decision: Reparations must be paid to the German Government and not to the individual owners. They must be paid in a lump sum to be determined by an expert commission. (Report of commission subsequently embodied in a Court order.)

5. THE LOTUS, September 27, 1927 (Series A, No. 10)
   Turkey *vs.* France

Question: Does Turkey owe France an indemnity for the arrest and prosecution of M. Demos in Turkish courts for involuntary manslaughter in connection with the sinking of the Turkish collier "Boz-Kourt" on the high seas in a collision with the French mail steamer "Lotus" on August 2, 1926? On the territory of which State did the collision take place? Do Turkish or French courts have jurisdiction?

Decision: Jurisdiction concurrent, since offense took place on both territories. Turkish courts may act in the absence of a definite prohibition by some rule of international law. Assertion of their jurisdiction no violation of international law in present instance.

6. GERMAN MINORITIES IN UPPER SILESIA, April 26, 1928 (Series A, No. 15)
   Germany *vs.* Poland

Question: Under the German-Polish convention of 1922, does an individual have the right, subject to no verification, to declare himself a member of a minority and to choose the school and the language of instruction for his children?

Decision: Right upheld.

7. JUGOSLAV LOANS, July 12, 1929 (Series A, No. 20)
   France *vs.* Jugoslavia

Question: Is Jugoslavia obliged to pay its loans issued in France in paper francs or in gold francs?

Decision: Payment in gold required by terms of the bonds.

8. BRAZILIAN LOANS, July 12, 1929 (Series A, No. 21)
   France *vs.* Brazil
   (Same question and decision as 7)

9. ODER RIVER COMMISSION, September 10, 1929 (Series A, No. 23)
   Germany *vs.* Poland

Question: Does the jurisdiction of the International Commission of the Oder extend, under the provisions of the Treaty of Versailles, to the sections of the tributaries of the Oder, *i.e.*, the Warthe (Warta) and the Netze (Notec) which are situated in Polish territory?

Decision: Yes; jurisdiction extends under Treaty to limits of navigability of all tributaries.

10. FREE ZONES OF GEX AND UPPER SAVOY, June 7, 1932 (Series A, No. 24)
    France *vs.* Switzerland

Question: Did Article 435 of the Treaty of Versailles constitute an abrogation or signify an intention to abrogate the treaties of 1815 respecting the free zones of Upper Savoy and the district of Gex?

Decision: No; France is bound by the 1815 treaties.

11. MEMEL DISPUTE, June 24, 1932 (Series A, No. 25)
    Great Britain, France, Italy, and Japan *vs.* Lithuania

Question: Does Article 17 of the Memel Convention of May 8, 1924, require that a dispute arising under the Convention must first be submitted to the Council of the League in order to fall within the jurisdiction of the Court?

Decision: No; the Convention provides two possible ways of dealing with disputes arising under its terms. Neither is a condition precedent to having recourse to the other.

B. ADVISORY OPINIONS

1. WORKERS' DELEGATE TO THE CONFERENCE OF THE INTERNATIONAL LABOR ORGANIZATION, Opinion requested by Council, May 12, 1922; Opinion rendered July 31, 1922 (Series B, No. 1)

Question: Was the workers' delegate from The Netherlands at the third session of the I.L.O. Conference "representative," i.e., nominated by the Government of The Netherlands in accordance with Article 389 of the Treaty of Versailles?

Opinion: Yes; each government determines for itself the "representativeness" of the workers' delegates.

2. COMPETENCE OF THE INTERNATIONAL LABOR ORGANIZATION, Request, May 12, 1922; Opinion, August 12, 1922 (Series B, No. 2)

Question: Is the I.L.O. competent to consider international regulation of conditions of labor in agriculture?

Opinion: Yes; its competence is clear and indisputable.

SAME, Request, July 18, 1922; Opinion, August 12, 1922 (Series B, No. 3)
Question: Is the I.L.O. competent to examine proposals for the organization of methods of agricultural production?

Opinion: Only in so far as they relate to labor problems.

SAME, Request, March 17, 1926; Opinion, July 23, 1926 (Series B, No. 13)
Question: Is the I.L.O. competent to consider the regulation, incidentally, of the personal work of employers?

Opinion: Yes, where it duplicates that of employees.

3. TUNISIAN NATIONALITY DECREES, Request, October 4, 1922; Opinion, February 7, 1923 (Series B, No. 4)

Question: Are questions arising under the French nationality decrees of November 8, 1921, in Tunis and Morocco, within French domestic jurisdiction or are they of an international nature?

Opinion: These questions are of an international nature since they involve the interpretation of treaties between France and Great Britain. The League Council is therefore competent to deal with them.

4. EASTERN KARELIA, Request, April 21, 1923; Opinion, July 23, 1923 (Series B, No. 5)

Question: Do Articles 10 and 11 of the Russian-Finnish Treaty of October 14, 1920, or the annexed declaration of the Russian delegation regarding the autonomy of Eastern Karelia, constitute obligations of an international character obligating Russia to carry out the provisions contained therein?

Opinion: The Court refused to give an opinion on the ground that one of the parties, i.e., the Soviet Government, had refused to recognize the jurisdiction of the League or the Court over the dispute.

5. GERMAN NATIONALS IN POLAND, Request, February 3, 1923; Opinion, September 10, 1923 (Series B, No. 6)

Question: Does Polish non-recognition of private contracts entered into by former German nationals residing in Poland fall within the competence of the League under the Minorities Treaty of June 28, 1919, and is such non-recognition a breach of Poland's obligations under the Treaty?

Opinion: Both questions answered in the affirmative.

SAME, Request, February 7, 1923; Opinion, September 15, 1923 (Series B, No. 7)

Question: Is the Council competent under the Minorities Treaty to consider disputes arising out of the acquisition of Polish nationality by former Germans in Poland? May the Polish Government under the Treaty require that the parents of the persons affected must not only have resided habitually at the birthplace of such persons at the time of birth but also have resided there habitually on January 10, 1920, the date of the coming into force of the Treaty?

Opinion: First question answered in affirmative, second in negative.

6. THE JAWORZINA QUESTION, Request, September 27, 1923; Opinion, December 6, 1923 (Series B, No. 8)

Question: Is the question of the delimitation of the Polish-Czechoslovak frontier still open, and if so to what extent?

Opinion: The question of the delimitation of the frontier has been definitely settled by the decision of the Conference of Ambassadors of July 28, 1920, but the right of the Delimitation Commission to propose modifications of the line thus fixed has not been exhausted.

7. THE MONASTERY OF SAINT-NAOUM, Request, June 17, 1924; Opinion, September 4, 1924 (Series B, No. 9)

Question: Have the Principal Allied Powers, by the decision of the Conference of Ambassadors of December 6, 1922, exhausted in regard to the frontier between Albania and Jugoslavia at the Monastery of Saint-Naoum, the mission which is contemplated by the resolution of the League Assembly of October 2, 1924?

Opinion: Yes; the decision of the Conference awarding the Monastery to Albania is final and definitive.

8. EXCHANGE OF GREEK AND TURKISH POPULATIONS, Request, December 13, 1924; Opinion, February 21, 1925 (Series B, No. 10)

Question and Opinion: (interpretation of the word "established" as used in Article 2 of the Convention of Lausanne to refer to residents exempted from compulsory exchange)

SAME, Request June 5, 1928; Opinion, August 28, 1928 (Series B, No. 16)

Question: Is it for the Mixed Commission for the Exchange of Greek and Turkish populations to decide whether the conditions laid down in the agreement of December 1, 1926, for the submission of questions to arbitration are or are not fulfilled—or is it for the arbitrator to decide this? To whom does the right of referring a question to the arbitrator belong?

Opinion: It is for the Mixed Commission to decide whether the conditions are fulfilled and only the Commission can refer questions to arbitration.

9. DANZIG POSTAL SERVICE, Request, March 14, 1925; Opinion, May 16, 1925 (Series B, No. 11)

Question: Are Polish postal authorities in Danzig entitled to deliver postal matter from Poland throughout the city or merely in the Polish post-office?

Opinion: In accordance with general postal usage, they are entitled to deliver mail throughout the city.

10. MOSUL BOUNDARY DISPUTE, Request, September 23, 1925; Opinion, November 21, 1925 (Series B, No. 12)

Question: What is the character of the action to be taken by the Council of the League under Article 3 of the Treaty of Lausanne? Must action be taken by unanimity or by a majority vote?

Opinion: The Treaty entrusts the Council with the task of determining the frontier definitively. Council decisions require unanimity but this principle is qualified by the rule that the votes recorded by the representatives of the disputants do not affect the required unanimity.

11. EUROPEAN COMMISSION OF THE DANUBE, Request, December 9, 1926; Opinion, December 8, 1927 (Series B, No. 14)

Question and Opinion: (Delimitation of the geographical extent and scope of the powers of the Commission)

12. JURISDICTION OF THE DANZIG COURTS, Request, September 22, 1927; Opinion, March 3, 1928 (Series B, No. 15)

Question: Do the Danzig courts have jurisdiction over cases involving pecuniary claims brought against the Polish Railways by Danzig railway officials who have passed into the Polish service?

Opinion: Yes; Danzig courts have not exceeded their powers.

13. THE GRECO-BULGARIAN COMMUNITIES, Request, January 16, 1930; Opinion, July 31, 1930 (Series B, No. 17)

Question and Opinion: (Definition of the terms "communities" and "dissolution of communities" in the Greco-Bulgarian Convention of November 27, 1919)

14. MEMBERSHIP OF DANZIG IN THE I.L.O., Request, May 15, 1930; Opinion, August 26, 1930 (Series B, No. 18)

Question: Is Danzig eligible to membership in the International Labor Organization?

Opinion: Yes, on condition of the conclusion of an agreement between Danzig and Poland giving the Free City the right to become a member, since Danzig foreign policy is under Polish control.

15. ACCESS TO GERMAN MINORITY SCHOOLS IN POLISH UPPER SILESIA, Request, January 24, 1931; Opinion, May 15, 1931 (Series B, No. 19)

Question: Can the children who were formerly excluded from the German minority schools on the basis of the language tests provided for in the Council's resolution of March 12, 1927, be now refused access to such schools?

Opinion: No; the language tests were exceptional and were not intended to replace option by declaration as provided for in the Convention of 1922.

APPENDIX V

16. AUSTRO-GERMAN CUSTOMS UNION PROJECT, Request, May 19, 1931; Opinion, September 5, 1931 (Series B, No. 20)

Question: Would a customs union between Germany and Austria on the basis of the principles laid down in the Protocol of March 19, 1931, be compatible with Article 88 of the Treaty of St. Germain and with the terms of the Financial Protocol signed at Geneva on October 4, 1922?

Opinion: No; such a union would be in violation of Austria's obligations under the Financial Protocol.

17. POLISH-LITHUANIAN RAILWAY TRAFFIC, Request, January 24, 1931; Opinion, October 15, 1931 (Series B, No. 21)

Question: Do the international engagements in force oblige Lithuania to take the necessary measures to open railway traffic with Poland?

Opinion: No; an engagement to negotiate does not imply an obligation to reach an agreement.

18. POLISH WAR VESSELS AT DANZIG, Request, September 19, 1931; Opinion, December 11, 1931 (Series B, No. 22)

Question: Under existing international obligations, what are the rights of Polish war vessels as regards access to, or anchorage in, the port of Danzig?

Opinion: Polish war vessels enjoy no special privileges under existing engagements.

19. POLISH NATIONALS IN DANZIG, Request, May 22, 1931; Opinion, February 4, 1932 (Series B, No. 23)

Question: Is Poland entitled to submit to the organs of the League questions of the treatment of Polish nationals in Danzig arising out of the application of the Constitution and laws of Danzig to such persons and what is the correct interpretation of the provisions of existing international obligations relating to such questions?

Opinion: Poland enjoys the right claimed. Existing obligations are purely negative and designed to prevent discrimination against Polish nationals in Danzig. They do not confer any positive privileges which Polish nationals may claim.

20. THE GRECO-BULGARIAN AGREEMENT OF December 9, 1927, Request, September 19, 1931; Opinion, March 8, 1932 (Series B, No. 24)

Question: Is Greece, in agreeing to the Hoover Moratorium Plan, entitled to connect the Bulgarian reparation debt and the Greek emigration debt and to set one off against the other?

Opinion: Under the agreement of December 9, 1927, there was no clause forbidding the setting off of one debt against the other, provided both debts fell within the categories covered by the Hoover Moratorium.

APPENDIX VI

COVENANT OF THE LEAGUE OF NATIONS[1]

THE HIGH CONTRACTING PARTIES,

In order to promote international cooperation and to achieve international peace and security.

by the acceptance of obligations not to resort to war,

by the prescription of open, just and honourable relations between nations,

by the firm establishment of the understandings of international law as the actual rule of conduct among Governments, and

by the maintenance of justice and a scrupulous respect for all treaty obligations in the dealings of organised peoples with one another,

Agree to this Covenant of the League of Nations.

ARTICLE 1

1. The original Members of the League of Nations shall be those of the Signatories which are named in the Annex to this Covenant and also such of those other States named in the Annex as shall accede without reservation to this Covenant. Such accession shall be effected by a Declaration deposited with the Secretariat within two months of the coming into force of the Covenant. Notice thereof shall be sent to all other Members of the League.

2. Any fully self-governing State, Dominion or Colony not named in the Annex may become a Member of the League if its admission is agreed to by two-thirds of the Assembly, provided that it shall give effective guarantees of its sincere intention to observe its international obligations, and shall accept such regulations as may be prescribed by the League in regard to its military, naval and air forces and armaments.

3. Any Member of the League may, after two years' notice of its intention so to do, withdraw from the League, provided that all its international obligations and all its obligations under this Covenant shall have been fulfilled at the time of its withdrawal.

ARTICLE 2

The action of the League under this Covenant shall be effected through the instrumentality of an Assembly and of a Council, with a permanent Secretariat.

ARTICLE 3

1. The Assembly shall consist of Representatives of the Members of the League.

2. The Assembly shall meet at stated intervals and from time to time as occasion may require at the Seat of the League, or at such other place as may be decided upon.

3. The Assembly may deal at its meetings with any matter within the sphere of action of the League or affecting the peace of the world.

[1] The Covenant is given with annotations as found in *Ten Years of World Cooperation*. Amendments in force are included in the text in italics; other proposed amendments have been added in footnotes. The paragraphs are given as officially numbered by an Assembly resolution of September 21, 1926.

4. At meetings of the Assembly, each Member of the League shall have one vote, and may have not more than three Representatives.

ARTICLE 4

1. The Council shall consist of Representatives of the Principal Allied and Associated Powers,[2] together with Representatives of four other Members of the League. These four Members of the League shall be selected by the Assembly from time to time in its discretion. Until the appointment of the Representatives of the four Members of the League first selected by the Assembly, Representatives of Belgium, Brazil, Spain and Greece shall be Members of the Council.

2. With the approval of the majority of the Assembly, the Council may name additional Members of the League, whose Representatives shall always be Members of the Council;[3] the Council with like approval may increase the number of Members of the League to be selected by the Assembly for representation on the Council.[4]

2 bis.[5] *The Assembly shall fix by a two-thirds majority the rules dealing with the election of the non-permanent Members of the Council, and particularly such regulations as relate to their term of office and the conditions of re-eligibility.*

3. The Council shall meet from time to time as occasion may require, and at least once a year, at the Seat of the League, or at such other place as may be decided upon.

4. The Council may deal at its meetings with any matter within the sphere of action of the League or affecting the peace of the world.

5. Any Member of the League not represented on the Council shall be invited to send a Representative to sit as a member at any meeting of the Council during the consideration of matters specially affecting the interests of that Member of the League.

6. At meetings of the Council, each Member of the League represented on the Council shall have one vote, and may have not more than one Representative.

ARTICLE 5

1. Except where otherwise expressly provided in this Covenant or by the terms of the present Treaty, decisions at any meeting of the Assembly or of the Council shall require the agreement of all the Members of the League represented at the meeting.

2. All matters of procedure at meetings of the Assembly or of the Council, including the appointment of Committees to investigate particular matters, shall be regulated by the Assembly or by the Council and may be decided by a majority of the Members of the League represented at the meeting.

3. The first meeting of the Assembly and the first meeting of the Council shall be summoned by the President of the United States of America.

[2] The Principal Allied and Associated Powers are the following: The United States of America, the British Empire, France, Italy, and Japan (see Preamble of the Treaty of Peace with Germany).

[3] In virtue of this paragraph of the Covenant, Germany was nominated as a permanent Member of the Council on September 8, 1926.

[4] The number of Members of the Council selected by the Assembly was increased to six instead of four by virtue of a resolution adopted at the third ordinary meeting of the Assembly on September 25, 1922. By a resolution taken by the Assembly on September 8, 1926, the number of Members of the Council selected by the Assembly was increased to nine.

[5] This amendment came into force on July 29, 1926, in accordance with Article 26 of the Covenant.

APPENDIX VI

ARTICLE 6

1. The permanent Secretariat shall be established at the Seat of the League. The Secretariat shall comprise a Secretary-General and such secretaries and staff as may be required.

2. The first Secretary-General shall be the person named in the Annex; thereafter the Secretary-General shall be appointed by the Council with the approval of the majority of the Assembly.

3. The secretaries and staff of the Secretariat shall be appointed by the Secretary-General with the approval of the Council.

4. The Secretary-General shall act in that capacity at all meetings of the Assembly and of the Council.

5.[6] *The expenses of the League shall be borne by the Members of the League in the proportion decided by the Assembly.*

ARTICLE 7

1. The Seat of the League is established at Geneva.

2. The Council may at any time decide that the Seat of the League shall be established elsewhere.

3. All positions under or in connection with the League, including the Secretariat, shall be open equally to men and women.

4. Representatives of the Members of the League and officials of the League when engaged on the business of the League shall enjoy diplomatic privileges and immunities.

5. The buildings and other property occupied by the League or its officials or by Representatives attending its meetings shall be inviolable.

ARTICLE 8

1. The Members of the League recognise that the maintenance of peace requires the reduction of national armaments to the lowest point consistent with national safety and the enforcement by common action of international obligations.

2. The Council, taking account of the geographical situation and circumstances of each State, shall formulate plans for such reduction for the consideration and action of the several Governments.

3. Such plans shall be subject to reconsideration and revision at least every ten years.

4. After these plans shall have been adopted by the several Governments, the limits of armaments therein fixed shall not be exceeded without the concurrence of the Council.

5. The Members of the League agree that the manufacture by private enterprise of munitions and implements of war is open to grave objections. The Council shall advise how the evil effects attendant upon such manufacture can be prevented, due regard being had to the necessities of those Members of the League which are not able to manufacture the munitions and implements of war necessary for their safety.

6. The Members of the League undertake to interchange full and frank information as to the scale of their armaments, their military, naval and air programmes, and the condition of such of their industries as are adaptable to warlike purposes.

ARTICLE 9

A permanent Commission shall be constituted to advise the Council on the execution of the provisions of Articles 1 and 8 and on military, naval and air questions generally.

[6] This paragraph came into force August 13, 1924, in accordance with Article 26.

APPENDIX VI

ARTICLE 10

The Members of the League undertake to respect and preserve as against external aggression the territorial integrity and existing political independence of all Members of the League. In case of any such aggression or in case of any threat or danger of such aggression the Council shall advise upon the means by which this obligation shall be fulfilled.

ARTICLE 11

1. Any war or threat of war, whether immediately affecting any of the Members of the League or not, is hereby declared a matter of concern to the whole League, and the League shall take any action that may be deemed wise and effectual to safeguard the peace of nations. In case any such emergency should arise the Secretary-General shall on the request of any Member of the League forthwith summon a meeting of the Council.

2. It is also declared to be the friendly right of each Member of the League to bring to the attention of the Assembly or of the Council any circumstance whatever affecting international relations which threatens to disturb international peace or the good understanding between nations upon which peace depends.

ARTICLE 12[7]

1. The Members of the League agree that if there should arise between them any dispute likely to lead to a rupture they will submit the matter either to arbitration *or judicial settlement* or to enquiry by the Council and they agree in no case to resort to war until three months after the award by the arbitrators *or the judicial decision* or the report by the Council.

2. In any case under this Article, the award of the arbitrators *or the judicial decision* shall be made within a reasonable time, and the report of the Council shall be made within six months after the submission of the dispute.

ARTICLE 13[7]

1. The Members of the League agree that whenever any dispute shall arise between them which they recognise to be suitable for submission to arbitration *or judicial settlement*, and which cannot be satisfactorily settled by diplomacy, they will submit the whole subject-matter to arbitration *or judicial settlement*.

2. Disputes as to the interpretation of a treaty, as to any question of international law, as to the existence of any fact which, if established, would constitute a breach of any international obligation, or as to the extent and nature of the reparation to be made for any such breach, are declared to be among those which are generally suitable for submission to arbitration *or judicial settlement*.

3. *For the consideration of any such dispute, the court to which the case is referred shall be the Permanent Court of International Justice, established in accordance with Article 14, or any tribunal agreed on by the parties to the dispute or stipulated in any convention existing between them.*

4. The Members of the League agree that they will carry out in full good faith any award *or decision* that may be rendered, and that they will not resort to war against a Member of the League which complies therewith. In the event of any failure to carry out such an award *or decision*, the Council shall propose what steps should be taken to give effect thereto.

[7] The amendments printed in italics relating to these articles came into force on September 26, 1924, in accordance with Article 26 of the Covenant.

The Council shall formulate and submit to the Members of the League for adoption plans for the establishment of a Permanent Court of International Justice. The Court shall be competent to hear and determine any dispute of an international character which the parties thereto submit to it. The Court may also give an advisory opinion upon any dispute or question referred to it by the Council or by the Assembly.

ARTICLE 15

1.[8] If there should arise between Members of the League any dispute likely to lead to a rupture, which is not submitted to arbitration *or judicial settlement* in accordance with Article 13, the Members of the League agree that they will submit the matter to the Council. Any party to the dispute may effect such submission by giving notice of the existence of the dispute to the Secretary-General, who will make all necessary arrangements for a full investigation and consideration thereof.

2. For this purpose the parties to the dispute will communicate to the Secretary-General, as promptly as possible, statements of their case with all the relevant facts and papers, and the Council may forthwith direct the publication thereof.

3. The Council shall endeavour to effect a settlement of the dispute and, if such efforts are successful, a statement shall be made public giving such facts and explanations regarding the dispute and the terms of settlement thereof as the Council may deem appropriate.

4. If the dispute is not thus settled, the Council either unanimously or by a majority vote shall make and publish a report containing a statement of the facts of the dispute and the recommendations which are deemed just and proper in regard thereto.

5. Any Member of the League represented on the Council may make public a statement of the facts of the dispute and of its conclusions regarding the same.

6. If a report by the Council is unanimously agreed to by the Members thereof other than the Representatives of one or more of the parties to the dispute, the Members of the League agree that they will not go to war with any party to the dispute which complies with the recommendations of the report.

7. If the Council fails to reach a report which is unanimously agreed to by the members thereof, other than the Representatives of one or more of the parties to the dispute, the Members of the League reserve to themselves the right to take such action as they shall consider necessary for the maintenance of right and justice.

8. If the dispute between the parties is claimed by one of them, and is found by the Council, to arise out of a matter which by international law is solely within the domestic jurisdiction of that party, the Council shall so report, and shall make no recommendation as to its settlement.

9. The Council may in any case under this Article refer the dispute to the Assembly. The dispute shall be so referred at the request of either party to the dispute provided that such request be made within fourteen days after the submission of the dispute to the Council.

10. In any case referred to the Assembly, all the provisions of this Article and of Article 12 relating to the action and powers of the Council shall apply to the action and powers of the Assembly, provided that a report made by the Assembly, if concurred in by the Representatives of those Members of the League represented on the Council and of a majority of the other Members of the League, exclusive in each case of the Representatives of the parties to the dispute, shall have the same force as a report by the Council concurred in by

---

[8] The amendment to the first paragraph of this article came into force on September 26, 1924, in accordance with Article 26 of the Covenant.

all the members thereof other than the Representatives of one or more of the parties to the dispute.

ARTICLE 16

1[9]. Should any Member of the League resort to war in disregard of its covenants under Articles 12, 13 or 15, it shall *ipso facto* be deemed to have committed an act of war against all other Members of the League, which hereby undertake immediately to subject it to the severance of all trade or financial relations, the prohibition of all intercourse between their nationals and the nationals of the covenant-breaking State, and the prevention of all financial, commercial or personal intercourse between the nationals of the covenant-breaking State and the nationals of any other State, whether a Member of the League or not.

2. It shall be the duty of the Council in such case to recommend to the several Governments concerned what effective military, naval or air force the Members of the League shall severally contribute to the armed forces to be used to protect the covenants of the League.

3. The Members of the League agree, further, that they will mutually support one another in the financial and economic measures which are taken under this Article, in order to minimise the loss and inconvenience resulting from the above measures, and that they will mutually support one another in resisting any special measures aimed at one of their number by the covenant-breaking State, and that they will take the necessary steps to afford passage through their territory to the forces of any of the Members of the League which are co-operating to protect the covenants of the League.

4. Any Member of the League which has violated any covenant of the League may be declared to be no longer a Member of the League by a vote of the Council concurred in by the Representatives of all the other Members of the League represented thereon.

ARTICLE 17

1. In the event of a dispute between a Member of the League and a State which is not a Member of the League, or between States not Members of the League, the State or States

[9] The following proposal for the amendment of paragraph 1 of Article 16 now awaits ratification:

"Should any Member of the League resort to war in disregard of its covenants under Articles 12, 13 or 15, it shall *ipso facto* be deemed to have committed an act of war against all other Members of the League, *which hereby undertake immediately to subject it to the severance of all trade or financial relations and to prohibit all intercourse at least between persons resident within their territories and persons resident within the territory of the covenant-breaking State and, if they deem it expedient, also between their nationals and the nationals of the covenant-breaking State, and to prevent all financial, commercial or personal intercourse at least between persons resident within the territory of that State and persons resident within the territory of any other State, whether a Member of the League or not, and, if they deem it expedient, also between the nationals of that State and the nationals of any other State whether a Member of the League or not.*

"*It is for the Council to give an opinion whether or not a breach of the Covenant has taken place. In deliberations on this question in the Council, the votes of Members of the League alleged to have resorted to war and of Members against whom such action was directed shall not be counted.*

"*The Council will notify to all Members of the League the date which it recommends for the application of the economic pressure under this Article.*

"*Nevertheless, the Council may, in the case of particular Members, postpone the coming into force of any of these measures for a specified period where it is satisfied that such a postponement will facilitate the attainment of the object of the measures referred to in the preceding paragraph, or that it is necessary in order to minimise the loss and inconvenience which will be caused to such Members.*"

It is proposed also to delete the words "in such case" in the following paragraph.

not Members of the League shall be invited to accept the obligations of membership in the League for the purposes of such dispute, upon such conditions as the Council may deem just. If such invitation is accepted, the provisions of Articles 12 to 16 inclusive shall be applied with such modifications as may be deemed necessary by the Council.

2. Upon such invitation being given the Council shall immediately institute an enquiry into the circumstances of the dispute and recommend such action as may seem best and most effectual in the circumstances.

3. If a State so invited shall refuse to accept the obligations of membership in the League for the purposes of such dispute, and shall resort to war against a Member of the League, the provisions of Article 16 shall be applicable as against the State taking such action.

4. If both parties to the dispute when so invited refuse to accept the obligations of membership in the League for the purposes of such dispute, the Council may take such measures and make such recommendations as will prevent hostilities and will result in the settlement of the dispute.

ARTICLE 18

Every treaty or international engagement entered into hereafter by any Member of the League shall be forthwith registered with the Secretariat and shall as soon as possible be published by it. No such treaty or international engagement shall be binding until so registered.

ARTICLE 19

The Assembly may from time to time advise the reconsideration by Members of the League of treaties which have become inapplicable and the consideration of international conditions whose continuance might endanger the peace of the world.

ARTICLE 20

1. The Members of the League severally agree that this Covenant is accepted as abrogating all obligations or understandings *inter se* which are inconsistent with the terms thereof, and solemnly undertake that they will not hereafter enter into any engagements inconsistent with the terms thereof.

2. In case any Member of the League shall, before becoming a Member of the League, have undertaken any obligation inconsistent with the terms of this Covenant, it shall be the duty of such Member to take immediate steps to procure its release from such obligations.

ARTICLE 21

Nothing in this Covenant shall be deemed to affect the validity of international engagements, such as treaties of arbitration or regional understandings like the Monroe doctrine, for securing the maintenance of peace.

ARTICLE 22

1. To those colonies and territories which as a consequence of the late war have ceased to be under the sovereignty of the States which formerly governed them and which are inhabited by peoples not yet able to stand by themselves under the strenuous conditions of the modern world, there should be applied the principle that the well-being and development of such peoples form a sacred trust of civilisation and that securities for the performance of this trust should be embodied in this Covenant.

2. The best method of giving practical effect to this principle is that the tutelage of such peoples should be intrusted to advanced nations who, by reason of their resources, their experience or their geographical position, can best undertake this responsibility, and

who are willing to accept it, and that this tutelage should be exercised by them as Mandatories on behalf of the League.

3. The character of the mandate must differ according to the stage of the development of the people, the geographical situation of the territory, its economic conditions and other similar circumstances.

4. Certain communities formerly belonging to the Turkish Empire have reached a stage of development where their existence as independent nations can be provisionally recognised subject to the rendering of administrative advice and assistance by a Mandatory until such time as they are able to stand alone. The wishes of these communities must be a principal consideration in the selection of the Mandatory.

5. Other peoples, especially those of Central Africa, are at such a stage that the Mandatory must be responsible for the administration of the territory under conditions which will guarantee freedom of conscience and religion, subject only to the maintenance of public order and morals, the prohibition of abuses such as the slave trade, the arms traffic and the liquor traffic, and the prevention of the establishment of fortifications or military and naval bases and of military training of the natives for other than police purposes and the defence of territory, and will also secure equal opportunities for the trade and commerce of other Members of the League.

6. There are territories, such as Southwest Africa and certain of the South Pacific islands, which, owing to the sparseness of their population, or their small size, or their remoteness from the centres of civilisation, or their geographical contiguity to the territory of the Mandatory, and other circumstances, can be best administered under the laws of the Mandatory as integral portions of its territory, subject to the safeguards above mentioned in the interests of the indigenous population.

7. In every case of mandate, the Mandatory shall render to the Council an annual report in reference to the territory committed to its charge.

8. The degree of authority, control or administration to be exercised by the Mandatory shall, if not previously agreed upon by the Members of the League, be explicitly defined in each case by the Council.

9. A permanent Commission shall be constituted to receive and examine the annual reports of the Mandatories, and to advise the Council on all matters relating to the observance of the mandates.

ARTICLE 23

Subject to and in accordance with the provisions of international conventions existing or hereafter to be agreed upon, the Members of the League:

(a) will endeavour to secure and maintain fair and humane conditions of labor for men, women, and children, both in their own countries and in all countries to which their commercial and industrial relations extend, and for that purpose will establish and maintain the necessary international organisations;

(b) undertake to secure just treatment of the native inhabitants of territories under their control;

(c) will entrust the League with the general supervision over the execution of agreements with regard to the traffic in women and children and the traffic in opium and other dangerous drugs;

(d) will entrust the League with the general supervision of the trade in arms and ammunition with the countries in which the control of this traffic is necessary in the common interest;

(e) will make provision to secure and maintain freedom of communications and of transit and equitable treatment for the commerce of all Members of the League. In this connection, the special necessities of the regions devastated during the war of 1914–1918 shall be borne in mind;

(f) will endeavour to take steps in matters of international concern for the prevention and control of disease.

ARTICLE 24

1. There shall be placed under the direction of the League all international bureaux already established by general treaties if the parties to such treaties consent. All such international bureaux and all commissions for the regulation of matters of international interest hereafter constituted shall be placed under the direction of the League.

2. In all matters of international interest which are regulated by general conventions but which are not placed under the control of international bureaux or commissions, the Secretariat of the League shall, subject to the consent of the Council and if desired by the parties, collect and distribute all relevant information and shall render any other assistance which may be necessary or desirable.

3. The Council may include as part of the expenses of the Secretariat the expenses of any bureau or commission which is placed under the direction of the League.

ARTICLE 25

The Members of the League agree to encourage and promote the establishment and co-operation of duly authorised voluntary national Red Cross organisations having as purposes the improvement of health, the prevention of disease and the mitigation of suffering throughout the world.

ARTICLE 26[10]

1. Amendments to this Covenant will take effect when ratified by the Members of the League whose Representatives compose the Council and by a majority of the Members of the League whose Representatives compose the Assembly.

2. No such amendment shall bind any Member of the League which signifies its dissent therefrom, but in that case it shall cease to be a Member of the League.

ANNEX

I. ORIGINAL MEMBERS OF THE LEAGUE OF NATIONS, SIGNATORIES OF THE TREATY OF PEACE

United States of America
Belgium
Bolivia
Brazil

British Empire
Canada
Australia
South Africa

[10] The following amendment has been offered to replace Article 26, and now awaits ratification:

"*Amendments to the present Covenant the text of which shall have been voted by the Assembly on a three-fourths majority, in which there shall be included the votes of all the Members of the Council represented at the meeting, will take effect when ratified by the Members of the League whose Representatives composed the Council when the vote was taken and by the majority of those whose Representatives form the Assembly.*

"*If the required number of ratifications shall not have been obtained within twenty-two months after the vote of the Assembly, the proposed amendment shall remain without effect.*

"*The Secretary-General shall inform the Members of the taking effect of an amendment.*

"*Any Member of the League which has not at that time ratified the amendment is free to notify the Secretary-General within a year of its refusal to accept it, but in that case it shall cease to be a Member of the League.*"

APPENDIX VI

New Zealand	Japan
India	Liberia
China	Nicaragua
Cuba	Panama
Ecuador	Peru
France	Poland
Greece	Portugal
Guatemala	Roumania
Haiti	Serb-Croat-Slovene State
Hedjaz	Siam
Honduras	Czechoslovakia
Italy	Uruguay

STATES INVITED TO ACCEDE TO THE COVENANT

Argentine Republic	Persia
Chile	Salvador
Colombia	Spain
Denmark	Sweden
Netherlands	Switzerland
Norway	Venezuela
Paraguay	

II. FIRST SECRETARY-GENERAL OF THE LEAGUE OF NATIONS
The Honorable Sir James Eric Drummond, K. C. M. G., C. B.

INDEX

A

Aaland Islands, 305, 307, 771–772
Abd-el-Krim, 393
Abyssinia, 101, 102, 117, 391, 392, 509, 598, 604
Adjudication, 216*f.*, 765–771
Administration, colonial, 589*f.*
and politics, 248–250
Afghanistan, 117
Aggression, 511*f.*
(*See also* "War guilt")
Agriculture, International Institute of, 247
Air, jurisdiction over, 139–140
Air fleets of world, 524
Alaska, 139, 396
boundary dispute (1903), 206–207
Albania, 118, 442, 457, 458, 508, 628, 774
Alexander I, 88–90
Alexander VI, 70
Alexander the Great, 22
Alfred the Great, 284
Aliens, enemy, 151
protection of, 133–134
Alliances, 665, 723
Anglo-Japanese, 461, 463, 466
Dual, 104, 432–433, 435
Holy, 92, 238–240
post-war, 724–725
Triple, 103, 306, 440, 441, 453
Alsace-Lorraine, 100, 304, 306, 327, 437
Althusius, Johannes, 51
Ambassadors (*see* Diplomatic agents)
American Revolution, 84
Amphictyonic Council, 19–20, 233, 234
Amritsar Massacre, 634
Andorra, 111, 118
Angell, Norman, quoted, 823
Anglo-Egyptian Sudan, 383, 601
Anglo-French Naval Compromise of 1928, 693–694
Anglo-Japanese Alliance, 461, 463, 466
Anschluss, 307, 366, 450–451, 458, 553
Aquinas, Thomas, 50

Arbitration, 208*f.*
among Greeks, 19–20
and the League of Nations, 764–765, 794–795
Papal, 41
United States practice, 212*f.*, 227
and war, 663–664
Arbitration treaties, 211*f.*, 227–228
Knox, 213–214
Root, 213
United States Senate and, 213*f.*
Aristotle, 1, 49
Armaments, and diplomacy, 516*f.*
expenditures on, 661
makers of, 736–738
and nationalism, 329
need of, 515–519
and State power, 517*f.*
Aryanism, 297–298
Assyria, 12, 13, 824
Australia, 383, 388
Austria, 117, 450, 458
economic dilemma, 552, 553
loans to, 366
minorities in, 313
war potential of, 526*f.*
Austria-Hungary, 440*f.*
army, 521–522
creation of, 100
destruction of, 107
foreign trade, 522–525
in Great War, 440*f.*
merchant marine, 522–525
minorities, 311
navy, 521–525
population, 520–521, 523–525
steel production, 522–525
Austro-German Customs Union, 125–126
Autarchy, 551*f.*, 568
Avenol, Joseph, 266

B

Babylonia, 9, 10, 13
Balance of power, 54–59, 507